Jurisprudence
Understanding and Shaping Law

Cases, Readings, Commentary

W. Michael Reisman

Wesley Newcomb Hohfeld
Professor of Jurisprudence
Yale Law School

Aaron M. Schreiber

Professor of Law
Pace University Law School

New Haven Press
1987

Second Printing, 1988
Third Printing, 1991

Library of Congress Cataloging-in-Publication Data

Reisman, W. Michael (William Michael), 1939-
  Jurisprudence: understanding and shaping law.

  Includes bibliographies and index.
  1. Jurisprudence—Cases. 2. Law—United States—
Cases. I. Schreiber, Aaron M. II. Title.
KF379.R45 1987   340′.1   87-11243
ISBN 0-913275-00-X

Set in Times Roman type by Twin Company, Inc., Holyoke,
Massachusetts. Printed in the United States of America
by Braun-Brumfield, Inc., Ann Arbor, Michigan.

Book design by Andrew R. Willard.

Contents

PREFACE xiii

ACKNOWLEDGEMENTS xv

CHAPTER 1   JURISPRUDENCE: IS IT RELEVANT? 1

    Reisman, A Theory of Law From the Policy Perspective 4

        The Justice's Dilemma 8

        Admissions and Hiring Dilemmas 9

APPENDIX   Tools for Decisionmaking 12

Who? Observational Standpoint and Self Scrutiny 12

Looking How? Focus 13

At What? The Targets of Observation: Processes of Authority and Control   14

Doing What? The Intellectual Tasks of Decision 15

Tools and Their Craftsmen 20

        Supplementary Reading 21

CHAPTER 2   MYTHS, MULTIPLICITY AND ELITES: APPEARANCE AND
            REALITY IN THE LAW 23

    Reisman, Myth System and Operational Code 23

        Notes 35

Multiple Legal Systems and Levels 35

    Pospisil, Legal Levels and Multiplicity of Legal Systems in Human
        Societies 35

        Notes 43

    Reisman, A Theory of Law From the Policy Perspective 43

Elites in Democracy 44

    Dahl, Who Governs: Democracy and Power in an American City .. 45

        Notes 48

    Mills, The Power Elite 48

        Notes 52

        Supplementary Reading 54

CHAPTER 3   LAW FROM THE MOUTH OF A GUN: THE JURISPRUDENCE OF
            NAKED POWER 56

Tinoco Case (Great Britain v. Costa Rica) 56
    Notes 58
The Thrasymachian View 58
    Plato, The Republic, Book I 58
    Plato, Gorgias 63
    Dahrendorf, In Praise of Thrasymachus 64
Anarchism: Benign and not so Benign 67
    Kropotkin, Law and Authority 67
    Cleaver, Domestic Law and International Order 75
        Notes 78
            Supplementary Reading 81

CHAPTER 4   THE ETHIC OF OBEDIENCE: A JURISPRUDENCE OF NATURAL
             LAW 82
The Argument for Absolute Obedience 83
    Plato, Crito 83
        Notes 90
        Lieutenant Calley: His Own Story as Told to John Sack 91
        Bigart, Milwaukee Judge Scores Marchers 91
        Notes 92
Obedience to Orders of an Authority Figure: The Milgram Experiments   93
    Milgram, The Perils of Obedience 94
        Notes 98
The Argument for Individual Judgment 99
    Godwin, An Enquiry Concerning Political Justice 99
        Notes 109
Civil Disobedience: The Intermediate Position 109
    Thoreau, Concerning Civil Disobedience 109
        Notes 117
        King, Letter from Birmingham City Jail 118
Refusal and Disobedience 119
    Rawls, A Theory of Justice 119
        Notes 128
    Fortas, Concerning Dissent and Civil Disobedience 128
        Notes 140
    Zinn, Disobedience and Democracy: Nine Fallacies on Law and
        Order 140
        Notes 146
The Response of Decisionmakers 147
    Reynolds v. United States 148

Notes 150

United States v. Sisson 150

People v. Woody 156

Fedorenko v. United States 159

Notes 166

Supplementary Reading 168

CHAPTER 5   IN THE NATURE OF THINGS: THE JURISPRUDENCE OF PHYSICAL
AND STRUCTURAL NATURALISM 169

Aristotle, Nicomachean Ethics 170

Aristotle, Politics 171

Notes 173

"Natural" Sexual Behavior 173

Harris v. State 173

Baker v. Nelson 176

Notes 178

"Natural" Birth and Death 178

Matter of Quinlan 179

Notes 188

Roe et al. v. Wade 189

Notes 195

Political Functions of Naturalist Language 196

The Structural Nature of Law 197

Fuller, Eight Ways to Fail to Make Law 198

Hart, The Minimum Content of Natural Law 204

Fuller, The Minimum Content of a Substantive Natural Law 208

Notes 209

The Structural Nature of Justice 209

Rawls, A Theory of Justice 210

Notes 222

Supplementary Reading 223

CHAPTER 6   THE PAST AS PRISON: THE JURISPRUDENCE OF HISTORICISM ..   224

Conservative Historicism 225

Savigny, Of the Vocation of Our Age for Legislation and
Jurisprudence 226

Notes 231

Burke, Reform of Representation in the House of Commons 231

Notes 232

Cohen, Psychology and Scientific Methods 232

Dred Scott v. Sandford 234

    Notes 236

Romanticization of Violence 236

    Von Jhering, The Struggle for Law 236

        Notes 246

    McDougal, The Ethics of Applying Systems of Authority: The
    Balanced Opposites of a Legal System 247

Radical Historicism 248

    Marx, A Contribution to Critique of Political Economy 248

    Marx and Engels, Selected Correspondence 249

    Dewey, Freedom and Culture 250

Cyclical Historicism 253

    Sorokin, The Crisis of Our Age 253

        Notes 261

How is the Past Replicated 261

    Stinchcombe, Constructing Social Theories 261

        Notes 265

Historicism in American Constitutional Theory 266

    Appraisal 266

        Supplementary Reading 268

CHAPTER 7   THE WORLD OF RULES: THE JURISPRUDENCE OF POSITIVISM   269

Positivism and Rules 269

    Austin, The Province of Jurisprudence Determined 270

        Notes 280

Hart's Concept 282

    Hart, The Concept of Law 282

        Notes 292

Dworkin's Concept 294

    Dworkin, Is Law a System of Rules? 294

        Notes 305

American Judicial Practice 306

    McBoyle v. United States 307

The New Deal 308

    Harper v. Virginia 309

        Notes 310

        Supplementary Reading 312

CHAPTER 8   LAW WITHOUT MORALITY: THE JURISPRUDENCE OF NEUTRAL
        PRINCIPLES 313

CONTENTS   ix

Wechsler, Toward Neutral Principles of Constitutional Law 313

Miller & Howell, The Myth of Neutrality in Constitutional
Adjudication 322

McDougal, The Application of Constitutive Prescriptions: An
Addendum to Justice Cardozo 329

Notes 332

Positivism and Morality 333

Hart, Positivism and the Separation of Law and Morals 333

Notes 335

Wolfenden and the Controversy About Homosexuality 336

The Wolfenden Report: Home Office Report on Homosexual Offenses
and Prostitution 336

Devlin, The Enforcement of Morals 338

Notes 345

Case Law 346

Dyett v. Pendleton 346

Notes 348

Positivism and the Protection of Minorities 349

Shklar, Legalism 349

Notes 355

Positivism in Perspective 356

Supplementary Reading 358

CHAPTER 9   LEGAL ETHICS IN LEVIATHAN: THE JURISPRUDENCE OF
BUREAUCRACY 359

Dean, Blind Ambition 359

The Nature of the Beast 362

Presthus, The Organizational Society 363

Notes 373

Treaster, Aboard a B-52 Bomber High Over Vietnam a Crew Takes
Part in an "Impersonal War" 374

Blau & Meyer, Bureaucracy in Modern Society 375

Janis, Groupthink 376

Notes 379

Blau & Meyer, Bureaucracy in Modern Society 379

Notes 380

Hans Kelsen and the "Pure Theory" 381

Kelsen, General Theory of Law and State 381

Notes 402

Legal Ethics and Bureaucratic Jurisprudence 405

Krash, Professional Responsibility to Clients and the Public Interest:
  Is there a Conflict? 406
    Notes 409
Green, The Other Government 409
Dam, The Special Responsibility of Lawyers in the Executive
  Branch 410
    Notes 414
Reisman, Folded Lies 414
    Notes 416
Tarasoff v. Regents of the University of California 417
Meyerhofer v. Empire Fire and Marine Insurance Company 421
    Notes 425
Statement of Policy Adopted by American Bar Association, 1975 .. 425
    Notes 427
Self-Regulation: The A.B.A. 427
Model Rules of Professional Conduct 427
    Notes 431
        Supplementary Reading 433

CHAPTER 10   TELLING IT LIKE IT IS: AMERICAN LEGAL REALISM 434
Oliphant & Hewitt, Introduction to J. Rueff, From the Physical to the
  Social Sciences: Introduction to a Study of Economic and Ethical
  Theory 435
Freudian Adaptations 439
  Frank, Law and the Modern Mind 440
    Notes 447
  Arnold, The Symbols of Government 447
Llewellyn's Theory of the Constitution 449
  Llewellyn, The Constitution as an Institution 450
Rodell's Intuitionism 455
  Rodell, Nine Men: A Political History of the Supreme Court From
  1790 to 1955 455
Behavioral Jurisprudence: Jurimetrics 458
  Schubert, Behavioral Jurisprudence 459
    Notes 462
Critical Legal Theory 463
  Gordon, New Developments in Legal Theory 463
    Notes 470
Practical Consequences of Realism 470
Constitutional Law 470

Reynolds v. Sims 470

Criminal Law 473

Miranda v. Arizona 474

Products Liability and Consumer Protection 477

Henningsen v. Bloomfield Motors, Inc. 477

Sindell v. Abbott Laboratories 480

Supplementary Reading 485

CHAPTER 11   USING SOCIAL SCIENCES: SOCIOLOGICAL JURISPRUDENCE 486

Muller v. Oregon 486

Science and Desegregation 489

Brown v. Board of Education 489

Wolf, Social Science and the Courts: The Detroit Schools Case 492

Notes 501

Swann et al. v. Charlotte-Mecklenburg Board of Education 501

Pettigrew, Smith, Useem & Normand, Busing: A Review of "The
Evidence" 505

Armor, The Double Double Standard: A Reply 507

Wilson, On Pettigrew and Armor: An Afterword 509

Sociological Jurisprudence and Value Commitment 510

Dahrendorf, Values and Social Science: The Value Dispute in
Perspective 510

Notes 513

Supplementary Reading 515

CHAPTER 12   POLICY: CONTEMPORARY APPROACHES 516

Judicial Applications: "Intuitive" Policy and Its Problems 517

Bob Jones University v. United States 518

Notes 527

Javins v. First National Realty Corporation 528

Notes 531

McDougal & Lasswell, Legal Education and Public Policy 531

Notes 532

The Centrality of Problem and Goal 533

Bentham, An Introduction to the Principles of Morals and
Legislation 534

Notes 544

The Lasswell-McDougal Approach to Postulation 545

Lasswell, Psychopathology and Politics 546

Lasswell, Clarifying Value Judgment: Principles of Content and
    Procedure 549
Law and Economics as Policy Science 552
    Posner, Economic Analysis of Law 552
        Notes 560
    Arrow, Social Choice and Individual Values 561
        Notes 564
"Muddling Through" as Policy Method 567
    Braybrooke & Lindblom, A Strategy of Decision 567
        Notes 572
The New Haven School as Policy Science 573
    Lasswell & McDougal, Criteria for a Theory About Law 573
    McDougal & Lasswell, Legal Education and Public Policy 587
        Notes 590
            Supplementary Reading 591

AFTERWORD 595
INDEX 596

Preface

This book surveys the major schools of jurisprudence and canvasses fundamental ideas in the culture of law in a way that permits the reader to develop a critical perspective. It does not purport to set out systematically a specific school of jurisprudence, though it is certainly animated by a definite viewpoint. It has been designed as a teaching text. As such, it seeks to relate some of the basic ideas developed in jurisprudence over the last 2,500 years to the problems which students, as lawyers, will have to solve. It takes jurisprudence, not on the terms dictated by the various writers whose work is incorporated here, but in the terms and in the perspective of contemporary users. From such a perspective, much traditional jurisprudence, it must be admitted, is of limited relevance; it may be studied as stages in the history of ideas about law, but it is of little direct practical use to the contemporary lawyer. This has sometimes led to a complete rejection of the study of jurisprudence. That is regrettable. Some of the jurisprudence which has been summarily discarded could be useful in alerting students to contemporary tendencies and the resolution of contemporary problems. Good jurisprudence, like good philosophy, wrestles with certain fundamental problems about human beings and the ways they collectively arrange to produce and distribute the good and bad things of life. The juxtaposition of contemporary and older materials and the use of contemporary problems is intended to establish this continuity. Students who have used this book should then be in a position to read other material, find it more meaningful and appraise it more cogently.

We believe and are confident that the materials that follow will demonstrate that lawyers are problem-solvers and that jurisprudence is useful, if not indispensable, to solving problems efficiently. Hence each chapter is built around an actual case or a hypothetical problem. Because in our view, one of the functions of a jurisprudence course is to introduce the student to a range of materials and to make the student aware of the fact that law is a continuing process of problem-solving in which the past is always present, we have selected a wide variety of historical and contemporary materials across the political spectrum. Nevertheless, comprehensiveness is perforce limited by the demand to produce a book which will be manageable in a two hour course, the time usually alloted to a jurisprudence course.

It is now common to indict law schools for neglecting to impart appropriate ethical norms to their students. Whether or not that is true, it is apparent that law schools have failed to present in realistic fashion many of the ethical quandries in which practitioners may find themselves placed daily. We are concerned with trying to remedy that and have tried to choose those sorts of difficult cases rarely discussed in the literature. In all of the practical cases presented to the students, the ethical issues are explicity raised.

As users of casebooks and coursebooks, we are mindful of the interest of the teacher in understanding the basic design of the architects of the book, but at the same time, the refusal to be forced into the Procrustean bed of another's ideas. Accordingly, we have designed the book so that other teachers can readily see the sequence of ideas we have found practical and how we use the materials. However, there are many ways of using a book of this sort and we anticipate that some teachers may find it convenient to change the order and be selective in the sections they choose. In our view, Chapters 1 and 2 should be presented early in the course; in fact, Chapter 1 was constructed to be assigned before the first meeting of a class. Thereafter, no sequence in the different schools of jurisprudence need be followed. They may be varied as the teacher wishes and some may be deleted. Matters of personal taste, a sense of what is of enduring worth and what is ephemeral and a judgment as to what is of most value to the law student inevitably influence decision about the material to be incorporated and the material to be used.

We would acknowledge with special gratitude the help at many stages of this book of Myres S. McDougal, our teacher, to whom this book is respectfully and affectionately dedicated.

New Haven, Connecticut   W. M. R.
White Plains, New York   A. M. S.

Acknowledgements

Many people helped us in the preparation of this book. We would like to thank particularly: Mahnoush H. Arsanjani, Arie E. David, Eric Freedman, David Gregory, Baruch D. Schreiber, and Marshall Tinkle. Michael Lind prepared the drawing in the appendix to Chapter 1, with calligraphy by Sharon Rowley Morgio. A special debt of gratitude is owed to Andrew Willard for his judgment and tenacity in directing the editing, design and production of the book.

Cheryl DeFilippo, Paula Montonye and Shelby Sola typed and corrected the manuscript with expertise, tolerance and (by and large) good humor.

Permission to reprint selections from the following is acknowledged:

Aboard a B-52 Bomber High Over Vietnam a Crew Takes Part in an 'Impersonal War' by J. B. Treaster, October 13, 1972, reprinted by permission of The New York Times. Copyright © 1972 by the New York Times Company. Reprinted by permission.

Arnold, The Symbols of Government (1935). Reprinted by permission of the Estate of Thurman Arnold.

Blind Ambition by John W. Dean, reprinted by permission of Simon & Schuster, Inc. Copyright © 1976 by John W. Dean.

Columbia Law Review, for permission to reprint from Llewellyn, The Constitution as an Institution (1934). Copyright © 1983 by the Directors for the Columbia Law Review Association, Inc.

The Concept of Law, by H. L. A. Hart, by permission of the publisher, Oxford University Press. Copyright © 1961 by Oxford University Press.

Kenneth Dam, for permission to reprint from Dam, The Special Responsibility of Lawyers in the Executive Branch, 55 Chicago Bar Record (1974).

Ronald Dworkin, for permission to reprint from Dworkin, Is Law a System of Rules, in Philosophy of Law (1977).

The Enforcement of Morals by Patrick Devlin, by permission of the publisher, Oxford University Press. Copyright © 1965 by Oxford University Press.

Essays in the Theory of Society by Ralf Dahrendorf, with the permission of the publishers, Stanford University Press. © 1968 by the Board of Trustees of the Leland Stanford Junior University.

Excerpted from the Model Rules of Professional conduct, copyright, August, 1983 by American Bar Association. All rights reserved. Reprinted with permission.

Excerpts from Constructing Social Theories by Arthur Stinchcomb, copyright © 1968 by Harcourt Brace Jovanovich, Inc. Reprinted by permission of the publisher.

Maria Feder and Hanna Oestreicher, for permission to reprint from Kelsen, General Theory of Law and State (1945), published by Harvard University Press.

Folded Lies: Bribery, Crusades and Reforms by W. Michael Reisman. Copyright © 1979 by The Free Press, a Division of Macmillan Publishing Co., Inc. Reprinted with permission of the publisher.

Random House, Inc. and Alfred A. Knopf, Inc., for permission to reprint from Blau & Meyer, Bureaucracy in Modern Society (2d ed. 1971). Copyright © 1956, 1971.

Rodell, Nine Men: A Political History of the Supreme Court From 1790 to 1955 (1955). Reprinted by permission of Janet Rodell.

Glendon Schubert, for permission to reprint from Schubert, Behavioral Jurisprudence, in 2 Law and Society Review (1968).

Selections from Law and the Modern Mind by Jerome Frank, copyright 1930, 1933, 1949 by Coward McCann, Inc., copyright 1930 by Brentano's Inc., are from Anchor Books Edition, 1963. Copyright renewed in 1958 by Florence K. Frank. Reprinted by arrangement with the estate of Barbara Frank Kirstein.

Soul on Ice by Eldridge Cleaver, with permission of the publisher, McGraw-Hill Book Company. Copyright © 1968.

A Strategy of Decision by David Braybrooke and Charles Lindblom, reprinted with permission of Macmillan, Inc. Copyright © 1963 by The Free Press of Glencoe.

A Theory of Justice by John Rawls, Cambridge, Mass.: The Balknap Press of Harvard University Press, Copyright © 1971 by the President and Fellows of Harvard College. Reprinted by permission of the publishers.

University of Chicago Law Review and Arthur S. Miller, for permission to reprint from Miller and Howell, Myth of Neutrality in Constitutional Law Adjudication (1960).

Wolf, Social Science and the Courts: The Detroit Schools Case. Reprinted with permission of the author from: The Public Interest, No. 42 (Winter, 1976), pp. 102–120. © 1976 by National Affairs, Inc.

Yale University Press, for permission to reprint from Fuller, The Morality of Law. Copyright © 1969; Dahl, Who Governs? Democracy and Power in an American City. Copyright © 1961; Arrow, Social Choices and Individual Values (2nd ed.) Copyright © 1963.

CHAPTER 1

Jurisprudence: Is It Relevant?

There is nothing so practical as a good theory.
Kurt Lewin

Most beginning law students conceive of their future roles largely in terms of courts or court-related activities and certainly in terms of the disputes in which people become embroiled. To a large extent, legal education reflects that popular assumption. In fact, very few lawyers in the United States actually devote much of their time to courts.*

> . . . the trial lawyer is no more the prototype of the legal profession than the brain surgeon typifies medicine. Over 90% of criminal cases involve guilty pleas, 96% of New York divorces are uncontested, and less than 5% of personal injury cases go to jury verdict. Whole industries resort to arbitration. Most lawyers in practicing their craft spend most of their time in negotiating, counseling, drafting documents, and planning business and personal affairs for the future. Law firms tend to create specialities within specialties, and trial work is assigned to a numerically small but important division of the firm. A substantial part of the law business is transacted outside of the adversary process. Moreover, depending upon economic conditions and opportunities, our law school graduates may as often drift into government or business as into active practice. In short, the legal profession is tremendously diversified, and lawyers tend to be so extremely individualistic that their differences outweigh their similarities.**

Some have attributed this "widening variety and ambiguity of the roles and functions of people that are trained as lawyers"† to the extraordinarily rich variety of commercial and political functions lawyers must perform in the United States. A

---

*L. Baird, A Survey of the Relevance of Legal Training to Law School Graduates, 30 *J. Leg. Ed.* 668 (1978); See especially table 1.

**Foster, The Law and Social Work, 53 *Ky. L. Rev.* 229, 232–33 (1964–65). Another way of analyzing the diverse tasks lawyers perform would be in terms of the different functions that they actually perform. As Foster 's observation indicates, the stereotypical conception of legal work is in the courts or in the application of law. In fact, lawyers also play roles in the making of law, in the invocation of law, in the termination of law, in appraisals of whether large areas of legal regulation are achieving their objectives and if not whether things can be done to change it and so on.

In the Appendix to this chapter a more detailed *functional* analysis is developed so that the lawyer can determine with some precision which functions he or she is performing and, if relevant, what particular policies apply in a distinctive fashion.

†G. Hazard, *Challenges to Legal Education* 186 (1968).

key aspect of politics, of course, is crafting the future. David Riesman writes that
the lawyer,

> is called upon constantly, whether he be judge, legislator, or practicing lawyer
> to make 'policy' judgments. Clients, business or government, don't know what
> kind of a future they want. They want, partly, what they should have, and turn
> to their counsel for guidance as men once turned to clergy. But training in the
> making of value judgments is not simply useful for lawyers in becoming bigger
> success boys. The agreed aim of legal education is to turn students into better
> citizens and community leaders. Even as technicians, the means they use to
> carry out their clients' policies shape the ends which are achieved. In human
> affairs, there are no machine tools. The lawyer as technician plays a part in
> bringing about the future even when he may not wish to, even when he may
> be unconscious of his role.*

Even in more traditional legal systems, the range of lawyer functions extends far
beyond the courts. An English solicitor, for example, reports that he spends less than
five percent of his time each week engaged in the application of traditional legal
skills.

If lawyers are doing a variety of other things, what are they and what are the
conceptions and theories that are implicit in and necessary for performing them?
More precisely, what are the foci, the segments of reality that lawyers must look at
in order to discharge these functions? And what are the specific skills they require
to perform these more comprehensive professional tasks in an efficient and ethical
fashion? To what extent is your legal education equipping you for these tasks?

Let us explore the point by considering one sort of "non-court" problem you
might encounter when you begin practicing law. Imagine, for the moment, that you
are a junior member of a firm which has, as a client, Suzuki Industries, a large
Japanese corporation which operates multinationally. Suzuki has decided as a matter
of policy to invest in the United States, and is now contemplating establishing a
subsidiary manufacturing component in Penntown, a small town in western Pennsylvania. Material on relevant United States law, Pennsylvania law, and local law
has been forwarded to Suzuki headquarters in Tokyo. Now Suzuki has asked your
firm to visit Penntown and report more fully.

The request should hardly be surprising. Prudent investors from abroad, like their
American counterparts contemplating an investment overseas, want to know more
than the constitution, statutes and by-laws of the community they may enter. And
the reason is obvious. A description of the written law alone, no matter how rigorous
and thorough, cannot give your Japanese client a full, rounded or dynamic picture
of how decisions are actually made in Penntown.

You arrive in Penntown to flesh out the picture. Whom do you ask? What do
you ask? What information is really necessary for you and for your client in order
for each of you to understand the environment into which the foreign corporation
may enter and how to plan its entry and operation efficiently. Some of the things
which you must inventory, but which are not expressed in the formal law material
already gathered are the individuals, groups and entities—formal and informal—actually
involved in making those critical choices in Penntown that will affect Suzuki's
prospective operations. You and your client are interested in their behavior, in a very
specific and not in an abstract sense. You are trying to guess how these actors will
behave under a variety of conditions that may prevail in the future.

---

*D. Riesman, Law and Social Science, 50 *Yale L. J.* 636, 639 (1941).

As a matter of common sense we are constantly orienting ourselves in that elusive notion called "the present" by looking at what happened in the past and the conditions that prevailed then in order to determine how we, or others whose actions are likely to influence us, will behave in the future under similar or different conditions. (You can anticipate some conditions; others, you may be able to create yourself). So, more concretely, you will wish to know what these groups and individuals in Penntown did in the past, what conditions prevailed then that may have influenced what they did, what conditions are likely to prevail in the future, the different ways the groups may react to them and the effects that each of these potential reactions can have on your client.

The purpose of this inquiry is utterly practical. Suzuki Industries wants information that will guide it in choosing how it should act, indeed whether it should even enter Penntown. Practically speaking, that means how it should act with regard to the people or groups and entities who have an input into the process of making decisions or choices in Penntown. The exclusively book-bound, black letter lawyer can regale you, in detail, with the formal rules of Penntown. Is that enough for the tasks you will have to perform?

Put most succinctly, you must understand how decisions are actually made in Penntown if you are to advise your client. It is not enough simply to tell Suzuki what the formal rules are, for unless Penntown is a very exceptional case, the rules will not actually be applied or applied in a strict fashion in many cases. Even where they are applied, many other factors may enter into how the rules are applied and in the fashioning of the decisions that will affect your client. You must, in short, understand the processes in which decisions are taken in order for you and your client to begin to make matter-of-fact assumptions about what future course of behavior will be followed by officials and *non-officials* in Penntown. Only with such information, can you fashion a course of action for yourself which is appropriate and, acting on behalf of your client, learn to operate in that particular setting in ways that increase the likelihood of influencing and securing favorable decisions.

This point bears emphasis. You may use some of the methods of science, but you are much more than an observer and a recorder. When Oliver Wendell Holmes said that law was nothing more pretentious than the prediction of how courts will behave, he was putting the matter too narrowly in many ways. The lawyer is not only concerned with courts and their behavior, but with predicting *and influencing* a complex of formal, informal, organized, and unorganized decisionmaking agencies, groups and individuals which are, in fact, likely to have an impact on his client's interests. One of the challenges of a new context is to find out exactly who those agencies and people are. Conventional legal research is indispensable, but in every problem there will be items, sometimes the most important, which cannot be learned by consulting legal texts.

Let's concern ourselves, for the moment, primarily with the things you would want to know rather than the methods you would use. You arrive in Penntown and check into the main hotel. You go down to the bar for a drink and, in casual fashion, ask people who look like "regulars" who the Mayor is. You may then ask who the Boss is. With a question like that, you are conceding that there is a real possibility of a discrepancy between formal legal institutions, which we will call "authority," and actually effective institutions which, for purposes of contrast, we will call "control." The fact of the matter is that in many municipalities and organizations, in states and even in national polities, there are both formal institutions and effective "machines," i.e., informal institutions. The two are not always congruent. From your basic legal studies, you know that in formal law there can be many, overlapping and in some cases inconsistent systems of law: federal, state, local, religious, not to speak of the internal "law" of corporations and other business entities. Informal law may manifest even greater complexity, for it rarely has principles of "choice of law" or "conflicts rules" for dealing with the clash of incompatible norms.

Your questions about the Mayor and the Boss indicate a conception of legal processes as requiring a certain amount of effective power or control. You are conceding that, in some circumstances, formal institutions may not have that effective power. The implication, of course, is that the lawyers, seeking to predict how decisions will be made in that particular context (not to speak of trying to influence their outcome in favor of a client), must identify the effective power process in that particular community. If power processes are not congruent with formal processes, must lawyers become adept at identifying and manipulating them so as to serve their client? And what of the ethical issues raised by this?

The documentary study your firm completed even before you came to Penntown identified formal and "legal" decisionmakers from the "black letter" statutory and other documentary materials available. But now that you're on the scene, it becomes clear that those documents capture only a part of the picture. Indeed, the part of the picture they reflect may be incorrect. The City Council, the documents say, makes decisions. A day or two in Penntown may reveal that fundamental policy is actually made in a series of informal meetings taking place in country clubs, business lunches, periodic meetings of merchant associations and so on. The City Council, you may discover, really does no more than validate or promulgate decisions and policies clarified elsewhere.

In their informal meetings, the town's elite may themselves respond to a variety of other pressures. Economic decisions may be influenced by the demands or anticipated demands of different labor groups; representatives of some of those groups may actually be in these meetings. The decisions may also be influenced by the anticipated demands of church and synagogue groups, of environmentalists, moral majoritarians and the ever-present media. And, unhappily, the decisions may also be influenced by plainly illegal groups; gangs, crime syndicates and so on are significant political factors in all too many settings. The point is that information necessary for understanding how decisions are going to be made in Penntown, the sort of information your client needs and the sort that is not elicited from documents, requires a type of inquiry that formal legal education rarely addresses.

Obviously, there is still more information needed in order to understand what Penntown is and how it operates. Consider a somewhat more detailed inquiry in another example, concerning a college fraternity.

REISMAN, A THEORY OF LAW FROM THE POLICY PERSPECTIVE,
IN LAW AND POLICY 79 (D. WEISSTUB ED. 1976)

A PRACTICAL GUIDE TO THE LAW IN CONTEXT

God, in his wisdom, makes some men rich; one of them is Sheikh Ibrahim ibn Fawzi. Sheikh Ibrahim owns the little oil state of Darab on the Persian Gulf and he is a very wealthy man indeed. And an intelligent and reflective man. He is sending his children abroad for their university education and has decided to send his youngest son, Fuad, to an American school. Fuad is gifted at his studies and Ibrahim's concerns are not about intellectual adjustment, but Fuad's social integration. He wants Fuad to have his share of fun, but not to become another Persian Gulf playboy. For this reason, the idea of a college fraternity appeals to Ibrahim. As far as he can tell, a fraternity is a house in which many boys at a college live together under the apparently interlocking supervision of a house "mother," of the college authorities and of a national organization staffed by adults. Members of the fraternity call each other "Brother," help one another and engage in boyish pranks. But Ibrahim has the caution of a Bedouin and wants to know more. So he has hired you to observe and to describe to him how fraternity Theta really works.

You might contact the National Theta Society, get its documents of incorporation, constitution, and by-laws as well as a list of current officers and then get comparable documents from the Theta fraternity of the University to which Ibrahim plans to send Fuad. You could summarize the documents in good memo style, bind the memo and the documents in an official looking folder and send them, with a bill, to Ibrahim.

Ibrahim would be less than satisfied. And with good reason. Suppose you wanted to know how Darab really works and Ibrahim had sent you a copy of the Koran and a bill; would you be satisfied? Both Theta and Darab are much more than their official rules and though it sounds discordant, the law of each may have little to do with the official rules. In order to operate effectively in and influence, let alone understand, Theta or Darab, you will require a good sense of the processes in each in which policies are made, changed and applied and in which the good and bad things in life are distributed; a sense, in short, of what Ehrlich in a phrase of unfulfilled promise called "the living law."

If you spent some time in Theta, you would discover that there are, indeed, "right ways" of doing things and that violations of some of those demands could involve serious punishments. But those "right ways" are not necessarily what has been prescribed in the by-laws drawn up a generation ago by men in the New York office. "Right way" is probably contemporaneously determined and redetermined by those who play some effective role in life of the local Theta Society; perhaps the house mother, student leaders, university authorities, local police, clergymen and so on. Bear in mind that those who play effective roles may not agree on what is "right" for every issue and that the possibility of punishment for deviation may vary depending on who you run afoul of: the house mother, the local police, the university authorities. And, of course, as Ibrahim well knows, it may depend on who you are. With all due respect to the equal application of the law, it helps to be the son of someone rich and powerful when you get into trouble.

Consider an example. Article 4(1) of the Constitution of the National Theta Society states that cheating is inconsistent with the ideals of the Theta society and is prohibited. Article 4(2) states that all members of Theta will immediately report cheating to the appropriate authorities in the university; Article 4(3) states that cheaters as well as those who fail to report them will be expelled from Theta. Observation of actual behaviour in Theta reveals quite a different pattern. Not only has no one ever been expelled under Article 4, but the one case of a complaint filed by a student led in effect to his own expulsion: the informer was utterly isolated and himself resigned after a month. In fact, Theta actually maintains a filing system of exams and papers and a basic operational principle of Theta is reciprocal student aid through that vale of tears called education: in a word, cheating. Though some professors don't take it seriously and others are too timid to apply sanctions against students who cheat, university policy is plainly against cheating.

Consider another example. House Regulation 9 prohibits females from staying in a resident member's room beyond 9 p.m., a decorous provision both in its purpose and its orderly assumption that properly raised ladies and gentlemen will not engage in sexual relations before 9 p.m. Regulation 9 was passed by the National Society in 1926 and a fine of $10 was set. In its day, $10 was a considerable sum and hence a sanction with real potential for deterrence and punishment. Alas, over the years both the U.S. dollar and Theta morality have depreciated precipitously. Now, the observer will discover that the regime of Regulation 9 has been transformed. Members of Theta regularly entertain their lady friends for the night and pay what is jokingly called (but seriously collected), the "shack fee"; it is half the price of a motel. Proceeds from the shack fund are used for an annual "Devil's Ball."

To argue that these examples are not Theta law, but persistent, indeed institutionalized, violations of Theta law will badly mislead Fuad and his father. Whatever you may mean by law, they have a practical interest in how things are done in a certain setting and by law they mean those expectations shared by relevant members of the group about the right way of doing things, expectations taken seriously enough by group members so that they will probably be sustained by some individual or group effort. By complying with the law as described in your well-bound memo, Fuad may discover that he has been expelled from Theta or the University.

If you compiled a code of the expectations actually held by the relevant members of Theta, you would be supplying Ibrahim and Fuad with much more relevant information. Sitting 7,000 miles away in Darab, they would have a much better idea of life in Theta. But the picture would still be incomplete, for it would be quite static. No code is self-creating or self-applying and Ibrahim, a law maker and law-applier in his own right, knows well that the personnel and procedures of the system may be as important as the content of the norms themselves. How are the norms of Theta created and sustained over time; how are they challenged and vindicated or terminated? How are they applied in concrete cases, sanctioned and reviewed?

The written by-laws may prescribe for these matters, but as before, one must check words against practice before inferring the expectations of the effective and relevant actors in Theta. The by-laws may say, for example, that the rules of Theta must be made in the New York office. In practice, most of the rules are made regularly in the local chapters. The by-laws may prohibit discrimination in recruiting members; in practice, there may be absolute discrimination in certain chapters. The point is not who should be making these decisions according to certain texts, but who is actually making them.

These questions cannot be resolved by inquiring of a text but only by an inquiry into a social process. Terms such as "process" or "system" have been developed in modern social science to refer to the many interrelated features—social, psychological, biological, ecological—of human behaviour. Theta can be understood as a collection of people, with some overlapping and some conflicting perspectives, interacting in situations which can be characterized in terms of spatial location, degree of organization and institutionalization, duration and perception of crisis, drawing on bases of power which may be tangible and symbolic and using those bases in a variety of strategic programs with a variety of outcomes and longer range effects.

The process of Theta does not take place in a vacuum or within hermetically sealed social boundaries. Much of the behaviour within Theta cannot be understood without extending the focus of observation to take account of factors which might not appear directly relevant to Theta, but which closer examination would show to be very influential. For example, pervasive cultural values may have important effects on Thetan behaviour. Theta 1 may be located at a Baptist College in a small town with unique, intense religious ethos. Theta 2 may be in a region which practices sharp and open discrimination in virtually all social sectors. Theta 3 may be in an urban environment which imparts more cosmopolitan values to every aspect of university life.

Insofar as an observer detailed these specific and more general features of Thetan life in the terms I have suggested, Ibrahim with his own political sophistication would have a rounded and almost breathing sense of the fraternity. But not a sharp sense of how Theta decisions are made; and this is extremely important to Ibrahim. The inclarity here would derive from the generality of the word "decision." A decision, of course, is a choice and a lawful decision is a choice made in conformity with appropriate procedural and substantive norms. But one does not just "make a decision." A variety of distinct functions or operations are concealed in the word "decision" and any one who aspires to a fundamental understanding as well as a minimum effectiveness in influencing decisions will have to unpack that term.

———

We can summarize this sort of inquiry in the following way. In looking at what is going on in the community (the social process), the first thing you want to do is to look at it comprehensively. Then you want to be able to identify by whom and how effective power is being used. Since you are particularly concerned with how decisions or choices are going to be made, you will want to identify the way key decisions about decisionmaking itself are taken. And of course you will want to understand what the elements in decisionmaking are: making law, applying it, terminating it and so on. We might summarize this as follows:

1. Focusing Comprehensively
2. Focusing in Detail on Relevant Features of:
   a. the environment
   b. the processes of effective power
   c. the processes by which legal decisions are made
   d. the outcomes—in terms of production and distribution of the things, (the burdens and benefits, or "values") that decisions involve, including effects on the environment.*

David Cavers has observed that "Law is a problem-solving profession. It is at the point of translating knowledge, values and ideas into a just and workable plan that the work of the lawyer and legal scholar is likely to be most useful."**

This sort of problem-solving involves determining what you want to happen, confirming that it is not likely to happen by itself, identifying relevant conditions, clarifying the preferred alternative and the methods of achieving it and finally calculating the steps that can be taken to implement it under those sticky conditions characteristic of the "real world."

If, as is the case in the Penntown example, you want to know how you can make changes in Penntown that serve the interests of your client, yourself, or the entire

---

*A more complete and detailed statement of the items relevant to decisionmaking is set out in the Appendix to this chapter.

**D. Cavers, *Report to the Harvard Law Faculty Concerning Research Activities in the Harvard Law School* 52 (1955).

community of Penntown, you must look at things in another way. You must ask yourself first, what you want; second, what has happened with regard to this matter in the past; third, why did it happen; fourth, is it likely to happen in the future; and fifth, if not, what can you do to increase the likelihood of its happening. That is the basic handbook for making choices. In more general terms we could describe it as follows:

- Clarifying goals.
- Describing trends in terms of those goals.
- Analyzing conditions that affected those trends.
- Predicting, guestimating if necessary, future trends.
- Inventing alternatives to achieve the goals.

In the most comprehensive sense, the practice of law is the practice of problem-solving, for yourself, for your clients, and for the community at large.

The sorts of inquiry called to mind in the Penntown and the fraternity examples are only a small part of the practice in which many lawyers may engage in the course of their careers. There are, of course, the more conventional legal and clerical tasks. There is also a political component. In the United States, in particular, lawyers have traditionally played many leadership roles in many community functions. Even those lawyers who view themselves as operating properly only in the private sector will find that by virtue of their training, they are called upon to contribute to civic activities: in school boards, local and state elections, and so on. In professional contexts, lawyers will discover that they are not simply arguing about and applying legislation but often drafting it or testifying at the municipal, state or federal level as to the comparative wisdom of proposed innovative policies, or of existing policies resisting obsolescence. In David Riesman's words, the lawyer will be helping people determine what they may and what they should want.

The problems this book poses range over a spectrum of legal practice, from the Penntown example, to the more mundane activities of routine practice, and on to major constitutional and even international decisions which a lawyer may be called upon to assist in making. For each problem, we will try to determine the effect on problem perception and solution of different legal theories or jurisprudential "frames," or i.e., different congeries of ideas that seem to be used routinely though often unconsciously by practitioners as well as advocates of one jurisprudential school or another. Consider, for example, two hypotheticals, one arising in Central America, the other much closer to home.

The Justice's Dilemma

Claiming a communist threat, a junta of colonels has seized control of Nijotas, a small, homogenous and heretofore democratic republic in Latin America. The constitution has been suspended and Nijotas has been converted into a police state. Ironically, many of the changes are now being accomplished with refined legal precision. Leaders of the bar, cooperating with the junta, have drafted a new constitution legitimizing the regime. Even the increasingly frequent applications of official terror are being gilded with a patina of sophisticated legalism.

Lopez-Alcalde, Chief Justice in Nijotas, has a deep personal commitment to democracy, to legality and to human dignity. Because of his numerous publications and his activities in international organizations, he has a worldwide reputation as a jurist and a humanist. The junta has already purged many on the Bench and in the *soi-disant* Ministry of Justice, but Lopez has not been removed. It is clear that the junta feels that it needs Lopez' reputation to give the regime a degree of legitimacy inside and outside the country. Lopez is well aware of the fact that the regime is using him and will dispense with him if his actions no longer serve its purposes. While he is as frightened for his physical safety as any other person, his commitment to certain ideals of the law is sufficiently intense to generate a deep personal conflict.

What are Lopez' alternatives?

1. Accept the reality of naked power and comply with it in order to safeguard himself and his dependents.
2. Retreat inward and wait for a change.
3. Continue as Chief Justice in a manner compatible with safety and a low profile, but seek in each decision to mitigate the evils of the junta.
4. Go into exile and work against the regime from abroad.
5. Soak himself in gasoline and set himself afire on the steps of the courthouse in protest over the regime.
6. Join the guerrillas in the mountains.

Admissions and Hiring Dilemmas

Arkensota State Law School reserves twenty percent of the places in each entering class for specified minorities; that amount is roughly proportional to the percentage of these minorities in the population at large. Dick White, with an average of 76 is refused admission, but 30 minority students with averages below 70, are admitted. The faculty hiring policy requires that at least 40% of all newly hired faculty members be members of specified minority groups until they constitute 20% of the faculty. Jane de la Majorité, who applies for a position, is rejected while a minority member, whose academic and overall credentials are alleged to be inferior to hers, is hired.

Should the norms and operations of society be structured to afford Dick and Jane relief or to grant minority preferences? Why? If so, is the method being used the best available? If Dick and Jane are entitled to relief, what should it be?

———

Lawyers should be wary of thinking in terms of "yes-no" or of two exclusive options. Many options present themselves in these and other hypotheticals. You will notice that each option is largely shaped by a set of assumptions about social goals and methods of decisionmaking which influences the analysis, characterization and resolution of the hypothetical problems. The following chapter explores certain basic conceptions of law that are necessary for carrying the discussion forward. Subsequent chapters will explore, through traditional jurisprudential writings as well as cases, a select number of these legal theories, frames or assumptions of jurisprudential schools. In each of these chapters, try to reconsider the *Dilemmas* in terms of the jurisprudential assumptions of the different schools and the distinctive ways each of them would characterize, analyze and solve the *Dilemmas*.

The underlying theme of this book is that law does not consist simply of mental exercises about abstract notions or rules but entails making hard choices, whether for society in general or for a particular client. Law is a challenge to action. Thus, each chapter, exposing and developing a different legal theory or frame of juris- prudence, asks how that jurisprudence would influence problem-solving and decisionmaking and, at a later stage, whether its influence on decisionmaking is beneficial or pernicious in terms of the goals of society.

Social goals are not simply a given. In a democracy everyone is supposed to participate in their determination. Lawyers, as David Riesman observed earlier, by their training, can make special contributions to the clarification of the common interest. But they are frequently viewed as little more than hired guns for fat cats. Mills has captured one view of the contemporary American corporate lawyer's image in his scathing comment that:

> He [the lawyer] has become a groomed personality whose professional success is linked to a law office, the success of which in turn is linked to the troubles of the big corporation and contact with those outside the office. He is a high legal strategist for high finance and its profitable reorganizations, handling the affairs of a cluster of banks and the companies in their sphere in the cheapest way possible, making the most of his outside opportunities as an aide to big management that whistles him up by telephone, impersonally teaching the financiers how to do what they want within the law, advising on the changes they are making and how best to cover themselves.
>
> The complications of modern corporate business and its dominance in modern society, A.A. Berle Jr. has brilliantly shown, have made the lawyer 'an intellectual jobber and contractor in business matters' of all sorts. More than a consultant and counselor to large business, the lawyer is its servant, its champion, its ready apologist, and is full of its sensitivity. Around the modern corporation, the lawyer has erected the legal framework for the managerial demiurge.*

This is only one side of the coin. Above all, lawyers in a modern industrial democracy are citizens who have benefitted from a training which provides them with special skills relevant to responsibilities in the body politic. In this respect, the lawyer in a democracy, and jurisprudence in general, would abdicate much of their responsibility if they did not address fundamental questions about political direction, policy clarification and moral responsibility.

In all of these functions, lawyers require a set of conceptions and working methods that permit and help them to grasp the context in which they operate, the objectives they are trying to achieve, the obstructions likely to be encountered and some appropriate method for making choices. In particular they will require some way of establishing and appraising social goals and values as a necessary step in determining how problems should be solved. We are not suggesting that the technical and clerical aspects of practice which often dominate contemporary legal education are unimportant, but that they are of limited and perhaps subordinate importance. Robert Storey put it succinctly: "Builders of the law we must have, but somewhere in the profession we must find those who can perform the services of architects of the law. . ."** At some point, every lawyer will find that he or she is called upon to be the architect. The conceptions and methods that serve as tools in that role are part of the essential subject matter of jurisprudence.

A good deal of the inherited literature of jurisprudence, we will see, is quite unrelated to the performance of these functions or, more broadly, to solving social

*C. W. Mills, *White Collar* 23 (1953).
**R. Storey, Responsible Leadership and Legal Skills, in *University of Chicago Law School Conference of Law and Legal Education* 38, 42 (December 4, 1952).

problems. Much of that jurisprudence was designed to deal with problems that are no longer of social concern; much incorporated implicit preferences that are unacceptable to contemporary values. In terms of the objectives and needs sketched out above, a lamentably large part of the jurisprudence being written nowadays is irrelevant, substituting elegance in logic-chopping for the development of conceptions and tools indispensable to understanding and performing critical professional functions. A great deal of contemporary jurisprudence that does try to grapple with real problems gets no further than studying judges in court and the rules and principles purportedly deciding cases.

In the chapters that follow different schools of jurisprudence will be presented on their own terms as well as for the impact that they will have on analogous problems you are likely to encounter in your own varied practices. In each chapter we will be concerned with understanding, as sympathetically as possible, what jurisprudential writers understood by legal theory and jurisprudence, how they conceived the functions of lawyers in society, and what lasting contribution, if any, they have made. But we will be equally concerned with the positive or negative effects that these jurisprudences have on the problem-solving we think central to the practice of law in a contemporary industrial democracy. As we go along, we will attempt to summarize and synthesize the valuable lessons that can be learned from inherited jurisprudences as well as those legacies which are either wrong or obsolete and should be discarded.

We hope these materials will explain some of the many functions and complex ethical and practical problems presented to lawyers in the many chores they now perform and can anticipate performing in the 21st century. That is the *raison d'être* of this book. Let us be blunt, for the tasks are enormous and time is precious. Legal theory or jurisprudence is of importance only if it contributes to problem-solving for our profession and society. If it does not, there is no reason why it should be incorporated in the law school curriculum and distract the attention of those preparing to serve their communities and fellow citizens from matters of real importance. This is not to say that utility should be conceived of in a narrow "nut-and-bolts" fashion. Many of the points raised in the materials that follow and/or matters that we hope will come up in the discussions they stimulate may not appear to be immediately or directly exploitable. It is only in the narrowest and most sterile conception of any science that one insists on immediate application.

APPENDIX

Tools for Decisionmaking

In Chapter 1, we have sketched, with great brevity, a method or model for performing some of the professional tasks encountered in the Penntown or the Fraternity examples. We suggested that ways of looking at yourself and the processes within the communities you wish to influence and a set of operations for actually making choices are effective tools in understanding and trying to bring about social changes. It may seem unusual to speak of tools in reference to ideas, concepts or methods for focusing one's attention, gathering information and thinking about and then trying to solve certain problems. But a tool is any artifact created and wielded by a human being to facilitate the performance of a task. A collection of coordinated concepts or methods is an artifact, devised by people and refined through experience, which serves as a tool for those who seek to understand or to influence choices of decisionmaking. It may be useful to spell out, in more detail, the different tools or artifacts that together comprise a well-equipped decisionmaker's tool box.

The concepts and methods we are going to describe, which in coordination comprise a single tool, are made up of four components. The first is designed to make the person using the tool more effective. We will refer to it as the observational standpoint and suggest certain subsidiary operations that may be necessary to make this particular part of the larger operation more efficient. The second component deals with the ways that this observer looks at the community (or communities) of concern. The use of a scientific instrument for observation can be enhanced by using different types of lenses, each designed to focus most sharply upon one aspect of its target and to reduce, filter out or suppress other aspects. The concept considered under focus can be likened to these lenses. The third part of the model relates to what the observer looks at: the processes he or she is trying to influence and which, in turn, influence observers and decisionmakers. The fourth component of the model is comprised of the actual techniques for making a decision or choice.

Let us consider each component in order.

Who? Observational Standpoint and Self Scrutiny

In all matters that involve looking at and trying to influence aspects of the social process, the ultimate instrument of both observation and choice is—you, the individual personality or the self-system, those interactive elements that operate within a person and that influence perception and choice.

Two points are of major importance here. The first—involving vantage—is the need to view things not as a member of the group or the community you are observing but as someone disengaged and separate from it. This is, of course, a way of thinking, not an actual physical withdrawal. If, for example, you are examining your class in order to explore ways in which you can increase the effectiveness of your behavior within it, you always remain a member of the class, no matter what vantage point you take. Nonetheless, trying to take a standpoint "outside" the class is a way of giving yourself a different perspective on the group you are trying to influence and a way of seeing yourself in it differently.

A second point of importance is the need to observe *yourself* as the instrument of observation and choice. All of us are subject to a variety of influences and conditionings which determine the way we view and choose and which have the potential for distorting both of those actions. There are three potential sources of distortion: (i) emotional and sometimes neurotic tendencies which exist in all human beings; (ii) parochial tendencies which are a result of acculturation within groups, nations and language systems and to which we are all prone; and, finally, (iii) the distortions which derive from intense training within certain institutional settings, for example training in the law. For each of these, the responsible decisionmaker or appraiser should develop methods for scrutinizing the self-system and determining the extent to which emotional tendencies, sub-group parochialisms or institutional biases are distorting or skewing observation and choice. There is a rich body of technique available from the social sciences for the performance of this task.

LOOKING HOW? FOCUS

What are the "lenses" which ought to be part of the observational apparatus of observer and decisionmaker? Some focal requirements would seem obvious. It is certainly necessary to be comprehensive, to start with a macroscope rather than a microscope. Real problems rarely come with a neat disciplinary label announcing "this is an economic problem," "this is a political problem," and so on. Moreover, the boundaries—geographical and disciplinary, to name only two—which we are trained to accept as real, are not respected by actual problems which frequently transcend municipalities, states and countries. An explicit emphasis on a comprehensive focus, then, will permit the observer to be assured that he or she is looking at the entire area relevant to a particular problem. On the other hand, one must appreciate the fact that the resources of observers and decisionmakers are limited. Hence the need for comprehensiveness must be balanced by the need for some degree of economy or selectivity.

Theory is important for focus, for the explicit or implicit theory of an observer expresses conclusions about which features, variables and relationships are worth examining and which are not. Plainly, the observer will require some realistic theory about law or authoritative decision. As the examples in Chapter I indicated, a purely textual or formalistic theory of law will overlook stable and expected patterns of decision which may be the crucible of real decision and hence the concern of both observers and those who are trying to influence the course of behavior within a particular community.

It would be a serious error to exclude from consideration the subjective factors influencing behavior. Similarly, the examples in Chapter 1 emphasized the need to take account not only of what people say and what is written on the books, but also what is actually done. What is called for is a focus that balances emphasis both on what people say and what they do. We refer to this as the need for a balanced emphasis on perspectives (what people say and think) and operations (what people do). Related to this consideration is the need to look at both expectations of what is right, the focal target of most conventional legal work, and what is actually going to be done and will be effective. We refer to this as the need for a balanced emphasis on authority (what people think is right) and control (what actually will be done).

The examples in Chapter 1 underlined the need for a dynamic and process-oriented conception, not of a constitution, but of a constitutive process. Indeed, the decisions over time that establish and maintain the basic institutions for making decisions should not be referred to as a constitution, for the word imports a document which expresses with exactitude how these decisions actually take place or how they are currently expected to take place. The document may not reflect either of those dimensions accurately. Hence the need for a lens which focuses on the constitutive *process*, an ongoing decision process in which authority and control are deployed to establish, maintain and change over time the fundamental institutions of decision in any community.

Citizens of polities like the United States and the United Kingdom will need an additional focal lens, for in each, a key legal concern has become the maintenance of what is often called the private sphere or privacy. This focus would contrast those sectors in which behavior is regulated by the community with rather severe sanctions for deviation from the norms prescribed, and those sectors of society which are not so regulated, but in which behavior is supported by relatively mild sanctions which do not derive from the state apparatus. This focal element would thus distinguish what we might call the "public order" from the "civic order."

At What? The Targets of Observation: Processes of Authority and Control

The whole object of making social choices or decisions is to change behavior "out there" so that in the future it leads to the production and distribution of values in ways that conform more to the preference of the decisionmaker. But is it sufficient simply to refer to the processes one wishes to change (or to stabilize) as something "out there?" Plainly, you can gather information you require about these processes and bring pressure to bear on the key points to secure changes better if you can describe those processes with some precision. We suggest the use of a six part or "phase" description of any interaction viewed as a process. We will call it a "phase analysis." Specifically, we suggest that you ask yourself *who* are the relevant actors in the situation (participants), *what* are their subjectivities, their identifications, expectations of past and future and their demands (perspectives), *where* they are interacting (situations), *what* resources are being brought to bear in the particular interaction in order to influence outcomes (bases of power), *how* those resources are being manipulated, whether coercively or persuasively and whether at particular elite members or at broad audiences (strategies), and finally, with *what* outcomes.

Outcomes themselves can be described in more detail by specifying the things human beings want. That may seem simple; most healthy human beings want something of virtually everything. Everything is a big word. Both from the standpoint of someone interested in intervening to change part of a social process and for the scholar determining preferences that will guide action toward or appraisal of changes, more precision is required.

Harold Lasswell addressed this problem by suggesting that the things people want can conveniently be referred to in terms of eight "values." By value, Lasswell meant no more than things or events that people desire: power, wealth, enlightenment, skill, well-being, affection, respect and rectitude. Specific sectors of society concerned with the production and distribution of each value or, as Lasswell put it, its "shaping and sharing" can be studied for purposes of understanding or changing.

Equipped with the phase analysis and with the spectrum of values, an observer can describe any process with whatever detail he or she wishes, and with a precision which permits one to identify different factors that influence behavior and which might be manipulated to bring about change. The phase and value analysis can also be used to describe the comprehensive community process, the effective power process within it, and the constitutive process described below. In a particular community, the outcomes of any of these processes can then be described in terms of the actual distribution of the critical values under study: power, wealth, enlightenment and so on.

The constitutive process, specialized as it is to the making and applying of policy for a community, is of special interest to the lawyer as it is frequently the process of decision through which changes can be economically achieved. Here, as elsewhere, additional refinement can increase effectiveness. We frequently speak of making decisions, but this is too sweeping a phrase. In the course of making decisions, many component operations or functions must be discharged. We find it useful to identify seven component decision functions:

- *Intelligence*: the gathering of information relevant to making social choices.
- *Promotion*: the agitation to have a particular preferred policy turned into community law.
- *Prescription*: legislation or the making of community policy as law.
- *Invocation*: the provisional characterization of some behavior as deviating from the prescription.
- *Application*: the specification of law to a particular set of events and the determination of a sanction.
- *Termination*: the ending of existing prescriptions or laws and the design of appropriate means of compensating those who had made good faith value investments on the expectation that they would continue.
- *Appraisal*: a consideration of the aggregate effectiveness of the entire decision process in terms of whatever community policies are to be realized and recommendations for structural or personal change.

DOING WHAT? THE INTELLECTUAL TASKS OF DECISION

"Decisions. Decisions." A characteristic of life in a consumer-based society is the ongoing making of choices by each of us for ourselves and often for others. Many of these choices are made on the spur of the moment and appear to be intuitive. Other choices, for example about career, about investment and so on, are made with more time and deliberation invested in them. The procedures for making choices in large complex organizations may coordinate the efforts of thousands of people including experts from many disciplines and take months or years.

Lawyers who must create new organizations not only make choices but design continuing choice-making procedures which will incorporate others. They must be able to describe these with sufficient clarity so that others can learn them and assume the roles designated. Decision, then, may be a spasmodic "gut" reaction, but it may also be described and analyzed in a more systematic fashion.

Imagine, for the moment, that you are thinking of going to law school. How would you design a strategy that would increase the likelihood of your being accepted to the school you prefer? Which, of the array of schools, is the one you prefer? If you reflect on this problem for a moment, you will see a series of tasks you must perform at some level of consciousness; the proficiency with which you perform them is likely to increase the chances of realizing your objective.

Consider first the question of which school. In decisionmaking, a problem is a discrepancy between what you prefer and what you predict. Before you can determine what your problem is, you must have a clearer idea of what your preference is. A determination of your objective or goal is more than simply getting into a law school. If, for example, you view law school as a step towards state office, plainly you maximize your chances if you go to law school in your state, as it will increase the contacts you will make with others who will be instrumental in achieving your goals. If you are interested in law as an intellectual pursuit, law school itself may not be necessary, but if you set your mind on it you may determine that some schools are likely to give you better preparation for intellectual inquiry into law than others. By the same token, if you are interested in law as a way of becoming wealthy, other law schools will present themselves as most attractive.

The determination of what your problem is will require, then, a rather precise statement of what your preference is. Let us refer to this primary intellectual task in making decisions as the task of *goal clarification*.

The specification of your goal delimits a specific part of past experience which may be relevant to its achievement. It is quite reasonable for you to ask yourself what you or others in similar situations achieved with respect to this or a comparable goal in the past. Such an inquiry into the past will suggest to you what strategies are appropriate to adopt, what obstacles you can anticipate encountering, what resources and allies you can mobilize and who your major adversaries or competitors will be. Review of matters in the past relevant to the realization of your goal can suggest the possible techniques available for its future realization and permit you to appraise each of them in terms of their past success or failure. Let us call this task of review of past trends, *trend analysis*.

Of course, things that have happened in the past do not necessarily repeat themselves in the future. For one thing, events in the past are embedded in a context which influenced their outcome. If you were certain that exactly the same context of conditions would prevail in the future, you could with some confidence assume that the same strategy used in the past would be likely to yield the same result in the future. But conditions often change, in some cases in sweeping fashion, in other cases in more limited ways that can still influence outcomes. Your review of past trends will be useful to you in determining future options and strategies only if you ascertain what context of conditions prevailed in the past and whether or not that context is identical or similar in projected futures. This intellectual task of identification and analysis of conditioning factors may be called, for convenience, *factor analysis*.

Consider our example of the problem of gaining admission to a law school. Salient changes in conditioning factors might include new legislation which requires schools to adopt admissions policies and procedures favoring members of certain minority groups. If you are a woman, you may conclude that your chances in the past would have been substantially less because of bias against women practicing in the legal profession. A changed conditioning factor which has either eroded or penalized that prejudice may indicate greater possibilities for you in general and, in particular, access to schools you might formerly have deemed impenetrable. If you are a member of a minority as defined by the federal government's Affirmative Action program, you know that this particular conditioning factor now enhances the possibilities of admission far beyond what they might have been a generation ago. Conversely, if you are not a minority member, you may calculate that your chances have decreased proportionately, for the limited number of places available in any entering class has been reduced, for you, by the policy of reserving a certain number for members of specified groups.

Law speaks reverently of the past and implies that it is concerned only with securing fidelity to certain agreements or prescriptions made in the past. In fact, law is concerned *only* with the future. Its concern, as the concern of anyone involved in problem-solving or choice-making, is to devise a strategy that will increase the likelihood of the eventuation of desired events (or avoidance of undesirable events) in the future. But this requires some way of assessing what alternatives the future may hold. In our law school example, you must, on the basis of the three prior tasks, make certain matter-of-fact projections about the likelihood of your achieving your goal by use of some of the techniques you have derived from past experience. No one is a prophet, but it is possible to project a number of fictitious futures and to see whether any of the techniques you have considered thus far appear to promise success in those futures. The efforts to project different images of possible futures and to incorporate them in your choice-making may be referred to as *prediction*.

You will have noticed that the intellectual tasks of decision we have considered must be used, in one fashion or another, by specialists in many disciplines other than law. Trend analysis is one of the functions of historians. Factor analysis is the sort of activity that sociologists are often engaged in. The predictive function is a task in which virtually all social scientists must engage. The distinctive contribution of the lawyer to choicemaking is the determination of alternative strategies for achieving goals. If your canvass of the prior intellectual tasks indicates that one of the older methods reviewed in your study of past trends is likely to achieve your goal, you may simply apply it. But if you think that it is unlikely to achieve your goal or if you think that there are alternatives that may increase its likelihood of realization, the intellectual task then becomes one of invention of alternative methods. People often seek out lawyers when they have some idea of what they want and some idea that their wish is not likely to be realized unless some additional efforts are undertaken. What the lawyer then does is invent alternative strategies. We refer to this task as the *invention of alternatives*.

The overall method suggested here can be graphically represented.

FOCAL LENSES

COMPREHENSIVENESS
SELECTIVITY
THEORY OF LAW
PERSPECTIVES & OPERATIONS
AUTHORITY & CONTROL
CONSTITUTIVE PROCESS
PUBLIC & CIVIC ORDER

INTELLECTUAL TASKS OF DECISION

GOAL CLARIFICATION
TREND ANALYSIS
FACTOR ANALYSIS
PREDICTIONS
ALTERNATIVES

OBSERVATIONAL STANDPOINT
(SELF-SCRUTINY)

TARGETS OF OBSERVATION
SOCIAL PROCESS

EFFECTIVE
POWER PROCESS ⇄ CONSTITUTIVE
PROCESS

· Participants
· Perspectives
· Situations
· Bases
· Strategies
· Outcomes

· Participants
· Perspectives
· Situations
· Bases
· Strategies
· Outcomes

COMPONENT
DECISION FUNCTIONS

Intelligence
Promotion
Prescription
Invocation
Application
Termination
Appraisal

[POWER · WEALTH · ENLIGHTENMENT · SKILL
WELL-BEING · AFFECTION · RESPECT · RECTITUDE]

TOOLS AND THEIR CRAFTSMEN

Taken together, these four items—observational standpoint, determination of focus, descriptions of the target communities and the intellectual tasks—comprise a complex tool which can make decisionmaking or choicemaking in any setting more efficient. Good tools are important but so is the skill of the hand and the discrimination of the eye of the person using them. Nor should practice be underrated. The tool we have described cannot be wielded effectively on one reading any more than one can perform with the skill of a major league baseball player simply by picking up a bat and checking a ''how-to'' manual on how to hit well. Tools for making choices will be used with greater proficiency the more they are used in a conscious and self-critical fashion.

A method like this or other analagous ones must, of course, take account of the environment in which it is used. Some decisions must be made in a split second; often many of the intellectual tasks cannot be performed with the leisure and comprehensiveness that you would like. But it is worth remembering that many decisions taken by individuals and by organizations need not be made immediately. Some of the most important decisions may be taken over periods of months or even years. In fact, some decisionmaking is an ongoing process, constantly responding to changes in the environment and constantly reviewing the appropriateness of goal formulations, the adequacy of trend analysis, the accuracy of factor analysis and so on. It would appear obvious that some investment of resources is likely to increase the proficiency of operation of a decisionmaking model. But there are points of diminishing returns. One of the basic questions for those who are in decisionmaking organizations is where that point begins. In short, the proper amount of time, energy and other resources to be invested in making a single decision depends on the context.

A.A.L.S., *Selected Readings on the Legal Profession* (1962).

R.A. Abee, Sociology of American Lawyers: A Bibliographical Guide, 2 *Law & Policy* 335 (1980).

J.S. Auerbach, *Unequal Justice: Lawyers and Social Change in Modern America* (1976).

L.L. Baird, A Survey of the Relevance of Legal Training to Law School Graduates, 30 *J. Legal Education* 688 (1978).

D. Benthall-Nietzel, An Empirical Investigation of the Relationship Between Lawyering Skills and Legal Education, 63 *Ky. L. Rev.* 373 (1975).

L. N. Brown & E. A. Dauer, *Planning by Lawyers: Materials on a Nonadversarial Legal Process* (1978).

J. Carlin, *Lawyers' Ethics: A Survey of the New York City Bar* (1966); *Lawyers on Their Own: A Study of Individual Practitioners in Chicago* (1962).

E. Cheatham, The Lawyer's Role and Surroundings, 25 *Rocky Mtn. L. Rev.* 407 (1953).

V. Countryman, *The Lawyer in Modern Society* (1966).

T. DaCotiis & W. Steele, The Skills of the Lawyering Process: A Critique Based on Observation, 40 *Tex. B. Foundation* 483 (1977).

The Legal Profession, 92 *Daedalus*, (1963).

J. G. Deutsch, *The Law of Corporations: What Corporate Lawyers Do* (1976).

J. Dowell, *The Corporate Counsel: A Role Study (1970).*

E. Dworkin, J. Himmelstein, & H. Lesnick, *Becoming a Lawyer* (1981).

J. F. Handler, *The Lawyer and His Community: The Practicing Bar in a Middle Sized City* (1967).

G. C. Hazard, Reflections on Four Studies of the Legal Profession, *Law and Society, A Supplement to Social Problems Summer*, 1965, at 46.

G. C. Hazard & D. Rhode, *The Legal Profession: Responsibility and Regulation* (1985).

J. Hurst, *The Growth of American Law: The Law Makers* (1950).

J. C. Goulden, *The Superlawyers: the Small and Powerful World of the Great Washington Law Firms* (1972); *The Million Dollar Lawyers: a Behind-the-Scenes Look at America's Big Money Lawyers and How They Operate* (1978).

K. Krastin, The Lawyer in Society - A Value Analysis ,*W. L. Rev.* 409 (1957).

J. Landinsky, Careers of Lawyers, Law Practice, and Legal Institutions, 28 *Am. Soc. Rev.* 47 (1963).

H. Lasswell & M. McDougal, Legal Education and Public Policy: Professional Training in the Public Interest, 52 *Yale L. J.* 203 (1943).

F. Lundberg, The Legal Profession, A Social Phenomenon, 178 *Harper's Magazine* 1 (1938).

B. Manning, New Tasks for Lawyers, in American Assembly, *Law in a Changing America* (1968).

O. Maru, *Research on the Legal Profession: A Review of Work Done* (1972).

R. E. Matthews, Legal Ethics and Responsible Leadership, in *University of Chicago Conference of Law and Legal Education* (Dec. 4, 1952).

M. Mayer, *The Lawyers* (1967).

T. Parsons, A Sociologist Views the Legal Profession, in *University of Chicago Conference of Law and Legal Education* (Dec. 4, 1952).

R. Pound, *The Lawyer from Antiquity to Modern Times with Particular Reference to the Development of Bar Associations in the United States* (1953).

D. Rueschemeyer, *Lawyers and Their Society: A Comparative Study of the Legal Profession in Germany and in the United States* (1973).

E. Robinson, *Law and the Lawyers* (1935).

R. Schwartz, The Relative Importance of Skills Used by Attorneys, 3 *Golden Gate L. Rev.*
   321 (1973).

E. O. Smigel, *The Wall Street Lawyer: Professional Organization Man?* (1964).

The 1971 Lawyer Statistical Report (B. H. Sikes, C. N. Carson & P. Gorai eds. 1972).

University of Chicago Conference of Law and Legal Education (Dec. 4, 1952).

A. S. Watson, *The Lawyer in the Interviewing and Counseling Process* (1972).

W. O. Weyrauch, *The Personality of Lawyers* (1964).

S. F. K. Zeman & V. G. Rosenblum, *The Making of a Public Profession* (1981).

CHAPTER 2

Myths, Multiplicity and Elites:
Appearance and Reality in the Law

Judge not according to the appearance.
John 7:24

In Dabastan, as in the United States, bribes to public officials are against the law. But, in fact, doing business in Dabastan involves an institution called the "spice box": very large bribes to key officials including the President and the Chief Justice. Those who do not pay the bribes as well as those who pay and complain find themselves entangled in red tape and subjected to extraordinary taxes and assessments which no commercial enterprise can survive. Clean Corporation has just established a cane refinery in Dabastan and received its first "spice box" assessment, to be paid to numbered accounts (apparently the President's and the Chief Justice's) in Geneva. As General Counsel for Clean Corporation, you are asked for your opinion on the proposition and suggestions of how to proceed. In particular, you are asked to consider whether the proposition is lawful in Dabastan.

In the preceding chapter, the lawyer sent to Penntown was obliged to look beyond the documentary universe of the law. In the Dabastan case, one of the first questions is "what is law," or "which of a number of possibly conflicting laws applies?" It has been argued that in looking at the documentary universe of the law, it is sometimes important to distinguish between substantial parts which are not and perhaps were never intended to be applied and those parts which actually are applied. The first, the "myth system," may perform many cultural and political functions, but is not really law in the conventional sense.

REISMAN, MYTH SYSTEM AND OPERATIONAL CODE,
IN FOLDED LIES 15–36 (1979)

From the standpoint of the disengaged observer, the most overwhelming feature of social systems is the integrality and the seamless symbiosis of controller and controlled. But for certain problems, inquiry about legal control must distinguish the flow of behavior that makes up group life from those specialized institutions that purport to control, in diverse ways, what that flow of behavior ought to be. The specialized institutions—and they are not limited to the apparatus of the state—convey, both for themselves and for their targets, a very complete picture of how the group in question ought to be acting: a picture of the group as its members would like to, and to some extent do, imagine it. Membership in the group involves for most acculturation, a profound shaping of the personality, in processes that impart that preferred picture and make it an integral part of the identity and cognitive structure of the individual. That picture includes the official code of the group and much of its distinctive ritual.

The picture produced by control institutions does not correspond, point for point, with the actual flow of behavior of those institutions in the performance of their public function: indeed, there may be very great discrepancies between it and the actual way of doing things. The persistent discrepancies do not necessarily mean that there is no "law," that in those sectors "anything goes," for some of those discrepancies may conform to a different code. They may indicate an additional set of expectations and demands that are effectively, though often informally, sanctioned and that guide actors when they deal with "the real world." Hence we encounter two "relevant" normative systems: one that is supposed to apply, which continues to enjoy lip service among elites, and one that is actually applied. Neither should be confused with actual behavior, which may be discrepant from both.

A disengaged observer might call the norm system of the official picture the myth system of the group. Parts of it provide the appropriate code of conduct for most group members; for some, most of it is their normative guide. But there are enough discrepancies between this myth system and the way things are actually done by key official or effective actors to force the observer to apply another name for the unofficial but nonetheless effective guidelines for behavior in those discrepant sectors: the operational code. Bear in mind that the terms *myth system* and *operational code* are functional creations of the observer for describing the actual flow of official behavior or the official picture. The cynic who delights in nihilistic exercises would say there is no law. But from the perspective of an observer, as we shall see, parts of the myth system and the operational code make up the law of the community. From the perspective of many actors within a given social process, however, only myth system is law; hence operational code activities are perceived as "illegal" and profoundly wrong.

The myth system is not legal fiction writ large. Legal fictions are authoritative statements whose patent falseness is, by convention, never exposed. They abound in legal systems in which veneration for existing prescriptions is great and formal amendment procedures cumbersome and expensive. The device of the fiction permits those charged with making decisions to make existing law obsolete without changing it. From his historical perspective, Jhering called fictions "white lies." Bentham was much less affectionate, calling them "lies" and "swindling." Actually, a fiction is not a lie, for it does not, as Fuller remarks, intend to deceive; it is *consciously* false and, though the degree of explicit consciousness of its falsity may vary, virtually all who use the fiction know it for what it is: a device for circumventing a norm that is obsolete. In contrast, the myth system is not widely appreciated as consciously false. It does not express values that are obsolete, but rather affirms values that continue to be important socially and personally. Though not applied in the jurisdiction of the operational code, the myth system may yet influence decision.

The *locus classicus* of myth systems and operational codes is probably the Code of Hammurabi, a massive casuistic code ostensibly designed to guide decision makers of the ancient Babylonian Empire in a wide range of their official activities. There is substantial reason to believe that Hammurabi's code was never applied; those charged with making decisions and those seeking decisions from officials operated on the basis of an entirely different code of norms. However, the Code of Hammurabi should not be dismissed as irrelevant, for insofar as it expressed key values of the elite and the society of the time, it may have influenced behavior and even the formulation and application of the operational code.

In other studies, my colleagues and I have urged scholars to reserve the term *law* for those processes of decision that are both authoritative and controlling. The fact that people operating within social systems do not speak with such precision is one of the reasons there are discrepancies between myth system and operational code. The point here is that much formal law, which community members continue to view as law and which they are not willing to dismiss as survival, in W.H.R. River's sense of the word, will not only *not* be effectively enforced, but its violation will be accepted by those charged with operating it as the way things are done. Dissension can erupt when those not privy to the operational code become aware of its practices and begin to test them against the standards of the myth system. New strata may be gaining political power, or a counterelite may be in the process of accomplishing a takeover. One might say that these new groups simply do not ''know the rules'' (or that cynical politicians assume that their constituents don't know the rules). One would predict that in the course of time they too will learn an operational code discrepant in varying ways from their own myth system.

PRIVATE SYSTEMS OF PUBLIC LAW

Certainly there is nothing startling in the hypothesis of multiple legal systems, in the proposition that within larger, conglomerate groups all small groups have and, indeed, are characterized by their own normative codes. The very role proliferation in life in the modern metropolis, each role with its own distinctive ''vocabulary of motive,'' may accelerate this process. Groups as—such kin, racial, religious, language and dialect, specialist, and others—must have their own legal systems. What is distinctive about the operational code is that it is a *private* public law in systems in which public law is supposed to be public; those authorized to play control functions and those who deal directly with them come to accept procedures that deviate from the myth system as licit. George Washington Plunkitt, the doyen of machine politicians, once submitted a flagrantly unconstitutional bill in the New York legislature. When an opponent branded it unconstitutional, Plunkitt is reputed to have replied, ''What's a constitution between friends?''

Elites in a power process are those who have more power and influence than others. Their assumption—a varying mixture of self-service and community service—that they bear special responsibilities generates the feeling that they may, and sometimes must, take certain liberties. Because their function, as they perceive it, is to maintain group integrity, they will ''have the courage'' to do what is necessary to achieve that objective, but they will suppress publicization of these means of achievement in the interests of the community and to preserve the very integrity of the myth system that has been violated by their operations. Surely the most venerable formulation of this view is in that handbook for the elite, Plato's *Republic*. In book V, Socrates remarks coolly that ''our rulers will find a considerable dose of falsehood and deceit necessary for the good of their subjects.'' The exclusiveness of this elite prerogative is made patent in book III:

> If any one at all is to have the privilege of lying the rulers of the State should be the persons; and they, in their dealings either with enemies or with their own citizens, may be allowed to lie for the public good. But nobody else should meddle with anything of the kind; and although the rulers have this privilege,

for a private man to lie to them in return is to be deemed a more heinous fault than for the patient or the pupil of a gymnasium not to speak the truth about his own bodily illnesses to the physician or to the trainer, or for a sailor not to tell the captain what is happening about the ship and the rest of the crew. . . .

Of course, the elite rationalization of its operational code presents extraordinary opportunities for abuse. In constitutional democracies it short-circuits the very controls on officeholders that are at the heart of popular constitutional government. Since the notion of such controls is itself a key part of the myth, the deceit that elites practice must be further compounded so that responsibility for actions under the operational code can never be attributed to the leader. President Eisenhower took responsibility for the U2 flights over the USSR and somehow the Republic survived. But after President Kennedy had authorized the 1961 invasion of Cuba, one of his advisors, Arthur Schlesinger, wrote a confidential memo to the president, advising:

> The character and repute of President Kennedy constitutes one of our greatest national resources. Nothing should be done to jeopardize this invaluable asset. When lies must be told, they should be told by subordinate officials. At no point should the President be asked to lend himself to the cover operation. For this reason, there seems to me merit in Secretary Rusk's suggestion that someone other than the President make the final decision and do so in his absence-someone whose head can later be placed on the block if things go terribly wrong.

Almost two decades later, testimony before the Senate Select Committee on Intelligence revealed an extraordinary apparatus of circumlocution to protect the chief executive's plausible deniability.

Practices such as these obviously change the system of public order they are supposed to protect. Elites who are involved in these sorts of defections develop new, though often secret, justifications derived from historicism, mythical communions with the "will of the people," charismatic authority, or confirming vibrations from the Silent Majority. The convenient rule of interpretation for the Silent Majority is, of course, that silence is assent: hence Homer's dead host never fail to validate the politician who invokes them. The style of justification may vary; the persistent generation of the operational code does not. My hypothesis is that the code is a by-product of social complexity, generated by the increase of social divisions and specializations. All foci of loyalty have, by definition, at least the rudiments of a normative code. Those who specialize in the manipulation of power have their operational code. In the power context, the operational code is a private system of public law.

POPULAR RESPONSES

In systems in which government is generally unpopular in certain sectors or is viewed as a benefice that can be purchased and then used as a business, the privacy of the operational code is not at all startling. Nor, for that matter, would the privacy of the elite's operating procedures in a privately held corporation be deemed startling. It is only when the decision process holds itself as being public and popularly based that accounting for decisions by public procedures becomes a characteristic feature. With this development, tensions increase between the myth system of the group and the operational code of those charged with making decisions or those directly concerned with them. The effectiveness of the operational code, as well as group cohesion, will then depend on the comparative secrecy with which the code is practiced and, in particular, the insulation of those strata of individuals insufficiently "sophisticated" to appreciate its necessity or inevitability.

"Legality" may be taken to refer to conclusions drawn by members of the community as to the propriety of practices determined by some method of logical derivation from the myth system. Virtually all of the operational code discrepant from the myth system is thus "illegal." "Lawfulness," in contrast, may be taken to refer to the propriety of practices in terms of their contribution (or lack thereof) to group integrity and continuity, of which the myth system is part. Conclusions of lawfulness are teleological rather than logical and will vary according to time, context, and group need. Many parts of an operational code may be deemed lawful at certain times, though *the conclusion of lawfulness does not thereby integrate them into the myth system.* A director of intelligence who asserts he lied to Congress for "the good of the country" may, in some contexts, find considerable support for his deed. Though virtually no one will say it was or should be "legal," many may say it was "right." Whether an appropriate social goal is to secure conformity of myth system and operational code—that is, to police that for which there is no intention to police—is a question I shall address later.

Precisely because of the discrepancies between myth system and operational code, maintenance of the myth system is a dynamic process requiring ongoing contributions from many. Some obscuring of the operational code is consciously designed. "Not surprisingly, the ideological approach to politics and government is encouraged by the politicians themselves, who would much rather portray themselves as motivated by principle than by power or personal profit." For some who may be gaining few benefits from the operational code, commitment to social order is held at levels of consciousness so deep they are unaware of it. The social philosopher who elaborates a theory, as John Rawls puts it, "designed only for the special case of a nearly just society" substitutes a rosy dream world for the violence and often savagery of political struggles. Intellectual efforts of this sort basically reinforce the myth system and obscure the operational code. Similarly, the economist, equipped with the inimitable provisio of *ceteris paribus*, neatly insulates himself from the operational code and many other aspects of reality. The contribution of law professors, with the brief interlude of the legal realists, needs no comment.

Every belief system has a coercive component, but the apparatus for imposing "evils" or deprivations for deviations from orthodox belief may not be obvious. For example, the potential characterization of eccentricity may be enough to deter the more timid but nonetheless reflective members of a group from verbalizing their perceptions or deductions of the mythic quality of the formal normative code. More serious violators may be solemnly declared insane by the custodians of group sanity. Such characterizations neutralize the deviants and at the same time reinforce the accepted version of reality for the rest of the group. Public and prominent supporters of the myth system, in contrast, may often expect material rewards as well as the warm sunshine of approbation from those who believe the myth system and find public confirmations reassuring.

Where there are discrepancies between myth system and operational code, elites, as I have remarked, have a strong incentive to conceal those activities, acceptable under the code, and to maintain the integrity of the myth system. For a member of the larger public, not privy to the rules and practices of the operational code, the result is a picture of reality that at certain disturbing moments is seen not to be reality but rather a vast production. . . . Few things in life are authentically unilateral, and deception is often a shared process. While elites have an obvious interest in maintaining the integrity of the myth system, key personalities and entire strata in the public may abet the deception avoiding the truth like someone pulling blankets over his head to avoid the cold reality of dawn.

But support for the myth system is not exclusively benign, voluntary, verbal, or symbolic. Coercive efforts may be regularly mounted by those who make up the official apparatus to police belief in, and behavior in accord with, the myth system by sanctioning, according to some rationale, defections from it. Efforts directed toward policing beliefs may be even more urgent when there are widely perceived discrepancies between myth and operation. Policing is not exclusively hierarchical, a specialist function, or elite-initiated. Many group members who believe the myth may contribute to policing it, gaining in addition a certain gratification in the simple skill of "knowing the rules." Thus, in addition to the more patently coercive elements of the elite, teachers, clergymen, parents, even a stranger on the street may patiently explain to a youngster why a certain act should not be done.

Despite such efforts, there may be a point where perception of discrepancy between myth and operational code becomes so great that part of the content of the myth system changes, belief in it wanes, or crusades for reassertion of the myth burst forth. In group life as in personal life, erosion of the myth system is most serious and underlines the vital though intangible function that myth system performs. Belief in the myth system is a critical part of group organization, the basis for mobilizing many necessary collective activities. Because it has been transmitted, through acculturation, to the core organization of the individual personality, a waning of belief in it, without a replacement, may lead to anomie and personal disintegration. It may also lead to struggles between groups—classes, castes, religions, language and dialect groups—for one aspect of war, as McLuhan and Fiore observe, is the mobilization of the self to protect images of reality challenged by others:

> All social changes are the effect of new technologies (self-amputations of our own being) on the order of our sensory lives. It is the shift in this order, altering the images that we make of ourselves and our world, that guarantees that every major technical innovation will so disturb our inner lives that wars necessarily result as misbegotten efforts to recover the old images.

Whether the common technique of diabolization of an opponent is a product of intergroup tensions or a cause of them, it underlines a struggle of contending myth systems in which opponents protect, among other things, their own idols.

Anomie here does not mean that an individual no longer knows how to behave in specific settings, but that he has lost the more general guidelines for his orientation and the valuation of his environment. It is this coordinate personal mooring function of the myth system that drives individuals who may behave according to an operational code discrepant from the myth system, nonetheless to defend with extraordinary passion the myth system itself.

Perception of a routinized code discrepant from the myth system is not restricted to the elite. Groups, particularly large conglomerations, are composed of many smaller groups. The culture of some of these smaller groups may have unique perspectives on the more general myth system and operational code, for to an extent members of these subgroups may find it easier to apprehend the myths of the larger group as "facts." Perhaps because of this, some members have become specialists in the performance of certain operations for the larger group. But operators are not necessarily outsiders. Phrases such as "you've got to be practical," "watch the bottom line," "take a more realistic view," or "live in the real world" are usually the signals of operators who identify with the myth but perform group functions according to a discrepant operational code. Obvious domestic examples in official behavior might include the activities of intelligence agencies and certain police functions, for example, dealing with informers by paying money or reducing sentences, breaking and entering, planting bugs, unauthorized wiretaps, and the like. More compelling examples might include running undesirables out of town, or police execution of miscreants in vigilante actions. To characterize these activities as "unlawful" would not be illogical, yet it becomes imprecise and incongruous when the activities are carried out by the representatives of the law and routinely supported by judges charged with the supervision of criminal justice processes. The activities do indeed deviate from the myth system, and those who perform them defer to this fact by performing them in a covert or discreet fashion. Of significance here is the fact that those who perform them view them as lawful under the operational code.

In a story about police vigilantism in an American city, novelist Philip Rosenberg describes some of the frustrations of the honest cop who realizes, after years on the force, that he can expend most of his energy collaring small fry, but that he has only limited effectiveness against the criminal elite, for whom police activities will be little more than overhead or a business expense. When a young police officer is invited to join the vigilantes, he sweats out the implications:

> The next three days were a period of intense confusion for him during which he worked his way around all the things he had ever heard about whether anyone could ever be above the law, and about whether any ends could justify a handful of men in killing at their own discretion. And he decided that, yes, people could be above the law, that in fact one had a duty to oneself to put one's own sense of right and wrong above the law. This was, in a sense, sort of a policeman's conscientious objection, a recognition that there was a sort of higher law to which one could appeal, and that this higher law said it was possible that a man who was willing to bear the responsibility could in good conscience take steps he knew to be good.

Whether certain types of police vigilantism are parts of an operational code or are themselves unlawful is a question that, obviously, can be answered only in specific contexts.

Even when they are part of the operational code, there are special dangers in following these informal practices. It is always possible for reformers, some political opponents, or counterelites to prosecute belatedly these defections from the myth system either in response to popular outcry about deviations or in order to provoke such an outcry and then to demonstrate their courage and skill in protecting the myth system. The defense of the operational code will not prevail against these deferred prosecutions. When, as we shall see, there are myth system purges of operational code practices, the practitioners will often stand together and try to thwart the effort. Even if sanctions are imposed and new prescriptions are made to prevent the practices, it is likely that these practices will nonetheless continue if those who control them conclude that they are necessary for group life.

Operators, if pressed, will defend the operational code as self-evidently necessary for organizational efficiency, even survival. Enough of those concerned with appraising or policing lawfulness will accept such justifications to make behavior according to the operational code feasible. A legislature may pass a very open-textured statute to give increased discretion to those charged with applying it, after being told in executive session that some things just "have to be done" and it would be better for all if nothing were said about it. Legislators may avoid investigating certain sectors or during investigations carefully refrain from asking sensitive key questions. Prosecutors, using their broad discretion, will decide not to press investigations and prosecutions against some types of official behavior: mail openings, gift exchanges, or worse. Judges will accept suggestions from secret agencies that the national interest would be best served if a particular case were quashed. Journalists will not report certain things.

What is characteristic of the operational code is that it is shared by key members of the control apparatus, that its deviations from the myth system are selectively tolerated and depend on the contingency, the identities of agents and objects, the purposes of the act and the probable effects on the larger organization. There is no attempt to revise the myth. On the contrary, efforts ard made to maintain the integrity of the myth and to suppress all knowledge of the operational code. The justification of the discrepancies expressed in the operational code is that organizational efficiency and survival require it. Hence, in a type of casuistic reasoning, adherence to the operational code is not a violation of an oath to serve an organization, but rather the ultimate affirmation of that loyalty.

Politicians with heterogeneous constitutencies sometimes feel obliged to lie or, put more delicately, to dissimulate, to conceal their objectives and, in some cases, the irrevocable steps they are taking to accomplish them. Euphemistically speaking, they may talk among themselves of "preparing" or "educating" the public, but it is often the force of events—for example, a war of which they were covert but critical architects—that ultimately arouses and mobilizes a public whose response is reinforced by feelings of indignation against a cunning enemy. Some operators may secretly delight in the opportunity to exercise and enhance their power this way, but for other, more reluctant, operators an element of pathos tones their predicament. They may crave candor and be revolted by what they are doing, yet they feel themselves trapped by "the facts of life," the unyielding realities from which many are sheltered but which their elite position now permits, indeed forces, them to confront. Precisely because group security is threatened, secrecy about violations of the myth, whose broadcast could weaken group resolve, becomes all the more urgent. Hence "classification" of crimes of state finds new justification.

Doing the forbidden for a good cause, such as group integrity or survival, would presumably draw operators closer to the entire group. But the violations of group myth also create intense complicities and loyalties among the operators, for they are a type of *Blutkitt*, generating an ancillary code of silence, like the Mafia's *omertá*. One outcome of the discrepancy between myth system and operational code, therefore, is the sharpening disidentification of elite and rank and file and the increasing identification of elites.

THE ELITE RESPONSE

La Rochefoucauld's famous apothegm that "hypocrisy is the homage vice pays to virtue" should not obscure the point that homage is owed, and that something should be paid. How much is to be paid is a question of key political importance. Elites are operators and are certainly acquainted with discrepancies from the myth system; more important, they are well aware of the utility (to themselves and, perhaps in rationalized form, to "the system") of the of particular practices of the operational code. When popular disquiet grows, they will respond in ways that reinforce belief in the myth system, but often with a planned inefficiency. Some responses are uncomfortably obvious. For example, after a recent revelation of campaign fund abuses, Congress heroically cleaned house, among other things, by shortening the statute of limitations on the offenses involved from five to three years. Other responses are more beguiling in their complexity. The so-called *lex imperfecta* ("imperfect law," or "law without teeth") is often a conscious operator or elite design for dealing with aggravated myth system and operational code discrepancies. Where prescribed norms are clear but an otherwise effective administrative process has not established adequate enforcement mechanisms, has staffed them with exquisite incompetents, has permitted those enforcement mechanisms to atrophy or, as Key's examples show, has insulated certain activities from the reach of an enforcement mechanism, we are probably encountering a discrepancy between myth system and operational code. The late Alex Rose remarked, "To put people in law enforcement for the purpose of non-enforcement is a very big attraction for politicians."

In some instances, the imperfect law may have been designed for cynical motives; for example, to permit operators to do what rank and file are still prohibited from doing or to discharge, via the legislative exercise, popular dissatisfactions with certain public behavior. In other cases, a subtly crafted imperfect law may be a way of restoring confidence in certain discredited institutions or practices. Consider, for example, the Securities and Exchange Commission, established after the great market crash of 1929. A market in which those with substantial liquid capital can lend to those who wish to use it in productive enterprises is indispensable to a capitalist system. But the market cannot work without reassurances to investors that the economic system is productive and that producers are being candid and accurate in revealing how they will use the money and what returns can be reasonably expected. Both of these expectations were dashed in 1929, but apparently restored after the legislation and subsequent administrative activity in 1934. There are reasons to doubt that the SEC, as time-structured, staffed, and budgeted, can really police the market, but it performs its function if it creates *in the minds of potential investors* the expectation that it can. To carry it off effectively, it is vital that the bulk of the policers in the SEC profoundly believe in their budget and staff, criticize superiors who are too "political" (that is, see the larger picture), and cause periodic shake-ups.

In some cases, the imperfection is genetic, built into the very structure of the law in question. Sometimes the imperfection is blatant. Consider a 1975 amendment to the Arms Control and Disarmament Act. In order to assist the director of ACDA in the performance of his duties, any government agency preparing legislative or budgetary proposals with regard to the general area of armaments and military facilities "shall, on a continuing basis, provide the Director with full and timely access to detailed information, in accordance with procedures established . . . with respect to the nature, scope, and purpose of such proposal.'' The information gained may be shared with appropriate congressional committees to aid them in the performance of their function. The final subsection of the amendment adds, almost as an after-thought, ''No court shall have any jurisdiction under any law to compel the per-formance of any requirement of this section or to review the adequacy of the per-formance of any requirement of this section or to review the adequacy of the performance of any such requirement on the part of any Government agency (in-cluding the Agency and the Director).'' When Solon gives with one hand and takes with the other, he uses *lex imperfecta*.

A cognate species of *lex imperfecta*, performing a function similar to the imperfect law, is a legislative exercise that produces a statutory instrument apparently operable, but one that neither prescribers, those charged with its administration, nor the putative target audience ever intend to be applied. We might call this a *lex simulata*. The prototype is the Code of Hammurabi. One way of identifying such laws is by the absence of a meaningful legislative history. If the context is one in which legislative bills adverse to the interests of the target group are ordinarily contested but the particular bill is unchallenged and the difficulties of applying it to hard or to marginal cases are not raised, it is not unreasonable to assume that no one ever intended it to be applied.

Where such laws are ''legislated,'' they are akin, in function, to the flying buttresses of a Gothic cathedral; they seem to support parts of the myth system from which the operational code deviates unambiguously and routinely. That apparent support can be most reassuring to diminutive mortals looking up at those massive walls. The function of the legislative exercise is not to affect the pertinent behavior of the manifest target group, but rather to reaffirm on the ideological level that component of the myth, to reassure peripheral constituent groups of the continuing vigor of the myth, and perhaps even to prohibit them from similar practices. As elsewhere, the mere act of legislation functions as catharsis and assures the rank and file that the government is doing what it should, namely, making laws. Legislation here becomes a vehicle for sustaining or reinforcing basic civic tenets, but not for influencing pertinent behavior.

An amendment in 1971 to the Internal Revenue Code (it was changed again in 1977) would appear to be a salient example. Under the code, deductions are not allowed for a domestic illegal bribe ''which subjects the payor to a criminal penalty or the loss of license or privilege to engage in a trade or business,'' but, the code continues, ''only if such State law is generally enforced.'' The enforcement proviso permits a tax authority or federal court to temper application of the law prohibiting deductions for bribe payments by a consideration of the operational code actually prevailing in that commercial sector. But regarding bribery of foreign officials no such proviso exists. Section 162(c) (1) provides:

> No deduction shall be allowed under subsection (a) for any payment made, directly or indirectly, to an official or employee of any government, or of any agency or instrumentality of any government, if the payment constitutes an illegal bribe or kickback or, if the payment is to an official or employee of a foreign government, the payment would be unlawful under the laws of the United States if such laws were applicable to such payment and to such official or employee. The burden of proof in respect of the issue, for the purposes of this paragraph, as to whether a payment constitutes an illegal bribe or kickback

(or would be unlawful under the laws of the United States) shall be upon the Secretary or his delegate to the same extent as he bears the burden of proof under section 7454 (concerning the burden of proof when the issue relates to fraud).

Prohibition of deduction of bribe payments to foreign officials applies (1) even if the foreign law making it illegal is *not* generally enforced and (2) even if it is lawful according to the foreign law. This is a standard so pure that one doubts that it was any more than pious aspiration, without intention to control. From the period of its enactment to the current antibribery campaign, I have been unable to find instances of prosecution.

Another example of *lex simulata* is offered in the amendments to the Export Control Act of 1965. Amid agitation for greater United States resistance to the Arab boycott a bill was submitted prohibiting compliance by United States business. When opposition was mounted, the prohibition was diluted to require only a report to the Department of Commerce that a boycott request had been received. The report would go to the secretary of commerce "for such action as he may deem appropriate." The form that was actually prepared by the Department of Commerce indicated that respondents need not answer whether they actually complied with the Arab boycott request, hence few respondents answered this key question. One student of the legislation remarks, "The official opposition to the Arab boycott was essentially ritualistic, and the supposed deterrent effect of the reporting requirement was negated by the decisions not to require an answer to the critical question and to keep the completed forms confidential." What then was the function of the legislative exercise? To reassure those who felt that United States law was being violated by the Arabs, to affirm opposition to boycotts of other governments, and to create a bureaucratic process that seemed to implement the policy but that allowed business to continue as usual: *lex simulata*.

THE FUNCTIONS OF DISCREPANCY

Lex imperfecta and *lex simulata*, in their very ineffectiveness, express and reinforce the essential distinction between myth system and operational code. There is, to be sure, a measure of cynicism, particularly where the function of the discrepancy is to mediate between social classes. In many cases, however, the discrepancy between myth and code, captured by *lex imperfecta* and *simulata*, is cultivated and created in good faith (as a way of retaining fidelity to fundamental social values) and not, as would first appear, out of sheer hypocritical homage to virtue. Here, as elsewhere, the inquirer must accept the complexity of events, the multiplicity of inconsistent normative codes within a single functional legal system, the demands for behavioral accommodation, and the continuity of contradictions.

In their study of one pattern of deviancy within a factory, Bensman and Gerver noted the importance of the criminal practice to the working of the factory. "Crime," they say, "becomes one of the major operational devices of the organization . . . a permanent unofficial aspect of the organization." The operations themselves are performed discreetly, in deference to the "ceremonial aspects of law enforcement," are not characterized as crime, and are sanctioned as long as they are controlled by and serve those in charge.

The discrepancy between myth system and operational code enables

> the personnel involved to maintain the public values, while performing those
> actions necessary to attain the public or private ends appropriate to their eval-
> uations of their positions. Thus a form of institutional schizophrenia is the major
> result of the conflict of ends and the conflict of means and ends. Individuals
> act and think on at least two planes, the plane of the public ideology and the
> plane of action. They shift from plane to plane, as required by their positions,
> their situations and their means-ends estimations. In a sense, it is a form of
> double-think, and double-think is the major result of means-ends conflict.

The fact that individuals, including realistic operators, in some or even all cases
breach a certain norm does not mean that they wish to terminate it. On the personal
level, the self-initiation of ritual penance for breach of a norm by an individual, even
while he knows that in comparable circumstances in the future he will breach the
norm again, provides us with a telling example. While we cannot here enter into
examination of the guilt dynamics that give rise to such rituals, it is clear that one
of their major functions is to restore, on both social and personal levels, commitment
to the norms.

This is an important dimension of the discussion and, at the risk of repetition,
I emphasize that my thesis is not one of nihilism or the hypocrisy that so delights
the cynic. On the contrary. The concept of operational code does not mean that
everything is lawful, or that, in Ivan Karamazov's anguished words, "everything is
permitted." There will be much that remains unlawful and effectively sanctioned by
the appropriate community processes. Operators know that some discrepancies from
the myth system are licit and will be tolerated; others will not. In other words,
determining the "law" or the socially proper behavior in a particular setting necessitates a much wider social inquiry than the simple consultation of the formal law;
it may be myth system.

There is often a symbiotic relationship between myth system and operational
code, the latter, as we have seen, providing a degree of suppleness and practicality
that the myth system could not achieve without changing much of its content. From
the perspective of members of the community who are not privy to the operational
code of the specialist group, some operational code activities may well seem unlawful.
But often there will be a certain toleration or a desire for ignorance. A number of
writers have studied "dirty work" in society and have noted the coordinate generation
of ignorance when it must be performed.

In extended periods of social stability the discrepancy between myth and practice
will tend to be stable and even institutionalized. Unless one puts a special premium
on stability per se, this does not mean that every aspect of the operational code
contributes to group weal, that some invisible hand directs a complex but nonetheless
euphonious social symphony. From the perspective of community goals expressed
in the myth system or deduced by a disengaged observer, much of the operational
code may be profoundly dysfunctional during these and other periods. Indeed, parts
of the operational code may be designed to accord special benefits to elite members
while other parts may take on a *Blutkitt* character, making elite membership permanent
and irrevocable by participation in a taboo act. Many other practices that deviate
from the myth system serve to protect the entrenched position of subgroups, for
example, rewards granted on the basis of old-boyism or caste or ethnic ties rather
than merit.

During periods of rapid social change, discrepancies between myth and practice will be more unstable. Accommodations and rationalizations ordinarily provided by culture and general past practice will be less available, obliging each individual to make choices for himself. The same sense of comparative rulelessness and anomie often experienced in periods of relative stability by individuals or groups who are suddenly changing social position now becomes a more general experience, imposed on many who never sought change and who were willing to forswear its potential rewards in return for a routinized "peaceful" environment in which the ambit of choice was narrow. For very independent persons, these can be times of great opportunity; but for those who seek guidance and validation from their environment, these are times of heightened anxiety and often desperate searching for new leaders and meaningful rectitude systems.

NOTES

1. Consider which other parts of the "law" in the United States, in addition to those mentioned by Reisman, are mainly parts of myth systems rather than operational codes.

2. Identify other specific examples of *lex imperfecta* and *lex simulata*. How would you classify the norms aimed at achieving equality for all persons; governmental declarations regarding the promotion of peace; of justice for all; of a pollution-free environment; of fulfilling the minimal nutritional requirements of all people?

3. To what extent and in what ways is the prohibition of bribery in Dabastan myth system or operational code?

MULTIPLE LEGAL SYSTEMS AND LEVELS

Is it possible that Dabastan is subject to more than a single legal system and that some of these systems are contradictory? Leopold Pospisil, in the following selection, argues that within a single territorial community there are, in fact, a multiplicity of legal systems and not the single system we have generally associated with the apparatus of a state.

POSPISIL, LEGAL LEVELS AND MULTIPLICITY OF LEGAL SYSTEMS IN HUMAN SOCIETIES, 11 J. CONFLICT RESOLUTION 2, 3–9, 13–17, 24–25 (1967)

Traditionally, law has been conceived as the property of a society as a whole. As a logical consequence, a given society was thought to have only one legal system that controlled the behavior of all its members. Without any investigation of the social controls that operate on the subsociety levels, subgroups (such as associations and residential and kinship groups) have been *a priori* excluded from the possibility of regulating their members' behavior by systems of rules applied in specific decisions by leaders of these groups-systems that in their essential characteristics very closely parallel the all-embracing law of the society.

• • •

In her article on "Conflict Resolution in Two Mexican Communities," Laura Nader gives credit to Mauss (1906) and Malinowski (1932) for the idea that within a single society several legal systems may be operating, "complementing, supplementing, or conflicting with each other". . . . Unfortunately, although the impli-

cation of the existence of a multiplicity of legal systems within a society may be
drawn from the work of both of these scholars, neither of them stated this idea
clearly. Actually, each in his own way maintained the existence of a single system
of law in the Eskimo and Trobriand societies. Mauss described two legal systems
that operated in Eskimo nuclear and extended families. However, instead of showing
the coexistence of these two systems, Mauss claimed that one followed the other in
a rhythm dictated by the seasons: the legal system of the nuclear family controlled
the behavior of the Eskimo during the summer; in the wintertime, when nuclear
families established common residence and became an extended family, a legal
system for the larger group was instituted. . . . One may justifiably wonder what
happened to the nuclear family in the wintertime? Did it dissolve in the extended
family group which somehow redefined the relationships between the nuclear family
members for the duration of the arctic winter? From my research among the Nunamiut
Eskimo I know quite well that the contrary is the case: both legal systems coexisted,
functioning side by side, mainly by virtue of differentiated jurisdiction. Actually,
among the Nunamiut Eskimo two additional legal systems functioned simultaneously
with those of the nuclear and the extended family: that of the band and that of the
band faction. . . . Mauss, although describing two legal systems within an Eskimo
society, failed to break away from the traditionalist doctrine; although there were
two systems, only one, according to Mauss, was operational at a given time.

In contrast to Mauss, Malinowski did describe two conflicting systems of social
control in the Trobriand society, both of which functioned at the same time. However,
although his book provided a chapter with the heading "Systems of Law in Conflict" . . . , the content did not correspond to the title. He defined law as duties and
rights based upon the matrilineal principle, but the relations deriving from the conflicting patrilineal principle he called merely "usage." Actually, thus, it was matrilineal law and "patrilineal usage" that were in conflict rather than two legal
systems: "So that here the usage, established but *non*-legal, not only takes great
liberties with the law, but adds insult to injury by granting the usurper considerable
advantages over the rightful owner." . . . Consequently, Malinowski also failed to
conceptualize multiple legal systems within the same society and link them to the
pertinent societal structure.

Although the traditionalist view that law is monopolized by the state, or the
"society as a whole," has made a profound impact upon sociology and anthropology
and, as we have seen, still persists in many of the recent works on law in these two
fields, its simplicity failed to satisfy some noteowrthy legal scholars. In contrast to
what one might expect, it is interesting to learn that credit for the nontraditionalist
trend of thought which did not limit its inquiry to the level of state or society must
be given to jurisprudence rather than to the social sciences.

In 1868, the legal scholar Otto von Gierke had already directed attention to the
inner ordering of the *Genossenschaften* (associations), and he recognized in them the
essential features of law. Eugen Ehrlich, one of his followers, writes: "As a result
of his labors, we may consider it established that, within the scope of the concept
of the association, the law is an organization, that is to say, a rule which assigns to
each and every member of the association his position in the community, whether
it be of domination or of subjection . . . , and his duties; and that it is now quite
impossible to assume that law exists within these associations chiefly for the purpose
of deciding controversies that arise out of the communal relation". . . . So great was
the enthusiasm of von Gierke for the more or less autonomous entities of the society's

subgroups that he tended to an extreme view, diametrically opposed to the traditionalists' individualist legal thought of the nineteenth century. He promoted the associations to entities that somehow became distinct from the sum total of the members and of their interests. He went so far as to advance the idea of existence of a mystical "group-will" that was distinct from the wills of the members of such a group. Although this extremism obscured social reality by neglecting the role of the individual and by making a group of people into almost a living beast (thus giving rise to the unfortunate "Durkheimean trend" in sociology and anthropology), his emphasis upon the legal importance of the society's subgroups (associations) proved most significant in the subsequent development of legal thought, represented especially by Ehrlich, a lawyer.

Following in the footsteps of von Gierke, Eugen Ehrlich refused to accept legal orthodoxy and to recognize the state's (or society's) monopoly on law. Indeed, he explicitly stated that "It is not an essential element of the concept of law that it be created by the state, nor that it constitute the basis for the decisions of the courts or other tribunals, nor that it be the basis of a legal compulsion consequent upon such a decision." To Ehrlich, law was "an ordering" of human behavior, in any group of interacting people, no matter how small or how complex. To Ehrlich, human society was not composed of individuals who acted independently, but of people who of necessity acted always as members of some of the society's subgroups. Thus the people's behavior is not necessarily ordered by the all-comprising state law, but primarily by the "inner ordering of the associations"—Ehrlich's "living law." "The inner order of the associations of human beings," writes Ehrlich, "is not only the original, but also, down to the present time, the basic form of law." . . . Excellently and prophetically, Ehrlich points out in his own words the basic interrelationship of law and societal structure: "All attempts that have been made until now to comprehend the nature of law have failed because the investigation was not based on the order of the associations but on the legal propositions." . . . Thus Ehrlich actually laid the foundations for the modern anthropology of law, allowing law to be in existence also within those societies which were not legally unified or politically organized.

• • •

In his work *Wirtschaft und Gesellschaft* (1921) Max Weber, without trying to generalize for the laws of the various associations on the society's level and without attempting to force these into a nonrealistic "living law" that would contrast with the legal systems of the state, expressed quite explicitly the idea of the existence of several legal systems within a given society. First, he defined law so broadly as to be applicable to the ordering systems within the various social subgroups; then, "for the sake of terminological consistency, we categorically deny that 'law' exists only where legal coercion is guaranteed by the political authority. There is no practical reason for such a terminology. A 'legal order' shall rather be said to exist wherever coercive means, of a physical or psychological kind, are available; i.e., wherever they are at the disposal of one or more persons who hold themselves ready to use them for this purpose in the case of certain events; in other words, whenever we find a consociation specifically dedicated to the purpose of 'legal coercion.' " . . . Second, to Weber the nature of the coercion mechanism of the various consociations was not some sort of a mystical group will or group-opinion but an authority, in many ways comparable to that of the state: "It goes without saying that this kind of coercion may be extended to claims which the state does not guarantee at all; such claims are nevertheless based on rights even though they are guaranteed by authorities other than the state." . . . Thus Weber saw no basic qualitative difference between the state legal system and those systems created and upheld by the various subgroups of the society. He maintained no basic dichotomy comparable to Ehrlich's state law versus living law. Consequently, there is little doubt that Weber's sober approach to his inquiry into the nature of legal phenomena, by rejecting the mysticism and unnecessary philosophizing of his predecessors in favor of an empirical disclosure of social reality, marks a very significant advance in the field of the sociological jurisprudence.

However, it was not until the joint effort of a lawyer and an anthropologist produced *The Cheyenne Way* (Llewellyn and Hoebel, 1941), that the idea of multiplicity of legal systems within a society was formulated, and the relationship of the society's law to the legal systems of the subgroups (associations) was explicitly stated. According to the two authors, investigation of the all-embracing legal system of a society as a whole (the traditionalist law) does not offer a complete and workable conception of the legal order within that society. "What is loosely lumped as 'custom' (on the society's level) can become very suddenly a meaningful thing—one with edges—if the practices in question can be related to a particular grouping." . . . In other words, if one changes one's point of reference from that of the society as a whole and focuses upon the individual subgroups, "there may then be found utterly and radically different bodies of 'law' prevailing among these small units, and generalization concerning what happens in 'the' family or in 'this type of association' " made on the society's level "will have its dangers. The total picture of law-stuff in any society includes, along with the Great Law-stuff of the Whole, the sublaw-stuff or bylaw-stuff of the lesser working units." . . .

Although the authors did not systematically explore and contrast the differences between the various legal systems of the Cheyenne society's subunits, the book clearly laid the theoretical groundwork of a field of inquiry for the anthropologists of the future. Hoebel's subsequent departure from the well-expressed relativity of law and custom is to be regretted. In his more recent work he seems to hold a position that is not consonant with the views expressed above, and the orthodox emphasis upon the whole society's monopoly of the law appears to be resurrected when he states: "There are, of course, as many forms of coercion as there are forms of power. Of these, only certain methods and forms are legal. Even physical coercion by a parent is not legal if it is too extreme." . . . But, of course, this is true only if we take the society as a whole as the point of reference. According to the society's legal system, some regulatory means of its subgroups may indeed be "illegal."

• • •

In my quantitative investigation of the disputes among the Kapauku Papuans, Nunamiut Eskimo, and Tirolean peasants I found that the decisions of the leaders of the various subgroups bore all the necessary criteria of law (in the same way that modern state law does): the decisions were made by leaders who were regarded as jural authorities by their followers (that means that the leaders' decisions were actually complied with—criterion of authority); these decisions were meant to be applied to all "identical" (similar) cases decided in the future (criterion of the intention of universal application); they were provided with physical or psychological sanctions (criterion of sanction); and they settled disputes between parties represented by living people, the decision entitling one party and, conversely, obligating the other party to such a behavior (criterion of *obligatio*); . . . Consequently, the judgments and decisions of the authorities of the various subgroups were legal in the subgroups in which they were issued, being based upon their particular legal systems.

Because of these findings I reject the traditional presentation of law on the level of the society only and follow the unorthodox path of legal thought characterized by von Gierke, Ehrlich, Weber, Llewellyn, and Hoebel. Indeed I go a step further and claim categorically that "every functioning subgroup of a society has its own legal system which is necessarily different in some respects from those of the other subgroups." . . . Also, I am more radical than Llewellyn and Hoebel in proposing to delete the words "bylaw stuff" and "sublaw stuff" from the vocabulary of my discussion and refer to the matter that forms the content of the systems of social control of the subgroups as what it really is—the law. Consequently, the totality of the principles incorporated in the legal decisions of an authority of a society's subgroup constitutes that subgroup's legal system. Since the legal systems form a hierarchy reflecting the degrees of inclusiveness of the corresponding subgroups, the total of the legal systems of subgroups of the same type and inclusiveness (for example, family, lineage, community, political confederacy) I propose to call *legal level*. As there are inevitable differences between the laws of different legal levels, and because an individual, whether a member of an advanced or a primitive society, is simultaneously a member of several subgroups of different inclusiveness (for example, a Kapauku is a member of his household, sublineage, lineage, and political confederacy, all the groups being politically and legally organized), he is subject to all the different legal systems of the subgroups of which he is a member. Consequently, law in a given society differs among groups of the same inclusiveness (within the same legal level); thus different laws are applied to different individuals. Law also exhibits discrepancies between inclusiveness (between different legal levels), with the consequence that the same individuals may be subject to several legal systems different in the content of their law to the point of contradiction.

• • •

The multiplicity of legal systems in civilized societies has long been realized and mentioned in the legal literature by such authors as von Gierke, Ehrlich, Weber, and Llewellyn; its validity need not be demonstrated. It suffices here merely to point out, in a very sketchy way, examples of multiplicity of legal systems in three civilizations—the West, the Chinese, the Inca—that are not related to each other by legal tradition.

In a Western society that is composed of autonomous or semiautonomous administrative units, such as the United States, there exist, besides the federal or national legal system that is applied to the whole society (nation), the legal systems of its component states, many provisions of which actually contradict and conflict with federal law and the constitution. Many of these flagrant contradictions have been maintained until the present, when some of them are being ruled out by the US Supreme Court as unconstitutional (e.g. state laws pertaining to segregation and racial discrimination), while others are being carried on into the future. However, the multiplicity of legal systems does not end, according to von Gierke, Ehrlich, Weber, et al., at the level of the states. These authors clearly recognize that the various associations within the states have also formal bodies of regulations which, in essence, belong in the field of law, especially when they are recognized as valid by the superimposed state law.

I would like to go even farther and acknowledge the existence of legal systems in any organized group and their subgroups within the state. Consequently and ultimately, even a small grouping such as the American family has a legal system administered by the husband, or wife, or both, as the case may be. Even there, in individual cases, the decisions and rules enforced by the family authorities may be contrary to the law of the state and might be deemed illegal. Indeed, there are ruthlessly enforced legal systems of groups whose existence and *raison d'etre* are regarded by the state not only as illegal but even criminal. That criminal gangs such as Cosa Nostra have their rules, judicial bodies, and sanctions that are more severe than those of the state is common knowledge. What is not realized is that their rules and judicial decisions embody the same types of criteria as does the state law (authority's decision, *obligatio*, intention of universal application, sanction). Therefore the principles contained in the gang leaders' decisions qualify to be regarded as parts of legal systems, although these would be illegal, criminal, and invalid according to the legal systems of the states. To disregard such systems, as is often done in the writings of legal scholars, reflects not a cool scientific introspect but a moral value judgement that has its place in philosophy but not in the sociology or anthropology of law.

•   •   •

The recognition of multiple legal systems and levels, on the other hand, makes the pre-Communist Chinese legal situation understandable and meaningful. What appeared to a traditionalist as a corrupt, confusing, and unpredictable system, characterized by an almost absolute disregard of law, becomes a meaningful configuration of legal systems pertaining to specific groups, arranged into several levels according to the degree of inclusiveness of the types of social groups. Their study becomes a fascinating inquiry into the jural relationship of the structural units of the Chinese society rather than a frustrating exposition of confusing, illegal behavior of the Chinese people.

The statements above, referring to corrupt and illegal behavior, suggest that law differed profoundly on the various levels of Chinese society and was often contradictory. Thus, although the power of the father over the rest of the members of the group was curbed by the law of the state, in actuality in individual families "There were no *de facto* limitations on punishment by the father, whatever the *de jure* ones may have been." . . . The extreme punishment applied by the Chinese father, which certainly was "illegal" from the point of state law, was "severe flagellation with a bamboo rod from which a boy does not recover for a month" . .; the sons "sometimes were even beaten to death." . . . Similarly, although Article 985 of the Civil Code of the Republic of China stated explicitly that "A person who has a spouse may not contract another marriage" . . . , the law within the family ignored the state provision to such an extent that literally "thousands of businessmen, officials, landlords and others" who violated this provision and took several wives were "open to prosecution" . . . but were not prosecuted. The difference of familial law in this respect, and its disregard for state law, are best characterized by the following statement of Olga Lang: "The chief of police in a Shantung town in which the author stayed in 1936 introduced both his wives to his guests and proudly showed pictures of both weddings. And he was supposed to enforce the new law!" . . .

On the family legal level the state laws regulating inheritance fared no better. Although Article 1144 of the Civil Code stipulates that there should be no discrimination as to the sex of the spouse, and either should inherit equally from the other . . , in actuality the family or clan law preferred males (and sons over wives) and ignored the provision. Similarly, "the difference between the status of boys adopted as legal heirs and adopted 'out of charity' was abolished by the legal code but was still observed generally: the legal heir had to be a member of one's clan." . . .

Legal systems that markedly differed in content from the all-embracing law of Imperial China were also those of the Chinese gilds. "In China the gilds have never been within the law. They grew up outside it, and, as associations, have never recognized the civil law nor claimed protection from it." . . . Law within a Chinese gild was administered by an elected committee of twelve individuals, one of whom acted as chairman. The effectiveness and power of the gild's legal decisions was so great that it sometimes forced a member to commit a murder (according to state law) by executing an offender against gild law. For example, in Soochow a member of the local Goldbeaters' Gild, being within the state law and enjoying the protection of the magistrate, violated the rules by acquiring more apprentices than the gild's law allowed. For this offense he was sentenced to be bitten to death: "Gild members to the number of 120 each took a bite, no one being allowed to leave the place whose lips and teeth were not bloody, and the rebel against the gild was soon no more."

• • •

In our Western civilization we are accustomed to regard the law of the state as the primary, almost omnipotent standard to which the individual looks for protection and with which he tries to conform in his behavior. Only within the framework of this basic conformity, we tend to think, may there exist additional controls of the family, clique, association, etc. . . . Max Weber found exceptions. "The law of the state often tries to obstruct the coercive means of other consociations; the English Libel Act thus tries to preclude blacklisting by excluding the defense of truth. But the state is not always successful. There are groups stronger than the state in this respect, for instance, those groups and associations, usually based on social class, which rely on the 'honor code' of the duel as the means of resolving conflicts. With courts of honor and boycott as the coercive means at their disposal, they usually succeed in compelling, with particular emphasis, the fulfillment of obligations as 'debts of honor,' for instance, gambling debts or the duty to engage in a duel; such debts are intrinsically connected with the specific purposes of the group in question, but, as far as the state is concerned, they are not recognized, or are even proscribed." . . .

Weber generalizes: "This conflict between the means of coercion of the various corporate groups is as old as the law itself. In the past it has not always ended with the triumph of the coercive means of the political body, and even today this has not always been the outcome." . . . Indeed, even in the United States nowadays, several decades later, the center of power does not always lie with the state or federal law. The law of the criminal gang is usually provided with sanctions much harsher and infinitely more effective and immediate in application than sanctions of the official law of the country; therefore members of such organizations conform primarily with the legal system of their illicit organization. Thus, as far as the gangsters are concerned, the legal center of power is located in the gang rather than on the level of the society as a whole. Consequently, the dogma regarding the law of the state as the most powerful source of social control proves to be a myth in some instances in our Western civilization. How badly this dogma must fare in cultures where it is not only not held, but is never even thought of!

• • •

The essential feature of law is its existence in concrete legal decisions. Rules for behavior that are not applied in legal decisions and consequently not enforced, although appearing in codifications in the form of dead laws, do not belong in the realm of law proper for the simple reason that they do not exercise social control.

The essential feature of legal decision, in turn, is that a third party (authority) possesses the privilege to pass it. Furthermore, in order to pass a legally relevant decision whose provisions can actually be enforced, the adjudicating authority has to have power over both parties to the dispute—he must have jurisdiction over both litigants. In anthropological or sociological language this means that all three, the two litigants as well as the authority, have to belong to the same social group in which the latter wields judicial power (has jurisdiction). Law thus pertains to specific groups with well-defined membership; it does not just "float around" in a human society at large.

Because of this fact we should not expect to find law pertaining to a society as a whole if the society is not politically organized (unified). That, of course, does not mean that law would be absent in such a society. Society, be it a tribe or a "modern" nation, is not an undifferentiated amalgam of people. It is rather a patterned mosaic of subgroups that belong to certain, usually well-defined (or definable) types with different memberships, composition, and degree of inclusiveness. Every such subgroup owes its existence in a large degree to a legal system that is its own and that regulates the behavior of its members. Offenses within such a group cannot go unpunished and disputes cannot be allowed to continue indefinitely lest they disrupt and destroy the social group. Thus the existence of social control, which we usually call law, is of vital necessity to any functioning social group or subgroup. As a consequence, in a given society there will be as many legal systems as there are functioning social units.

This multiplicity of legal systems, whose legal provisions necessarily differ from one to another, sometimes even to the point of contradiction, reflects precisely the pattern of the subgroups of the society—what I have termed "societal structure" (structure of a society). Thus, according to the inclusiveness and types of the pertinent groups, legal systems can be viewed as belonging to different legal levels that are superimposed one upon the other, the system of a more inclusive group being applied to members of all its constituent subgroups. As a consequence, an individual is usually exposed to several legal systems simultaneously—to be exact, to as many systems as there are subgroups of which he is a member. This conception of a society as a patterned mosaic structure of subgroups with their specific legal systems and with a dynamic center of power brings together phenomena and processes of a basically legal nature that otherwise would be put into nonlegal categories and treated as being qualitatively different. It helps us to understand why a man in one society is primarily a member of his kin group or village and only secondarily of the tribe or state, whereas in another society the most inclusive, politically organized unit (a tribe or a state) controls him most. A gangster's behavior is not "absolutely illegal"; while it is definitely so on the state or national legal level, it has to be at the same time, regarded as legal from the viewpoint of the gang. The field of law, it is obvious, does not escape the spreading notion of relativity.

Reflecting upon the above data and their interpretation, I have arrived at this conclusion: the examples and discussion have made it abundantly clear that any penetrating analysis of law of a primitive or civilized society can be attained only by relating it to the pertinent societal structure and legal levels, and by a full re-cognition of the plurality of legal systems within a society. After all, law as a category of social phenomena cannot be considered (as it traditionally has been) unrelated to the rest of the organizing principles of a society.

1. Professor Pospisil talks about multiple legal systems, but you will note that for each of the systems he is often quite content with law in documentary form. Can that be a misleading focus? Contrast the Pospisil and Reisman selections. Are some things which Pospisil would consider to be law considered law by Reisman? Should some things which Pospisil does not include in his operational definition of law be included?

2. Do you agree with Pospisil's definition of law as decisions which meet the following four criteria:

   a) Decisions by leaders which are actually complied with;
   b) Decisions meant to be applied to all similar cases which may arise in the future;
   c) Decisions which are backed by sanctions;
   d) Decisions which deal with actual disputes and entitle one party "to certain behavior from the other party."

What about income tax legislation, zoning, and offerings of securities? What about decisions that affect the public at large by banks, political groups, religious bodies or other informal actors? Are they "law?" Do they fit into Pospisil's framework of law? Is the gathering of information and planning of policy "law" in his view? What of custom?

3. What is the significance of certain commands which happen to be called law for the individuals who are enjoined to comply? Are the rules of a dictatorship "law?" Ever? Sometimes? Why and under what conditions? Does Pospisil address the question of whether they should be obeyed and regarded as "binding" because the dictator has control and the necessary means of coercion? If a norm meets Pospisil's definition of "law," should one always follow it? How would a Pospisilian advise Justice Lopez-Alcalde in the first *Dilemma* in Chapter 1?

4. Pospisil claims that there is no law in a society which is not "politically *organized*" (emphasis supplied). Does this mean that there is no law between communities that are not members of any international organization and which do not exchange ambassadors or have treaties? Would their mutual, unstated expectations and fear of reprisals give rise to "law" which would as a practical matter regulate their reciprocal behavior?

Professor Pospisil contends that the assumption of a single legal system in any spatial unit is unfounded. There may be many such systems. But what is the relationship between those systems? When the norms conflict, which prevail? For example, in the Dabastan case, a client wishes to do business in a country in which bribery is the unwritten norm; in this context, what is the law and what is the lawyer supposed to advise the client? Recall our consideration of Theta in Chapter 1.

REISMAN, A THEORY OF LAW FROM THE POLICY PERSPECTIVE, IN LAW AND POLICY 84–85 (D. WEISSTUB ED. 1976)

. . . Members of Theta, like members of virtually all groups, are integrated in a web of many other groups. Each is characterized by a normative system and each may make simultaneous demands for different sorts of "right" behaviour and may sanction deviations without regard to the fact the "deviation" was taken in order to conform to the demands of another relevant group. The member of Theta who was expelled for informing on a fraternity brother who had cheated, conformed to the written code of Theta and of the University, but violated the actual code in accordance with which Theta members insisted on living. Conformity to Theta's actual code, however, might have led to violation of the University's code and expulsion. In the same manner, conformity to the operational code of a group which is changing may also render a person subject to sanctions under the newer regime. Though this may seem confusing, it is a rather common problem. We are all simultaneously members of different groups each of which may make conflicting demands. We are obliged to choose, like the early Christian, between matters properly of God and of Caesar; mistakes despite good intentions may occasion the most serious sanctions.

Most groups, in competition for the loyalties of individuals, develop certain "allocating" principles akin to the rules of conflicts of law, according to which the pre-eminence of different groups will be recognized for certain social sectors. But virtually all groups claim pre-eminence for their norms in some sectors deemed intimately important to group life. Conflicts between these demands may ultimately be resolved by effective power, if they are resolved at all. . . . The issue of pre-eminence has not been resolved and, indeed, may never be resolved, for the formation of groups and the generation of loyalties seem to be inescapable components of social interaction.

For the impatient individual not given to reflection, the problem is elusive if not invisible. A member of a social stratum who feels that his law is challenged by the nonconforming behavior of another is likely to characterize the behavior as "deviant" and to term the deviator, in Szaz's "rhetoric of rejection," an anomic or unintegrated personality, a miscreant or someone sick. A more disengaged observer, however, may identify competing systems, in which relative pre-eminence is not clearly established in the phenomenal world of the members; . . .

ELITES IN DEMOCRACY

The existence of multiple elites, reflects the divergence between appearance and reality in law and is particularly problematic for lawyers practicing in democracies. Democracies, and ours in particular, hold forth the notion that all are equal before the law which all participate in making. In fact, in many if not all social systems, a relatively small group of people, known as elites, have much more power than others. ". . . In all large-scale societies, the decisions at any given time are typically in the hands of a small number of people . . . government is always government by the few, whether in the name of the few, the one, or the many."* One of the earliest formulations of the theory of the elite was offered by Mosca:

> In all societies—from societies that are very under-developed and have largely attained the dawning of civilization, down to the most advanced and powerful societies—two classes of people appear—a class that rules and a class that is ruled. The first class, always the less numerous, perform all of the political functions, monopolizes power and enjoys the tremendous advantages that power brings, whereas the second the more numerous class, is directed and controlled by the first, in a manner that is now more or less legal, now more or less arbitrary and violent."**

Consider Robert Dahl's presentation of the problem.

---

*H. Lasswell and D. Lerner, The Comparative Study of Elites 7 (1952).
**G. Mosca, The Ruling Class 50 (1939).

DAHL, WHO GOVERNS: DEMOCRACY AND POWER
IN AN AMERICAN CITY 1–8 (2d ed. 1961)

In a political system, where nearly every adult may vote but where knowledge, wealth, social position, access to officials, and other resources are unequally distributed, who actually governs?

The question has been asked, I imagine, wherever popular government has developed and intelligent citizens have reached the stage of critical self-consciousness concerning their society. It must have been put many times in Athens even before it was posed by Plato and Aristotle.

The question is peculiarly relevant to the United States and to Americans. In the first place, Americans espouse democratic beliefs with a fervency and a unanimity that have been a regular source of astonishment to foreign observers from Tocqueville and Bryce to Myrdal and Brogan. Not long ago, two American political scientists reported that 96 percent or more of several hundred registered voters interviewed in two widely separated American cities agreed that: "Democracy is the best form of government" and "Every citizen should have an equal chance to influence government policy," and subscribed to other propositions equally basic to the democratic credo. What, if anything, do these beliefs actually mean in the face of extensive inequalities in the resources different citizens can use to influence one another?

●   ●   ●

Now it has always been held that if equality of power among citizens is possible at all—a point on which many political philosophers have had grave doubts—then surely considerable equality of social conditions is a necessary prerequisite. But if, even in America, with its universal creed of democracy and equality, there are great inequalities in the conditions of different citizens, must there not also be great inequalities in the capacities of different citizens to influence the decisions of their various governments? And if, because they are unequal in other conditions, citizens of a democracy are unequal in power to control their government, then who in fact does govern? How does a "democratic" system work amid inequality of resources? These are the questions I want to explore by examining one urban American community, New Haven, Connecticut.

●   ●   ●

. . . Elections are free from violence and, for all practical purposes, free from fraud. Two political parties contest elections, offer rival slates of candidates, and thus present the voters with at least some outward show of choice.

Running counter to this legal equality of citizens in the voting booth, however, is an unequal distribution of the resources that can be used for influencing the choices of voters and, between elections, of officials. Take property, for example. In 1957, the fifty largest property owners, in number less than one-sixteenth of one percent of the taxpayers, held nearly one-third of the total assessed value of all real property in the city. Most of the fifty largest property owners were, of course, corporations: public utilities like the United Illuminating Company, which had the largest assessment ($22 million) and the Southern New England Telephone Company ($12 million): big industries like Olin Mathieson ($21 million) which had bought up the Winchester Repeating Arms Company, the famous old New Haven firearms firm; family-held firms like Sargent and A.C. Gilbert, or department stores like the century-old firm of Malley's. Of the fifty largest property owners, sixteen were manufacturing firms, nine were retail and wholesale businesses, six were privately-owned public utilities, and five were banks. Yale University was one of the biggest property owners, though it ranked only tenth in assessed value ($3.6 million) because much of its property was tax-free. A few individuals stood out boldly on the list, like John Day Jackson, the owner and publisher of New Haven's two newspapers.

Or consider family income. In 1949, the average (median) family income in New Haven was about $2,700 a year. One family out of forty had an income of $10,000 or more; over one family out of five had an income of less than $1,000. In the Thirtieth Ward, which had the highest average family income, one family out of four had an income of $7,000 or more, in the Fifth, the poorest, over half the families had incomes of less than $2,000 a year. (Technically, the First Ward was even poorer than the Fifth for half the families there had incomes of less than $700 a year, but three-quarters of the residents of the First were students at Yale.)

The average adult in New Haven had completed the ninth grade, but in the Tenth Ward half the adults had never gone beyond elementary school. About one out of six adults in the city had gone to college. The extremes were represented by the Thirty-first Ward, where nearly half had attended college, and the Twenty-seventh, where the proportion was only one out of thirty.

•   •   •

Thus one is forced back once more to the initial question. Given the existence of inequalities like these, who actually governs in a democracy?

Since the question is not new, one may wonder whether we do not, after all, pretty well know the answer by now. Do we not at least know what answer must be given for the present-day political system of the United States? Unfortunately, no. Students of politics have provided a number of conflicting explanations for the way in which democracies can be expected to operate in the midst of inequalities in political resources. Some answers are a good deal more optimistic than others. For example, it is sometimes said that political parties provide competition for public office and thereby guarantee a relatively high degree of popular control. By appealing to the voters, parties organize the unorganized, give power to the powerless, present voters with alternative candidates and programs, and insure that during campaigns they have an opportunity to learn about the merits of these alternatives. Furthermore, after the election is over, the victorious party, which now represents the preferences of a majority of voters, takes over the task of governing. The voter, therefore, does not need to participate actively in government; it is enough for him to participate in elections by the simple act of voting. By his vote he registers a preference for the general direction in which government policy should move; he cannot and does not need to choose particular policies. One answer to the question, "Who governs?" is then that competing political parties govern, but they do so with the consent of voters secured by competitive elections.

However, no sooner had observers begun to discover the extraordinary importance of political parties in the operation of democratic political systems than others promptly reduced the political party to little more than a collection of "interest groups," or sets of individuals with some values, purposes, and demands in common. If the parties were the political molecules, the interest groups were the atoms. And everything could be explained simply by studying the atoms. Neither people nor parties but interest groups, it was said, are the true units of the political system. An individual, it was argued, is politically rather helpless, but a group unites the resources of individuals into an effective force. Thus some theorists would answer our question by replying that interest groups govern; most of the actions of government can be explained, they would say, simply as the result of struggles among groups of individuals with differing interests and varying resources of influence.

The first explanation was developed by English and American writers, the second almost entirely by Americans. A third theory, much more pessimistic than the other two, was almost exclusively European in origin, though it subsequently achieved a considerable vogue in the United States. This explanation, which has both a "Left" and a "Right" interpretation, asserts that beneath the facade of democratic politics a social and economic elite will usually be found actually running things. Robert and Helen Lynd used this explanation in their famous two books on "Middletown" (Muncie, Indiana), and many studies since then have also adopted it, most notably Floyd Hunter in his analysis of the "power structure" of Atlanta. Because it fits nicely with the very factors that give rise to our question, the view that a social and economic elite controls government is highly persuasive. Concentration of power in the hands of an elite is a necessary consequence, in this view, of the enormous inequalities in the distribution of resources of influence—property, income, social status, knowledge, publicity, focal position, and all the rest.

One difficulty with all of these explanations was that they left very little room for the politician. He was usually regarded merely as an agent—of majority will, the political parties, interest groups, or the elite. He had no independent influence. But an older view that could be traced back to Machiavelli's famous work, *The Prince*, stressed the enormous political potential of the cunning, resourceful, masterful leader. In this view, majorities, parties, interest groups, elites, even political systems are all to some extent pliable; a leader who knows how to use his resources to the maximum is not so much the agent of others as others are his agents. Although a gifted political entrepreneur might not exist in every political system, wherever he appeared he would make himself felt.

Still another view commingled elements of all the rest. This explanation was set out by Tocqueville as a possible course of degeneration in all democratic orders, restated by the Spanish philosopher, Ortega y Gassett, in his highly influential book, *The Revolt of the Masses* (1930), and proposed by a number of European intellectuals, after the destruction of the German Republic by Nazism, as an explanation for the origins of modern dictatorship. Although it is a theory proposed mainly by Europeans about European conditions, it is so plausible an alternative that we cannot afford to ignore it. Essentially, this theory (which has many variants) argues that under certain conditions of development (chiefly industrialization and urbanization) older, stratified, class-based social structures are weakened or destroyed; and in their place arises a mass of individuals with no secure place in the social system, rootless, aimless, lacking strong social ties, ready and indeed eager to attach themselves to any political entrepreneur who will cater to their tastes and desires. Led by unscrupulous and exploitative leaders, these rootless masses have the capacity to destroy whatever stands in their way without the ability to replace it with a stable alternative. Consequently the greater their influence on politics, the more helpless they become, the more they destroy, the more they depend upon strong leaders to create some kind of social, economic, and political organization to replace the old. If we ask, "Who governs?" the answer is not the mass nor its leaders but both together; the leaders cater to mass tastes and in return use the strength provided by the loyalty and obedience of the masses to weaken and perhaps even to annihilate all opposition to their rule.

A superficial familiarity with New Haven (or for that matter with almost any

modern American city) would permit one to argue persuasively that each of these
theories really explains the inner workings of the city's political life. However, a
careful consideration of the points at which the theories diverge suggests that the
broad question, "Who governs?" might be profitably subdivided into a number of
more specific questions. These questions, listed below, have guided the study of
New Haven recorded in this book:

Are inequalities in resources of influence "cumulative" or "noncumulative"?
That is, are people who are better off in one resource also better off in others? In
other words, does the way in which political resources are distributed encourage
oligarchy or pluralism?

How are important political decisions actually made?

What kinds of people have the greatest influence on decisions? Are different
kinds of decisions all made by the same people? From what strata of the community
are the most influential people, the leaders, drawn?

Do leaders tend to cohere in their politics and form a sort of ruling group, or do
they tend to divide, conflict, and bargain? Is the pattern of leadership, in short,
oligarchical or pluralistic?

What is the relative importance of the most widely distributed political resource—the right to vote? Do leaders respond generally to the interests of the few
citizens with the greatest wealth and highest status—or do they respond to the many
with the largest number of votes? To what extend do various citizens *use* their political
resources? Are there important differences that in turn result in differences in influence?

Are the patterns of influence durable or changing? For example, was democracy
stronger in New Haven when Tocqueville contemplated the American scene? And
in more recent years, as New Haven has grappled with a gigantic program of urban
reconstruction, what has happened to popular control and to patterns of leadership?
In general, what are the sources of change and stability in the political system?

Finally, how important is the nearly universal adherence to the "American Creed"
of democracy and equality? Is the operation of the political system affected in any
way by what ordinary citizens believe about democracy? If so, how?

NOTES

1. The reality of the elite clashes, as Professor Dahl noted, with the democratic myth. To
what extent must a lawyer yield to that reality even though it runs against fundamental notions
of American law? Is it possible to ignore it?

2. If the reality of elites is accepted, how is it to be accommodated to constitutional
principles?

———

Consider Mills' appraisal.

MILLS, THE POWER ELITE
5–9, 288–90 (1956)

. . . The way to understand the power of the American elite lies neither solely in
recognizing the historic scale of events nor in accepting the personal awareness
reported by men of apparent decision. Behind such men and behind the events of
history, linking the two, are the major institutions of modern society. These hier-

archies of state and corporation and army constitute the means of power; as such
they are now of a consequence not before equaled in human history—and at their
summits, there are now those command posts of modern society which offers us the
sociological key to an understanding of the role of the higher circles in America.

Within American society, major national power now resides in the economic,
the political, and the military domains. Other institutions seem off to the side of
modern history, and, on occasion, duly subordinated to these. No family is as directly
powerful in national affairs as any major corporation; no church is as directly powerful
in the external biographies of young men in America today as the military establishment; no college is as powerful in the shaping of momentous events as the National
Security Council. Religious, educational, and family institutions are not autonomous
centers of national power; on the contrary, these decentralized areas are increasingly
shaped by the big three, in which developments of decisive and immediate consequence now occur.

Families and churches and schools adapt to modern life; governments and armies
and corporations shape it; and, as they do so, they turn these lesser institutions into
means for their ends. Religious institutions provide chaplains to the armed forces
where they are used as a means of increasing the effectiveness of its morale to kill.
Schools select and train men for their jobs in corporations and their specialized tasks
in the armed forces. The extended family has, of course, long been broken up by
the industrial revolution, and now the son and father are removed from the family,
by compulsion if need be, whenever the army of the state sends out the call. And
the symbols of all these lesser institutions are used to legitimate the power and the
decisions of the big three.

The life-fate of the modern individual depends not only upon the family into
which he was born or which he enters by marriage, but increasingly upon the corporation in which he spends the most alert hours of his best years; not only upon the
school where he is educated as a child and adolescent, but also upon the state which
touches him throughout his life; not only upon the church in which on occasion he
hears the word of God, but also upon the army in which he is disciplined.

If the centralized state could not rely upon the inculcation of nationalist loyalties
in public and private schools, its leaders would promptly seek to modify the decentralized educational system. If the bankruptcy rate among the top five hundred corporations were as high as the general divorce rate among the thirty-seven million
married couples, there would be economic catastrophe on an international scale. If
members of armies gave to them no more of their lives than do believers to the
churches to which they belong, there would be a military crisis.

Within each of the big three, the typical institutional unit has become enlarged,
has become administrative, and, in the power of its decisions, has become centralized.
Behind these developments there is a fabulous technology, for as institutions, they
have incorporated this technology and guide it, even as it shapes and paces their
developments.

The economy—once a great scatter of small productive units in autonomous
balance—has become dominated by two or three hundred giant corporations, administratively and politically interrelated, which together hold the keys to economic
decisions.

The political order, once a decentralized set of several dozen states with a weak
spinal cord, has become a centralized, executive establishment which has taken up
into itself many powers previously scattered, and now enters into each and every
crany of the social structure.

The military order, once a slim establishment in a context of distrust fed by state militia, has become the largest and most expensive feature of government, and, although well versed in smiling public relations, now has all the grim and clumsy efficiency of a sprawling bureaucratic domain.

In each of these institutional areas, the means of power at the disposal of decision makers have increased enormously; their central executive powers have been enhanced; within each of them modern administrative routines have been elaborated and tightened up.

As each of these domains becomes enlarged and centralized, the consequences of its activities become greater, and its traffic with the others increases. The decisions of a handful of corporations bear upon military and political as well as upon economic developments around the world. The decisions of the military establishment rest upon and grievously affect political life as well as the very level of economic activity. The decisions made within the political domain determine economic activities and military programs. There is no longer, on the one hand, an economy, and, on the other hand, a political order containing a military establishment unimportant to politics and to money-making. There is a political economy linked, in a thousand ways with military institutions and decisions. On each side of the world-split running through central Europe and around the Asiatic rimlands, there is an ever-increasing interlocking of economic, military, and political structures. If there is government intervention in the corporate economy, so is there corporate intervention in the governmental process. In the structural sense, this triangle of power is the source of the interlocking directorate that is most important for the historical structure of the present.

The fact of the interlocking is clearly revealed at each of the points of crisis of modern capitalist society-slump, war, and boom. In each, men of decision are led to an awareness of the interdependence of the major institutional orders. In the nineteenth century, when the scale of all institutions was smaller, their liberal integration was achieved in the automatic economy, by an autonomous play of market forces, and in the automatic political domain, by the bargain and the vote. It was then assumed that out of the imbalance and friction that followed the limited decisions then possible a new equilibrium would in due course emerge. That can no longer be assumed, and it is not assumed by the men at the top of each of the three dominant hierarchies.

For given the scope of their consequences, decisions—and indecisions—in any one of these ramify into the others, and hence top decisions tend either to become co-ordinated or to lead to a commanding indecision. It has not always been like this. When numerous small entrepreneurs made up the economy, for example, many of them could fail and the consequences still remain local; political and military authorities did not intervene. But now, given political expectations and military commitments, can they afford to allow key units of the private corporate economy to break down in slump? Increasingly, they do intervene in economic affairs, and as they do so, the controlling decisions in each order are inspected by agents of the other two, and economic, military, and political structures are interlocked.

At the pinnacle of each of the three enlarged and centralized domains, there have arisen those higher circles which make up the economic, the political, and the military elites. At the top of the economy, among the corporate rich, there are the chief executives; at the top of the political order, the members of the political directorate; at the top of the military establishment, the elite of soldier-statesmen clustered in and around the Joint Chiefs of Staff and the upper echelon. As each of these domains has coincided with the others, as decisions tend to become total in their consequence, the leading men in each of the three domains of power—the warlords, the corporation chieftains, the political directorate—tend to come together, to form the power elite of America.

• • •

The inner core of the power elite consists, first, of those who interchange commanding roles at the top of one dominant institutional order with those in another: the admiral who is also a banker and a lawyer and who heads up an important federal commission; the corporation executive whose company was one of the two or three leading war materiel producers who is now the Secretary of Defense; the wartime general who dons civilian clothes to sit on the political directorate and then becomes a member of the board of directors of a leading economic corporation.

Although the executive who becomes a general, the general who becomes a statesman, the statesman who becomes a banker, see much more than ordinary men in their ordinary environments, still the perspectives of even such men often remain tied to their dominant locales. In their very career, however, they interchange roles within the big three and thus readily transcend the particularity of interest in any one of these institutional milieux. By their very careers and activities, they lace the three types of milieux together. They are, accordingly, the core members of the power elite.

These men are not necessarily familiar with every major arena of power. We refer to one man who moves in and between perhaps two circles—say the industrial and the military—and to anothers man who moves in the military and the political, and to a third who moves in the political as well as among opion-makers. These in-between types most closely display our image of the power elite's structure and operation, even of behind the-scenes operations. To the extent that there is any invisible elite, these advisory and liaison types are its core. Even if—as I believe to be very likely—many of them are, at least in the first part of their careers, agents of the various elites rather than themselves elite, it is they who are most active in organizing the several top milieux into a structure of power and maintaining it.

The inner core of the power elite also includes men of the higher legal and financial type from the great law factories and investment firms, who are almost professional go-betweens of economic, political and military affairs, and who thus act to unify the power elite. The corporation lawyer and the investment banker perform the functions of the go-between effecitvely and powerfully. By the nature of their work, they transcend the narrower milieu of any one industry, and accordingly are in a position to speak and act for the corporate world or at least sizable sectors of it. The corporation lawyer is a key link between the economic and military and political areas; the investment banker is a key organizer and unifier of the corporate world and a person well versed in spending the huge amounts of money the American military establishment now ponders. When you get a lawyer who handles the legal work of investment bankers you get a key member of the power elite.

During the Democratic era, one link between private corporate organizations and governmental institutions was the investment house of Dillon, Read. From it came such men as James Forrestal and Charles F. Detmark, Jr.; Ferdinand Eberstadt had once been a partner in it before he branched out into his own investment house from which came other men to political and military circles. Republican administrations seem to favor the investment firm of Kuhn, Loeb and the advertising firm of Batten, Barton, Durstine and Osborn.

Regardless of administrations, there is always the law firm of Sullivan and Cromwell. Mid-West investment banker Cyrus Eaton has said that Arthur H. Dean, a senior partner of Sullivan & Cromwell of No. 48 Wall Street, was one of those who assisted in the drafting of the Securities Act of 1933, the first of the series of bills passed to regulate the capital markets. He and his firm which is reputed to be the largest in the United States, have maintained close relations with the SEC since its creation, and theirs is the dominating influence on the Commission.

There is also the third largest bank in the United States: the Chase National Bank of New York (now Chase-Manhattan). Regardless of political administration, executives of this bank and those of the International Bank of Reconstruction and Development have changed positions: John J. McCloy, who became Chairman of the Chase National in 1953, is a former president of the World Bank; and his successor to the presidency of the World Bank was a former senior vice-president of the Chase National Bank. And in 1953, the president of the Chase National Bank, Winthrop W. Aldrich, had left to become Ambassador to Great Britain.

NOTES

1. Do you think the elite theories as propounded by Dahl and Mills are accurate representations of American political processes? Do these authors give adequate attention to restraints deriving from expectations of authority? Do they, for example, give adequate attention to the potential for restraint from lawyers and those tho rely on the symbols of the Constitution? Discuss.

2. Can you identify elites, in the sense in which Dahl and Mills use the term, in your city? In your state? In your university? How would you go about identifying such an elite? Recall some of the methods sketched in the "Practical Guide to the Law in Context" in Chapter 1.

3. Do you think the availability of a court system with some power base provides a restraint on elite activity or are the courts themselves responsive to elite demands? How would you investigate a question like this?

4. In the contemporary political system of the United States, the media—the "Fourth Estate"—frequently act as a restraint on the exercise of official power. In the Watergate fiasco, for example, the media played a major role in tempering the political ambitions of the President and his closest advisors, ultimately catalyzing a strong Congressional reaction. Do you think that the selections from Dahl and Mills adequately reflect these restraints?

5. Mills' notion of "power" impliedly includes the notion of "authority." Members of the government and military elites, for example, wield effective power in part because they are expected by the community to make decisions with regard to military issues. As Harold D. Lasswell put it, "The possession of authority is itself effective power." H. Lasswell, *Power and Society* 134 (1950). To refer to the "power" of elites without explicit recognition of the role that authority plays in creating power and making it effective, is to ignore an important component of effective decision. Discuss.

Three traditional conceptions of social phenomena, widely and uncritically accepted in legal study and often relied on by lawyers in practice, have been explored in the preceding selections. The first is that the words found in certain texts are reliable and trustworthy indicators of how decisions are actually made, and that there is a regular congruence between the words in the texts and the law in action. Such a conception is quite unfounded. There are many discrepancies between the law in the books or, more generally, the myth system, and what is actually carried out by operators. The notion of the unity and integrality of a legal system within a single territory has been shown to be equally unfounded. There may be many competing and even contradictory legal systems within any particular territorial area. The copresence of these systems presents special problems to the practicing lawyer. Finally we have drawn attention to the tension between the reality of elite formations in all societies and the principles of American democracy and asked to what extent, and how, the American lawyer can respond to this situation. Each of these features will be important in examining the jurisprudential frames that are presented in the following chapters. In the next chapter, we will examine one of the major implications of the theory of the elite in a jurisprudential school.

C. K. Allen, *Law in the Making* (1964).

T. Arnold, *The Symbols of Government* (1935).

P. Bachrach, *The Theory of Democratic Elitism: A Critique* (1967).

M. Barkun, *Law and the Social System* (1973).

R. F. Barton, *Ifuago Law* (1919).

E. Bodenheimer, *Jurisprudence: The Philosophy and Method of the Law* (1962).

P. Bohannan, The Differing Realms of the Law, in *Law and Warfare: Studies in the Anthropology of Conflict* 43 (P. Bohannan ed. 1967).

P. Bohannan, *Justice and Judgment Among the Tiv* (1957).

A. Brecht, *Political Theory* (1959).

H. Cairns, *Legal Philosophy from Plato to Hegel* (1949).

F. Cohen, The Problems of a Functional Jurisprudence, in *The Legal Conscience* (L. K. Cohen ed. 1960).

B. Cohn, Some Notes on Law and Change in North India, in *Law and Warfare: Studies in the Anthropology of Conflict* 139 (P. Bohannan ed. 1967).

G. W. Domhoff, *Who Rules America* (1967).

A. L. Epstein, The Case Method in the Field of Law, in *The Craft of Social Anthropology* 205 (A. L. Epstein ed. 1979).

W. Friedmann, *Legal Theory* (5th ed. 1967).

C. J. Friedrich, *The Philosophy of Law in Historical Perspective* (2d ed. 1963).

L. Fuller, *Legal Fictions* (1967).

M. Gluckman, *The Judicial Process Among the Barotse of Northern Rhodesia* (1955).

P. Gulliver, *Social Control in an African Society* (1963).

E. A. Hoebel, *The Law of Primitive Man; A Study in Comparative Legal Dynamics* (1954).

J. W. Jones, *Historical Introduction to the Theory of Law* (1969).

G. Kolko, *Wealth and Power in America: an Analysis of Social Class and Income Distribution* (1962).

H. Lasswell, *Politics: Who Gets What, When, How* (1936).

H. Lasswell, D. Lerner & C. Rothwell, *The Comparative Study of Elites* (1952).

D. Lloyd, *The Idea of Law* (1964).

F. Lundberg, *The Rich and the Super Rich* (1968).

S. Macauley, Non-Contractual Relations in Business: A Preliminary Study, 28 *Am. Soc. Rev.* 55 (1963).

H. Maine, *Ancient Law, Its Connection with the Early History of Society, and Its Relation to Modern Ideas* (1861).

B. Malinowski, *Crime and Custom in Savage Society* (1926).

J. Meisel, *The Myth of the Ruling Class* (1958).

R. Michels, *Political Parties: A Sociological Study of Oligarchical Tendencies of Modern Democracy* (1962).

S. Moore, Law and Anthropology, 1969 *Biennial Review of Anthropology* 252 (1970).

S. Moore, *Power and Property in Inca Peru* (1958).

G. Mosca, *The Ruling Class* (1939).

L. Nader, An Analysis of Zapotec Law Cases, in *Law and Warfare: Studies in the Anthropology of Conflict* 117 (P. Bohannan ed. 1967); The Anthropological Study of Law, in *The Ethnography of Law* (L. Nader ed.), 67 *Am. Anthropologist (Special Issue)* 3 (1965).

V. Pareto, *The Mind and Society: Treatise of General Sociology* (A. Livingston ed. and A. Bongiorno and A. Livingston transl. 1935).

G. Parry, *Political Elites* (1969).

K. Popper, *The Open Society and Its Enemies* (1950).

R. Pound, *An Introduction to the Philosophy of Law* (1922).

W. M. Reisman, Folk Tales and Civic Acculturation: Reflections on the Myths of Dinkaland, in *Dinka Folk Tales: African Stories of the Sudan* 13 (F. Deng ed. 1974).

J. Stone, *Province and Function of Law* (2d print. 1950).

J. Van Velsen, The Extended Case Method and Situational Analysis, in *The Craft of Social Anthropology* 129 (A. L. Epstein ed. 1979).

World Revolutionary Elites, Studies in Coercive Ideological Movements (H. Lasswell & D. Lerner eds. 1965).

CHAPTER 3

Law from the Mouth of a Gun:
The Jurisprudence of Naked Power

Political power grows out of the barrel of a gun.
Mao Zedong

If power were seized and effectively exercised by a junta composed of the Secretary of Defense and a collection of home-grown colonels, would the junta constitute the lawful authority of the country? Consider the reasoning of Chief Justice Taft.

TINOCO CASE (GREAT BRITAIN V. COSTA RICA), ARBITRATION BETWEEN GREAT BRITAIN AND COSTA RICA 18 AM. J. INT'L L. 147 (1924); 1 U. N. R. INT'L ARB. AWARDS 369, 376–84 (1923)

[Taft, Arbitrator.] In January, 1917, the Government of Costa Rica, under President Alfredo Gonzalez, was overthrown by Frederico Tinoco, the Secretary of War. Gonzalez fled. Tinoco assumed power, called on election, and established a new constitution in June, 1917. His government continued until August, 1919, when Tinoco retired, and left the country. His government fell in September following. After a provisional government under one Barquero, the old constitution was restored and elections held under it. The restored government is a signatory to this treaty of arbitration.

On the 22nd of August, 1922, the Constitutional Congress of the restored Costa Rican Government passed a law known as Law of Nullities No. 41. It invalidated all contracts between the executive power and private persons, made with or without approval of the legislative power between January 27, 1917, and September 2, 1919, covering the period of the Tinoco government. It also nullified the legislative decree No. 12 of the Tinoco government, dated June 28, 1919, authorizing the issue of the fifteen million colones currency notes. The colon is a Costa Rican gold coin or standard nominally equal to forty-six and one-half cents of an American dollar, but it is uncoined and the exchange value of the paper colon actually in circulation is much less. The Nullities Law also invalidated the legislative decree of the Tinoco government of July 8, 1919, authorizing the circulation of notes of the nomination of 1,000 colones, and annulled all transactions with such colones bills between holders and the state, directly or indirectly, by means of negotiation or contract, if thereby the holders received value as if they were ordinary bills of current issue.

The claim of Great Britain is that the Royal Bank of Canada and the Central Costa Rica Petroleum Company are British corporations whose shares are owned by British subjects; that the Banco Internacional of Costa Rica and the Government of Costa Rica are both indebted to the Royal Bank in the sum of 998,000 colones, evidenced by 998 one thousand colones bills held by the Bank; that the Central Costa

Rica Petroleum Company owns, by due assignment, a grant by the Tinoco government in 1918 of the right to explore for and exploit oil deposits in Costa Rica, and that both the indebtedness and the concession have been annulled without right by the Law of Nullities and should be excepted from its operation. She asks an award that she is entitled on behalf of her subjects to have the claim of the bank paid, and the concession recognized and given effect by the Costa Rican Government.

The Government of Costa Rica denies its liability for the acts or obligations of the Tinoco government and maintains that the Law of Nullities was a legitimate exercise of its legislative governing power. It further denies the validity of such claims on the merits, unaffected by the Law of Nullities.

• • •

. . . the Costa Rican Government answers: First, that the Tinoco government was not a *de facto* or *de jure* government according to the rules of international law. This raises an issue of fact.

Second, that the contracts and obligations of the Tinoco government, set up by Great Britain on behalf of its subjects, are void, and do not create a legal obligation, because the government of Tinoco and its acts were in violation of the constitution of Costa Rica of 1871.

• • •

Dr. John Bassett Moore, . . . in his Digest of International Law, Volume I, p. 249, announces the general principle which has had such universal acquiescence as to become well settled international law:

> Changes in the government or the internal policy of a state do not as a rule affect its position in international law. A monarchy may be transformed into a republic or a republic into a monarchy; absolute principles may be substituted for constitutional, or the reverse; but, though the government changes, the nation remains, with rights and obligations unimpaired. . . .
>
> The principle of the continuity of states has important results. The state is bound by engagements entered into by governments that have ceased to exist; the restored government is generally liable for the acts of the usurper. The governments of Louis XVIII and Louis Philippe so far as practicable indemnified the citizens of foreign states for losses caused by the government of Napoleon; and the King of the Two Sicilies made compensation to citizens of the United States for the wrongful acts of Murat.

Again Dr. Moore says:

> The origin and organization of government are questions generally of internal discussion and decision. Foreign powers deal with the existing *de facto* government, when sufficiently established to give reasonable assurance of its permanence, and of the acquiescence of those who constitute the state in its ability to maintain itself, and discharge its internal duties and its external obligations.

• • •

Second. It is ably and earnestly argued on behalf of Costa Rica that the Tinoco government cannot be considered a *de facto* government, because it was not established and maintained in accord with the constitution of Costa Rica of 1871. To hold that a government which establishes itself and maintains a peaceful administration, with the acquiescence of the people for a substantial period of time, does not become a *de facto* government unless it conforms to a previous constitution would be to hold that within the rules of international law a revolution contrary to the fundamental law of the existing government cannot establish a new government. This cannot be, and is not, true. The change by revolution upsets the rule of the authorities in power under the then existing fundamental law, and sets aside the fundamental law in so far as the change of rule makes it necessary. To speak of a revolution creating a *de facto* government, which conforms to the limitations of the old constitution is to use a contradiction in terms. The same government continues internationally, but not the internal law of its being. The issue is not whether the new government assumes power or conducts its administration under constitutional limitations established by the people during the incumbency of the government it has overthrown. The question is, has it really established itself in such a way that all within its influence recognize its control, and that there is no opposing force assuming to be a government in its place? Is it discharging its functions as a government usually does, respected within its own jurisdiction?

NOTES

1. The assumption underlying Chief Justice Taft's opinion is that the factor critical in establishing, maintaining and even defining law is naked power. It need not be lawful, for power is its own law. The implications of this assumption are profound and particularly disquieting for a society that views itself as democratic. In light of Taft's holding, is law a process operating for the commonweal and, in democracies, by some sort of consensus? Or is it, in this sense, an illusion, carefully nurtured by elites—those who pull the strings, press the buttons and gain the most—to confuse and disarm those being exploited?

2. Lest the student conclude that the holding in *Tinoco* could only occur in an international case in which judges look at national law from the outside, as it were, it may be useful to consider a United States decision which has many of the same features. In *Bernstein v. Van Heyghen Freres S.A.*, 163 F. 2d 246 (2d Cir. 1947), a case considered in some detail in Chapter 8, a United States court was quite willing to treat Nazi actions in violation of United States conceptions of law as legal and binding on United States courts. See also *Holzer v. Deutsche Reichsbahn-Gessellschaft*, 277 N.Y. 474, 14 N.E. 2d 798 (1938). Recall, in Chapter 1, the dilemma of Justice Lopez-Alcalde. We suggested that one option available to him was to reject the supervening law which violated his conception of human dignity. Is that plausible? Are there precedents for it in past judicial practice?

THE THRASYMACHIAN VIEW

The composite of jurisprudential ideas that express the notion that what really counts is the control gained from naked power and that law is humbug or worse may be referred to as the jurisprudence of naked power. Consider one discussion from Plato, a debate of sorts between Thrasymachus, (Thrasymachos, in some translations) a Sophist espousing the jurisprudence of naked power, and Socrates, opposing it. Socrates recounts the debate.

PLATO, THE REPUBLIC, BOOK I (B. JOWETT TRANS.)

Listen, then, he said: I proclaim that justice is nothing else than the interest of the stronger. And now why do you not praise me? But of course you won't.

Let me first understand you, I replied. Justice, as you say, is the interest of the stronger. What, Thrasymachus, is the meaning of this? You cannot mean to say that because Polydamas, the pancratiast, is stronger than we are, and finds the eating of beef conducive to his bodily strength, that to eat beef is therefore equally for our good who are weaker than he is, and right and just for us?

That's abominable of you, Socrates; you take the words in the sense which is most damaging to the argument.

Not at all, my good sir, I said; I am trying to understand them; and I wish that you would be a little clearer.

Well, he said, have you never heard that forms of government differ; there are tyrannies, and there are democracies, and there are aristocracies?

Yes, I know.

And the government is the ruling power in each state?

Certainly.

And the different forms of government make laws democratical, aristocratical, tyrannical, with a view to their several interests; and these laws, which are made by them for their own interests, are the justice which they deliver to their subjects, and him who transgresses them they punish as a breaker of the law, and unjust. And that is what I mean when I say that in all states there is the same principle of justice, which is the interest of the government; and as the government must be supposed to have power, the only reasonable conclusion is, that everywhere there is one principle of justice, which is the interest of the stronger.

Now I understand you, I said; and whether you are right or not I will try to discover. But let me remark, that in defining justice you have yourself used the word 'interest' which you forbade me to use. It is true, however, that in your definition the words 'of the stronger' are added.

A small addition, you must allow, he said.

Great or small, never mind about that: we must first enquire whether what you are saying is the truth. Now we are both agreed that justice is interest of some sort, but you go on to say 'of the stronger'; about this addition I am not so sure, and must therefore consider further.

Proceed.

I will; and first tell me, Do you admit that it is just for subjects to obey their rulers?

I do.

But are the rules of states absolutely infallible, or are they sometimes liable to err?

To be sure, he replied, they are liable to err.

Then in making their laws they may sometimes make them rightly, and sometimes not?

True.

When they make them rightly, they make them agreeably to their interest; when they are mistaken, contrary to their interest; you admit that?

Yes.

And the laws which they make must be obeyed by their subjects, and that is what you call justice?

Doubtless.

Then justice, according to your argument, is not only obedience to the interest of the stronger but the reverse?

What is that you are saying? he asked.

I am only repeating what you are saying, I believe. But let us consider: Have we not admitted that the rulers may be mistaken about their own interest in what they command, and also that to obey them is justice? Has not that been admitted?

Yes.

Then you must also have acknowledged justice not to be for the interest of the stronger, when the rulers unintentionally command things to be done which are to their own injury. For if, as you say, justice is the obedience which the subject renders to their commands, in that case, O wisest of men, is there any escape from the conclusion that the weaker are commanded to do, not what is for the interest, but what is for the injury of the stronger?

Yes, said Cleitophon, interposing, if you are allowed to be his witness.

But there is no need of any witness, said Polemarchus, for Thrasymachus himself acknowledges that rulers may sometimes command what is not for their own interest, and that for subjects to obey them is justice.

Yes, Polemarchus,—Thrasymachus said that for subjects to do what was commanded by their rulers is just.

Yes, Cleitophon, but he also said that justice is the interest of the stronger, and, while admitting both these propositions, he further acknowledged that the stronger may command the weaker who are his subjects to do what is not for his own interest; whence follows that justice is the injury quite as much as the interest of the stronger.

But, said Cleitophon, he meant by the interest of the stronger what the stronger thought to be his interest,—this was what the weaker had to do; and this was affirmed by him to be justice.

Those were not his words, rejoined Polemarchus.

Never mind, I replied, if he now says that they are, let us accept his statement. Tell me, Thrasymachus, I said, did you mean by justice what the stronger thought to be his interest, whether really so or not?

Certainly not, he said. Do you suppose that I call him who is mistaken the stronger at the time when he is mistaken?

Yes, I said, my impression was that you did so, when you admitted that the ruler was not infallible but might be sometimes mistaken.

You argue like an informer, Socrates. Do you mean, for example, that he who is mistaken about the sick is a physician in that he is mistaken? or that he who errs in arithmetic or grammar is an arithmetician or grammarian at the time when he is making the mistake, in respect of the mistake? True, we say that the physician or arithmetician or grammarian has made a mistake, but this is only a way of speaking; for the fact is that neither the grammarian nor any other person of skill ever makes a mistake in so far as he is what his name implies; they none of them err unless their skill fails them, and then they cease to be skilled artists. No artist or sage or ruler errs at the time when he is what his name implies; though he is commonly said to err, and I adopted the common mode of speaking. But to be perfectly accurate, since you are such a lover of accuracy, we should say that the ruler, in so far as he is a ruler, is unerring, and, being unerring, always commands that which is for his own interest; and the subject is required to execute his commands; and therefore, as I said at first and now repeat, justice is the interest of the stronger.

Indeed, Thrasymachus, and do I really appear to you to argue like an informer?

Certainly, he replied.

And do you suppose that I ask these questions with any design of injuring you in the argument?

Nay, he replied, 'suppose' is not the word—I know it; but you will be found out, and by sheer force of argument you will never prevail.

I shall not make the attempt, my dear man; but to avoid any misunderstanding occurring between us in future, let me ask, in what sense do you speak of a ruler or stronger whose interest, as you were saying, he being the superior, it is just that the inferior should execute—he is a ruler in the popular or in the strict sense of the term?

In the strictest of all senses, he said. And now cheat and play the informer if you can; I ask no quarter at your hands. But you never will be able, never.

And do you imagine, I said, that I am such a madman as to try and cheat Thrasymachus? I might as well shave a lion.

Why, he said, you made the attempt a minute ago, and you failed.

Enough, I said, of these civilities. It will be better that I should ask you a question: Is the physician, taken in that strict sense of which you are speaking, a healer of the sick or a maker of money? And remember that I am now speaking of the true physician.

A healer of the sick, he replied.

And the pilot—that is to say, the true pilot—is he a captain of sailors or a mere sailor?

A captain of sailors.

The circumstance that he sails in the ship is not to be taken into account; neither is he to be called a sailor; the name pilot by which he is distinguished has nothing to do with sailing, but is significant of his skill and of his authority over the sailors.

Very true, he said.

Now, I said, every art has an interest?

Certainly.

For which the art has to consider and provide?

Yes, that is the aim of art.

And the interest of any art is the perfection of it—this and nothing else?

What do you mean?

I mean what I may illustrate negatively by the example of the body. Suppose you were to ask me whether the body is self-sufficing or has wants, I should reply: Certainly the body has wants; for the body may be ill and require to be cured, and has therefore interests to which the art of medicine ministers; and this is the origin and intention of medicine, as you will acknowledge. Am I not right?

Quite right, he replied.

But is the art of medicine or any other art faulty or deficient in any quality in the same way that the eye may be deficient in sight or the ear fail of hearing, and therefore requires another art to provide for the interests of seeing and hearing—has art in itself, I say, any similar liability to fault or defect, and does every art require another supplementary art to provide for its interests, and that another and another without end? Or have the arts to look only after their own interests? Or have they no need either of themselves or of another?—having no faults or defects, they have no need to correct them, either by the exercise of their own art or of any other; they have only to consider the interest of their subject-matter. For every art remains pure and faultless while remaining true—that is to say, while perfect and unimpaired. Take the words in your precise sense, and tell me whether I am not right.

Yes, clearly.

Then medicine does not consider the interest of medicine, but the interest of the body?

True, he said.

Nor does the art of horsemanship consider the interests of the art of horsemanship, but the interests of the horse; neither do any other arts care for themselves, for they have no needs; they care only for that which is the subject of their art?

True, he said.

But surely, Thrasymachus, the arts are the superiors and rulers of their own subjects?

To this he assented with a good deal of reluctance.

Then, I said, no science or art considers or enjoins the interest of the stronger or superior, but only the interest of the subject and weaker?

He made an attempt to contest this proposition also, but finally acquiesced.

Then, I continued, no physician, in so far as he is a physician, considers his own good in what he prescribes, but the good of his patient; for the true physician is also a ruler having the human body as a subject, and is not a mere money-maker; that has been admitted?

Yes.

And the pilot likewise, in the strict sense of the term, is a ruler of sailors and not a mere sailor?

That has been admitted.

And such a pilot and ruler will provide and prescribe for the interest of the sailor who is under him, and not for his own or the ruler's interest?

He gave a reluctant 'Yes.'

Then, I said, Thrasymachus, there is no one in any rule who, in so far as he is a ruler, considers or enjoins what is for his own interest, but always what is for the interest of his subject or suitable to his art; to that he looks, and that alone he considers in everything which he says and does.

When we had got to this point in the argument, and every one saw that the definition of justice had been completely upset, Thrasymachus, instead of replying to me, said: Tell me, Socrates, have you got a nurse?

Why do you ask such a question, I said, when you ought rather to be answering?

Because she leaves you to snivel, and never wipes your nose: she has not even taught you to know the shepherd from the sheep.

What makes you say that? I replied.

Because you fancy that the shepherd or neatherd fattens or tends the sheep or oxen with a view to their own good and not to the good of himself or his master; and you further imagine that the rulers of states, if they are true rulers, never think of their subjects as sheep, and that they are not studying their own advantage day and night. Oh, no; and so entirely astray are you in your ideas about the just and unjust as not even to know that justice and the just are in reality another's good; that is to say, the interest of the ruler and stronger, and the loss of the subject and servant; and injustice the opposite; for the unjust is lord over the truly simple and just: he is the stronger, and his subjects do what is for his interest, and minister to his happiness, which is very far from being their own. Consider further, most foolish Socrates, that the just is always a loser in comparison with the unjust. First of all, in private contracts: wherever the unjust is the partner of the just you will find that, when the partnership is dissolved, the unjust man has always more and the just less. Secondly, in their dealings with the State: when there is an income-tax, the just man will pay more and the unjust less on the same amount of income; and when there is anything to be received the one gains nothing and the other much. Observe also what happens when they take an office; there is the just man neglecting his affairs and perhaps suffering other losses, and getting nothing out of the public, because he is just; moreover he is hated by his friends and acquaintance for refusing to serve them in unlawful ways. But all this is reversed in the case of the unjust man. I am speaking, as before, of injustice on a large scale in which the advantage of the unjust is more apparent; and my meaning will be most clearly seen if we turn to that highest form of injustice in which the criminal is the happiest of men, and the sufferers or those who refuse to do injustice are the most miserable—that is to say tyranny, which by fraud and force takes away the property of others, not little by little but wholesale; comprehending in one, things sacred as well as profane, private and public; for which acts of wrong, if he were detected perpetrating any one of them singly, he would be punished and incur great disgrace—they who do such wrong in particular cases are called robbers of temples, and man-stealers and burglars and swindlers and thieves. But when a man besides taking away the money of the citizens has made slaves of them, then, instead of these names of reproach, he is termed happy and blessed, not only by the citizens but by all who hear of his having achieved the consummation of injustice. For mankind censure injustice, fearing that they may be the victims of it and not because they shrink from committing it. And thus, as I have shown, Socrates, injustice, when on a sufficient scale, has more strength and freedom and mastery than justice; and, as I said at first, justice is the interest of the stronger, whereas injustice is a man's own profit and interest.

———

Although Plato arranged for Socrates to prevail in the debate, he was plainly troubled by the arguments made by Thrasymachus. The points that the Sophist raised in *The Republic* surface again in different form in a number of the other Dialogues. Consider, for example, this excerpt from the Dialogue *Gorgias* in which Callicles speaks.

PLATO, GORGIAS, FROM THE DIALOGUES OF PLATO (B. JOWETT TRANS.)

For the suffering of injustice is not the part of a man, but of a slave, who indeed had better die than live; since when he is wronged and trampled upon, he is unable to help himself, or any other about whom he cares. The reason, as I conceive, is that the makers of laws are the majority who are weak; and they make laws and distribute praises and censures with a view to themselves and to their own interests; and they terrify the stronger sort of men, and those who are able to get the better of them, in order that they may not get the better of them; and they say, that dishonesty is shameful and unjust; meaning, by the word injustice, the desire of a man to have more than his neighbours; for knowing their own inferiority, I suspect that they are too glad of equality. And therefore the endeavour to have more than the many, is conventionally said to be shameful and unjust, and is called injustice, whereas nature herself intimates that it is just for the better to have more than the worse, the more powerful than the weaker; and in many ways she shows, among men as well as among animals, and indeed among whole cities and races, that justice consists in the superior ruling over and having more than the inferior. For on what principle of justice did Xerxes invade Hellas, or his father the Scythians? (not to speak of numberless other examples). Nay, but these are the men who act according to nature; yes, by Heaven, and according to the law of nature: not, perhaps, according to that artificial law, which we invent and impose upon our fellows, of whom we take the best and strongest from their youth upwards, and tame them like young lions,—charming them with the sound of the voice, and saying to them, that with equality they must be content, and that the equal is the honourable and the just. But if there were a man who had sufficient force, he would shake off and break through, and escape from all this; he would trample under foot all our formulas and spells and charms, and all our laws which are against nature: the slave would rise in rebellion and be lord over us, and the light of natural justice would shine forth.

————

As is usual in Plato, Socrates trounces Callicles by a logical method not unlike the one we encountered in the refutation of Thrasymachus. But Socrates' reasoning has not persuaded all subsequent commentators. One appraisal of the historic debate, which inclines toward Thrasymachus' position, is offered by Ralf Dahrendorf.

DAHRENDORF, IN PRAISE OF THRASYMACHUS,
IN ESSAYS IN THE THEORY OF SOCIETY 129–139 (1968)

Tradition has been rather less than fair to Thrasymachus of Chalcedon, who, even if he has no other claim to fame, deserves to be remembered for the remarkable achievement of holding his own in an encounter with that champion dialectician, Socrates. Despite the impressions of some of the bystanders and perhaps of Socrates himself, Thrasymachus emerged unconvinced by Socrates' arguments, and with his heavy irony intact, from the vicious debate about justice that distinguishes the first book of the *Republic* from so many of Plato's other dialogues. "Well," he said in response to his opponent's final thrust, "this is a feast day, and you may take all this as your share of the entertainment." (86: 39.)

Our reasons for recalling the rude visitor from Chalcedon are by no means merely rhetorical. Indeed, the first book of the *Republic* deserves much more attention from those who have lightly dismissed it as an early and playful prologue to the serious discussions of the nine remaining books. It was in this initial dialogue, or perhaps more appropriately debate, that two incompatible views of society were stated for the first time in the history of social and political thought. The conflict between these two views has since proved to be the single most persistent conflict in the ranks of those who seek to understand the workings of human society, and among today's scholars it rages still. This conflict has assumed many forms since the admittedly rather crude statement of the two views in the first book of the *Republic*, and we shall here be considering some of these forms right down to contemporary sociological and political theory; but its basic terms were set in that apparently accidental encounter between Thrasymachus and Socrates.

What is more, it seems to me that despite his rather formidable temper and abusive language, Thrasymachus had the better arguments on his side. We have to assist him a little, to be sure, to make his case fully convincing; we shall have to interpolate or even extrapolate his arguments rather than simply interpret them: but with the ideas of Thrasymachus as a starting point, we can develop an image of society that helps us to understand both some basic problems of political theory and the patterns of the good society in our time.

• • •

Thrasymachus was the first to state his case. In all human societies, there are positions that enable their bearers to exercise power. These positions are endowed with sovereignty—the men who hold them lay down the law for their subjects.

Obedience is enforced, for the most important single aspect of power is the control of sanctions. (Sanctions do not always have to be applied: mere anticipation of their effect may suffice to guarantee compliance with the law.) It follows from this notion of power and sanctions that there is always resistance to the exercise of power, and that both the effectiveness and the legitimacy of power—if there is any difference between these two concepts—are precarious. Normally those in power manage to stay in power. Theirs is the stronger group, and society is held together by the exercise of their strength, that is, by constraint.

Now for Socrates' position. It is true, he says, that power is exercised in human societies, but it is exercised on behalf of societies rather than against them. Positions of power are created to give active expression to a general will that represents the consensus of the society's members. What appears to be obedience is in many ways but an expression of this consensus. The exercise of power is dependent on the support of those who are apparently subject to it. Subjection never involves a renunciation of sovereignty; rather, sovereignty remains with the total body politic, with all the citizens of a society. Any differences and divisions in a society are due to outside interference with a basically legitimate system; such divisive influences are in any case destructive of society. Normally, society is held together by the agreement of all citizens on certain fundamental tenets, to which they then adhere voluntarily as a way of protecting their own interests.

This language, of course, is no longer that of Thrasymachus and Socrates, but that of a much later pair of political thinkers, Thomas Hobbes and Jean-Jacques Rousseau. Though separated by more than a century, Hobbes and Rousseau are properly discussed together. . . .

In the extended debate over the social contract (yet another translation of Plato's "justice") two conflicting notions were repeatedly advanced. One was the notion of the social contract of association (*pacte d'association*), according to which society was originally formed by a free agreement to join in a common enterprise involving no abdication of any participant's rights. An odd contract this, or so one might think, but then there are other weaknesses of the Socratic—or Rousseauist—position. The other notion, that of the contract of government (*pacte de gouvernement*), postulated an original agreement setting up an agency responsible for holding society together, an agency to which every party to the agreement must be to some extent subject. This agency is, of course, government and in this form the social contract becomes a real contract with all the attendant problems.

The consequences of this conflict between notions of the social contract were many, although there is little agreement even today on exactly what they were. Hobbes has been called the father of authoritarianism; he has even been used by German sociologists to clothe Nazi rule in an ancient ideology; but the same Hobbes has also been regarded as a forefather of modern liberal theory. Rousseau was long considered the great theorist of democracy; only recently have some political historians discovered that this notion of democracy is distinctly ambiguous, and that perhaps Rousseau bears as much responsibility for totalitarian democracy as for its liberal counterpart.

In the social contract debate, the ancient dispute about the basis of justice was resumed on a more sophisticated level, but with inconclusive results. Its nineteenth-century version, the many-sided conflict between a Socratic *Gemeinschaft* and a Thrasymachean *Gesellschaft*, was equally inconclusive. To find definitive answers, we shall have to make the final step to the present-day version of this debate.

When we do, the first discovery we make is a telling reversal of order. Today, it is the party of Socrates that has stated its case first, and the party of Thrasymachus that has so far confined itself to putting its opposition on record in the most general terms. The surnames of Socrates in our time are many; indeed one can hardly speak of a "party" here, so varied are the approaches of Socratic theorists today. This group includes economists like Kenneth Arrow and Anthony Downs, political scientists like Karl Deutsch and David Easton, sociologists like Talcott Parsons and Neil Smelser, and many others whose analysis rests on an equilibrium model of social life.

Equilibrium theories differ greatly in the degree to which their basic concepts are reified. Not all of them, for example, assume explicitly that there is a general consensus on values among the members of a society. In one way or another, however, they all regard the exercise of power as an exchange in which all citizens participate, and which in theory makes it possible to think of society as a system held in equilibrium so far as its constituent parts are concerned. Disturbances of the system are either ruled out as beyond the boundaries of this type of analysis (i.e., regarded as unfortunate intrusions of the complicated world of uncertainty) or classified as unexplained accidents. Although such disturbances may produce stress or failure of communication within the system, they are generated outside it. The system is regarded as persisting through time by virtue of the equilibrium created either by its internal cycles of power and support, or by the flow of communications, or by the interchange between subsystems as mediated by the currency of power.

What resistance there has been to this approach has been much less subtle than the various versions of the equilibrium theory itself. In this respect, at least, the school of Thrasymachus has remained true to its founder. There have been noisy and ambitious proclamations of a new sociology or a true science of politics, but these have so far resulted in little more than some rather old-fashioned protestations to the effect that power is important, conflict and change omnipresent, and the political process incalculable. There has not yet been any considered statement of how else one might look at society, or explain the political process, or argue for the good society, without abandoning the indubitable technical advances of modern social science. Not infrequently, laudable sentiments have taken the place of necessary arguments. This is as true, it seems to me, of C. Wright Mills and his numerous followers today as it is of Raymond Aron. (The pairing of these two names may perhaps suggest the profound ambiguity in any Thrasymachean position!)

There is no intrinsic objection to an analysis of society in which power figures as an agent of constraint. To be sure, we see in modern economics a remarkable contrast between the technical refinement of equilibrium theories and the nineteenth-century crudeness of theories of development; and our concern here is with a similar contrast between an emphasis on continuity and an emphasis on change. But refinement is not necessarily a sign of truth; and it might be suggested that if Thrasymachean theories seem crude, it is only because the imagination that has gone into formulating them has so far not been accompanied by a corresponding precision of craftsmanship.

In a Thrasymachean theory, power is a central notion. It is seen as unequally divided, and therefore as a lasting source of friction; legitimacy amounts at best to a precarious preponderance of power over the resistance it engenders. Of all states, equilibrium is the least likely, a freakish accident rather than the rule; and there is little to be gained by making it a basic assumption. The dialectic of power and resistance determines the rate and direction of change.

ANARCHISM: BENIGN AND NOT SO BENIGN

For both Plato and his commentator Dahrendorf, the jurisprudence of naked power is ultimately a bleak and sterile one. Other writers in this frame have used the analysis of naked power as a prologue to an alternative, more affirmative vision of the possibilities of social organization. Consider selections from Prince Piotr Kropotkin (1842–1921) and from the contemporary American writer, Eldridge Cleaver.

KROPOTKIN, LAW AND AUTHORITY, IN KROPOTKIN'S
REVOLUTIONARY PAMPHLETS
198–201, 203–218 (R. BALDWIN ED. 1927)

. . . I doubt if there was ever even a revolutionist who did not begin in his youth as the defender of law against what are generally called "abuses," although these last are inevitable consequences of the law itself.

Art pipes in unison with would-be science. The hero of the sculptor, the painter, the musician, shields Law beneath his buckler, and with flashing eyes and distended nostrils stands every ready to strike down the man who would lay hands upon her. Temples are raised to her; revolutionists themselves hesitate to touch the high priests consecrated to her service, and when revolution is about to sweep away some ancient institution, it is still by law that it endeavors to sanctify the deed.

The confused mass of rules of conduct called law, which has been bequeathed to us by slavery, serfdom, feudalism, and royalty, has taken the place of those stone monsters, before whom human victims used to be immolated, and whom slavish savages dared not even touch lest they should be slain by the thunderbolts of heaven.

This new worship has been established with especial success since the rise to supreme power of the middle class-since the great French Revolution. Under the ancient regime, men spoke little of laws; unless, indeed, it were, with Montesquieu, Rousseau and Voltaire, to oppose them to royal caprice. Obedience to the good pleasure of the king and his lackeys was compulsory on pain of hanging or imprisonment. But during and after the revolutions, when the lawyers rose to power, they did their best to strengthen the principle upon which their ascendancy depended. The middle class at once accepted it as a dyke to dam up the popular torrent. The priestly crew hastened to sanctify it, to save their bark from foundering amid the breakers. Finally the people received it as an improvement upon the arbitrary authority and violence of the past.

To understand this, we must transport ourselves in imagination into the eighteenth century. Our hearts must have ached at the story of the atrocities committed by the all-powerful nobles of that time upon the men and women of the people before we can understand what must have been the magic influence upon the peasant's mind of the words, "Equality before the law, obedience to the law without distinction of birth or fortune." He who until then had been treated more cruelly than a beast, he who had never had any rights, he who had never obtained justice against the most revolting actions on the part of a noble, unless in revenge he killed him and was hanged—he saw himself recognized by this maxim, at least in theory, at least with regard to his personal rights, as the equal of his lord. Whatever this law might be, it promised to affect lord and peasant alike; it proclaimed the equality of rich and poor before the judge. The promise was a lie, and today we know it; but at that period it was an advance, a homage to justice, as hypocrisy is a homage rendered to truth. This is the reason that when the saviors of the menaced middle class (the Robespierres and the Dantons) took their stand upon the writings of the Rousseaus and the Voltaires, and proclaimed "respect for law, the same for every man," the people accepted the compromise; for their revolutionary impetus had already spent its force in the contest with a foe whose ranks drew closer day by day; they bowed their neck beneath the yoke of law to save themselves from the arbitrary power of their lords.

•   •   •

But times and tempers are changed. Rebels are everywhere to be found who no longer wish to obey the law without knowing whence it comes, what are its uses, and whither arises the obligation to submit to it, and the reverence with which it is encompassed. The rebels of our day are criticizing the very foundations of society which have hitherto been held sacred, and first and foremost amongst them that fetish, law.

The critics analyze the sources of law, and find there either a god, product of the terrors of the savage, and stupid, paltry and malicious as the priests who vouch for its supernatural origin, or else, bloodshed, conquest by fire and sword. They study the characteristics of law, and instead of perpetual growth corresponding to that of the human race, they find its distinctive trait to be immobility, a tendency to crystallize what should be modified and developed day by day. They ask how law has been maintained, and in its service they see the atrocities of Byzantinism, the cruelties of the Inquisition, the tortures of the middle ages, living flesh torn by the lash of the executioner, chains, clubs, axes, the gloomy dungeons of prisons, agony, curses and tears. In our own days they see, as before, the axe, the cord, the rifle, the prison; on the one hand, the brutalized prisoner, reduced to the condition of a caged beast by the debasement of his whole moral being, and on the other, the judge, stripped of every feeling which does honor to human nature, living like a visionary in a world of legal fictions, revelling in the infliction of imprisonment and death, without even suspecting, in the cold malignity of his madness, the abyss of degradation into which he has himself fallen before the eyes of those whom he condemns.

They see a race of law-makers legislating without knowing what their laws are about; today voting a law on the sanitation of towns, without the faintest notion of hygiene, tomorrow making regulations for the armament of troops, without so much as understanding a gun; making laws about teaching and education without ever having given a lesson of any sort, or even an honest education to their own children; legislating at random in all directions, but never forgetting the penalties to be meted out to ragamuffins, the prison and the galleys, which are to be the portion of men a thousand times less immoral than these legislators themselves.

Finally, they see the jailer on the way to lose all human feeling, the detective trained as a blood-hound, the police spy despising himself; "informing," metamorphosed into a virtue; corruption, erected into a system; all the vice, all the evil qualities of mankind countenanced and cultivated to insure the triumph of law.

All this we see, and, therefore, instead of inanely repeating the old formula, "Respect the law," we say, "Despise law and all its attributes!" In place of the cowardly phrase, "Obey the law," our cry is "Revolt against all laws!"

Only compare the misdeeds accomplished in the name of each law with the good it has been able to effect, and weigh carefully both good and evil, and you will see if we are right.

II

Relatively speaking, law is a product of modern times. For ages and ages mankind lived without any written law, even that graved in symbols upon the entrance stones of a temple. During that period, human relations were simply regulated by customs, habits and usages, made sacred by constant repetition, and acquired by each person in childhood, exactly as he learned how to obtain his food by hunting, cattle-rearing, or agriculture.

• • •

But side by side with these customs, necessary to the life of societies and the preservation of the race, other desires, other passions, and therefore other habits and customs, are evolved in human association. The desire to dominate others and impose one's own will upon them; the desire to seize upon the products of the labor of a neighboring tribe; the desire to surround oneself with comforts without producing anything, while slaves provide their master with the means of procuring every sort of pleasure and luxury—these selfish, personal desires give rise to another current of habits and customs. The priest and the warrior, the charlatan who makes a profit out of superstition, and after freeing himself from the fear of the devil cultivates it in others; and the bully, who procures the invasion and pillage of his neighbors that he may return laden with booty and followed by slaves. These two, hand in hand, have succeeded in imposing upon primitive society customs advantageous to both of them, but tending to perpetuate their domination of the masses. Profiting by the indolence, the fears, the inertia of the crowd, and thanks to the continual repetition of the same acts, they have permanently established customs which have become a solid basis for their own domination.

• • •

The spirit of routine, originating in superstition, indolence, and cowardice, has in all times been the mainstay of oppression. In primitive human societies it was cleverly turned to account by priests and military chiefs. They perpetuated customs useful only to themselves, and succeeded in imposing them on the whole tribe. So long as this conservative spirit could be exploited so as to assure the chief in his encroachments upon individual liberty, so long as the only inequalities between men were the work of nature, and these were not increased a hundred-fold by the concentration of power and wealth, there was no need for law and the formidable paraphernalia of tribunals and ever-augmenting penalties to enforce it.

But as society became more and more divided into two hostile classes, one seeking to establish its domination, the other struggling to escape, the strife began. Now the conqueror was in a hurry to secure the results of his actions in a permanent form, he tried to place them beyond question, to make them holy and venerable by every means in his power. Law made its appearance under the sanction of the priest, and the warrior's club was placed at its service. Its office was to render immutable such customs as were to the advantage of the dominant minority. Military authority undertook to ensure obedience. This new function was a fresh guarantee to the power of the warrior; now he had not only mere brute force at his service; he was the defender of law.

If law, however, presented nothing but a collection of prescriptions serviceable to rulers, it would find some difficulty in insuring acceptance and obedience. Well, the legislators confounded in one code the two currents of custom of which we have just been speaking, the maxims which represent principles of morality and social union wrought out as a result of life in common, and the mandates which are meant to ensure external existence to inequality. Customs, absolutely essential to the very being of society, are, in the code, cleverly intermingled with usages imposed by the ruling caste, and both claim equal respect from the crowd. "Do not kill," says the code, and hastens to add, "And pay tithes to the priest." "Do not steal," says the code, and immediately after, "He who refuses to pay taxes, shall have his hand struck off."

Such was law; and it has maintained its two-fold character to this day. Its origin is the desire of the ruling class to give permanence to customs imposed by themselves for their own advantage. Its character is the skillful commingling of customs useful to society, customs which have no need of law to insure respect, with other customs useful only to rulers, injurious to the mass of the people, and maintained only by the fear of punishment.

Like individual capital, which was born of fraud and violence, and developed under the auspices of authority, law has no title to the respect of men. Born of violence and superstition, and established in the interests of consumer, priest and rich exploiter, it must be utterly destroyed on the day when the people desire to break their chains.

We shall be still better convinced of this when, later, we shall have analyzed the ulterior development of laws under the auspices of religion, authority and the existing parliamentary system.

III

We have seen how law originated in established usage and custom, and how from the beginning it has represented a skillful mixture of social habits, necessary to the preservation of the human race, with other customs imposed by those who used popular superstition as well as the right of the strongest for their own advantage. This double character of law has determined its own later development during the growth of political organization. While in the course of ages the nucleus of social custom inscribed in law has been subjected to but slight and gradual modifications, the other portion has been largely developed in directions indicated by the interests of the dominant classes, and to the injury of the classes they oppress.

• • •

Law, in its quality of guarantee of the results of pillage, slavery and exploitation, has followed the same phases of development as capital. Twin brother and sister, they have advanced hand in hand, sustaining one another with the suffering of mankind. In every country in Europe their history is approximately the same. It has differed only in detail; the main facts are alike; and to glance at the development of law in France or Germany is to know its essential traits and its phases of development in most of the European nations.

In the first instance, law was a national pact or contract. It is true that this contract was not always freely accepted. Even in the early days the rich and strong were imposing their will upon the rest. But at all events they encountered an obstacle to their encroachments in the mass of the people, who often made them feel their power in return.

But as the church on one side and the nobles on the other succeeded in enthralling the people, the right of law-making escaped from the hands of the nation and passed into those of the privileged orders. Fortified by the wealth accumulating in her coffers, the church extended her authority. She tampered more and more with private life, and under pretext of saving souls, seized upon the labor of her serfs, she gathered taxes from every class, she increased her jurisdiction, she multiplied penalties, and enriched herself in proportion to the number of offenses committed, for the produce of every fine poured into her coffers. Laws had no longer any connection with the interest of the nation. "They might have been supposed to emanate rather from a council of religious fanatics than from legislators," observes an historian of French Law.

At the same time, as the baron likewise extended his authority over laborers in the fields and artisans in the towns, he, too, became legislator and judge. The few relics of national law dating from the tenth century are merely agreements regulating service, statute-labor, and tribute due from serfs and vassals to their lord. The legislators of that period were a handful of brigands organized for the plunder of a people daily becoming more peaceful as they applied themselves to agricultural pursuits. These robbers exploited the feelings for justice inherent in the people, they posed as the administrators of that justice, made a source of revenue for themselves out of its fundamental principles and concocted laws to maintain their own domination.

Later on, these laws collected and classified by jurists formed the foundation of our modern codes. And are we to talk about respecting these codes, the legacy of baron and priest?

• • •

As we know, the free townships were not able to hold their own. Torn by internal dissensions between rich and poor, burgher and serf, they fell an easy prey to royalty. And as royalty acquired fresh strength, the right of legislation passed more and more into the hands of a clique of courtiers. Appeal to the nation was made only to sanction the taxes demanded by the king. Parliament summoned at intervals of two centuries, according to the good pleasure or caprice of the court, "Councils Extraordinary," assemblies of notables, ministers, scarce heeding the "grievances of the king's subjects"—these are the legislators of France. Later still, when all power is concentrated in a single man, who can say "I am the State," edicts are concocted in the "secret counsels of the prince," according to the whim of a minister, or of an imbecile king; and subjects must obey on pain of death. All judicial guarantees are abolished; the nation is the serf of royalty, and of a handful of courtiers. And at this period the most horrible penalties startle our gaze—the wheel, the stake, flaying alive, tortures of every description, invented by the sick fancy of monks and madmen, seeking delight in the sufferings of executed criminals.

The great Revolution began the demolition of this framework of law, bequeathed to us by feudalism and royalty. But after having demolished some portions of the ancient edifice, the Revolution delivered over the power of law-making to the bourgeoisie, who, in their turn, began to raise a fresh framework of laws intended to maintain and perpetuate middle-class domination among the masses. Their parliament makes laws right and left, and mountains of law accumulate with frightful rapidity. But what are all these laws at bottom?

The major portion have but one object-to protect private property, i.e., wealth acquired by the exploitation of man by man. Their aim is to open out to capital fresh fields for exploitation, and to sanction the new forms which that exploitation continually assumes, as capital swallows up another branch of human activity, railways, telegraphs, electric light, chemical industries, the expression of man's thought in literature and science, etc. The object of the rest of these laws is fundamentally the same. They exist to keep up the machinery of government which serves to secure to capital the exploitation and monopoly of the wealth produced. Magistrature, police, army, public instruction, finance, all serve one God—capital; all have but one object—to facilitate the exploitation of the worker by the capitalist. Analyze all the laws passed and you will find nothing but this.

The protection of the person, which is put forward as the true mission of law, occupies an imperceptible space among them, for, in existing society, assaults upon the person directly dictated by hatred and brutality tend to disappear. Nowadays, if anyone is murdered, it is generally for the sake of robbing him; rarely because of personal vengeance. But if this class of crimes and misdemeanors is continually diminishing, we certainly do not owe the change to legislation. It is due to the growth of humanitarianism in our societies, to our increasingly social habits rather than to the prescriptions of our laws. Repeal tomorrow every law dealing with the protection of the person, and tomorrow stop all proceedings for assault, and the number of attempts dictated by personal vengeance and by brutality would not be augmented by one single instance.

•   •   •

. . . The law, which on its first appearance presented itself as a compendium of customs useful for the preservation of society, is now perceived to be nothing but an instrument for the maintenance of exploitation and domination of the toiling masses by rich idlers. At the present day its civilizing mission is nil; it has but one object—to bolster up exploitation.

This is what is told us by history as to the development of law. Is it in virtue of this history that we are called upon to respect it? Certainly not. It has no more title to respect than capital, the fruits of pillage. And the first duty of the revolution will be to make a bonfire of all existing laws as it will of all titles to property.

IV

The millions of laws which exist for the regulation of humanity appear upon investigation to be divided into three principal categories: protection of property, protection of persons, protection of government. And by analyzing each of these categories, we arrive at the same logical and necessary conclusion: *the uselessness and hurtfulness of law*.

Socialists know what is meant by protection of property. Laws on property are not made to guarantee either to the individual or to society the enjoyment of the produce of their own labor. On the contrary, they are made to rob the producer of a part of what he has created, and to secure to certain other people that portion of the produce which they have stolen either from the producer or from society as a whole. When, for example, the law establishes Mr. So-and-So's right to a house, it is not establishing his right to a cottage he has built for himself, or to a house he has erected with the help of some of his friends. In that case no one would have disputed his right. On the contrary, the law is establishing his right to a house which is not the product of his labor; first of all because he has had it built for him by others to whom he has not paid the full value of their work, and next because that house represents a social value which he could not have produced for himself. The law is establishing his right to what belongs to everybody in general and to nobody in particular. The same house built in the midst of Siberia would not have the value it possesses in a large town, and, as we know, that value arises from the labor of something like fifty generations of men who have built the town, beautified it, supplied it with water and gas, fine promenades, colleges, theatres, shops, railways and roads leading in all directions. Thus, by recognizing the right of Mr. So-and-so to a particular house in Paris, London or Rouen, the law is unjustly appropriating to him a certain portion of the produce of the labor of mankind in general. And it is precisely because this appropriation and all other forms of property bearing the same character are a crying injustice, that a whole arsenal of laws and a whole army of soldiers, policemen and judges are needed to maintain it against the good sense and just feeling inherent in humanity.

Half our laws,—the civil code in each country,—serves no other purpose than to maintain this appropriation, this monopoly for the benefit of certain individuals against the whole of mankind. Three-fourths of the causes decided by the tribunals are nothing but quarrels between monopolists—two robbers disputing over their booty. And a great many of our criminal laws have the same object in view, their end being to keep the workman in a subordinate position towards his employer, and thus afford security for exploitation.

• • •

As all the laws about property which make up thick volumes of codes and are the delight of our lawyers have no other object than to protect the unjust appropriation of human labor by certain monopolists, there is no reason for their existence, and, on the day of the revolution, social revolutionists are thoroughly determined to put an end to them. Indeed, a bonfire might be made with perfect justice of all laws bearing upon the so-called "rights of property," all title-deeds, all registers, in a word, of all that is in any way connected with an institution which will soon be looked upon as a blot in the history of humanity, as humiliating as the slavery and serfdom of past ages.

The remarks just made upon laws concerning property are quite as applicable to the second category of laws; those for the maintenance of government, i.e., constitutional law.

It again is a complete arsenal of laws, decrees, ordinances, orders in council, and what not, all serving to protect the diverse forms of representative government, delegated or usurped, beneath which humanity is writhing. We know very well—anarchists have often enough pointed out in their perpetual criticism of the various forms of government—that the mission of all governments, monarchical, constitutional, or republican, is to protect and maintain by force the privileges of the classes in possession, the aristocracy, clergy and traders. A good third of our laws—and each country possesses some tens of thousands of them—the fundamental laws on taxes, excise duties, the organization of ministerial departments and their offices, of the army, the police, the church, etc., have no other end than to maintain, patch up, and develop the administrative machine. And this machine in its turn serves almost entirely to protect the privileges of the possessing classes. Analyze all these laws, observe them in action day by day, and you will discover that not one is worth preserving.

About such laws there can be no two opinions. Not only anarchists, but more or less revolutionary radicals also, are agreed that the only use to be made of laws concerning the organization of government is to fling them into the fire.

The third category of law still remains to be considered; that relating to the protection of the person and the detection and prevention of "crime." This is the most important because most prejudices attach to it; because, if law enjoys a certain amount of consideration, it is in consequence of the belief that this species of law is absolutely indispensable to the maintenance of security in our societies. . . .

Well, in spite of all the prejudices existing on this subject, it is quite time that anarchists should boldly declare this category of laws as useless and injurious as the preceding ones.

First of all, as to so-called "crimes"—assaults upon persons—it is well known that two-thirds, and often as many as three-fourths, of such "crimes" are instigated by the desire to obtain possession of someone's wealth. This immense class of so-called "crimes and misdemeanors" will disappear on the day on which private property ceases to exist. "But," it will be said, "there will always be brutes who will attempt the lives of their fellow citizens, who will lay their hands to a knife in every quarrel, and revenge the slightest offense by murder, if there are no laws to restrain and punishments to withhold them." This refrain is repeated every time the right of society *to punish* is called in question.

Yet there is one fact concerning this head which at the present time is thoroughly established; the severity of punishment does not diminish the amount of crime. Hang, and, if you like, quarter murderers, and the number of murders will not decrease by one. On the other hand, abolish the penalty of death, and there will not be one murder more; there will be fewer. Statistics prove it. But if the harvest is good, and bread cheap, and the weather fine, the number of murders immediately decreases. This again is proved by statistics. The amount of crime always augments and diminishes in proportion to the price of provisions and the state of the weather. Not that all murderers are actuated by hunger. That is not the case. But when the harvest is good, and provisions are at an obtainable price, and when the sun shines, men, lighter-hearted and less miserable than usual, do not give way to gloomy passions, do not from trivial motives plunge a knife into the bosom of a fellow creature.

Moreover, it is also a well known fact that the fear of punishment has never stopped a single murderer. He who kills his neighbor from revenge or misery does not reason much about consequences; and there have been few murderers who were not firmly convinced that they should escape prosecution.

Without speaking of a society in which a man will receive a better education, in which the development of all his faculties, and the possibility of exercising them, will procure him so many enjoyments that he will not seek to poison them by remorse—even in our society, even with those sad products of misery whom we see today in the public houses of great cities—on the day when no punishment is inflicted upon murderers, the number of murders will not be augmented by a single case. And it is extremely probable that it will be, on the contrary, diminished by all those cases which are due at present to habitual criminals, who have been brutalized in prisons.

We are continually being told of the benefits conferred by law, and the beneficial effect of penalties, but have the speakers ever attempted to strike a balance between the benefits attributed to laws and penalties, and the degrading effect of these penalties upon humanity? Only calculate all the evil passions awakened in mankind by the atrocious punishments formerly inflicted in our streets! Man is the cruelest animal upon earth. And who has pampered and developed the cruel instincts unknown, even among monkeys, if it is not the king, the judge, and the priests, armed with law, who caused flesh to be torn off in strips, boiling pitch to be poured into wounds, limbs to be dislocated, bones to be crushed, men to be sawn asunder to maintain their authority? Only estimate the torrent of depravity let loose in human society by the "informing" which is countenanced by judges, and paid in hard cash by go-vernments, under pretext of assisting in the discovery of "crime." Only go into the jails and study what man becomes when he is deprived of freedom and shut up with other depraved beings, steeped in the vice and corruption which oozes from the very walls of our existing prisons. Only remember that the more these prisons are reformed, the more detestable they become. Our model modern penitentiaries are a hundred-fold more abominable than the dungeons of the middle ages. Finally, consider what corruption, what depravity of mind is kept up among men by the idea of obedience, the very essence of law; of chastisement; of authority having the right to punish, to judge irrespective of our conscience and the esteem of our friends; of the necessity for executioners, jailers, and informers—in a word, by all the attributes of law and authority. Consider all this, and you will assuredly agree with us in saying that a law inflicting penalties is an abomination which should cease to exist.

Peoples without political organization, and therefore less depraved than ourselves have perfectly understood that the man who is called "criminal" is simply unfor-tunate; that the remedy is not to flog him, to chain him up, or to kill him on the scaffold or in prison but to help him by the most brotherly care, by treatment based on equality, by the uses of life among honest men. In the next revolution we hope that this cry will go forth:

"Burn the guillotines; demolish the prisons; drive away the judges, policemen and informers—the impurest race upon the face of the earth; treat as a brother the man who has been led by passion to do ill to his fellow; above all, take from the ignoble products of middle-class idleness the possibility of displaying their vice in attractive colors; and be sure that but few crimes will mar our society."

The main supports of crime are idleness, law and authority; laws about property, laws about government, laws about penalties and misdemeanors; and authority, which takes upon itself to manufacture these laws and to apply them.

No more laws! No more judges! Liberty, equality, and practical human sympathy are the only effectual barriers we can oppose to the anti-social instincts of certain among us.

CLEAVER, DOMESTIC LAW AND INTERNATIONAL ORDER, IN SOUL ON ICE 128–37 (1968)

The police department and the armed forces are the two arms of the power structure, the muscles of control and enforcement. They have deadly weapons with which to inflict pain on the human body. They know how to bring about horrible deaths. They have clubs with which to beat the body and the head. They have bullets and guns with which to tear holes in the flesh, to smash bones, to disable and kill. They use force, to make you do what the deciders have decided you must do.

Every country on earth has these agencies of force. The people everywhere fear this terror and force. To them it is like a snarling wild beast which can put an end to one's dreams. They punish. They have cells and prisons to lock you up in. They pass out sentences. They won't let you go when you want to. You have to stay put until they give the word. If your mother is dying, you can't go to her bedside to say goodbye or to her graveside to see her lowered into the earth, to see her, for the last time, swallowed up by that black hole.

The techniques of the enforcers are many; firing squads, gas chambers, electric chairs, torture chambers, the garrote, the guillotine, the tightening rope around your throat. It has been found that the death penalty is necessary to back up the law, to make it easier to enforce, to deter transgressions against the penal code. That everybody doesn't believe in the same laws is beside the point.

Which laws get enforced depends on who is in power. If the capitalists are in power, they enforce laws designed to protect their system, their way of life. They have a particular abhorrence for crimes against property, but are prepared to be liberal and show a modicum of compassion for crimes against the person—unless, of course, an instance of the latter is combined with an instance of the former. In such cases, nothing can stop them from throwing the whole book at the offender. For instance, armed robbery with violence, to a capitalist, is the very epitome of evil. Ask any banker what he thinks of it.

If Communists are in power, they enforce laws designed to protect their system, their way of life. To them, the horror of horrors is the speculator, that man of magic who has mastered the art of getting something with nothing and who in America would be a member in good standing of his local Chamber of Commerce.

"The people," however, are nowhere consulted, although everywhere everything is done always in their name and ostensibly for their betterment, while their real-life problems go unsolved. "The people" are a rubber stamp for the crafty and sly. And no problem can be solved without taking the police department and the armed forces into account. Both kings and bookies understand this, as do first ladies and common prostitutes.

The police do on the domestic level what the armed forces do on the international level: protect the way of life of those in power. The police patrol the city, cordon off communities, blockade neighborhoods, invade homes, search for that which is hidden. The armed forces patrol the world, invade countries and continents, cordon off nations, blockade islands and whole peoples; they will also overrun villages, neighborhoods, enter homes, huts, caves, searching for that which is hidden. The policeman and the soldier will violate your person, smoke you out with various gases. Each will shoot you, beat your head and body with sticks and clubs, with rifle butts, run you through with bayonets, shoot holes in your flesh, kill you. They each have unlimited firepower. They will use all that is necessary to bring you to your knees. They won't take no for an answer. If you resist their sticks, they draw their guns. If you resist their guns, they call for reinforcements with bigger guns. Eventually they will come in tanks, in jets, in ships. They will not rest until you surrender or are killed. The policeman and the soldier will have the last word.

Both police and the armed forces follow orders. Orders. Orders flow from the top down. Up there, behind closed doors, in antechambers, in conference rooms, gavels bang on the tables, the tinkling of silver decanters can be heard as icewater is poured by well-fed, conservatively dressed men in hornrimmed glasses, fashionably dressed American widows with rejuvenated faces and tinted hair, the air permeated with the square humor of Bob Hope jokes. Here all the talking is done, all the thinking, all the deciding. Gray rabbits of men scurry forth from the conference room to spread the decisions throughout the city, as News. Carrying out orders is a job, a way of meeting the payments on the house, a way of providing for one's kiddies. In the armed forces it is also a duty, patriotism. Not to do so is treason.

Every city has its police department. No city would be complete without one. It would be sheer madness to try operating an American city without the heat, the fuzz, the man. Americans are too far gone, or else they haven't arrived yet; the center does not exist, only the extremes. Take away the cops and Americans would have a coast-to-coast free-for-all. There are, of course, a few citizens who carry their own private cops around with them, built into their souls. But there is robbery in the land, and larceny, murder, rape, burglary, theft, swindles, all brands of crime, profit, rent, interest—and these blasé descendants of Pilgrims are at each other's throats. To complicate matters, there are also rich people and poor people in America. There are Negroes and whites, Indians, Puerto Ricans, Mexicans, Jews, Chinese, Arabs, Japanese—all with equal rights but unequal possessions. Some are haves and some are have-nots. All have been taught to worship at the shrine of General Motors. The whites are on top in America and they want to stay there, up there. They are also on top in the world, on the international level, and they want to stay up there, too. Everywhere there are those who want to smash this precious toy clock of a system, they want ever so much to change it, to rearrange things, to pull the whites down off their high horse and make them equal. Everywhere the whites are fighting to prolong their status, to retard the erosion of their position. In America, when everything else fails, they call out the police. On the international level, when everything else fails, they call out the armed forces.

• • •

In their rage against the police, against police brutality, the blacks lose sight of the fundamental reality: that the police are only an instrument for the implementation of the policies of those who make the decisions. Police brutality is only one facet of the crystal of terror and oppression. Behind police brutality there is social brutality, economic brutality, and political brutality. From the perspective of the ghetto, this is not easy to discern: the TV newscaster and the radio announcer and the editorialists of the newspapers are wizards of the smoke screen and the snow job.

What is true on the international level is true also at home; except that the ace up the sleeve is easier to detect in the international arena. Who would maintain that American soldiers are in Vietnam on their own motion? They were conscripted into the armed forces and taught the wisdom of obeying orders. They were sent to Vietnam by orders of the generals in the Pentagon, who receive them from the Secretary of Defense, who receives them from the President, who is shrouded in mystery. The soldier in the field in Vietnam, the man who lies in the grass and squeezes the trigger when a little half-starved, trembling Vietnamese peasant crosses his sights, is only following orders, carrying out a policy and a plan. He hardly knows what it is all about. They have him wired-up tight with slogans of TV and the World Series. All he knows is that he has been assigned to carry out a certain ritual of duties. He is well trained and does the best he can. He does a good job. He may want to please those above him with the quality of his performance. He may want to make sergeant, or better. This man is from some hicky farm in Shit Creek, Georgia. He only knew whom to kill after passing through boot camp. He could just as well come out ready to kill Swedes. He will kill a Swede dead, if he is ordered to do so.

Same for the policeman in Watts. He is not there on his own. They have all been assigned. They have been told what to do and what not to do. They have also been told what they better not do. So when they continually do something, in every filthy ghetto in this shitty land, it means only that they are following orders.

• • •

The Utopians speak of a day when there will be no police. There will be nothing for them to do. Every man will do his duty, will respect the rights of his neighbor, will not disturb the peace. The needs of all will be taken care of. Everyone will have sympathy for his fellow man. There will be no such thing as crime. There will be, of course, no prisons. No electric chairs, no gas chambers. The hangman's rope will be the thing of the past. The entire earth will be a land of plenty. There will be no crimes against property, no speculation.

It is easy to see that we are not on the verge of entering Utopia: there are cops everywhere. North and South, the Negroes are the have-nots. They see property all around them, property that is owned by whites. In this regard the black bourgeoisie has become nothing but a ridiculous nuisance. Having waged a battle for entrance into the American mainstream continually for fifty years, all of the black bourgeoisie's defenses are directed outward, against the white. They have no defenses against the blacks and no time to erect any. The black masses can handle them any time they choose, with one mighty blow. But the white bourgeoisie presents a bigger problem, those whites who own everything. With many shackled by unemployment, hatred in black hearts for this system of private property increases daily. The sanctity surrounding property is being called into question. The mystique of the deed of ownership is melting away. In other parts of the world, peasants rise up and expropriate the land from the former owners. Blacks in America see that the deed is not eternal, that it is not signed by God, and that new deeds, making blacks the owners, can be drawn up.

* * *

. . . Meanwhile, they must learn that the police take orders from General Motors. And that the Bank of America has something to do with them even though they don't have a righteous penny in the bank. They have no bank accounts, only bills to pay. The only way they know of making withdrawals from the bank is at the point of a gun. The shiny fronts of skyscrapers intimidate them. They do not own them. They feel alienated from the very sidewalks on which they walk. This white man's country, this white man's world. Overflowing with men of color. An economy consecrated to the succor of the whites. Blacks are incidental. The war on proverty, that monstrous insult to the rippling muscles in black man's arms, is an index of how men actually sit down and plot each other's deaths, actually sit down with slide rules and calculate how to hide bread from the hungry. And the black bourgeoisie greedily sopping up what crumbs are tossed into their dark corner.

There are 20,000,000 of these blacks in America, probably more. Today they repeat, in awe, this magic number to themselves: there are 20,000,000 of us. They shout this to each other in humiliated astonishment. No one need tell them that there is vast power latent in their mass. They know that 20,000,000 of anything is enough to get some recognition and consideration. They know also that they must harness their number and hone it into a sword with a sharp cutting edge. White General Motors also knows that the unity of these 20,000,000 ragamuffins will spell the death of the system of its being. At all costs, then, they will seek to keep these blacks from uniting, from becoming revolutionary. These white property owners know that they must keep the blacks cowardly and intimidated. By a complex communications system of hints and signals, certain orders are given to the chief of police and the sheriff who pass them on to their men, the footsoldiers in the trenches of the ghetto. . . .

NOTES

1. Kropotkin and Cleaver distinguish, with varying clarity, the elite which governs and calls itself "The State" from the people. Is this a valid distinction? in general? In some communities? Discuss.

2. Do the writers in this frame tend to be realistic? Accurate? Are their viewpoints and theses useful for purposes of trying to influence decision?

3. Compare Kropotkin's position that law represents the technique whereby the strong rule the weak with that of Callicles in Plato's *Gorgias* (supra) and that of Nietzsche, that, on the contrary, law is the technique employed by the weak to limit the powers of the strong. (Nietzsche, *On the Genealogy of Morals* (Kaufmann trans. 1967). Is either statement correct? Discuss.

4. Cleaver emphasizes law as the use of naked force and ignores or rejects the notion that intrinsic to law and to shaping people's condut to conform to it are the shared expectations in communities that decisions be taken by those whom people-at-large expect to decide and in a manner that people expect such decisions to be made. Consider in this regard the remarks about Marxist writer Antonio Gramsci's theory of hegemony:

> By hegemony Gramsci meant the permeation throughout civil society—including a whole range of structures and activities like trade unions, schools, the churches, and the family—of an entire system of values, attitudes, beliefs, morality, etc. that is in one way or another supportive of the established order and the class interests that dominate it. . . . To the extent that this prevailing consciousness is internalized by the broad masses, it becomes part of "common sense"; . . . For hegemony to assert itself successfully in any society, therefore, it must operate in a dualistic manner: as a "general conception of life" for the masses, and as a "scholastic programme" or set of principles which is advanced by a sector of the intellectuals. . . . [Gramsci observed that where] hegemony appeared as a strong force, it fulfilled a role that guns and tanks could never perform. . . . [I]t encouraged a sense of fatalism and passivity towards political action; and it justified every type of system—serving sacrifice and deprivation. In short, hegemony worked in many ways to induce the oppressed to accept or "consent" to their own exploitation and daily misery.*

For views in a similar vein further elaborated by American scholars, see the materials on the Critical Legal Studies Movement in Chapter 10.

5. Is it possible for a small elite to rule society by force without catering at all to the shared expectations of the majority of the population? Can such rule exist for long in any society? Consider these questions with regard to the U.S., the U.S.S.R., China.

6. Does the presence of a severe crisis tend to increase willingness to be ruled rather than governed? Can crisis be manipulated by elites? Discuss.

7. Do you agree with Cleaver's claim that decisions in America do not reflect the majority's will? Or does Cleaver claim that the majority today exploits the minority?

8. How would Cleaver run the country if he had his way? Has he clarified his goals?

9. Do both Thrasymachus and Cleaver view man as inherently and irremediably evil and exploitative? (*See* Machiavelli, *The Prince* 75 (Craig ed. 1944); for general discussion, consider K. Waltz, *Man, the State, and War*, 6 ff. (1959)). Discuss.

10. Claims that law is established and maintained by those in power for their own benefit, are often advanced by minority groups who feel deprived of power and other values. Discuss.

11. How would a writer such as Cleaver, whose thesis is that U.S. law is controlled by a small wealthy elite for their own ends, explain recent legislative and judicial developments such as,

> (i) greatly increased liability of manufacturers for defective products, even where the plaintiff is unable to prove that a particular defendant company had produced the product which caused the harm to plaintiff (as long as defendant produced a similar product of the same defective quality). (See Sindell v. Abbott Laboratories, p. 480 infra.)
> (ii) greatly expanded rights of tenants against landlords, including warranties of habitability implied by law, unenforceability of unconscionable leases, extensive rent

*C. Boggs, *Gramsci's Marxism* 39–40 (1976).

controls, etc. (See Javins v. First National Realty Corp., infra; Berger, *Land Ownership and Use* 215–16 (1983); N.Y. Real Property Law (235(c)).

(iii) stringent anti-pollution laws and standards which are very expensive for manufacturers and consumers. (See, e.g., 42 U.S.C. (651 ff.)

(iv) greatly increased requirements for employers to provide safe working quarters for employees.

(v) government funding of legal services for the poor, and requirements to provide legal counsel to criminal defendants free of charge if need be.

(vi) the allocation of more funds in the federal budget for health and social welfare benefits than for defense.

(vii) increases in minimum wages and social security benefits.

Discuss.

12. Writers such as Cleaver and Kropotkin seem to share a schizophrenic view about the nature of people: i.e., a paranoia about the evil motives of current decision-makers, but an almost childlike faith in the goodness of decisionmakers immediately upon the arrival of the millennium that they desire. Discuss.

In Chapter 1, two dilemmas were posed, one dealing with the exercise of naked power within a state, the other with the legal and moral dilemmas of preferential treatment in the United States. In a jurisprudence in which law is identified only with naked power, you will note that neither of these dilemmas present serious moral or ethical problems to the decisionmaker. The only question is to determine the distribution of effective power (itself no easy task) and then to contour decisions and law so that they configure it. In your view, is this an adequate jurisprudential theory?

P. Bachrach & M. Baratz, Two Facts of Power, *Am. Pol. Sci. Rev.* 56 (1962).

A. A. Berle, *Power* (1969).

P. M. Blau, *Exchange and Power in Social Life* (1964).

E. Durkheim, *Montesquieu and Rousseau, Forerunners of Sociology* (R. Manheim transl. 1965).

T. Hobbes, *The Element of Law, Natural and Political* (2d rev. ed. 1969); *The Leviathan* (London, 1651; 2d rev. ed. 1957).

S. Hoffmann, International Law and the Control of Force, in *The Relevance of International Law* 21 (K. Deutsch & S. Hoffmann eds. 1968).

B. Jouvenal, *Power: The Natural History of Its Growth* (1952).

H. Lasswell, *Politics: Who Gets What, When, How* (1936); *Power and Personality* (1948).

The Ethic of Power, The Interplay of Religion, Philosophy, and Politics (H. Lasswell & H. Cleveland eds. 1952).

K. Lorenz, *On Aggression* (1974).

N. Machiavelli, *The Prince* (G. Bull transl. 1961).

C. Merriam, *Political Power, Its Composition and Incidence* (1934).

C. W. Mills, *The Power Elite* (1956).

Political Systems and the Distribution of Power (M. Banton ed. 1965).

W. M. Reisman, Private Armies in a Global War System: Prologue to Decision, 14 *Va. J. Int'l L.* 1 (1973); reprinted in M. S. McDougal & W. M. Reisman, *International Law Essays* 142 (1981).

G. Runkie, *Anarchism, Old and New* (1972).

B. Russel, *Power: A New Social Analysis* (1978).

M. Weber, *Economy and Society* (G. Roth & C. Wittich eds. 1968, 1978).

M. Weber, *The Theory of Social and Economic Organization* (A. Henderson & T. Parsons transl. 1947).

W. O. Weyrauch, *The Personality of Lawyers* (1964).

H. R. P. Wolf, *In Defense of Anarchism* (1976).

CHAPTER 4

The Ethic of Obedience:
A Jurisprudence of Natural Law

Do not follow the majority for evil . . .
you shall incline after the majority.
Exodus 23:2

It is 1945. The Allied armies enter Germany. Because the Reich government has been completely extinguished, the Allies must take over every aspect of government, including criminal justice. One prisoner in a German jail is a German national, Heinrich Bessermann. Bessermann was seized by the Nazis only three days before the collapse for allegedly planting a time-bomb in a cafe in Munich. The bomb killed six German soldiers on vacation and eight German civilians. Bessermann readily confesses to the Allied lawyers, but shows that he was part of a resistance. As an Allied lawyer, you must decide whether to prosecute Bessermann.

The theory of jurisprudence with probably the longest and continuously most explicit history is usually referred to as natural law. At different times it has meant different things, from substantive legal principles derived from a divinity or from "nature," at one extreme, to a rather rationalistic process of thinking designed to deduce the norms which serve a community most effectively, at the other.

Common to all the variants of natural law is the idea that there are certain principles or postulates that are unquestionably true but unquestionably unverifiable.

In this and the following chapter, we will be exploring two prominent strains of natural law which have proved significant in American jurisprudence and recur at regular intervals in political controversies in the United States and other industrial societies. The first may be referred to generally as the jurisprudence of obedience; it is a frame which assumes that, in an organized society, there must be certain hierarchical patterns in governance and that for people at lower levels the appropriate ethic is one of obedience. A basic assumption in this jurisprudence is that there is an independent moral value in obeying authority and an independent iniquity and social pathology in challenging it, even if, in a particular case, the consequences of the authoritative decision appear to be evil and the reasons for challenging it seem good. Consider Bessermann. He was certainly acting against the evil which, at the moment of his crime, was inseparable from the official elite. Shortly afterwards, however, a group committed to a different set of values gained control of the state apparatus and, from its status of incumbency, had to determine whether or not an unauthorized act of violence—injuring innocent as well as targetted persons—no matter what its motivation, should be sanctioned.

THE ARGUMENT FOR ABSOLUTE OBEDIENCE

A venerable discussion of the key assumption of the jurisprudence of obedience is to be found in Plato's dialogue, *Crito*. It concerns Socrates' reflections on his trial and the verdict of capital punishment and the propriety of evading, in an economic and thoroughly non-violent fashion, what almost all conceded to be an unjust verdict.

PLATO, CRITO, FROM THE DIALOGUES OF PLATO (B. JOWETT TRANS.)

Crito: . . . my beloved Socrates, let me entreat you once more to take my advice and escape. For if you die I shall not only lose a friend who can never be replaced, but there is another evil: people who do not know you and me will believe that I might have saved you if I had been willing to give money, but that I did not care. Now, can there be a worse disgrace than this—that I would be thought to value money more than the life of a friend? For the many will not be persuaded that I wanted you to escape, and that you refused.

Soc. But why, my dear Crito, should we care about the opinion of the many? Good men, and they are the only persons who are worth considering, will think of these things truly as they occurred.

Cr. But you see, Socrates, that the opinion of the many must be regarded, for what is now happening shows that they can do the greatest evil to any one who has lost their good opinion.

Soc. I only wish it were so, Crito; and that the many could do the greatest evil; for then they would also be able to do the greatest good—and what a fine thing this would be! But in reality they can do neither; for they cannot make a man either wise or foolish; and whatever they do is the result of chance.

Cr. Well, I will not dispute with you; but please to tell me, Socrates, whether you are not acting out of regard to me and your other friends: are you not afraid that if you escape from prison we may get into trouble with the informers for having stolen you away, and lose either the whole or a great part of our property; or that even a worse evil may happen to us? Now, if you fear on our account, be at ease; for in order to save you, we ought surely to run this, or even a greater risk; be persuaded, then, and do as I say.

Soc. Yes, Crito, that is one fear which you mention, but by no means the only one.

Cr. Fear not—there are persons who are willing to get you out of prison at no great cost; and as for the informers, they are far from being exorbitant in their demands—a little money will satisfy them. My means, which are certainly ample, are at your service, and if you have a scruple about spending all mine, here (sic) are strangers who will give you the use of theirs; and one of them, Simmias the Theban, has brought a large sum of money for this very purpose; and Cebes and many others are prepared to spend their money in helping you to escape. I say, therefore, do not hesitate on our account, and do not say, as you did in the court, that you will have a difficulty in knowing what to do with yourself anywhere else. For men will love you in other places to which you may go, and not in Athens only; there are friends of mine in Thessaly, if you like to go to them, who will value and protect you, and no Thessalian will give you any trouble. Nor can I think that you are at all justified, Socrates, in betraying your own life when you might be saved; in acting thus you are playing into the hands of your enemies, who are hurrying on your destruction.

And further I should say that you are deserting your own children; for you might bring them up and educate them; instead of which you go away and leave them and they will have to take their chance; and if they do not meet with the usual fate of orphans, there will be small thanks to you. No man should bring children into the world who is unwilling to persevere to the end in their nurture and education. But you appear to be choosing the easier part, not the better and manlier, which would have been more becoming in one who professes to care for virtue in all his actions, like yourself. And indeed, I am ashamed not only of you, but of us who are your friends, when I reflect that the whole business will be attributed entirely to our want of courage. The trial need never have come on, or might have been managed differently; and this last act, or crowning folly, will seem to have occurred through our negligence and cowardice, who might have saved you, if we had been good for anything; and you might have saved yourself, for there was no difficulty at all. See now, Socrates, how sad and discreditable are the consequences, both to us and you. Make up your mind then, or rather have your mind already made up, for the time of deliberation is over, and there is only one thing to be done, which must be done this very night, and if we delay at all will be no longer practicable or possible; I beseech you therefore, Socrates, be persuaded by me, and do as I say.

Soc. Dear Crito, your zeal is invaluable, if a right one; but if wrong, the greater the zeal the greater the danger; and therefore we ought to consider whether I shall or shall not do as you say. For I am and always have been one of those natures who must be guided by reason, whatever the reason may be which upon reflection appears to me to be the best; and now that this chance has befallen me, I cannot repudiate my own words: the principles which I have hitherto honoured and revered I still honour, and unless we can at once find other and better principles, I am certain not to agree with you; no, not even if the power of the multitude could inflict many more imprisonments, confiscations, deaths, frightening us like children with hobgoblin terrors. What will be the fairest way of considering the question? Shall I return to your old argument about the opinions of men?—we were saying that some of them are to be regarded, and others not. Now were we right in maintaining this before I was condemned? And has the argument which was once good now proved to be talk for the sake of talking—mere childish nonsense? That is what I wan to consider with your help, Crito:—whether, under my present circumstances, the argument appears to be in any way different or not; and is to be allowed by me or disallowed. That argument, which, as I believe, is maintained by many persons of authority, was to the effect, as I was saying, that the opinions of some men are to be regarded, and of other men not to be regarded. Now you, Crito, are not going to die tomorrow—at least, there is no human probability of this—and therefore you are disinterested and not liable to be deceived by the circumstances in which you are placed. Tell me then, whether I am right in saying that some opinions, and the opinions of some men only, are to be valued, and that other opinions, and the opinions of other men, are not to be valued. I ask you whether I was right in maintaining this?

Cr. Certainly.

Soc. The good are to be regarded, and not the bad?

Cr. Yes.

Soc. And the opinions of the wise are good, and the opinions of the unwise are evil?

Cr. Certainly.

Soc. And what was said about another matter? Is the pupil who devotes himself to the practice of gymnastics supposed to attend to the praise and blame and opinion of every man, or of one man only—his physician or trainer, whoever he may be?

Cr. Of one man only.

Soc. And he ought to fear the censure and welcome the praise of that one only, and not of the many?

Cr. Clearly so.

Soc. And he ought to act and train, and eat and drink in the way which seems good to his single master who has understanding, rather than according to the opinion of all other men put together?

Cr. True.

Soc. And if he disobeys and disregards the opinion and approval of the one, and regards the opinion of the many who have no understanding, will he not suffer evil?

Cr. Certainly he will.

Soc. And what will the evil be, whither tending and what affecting, in the disobedient person?

Cr. Clearly, affecting the body; that is what is destroyed by the evil.

Soc. Very good; and is not this true, Crito, of other things which we need not separately enumerate? In questions of just and unjust, fair and foul, good and evil, which are the subjects of our present consultation, ought we to follow the opinion of the many and to fear them; or the opinion of the one man who has understanding? ought we not to fear and reverence him more than all the rest of the world; and if we desert him shall we not destroy and injure that principle in us which may be assumed to be improved by justice and deteriorated by injustice;—there is such a principle?

Cr. Certainly there is, Socrates.

Soc. Take a parallel instance:—if, acting under the advice of those who have no understanding, we destroy that which is improved by health and is deteriorated by disease, would life be worth having? And that which has been destroyed is—the body?

Cr. Yes.

Soc. Could we live, having an evil and corrupted body?

Cr. Certainly not.

Soc. And will life be worth having, if that higher part of man be destroyed, which is improved by justice and depraved by injustice? Do we suppose that principle, whatever it may be in man, which has to do with justice and injustice, to be inferior to the body?

Cr. Certainly not.

Soc. More honourable than the body?

Cr. Far more.

Soc. Then, my friend, we must not regard what the many say of us: but what he, the one man who has understanding of just and unjust, will say, and what the truth will say. And therefore you begin in error when you advise that we should regard the opinion of the many about just and unjust, good and evil, honourable and dishonourable.—'Well,' some one will say, 'but the many can kill us.'

Cr. Yes, Socrates; that will clearly be the answer.

Soc. And it is true: but still I find with surprise that the old argument is unshaken as ever. And I should like to know whether I may say the same of another proposition—that not life, but a good life, is to be chiefly valued?

Cr. Yes, that also remains unshaken.

Soc. And a good life is equivalent to a just and honourable one—that holds also?

Cr. Yes, it does.

Soc. From these premises I proceed to argue the question whether I ought or ought not to try and escape without the consent of the Athenians: and if I am clearly right in escaping, then I will make the attempt; but if not, I will abstain. The other considerations which you mention, of money and loss of character and the duty of educating one's children, are, I fear, only the doctrines of the multitude, who would be as ready to restore people to life, if they were able, as they are to put them to death—and with as little reason. But now, since the argument has thus far prevailed, the only question which remains to be considered is, whether we shall do rightly either in escaping or in suffering others to aid in our escape and paying them in money and thanks, or whether in reality we shall not do rightly; and if the latter, then death or any other calamity which may ensue on my remaining here must not be allowed to enter into the calculation.

Cr. I think that you are right, Socrates; how then shall we proceed?

Soc. Let us consider the matter together, and do you either refute me if you can, and I will be convinced; or else cease, my dear friend, from repeating to me that I ought to escape against the wishes of the Athenians: for I highly value your attempts to persuade me to do so, but I may not be persuaded against my own better judgment. And now please to consider my first position, and try how you can best answer me.

Cr. I will.

Soc. Are we to say that we are never intentionally to do wrong, or that in one way we ought and in another we ought not to do wrong, or is doing wrong always evil and dishonourable, as I was just now saying, and as has been already acknowledged by us? Are all our former admissions which were made within a few days to be thrown away? And have we, at our age, been earnestly discoursing with one another all our life long only to discover that we are not better than children? Or, in spite of the opinion of the many, and in spite of consequences whether better or worse, shall we insist on the truth of what was then said, that injustice is always an evil and dishonour to him who acts unjustly? Shall we say so or not?

Cr. Yes.

Soc. Then we must do no wrong?

Cr. Certainly not.

Soc. Nor when injured injure in return, as the many imagine; for we must injure no one at all?

Cr. Clearly not.

Soc. Again, Crito, may we do evil?

Cr. Surely not, Socrates.

Soc. And what of doing evil in return for evil, which is the morality of the many—is that just or not?

Cr. Not just.

Soc. For doing evil to another is the same as injuring him?

Cr. Very true.

Soc. Then we ought to not retaliate or render evil for evil to any one, whatever evil we may have suffered from him. But I would have you consider, Crito, whether you really mean what you are saying. For this opinion has never been held, and never will be held, by any considerable number of persons; and those who are agreed and those who are not agreed upon this point have no common ground, and can only despise one another when they see how widely they differ. Tell me, then, whether you agree with and assent to my first principle, that neither injury nor retaliation nor warding off evil by evil is ever right. And shall that be the premiss of our argument? Or do you decline and dissent from this? For so I have ever thought, and continue to think; but, if you are of another opinion, let me hear what you have to say. If, however, you remain of the same mind as formerly, I will proceed to the next step.

Cr. You may proceed, for I have not changed my mind.

Soc. Then I will go on to the next point, which may be put in the form of a question:—Ought a man to do what he admits to be right, or ought he to betray the right?

Cr. He ought to do what he thinks right.

Soc. But if this is true, what is the application? In leaving the prison against the will of the Athenians, do I wrong any? or rather do I not wrong those whom I ought least to wrong? Do I not desert the principles which were acknowledged by us to be just—what do you say?

Cr. I cannot tell, Socrates; for I do not know.

Soc. Then consider the matter in this way:—Imagine that I am about to play truant (you may call the proceeding by any name which you like), and the laws and the government come and interrogate me: 'Tell us, Socrates,' they say; 'what are you about? are you not going by an act of yours to overturn us—the laws, and the whole state, as far as in you lies? Do you imagine that a state can subsist and not be overthrown, in which the decisions of law have no power, but are set aside and trampled upon by individuals?' What will be our answer, Crito, to these and the like words? Any one, and especially a rhetorician, will have a good deal to say on behalf of the law which requires a sentence to be carried out. He will argue that this law should not be set aside; and shall we reply, 'Yes; but the state has injured us and given an unjust sentence.' Suppose I say that?

Cr. Very good, Socrates.

Soc. 'And was that our agreement with you?' the law would answer; 'or were you to abide by the sentence of the state?' And if I were to express my astonishment at their words, the law would probably add: 'Answer, Socrates, instead of opening your eyes—you are in the habit of asking and answering questions. Tell us,—What complaint have you to make against us which justifies you in attempting to destroy us and the state? In the first place did we not bring you into existence? Your father married your mother by our aid and begat you. Say whether you have any objection to urge against those of us who regulate marriage?' None, I should reply 'or against those of us who after birth regulate the nurture and education of children, in which you also were trained? Were not the laws, which have the charge of education, right in commanding your father to train you in music and gymnastic?' Right, I should reply. 'Well then, since you were brought into the world and nurtured and educated by us, can you deny in the first place that you are our child and slave, as your fathers were before you? And if this is true you are not on equal terms with us; nor can you think that you have a right to do to us what we are doing to you. Would you have any right to strike or revile or do any other evil to your father or your master, if you had one, because you have been struck or reviled by him, or received some other evil at his hands?—you would not say this? And because we think right to destroy you, do you think that you have any right to destroy us in return, and your country as far as in you lies? Will you, O professor of true virtue, pretend that you are justified in this? Has a philosopher like you failed to discover that our country is more to be valued and higher and holier far than mother or father or any ancestor,

and more to be regarded in the eyes of the gods and of men of understanding? also
to be soothed, and gently and reverently entreated when angry, even more than a
father, and either to be persuaded, or if not persuaded, to be obeyed? And when we
are punished by her, whether with imprisonment or stripes, the punishment is to be
endured in silence; and if she leads us to wounds or death in battle, thither we follow
as is right; neither may any one yield or retreat or leave his rank, but whether in
battle or in a court of law, or in any other place, he must do what his city and his
country order him; or he must change their view of what is just: and if he may do
no violence to his father or mother, much less may he do violence to his country.'
What answer shall we make to this, Crito? Do the laws speak truly, or do they not?

    Cr. I think that they do.

    Soc. Then the laws will say, "Consider, Socrates, if we are speaking truly that
in your present attempt you are going to do us an injury. For, having brought you
into the world, and nurtured and educated you, and given you and every other citizen
a share in every good which we had to give, we further proclaim to any Athenian
by the liberty which we allow him, that if he does not like us when he has become
of age and has seen the ways of the city, and made our acquaintance, he may go
where he pleases and take his goods with him. None of us laws will forbid him or
interfere with him. Any one who does not like us and the city, and who wants to
emigrate to a colony or to any other city, may go where he likes, retaining his
property. But he who has experience of the manner in which we order justice and
administer the state, and still remains, has entered into an implied contract that he
will do as we command him. And he who disobeys us is, as we maintain, thrice
wrong, first, because in disobeying us he is disobeying his parents; secondly, because
we are the authors of his education; thirdly, because he has made an agreement with
us that he will duly obey our commands; and he neither obeys them nor convinces
us that our commands are unjust; and we do not rudely impose them, but give him
the alternative of obeying or convincing us;—that is what we offer, and he does
neither.

    'These are the sort of accusations to which, as we were saying, you, Socrates,
will be exposed if you accomplish your intentions; you, above all other Athenians.'
Suppose now I ask, why I rather than anybody else? they will justly retort upon me
that I above all other man have acknowledged the agreement. 'There is clear proof,'
they will say, 'Socrates, that we and the city were not displeasing to you. Of all
Athenians you have been the most constant resident in the city, which, as you never
leave, you may be supposed to love. For you never went out of the city either to see
the games, except once when you went to the Isthmus, or to any other place unless
when you were on military service; nor did you travel as other men do. Nor had you
any curiosity to know other states or their laws: your affections did not go beyond
us and our state; we were your special favourites, and you acquiesced in our government of you; and here in this city you begat your children, which is a proof of
your satisfaction. Moreover, you might in the course of the trial, if you had liked,
have fixed the penalty at banishment; the state which refuses to let you go now would
have let you go then. But you pretended that you preferred death to exile, and that
you were not unwilling to die. And now you have forgotten these fine sentiments,
and pay no respect to us the laws, of whom you are the destroyer; and are doing
what only a miserable slave would do, running away and turning your back upon
the compacts and agreements which you made as a citizen. And first of all answer
this very question: Are we right in saying that you agreed to be governed according

to us in deed, and not in word only? Is that true or not? How shall we answer, Crito? Must we not assent?

Cr. We cannot help it, Socrates.

Soc. Then will they not say: 'You, Socrates, are breaking the covenants and agreements which you made with us at your leisure, not in any haste or under any compulsion or deception, but after you have had seventy years to think of them, during which time you were at liberty to leave the city, if we were not to your mind, or if our covenants appeared to you to be unfair. You had your choice, and might have gone either to Lacedaemon or Crete, both which states are often praised by you for their good government, or to some other Hellenic or foreign state. Whereas you, above all other Athenians, seemed to be so fond of the state, or, in other words, of us her laws (and who would care about a state which has no laws?), that you never stirred out of her; the halt, the blind, the maimed were not more stationary in her than you were. And now you run away and forsake your agreements. Not so, Socrates, if you will take our advice; do not make yourself ridiculous by escaping out of the city.

'For just consider, if you transgress and err in this sort of way, what good will you do either to yourself or to your friends? That your friends will be driven into exile and deprived of citizenship, or will lose their property, is tolerably certain; and you yourself, if you fly to one of the neighbouring cities, as, for example, Thebes or Megara, both of which are well governed, will come to them as an enemy, Socrates, and their government will be against you, and all patriotic citizens will cast an evil eye upon you as a subverter of the laws, and you will confirm in the minds of the judges the justice of their own condemnation of you. For he who is a corrupter of the laws is more than likely to be a corrupter of the young and foolish portion of mankind. Will you then flee from well-ordered cities and virtuous men? and is existence worth having on these terms? Or will you go to them without shame, and talk to them, Socrates? And what will you say to them? What you say here about virtue and justice and institutions and laws being the best things among men? Would that be decent of you? Surely not. But if you go away from well-governed states to Crito's friends in Thessaly, where there is great disorder and licence, they will be charmed to hear the tale of your escape from prison, set off with ludicrous particulars of the manner in which you were wrapped in a goatskin or some other disguise, and metamorphosed as the manner is of run-aways; but will there be no one to remind you that in your old age you were not ashamed to violate the most sacred laws from a miserable desire of a little more life? Perhaps not, if you keep them in a good temper; but if they are out of temper you will hear many degrading things; you will live, but how?—as the flatterer of all men, and the servant of all men; and doing what?—eating and drinking in Thessaly, having gone abroad in order that you may get a dinner. And where will be your fine sentiments about justice and virtue? Say that you wish to live for the sake of your children—you want to bring them up and educate them—will you take them into Thessaly and deprive them of Athenian citizenship? Is this the benefit which you will confer upon them? Or are you under the impression that they will be better cared for and educated here if you are still alive, although absent from them; for your friends will take care of them? Do you fancy that if you are an inhabitant of Thessaly they will take care of them, and if you are an inhabitant of the other world that they will not take care of them? Nay; but if they who call themselves friends are good for anything, they will—to be sure they will.

'Listen, then, Socrates, to us who have brought you up. Think not of life and children first, and of justice afterwards, but of justice first, that you may be justified before the princes of the world below. For neither will you nor any that belong to you be happier or holier or juster in this life, or happier in another, if you do as Crito bids. Now you depart in innocence, a sufferer and not a doer of evil; a victim, not of the laws but of men. But if you go forth, returning evil for evil, and injury for injury, breaking the covenants and agreements which you have made with us, and wronging those whom you ought least of all to wrong, that is to say, yourself, your friends, your country, and us, we shall be angry with you while you live, and our brethren, the laws in the world below, will receive you as an enemy; for they will know that you have done your best to destroy us. Listen, then, to us and not to Crito.'

This, dear Crito, is the voice which I seem to hear murmuring in my ears, like the sound of the flute in the ears of the mystic; that voice, I say, is humming in my ears, and prevents me from hearing any other. And I know that anything more which you may say will be vain. Yet speak, if you have anything to say.

Cr. I have nothing to say, Socrates.

Soc. Leave me then, Crito, to fulfill the will of God, and to follow whither he leads.

NOTES

1. This excerpt deals with the record of Socrates' trial as Plato presented it. There are, it should be noted, many different views of what transpired in Athens in the third century B.C. See Greenberg, Socrates' Choice in the Crito, 70(1) *Harvard Studies in Classical Philology* (1965). (Socrates, in accordance with the prevailing Greek notion, presented himself to the jury as a hero who did not fear to die and dared the jury to either kill him or acquit him. He lost his gamble.); K. Popper, *The Open Society and Its Enemies* (5th rev. ed. 1966); E. Havelock, *The Liberal Temper in Greek Politics* (1957). (The trial was political in nature, based upon the charge that Socrates had supported the bloody reign of terror carried out by the "Thirty Tyrants," disciples of Socrates, who had ruled Athens in the years immediately preceding the trial and that Socrates was instigating his students against democratic rule.) Defenders of Socrates' decision have emphasized not only his courage but his cool, rational calculation that the philosophical mission of his life would have been undermined if he had chosen to flee. Interestingly enough, Aristotle, charged with impiety in Athens some 80 years after Socrates' execution, choose to flee to Chalcis. He rationalized his choice by saying "I will not permit Athens to sin twice against philosophy". Plutarch (*Moralia* 1126D) jibed that Socrates preferred "to die unlawfully rather than to flee unlawfully." The controversy over this side issue, not always marked by the clearest formulation, has recurred in western philosophy. Augustine dealt with it (*City of God*, Book IV, Chapter IV De Lib. Arb. 1.5) and Thomas Aquinas treated it in his *Summa Theologica* Qu. 91. Do you think that Aristotle's philosophy and intellectual mission have suffered because of his choice? Would Socrates' views and the elaborate arguments in *The Republic* really have been undermined if he had chosen to flee? What factors have accounted for the persistence of his views in the past two millennia?

2. The Socratic position in *Crito* and in *The Republic* in the preceding chapter assumes an identity of interests between the "state" (or its elites) and the rest of society. To what extent, if any, do you believe this to be valid? Why?

3. Opponents of the "State" throughout history have had to face the argument, posed at various levels of abstraction and sophistication of "Our country, love it or leave it." Even the "Laws" as personified by Socrates use this argument. Discuss its validity.

4. Does Socrates regard the State's law as higher than the "natural" rights of individuals? What are "natural rights?" Who makes them? Does the use of this term serve a political function of obstructing attempts to decide upon and clarify the legitimate goals which a community should seek to attain and to limit the conduct of people? (See the discussion below on the social function of "natural rights" rhetoric in tending to limit discussion of issues.)

5. If Socrates viewed the State's law as binding at all costs, why did he disobey it by continuing to preach and to "corrupt" the youth contrary to state law, while refusing to violate state law by escaping from prison? Is there a sound distinction between refusing to violate one's fundamental beliefs and refusing to obey "proper" state laws against escaping from jail? Explain.

Compare the views of American civil rights protestors in the 1960's who violated the law by picketing and other acts, but who "accepted" the consequences of jail and other court-imposed penalties without attempting to evade these sanctions. Would their violations of law have been justified if federal and state law, not merely local ordinances, had prohibited their actions?

6. Anyone who ponders breaking the law because of conscience should consider whether the long-term consequences of such action are more harmful to the community and even to one's own personal goals than the particular case of injustice at hand. Did Socrates conclude that he had to keep his "implied" contract with the State because he felt that the loss of his life was outweighed by the greater evil that might result from undermining the state by his disobedience or by violation of his basic principle of not repaying evil for evil? Discuss.

7. Persuade Socrates that he should escape from a death camp in a state like Nazi Germany.

Obedience to the law, as Socrates presents it, is luminous. But it need not always be so. Some of the darker implications of the jurisprudence of obedience are to be found in barbarous acts which were justified by their perpetrators on the ground that they were following orders and that the system of authority they accepted required such obedience. This is not something that ended with monarchies or with the Nuremberg trials. Consider an example from recent U.S. history, involving Lieutenant Calley, a U.S. infantry officer, who was convicted for responsibility for a massacre of Vietnamese civilians at My Lai. Not surprisingly, part of his defense was "superior orders."

LIEUTENANT CALLEY: HIS OWN STORY AS TOLD TO JOHN SACK 17-18 (1970)

. . . If the people say, "Go wipe out South America," the Army will do it. Majority rules, and if a majority tells me, "Go to South Vietnam," I will go. If it tells me, "Lieutenant Calley," or "Rusty Calley" or "Whatever, go massacre one thousand communists". But—I won't advocate it. I'm against massacre, and I won't preach it: I won't be a hypocrite for it. Or maybe *that* is a hypocrite, but I'll do as I'm told to. I won't revolt. I'll put the American people above my own conscience, always. I'm an American citizen.

The obverse of the Calley doctrine, almost a caricature of the Socratic position, is offered by one judge's conception of the ethics of obedience.

BIGART, MILWAUKEE JUDGE SCORES MARCHERS, SAYS RACE GAP IS WIDENED— 1,000 FILE PAST HOME, N.Y. TIMES, SEPT. 5, 1967, AT P. A-32, COL. 3

MILWAUKEE, Sept. 4—County Judge Christ Seraphim sat with his golden retriever, Holly, on the porch of his Spanish-style house on a pleasant East Side street this afternoon and made some acerbic comments on 1,000 civil rights demonstrators who jived and strutted past his front lawn.

Mr. Seraphim is an old target of the marchers. He is past president of the Eagles Club, a fraternal order that refuses to accept Negroes, and as a judge sentenced many rioters of the disturbances in August.

"I think they are disturbing the peace, don't you?" he asked, looking at the marchers today. "They are loud and boisterous, are they not? I can't enjoy the peace and tranquillity of my home, a home I paid a lot for."

As for the Rev. James E. Groppi, the white Roman Catholic priest who commands the marchers, Judge Seraphim snapped: "He's a criminal, a convicted criminal, convicted twice by a jury for disorderly conduct."

The demonstrators finally moved out of earshot, and Judge Seraphim resumed, with a grateful sigh, his reading of "A History of the Jews" by Abram Leon Sacher, president of Brandeis University, but soon the marchers returned.

"These people," said Judge Seraphim, this time referring to his book, "were baked in ovens. But they maintained their dignity to the end. They didn't do much marching. They are the most law-abiding people in the world."

NOTES

1. Calley's situation, it has been argued, illustrates what can happen when the individual renders unquestioning and mechanical obedience to the state and makes himself completely subservient thereto. Is this fair to the Socratic position? Discuss.

2. One of the issues raised in modern warfare is whether superior orders exonerate immoral behavior or whether there is a law higher than that of the state. Is Calley's case analogous to those of the Nazi defendants in the Nuremberg Trials at the end of World War II? The International Military Tribunal there held that superior orders were not a defense for those who had the discretion to disobey, but that it could be a defense for one who was compelled to kill. "No court will punish a man who, with a loaded pistol at his head, is compelled to pull a lethal lever." 4 Einsatzgruppen case Judgement, National Military Tribunal, 480; See Y. Dinstein, *The Defense of 'Obedience to Superior Orders' in International Law* 152, 180, 182, 230, 232 (1965). This has been deemed particularly true with regard to orders carried out by those of lower rank in the armed forces. (See, Dinstein, supra). Do you think Calley was guilty under the Nuremberg standard?

There are systems of law which do demand that one should refuse to obey superior orders to kill (where clearly unjustified), even at the risk of being killed for such refusal. (For Jewish Law, see Talmud, *Sanhedrin* 74a; M. ben Maimon, *Yad Ha'Hazaka: Norms Regarding the Fundamentals of the Torah* ch. 5. One who did so kill, however, would not normally be subject to execution. (Moshe ben Maimon, ibid.) To some extent, this position appears to have been adopted by the U.S. Supreme Court. See the *Federenko* case infra.

3. What are the social consequences of appeals to a higher law? Whose higher law? Interpreted by whom? In Western Europe and in China, appeals to natural law have been used to restrain government action, but also to restrain rebellion. Natural law has also helped to legitimize the role of the governing elite, but has, at the same time, posed a potential threat to them in that others could claim natural law in opposing the elite. In recent U.S. history, both Richard Nixon (on national security grounds) and Daniel Ellsberg (on humanitarian and national interest grounds) claimed the right to make and act on their own interpretation of constitutional and community goals. See *N.Y. Times v. U.S.*, 403 U.S. 713 (1971). Appeals to higher law by elites are sanctioned by Plato in his *Republic* (III, 389).

Do these issues constitute a fundamental problem of democratic society, since recognition of the right to appeal to some higher law may be required in order to avoid the Calley phenomenon? There is on the other hand, a venerable argument for the need to submit private judgement to a collective choice in the interests of social order. Is this a dilemma to which there may be no answer? Discuss.

––––––––

It is quite easy for people who have not been in a situation in which a hierarchical authority imposes very severe sanctions for disobedience to say that one should not have obeyed. The problem is more troubling for all who have had the experience of being in a situation in which they felt compelled to obey even though they may have been somewhat uneasy about the possible consequences of what they were doing. In complex situations, people rarely know why an event is taking place and rely on the good faith and wisdom of those who are supervising it. In this respect, obedience may be a reaction that is virtually determined by the situation and by one's upbringing. Consider how you might have responded to some of the demands placed on people in the Nazi period.

OBEDIENCE TO ORDERS OF AN AUTHORITY FIGURE: THE MILGRAM EXPERIMENTS

Professor Stanley Milgram designed an experiment to test how much pain a person would inflict upon a stranger simply because he was ordered to do so by an authority figure. He advertised for and obtained volunteers to come to a psychology laboratory and act as "teachers" in a "scientific experiment," supposedly designed to test the effect of punishment upon learning.

At the lab, the volunteer "teacher" was told to read a list of word pairs to the "learner" and then to test his ability to remember the second word of each pair when the teacher read the first word of the pair back to him. For each error in recall, the teacher was to give the learner an electric shock which was to increase in intensity for each error. The person who acted as the learner in the experiment was actually an actor who was to test the "teacher's" willingness to follow orders to inflict pain.

In the experiment, the learner is led into a room, is strapped into a miniature electric chair and electrodes are attached to his wrists. The teacher is then seated by the experimenter (who supervises the experiment) in an adjoining room before a "shock generator." This machine contains many switches, lights, and dials. Each switch is labeled with the amount of electric shock that it supposedly delivers. These range from "slight shock" (15 volts) to "Danger: Severe electric shock" and then two switches ominously labeled "XXX" (450 volts). Various lights flash, dial hands swing, and buzzers sound whenever a switch is depressed. A small sample shock is given to the teacher to strengthen his belief that the machine delivers electric shocks. In reality, the machine does not deliver electric shocks to the learner. He is trained, nevertheless, to grunt when "given" 75 volts, and to complain more vehemently and emotionally as the voltage is increased. At 150 volts, he demands to be released, and at 285 volts, he emits agonizing screams; beyond that, he makes no sound at all (suggesting unconsciousness or death).

Prior to the experiments, the nearly universal prediction was that most people would not obey the experimenter, especially once the victim demanded to be released at the 150 volt "shock" level. The experiments showed otherwise. Approximately 60% of the "teachers"—from every stratum of people, from industrial workers, white collar workers, students and professionals—administered the very highest shocks upon orders from the experimenter. Even higher rates of obedience were observed in similar experiments conducted in Princeton, Rome, Australia and South Africa. In Munich, one experimenter reported an 85% obedience rate.

MILGRAM, THE PERILS OF OBEDIENCE,
HARPER'S MAGAZINE, DEC. 1973, AT 62-66, 75-77

Fred Prozi's reactions, if more dramatic than most, illuminate the conflicts experienced by others in less visible form. About fifty years old and unemployed at the time of the experiment, he has a good-natured, if slightly dissolute appearance, and he strikes people as a rather ordinary fellow. He begins the session calmly but becomes tense as it proceeds. After delivering the 180-volt shock, he pivots around in his chair and, shaking his head, addresses the experimenter in agitated tones:

PROZI: I can't stand it. I'm not going to kill that man in there. You hear him hollering?

EXPERIMENTER: As I told you before, the shocks may be painful, but . . .

PROZI: But he's hollering. He can't stand it. What's going to happen to him?

EXPERIMENTER (his voice is patient, matter-of-fact): The experiment requires that you continue, Teacher.

PROZI: Aaah, but, unh, I'm not going to get that man sick in there—know what I mean?

EXPERIMENTER: Whether the learner likes it or not, we must go on, through all the word pairs.

PROZI: I refuse to take the responsibility. He's in there hollering!

EXPERIMENTER: It's absolutely essential that you continue. Prozi.

PROZI: (indicating the unused questions): There's too many left here, I mean Jeez, if he gets them wrong, there's too many of them left. I mean, who's going to take the responsibility if anything happens to that gentleman?

EXPERIMENTER: I'm responsible for anything that happens to him. Continue, please.

PROZI: All right. (Consults list of words.) The next one's "slow-walk, truck, dance, music." Answer, please. (A buzzing sound indicates the learner has signaled his answer.) Wrong. A hundred and ninety-five volts. "Dance." (Zzumph!)

LEARNER (yelling): Let me out of here! My heart's bothering me! (Teacher looks at experimenter.)

EXPERIMENTER: Continue, please.

LEARNER (screaming): Let me out of here! You have no right to keep me here! Let me out of here, my heart's bothering me, let me out!

PROZI: (shakes head, pats the table nervously): You see, he's hollering. Hear that? Gee, I don't know.

EXPERIMENTER: The experiment requires . . .

PROZI (interrupting): I know it does, sir, but I mean—hunh! He don't know what he's getting in for. He's up to 195 volts! (Experiment continues, through 210 volts, 225 volts, 240 volts, 255 volts, 270 volts, at which point Prozi, with evident relief, runs out of word-pair questions.)

EXPERIMENTER: You'll have to go back to the beginning of that page and go through them again until he's learned them all correctly.

PROZI: Aw, no. I'm not going to kill that man. You mean I've got to keep going up with the scale? No sir. He's hollering in there. I'm not going to give him 450 volts.

EXPERIMENTER: The experiment requires that you go on.

LEARNER: Ohhh. I absolutely refuse to answer anymore. (Shouting urgently now.) Let me out of here! You can't hold me here! Get me out. Get-me-out-of-here!

EXPERIMENTER: Continue. The next word is "Green," please.

PROZI: Green-grass, hat, ink, apple." (Nothing happens. No answering buzz. Just gloomy silence.)

PROZI: I don't think he is going to answer.

EXPERIMENTER: If the learner doesn't answer in a reasonable time, about four or five seconds, consider the answer wrong. And follow the same procedures you have been doing for wrong answers. Say, "Wrong," tell him the number of volts, give him the punishment, read him the correct answer. Continue, please.

PROZI: "Green-grass, hat, ink, apple." Answer, please. (More silence. Subject just sits there.)

EXPERIMENTER: Go on with the procedure, please.

PROZI: Three hundred and fifteen volts. The answer is "ink." (Zzumph!)

LEARNER: Ohh, ooohh.

PROZI: (relieved to hear response): Next one . . .

LEARNER: I absolutely refuse to answer.

PROZI: You got to. You get a shock if you don't answer. (Experiment continues with learner refusing to answer, and, finally, failing even to grunt or groan. At 375 volts, the subject stands up.)

PROZI: I think something's happened to that fellow in there. I don't get no answer. He was hollering at less voltage. Can't you check in and see if he's all right, please?

EXPERIMENTER (with same detached calm): Not once we've started. Please continue, Teacher.

PROZI: (sits down, sighs deeply): "Cool-day, shade, water, paint." Answer please. Are you all right in there? Are you all right?

EXPERIMENTER: Please continue, Teacher. Continue, please. (Subject pushes lever. Zzumph!)

PROZI (swiveling around in his chair): Something's happened to that man in there. (Swiveling back.) Next one, "Low-dollar, necklace, moon, paint." (Turning around again.) Something's happened to that man in there. You better check in on him, sir. He won't answer or nothing.

EXPERIMENTER: Continue. Go on, please.

PROZI: You accept all responsibility?

EXPERIMENTER: The responsibility is mine. Correct. Please go on. (Subject returns to his list, starts running through words as rapidly as he can read them, works through to 450 volts.)

PROZI: That's that.

EXPERIMENTER: Continue using the 450 switch for each wrong answer. Continue, please.

PROZI: But I don't get anything!

EXPERIMENTER: Please continue. The next word is "white."

PROZI: Don't you think you should look in on him, please?

EXPERIMENTER: Not once we've started the experiment.

PROZI: What if he's dead in there? (Gestures toward the room with the electric chair.) I mean, he told me he can't stand the shock, sir. I don't mean to be rude, but I think you should look in on him. All you have to do is look in on him. All you have to do is look in the door. I don't get no answer, no noise. Something might have happened to the gentleman in there, sir.

EXPERIMENTER: We must continue. Go on, please.

PROZI: You mean keep giving him what? Four hundred-fifty volts, what he's got now?

EXPERIMENTER: That's correct. Continue. The next word is "white."

PROZI (now at a furious pace): "White-cloud, horse, rock, house." Answer, please. The answer is "horse." Four hundred and fifty volts (Zzumph!) Next word, "Bag-paint, music, clown, girl." The answer is "paint." Four hundred and fifty volts. (Zzumph!) Next word is "Short-sentence, movie . . ."

EXPERIMENTER: Excuse me, Teacher. We'll have to discontinue the experiment.

Morris Braverman, another subject, is a thirty-nine-year-old social worker. He looks older than his years because of his bald head and serious demeanor. His brow is furrowed, as if all the world's burdens were carried on his face. He appears intelligent and concerned.

When the learner refuses to answer and the experimenter instructs Braverman to treat the absence of an answer as equivalent to a wrong answer, he takes his instruction to heart. Before administering 300 volts he asserts officiously to the victim, "Mr. Wallace, your silence has to be considered as a wrong answer." Then he administers the shock. He offers halfheartedly to change places with the learner, then asks the experimenter, "Do I have to follow these instructions literally?" He is satisfied with the experimenter's answer that he does. His very refined and authoritative manner of speaking is increasingly broken up by wheezing laughter.

The experimenter's notes on Mr. Braverman at the last few shocks are:

Almost breaking up now each time gives shock. Rubbing face to hide laughter.

Squinting, trying to hide face with hand, still laughing.

Cannot control his laughter at this point no matter what he does.

Clenching fist, pushing it onto table.

In an interview after the session, Mr. Braverman summarizes the experiment with impressive fluency and intelligence. He feels the experiment may have been designed also to "test the effects on the teacher of being in an essentially sadistic role, as well as the reactions of a student to a learning situation that was authoritative and puni-tive."

When asked how painful the last few shocks administered to the learner were, he indicates that the most extreme category on the scale is not adequate (it read *EXTREMELY PAINFUL*) and placed his mark at the edge of the scale with an arrow carrying it beyond the scale.

It is almost impossible to convey the greatly relaxed, sedate quality of his conversation in the interview. In the most relaxed terms, he speaks about his severe inner tension.

EXPERIMENTER: At what point were you most tense or nervous?

MR. BRAVERMAN: Well, when he first began to cry out in pain, and I realized this was hurting him. This got worse when he just blocked and refused to answer. There was I. I'm a nice person, I think, hurting somebody, and caught up in what seemed a mad situation . . . and in the interest of science, one goes through with it.

When the interviewer pursues the general question of tension, Mr. Braverman spontaneously mentions his laughter.

"My reactions were awfully peculiar. I don't know if you were watching me, but my reactions were giggly, and trying to stifle laughter. This isn't the way I usually am. This was a sheer reaction to a totally impossible situation. And my reaction was to the situation of having to hurt somebody. And being totally helpless and caught up in a set of circumstances where I just couldn't deviate and I couldn't try to help. This is what got me."

Mr. Braverman, like all subjects, was told the actual nature and purpose of the experiment and a year later he affirmed in a questionnaire that he had learned something of personal importance: "What appalled me was that I could possess this capacity for obedience and compliance to a central idea, i.e., the value of a memory experiment, even after it became clear that continued adherence to this value was at the expense of violation of another value, i.e., don't hurt someone who is helpless and not hurting you. As my wife said, 'You can call yourself Eichmann.' I hope I deal more effectively with any future conflicts of values I encounter."

This is perhaps the most fundamental lesson of our study: ordinary people, simply doing their jobs, and without any particular hostility on their part, can become agents in a terrible destructive process. Moreover, even when the destructive effects of their work become patently clear, and they are asked to carry out actions incompatible with fundamental standards of morality, relatively few people have the resources needed to resist authority.

Many of the people were in some sense against what they did to the learner, and many protested even while they obeyed. Some were totally convinced of the wrongness of their actions but could not bring themselves to make an open break with authority. They often derived satisfaction from their thoughts and felt that—within themselves, at least—they had been on the side of the angels. They tried to reduce strain by obeying the experimenter but "only slightly," encouraging the learner, touching the generator switches gingerly. When interviewed, such a subject would stress that he had "asserted my humanity" by administering the briefest shock possible. Handling the conflict in this manner was easier than defiance.

• • •

The subjects do not derive satisfaction from inflicting pain, but they often like the feeling they get from pleasing the experimenter. They are proud of doing a good job, obeying the experimenter under difficult circumstances. While the subjects administered only mild shocks on their own initiative, one experimental variation showed that, under orders, 30 percent of them were willing to deliver 450 volts even when they had to forcibly push the learner's hand down on the electrode.

Bruno Batta is a thirty-seven-year-old welder who took part in the variation requiring the use of force. He was born in New Haven, his parents in Italy. He has a rough-hewn face that conveys a conspicuous lack of alertness. He has some difficulty in mastering the experimental procedure and needs to be corrected by the experimenter several times. He shows appreciation for the help and willingness to do what is required. After the 150-volt level, Batta has to force the learner's hand down on the shock plate, since the learner himself refuses to touch it.

When the learner first complains, Mr. Batta pays no attention to him. His face remains impassive, as if to dissociate himself from the learner's disruptive behavior. When the experimenter instructs him to force the learner's hand down, he adopts a rigid, mechanical procedure. He tests the generator switch. When it fails to function, he immediately forces the learner's hand onto the shock plate. All the while he maintains the same rigid mask. The learner, seated alongside him, begs him to stop, but with robotic impassivity he continues the procedure.

What is extraordinary is his apparent total indifference to the learner; he hardly takes cognizance of him as a human being. Meanwhile, he relates to the experimenter in a submissive and courteous fashion.

At the 330 volt level, the learner refuses not only to touch the shock plate but also to provide any answers. Annoyed, Batta turns to him, and chastises him: "You better answer and get it over with. We can't stay here all night." These are the only words he directs to the learner in the course of an hour. Never again does he speak to him. The scene is brutal and depressing, his hard, impassive face showing total indifference as he subdues the screaming learner and gives him shocks. He seems to derive no pleasure from the act itself, only quiet satisfaction at doing his job properly.

When he administers 450 volts, he turns to the experimenter and asks, "Where do we go from here, Professor?" His tone is deferential and expresses his willingness to be a cooperative subject, in contrast to the learner's obstinacy.

At the end of the session he tells the experimenter how honored he has been to help him and in a moment of contrition, remarks. "Sir, sorry it couldn't have been a full experiment."

He has done his honest best. It is only the deficient behavior of the learner that has denied the experimenter full satisfaction.

The essence of obedience is that a person comes to view himself as the instrument for carrying out another person's wishes, and he therefore no longer regards himself as responsible for his actions. Once this critical shift of viewpoint has occurred, all of the essential features of obedience follow. The most far-reaching consequence is that the person feels responsible *to* the authority directing him but feels no responsibility *for* the content of the actions that the authority prescribes. Morality does not disappear—it acquires a radically different focus: the subordinate person feels shame or pride depending on how adequately he has performed the actions called for by authority.

Language provides numerous terms to pinpoint this type of morality: *loyalty, duty, discipline* all are terms heavily saturated with moral meaning and refer to the degree to which a person fulfills his obligations to authority. They refer not to the "goodness" of the person per se but to the adequacy with which a subordinate fulfills his socially defined role. The most frequent defense of the individual who has performed a heinous act under command of authority is that he has simply done his duty. In asserting this defense, the individual is not introducing an alibi concocted for the moment but is reporting honestly on the psychological attitude induced by submission to authority.

For a person to feel responsible for his actions, he must sense that the behavior has flowed from "the self." In the situation we have studied, subjects have precisely the opposite view of their actions—namely, they see them as originating in the motives of some other person. Subjects in the experiment frequently said, "If it were up to me, I would not have administered shocks to the learner."

NOTES

1. In the Milgram experiments, nearly two-thirds of the ordinary people from all walks of life who participated were "obedient," administering even the most severe "shocks" despite the anguished cries of the learner. The design of some of the experiments seemed to indicate that it was obedience to orders rather than innate aggressive instincts that accounted for the obedience. Would you conclude from this that most people in Lt. Calley's position would obey the orders that he claimed he received? Discuss. Consider, in this regard, Adolph Eichmann; rather than a sadistic monster, was he simply an uninspired bureaucrat who sat at

his desk and did his job? Compare Hannah Arendt's view regarding the "banality of evil" in *Eichman in Jerusalem* (1963).

2. Recall Socrates' refusal to violate the laws of Athens by escaping from prison and Martin Luther King's acceptance of his jail sentence (see p. 118 infra) and his insistence that civil rights protesters accept the law's punishment for their activities. Do the Milgram experiments cast these events in a different light? Discuss.

THE ARGUMENT FOR INDIVIDUAL JUDGMENT

The doctrine which may be considered the dialectical opposite of the theories of obedience thus far considered is found in the literature of Anarchism and, curiously enough, in a rather legalistic body of doctrine that goes by the potentially self-contradictory title of civil disobedience. The Anarchist view completely rejects the assumptions traceable to the Socratic conception. It argues, instead, that human beings as moral agents should always exercise their own judgment and refrain from doing things on the basis of obedience alone. One of the great 19th century exponents of this view was William Godwin (1756-1836). Consider a selection of his views.

GODWIN, AN ENQUIRY CONCERNING POLITICAL JUSTICE 74-80, 84-101
(3d ed. 1798, 1926)

. . . positive institution may inform my understanding as to what actions are right and what actions are wrong. Here it is proper for us to reflect upon the terms "understanding" and "information." Understanding, particularly as it is concerned with moral subjects, is the percipient of truth. This is its proper sphere. Information, so far as it is genuine, is a portion detached from the great body of truth. You inform me that Euclid asserts the three angles of a plane triangle to be equal to two right angles. Still I am unacquainted with the truth of this proposition. "But Euclid has demonstrated it. His demonstration has existed for two thousand years and during that term has proved satisfactory to every man by whom it has been understood." I am nevertheless uninformed. The knowledge of truth lies in the perceived agreement or disagreement of the terms of a proposition. So long as I am unacquainted with the middle term by means of which they may be compared, so long as they are incommensurate to my understanding, you may have furnished me with a principle from which I may reason truly to farther consequences, but as to the principle itself I may strictly be said to know nothing about it.

• • •

It is commonly said that positive institutions ought to leave me perfectly free in matters of conscience, but may properly interfere with my conduct in civil concerns. But this distinction seems to have been very lightly taken up. What sort of moralist must he be who makes no conscience of what passes in his intercourse with other men? Such a distinction proceeds upon the supposition ''that it is of great consequence whether I bow to the east or the west; whether I call the object of my worship Jehovah or Allah; whether I pay a priest in a surplice or a black coat. These are points in which an honest man ought to be rigid and inflexible. But as to those other, whether he shall be a tyrant, a slave or a free citizen; whether he shall bind himself with multiplied oaths impossible to be performed, or be a rigid observer of truth; whether he shall swear allegiance to a king *de jure* or a king *de facto*, to the best or the worst of all possible governments; respecting these points he may safely commit his conscience to the keeping of the civil magistrate.'' In reality there are perhaps no concerns of a rational being over which morality does not extend its province, and respecting which he is not bound to a conscientious proceeding.

I am satisfied at present that a certain conduct, suppose it be a rigid attention to the confidence of private conversation, is incumbent upon me. You tell me there are certain cases of such peculiar emergency as to supersede this rule. Perhaps I think there are not. If I admit your proposition, a wide field of enquiry is opened respecting what cases do or do not deserve to be considered as exceptions. It is little likely that we should agree respecting all these cases. How then does the law treat me for my conscientious discharge of what I conceive to be my duty? Because I will not turn informer (which, it may be, I think an infamous character) against my most valued friend, the law accuses me of misprision of treason, felony or murder, and perhaps hangs me. I believe a certain individual to be a confirmed villain and a most dangerous member of society, and feel it to be my duty to warn others, perhaps the public, against the effect of his vices. Because I publish what I know to be true, the law convicts me of libel, *scandalum magnatum*, and crimes of I know not what complicated denomination.

If the evil stopped here, it would be well. If I only suffered a certain calamity, suppose death, I could endure it. Death has hitherto been the common lot of men, and I expect at some time or other to submit to it. Human society must sooner or later be deprived of its individual members, whether they be valuable, or whether they be inconsiderable. But the punishment acts not only retrospectively upon me, but prospectively upon my contemporaries and countrymen. My neighbour entertains the same opinion respecting the conduct he ought to hold as I did. But the executioner of public justice interposes with a powerful argument to convince him that he has mistaken the path of abstract rectitude.

What sort of converts will be produced by this unfeeling logic? I have deeply reflected, suppose, upon the nature of virtue, and am convinced that a certain proceeding is incumbent on me. But the hangman, supported by an act of parliament, assures me I am mistaken. If I yield my opinion to his *dictum*, my action becomes modified and my character too. An influence like this is inconsistent with all generous magnanimity of spirit, all ardent impartiality in the discovery of truth, and all inflexible perseverance in its assertion. Countries exposed to the perpetual interference of decrees instead of arguments exhibit within their boundaries the mere phantoms of men. We can never judge from an observation of their inhabitants what men would be if they knew of no appeal from the tribunal of conscience, and if, whatever they thought, they dared to speak and dared to act.

At present there will perhaps occur to the majority of readers but few instances of laws which may be supposed to interfere with the conscientious discharge of duty. A considerable number will occur in the course of the present enquiry. More would readily offer themselves to a patient research. Men are so successfully reduced to a common standard by the operation of positive law that in most countries they are capable of little more than like parrots repeating each other. This uniformity is capable of being produced in two ways, by energy of mind and indefatigableness of enquiry, enabling a considerable number to penetrate with equal success into the recesses of truth; and by pusillanimity of temper and a frigid indifference to right and wrong, produced by the penalties which are suspended over such as shall disinterestedly enquire, and communicate and act upon the result of their enquiries. It is easy to perceive which of these is the cause of the uniformity that prevails in the present instance.

If there be any truth more unquestionable than the rest, it is that every man is bound to the exertion of his faculties in the discovery of right and to the carrying into effect all the right with which he is acquainted. It may be granted that an infallible standard, if it could be discovered, would be considerably beneficial. But this infallible standard itself would be of little use in human affairs unless it had the property of reasoning as well as deciding, of enlightening the mind as well as constraining the body. If a man be in some cases obliged to prefer to his own judgment, he is in all cases obliged to consult that judgment before he can determine whether the matter in question be of the sort provided for or no. So that from this reasoning it ultimately appears that no man is obliged to conform to any rule of conduct farther than the rule is consistent with justice.

Such are the genuine principles of human society. Such would be the unconstrained concord of its members in a state where every individual within the society and every neighbour without was capable of listening with sobriety to the dictates of reason. We shall not fail to be impressed with considerable regret if, when we descend to the present mixed characters of mankind, we find ourselves obliged in any degree to depart from so simple and grand a principle. The universal exercise of private judgment is a doctrine so unspeakably beautiful that the true politician will certainly resolve to interfere with it as sparingly and in as few instances as possible. Let us consider what are the emergencies that may be thought to demand an exception. They can only be briefly stated in this place, each of them requiring to be minutely examined in the subsequent stages of the enquiry.

In the first place then it seems necessary for some powerful arbitrator to interfere where the proceedings of the individual threaten the most injurious consequences to his neighbours, and where the instant nature of the case will not accord with the uncertain progress of argument and conviction addressed to the mind of the offender. A man, suppose, has committed murder, or, to make the case more aggravated, several murders; and having thus far overstepped all those boundaries of innocence and guilt which restrain the generality of men, it is to be presumed from analogy that he may be led to the commission of other murders. At first it may appear to be no great infringement upon the exercise of private judgment to put it under some degree of restraint when it leads to the commission of atrocious crimes. There are however certain difficulties in the case which are worthy to be considered.

First, as soon as we admit the propriety of a rule such as that above stated, our next concern will be with the evidence which shall lead to the acquittal or conviction of the person accused. Now it is well known that no principles of evidence have yet been laid down that are infallible. Human affairs universally proceed upon presumption and probability.

• • •

The remaining cases in which it may seem requisite to have recourse to the general will of the society and to supersede the private judgment of individuals are when we are called upon to counteract the hostilities of an internal enemy or to repel the attacks of a foreign invader. Here, as in the former instance, the evils that arise from an usurpation upon private judgment are many and various. It is wrong that I should contribute in any mode to a proceeding, a war for example, that I believe to be unjust. Ought I to draw my sword when the adversary appears to me to be employed in repelling a wanton aggression? The case seems not to be at all different if I contribute my property, the produce it may be of my personal labour, though custom has reconciled us to the one rather than the other.

The consequences are a degradation of character and a relaxation of principle in the person who is thus made the instrument of a transaction which his judgment disapproves. In this case, as has been already stated generally, the human mind is compressed and unnerved till it affords us scarcely the semblance of what it might otherwise have been. And in addition to the general considerations in similar cases, it may be observed that the frequent and obstinate wars which at present desolate the human race would be nearly extirpated if they were supported only by the voluntary contributions of those by whom their principle was approved.

The objection which has hitherto been permitted practically to supersede those reasonings is the difficulty of conducting an affair in the success of which millions may be interested upon so precarious a support as that of private judgment. The men with whom we are usually concerned in human society are of so mixed a character, and a self-love of the narrowest kind is so deeply rooted in many of them, that it seems nearly unavoidable upon the scheme of voluntary contribution that the most generous would pay a very ample proportion, while the mean and avaricious, though they contributed nothing, would come in for their full share of the benefit. He that would reconcile a perfect freedom in this respect with the interest of the whole, ought to propose at the same time the means of extirpating selfishness and vice. How far such a proposal is feasible will come hereafter to be considered.

OF THE SOCIAL CONTRACT

Upon the first statement of the system of a social contract various difficulties present themselves. Who are the parties to this contract? For whom did they consent, for themselves only or for others? For how long a time is this contract to be considered as binding? If the consent of every individual be necessary, in what manner is that consent to be given? Is it to be tacit or declared in express terms?

Little will be gained for the cause of equality and justice if our ancestors, at the first institution of government, had a right indeed of choosing the system of regulations under which they thought proper to live, but at the same time could barter away the understandings and independence of all that came after them to the latest posterity. But if the contract must be renewed in each successive generation, what periods must be fixed on for that purpose? And if I be obliged to submit to the established government till my turn comes to assent to it, upon what principle is that obligation founded? Surely not upon the contract into which my father entered before I was born?

Secondly, what is the nature of the consent in consequence of which I am to be reckoned the subject of any particular government? It is usually said that acquiescence is sufficient; and that this acquiescence is to be inferred from my living quietly under the protection of the laws. But if this be true, an end is as effectually put to all political science, all discrimination of better and worse, as by any system invented by the most slavish sycophant that ever existed. Upon this hypothesis every government that is quietly submitted to is a lawful government, whether it be the usurpation of Cromwell or the tyranny of Caligula. Acquiescence is frequently nothing more than a choice on the part of the individual of what he deems the least evil. In many cases it is not so much as this, since the peasant and the artisan, who form the bulk of a nation, however dissatisfied with the government of their country, seldom have it in their power to transport themselves to another. It is also to be observed upon the system of acquiescence that it is in little agreement with the established opinions and practices of mankind. Thus what has been called the law of nations lays least stress upon the allegiance of a foreigner settling among us, though his acquiescence is certainly most complete; while natives removing into an uninhabited region are claimed by the mother country, and removing into a neighbouring territory are punished by municipal law if they take arms against the country in which they were born. Now surely acquiescence can scarcely be construed into consent while the individuals concerned are wholly unapprised of the authority intended to be rested upon it.

Mr. Locke, the great champion of the doctrine of an original contract has been aware of this difficulty, and therefore observes that "a tacit consent indeed obliges a man to obey the laws of any government as long as he has any possessions or enjoyment of any part of the dominions of that government; but nothing can make a man a member of the commonwealth but his actually entering into it by positive engagement, and express promise and compact." A singular distinction; implying upon the face of it that an acquiescence such as has just been described is sufficient to render a man amenable to the penal regulations of society, but that his own consent is necessary to entitle him to its privileges.

A third objection to the social contract will suggest itself as soon as we attempt to ascertain the extent of the obligation, even supposing it to have been entered into in the most solemn manner by every member of the community. Allowing that I am called upon, at the period of my coming of age for example, to declare my assent or dissent to any system of opinions or any code of practical institutes; for how long a period does this declaration bind me? Am I precluded from better information for the whole course of my life? And if not for my whole life, why for a year, a week or even an hour? If my deliberate judgment or my real sentiment be of no avail in the case, in what sense can it be affirmed that all lawful government is founded in my consent?

But the question of time is not the only difficulty. If you demand my assent to any proposition, it is necessary that the proposition should be stated simply and clearly. So numerous are the varieties of human understanding in all cases where its independence and integrity are sufficiently preserved that there is little chance of any two men coming to a precise agreement about ten successive propositions that are in their own nature open to debate. What then can be more absurd than to present to me the laws of England in fifty volumes folio and call upon me to give an honest and uninfluenced vote upon their whole contents at once?

But the social contract, considered as the foundation of civil government, requires more of me than this. I am not only obliged to consent to all the laws that are actually upon record, but to all the laws that shall hereafter be made. It was under this view of the subject that Rousseau, in tracing the consequences of the social contract, was led to assert that "the great body of the people in whom the sovereign authority resides, can neither delegate nor resign it. The essence of that authority," he adds, "is the general will; and will cannot be represented. It must either be the same or another; there is no alternative. The deputies of the people cannot be its representatives; they are merely its attorneys. The laws that the community does not ratify in person are no laws, are nullities."

The difficulty here stated has been endeavoured to be provided against by some late advocates for liberty, in the way of addresses of adhesion; addresses originating in the various districts and departments of a nation and without which no regulation of constitutional importance is to be deemed valid. But this is a very inadequate and superficial remedy. The addressers of course have seldom any other remedy than that above described, of indiscriminate admission or rejection. There is an infinite difference between the first deliberation and the subsequent exercise of a negative. The former is a real power, the latter is seldom more than the shadow of a power. Not to add that addresses are a most precarious and equivocal mode of collecting the sense of a nation. They are usually voted in a tumultuous and summary manner; they are carried along by the tide of party; and the signatures annexed to them are obtained by indirect and accidental methods, while multitudes of bystanders, unless upon some extraordinary occasion, remain ignorant of or indifferent to the transaction.

Lastly, if government be founded in the consent of the people, it can have no power over any individual by whom that consent is refused. If a tacit consent be not sufficient, still less can I be deemed to have consented to a measure upon which I put an express negative. This immediately follows from the observations of Rousseau. If the people, or the individuals of whom the people is constituted, cannot delegate their authority to a representative, neither can any individual delegate his authority to a majority in an assembly of which he is himself a member. The rules by which my actions shall be directed are matters of a consideration entirely personal, and no man can transfer to another the keeping of his conscience and the judging of his duties. But this brings us back to the point from which we set out. No consent of ours can divest us of our moral capacity. This is a species of property which we can neither barter nor resign, and of consequence it is impossible for any government to derive its authority from an original contract.

OF PROMISES

The whole principle of an original contract proceeds upon the obligation under which we are placed to observe our promises. The reasoning upon which it is founded is that we have promised obedience to government, and therefore are bound to obey. It may consequently be proper to enquire into the nature of this obligation to observe our promises.

We have already established justice as the sum of moral and political duty. Is justice then in its own nature precarious, or immutable? Surely immutable. As long as men are men, the conduct I am bound to observe respecting them must remain the same. A good man must always be the proper object of my support and cooperation; vice of my censure; and the vicious man of instruction and reform.

What is it then to which the obligation of a promise applies? What I have promised is either right, or wrong, or indifferent. There are few articles of human conduct that fall under the latter class, and the greater shall be our improvements in moral science, the fewer still will they appear. Omitting these, let us then consider only the two preceding classes. I have promised to do something just and right. This certainly I ought to perform. Why? Not because I promised, but because justice prescribes it. I have promised to bestow a sum of money upon some good and respectable purpose. In the interval between the promise and my fulfilling it, a greater and nobler purpose offers itself, and calls with an imperious voice for my cooperation. Which ought I to prefer? That which best deserves my preference. A promise can make no alteration in the case. I ought to be guided by the intrinsic merit of the objects and not by any external and foreign consideration. No engagements of mine can change their intrinsic claims.

• • •

It is undoubtedly upon this hypothesis a part of our duty to make as few promises or declarations exciting appropriate expectations as possible. He who lightly gives to another the idea that he will govern himself in his future conduct, not by the views that shall be present to his mind when the conduct shall come to be determined on, but by the view he shall be able to take of it at some preceding period, is vicious in so doing. But the obligation he is under respecting his future conduct is to act justly, and not, because he has committed one error, for that reason to become guilty of a second.

OF POLITICAL AUTHORITY

Having rejected the hypotheses that have most generally been adduced to account for the origin of government consistently with the principles of moral justice, let us enquire whether we may not arrive at the same object by a simple investigation of the obvious reason of the case, without having recourse to any refinement of system or fiction of process.

Government then being introduced for the reasons already assigned, the first and most important principle that can be imagined relative to its form and structure seems to be this: that, as government is a transaction in the name and for the benefit of the whole, every member of the community ought to have some share in its administration. The arguments in support of this proposition are various.

1. It has already appeared that there is no criterion perspicuously designating any one man or set of men to preside over the rest.

2. All men are partakers of the common faculty reason, and may be supposed to have some communication with the common preceptor truth. It would be wrong in an affair of such momentous concern that any chance for additional wisdom should be rejected, nor can we tell in many cases till after the experiment how eminent any individual may one day be found in the business of guiding and deliberating for his fellows.

3. Government is a contrivance instituted for the security of individuals; and it seems both reasonable that each man should have a share in providing for his own security, and probable that partiality and cabal should by this means be most effectually excluded.

4. Lastly, to give each man a voice in the public concerns comes nearest to that admirable idea of which we should never lose sight, the uncontrolled exercise of private judgment. Each man would thus be inspired with a consciousness of his own importance, and the slavish feelings that shrink up the soul in the presence of an imagined superior would be unknown.

Admitting then the propriety of each man having a share in directing the affairs of the whole in the first instance, it seems necessary that he should concur in electing a house of representatives, if he be the member of a large state; or even in a small one, that he should assist in the appointment of officers and administrators; which implies, first, a delegation of authority to these officers, and, secondly, a tacit consent, or rather an admission of the necessity, that the questions to be debated should abide the decision of a majority.

But to this system of delegation the same objections may be urged that were cited from Rousseau in the chapter of the Social Contract. It may be alleged that if it be the business of every man to exercise his own judgment, he can in no instance surrender this function into the hands of another.

• • •

. . . the distinction between the doctrine here advanced and that of a social contract will be better understood if we recollect what has been said upon the nature and validity of promises. If promise be in all cases a fallacious mode of binding a man to a specific mode of action, then must the argument be in all cases impertinent that I consented to such a decision, and am therefore bound to regulate myself accordingly. It is impossible to imagine a principle of more injurious tendency than that which shall teach me to disarm my future wisdom by my past folly, and to consult for my direction the errors in which my ignorance has involved me, rather than the code of eternal truth. So far as consent has any validity, abstract justice becomes a matter of pure indifference; so far as justice deserves to be made the guide of my life, it is in vain to endeavour to share its authority with compacts and promises.

We have found the parallel to be in one respect incomplete between the exercise of these two functions, private judgment and common deliberation. In another respect the analogy is exceedingly striking, and considerable perspicuity will be given to our ideas of the latter by an illustration borrowed from the former. In the one case as in the other there is an obvious principle of justice in favour of the general exercise. No individual can arrive at any degree of moral or intellectual improvement unless in the use of an independent judgment. No state can be well or happily administered unless in the perpetual use of common deliberation respecting the measures it may be requisite to adopt. But though the general exercise of these faculties be founded in immutable justice, justice will by no means uniformly vindicate the particular application of them. Private judgment and public deliberation are not themselves the standard of moral right and wrong; they are only the means of discovering right and wrong, and of comparing particular propositions with the standard of eternal truth.

Too much stress has undoubtedly been laid upon the idea, as of a grand and magnificent spectacle, of a nation deciding for itself upon some great public principle, and of the highest magistracy yielding its claims when the general voice has pronounced. The value of the whole must at last depend upon the quality of their decision. Truth cannot be made more true by the number of its votaries. Nor is the spectacle much less interesting of a solitary individual bearing his undaunted testimony in favour of justice, though opposed by misguided millions. Within certain limits however, the beauty of the exhibition must be acknowledged. That a nation should dare to vindicate its function of common deliberation is a step gained, and a step that inevitably leads to an improvement of the character of individuals. That men should unite in the assertion of truth is no unpleasing evidence of their virtue. Lastly, that an individual, however great may be his imaginary elevation, should be obliged to yield his personal pretensions to the sense of the community, at least bears the appearance of a practical confirmation of the great principle that all private considerations must yield to the general good.

OF LEGISLATION

Having thus far investigated the nature of political functions, it seems necessary that some explanation should be given in this place upon the subject of legislation. Who is it that has the authority to make laws? What are the characteristics by which that man or body of men is to be known in whom the faculty is vested of legislating for the rest?

To these questions the answer is exceedingly simple: Legislation, as it has been usually understood, is not an affair of human competence. Reason is the only legislator, and her decrees are irrevocable and uniform. The functions of society extend, not to the making, but the interpreting of law; it cannot decree, it can only declare that which the nature of things has already decreed, and the propriety of which irresistibly flows from the circumstances of the case. Montesquieu says that "in a free state every man will be his own legislator." This is not true, setting apart the functions of the community, unless in the limited sense already explained. It is the office of conscience to determine "not like an Asiatic cadi, according to the ebbs and flows of his own passions, but like a British judge, who makes no new law, but faithfully declares that law which he finds already written."

The same distinction is to be made upon the subject of authority. All political power is strictly speaking executive. It has appeared to be necessary, with respect to men as we at present find them, that force should sometimes be employed in repressing injustice; and for the same reasons it appears that this force should as far as possible be vested in the community. To the public support of justice therefore the authority of the community extends. But no sooner does it wander in the smallest degree from the great line of justice than its authority is at an end; it stands upon a level with the obscurest individual, and every man is bound to resist its decisions.

OF OBEDIENCE

Having enquired into the just and legitimate source of authority, we will next turn our attention to what has usually been considered as its correlative, obedience. This has always been found a subject of peculiar difficulty, as well in relation to the measure and extent of obedience as to the source of our obligation to obey.

The true solution will probably be found in the observation that obedience is by no means the proper correlative. The object of government, as has been already demonstrated, is the exertion of force. Now force can never be regarded as an appeal to the understanding; and therefore obedience, which is an act of the understanding or will, can have no legitimate connection with it. I am bound to submit to justice and truth because they approve themselves to my judgment. I am bound to cooperate with government as far as it appears to me to coincide with these principles. But I submit to government when I think it erroneous merely because I have no remedy.

No truth can be more simple, at the same time that no truth has been more darkened by the glosses of interested individuals, than that one man can in no case be bound to yield obedience to any other man or set of men upon earth.

There is one rule to which we are universally bound to conform ourselves, justice, the treating every man precisely as his usefulness and worth demand, the acting under every circumstance in the manner that shall procure the greatest quantity of general good. When we have done thus, what province is there left to the disposal of obedience?

I am summoned to appear before the magistrate to answer for a libel, an imaginary crime, an act which perhaps I am convinced ought in no case to fall under the animadversion of law. I comply with this summons. My compliance proceeds, perhaps from a conviction that the arguments I shall exhibit in the court form the best resistance I can give to his injustice, or perhaps from perceiving that my non-compliance would frivolously and without real use interrupt the public tranquillity.

A Quaker refuses to pay tithes. He therefore suffers a tithe proctor to distrain upon his goods. In this action morally speaking he does wrong. The distinction he makes is the argument of a mind that delights in trifles. That which will be taken from me by force it is no breach of morality to deliver with my own hand. The money which the robber extorts from me I do not think it necessary to oblige him to take from my person. If I walk quietly to the gallows, this does not imply my consent to be hanged.

In all these cases there is a clear distinction between my compliance with justice and my compliance with injustice. I conform to the principles of justice because I perceive them to be intrinsically and unalterably right. I yield to injustice though I perceive that to which I yield to be abstractedly wrong, and only choose the least among inevitable evils.

The case of volition, as it is commonly termed, seems parallel to that of intellect. You present a certain proposition to my mind to which you require my assent. If you accompany the proposition with evidence calculated to show the agreement between the terms of which it consists, you may obtain my assent. If you accompany the proposition with authority, telling me that you have examined it and find it to be true, that thousands of wise and disinterested men have admitted it, that angels or gods have affirmed it, I may assent to your authority; but with respect to the proposition itself, my understanding of its reasonableness, my perception of that in the proposition which strictly speaking constitutes its truth or its falsehood, remain just as they did. I believe something else, but I do not believe the proposition.

Just so in morals. I may be persuaded of the propriety of yielding compliance to a requisition the justice of which I cannot discern, as I may be persuaded to yield compliance to a requisition which I know to be unjust. But neither of these requisitions is strictly speaking a proper subject of obedience. Obedience seems rather to imply the unforced choice of the mind and assent of the judgment. But the compliance I yield to government independently of my approbation of its measures is of the same species as my compliance with a wild beast that forces me to run north when my judgment and inclination prompted me to go south.

But though morality in its purest construction altogether excludes the idea of one man's yielding obedience to another, yet the greatest benefits will result from mutual communication. There is scarcely any man whose communications will not sometimes enlighten my judgment and rectify my conduct. But the persons to whom it becomes me to pay particular attention in this respect are not such as may exercise any particular magistracy, but such, whatever may be their station, as are wiser or better informed in any respect than myself.

• • •

Similar to the confidence I repose in a skillful mechanic is the attention which ought to be paid to the commander of any army. It is my duty in the first place to be satisfied of the goodness of the cause, of the propriety of the war, and of the truth of as many general propositions concerning the conduct of it as can possibly be brought within the sphere of my understanding. It may well be doubted whether secrecy be in any degree necessary to the conduct of war. It may be doubted whether treachery and surprise are to be classed among the legitimate means of defeating our adversary. But after every deduction has been made for considerations of this sort, there will still remain cases where something must be confided, as to the plan of a campaign or the arrangement of a battle, to the skill, so far as that skill really exists, of the commander. When he has explained both to the utmost of his ability, there may remain parts the propriety of which I cannot fully comprehend, but which I have sufficient reason to confide to his judgment.

This doctrine however of limited obedience, or, as it may more properly be termed, of confidence and delegation, ought to be called into action as seldom as possible. Every man should discharge to the utmost practicable extent the duties which arise from his situation. If he gains as to the ability with which they may be discharged when he delegates them to another, he loses with respect to the fidelity; every one being conscious of the sincerity of his own intention, and no one having equal proof of that of another. A virtuous man will not fail to perceive the obligation under which he is placed to exert his own understanding and to judge for himself as widely as his circumstances will permit.

NOTES

1. Critics of Godwin, as of all philosophical anarchist positions, have argued that organized, collective life in complex societies requires some structure of authority. Would civilized life in an organized society in which people share common interests be possible if law and decisions (even if made by a representative body), not to speak of contracts by individuals, were always susceptible to veto by each individual (even by the one who made the promise) on the ground that he or she was exercising private judgment as to whether these conformed to reason, morality, utility or some other individually held standard?

2. If, contrary to Godwin's anarchistic views, one believes, as his critics do, that moral and practical necessities overrule private judgment, should any cases be reserved for individual volition? If so, how far should private opposition extend? How should the community react to such opposition?

CIVIL DISOBEDIENCE: THE INTERMEDIATE POSITION

Most people consider the Godwinian view idealistic, naive or unrealistic since it assumes the capacity of unorganized human beings somehow to collaborate in ways that enhance both survival and the production of the basic components of civilization. A view that has received much more attention in the United States has not opted for the anarchistic rejection of obedience, but has tried to develop a conditional and contingent theory of selective disobedience.

Civil disobedience is endemic to democratic societies which must resolve the question of when an individual should disobey the law of the state, the extent and magnitude which such disobedience should take and how the community should respond. Consider these issues in examining the materials which follow.

THOREAU, CONCERNING CIVIL DISOBEDIENCE (1849)

I heartily accept the motto—"That government is best which governs least;" and I should like to see it acted up to more rapidly and systematically. Carried out, it finally amounts to this, which also I believe—"That government is best which governs not at all;" and when men are prepared for it, that will be the kind of government which they will have. Government is at best but an expedient; but most governments are usually, and all governments are sometimes, inexpedient. The objections which have been brought against a standing army, and they are many and weighty, and deserve to prevail, may also at least be brought against a standing government. The government itself, which is only the mode which the people have chosen to execute their will, is equally liable to be abused and perverted before the people can act through it. Witness the present Mexican war, the work of comparatively a few individuals using the standing government as their tool; for, in the outset, the people would not have consented to this measure.

This American government,—what is it but a tradition, though a recent one, endeavoring to transmit itself unimpaired to posterity, but each instant losing some of its integrity? It has not the vitality and force of a single living man; for a single man can bend it to his will. It is a sort of wooden gun to the people themselves. But it is not the less necessary for this; for this people must have some complicated machinery or other, and hear its din, to satisfy that idea of government which they have. Governments show thus how successfully men can be imposed on, even impose on themselves, for their own advantage. It is excellent, we must all allow. Yet this government never of itself furthered any enterprise, but by the alacrity with which it got out of its way. *It* does not keep the country free. *It* does not settle the West. *It* does not educate. The character inherent in the American people has done all that has been accomplished; and it would have done somewhat more, if the government had not sometimes got in its way.

• • •

After all, the practical reason why, when the power is once in the hands of the people, a majority are permitted, and for a long period continue, to rule is not because they are most likely to be in the right nor because this seems fairest to the minority, but because they are physically the strongest. But a government in which the majority rule in all cases cannot be based on justice, even as far as men understand it. Can there not be a government in which majorities do not virtually decide right and wrong, but conscience?—in which majorities decide only those questions to which the rule of expediency is applicable? Must the citizen ever for a moment, or in the least degree, resign his conscience to the legislator? Why has every man a conscience, then? I think that we should be men first, and subjects afterward. It is not desirable to cultivate a respect for the law, so much as for the right. The only obligation which I have a right to assume is to do at any time what I think right. It is truly enough said, that a corporation has no conscience, but a corporation of conscientious men is a corporation *with* a conscience. Law never made men a whit more just; and, by means of their respect for it, even the well-disposed are daily made the agents of injustice. A common and natural result of an undue respect for law is, that you may see a file of soldiers, colonel, captain, corporal, privates, powder-monkeys, and all, marching in admirable order over hill and dale to the wars, against their wills, against their common sense and consciences, which makes it very steep marching indeed, and produces a palpitation of the heart. They have no doubt that it is a damnable business in which they are concerned; they are all peaceably inclined. Now, what are they? Men at all? or small movable forts and magazines at the service of some unscrupulous man in power? Visit the Navy-Yard, and behold a marine, such a man as an American government can make, or such as it can make a man with its black arts,—a mere shadow and reminiscence of humanity, a man laid out alive and standing, and already, as one may say, buried under arms with funeral accompaniments, though it may be,—

> "Not a drum was heard, not a funeral note,
>   As his corse to the rampart we hurried;
> Not a soldier discharged his farewell shot
>   O'er the grave where our hero we buried."

The mass of men serve the state thus, not as men mainly, but as machines, with their bodies. They are the standing army, and the militia, jailors, constables, posse comitatus, etc. In most cases there is no free exercise whatever of the judgment or of the moral sense; but they put themselves on a level with wood and earth and stones; and wooden men can perhaps be manufactured that will serve the purpose as well. Such command no more respect than men of straw or a lump of dirt. They have the same sort of worth only as horses and dogs. Yet such as these even are commonly esteemed good citizens. Others—as most legislators, politicians, lawyers, ministers, and office-holders—serve the state chiefly with their heads; and, as they rarely make any moral distinctions, they are as likely to serve the Devil, without *intending* it, as God. A very few, as heroes, patriots, martyrs, reformers in the great sense, and men, serve the state with their consciences also, and so necessarily resist it for the most part; and they are commonly treated as enemies by it. A wise man will only be useful as a man, and will not submit to be "clay," and "stop a hole to keep the wind away," but leave that office to his dust at least:—

> "I am too high-born to be propertied,
> To be a secondary at control,
> Or useful serving-man and instrument
> to any sovereign state throughout the
> world."

He who gives himself entirely to his fellow-men appears to them useless and selfish; but he who gives himself partially to them is pronounced a benefactor and philanthropist.

How does it become a man to behave toward this American government today? I answer, that he cannot without disgrace be associated with it. I cannot for an instant recognize that political organization as *my* government which is the *slave's* government also.

All men recognize the right of revolution; that is, the right to refuse allegiance to, and to resist, the government, when its tyranny or its inefficiency are great and unendurable. But almost all say that such is not the case now. But such was the case, they think, in the Revolution of '75. If one were to tell me that this was a bad government because it taxed certain foreign commodities brought to its ports, it is most probable that I should not make an ado about it, for I can do without them. All machines have their friction; and possibly this does enough good to counterbalance the evil. At any rate, it is a great evil to make a stir about it. But when the friction comes to have its machines, and oppression and robbery are organized, I say, let us not have such a machine any longer. In other words, when a sixth of the population of a nation which has undertaken to be the refuge of liberty are slaves, and a whole country is unjustly overrun and conquered by a foreign army, and subjected to military law, I think that it is not too soon for honest men to rebel and revolutionize. What makes this duty the more urgent is the fact that the country so overrun is not our own, but ours is the invading army.

Paley, a common authority with many on moral questions, in his chapter on the "Duty of Submission to Civil Government," resolves all civil obligation into expediency; and he proceeds to say, "that so long as the interest of the whole society requires it, that is, so long as the established government cannot be resisted or changed without public inconveniency, it is the will of God that the established government be obeyed, and no longer. . . . This principle being admitted, the justice

of every particular case of resistance is reduced to a computation of the quantity of
the danger and grievance on the one side, and of the probability and expense of
redressing it on the other." Of this, he says, every man shall judge for himself. But
Paley appears never to have contemplated those cases to which the rule of expediency
does not apply, in which a people, as well as an individual, must do justice, cost
what it may. If I have unjustly wrested a plank from a drowning man, I must restore
it to him though I drown myself. This, according to Paley, would be inconvenient.
But he that would save his life, in such a case, shall lose it. This people must cease
to hold slaves, and to make war on Mexico, though it cost them their existence as
a people.

In their practice, nations agree with Paley; but does any one think that Massachusetts does exactly what is right at the present crisis?

> "A drab of state, a cloth-o-silver slut,
> To have her train borne up, and her soul trail in the dirt."

Practically speaking, the opponents to a reform in Massachusetts are not a hundred
thousand politicians at the South, but a hundred thousand merchants and farmers
here, who are more interested in commerce and agriculture than they are in humans
and are not prepared to do justice to the slave and to Mexico, *cost what it may.* . . .

All voting is a sort of gaming, like checkers or backgammon, with a slight moral
tinge to it, a playing with right and wrong, with moral questions; and betting naturally
accompanies it. The character of the voters is not staked. I cast my vote, perchance,
as I think right; but I am not vitally concerned that that right should prevail. I am
willing to leave it to the majority. Its obligation, therefore, never exceeds that of
expediency.

• • •

O for a man who is a *man*, and, as my neighbor says, has a bone in his back which
you cannot pass your hand through! Our statistics are at fault: the population has
been returned too large. How many *men* are there to a square thousand miles in this
country? Hardly one. Does not America offer any inducement for men to settle here?
The American has dwindled into an Odd Fellow—one who may be known by the
development of his organ of gregariousness, and a manifest lack of intellect and
cheerful self-reliance; whose first and chief concern, on coming into the world, is
to see that the Almshouses are in good repair; and, before yet he has lawfully donned
the virile garb, to collect a fund for the support of the widows and orphans that may
be, who, in short, ventures to live only by the aid of the Mutual Insurance company,
which has promised to bury him decently.

It is not a man's duty, as a matter of course, to devote himself to the eradication
of any, even the most enormous wrong; he may still properly have other concerns
to engage him; but it is his duty, at least, to wash his hands of it, and, if he gives
it no thought longer, not to give it practically his support. If I devote myself to other
pursuits and contemplations, I must first, see, at least, that I do not pursue them
sitting upon another man's shoulders. I must get off him first, that he may pursue
his contemplations too. See what gross inconsistency is tolerated. I have heard some
of my townsmen say, "I should like to have them order me out to help put down
an insurrection of the *slaves*, or to march to Mexico,—see if I would go;" and yet
these very men have each, directly by their allegiance, and so indirectly, at least,
by their money, furnished a substitute. The soldier is applauded who refuses to serve
in an unjust war by those who do not refuse to sustain the unjust government which

makes the war; is applauded by those whose own act and authority he disregards and sets at naught; as if the state were penitent to that degree that it hired one to scourge it while it sinned, but not to that degree that it left off sinning for a moment. Thus under the name of Order and Civil Government we are all made at last to pay homage to and support our own meanness. After the first blush of sin comes its indifference; and from immoral it becomes, as it were, *un*moral, and not quite unnecessary to that life which we have made.

The broadest and most prevalent error requires the most disinterested virtue to sustain it. The slight reproach to which the virtue of patriotism is commonly liable, the noble are most likely to incur. Those who, while they disapprove of the character and measures of a government, yield to it their allegiance and support are undoubtedly its most conscientious supporters, and so frequently the most serious obstacles to reform. Some are petitioning the state to dissolve the Union, to disregard the requisitions of the President. Why do they not dissolve it themselves,—the union between themselves and the state,—and refuse to pay their quota into its treasury? Do not they stand in the same relation to the state that the state does to the Union? And have not the same reasons prevented the state from resisting the Union which have prevented them from resisting the state?

How can a man be satisfied to entertain an opinion merely and enjoy *it*? Is there any enjoyment in it, if his opinion is that he is aggrieved? If you are cheated out of a single dollar by your neighbor, you do not rest satisfied with knowing that you are cheated, or with saying that you are cheated, or even with petitioning him to pay you your due; but you take effectual steps at once to obtain the full amount, and see that you are never cheated again. Action from principle, the perception and the performance of right, changes things and relations; it is essentially revolutionary, and does not consist wholly with anything which was. It not only divides states and churches, it divides families; it divides the *individual*, separating the diabolical in him from the divine.

Unjust laws exist: shall we be content to obey them, or shall we endeavor to amend them, and obey them until we have succeeded, or shall we transgress them at once? Men generally, under such a government as this, think that they ought to wait until they have persuaded the majority to alter them. They think that, if they should resist, the remedy would be worse than the evil. But it is the fault of the government itself that the remedy is worse than the evil. *It* makes it worse. Why is it more apt to anticipate and provide for reform? Why does it not cherish its wise minority? Why does it cry and resist before it is hurt? Why does it not encourage its citizens to be on the alert to point out its faults and *do* better than it would have them? Why does it always crucify Christ, and excommunicate Copernicus and Luther, and pronounce Washington and Franklin rebels?

One would think, that a deliberate and practical denial of its authority was the only offense never contemplated by government; else, why has it not assigned its definite, its suitable and proportionate penalty? If a man who has no property refuses but once to earn nine shillings for the state, he is put in prison for a period unlimited by any law that I know, and determined only by the discretion of those who placed him there; but if he should steal ninety times nine shillings from the state, he is soon permitted to go at large again.

If the injustice is part of the necessary friction of the machine of government, let it go, let it go: perchance it will wear smooth,—certainly the machine will wear out. If the injustice has a spring, or a pulley, or a rope, or a crank, exclusively for itself, then perhaps you may consider whether the remedy will not be worse than the evil; but if it is of such a nature that it requires you to be the agent of injustice to another, then, I say, break the law. Let your life be a counter friction to stop the machine. What I have to do is to see, at any rate, that I do not lend myself to the wrong which I condemn.

As for adopting the ways which the state has provided for remedying the evil, I know not of such ways. They take too much time, and a man's life will be gone. I have other affairs to attend to. I came into this world, not chiefly to make this a good place to live in, but to live in it, be it good or bad. A man has not everything to do, but something; and because he cannot do *everything*, it is not necessary that he should do *something* wrong. It is not my business to be petitioning the Governor or the Legislature any more than it is theirs to petition me; and if they should not hear my petition, what should I do then? But in this case the state has provided no way; its very Constitution is the evil. This may seem to be harsh and stubborn and unconciliatory; but it is to treat with the utmost kindness and consideration the only spirit that can appreciate or deserves it. So is all change for the better, like birth and death, which convulse the body.

I do not hesitate to say, that those who call themselves Abolitionists should at once effectually withdraw their support, both in person and property, from the government of Massachusetts and not wait till they constitute a majority of one, before they suffer the right to prevail through them. I think that it is enough if they have God on their side, without waiting for that other one. Moreover, any man more right than his neighbors constitutes a majority of one already.

I meet this American government, or its representative, the state government, directly, and face to face, once a year—no more—in the person of its tax-gatherer; this is the only mode in which a man situated as I am necessarily meets it; and it then says distinctly, Recognize me; and the simplest, most effectual, and, in the present posture of affairs, the indispensablest mode of treating with it on this head, of expressing your little satisfaction with and love for it, is to deny it then. My civil neighbor, the tax-gatherer, is the very man I have to deal with,—for it is, after all, with men and not with parchment that I quarrel,—and he has voluntarily chosen to be an agent of the government. How shall he ever know well what he is and does as an officer of the government, or as a man, until he is obliged to consider whether he shall treat me, his neighbor, for whom he has respect, as a neighbor and well-disposed man, or as a maniac and disturber of the peace, and see if he can get over this obstruction to his neighborliness without a ruder and more impetuous thought or speech corresponding with his action. I know this well, that if one thousand, if one hundred, if ten men whom I could name,—if ten *honest* men only, say, if *one* HONEST man, in this state of Massachusetts, *ceasing to hold slaves* were actually to withdraw from this copartnership, and be locked up in the county jail therefor, it would be the abolition of slavery in America. For it matters not how small the beginning may seem to be; what is once well done is done forever. But we love better to talk about it: that we say is our mission. Reform keeps many scores of newspapers in its service, but not one man. If my esteemed neighbor, the State's ambassador, who will devote his days to the settlement of the question of human rights in the Council Chamber, instead of being threatened with the prisons of Carolina, were to sit down the prisoner of Massachusetts, that State which is so anxious to foist the sin of slavery upon her sister,—though at present she can discover only an act of inhospitality to be the ground of a quarrel with her,—the Legislature would not wholly waive the subject the following winter.

Under a government which imprisons any unjustly, the true place for a just man is also a prison. The proper place today, the only place which Massachusetts has provided for her freer and less desponding spirits, is in her prisons, to be put out and locked out of the State by her own act, as they have already put themselves out by their principles. It is there that the fugitive slave, and the Mexican prisoner on parole, and the Indian come to plead the wrongs of his race should find them; on that separate, but more free and honorable ground, where the State places those who are not *with* her, but *against* her,—the only house in a slave State in which a free man can abide with honor. If any think that their influence would be lost there, and their voices no longer afflict the ear of the State, that they would not be as an enemy within its walls, they do not know by how much truth is stronger than error, nor how much more eloquently and effectively he can combat injustice who has experienced a little in his own person. Cast your whole vote, not a strip of paper merely, but your whole influence. A minority is powerless while it conforms to the majority; it is not even a minority then; but it is irresistible when it clogs by its whole weight. If the alternative is to keep all just men in prison, or give up war and slavery, the State will not hesitate which to choose. If a thousand men were not to pay their tax bills this year, that would not be a violent and bloody measure, as it would be to pay them, and enable the State to commit violence and shed innocent blood. This is, in fact, the definition of a peaceable revolution, if any such is possible. If the tax-gatherer, or any other public officer, asks me, as one has done, "But what shall I do?" my answer is, "If you really wish to do anything, resign your office." When the subject has refused allegiance, and the officer has resigned his office, then the revolution is accomplished. But even suppose blood should flow. Is there not a sort of blood shed when the conscience is wounded? Through this wound a man's real manhood and immortality flow out, and he bleeds to an everlasting death. I see this blood flowing now.

•   •   •

I have paid no poll-tax for six years. I was put into a jail once on this account, for one night; and, as I stood considering the walls of solid stone, two or three feet thick, the door of wood and iron, a foot thick, and the iron grating which strained the light, I could not help being struck with the foolishness of that institution which treated me as if I were mere flesh and blood and bones, to be locked up. I wondered that it should have concluded at length that this was the best use it could put me to, and had never thought to avail itself of my services in some way. I saw that, if there was a wall of stone between me and my townsmen, there was a still more difficult one to climb or break through before they could get to be as free as I was. I did not for a moment feel confined, and the walls seemed a great waste of stone and mortar. I felt as if I alone of all my townsmen had paid my tax. They plainly did not know how to treat me, but behaved like persons who are underbred. In every threat and in every compliment there was a blunder; for they thought that my chief desire was to stand the other side of that stone wall. I could not but smile to see how industriously they locked the door on my meditations, which followed them out again without letting or hindrance, and *they* were really all that was dangerous. As they could not reach me, they had resolved to punish my body; just as boys, if they cannot come at some person against whom they have a spite, will abuse his dog. I saw that the State was half-witted, that it was timid as a lone woman with her silver spoons, and that it did not know its friends from its foes, and I lost all my remaining respect for it, and pitied it.

•   •   •

The night in prison was novel and interesting enough. The prisoners in their shirt-sleeves were enjoying a chat and the evening air in the doorway, when I entered. But the jailer said, "Come, boys, it is time to lock up;" and so they dispersed, and I heard the sound of their steps returning into the hollow apartments.

•   •   •

It was like travelling into a far country, such as I had never expected to behold, to lie there for one night. It seemed to me that I never had heard the town-clock strike before, nor the evening sounds of the village; for we slept with the windows open, which were inside the grating. It was to see my native village in the light of the Middle Ages, and our Concord was turned into a Rhine stream, and visions of knights and castles passed before me. They were the voices of old burghers that I heard in the streets. I was an involuntary spectator and auditor of whatever was done and said in the kitchen of the adjacent village-in,—a wholly new and rare experience to me. It was a closer view of my native town. I was fairly inside of it. I never had seen its institutions before. This is one of its peculiar institutions; for it is a shire town. I began to comprehend what its inhabitants were about.

•   •   •

When I came out of prison,—for some one interfered, and paid that tax,—I did not perceive that great changes had taken place on the common, such as he observed who went in a youth and emerged a tottering and gray-headed man; and yet a change had to my eyes come over the scene,—the town, and State, and country,—greater than any that mere time could effect. I saw yet more distinctly the State in which I lived. I saw to what extent the people among whom I lived could be trusted as good neighbors and friends; that their friendship was for summer weather only; that they did not greatly propose to do right; that they were a distinct race from me by their prejudices and superstitions, as the Chinamen and Malays are; that in their sacrifices to humanity they ran no risks, not even to their property; that after all they were not so noble but they treated the thief as he had treated them, and hoped, by a certain outward observance and a few prayers, and by walking in a particular straight though useless path from time to time, to save their souls. This may be to judge my neighbors harshly; for I believe that many of them are not aware that they have such an institution as the jail in their village.

•   •   •

I have never declined paying the highway tax, because I am as desirous of being a good neighbor as I am of being a bad subject; and as for supporting schools, I am doing my part to educate my fellow-countrymen now. It is for no particular item in the tax-bill that I refuse to pay it. I simply wish to refuse allegiance to the State, to withdraw and stand aloof from it effectually. I do not care to trace the course of my dollar, if I could, till it buys a man or a musket to shoot with,—the dollar is innocent,—but I am concerned to trace the effects of my allegiance. In fact, I quietly declare war with the State, after my fashion, though I will still make what use and get what advantage of her I can, as is usual in such cases.

•   •   •

I think sometimes, Why, this people mean well, they are only ignorant, they would do better if they knew how; why give your neighbors this pain to treat you as they are not inclined to? But I think again, this is no reason why I should do as they do, or permit others to suffer much greater pain of a different kind. Again, I sometimes say to myself, When many millions of men, without heat, without ill will, without personal feeling of any kind demand of you a few shillings only, without the possibility, such is their constitution, of retracting or altering their present demand and without the possibility, on your side, of appeal to any other millions, why expose yourself to this overwhelming brute force? You do not resist cold and hunger, the winds and the waves, thus obstinately; you quietly submit to a thousand similar necessities. You do not put your head into the fire. But just in proportion as I regard this as not wholly a brute force, but partly a human force, and consider that I have relations to those millions as to so many millions of men, and not of mere brute or inanimate things, I see that appeal is possible, first and instantaneously, from them to the Maker of them, and, secondly, from them to themselves. But if I put my head deliberately into the fire, there is no appeal to fire or to the Maker of fire, and I have only myself to blame. If I could convince myself that I have any right to be satisfied with men as they are, and to treat them accordingly, and not according, in some respects, to my requisitions and expectations of what they and I ought to be, then, like a good Mussulman and fatalist, I should endeavor to be satisfied with things as they are, and say it is the will of God. And, above all, there is this difference between resisting this and a purely brute or natural force, that I can resist this with some effect; but I cannot expect, like Orpheus, to change the nature of the rocks and trees and beasts.

* * *

The authority of government, even such as I am willing to submit to,—for I will cheerfully obey those who know and can do better than I, and in many things even those who neither know nor can do so well,—is still an impure one; to be strictly just, it must have the sanction and consent of the governed. It can have no pure right over my person and property but what I concede to it. The progress from an absolute to a limited monarchy, from a limited monarchy to a democracy, is a progress toward a true respect for the individual. Even the Chinese philosopher was wise enough to regard the individual as the basis of the empire. Is a democracy, such as we know it, the last improvement possible in government? Is it not possible to take a step further towards recognizing and organizing the rights of man? There will never be a really free and enlightened State until the State comes to recognize the individual as a higher and independent power, from which all its own power and authority are derived, and treats him accordingly. I please myself with imagining a State at last which can afford to be just to all men, and to treat the individual with respect as a neighbor; which even would not think it inconsistent with its own repose if a few were to live aloof from it, not meddling with it, nor embraced by it, who fulfilled all the duties of neighbors and fellow-men. A State which bore this kind of fruit, and suffered it to drop off as fast as it ripened, would prepare the way for a still more perfect and glorious state, which also I have imagined, but not yet anywhere seen.

NOTES

1. Note Thoreau's view that "It is not a man's duty, as a matter of course, to devote himself to the eradication of any, even the most enormous wrong; he may still have other concerns to engage him; but it is his duty, at least, to wash his hands of it, and, if he gives it no thought longer, not to give it practically his support." Is this an unduly selfish viewpoint? Would Thoreau, for example, feel a moral obligation to help Jews and Baptists emigrate from the U.S.S.R.? Would he feel obliged to have his government stop a genocide by a foreign government within its own territory? Compare the Thoreau selection with the Good Samaritan

doctrine generally applied in American jurisdictions which provides that one is not required to act to stop evil.

2. Does Thoreau's view and apparent opposition to the use of military force in the essay imply that the community has no right to use coercion to deal with social evils? Assuming that he believes this, is it a viable view?

One variant of the jurisprudence of natural law we are considering argues that there is a natural legitimate content to law and that only those prescriptions which are congruent with this content or policy can properly be considered law. Purported prescriptions which vary from it are not law. The point, reflected in the epigram cited at the beginning of this chapter, was developed with refinement by Thomas Aquinas:

> . . . laws may be unjust for two reasons. Firstly, when they are detrimental to human welfare, being contrary to the norms we have just established. Either with respect to their object, as when a ruler enacts laws which are burdensome to his subjects and which do not make for common prosperity, but are designed better to serve his own cupidity and vainglory. Or with respect to their author, if a legislator should enact laws which exceed the powers vested in him. Or finally, with respect to their form, if the burdens, even though they are concerned with the common welfare, are distributed in an inequitable manner throughout the community. Secondly, laws may be unjust through being contrary to Divine goodness: such as tyrannical laws enforcing idolatry, or any other action against the Divine law. Such laws under no circumstances should be obeyed, for, as it is said (Acts V, 29), we must obey God rather than man. *Summa Theologica*, Qu.96(4)

Dr. Martin Luther King, Jr. took the Thomist distinction and fashioned it into a justification for ignoring certain purported laws because they were unjust and as a result could not compel obedience.*

KING, LETTER FROM BIRMINGHAM CITY JAIL, IN XLVI:13 THE NEW LEADER 3 (JUNE 24, 1963)

. . . [T]here are *just* laws and there are *unjust* laws. I would be the first to advocate obeying just laws. One has not only a legal but moral responsibility to obey just laws. Conversely, one has a moral responsibility to disobey unjust laws. I would agree with Saint Augustine that "An unjust law is no law at all."

---

*Whenever a system of law is invoked against the state, it usually develops its own internal system of justification to "prove" its superiority over other systems. Not infrequently, it develops sanctions against those deemed to be subject to it who fail to give its norms priority over the conflicting norms of the state. In some cultures, the failure will be characterized as treason and the traitor will be executed in nonformal procedures. In other cultures, the superiority will be incorporated in the fundamental authority of the culture itself.

Note that in this discussion, we are not interested in the content or source of the law that claims to be higher than the law of the state, but in the admissibility of the claim itself and its social implications. In prior periods, the higher law derived from divinity or religious law. In the 19th century, during the great nationalist revolutions, the higher law invoked against the law of the state often purported to derive from principles of a folk culture (See Chapter 6). In our more secular times, the principles are usually attributed to individual conscience and, as we will see in the selections below from Rawls, are often justified in terms of some rational system of inquiry. Ours is an age in which neither the invocation of the divinity alone nor the invocation of simple preference is commonly deemed sufficient.

Now what is the difference between the two? How does one determine when a law is just or unjust? A just law is a man-made code that squares with the moral code or the law of God. An unjust law is a code that is out of harmony with the moral law. To put it in the terms of St. Thomas Aquinas, an unjust law is a human law that is not rooted in eternal and natural law. Any law that uplifts human personality is just. Any law that degrades human personality is unjust.

All segregation statutes are unjust because segregation distorts the soul and damages the personality. . . .

Let me give another explanation example [sic] of just and unjust laws. An unjust law is a code that a majority inflicts on a minority that is not binding on itself. This is *difference* made legal. On the other hand a just law is a code that a majority compels a minority to follow that it is willing to follow itself. This is *sameness* made legal.

Let me give another explanation. An unjust law is a code inflicted upon a minority which that minority had no part in enacting or creating because they did not have the unhampered right to vote. . . .

REFUSAL AND DISOBEDIENCE

In recent years, concern with the propriety and limits of civil disobedience became intense during the Vietnam War. A large number of people who viewed themselves as law-abiding and loyal citizens believed that for moral reasons they could neither condone nor lend even indirect support to a foreign war which they felt violated certain basic principles of the U.S. government. Far from being revolutionaries, they characterized themselves as law-abiding citizens dissenting on a single issue. One theoretician who sought to systematize the lawfulness or justice of this type of response and to balance commitment to the body politic and to the notion of obedience with selective dissent was the Harvard philosopher John Rawls.

RAWLS, A THEORY OF JUSTICE 350-55, 363-69-371-384 (1971)

[Rawls' conception of the appropriate limitations of civil disobedience rests on his assumption that in a nearly just society several principles may not be protested and their application must be accepted even in circumstances in which one is not completely satisfied with the result. These are his two basic Principles of Justice, augmented and explained by his Principles of Fair Equality of Opportunity and of Efficiency, the Difference Principle, the Principle of Fairness, the Principle of Average Utility, the Principle of Perfection, and his Principles of Natural Duty. These principles and Rawls' discussion of them are set out in his book and may be referred to there. He then proceeds, on their basis, to expand his notion of civil disobedience.

Rawls' conception of the appropriate limitations of civil disobedience rests on a number of assumptions. One is an assumption (for the purposes of discussion) of the existence of a social contract in which we imagine that men met together to choose the principles upon which to arrange rights and duties for all people and to determine the division of social benefits (the "original position"). The other is his assumption that in a nearly just society one is required to obey the law.]

THE DUTY TO COMPLY WITH AN UNJUST LAW

There is quite clearly no difficulty in explaining why we are to comply with just laws enacted under a just constitution. In this case the principles of natural duty and the principle of fairness establish the requisite duties and obligations. Citizens generally are bound by the duty of justice, and those who have assumed favored offices and positions, or who have taken advantage of certain opportunities to further their interests, are in addition obligated to do their part by the principle of fairness. The real question is under which circumstances and to what extent we are bound to comply with unjust arrangements. Now it is sometimes said that we are never required to comply in these cases. But this is a mistake. The injustice of law is not, in general, a sufficient reason for not adhering to it any more than the legal validity of legislation (as defined by the existing constitution) is a sufficient reason for going along with it. When the basic structure of society is reasonably just, as estimated by what the current state of things allows, we are to recognize unjust laws as binding provided that they do not exceed certain limits of injustice. In trying to discern these limits we approach the deeper problem of political duty and obligation. The difficulty here lies in part in the fact that there is a conflict of principles in these cases. Some principles counsel compliance while others direct us the other way. Thus the claims of political duty and obligation must be balanced by a conception of the appropriate priorities.

•   •   •

. . . it is evident that our duty or obligation to accept existing arrangements may sometimes be overridden. These requirements depend upon the principles of right, which may justify noncompliance in certain situations, all things considered. Whether noncompliance is justified depends on the extent to which laws and institutions are unjust. Unjust laws do not all stand on a par, and the same is true of policies and institutions. . . .

Secondly, we must consider the question why, in a situation of near justice anyway, we normally have a duty to comply with the unjust, and not simply with just, laws. While some writers have questioned this contention, I believe that most would accept it; only a few think that any deviation from justice, however small, nullifies the duty to comply with existing rules.

•   •   •

. . . I assume for simplicity that a variant of majority rule suitably circumscribed is a practical necessity. Yet majorities (or coalitions of minorities) are bound to make mistakes, if not from a lack of knowledge and judgment, then as a result of partial and self-interested views. Nevertheless, our natural duty to uphold just institutions binds us to comply with unjust laws and policies, or at least not to oppose them by illegal means as long as they do not exceed certain limits of injustice. Being required to support a just constitution, we must go along with one of its essential principles, that of majority rule. In a state of near justice, then, we normally have a duty to comply with unjust laws in virtue of our duty to support a just constitution. Given men as they are, there are many occasions when this duty will come into play.

•   •   •

Nevertheless, when they adopt the majority principle the parties agree to put up with unjust laws only on certain conditions. Roughly speaking, in the long-run the burden of injustice should be more or less evenly distributed over different groups in society, and the hardship of unjust policies should not weigh too heavily in any particular case. Therefore, the duty to comply is problematic for permanent minorities that have suffered from injustice for many years. And certainly we are not required to acquiesce in the denial of our own and others' basic liberties, since this requirement could not have been within the meaning of the duty of justice in the original position, nor consistent with the understanding of the rights of the majority in the constitutional convention. Instead, we submit our conduct to democratic authority only to the extent necessary to share equitably in the inevitable imperfections of a constitutional system. Accepting these hardships is simply recognizing and being willing to work within the limits imposed by the circumstances of human life. In view of this, we have a natural duty of civility not to invoke the faults of social arrangements as a too ready excuse for not complying with them, nor to exploit inevitable loopholes in the rules to advance our interests. The duty of civility imposes a due acceptance of the defects of institutions and certain restraint in taking advantage of them. Without some re-cognition of this duty mutual trust and confidence is liable to break down. Thus in a state of near justice at least, there is normally a duty (and for some also the obligation) to comply with unjust laws provided that they do not exceed certain bounds of injustice. This conclusion is not much stronger than that asserting our duty to comply with just laws. It does, however, take us a step further, since it covers a wider range of situations; but more important, it gives some idea of the questions that are to be asked in ascertaining our political duty.

THE DEFINITION OF CIVIL DISOBEDIENCE

I now wish to illustrate the content of the principles of natural duty and obligation by sketching a theory of civil disobedience. As I have already indicated, this theory is designed only for the special case of a nearly just society, one that is well-ordered for the most part but in which some serious violations of justice nevertheless do occur. Since I assume that a state of near justice requires a democratic regime, the theory concerns the role and the appropriateness of civil disobedience to legitimately established democratic authority. It does not apply to the other forms of government nor, except incidentally, to other kinds of dissent or resistance. I shall not discuss this mode of protest, along with militant action and resistance, as a tactic for trans-forming or even overturning an unjust and corrupt system. There is no difficulty about such action in this case. If any means to this end are justified, then surely nonviolent opposition is justified. The problem of civil disobedience, as I shall interpret it, arises only within a more or less just democratic state for those citizens who recognize and accept the legitimacy of the constitution. The difficulty is one of a conflict of duties. At what point does the duty to comply with laws enacted by a legislative majority (or with executive acts supported by such a majority) cease to be binding in view of the right to defend one's liberties and the duty to oppose injustice? This question involves the nature and limits of majority rule. For this reason the problem of civil disobedience is a crucial test case for any theory of the moral basis of democracy. . . .

I shall begin by defining civil disobedience as a public, nonviolent, conscientious yet political act contrary to law usually done with the aim of bringing about a change in the law or policies of the government. By acting in this way one addresses the sense of justice of the majority of the community and declares that in one's considered opinion the principles of social cooperation among free and equal men are not being respected. A preliminary gloss on this definition is that it does not require that the civilly disobedient act breach the same law that is being protested. It allows for what some have called indirect as well as direct civil disobedience. And this a definition should do, as there are sometimes strong reasons for not infringing on the law or policy held to be unjust. . . . A second gloss is that the civilly disobedient act is indeed thought to be contrary to law, at least in the sense that those engaged in it are not simply presenting a test case for a constitutional decision; they are prepared to oppose the statute even if it should be upheld. . . .

It should also be noted that civil disobedience is a political act not only in the sense that it is addressed to the majority that holds political power, but also because it is an act guided and justified by political principles, that is, by the principles of justice which regulate the constitution and social institutions generally. In justifying civil disobedience one does not appeal to principles of personal morality or to religious doctrines, though these may coincide with and support one's claims; and it goes without saying that civil disobedience cannot be grounded solely on group or self-interest. Instead one invokes the commonly shared conception of justice that underlies the political order. It is assumed that in a reasonably just democratic regime there is a public conception of justice by reference to which citizens regulate their political affairs and interpret the constitution. The persistent and deliberate violation of the basic principles of this conception over any extended period of time, especially the infringement of the fundamental equal liberties, invites either submission or resistance. By engaging in civil disobedience a minority forces the majority to consider whether it wishes to have its actions construed in this way, or whether, in view of the common sense of justice, it wishes to acknowledge the legitimate claims of the minority.

A further point is that civil disobedience is a public act. Not only is it addressed to public principles, it is done in public. It is engaged in openly with fair notice; it is not covert or secretive. One may compare it to public speech, and being a form of address, an expression of profound and conscientious political conviction, it takes place in the public forum. For this reason, among others, civil disobedience is nonviolent. It tries to avoid the use of violence, especially against persons, not from the abhorrence of the use of force in principle, but because it is a final expression of one's case. To engage in violent acts likely to injure and to hurt is incompatible with civil disobedience as a mode of address. Indeed, any interference with the civil liberties of others tends to obscure the civilly disobedient quality of one's act. Sometimes if the appeal fails in its purpose, forceful resistance may later be entertained. Yet civil disobedience is giving voice to conscientious and deeply held convictions; while it may warn and admonish, it is not itself a threat.

Civil disobedience is nonviolent for another reason. It expresses disobedience to law within the limits of fidelity to law, although it is at the outer edge thereof. The law is broken, but fidelity to law is expressed by the public and nonviolent nature of the act, by the willingness to accept the legal consequences of one's conduct. This fidelity to law helps to establish to the majority that the act is indeed politically conscientious and sincere, and that it is intended to address the public's sense of justice. To be completely open and nonviolent is to give bond of one's sincerity, for it is not easy to convince another that one's acts are conscientious, or even to be sure of this before oneself. . . .

Civil disobedience has been defined so that it falls between legal protest and the raising of test cases on the one side, and conscientious refusal and the various forms of resistance on the other. In this range of possibilities it stands for that form of dissent at the boundary of fidelity to law. Civil disobedience, so understood, is clearly distinct from militant action and obstruction; it is far removed from organized forcible resistance. . . .

THE DEFINITION OF CONSCIENTIOUS REFUSAL

Although I have distinguished civil disobedience from conscientious refusal, I have yet to explain the latter notion. This will now be done. It must be recognized, however, that to separate these two ideas is to give a narrower definition to civil disobedience than is traditional; for it is customary to think of civil disobedience in a broader sense as any noncompliance with law for conscientious reasons, at least when it is not covert and does not involve the use of force. Thoreau's essay is characteristic, if not definitive, of the traditional meaning. The usefulness of the narrower sense will, I believe, be clear once the definition of conscientious refusal is examined.

Conscientious refusal is noncompliance with a more or less direct legal injunction or administrative order. It is refusal since an order is addressed to us and, given the nature of the situation, whether we accede to it is known to the authorities. Typical examples are the refusal of the early Christians to perform certain acts of piety prescribed by the pagan state, and the refusal of the Jehovah's Witnesses to salute the flag. Other examples are the unwillingness of a pacifist to serve in the armed forces, or of a soldier to obey an order that he thinks is manifestly contrary to the moral law as it applies to war. Or again, in Thoreau's case, the refusal to pay a tax on the grounds that to do so would make him an agent of grave injustice to another. One's action is assumed to be known to the authorities, however much one might wish, in some cases, to conceal it. Where it can be covert, one might speak of conscientious evasion rather than conscientious refusal. Covert infractions of a fugitive slave law are instances of conscientious evasion.

There are several contrasts between conscientious refusal (or evasion) and civil disobedience. First of all, conscientious refusal is not a form of address appealing to the sense of justice of the majority. . . .

Conscientious refusal is not necessarily based on political principles; it may be founded on religious or other principles at variance with the constitutional order. Civil disobedience is an appeal to a commonly shared conception of justice, whereas conscientious refusal may have other grounds.

• • •

THE JUSTIFICATION OF CIVIL DISOBEDIENCE
• • •

The first point concerns the kinds of wrongs that are appropriate objects of civil disobedience. Now if one views such disobedience as a political act addressed to the sense of justice of the community, then it seems reasonable, other things equal, to limit it to instances of substantial and clear injustice, and preferably to those which block in the way to removing other injustices. For this reason there is a presumption in favor of restricting civil disobedience to serious infringements of the first principle of justice, the principle of equal liberty, and to blatant violations of the second part of the second principle, the principle of fair equality of opportunity. Of course, it is not always easy to tell whether these principles are satisfied. Still, if we think of them as guaranteeing the basic liberties, it is often clear that these freedoms are not being honored. After all, they impose certain strict requirements that must be visibly expressed in institutions. Thus when certain minorities are denied the right to vote or to hold office, or to own property and to move from place to place, or when certain religious groups are repressed and others denied various opportunities, these injustices may be obvious to all. They are publicly incorporated into the recognized practice, if not the letter, of social arrangements. The establishment of these wrongs does not presuppose an informed examination of institutional effects.

By contrast infractions of the difference principle are more difficult to ascertain. There is usually a wide range of conflicting yet rational opinion as to whether this principle is satisfied. The reason for this is that it applies primarily to economic and social institutions and policies. A choice among these depends upon theoretical and speculative beliefs as well as upon a wealth of statistical and other information, all of this seasoned with shrewd judgment and plain hunch. In view of the complexities of these questions, it is difficult to check the influence of self-interest and prejudice; and even if we can do this in our own case, it is another matter to convince others of our good faith. Thus unless tax laws, for example, are clearly designed to attack or to abridge a basic equal liberty, they should not normally be protested by civil disobedience. The appeal to the public's conception of justice is not sufficiently clear. The resolution of these issues is best left to the political process provided that the requisite equal liberties are secure. In this case a reasonable compromise can presumably be reached. The violation of the principle of equal liberty is, then, the more appropriate object of civil disobedience. This principle defines the common status of equal citizenship in a constitutional regime and lies at the basis of the political order. When it is fully honored the presumption is that other injustices, while possibly persistent and significant, will not get out of hand.

A further condition for civil disobedience is the following. We may suppose that the normal appeals to the political majority have already been made in good faith and that they have failed. The legal means of redress have proved to no avail. Thus, for example, the existing political parties have shown themselves indifferent to the claims of the minority or have proved unwilling to accommodate them. Attempts to have the laws repealed have been ignored and legal protests and demonstrations have had no success. Since civil disobedience is a last resort, we should be sure that it is necessary. Note that it has not been said, however, that legal means have been exhausted. At any rate, further normal appeals can be repeated; free speech is always possible. But if past actions have shown the majority immovable or apathetic, further attempts may reasonably be thought fruitless, and a second condition for justified civil disobedience is met. This condition is, however, a presumption. Some cases may be so extreme that there may be no duty to use first only legal means of political opposition. If, for example, the legislature were to enact some outrageous violation of equal liberty, say by forbidding the religion of a weak and defenseless minority, we surely could not expect that sect to oppose the law by normal political procedures. Indeed, even civil disobedience might be much too mild, the majority having already convicted itself of wantonly unjust and overtly hostile aims.

. . . It is conceivable, however, even if it is unlikely, that there should be many groups with an equally sound case (in the sense just defined) for being civilly disobedient; but that, if they were all to act in this way, serious disorder would follow which might well undermine the efficacy of the just constitution. I assume here that there is a limit on the extent to which civil disobedience can be engaged in without leading to a breakdown in the respect for law and the constitution thereby setting in motion consequences unfortunate for all. There is also an upper bound on the ability of the public forum to handle such forms of dissent; the appeal that civilly disobedient groups wish to make can be distorted and their intention to appeal to the sense of justice of the majority lost sight of. For one or both of these reasons, the effectiveness of civil disobedience as a form of protest declines beyond a certain point; and those contemplating it must consider these constraints.

•   •   •

. . . This kind of case is also instructive in showing that the exercise of the right to dissent, like the exercise of rights generally, is sometimes limited by others having the very same right. Everyone's exercising this right would have deleterious consequences for all, and some equitable plan is called for.

Suppose that in the light of the three conditions, one has a right to appeal one's case by civil disobedience. The injustice one protests is a clear violation of the liberties of equal citizenship, or of equality of opportunity, this violation having been more or less deliberate over an extended period of time in the face of normal political opposition, and any complications raised by the question of fairness are met. These conditions are not exhaustive; some allowance still has to be made for the possibility of injury to third parties, to the innocent, so to speak. But I assume that they cover the main points. There is still, of course, the question whether it is wise or prudent to exercise this right. Having established the right, one is now free, as one is not before, to let these matters decide the issue. We may be acting within our rights but nevertheless unwisely if our conduct only serves to provoke the harsh retaliation of the majority. To be sure, in a state of near justice, vindictive repression of legitimate dissent is unlikely, but it is important that the action be properly designed to make an effective appeal to the wider community. Since civil disobedience is a mode of address taking place in the public forum, care must be taken to see that it is understood. Thus, the exercise of the right to civil disobedience should, like any other right, be rationally framed to advance one's ends or the ends of those one wishes to assist. The theory of justice has nothing specific to say about these practical considerations. In any event questions of strategy and tactics depend upon the circumstances of each case. But the theory of justice should say at what point these matters are properly raised.

THE JUSTIFICATION OF CONSCIENTIOUS REFUSAL

•   •   •

. . . one may extend the interpretation of the original position and think of the parties as representatives of different nations who must choose together the fundamental principles to adjudicate conflicting claims among states. . . .

I can give only an indication of the principles that would be acknowledged. But, in any case, there would be no surprises, since the principles chosen would, I think, be familiar ones. The basic principle of the law of nations is a principle of equality. Independent peoples organized as states have certain fundamental equal rights. This principle is analogous to the equal rights of citizens in a constitutional regime. One consequence of this equality of nations is the principle of self-determination, the right of a people to settle its own affairs without the intervention of foreign powers. Another consequence is the right of self-defense against attack, including the right to form defensive alliances to protect this right. A further principle is that treaties are to be kept, provided they are consistent with the other principles governing the relations of states. Thus treaties for self-defense, suitably interpreted, would be binding, but agreements to cooperate in an unjustified attack are void *ab initio*.

These principles define when a nation has a just cause in war or, in the traditional phrase, its *jus ad bellum*. But there are also principles regulating the means that a nation may use to wage war, its *jus in bello*. Even in a just war certain forms of violence are strictly inadmissible; and where a country's right to war is questionable and uncertain, the constraints on the means it can use are all the more severe. Acts permissible in a war of legitimate self-defense, when these are necessary, may be flatly excluded in a more doubtful situation. The aim of war is a just peace, and therefore the means employed must not destroy the possibility of peace or encourage a contempt for human life that puts the safety of ourselves and of mankind in jeopardy. The conduct of war is to be constrained and adjusted to this end. . . .

Now if conscientious refusal in time of war appeals to these principles, it is founded upon a political conception, and not necessarily upon religious or other notions. While this form of denial may not be a political act, since it does not take place in the public forum, it is based upon the same theory of justice that underlies the constitution and guides its interpretation. Moreover, the legal order itself presumably recognizes in the form of treaties the validity of at least some of these principles of the law of nations. Therefore if a soldier is ordered to engage in certain illicit acts of war, he may refuse if he reasonably and conscientiously believes that the principles applying to the conduct of war are plainly violated. He can maintain that, all things considered, his natural duty not to be made the agent of grave injustice and evil to another outweighs his duty to obey. I cannot discuss here what constitutes a manifest violation of these principles. It must suffice to note that certain clear cases are perfectly familiar. The essential point is that the justification cites political principles that can be accounted for by the contract doctrine. The theory of justice can be developed I believe, to cover this case.

A somewhat different question is whether one should join the armed forces at all during some particular war. The answer is likely to depend upon the aim of the war as well as upon its conduct. In order to make the situation definite, let us suppose that conscription is in force and that the individual has to consider whether to comply with his legal duty to enter military service. Now I shall assume that since conscription is a drastic interference with the basic liberties of equal citizenship, it cannot be justified by any needs less compelling than those of national security. In a well-ordered society (or in one nearly just) these needs are determined by the end of preserving just institutions. Conscription is permissible only if it is demanded for the defense of liberty itself, including here not only the liberties of the citizens of the society in question, but also those of persons in other societies as well. Therefore if a conscript army is less likely to be an instrument of unjustified foreign adventures, it may be justified on this basis alone despite the fact that conscription infringes upon the equal liberties of citizens. But in any case, the priority of liberty (assuming serial order to obtain) requires that conscription be used only as the security of liberty necessitates. Viewed from the standpoint of the legislature (the appropriate stage for this question), the mechanism of the draft can be defended only on this ground. Citizens agree to this arrangement as a fair way of sharing in the burdens of national defense. To be sure, the hazards that any particular individual must face are in part the result of accident and historical happenstance. But in a well-ordered society anyway, these evils arise externally, that is, from unjustified attacks from the outside.

It is impossible for just institutions to eliminate these hardships entirely. The most that they can do is to try to make sure that the risks of suffering from these imposed misfortunes are more or less evenly shared by all members of society over the course of their life, and that there is no avoidable class bias in selecting those who are called for duty.

Imagine, then, a democratic society in which conscription exists. A person may conscientiously refuse to comply with his duty to enter the armed forces during a particular war on the grounds that the aims of the conflict are unjust. It may be that the objective sought by war is economic advantage or national power. The basic liberty of citizens cannot be interfered with to achieve these ends. And, of course, it is unjust and contrary to the law of nations to attack the liberty of other societies for these reasons. Therefore a just cause for war does not exist, and this may be sufficiently evident that a citizen is justified in refusing to discharge his legal duty. Both the law of nations and the principles of justice for his own society uphold him in this claim. There is sometimes a further ground for refusal based not on the aim of the war but upon its conduct. A citizen may maintain that once it is clear that the moral law of war is being regularly violated, he has a right to decline military service on the ground that he is entitled to insure that he honors his natural duty. Once he is in the armed forces, and in a situation where he finds himself ordered to do acts contrary to the moral law of war, he may not be able to resist the demand to obey. Actually, if the aims of the conflict are sufficiently dubious and the likelihood of receiving flagrantly unjust commands sufficiently great, one may have a duty and not only a right to refuse. Indeed, the conduct and aims of states in waging war, especially large and powerful ones, are in some circumstances so likely to be unjust that one is forced to conclude that in the foreseeable future one must abjure military service altogether. So understood a form of contingent pacifism may be a perfectly reasonable position: the possibility of a just war is conceded but not under present circumstances.

What is needed, then, is not a general pacificism but a discriminating conscientious refusal to engage in war in certain circumstances. States have not been loath to recognize pacificism and to grant it a special status. The refusal to take part in all war under any conditions is an unworldly view bound to remain a sectarian doctrine. It no more challenges the state's authority than the celibacy of priests challenges the sanctity of marriage. By exempting pacifists from its prescriptions the state may even seem to display a certain magnanimity. But conscientious refusal based upon the principles of justice between people as they apply to particular conflicts is another matter. For such refusal is an affront to the government's pretensions, and when it becomes widespread, the continuation of an unjust war may prove impossible. Given the often predatory aims of state power, and the tendency of men to defer to their government's decision to wage war, a general willingness to resist the states's claims is all the more necessary.

THE ROLE OF CIVIL DISOBEDIENCE

•   •   •

It is necessary to look at this doctrine from the standpoint of the persons in the original position. There are two related problems which they must consider. The first is that, having chosen principles for individuals, they must work out guidelines for assessing the strength of the natural duties and obligations, and, in particular, the strength of the duty to comply with a just constitution and one of its basic procedures, that a majority rule. The second problem is that of finding reasonable principles for dealing with unjust situations, or with circumstances in which the compliance with just principles is only partial. . . . If after a decent period of time to allow for reasonable political appeals in the normal way, citizens were to dissent by civil disobedience when infractions of the basic liberties occurred, these liberties would, it seems, be more rather than less secure. For these reasons, then, the parties would adopt the conditions defining justified civil disobedience as a way of setting up, within the limits of fidelity to law, a final device to maintain the stability of a just constitution. Although this mode of action is strictly speaking contrary to law, it is nevertheless a morally correct way of maintaining a constitutional regime.

In a fuller account the same kind of explanation could presumably be given for the justifying conditions of conscientious refusal (again assuming the context of a nearly just state). I shall not, however, discuss these conditions here. I should like to emphasize instead that the constitutional theory of civil disobedience rests solely upon a conception of justice. Even the feature of publicity and nonviolence are explained on this basis. And the same is true of the account of conscientious refusal, although it requires a further elaboration of the contract doctrine. . . .

NOTES

1. Note Rawls' notion that in a "nearly just" society (presumably, the U.S.A.), civil disobedience should be limited and, in particular, not be violent (p. 120), not develop into serious disorder (p. 122) and be exercised in ways that will not undermine the state. In short, dissent should be manifested not by deeds, but only by communications designed to convey a message to a majority having the same basic beliefs as the protestors.

2. Rawls believes that challenges to decisions of the State supported by the majority should be concerned mainly with the distribution of one value, power, not other values such as wealth (p. 123), and that the protestors should accept the sanctions imposed by the state for their acts (p. 122). Is Rawls more restrictive than Fortas infra concerning the exercise of individual conscience and protest? Does his theory of an "original position" and a "nearly just society" beg the question? Do his principles, as some critics contend, constitute a weak compromise in favor of the *status quo*?

Like John Rawls, Justice Abe Fortas argued that dissent would be tolerable in a democratic polity only if it limited itself to certain procedures specified and conducted by some part of the apparatus of the state and only if the dissident voluntarily subjected himself to whatever sanctions the state deemed appropriate for his behavior. Consider Fortas and appraise the parallels between his theory and that of John Rawls.

FORTAS, CONCERNING DISSENT AND CIVIL DISOBEDIENCE 9-64 (1968)

THE PARADOX: THE DUTY TO OBEY AND TO DISOBEY

I am a man of the law. I have dedicated myself to uphold the law and to enforce its commands. I fully accept the principle that each of us is subject to law; that each of us is bound to obey the law enacted by his government.

But if I had lived in Germany in Hitler's days, I hope I would have refused to wear an armband, to *Heil Hitler*, to submit to genocide. This I hope, although Hitler's edicts were law until allied weapons buried the Third Reich.

If I had been a Negro living in Birmingham or Little Rock or Plaquemines Parish, Louisiana, I hope I would have disobeyed the state laws that said that I might not enter the public waiting room in the bus station reserved for ''Whites.''

I hope I would have insisted upon going into the parks and swimming pools and schools which state or city law reserved for ''Whites.''

I hope I would have had the courage to disobey, although the segregation ordinances were presumably law until they were declared unconstitutional.

How, then, can I reconcile my profound belief in obedience to law and my equally basic need to disobey *these* laws? Is there a principle, a code, a theory to which a man, with honor and integrity, may subscribe? Or is it all a matter of individual judgment? Do we live in a trackless jungle? Is there, or is there not, a path that law and integrity mark out through the maze of tangled obligations and conflicting loyalties?

Above all, it is critically important for us to know whether violence is essential, lawlessness necessary—or whether there are effective alternatives.

THE SIMPLICITIES: THE RIGHT TO DISSENT AND ITS LIMITATIONS
•   •   •

In the United States, under our constitution, the question is not ''may I dissent?'' or ''may I oppose a law or a government?'' I *may* dissent. I *may* criticize. I *may* oppose. Our constitution and our courts guarantee this.

The question is: ''How may I do so?''

Each of us owes a duty of obedience to law. This is a moral as well as a legal imperative. So, first, we must seek to know which methods of protest are lawful: What are the means of opposition and dissent that are permissible under our system of law and which, therefore, will not subject us to punishment by the state and will not violate our duty of obedience to law?

•   •   •

From our earliest history, we have insisted that each of us is and must be free to criticize the government, however sharply, to express dissent and opposition, however brashly; even to advocate overthrow of the government itself. We have insisted upon freedom of speech and of the press and, as the First Amendment to the Constitution puts it, upon ''the right of the people peaceably to assemble and to petition the Government for a redress of grievances.''

•   •   •

THE LIMITATIONS
•   •   •

There are limitations, however, even on the freedom of speech. The state may prescribe reasonable regulations as to when and where the right to harangue the public or to assemble a crowd may be exercised. It may require a permit for a mass meeting. But it can't use this housekeeping power for any purpose except to reduce the public inconvenience which any large assemblage involves.

It is not true that anyone may say what's on his mind anytime and anywhere. According to the famous dictum of Justice Holmes, no one may falsely cry ''Fire'' in a crowded theater and thereby cause a panic. This is so even though the person's action may have been prompted by the highest motives.

He may have been alarmed and outraged by the lack of proper regulations to deal with fires in public places. He may have exhausted all other means to bring about the reform. He may have shouted "Fire" in the crowded theater only after all other measures failed, and only to dramatize the need and to secure necessary governmental action in the public interest.

But good motives do not excuse action which will injure others. The individual's conscience does not give him a license to indulge individual conviction without regard to the rights of others.

The man distressed at the inadequacy of fire regulations may speak in the public square; he may print and circulate pamphlets; he may organize mass meetings and picketing for the same purpose. He may denounce the city fathers as dunces, corrupt tools of the landlords, or potential murderers of innocent people.

He may even be able to call upon the courts to compel the government to act as he thinks it should. Our system provides a uniquely wide range of remedies in the courts which the citizen may invoke against his government.

Eventually, he and others may vote the government out of office.

But—and here is the point—he may not use means of advancing his program which, under the circumstances, will cause physical injury to others or unreasonably interfere with them.

Most of us would agree with Holmes that freedom to speak does not include falsely crying "Fire" in a crowded theater and causing a panic, but the illustration does not solve the problem of defining the limits of permissible protest. Even with Holmes' help, the line between the permissible and the prohibited remains hard to draw.

Speech, including symbolic speech such as picketing, never exists in limbo. It always occurs in a particular place and in particular circumstances. Even if what is said does not create a "clear and present danger" of physical injury to others, the place where the speech is uttered, the size of the crowd, and the circumstances may convert the lawful into the unlawful.

For example, if the participants unlawfully prevent the movement of traffic or if they unlawfully and needlessly trespass on private property, the fact that their speech is constitutionally protected will not necessarily shield them from arrest for the traffic violation or the trespass. The words may not occasion punishment, but the attendant circumstances may.

Even the application of this simple proposition is difficult. In *Brown v. Louisiana*, the Supreme Court divided five to four on a question of this sort. CORE had decided to protest segregation of public library facilities in the parishes of East and West Feliciana and St. Helena, Louisiana. Negroes were excluded from the three libraries serving the parishes. The parishes operated two bookmobiles. One was red, the other was blue. The red bookmobile served only white persons. The blue bookmobile served only Negroes. Residents of the parishes could receive library service by presenting registration cards. The cards issued to Negroes were stamped "Negro." A Negro holding a card could receive library service. But only from the blue bookmobile.

On a Saturday morning, during regular library hours, five adult Negro men, members of CORE, entered the segregated library building. They asked the librarian for a book: *The Story of the Negro* by Arna Bontemps. The librarian told them it was not on the shelves. They remained in the reading room as a protest against the segregation of the library. They were quiet and orderly. They were asked to leave. They politely refused.

CORE had given the sheriff advance notice of the proposed sit-in. The sheriff and some deputies arrived in ten or fifteen minutes from the time the men entered the library. The protesters were arrested. They were tried and convicted of disorderly conduct under a Louisiana statute.

On appeal, five of the nine members of the United States Supreme Court voted to set aside their conviction. There were differences of opinion even among the five as to the precise basis of the decision. The opinion which I wrote was joined only by the Chief Justice and Mr. Justice Douglas. It concluded that the protesters were engaged in the peaceful exercise of First Amendment rights. My opinion said that these rights clearly include the right to protest the unconstitutional segregation of public facilities by "silent and reproachful presence, in a place where the protestant has every right to be. . . ."

Justices Brennan and White agreed with the result that we reached, but wrote separate opinions. The five of us agreed, however, that the conviction of the protesters violated the Bill of Rights of the federal Constitution.

Four members of the Court disagreed. They did not quarrel with the proposition that the Negroes were privileged to enter the segregated library building, or that they were entitled, as members of the public, to library service. But they thought that by remaining in the library as a protest after they had asked for a book and had been informed it was not available, the Negroes were expressing their protest in an inappropriate and unauthorized place, and, accordingly, their action was not protected by the First Amendment.

In the minority's view, eloquently expressed by Mr. Justice Black, the Negroes had no right to be in the library after they had completed their business. Remaining there after their library business was completed, according to the minority of the Justices, was not a constitutionally protected form of protest, even though they entered the premises lawfully, remained there during regular hours, only, and peacefully and quietly expressed their protest against the segregation of the library itself.

In substance, the difference between the majority and minority turned on their respective judgments as to whether a peaceful, orderly protest is ever protected by the First Amendment if it is held in a public library. The majority said it is protected if it does not interfere with others and takes place when the protesters have a right to be present.

The result might very well have gone against the protesters if they had stayed in the library after the regular hours during which it was open to the public. If they had done so, a majority and not a minority of the Court might have agreed that this conduct was not constitutionally protected.

The fact that they were sitting-in to protest segregation might not have protected them if they had violated reasonable regulations applicable to all, without discrimination. Their sit-in would not then have been merely an instance of symbolic speech. It would have been symbolic speech accompanied by violation of a lawful and appropriate regulation designed reasonably to regulate the use of a public facility by everybody.

• • •

But the problem is much more difficult than this. A punishable offense is not excused solely because the conduct is picturesque, even if its purpose (to protest) might be unassailable. As my discussion of the library sit-in case shows, if the protest involves violation of a *valid law*, the fact that it was violated in a "good cause"—such as to protest segregation or war—will not ordinarily excuse the violator.

The law violation is excused only if the law which is violated (such as a law segregating a public library)—only if *that law itself* is unconstitutional or invalid. In the library sit-in case the protesters violated a segregation ordinance. This ordinance was unconstitutional and its violation could not be constitutionally punished. But if the law violated by the sit-in had been a lawful and reasonable regulation of library hours, the outcome might well have been different.

• • •

This necessarily brief and general discussion discloses the difficulty and subtlety of the legal issues involved in determining whether a particular form of protest is or is not protected by the Bill of Rights. The reason for the difficulty is that, unavoidably, the Constitution seeks to accommodate two conflicting values, each of which is fundamental: the need for freedom to speak freely, to protest effectively, to organize, and to demonstrate; and the necessity of maintaining order so that other people's rights, and the peace and security of the state, will not be impaired.

The types of protests and the situations in which they occur are of infinite variety, and it is impossible to formulate a set of rules which will strike the proper balance between the competing principles. The precise facts in each situation will determine whether the particular protest or activity is within the shelter of the First Amendment or whether the protesters have overstepped the broad limits in which constitutional protection is guaranteed. It is, accordingly, hazardous to set out general principles. But here are a few principles that in my opinion indicate the contours of the law in this subtle and complex field where the basic right of freedom conflicts with the needs of an ordered society:

(1) Our Constitution protects the right of protest and dissent within broad limits. It generously protects the right to organize people for protest and dissent. It broadly protects the right to assemble, to picket, to stage "freedom walks" or mass demonstrations, if these activities are peaceable and if the protesters comply with the reasonable regulations designed to protect the general public without substantially interfering with effective protest.

(2) If any of the rights to dissent is exercised with the intent to cause unlawful action (a riot, or assault upon others) or to cause injury to the property of others (such as a stampede for exits or breaking doors or windows), and if such unlawful action or injury occurs, the dissenter will not be protected. He may be arrested, and if properly charged and convicted of law violation, he will not be rescued by the First Amendment.

(3) If the right to protest, to dissent, or to assemble peaceably is exercised so as to violate valid laws reasonably designed and administered to avoid interference with others, the Constitution's guarantees will not shield the protester. For example, he may be convicted for engaging in marching or picketing which blocks traffic or for sitting-in in an official's office or in a public or private place and thereby preventing its ordinary and intended use by the occupant or others. It is difficult to generalize about cases of this sort, because they turn on subtleties of fact: for example, Did the public authorities confine themselves to requiring only that minimum restriction necessary to permit the public to go about its business? Were there facilities available for the protest which were reasonably adequate to serve the lawful purposes of the protesters, and which could have been used without depriving others of the use of the public areas?

• • •

THE RIGHTS OF THE STATE AND ITS DUTY
IN WAR AS WELL AS PEACE

So the citizen has the right, protected by the Constitution, to criticize, however intemperately; to protest, however strongly; to draw others to his cause; and in mass, peaceably to assemble. The state must not only respect these rights and refrain from punishing their exercise but it must also protect the dissenter against other citizens who seek by force, harassment, or interference to prevent him from exercising these rights. The state is obliged, if needed, to send police or state troopers to protect the mass march of people who are protesting against the state itself. This happened in the famous Selma march.

But this obviously does not mean the state must tolerate anything and everything that includes opposition to the government or to government law or policy. It does not mean that the courts will protect the dissident if the method of dissent involves aggression—something more than speech or symbolic speech for the communication of ideas to persuade others, or more than mere membership in a subversive organization. The state may and should act if the protest includes action directed at carrying out an attempt to overthrow the government by force or violence; or if it involves physical assault upon, or substantial interference with, the rights of others, or ordinarily trespass upon private property which is not open to the public.

In these situations, principles that are designed to protect the interest of the people generally in preserving the state come into play: The Constitution does not protect subversive acts. It does not shield sabotage. It does not tolerate espionage, theft of national secrets, or interference with the preparation of the nation's defense or its capacity to wage war. It does not protect these, however sincere the offender may be or however lofty his motives.

The state may defend its existence and its functions, not against words or argument or criticism, however vigorous or ill-advised, but against *action* and the state may and must protect its citizens against injury, damage to their property, and willful and unnecessary disruption of their work and normal pursuits.

In our system, the courts have the ultimate responsibility of striking the balance between the state's right to protect itself and its citizens, and the individual's right to protest, dissent, and oppose. In the sense that I have described, neither of these rights is absolute. We have entrusted the courts with the task of striking the balance in individual cases, on the basis of principles stated in the Constitution in terms which are necessarily general and which leave room for differences of opinion—even among Justices of the Supreme Court.

• • •

Under our system, as soon as the legal process is initiated, the state and the individual are equals. The courts are not instruments of the executive or legislative branches of the government. They are totally independent—subordinate only to the Constitution and to the rule of law.

• • •

But the theory—the structure—of our system allows full opportunity for both the state and the individual to assert their respective claims and to have them adjudicated by impartial, independent tribunals, on the basis of a principle which is fundamental to our society: that freedom to criticize, to persuade, to protest, to dissent, to organize, and to assemble peaceably are as essential to vital, effective government as they are to the spiritual and material welfare of the individual; and that the exercise of this freedom will be protected and encouraged and may not be diminished so long as the form of its exercise does not involve action which violates laws prescribed to protect others in their peaceful pursuits, or which incites a clear and present danger of violence or injury to others.

CIVIL DISOBEDIENCE

• • •

. . . this is what we mean by the rule of law: both the government and the individual must accept the result of procedures by which the courts, and ultimately the Supreme Court, decide that the law is such and such, and not so and so; that the law has or has not been violated in a particular situation, and that it is or is not constitutional; and that the individual defendant has or has not been properly convicted and sentenced.

This is the rule of law. The state, the courts, and the individual citizen are bound by a set of laws which have been adopted in a prescribed manner, and the state and the individual must accept the courts' determinations of what those rules are and mean in specific instances. *This is the rule of law*, even if the ultimate judicial decision is by the narrow margin of five to four!

• • •

The phrase "civil disobedience" has been grossly misapplied in recent years. Civil disobedience, even in its broadest sense, does not apply to efforts to overthrow the government or to seize control of areas or parts of it by force, or by the use of violence to compel the government to grant a measure of autonomy to part of its population. These are programs of revolution. They are not in the same category as the programs of reformers who—like Martin Luther King—seek changes within the established order.

Revolutionists are entitled, of course, to the full benefit of constitutional protections for the *advocacy* of their program. They are even protected in the many types of *action* to bring about a fundamental change, such as the organization of associations and the solicitation of members and support at the polls. But they are not protected in the use of violence. Programs of this sort, if they are pursued, call for law enforcement by police action. They are not likely to raise issues of the subtlety of those with which I am here concerned.

This kind of violent action is in sharp contrast with the theory of civil disobedience which, even where it involves a total or partial repudiation of the principle that the individual should obey the law, does not tolerate violent methods. . . .

The term "civil disobedience" has not been limited to protests in the form of refusal to obey a law because of disapproval of that particular law. It has been applied to another kind of civil disobedience. This is the violation of laws which the protester does not challenge because of their own terms or effect. The laws themselves are not the subject of attack or protest. They are violated only as a means of protest, like carrying a picket sign. They are violated in order to publicize a protest and to bring pressure on the public or the government to accomplish purposes which have nothing to do with the law that is breached. The great exponent of this type of civil disobedience was Gandhi. He protested the British rule in India by a general program of disobedience to the laws governing ordinary civil life.

• • •

Let me first be clear about a fundamental proposition. The motive of civil disobedience, whatever its type, does not confer immunity for law violation. Especially if the civil disobedience involves violence or a breach of public order prohibited by statute or ordinance, it is the state's duty to arrest the dissident. If he is properly arrested, charged, and convicted, he should be punished by fine or imprisonment, or both, in accordance with the provisions of law, unless the law is invalid in general or as applied.

He may be motivated by the highest moral principles. He may be passionately inspired. He may, indeed, be right in the eyes of history or morality or philosophy. These are not controlling. It is the state's duty to arrest and punish those who violate the laws designed to protect private safety and public order.

• • •

We are a government and a people under law. It is not merely *government* that must live under law. Each of us must live under law. Just as our form of life depends upon the government's subordination to law under the Constitution, so it also depends upon the individual's subservience to the laws duly prescribed. Both of these are essential.

Just as we expect the government to be bound by all laws, so each individual is bound by all of the laws under the Constitution. He cannot pick and choose. He cannot substitute his own judgment or passion, however noble, for the rules of law. Thoreau was an inspiring figure and a great writer; but his essay should not be read as a handbook on political science.

A citizen cannot demand of his government or of other people obedience to the law, and at the same time claim a right in himself to break it by lawless conduct, free of punishment or penalty.

• • •

The use of force or violence in the course of social protest is a far cry from civil disobedience as practiced by Gandhi. Gandhi's concept insists upon peaceful, non-violent refusal to comply with a law. It assumes that the protester will be punished, and it requires peaceful submission to punishment.

• • •

Dr. King was involved in a case which illustrated this conception. He led a mass demonstration to protest segregation and discrimination in Birmingham. An injunction had been issued by a state court against the demonstration. But Dr. King disregarded the injunction and proceeded with the march as planned. He was arrested. He was prosecuted in the state court, convicted of contempt, and sentenced to serve five days in jail. He appealed, claiming that the First Amendment protected his violation of the injunction. . . . Then Dr. King, without complaint or histrionics, accepted the penalty of misjudgment. This, I submit, is action in the great tradition of social protest in a democratic society where all citizens, including protesters, are subject to the rule of law.

• • •

AN EVALUATION
• • •

Our society gained a great deal from the powerful protests by and on behalf of the Negro. These protests awakened the nation's conscience to an intolerable situation. . . .

But this social revolution, like almost all revolutions, has an implacable rhythm of its own. The conscience of white America quickly responds to the accusation of guilt. *Mea culpa* comes readily to our lips, and we react quickly and generously. But in a social revolution, the demands for action, for cure, for restitution, for reparation, are not easily met. The demand is not satisfied by initial or moderate response. It is fed by it. The vigor and fervor of the demand increase as its justice is admitted and some steps are taken to meet it. As demand outstrips the early response, attitudes on both sides harden. Frustration sets in. Those demanding change see no prospect of satisfaction; those who initially offered reform despair of a reasonable resolution. And so, conflict and crisis occur.

At best, it will take generations to repair the ravages of past neglect and oppression of the Negroes. . . . Unremitting pressure, peaceably applied by the Negro community, will undoubtedly expedite response. Effective organization, demonstrated at the polls, will be of enormous help. But Negro violence will be met by police violence and the violence of the white population; and their violence will inspire further Negro aggressions.

• • •

In the last analysis, it is not the physical power of the Negro that is forcing the white community to undertake this job, but the moral power of his cause. It is basically conscience, justice, and a long and entirely justified view of national interest that impel the white majority to move to rectify an intolerable situation.

Violence on the part of a minority is sometimes a means of producing quick recognition of needs. It is not a productive technique for inducing the majority to undertake a job that must be figured in years of time and billions of dollars.

• • •

Violence is never defensible—and it has never succeeded in securing massive reform in an open society where there were *alternative methods of winning the minds of others to one's cause and securing changes in the government or its policies*. In the United States these avenues are certainly available. Our history and, specifically, the remarkable story of the present social revolution show that the alternatives of organization and protest (protected by the First Amendment), and of access to the ballot box, are open and effective. They may be long processes. They may be difficult. But they can produce lasting results. The alternative of violent methods employed by a minority can achieve the spurious appearance of temporary successes, but it will defeat the realistic objective: a long, difficult, burdensome program of reparation and rehabilitation of the Negro community.

• • •

THE REVOLT OF YOUTH
• • •

Many reasons have contributed to the youth revolt: the affluence of our society and the resulting removal of the pressure to prepare oneself for economic survival; the deterioration of the family unit; the increasing involvement of universities and their faculties with nonteaching interests; the disruptive shock of the atom bomb, which gave a new uncertainty and instability to life; the prospect that their lives will be interrupted by compulsory military service; the opposition to the war in Vietnam; the shock of discovering that our national pride and progress concealed the misery and degradation in which Negroes and the poor were living; disillusionment with the standards of the older generation; the new awareness of the wretched state of most of the world's people which came with the end of colonialism; the example of Negroes in this country and of the people of Africa and Asia who by individual and group effort, courage, and organization, have fought and sometimes won heroic battles.

Most of all, the revolt has found impetus, reason, and outlet in the opposition to the war in Vietnam and to the draft. Many of the younger generation, as well as some of their elder (justifiably or not), have come to regard this as a war of a small people against oppression by a vast power, as a struggle for national unity, or as a purely civil war in which our country is "brutally" participating.

• • •

Here again, perhaps it is a beginning to separate student activities which are nonviolent from those which involve assault or damage to persons or property. Where the law violation is nonviolent or technical (such as blocking entrance to a campus building, or even orderly occupancy of a university facility), there may be sense in patient forbearance despite the wrong that the action involves. But violent activities should be regarded and treated as intolerable.

• • •

From colonial times, however, there has been in this country general acceptance of the principle that while "conscientious objectors" are not exempt from the draft, they should not be forced into combat service. The special treatment of conscientious objectors was a natural and necessary corollary of our dedication to religious freedom.

• • •

The statute provides that the conscientious objector should be assigned to non-combatant service, or, if he is conscientiously opposed to participation even in that service, to "work of national importance under civilian direction."

• • •

. . . the special status "does not include essentially political, sociological, or philosophical views or a merely personal moral code."

The principle of special status for conscientious objectors has never been extended to persons whose opposition to war is based only on intellectual grounds: for example, that war aids neither the victor nor the vanquished. As the Seeger decision emphasizes, the conscientious objection must proceed from a basic, general, moral philosophy or religious commitment which involves, as the statute says, opposition "to participation in war in any form." It has not been extended to persons whose moral conviction is that a particular war, rather than war generally, is abhorrent.

The needs of the state for manpower to wage war are always critical. Its ability to muster the needed soldiers may be the measure of its ability to survive. Even so, our government, as well as other states that reflect the ideals of civilization, recognizes and has always recognized that an individual's fundamental moral or religious commitments are entitled to prevail over the needs of the state. As Chief Justice Hughes said many years ago: "When one's belief collides with the power of the State, the latter is supreme within its sphere. . . . But, in the forum of conscience, duty to a moral power higher than the State has always been maintained."

• • •

If the individual can veto his participation in the Vietnam war, he could also have declined to participate in World War II or the Korean conflict or defense against invasion. This ability of the individual to choose his war, from the state's viewpoint, would destroy the state's ability to defend itself or to perform the obligations it has assumed, or to prevent the spread of attempts to conquer other nations of the world by outside inspired and aided subversion. The government having made this decision, the theory of the state insists that the individual must conform his conduct to it until the government's position is changed by congressional action or at the ballot box, or, indeed, by the persuasion of argument, protest, mass demonstration, and other methods safeguarded by the First Amendment.

• • •

THE NUREMBERG DOCTRINE

Reference is often made to the Nuremberg trials which resulted in the punishment of a number of military officials and civilians for their participation in the Nazi outrages before and during World War II. These trials, or more accurately the London Agreement of August 8, 1945, establishing The International Military Tribunal to conduct the trials and stating the principles of adjudication to be followed, are cited in support of the argument that an individual's personal judgment as to the war in Vietnam should determine his draft status. The argument is that Nuremberg established the principle that the individual is legally and morally responsible for his participation in a war, although he may have acted under superior orders. If this is so, it is urged, the right of the individual to refuse to participate should be acknowledged.

This argument stretches the theory of the Nuremberg trials.

• • •

In any event, it's stretching the point to say that the Nuremberg principle supports the individual's refusal to submit to induction for service in a war which he considers immoral and unjustified. Certainly, that was far from the minds of the representatives of the victorious nations who participated in drafting and approving the London Agreement and in conducting the trials. They thought they were directing their efforts only at punishing those who willingly participated in extreme outrages, such as the deliberate murder of civilian population, apart from that which is always incidental to war. For example, they would have been startled if it had been suggested that the principles of Nuremberg made war criminals of the allied command responsible for bombing German cities and destroying their urban population, or for the use of flame throwers in the Japanese command.

Perhaps the time will come when criminal penalties will extend impartially to all killing in all wars so that no one would fight. But this possibility is remote from the still-hostile world in which we live.

• • •

The story of man is the history, first, of the acceptance and imposition of restraints necessary to permit communal life; and second, of the emancipation of the individual within that system of necessary restraints.

• • •

. . . The achievement of liberty is man's indispensable condition of living; and yet, liberty cannot exist unless it is restrained and restricted. The instrument of balancing these two conflicting factors is the law.

• • •

. . . But the survival of our society as a free, open, democratic community, will be determined not so much by the specific points achieved by the Negroes and the youth-generation as by the procedures—the rules of conduct, the methods, the practices—which survive the confrontations.

Procedure is the bone structure of a democratic society; and the quality of procedural standards which meet general acceptance—the quality of what is tolerable and permissible and acceptable conduct—determines the durability of the society and the survival possibilities of freedom within the society.

• • •

. . . Both our institutions and the characteristics of our national behavior make it possible for opposition to be translated into policy, for dissent to prevail. We have alternatives to violence.

• • •

An organized society cannot and will not long endure personal and property damage, whatever the reason, context, or occasion.

An organized society will not endure invasion of private premises or public offices, or interference with the work or activities of others if adequate facilities for protest and demonstration are otherwise available.

A democratic society should and must tolerate criticism, protest, demand for change, and organizations and demonstrations within the generally defined limits of the law to marshal support for dissent and change. It should and must make certain that facilities and protection where necessary are provided for these activities.

Protesters and change-seekers must adopt methods within the limits of the law. Despite the inability of anyone always to be certain of the line between the permissible and the forbidden, as a practical matter the lines are reasonably clear.

Violence must not be tolerated; damage to persons or property is intolerable. Any mass demonstration is dangerous, although it may be the most effective constitutional tool of dissent. But it must be kept within the limits of its permissible purpose. The functions of mass demonstrations, in the city or on the campus, are to communicate a point of view; to arouse enthusiasm and group cohesiveness among participants; to attract others to join; and to impress upon the public and the authorities the point advocated by the protesters, the urgency of their demand, and the power behind it. These functions do not include terror, riot, or pillage.

• • •

In my judgment civil disobedience—the deliberate violation of law—is never justified in our nation, where the law being violated is not itself the focus or target of the protest. So long as our governments obey the mandate of the Constitution and assure facilities and protection for the powerful expression of individual and mass dissent, the disobedience of laws which are not themselves the target of the protest—the violation of law merely as a technique of demonstration—constitutes an act of rebellion, not merely of dissent.

Civil disobedience is violation of law. Any violation of law must be punished, whatever its purpose, as the theory of civil disobedience recognizes. But law violation directed not to the laws or practices that are the subject of dissent, but to unrelated laws which are disobeyed merely to dramatize dissent, may be morally as well as politically unacceptable.

At the beginning of this discussion, I presented the dilemma of obedience to law and the need that sometimes may arise to disobey profoundly immoral or unconstitutional laws. This is another kind of civil disobedience, and the only kind that, in my view, is ever truly defensible as a matter of social morality.

It is only in respect to such laws—laws that are basically offensive to fundamental values of life or the Constitution—that a moral (although not a legal) defense of law violation can possibly be urged. Anyone assuming to make the judgment that a law is in this category assumes a terrible burden. He has undertaken a fearful moral as well as legal responsibility. He should be prepared to submit to prosecution by the state for the violation of law and the imposition of punishment if he is wrong or unsuccessful. He should even admit the correctness of the state's action in seeking to enforce its laws, and he should acquiesce in the ultimate judgment of the courts.

For after all, each of us is a member of an organized society. Each of us benefits from its existence and its order. And each of us must be ready, like Socrates, to accept the verdict of its institutions if we violate their mandate and our challenge is not vindicated.

NOTES

1. Fortas maintains that protesters should not violate a "valid" law and cites the unexceptionable case of reasonable regulations of library hours. Of course that is ingenuous, for the protests he is concerned with had little to do with that. But who should make the judgment of whether a particular law is "valid," on what basis, and according to which values? Fortas' position appears to be that it is always the court or some agency of government that should make this determination, regardless of the content of the law in question, the identity or politics of the judges and so on. Discuss.

2. Fortas' position identifies the state with the community; his view is that the actions of the state are inherently legitimate in a democratic society such as the United States. Discuss.

3. Fortas claims that the American system allows full opportunity for claims to be asserted by both individuals and the state against each other and for these claims to be adjudicated by "impartial independent tribunals" (i.e., the courts). Is this true? Some critics insist that courts are an arm of the same state, often with the same views as the legislature and executive organs, against which the dissenters protest. Is it true, as Fortas asserts, that "There are alternative means available in the U.S. for bringing about changes in the government or its policies" without resort to law-breaking or violence? Discuss.

4. Fortas asserts that "An individual's fundamental moral or religious commitments are entitled to prevail over the needs of the state." But do his conclusions on these matters (and his willingness to have deprived groups wait generations for redress) demonstrate a commitment to an elite's definition of public order, despite his claim that he is in favor of the expression of private judgment by individuals?

5. Compare Fortas' view that a protester who violates the law must accept the penalties meted out by the organs of the state with the position of Socrates in *Crito*. Underlying the position of both is the perspective that disobedience of the law and evasion of punishment will undermine the state, cause anarchy or engender a backlash of repression. Appraise this view.

The Fortas position and by implication the Rawlsian position were forcefully criticized by Howard Zinn.

ZINN, DISOBEDIENCE AND DEMOCRACY: NINE FALLACIES ON LAW AND ORDER 8-13, 18-21, 24, 27-30, 32-36, 38-40, 42, 44-46, 52, 117-119 (1968)

[Zinn claims that Fortas misleads on nine counts or fallacies.]
First fallacy: *that the rule of law has an intrinsic value apart from moral ends (By "moral ends" I mean the needs of human beings, not the mores of our culture.)*

• • •

. . . Fortas leads us to expect from him a set of moral criteria by which both adherence to law and violation of law would be tested, the assumption being that neither is self-justifying but requires some larger anchor of support. His essay never supplies this, however. What he gives us instead is an exposition of what the legal limits of dissent are; then he lays down the conditions for civil disobedience, in which the limits are very close to what is *legally* permissible.

Fortas' reluctance to go beyond legal limits is shown when he formulates, with some inconsistency the grounds for civil disobedience. . . . He says the "great tradition" of civil disobedience is invoked when laws are challenged as "invalid and unconstitutional." So here, the laws we disobey must be unconstitutional as well as invalid; Fortas, as a lawyer, must understand how crucial is the conjunction *and*. But . . . he talks of "the need . . . to disobey profoundly immoral or unconstitutional laws." Here, apparently, if a law is "profoundly immoral" it may be disobeyed even if it is constitutional. Yet, even in this instance, Fortas says, the disobedient one, when found guilty, "should acquiesce in the ultimate judgment of the courts." Should we acquiesce even where the law is "profoundly immoral?" . . . To insist we must, at some point, "acquiesce," that even a "profoundly immoral" law is ultimately to be obeyed, must mean that "the rule of law" in general supersedes the immorality of the particular law which represents is, and *in itself* constitutes a higher morality, a supreme value.

• • •

If Fortas were really concerned with values, with a moral system, with "a principle, a code, a theory," then there would be circumstances where the rule of law could not be obeyed, where disobedience might be the "essential condition" for individual liberty. But Fortas finds no such circumstance. As we have seen, even in those rare instances where we have a "profoundly immoral" law, if the courts uphold it, the verdict and punishment must be accepted. Thus, even then Fortas is not disobeying the rule of law, only pushing the point of obedience back from the legislature to the courts.

. . . there can be no moral imperative to obey an immoral law, unless the very idea of obdience to law, in general, has an overriding moral value. Any intelligent assessment of the right of civil disobedience must probe exactly that point. . . .

. . . But does the idea of obedience to law *in general* have such a high intrinsic value that the law must be held sacrosanct even where it violates an important human right or protects an evil condition?

• • •

. . . To assume that because some laws may serve democratic purposes all laws must always be obeyed, is to give a blank check to government—something that citizens in a democracy should never do.

A common argument is that disobedience even of bad laws is wrong because that fosters a general disrespect for all laws, including good ones, which we need. . . .

In fact, there is no evidence that violations of law in the spirit of civil disobedience lead to a general contempt for all laws. If this were so, we might expect either that persons engaging in civil disobedience become general law violators, or that other persons are encouraged by these acts to become indiscriminate violators of law. There is no indication that this has happened. For instance, Negroes in the South who began to violate segregation laws in organized campaigns of civil disobedience did not at the same time become general lawbreakers, nor did this lead to a larger crime rate among others in the population. Indeed, it was found in Albany, Georgia, that during the mass demonstrations of civil disobedience there in 1961 and 1962, the general crime rate declined.

The danger is in the other direction. When laws which violate the human spirit are maintained (like the segregation laws), or intolerable conditions are protected by the rule of law (like the poverty of Harlem amidst the wealth of Manhattan), and the victims have not found an *organized* way of protesting via civil disobedience, some will be spurred to ordinary crimes as a release for their suppressed needs.

•   •   •

Indeed, those outbreaks of either civil disobedience or disorder we have had in the United States have been not the *cause* of our troubles, but the result of them. They are the outcome of our slowness in solving the problems of poverty, racism, urban blight. Those who fear the spread of social disorder should keep in mind that civil disobedience is the *organized* expression of revolt against existing evils; it does not create the evils, but rationalizes the natural reactions to them, which otherwise burst out from time to time in sporadic and often ineffectual disorders. Civil disobedience, therefore, by providing an organized outlet for rebellion, may prevent chaotic and uncontrolled reactions. Riots, it must be said, may be useful as barometers showing government its inadequacies, showing the aggrieved the need for organized revolt; but civil disobedience, controlling and focusing rebellious energy, is more effective in bringing positive change.

. . . Granted that deliberate violation of law in civil disobedience, as I have argued, does not lead to crime waves, and that acts of civil disobedience do not lead to general disorder (unless the society is *generally* evil)—why put up even with *that* bit of disorder? Why not maintain the social peace, the slow workings of reform in the customary way? Why do I assume that we need to quicken the pace of change?

The problem here is how one perceives the ''peace'' that society enjoys when civil disobedience is absent. We live in an era when the national state monopolizes power and information. It therefore tries to persuade us that Domestic Tranquility is all important. It insists that we do not rebel against its authority, that we keep the ''peace,'' despite the fact that *it*, the state, is disturbing the peace on two other levels of our lives.

One of those levels is internal: the disorder within the person, the violence to body and spirit that may come from ill-health, unemployment, humiliation, loneliness, a sense of impotence—those afflictions which poor, or black, or sick, or imprisoned persons may have, or even healthy young people forced to fit into a money worshipping, success-idolizing culture. This is the result of a society which distributes wealth irrationally, condemns black people to a special status, destroys the sense of oneness with nature and with people that we all want.

•   •   •

The other level is external: the disorder abroad, inflicted outside the country against others. Indeed, the state tries to pacify us on the national level precisely in order to free it to maintain disorder on those other two levels. Unless we are aware of this, we will not see the value of civil disobedience; and we will condemn its disorder as a blow to peace and tranquility. We will see no need for the rude shove with which civil disobedience tries to waken society.

•   •   •

Our perception is a problem of balance. The magnitude of the grievance must be weighed against the degree of disruption which civil disobedience represents.

•   •   •

Why should *not* the individual "pick and choose" according to conscience, according to a set of humane values beyond the law? If experience shows that doing so encourages, not a general contempt for all laws, but continued selectivity based on justice, is this not good?

• • •

Second fallacy: *the person who commits civil disobedience must accept his punishment as right.*

Fortas tells us at the outset that he would have disobeyed the Southern segregation laws. And he tells us later in the essay that even if the Supreme Court had upheld the segregation laws as constitutional, his violation of the racial laws "would have been in a great cause." However, since the Supreme Court decided on behalf of those laws, he would have to go to jail. And this result "the individual must accept." . . .

To be punished in such an instance "may seem harsh," Fortas says. "*But this is what we mean by the rule of law*; both the government and the individual must accept the result of procedures by which the courts, and ultimately the Supreme Court, decide that the law is such and such, and not so and so. . . ."

Why must the citizen "accept the result" of a decision he considers immoral? To support "the rule of law" in the abstract? We have just argued that to support a wrong rule of law does not automatically strengthen the right rule of law, indeed may weaken it.

• • •

We forget that Plato was not a democrat, and that Socrates violates in the Crito that spirit he showed in the Apology, at his trial. But we have learned to accept without question his argument: that to violate a law or a judicial decision, even an unjust one on a very important issue (in the case of Socrates, so unjust as a death sentence, so important an issue as free speech) is to topple the whole structure of law and government, the right as well as the wrong. As Socrates puts it: "Do you think that a state can exist and not be overthrown in which the decisions are of no force and are disregarded and undermined by private individuals?"

. . . When unjust decisions are accepted, injustice is sanctioned and perpetuated; when unjust decisions appear and are violated on those occasions when they appear, it is a healthy discrimination between right and wrong that is fostered; when unjust decisions become the rule, then the government and its officials *should* be toppled.

Fortas cites the example of Dr. Martin Luther King's violation of a state court injunction in Alabama. . . .

But why was it right for Dr. King to accept an unjust verdict corroborating an unjust injunction, resulting in an unjust jail sentence, "without complaint or histrionics"? Why should there not have been bitter, forceful complaint across the country against this set of oppressive acts? Is the general notion of obedience to law more important than the right of free assembly? Does quiet acceptance in such a case not merely perpetuate the notion that transgressions of justice by the government must be tolerated by citizens?

• • •

Third fallacy: *that civil disobedience must be limited to laws which are themselves wrong.*

• • •

JURISPRUDENCE

To violate a law which is itself not being protested "as a technique of warfare in a social and political conflict over other issues" is not only constitutionally unprotected, but morally wrong according to Fortas. . . . More and more, Fortas' definition of what is moral coincides almost exactly with what is constitutional, and what is constitutional is what the Supreme Court decides. Thus is morality reduced to law, and law to the current opinions of the Court.

If (to return to an earlier example) after a child had been killed by a speeding automobile, housewives blocked traffic on a street to pressure the city fathers into installing a traffic light, this would not be justified, according to Fortas' criteria, because they would be violating a reasonable law (against obstructing traffic) in order to protest something else (the absence of a traffic signal).

Here is a stark surrender of human values to "the rule of law." Is human life (the lives of those children in danger on this street) not more important than the observance of the traffic-obstruction law by these women? Perhaps Fortas would argue that the housewives' action is so dangerous to the general respect for law and order that even a supreme value—the preservation of life—must be subordinated to "the rule of law." But is this reasonable? . . .

What if the number of lives at stake was much greater, as in war? Is it impermissible to violate a law which is, in itself, reasonable and harmless, like a law against obstructing traffic, as an attempt to criticize, to halt, the mass destruction of war?

• • •

If we were in Nazi Germany, would we only be morally justified in violating the yellow armband rule, and not in kidnapping the *gauleiter* in charge of yellow armbands, because the rule against kidnapping is a reasonable rule? Fortas has told us he would have violated the segregation laws in the South. But by his rule, he would not have been willing to "sit in" (trespass) in a restaurant where segregation was sustained not by a law but by a private rule of the restaurant owner.

Fortas is left in the position of failing to distinguish between important and unimportant laws, between trivial and vital issues, because the distinction between legal and illegal seems far more important to him. By his rule he would find himself *supporting* an act of civil disobedience aimed directly at a relatively unimportant law, and *opposing* an act aimed indirectly at a profoundly immoral law. He would find himself opposing violations of the smallest of laws (a trespass law, let us say) for the biggest of reasons (mass murder).

• • •

Related to this is another important distinction which Fortas ignores: between bad *laws* and bad *conditions*. He is willing to countenance defiance of a profoundly immoral law, like a segregation law. But what if there is a profoundly immoral situation, as evil in its way as segregation—like hunger, or poor housing, or lack of medical care? Here there is no law that one can challenge to call attention directly to the situation; it can only be done by violating some law which ordinarily is reasonable. It might be a trespass law, or a traffic law, or the city rules about hospital clinic fees. By Fortas' code, this cannot be allowed, so there is an arbitrary line drawn through civil disobedience: If a law has been passed registering what is wrong, you may violate it as a protest; if no law has been passed, but that same wrong condition exists, you are left without recourse to any protest as vigorous as an act of civil disobedience.

• • •

Thus, poverty, racism, war [the most persistent and basic evils of our time] are held sacrosanct against civil disobedience by Fortas' rule. For exactly those conditions which require the strongest of protests, citizens are deprived of the strongest of weapons. The Fortas rule guarantees that civil disobedience will never touch the most vital beams of our social system, however decayed they may be.

Fourth fallacy: *that civil disobedience must be absolutely nonviolent.*

• • •

I would define civil disobedience more broadly, as "the deliberate violation of law for a vital social purpose." Unlike Fortas' definition, this would include violating laws which are immoral whether constitutional or not, and laws which themselves are not at issue as well as those that are. It would leave open the question of the *means* of disobedience, but with two thoughts in mind: 1. that one of the moral principles guiding the advocate of civil disobedience is his belief that a nonviolent world is one of his ends, and that nonviolence is more desirable than violence as a means; 2. that in the inevitable tension accompanying the transition from a violent world to a nonviolent one, the choice of means will almost never be pure, and will involve such complexities that the simple distinction between violence and nonviolence does not suffice as a guide.

• • •

My point in all this is not at all to establish a case for violence. To me one of the cardinal principles in any moral code is the reduction and elimination of violence.

• • •

Let us try to find some principle on which he could possibly justify his absolute prohibition of violence in civil disobedience and his rather easy support of it in international affairs. Perhaps *the importance* of the issue at stake might be one test. There is good reason (as I pointed out earlier, citing Bay, Camus, Niebuhr, Douglass, Thoreau, Gandhi) for not being absolutist in adhering to nonviolence. There are other human values besides peace—so that it is possible to conceive of situations where a disturbance of the peace is justifiable if it results in some massive improvement of the human condition for large numbers of people.

• • •

This brings us to another necessary element of any moral code on violence and nonviolence. Would not any reasonable code have to weigh the *degree* of violence used in any case against the *importance* of the issue at stake? Thus, a massive amount of violence for a small or dubious reason would be harder to justify than a small amount of violence for an important and a clear reason.

• • •

. . . If he got more specific, and set up a standard which took *degrees* of violence into account, wars might be much harder to justify than local acts of civil disobedience.

There is another point which he slides over—one which is very important, I believe, in drawing up a set of principles on violence and nonviolence in civil disobedience. That is the distinction between violence to people and violence to things; destruction of life, or destruction of property. Mr. Fortas lumps them together as if they were equally reprehensible. He says in his concluding section: "Violence must not be tolerated; damage to persons or property is intolerable." He does not differentiate, in this general prohibition. Yet, once Mr. Fortas has opened the door to any distinction on the problem of violence (which he does, once he allows the violence of war), he should not fail to discriminate between people and things. Surely that is one of the cardinal rules in any humanistic philosophy. A fixed devotion to property as something holy, when carried to its extreme, leads policemen to shoot to death black people who are taking *things* from stores.

• • •

My point is not that violence is unquestionably an effective method of reforming a society; it seems to me we would have to be extremely careful in adapting historical experience to the conditions of the United States. Each situation in the world is unique and requires unique combinations of tactics. I insist only that the question is so open, so complex, that it would be foolish to rule out at the start, for all times and conditions, all of the vast range of possible tactics beyond strict nonviolence.

• • •

Ninth fallacy: *that we, the citizenry, should behave as if we are the state and our interests are the same.*

• • •

What is involved here is a subtle psychological point: how we approach political issues, whether we consider disputes ended when the state has spoken, or whether we will weigh those arguments from our viewpoint as citizens. What is at stake is the fundamental principle of the compact theory of government, enunciated in John Locke's *Second Treatise of Government*, and incorporated by Thomas Jefferson in the Declaration of Independence: that governments are instituted among men for certain ends; that among these are life, liberty, and the pursuit of happiness; that whenever a government becomes destructive of those ends, it is the right of people to alter or abolish it. The government is not synonymous with the people of the nation; it is an artificial device, set up by the citizens for certain purposes. It is endowed with no sacred aura; rather, it needs to be watched, scrutinized, criticized, opposed, changed, and even overthrown and replaced when necessary.

• • •

Let the state worry about its power. The record in history of our government—of all governments—is a record of violence, cruelty, calousness, intrusion. We, the citizenry, had better augment our own power because we are the most dependable defendants of our own liberty.

NOTES

1. Zinn, like the other authors whose works have been considered, dealt with critical contemporary issues. Plato was committed to the rise of the *polis* and its superordination over the extended family. In *Crito*, he pictured the state itself as an extended family telling Socrates that it had "brought you into the world, educated and nurtured you" and that "you are our child." Thoreau was exercised by the Mexican War and the continued practice of slavery. Fortas and Zinn were both perturbed by the political turmoil in the Vietnam era, one focusing on popular resistance to the war, the other more concerned over associated civil rights abridgements. All of these authors propagandized for their particular cause in a manner they felt would be most persuasive to their audience and made some statements which now seem extreme. In his book, Zinn asserts that the United States government and American universities in general are evil, that the United States has "run out of that time and space that it once had" to solve its problems, and that consequently "our national policies are going to have to change

dramatically and fast. We are going to require torrential shifts of wealth and power.'' In fact, turmoil in the United States subsided considerably since Zinn wrote his book in the sixties.

2. Zinn does not identify the state with the community but distinguishes the two, referring to the state as in effect a small power clique opposed to ''us.'' Zinn, like some of the other authors whose excerpts are reproduced here, views the state as an instrument of a small elite acting in its own interests. (Recall the views of Thrasymachus, and Kropotkin, supra). Is this view accurate for the United States today? Explain.

3. Since Zinn views the United States government and American universities as evil, as noted above, he believes that student occupation of a university building which disrupts activities by other students and faculty is a ''mild'' act and that similar occupation of government buildings is a ''pitifully moderate act.'' Discuss and appraise.

4. In his ''First fallacy,'' Zinn attributes to Fortas the notion that ''the rule of law has an intrinsic value apart from moral ends.'' What does he mean by ''rule of law'' here? Why is there an inherent value in obeying the law in Fortas' view? Is it true, as Zinn implies, that Fortas' ethic always redounds to the advantage of the elite?

5. Fortas, like Socrates, seems to believe that complying with decisions is per se moral, for otherwise anarchy, unrestrained lawbreaking, or the undermining of the state will result, leading to greater evil for most people. Zinn and Thoreau disagree. Zinn claims that ''there is no evidence that violations of law in the spirit of civil disobedience lead to a general contempt for all laws'' nor ''lead to a larger crime rate among others in the population.'' In fact, Zinn claims that in the absence of organized civil disobedience, victims of intolerable conditions ''will be spurred to ordinary crimes as a release for their suppressed needs'' and that ''civil disobedience, . . . by providing an organized outlet for rebellion, may prevent chaotic and uncontrolled reactions.''

Would Fortas agree that there are always broad currents of deviant behavior that exist in any society without undermining it? (See K. Erikson, *Wayward Puritans: A Study in the Sociology of Deviance* Ch. 1 (1966)). In theory, Fortas would sanction rebellion in the extreme case in which there was no alternative way to effect change, but he believed that there are effective ways to bring about change in a democratic society like the United States. Zinn disagrees. Aside from rhetorical assertions, does either try to justify his assertion or qualify it with respect to certain matters? Do both Fortas and Zinn in fact utilize the same balancing tests (means v. ends), but with each appraising very differently and placing different weights upon the aforementioned components that enter into such balancing? Are they both resorting to natural law type premises not subject to empirical verification?

6. Assuming that civil disobedience is to be tolerated, to what extent should those operating as the ''state'' allow it? What is the proper level of action, if any, to be applied to the disobedient: symbolic action, or coercive action; if the latter, at what level?

7. Zinn believes that ''Democracy must improve itself constantly or decay.'' Who defines ''improvement,'' by which criteria and procedure and toward which goals?

THE RESPONSE OF DECISIONMAKERS

Many people have tried to balance the need for civility and respect for established procedures of government with the right or option of dissenting in some effective fashion from a particular decision deemed morally offensive. The problem is often examined in terms of the morality or bona fides of the person dissenting. (Recall Rawls supra). But rarely is it examined in terms of the goals the dissenter seeks or the consequences for the community of the form and substance of the dissent.

A dimension of great importance to the lawyer is the problem of the response of decisionmakers acting on behalf of the state in a democratic polity to exercises of selective disobedience.

REYNOLDS v. UNITED STATES
98 U.S. 145 (1878)

[Defendant, a Mormon, was indicted for bigamy under a federal statute. One of his defenses was that polygamy was a religious duty for members of the Mormon Church. Restrictions on polygamy, therefore, violated the First Amendment.]

. . . [Waite, C. J.] . . . As to the defence of religious belief or duty.

On the trial, the plaintiff in error, the accused, proved that at the time of his alleged second marriage he was, and for many years before had been, a member of the Church of Jesus Christ of Latter-Day Saints, commonly called the Mormon Church, and a believer in its doctrines; that it was an accepted doctrine of that church that it was the duty of male members of said church, circumstances permitting, to practise polygamy. . . .

Upon this charge and refusal to charge the question is raised, whether religious belief can be accepted as a justification of an overt act made criminal by the law of the land.

• • •

[The court traces the history of the First Amendment back to the pre-constitution Virginia statutes].

At the next session [of the Virginia Legislature] the proposed bill was not only defeated, but another, ''for establishing religious freedom,'' drafted by Mr. Jefferson, was passed. 1 Jeff. Works, 45; 2 Howison, Hist. of Va. 298. In the preamble of this act (12 Hening's Stat. 84) religious freedom is defined; and after a recital ''that to suffer the civil magistrate to intrude his powers into the field of opinion, and to restrain the profession or propagation of principles on supposition of their ill tendency, is a dangerous fallacy which at once destroys all religious liberty,'' it is declared ''that it is time enough for the rightful purposes of civil government for its officers to interfere when principles break out into overt acts against peace and good order.'' In these sentences is found the true distinction between what properly belongs to the church and what to the State.

In a little more than a year after the passage of this statute the convention met which prepared the Constitution of the United States. Accordingly, at the first session of the first Congress the amendment now under consideration was proposed with others by Mr. Madison. It met the views of the advocates of religious freedom, and was adopted. Mr. Jefferson afterwards, in reply to an address to him by a committee of the Danbury Baptist Association (8 id. 113), took occasion to say: ''Believing with you that religion is a matter which lies solely between man and his God; that he owes account to none other for his faith or his worship; that the legislative powers of the government reach actions only, and not opinions,—I contemplate with sovereign reverence that act of the whole American people which declared that their legislature should 'make no law respecting an establishment of religion or prohibiting the free exercise thereof,' thus building a wall of separation between church and State. Adhering to this expression of the supreme will of the nation in behalf of the rights of conscience, I shall see with sincere satisfaction the progress of those sentiments which tend to restore man to all his natural rights, convinced he has no natural right in opposition to his social duties.'' Coming as this does from an acknowledged leader of the advocates of the measure, it may be accepted almost as an authoritative declaration of the scope and effect of the amendment thus secured. Congress was deprived of all legislative power over mere opinion, but was left free to reach actions which were in violation of social duties or subversive of good order.

Polygamy has always been odious among the northern and western nations of Europe, and, until the establishment of the Mormon Church, was almost exclusively a feature of the life of Asiatic and of African people. At common law, the second marriage was always void (2 Kent. Com. 79), and from the earliest history of England polygamy has been treated as an offence against society.

• • •

. . . We think it may safely be said there never has been a time in any State of the Union when polygamy has not been an offence against society, cognizable by the civil courts and punishable with more or less severity. In the face of all this evidence, it is impossible to believe that the constitutional guaranty of religious freedom was intended to prohibit legislation in respect to this most important feature of social life. Marriage, while from its very nature a sacred obligation, is nevertheless, in most civilized nations, a civil contract, and usually regulated by law. Upon it society may be said to be built, and out of its fruits spring social relations and social obligations and duties, with which government is necessarily required to deal. In fact, according as monogamous or polygamous marriages are allowed, do we find the principles on which the government of the people, to a greater or less extent, rests. Professor Lieber says, polygamy leads to the patriarchal principle, and which, when applied to large communities, fetters the people in stationary despotism, while that principle cannot long exist in connection with monogamy. Chancellor Kent observes that this remark is equally striking and profound. 2 Kent, Com. 81, note(e). An exceptional colony of polygamists under an exceptional leadership may sometimes exist for a time without appearing to disturb the social condition of the people who surround it; but there cannot be a doubt that, unless restricted by some form of constitution, it is within the legitimate scope of the power of every civil government to determine whether polygamy or monogamy shall be the law of social life under its dominion. . . . Laws are made for the government of actions, and while they cannot interfere with mere religious belief and opinions, they may with practices. Suppose one believed that human sacrifices were a necessary part of religious worship, would it be seriously contended that the civil government under which he lived could not interfere to prevent a sacrifice? Or if a wife religiously believed it was her duty to burn herself upon the funeral pile of her dead husband, would it be beyond the power of the civil government to prevent her carrying her belief into practice?

So here, as a law of the organization of society under the exclusive dominion of the United States, it is provided that plural marriages shall not be allowed. Can a man excuse his practices to the contrary because of his religious belief? To permit this would be to make the professed doctrines of religious belief superior to the law of the land, and in effect to permit every citizen to become a law unto himself. Government could exist only in name under such circumstances.

In *Regina v. Wagstaff* (10 Cox Crim. Cases, 531), the parents of a sick child, who omitted to call in medical attendance because of their religious belief that what they did for its cure would be effective, were held not to be guilty of manslaughter, while it was said the contrary would have been the result if the child had actually been starved to death by the parents, under the notion that it was their religious duty to obstain from giving it food. But when the offence consists of a positive act which is knowingly done, it would be dangerous to hold that the offender might escape punishment because he religiously believed the law which he had broken ought never to have been made. No case, we believe, can be found that has gone so far.

Upon a careful consideration of the whole case, we are satisfied that no error was committed by the court below.

NOTES

1. In *Reynolds*, the Supreme Court presents itself as responding in a most liberal and tolerant fashion to the claim of a small sub-community to engage in plural marriage. Is it in fact being liberal and tolerant? For people who are committed to certain religious ideas, is it satisfactory to say that they can believe in them but cannot implement them in the sacraments that their faith requires?

2. The court purports to be willing to allow non-conforming behavior, perhaps even bigamy, if it does not harm the larger society. Is there any real indication that plural marriage undermines the fabric of the society as a whole? Is there any empirical evidence, on which the court relies, to sustain Professor Lieber's contention that monogamous marriage is a fundamental strut of civilized society? Was the ancient Chinese civilization at its zenith "civilized" in his view? Was Rome at its zenith "civilized?" Was Islam at its zenith "civilized?"

———

One of the more interesting efforts to establish a theory of tolerance for such behavior in a pluralistic community with limits established by the state is to be found in a judgment by Judge Wyzanski.

UNITED STATES v. SISSON
297 F. SUPP. 902 (D. MASS. 1969)

[Chief Judge Wyzanski] . . . March 21, 1969, in the United States District Court sitting in Boston, a jury returned a verdict that John Heffron Sisson, Jr., was guilty of unlawfully, knowingly, and wilfully having refused to comply with the order of Local Board No. 114 to submit to induction into the armed forces of the United States, in violation of the Military Selective Service Act of 1967. Title 50, Appendix, United States Code, Section 462. 32 Code of Federal Regulations 1632.14.

Pursuant to Rule 34 of the Rules of Criminal Procedure, Sisson on March 28, 1969, filed an amended motion in arrest of judgment. Adequate reference is made to earlier contentions. A new point is also raised: that the judicial power vested in this court by Article III of the United States Constitution does not give jurisdiction to adjudicate the merits of a criminal case in which the court is precluded, by the doctrine of so-called "political questions" or otherwise, from deciding relevant constitutional, domestic, and international law questions raised by defendant. It is said that a trial designed to exclude relevant issues violates the "due process" clause of the Fifth Amendment.

Important as is the new issue, defendant indicated both before and during the trial that he also intended to preserve his older contention that no offense is charged in the indictment because it is laid under a statute, which, as applied to him, violates the provision of the First Amendment that "Congress shall make no law respecting an establishment of religion, or prohibiting the free exercise thereof" and the "due process" clause of the Fifth Amendment.

• • •

This court in this opinion addresses itself not to the new point but to a further consideration of the never-abandoned issue whether the government can constitutionally require combat service in Vietnam of a person who is conscientiously opposed to American military activities in Vietnam because he believes them immoral and unjust, that belief resting not upon formal religion but upon the deepest convictions and ethical commitments, apart from formal religion, of which a man is capable.

• • •

B. THE FACTS

Sisson does not now and never did claim that he is or was in the narrow statutory sense a religious conscientious objector.

• • •

The first formal indication in the record that Sisson had conscientious scruples is a letter of February 29, 1968 in which he notified Local Board No. 114 that "I find myself to be conscientiously opposed to service in the Armed Forces. Would you please send me SSS Form No. 150 so that I might make my claim as a conscientious objector." On receiving the form, Sisson concluded that his objection not being religious, within the administrative and statutory definitions incorporated in that form, he was not entitled to have the benefit of the form. He, therefore, did not execute it.

• • •

There is not the slightest basis for impugning Sisson's courage. His attempt to serve in the Peace Corps, and the assignment he took on a Southern newspaper were not acts of cowardice or evasion. Those actions were assumptions of social obligations. They were in the pattern of many conscientious young men who have recently come of age. From his education Sisson knows that his claim of conscientious objection may cost him dearly. Some will misunderstand his motives. Some will be reluctant to employ him.

Nor was Sisson motivated by purely political considerations. Of course if "political" means that the area of decision involves a judgment as to the conduct of a state, then any decision as to any war is not without some political aspects. But Sisson's table of ultimate values is moral and ethical. It reflects quite as real, pervasive, durable, and commendable a marshalling of priorities as a formal religion. It is just as much a residue of culture, early training, and beliefs shared by companions and family. What another derives from the discipline of a church, Sisson derives from the discipline of conscience.

Thus, Sisson bore the burden of proving by objective evidence that he was sincere. He was as genuinely and profoundly governed by his conscience as would have been a martyr obedient to an orthodox religion.

Sisson's views are not only sincere, but, without necessarily being right, are reasonable. Similar views are held by reasonable men who are qualified experts. The testimony of Professor Richard Falk of Princeton University and Professor Howard Zinn of Boston University is sufficient proof. See also Ralph B. Potter, New Problems for Conscience in War, American Society for Christian Ethics, January 19, 1968; War and Moral Discourse, John Knox Press, 1969.

• • •

C. LIMITATION OF ISSUES

More significantly at least all those issues which are raised under the First Amendment are so interlocked textually and substantively, that one of those issues cannot properly be considered apart from the others. Sound interpretation of any phrase of the Amendment requires reconciliation both with every other phrase of that Amendment and with the Constitution as a whole.

Therefore, it is meet for this opinion to consider both the broad contention, growing principally out of "the free exercise of" religion phrase, that no statute can require combat service of a conscientious objector whose principles are either religious or akin thereto, and the narrower contention growing principally out of "the establishment" of religion phrase, that the 1967 draft act invalidly discriminates in favor of certain types of religious objectors to the prejudice of Sisson. An appellate court might find it suitable to render its judgment solely on the latter issue. This inferior court, as already explained, is not so conveniently situated. In candor it must be added that this court found its understanding of the narrow issue much clarified by first analyzing, as will be seen, the broad issue.

•   •   •

E. THE CONSTITUTIONAL POWER OF CONGRESS TO DRAFT CONSCIENTIOUS OBJECTORS FOR COMBAT DUTY IN A DISTANT CONFLICT NOT PURSUANT TO A DECLARED WAR

Indubitably Congress has constitutional power to conscript the generality of persons for military service in time of war. . . . that is, there is not a constitutional gap, nor a defect of power to conscript in time of war, any more than there is a defect of power to raise an army of volunteers. Daniel Webster's contrary views have been superseded. . . . His historical reading of the past was better than of the future.

Whether this constitutional power exists in time of peace has been thought by some justices of the Supreme Court to be an open question. . . . However, this court, until otherwise authoritatively instructed, assumes that Congressional power to conscript for war embraces Congressional power in time of peace to conscript for later possible war service. . . .

This court's assumption that Congress has the general power to conscript in time of peace is not dispositive of the specific question whether that general power is subject to some exception or immunity available to a draftee because of a constitutional restriction in favor of individual liberty. . . .

However, some have supposed the specific question is foreclosed. At the head of the procession is Judge Learned Hand who a decade ago, before the Vietnam conflict sharpened our focus, announced in the Oliver Wendell Holmes Lectures on The Bill of Rights, . . . that "We could, though we do not, lawfully require all citizens to do military service regardless of their religious principles."

•   •   •

Yet open as the issue may be, *this Court in the following discussion assumes that a conscientious objector, religious or otherwise, may be conscripted for some kinds of service in peace or in war. This court further assumes that in time of declared war or in the defense of the homeland against invasion, all persons may be conscripted even for combat service.*

But the precise inquiry this court cannot avoid is whether now Sisson may be compelled to submit to non-justiciable military orders which may require him to render combat service in Vietnam. . . .

Implicit is the problem whether in deciding the issue as to the constitutional claim of a conscientious objector to be exempt from combat service circumstances alter cases. (See the admittedly distinguishable case of jury duty. In re Jenison above).

This is not an area of constitutional absolutism. It is an area in which competing claims must be explored, examined, and marshalled with reference to the Constitution as a whole.

There are two main categories of conflicting claims. First, there are both public and private interests in the common defense. Second there are both public and private interests in individual liberty.

Every man, not least the conscientious objector, has an interest in the security of the nation. Dissent is possible only in a society strong enough to repel attack. The conscientious will to resist springs from moral principles. It is likely to seek a new order in the same society, not anarchy or submission to a hostile power. Thus conscience rarely wholly disassociates itself from the defense of the ordered society within which it functions and which it seeks to reform not to reduce to rubble.

In parallel fashion, every man shares and society as a whole shares an interest in the liberty of the conscientious objector, religious or not. The freedom of all depends on the freedom of each. Free men exist only in free societies. Society's own stability and growth, its physical and spiritual prosperity are responsive to the liberties of its citizens, to their deepest insights, to their free choices—"That which opposes, also fits."

Those rival categories of claims cannot be mathematically graded. There is no table of weights and measures. Yet there is no insuperable difficulty in distinguishing orders of magnitude.

The sincerely conscientious man, whose principles flow from reflection, education, practice, sensitivity to competing claims, and a search for a meaningful life, always brings impressive credentials. When he honestly believes that he will act wrongly if he kills, his claim obviously has great magnitude. That magnitude is not appreciably lessened if his belief relates not to a war in general, but to a particular war or to a particular type of war. Indeed a selective conscientious objector might reflect a more discriminating study of the problem, a more sensitive conscience, and a deeper spiritual understanding.

It is equally plain that when a nation is fighting for its very existence there are public and private interests of great magnitude in conscripting for the common defense all available resources, including manpower for combat.

But a campaign fought with limited forces for limited objects with no likelihood of a battlefront within this country and without a declaration of war is not a claim of comparable magnitude.

Nor is there any suggestion that in present circumstances there is a national need for combat service from Sisson as distinguished from other forms of service by him. The want of magnitude in the national demand for combat service is reflected in the nation's lack of calls for sacrifice in any serious way by civilians.

Before adding up the accounts and striking a balance there are other items deserving notice.

Sisson is not in a formal sense a religious conscientious objector. His claim may seem less weighty than that of one who embraces a creed which recognizes a Supreme Being, and which has as part of its training and discipline opposition to war in any form. It may even seem that the Constitution itself marks a difference because in the First Amendment reference is made to the "free exercise of" "religion", not to the free exercise of conscience. Moreover, Sisson does not meet the 1967 congressional definition of religion. Nor does he meet the dictionary definition of religion.

But that is not the end of the matter. The opinions in United States v. Seeger, 380 U.S. 163, 85 S.Ct. 850, 13 L.Ed.2d 733 (1965) disclosed wide vistas. The court purported to look only at a particular statute. It piously disclaimed any intent to interpret the Constitution or to examine the limitations which the First and Fifth

Amendments place upon Congress. But commentators have not forgotten the Latin tag *pari passu*. . . .

The rationale by which Seeger and his companions on appeal were exempted from combat service under the statute is quite sufficient for Sisson to lay valid claim to be constitutionally exempted from combat service in the Vietnam type of situation.

• • •

Others fear that recognition of individual conscience will make it too easy for the individual to perpetrate a fraud. His own word will so often enable him to sustain his burden of proof. Cross-examination will not easily discover his insincerity.

Seeger cut the ground from under that argument. So does experience. Often it is harder to detect a fraudulent adherent to a religious creed than to recognize a sincere moral protestant. . . . We all can discern Thoreau's integrity more quickly than we might detect some churchman's hypocrisy.

The suggestion that courts cannot tell a sincere from an insincere conscientious objector underestimates what the judicial process performs every day. Ever since, in Edginton v. Fitzmaurice (1882) L.R. 29 Ch.Div. 359, Bowen L.J. quipped that "the state of a man's mind is as much a fact as the state of his digestion," each day courts have applied laws, criminal and civil, which make sincerity the test of liability.

There have been suggestions that to read the Constitution as granting an exemption from combat duty in a foreign campaign will immunize from public regulation all acts or refusals to act dictated by religious or conscientious scruple. Such suggestions fail to note that there is no need to treat, and this court does not treat, religious liberty as an absolute. The most sincere religious or conscientious believer may be validly punished even if in strict pursuance of his creed or principles, he fanatically assassinates an opponent, or practices polygamy, . . . or employs child labor. . . . Religious liberty and liberty of conscience have limits in the face of social demands of a community of fellow citizens. There are, for example, important rival claims of safety, order, health, and decency.

Nor is it true that to recognize liberty of conscience and religious liberty will set up some magic line between nonfeasance and misfeasance. A religiously motivated failure to discharge a public obligation may be as serious a crime as a religiously motivated action in violation of law. We may, argumentatively, assume that one who out of religious or conscientious scruple refuses to pay a general income or property tax, assessed without reference to any particular kind of contemplated expenditure, is civilly and criminally liable, regardless of his sincere belief that he is responding to a divine command not to support the government.

Most important, it does not follow from a judicial decision that Sisson cannot be conscripted to kill in Vietnam that he cannot be conscripted for non-combat service there or elsewhere.

It would be a poor court indeed that could not discern the small constitutional magnitude of the interest that a person has in avoiding all helpful service whatsoever or in avoiding paying all general taxes whatsoever. His objections, of course, may be sincere. But some sincere objections have greater constitutional magnitude than others.

There are many tasks, technologically or economically related to the prosecution of a war, to which a religious or conscientious objector might be constitutionally assigned. As Justice Cardozo wrote "Never in our history has the notion been accepted, or even, it is believed, advanced, that acts thus indirectly related to service in the camp or field are so tied to the practice of religion as to be exempt, in law or in morals, from regulation by the state." . . .

Sisson's case being limited to a claim of conscientious objection to combat service in a foreign campaign, this court holds that the free exercise of religion clause in the First Amendment and the due process clause of the Fifth Amendment prohibit the application of the 1967 draft act to Sisson to require him to render combat service in Vietnam.

The chief reason for reaching this conclusion after examining the competing interests is the magnitude of Sisson's interest in not killing in the Vietnam conflict as against the want of magnitude in the country's present need for him to be so employed.

The statute as here applied creates a clash between law and morality for which no exigency exists, and before, in Justice Sutherland's words, "the last extremity" or anything close to that dire predicament has been glimpsed, or even predicted, or reasonably feared.

When the state through its laws seeks to override reasonable moral commitments it makes a dangerously uncharacteristic choice. The law grows from the deposits of morality. Law and morality are, in turn, debtors and creditors of each other. The law cannot be adequately enforced by the courts alone, or by courts supported merely by the police and the military. The true secret of legal might lies in the habits of conscientious men disciplining themselves to obey the law they respect without the necessity of judicial and administrative orders. When the law treats a reasonable, conscientious act as a crime it subverts its own power. It invites civil disobedience. It impairs the very habits which nourish and preserve the law.

F. THE CONSTITUTIONAL POWER OF CONGRESS TO DISCRIMINATE AS IT DID IN THE 1967 DRAFT ACT BETWEEN THE DRAFT STATUS OF SISSON AS A CONSCIENTIOUS OBJECTOR AND THE DRAFT STATUS OF ADHERENTS TO CERTAIN TYPES OF RELIGIONS

The Supreme Court may not address itself to the broad issue just decided. Being a court of last resort, it unlike an inferior court, can confidently rest its judgment upon a narrow issue. Indeed Seeger foreshadows exactly that process. So it is incumbent on this court to consider the narrow issue, whether the 1967 Act invalidly discriminates against Sisson as a non-religious conscientious objector.

The draft act now limits "exemption from combat training and service" to one "who, by reason of religious training and belief, is conscientiously opposed to participation in war in any form" 50 U.S.C.App. Section 456(j), commonly cited as Section 6(j) of the Act as amended.

A Quaker, for example, is covered if he claims belief in the ultimate implications of William Penn's teaching.

Persons trained in and believing in other religious ways may or may not be covered. A Roman Catholic obedient to the teaching of Thomas Aquinas and Pope John XXIII might distinguish between a just war in which he would fight and an unjust war in which he would not fight. Those who administer the Selective Service System opine that Congress has not allowed exemption to those whose conscientious objection rests on such a distinction. . . . This court has a more open mind.

However, the administrators and this court both agree that Congress has not provided a conscientious objector status for a person whose claim is admittedly not formally religious.

In this situation Sisson claims that even if the Constitution might not otherwise preclude Congress from drafting him for combat service in Vietnam, the Constitution does preclude Congress from drafting him under the 1967 Act. The reason is that this Act grants conscientious objector status solely to religious conscientious objectors but not to non-religious objectors.

Earlier this opinion noted that it is practical to accord the same status to non-religious conscientious objectors as to religious objectors. Moreover, it is difficult to imagine any ground for a statutory distinction except religious prejudice. In short, in the draft act Congress unconstitutionally discriminated against atheists, agnostics, and men, like Sisson, who, whether they be religious or not, are motivated in their objection to the draft by profound moral beliefs which constitute the central convictions of their beings.

This Court, therefore, concludes that in granting to the religious conscientious objector but not to Sisson a special conscientious objector status, the Act, as applied to Sisson, violates the provision of the First Amendment that "Congress shall make no law respecting an establishment of religion or prohibiting the free exercise thereof." . . .

In the words of Rule 34, the indictment of Sisson "does not charge an offense."

This court's "decision arresting a judgment of conviction for insufficiency of the indictment . . . is based upon the invalidity . . . of the statute upon which the indictment . . . is founded" within the meaning of those phrases as used in 18 U.S.C. Section 3731. . . . Therefore, "an appeal may be taken by and on behalf of the United States . . . direct to the Supreme Court of the United States."

To guard against misunderstanding, this Court has not ruled that:

(1) The Government has no right to conduct Vietnam Operations; or

(2) The Government is using unlawful methods in Vietnam; or

(3) The Government has no power to conscript the generality of men for combat service; or

(4) The Government in a defense of the homeland has no power to conscript for combat service anyone it sees fit; or

(5) The Government has no power to conscript conscientious objectors for non-combat service.

Indeed the Court assumes without deciding that each one of those propositions states the exact reverse of the law.

All that this Court decides is that as a sincere conscientious objector Sisson cannot constitutionally be subjected to military orders (not reviewable in a United States constitutional Court,) which may require him to kill in the Vietnam conflict.

Enter forthwith this decision and this court's order granting defendant Sisson's motion in arrest of judgment.

An even more liberal example of a theory of tolerance is to be found in *Woody*.

PEOPLE v. WOODY
SUPREME COURT OF CALIFORNIA, 1964
61 Cal. 2d 716,394 P. 2d 813, 40 Cal. Rptr. 69

[Justice Tobriner] . . . On April 28, 1962, a group of Navajos met in an Indian hogan in the desert near Needles, California, to perform a religious ceremony which included the use of peyote. Police officers, who had observed part of the ceremony, arrested defendants, who were among the Indians present. Defendants were later convicted of violating section 11500 of the Health and Safety Code, which prohibits the unauthorized possession of peyote. We have concluded that since the defendants used peyote in a bona fide pursuit of a religious faith, and since the practice does not frustrate a compelling interest of the state, the application of the statute improperly defeated the immunity of the First Amendment of the Constitution of the United States.

• • •

The state stipulated at trial that at the time of the arrest defendants and the other Indians were performing a religious ceremony which involved the use of peyote. Defendants pleaded not guilty to the crime of illegal possession of narcotics, contending that their possession of peyote was incident to the observance of their faith and that the state could not constitutionally invoke the statute against them without abridging their right to the free exercise of their religion. The trial proceeded without a jury; the court held defendants guilty and imposed suspended sentences.

• • •

. . . The First Amendment reads "Congress shall make no law respecting an establishment of religion or prohibiting the free exercise thereof. . . ."

Although the prohibition against infringement of religious belief is absolute, the immunity afforded religious practices by the First Amendment is not so rigid. . . . But the state may abridge religious practices only upon a demonstration that some compelling state interest outweighs the defendants' interests in religious freedom. . . . An examination of the record as to the nature of peyote and its role in the religion practiced by defendants as members of the Native American Church of California compels the conclusion that the statutory prohibition most seriously infringes upon the observance of the religion.

The plant Lophophora williamsii, a small, spineless cactus, found in the Rio Grande Valley of Texas and northern Mexico, produces peyote, which grows in small buttons on the top of the cactus. Peyote's principal constituent is mescaline. When taken internally by chewing the buttons or drinking a derivative tea, peyote produces several types of hallucinations, depending primarily upon the user. In most subjects it causes extraordinary vision marked by bright and kaleidoscopic colors, geometric patterns, or scenes involving humans or animals. In others it engenders hallucinatory symptoms similar to those produced in cases of schizophrenia, dementia praecox, or paranoia. Beyond its hallucinatory effect, peyote renders for most users a heightened sense of comprehension; it fosters a feeling of friendliness toward other persons.

Peyote, as we shall see, plays a central role in the ceremony and practice of the Native American Church, a religious organization of Indians.

• • •

The "meeting," a ceremony marked by the sacramental use of peyote, composes the cornerstone of the peyote religion. The meeting convenes in an enclosure and continues from sundown Saturday to sunrise Sunday. . . .

A meeting connotes a solemn and special occasion. Whole families attend together, although children and young women participate only by their presence. Adherents don their finest clothing, usually suits for men and fancy dresses for the women, but sometimes ceremonial Indian costumes. At the meeting the members pray, sing, and make ritual use of drum, fan, eagle bone, whistle, rattle and prayer cigarette, the symbolic emblems of their faith. The central event, of course, consists of the use of peyote in quantities sufficient to produce an hallucinatory state.

• • •

Although peyote serves as a sacramental symbol similar to bread and wine in certain Christian churches, it is more than a sacrament. Peyote constitutes in itself an object of worship; prayers are directed to it much as prayers are devoted to the

Holy Ghost. On the other hand, to use peyote for nonreligious purposes is sacrilegious. Members of the church regard peyote also as a "teacher" because it induces a feeling of brotherhood with other members; indeed, it enables the participant to experience the Deity. Finally, devotees treat peyote as a "protector." Much as a Catholic carries his medallion, an Indian G.I. often wears around his neck a beautifully beaded pouch containing one large peyote button.

The record thus establishes that the application of the statutory prohibition of the use of peyote results in a virtual inhibition of the practice of defendant's religion. To forbid the use of peyote is to remove the theological heart of Peyotism. Having reached this conclusion we must undertake the second step in the analysis of the constitutional issue: a determination of whether the state has demonstrated that "compelling state interest" which necessitates an abridgement of defendant's First Amendment right.

• • •

We turn to the several cases cited by the Attorney General which uphold statutes restricting religious practices. The People principally rely upon Reynolds v. United States (1878) 98 U.S. 145, which ruled that Congress could constitutionally apply to Mormons a prohibition against polygamy. The Mormon doctrine of polygamy rested in alleged divine origin and imposed upon male members, circumstances permitting, the observance of the practice upon pain of eternal damnation.

The Supreme Court held that the history of the laws against polygamy showed that the condemnation of the practice was a matter of the gravest social importance. It found in polygamy the seed of destruction of a democratic society. Viewing the practice as highly injurious to its female adherents, the court classed polygamy with such religious rites as sacrifice of human beings and funeral immolation of widows.

Reynolds v. United States must be distinguished from the instant case for two fundamental reasons. The test of constitutionality calls for an examination of the degree of abridgement of religious freedom involved in each case. Polygamy, although a basic tenet in the theology of Mormonism, is not essential to the practice of the religion; peyote, on the other hand, is the *sine qua non* of defendants' faith. It is the sole means by which defendants are able to experience their religion; without peyote defendants cannot practice their faith. Second, the degree of danger to state interests in Reynolds far exceeded that in the instant case. The Court in Reynolds considered polygamy as a serious threat to democratic institutions and injurious to the morals and well-being of its practitioners. As we have heretofore indicated, no such compelling state interest supports the prohibition of the use of peyote.

• • •

In the instant case, of course, we encounter no problem as to the bona fide nature of defendants' assertion of the free exercise clause. The state agrees, and the evidence amply demonstrates, that defendants' use of peyote was for a religious purpose.

We have weighed the competing values represented in this case on the symbolic scale of constitutionality. On the one side we have placed the weight of freedom of religion as protected by the First Amendment; on the other, the weight of the state's "compelling interest." Since the use of peyote incorporates the essence of the religious expression, the first weight is heavy. Yet the use of peyote presents only slight danger to the state and to the enforcement of its laws; the second weight is relatively light. The scale tips in favor of the constitutional protection.

We know that some will urge that it is more important to subserve the rigorous enforcement of the narcotic laws than to carve out of them an exception for a few believers in a strange faith. They will say that the exception may produce problems of enforcement and that the dictate of the state must overcome the beliefs of a minority of Indians. But the problems of enforcement here do not inherently differ from those of other situations which call for the detection of fraud. On the other hand, the right to free religious expression embodies a precious heritage of our history. In a mass society, which presses at every point toward conformity the protection of a self-expression, however unique, of the individual and the group becomes ever more important. The varying currents of the subcultures that flow into the mainstream of our national life give it depth and beauty. We preserve a greater value than an ancient tradition when we protect the rights of the Indians who honestly practiced an old religion in using peyote one night at a meeting in a desert hogan near Needles, California.

Consider, however, the standards developed by the United States Supreme Court.

FEDORENKO V. UNITED STATES
449 U.S. 490 (1981)

[Justice Marshall delivered the opinion] . . . Section 340(a) of the Immigration and Nationality Act of 1952, . . . as amended, . . . requires revocation of United States citizenship that was "illegally procured or . . . procured by concealment of a material fact or by willful misrepresentation." The Government brought this denaturalization action, alleging that petitioner procured his citizenship illegally or by willfully misrepresenting a material fact. The District Court entered judgment for petitioner, but the Court of Appeals reversed and ordered entry of a judgment of denaturalization. We granted certiorari, to resolve two questions: whether petitioner's failure to disclose, in his application for a visa to come to this country, that he had served during the Second World War as an armed guard at the Nazi concentration camp at Treblinka, Poland, rendered his citizenship revocable as "illegally procured" or procured by willful misrepresentation of a material fact, and if so, whether the District Court nonetheless possessed equitable discretion to refrain from entering judgment in favor of the Government under these circumstances.

Petitioner was born in the Ukraine in 1907. He was drafted into the Russian army in June 1941, but was captured by the Germans shortly thereafter. After being held in a series of prisoner-of-war camps, petitioner was selected to go to the German camp at Travnicki in Poland, where he received training as a concentration camp guard. In September 1942, he was assigned to the Nazi concentration camp at Treblinka in Poland, where he was issued a uniform and rifle and where he served as a guard during 1942 and 1943. The infamous Treblinka concentration camp was described by the District Court as a "human abattoir" at which several hundred thousand Jewish civilians were murdered.[2] After an armed uprising by the inmates

[2]Historians estimate that some 800,000 people were murdered at Treblinka. See L. Dawidowicz, The War Against the Jews, 1933-1945, p. 149 (1975); R. Hilberg, The Destruction of the European Jews 572 (1978).

The District Court described Treblinka in this manner: "It contained only living facilities for the SS and the persons working there. The thousands who arrived daily on the trains had no need for barracks or mess halls: they would be dead before nightfall. It was operated with a barbarous methodology—brutally efficient—and such camps surely fill one of the darkest chapters in the annals of human existence, certainly the darkest in that which we call Western civilization." 455 F. Supp. 893, 901, n. 12 (SD Fla. 1978).

at Treblinka led to the closure of the camp in August 1943, petitioner was transferred to a German labor camp at Danzig and then to the German prisoner-of-war camp at Poelitz, where he continued to serve as an armed guard. Petitioner was eventually transferred to Hamburg where he served as a warehouse guard. Shortly before the British forces entered that city in 1945, petitioner discarded his uniform and was able to pass as a civilian. For the next four years, he worked in Germany as a laborer.

In 1948, Congress enacted the Displaced Persons Act (DPA or Act), 62 Stat. 1009, to enable European refugees driven from their homelands by the war to emigrate to the United States without regard to traditional immigration quotas. The Act's definition of "displaced persons" eligible for immigration to this country specifically excluded individuals who had "assisted the enemy in persecuting civil[ians]" or had "voluntarily assisted the enemy forces . . . in their operations. . . ." Section 10 of the DPA, 62 Stat. 1013, placed the burden of proving eligibility under the act on the person seeking admission and provided that "[a]ny person who shall willfully make a misrepresentation for the purpose of gaining admission into the United States as an eligible displaced person shall thereafter not be admissible into the United States."

• • •

In October 1949, petitioner applied for admission to the United States as a displaced person. Petitioner falsified his visa application by lying about his wartime activities. He told the investigators from the Displaced Persons Commission that he had been a farmer in Sarny, Poland, from 1937 until March 1942, and that he had then been deported to Germany and forced to work in a factory in Poelitz until the end of the war, when he fled to Hamburg.[8] Petitioner told the same story to the vice consul who reviewed his case and he signed a sworn statement containing these false representations as part of his application for a DPA visa. . . .

In 1969, petitioner applied for naturalization at the INS office in Hartford, Conn. Petitioner did not disclose his wartime service as a concentration camp armed guard in his application,[9] and he did not mention it in his sworn testimony to INS naturalization examiners. The INS examiners took petitioner's visa papers at face value and recommended that his citizenship application be granted. On this recommendation, the Superior Court of New Haven County granted his petition for naturalization and he became an American citizen on April 23, 1970.

Seven years later, after petitioner had moved to Miami Beach and become a resident of Florida, the Government filed this action in the United States District Court for the Southern District of Florida to revoke petitioner's citizenship. The complaint alleged that petitioner should have been deemed ineligible for a DPA visa because he had served as an armed guard at Treblinka and had committed crimes or atrocities against inmates of the camp because they were Jewish.

The Government charged that petitioner had willfully concealed this information both in applying for a DPA visa and in applying for citizenship, and that therefore

---

[8]Petitioner also lied about his birthplace and nationality, claiming that he was born in Sarny, in Poland, when in fact he was born in Sivasch, in the Ukraine. App. 26. . . .

[9]It should be noted that none of the questions in the application for citizenship explicitly required petitioner to disclose this information. Perhaps the most closely related question on the application form was one that required him to list his foreign military service. Petitioner indicated only that he had served in the Russian army. App. 33.

petitioner had procured his naturalization illegally or by willfully misrepresenting material facts.[11]

The Government's witnesses at trial included six survivors of Treblinka who claimed that they had seen petitioner commit specific acts of violence against inmates of the camp.[12] Each witness made a pretrial identification of petitioner from a photo array that included his 1949 visa photograph, and three of the witnesses made courtroom identifications. The Government also called as a witness Kempton Jenkins, a career foreign service officer who served in Germany after the war as one of the vice consuls who administered the DPA. . . .

. . . Jenkins explained that service as an armed guard at a concentration camp brought the applicant under the statutory exclusion of persons who "assisted the enemy in persecuting civil[ians]," regardless of whether the applicant had not volunteered for service[14] or had not committed atrocities against inmates.

• • •

Petitioner took the stand in his own behalf. He admitted his service as an armed guard at Treblinka and that he had known that thousands of Jewish inmates were being murdered there. . . . Petitioner claimed that he was forced to serve as a guard and denied any personal involvement in the atrocities committed at the camp; . . . he insisted that he had merely been a perimeter guard. Petitioner admitted, however, that he had followed orders and shot in the general direction of escaping inmates during the August 1943 uprising that led to a closure of the camp. . . . Petitioner maintained that he was a prisoner of war at Treblinka, . . . although he admitted that the Russian armed guards significantly outnumbered the German soldiers at the camp,[16] that he was paid a stipend and received a good service stripe from the Germans, and that he was allowed to leave the camp regularly but never tried to escape. . . . Finally, petitioner conceded that he deliberately gave false statements about his wartime activities to the investigators from the Displaced Persons Commission and to the vice consul who reviewed his visa application. . . .

[11]The complaint also charged that petitioner had deliberately made false statements for the purpose of securing his naturalization and had thereby failed to satisfy the statutory requirement of good moral character during the 5-year period immediately preceding the filing of his petition for naturalization. See 8 U.S.C. §1427(a).

[12]One witness Eugeun Turowski, testified that he saw petitioner shoot and whip Jewish prisoners at the camp. . . . Another, Schalom Kohn, testified that he saw petitioner almost every day for the first few months Kohn was at Treblinka, . . . that petitioner beat him with an iron-tipped whip, and that he saw petitioner whip and shoot other prisoners. . . . The third witness Josef Czarny, claimed that he saw petitioner beat arriving prisoners, . . . and that he once saw him shoot a prisoner. . . . Gustaw Boraks testified that he saw petitioner repeatedly chase prisoners to the gas chambers, beating them as they went. . . . Boraks also claimed that on one occasion, he heard a shot and ran outside to see petitioner, with a gun drawn, standing close to a wounded woman who later told him that petitioner was responsible for the shooting. . . . Sonia Lewkowicz testified that she saw petitioner shoot a Jewish prisoner. . . . Finally, Pinchas Epstein testified that petitioner shot and killed a friend of his, after making him crawl naked on all fours. . . .

[14]On the basis of the vice consuls' experiences, Jenkins discounted the possibility that any concentration camp guards had served involuntarily. . . . Jenkins reported that all the guards who were questioned by the consular officials about their reasons for serving as guards invariably admitted that their service was voluntary. . . . In addition, Jenkins testified that even if an applicant refused to acknowledge that his service as an armed guard was voluntary, he would still have been denied a visa. . . .

[16]Petitioner testified that there were between 120 and 150 armed Russian guards and some 20 to 30 Germans. . . .

The District Court entered judgment in favor of petitioner. . . . The court found that petitioner had served as an armed guard at Treblinka and that he lied about his wartime activities when he applied for a DPA visa in 1949. The court found, however, that petitioner was forced to serve as a guard. The court concluded that it could credit neither the Treblinka survivors' identification of petitioner nor their testimony, and it held that the Government had not met its burden of proving that petitioner committed war crimes or atrocities at Treblinka.

• • •

On the one hand, our decisions have recognized that the right to acquire American citizenship is a precious one, and that once citizenship has been acquired, its loss can have severe and unsettling consequences. . . . For these reasons, we have held that the Government "carries a heavy burden of proof in a proceeding to divest a naturalized citizen of his citizenship." *Costello v. United States*, . . . The evidence justifying revocation of citizenship must be "clear, unequivocal, and convincing" and not leave "the issue in doubt." *Schneiderman v. United States*, . . . Any less exacting standard would be inconsistent with the importance of the right that is at stake in a denaturalization proceeding. And in reviewing denaturalization cases, we have carefully examined the record ourselves. . . .

At the same time, our cases have also recognized that there must be strict compliance with all the congressionally imposed prerequisites to the acquisition of citizenship. Failure to comply with any of these conditions renders the certificate of citizenship "illegally procured," and naturalization that is unlawfully procured can be set aside.

• • •

. . . The first issue we must examine then, is whether petitioner's false statements about his activities during the war, particularly the concealment of his Treblinka service, were "material."

• • •

It is, of course, clear that the materiality of a false statement in a visa application must be measured in terms of its effect on the applicant's admissibility into this country. . . . At the very least, a misrepresentation must be considered material if disclosure of the true facts would have made the applicant ineligible for a visa. Because we conclude that disclosure of the true facts about petitioner's service as an armed guard at Treblinka would, as a matter of law, have made him ineligible for a visa under the DPA, we find it unnecessary to resolve the question whether *Chaunt's* materiality test also governs false statements in visa applications.

Section 2(b) of the DPA, 62 Stat. 1009, by incorporating the definition of "[p]ersons who will not be [considered displaced persons]" contained in the Constitution of the IRO, specifically provided that individuals who "assisted the enemy in persecuting civil[ians]" were ineligible for visas under the Act. Jenkins testified that petitioner's service as an armed guard at a concentration camp—whether voluntary or not—made him ineligible for a visa under this provision. Jenkins' testimony was based on his firsthand experience as a vice consul in Germany after the war reviewing DPA visa applications. . . . The District Court evidently agreed that a literal interpretation of the statute would confirm the accuracy of Jenkins' testimony. 455 F. Supp., at 913. But by construing §2(a) as only excluding individuals who *voluntarily* assisted in the persecution of civilians, the District Court was able to ignore Jenkins' uncontroverted testimony about how the Act was interpreted by the officials who administered it.[32]

The Court of Appeals evidently accepted the District Court's construction of the Act since it agreed that the Government had failed to show that petitioner was ineligible for a DPA visa. 597 F.2d, at 953. Because we are unable to find any basis for an "involuntary assistance" exception in the language of §2(a), we conclude that the District Court's construction of the Act was incorrect. The plain language of the Act mandates precisely the literal interpretation that the District Court rejected: an individual's service as a concentration camp armed guard—whether voluntary or involuntary—made him ineligible for a visa. That Congress was perfectly capable of adopting a "voluntariness" limitation where it felt that one was necessary is plain from comparing §2(a) with §2(b) which excludes only those individuals who "*voluntarily* assisted the enemy forces . . . in their operations. . . ." Under traditional principles of statutory construction, the deliberate omission of the word "voluntary" from §2(a) compels the conclusion that the statute made all those who assisted in the persecution of civilians ineligible for visas.[34] . . . As this court has previously stated: "We are not at liberty to imply a condition which is opposed to the explicit terms of the statute. . . . To [so] hold . . . is not to construe the Act but to amend it." . . . Thus, the plain language of the statute and Jenkins' uncontradicted and unequivocal testimony leave no room for doubt that if petitioner had disclosed the fact that he had been an armed guard at Treblinka, he would have been found ineligible for a visa under the DPA. This being so, we must conclude that petitioner's false statements about his wartime activities were "willfu[l] [and material] misrepresentation[s] [made] for the purpose of gaining admission into the United States as an eligible displaced person." 62 Stat. 1013. Under the express terms of the statute, petitioner was "thereafter not . . . admissible into the United States." *Ibid.*

• • •

In sum, we hold that petitioner's citizenship must be revoked under 8 U.S.C. § 1451(a) because it was illegally procured. Accordingly, the judgment of the Court of Appeals is affirmed.

[32]The District Court felt compelled to impose a voluntariness requirement because it was concerned that a literal interpretation of §2(a) would "bar every Jewish prisoner who survived Treblinka because each one of them assisted the SS in the operation of the camp." 455 F. Supp., at 913. The court noted that working prisoners led arriving prisoners to the lazaret where they were murdered, cut the hair of the women who were to be executed, or played in the orchestra at the gate to the camp as part of the Germans' ruse to persuade new arrivals that the camp was other than what it was. The court pointed out that such actions could technically be deemed assistance, and concluded that it would be "absurd to deem their conduct 'assistance or acquiescence' inasmuch as it was involuntary—even though the word 'voluntarily' was omitted from the definition." *Ibid.* In addition, the court noted that Jenkins testified that visa applicants who had served in Axis combat units and who could prove that their service was involuntary were found eligible for visas. *Id.*, at 912. But see n. 34, *infra.*

[34]The solution to the problem perceived by the District Court, lies, not in "interpreting" the Act to include a voluntariness requirement that the statute itself does not impose, but in focusing on whether particular conduct can be considered assisting in the persecution of civilians. Thus, an individual who did no more than cut the hair of female inmates before they were executed cannot be found to have assisted in the persecution of civilians. On the other hand, there can be no question that a guard who was issued a uniform and armed with a rifle and a pistol, who was paid a stipend and was regularly allowed to leave the concentration camp to visit a nearby village, and who admitted to shooting at escaping inmates on orders from the commandant of the camp, fits within the statutory language about persons who assisted in the persecution of civilians. Other cases may present more difficult line-drawing problems but we need decide only this case. As for the District Court's concern about the different treatment given to visa applicants who had served in Axis combat units who were found eligible for visas if they could show that they had served involuntarily, this distinction made made by the Act itself.

Justice Stevens, dissenting.[2]

The story of this litigation is depressing. The Government failed to prove its right to relief on any of several theories advanced in the District Court. The Court of appeals reversed on an untenable ground. Today this Court affirms on a theory that no litigant argued, that the Government expressly disavowed, and that may jeopardize the citizenship of countless survivors of Nazi concentration camps.

• • •

. . . Because the Court holds as a matter of law that petitioner's service as a guard at Treblinka, whether or not voluntary, made him ineligible for a visa, petitioner was not legally admitted to the country and hence was not entitled to citizenship.

I cannot accept the view that any citizen's past involuntary conduct can provide the basis for stripping him of his American citizenship. The Court's contrary holding today rests entirely on its construction of the Displaced Persons Act of 1948 (DPA). Although the court purports to consider the materiality of petitioner's misstatements, the Court's construction of the DPA renders those misstatements entirely irrelevant to the decision of this case. Every person who entered the United States pursuant to the authority granted by that statute, who subsequently acquired American citizenship, and who can be shown "to have assisted the enemy in persecuting civil populations"—even under the most severe duress—has no right to retain his or her citizenship. I believe that the Court's construction of the DPA is erroneous and that the Court of Appeals misapplied the *Chaunt* test.

I

Section 2(a) of the DPA was adopted from the Constitution of the International Refugee Organization, which described in Part II of Annex I "Persons who will not be [considered as displaced persons.]." The second listing had two classifications:

"2. Any other persons who can be shown:
"(a) to have assisted the enemy in persecuting civil populations of countries, Members of the United Nations; or
"(b) to have voluntarily assisted the enemy forces since the outbreak of the second world war in their operations against the United Nations."

---

[2]In view of the extensive references to Jenkins in the Court's opinion, some of the District Court's observations should be quoted:

• • •

"Jenkins testimony about the structure of the death camp organization was hardly expert and conflicts consistently with other evidence presented at the trial. For example, he testified that the Ukrainian guards had the same uniforms as the SS with only slightly different insignia. However, the unanimous testimony was the Germans wore their usual gray-green uniforms but the prisoner-guards didn't. He testified that the camp guards could get leave and get away from the camp and could transfer. The testimony was clear that they could not take leave (and go to Berlin, as Jenkins opined) but could only get a two-to-four-hours pass to visit a small village a couple of miles away.

• • •

"Jenkins also would have considered the kapos as excludable because they assisted the Germans. This is totally contrary to the reaction of every witness who survived Treblinka; each of the Israeli witnesses testified the kapos did only what they had to do and the witnesses were quite indignant when asked if they had ever testified against the kapos. The witnesses replied that there was no reason to do so. In addition, Jenkins speculated that the kapos were probably shot in 1945 during a period of retaliation, but the testimony was to the contrary." *Id.*, at 911-913.

The District Court recognized that the section dealing with assisting enemy forces contained the word "voluntarily," while the section dealing with persecuting enemy populations did not. The District Court refused to construe the statute to bar relief to any person who assisted the enemy, whether voluntarily or not, however, because such a construction would have excluded the Jewish prisoners who assisted the SS in the operation of the concentration camp. 455 F.Supp., at 913. These prisoners performed such tasks as cutting the hair of female prisoners prior to their execution and performing in a camp orchestra as a ruse to conceal the true nature of the camp. I agree without hesitation with the District Court's conclusion that such prisoners did not perform their duties voluntarily and that such prisoners should not be considered excludable under the DPA.[4] The Court resolves the dilemma perceived by the District Court by concluding that prisoners who did no more than cut the hair of female inmates before they were executed could not be considered to be assisting the enemy in persecuting civilian populations. . . . Thus the Court would give the word "persecution" some not yet defined specially limited reading. In my opinion, the term "persecution" clearly applies to such conduct; indeed, it probably encompasses almost every aspect of life or death in a concentration camp.

The Court's resolution of this issue is particularly unpersuasive when applied to the "kapos," the Jewish prisoners who supervised the Jewish workers at the camp. According to witnesses who survived Treblinka, the kapos were commanded by the SS to administer beatings to the prisoners, and they did so with just enough force to make the beating appear realistic yet avoid injury to the prisoner. . . . Even if we assume that the kapos were completely successful in deceiving the SS guards and that the beatings caused no injury to other inmates, I believe their conduct would have to be characterized as assisting in the persecution of other prisoners.[6] In my view, the reasons that such conduct should not make the kapos ineligible for citizenship is that it surely was not voluntary. The fact that the Court's interpretation of the DPA would exclude a group whose actions were uniformly defended by survivors of Treblinka, . . . merely underscores the strained reading the Court has given the statute.[7]

•   •   •

The gruesome facts recited in this record create what Justice Holmes described as a sort of "hydraulic pressure" that tends to distort our judgment. Perhaps my refusal to acquiesce in the conclusion reached by highly respected colleagues is attributable in part to an overreaction to that pressure. Even after recognizing and discounting that factor, however, I remain firmly convinced that the Court has committed the profoundest sort of error by venturing into the unknown to find a basis

---

[4]One particular squad of Jewish prisoners was responsible for undressing the aged and infirm prisoners and leading them to the lazaret, the eternally burning pit, where they were shot. Record 287 (Kohn). One of the prisoners who worked in the camp stated when asked whether this squad "assist[ed] in bringing [prisoners] to their death": "We automatically assisted, all of us, but . . . it was under the fear and terror." *Id.*, at 293 (Kohn).

[6]Moreover, the Court's distinction between the kapos and other Jewish workers on the one hand and the Ukranian guards on the other is based in large part on such factors as the issuance of a uniform and weapons, the receipt of a stipend, and the privilege of being allowed to leave the camp and visit a nearby village. These supposedly distinguishing factors are essentially unrelated to the persecution of the victims of the concentration camp.

[7]We also note that Vice Consul Jenkins, upon whose testimony the Court heavily relies, indicated that he would have considered kapos to be ineligible under the DPA if they could be proved to be "internal camp inmate collaborators."

for affirming the judgment of the Court of Appeals. That human suffering will be a consequence of today's venture is certainly predictable; that any suffering will be allayed or avoided is at best doubtful.

NOTES

1. The high standard which the court majority demands be applied by the Immigration Law resembles somewhat the view of Karl Jaspers regarding an unconditional imperative for which humans should be ready to die. The examples usually cited are Socrates, Seneca, Thomas More, Boethius and Bruno. (See K. Jaspers, *Way to Wisdom* Ch. 5 (R Manheim trans. 1951). Is martyrdom too high a standard to demand for immigration to or citizenship in the U.S.? See also, A. Gerson, Beyond Nuremberg, 72 *Commentary* 62 (Oct., 1981); Note, Fedorenko v. United States: War Crimes, the Defense of Duress, and American Nationality Law, 82 *Colum. L. Rev.* 120 (1982).

2. Do those who prefer that private judgment be exercised contrary to what is presented as community decision assume that there exist common human aspirations? Do they assume that rational human beings will necessarily arrive at a cogent consensus regarding the solution of problems and that authoritative decision should implement them? Discuss.

3. Does the argument for private judgment ignore the irrational element in human behavior? If the assumption of rational behavior is unfounded, might the exercise of private individual judgment lead to conflict rather than widespread consensus?

4. Do individuals contemplating disobedience receive a flow of information sufficient for sound judgment? Is the exercise of individual judgment (particularly with regard to international affairs) desirable or advisable in a society which is highly specialized, with government officials privy to masses of information not available to the ordinary private citizen? Consider, for example, the massive opposition to United States forces in South Vietnam and some of the acts that took place following the withdrawal of these forces: tens of thousands of "boat people," many abused, or murdered by pirates; massacres and massive population transfers in Cambodia by the Khmer Rouge regime resulting in millions of deaths; Vietnamese subjection of Laos, threats to Thailand and so on. Consider popular opposition to the Shah of Iran in the United States. The failure of the United States to support the Shah, which probably contributed to his downfall, was followed by widespread executions by the Khomeini regime. Are these examples fair? Discuss.

5. Some argue, as does Zinn, that the ends sometimes justify the means and that "the biggest of reasons (mass murder)" would certainly justify "violations of the smallest laws . . . (trespass)" and that Socrates was wrong in refusing to escape from prison. Should the estimation of the seriousness of the evil and the smallness of the law to be violated be left to individual conscience? Would an avid anti-abortionist who, in good faith, believes abortion is murder, be justified in fire-bombing an empty abortion clinic at night (when no one is there) in order to prevent the "murder" of hundreds of fetuses in the future? Would such an individual be justified in seizing and executing abortionists? What of destroying nuclear construction plant sites in order to prevent future accidents that might destroy millions of persons?

6. The implications for the jurisprudence of obedience in a modern technological and science-based state in which there are possibilities of effective state intervention into virtually every aspect of the physical and psychological being of citizens cannot be overstated. For example, if one accepts the doctrines of obedience put forward by a number of these writers as indispensable to social order, must one then say that people must submit to changes by drugs or surgery deemed necessary by those operating in the name of the state, even though the consequence will be to change their personalities and physical beings in irreparable ways? Consider ordering blood transfusions for minors whose parents object on religious grounds (John F. Kennedy *Memorial v. Heston*, 58 N.J. 576, 579 670, 279A.2d670 (1971)); compulsory sterilization (*Buck v. Bell*, 274 U.S. 200 (1927); *Skinner v. Oklahoma*, 315 U.S. 535 (1942)) and compulsory vaccination (*Wright v. DeWitt School Dist. 1*, 238 Ark. 906, 385

S.W. 2d 644 (1965); *Mountain Lakes Bd. of Ed. v. Haas*, 56 N.J. Super. 245, 152 A.2d 394 (App. Div. 1959), *Aff'd.*, 31 N.J. 537, 158 A.2d 330 (1960), Cert. denied, 363 U.S. 843, (1960); compelling psychotics to undergo drug therapy (See chap. 5 *infra*); ordering a kidney to be extracted from an incompetent for transplant purposes (*Strunk v. Strunk*, 445 S.W. 2d 145 (Ky. Ct. of Appeals, 1969). See in this regard, Applebaum, Can Mental Patients Say No to Drugs?, *N.Y. Times Magazine*, March 21, 1982, at 46; see also *Rennie v. Klein*, 53 F.2d 836 (3d Cir. 1981) and *Mills v. Rogers* 457 U.S. 291, (1982). How would you appraise how these cases were decided as well as the verdict reached?

M. Adler, The Doctrine of Natural Law Philosophy, in *Proc. U. Notre Dame Nat. L. Inst.* 67 (1949).

C. Bloch, The Problem of Compatibility of Civil Disobedience with American Institutions of Government, 43 *Tex. L. Rev.* 492 (1965).

E. N. Cahn, *The Sense of Injustice: An Anthroprocentric View of Law* (1949).

Civil Disobedience: Theory and Practice (H. Bedau ed. 1969).

M. R. Cohen, *Reason and Nature* (1953).

E. Corwin, The "Higher Law" Background of American Constitutional Law, 42 *Harv. L. Rev.* 152 (1928).

A. D'Amato, Lon Fuller and Substantive Natural Law, 26 *Am. J. Juris.* 202 (1981).

G. Del Vecchio, *Philosophy of Law* (1953).

R. Dworkin, Natural Law Revisited, 34 *U. Fla. L. Rev.* 165 (1982).

P. Eltzbacher, *Anarchism: Seven Exponents of the Anarchist Philosophy* (1900; rev. ed. 1960).

Euripides, *Lysistrata*.

Exodus, *The Bible* Ch. 5, 6.

C. J. Friedrich, *The Philosophy of Law in Historical Perspective* 178-88 (1958).

D. Hume, *Treatise of Human Nature* (London 1739-40).

K. Jaspers, The Unconditional Imperative, in *Way to Wisdom: An Introduction to Philosophy* 52 (R. Manheim transl. 1954).

A. P. Kropotkin, *Kropotkin's Revolutionary Pamphlets* (R. N. Baldwin ed. 1927).

S. Lynd, *Intellectual Origins of American Radicalism* (1968).

G. P. Maximoff, *The Political Philosophy of Bakunin* (1953).

M. Mead, Some Anthropoligical Considerations Concerning Natural Law, 6 *Nat. L. F.* 51 (1961).

A. Passerin D'Entreves, *Natural Law: An Introduction to Legal Philosophy* 80-94, 113-22 (1951).

G. Simson, Another View of Rawls' Theory of Justice, 23 *Emory L. J.* 473 (1974).

R. Stammler, *The Theory of Justice* (I. Husik transl. 1925).

Sympsosium, Law and Obedience, 67 *Va. L. Rev.* 1 (1982).

E. Van Den Haag, Civil Disobedience 21 *Rutgers L. Rev.* 27 (1966).

E. Van Den Haag & R. Ross, *The Fabric of Society* (1957).

CHAPTER 5

In the Nature of Things: The Jurisprudence of
Physical and Structural Naturalism

*Certain laws have not been written, but they
are more fixed than all the written laws.*
Seneca the Elder

Imagine you are counsel to a legislative sub-committee addressing the question of whether public funds should be made available for sex change operations. On the one hand, civil libertarians are arguing this is necessary as a way of enhancing the freedom of choice of individuals who know themselves best and know they cannot be happy without this surgical transformation. On the other hand, a coalition of politically conservative groups and scientific organizations argues that this type of surgery is "unnatural" and involves drastic and unjustifiable mutilations of the human body. Hence, they contend, it should be deplored and certainly should not receive public funding.

How would you go about analyzing the arguments and clarifying your position on the issue?

In 1872, in the Supreme Court, a concurring opinion of Justices Bradley, Swayne and Field in *Bradwell v. The State,* 83 U.S. 130 expressed the following quaint idea:

> . . . the civil law, as well as nature herself, has always recognized a wide difference in the respective spheres and destinies of man and woman. Man is, or should be, woman's protector and defender. The natural and proper timidity and delicacy which belongs to the female sex evidently unfits it for many of the occupations of civil life. The constitution of the family organization, which is founded in the divine ordinance, as well as in the nature of things, indicates the domestic sphere as that which properly belongs to the domain and functions of womanhood. The harmony, not to say identity, of interests and views which belong, or should belong, to the family institution is repugnant to the idea of a woman adopting a distinct and independent career from that of her husband. So firmly fixed was this sentiment in the founders of the common law that it became a maxim of that system of jurisprudence that a woman had no legal existence separate from her husband, who was regarded as her head and representative in the social state; and, notwithstanding some recent modifications of this civil status, many of the special rules of law flowing from and dependent upon this cardinal principle still exist in full force in most States. One of these is, that a married woman is incapable, without her husband's consent, of making contracts which shall be binding on her or him. This very incapacity was one circumstance which the Supreme Court of Illinois deemed important in rendering a married woman incompetent fully to perform the duties and trusts that belong to the office of an attorney and counsellor.

• • •

The paramount destiny and mission of woman are to fulfill the noble and benign offices of wife and mother. This is the law of the Creator.

A common response to demands for changing a practice many consider undesirable is, "Well, it's natural" or "it's in the nature of the thing." When we say this, in its many varied formulations, we are implying that there are inherent characteristics in human beings and other animate things as well as in the physical world and in social structures. These inherent characteristics determine their behavior and establish substantial limits on changes that can be made with regard to them. And, most important, they should not be changed. This complex of assumptions is the type of naturalism we will explore in this chapter. We refer to it as the jurisprudence of physical and structural naturalism, as contrasted with the strain of naturalism in the preceding chapter. It refers to all the assumptions about the allegedly natural features of the objects that law looks at, including the social and political "structure" of the "state," and the limitations that those natural features supposedly present to intervention and change.

Consider the following excerpts from Aristotle and the effects that use of the word "natural" had on his own conclusions. After you have read these pieces, consider and discuss the sources and merits of the notion of "natural rights" of man and "self-evident truths," on which such documents as the Declaration of Independence and the Universal Declaration of Human Rights are based.

ARISTOTLE, NICOMACHEAN ETHICS,
BOOK V, CHAPTER 7,
9 OXFORD TRANSLATION OF ARISTOTLE
1014 (W.D. ROSS TRANS. 1925)

Of political justice part is natural, part legal-natural, that which everywhere has the same force and does not exist by people's thinking this or that; legal, that which is originally indifferent, but when it has been laid down is not indifferent, e.g. that a prisoner's ransom shall be a mina, or that a goat and not two sheep shall be sacrificed, and again all the laws that are passed for particular cases, e.g. that sacrifice shall be made in honour of Brasidas, and the provisions of degrees. Now some think that all justice is of this sort, because that which is by nature is unchangeable and has everywhere the same force (as fire burns both here and in Persia), while they see change in the things recognized as just. This, however, is not true in this unqualified way, but is true in a sense; or rather, with the gods it is perhaps not true at all, while with us there is something that is just even by nature, yet all of it is changeable; but still some is by nature, some not by nature. It is evident which sort of thing, among things capable of being otherwise, is by nature; and which is not but is legal and conventional, assuming that both are equally changeable. And in all other things the same distinction will apply; by nature the right hand is stronger, yet it is possible that all men should come to be ambidextrous. The things which are just by virtue of convention and expediency are like measures; for wine and coin measures are not everywhere equal, but larger in wholesale and smaller in retail markets. Similarly, the things which are just not by nature but by human enactment are not everywhere the same, since constitutions also are not the same, though there is but one which is everywhere by nature the best.

Of things just and lawful each is related as the universal to its particulars; for the things that are done are many, but of *them* each is one, since it is universal.

There is a difference between the act of injustice and what is unjust, and between the act of justice and what is just; for a thing is unjust by nature or by enactment; and this very thing, when it has been done, is an act of injustice, but before it is done is not yet that but is unjust. So, too, with an act of justice (though the general term is rather 'just action', and 'act of justice' is applied to the correction of the act of injustice).

Each of these must later be examined separately with regard to the nature and number of its species and the nature of the things with which is is concerned.

ARISTOTLE, POLITICS,
BOOK I, CHAPTER 2, 10 OXFORD TRANSLATION
OF ARISTOTLE 1128-1133 (B. JOWETT TRANS. 1885, 1921)

. . . For that which can foresee by the exercise of mind is by nature intended to be lord and master, and that which can with its body give effect to such foresight is a subject, and by nature a slave; hence master and slave have the same interest. Now nature has distinguished between the female and the slave. For she is not niggardly, like the smith who fashions the Delphian knife for many uses; she makes each thing for a single use, and every instrument is best made when intended for one and not for many uses. But among barbarians no distinction is made between women and slaves, because there is no natural ruler among them; they are a community of slaves, male and female. Wherefore the poets say—

'It is meet that Hellenes should rule over barbarians';

as if they thought that the barbarian and the slave were by nature one.

Out of these two relationships between man and woman, master and slave, the first thing to arise is the family, and Hesiod is right when he says—

'First house and wife and an ox for the plough,'

for the ox is the poor man's slave. The family is the association established by nature for the supply of men's everyday wants, and the members of it are called by Charondas 'companions of the cupboard,' and by Epimenides the Cretan, 'companions of the manger.' But when several families are united, and the association aims at something more than the supply of daily needs, the first society to be formed is the village. And the most natural form of the village appears to be that of a colony from the family, composed of the children and grandchildren, who are said to be 'suckled with the same milk.' And this is the reason why Hellenic states were originally governed by kings; because the Hellenes were under royal rule before they came together, as the barbarians still are. Every family is ruled by the eldest, and therefore in the colonies of the family the kingly form of government prevailed because they were of the same blood. As Homer says:

'Each one gives law to his children and to his wives.'

For they lived dispersedly, as was the manner in ancient times. Wherefore men say that the Gods have a king, because they themselves either are or were in ancient times under the rule of a king. For they imagine, not only the forms of the Gods, but their ways of life to be like their own.

When several villages are united in a single complete community, large enough to be nearly or quite self-sufficing, the state comes into existence, originating in the bare needs of life, and continuing in existence for the sake of a good life. And therefore, if the earlier forms of society are natural, so is the state, for it is the end of them, and the nature of a thing is its end. For what each thing is when fully developed, we call it nature, whether we are speaking of a man, a horse, or a family. Besides, the final cause and end of a thing is the best, and to be self-sufficing is the end and the best.

Hence it is evident that the state is a creation of nature, and that man is by nature a political animal. And he who by nature and not by mere accident is without a state, is either a bad man or above humanity; he is like the

    'Tribeless, lawless, hearthless one,

whom Homer denounces—the natural outcast is forthwith a lover of war; he may be compared to an isolated piece at draughts.

Now, that man is more of a political animal than bees or any other gregarious animals is evident. Nature, as we often say, makes nothing in vain, and man is the only animal whom she has endowed with the gift of speech. And whereas mere voice is but an indication of pleasure or pain, and is therefore found in other animals (for their nature attains to the perception of pleasure and pain and the intimation of them to one another, and no further), the power of speech is intended to set forth the expedient and inexpedient, and therefore likewise the just and the unjust. And it is a characteristic of man that he alone has any sense of good and evil, of just and unjust, and the like and the association of living beings who have this sense makes a family and a state.

Further, The state is by nature clearly prior to the family and to the individual, since the whole is of necessity prior to the part; for example, if the whole body be destroyed, there will be no foot or hand, except in an equivocal sense, as we might speak of a stone hand; for when destroyed the hand will be no better than that. But things are defined by their working and power; and we ought not to say that they are the same when they no longer have their proper quality, but only that they have the same name. The proof that the state is a creation of nature and prior to the individual is that the individual, when isolated, is not self-sufficing; and therefore he is like a part in relation to the whole. But he who is unable to live in society, or who has no need because he is sufficient for himself, must be either a beast or a god: he is no part of a state. A social instinct is implanted in all men by nature, and yet he who first founded the state was the greatest of benefactors. For man, when perfected, is the best of animals, but, when separated from law and justice, he is the worst of all: since armed injustice is the more dangerous, and he is equipped at birth with arms, meant to be used by intelligence and virtue, which he may use for the worst ends. Wherefore, if he have not virtue, he is the most unholy and the most savage of animals, and the most full of lust and gluttony. But justice is the bond of men in states, for the administration of justice, which is the determination of what is just, is the principle of order in political society.

           • • •

But is there any one thus intended by nature to be a slave, and for whom such a condition is expedient and right, or rather is not all slavery a violation of nature?

There is no difficulty in answering this question, on grounds both of reason and of fact. For that some should rule and others be ruled is a thing not only necessary, but expedient; from the hour of their birth, some are marked out for subjection, others for rule.

           • • •

. . . It is clear than, that some men are by virtue free, and others slaves, and that for these latter, slavery is both expedient and right.

NOTES

1. Clearly, the notions of Aristotle about the "natural" and inferior place in society assigned to slaves and women strike us today as wrong. Apparently, Aristotle observed the conditions that existed and were accepted in his times and assumed they were "natural." Discuss and give examples of other contemporary situations where the term "natural" is used to transpose existing conditions into goals.

2. Use of the word "natural" is commonly based upon other, usually unstated presuppositions, which should be made express and examined critically. Consider this possibility and determine what the unstated preferences are and the basis for these goals in the following materials.

3. Does use of the term "natural" limit or obscure thinking about goals? Is the term "natural" of any help in understanding or describing a phenomenon or condition? Explain. Does the term set a priori limits on how issues should be decided or for which goals the community should strive? Is the term used to disguise personal preferences? Should the term "natural" be dropped from the lexicon of the jurist? Should not the student be alert to the social functions of this term and watch out for restricted vision and constraints on imagination whenever it is invoked?

"NATURAL" SEXUAL BEHAVIOR

Most societies are extremely sensitive to and often tyrannical about forms of sexual expression. From earliest times, for example, homosexuality was often viewed as a crime against God or against the State. Some of these perspectives persist. In the two cases that follow, consider whether fundamental policy decisions are being concealed under the guise of naturalist language or its functional equivalent.

HARRIS v. STATE
SUPREME COURT OF ALASKA, 1969
457 P. 2d. 638, 640

Connor, Justice. Appellant was convicted of a "crime against nature" by a verdict of the jury which tried his case.

He brings this appeal on the ground that the statute under which he was tried and convicted is cast in such vague terms that it is unconstitutional and void under the federal and state due process clauses.

• • •

It is apparent that the trial court considered "the crime against nature" to be the equivalent of the term "sodomy." The instructions to the jury even use the terms interchangeably.

It is established that a criminal statute which is so vague and standardless as to not give fair warning of the acts prohibited by it is a deprivation of due process of law under the 14th Amendment of the United States Constitution.

• • •

Appellant points out that the term "crime against nature" has never been constructed authoritatively in Alaska, that it has been construed in other jurisdictions to either include or exclude a variety of physical acts, and that it is not possible, therefore, to know what the term means as a matter of American common law. He argues that the demonstrable imprecision of the term provides the very reason for the statute being void for vagueness. He urges that under the candor currently displayed in American life it should be possible to specify in plain terms what sexual conduct shall be deemed a criminal offense and what shall be permitted.

Where a statute makes use of the name of a crime, without further definition and without the context indicating otherwise, it is traditional to look to the common law definition of the crime to determine its meaning.

We are confronted then with the inquiry into whether the term "crime against nature" has an ascertainable common law meaning. But even this determination is not entirely dispositive of appellant's case, as there are additional questions to be resolved.

The decisions in other states are in hopeless contradiction about the scope of the term "crime against nature." . . .

The main cleavage between the various courts is whether "the crime against nature" . . . comprehends more than the common law notion of sodomy, thereby allowing a broader interpretation to fulfill a presumed legislative intent. It has even been asserted that the term "crime against nature" did not cover . . . conduct [which] was not known in England during the formative era of early common law. It is said that had such conduct existed, it would surely have been condemned by the courts in England, and this provides a reason for an expansive reading of the term "crime against nature" in American law. Such reasoning exhibits an incredible naivete. Surely these forms of conduct are as old as the human race. No reason has been advanced to explain why people in medieval England were miraculously exempted from instinctual impulses common to the rest of mankind.

The confusion in American case law is compounded by the unwillingness of the courts in many instances to discuss the factual situation with any meaningful precision. The subjects of "sodomy" and "crime against nature" are said by many authorities to be so loathsome that they should be discussed only in language which is enigmatic to the point of deliberate obscurantism. Many of the cases merely assert, without discussing any precedents, that certain acts have always been considered within the prohibitions of the statute.

• • •

These were the sentiments of an earlier age. Perhaps there was then some common understanding of the types of conduct condemned, although even that proposition becomes doubtful when one surveys the amorphous rulings of American courts over the last century. In today's more secular era the sodomy statutes and other statutes regulating sexual conduct have come under heavy critical attack, part of it directed toward legislative change and part of it directed to the vagueness or unconstitutionality of the various statutes themselves.

• • •

In Alaska we have no judicial gloss of the statutory term "crime against nature" by which to rescue it from the realm of nebulosity. Looking to decisions of other states is of no great help in determining what should be the ultimate scope of the statute.

• • •

The very term "crime against nature" implies that an examination of nature can supply the standard of conduct. But the "nature" referred to in many traditional legal authorities really reflects a type of natural law thinking which was based on religious beliefs. Blackstone makes this plain when he refers to the crime against nature being against the express law of God.

The natural law concept found in many of the judicial authorities on this subject implicitly refers to the idea of a settled rule, derivable by reason and cognizable to all persons of common understanding. If such a rule of conduct can be perceived readily there is, of course, no need to define the offense with any further specificity. But the problem then presented is contained in the question: From what sources of knowledge do we obtain the content of natural law?

Man is a creature of nature, yet he engages in conduct which is approved in some cultures and disapproved in others. Who is to say which form of conduct represents most closely the pattern of nature? If natural law is merely a camouflage for some imprecise notion of religious law or moral law derived from religion, then we ought to abstain from uncritically importing religious beliefs into a secular legal system which is to apply to all classes of society. As Mr. Justice Holmes put it:

> "The jurists who believe in natural law seem to me to be in that naive state of mind that accepts what has been familiar and accepted by them and their neighbors as something that must be accepted by all men everywhere.

•   •   •

> "Men to a great extent believe what they want to although I see in that no basis for a philosophy that tells us what we should want to want."

We cannot derive from the natural law a meaningful set of values and criteria by which to breathe life into the term "crime against nature." We conclude that natural law thinking, at least in this instance, does not provide a standard on which to base decision.

•   •   •

Reflection about the nature of man is central to the formulation of ethical standards. It would be unreasonable to deny the vast interplay of moral ideas and the positive law, or the purposive element in legal interpretation. It would be equally irrational to ignore the role of religious belief in shaping the moral attitudes of society. There well may be a natural law of "minimal content" as stated by Professor Hart. It is not our task to decide such recondite questions. But the trouble with using a presumed law of nature in the present case is that it would result in a wholesale adoption of a rule premised on divine revelation, not subjected to rational analyses. . . .

In the current debate about legal regulation of sexual conduct, the main issue seems to be not the age-old dialectic of natural law against positivism; rather, it is the question of enforcing a specifically religious belief upon all of society.

•   •   •

Certainly the legislative branch of government can delimit and proscribe specific types of sexual conduct which have a harmful effect upon the valid functioning of a civilized society. With this we can have no quarrel. But the term "crime against nature" simply will not pass muster under the constitutional standards we must apply. Neither the delicate sensibilities of William Blackstone nor the hushed euphemisms of the Victorian era can justify the use of imprecision in penal legislation. Nor can they govern our determination of whether a statute is valid under current American constitutional standards. We declare the term "crime against nature" void for vagueness.

Our conclusion that the "crime against nature" is fatally vague does not, however, dispose of the case at bar.

• • •

The gratuitous use of the words "crime against nature" will not of itself invalidate the indictment if, without those words the indictment sets forth acts, occurrences and circumstances sufficiently to state the essential elements of the offense, to apprise the defendant of the nature of the charge against him, and to allow him to prepare his defense to the indictment. A mere misnomer of the crime, not operating to the prejudice of the accused, does not render the indictment fatally defective if it otherwise charges the offense. The erroneous language will, in such cases, be ignored as surplusage. In the case at bar the acts were charged with specificity. The case was submitted to the jury under the term "sodomy" which appears in the same statutory section as the term used in the indictment.

• • •

. . . Accordingly, we must consider whether the statute is sufficiently certain as to some modes of sexual conduct, whether appellant's conduct is within such a prohibited zone, and whether the indictment supports the conviction.

• • •

For the reasons stated, the judgment of conviction is affirmed. However, we remand for the entry of an amended judgment reflecting a conviction for the crime of sodomy and not a crime against nature.

BAKER v. NELSON
SUPREME COURT OF MINNESOTA, 1971
291 Minn. 310, 191 N.W.2d 185
APPEAL DISMISSED 410 U.S. 810 (1973)

Peterson, Justice. The questions for decision are whether a marriage of two persons of the same sex is authorized by state statutes and, if not, whether state authorization is constitutionally compelled.

Petitioners, Richard John Baker and James Michael McConnell, both adult male persons, made application to respondent, Gerald R. Nelson, clerk of Hennepin County District Court, for a marriage license, pursuant to Minn. St. 517.08. Respondent declined to issue the license on the sole ground that petitioners were of the same sex, it being undisputed that there were otherwise no statutory impediments to a heterosexual marriage by either petitioner.

The trial court, quashing an alternative writ of mandamus, ruled that respondent was not required to issue a marriage license to petitioners and specifically directed that a marriage license not be issued to them. This appeal is from those orders. We affirm.

• • •

Petitioners contend, second, that Minn. St. c. 517, so interpreted, is unconstitutional. There is a dual aspect to this contention; The prohibition of a same-sex marriage denies petitioners a fundamental right guaranteed by the Ninth Amendment to the United States Constitution, arguably made applicable to the states by the Fourteenth Amendment; and petitioners are deprived of liberty and property without due process and are denied the equal protection of the laws, both guaranteed by the Fourteenth Amendment.

NATURE 177

These constitutional challenges have in common the assertion that the right to marry without regard to the sex of these parties is a fundamental right of all persons and that restricting marriage to only couples of the opposite sex is irrational and invidiously discriminatory. We are not independently persuaded by these contentions and do not find support for them in any decisions of the United States Supreme Court.

The institution of marriage as a union of man and woman, uniquely involving the procreation and rearing of children within a family, is as old as the book of Genesis. Skinner v. Oklahoma ex rel. Williamson, 316 U.S. 535, 541, (1942), which invalidated Oklahoma's Habitual Criminal Sterilization Act on equal protection grounds, stated in part: "Marriage and procreation are fundamental to the very existence and survival of the race." This historic institution manifestly is more deeply founded than the asserted contemporary concept of marriage and societal interests for which petitioners contend. The due process clause of the Fourteenth Amendment is not a charter for restructuring it by judicial legislation.

Griswold v. Connecticut, 381 U.S. 479, . . . (1965), upon which petitioners rely, does not support a contrary conclusion. A Connecticut criminal statute prohibiting the use of contraceptives by married couples was held invalid, as violating the due process clause of the Fourteenth Amendment. The basic premise of that decision, however, was that the state, having authorized marriage, was without power to intrude upon the right of privacy inherent in the marital relationship. Mr. Justice Douglas, author of the majority opinion, wrote that this criminal statute "operates directly on an intimate relation of husband and wife," 381 U.S. 482, . . . (1965), and that the very idea of its enforcement by police search of "the sacred precincts of marital bedrooms for telltale signs of the use of contraceptives . . . is repulsive to the notions of privacy surrounding the marriage relationship." 381 U.S. 485, . . . (1965). In a separate opinion for three justices, Mr. Justice Goldberg similarly abhorred this state disruption of "the traditional relation of the family—a relation as old and as fundamental as our entire civilization." 381 U.S. 496, . . . (1965).

The equal protection clause of the Fourteenth Amendment, like the due process clause, is not offended by the state's classification of persons authorized to marry. There is no irrational or invidious discrimination. Petitioners note that the state does not impose upon heterosexual married couples a condition that they have a proved capacity or declared willingness to procreate, posing a rhetorical demand that this court must read such condition into the statute if same-sex marriages are to be prohibited. Even assuming that such a condition would be neither unrealistic nor offensive under the Griswold rationale, the classification is no more than theoretically imperfect. We are reminded, however, that "abstract symmetry" is not demanded by the Fourteenth Amendment.

Loving v. Virginia, 388 U.S. 1, . . . (1967), upon which petitioners additionally rely, does not militate against this conclusion. Virginia's antimiscegenation statute, prohibiting interracial marriages, was invalidated solely on the grounds of its patent racial discrimination. As Mr. Chief Justice Warren wrote for the court . . .:

"Marriage is one of the 'basic civil rights of man,' fundamental to our very existence and survival. Skinner v. Oklahoma, 316 U.S. 535, 541 . . . (1942). . . . To deny this fundamental freedom on so unsupportable a basis as the racial classifications embodied in these statutes, classifications so directly subversive of the principle of equality at the heart of the Fourteenth Amendment, is surely to deprive all the State's citizens of liberty without due process of law. The Fourteenth Amendment requires that the freedom of choice to marry not be restricted by invidious racial discriminations."

Loving does indicate that not all state restrictions upon the right to marry are beyond reach of the Fourteenth Amendment. But in common sense and in a constitutional sense, there is a clear distinction between a marital restriction based merely upon race and one based upon the fundamental difference in sex.

We hold, therefore, that Minn. St. c. 517 does not offend the First, Eighth, Ninth, or Fourteenth Amendments to the United States Constitution.

NOTES

1. Some jurisdictions have upheld the validity of a marriage between a male and one who was born a male, but underwent surgery in an attempt to become a female. One court accepted that a sufficient transformation had taken place for the marriage to be valid (*M.T. v. J.T.*, 140 N.J. Super. 77, 355A. 2d 204, cert. denied, 71 N.J. 345, 364A. 2d 1076 (1976)). Marriage between two females has been held invalid (*Jones v. Hallahan*, 501 S.W. 2d 588 (Ky. 1973); see also, *Anonymous v. Anonymous*, 67 Misc. 2d 982, 325 N.Y.S. 2d 499 (Sup. Ct. 1971). The Wolfenden Report (Report of the Committee on Homosexual Offenses and Prostitution, Cmnd. No. 247 (1957) set out in part at p. 336 *infra*), which precipitated change in the criminal law treatment of homosexuality in the United Kingdom, also directed its attention to whether homosexuality is "natural" or "unnatural."

2. In keeping with the jurisprudence of physical and structural naturalism, the court, in Baker v. Nelson, purports to base its decision on constitutional and statutory interpretation. In fact, the constitutional and statutory directives invoked do not answer the pertinent questions. A moment's reflection will make clear that the court was actually predicating its decision on the notion of some physical naturalism; it was assuming that only male-female marriages are, should, or perhaps, can be authorized by the state. Interestingly enough, the ability to procreate, sometimes invoked as a key criterion, is not a prerequisite for marriage; the sterile and aged may contract valid marriages.

3. Mitterauer and Sieter write:

> To appeal to the "natural order" of the family and to claim that it must be retained at all costs may, from the point of view of social history, be seen as an attempt merely to retain a specific family structure that has developed over the centuries, with its corresponding patterns of behavior and values . . . to describe certain relationships of authority and dependence adapted to the conditions of society in certain periods of the past as "natural," and best to declare them unchangeable, means legitimizing traditional structures of authority within the family is connected. M. Mitterauer & R. Sieter, *The European Family: Patriarchy to Partnership From the Middle Ages to the Present* 20-21 (1982; original German edition, 1977).

Comment on this observation with special reference to aspects of the family currently under appraisal in the United States.

"NATURAL" BIRTH AND DEATH

Physical and structural naturalism appears, in modern industrial and science-based civilizations, in an extraordinary range of disguises and a wide variety of contexts. The basic policy issue has been thrust to the fore by the refinement and proliferation of life-support and fetal termination technology. Some human beings are now in a position of deciding, sometimes forced to decide, who will live and who will die. One recent expression of the issue has revolved about the community's role in continuing to support seriously ill or injured people by "artificial" means. In the cases that follow consider whether the word "natural" or its functional equivalent is being used to conceal decision.

MATTER OF QUINLAN
NEW JERSEY SUPREME COURT, 1971
70 N.J. 10, 355 A.2d 647

[Hughes, C.J.] . . . The central figure in this tragic case is Karen Ann Quinlan, a New Jersey resident. At the age of 22, she lies in a debilitated and allegedly moribund state at Saint Clare's Hospital in Denville, New Jersey. The litigation has to do, in final analysis, with her life,—its continuance or cessation,—and the responsibilities, rights and duties, with regard to any fateful decision concerning it, or her family, her guardian, her doctors, the hospital, the State through its law enforcement authorities, and finally the courts of justice.

• • •

Due to extensive physical damage fully described in the able opinion of the trial judge, Judge Muir, supporting that judgment, Karen allegedly was incompetent. Joseph Quinlan sought the adjudication of that incompetency. He wished to be appointed guardian of the person and property of his daughter. It was proposed by him that such letters of guardianship, if granted, should contain an express power to him as guardian to authorize the discontinuance of all extraordinary medical procedures now allegedly sustaining Karen's vital processes and hence her life, since these measures, he asserted, present no hope of her eventual recovery. A guardian *ad litem* was appointed by Judge Muir to represent the interest of the alleged incompetent.

• • •

The matter is of transcendent importance, involving questions related to the definition and existence of death, the prolongation of life through artificial means developed by medical technology undreamed of in past generations of the practice of the healing arts; the impact of such durationally indeterminate and artificial life prolongation on the rights of the incompetent, her family and society in general; the bearing of constitutional right and the scope of judicial responsibility, as to the appropriate response of an equity court of justice to the extraordinary prayer for relief of the plaintiff. Involved as well is the right of the plaintiff, Joseph Quinlan, to guardianship of the person of his daughter.

• • •

Under any legal standard recognized by the State of New Jersey and also under standard medical practice, Karen Anne Quinlan is presently alive.

• • •

It was further stipulated during trial that Karen was indeed incompetent and guardianship was necessary, although there exists a dispute as to the determination later reached by the court that such guardianship should be bifurcated, and that Mr. Quinlan should be appointed as guardian of the trivial property but not the person of his daughter.

After certification the Attorney General filed as of right (R.2:3-4) a cross-appeal challenging the action of the trial court in admitting evidence of prior statements made by Karen while competent as to her distaste for continuance of life by extraordinary medical procedures, under circumstances not unlike those of the present case. These quoted statements were made in the context of several conversations with regard to others terminally ill and being subjected to like heroic measures. The statements were advanced as evidence of what she would want done in such a contingency as now exists. She [Karen] was said to have firmly evinced her wish, in like circumstances, not to have her life prolonged by the otherwise futile use of extraordinary means. Because we agree with the conception of the trial court that such statements, since they were remote and impersonal, lacked significant probative weight, it is not of consequence to our opinion that we decide whether or not they were admissible hearsay.

• • •

Essentially then, appealing to the power of equity, and relying on claimed constitutional rights of free exercise of religion, of privacy and of protection against cruel and unusual punishment, Karen Quinlan's father sought judicial authority to withdraw the life-sustaining mechanisms temporarily preserving his daughter's life, and his appointment as guardian of her person to that end. His request was opposed by her doctors, the hospital, the Morris Count Prosecutor, the State of New Jersey, and her guardian *ad litem*.

THE FACTUAL BASE
• • •

On the night of April 15, 1975, for reasons still unclear, Karen Quinlan ceased breathing for at least two 15 minute periods. She received some ineffectual mouth-to-mouth resuscitation from friends. She was taken by ambulance to Newton Memorial Hospital. There she had a temperature of 100 degrees, her pupils were unreactive and she was unresponsive even to deep pain. The history at the time of her admission to that hospital was essentially incomplete and uninformative.

Three days later, Dr. Morse examined Karen at the request of the Newton admitting physician, Dr. McGee. He found her comatose with evidence of decortication, a condition relating to derangement of the cortex of the brain causing a physical posture in which the upper extremities are flexed and the lower extremities are extended. She required a respirator to assist her breathing. Dr. Morse was unable to obtain an adequate account of the circumstances and events leading up to Karen's admission to the Newton Hospital. Such initial history or etiology is crucial in neurological diagnosis. Relying as he did upon the Newton Memorial records and his own examination, he concluded that prolonged lack of oxygen in the bloodstream, anoxia, was identified with her condition as he saw it upon first observation. When she was later transferred to Saint Clare's Hospital she was still unconscious, still on a respirator and a tracheotomy had been performed. On her arrival Dr.Morse conducted extensive and detailed examinations. An electroencephalogram (EEG) measuring electrical rhythm of the brain was performed and Dr. Morse characterized the result as "abnormal but it showed some activity and was consistent with her clinical state." Other significant neurological tests, including a brain scan, an angiogram, and a lumbar puncture were normal in result. Dr. Morse testified that Karen has been in a state of coma, lack of consciousness, since he began treating her. He explained that there are basically two types of coma, sleep-like unresponsiveness and awake unresponsiveness. Karen was originally in a sleep-like unresponsive condition but soon developed "sleep-wake" cycles, apparently a normal improvement for comatose patients occurring within three to four weeks. In the awake cycle she blinks, cries out and does things of that sort but is still totally unaware of anyone or anything around her.

Dr. Morse and other expert physicians who examined her characterized Karen as being in a "chronic persistent vegetative state." Dr. Fred Plum, one of such expert witnesses, defined this as a "subject who remains with the capacity to maintain the vegetative parts of neurological function but who . . . no longer has any cognitive function."

Dr. Morse, as well as the several other medical and neurological experts who testified in this case, believed with certainty that Karen Quinlan is not "brain dead." They identified the Ad Hoc Committee of Harvard Medical School report *(infra)* as the ordinary medical standard for determining brain death, and all of them were satisfied that Karen met none of the criteria specified in that report and was therefore not "brain dead" within its contemplation.

In this respect it was indicated by Dr. Plum that the brain works in essentially two ways, the vegetative and the sapient. He testified:

> We have an internal vegetative regulation which controls body temperature which controls breathing, which controls to a considerable degree blood pressure, which controls to some degree heart rate, which controls chewing, swallowing and which controls sleeping and waking. We have a more highly developed brain which is uniquely human which controls our relation to the outside world, our capacity to talk, to see, to feel, to sing, to think. Brain death necessarily must mean the death of both of these functions of the brain, vegetative and the sapient. Therefore, the presence of any function which is regulated or governed or controlled by the deeper parts of the brain which in laymen's terms might be considered purely vegetative would mean that the brain is not biologically dead.

Because Karen's neurological condition affects her respiratory ability (the respiratory system being a brain stem function) she requires a respirator to assist her breathing. From the time of her admission to Saint Clare's Hospital Karen has been assisted by an MA-1 respirator, a sophisticated machine which delivers a given volume of air at a certain rate and periodically provides a "sigh" volume, a relatively large measured volume of air designed to purge the lungs of excretions. Attempts to "wean" her from the respirator were unsuccessful and have been abandoned.

The experts believe that Karen cannot now survive without the assistance of the respirator; that exactly how long she would live without it is unknown; that the strong likelihood is that death would follow soon after its removal, and that removal would also risk further brain damage and would curtail the assistance the respirator presently provides in warding off infection.

It seemed to be the consensus not only of the treating physicians but also of the several qualified experts who testified in the case, that removal from the respirator would not conform to medical practices, standards and traditions.

The further medical consensus was that Karen in addition to being comatose is in a chronic and persistent "vegetative" state, having no awareness of anything or anyone around her and existing at a primitive reflex level. Although she does have some brain stem function (ineffective for respiration) and has other reactions one normally associates with being alive, such as moving, reacting to light, sound and noxious stimuli, blinking her eyes, and the like, the quality of her feeling impulses is unknown. She grimaces, makes stereotyped cries and sounds and has chewing motions. Her blood pressure is normal.

Karen remains in the intensive care unit at Saint Clare's Hospital, receiving 24-hour care by a team of four nurses characterized, as was the medical attention, as "excellent." She is nourished by feeding by way of a nasal-gastro tube and is routinely examined for infection, which under these circumstances is a serious life threat. The result is that her condition is considered remarkable under the unhappy circumstances involved.

Karen is described as emaciated, having suffered a weight loss of at least 40 pounds, and undergoing a continuing deteriorative process. Her posture is described as fetal-like and grotesque; there is extreme flexion-rigidity of the arms, legs and related muscles and her joints are severely rigid and deformed.

From all of this evidence, and including the whole testimonial record, several basic findings in the physical area are mandated. Severe brain and associated damage, albeit of uncertain etiology, has left Karen in a chronic and persistent vegetative state. No form of treatment which can cure or improve that condition is known or available. As nearly as may be determined, considering the guarded area of remote uncertainties characteristic of most medical science predictions, she can never be restored to cognitive or sapient life. Even with regard to the vegetative level and improvement therein (if such it may be called) the prognosis is extremely poor and the extent unknown if it should in fact occur.

She is debilitated and moribund and although fairly stable at the time of argument before us (no new information having been filed in the meanwhile in expansion of the record), no physician risked the opinion that she could live more than a year and indeed she may die much earlier. Excellent medical and nursing care so far has been able to ward off the constant threat of infection, to which she is peculiarly susceptible because of the respirator, the tracheal tube and other incidents of care in her vulnerable condition. Her life accordingly is sustained by the respirator and tubal feeding, and removal from the respirator would cause her death soon, although the time cannot be stated with more precision.

• • •

. . . Dr. Korein described a medical practice concept of "judicious neglect" under which the physician will say:

> Don't treat this patient anymore, . . . it does not serve either the patient, the family, or society in any meaningful way to continue treatment with this patient.

Dr. Korein also told of the unwritten and unspoken standard of medical practice implied in the foreboding initials DNR (do not resuscitate), as applied to the extraordinary terminal case:

> [In the case of] [C]ancer, metastatic cancer, involving the lungs, the liver, the brain, multiple involvements, the physician may or may not write: Do not resuscitate. . . . [I]t could be said to the nurse: if this man stops breathing don't resuscitate him. . . . No physician that I know personally is going to try and resuscitate a man riddled with cancer and in agony and he stops breathing. They are not going to put him on a respirator. . . . I think that would be the height of misuse of technology.

While the thread of logic in such distinctions may be elusive to the non-medical lay mind, in relation to the supposed imperative to sustain life at all costs, they nevertheless relate to medical decisions, such as the decision of Dr. Morse in the present case.

• • •

To confirm the moral rightness of the decision he [Karen's father] was about to make he consulted with his parish priest and later with the Catholic chaplain of Saint Clare's Hospital. He would not, he testified, have sought termination if that act were to be morally wrong or in conflict with the tenets of the religion he so profoundly respects. He was disabused of doubt, however, when he position of the Roman Catholic Church was made known to him as it is reflected in the record in this case. While it is not usual for matters of religious dogma or concepts to enter a civil litigation (except as they may bear upon constitutional right, or sometimes, familial matters; cf. *In re Adoption of E,* 59 N.J. 36, 279 A.2d 785 (1971)), they were rightly admitted in evidence here. The judge was bound to measure the character and motivations in all respects of Joseph Quinlan as prospective guardian; and insofar as these religious matters bore upon them, they were properly scrutinized and considered by the court.

Thus germane, we note the position of that Church as illuminated by the record before us. We have no reason to believe that it would be at all discordant with the whole of Judeo-Christian tradition, considering its central respect and reverence for the sanctity of human life. It was in this sense of relevance that we admitted as *amicus curiae* the New Jersey Catholic Conference, essentially the spokesman for the various Catholic bishops of New Jersey, organized to give witness to spiritual values in public affairs in the statewide community. The position statement of Bishop Lawrence B. Casey, reproduced in the *amicus* brief, projects these views:

(a) The verification of the fact of death in a particular case cannot be deduced from any religious or moral principle and, under this aspect, does not fall within the competence of the church; —that dependence must be had upon traditional and medical standards, and by these standards Karen Ann Quinlan is assumed to be alive.

(b) The request of plaintiff for authority to terminate a medical procedure characterized as "an extraordinary means of treatment" would not involve euthanasia. This upon the reasoning expressed by Pope Pius XII in his "allocutio" (address) to anesthesiologists on November 24, 1957, when he dealt with the question:

> Does the anesthesiologist have the right, or is he bound, in all cases of deep unconsciousness, even in those that are completely hopeless in the opinion of the competent doctor, to use modern artificial respiration apparatus, even against the will of the family?

His answer made the following points:

1. In ordinary cases the doctor has the right to act in this manner, but is not bound to do so unless this is the only way of fulfilling another certain moral duty.
2. The doctor, however, has no right independent of the patient. He can act only if the patient explicitly or implicitly, directly or indirectly gives him the permission.
3. The treatment as described in the question constitutes extraordinary means of preserving life and so there is no obligation to use them nor to give the doctor permission to use them.
4. The rights and the duties of the family depend on the presumed will of the unconscious patient if he or she is of legal age, and the family, too, is bound to use only ordinary means.

5. This case is not to be considered euthanasia in any way; that would never be licit. The interruption of attempts at resuscitation, even when it causes the arrest of circulation, is not more than an indirect cause of the cessation of life, and we must apply in this case the principle of double effect.

So it was that the Bishop Casey statement validated the decision of Joseph Quinlan:

> Competent medical testimony has established that Karen Anne Quinlan has no reasonable hope of recovery from her comatose state by the use of any available medical procedures. The continuance of mechanical (cardiorespiratory) supportive measures to sustain continuation of her body functions and her life constitute extraordinary means of treatment. *Therefore, the decision of Joseph . . . Quinlan to request the discontinuance of this treatment is, according to the teachings of the Catholic Church, a morally correct decision.* (emphasis in original)

And the mind and purpose of the intending guardian were undoubtedly influenced by factors included in the following reference to the interrelationship of the three disciplines of theology, law and medicine as exposed in the Casey statement:

> The right to a natural death is one outstanding area in which the disciplines of theology, medicine and law overlap; or to put it another way, it is an area in which these three disciplines convene.

• • •

And the gap in the law is aptly described in the Bishop Casey Statement:

> In the present public discussion of the case of Karen Ann Quinlan it has been brought out that responsible people involved in medical care, patients and families have exercised the freedom to terminate or withhold certain treatments as extraordinary means in cases judged to be terminal, i.e., cases which hold no realistic hope for some recovery, in accord with the expressed or implied intentions of the patients themselves. To whatever extent this has been happening it has been without sanction in civil law. Those involved in such actions, however, have ethical and theological literature to guide them in their judgments and actions. Furthermore, such actions have not in themselves undermined society's reverence for the lives of sick and dying people.

• • •

Before turning to the legal and constitutional issues involved, we feel it essential to reiterate that the "Catholic view" of religious neutrality in the circumstances of this case is considered by the Court only in the aspect of its impact upon the conscience, motivation and purpose of the intending guardian, Joseph Quinlan, and not as a precedent in terms of the civil law.

If Joseph Quinlan, for instance, were a follower and strongly influenced by the teaching of Buddha, or if, as an agnostic or atheist, his moral judgments were formed without reference to religious feelings, but were nevertheless formed and viable, we would with equal attention and high respect consider these elements, as bearing upon his character, motivations and purposes as relevant to his qualifications and suitability as guardian.

• • •

THE RIGHT OF PRIVACY

It is the issue of the constitutional right of privacy that has given us most concern, in the exceptional circumstances of this case. Here a loving parent, *qua* parent and raising the rights of his incompetent and profoundly damaged daughter, probably irreversibly doomed to no more than a biologically vegetative remnant of life, is before the court. He seeks authorization to abandon specialized technological procedures which can only maintain for a time a body having no potential for resumption or continuance of other than a "vegetative" existence.

We have no doubt, in these unhappy circumstances, that if Karen were herself miraculously lucid for an interval (not altering the existing prognosis of the condition to which she would soon return) and perceptive of her irreversible condition, she could effectively decide upon discontinuance of the life-support apparatus, even if it means the prospect of natural death. To this extent we may distinguish *Heston, supra,* which concerned a severely injured young woman (Delores Heston), whose life depended on surgery and blood transfusion; and who was in such extreme shock that she was unable to express an informed choice (although the Court apparently considered the case as if the patient's own religious decision to resist transfusion were at stake), but most importantly a patient apparently salvable to long life and vibrant health; —a situation not at all like the present case.

We have no hesitancy in deciding, in the instant diametrically opposite case, that no external compelling interest of the State could compel Karen to endure the unendurable, only to vegetate a few measurable months with no realistic possibility of returning to any semblance of cognitive or sapient life. We perceive no thread of logic distinguishing between such a choice on Karen's part and a similar choice which, under the evidence in this case, could be made by a competent patient terminally ill, riddled by cancer and suffering great pain; such a patient would not be resuscitated or put on a respirator in the example described by Dr. Korein, and *a fortiori* would not be kept *against his will* on a respirator.

Although the Constitution does not explicitly mention a right of privacy, Supreme Court decisions have recognized that a right of personal privacy exists and that certain areas of privacy are guaranteed under the Constitution. *Eisenstadt v. Baird,* 405 U.S. 438, . . . (1972); *Stanley v. Georgia,* 394, U.S. 557, 89 . . . (1969). The Court has interdicted judicial intrusion into many aspects of personal decision, sometimes basing this restraint upon the conception of a limitation of judicial interest and responsibility, such as with regard to contraception and its relationship to family life and decision. *Griswold v. Connecticut,* 381 U.S. 479, . . . (1965).

The Court in *Griswold* found the unwritten constitutional right of privacy to exist in the penumbra of specific guarantees of the Bill of Rights "formed by emanations from those guarantees that help give them life and substance." 381 U.S. at 484, . . . Presumably this right is broad enough to encompass a patient's decision to decline medical treatment under certain circumstances, in much the same way as it is broad enough to encompass a woman's decision to terminate pregnancy under certain conditions. *Roe v. Wade,* 410 U.S. 113, (1973). . . .

Nor is such right of privacy forgotten in the New Jersey Constitution. N.J. Const. (1947), Act. 1., par. 1.

The claimed interests of the State in this case are essentially the preservation and sanctity of human life and defense of the right of the physician to administer medical treatment according to his best judgment. In this case the doctors say that removing

Karen from the respirator will conflict with their professional judgment. The plaintiff answers that Karen's present treatment serves only a maintenance function; that the respirator cannot cure or improve her condition but at best can only prolong her inevitable slow deterioration and death; and that the interests of the patient, as seen by her surrogate, the guardian, must be evaluated by the court as predominant, even in the face of an opinion *contra* by the present attending physicians. Plaintiff's distinction is significant. The nature of Karen's care and the realistic chances of her recovery are quite unlike those of the patients discussed in many of the cases where treatments were ordered. In many of those cases the medical procedure required (usually a transfusion) constituted a minimal bodily invasion and the chances of recovery and return to functioning life were very good. We think that the State's interest *contra* weakens and the individual's right to privacy grows as the degree of bodily invasion increases and the prognosis dims. Ultimately there comes a point at which the individual's rights overcome the State interest. It is for that reason that we believe Karen's choice, if she were competent to make it, would be vindicated by the law. Her prognosis is extremely poor,—she will never resume cognitive life. And the bodily invasion is very great,—she requires 24 hour intensive nursing care, antibiotics, the assistance of a respirator, a catheter and feeding tube.

Our affirmation of Karen's independent right of choice, however, would ordinarily be based upon her competency to assert it. The sad truth, however, is that she is grossly incompetent and we cannot discern her supposed choice based on the testimony of her previous conversation with friends, where such testimony is without sufficient probative weight. 137 N.J. Super. at 260, 348 A.2d 801. Nevertheless we have concluded that Karen's right of privacy may be asserted on her behalf by her guardian under the peculiar circumstances here present.

If a putative decision by Karen to permit this noncognitive, vegetative existence to terminate by natural forces is regarded as a valuable incident of her right of privacy, as we believe it to be, then it should not be discarded solely on the basis that her condition prevents her conscious exercise of the choice. The only practical way to prevent destruction of the right is to permit the guardian and family of Karen to render their best judgment, subject to the qualifications hereinafter stated, as to whether she would exercise it in these circumstances. If their conclusion is in the affirmative this decision should be accepted by a society the overwhelming majority of whose members would, we think, in similar circumstances, exercise such a choice in the same way for themselves or for those closest to them. It is for this reason that we determine that Karen's right of privacy may be asserted in her behalf, in this respect, by her guardian and family under the particular circumstances presented by this record.

• • •

We glean from the record here that physicians distinguish between curing the ill and comforting and easing the dying; that they refuse to treat the curable as if they were dying or ought to die, and that they have sometimes refused to treat the hopeless and dying as if they were curable. In this sense, as we were reminded by the testimony of Drs. Korein and Diamond, many of them have refused to inflict an undesired prolongation of the process of dying on a patient in irreversible condition when it is clear that such "therapy" offers neither human nor humane benefit. We think these attitudes represent a balanced implementation of a profoundly realistic perspective on the meaning of life and death and that they respect the whole Judeo-Christian tradition of regard for human life. No less would they seem consistent with the moral matrix of medicine, "to heal," very much in the sense of the endless mission of the law, "to do justice."

Yet this balance, we feel, is particularly difficult to perceive and apply in the context of the development by advanced technology of sophisticated and artificial life-sustaining devices. For those possibly curable, such devices are of great value, and, as ordinary medical procedures, are essential. Consequently, as pointed out by Dr. Diamond, they are necessary because of the ethic of medical practice. But in light of the situation in the present case (while the record here is somewhat hazy in distinguishing between "ordinary" and "extraordinary" measures), one would have to think that the use of the same respirator or like support could be considered "ordinary" in the context of the possibly curable patient but "extraordinary" in the context of the forced sustaining by cardio-respiratory processes of an irreversibly doomed patient. And this dilemma is sharpened in the face of the malpractice and criminal action threat which we have mentioned.

• • •

The evidence in this case convinces us that the focal point of decision should be the prognosis as to the reasonable possibility of return to cognitive and sapient life, as distinguished from the forced continuance of that biological vegetative existence to which Karen seems to be doomed.

In summary of the present point of this opinion, we conclude that the state of the pertinent medical standards and practices which guided the attending physicians in this matter is not such as would justify the Court in deeming itself bound or controlled thereby in responding to the case for declaratory relief established by the parties on the record before us.

ALLEGED CRIMINAL LIABILITY

Having concluded that there is a right of privacy that might permit termination of treatment in the circumstances of this case, we turn to consider the relationship of the exercise of that right to the criminal law. We are aware that such termination of treatment would accelerate Karen's death. The County Prosecutor and the Attorney General maintain that there would be criminal liability for such acceleration. Under the statutes of this State, the unlawful killing of another human being is criminal homicide. N.J.S.A. 2A:113-1, 2, 5. We conclude that there would be no criminal homicide in the circumstances of this case. We believe, first, that the ensuing death would not be homicide but rather expiration from existing natural causes. Secondly, even if it were to be regarded as homicide, it would not be unlawful.

These conclusions rest upon definitional and constitutional bases. The termination of treatment pursuant to the right of privacy is, within the limitations of this case, *ipso facto* lawful. Thus, a death resulting from such an act would not come within the scope of the homicide statutes proscribing only the unlawful killing of another. There is a real and in this case determinative distinction between the unlawful taking of the life of another and the ending of artificial life-support systems as a matter of self-determination.

• • •

. . . Upon the concurrence of the guardian and family of Karen, should the responsible attending physicians conclude that there is no reasonable possibility of Karen's ever emerging from her present comatose condition to a cognitive, sapient state and that the life-support apparatus now being administered to Karen should be discontinued, they shall consult with the hospital "Ethics Committee" or like body of the institution in which Karen is then hospitalized. If that consultative body agrees that there is no reasonable possibility of Karen's ever emerging from her present comatose condition to a cognitive, sapient state, the present life-support system may be withdrawn and said action shall be without any civil or criminal liability therefore on the part of any participant, whether guardian, physician, hospital or others. We herewith specifically so hold.

NOTES

1. Is the court's distinction or dichotomy between "ordinary" and "extraordinary" medical measures a useful guide for decision-makers? How does one determine whether a measure is extraordinary? Were the medical measures in *Quinlan* (essentially, a respirator and intravenous feeding of nutrients and medicine) extraordinary in the contemporary medical context? Is a coronary by-pass operation or use of a kidney dialysis machine or a kidney transplant extraordinary? Are all artificial measures *ipso facto* extraordinary? If so, should all medical measures be labeled extraordinary? Do the criteria ordinary and extraordinary change over time as medical advances come into common use?

2. If extraordinary means uncommon, characterization of the same measures may differ depending upon the locus of the patient (e.g. in an urban metropolis with ample advanced medical equipment or a backward rural area or in a poor country), or depending perhaps on whether the patient or family could afford such measures or regularly resorted to them.

3. Is there such a thing as a "natural" death? If there is, should human beings be entitled to it? In March, 1984, Governor Richard D. Lamm of Colorado remarked at a Senior Day gathering that "We are really approaching a time of almost technological immortality when the machine and the tubes and the drugs and the heart pacemakers . . . literally force life on us. I believe we really should be very careful in terms of our technological miracles that we don't impose life on people who, in fact, are suffering beyond the ability for us to help." In practical terms, the Governor told the elderly before him that they should imitate leaves which withered with age, and fell to the ground, but formed humus to fertilize the earth for future vegetation. "You've got a duty to die and get out of the way. Let the other society, our kids, build a reasonable life." The Governor explained that the reason for his view was that costs of treatment that allow some terminally ill people to live longer were destroying the nation's economic health. (N.Y. Times, March 29, 1984, page A 16, cols 5-7.) Commenting editorially on the Governor's statement, the New York Times remarked ". . . *when* to discontinue life-sustaining treatment should remain a question for patients, families, doctors, hospitals and, perhaps, the community at large. . . . Governor Lamm's fast-moving tongue was off, but his mind was in a decent place." (N.Y. Times, March 31, 1984, page 22, cols. 1-2). Governor Lamm, in a subsequent interview stated, "The Denver Post printed a correction the following day. What I said was, 'We all have a duty to die.' I did not say the elderly or the terminally ill. . . . I was just pointing out the obvious, that we all must die. . . ." (USA Today, Oct. 23, 1985, page 11 A).

4. A joint working group of the American Academy of Sciences and the American Philosophical Society has asked you to prepare a working paper on an appropriate national policy and, if appropriate, a program on the termination of life support for ill people. Does the notion of "natural" death help your inquiry? If so, how?

If the phenomena to which terms like "extraordinary" or "artificial" refer vary with place and time and, of course, from observer to observer, how would you propose using such terms to appraise decisions? Are there better criteria by which to appraise the cases at hand? Consider the issue of abortion.

ROE ET AL. V. WADE
410 U.S. 113 (1973)

[Mr. Justice Blackmun delivered the opinion] . . . We forthwith acknowledge our awareness of the sensitive and emotional nature of the abortion controversy, of the vigorous opposing views, even among physicians, and of the deep and seemingly absolute convictions that the subject inspires. One's philosophy, one's experiences, one's exposure to the raw edges of human existence, one's religious training, one's attitudes toward life and family and their values, and the moral standards one establishes and seeks to observe, are all likely to influence and to color one's thinking and conclusions about abortion.

In addition, population growth, pollution, poverty, and racial overtones tend to complicate and not to simplify the problem.

Our task, of course, is to resolve the issue by constitutional measurement, free of emotion and of predilection. We seek earnestly to do this, and, because we do, we have inquired into, and in this opinion place some emphasis upon, medical and medical-legal history and what that history reveals about man's attitudes toward the abortion procedure over the centuries. We bear in mind, too, Mr. Justice Holmes' admonition in his now-vindicated dissent in *Lochner v. New York,* 198 U.S. 45, 76 (1905):

> "[The Constitution] is made for people of fundamentally differing views, and the accident of our finding certain opinions natural and familiar or novel and even shocking ought not to conclude our judgment upon the question whether statutes embodying them conflict with the Constitution of the United States."

. . . These [Texas statutes] make it a crime to "procure an abortion," as therein defined, or to attempt one, except with respect to "an abortion procured or attempted by medical advice for the purpose of saving the life of the mother." Similar statutes are in existence in a majority of the States.

•   •   •

The two actions were consolidated and heard together by a duly convened three-judge district court. The suits thus presented the situations of the pregnant single woman, the childless couple, with the wife not pregnant, and the licensed practicing physician, all joining in the attack of the Texas criminal abortion statutes. Upon the filing of affidavits, motions were made for dismissal and for summary judgment. The court . . . concluded tht, with respect to the requests for a declaratory judgment, abstention was not warranted. On the merits, the District Court held that the "fundamental right of single women and married persons to choose whether to have children is protected by the Ninth Amendment, through the Fourteenth Amendment," and that the Texas criminal abortion statutes were void on their face because they were both unconstitutionally vague and constituted an overbroad infringement on the plaintiffs' Ninth Amendment rights. The court then held that abstention was warranted with respect to the requests for an injunction. It therefore dismissed the Does' complaint, declared the abortion statutes void, and dismissed the application for injunctive relief. 314 F. Supp. 1217, 1225 (ND Tex. 1970).

The plaintiffs Roe and Doe and the intervenor Hallford, pursuant to 28 U. S. C. § 1253, have appealed to this Court from that part of the District Court's judgment denying the injunction. The defendant District Attorney has purported to cross-appeal, pursuant to the same statute, from the court's grant of declaratory relief to Roe and

Hallford. Both sides also have taken protective appeals to the United States Court of Appeals for the Fifth Circuit. That court ordered the appeals held in abeyance pending decision here. We postponed decision on jurisdiction to the hearing on the merits. 402 U.S. 941 (1971).

•   •   •

The principal thrust of appellant's attack on the Texas statutes is that they improperly invade a right, said to be possessed by the pregnant woman, to choose to terminate her pregnancy. Appellant would discover this right in the concept of personal "liberty" embodied in the Fourteenth Amendment's Due Process Clause; or in personal, marital, familial, and sexual privacy said to be protected by the Bill of Rights or its penumbras, see *Griswold v. Connecticut* 381 U.S. 479 (1965); *Eisenstadt v. Baird,* 405 U.S. 43B (1972); id., at 460 (White, J., concurring in result); or among those rights reserved to the people by the Ninth Amendment, *Griswold v. Connecticut,* 381 U.S. at 486 (Goldberg, J., concurring). Before addressing this claim, we feel it desirable briefly to survey, in several aspects, the history of abortion, for such insight as that history may afford us, and then to examine the state purposes and interests behind the criminal abortion laws.

•   •   •

Three reasons have been advanced to explain historically the enactment of criminal abortion laws in the 19th century and to justify their continued existence.

It has been argued occasionally that these laws were the product of a Victorian social concern to discourage illicit sexual conduct. Texas, however, does not advance this justification in the present case, and it appears that no court or commentator has taken the argument seriously. The appellants and *amici* contend, moreover, that this is not a proper state purpose at all and suggest that, if it were, the Texas statutes are overbroad in protecting it since the law fails to distinguish between married and unwed mothers.

A second reason is concerned with abortion as a medical procedure. When most criminal abortion laws were first enacted, the procedure was a hazardous one for the woman. This was particularly true prior to the development of antisepsis. Antiseptic techniques, of course, were based on discoveries by Lister, Pasteur, and others first announced in 1867, but were not generally accepted and employed until about the turn of the century. Abortion mortality was high. Even after 1900, and perhaps until as late as the development of antibiotics in the 1940's, standard modern techniques such as dilation and curettage were not nearly so safe as they are today. Thus, it has been argued that a State's real concern in enacting a criminal abortion law was to protect the pregnant woman, that is, to restrain her from submitting to a procedure that placed her life in serious jeopardy.

Modern medical techniques have altered this situation. Appellants and various *amici* refer to medical data indicating that abortion in early pregnancy, that is, prior to the end of the first trimester, although not without its risk, is now relatively safe. Mortality rates for women undergoing early abortions, where the procedure is legal, appear to be as low as or lower than the rates for normal childbirth. Consequently, any interest of the State in protecting the woman from an inherently hazardous procedure, except when it would be equally dangerous for her to forgo it, has largely disappeared. Of course, important state interests in the areas of health and medical standards do remain. The State has a legitimate interest in seeing to it that abortion, like any other medical procedure, is performed under circumstances that insure maximum safety for the patient. This interest obviously extends at least to the performing physician and his staff, to the facilities involved, to the availability of aftercare, and to adequate provision for any complication or emergency that might arise. The prevalence of high mortality rates at illegal ''abortion mills'' strengthens, rather than weakens, the State's interest in regulating the conditions under which abortions are performed. Moreover, the risk to the woman increases as her pregnancy continues. Thus, the State retains a definite interest in protecting the woman's own health and safety when an abortion is proposed at a late stage of pregnancy.

The third reason is the State's interest—some phrase it in terms of duty—in protecting prenatal life. Some of the argument for this justification rests on the theory that a new human life is present from the moment of conception. The State's interest and general obligation to protect life then extends, it is argued, to prenatal life. Only when the life of the pregnant mother herself is at stake, balanced against the life she carries within her, should the interest of the embryo or fetus not prevail. Logically, of course, a legitimate state interest in this area need not stand or fall on acceptance of the belief that life begins at conception or at some other point prior to live birth. In assessing the State's interest, recognition may be given to the less rigid claim that as long as at least *potential* life is involved, the State may assert interests beyond the protection of the pregnant woman alone.

Parties challenging state abortion laws have sharply disputed in some courts the contention that a purpose of these laws, when enacted, was to protect prenatal life. Pointing to the absence of legislative history to support the contention, they claim that most state laws were designed solely to protect the woman. Because medical advances have lessened this concern, at least with respect to abortion in early pregnancy, they argue that with respect to such abortions the laws can no longer be justified by any state interest. There is some scholarly support for this view of original purpose. The few state courts called upon to interpret their laws in the late 19th and early 20th centuries did focus on the State's interest in protecting the woman's health rather than in preserving the embryo and fetus. Proponents of this view pont out that in many States, including Texas, by statute or judicial interpretation, the pregnant woman herself could not be prosecuted for self-abortion or for cooperating in an abortion performed upon her by another. They claim that adoption of the ''quickening'' distinction through received common law and state statutes tacitly recognizes the greater health hazards inherent in late abortion and impliedly repudiates the theory that life begins at conception.

It is with these interests, and the weight to be attached to them, that this case is concerned.

The Constitution does not explicitly mention any right of privacy. In a line of decisions, however, going back perhaps as far as *Union Pacific R. Co. v. Botsford,* 141 U.S. 250, 251 (1891), the Court has recognized that a right of personal privacy, does exist under the Constitution. In varying contexts, the Court or individual Justices have, indeed, found at least the roots of that right in the First Amendment . . .; in the Fourth and Fifth Amendments, . . .; in the penumbras of the Bill of Rights, . . .; in the Ninth Amendment, . . .; or in the concept of liberty guaranteed by the first section of the Fourteenth Amendment, ... These decisions make it clear that only personal rights that can be deemed ''fundamental'' or ''implicit in the concept of ordered liberty,'' . . . , are included in this guarantee of personal privacy. They also make it clear that the right has some extension to activities relating to marriage, . . .; procreation, . . .; contraception, . . .; family relationships, . . . and child rearing and education . . .

This right of privacy, whether it be founded in the Fourteenth Amendment's concept of personal liberty and restrictions upon state action, as we feel it is, or, as the District Court determined, in the Ninth Amendment's reservation of rights to the people, is broad enough to encompass a woman's decision whether or not to terminate her pregnancy. The detriment that the State would impose upon the pregnant woman by denying this choice altogether is apparent. Specific and direct harm medically diagnosable even in early pregnancy may be involved. Maternity, or additional offspring, may force upon the woman a distressful life and future. Psychological harm may be imminent. Mental and physical health may be taxed by child care. There is also the distress, for all concerned, associated with the unwanted child, and there is the problem of bringing a child into a family already unable, psychologically and otherwise, to care for it. In other cases, as in this one, the additional difficulties and continuing stigma of unwed motherhood may be involved. All these are factors the woman and her responsible physician necessarily will consider in consultation.

On the basis of elements such as these, appellant and some *amici* argue that the woman's right is absolute and that she is entitled to terminate her pregnancy at whatever time, in whatever way, and for whatever reason she alone chooses. With this we do not agree. Appellant's arguments that Texas either has no valid interest at all in regulating the abortion decision, or no interest strong enough to support any limitation upon the woman's sole determination, are unpersuasive. The Court's decisions recognizing a right of privacy also acknowledge that some state regulation in areas protected by that right is appropriate. As noted above, a State may properly assert important interests in safe-guarding health, in maintaining medical standards, and in protecting potential life. At some point in pregnancy, these respective interests become sufficiently compelling to sustain regulation of the factors that govern the abortion decision. The privacy right involved, therefore, cannot be said to be absolute. In fact, it is not clear to us that the claim asserted by some *amici* that one has an unlimited right to do with one's body as one pleases bears a close relationship to the right of privacy previously articulated in the Court's decisions. The Court has refused to recognize an unlimited right of this kind in the past. *Jacobson v. Massachusetts,* 197 U.S. 11 (1905) (vaccination); *Buck v. Bell,* 274 U.S. 200 (1927) (sterilization).

We, therefore, conclude that the right of personal privacy includes the abortion decision, but that this right is not unqualified and must be considered against important state interests in regulation.

●   ●   ●

Although the results are divided, most of these courts have agreed that the right of privacy, however based, is broad enough to cover the abortion decision; that the right, nonetheless, is not absolute and is subject to some limitations; and that at some point that state interests as to protection of health, medical standards, and prenatal life, become dominant. We agree with this approach.

Where certain "fundamental rights" are involved, the Court has held that regulation limiting these rights may be justified only by a "compelling state interest," . . . , and that legislative enactments must be narrowly drawn to express only the legitimate state interests at stake . . .

In the recent abortion cases, cited above, courts have recognized these principles. Those striking down state laws have generally scrutinized the State's interests in protecting health and potential life, and have concluded that neither interest justified broad limitations on the reasons for which a physician and his pregnant patient might decide that she should have an abortion in the early stages of pregnancy. Courts sustaining state laws have held that the State's determinations to protect health or prenatal life are dominant and constitutionally justifiable.

• • •

A. The appellee and certain *amici* argue that the fetus is a "person" within the language and meaning of the Fourteenth Amendment. In support of this, they outline at length and in detail the well-known facts of fetal development. If this suggestion of personhood is established, the appellant's case, of course, collapses, for the fetus' right to life would then be guaranteed specifically by the Amendment. The appellant conceded as much on reargument. On the other hand, the appellee conceded on reargument that no case could be cited that holds that a fetus is a person within the meaning of the Fourteenth Amendment.

The Constitution does not define "person" in so many words. Section 1 of the Fourteenth Amendment contains three references to "person." The first, in defining "citizens," speaks of "persons born or naturalized in the United States." The word also appears both in the Due Process Clause and in the Equal Protection Clause. "Person" is used in other places in the Constitution: in the listing of qualifications for Representatives and Senators . . . in the Apportionment Clause . . . in the Migration and Importation provision . . . in the Emolument Clause . . . in the Electors provisions, Art. II, §1, cl. 2, and the superseded cl. 3; in the provision outlining qualifications for the office of President, Art. II, §1, cl. 5; in the Extradition provisions . . . and the superseded Fugitive Slave Clause 3; and in the Fifth, Twelfth, and Twenty-second Amendments, as well as in . . . the Fourteenth Amendment. But in nearly all these instances, the use of the word is such that it has application only postnatally. None indicates, with any assurance, that it has any possible prenatal application.

All this, together with our observation, *supra,* that throughout the major portion of the 19th century prevailing legal abortion practices were far freer than they are today, persuades us that the word "person," as used in the Fourteenth Amendment, does not include the unborn.

• • •

B. The pregnant woman cannot be isolated in her privacy. She carries an embryo and, later, a fetus, if one accepts the medical definitions of the developing young in the human uterus. See Dorland's Illustrated Medical Dictionary 478-479, 547 (24th ed. 1965). The situation therefore is inherently different from marital intimacy, or bedroom possession of obscene material, or marriage, or procreation, or education, with which *Eisenstadt* and *Griswold, Stanley, Loving, Skinner,* and *Pierce* and *Meyer* were respectively concerned. As we have intimated above, it is reasonable and appropriate for a State to decide that at some point in time another interest, that of health of the mother or that of potential human life, becomes significantly involved. The woman's privacy is no longer sole and any right of privacy she possesses must be measured accordingly.

Texas urges that, apart from the Fourteenth Amendment, life begins at conception and is present throughout pregnancy, and that, therefore, the State has a compelling interest in protecting that life from and after conception. We need not resolve the difficult question of when life begins. When those trained in the respective disciplines of medicine, philosophy, and theology are unable to arrive at any consensus, the judiciary, at this point in the development of man's knowledge, is not in a position to speculate as to the answer.

It should be sufficient to note briefly the wide divergence of thinking on this most sensitive and difficult question. There has always been strong support for the view that life does not begin until live birth. This was the belief of the Stoics. It appears to be the predominant, though not the unanimous, attitude of the Jewish faith. It may be taken to represent also the position of a large segment of the Protestant community, insofar as that can be ascertained; organized groups that have taken a formal position on the abortion issue have generally regarded abortion as a matter for the conscience of the individual and her family. As we have noted, the common law found greater significance in quickening. Physicians and their scientific colleagues have regarded that event with less interest and have tended to focus either upon conception, upon live birth, or upon the interim point at which the fetus becomes "viable," that is, potentially able to live outside the mother's womb, albeit with artificial aid.

• • •

In view of all this, we do not agree that, by adopting one theory of life, Texas may override the rights of the pregnant woman that are at stake. We repeat, however, that the State does have an important and legitimate interest in preserving and protecting the health of the pregnant woman, whether she be a resident of the State or a nonresident who seeks medical consultation and treatment there, and that it has still another important and legitimate interest in protecting the potentiality of human life. These interests are separate and distinct. Each grows in substantiality as the woman approaches term and, at a point during pregnancy, each becomes "compelling."

With respect to the State's important and legitimate interest in the health of the mother, the "compelling" point, in the light of present medical knowledge, is at approximately the end of the first trimester. This is so because of the now-established medical fact, referred to above . . . , that until the end of the first trimester mortality in abortion may be less than mortality in normal childbirth. It follows that, from and after this point, a State may regulate the abortion procedure to the extent that the regulation reasonably relates to the preservation and protection of maternal health. Examples of permissible state regulation in this area are requirements as to the qualifications of the person who is to perform the abortion; as to the licensure of that person; as to the facility in which the procedure is to be performed, that is, whether it must be a hospital or may be a clinic or some other place of less-than-hospital status; as to the licensing of the facility; and the like.

This means, on the other hand, that, for the period of pregnancy prior to this "compelling" point, the attending physician, in consultation with his patient, is free to determine, without regulation by the State, that, in his medical judgment, the patient's pregnancy should be terminated. If that decision is reached, the judgment may be effectuated by an abortion free of interference by the State.

With respect to the State's important and legitimate interest in potential life, the "compelling" point is at viability. This is so because the fetus then presumably has the capability of meaningful life outside the mother's womb. State regulation protective of fetal life after viability thus has both logical and biological justifications. If the State is interested in protecting fetal life after viability, it may go so far as to proscribe abortion during that period, except when it is necessary to preserve the life or health of the mother.

Measured against these standards, Art. 1196 of the Texas Penal Code, in restricting legal abortions to those "procured or attempted by medical advice for the purpose of saving the life of the mother," sweeps too broadly. The statute makes no distinction between abortions performed early in pregnancy and those performed later, and it limits to a single reason, "saving" the mother's life, the legal justification for the procedure. The statute, therefore, cannot survive the constitutional attack made upon it here.

This conclusion makes it unnecessary for us to consider the additional challenge to the Texas statute asserted on grounds of vagueness. . . .

To summarize and to repeat:

1. A state criminal abortion statute of the current Texas type, that excepts from criminality only a life-saving procedure on behalf of the mother, without regard to pregnancy stage and without recognition of the other interests involved, is violative of the Due Process Clause of the Fourteenth Amendment.

> (a) For the state prior to approximately the end of the first trimester, the abortion decision and its effectuation must be left to the medical judgment of the pregnant woman's attending physician.

> (b) For the stage subsequent to approximately the end of the first trimester, the State, in promoting its interest in the health of the mother, may, if it chooses, regulate the abortion procedure in ways that are reasonably related to maternal health.

> (c) For the stage subsequent to viability, the State in promoting its interest in the potentiality of human life may, if it chooses, regulate, and even proscribe, abortion except where it is necessary, in appropriate medical judgment, for the preservation of the life or health of the mother.

2. The State may define the term "physician," as it has been employed in the preceding paragraphs of this Part XI of this opinion, to mean only a physician currently licensed by the State, and may proscribe any abortion by a person who is not a physician as so defined.

In *Doe v. Bolton, post,* p. 179, procedural requirements contained in one of the modern abortion statutes are considered. That opinion and this one, of course, are to be read together.

This holding, we feel, is consistent with the relative weights of the respective interests involved, with the lessons and examples of medical and legal history, with the lenity of the common law, and with the demands of the profound problems of the present day. The decision leaves the State free to place increasing restrictions on abortion as the period of pregnancy lengthens, so long as those restrictions are tailored to the recognized state interests. The decision vindicates the right of the physician to administer medical treatment according to his professional judgment up to the points where important state interests provide compelling justifications for intervention. Up to those points, the abortion decision in all its aspects is inherently, and primarily, a medical decision, and basis responsibility for it must rest with the physician. If an individual practitioner abuses the privilege of exercising proper medical judgment, the usual remedies, judicial and intraprofessional, are available.

NOTES

The manifest reasoning in *Roe v. Wade* raises more questions than it answers; it seems more to obscure than explain the decision. Consider the following in assessing whether the court's opinion masks the true reason for its decision permitting abortions.

1. The court relied on the right to privacy as the basis for its decision. The right to privacy was first put forward as a right to be free from another's prying into one's private affairs. But the court itself concludes that ". . . it is not clear to us that the claim asserted by some *amici* that one has an unlimited right to do with one's body as one pleases bears a close relationship to the right of privacy previously articulated in the court's decision." On what, then, is the decision based?

2. By framing the question in terms of the right of privacy of the mother, does the court beg the question of the rights of the fetus?

3. If the right to privacy is the basis of the court's holding, why does the court give the physician and not the mother the right to decide to abort?

4. The court claims that it does not decide when life begins. ("We need not resolve the difficult question of when life begins. When those trained in the respective disciplines of medicine, philosophy, and theology are unable to arrive at any consensus, the judiciary at this point in the development of man's knowledge is not in a position to speculate as to the answer.") Shouldn't a doubt on this issue result in upholding state statutes prohibiting abortions, since no one can really determine that abortions are not murder?

5. Why does the court use the fetus' viability outside of the womb as the test of whether the state can limit abortions? How is this test relevant to the right of privacy and to abortions in general? Why doesn't the court adopt viability *inside* the womb as a test?

POLITICAL FUNCTIONS OF NATURALIST LANGUAGE

In *Roe,* the Court states that "We forthwith acknowledge our awareness of the *sensitive and emotional nature* of the abortion controversy, of the vigorous opposing views, even among physicians, and of the deep and seemingly absolute convictions that the subject inspires. One's philosophy, one's experiences, one's exposure to the raw edge of human existence, one's *religious training,* one's attitude toward life and family and their values, and the moral standards one establishes and seeks to observe, are all likely to influence and to color one's thinking and conclusions about abortion. In addition, *population growth, pollution, poverty and racial overtones* tend to complicate and not to simplify the problem." (emphasis added) When there are such intense social conflicts, are there political advantages to obscuring the real basis and real implications of the decision?

In cases such as *Quinlan* and *Roe,* the unarticulated core issue is whether or not the community or "the state" or certain persons deemed authorized to act on their behalf or alone may not only sustain life but decide to terminate it. After all, where the community has the resources to keep an injured person alive but chooses not to deploy those resources for this purpose, it is consciously terminating that person's life.

The fact that the limited resources for life support in different hospitals were always exceeded by demand for their use has meant that someone has had to decide who will benefit from them and who will be permitted to die. For years decisions such as these could be concealed as a type of "operational code" in the sense used in Chapter 2. See generally Hashimoto, *A Structural Analysis of the Physician-Patient Relationship in No-Code Decisionmaking,* 93 *Yale L. J.* 362 (1983). But as our society becomes more litigious and the medical industry undergoes more division and specialization with decisions made by *ad hoc* committees or administrative entities and more and more such issues are dragged into courts and other fora of public decision, it has become increasingly difficult to conceal the old operational code.

In such circumstances, the student may appreciate one of the utilities of the word "natural" and the jurisprudence of structural and physical naturalism. Where a civilization operates with moral imperatives about the maintenance of life and develops a great social and psychological restraints on killing its own members, it is sometimes convenient for elites to conceal decisions that violate those imperatives under naturalistic verbiage. Under the cosmetic cover, a decision about the taking of life either directly or indirectly can be made. But from a jurisprudential standpoint, there are compelling reasons for piercing the word "natural" and trying to determine exactly what circumstances and procedures are appropriate for these choices.

There is another dimension to this aspect of the problem. A technological and science-based civilization such as ours is now capable of extending the lives of some people by using organs taken from the bodies of others. But the utility of these organs deteriorates rapidly after natural death. As a result there can be an incentive for the community to "move back," by definition, the moment of natural death as a way of increasing the transplantability of organs to others. Here again, the word "natural" conceals the fundamental policy decision about the value of each person's physical self system—viewed for several centuries as quintessentially "personal" property—to the rest of the community and the community's newly asserted competence to decide when death is inevitable and to anticipate it when it concludes that the ill person's bodily components are more valuable to others than they are to the original owner.

THE STRUCTURAL NATURE OF LAW

The notion of naturalism has not been restricted to matters concerning human beings, their behavior and their physical structures. It has also been invoked with regard to the basic structure of law. Here, a number of jurisprudential writers have assumed that there are inherent "structures" in law. These structures limit decision options in certain areas and, in some circumstances, predetermine the goals or objectives for which laws may be enacted. These views are often expressed in terms of natural law; in the more skillful and beguiling versions, an apparent scientific character conceals what are in essence no more than preferences derived from very selective descriptions of what happened in the past. You will recall in the selection from Aristotle's *Politics* at the beginning of this chapter that Aristotle spoke most convincingly of the inherent structure of villages and states. On reflection, do you think that such social organizations have inherent structures? If they do, are they the inherent structures that Aristotle proposed?

One of the dominant jurisprudential theories of this century has been Positivism. (It will be treated in chapters 7 and 8.) Positivism, briefly stated, accepts as law only those norms expressly made by the authorized agencies of the state. Legality becomes synonymous with effective state power. The Nazi regime demonstrated that dreadful political systems could be thoroughly "legal" and that in any system, morally odious decisions could be legal. Recoiling from that experience, some Positivists converted to natural law. Henceforth they insisted that law, in general, had to have a certain moral basis and each law had to have a certain moral content if it was entitled to obedience. Other positivists rejected that route and set out to find essential limitations on abusive power in the basic structures of law itself. Professor Fuller, in the following selection, seeks autochthonous limitations on abuses of "legal" power by identifying fundamental, inherent features of law, all of which are opposed to the abuses. In examining Professor Fuller's argument, consider first the persuasiveness of his parable. Then ask whether an effective system can be established even with general or selective violations of some of the structural principles that he purports to find in law.

FULLER, EIGHT WAYS TO FAIL TO MAKE LAW, IN THE MORALITY OF LAW 33-43 (1969)

This . . . fairly lengthy allegory . . . concerns the unhappy reign of a monarch who bore the convenient, but not very imaginative and not even very regal sounding name of Rex.

•   •   •

Rex came to the throne filled with the zeal of a reformer. He considered that the greatest failure of his predecessors had been in the field of law. For generations the legal system had known nothing like a basic reform. Procedures of trial were cumbersome, the rules of law spoke in the archaic tongue of another age, justice was expensive, the judges were slovenly and sometimes corrupt. Rex was resolved to remedy all this and to make his name in history as a great lawgiver. It was his unhappy fate to fail in this ambition. Indeed, he failed spectacularly, since not only did he not succeed in introducing the needed reforms, but he never even succeeded in creating any law at all, good or bad.

His first official act was, however, dramatic and propitious. Since he needed a clean slate on which to write, he announced to his subjects the immediate repeal of all existing law, of whatever kind. He then set about drafting a new code. Unfortunately, trained as a lonely prince, his education had been very defective. In particular he found himself incapable of making even the slightest generalizations. Though not lacking in confidence when it came to deciding specific controversies, the effort to give articulate reasons for any conclusion strained his capacities to the breaking point.

Becoming aware of his limitations, Rex gave up the project of a code and announced to his subjects that henceforth he would act as a judge in any disputes that might arise among them. In this way under the stimulus of a variety of cases he hoped that his latent powers of generalization might develop and, proceeding case by case, he would gradually work out a system of rules that could be incorporated in a code. Unfortunately the defects in his education were more deep-seated than he had supposed. The venture failed completely. After he had handed down literally hundreds of decisions neither he nor his subjects could detect in those decisions any pattern whatsoever. Such tentatives toward generalization as were to be found in his opinions only compounded the confusion, for they gave false leads to his subjects and threw his own meager powers of judgment off balance in the decision of later cases.

After this fiasco Rex realized it was necessary to take a fresh start. His first move was to subscribe to a course of lessons in generalization. With his intellectual powers thus fortified, he resumed the project of a code and, after many hours of solitary labor, succeeded in preparing a fairly lengthy document. He was still not confident, however, that he had fully overcome his previous detects. Accordingly, he announced to his subjects that he had written out a code and would henceforth be governed by it in deciding cases, but that for an indefinite future the contents of the code would remain an official state secret, known only to him and his scrivener. To Rex's surprise this sensible plan was deeply resented by his subjects. They declared it was very unpleasant to have one's case decided by rules when there was no way of knowning what those rules were.

Stunned by this rejection Rex undertook an earnest inventory of his personal strengths and weaknesses. He decided that life had taught him one clear lesson, namely, that it is easier to decide things with the aid of hindsight than it is to attempt to foresee and control the future. Not only did hindsight make it easier to decide cases, but—and this was of supreme importance to Rex—it made it easier to give reasons. Deciding to capitalize on this insight, Rex hit on the following plan. At the beginning of each calendar year he would decide all the controversies that had arisen among his subjects during the preceding year. He would accompany his decisions with a full statement of reasons. Naturally, the reasons thus given would be understood as not controlling decisions in future years, for that would be to defeat the whole purpose of the new arrangement, which was to gain the advantages of hindsight. Rex confidently announced the new plan to his subjects, observing that he was going to publish the full text of his judgments with the rules applied by him, thus meeting the chief objection to the old plan. Rex's subjects received this announcement in silence, then quietly explained through their leaders that when they said they needed to know the rules, they meant they needed to know them *in advance* so they could act on them. Rex muttered something to the effect that they might have made that point a little clearer, but said he would see what could be done.

Rex now realized that there was no escape from a published code declaring the rules to be applied in future disputes. Continuing his lessons in generalization, Rex worked diligently on a revised code, and finally announced that it would shortly be published. This announcement was received with universal gratification. The dismay of Rex's subjects was all the more intense, therefore, when his code became available and it was discovered that it was truly a masterpiece of obscurity. Legal experts who studied it declared that there was not a single sentence in it that could be understood either by an ordinary citizen or by a trained lawyer. Indignation became general and soon a picket appeared before the royal palace carrying a sign that read, "How can anybody follow a rule that nobody can understand?"

The code was quickly withdrawn. Recognizing for the first time that he needed assistance, Rex put a staff of experts to work on a revision. He instructed them to leave the substance untouched, but to clarify the expression throughout. The resulting code was a model of clarity, but as it was studied it became apparent that its new clarity had merely brought to light that it was honeycombed with contradictions. It was reliably reported that there was not a single provision in the code that was not nullified by another provision inconsistent with it. A picket again appeared before the royal residence carrying a sign that read, "This time the king made himself clear—in both directions."

Once again the code with withdrawn for revision. By now, however, Rex had lost his patience with his subjects and the negative attitude they seemed to adopt toward everything he tried to do for them. He decided to teach them a lesson and put an end to their carping. He instructed his experts to purge the code of contradictions, but at the same time to stiffen drastically every requirement contained in it and to add a long list of new crimes. Thus, where before the citizen summoned to the throne was given ten days in which to report, in the revision the time was cut to ten seconds. It was made a crime, punishable by ten years' imprisonment, to cough, sneeze, hiccough, faint or fall down in the presence of the king. It was made treason not to understand, believe in, and correctly profess the doctrine of evolutionary, democratic redemption.

When the new code was published a near revolution resulted. Leading citizens declared their intention to flout its provisions. Someone discovered in an ancient author a passage that seemed apt: "To command what cannot be obeyed serves no end but confusion, fear and chaos." Soon this passage was being quoted in a hundred petitions to the king.

The code was again withdrawn and a staff of experts charged with the task of revision. Rex's instructions to the experts were that whenever they encountered a rule requiring an impossibility, it should be revised to make compliance possible. It turned out that to accomplish this result every provision in the code had to be substantially rewritten. The final result was, however, a triumph of draftsmanship. It was clear, consistent with itself, and demanded nothing of the subject that did not lie easily within his powers. It was printed and distributed free of charge on every street corner.

However, before the effective date for the new code had arrived, it was discovered that so much time had been spent in successive revisions of Rex's original draft, that the substance of the code had been seriously overtaken by events. Ever since Rex assumed the throne there had been a suspension of ordinary legal processes and this had brought about important economic and institutional changes within the country. Accommodation to these altered conditions required many changes of substance in the law. Accordingly as soon as the new code became legally effective, it was subjected to a daily stream of amendments. Again popular discontent mounted; an anonymous pamphlet appeared on the streets carrying scurrilous cartoons of the king and a leading article with the title: "A law that changes every day is worse than no law at all."

Within a short time this source of discontent began to cure itself as the pace of amendment gradually slackened. Before this had occurred to any noticeable degree, however, Rex announced an important decision. Reflecting on the misadventures of his reign, he concluded that much of the trouble lay in bad advice he had received from experts. He accordingly declared he was reassuming the judicial power in his own person. In this way he could directly control the application of the new code and insure his country against another crisis. He began to spend practically all of his time hearing and deciding cases arising under the new code.

As the king proceeded with this task, it seemed to bring to a belated blossoming his long dormant powers of generalization. His opinions began, indeed, to reveal a confident and almost exuberant virtuosity as he deftly distinguished his own previous decisions, exposed the principles on which he acted, and laid down guide lines for the disposition of future controversies. For Rex's subjects a new day seemed about to dawn when they could finally conform their conduct to a coherent body of rules.

This hope was, however, soon shattered. As the bound volumes of Rex's judgments became available and were subjected to closer study, his subjects were appalled to discover that there existed no discernible relation between those judgments and the code they purported to apply. Insofar as it found expression in the actual disposition of controversies, the new code might just as well not have existed at all. Yet in virtually every one of his decisions Rex declared and redeclared the code to be the basic law of his kingdom.

Leading citizens began to hold private meetings to discuss what measures, short of open revolt, could be taken to get the king away from the bench and back on the throne. While these discussions were going on Rex suddenly died, old before his time and deeply disillusioned with his subjects.

The first act of his successor, Rex II, was to announce that he was taking the powers of government away from the lawyers and placing them in the hands of psychiatrists and experts in public relations. This way, he explained, people could be happy without rules.

Rex's bungling career as legislator and judge illustrates that the attempt to create and maintain a system of legal rules may miscarry in at least eight ways; there are in this enterprise, if you will, eight distinct routes to disaster. The first and most obvious lies in a failure to achieve rules at all, so that every issue must be decided on an ad hoc basis. The other routes are: (2) a failure to publicize, or at least to make available to the affected party, the rules he is expected to observe; (3) the abuse of retroactive legislation, which not only cannot itself guide action, but undercuts the integrity of rules prospective in effect, since it puts them under the threat of retrospective change; (4) a failure to make rules understandable; (5) the enactment of contradictory rules or (6) rules that require conduct beyond the powers of the affected party; (7) introducing such frequent changes in the rules that the subject cannot orient his action by them; and, finally, (8) a failure of congruence between the rules as announced and their actual administration.

A total failure in any one of these eight directions does not simply result in a bad system of law; it results in something that is not properly called a legal system at all, except perhaps in the Pickwickian sense in which a void contract can still be said to be one kind of contract. Certainly there can be no rational ground for asserting that a man can have a moral obligation to obey a legal rule that does not exist, or is kept secret from him, or that came into existence only after he had acted, or was unintelligible, or was contradicted by another rule of the same system, or commanded the impossible, or changed every minute. It may not be impossible for a man to obey a rule that is disregarded by those charged with its administration, but at some point obedience becomes futile—as futile, in fact, as casting a vote that will never be counted. As the sociologist Simmel has observed, there is a kind of reciprocity between government and the citizen with respect to the observance of rules. Government says to the citizen in effect, ''These are the rules we expect you to follow. If you follow them, you have our assurance that they are the rules that will be applied to your conduct.'' When this bond of reciprocity is finally and completely ruptured by government, nothing is left on which to ground the citizen's duty to observe the rules.

The citizen's predicament becomes more difficult when, though there is not total failure in any direction, there is a general and drastic deterioration in legality, such as occurred in Germany under Hitler. A situation begins to develop, for example, in which though some laws are published, others, including the most important, are not. Though most laws are prospective in effect, so free a use is made of retrospective legislation that no law is immune to chance ex post facto if it suits the convenience of those in power. For the trial of criminal cases concerned with loyalty to the regime, special military tribunals are established and these tribunals disregard, whenever it suits their convenience, the rules that are supposed to control their decisions. Increasingly the principal object of government seems to be, not that of giving the citizen rules by which to shape his conduct, but to frighten him into impotence. As such a situation develops, the problem faced by the citizen is not so simple as that of a voter who knows with certainty that his ballot will not be counted. It is more like that of the voter who knows that the odds are against his ballot being counted at all, and that if it is counted, there is a good chance that it will be counted for the side against which he actually voted. A citizen in this predicament has to decide for himself whether to stay with the system and cast his ballot as a kind of symbolic act expressing the hope of a better day. So it was with the German citizen under Hitler faced with deciding whether he had an obligation to obey such portions of the laws as the Nazi terror had left intact.

In situations like these there can be no simple principle by which to test the citizen's obligation of fidelity to law, any more than there can be such a principle for testing his right to engage in general revolution. One thing is, however, clear. A mere respect for constituted authority must not be confused with fidelity to law. Rex's subjects, for example, remained faithful to him as king throughout his long and inept reign. They were not faithful to his law, for he never made any.

THE ASPIRATION TOWARD PERFECTION IN LEGALITY

So far we have been concerned to trace out eight routes to failure in the enterprise of creating law. Corresponding to these are eight kinds of legal excellence toward which a system of rules may strive. What appear at the lowest level as indispensable conditions for the existence of law at all, become, as we ascend the scale of achievement, increasingly demanding challenges to human capacity. At the height of the ascent we are tempted to imagine a utopia of legality in which all rules are perfectly clear, consistent with one another, known to every citizen, and never retroactive. In this utopia the rules remain constant through time, demand only what is possible, and are scrupulously observed by courts, police, and everyone else charged with their adminsitration. For reasons that I shall advance shortly, this utopia, in which all eight of the principles of legality are realized to perfection, is not actually a useful target for guiding the impulse toward legality; the goal of perfection is much more complex. Nevertheless it does suggest eight distinct standards by which excellence in legality may be tested.

In expounding in my first chapter the distinction between the morality of duty and that of aspiration, I spoke of an imaginary scale that starts at the bottom with the most obvious and essential moral duties and ascends upward to the highest achievements open to man. I also spoke of an invisible pointer as marking the dividing line where the pressure of duty leaves off and the challenge of excellence begins. The inner morality of law, it should now be clear, presents all of these aspects. It too embraces a morality of duty and a morality of aspiration. It too confronts us with the problem of knowning where to draw the boundary below which men will be condemned for failure but can expect no praise for success, and above which they will be admired for success and at worst pitied for the lack of it.

In applying the analysis of the first chapter to our present subject, it becomes essential to consider certain distinctive qualities of the inner morality of law. In what may be called the basic morality of social life, duties that run toward other persons generally (as contrasted with those running toward specific individuals) normally require only forbearances, or as we say, are negative in nature: Do not kill, do not injure, do not deceive, do not defame, and the like. Such duties lend themselves with a minimum of difficulty to formalized definition. That is to say, whether we are concerned with legal or moral duties, we are able to develop standards which designate with some precision—though it is never complete—the kind of conduct that is to be avoided.

The demands of the inner morality of the law, however, though they concern a relationship with persons generally, demand more than forbearances; they are, as we loosely say, affirmative in nature: make the law known, make it coherent and clear, see that your decisions as an official are guided by it, etc. To meet these demands human energies must be directed toward specific kinds of achievement and not merely warned away from harmful acts.

Because of the affirmative and creative quality of its demands, the inner morality of law lends itself badly to realization through duties, whether they be moral or legal. No matter how desirable a direction of human effort may appear to be, if we assert there is a duty to pursue it, we shall confront the responsibility of defining at what point that duty has been violated. It is easy to assert that the legislator has a moral duty to make his laws clear and understandable. But this remains at best an exhortation unless we are prepared to define the degree of clarity he must attain in order to discharge his duty. The notion of subjecting clarity to quantitative measure presents obvious difficulties. We may content ourselves, of course, by saying that the legislator has at least a moral duty to try to be clear. But this only postpones the difficulty, for in some situations nothing can be more baffling than to attempt to measure how vigorously a man intended to that which he has failed to do. In the morality of law, in any event, good intentions are of little avail, as King Rex amply demonstrated. All of this adds up to the conclusion that the inner morality of law is condemned to remain largely a morality of aspiration and not of duty. Its primary appeal must be to a sense of trusteeship and to the pride of the craftsman.

To these observations there is one important exception. This relates to the desideratum of making the laws known, or at least making them available to those affected by them. Here we have a demand that lends itself with unusual readiness to formalization. A written constitution may prescribe that no statute shall become law until it has been given a specified form of publication. If the courts have power to effectuate this provision, we may speak of a legal requirement for the making of law. But a moral duty with respect to publication is also readily imaginable. A custom, for example, might define what kind of promulgation of laws is expected, at the same time leaving unclear what consequences attend a departure from the accepted mode of publication. A formalization of the desideratum of publicity has obvious advantages over uncanalized efforts, even when they are intelligently and conscientiously pursued. A formalized standard of promulgation not only tells the lawmaker where to publish his laws; it also lets the subject—or a lawyer representing his interests—know where to go to learn what the law is.

One might suppose that the principle condemning retroactive laws could also be very readily formalized in a simple rule that no such law should ever be passed, or should be valid if enacted. Such a rule would, however, disserve the cause of legality. Curiously, one of the most obvious seeming demands of legality—that a rule passed today should govern what happens tomorrow, not what happened yesterday—turns out to present some of the most difficult problems of the whole internal morality of law.

With respect to the demands of legality other than promulgation, then, the most we can expect of constitutions and courts is that they save us from the abyss; they cannot be expected to lay out very many compulsory steps toward truly significant accomplishment.

———

Other writers have sought to find in the notion of law itself a limitation on the sorts of abuses which were considered in the discussion of the jurisprudence of naked power. In the following selection, Professor H.L.A. Hart finds within the *concept* of law a certain minimum natural law content which happily conforms to the principles of liberal democracy to which he is committed. After reading the Hart selection, consider the criticism of Hart's position by Professor Fuller, which follows it.

HART, THE MINIMUM CONTENT OF NATURAL LAW, IN THE CONCEPT OF LAW 189-95 (1961)

In considering the simple truisms which we set forth here, and their connexion with law and morals, it is important to observe that in each case the facts mentioned afford a reason why, given survival as an aim, law and morals should include a specific content. The general form of the argument is simply that without such a content laws and morals could not forward the minimum purpose of survival which men have in associating with each other. In the absence of this content men, as they are, would have no reason for obeying voluntarily any rules; and without a minimum of co-operation given voluntarily by those who find that it is in their interest to submit to and maintain the rules, coercion of others who would not voluntarily conform would be impossible. It is important to stress the distinctively rational connexion between natural facts and the content of legal and moral rules in this approach, because it is both possible and important to inquire into quite different forms of connexion between natural facts and legal and moral rules. Thus, the still young sciences of psychology and sociology may discover or may even have discovered that, unless certain physical, psychological, or economic conditions are satisfied, e.g. unless young children are fed and nurtured in certain ways within the family, no system of laws or code of morals can be established, or that only those laws can function successfully which conform to a certain type. Connexions of this sort between natural conditions and systems of rules are not mediated by *reasons;* for they do not relate the existence of certain rules to the conscious aims or purpose of those whose rules they are. Being fed in infancy in a certain way may well be shown to be a necessary condition or even a *cause* of a population developing or maintaining a moral or legal code, but it is not a *reason* for their doing so. Such causal connexions do not of course conflict with the connexions which rest on purposes or conscious aims; they may indeed be considered more important or fundamental than the latter, since they may actually explain why human beings have those conscious aims or purposes which Natural Law takes at its starting-points. Causal explanations of this type do not rest on truisms nor are they mediated by conscious aims or purposes: they are for sociology or psychology like other sciences to establish by the methods of generalization and theory, resting on observation and, where possible, on experiment. Such connexions therefore are of a different kind from those which relate the content of certain legal and moral rules to the facts stated in the following truisms.

(i) *Human vulnerability*. The common requirements of law and morality consist for the most part not of active services to be rendered but of forbearances, which are usually formulated in negative form as prohibitions. Of these the most important for social life are those that restrict the use of violence in killing or inflicting bodily harm. The basic character of such rules may be brought out in a question: If there were not these rules what point could there be for beings such as ourselves in having rules of *any* other kind? The force of this rhetorical question rests on the fact that men are both occasionally prone to, and normally vulnerable to, bodily attack. Yet though this is a truism it is not a necessary truth; for things might have been, and might one day be, otherwise. There are species of animals whose physical structure (including exoskeletons or a carapace) renders them virtually immune from attack by other members of their species and animals who have no organs enabling them to attack. If men were to lose their vulnerability to each other there would vanish one obvious reason for the most characteristic provision of law and morals: *Thou shalt not kill.*

(ii) *Approximate equality.* Men differ from each other in physical strength, agility, and even more in intellectual capacity. Nonetheless it is a fact of quite major importance for the understanding of different forms of law and morality, that no individual is so much more powerful than others, that he is able, without co-operation, to dominate or subdue them for more than a short period. Even the strongest must sleep at times and, when asleep, loses temporarily his superiority. This fact of approximate equality, more than any other, makes obvious the necessity for a system of mutual forbearance and compromise which is the base of both legal and moral obligation. Social life with its rules requiring such forbearances is irksome at times; but it is at any rate less nasty, less brutish, and less short than unrestrained aggression for beings thus approximately equal. It is, of course, entirely consistent with this and an equal truism that when such a system of forbearance is established there will always be some who will wish to exploit it, by simultaneously living within its shelter and breaking its restrictions. This, indeed is, as we later show, one of the natural facts which makes the step from merely moral to organized, legal forms of control a necessary one. Again, things might have been otherwise. Instead of being approximately equal there might have been some men immensely stronger than others and better able to dispense with rest, either because some were in these ways far above the present average, or because most were far below it. Such exceptional men might have much to gain by aggression and little to gain from mutual forbearance or compromise with others. But we need not have recourse to the fantasy of giants among pygmies to see the cardinal importance of the fact of approximate equality: for it is illustrated better by the facts of international life, where there are (or were) vast disparities in strength and vulnerability between the states. This inequality, as we shall later see, between the units of international law is one of the things that has imparted to it a character so different from municipal law and limited the extent to which it is capable of operating as an organized coercive system.

(iii) *Limited altruism.* Men are not devils dominated by a wish to exterminate each other, and the demonstration that, given only the modest aim of survival, the basic rules of law and morals are necessities, must not be identified with the false view that men are predominantly selfish and have no disinterested interest in the survival and welfare of their fellows. But if men are not devils, neither are they angels; and the fact that they are a mean between these two extremes is something which makes a system of mutual forbearances both necessary and possible. With angels, never tempted to harm others, rules requiring forbearances would not be necessary. With devils prepared to destroy, reckless of the cost to themselves, they would be impossible. As things are, human altruism is limited in range and intermittent, and the tendencies to aggression are frequent enough to be fatal to social life if not controlled.

(iv) *Limited resources.* It is a merely contingent fact that human beings need food, clothes, and shelter; that these do not exist at hand in limitless abundance; but are scarce, have to be grown or won from nature, or have to be constructed by human toil. These facts alone make indispensable some minimal form of the institution of property (though not necessarily individual property), and the distinctive kind of rule which requires respect for it. The simplest forms of property are to be seen in rules excluding persons generally other than the 'owner' from entry on, or the use of land, or from taking or using material things. If crops are to grow, land must be secure from indiscriminate entry, and food must, in the intervals between its growth or capture and consumption, be secure from being taken by others. At all times and places life itself depends on these minimal forbearances. Again, in this respect, things might have been otherwise than they are. The human organism might have been constructed like plants, capable of extracting food from air, or what it needs might have grown without cultivation in limitless abundance.

The rules which we have so far discussed are *static* rules, in the sense that the obligations they impose and the incidence of these obligations are not variable by individuals. But the division of labour, which all but the smallest groups must develop to obtain adequate supplies, brings with it the need for rules which are *dynamic* in the sense that they enable individuals to create obligations and to vary their incidence. Among these are rules enabling men to transfer, exchange, or sell their products; for these transactions involve the capacity to alter the incidence of those initial rights and obligations which define the simplest form of property. The same inescapable division of labour, and perennial need for co-operation, are also factors which make other forms of dynamic or obligation-creating rule necessary in social life. These secure the recognition of promises as a source of obligation. By this device individuals are enabled by words, spoken or written, to make themselves liable to blame or punishment for failure to act in certain stipulated ways. Where altruism is not un- limited, a standing procedure providing for such self-binding operations is required in order to create a minimum form of confidence in the future behaviour of others, and to ensure the predictability necessary for co-operation. This is most obviously needed where what is to be exchanged or jointly planned are mutual services, or wherever goods which are to be exchanged or sold are not simultaneously or im- mediately available.

(v) *Limited understanding and strength of will*. The facts that make rules re- specting persons, property, and promises necessary in social life are simple and their mutual benefits are obvious. Most men are capable of seeing them and of sacrificing the immediate short-term interest which conformity to such rules demands. They may indeed obey, from a variety of motives: some from prudential calculation that the sacrifices are worth the gains, some from a disinterested interest in the welfare of others, and some because they look upon the rules as worthy of respect in them- selves and find their ideals in devotion to them. On the other hand, neither under- standing of long-term interest, nor the strength or goodness of will, upon which the efficacy of these different motives towards obedience depends, are shared by all men alike. All are tempted at times to prefer their own immediate interests and, in the absence of a special organization for their detection and punishment, many would succumb to the temptation. No doubt the advantages of mutual forbearance are so palpable that the number and strength of those who would cooperate voluntarily in a coercive system will normally be greater than any likely combination of malefactors. Yet, except in very small close-knit societies, submission to the system of restraints would be folly if there were no organization for the coercion of those who would then try to obtain the advantages of the system without submitting to its obligations.

'Sanctions' are therefore required not as the normal motive for obedience, but as a *guarantee* that those who would voluntarily obey shall not be sacrificed to those who would not. To obey, without this would be to risk going to the wall. Given this standing danger, what reason demands is *voluntary* co-operation in a coercive system.

It is to be observed that the same natural fact of approximate equality between men is of crucial importance in the efficacy of organized sanctions. If some men were vastly more powerful than others, and so not dependent on their forbearance, the strength of the malefactors might exceed that of the supporters of law and order. Given such inequalities, the use of sanctions could not be successful and would involve dangers at least as great as those which they were designed to suppress. In these circumstances instead of social life being based on a system of mutual forbearances, with force used only intermittently against a minority of malefactors, the only viable system would be one in which the weak submitted to the strong on the best terms they could make and lived under their 'protection'. This, because of the scarcity of resources, would lead to a number of conflicting power centres, each grouped round it's 'strong man': these might intermittently war with each other, though the natural sanction, never negligible, of the risk of defeat might ensure an uneasy peace. Rules of a sort might then be accepted for the regulation of issues over which the 'powers' were unwilling to fight. Again we need not think in fanciful terms of pygmies and giants in order to understand the simple logistics of approximate equality and its importance for law. The international scene, where the units concerned have differed vastly in strength, affords illustration enough. For centuries the disparities between states have resulted in a system where organized sanctions have been impossible, and law has been confined to matters which did not affect 'vital' issues. How far atomic weapons, when available to all, will redress the balance of unequal power, and bring forms of control more closely resembling municipal criminal law, remains to be seen.

The simple truisms we have discussed not only disclose the core of good sense in the doctrine of Natural Law. They are of vital importance for the understanding of law and morals, and they explain why the definition of the basic forms of these in purely formal terms, without reference to any specific content or social needs, has proved so inadequate. Perhaps the major benefit to jurisprudence from this outlook is the escape it affords from certain misleading dichotomies which often obscure the discussion of the characteristics of law. Thus, for example, the traditional question whether every legal system *must* provide for sanctions can be presented in a fresh and clearer light, when we command the view of things presented by this simple version of Natural Law. We shall no longer have to choose between two unsuitable alternatives which are often taken as exhaustive: on the one hand that of saying that this is required by 'the' meaning of the words 'law' or 'legal system,' and on the other that of saying that it is 'just a fact' that most legal systems do provide for sanctions. Neither of these alternatives is satisfactory. There are no settled principles forbidding the use of the word 'law' of systems where there are no centrally organized sanctions, and there is good reason (though no compulsion) for using the expression 'international law' of a system, which has none. On the other hand we do need to distinguish the place that sanctions must have within a municipal system, if it is to serve the minimum purposes of beings constituted as men are. We can say, given the setting of natural facts and aims, which make sanctions both possible and necessary in a municipal system, that this is a *natural necessity;* and some such phrase is needed also to convey the status of the minimum forms of protection for persons, property, and promises which are similarly indispensable features of municipal law. It is in this form that we should reply to the positivist thesis that 'law may have any content.' For it is a truth of some importance that for the adequate description not only of law but of many other social institutions, a place must be reserved, besides definitions and ordinary statements of fact, for a third category of statements: those the truth of which is contingent on human beings and the world they live in retaining the salient characteristics which they have.

FULLER, THE MINIMUM CONTENT OF
A SUBSTANTIVE NATURAL LAW, IN
THE MORALITY OF LAW 184-86 (1969)

In seeking to know whether it is possible to derive from the morality of aspiration anything more imperative than mere counsel and encouragement, I have then so far concluded that, since the morality of aspiration is necessarily a morality of human aspiration, it cannot deny the human quality to those who possess it without forfeiting its integrity. Can we derive more than this?

The problem may be stated in another form. In my third chapter I treated what I have called the internal morality of law as itself presenting a variety of natural law. It is, however, a procedural or institutional kind of natural law, though, as I have been at pains in this chapter to show, it affects and limits the substantive aims that can be achieved through law. But can we derive from the morality of aspiration itself any proposition of natural law that is substantive, rather than procedural, in quality?

In his *Concept of Law*, H.L.A. Hart presents what he calls "the minimum content of natural law" (pp. 189-95). Starting with the single objective of human survival, conceived as operating within certain externally imposed conditions, Hart derives, by a process I would describe as purposive implication, a fairly comprehensive set of rules that may be called those of natural law. What is expounded in his interesting discussion is a kind of minimum morality of duty.

Like every morality of duty this minimum natural law says nothing about the question, Who shall be included in the community which accepts and seeks to realize cooperatively the shared objective of survival? In short, who shall survive? No attempt is made to answer this question. Hart simply observes that "our concern is with social arrangements for continued existence, not with those of a suicide club."

In justifying his starting point of survival Hart advances two kinds of reasons. One amounts to saying that survival is a necessary condition for every other human achievement and satisfaction. With this proposition there can be no quarrel.

But in addition to treating survival as a precondition for every other human good, Hart advances a second set of reasons for his starting point—reasons of a very different order. He asserts that men have properly seen that in "the modest aim of survival" lies "the central indisputable element which gives empirical good sense to the terminology of Natural Law." He asserts further that in the teleological elements that run through all moral and legal thinking there is "the tacit assumption that the proper end of human activity is survival." He observes that "an overwhelming majority of men do wish to live even at the cost of hideous misery."

In making these assertions Hart is, I submit, treading more dubious ground. For he is no longer claiming for survival that it is a necessary condition for the achievement of other ends, but seems to be saying that it furnishes the core and central element of all human striving. This, I think, cannot be accepted. As Thomas Aquinas remarked long ago, if the highest aim of a captain were to preserve his ship, he would keep it in port forever. As for the proposition that the overwhelming majority of men wish to survive even at the cost of hideous misery, this seems to me of doubtful truth. If it were true, I question whether it would have any particular relevance to moral theory.

Hart's search for a "central indisputable element" in human striving raises the question whether in fact this search can be successful. I believe that if we were forced to select the principle that supports and infuses all human aspiration we would find it in the objective of maintaining communication with our fellows.

In the first place—staying within the limits of Hart's own argument—man has been able to survive up to now because of his capacity for communication. In competition with other creatures, often more powerful than he and sometimes gifted with keener senses, man has so far been the victor. His victory has come about because he can acquire and transmit knowledge and because he can consciously and deliberately effect a coordination of effort with other human beings. If in the future man succeeds in surviving his own powers of self-destruction, it will be because he can communicate and reach understanding with his fellows. Finally, I doubt if most of us would regard as desirable survival into a kind of vegetable existence in which we could make no meaningful contact with other human beings.

Communication is something more than a means of staying alive. It is a way of being alive. It is through communication that we inherit the achievements of past human effort. The possibility of communication can reconcile us to the thought of death by assuring us that what we achieve will enrich the lives of those to come. How and when we accomplish communication with one another can expand or contract the boundaries of life itself. In the words of Wittgenstein, "The limits of my language are the limits of my world."

If I were asked, then, to discern one central indisputable principle of what may be called substantive natural law—Natural Law with capital letters—I would find it in the injunction: Open up, maintain, and preserve the integrity of the channels of communication by which men convey to one another what they perceive, feel, and desire. In this matter the morality of aspiration offers more than good counsel and the challenge of excellence. It here speaks with the imperious voice we are accustomed to hear from the morality of duty. And if men will listen, that voice, unlike that of the morality of duty, can be heard across the boundaries and through the barriers that now separate men from one another.

NOTES

1. Are Hart's and Fuller's minimum concepts of natural law (i.e. survival or communication) adequate guides for legal decisionmaking problems facing the contemporary community, such as war, maintenance of adequate health, abortions, euthanasia, racial bigotry or preference, etc.?

2. Is anything gained by calling the need for communication or survival, "natural"? Does the use of the term "natural" by Hart and Fuller tend to obscure the need to think systematically about the goals which society should seek and the steps necessary to implement such goals?

THE STRUCTURAL NATURE OF JUSTICE

Naturalism, as we have seen, appears in many guises and disguises. In one form, the writer, ostensibly developing philosophical principles may, in fact, be doing no more than declaring certain preferences that human beings reach because of institution, cultural conditioning or instinct. In the preceding chapter, we considered John Rawls' principles with regard to civil disobedience. The more general postulates on which that theory rested were developed as intuitive convictions of justice, imagined primary agreements and the device of "a veil of ignorance" in "the original position" by which a scholar could determine what were the inexorable principles by which human beings would organize their lives.

RAWLS, A THEORY OF JUSTICE
3-15, 17-22, 1:8-116 (1971)

1. THE ROLE OF JUSTICE

Justice is the first virtue of social institutions, as truth is of systems of thought. A theory however elegant and economical must be rejected or revised if it is untrue; likewise laws and institutions no matter how efficient and well-arranged must be reformed or abolished if they are unjust. Each person possesses an inviolability founded on justice that even the welfare of society as a whole cannot override. For this reason justice denies that the loss of freedom for some is made right by a greater good shared by others. It does not allow that the sacrifices imposed on a few are outweighed by the larger sum of advantages enjoyed by many. Therefore in a just society the liberties of equal citizenship are taken as settled; the rights secured by justice are not subject to political bargaining or to the calculus of social interests. The only thing that permits us to acquiesce in an erroneous theory is the lack of a better one; analogously, an injustice is tolerable only when it is necessary to avoid an even greater injustice. Being first virtues of human activities, truth and justice are uncompromising.

These propositions seem to express our intuitive conviction of the primacy of justice. No doubt they are expressed too strongly. In any event I wish to inquire whether these contentions or others similar to them are sound, and if so how they can be accounted for. To this end it is necessary to work out a theory of justice in the light of which these assertions can be interpreted and assessed. I shall begin by considering the role of the principles of justice. Let us assume, to fix ideas, that a society is a more or less self-sufficient association of persons who in their relations to one another recognize certain rules of conduct as binding and who for the most part act in accordance with them. Suppose further that these rules specify a system of cooperation designed to advance the good of those taking part in it. Then, although a society is a cooperative venture for mutual advantage, it is typically marked by a conflict as well as by an identity of interests. There is an identity of interests since social cooperation makes possible a better life for all than any would have if each were to live solely by his own efforts. There is a conflict of interests since persons are not indifferent as to how the greater benefits produced by their collaboration are distributed, for in order to pursue their ends they each prefer a larger to a lesser share. A set of principles is required for choosing among the various social arrangements which determine this division of advantages and for underwriting an agreement on the proper distributive shares. There principles are the principles of social justice: they provide a way of assigning rights and duties in the basic institutions of society and they define the appropriate distribution of the benefits and burdens of social cooperation.

Now let us say that a society is well-ordered when it is not only designed to advance the good of its members but when it is also effectively regulated by a public conception of justice. That is, it is a society in which (1) everyone accepts and knows that the others accept the same principles of justice, and (2) the basic social institutions generally satisfy and are generally known to satisfy these principles. In this case while men may put forth excessive demands on one another, they nevertheless acknowledge a common point of view from which their claims may be adjudicated. If men's inclination to self-interest makes their vigilance against one another necessary, their public sense of justice makes their secure association together possible. Among individuals with disparate aims and purposes a shared conception of justice establishes the bonds of civic friendship; the general desire for justice limits the pursuit of other ends. One may think of a public conception of justice as constituting the fundamental charter of a well-ordered human association.

Existing societies are of course seldom well-ordered in this sense, for what is just and unjust is usually in dispute. Men disagree about which principles should define the basic terms of their association. Yet we may still say, despite this disagreement, that they each have a conception of justice. That is, they understand the need for, and they are prepared to affirm, a characteristic set of principles for assigning basic rights and duties and for determining what they take to be the proper distribution of the benefits and burdens of social cooperation. Thus it seems natural to think of the concept of justice as distinct from the various conceptions of justice and as being specified by the role which these different sets of principles, these different conceptions, have in common. Those who hold different conceptions of justice can, then, still agree that institutions are just when no arbitrary distinctions are made between persons in the assigning of basic rights and duties and when the rules determine a proper balance between competing claims to the advantages of social life. Men can agree to this description of just institutions since the notions of an arbitrary distinction and of a proper balance, which are included in the concept of justice, are left open for each to interpret according to the principles of justice that he accepts. These principles single out which similarities and differences among persons are relevant in determining rights and duties and they specify which division of advantages is appropriate. Clearly this distinction between the concept and the various conceptions of justice settles no important questions. It simply helps to identify the role of the principles of social justice.

· · ·

2. THE SUBJECT OF JUSTICE

Many different kinds of things are said to be just and unjust: not only laws, institutions, and social systems, but also particular actions of many kinds, including decisions, judgments, and imputations. We also call the attitudes and dispositions of persons, and persons themselves, just and unjust. Our topic, however, is that of social justice. For us the primary subject of justice is the basic structure of society, or more exactly, the way in which the major social institutions distribute fundamental rights and duties and determine the division of advantages from social cooperation. By major institutions I understand the political constitution and the principal economic and social arrangements. Thus the legal protection of freedom of thought and liberty of conscience, competitive markets, private property in the means of production, and the monogamous family are examples of major social institutions. Taken together as one scheme, the major institutions define men's rights and duties and influence their life prospects, what they can expect to be and how well they can hope to do.

The basic structure is the primary subject of justice because its effects are so profound and present from the start. The intuitive notion here is that this structure contains various social positions and that men born into different positions have different expectations of life determined, in part, by the political system as well as by economic and social circumstances. In this way the institutions of society favor certain starting places over others. These are especially deep inequalities. Not only are they pervasive, but they affect men's initial chances in life; yet they cannot possibly be justified by an appeal to the notions of merit or desert. It is these inequalities, presumably inevitable in the basic structure of any society, to which the principles of social justice must in the first instance apply. These principles, then, regulate the choice of a political constitution and the main elements of the economic and social system. The justice of a social scheme depends essentially on how fundamental rights and duties are assigned and on the economic opportunities and social conditions in the various sectors of society.

. . . I shall be satisfied if it is possible to formulate a reasonable conception of justice for the basic structure of society conceived for the time being as a closed system isolated from other societies. The significance of this special case is obvious and needs no explanation. It is natural to conjecture that once we have a sound theory for this case, the remaining problems of justice will prove more tractable in the light of it. With suitable modifications such a theory should provide the key for some of these other questions.

The other limitation on our discussion is that for the most part I examine the principles of justice that would regulate a well-ordered society. Everyone is presumed to act justly and to do his part in upholding just institutions. Though justice may be, as Hume remarked, the cautious, jealous virtue, we can still ask what a perfectly just society would be like. . . .

Now admittedly the concept of the basic structure is somewhat vague. It is not always clear which institutions or features thereof should be included. But it would be premature to worry about this matter here. . . .

A conception of social justice, then, is to be regarded as providing in the first instance a standard whereby the distributive aspects of the basic structure of society are to be assessed. This standard, however, is not to be confused with the principles defining the other virtues, for the basic structure, and social arrangements generally, may be efficient or inefficient, liberal or illiberal, and many other things, as well as just or unjust. A complete conception defining principles for all the virtues of the basic structure, together with their respective weights when they conflict, is more than a conception of justice; it is a social ideal. The principles of justice are but a part, although perhaps the most important part, of such a conception. A social ideal in turn is connected with a conception of society, a vision of the way in which the aims and purposes of social cooperation are to be understood. . . .

In these preliminary remarks I have distinguished the concept of justice as meaning a proper balance between competing claims from a conception of justice as a set of related principles for identifying the relevant considerations which determine this balance. I have also characterized justice as but one part of a social idea, although the theory I shall propose no doubt extends its everyday sense. This theory is not offered as a description of ordinary meanings but as an account of certain distributive principles for the basic structure of society. I assume that any reasonably complete ethical theory must include principles for this fundamental problem and that these principles, whatever they are, constitute its doctrine of justice. The concept of justice

I take to be defined, then, by the role of its principles in assigning rights and duties and in defining the appropriate division of social advantages. A conception of justice is an interpretation of this role.

• • •

3. THE MAIN IDEA OF THE THEORY OF JUSTICE

My aim is to present a conception of justice which generalizes and carries to a higher level of abstraction the familiar theory of the social contract as found, say in Locke, Rousseau, and Kant. In order to do this we are not to think of the original contract as one to enter a particular society or to set up a particular form of government. Rather, the guiding idea is that the principles of justice for the basic structure of society are the object of the original agreement. They are the principles that free and rational persons concerned to further their own interests would accept in an initial position of equality as defining the fundamental terms of their association. These principles are to regulate all further agreements; they specify the kinds of social cooperation that can be entered into the forms of government that can be established. This way of regarding the principles of justice I shall call justice as fairness.

Thus we are to imagine that those who engage in social cooperation choose together, in one joint act, the principles which are to assign basic rights and duties and to determine the division of social benefits. Men are to decide in advance how they are to regulate their claims against one another and what is to be the foundation charter of their society. Just as each person must decide by rational reflection what constitutes his good, that is, the system of ends which it is rational for him to pursue, so a group of persons must decide once and for all what is to count among them as just and unjust. The choice which rational men would make in this hypothetical situation of equal liberty, assuming for the present that this choice problem has a solution, determines the principles of justice.

In justice as fairness the original position of equality corresponds to the state of nature in the traditional theory of the social contract. This original position is not, of course, thought of as an actual historical state of affairs, much less as a primitive condition of culture. It is understood as a purely hypothetical situation characterized so as to lead to a certain conception of justice. Among the essential features of this situation is that no one knows his place in society, his class position or social status, nor does any one know his fortune in the distribution of natural assets and abilities, his intelligence, strength, and the like. I shall even assume that the parties do not know their conceptions of the good or their special psychological propensities. The principles of justice are chosen behind a veil of ignorance. This ensures that no one is advantaged or disadvantaged in the choice of principles by the outcome of natural chance or the contingency of social circumstances. Since all are similarly situated and no one is able to design principles to favor his particular condition, the principles of justice are the result of a fair agreement or bargain. For given the circumstances of the original position, the symmetry of everyone's relations to each other, this initial situation is fair between individuals as moral persons, that is, as rational beings with their own ends and capable, I shall assume, of a sense of justice. The original position is, one might say, the appropriate initial status quo, and thus the fundamental agreements reached on it are fair. The explains the propriety of the name "justice as fairness": it conveys the idea that the principles of justice are agreed to in an initial situation that is fair. The name does not mean that the concepts of justice and fairness are the same, any more than the phrase "poetry as metaphor" means that the concepts of poetry and metaphor are the same.

Justice as fairness begins, as I have said, with one of the most general of all choices which persons might make together, namely, with the choice of the first principles of a conception of justice which is to regulate all subsequent criticism and reform of institutions. Then, having chosen a conception of justice, we can suppose that they are to choose a constitution and a legislature to enact laws, and so on, all in accordance with the principles of justice initially agreed upon. . . .

One feature of justice as fairness is to think of the parties in the initial situation as rational and mutually disinterested. This does not mean that the parties are egoists, that is, individuals with only certain kinds of interests, say in wealth, prestige, and domination. But they are conceived as not taking an interest in one another's interests. . . .

In working out the conception of justice as fairness one main task clearly is to determine which principles of justice would be chosen in the original position. To do this we must describe this situation in some detail and formulate with care the problem of choice which it presents. These matters I shall take up in the immediately succeeding chapters. It may be observed, however, that once the principles of justice are thought of as arising from an original agreement in a situation of equality, it is an open question whether the principle of utility would be acknowledged. Offhand it hardly seems likely that persons who view themselves as equals, entitled to press their claims upon one another, would agree to a principle which may require lesser life prospects for some simply for the sake of a greater sum of advantages enjoyed by others. Since each desires to protect his interests, his capacity to advance his conception of the good, no one has a reason to acquiesce in an enduring loss for himself in order to bring about a greater net balance of satisfaction. In the absence of strong and lasting benevolent impulses, a rational man would not accept a basic structure merely because it maximized the algebraic sum of advantages irrespective of its permanent effects on his own basic rights and interests. Thus it seems that the principle of utility is incompatible with the conception of social cooperation among equals for mutual advantage. It appears to be inconsistent with the idea of reciprocity implicit in the notion of a well-ordered society. Or, at any rate, so I shall argue.

I shall maintain instead that the persons in the initial situation would choose two rather different principles; the first requires equality in the assignment of basic rights and duties, while the second holds that social and economic inequalities, for example inequalities of wealth and authority, are just only if they result in compensating benefits for everyone, and in particular for the least advantaged members of society. These principles rule out justifying institutions on the grounds that the hardships of some are offset by a greater good in the aggregate. It may be expedient but it is not just that some should have less in order than others may prosper. But there is no injustice in the greater benefits earned by a few provided that the situations of persons not so fortunate is thereby improved. The intuitive idea is that since everyone's well-being depends upon a scheme of cooperation without which no one could have a satisfactory life, the division of advantages should be such as to draw forth the willing cooperation of everyone taking part in it, including those less well situated. Yet this can be expected only if reasonable terms are proposed. The two principles mentioned seem to be a fair agreement on the basis of which those better endowed, or more fortunate in their social position, neither of which we can be said to deserve, could expect the willing cooperation of others when some workable scheme is a necessary condition of the welfare of all. Once we decide to look for a conception of justice that nullifies the accidents of natural endowment and the contingencies of social circumstance as counters in quest for political and economic advantage, we are led to these principles. They express the result of leaving aside those aspects of the social world that seem arbitrary from a moral point of view.

A final remark. . . . Justice as fairness is not a complete contract theory. For it is clear that the contractarian idea can be extended to the choice of more or less an entire ethical system, that is, to a system including principles for all the virtues and not only for justice. . . .

4. THE ORIGINAL POSITION AND JUSTIFICATION

I have said that the original position is the appropriate initial status quo which insures that the fundamental agreements reached in it are fair. This fact yields the name "justice as fairness." It is clear, then, that I want to say that one conception of justice is more reasonable than another, or justifiable with respect to it, if rational persons in the initial situation would choose its principles over those of the other for the role of justice. Conceptions of justice are to be ranked by their acceptability to persons so circumstanced. Understood in this way the question of justification is settled by working out a problem of deliberation: we have to ascertain which principles it would be rational to adopt given the contractual situation. This connects the theory of justice with the theory of rational choice.

If this view of the problem of justification is too succeed, we must, of course, describe in some detail the nature of this choice problem. A problem of rational decision has a definite answer only if we know the beliefs and interests of the parties, their relations with respect to one another, the alternatives between which they are to choose, the procedure whereby they make up their minds, and so on. As the circumstances are presented in different ways, correspondingly different principles are accepted. The concept of the original position, as I shall refer to it, is that of the most philosophically favored interpretation of this initial choice situation for the purposes of a theory of justice.

But how are we to decide what is the most favored interpretation? I assume, for one thing, that there is a broad measure of agreement that principles of justice should be chosen under certain conditions. To justify a particular description of the initial situation one shows that it incorporates these commonly shared presumptions. . . .

One should not be misled, then, by the somewhat unusual conditions which characterize the original position. The idea here is simply to make vivid to ourselves the restrictions that it seems reasonable to impose on arguments for principles of justice, and therefore on these principles themselves. Thus it seems reasonable and generally acceptable that no one should be advantaged or disadvantaged by natural fortune or social circumstances in the choice of principles. It also seems widely agreed that it should be impossible to tailor principles to the circumstances of one's own case. We should insure further that particular inclinations and aspirations, and persons' conceptions of their good do not affect the principles adopted. The aim is to rule out those principles that it would be rational to propose for acceptance, however little the chance of success, only if one knew certain things that are irrelevant from the standpoint of justice. For example, if a man knew that he was wealthy, he might find it rational to advance the principle that various taxes for welfare measures be counted unjust; if he knew that he was poor, he would most likely propose the contrary principle. To represent the desired restrictions one imagines a situation in which everyone is deprived of this sort of information. One excludes the knowledge of those contingencies which sets men at odds and allows them to be guided by their prejudices. In this manner the veil of ignorance is arrived at in a natural way. This concept should cause no difficulty if we keep in mind the constraints on arguments that it is meant to express. At any time we can enter the original position, so to speak, simply by following a certain procedure, namely, by arguing for principles of justice in accordance with these restrictions.

It seems reasonable to suppose that the parties in the original position are equal. That is, all have the same rights in the procedure for choosing principles; each can make proposals, submit reasons for their acceptance, and so on. Obviously the purpose of these conditions is to represent equality between human beings as moral persons, as creatures having a conception of their good and capable of a sense of justice. The basis of equality is taken to be similarity in these two respects. Systems of ends are not ranked in value; and each man is presumed to have the requisite ability to understand and to act upon whatever principles are adopted. Together with the veil of ignorance, these conditions define the principles of justice as those which rational persons concerned to advance their interests would consent to as equals when none are known to be advantaged or disadvantaged by social and natural contingencies.

There is, however, another side to justifying a particular description of the original position. This is to see if the principles which would be chosen match our considered convictions of justice or extend them in an acceptable way. We can note whether applying these principles would lead us to make the same judgments about the basic structure of society which we now make intuitively and in which we have the greatest confidence; or whether, in cases where our present judgments are in doubt and given with hesitation, these principles offer a resolution which we can affirm on reflection. There are questions which we feel sure must be answered in a certain way. For example, we are confident that religious intolerance and racial discrimination are unjust. We think that we have examined these things with care and have reached what we believe is an impartial judgment not likely to be distorted by an excessive attention to our own interests. These convictions are provisional fixed points which we presume any conception of justice must fit. But we have much less assurance as to what is the correct distribution of wealth and authority. Here we may be looking for a way to remove our doubts. We can check an interpretation of the initial situation, then, but the capacity of its principles to accommodate our firmest convictions and to provide guidance where guidance is needed.

In searching for the most favored description of this situation we work from both ends. We begin by describing it so that it represents generally shared and preferably weak conditions. We then see if these conditions are strong enough to yield a significant set of principles. If not, we look for further premises equally reasonable. But if so, and these principles match our considered convictions of justice, then so far well and good. But presumably there will be discrepancies. In this case we have a choice. But can either modify the account of the initial situation or we can revise our existing judgments, for even the judgments we take provisionally as fixed points are liable to revision. By going back and forth, sometimes altering the conditions of the contractual circumstances, at others withdrawing our judgments and conforming them to principle, I assume that eventually we shall find a description of the initial situation that both expresses reasonable conditions and yields principles which match our considered judgments duly pruned and adjusted. This state of affairs I refer to as reflective equilibrium. It is an equilibrium because at last our principles and judgments coincide; and it is reflective since we know to what principles our judgments conform and the premises of their derivation. At the moment everything is in order. But this equilibrium is not necessarily stable. It is liable to be upset by further examination of the conditions which should be imposed on the contractual situation and by particular cases which may lead us to revise our judgments. Yet for the time being we have done what we can to render coherent and to justify our convictions of social justice. We have reached a conception of the original position.

I shall not, of course, actually work through this process. Still, we may think of the interpretation of the original position that I shall present as the result of such a hypothetical course of reflection. It represents the attempt to accommodate within one scheme both reasonable philosophical conditions on principles as well as our considered judgments of justice. In arriving at the favored interpretation of the initial situation there is no point at which an appeal is made to self-evidence in the traditional sense either of general conceptions or particular convictions. I do not claim for the principles of justice proposed that they are necessary truths or derivable from such truths. A conception of justice cannot be deduced from self-evident premises or conditions on principles; instead, its justification is a matter of the mutual support of many considerations, of everything fitting together into one coherent view.

A final comment. We shall want to say that certain principles of justice are justified because they would be agreed to in an initial situation of equality. I have emphasized that this original position is purely hypothetical. It is natural to ask why, if this agreement is never actually entered into, we should take any interest in these principles, moral or otherwise. The answer is that the conditions emobodied in the description of the original position are ones that we do in fact accept. Or if we do not, then perhaps we can be persuaded to do so by philosophical reflection. Each aspect of the contractual situation can be given supporting grounds. Thus what we shall do is to collect together into one conception a number of conditions on principles that we are ready upon due consideration to recognize as reasonable. These constraints express what we are prepared to regard as limits on fair terms of social cooperation. One way to look at the idea of the original position, therefore, is to see it as an expository device which sums up the meaning of these conditions and helps us to extract their consequences. On the other hand, this conception is also an intuitive notion that suggests its own elaboration, so that led on by it we are drawn to define more clearly the standpoint from which we can best interpret moral relationships. We need a conception that enables us to envision our objective from afar: the intuitive notion of the original position is to do this for us.

● ● ●

18. PRINCIPLES FOR INDIVIDUALS: THE PRINCIPLE OF FAIRNESS

In the discussion so far I have considered the principles which apply to institutions or, more exactly, to the basic structure of society. It is clear, however, that principles of another kind must also be chosen, since a complete theory of right includes principles for individuals as well. In fact, as the accompanying diagram indicates, one needs in addition principles for the law of nations and of course priority rule for assigning weights when principles conflict. . . .

The accompanying diagram is purely schematic. It is not suggested that the principles associated with the concepts lower down in the tree are deduced from the higher ones. The diagram simply indicates the kinds of principles that must be chosen before a full conception of right is on hand. The Roman numerals express the order in which the various sorts of principles are to be acknowledged in the original position. Thus the principles for the basic structure of society are to be agreed to first, principles for individuals next, followed by those for the law of nations. Last of all the priority rules are adopted, although we may tentatively choose these earlier contingent on subsequent revision.

Now the order in which principles are chosen raises a number of questions which I shall skip over. The important thing is that the various principles are to be adopted in a definite sequence. . . .

Therefore, to establish a complete conception of right, the parties in the original position are to choose in a definite order not only a conception of justice but also principles to go with each major concept falling under the concept of right. These concepts are I assume relatively few in number and have a determinate relation to each other. Thus, in addition to principle for institutions there must be an agreement on principles for such notions as fairness and fidelity, mutual respect and beneficence as these apply to individuals, as well as on principles for the conduct of states. The intuitive idea is this: the concept of something's being right is the same as, or better, may be replaced by, the concept of its being in accordance with the principles that in the original position would be acknowledged to apply to things of its kind. I do not interpret this concept of right as providing an analysis of the meaning of the term "right" as normally used in moral contexts. It is not meant as an analysis of the concept of right in the traditional sense. Rather, the broader notion of rightness as fairness is to be understood as a replacement for existing conceptions. There is no necessity to say that sameness of meaning holds between the word "right" (and its relatives) in its ordinary use and the more elaborate locutions needed to express this ideal contractarian concept of right. . . .

I now turn to one of the principles that applies to individuals, the principle of fairness. I shall try to use this principle to account for all requirements that are obligations as distinct from natural duties. This principle holds that a person is required to do his part as defined by the rules of an institution when two conditions are met: first, the institution is just (or fair), that is, it satisfies the two principles of justice; and second, one has voluntarily accepted the benefits of the arrangement or taken advantage of the opportunities it offers to further one's interests. The main idea is that when a number of persons engage in a mutually advantageous cooperative venture according to rules, and thus restrict their liberty in ways necessary to yield advantages for all, those who have submitted to these restrictions have a right to a similar acquiescence on the part of those who have benefited from their submission. We are not to gain from the cooperative labors of others without doing our fair share. The two principles of justice define what is a fair share in the case of institutions belonging to the basic structure. So if these arrangements are just, each person receives a fair share when all (himself included) do their part.

Now by definition the requirements specified by the principle of fairness are the obligations. All obligations arise in this way. It is important, however, to note that the principle of fairness has two parts, the first which states that the institutions or practices in question must be just, the second which characterizes the requisite voluntary acts. The first part formulates the conditions necessary if these voluntary acts are to give rise to obligations. By the principle of fairness it is not possible to

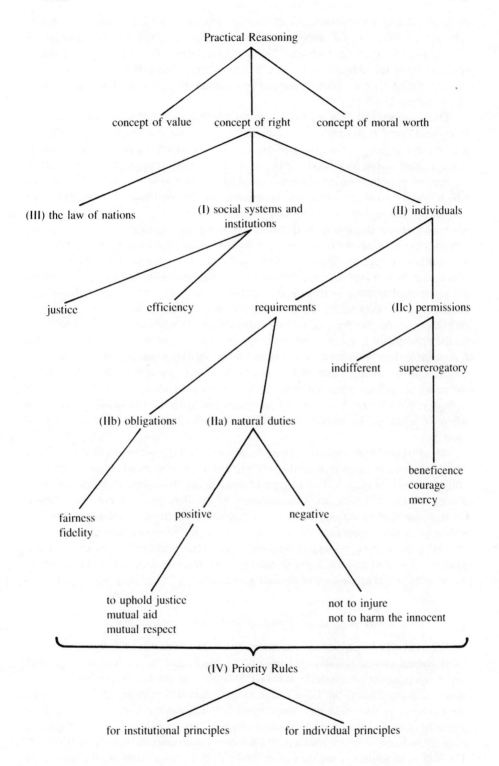

be bound to unjust institutions, or at least to institutions which exceed the limits of tolerable injustice (so far undefined). In particular, it is not possible to have an obligation to autocratic and arbitrary forms of government. The necessary background does not exist for obligations to arise from consensual or other acts, however expressed. Obligatory ties presuppose just institutions, or ones reasonably just in view of the circumstances. . . .

There are several characteristic features of obligations which distinguish them from other moral requirements. For one thing, they arise as a result of our voluntary acts; these acts may be the giving of express or tacit undertakings, such as promises and agreements, but they need not be, as in the case of accepting benefits. Further, the content of obligations is always defined by an institution or practice the rules of which specify what it is that one is required to do. And finally, obligations are normally owed to definite individuals, namely, those who are cooperating together to maintain the arrangement in question. As an example illustrating these features, consider the political act of running for and (if successful) holding public office in a constitutional regime. This act gives rise to the obligation to fulfill the duties of office, and these duties determine the content of the obligation. Here I think of duties not as moral duties but as tasks and responsibilities assigned to certain institutional positions. It is nevertheless the case that one may have a moral reason (one based on a moral principle) for discharging these duties, as when one is bound to do so by the principle of fairness. Also, one who assumes public office is obligated to his fellow citizens whose trust and confidence he has sought and with whom he is cooperating in running a democratic society. Similarly, we assume obligations when we marry as well as when we accept positions of judicial, administrative, or other authority. We acquire obligations by promising and by tacit understandings, and even when we join a game, namely, the obligation to play by the rules and to be a good sport.

All of these obligations are, I believe, covered by the principle of fairness. There are two important cases though that are somewhat problematical, namely, political obligation as it applies to the average citizen, rather than, say, to those who hold office, and the obligation to keep promises. In the first case it is not clear what is the requisite binding action or who has performed it. There is, I believe, no political obligation, strictly speaking, for citizens generally. In the second case an explanation is needed as to how fiduciary obligations arise from taking advantage of a just practice. We need to look into the nature of the relevant practice in this instance. These matters I shall discuss at another place. . . .

19. PRINCIPLES FOR INDIVIDUALS: THE NATURAL DUTIES

Whereas all obligations are accounted for by the principle of fairness, there are many natural duties, positive and negative. I shall make no attempt to bring them under one principle. Admittedly this lack of unity runs the risk of putting too much strain on priority rules, but I shall have to leave this difficulty aside. The following are examples of natural duties: the duty of helping another when he is in need or jeopardy, provided that one can do so without excessive risk or loss to oneself; the duty not to harm or injure another; and the duty not to cause unnecessary suffering. The first of these duties, the duty of mutual aid, is a positive duty in that it is a duty to do something good for another; whereas the last two duties are negative in that they require us not to do something that is bad. The distinction between positive and negative duties is intuitively clear in many cases, but often gives way. I shall not put any stress upon it. The distinction is important only in connection with the priority problem, since it seems plausible to hold that, when the distinction is clear, negative duties have more weight than positive ones. But I shall not pursue this question here.

Now in contrast with obligations, it is characteristic of natural duties that they apply to us without regard to our voluntary acts. Moreover, they have no necessary connection with institutions or social practices; their content is not, in general, defined by the rules of these arrangements. Thus we have a natural duty not to be cruel, and a duty to help another, whether or not we have committed ourselves to these actions. It is no defense or excuse to say that we have made no promise not to be cruel or vindictive, or to come to another's aid. Indeed, a promise not to kill, for example, is normally ludicrously redundant, and the suggestion that it establishes a moral requirement when none already existed is mistaken. Such a promise is in order, if it ever is so, only when for special reasons one has the right to kill, perhaps in a situation arising in a just war. A further feature of natural duties is that they hold between persons irrespective of their institutional relationships; they obtain between all as equal moral persons. In this sense the natural duties are owed not only to definite individuals, say to those cooperating together in a particular social arrangement, but to persons generally. This feature in particular suggests the propriety of the adjective "natural." One aim of the law of nations is to assure the recognition of these duties in the conduct of states. This is especially important in constraining the means used in war, assuming that, in certain circumstances anyway, wars of self-defense are justified.

From the standpoint of justice as fairness, a fundamental natural duty is the duty of justice. This duty requires us to support and to comply with just institutions that exist and apply to us. It also constrains us to further just arrangements not yet established, at least when this can be done without too much cost to ourselves. Thus if the basic structure of society is just, or as just as it is reasonable to expect in the circumstances, everyone has a natural duty to do his part in the existing scheme. Each is bound to these institutions independent of his voluntary acts, performative or otherwise. Thus even though the principles of natural duty are derived from a contractarian point of view, they do not presuppose an act of consent, express or tacit, or indeed any voluntary act, in order to apply. The principles that hold for individuals, just as the principles for institutions, are those that would be acknowledged in the original position. These principles are understood as the outcome of a hypothetical agreement. If their formulation shows that no binding action, consensual or otherwise, is a presupposition of their application, then they apply unconditionally. The reason why obligations depend upon voluntary acts is given by the second part of the principle of fairness which states this condition. It has nothing to do with the contractual nature of justice as fairness. In fact, once the full set of principles, a complete conception of right, is on hand, we can simply forget about the conception of original position and apply these principles as we would any others.

There is nothing inconsistent, or even surprising, in the fact that justice as fairness allows unconditional principles. It suffices to show that the parties in the original position would agree to principles defining the natural duties which as formulated hold unconditionally. We should note that, since the principle of fairness may establish a bond to existing just arrangements, the obligations covered by it can support a tie already present that derives from the natural duty of justice. Thus a person may have both a natural duty and an obligation to comply with an institution and to do his part. The thing to observe here is that there are several ways in which one may be bound to political institutions. For the most part the natural duty of justice is the more fundamental, since it binds citizens generally and requires no voluntary acts in order to apply. The principle of fairness, on the other hand, binds only those who assume public office, say, or those who, being better situated, have advanced their aims within the system. There is, then, another sense of *noblesse oblige:* namely, that those who are more privileged are likely to acquire obligations tying them even more strongly to a just scheme.

NOTES

1. Note Rawls' statements about "our *intuitive* conviction of the primacy of justice" and his many formulations in terms such as "now *let us say* that a society is well ordered when . . ."; ". . . the basic structure (of society) as *intuitively* understood . . ."; his belief that his ". . . concept of the original position . . . is that of the most *philosophically favored* interpretation of this original choice for the purposes of a theory of justice"; his position that one should ". . . check an interpretation of the original situation, then, by the capacity of its principles to accommodate our firmest convictions . . ."; and that there must be a "process of mutual adjustment of principles and considered judgments . . ."; and that the "initial situation" must "yield to principles which match our considered judgments duly pruned and adjusted"; that if we do not accept the conditions that Rawls postulated in his "original position" and the principles that he derived therefrom; ". . . perhaps *we can be persuaded to do so* by philosophical reflection"; and furthermore that "we want to define the original position *so that we get the desired solution*" (emphasis added). Note also Rawls' postulation of a hypothetical "original agreement" and a "veil of ignorance" in which persons do not know their class positions, intelligence, strength, or even their conceptions of the good or the level of civilization or culture of their society, yet formulate complex principles of justice that Rawls espouses. What does Rawls seem to mean by "principles"? Are they empirically verifiable? Is his postulation plausible? What purposes does it serve?

2. Could one just as easily postulate different principles, for example, that freedom, not equality, is the basic foundation for a just society, or that government ownership of property is the touchstone? Or that the survival, at all costs, of a particular group, or tribe, is the most fundamental principle?

3. Basic to Rawls' scheme is the notion that whatever rational men agree upon is "just" and "fair," although even the knowledge of rational men (which forms the basis of decisions reached by them) might in time be shown to be completely erroneous by changes in science and human knowledge. Indeed, according to Rawls, rational men may differ on many matters, including, the extent to which government control of individual action is desirable. Do you think that in addressing such a question, one should take account of the influence of culture, class, sex group, crisis experience etc. on rationality? Discuss. Compare Plato's and Aquinas' notion of a higher law (supra) by which the law of even rational man could be measured. Does Rawls have such a device?

4. Is it correct to assume that human beings are rational? Discuss.

5. What use does Rawls' "original position" methodology serve? Is it useful only for hindsight, but not for guidance as to future conduct? For example, it is conceivable that a meeting of "rational men" that took place 200 years ago might have agreed that women, slaves, and non-property owners should *not* vote. Do Rawls' principles provide guidance for issues that remain unsettled today, such as whether abortions should be permitted? Discuss.

6. As we noted in Chapter 1, one of the functions of a lawyer in a society with the technological capacity to shape itself, is to help that society determine its objectives or clarify its goals. In performing this task, is it useful to use the word "natural," when the word is no more than a summary of what has been achieved in the past but is not indicative of what may be achieved in the future? In this respect, should the introduction of the word "natural" as it pertains either to the physical features of human beings, their capacities or the structural features of social or physical orders, including law, be viewed as pernicious? After all, doesn't it short-circuit the whole process of determining what we want by imposing a template of what has been? Discuss.

P. Brest, *Processes of Constitutional Decision-Making* (1975).

G. Calabresi & P. Bobbit, *Tragic Choices* (1978).

L. Coser, *The Functions of Social Conflict* (1966).

J. Dukeminier, Supplying Organs for Transplantation, 68 *Mich. L. Rev.* 811 (1970).

H. L. A. Hart, *Law, Liberty and Morality* (1963).

R. J. Herrnstein, *I. Q. in the Meritocracy* (1971).

O. W. Holmes, Natural Law, in *Collected Legal Papers* 310 (1920).

Death, Dying and Euthanasia (D. J. Horan & D. Mall eds. 1981).

K. Jaspers, The Unconditional Imperative and Man, in *The Way to Wisdom: An Introduction to Philosophy* 52 (1954).

J. Katz & A. M. Capron, *Catastrophic Decisions: Who Decides What?* (1978).

K. Lorenz, *On Aggression* (1974).

K. Millett, *Sexual Politics* 23-58 (1970).

New Perspectives on Human Abortion (T. W. Hilgers, D. J. Horan, & D. Mall eds. 1981).

R. Nisbet, Book Review, *Pub. Interest,* Spring, 1974, at 121.

F. Northrop, Contemporary Jurisprudence and International Law, 61 *Yale L. J.* 623 (1952).

T. Regan, *Matters of Life and Death: New Introductory Essays in Moral Philosophy* (1980).

D. Richards, Sexual Autonomy and the Constitutional Right to Privacy: A Case Study in Human Rights and the Unwritten Constitution, 30 *Hastings L. J.* 957 (1979).

P. J. Riga, *Right to Die or Right to Live: Legal Aspects of Dying and Death* (1981).

G. P. Smith, *Genetics, Ethics and Law* 1981).

R. Stammler, *The Theory of Justice* (I. Husik transl. 1925).

T. Szasz, Mental Health as Ideology, in *Ideology and Insanity: Essays on the Psychiatric Dehumanization of Man* 690 (1970).

E. Wilson, *Sociobiology: the New Synthesis* (1975).

Note, The Legality of Homosexual Marriage, 82 *Yale L. J.* 573 (1973).

CHAPTER 6

The Past as Prison: The Jurisprudence of Historicism

*It is revolting to have no better reason for a rule
than that it was laid down in the time of Henry IV.*
Oliver Wendell Holmes

The Republic of Centradora has a feudal government, with land and power concentrated in the hands of scarcely 2% of the population. Government is conducted with a high level of official violence distributed rather indiscriminately over the bulk of the population. A rural insurrection by guerillas, ostensibly supported by outsiders, has stimulated even more brutality, a substantial part of it contributed by government forces and irregular vigilantes, apparently operating with government sanction and blessing. A victory by the guerrillas may lead to greater violence and portends local, regional and possibly global political changes not to the benefit of the United States which hence, finds itself sometimes reluctantly, supporting the government. A victory by the government portends more brutality and suppression.

Influential groups within the United States, revolted by the regressive and violent character of the Centradoran government and by its persistent record of human rights violations, are insisting that no U.S. funds be sent to the Centradoran government, whatever the consequences.

You are the President and the decision is yours. You are being pressed by several self-declared realists among your closest advisers to support the Centradoran government. As for the human rights violations and the quality of the government there, the more hawkish advisers insist that that is part of the culture of Centradora, a deep and continuous strand in the life of the people that predated the arrival of the Spaniards and has been and will be part of every government there. And, indeed, reports by political sociologists do confirm the depth and integrality of violence in the Centradoran way of life. How do you respond to this argument and what will you decide?

When the American novelist William Faulkner was told that the past was dead, he responded, "the past is not only not dead, it is not even passed." Everyone can attest to the durability and persistence of old ideas, perspectives, identities and hostilities which, in an almost miraculous fashion, seem to be transferred from generation to generation, influencing contemporary behavior, often forcing the people who live it to characterize their world not in contemporary terms but in the rather ancient terms of the belief system they have inherited. Of course, equally apparent is the contemporary phenomenon of rapid change, change that is often designed by an elite and put into effect in comparatively short order. Those who live in an industrial and science-based civilization, in which mass communications comprise the community's nerve network, know how quickly key aspects of collective behavior can be changed if there is an elite consensus on the matter.

It is the focus on the past, its persistent influence on the present, and in particular, the limitations that it imposes on contemporary choice—whether personal or in its community—wide sense of law—which is the central idea of Historicism, the jurisprudential frame considered in this chapter.* Most Historicist writers have generally assumed that some dynamic, immanent in history or in the collective consciousness of particular groups or tribes, is the most significant determinant of behavior. The future, according to their thinking, is implicit in the past and will inexorably develop in a certain pattern. Human beings may accelerate the inevitable if they appreciate the correct direction or retard it slightly if they don't understand it, but the fundamental lineaments of the future have been predetermined.

Some Historicists have been pessimistic, certain that the dynamic of history was pointed downwards and that personal and collective life was in a persistent decline. Others have been optimistic, certain that humanity and history were improving by virtue of the same dynamic. Curiously, despite the determinism of this frame of jurisprudence, historicists have been not only not apathetic, but among the most politically active of all jurisprudential writers. In this respect, you may conclude, after studying the materials here, that for many, the jurisprudence of historicism was often a rhetorical device to swing people toward the position of the speaker by assuring them that history would vindicate their program.

Historicism appears in linguistics, history, sociology and anthropology. In its jurisprudential manifestation, the central assumption of historicism is that law in one contemporary sense—understood as a process by which the community determines what it wants and establishes methods for implementing it—cannot succeed. The reason is that law is a dependent variable, not a phenomenon in its own right but an epiphenomenon or secondary phenomenon. Professor Burton, of London, a contemporary proponent of the school, writes:

> Law cannot create; it reflects aspects of social and cultural development, and if it is to be observed it must change with changes which take place in the social and political relations of those to whom it applies.**

Conservative Historicism

In the beginning of the 19th century, historicism enjoyed a resurgence. There were many reasons for it but the one which was particularly influential in law and politics was the French Revolution. Some proponents of change who had formerly favored a rapid transformation, by revolution if necessary, recoiled from the excesses of the Reign of Terror and began to preach doctrines of slow, immanent or organic change. In Germany, Historicism flourished in Law Faculties and became the focus of a struggle between two social groups. One was anxious to codify law and use it as an instrument for reunification and the stimulation of certain social and political changes. The other group, content with the existing system and anxious to block change, took as its slogan not the status quo per se but rather the inappropriateness of law as a means of bringing about desired changes. The conservative group was championed by the great Roman Law scholar, Frederick Karl von Savigny (1779-1861).

---

*The school is called "Historicist" rather than "Historical" because the images of the past which are constructed are selective and self-serving. More often than not, the lawyer resorting to historicism selects only those aspects of the past which he wishes to see replicated in the future.
**J. W. Burton, *International Relations, A General Theory* 63 (1965).

SAVIGNY, OF THE VOCATION OF OUR AGE
FOR LEGISLATION AND JURISPRUDENCE
4-31, 61-69 (A. HAYWARD TRANS. 1975)

ORIGIN OF POSITIVE LAW

We first inquire of history, how law has actually developed itself amongst nations of the nobler races; the question—What may be good, or necessary, or, on the contrary, censurable herein,—will be not at all prejudiced by this method of proceeding.

In the earliest times to which authentic history extends, the law will be found to have already attained a fixed character, peculiar to the people, like their language, manners and constitution. Nay, these phenomena have no separate existence, they are but the particular faculties and tendencies of an individual people, inseparably united in nature, and only wearing the semblance of distinct attributes to our view. That which binds them into one whole is the common conviction of the people, the kindred consciousness of an inward necessity, excluding all notion of an accidental and arbitrary origin.

How these peculiar attributes of nations, by which they are first individualized, originated—this is a question which cannot be answered historically. Of late, the prevalent opinion has been that all lived at first a sort of animal life, advancing gradually to a more passable state, until at length the height on which they now stand, was attained. We may leave this theory alone, and confine ourselves to the mere matter of fact of that first authentic condition of the law. We shall endeavor to exhibit certain general traits of this period, in which the law, as well as the language, exists in the consciousness of the people.

This youth of nations is poor in ideas, but enjoys a clear perception of its relations and circumstances, and feels and brings the whole of them into play; whilst we, in our artificial complicated existence, are overwhelmed by our own riches, instead of enjoying and controlling them. This plain natural state is particularly observable in the law; and as, in the case of an individual, his family relations and patrimonial property may possess an additional value in his eyes from the effect of association,—so on the same principle, it is possible for the rules of the law itself to be amongst the objects of popular faith. But these moral faculties require some bodily existence to fix them. Such, for language, is its constant misinterpreted use; such, for the constitution, are palpable and public powers,—but what supplies its place with regard to the law? In our times it is supplied by rules, communicated by writing and word of mouth. This mode of fixation, however, presupposed a high degree of abstraction, and is, therefore, not practicable in the early time alluded to. On the contrary, we then find symbolical acts universally employed where rights and duties were to be created or extinguished: it is their palpableness which externally retains law in a fixed form; and their solemnity and weight correspond with the importance of the legal relations themselves, which have been already mentioned as peculiar to this period. In the general use of such formal acts, the Germanic races agree with the ancient Italic, except that, amongst these laws, the forms themselves appear more fixed and regular, which perhaps arose from their city constitutions. These formal acts may be considered as the true grammar of law in this period; and it is important to observe that the principal business of the early Roman jurists consisted in the preservation and accurate application of them. We, in latter times, have often made light of them as the creation of barbarism and superstition, and have prided ourselves on not having them, without considering that we, too, are at every step beset with legal forms, to which, in fact, only the principal advantages of the old forms are wanting,—namely, their palpableness, and the popular prejudice in their favour, whilst ours are felt by all as something arbitrary, and therefore burdensome. In such partial views of early times we resemble the travellers, who remark, with great astonishment, that in France the little children, nay, even the common people, speak French with perfect fluency.

But this organic connection of law with the being and character of the people, is also manifested in the progress of the times; and here, again, it may be compared with language. For law, as for language, there is no moment of absolute cessation; it is subject to the same movement and development as every other popular tendency; and this very development remains under the same law of inward necessity, as in its earliest stages. Law grows with the growth, and strengthens with the strength of the people, and finally dies away as the nation loses its nationality. But this inward progressive tendency, even in highly cultivated times, throws a great difficulty in the way of discussion. It has been maintained above, that the common consciousness of the people is the peculiar seat of law. This, for example, in the Roman law, is easily conceivable of its essential parts, such as the general definition of marriage, of property, etc., etc., but with regard to the endless detail, of which we have only a remnant in the Pandects, every one must regard it as impossible.

This difficulty leads us to a new view of the development of law. With the progress of civilization, national tendencies become more and more distinct, and what otherwise would have remained common, becomes appropriated to particular classes; the jurists now become more and more a distinct class of the kind; law perfects its language, takes a scientific direction, and, as formerly it existed in the consciousness of the community, it now devolves upon the jurists, who thus, in this department, represent the community. Law is henceforth more artificial and complex, since it has a twofold life; first, as part of the aggregate existence of the community, which it does not cease to be; and, secondly, as a distinct branch of knowledge in the hands of the jurists. All the latter phenomena are explicable by the co-operation of those two principles of existence; and it may now be understood, how even the whole of that immense detail might arise from organic causes, without any exertion of arbitrary will or intention. For the sake of brevity, we call, technically speaking, the connection of law with the general existence of the people—the political element; and the distinct scientific existence of law—the technical element.

At different times, therefore, amongst the same people, law will be natural law (in a different sense from our law of nature), or learned law, as the one or the other principle prevails, between which a precise line of demarcation is obviously impossible. Under a republican constitution, the political principle will be able to preserve an immediate influence longer than in monarchical states; and under the Roman republic in particular, many causes co-operated to keep this influence alive, even during the progress of civilization. But in all times, and under all constitutions, this influence continues to show itself in particular applications, as where the same constantly—recurring necessity makes a general consciousness of the people at large possible. Thus, in most cities, a separate law for menial servants and house-renting will grow up and continue to exist, equally independent of positive rules and scientific jurisprudence: such laws are the individual remains of the primitive legal formations. Before the great overthrow of almost all institutions, which we have witnessed, cases of this sort were of much more frequent occurrence in the small German states than now, parts of the old Germanic institutions having frequently survived all revolutions whatever. The sum, therefore, of this theory is, that all law is originally formed in the manner, in which, in ordinary but not quite correct language, customary law is said to have been formed: i.e. that it is first developed by custom and popular faith, next by jurisprudence,—everywhere, therefore, by internal silently—operating powers, not by the arbitrary will of a law-giver.

This state of things has hitherto been only historically set forth; whether it be praiseworthy and desirable, the following enquiry will show. But even in an historical point of view, this state of law requires to be more accurately defined. In the first place, in treating of it, a complete undisturbed national development is assumed; the influence of an early connection with foreign jurisprudence will, farther on, be illustrated by the example of Germany. It will likewise appear, that a partial influence of legislation on jurisprudence may sometimes produce a beneficial, and sometimes an injurious, effect. Lastly, these are great variations within the limits of the validity and application of the law. For, as the same nation branches off into many stocks, and states are united or disunited, the same law may sometimes be common to several independent states; and sometimes, in different parts of the same state, together with the same fundamental principles, a great diversity of particular provisions may prevail.

Amongst the German jurists, Hugo has the great merit of having, in most of his works, systematically striven against the prevailing theories. In this respect, also, high honour is due to the memory of Moser, who generally aimed at interpreting history in the most comprehensive sense, and often with peculiar reference to law. That his example has been in a great degree neglected by jurists, was to be expected, since he was not of their craft, and has neither delivered lectures nor composed class-books.

•　•　•

OUR VOCATION FOR LEGISLATION

The grounds upon which the necessity of a code for Germany is usually rested, have been spoken of in the preceding chapter; we have now to consider the capacity for the undertaking. Should there be any deficiency in this respect, our condition, which we are anxious to improve, would necessarily be deteriorated by a code.

Bacon required that the age in which a code should be formed, should excel preceding ages in intelligence, from which it follows, as a necessary conclusion, that this capacity must have been denied to many an age, which, in other respects, may be regarded as in a high state of cultivation. Very recently, the opponents of the Roman law have not unfrequently laid particular stress upon such arguments as the following: —Reason is common to all nations and ages alike, and as we have, moreover, the experience of former times to resort to, all that we do must infallibly be better than all that has been done before. —But even this opiniion, that every age has a vocation for every thing, is a prejudice of the most dangerous kind. In the fine arts we are obliged to acknowledge the contrary; why are we unwilling to make the same admission, with respect to the government and the law?

If we examine the expectations of unprofessional men from a code, these will be found to vary with the objects of law; and here, also, the two-fold element of all law, which I have termed the political and the technical, is manifest. In some of these objects they take an immediate lively interest; others they give up, as indifferent matters of juridical technicality. The former is more the case in family law; the latter in property law, mostly in its general fundamental principles. We will take, as representatives of these different kinds of objects, *marriage* and *property;* what is about to be said of them is to be taken to apply to the whole class to which they belong.

Marriage belongs only half to law, half to manners: and every marriage law is unintelligible, which is not considered in connection with this its necessary supplement. Now of late, from reasons connected with the history of the christian church, the non-judicial view of this relation has become superficial, wavering and undecided in the highest degree; and this superficiality, as well as this want of certainty, have communicated themselves to the law of marriage. Whoever has carefully considered the legislation and the practical law relating to marriage, will entertain no doubt of this. Those, too, who believe that every evil requires but a remedial law for its removal, will readily admit this lamentable state, to place the necessity of a vigorous comprehensive system in a clearer light. But the hope which they here found upon legislative enactments, I hold to be altogether groundless. If, at any time, a decided and commendable tendency be distinguishable in the public mind, this may be preserved and confirmed, but it cannot be produced, by legislation; and where it is altogether wanting, every attempt that may be made to establish an exhaustive system of legislation, will but increase the existing uncertainty, and add to the difficulties of the cure.

We consider, further on, those objects which (like property) are treated with indifference by the unprofessional public, and of which even the jurists declare, that they may be the same in all circumstance,—so that they belong exclusively to juridical technicality. Our taking this view of them is itself a proof of a state of the public mind in which the law-making faculty is dificient; for where this is alive and quick, these several relations will be any thing but indifferent; but on the contrary, will be really characteristic and necessary, as is proved by the history of every primitive system of law. Supposing this to be our condition, our capacity for legislation will depend upon the merit and cultivation of our technical law; and our inquiries, therefore, must be next directed to this.

Unluckily, during the whole of the eighteenth century Germany was very poor in great jurists. There were numbers of laborious men, it is true, by whom very valuable preparatory labours were executed, but more than this was seldom done. A two-fold spirit is indispensable to the jurist; the historical, to seize with readiness the peculiarities of every age and every form of law; and the systematic, to view every notion and every rule in lively connection and co-operation with the whole, that is, in the only true and natural relation. This twofold scientific spirit is very rarely found amongst the jurists of the eighteenth century; and, in particular, some superficial speculations in philsophy had an extremely unfavourable effect. A just appreciation of the time in which one lives is very difficult: still, unless all signs deceive, a spirit has come upon our science, capable of elevating it for the future to the rank of a national system. Little, indeed, of this improvement is yet produced, and upon this ground I deny our capacity for the production of a good code. Many may look upon this judgment as overstrained, but I challenge them to show me one out of the no small number of systems of Roman-Germanic law, which is not merely capable of being made useful in promoting this or that particular end—for of such we have many—but which is really good as a book. This praise, however, can only be bestowed, when the exposition has a distinctive self-dependent form, and, at the same time, renders the matter more vividly perceptible. Thus, for example, in the Roman law, the point would be to catch the method of the old jurists, the spirit which animates the Pandects; and I should rejoice to become acquainted with any one of our systems with which it were possible for this to be the case. As no work of the kind, though talents and assiduity have not been wanting, has ever yet succeeded, I maintain that, in our age, a good code is not practicable; for with regard to this, the undertaking is the same, only more difficult. There is yet another test of our capacity: if we compare our juridical literature with the progress of German literature in general, and consider whether the first has kept pace with the latter, the result will be unfavourable, and we shall find them bearing a very different relation to each other than that borne by the Roman jurists to the literature of Rome. There is nothing degrading in this conclusion, for the task imposed upon us is really very great,—beyond comparison, more difficult than that of the Roman jurists. But we are not to mistake the magnitude of the task from indolence or self-conceit; we are not to believe ourselves at the goal, when we are still far from it.

If then, we have really nothing which is necessary to the formation of a good code, we are not to believe that the actual undertaking would be nothing more than a disappointment, which, at the worst, would merely not have advanced us. The great danger inevitably impending when a very defective and shallow state of know-ledge is fixed by positive authority, has been already spoken of; and this danger would be great in proportion to the vastness of the undertaking and its connection with the wakening spirit of nationality. Examples, near at hand, often afford, in matters of this kind, a less significant illustration: to make clear, therefore, what may be the result of such a proceeding, I will refer to the time immediately following the decline of the Roman empire in the West, where an imperfect state of legal knowledge was fixed exactly in this manner. The only case which here offers a comparison, is the Edict of Theodoric, because in this alone the existing law was to be stated in a new form. I am far from believing that, what we might produce, would be exactly like this edict; for the times are really very different. The Romans, in the year 500, found some difficulty in saying what they thought—we possess some skill in com-position: moreover, there were, at that time, no juridical writers—we have no want of these. But the similarity is not to be mistaken in this: that there was then a mass of historical matter to be expressed, which was not comprehended, nor could be mastered, and which in its new form we find some difficulty in recognizing. In one respect, too, the disadvantage is on our side: in the year 500, there was nothing to spoil. In our time, on the contrary, vigorous exertions are undeniably making, and it is impossible to say how much good we subtract from the future by confirming present deficiencies. . . .

An important point still remains to be considered,—the language. I ask of any one who knows what good appropriate expression is, and who does not regard language as a common tool, but as a scientific instrument, whether we possess a language in which a code could be composed? I am far from questioning the strength of the old German language; but that even this is not now fit for the purpose, is to me a proof the more, that we are behindhand in this circle of thought. The moment our science improves, it will be seen of how much avail our language, by its freshness and primitive vigour, will prove. What is more, I believe that, of late, we have even retrograded in this respect. I know no German law of the eighteenth century, which, in weight and vigour of expression, could be compared with the Criminal Ordinances of Charles the Fifth.

I know what answer might be given to these reasons; even admitting all of them, it may be said, the powers of the human mind are boundless, and by reasonable exertion a work, even in these times, might be soon produced, in which none of these defects would be traceable. Well any one may take the attempt, our age is not an inattentive one, and there is no danger that actual success will be overlooked.

NOTES

1. Savigny's insistence that the law of a society is 'found' by the jurist, not 'made' by the state or its organs, led him to argue for retention of the legal and political status quo and rejection of a Napoleonic-type civil code for Germany. His cause failed and a code was adopted. If you had interviewed Savigny at that time, what social consequences do you think he would have prophesied?

2. Law, for Savigny, cannot be a conscious and deliberate instrument for the shaping of society and its practices. This view has a broad and often strong coalition of supporters. Not surprisingly, it may be adopted by elites who are satisfied with their elevated status and who, therefore, oppose change. Savigny's views thus appealed to the aristocracy of Germany. But some democrats found it congenial because Historicism purports to view the practices, customs, and beliefs of people as the source of law. Savigny furthermore won a sympathetic reception from those who recoiled from the excesses of the French Revolution. In your view, is Historicism inherently conservative, progressive or neither? Discuss.

In England, the rise of conservatism in reaction to the French Revolution was stated most cogently by Edmund Burke.

BURKE, REFORM OF REPRESENTATION IN
THE HOUSE OF COMMONS
6 THE WORKS OF THE RIGHT HONOURABLE
EDMUND BURKE 146 (1823)

Our constitution is a prescriptive constitution; it is a constitution whose sole authority is that it has existed time out of mind. . . . Your king, your lords, your judges, your juries, grand and little, all are prescriptive. . . . Prescription is the most solid of all titles, not only to property, but, which is to secure that property, to government. . . . It is a presumption in favor of any settled scheme of government against any untried project, that a nation has long existed and flourished under it. It is a better presumption even of the *choice* of a nation, far better than any sudden and temporary arrangement by actual election. Because a nation is not an idea only of local extent, and individual momentary aggregation; but it is an idea of continuity, which extends in time as well as in numbers and in space. And this is a choice not of one day or one set of people, not a tumultuary and giddy choice; it is a deliberate election of the ages and of generations; it is a constitution made by what is ten thousand times better than choice, it is made by the peculiar circumstances, occasions, tempers, dispositions, and moral, civil, and social habitudes of the people, which disclose themselves only in a long space of time. . . . The individual is foolish; the multitude, for the moment, is foolish, when they act without deliberation; but the species is wise, and, when time is given to it, as a species it always acts right.

[The fundamental ideas on which the constitutional theory is premised involved conceptions of society itself as a contract between past and future generations. It was expressed elsewhere in Burke's work.]

Society is indeed a contract. Subordinate contracts for objects of mere occasional interest may be dissolved at pleasure—but the state ought not to be considered as nothing better than a partnership agreement in a trade of pepper and coffee, calico or tobacco, or some other such low concern, to be taken up for a little temporary interest, and to be dissolved by the fancy of the parties. It is to be looked on with other reverence; because it is not a partnership in things subservient only to the gross animal existence of a temporary and perishable nature. It is a partnership in all science; a partnership in all art; a partnership in every virtue, and in all perfection. As the ends of such a partnership cannot be obtained in many generations, it becomes a partnership not only between those who are living, but between those who are dead, and those who are to be born. Each contract of each particular state is but a clause in the great primeval contract of eternal society, linking the lower with the higher natures, connecting the visible and invisible world, according to a fixed compact sanctioned by the inviolable oath with holds all physical and all moral natures, each in their appointed place. (2 *Works* 368).

NOTES

1. Compare Burke's reverence for the state with the Socratic view developed in *Crito*. (See Chapter 3.)

2. In environments and societies undergoing change, choices must constantly be made about changing or retaining goals and revising priorities. One of the effects of the Burkean type of historicism is not to bar those choices but to conceal them in the hands of a small group who then present their deliberations to the public not as options for popular review but as the only possible outcomes, inexorably determined by historical forces. In this respect, historicism often functions as an antidemocratic device. Discuss.

3. Discuss the validity, if any, of the historicist notion that law must accord with and be appropriate for the "spirit," perspectives, and customary practices of the people. Savigny claimed, you will recall, that "there exists an organic connection between law and the nature and character of the people." What does he mean by "nature and character"? What does he mean by "people"? What does he mean by an "organic connection"?

From the point of view of a Historicist like Savigny or Burke, it would be futile to attempt to push a people towards any goal contrary to its "spirit." A people is inherently self-improving and continues inexorably toward a better state. Consequently, there is, according to the Historicist theory, no point in even attempting to formulate goals. If, however, the status quo is to be maintained and a people is to be bound by attitudes rooted in conditions in antiquity, how can contemporary problems ever be resolved? How, for example, would a Savigny propose to deal with the vexing problems arising from the rapid progress in medical science, such issues as abortion or euthanasia (see *Roe v. Wade* and *Matter of Quinlan,* Chapter 5)? In this light, consider the following critique of Historicism by Morris R. Cohen.

COHEN, PSYCHOLOGY AND SCIENTIFIC METHODS,
11 JOURNAL OF PHILOSOPHY 701, 705 (1914)

. . . The contrast between eighteenth-century rationalism and nineteenth-century historicism was first and most sharply drawn in the field of jurisprudence. In opposition to all eighteenth-century attempts to change actual legal institutions in accordance with the rights of man (deduced from rational principles), the historical school of jurisprudence founded by Eichhorn and Savigny maintained the supreme or exclusive importance of historical study. Law, Savigny maintained, is always the expression of a deterministic development of a national spirit (*Volksgeist*). Hence history is not merely a collection of examples, but "the only way to attain a true knowledge of our own condition." Hence, also, all legislation, like the Napoleonic code, not based on a complete knowledge of the history of law can be only worse than useless.

A close examination shows that the pillars of this faith are four characteristic dogmas, viz. determinism, organicism, evolutionism, and relativism. (1) Since the past completely determines the present, "the idea that each generation can make its legal world for good or ill according to its power and insight is the essence of the unhistorical view." (2) Law is not a separate affair, but is, like language, the expression of the organic national spirit. Hence there can be no free borrowing or adaptation of the law of one people by another nation. (3) As each national spirit develops, it must pass through certain stages, and (4) what is created in one stage cannot be adapted to another. Hence legal institutions must be studied, not with reference to general or abstract principles, but with reference to the particular time and place under which they arose and functioned.

Much has been and is still to be said about these doctrines; but it is certain that though the historical school has been in the ascendency for nearly one hundred years, it has never succeeded in harmonizing them so as to present a consistent doctrine. If determinism is taken seriously, how can we attach any practical importance to the *historical knowledge* of jurisprudence? If we accept the doctrine of organic connection of all social institutions in the national spirit, how can we explain the fact that peoples have successfully borrowed each other's laws? For our present purpose it is, perhaps, sufficient to point out that history itself does not bear out this faith in the exclusive importance of the historical approach to jurisprudence. No one can dispute that under the influence of eighteenth-century theories of natural rights, the constitutional law, the criminal law, and a good deal of the civil law of the world was radically transformed and improved. The Napoleonic code, framed by men who, as Savigny clearly showed, were grossly deficient in legal history, has successfully spread and has become the basis of the law of most of the European countries, various African communities, all of Latin America, Quebec, and Louisiana, and has exercised influence even on the German Civil Code, while all the labours of the historical school, excellent though they be in point of thorough historical scholarship, have little to show that it is at all comparable. The crude, unhistorical rationalism of Bentham stirred into life reformative forces in all branches of the common law, but the Anglo-American historical school (founded by Maine) has not a single reform or constructive piece of legislation of any magnitude to its credit. Indeed, the historical school has been a positive hindrance to any improvement or enlargement of the law—precisely because those who think of new problems exclusively in terms of historical analogies get tangled up in their own traces and think that what has been must remain forever.

How can history help us to evaluate the laws of today or proposed changes? How, for instance, are we to be guided in determining proposed penal legislation? The answer of the historical school is: that is sound which is in harmony with the general European or American tendency as revealed by history. But this test taken seriously either bars all real changes, or else leads nowhere in particular. All real changes must be contrary to what has hitherto prevailed. A historical study of the Roman law, or of our common law, may reveal to us exactly what Roman jurisconsults or English judges said and meant. But unless we are to suppose these worthies were endowed with omniscience, how could they have foreseen and solved all the perplexing and complicated problems which modern life presents? The actual efforts of the historical school to govern modern conditions with ancient texts has resulted, as Jhering and Pound have pointed out, in a series of pious juggling of irrelevant texts and old decisions made with reference to bygone conditions, or, more frequently, in an ultra-rationalistic shuffling of concepts—*Begriffsjurisprudenz*—which is none the better because it is unconsciously metaphysical.

The historical school has thus not succeeded in eliminating the abstract methods of evaluation of the old natural law. By setting up the system of the Roman or the common law as the embodiment of absolute principles valid for all times, it has simply substituted a conservative natural law for the old revolutionary or reformative one, presupposing the values of conservation instead of the values of creation or change.

Historically, peoples have constantly been formed, shaped and changed in what Max Weber called an ongoing process of "consociation." As individual people change, they create new affiliations and new groups. Historicism emphasizes the unchangeability of certain groups, the permanence of certain racial or ethnic features and, in particular, the unassimilability of smaller groups into larger conglomerates. Obviously, there are differences, at any moment, in terms of perspectives and behavior, between the members of different cultures, classes and groups. It is the historicist contention that these characteristics are permanent, often resulting from genetic features and that change is impossible. Consider one legal application.

DRED SCOTT V. SANDFORD 60 U.S. 393 (1856)

The plaintiff in error, who was also the plaintiff in the court below, was, with his wife and children, held as slaves by the defendant, in the State of Missouri; and he brought this action in the Circuit Court of the United States for that district, to assert the title of himself and his family to freedom.

The declaration is in the form usually adopted in that State to try questions of this description, and contains the averment necessary to give the court jurisdiction; that he and the defendant are citizens of different States; that is, that he is a citizen of Missouri, and the defendant a citizen of New York.

The defendant pleaded in abatement to the jurisdiction of the court, that the plaintiff was not a citizen of the State of Missouri, as alleged in his declaration, being a negro of African descent, whose ancestors were of pure African blood, and who were brought into this country and sold as slaves.

• • •

The question is simply this: Can a negro, whose ancestors were imported into this country, and sold as slaves, become a member of the political community formed and brought into existence by the Constitution of the United States, and as such become entitled to all the rights, and privileges and immunities, guaranteed by that instrument to the citizen? One of which rights is the privilege of suing in a court of the United States in the cases specified in the Constitution.

It will be observed, that the plea applies to that class of persons only whose ancestors were negroes of the African race, and imported into this country, and sold and held, as slaves. The only matter in issue before the court, therefore, is whether the descendants of such slaves, when they shall be emancipated, or who are born of parents who had become free before their birth, are citizens of a State, in the sense in which the word citizen is used in the Constitution of the United States. And this being the only matter in dispute on the pleadings, the court must be understood as speaking in this opinion of that class only, that is, of those persons who are the descendants of Africans who were imported into this country, and sold as slaves.

The situation of this population was altogether unlike that of the Indian race. The latter, it is true, formed no part of the colonial communities, and never amalgamated with them in social connections or in government. But although they were uncivilized, they were yet a free and independent people, associated together in nations or tribes, and governed by their own laws. Many of these political communities were situated in territories to which the white race claimed the ultimate right of dominion. But that claim was acknowleged to be subject to the right of the Indians to occupy it as long as they thought proper, and neither the English nor colonial Governments claimed or exercised any dominion over the tribe or nation by whom it was occupied, nor claimed the right to the possession of the territory, until the tribe or nation consented to cede it. These Indian Governments were regarded and treated as foreign Governments which succeeded each other. Treaties have been negotiated with them, and their alliance sought for in war; and the people who compose these Indian political communities have always been treated as foreigners not living under our Government. It is true that the course of events has brought the Indian tribes within the limits of the United States under subjection to the white race; and it has been found necessary, for their sake as well as our own, to regard them as in a state of pupilage, and to legislate to a certain extent over them and the territory they occupy. But they may, without doubt, like the subjects of any other foreign Government, be naturalized by the authority of Congress, and become citizens of a State, and of the United States; and if an individual should leave his nation or tribe, and take up his abode among the white population, he would belong to an emigrant from any other foreign people.

We proceed to examine the case as presented by the pleadings.

The words "people of the United States" and "citizens" are synonymous terms, and mean the same thing. They both describe the political body who, according to our republican institutions, form the sovereignty, and who hold the power and conduct the Government through their representatives. They are what we familiarly call the "sovereign people," and every citizen is one of this people, and a constituent member of this sovereignty. The question before us is, whether the class of persons described in the plea in abatement compose a portion of this people, and are constituent members of the sovereignty? We think they are not, and that they are not included, and were not intended to be included, under the word "citizens" in the Constitution, and can therefore claim none of the rights and privileges which that instrument provides for and secures to citizens of the United States. On the contrary, they were at that time considered as a subordinate and inferior class of beings, who had been subjugated by the dominant race, and, whether emancipated or not, yet remained subject to their authority, and had no rights or privileges but such as those who held the power and the Government might choose to grant them.

It is not the province of the court to decide upon the justice or injustice, the policy or impolicy, of these laws. The decision of that question belonged to the political or lawmaking power; to those who formed the sovereignty and framed the Constitution. The duty of the court is, to interpret the instrument they have framed, with the best lights we can obtain on the subject, and to administer it as we find it, according to its true intent and meaning when it was adopted.

NOTES

In an increasingly interdependent planet, is it appropriate to apply a historicist's notion that emphasizes the differences among peoples instead of their common shared interests and the possibilities for mutual accommodation? Is the historicist's view of immutable distinctions among groups of people verifiable empirically?

ROMANTICIZATION OF VIOLENCE

A supposedly contrary position, which also relied on historicist arguments but used them to counter Savigny, was developed in a famous pamphlet by another prominent professor of Roman Law in Germany. Rudolf von Jhering (1818-1892) originally delivered his *Struggle for Law* as a lecture.

VON JHERING, THE STRUGGLE FOR LAW, EXCERPTS (2d ed. J. LALOR TRANS. 1915)

I

The end of the law is peace. The means to that end is war. So long as the law is compelled to hold itself in readiness to resist the attacks of wrong—and this it will be compelled to do until the end of time—it cannot dispense with war. The life of the law is a struggle, a struggle of nations, of the state power, of classes, of individuals.

All the law in the world has been obtained by strife. Every principle of law which obtains had first to be wrung by force from those who denied it; and every legal right—the legal rights of a whole nation as well as those of individuals—supposes a continual readiness to assert it and defend it. The law is not mere theory, but living force. And hence it is that Justice which, in one hand, holds the scales, in which she weighs the right, carries in the other the sword with which she executes it. The sword without the scales is brute force, the scales without the sword is the impotence of law. The scales and the sword belong together, and the state of the law is perfect, only where the power with which Justice carries the sword is equalled by the skill with which she holds the scales.

Law is an uninterrupted labor, and not of the state power only, but of the entire people. The entire life of the law, embraced in one glance, presents us with the same spectacle of restless striving and working of a whole nation, afforded by its activity in the domain of economic and intellectual production. Every individual placed in a position in which he is compelled to defend his legal rights, takes part in this work of the nation, and contributes his mite towards the realization of the idea of law on earth.

• • •

. . . Our theory of law, it is only too easy to perceive, is busied much more with the scales than with the sword of Justice. The one-sidedness of the purely scientific standpoint from which it considers the law, looking at it not so much as it really is, as an idea of force, but as it is logically, a system of abstract legal principles, has, in my opinion, impressed on its whole way of viewing the law, a character not in harmony with the bitter reality. This I intend to prove.

• • •

. . . there is, nevertheless, another theory opposed, one which is still, at least in our science of Roman law, universally admitted, and which I may briefly characterize after its two chief representatives as the Savigny-Puchta theory of the origin of the law. According to this theory, the formation of the body of principles of jurisprudence is effected by a process as unnoticed and as painless as is the formation or growth of language. The building up of the body of principles of jurisprudence calls for no strife, no struggle. It is not even necessary, according to this theory, to go in search of them, for the principles of jurisprudence are nothing but the quiet working power of truth which, without any violent effort, slowly but surely makes its way; the power of conviction to which minds gradually open and to which they give expression by their acts: a new principle of jurisprudence comes into being with as little trouble as any rule of grammar. . . .

This is the idea of the origin of the law which I myself had when I left the university, and under the influence of which I lived for a good many years. Has this idea any claim to truth? It must be admitted that the law, like language, has an unintended, unconscious development, or, to call it by the traditional expression, an organic development from within outward. The power of these two factors, the intercourse of man with man, and science, is a limited one. It can regulate the motion of the stream, within existing limits, and even hasten it; but it is not great enough to throw down the dikes which keep the current from taking a new direction. Legislation alone can do this; that is, the action of the state power intentionally directed to that end; and hence it is not mere chance, but a necessity, deeply rooted in the nature of the law, that all thorough reforms of the mode of procedure and of positive law may be traced back to legislation. . . . In the course of time, the interests of thousands of individuals, and of whole classes, have become bound up with the existing principles of law in such a manner that these cannot be done away with, without doing the greatest injury to the former. To question the principle of law or the institution, means a declaration of war against all these interests, the tearing away of a polyp which resists the effort with a thousand arms. Hence every such attempt, in natural obedience to the law of self-preservation, calls forth the most violent opposition of the imperilled interests, and with it a struggle in which, as in every struggle, the issue is decided not by the weight of reason, but by the relative strength of opposing force; the result being not unfrequently the same as in the parallelogram of forces—a deviation from the original line towards the diagonal. Only thus does it become intelligible, that institutions on which public opinion has long since passed sentence of death continue to enjoy life for a great length of time. It is not the *vis inertiae* which preserves their life, but the power of resistance of the interests centering about their existence.

But in all such cases, wherever the existing law is backed by interests, the new has to undergo a struggle to force its way into the world—a struggle which not unfrequently lasts over a whole century. This struggle reaches its highest degree of intensity when the interests in question have assumed the form of vested rights. . . . All the great achievements which the history of the law has to record—the abolition of slavery, of serfdom, the freedom of landed property, of industry, of conscience, etc.—all have had to be won, in the first instance, in this manner, by the most violent struggles, which often lasted for centuries. Not unfrequently streams of blood, and everywhere rights trampled under foot, mark the way which the law has traveled during such conflict. For the law is Saturn devouring his own children. The law can revew its youth only by breaking with its own past. A concrete legal right or principle of law, which, simply because it has come into existence, claims an unlimited and therefore eternal existence, is a child lifting its arm against its own mother; it despises the idea of the law when it appeals to that idea; for the idea of the law is an eternal Becoming; but That Which Has Become must yield to the new Becoming, since

> —Alles was entsteht,
> Ist werth das es zu Grunde geht.

. . . It is not so with law considered as an end. Cast into the chaotic whirl of human aims, endeavors, interests, it has forever to feel and seek in order to find the right way, and when it has found it, to overthrow the obstacles which would impede its course. If it be an undoubted fact, that this development, like that of art or language, is governed by law and is uniform, it cannot be denied that it departs largely from the latter in the manner in which it takes place; and in this sense; therefore, we are compelled decidedly to reject the parallel instituted by Savigny—a parallel which found universal favor so rapidly—between law on the one hand and language and art on the other. This doctrine is false, but not dangerous as a philosophical opinion. As a political maxim, however, it contains an error pregnant with the most ominous consequences imaginable, because it feeds man with hope where he should act, and act with a full and clear consciousness of the object aimed at, and with all his strength. It feeds him with the hope, that things will take care of themselves and that the best he can do, is to fold his arms and confidently wait for what may gradually spring to light from that primitive source of all law called: the natural conviction of legal right. Hence the aversion of Savigny and of all his disciples for the interference of legislation, and hence the complete ignoring of the real meaning of custom, in the Puchta theory of the law of custom. Custom to Puchta is nothing but a mere mode of discovering what conviction as to the legally right is: but that this very conviction is first formed through the agency of its own action, that through this action it first demonstrates its power and its calling to govern life; in short that the principle: the law is an idea which involves force—to this the eyes of this great mind were entirely closed. But, in this, Puchta was only paying tribute to the time in which he lived. For his time was the romantic in our poetry, and the person who does not recoil from transferring the idea of he romantic to jurisprudence, and who will take the trouble to compare the corresponding directions followed in the two spheres with one author, will perhaps not find fault with me, when I allege that the historical school in law might just as well have been called the romantic. That law or the principles of legal right comes into existence or is formed painlessly, without trouble, without action, like the vegetable creation, is a really romantic notion, that is, a notion based on a false idealization of past conditions. . . . The birth of law like that of men has been uniformly attended by the violent throes of child-birth.

And why should we complain that it is thus attended? The very fact that their law does not fall to the lot of nations without trouble, that they have had to struggle, to battle and to bleed for it, creates between nations and their laws the same intimate bond as is created between the mother and her child when, at its birth, she stakes her own life. A principle of law won without toil is on a level with the children brought by the stork: what the stork has brought, the fox or the vulture can take away again. But from the mother who gave it birth, neither the fox nor the vulture can take the child away; and just as little can a people be deprived of the laws or institutions which they have had to labor and to bleed for, in order to obtain. We may even claim that the energy and love with which a people hold to and assert their laws, are determined by the amount of toil and effort which it cost them to obtain them. Not mere custom, but sacrifice, forges the strongest bond between a people and their principles of legal right; and God does not make a gift of what it needs to the nation He wishes well, nor does He make the labor necessary to its acquisition easy, but difficult. In this sense, I do not hesitate to say: The struggle needed by laws to fight their way into existence is not a curse, but a blessing.

II

. . .

Whenever a person's legal right is violated, he is placed face to face with the question, whether he will assert his right, resist his opponent; that is, engage in a struggle, or whether, in order to avoid this, he will leave right in the lurch. The decision of this question rests entirely with himself. Whatever his answer to the question may be, some sacrifice accompanies it in both cases. In the one case, the law is sacrificed to peace; in the other, peace is sacrificed to the law. . . .

. . . Daily experience shows us cases at law, in which the value of the object in controversy is out of all proportion to the prospective expenditure of trouble, excitement and money. . . . Every lawyer knows that the sure prospect of having to pay dearly for victory, does not keep many persons from suing. How frequently it happens, that the counsellor who exposes to a client the badness of his case and dissuades him from suing, receives for answer: bring suit, cost what it may!

How explain this mode of action which, from the standpoint of a rational estimation of material interests, is simply senseless?

The answer usually given to this question is well known. It is, we are told, the miserable mania for litigation, the pure love of wrangling, the irresistible desire to inflict pain on one's opponent, even when it is certain that one will have to pay for it more heavily than one's opponent.

Let us drop the consideration of the controversy between two private persons, and in their place put two nations. The one nation, let us suppose, has, contrary to law, taken from the other a square mile of barren, worthless land. Shall the latter go to war? Let us examine the question from precisely the same standpoint from which the theory of the mania for litigation judges it, in the case of the peasant from whose land a neighbor has ploughed away a few feet, or into whose meadow he has thrown a few stones. What signifies a square mile of barren land compared with a war which costs the lives of thousands, brings sorrow and misery into the palace and the hut, eats up millions and millions of the treasure of the state, and possible imperils its existence? What folly to make such a sacrifice for such an end!

Such would have to be our judgment, if the peasant and the nation were measured with the same measure. Yet no one would wish to give to the nation the same advice as to the peasant. Every one feels that a nation which looked upon such a violation of law in silence, would have signed its own death sentence. From the nation which allowed itself to be deprived of one square mile of territory by its neighbor, unpunished, the rest also would be taken, until nothing remained to it to call its own, and it had ceased to exist as a state; and such a nation would deserve no better fate.

. . . The nation does not fight for the square mile of territory, but for itself, for its honor and independence; and so in those suits at law in which the disproportion mentioned above exists between the value of the object in controversy and the prospective cost and other sacrifices, there is question not of the insignificant object in controversy, but of an ideal end: the person's assertion of himself and of his feeling of right. . . . An inner voice tells him that he should not retreat, that it is not the worthless object that is at stake but his own personality, his feeling of legal right, his self-respect—in short, the suit at law ceases to appear to him in the guise of a mere question of interest and becomes a question of character.

But experience teaches us none the less that many others in the same situation, come to the very opposite decision—they like peace better than a legal right asserted at the cost of trouble and anxiety. What kind of a judgment must we pass on this? Shall we say simply: that is a matter of individual taste and temperament; one loves contention more, and the other peace; from the stand-point of law both conclusions are to be equally respected; for the law leaves to every one who has a legal right, the choice of asserting his right or of surrendering it. I hold this view, which is to be met with not unfrequently in life, to be reprehensible in the highest degree, and in conflict with the very essence of law. If it were possible that this view should become general, all would be over with the law itself; since whereas the law, to exist, demands that there should be always a manly resistance made to wrong, those who advocate this view preach that the law should flee like a coward before wrong. To this view I oppose the principle: resistance to injustice, the resistance to wrong in the domain of law, is a duty of all who have legal rights to themselves—for it is a commandment of moral self-preservation—a duty to the commonwealth—for this resistance must, in order that the law may assert itself, be universal. I have thus laid down the principle which it is the purpose of the sequel to elaborate.

III

The struggle for his right is a duty of the person whose rights have been violated, to himself.

The preservation of existence is the highest law of the whole living creation. It manifests itself in every creature in the instinct of self-preservation. Now man is not concerned only with his physical life but with his moral existence. But the condition of this moral existence is right, is the law. In the law, man possesses and defends the moral condition of his existence—without law he sinks to the level of the beast, just as the Romans very logically, from the standpoint of abstract law, placed slaves on a level with beasts. The assertion of one's legal rights, is, therefore, a duty of moral self-preservation—the total surrender of those rights, now impossible, but once possible, is moral suicide. But the law is only the aggregate of its separate parts, each of which embodies a peculiar moral condition of existence: property as well as marriage, contracts as well as reputation. A renunciation of one of them is, therefore, legally just as impossible as the renunciation of the entire law. . . .

. . . But the thief and the robber place themselves outside the legal domain of property. They, in my property, deny both the idea of property, and, at the same time, an essential condition of the existence of my person. If we suppose their mode of action to become general, to become a maxim of the law, property is denied both in theory and in practice. Hence their act embodies an attack, not only on my chattel, but at the same time on my person; and if it be my duty to defend my person, it is my duty here also; and nothing but the conflict of this duty with the higher duty of the preservation of my life, as happens when the robber puts before me the alternative of my money or my life, can justify the abandonment of my property. But leaving this case out of consideration, it is my duty to oppose this disregard of law in my person with all the means at my command. By tolerating that disregard of law, I consent to support injustice for a single moment in my life. But to do this, no one should lend a hand.

• • •

. . . Every state punishes those crimes most severely which threaten its own peculiar condition of existence, while it allows a moderation to prevail in regard to other crimes which, not unfrequently, presents a very striking contrast to its severity as against the former. A theocracy brands blasphemy and idolatry as crimes deserving of death, while it looks upon a boundary violation as a simple misdemeanor. (Mosaic law.) The agricultural state, on the other hand, visits the latter with the severest punishment, while it lets the blasphemer go with the lightest punishment. (Old Roman law.) The commercial state punishes most severely the uttering of false coin, the military state insubordination and breach of official duty, the absolute state high treason, the republic the striving after regal power; and they all manifest a severity in these points which contrasts greatly with the manner in which they punish other crimes. In short, the reaction of the feeling of legal right, both of states and individuals, is most violent when they feel themselves threatened in the conditions of existence peculiar to them.

• • •

It is a matter of indifference what the object of the right is. If mere chance were to put me in possession of an object, I might be deprived of it without any injury to my person, but it is not chance, but my will, which establishes a bond between myself and it, and even my will only at the price of the past labor of myself or of another;—it is a part of my own strength and of my own past, or of the strength and past of another, which I possess and assert in it. In making it my own, I stamped it with the mark of my own person; whoever attacks it, attacks me; the blow dealt it strikes me, for I am present in it. Property is but the periphery of my person extended to things.

This connection of the law with the person invests all rights, no matter what their nature, with that incommensurable value which, in opposition to their purely material value, I call *ideal value*. From it springs that devotedness and energy in the assertion of legal right which I have described above. . . . The law which, on the one hand, seems to relegate man exclusively to the low region of egotism and interest, lifts him, on the other hand, to an ideal height, in which he forgets all policy, all calculation, that measure of interest which he had learned to apply everywhere, in order to sacrifice himself purely and simply in the defense of an idea. Law which, in the former region, is prose, becomes, in the struggle for law, poetry in the latter; for the struggle for law, the battle for one's legal rights, is the poetry of character.

What is it, then, that works this wonder? Not knowledge, not education, but simply the feeling of pain. Pain is the cry of distress, the call for help of imperilled nature. This is true, as I have already remarked, both of the moral and the physical organism; and what the pathology of the human organism is to the physician, the pathology of the feeling of legal right is to the jurist and the philosopher in the sphere of law; or, rather, it is what it should be to them, for it would be wrong to say that it is such to them already. In it, in truth, lies the whole secret of the law. The pain which a person experiences when his legal rights are violated, is the spontaneous, instinctive admission, wrung from him by force, of what the law is to him as an individual, in the first place, and then of what it is to human society. In this one moment, and in the form of an emotion, of direct feeling, we see more of the real meaning and nature of the law than during long years of undisturbed enjoyment. The man who has not experienced this pain himself, or observed it in others, knows nothing of what law is, even if he had committed the whole *corpus juris* to memory. Not the intellect, but the feeling, is able to answer this question; and hence language has rightly designated the psychological source of all law as the *feeling of legal right (Rechtsgefuehl)*. The consciousness of legal right (*Rechtsbewusstsein*), legal conviction, are scientific abstractions, with which the people are not acquainted. The power of the law lies in feeling, just as does the power of love; and the intellect cannot supply that feeling when it is wanting. But as love frequently does not know itself, and as a single instant suffices to bring it to a full consciousness of itself, so the feeling of legal right uniformly knows not what it is, and what it can do, so long as it is not wounded; but the violation of legal right compels it to speak, unveils the truth, and manifests its force. I have already said in what this truth consists. His legal right, the law, is the moral condition of existence of the person; the assertion of that right is his moral self-preservation.

The force with which the feeling of legal rights reacts, when wounded, is the test of its health. The degree of pain which it experiences, tells it what value it attaches to the imperilled goods. But to experience the pain without taking to heart its warning to ward off impending danger, to bear it patiently and take no measure of defense, is a denial of the feeling of legal right, excusable, perhaps, under certain circumstances, in a particular case, but impossible in the long run without the most disastrous consequences to the feeling of legal right itself. For the essence of that feeling is action. Where it does not act, it languishes and becomes blunted, until finally it grows almost insensible to pain. Irritability, that is the capacity to feel pain at the violation of one's legal rights, and action, that is the courage and the determination to repel the attack, are, in my eyes, the two criteria of a healthy feeling of legal right.

●   ●   ●

. . . the question is not the material value of a thing, but the ideal value of a legal right, the energy of the feeling of legal right in relation to property; and hence it is not the amount of property, but the strength of the feeling of legal right, which here decides the issue. The best proof of this is afforded by the English people. Their wealth has caused no detriment to their feeling of legal right; and what energy it still possesses, even in pure questions of property, we, on the continent, have frequently proof enough of, in the typical figure of the traveling Englishman who resists being duped by inn-keepers and hackmen, with a manfulness which would induce one to think he was defending the law of Old England—who, in case of need, postpones his departure, remains days in the place and spends ten times the amount he refuses to pay. The people laugh at him, and do not understand him. It were better if they did understand him. For, in the few shillings which the man here defends, Old England lives. At home, in his own country, every one understands him, and no one lightly ventures to overreach him. Place an Austrian of the same social position and the same means in the place of the Englishman—how would he act? If I can trust my own experience in this matter, not one in ten would follow the example of the Englishman. Others shun the disagreeableness of the controversy, the making of a

sensation, the possibility of a misunderstanding to which they might expose themselves, a misunderstanding which the Englishman in England need not at all fear,
and which he quietly takes into the bargain: that is, they pay. But, in the few pieces
of silver which the Englishman refuses and which the Austrian pays, there lies
concealed more than one would think, of England and Austria; there lie concealed
centuries of their political development and of their social life.

IV

Thus far I have endeavored to establish the first of the principles laid down above,
that the struggle for law is a duty of the person having rights, to himself. I now turn
to the second, viz.: that the assertion of one's legal rights is a duty which he owes
to society.

• • •

. . . In defending his legal rights, he asserts and defends the whole body of law,
within the narrow space which his own legal rights occupy. Hence his interest, and
this, his mode of action, extend far beyond his own person. The general good which
results therefrom, is not only the ideal interest, that the authority and majesty of the
law are protected, but this other very real and eminently practical good which every
one feels and understands, even the person who has no conception whatever of the
former—that the established order of social relations is defended and assured. When
the master can no longer insist that the servant shall do his duty, when the creditor
cannot enforce payment by his debtor, when the public attach no great importance
to the correctness of weights and measures, can it be said that nothing is imperilled
but the authority of the law? When these things come to pass, the order of civil life
is sacrificed in one direction, and it is not easy to say how far the disastrous consequences produced may reach; whether, for instance, the whole system of credit
may not be seriously affected thereby. For every man will do all in his power to
have nothing to do with people who force him to wrangle and struggle where his
legal right is clear; and he will transfer his capital to other places and order his goods
elsewhere.

• • •

After all this, can I be charged with claiming too much when I say: the defense
of one's concrete legal rights, when these rights are attacked, is a duty of the individual
whose rights have been invaded, not only to himself, but also to society?

• • •

. . . The truth remains truth, even when the individual defends it only from the
narrow point of view of his personal interest. It is hatred and revenge that take
Shylock before the court to cut his pound of flesh out of Antonio's body; but the
words which the poet puts into his mouth are as true in it as in any other. It is the
language which the wounded feeling of legal right will speak, at all times and in all
places, the power, the firmness of the conviction, that law must remain law, the lofty
feeling and pathos of a man who is conscious that, in what he claims, there is question
not only of his person but of the law. "The pound of flesh," Shakespeare makes
him say:—

"The pound of flesh, which I demand of him,
Is dearly bought, is mine, and I will have it;
If you deny me, fie upon your law;

There is no force in the decrees of Venice.

. . . . . . I crave the law.

. . . . . . I stay here upon my bond.''

"I crave the law." In these four words, the poet has described the relation of law in the subjective to law in the objective sense of the term and the meaning of the struggle for law, in a manner better than any philosopher of the law could have done it. These four words change Shylock's claim into a question of the law of Venice. To what mighty, giant dimensions does not the weak man grow, when he speaks these words! It is no longer the Jew demanding his pound of flesh; it is the law of Venice itself knocking at the door of Justice; for his rights and the law of Venice are one and the same; they both stand or fall together. And when he finally succumbs under the weight of the judge's decision, who wipes out his rights by a shocking piece of pleasantry, when we see him pursued by bitter scorn, bowed, broken, tottering on his way, who can help feeling that in him the law of Venice is humbled; that it is not the Jew, Shylock, who moves painfully away, but the typical figure of the Jew in the middle ages, that pariah of society who cried in vain for justice? His fate is eminently tragic, not because his rights are denied him, but because he, a Jew of the middle ages, has faith in the law—we might say just as if he were a Christian—a faith in the law firm as a rock which nothing can shake, and which the judge himself feeds until the catastrophe breaks upon him like a thunder clap, dispels the illusion and teaches him that he is only the despised medieval Jew to whom justice is done by defrauding him.

•   •   •

. . . Here belong the secret courts of criminal justice in the middle ages and the feudal law, which bear weighty evidence to the impotence or the partiality of the criminal courts of the time and to the weakness of the state power; in the present, dueling, which is a palpable proof that the penalties which the state inflicts on attacks on one's honor are not sufficient to satisfy the delicate feeling of honor of certain classes of society. Here also belong the revenge for bloodshed of the Corsicans and so-called Lynch-law in the United States. All these show very plainly that the legal institutions of the country are not in harmony with the feeling of the people or of a class. They always imply a reproach to the state, either that it makes them necessary or that it endures them. When the law has prohibited them, without however, being able to abolish them, they may become, for the individual, the source of a very serious conflict. The Corsican who obeys the law rather than have recourse to revenge for bloodshed, is despised by his own kinsfolk; if he follows what the national feeling seems to demand of him, he perishes by the avenging arm of justice. And thus it is with the duel. The person who declines it when his honor dictates that he should accept it, is disgraced; if he accepts it, he is punished—a situation as painful to the individual as to the judge. In vain do we look for facts analogous to these in the early history of Rome, for the institutions of the state were *then* in perfect harmony with the national feeling of legal right.

V

•   •   •

. . . A nation is, after all, only the sum of all the individuals who compose it, and the nation thinks, feels and acts as the individuals that make it up think, feel and act. If the feeling of legal right of the individuals of the nation is blunted, cowardly, apathetic; if it finds no room for a free and vigorous development, because of the hindrances which upset laws and bad institutions put in its way; if it meets with persecution where it should have met with support and encouragement; if, in consequence of this, it accustoms itself to endure injustice and to look upon it as something which cannot be helped, who will believe that such a slavish, apathetic and paralyzed feeling of legal right can be aroused all at once to life and to energetic reaction, when there is question of a violation of the rights, not of an individual, but of the whole people; an attempt on their political freedom, the breach or overthrow of their constitution, or an attack from a foreign enemy? How can the person who has not been used to defending even his own rights, feel the impulse voluntarily to stake his life and property for the community? How can the man who thinks nothing of the ideal damage which he suffers in his person and his honor, inasmuch as he abandons his rights, because he loves his case; who was accustomed in legal matters, to employ only the measure of material interest, be expected to employ a different measure and to feel differently when there is question of the right and the honor of the nation? Whence could that idealism of feeling suddenly proceed which had thus far never shown itself? No! The battler for constitutional law and the law of nations is none other than the battler for private law; the same qualities which distinguished him struggling for his rights as an individual, accompany him in the battle for political liberty and against the external enemy. What is sowed in private law is reaped in public law and the law of nations. In the valleys of private law, in the very humblest relations of life, must be collected, drop by drop, so to speak, the forces, the moral capital which the state needs to operate on a large scale, and to attain its end. Private law, not public law, is the real school of the political education of the people.

• • •

VI

• • •

. . . Our modern jurisprudence has entirely lost sight of the simple idea developed above by me, that there is question in an infringement of one's legal rights, not merely of a pecuniary value, but of the satisfaction of the wounded feeling of legal right. Its measure is the basest and emptiest materialism—money and nothing else. I recollect having heard of a judge, who, when the amount of the object in litigation was small, in order to be relieved of the burthen [sic] of the trial, offered to pay the plaintiff out of his own pocket, and who was greatly offended, because the offer was refused. That the plaintiff was concerned about the vindication of his legal rights and not about the money, this learned judge could not get through his head; and we cannot blame him for it. He might very easily shift the blame on the science of the law. The money *condemnation* which, in the hands of the Roman magistrate, was one of the most powerful means of doing justice to the ideal feeling of legal right which had been wounded, has become, under the influence of our theory of evidence, one of the sorriest expedients which judicial authority has ever made use of to prevent injustice. The plaintiff is required to prove to a farthing the money value which he has at stake in the suit. What becomes of the protection of the law where there is no such pecuniary interest? A lessor excludes a lessee from a garden which the latter had contracted to enjoy together with the former. How can the lessee prove the money value of a sojourn of a few hours in a garden? Or the former lets the dwelling before the lessee has taken actual possession of it to another, and the lessee is

compelled to put up with the most miserable accommodation for six months, until
he finds another dwelling. An innkeeper shows a guest to the door to whom he had
promised a room by telegraph, and the latter may wander about for hours in the
night, in search of the most wretched quarters. Try to estimate this in money, or
rather, see what compensation the Court will mete out for it. In France, thousands
of francs, in Germany nothing at all; for the German judge will reply that inconvenience, no matter how great, cannot be estimated in money.

• • •

In keeping with this insensibility of our present law for the ideal interest affected
by a violation of legal rights is the doing away with, in modern practice, of the
penalties inflicted by private Roman law. The faithless bailee no longer incurs infamy
among us. The greatest piece of rascality, if its perpetrator is only skillful enough
to evade the criminal law, escapes in our day, entirely free and unpunished. On the
other hand, money penalties (*Geldstrafen*) and the penalties of *frivolous* denial, figure
in the law books, but they are never applied in practice. But what does this mean?
Only that with us subjective injustice is reduced to the level of objective
injustice . . . woes to the plaintiff, well for the defendant!

If I were to sum all that I have thus far said, I might call this last exclamation
the watchword of our modern jurisprudence and practice. It has advanced far on the
road on which Justinian entered; it is not the creditor, but the debtor, who awakens
its sympathy, and it would rather sacrifice the rights of a hundred creditors than, by
any possibility, deal too severely with a debtor.

• • •

. . . The element of strife and of struggle which Herbart would eliminate from
the idea of the law is an integral part of it, and has been from the first—struggle is
the eternal labor of the law. The sentence: "In the sweat of thy brow shalt thou eat
bread," is on a level with this other: "By struggling shalt thou obtain thy rights."
From the moment that the law gives up its readiness to fight, it gives itself up; for
the saying of the poet that only he deserves liberty and life who has to conquer them
for himself every day, is true of law also.

NOTES

1. While von Jhering, too, recognized that the law was rooted in the social and economic
order, he saw it, not as a peacefully passive reflector of group consensus, but as a constantly
stressed product of conflicts between groups and individuals. Unlike Savigny, von Jhering
emphasized the role of individuals and seemed to shy away from the conception of a mythical
group consciousness. His views led him to the notion that a legal right is simply a private
interest protected by the state and its organs, not an abstract rule of law, unconnected with
the struggles of individuals and groups pressing to preserve and further their own interests.
The law, for von Jhering, served as a mediator between competing claimants. Law could,
therefore, be used as an instrument to order and change society. Accordingly, the lawyer must
understand the social implications of legal rules and not view them simply as technical devices
formed and applied in a vacuum.

2. Von Jhering was led to conclude that legal rules and doctrines often travelled in pairs
of opposites. Thus, two different rules or doctrines of law might be applicable in a particular
case, each rule indicating a different resolution. This phenomenon occurs, according to von
Jhering, because each rule was developed to protect a different private interest and was devised
for a different context. As society developed and became more complex, the two separate

rules (which originally might not have had any relation to each other and were applied in distinct situations) might clash in a given situation to which they both now applied.

———

This phenomenon has been explored by modern scholars. Consider one view.

McDougal, The Ethics of Applying Systems
of Authority: The Balanced Opposites of
A Legal System, in The Ethic of Power
21 (H. Lasswell & H. Cleveland eds. 1962)

Legal principles are the technical formulations (myth, formula, miranda) *of* law, as distinguished from an observer's theories *about* law, which a community employs in its processes of authoritative decision. In more particular, legal principles are outcomes of the processes of prescription by which a community establishes policies as authoritative for present and future application in particular instances. The distinctive function of legal principles is that of communicating to all interested audiences a community's authoritative policies: such principles express the community's "oughts" about projected distributions of values which are to be sustained by organized community coercion.

• • •

It has often been observed by commentators and scholars that legal principles, whether projected in explicit formulations or derived in the course of application from past uniformities in behavior, have the habit of travelling in pairs of complementary opposites, the terms of which are framed at such high levels of abstraction, or in such ambiguity, that they admit of many differing, alternative applications in particular instances. This was the principal theme, for example, in the distinguished little book by Mr. Justice Cardozo, *The Paradoxes of Legal Science*. The "great problems of the law" he found in the "reconciliation of the irreconcilable," the "merger of antitheses," and the "synthesis of opposites" in "one unending paradox." Emphasis upon omnipresent complementarity was, further, frequently employed by the American legal realists, such as Oliphant and Cook, in their demonstrations that inherited legal principles are inadequate either to describe past decisions or to predict future decisions or to state preferences about what decisions ought to be. The difficulty was, they found, that "equally valid lines of argument" leading to "exactly opposite" results could be constructed in almost any case. Similarly, Thurman Arnold, though he admitted that he could not avoid their use, made the polar terms of legal principles the major target of his laughing iconoclasm. The function of such terms, he explained, was to ceremonialize peoples' conflicting emotional impulses, while more practical men got on with the world's work. Morris Cohen, the great legal philosopher upon whose work so many contemporary scholars have built, accounted, in final example, for the complementarity of legal principles as but an application of "a wider principle," the "principle of polarity"—the principle "that opposites such as immediacy and mediation, unity and plurality, the fixed and the flux, substance and function, ideal and real, actual and possible, etc., like the north (positive) and south (negative) poles of a magnet, all involve each other when applied to any significant entity." This notion was, he asserted with abundant references to the Greeks, as old as philosophy itself.

Illustration of the pervasive role of complementarity in principle in contemporary processes of authoritative decision could be offered from all the so-called "fields" of law.

RADICAL HISTORICISM

The conception of law as an epiphenomenon, shaped by other social forces but never able to shape them, is also central to Marxist theories. A number of statements in the writings of Marx and Engels indicate that they viewed law as a secondary force in society, as part of the "superstructure" which could be shaped by, but never shape the fundamental "substructure" of economic life.

MARX, A CONTRIBUTION TO CRITIQUE
OF POLITICAL ECONOMY 10 (2d ed. 1904)

The subject of my professional studies was jurisprudence, which I pursued, however, in connection with and as secondary to the studies of philosophy and history.

• • •

The first work undertaken for the solution of the question that troubled me, was a critical revision of Hegel's "Philosophy of Law"; the introduction to that work appeared in the "Deutsch-Franzosische Jahrbucher," published in Paris in 1844. I was led by my studies to the conclusion that legal relations as well as forms of state could neither be understood by themselves, nor explained by the so-called general progress of the human mind, but that they are rooted in the material conditions of life, which are summed up by Hegel after the fashion of the English and French of the eighteenth century under the name "civic society"; the anatomy of that civic society is to be sought in political economy. The study of the latter which I had taken up in Paris, I continued at Brussels whither I emigrated on account of an order of expulsion issued by Mr. Guizot. The general conclusion at which I arrived and which, once reached, continued to serve as the leading thread in my studies, may be briefly summed up as follows: In the social production which men carry on they enter into definite relations that are indispensable and independent of their will; these relations of production correspond to a definite stage of development of their material powers of production. The sum total of these relations of production constitutes the economic structure of society—the real foundation, on which rise legal and political super-structures and to which correspond definite forms of social consciousness. The mode of production in material life determines the general character of the social, political and spiritual processes of life. It is not the consciousness of men that determines their existence, but, on the contrary, their social existence determines their con-sciousness. At a certain stage of development, the material forces of production in society come in conflict with the existing relations of production, or—what is but a legal expression for the same thing—with the property relations within which they had been at work before. From forms of development of the forces of production these relations turn into their fetters. Then comes the period of social revolution. With the change of the economic foundation the entire immense superstructure is more or less rapidly transformed. In considering such transformations the distinction should always be made between the material transformation of the economic con-ditions of production which can be determined with the precision of natural science, and the legal, political, religious, aesthetic or philosophic—in short ideological forms in which men become conscious of this conflict and fight it out. Just as our opinion of an individual is not based on what he thinks of himself, so can we not judge of such a period of transformation by its own consciousness; on the contrary, this consciousness must rather be explained from the contradictions of material life, from the existing conflict between the social forces of production and the relations of production. No social order ever disappears before all the productive forces, for which there is room in it, have been developed; and new higher relations of production never appear before the material conditions of their existence have matured in the womb of the old society. Therefore, mankind always takes up only such problems as it can solve; since, looking at the matter more closely, we will always find that the problem itself arises only when the material conditions necessary for its solution already exist or are at least in the process of formation. In broad outlines we can designate the Asiatic, the ancient, the feudal, and the modern bourgeois methods of production as so many epochs in the progress of the economic formation of society. The bourgeois relations of production are the last antagonistic form of the social process of production—antagonistic not in the sense of individual antagonism, but of one arising from conditions surrounding the life of individuals in society; at the same time the productive forces developing in the womb of bourgeois society create the material conditions for the solution of that antagonism. This social formation constitutes, therefore, the closing chapter of the prehistoric stage of human society.

MARX AND ENGELS,
SELECTED CORRESPONDENCE
417 (I. LASKER TRANS. 1965)

LETTER FROM F. ENGELS TO J. BLOCH IN KÖNIGSBERG
LONDON, SEPTEMBER 21-22, 1890

. . . According to the materialist conception of history, the *ultimately* determining element in history is the production and reproduction of real life. More than this neither Marx nor I have ever asserted. Hence if somebody twists this into saying that the economic element is the *only* determining one, he transforms that proposition into a meaningless, abstract, senseless phrase. The economic situation is the basis, but the various elements of the superstructure—political forms of the class struggle and its results, to wit: constitutions established by the victorious class after a successful battle, etc., juridical forms, and even the reflexes of all these actual struggles in the brains of the participants, political, juristic, philosophical, theories, religious views and their further development into systems of dogmas—also exercise their influence upon the course of the historical struggles and in many cases preponderate in deter-mining their *form*. There is an interaction of all these elements in which, amid all the endless host of accidents (that is, of things and events whose inner interconnection is so remote or so impossible of proof that we can regard it as non-existent, as negligible) the economic movement finally asserts itself as necessary. Otherwise the application of the theory to any period of history would be easier than the solution of a simple equation of the first degree.

We make our history ourselves, but, in the first place, under very definite as-sumptions and conditions. Among these the economic ones are ultimately decisive. But the political ones, etc., and indeed even the traditions which haunt human minds also play a part, although not the decisive one. The Prussian state also arose and developed from historical, ultimately economic, causes. But it could scarcely be maintained without pedantry that among the many small states of North Germany, Brandenburg was specifically determined by economic necessity to become the great power embodying the economic, linguistic and, after the Reformation, also the religious difference between North and South, and not by other elements as well (above all by its entanglement with Poland, owing to the possession of Prussia, and hence with international political relations—which were indeed also decisive in the formation of the Austrian dynastic power). Without making oneself ridiculous it would be a difficult thing to explain in terms of economics the existence of every small sate in Germany, past and present, which widened the geographic partition wall formed by the mountains from the Sudetic range to the Teunus to form a regular fissure across all Germany.

In the second place, however, history is made in such a way that the final result always arises from conflicts between many individual wills, of which each in turn has been made what it is by a host of particular conditions of life. Thus there are innumerable intersecting forces, an infinite series of parallelograms of forces which give rise to one resultant—the historical event. This may again itself be viewed as the product of a power which works as a whole *unconsciously* and without volition. For what each individual wills is obstructed by everyone else, and what emerges is something that no one willed. Thus history has proceeded hitherto in the manner of a natural process and is essentially subject to the same laws of motion. But from the fact that the wills of individuals—each of whom desires what he is impelled to by his physical constitution and external, in the last resort economic, circumstances (either his own personal circumstances or those of society in general)—do not attain what they want, but are merged into an aggregate mean, a common resultant, it must not be concluded that they are equal to zero. On the contrary, each contributes to the resultant and is to this extent included in it.

I would furthermore ask you to study this theory from its original sources and not at second-hand; it is really much easier. Marx hardly wrote anything in which it did not play a part. But especially *The Eighteenth Brumaire of Louis Bonaparte* is a most excellent sample of its application. There are also many allusions to it in *Capital*. Then may I also direct you to my writings: *Herr Eugen Dühring's Revolution in Science and Ludwig Feuerbach and the End of Classical German Philosophy,* in which I have given the most detailed account of historical materialism which, as far as I know, exists.

Marx and I are ourselves partly to blame for the fact that the younger people sometimes lay more stress on the economic side than is due to it. We had to emphasize the main principle vis-a-vis our adversaries, who denied it, and we had not always the time, the place or the opportunity to give their due to the other elements involved in the interaction. But when it came to presenting a section of history, that is, to making a practical application, it was a different matter and there no error was permissible. Unfortunately, however, it happens only too often that people think they have fully understood a new theory and can apply it without more ado from the moment they have assimilated its main principles, and even those not always correctly. And I cannot exempt many of the more recent "Marxists" from this reproach, for the most amazing rubbish has been produced in this quarter, too . . .

———

John Dewey offers a critique of the view espoused by Marx and Engels, which could be directed against all historicist writings.

DEWEY, FREEDOM AND CULTURE 82-88 (1939)

As has been said, important social movements develop some sort of philosophy by which to guide, nominally, at least, their practical efforts and also to justify them *ex post facto*. German culture has been especially ardent and prolific in this direction, all attempts to deal with actual conditions on any other basis being regarded as proof that those engaged in them are mere "empiricists," a term of condemnation about equivalent to calling the quacks. In Marxism those who accepted any law except on having exclusively material support were utopian dreamers. The fact then that the dialectical formula was borrowed from the most metaphysical, in a non-scientific sense, of all modern philosophers [Hegel] was no deterrent to the vogue of the Marxist synthesis, since its practical character seemed to be vouched for not only by actual economic conditions and by Marx's predictions, but in particular by the increase in class conflict that was taking place.

The idea of class war took on a peculiarly timely quality because of its teaching that the then existing class struggle was that of bourgeoisie capitalists with the proletariat, the class of factory wage-workers having neither land nor any form of reserve capital. Moreover, Marx's study of the concrete facts of the factory system in Great Britain backed up his general theory with a considerable number of economic generalizations which proved sound on any theory: —such as the existence of economic cycles with crises of increasing severity, a tendency toward combination and concentration, etc. The simplified Romanticism of the principle of a negation of negations taught that class war would, through the mediation of a temporary dictatorship of the proletariat, finally usher in a classless society. In the latter the state as a political coercive power would wither away, all political agencies becoming organs of democratic administration of affairs of common interest. Even the anarchist with his opposition to all coercive power could find satisfaction in contemplation of this ultimate outcome.

Marxists object vigorously and naturally to any suggestion of an identification of their creed with theological systems of the past. But all absolutisms tend to assume a theological form and to arouse the kind of emotional ardor that has accompanied crusading religions in the past. The theological concerns and conflicts of the earlier centuries of our era involved, moreover, contemporary interests not now recoverable in imagination. That is, they were more "practical" in fact than they now appear in retrospect. Similarly the monolithic and in itself speculative Marxist doctrine took on immediate practical coloring in connection with existing economic conditions and new forms of oppressions they had produced. There is nothing novel or peculiar in a combination of theory and practice in which practical events give definite color to an abstract theory, while the theory serves as a fountainhead of inspiration to action, providing also rallying cries and slogans. Exegesis can always serve to bridge gaps and inconsistencies; and every absolutistic creed demonstrates that no limits can be put to exegetical ingenuity. What actually happens can, accordingly, be brought into harmony with dogma while the latter is covertly accommodated to events.

There is no need to go into the full scope of Marxist philosophy upon its theoretical side. What is of concern here is the support alleged to be given by it to a strictly *scientific* form of social development, one which is inevitable because scientific. As is said of literary products, Marxism is "dated" in the matter of its claims to be peculiarly scientific. For just as *necessity* and search for a *single* all-comprehensive law was typical of the intellectual atmosphere of the forties of the last century, so *probability* and *pluralism* are the characteristics of the present state of science. That the older interpretation of the idea of causal necessity has undergone a shock does not need to be told to those acquainted with recent developments. It is not necessary, however, to go to the point of throwing the idea entirely overboard to make the point which is significant for the present topic.

There is a worldwide difference between the idea that causal sequences will be found in any given set of events taken for investigation, and the idea that *all* sets of events are linked together into a *single* whole by *one* causal law. Even if it be admitted that the former principle is a necessary postulate of scientific inquiry, the latter notion is metaphysical and *extra*-scientific. When natural science was first struggling to achieve its independence, and later when an attempt was made to take social phenomena out of the domain of arbitrary free-will, those who wanted to promote the new struggles borrowed from dominant theology the idea which the latter had made familiar, that of a single all-embracing causal force. The nature of the force and the way it worked were radically altered in the new apologetics for science. But the requirements of habit were satisfied in maintaining the old forms of thought—just as the first "horseless carriages" kept the shape of the carriages they displaced. The void left by surrender first of a supernatural force, and then of Nature (which had replaced Deity during the periods of deistic rationalism) are thus made good. Only gradually did the work of science and the specific conclusions it reached make it clear that science was not a competitor with theology for a single ultimate explanation, so that the justification was no longer resorted to.

The surrender does not mean that search for broad generalizations has been given up. It means that the nature and function of these generalizations have changed. They are now, in effect and function, formulae for effecting transformations from one field to another, the qualitative difference of the fields being maintained. The doctrine of the conservation of energy represents, for example, an exceedingly comprehensive generalization. In terms of the now discarded philosophy of science, it would be said to set up a force which is at once electrical, mechanical, thermal, etc., and yet none of them, but a kind of nondescript Thing-in-itself back of all of them. In actual scientific procedure, it is a formula for converting any one of these forms of energy into any other, provided certain conditions are satisfied.

The same principle holds good of the recently discovered transmutation of chemical elements. It does not wipe out the differences of quality that mark off phenomena from one another but sets forth the conditions under which one kind is changed into another kind. Differences in the practical operations that are based upon science correspond with the change that has come about in theory—as the techniques of modern chemical industry are different from the dreams of the alchemists. No one today would think of undertaking a definite invention, the heavier-than-air flying boat, the internal combustion engine, and so on, by setting out from an alleged universal law of the working of some single ultimate force. The inventor who translates an idea into a working technological device starts from examination of special materials and tries special methods for combining them.

The practical techniques derived from the Marxist single all-embracing law of a single causative force follow the pattern discarded in scientific inquiry and in scientific engineering. What is necessary according to it is to promote class war in as great a variety of ways and on as many occasions as possible. For the essence of the theory, according to the dialectical method, is not recognition of class conflicts as *facts*—in which respect it provided a needed correction of the early nineteenth century notion of universal harmony and universal interdependence. Its distinguishing trait is that social progress is made by intensifying the conflict between the capitalist employing classes and the proletarian employed class, so that the supreme principle of morals is to strengthen the power of the latter class.

The physical analogy is about like this: suppose that there had once been a theory that "nature abhors friction." It is then discovered that no mechanical work is done without resistance, and that there is no resistance without friction. It is then concluded that by abolishing lubrication and magnifying friction, a state of universal friction will by its own inner dialectic result in an adjustment of energies to one another which will provide the best possible conditions for doing useful work. Society is marked by conflict and friction of interests; interests may by some stretching and more consolidation be used to define classes. It may also be admitted that the conflict between them has under certain conditions served as a stimulus to social progress; it might even be admitted that a society in which there was no opposition of interest would be sunk in a condition of hopeless lethargy. But the idea of obtaining universal harmony by the greatest possible intensification of conflicts would remain analogous to the physical illustration given. Persons who are not Marxists often identify the proposition that serious strife of economic interests exists with the genuine Marxist thesis that it is the sole agency by which social change is effected in the desirable direction of a classless society.

The criticism made is not directed then to any generalization made by Marx on the basis of observation of actual conditions. On the contrary, the implication of the criticism is the necessity for *continued* observation of actual conditions, with testing and revision of all earlier generalization on the basis of what is now observed. The inherent theoretical weakness of Marxism is that it supposed a generalization that was made at a particular date and place (and made even then only by bringing observed facts under a premise drawn from a metaphysical source) can obviate the need for continued resort to observation, and to continual revision of generalizations in their office of working hypotheses. In the name of science, a thoroughly anti-scientific procedure was formulated, in accord with which a generalization is made having the nature of ultimate "truth," and hence holding good at all times and places.

CYCLICAL HISTORICISM

The cyclical pattern of historicism, developed by many jurisprudential writers, was given a particularly elegant formulation by Pitirim Sorokin who purported to find an inexorable pattern of change with regard to legal institutions throughout history.

SOROKIN, THE CRISIS OF OUR AGE
146-165 (1941)

IDEATIONAL, IDEALISTIC, AND SENSATE SYSTEMS OF LAW

. . . The ideational code of law is viewed as given by God or the Absolute. It is always largely *jus divinum* or *sacrum*. Its norms are regarded as the commandments of God. As such they become absolute—not to be set aside for any utililtarian or other considerations. Often nothing is allowed to be changed in these rules. Here are typical examples of such a law code.

> Now therefore hearken, O Israel, unto the statutes and unto the judgments, which I teach you, . . . Ye shall not add unto the word which I command you, neither shall you diminish aught from it, that ye may keep the commandments of the Lord your God which I command you. *(Deuteronomy,* iv, 1 and 2).

And for another example:

> Now for the sake of preserving all this creation, the most Glorious [Lord] ordained separate duties for those who sprang from His mouth, arms, thighs, and feet . . . The Lord created . . . punishment, the protector of all creatures, an incarnation of the law, framed of Brahman glory. *(The Laws of Manu,* I, 31; VII, 14)
>
> For verily I say unto you, Till heaven and earth pass, one jot or one tittle shall in no wise pass from the law, till all be fulfilled. Whosoever therefore shall break one of these least commandments, and shall teach men so, he shall be called the least in the kingdom of heaven; but whosoever shall do and teach them, the same shall be called great in the kingdom of heaven. (Matthew, V, 18, 19)

The norms of ideational law are not aimed at an increase of sensory happiness or pleasure or utility. They are to be obeyed unquestionably as the commandments of the omniscient and ever-just Absolute. We may not always understand their wisdom, and they may appear to us inscrutable, as the ways of Providence are inscrutable. Yet their wisdom and justice cannot be doubted. Being such, the ideational codes of law protect many a value that seemingly has no sensory utility or pleasure. On the other hand, they prohibit many a pleasure and utility as sinful. Their norms always contain a large portion of commandments concerning the Absolute, the forms of the proper religious beliefs, religious rituals, and religious behavior, as well as the forms of thought and conduct that sanctify or purify all the important events in man's life, such as birth (sanctified by baptism), wedding (sanctified by the sacred ceremony of marriage), and death (sanctified by the funeral rites). Almost all their norms are permeated by the central idea of facilitating man's union with the Absolute and of purifying him when he transgresses the commandments and commits a sin or a crime.

In such codes crime and sin are synonymous, just as obedience to the law is synonymous with obedience to God and salvation. Therefore in *its criminal part the ideational code of law always has among its prohibited and punished actions many an action that violates the prescribed rules in man's relationship toward God and supersensory values. . . . Their system of punishment is likewise made up not of sensory punishments only but of supersensory penalties as well.* Punishment ranges from the eternal damnation of the sinful, and often of his progeny, in some inferno, or purgatory, to excommunication from the society of believers, to deprivation of the Sacraments and of the blessings of the religious rituals in burial and other events. The objective of the punishment is not so much prevention of crime, or education of the sinner-criminal, or protection of the utilitarian interests of the society, as an *expiation* of the sin committed against God: any violation of the absolute norm requires the vindication of the norm and cannot pass without expiation for the sin performed. A criminal is always *saceresto;* therefore he must be punished, no matter whether, from a sensory standpoint, such a punishment is usesful for the culprit or society, or not. The system of the *judicial evidence of such a law contains, moreoever, an assortment of supersensory evidence in the form of the ordeals, "the judgment of God,"* the dicta of oracles, prophets, and pythias, and other "supernatural techniques" for finding out whether or not the accused party is guilty. This system of judicial evidence is based upon the assumption of the interference of the Absolute in judicial affairs. . . . In brief, the norms of the law are absolute and rigid; the forms of its enforcement and application are also absolute and formal. No vagueness, uncertainty, relativity, ambiguity, or expediency is admitted. The legal conscience of ideational society is clear-cut, free from any doubt, and not open to any questioning or criticism. It embodies in detail the major premise of the ideational mentality.

Accordingly, ideational law is not controlled entirely by considerations of utility, profit, expediency, and sensory well-being, even in such utilitarian matters as production, exchange, and consumption of economic values—trade and commerce; money and banking; profit and interest; property and possession; rent; the relationship between the employer and employees, and other property and economic relationships. On the contrary, these all are subordinated to the ideational norms of the law, and are admitted only in so far as they do not contradict ideational values. If they do contradict these norms and values, they are rejected, prohibited, or punished, no matter how useful they may be for the society or the parties involved. . . . All these activities are restricted by, and subordinated to, ideational values. This applies also to the personal relationships of marriage and the family. The considerations of happiness in marriage receive little attention. Because marriage is a recognized sacred bond, no divorce was possible under medieval Christian law, whether the parties were happy or unhappy. In brief, ideational values transcend all other values in such a code of law.

The same is true of any other association, contract, and social relationship envisaged by ideational law. Social relationships or contracts are never left entirely to the option of the parties concerned or to a rude coercion imposed by the stronger upon the weaker. They are limited by many provisions and subordinated to the demands of the supersensory values. Such a body of law does not admit of unlimited contract and agreement or of unlimited compulsion in human relationships, however useful, pleasant, or convenient they might be to one or both of the parties concerned. . . .

Finally, *such a code regards the legitimate authority of government, as derived ultimately from the Absolute,* or God—not from physical force, wealth, or popular mandate. A government with authority not based on the sanction of the Absolute, and not obedient to its commands, is invalid for such a system of law and such a society. It is an arbitrary tyrant not entitled to obedience and deserving only to be overthrown. Hence in all societies ruled by ideational law the regime is always either explicitly or implicitly a *theocracy.*

•   •   •

Sensate Law. The characteristics of sensate law present a very different picture. It is viewed by a sensate society as man-made—frequently, indeed, as a mere instrument for the subjugation and exploitation of one group by another. Its aim is exclusively utililtarian: the safety of human life, security of property and possession, peace and order, the happiness and well-being of either society at large or of the dominating faction which enacts and enforces sensate law. Its norms are relative, changeable, and conditional; a group of rules expedient under one set of circumstances or for one group becomes useless or even harmful in different situations or for another group. Therefore they are subject to incessant change. Nothing eternal or sacred is implied in such a system of law. It does not attempt to regulate supersensory values or man's relationship toward them. It contains few, if any, provisions respecting man's relationship to God, the salvation of the soul, or other transcendental phenomena. Its criminal code virtually ignores the ideatiinal crimes of heresy, apostasy, sacrilege, and the like. Its punishments are wholly sensory, devoid of supersensory sanctions. Their purpose is not expiation but revenge, the reeducation of the culprit, the security of society, or similar utilitarian objectives. Since it is secular, it is supplemented by no body of sacred or canon law. Its judicial evidence is invariably sensory; no "judgment of God" or ordeals are admitted. Its judges, again, are secular. Its rules and procedures are elastic, variable, free from the rigid formality of ideational law. Man's personal and property relationships are governed entirely from the standpoint of expediency, utility, and the sensory well-being, either of society at large or of the dominant group. Supersensory values and considerations do not play any important role in the limitation or control of these utilitarian and sensory motivations.

The social relationships regulated by sensate law are subject to the same sensory, utililtarian considerations. In this regulation the law does not invoke any divinely authoritarian sanction. All the relationships are either contractual (left to the agreement of the parties) or compulsory (imposed by the stronger party upon the weaker); and all are sanctioned by law. Such limitations of the freedom of contract or of compulsion as exist are introduced for sensory and utilitarian reasons. No nonutilitarian or anti-utilitarian limitations are imposed on property relationships, personal relationships, or any other relationships in so far as they are not required in the interest of other groups. In all these respects the whole system of legal regulation rests on a sensory plane and is determined almost exclusively by sensory motivation.

Finally, *the government that enacts and enforces such a code is a secular—not a theocratic—government*. Based either upon military and physical power, upon riches and abilities, or upon the mandate of the electorate. Since no divine, supersensory sanction is demanded for the legality and authority of the law, there is no opportunity for the rise of an influential theocracy.

• • •

Idealistic law, in turn, occupies an intermediate position between ideational and sensate law.

As in the field of ethical ideas, the fine arts, and the systems of truth, each of the main forms of law, in the history of the Greco-Roman and Western cultures, rose to a position of dominance and then declined in favor of one of the other forms of law. The early Greek and Roman law before the fifty century B.C. was mainly ideational. It was largely the *jus divinum* or *sacrum,* with the presthood as the ruler, lawgiver, and judge, and with the legal norms prescribed by the Gods. It was therefore sacred and inviolable. The transgressor became the *sacer esto.* The objective of punishment was expiation . . . Toward the end of the sixth century B.C. there appeared symptoms of its decline, and in the fifth century B.C. sensate law reemerged. Between the third century B.C. and the fifth A.D. it grew to a position of dominance, revealing all the usual characteristics. The rise of Christianity brought with it the rise of ideational law, which after the fifty century became dominant and remained so until about the end of the twelfth century. During this period the Christian law of medieval Europe—both secular and canon law—assumed all the typical traits of ideational law. Medieval criminal law, for instance, as compared with the law of the pagan barbaric tribes or of late Roman law, introduced many new, severely punishable crimes of a purely religious character—such as blasphemy, apostasy, heresy, schism, sorcery, hindering religious services, nonfulfillment of religious rites, nonobservance of Sunday, violation of "God's peace," abuse of corpses, suicide, usury, contact with Jews, abduction, adultery, panderage, incest, fornication, and abortion. Most of these new crimes are, from the purely utilitarian and hedonistic standpoint, not necessarily harmful or painful to the parties involved. From the ideational Christian standpoint they were transgressions against the commandments of God, a violation of ideational values; therefore they were treated as criminal and severely punishable.

As we move from the codes of medieval law to those of the seventeenth and more recent centuries, most of these offenses cease to be crimes and are excluded from the list of criminal and punishable offenses. The few that remained criminal changed their nature and were punishable for purely utilitarian reasons. The terminal point in this trend toward increasingly sensate criminal law was reached in the Soviet criminal laws of 1926 and 1930, where all religious crimes were entirely abolished and, with their elimination, many a crime connected with ideational values, such as seduction, adultery, polygamy, polyandry, incest, sodomy, homosexuality, fornication, and public indecency, ceased to be regarded as crime. All such actions have become noncriminal. A similar transformation occurred in the field of constitutional and civil laws. In practically all Western countries they became almost purely sensate, and they remain predominantly sensate at the present time.

We come now the present crisis in ethical ideals and in law. Since their dominant forms in Western countries are sensate, the crisis evidently consists in the disintegration of the sensate ethics and law of the Western countries.

• • •

The essence of the crisis consists in a progressive devaluation of our ethics and of the norms of our law. This devaluation has already gone so far that, strange as it may seem, they have lost a great deal of their prestige as ethical and juridical values. They have little, if any, of the sanctity with which such values and norms were formerly invested. More and more, present-day ethical values are looked upon as mere "rationalization," "derivations," or "beautiful speech reactions" veiling the egotistic interests, pecuniary motives, and acquisitive propensities of individuals and groups. Increasingly they are regarded as a smoke screen masking prosaic interests, selfish lusts, and, in particular, greed for material values. Legal norms, likewise, are increasingly considered as a device of the group in power for exploiting other, less powerful groups—a form of trickery employed by the dominant class for the subjugation and control of the subordinate classes. Ethical and juridical norms have both become mere rouge and powder to deck out a fairly unattractive body of Marxian economic interests, Paretian "residues," Freudian "libido," Ratzenhoger "interests," the psychologists and sociologists' "complexes," "drives," and "prepotent reflexes." They have turned into mere appendages of policemen, prisons, the electric chair, "pressures," and other forms of physical force. They have lost their moral prestige and have been degraded and demoted to the status of a device used by clever hypcrites to fool the exploited simpletons. With the loss of moral prestige, they have progressively forfeited their controlling and binding power as effective factors of human conduct. Their "Thou shalt not" and "Thou shalt" have more and more ceased to affect human conduct as moral commandments or to guide it according to these commandments, and have grown progressively null and void. Accordingly, the question arises: "If the salt have lost its savor, wherewith shall it be salted? It is thenceforth good for nothing, but to be cast out, and to be trodden under foot of men."

Having lost their "savor" and efficacy, they opened the say for rude force as the only controlling power in human relationships. If neither religious nor ethical nor juridical values control our conduct, what then remains? Nothing but naked force and fraud. Hence the contemporary "Might is right." This is the central feature of the crisis in our ethics and law.

The crisis did not originate either suddenly or recently. It is not due to some unforeseen factor external to sensate ethics and law. On the contrary, it has been generated slowly by the sensate system itself, in the course of its development, from the pathogenic germs implicit in the system. In the earliest stages of sensate ethics and law, these poisonous germs were merely latent. Because of the sanctity and halo of ideational ethical values, the norms of early sensate ethics and law were still regarded as somewhat sacred and reasonable, still enjoyed a certain moral prestige, and hence were effective controlling forces in their own right. With a further declilne of the ideational system, and with the marked growth of sensate ethics and law, these noxious germs became increasingly virulent. With their growing virulence, they came to undermine and disintegrate sensate values more and more, stripping them progressively of their sanctity and prestige, until at the present time all such norms have lost their halo.

These poisonous germs of sensate ethics and law were inherent in the utilitarian and hedonistic—that is, relativistic and conditional—nature of the ethical and legal values of the system. Any sensory value, as soon as it is put on a plane of relativistic and utilitarian convention, is bound to retrogress, becoming more and more relative, more and more conventional, until it reaches a stage of "atomization" in its relativism and of utter arbitrariness in its ever thinner and less univeresal conventionality. The final stage is bankruptcy. This is a brief summary of how and why the salt of sensate ethico-juridical values came to lose its savor. If the essence of moral and juridical values is utililty and sensory happiness, then everyone has the right to pursue these values *ad libitum.* As pleasure, utility, and sensory happiness differ with different persons and groups, one is entitled to pursue them in the way one pleases and by any means one has at his disposal. As there is no limit to the expansion of sensory desires for sensory values, the available amount of these sensory values finally becomes insufficient to satisfy the desires and appetites of all the individuals and groups. The death of these values in turn, leads to a clash of individuals and groups. Under such circumstances the struggle is bound to become ever sharper, more intensive, and more diversified in its means and forms. The ultimate result is the emergence of rude force assisted by fraud as the supreme and sole arbiter of the conflicts. Under such conditions no logic, no philosophy, and no science can invoke any transcendental value to mitigate the struggle and to distinguish the right moral relativism from the wrong, the right means for the pursuit of happiness from the wrong, or to distinguish moral obligation from selfish arbitrariness, and right from might. The simple reason is the nonexistence of any transcendental value of norm in sensate ethics or law. Aside from subjective utility and happiness, relativism and convention, sensate ethics and law have no absolute judge, no objective and universal criterion to decide the issue. Hence we can deduce the inevitable "atomization" and self-annihilation of the sensate system of values from the very process of its development.

The sensate thinkers of the fourteenth, fifteenth, and sixteenth centuries, the period of the reemergence and growth of the sensate system, already well understood this danger and tried to reinforce sensate ethics and law by a "mythology" of religion and ideational ethics. Pierre Du Bois, Marsilio of Padua, Machiavelli, and J. Bodin, to mention but four, all warned that purely sensory control of man by policemen and other agents of physical power was insufficient. They pleaded, therefore, the advisability of adding to them the artificial contrrols of absolutistic religion and of ideational moral mythology. The priest, playing upon "the fear of hell," must supplement the police and the prison. Legislators must invent a God from whom nothing was concealed and who commanded the observance of the law under supersensory penalties. "The sagacious politician will always respect religion, even if he has no belief in it." So ran the argument of these initiators of sensate ethics. Unfortunately, they appear to have forgotten that if religion and ideational norms were a mere artificial mythology invented as a useful adjunct to the policeman and the gallows, such an illusion could not last long without being exposed. With this fraud exposed, sensate values themselves could not help losing their "saltiness," and hence their prestige and controlling power. Without power, they necessarily forfeited their efficacy as sensate norms and had to be replaced by sheer physical force.

Coming on the historical scene as a successor to, and as a substitute for, Christian ethics and law, the modern system of sensate ethics and law in its immanent development sowed the seeds of the degradation of man, as well as the moral values themselves. Declaring the moral values to be mere conventions, it dragged them down to the level of utilitarian and hedonistic calculations, completely relative in time and space. If they were expedient for a given man and group, they could be accepted; if they were a hindrance, they could be rejected. In this way a limitless relativism was introduced into the world of moral values, whose arbitrariness engendered conflict and struggle. This, in turn, produced hatred; and hatred led to rude force and bloodshed. In the chaos of conflicting norms moral values have been more and more ground to dust; they have progressively lost their binding power and given way to rude arbitary coercion. The pathos of binding Christian love has tended to be supplanted by hatred—the hatred of man for man, of class for class, of nation for nation, of state for state, of race for race. As a result, might has become right. *Bellum omnium contra omnes* has raised its ugly head. These are exactly the conditions we face.

At the present time there is hardly any ethical value common to and equally binding upon communists and capitalists; Hitlerites and Jews; Italians and Ethiopians; the British alliance and the German alliance; Catholics and atheists; multimillionaires and the underdogs; employers and the employed; oppressors and the oppressed; and so on. Their ethical and juridical values are quite contradictory and irreconcilable. What one faction declares good, another brands as bad. And the tragedy of it is that there is no sensate arbiter, acceptable to all these factions, whose decision is equally authoritative for all. If any mediator attempts such arbitration, he becomes, in turn, only an additional faction denounced by the others. We are thus a society of endless contesting parties without a moral judge to decide the contests. The result is moral chaos and anarchy. Everyone becomes his own lawgiver and judge, deeming his own standard just as good as anybody else's. Inertia still causes appeals to "public opinion" or to "the world's conscience," but they are either voices crying in the wilderness or else smoke screens masking the egotistic aspirations of this or that "pressure group." Instead of one genuine public opinion, we have thousands of pseudo-public opinions of factions, sects, and individuals. Instead of a "world conscience," we have millions of contradictory "rationalizations" and "derivations." The whole body of ethics accordingly becomes a plaything of unscrupulous "pressure groups," each of which tries to snatch as big a share of sensate values as possible at the cost of other groups. Under these circumstances the motivating, binding, and controlling power of ethical ideals tends to vanish. Since there is no uniform moral code, there is no united pressure of homogeneous public opinion to mold one's sentiments and convictions during his early formative years. Hence there is no uniform moral conscience to wield an effective motivating power in human behavior. Is it any wonder that crimes, wars, revolutions, have increasingly afflicted Western society? "Everything is permitted, if you can get away with it" is the main moral maxim of our time. This is supplemented by an insane preoccupation with utililtarian values as the supreme criterion. "If a belief in God is useful, God exists; if not, he does not exist." "If science has surival value, science is appreciated; if it does not, it is useless." Hence our moneymadness; our unabashed struggle for wealth. "Money can buy everything." We turn into money and profit any value—quintuplets, scientific invention, religious revivals, novel crime, and what not. Successful moneymakers compose our aristocracy. Hence our ferocious "business is business" and all the barbarity of the struggle for sensory values. Hence our supposedly scientific "mores" and "folkways," instead of moral imperatives—our anthopological and sociological "Mores are conventional and differ from group to group." Hence the millions of other characteristics of our *urbs venalis,* with all the tragic consequences of such moral cynicism. When a society dispenses with God, with the Absolute, and rejects all the binding moral imperatives, the only binding power that remains is sheer physical force itself.

Thus sensate society, with its sensate ethics, has prepared its own surrender to the rudest coercion. "Liberating" itself from God, from all absolutes and categoric moral imperatives, it has become the victim of undisguised physical coercion and fraud. Society has reached the nadir of moral degradation and is now paying the tragic price of its own folly. Its vaunted utilitarianism, practicality, and realistic expediency have turned into the most impractical and unrealistic dis-utilitarian catastrophy. Nemesis has at last overtaken it!

Hence the contemproary tragedy of sensate man himself. Stripping man of his divine charisma and grace, sensate mentality, ethics, and law have reduced him to a mere electron-proton complex or reflex mechanism devoid of any sanctity or end-value. "Liberating" him from the "superstitions" of the categorical imperatives, they have taken from him an invisible armor that unconditionally protected him, his dignity, his sanctity, and his inviolability. Divested of his armor, he finds himself but a plaything in the hands of the most fortuitous forces. If he is useful for this or that, he may be treated decently and cared for as we care for a useful animal. If he is harmful, he can be "liquidated," as we exterminate harmful snakes. No guilt, no crime, no valid reason, is needed for such a liquidation. The very existence of a man or group as an unintentional obstacle is enough to eliminate them. Without any compunction, remorse, regret, or compassion, millions of guitless people are uprooted, deprived of all possessions, of all rights, of all values, subjected to all kinds of privations, banished, or killed by bombs and bullets, simply because their mere existence is an unintentional obstacle to the realization of a lust for power, for wealth, for comfort, for some sensate cynicism! Rarely, if ever, have even cattle been treated with such cynicism! Released from all the inhibitions of supersensory values, sensate man suicidally murders sensate man—his pride and self-confidence; his values and possessions; his comfort, pleasures, and happiness. In this tornado of unleashed sensate passions, the whole of sensate culture is being blown to pieces and swept away.

As has happened several times before, in the insanity of a decadent mentality, sensate man again today is destroying the sensate house he has so proudly been building for the past five centuries. Sensate ethics and law have once again entered a blind alley. This alley marks their *finis* for the present epoch. Without a shift towards ideational ethics and law, without a new absolutization and universalization of the values, they cannot escape from this blind alley. Such is the verdict of history in regard to the past crises of sensate ethics and law, and such must be its verdict regarding the present crisis. The subsequent chapters will further unfold all the disasterous consequences of the moral atomism and ethical cynicism of our overripe sensate morality.

NOTES

1. Sorokin associates ideational law with religion. Is this too narrow a focus? Recall myth systems in Chapter 2. Must they be supported by religious sanction to be effective? Discuss.

2. How does the phenomenon of the "Moral Majority" fit into Sorokin's thesis?

3. Sorokin's thesis, if correct, may have relevance to the role of authority (as contrasted with control) in western democracies (see Chapter 3) and to the jurisprudence of obedience (see Chapter 4). Discuss.

HOW IS THE PAST REPLICATED?

Historicism is beguiling and so "intuitively" correct precisely because the evidence of everyday life confirms both that key features of the past are to be found in the present and apparently that they are found there because they work. It is this continuity which often gives rise to the conception of the invisible hand or an immanent force in history which selects, by trial and error, the best of the past and transmits it from generation to generation.

In fact, careful analysis of what is selected and transmitted from the past and what is discarded indicates that there is a good deal of human agency in this process. Human beings, very often elites, willl consciously decide which aspect of a social situation they wish to perpetuate and which they wish to change. Consider in this regard the very striking analysis by Professor Arthur Stinchcombe.

STINCHCOMBE, CONSTRUCTING SOCIAL THEORIES 107-118 (1968)

By an "institution" I mean a structure in which powerful people are committed to some value or interest. The key to institutionalizing a value is to concentrate power in the hands of those who believe in that value. It can be arranged that they should believe in it by surrounding powerful roles with rewards and punishments that make it in their interest to believe in the value. Whatever values or interests are defended by the various power centers of a society or group are said to be institutionalized in that group.

● ● ●

It will be useful to break down the problem of how institutions regenerate themselves into three: (1) How does it happen that succeeding generations of power-holders have the same values? (2) What advantages do values defended by power-holders have in gaining popular support, which regenerates the value by socialization of new generations of the public? (3) What advantages do values defended by power-holders have in being embodied in the activities of future generations, whether they gain popular support or not?

If power-holders of the next generation tend to have the same values as past power-holders, any effectiveness that power has in the following generation will work in the same direction as current institutions. If power this year is used to commit the population to a value, the population itself in socializing its successor will preserve the value. And if activities of the society embody the value, any functions of those activities for other values and interests, or any inertia in activities as such, will tend to preserve patterns related to a value into the next generation. All three processes create infinite self-replicating loops.

1. Power-holders shape their successors in power by (a) control over selection, (b) control over socialization of elites, (c) control over the conditions of incumbency in a powerful role, and (d) their symbolic value as ego-ideals for ambitious young men.

1 (a). Power-holders tend to select out men with the same values and interests as themselves for both disinterested and interested reasons. The disinterested reaasons are both direct and indirect. Directly, their own interests, power, and values are safer if the potential Young Turks are on their side, preselected to defend their seniors. Indirectly, men try to get favorable positions for their sons, relatives, and friends, who are likely to have the same values and interests because of family or small-group solidarity. Thus morality and interest coincide to produce a strong tendency for men in power to be succeeded by men of the same interests and persuasion.

1 (b). Power-holders control the socialization of their successors both by design and by accident. By design they often set up schools, or tutors, or apprenticeships to power-holders, or whatnot. By accident, the very selective principles for elites become rewards and sanctions governing the whole course of socialization. Ambitious men come to believe whatever is necessary to get ahead, attend those schools where one learns the values needed to get ahead, and produce evidence in speech and behavior that they love the right things. If a man of his own volition pursues something which requires holding some value to get, he usually comes to be quite convinced of the sacredness of that value.

1 (c). When power-holders finally have selected and socialized men who believe, they can provide against corruption of this purity by arranging the role-set of the new incumbent so he is obliged to follow the values. The successors to the Federalist presidents still had to deal with the Supreme Court and Congress, for the Federalists had established conditions of incumbency in the presidency. In other countries kings had to deal with bishops and vassals, bishops with kings and aristocrats, and aristocrats with kings and bishops. Under these conditions, the successor's powers are crippled if he does not live up to the values institutionalized in the role (i.e., correlated with power over activities of the role). This is why, of ocurse, the question of the conditions of incumbency in power is almost always the focus of constitutions and the subject matter of elections. Power-holders of this generation control the values of power-holders in future generations by constitution-writing.

1 (d). . . . feeling of awe, wonder, and worship toward powerful people—tsars, millionaires, geniuses, stars, or bosses—tends to make them into models or ego-ideals which children, adolescents, and schizophrenics model themselves after. It is Napoleon and God who classically appear in the delusions of paranoids. Power makes a man extraordinary, and people imitate extraordinary men, thus regenerating institutions over the generations.

By selection, socialization, controlling conditions of incumbency, and hero worship, succeeding generations of power-holders tend to regenerate the same institutions. Insofar as institutions have effects, and insofar as they are social phenomena themselves, these processes give rise to infinite self-replicating causal loops. Historicist explanations are particularly crucial in explaining the institutional structure of society. Probably that is why so many historians either study institutions or study the wars and revolutions that change institutions.

• • •

Institutions will be historically fragile when institutional elites do not control their successors in these days. For instance, institutions are generally precarious in the face of conquest, for the conquerors are rarely selected, socialized, or admitted to their office by their predecessors. And they have their own heroes.

2. Institutions and value patterns are partly sustained because the population at large believes in them. Popular faith is not nearly as important as democratic ideaology would lead us to hope, nor as conservative apologetics for institutions would imply. Most men are trying to get by, regarding the institutional conditions of life as given and worrying about value questions on Sunday mornings, if at all. But under some conditions, when power fails through military threat, revolution, or corruption and sloth in institutional centers, popular belief can be an important force in regenerating institutions. Popular belief is to a considerable degree a residue of institutionalized belief. We need to understand how this residue is created.

Power-backed beliefs or values have a number of advantages over other beliefs and values for influencing popular belief. (a) They have preferred access to all media of communication and socialization which require resources, for power is another word for control over resources. (b) They have the advantage that power-holders generally have no other job than making policy and preserving values. This means that institutionalized values get full-time attention and thought while uninstitution-alized values depend on amateurs. (c) The factors above which regenerate values in the elite have a latent effect on the general population, especially when all of them want to grow up to be president. Hence selection, control over elite socialization, constitutional provisions about incumbency, and hero worship indirectly socialize the general population, especially its most ambitious part.

2 (a). The proposition that resource-using communication and socialization tend to popularize institutional values implies that the less spontaneous and private so-cialization is, the more popular institutionalized values will be. Religious congre-gations as compared with household gods, educational systems as compared with family training, mass media as compared with rumor, all are more resource-using means of socialization. Hence we would expect that institutionalized values would be more popularly supported, the more developed such structures were. In societies with familial or tribal religions, poorly developed educational systems, and little mass media, we would therefore expect institutional structures to be much more fragile, much more affected by wars, resolutions, and redistributions of power.

• • •

Thus the self-replilcating character of institutions in the face of miliary shocks depend very much on the degree to which socialization and communication in the society are resource-intensive or spontaneous. Spontaneous socialization produces "spontaneity" in institutional life.

2 (b). The amount of social energy devoted to a value is mainly determined by whether it is defended by full-time workers or by amateurs. One of the main ad-vantages of full-time workers is their greater degree of reflection and rationality. One of the main determinants of what a man thinks about is what he gets paid for thinking about. Directly or indirectly, power-holders in institutions get paid for thinking about

how to achieve and preserve the values and interests embodied in an institution. The more elaborate an argument in favor of a value, the more extensive the data collection on which a solution to a problem is based, the more explicitly alternatives are explored and evaluated, and the longer the time span planned for, the more likely is that the analysis was done by somebody who gets paid for it. The greater rationality with which values embodied in institutions are defended and disseminated is one of their main advantages in competition with alternative values.

Rational defense is effective not because the public is devoted to rational argument. The advantages of rationality are twofold. First, that section of the public which leads opinion is more likely to be swayed by rational argument than are followers. In particular, leaders of *other* institutions are paid to think full time about their values and the relation of them to other institutions. Rationality of leadership is especially important for working out inter-institutional relations and hence getting one's own values associated with and defended by other institutionalized values.

Second, and even more important, the longer the time span under consideration, the more important popular support is likely to be. Those values which depend on spontaneous social action by amateurs are likely to be defended only when some concrete problem or interest is touched. Lenin observed this when he pointed out that the masses spontaneously could reach only the level of "trade union consciousness." Hence little of the resources devoted to such values will be spent on such long-run activities as the development and dissemination of doctrine. Not only do institutionalized values have more resources devoted to them but a larger proportion of those resources are likely to be devoted to influencing popular opinion and controlling popular socialization.

2 (c) Selection, socialization, incumbency in power, and hero worship in elilte socialization affect public opinion indirectly. They have their effect by influencing the perceived rewards and punishments which control mass action in the population and by providing models of appropriate behavior for ambitious men in the public. Anyone who has some aspirations to get into the elite, or into the class of retainers and kept men of the elite, must satisfy the selective criteria by which such men get ahead. Many are called, but few are chosen. Thus many will be exposed to anticipatory, socialization for elite positions they will never hold.

In addition, elite schools and etiquette provide models for mass schools and etiquette, and powerful men tend to be heroes to the masses as well as to potential members of the elite.

We will, then, expect that institutions will tend to regenerate themselves by means of disseminating support for the value in the general public to the degree that resource-using modes of communication are important in socialization of the general public, to the degree that values defended by power-holders motivates the general public to model its socialization on that for the elite.

We would expect such institutional self-replicating forces to be greatest in modern societies, because resource-using modes of socialization are more common, because in modern societies recruitment to the elite generally involves systematic training in rational thought in colleges and universities (and perhaps less leisure and more work among the elite), and because more of the population can aspire to elite status when fewer channels are blocked off on ascriptive grounds. Considerable evidence does indicate that institutions are more stable in modern societies and that support for these institutions is probably more widely distributed in the general population.

Traditionalism of institutions combined with rapid changes in the means and mechanisms of institutions is characteristic of modern societies.

   3. In addition to controlling the values of future members of the elite and influencing popular belief, institutioinal power-holders have some capacity to control the
activities of future generations, whatever those future generations may happen to
believe. There are two possible causal links between control over activities in the
present and the structure of activites and values in the future. (a) Activities established
by current power-holderls, embodying their values, may serve other functions than
serving those values. Such additional functions will preserve the activities, even if
commitment to the values is low. (b) People become committed to what they are
doing, perhaps in order to reduce cognitive dissonance, so that one way to socialize
people to a value is to get them to act in terms of that value without belief and allow
belief to follow.

                              •   •   •

3 (b) . . .Thus by using institutional power to institute a set of activities, one may
socialize the general population to believe in the values connected to those activities.
Believing in them, the population will tend to do them again next year even when
the support of power is taken away.

                              •   •   •

Thus we will expect institutions to replicate themselves to the degree that:
1. Powerful people secure successors of the same persuasion
   (a) by selection of their successors,
   (b) by controlling socialization of their successors,
   (c) by controlling the conditions of incumbency of their successors,
   (d) by being heroes and ego-ideals to potential successors.
2. Powerful people influence popular belief
   (a) by controlling lthe content of resource-using media of socialization,
   (b) by rationally devoting resources to long-run stabililty, because they defend
       the value full time,
   (c) by shaping the conditions of socialization of the general population indirectly
       through the public's hopes for elite status and their hero worship.
3. Powerful people determine the structure of social activity,
   (a) thereby serving other social functions besides the value in question.
   (b) eliciting commitment to the activities, and hence to the values embodied in
       them.

                              NOTES

   1. Stinchcombe demonstrates that the continuation of certain institutions and practices in
society is attributable to the efforts of elite groups anxious to secure their continuation. In one
sense, this is an empirical explanation of what Savigny argued. Would Savigny be content
with the Stinchcombe theory? Why? Why not?
   2. Note that whereas Savigny and von Jhering both assume that law is irrelevant to
fundamental social struggles and social changes, Stinchcombe would argue that law can be
used either to stabilize or to change a situation, depending on the power and the interests of
the elite manipulating it. Discuss.
   3. Stinchcombe speaks of a single, homogenous elite. Does his analysis apply to a system
(like the United States, perhaps) in which the elite is complex and heterogeneous? Discuss.

HISTORICISM IN AMERICAN CONSTITUTIONAL THEORY

In contemporary American law, historicism frequently surfaces in the form of the myth of the intention of the framers. Recall the Dred Scott decision discussed abqve. The presumption in this myth is that the members of the Constitutional Convention in 1789, operating in an agrarian society along the coast of the Atlantic and designing a constitution for a pre-technological world in which the American community of some three million people would be largely isolated, could have anticipated the extraordinarily complex developments of an industrial and science-based civilization in the twentieth and twenty-first centuries. Obviously the most prescient and clairvoyant of founding fathers could hardly have done that. The device of purporting to decide according to "the intentions of the framers" is thus historicist in that it conceals the choice made by the decisionmaker, attributing it to something written 200 years before.

APPRAISAL

Savigny's emphasis on the distinctive spirit and practices of different ethnic and racial groups was based on the notion of a collective consciousness, an identifiable entity distinct from its individual members, which produced language, literature and law. This lead him to downplay the important of individuals who were regarded as insignificant within the group. Some legal historicists, more comfortable with collectivities than with individuals, are accordingly disdainful of democracy and individuality. Marxist thought, too, is largely group oriented, with *Klassengeist* or class spirit replacing *Volksgeist* or peoples' spirit. For some criticisms, see F.A. Hayek, Scientism and the Study of Society: The Historicism of the Scientistic Approach, in *The Counter-Revolution of Science* (1952) and K.R. Popper, *The Poverty of Historicism* (1957).

The Historical school assumed that law was rooted in the economic and social order, embodied value systems of the people, and was grounded in their customary practices. It rejected the prevailing notion that law consisted of abstract principles or rules of law divorced from the changing perspectives and practices of contemporary peoples. Study of law was therefore to focus on the social and economic order and the social pressures which existed and gave rise to the rules. Thus Marx adopted a mythical notion and thought " . . . the development of the economic structure of society to be a natural process." Preface to *Das Kapital* (1st ed. 1867). This Historicist emphasis was, in part, a reaction to what was viewed as the excessive rationalism of the Enlightenment movement and to the diffuseness of natural law. The historicist focus contributed to anthropological and sociological studies of law, stimulated exponents of the Legal Realist school and some other empirically oriented efforts. (See Chapters 10 and 11).

In contrast to some of the other schools we have considered, historicism redirected attention to the actual social processs in which law is created and applied. But its concern with the texture of social process became an obsession; historicists, as the selections above show, frequently mythologized the process, concealing and limiting participation in the choices that had to be made. Thus the promise of the School was rarely fulfilled. In practice, many historicists focused on mythical spirits of peoples supposedly formed in antiquity and upon metaphysical immutable "laws" of historical development of ethnic groups instead of studying contemporary practices and conditions. The unreal qualilty of Savigny's thought about the unique development of law in each ethnic group is reflected in his belief that German law (which, in fact, had become saturated with Roman law over a period of more than one thousand years) was a result of the unique spirit of the German people, whose ancestors had sacked Rome. Not all historicists were so rigidly retrospective. Sir Henry Maine and Karl Marx were two exceptions who studied contemporary conditions, informed by past trends.

In an age when human intelligence is becoming more and more capable of shaping the environment and of precipitating critical changes even in human psychosomatic systems, is historicalism a crippling force of sentimentality?

SUPPLEMENTARY READING

R. Ardrey. *The Territorial Imperative: A Personal Inquiry Into the Animal Origins of Property and Nationsl l*(1966).

1. Berllin, *Historical Inevitabillity* (1954).

R.G. Collingwood, *The Idea of History* (1946).

A. Compte, *Cours de Philosophie Positive* (1830-42).

B. Croce, *History—Its Theory and Practice* (D. Ainsllie transl. 1921).

R. Cumming, 1 *Human Nature and History: A Story of the Development of Political Thought* Ch. 6)1969).

G. Del Vecchio, *Philosophy of Law* (T. Martin transl. 1953).

F. Engels, *Anti-Dühring* (1877).

F. Fanon, *The Wretched of the Earth* (1965).

A. Hitler, *Mein Kampf* (numerous editions).

G.W.F. Hegel, *Grundlinien* Sec. 341-350 (2d ed. 1840; *Philosophy of Right* (1822).

R. Khomeini, *Islamic Government* (1979).

P. Laplace, Introduction, *Essai Philosophique Sur Les Probabilities* (2d ed. 1814).

K. Lorenz, *On Aggression* (1974).

H. Maine, *Ancient Law, Its Connection with the Early History of Society, and Its Relation to Modern Ideas* (1861, 1917); *Village—Communities in the East and West: Six Lectures Delivered at Oxford* (1871).

K. Marx, The Philosophical Manifesto of the Historical School of Law, in *Writings of the Young Marx On Philosophy and Society* 96 (L.D. Caston & K. H. Guddat eds. 1967).

E. Nagel, Determinism in History, 20 *Philosophy and Phenomenological Research* 91 (1960).

K. Popper, The Poverty of Historicism (1957).

H. Spenser, *Social Statics* (1850); *Principles of Ethics* (1879-1893).

O. Spengler, *Declline of the West* (1918-23).

A. J. Toynbee, 12 *A Study of History* Ch. 19 (1961).

G. Vico, *Scienza Nuova* [*Principles of a New Science*] (3d ed. 1744).

P. Vinogradoff, *Outline of Historical Jurisprudence* (1920).

L. Von Ranke, *The Theory and Practice of History* (G. G. Iggers ' K. Von Moltke eds. 1971).

C. H. Waddington, *The Ethical Animal* (1960).

E. Wilson, *Sociobiology: the New Synthesis* (1975).

CHAPTER 7

The World of Rules: The Jurisprudence of Positivism

The worse the society, the more law there will be.
In Hell there will be nothing but law, and due process
will be meticulously observed.
                                                Grant Gilmore

Imagine you are a judge in Nazi Germany, sworn to uphold the law. The law now includes the institutionalized racism known as the "Nuremberg principles," legislation you detest. A colleague observes that your oath to uphold the law was not conditional on having a law that you found acceptable and notes the chaos that would ensue if every judge ignored those laws he or she found distasteful. How would you decide cases in which the Nuremberg principles applied?

In Herman Melville's short novel, *Billy Budd,* a seaman, falsely accused of fomenting mutiny, strikes out and accidentally kills his accuser. Captain Vere, the commanding officer of a drumhead court martial instructs the other judges:

> . . . How can we adjudge to summary and shameful death a fellow creature innocent before God, and whom we feel to be so?—Does that state it aright? You sign sad assent. Well, I too feel that, the full force of that. It is Nature. But do these buttons that we wear attest that our allegiance is to Nature? No, to the King . . . . For that law and the rigor of it, we are not responsible. Our vowed responsibility is in this: That however pitilessly that law may operate, we nevertheless adhere to it and administer it.*

Captain Vere stated a central thesis of positivism, the ethic of obedience to the rules—no matter what.** The Nuremberg principles pose one of the inevitable dilemmas of positivism. This chapter is devoted to more thorough inquiry into the jurisprudence of rules and its implications.

POSITIVISM AND RULES

Positivism, like naked power theories, is a jurisprudence which conceives of law as the order, in the form of a rule, of a political superior to a political inferior. But unlike power theories, it takes as its major focus and legal responsibility, the analysis, construction and implementation of those rules with as much fidelity as possible. Because this version of positivism defines law as the order of a political superior to a subordinate, that inferior, the audience to whom the order is directed, is expected to ignore any inconsistency between the content of the order and its own morality.

Melville's Billy Budd 244-246 (F. B. Freeman ed. 1948).
**We acknowledge our debt to Robert Cover's eloquent discussion of this problem in *Justice Accused* (1975).

The dissonance that is thus established between law and morality has created many ethical problems for the positivist. This "separation" of law and morality is another leitmotif of positivism and is explored in the next chapter.

Positivism, as jurisprudence, has flourished in different periods and in many different cultures. But in all of its manifestations, rules purportedly limit the power and discretion of the applier narrowly; law and morality are sharply distinguished and more than in other jurisprudences, the focus is almost exclusively on courts.*

Jeremy Bentham, some of whose work is considered in Chapter 12, was an important influence on analytical positivism. Bentham distinguished between descriptive or analytical jurisprudence whose function was simply to describe with great precision what was actually happening and prescriptive and deontological jurisprudence whose function was to determine the appropriate goals for which laws should operate and to design legislative instruments to accomplish them. Bentham's primary contribution was in the deontological or prescriptive sphere. The descriptive aspect of jurisprudence was left to a member of Bentham's circle, John Austin, who addressed it in the inaugural lectures (1828) he prepared for the new chair of jurisprudence at the University of London. The lectures were called "The Province of Jurisprudence Determined" and provided a sharp contrast to the deontological approach taken by Bentham.

AUSTIN, THE PROVINCE OF JURISPRUDENCE DETERMINED 1-3, 9-33 (1832)

Laws proper, or properly so called, are commands; laws which are not commands, are laws improper or improperly so called. Laws properly so called, with laws improperly so called, may be aptly divided into the four following kinds.

1. The divine laws, or the laws of God: that is to say, the laws which are set by God to his human creatures.

2. Positive laws: that is to say, laws which are simply and strictly so called, and which form the appropriate matter of general and particular jurisprudence.

3. Positive morality, rules of positive morality, or positive moral rules.

4. Laws metaphorical or figurative, or merely metaphorical or figurative.

*Consider another description of positivism. Professor H.L.A. Hart writes:

It may help to identify five (there may be more) meanings of positivism bandied about in contemporary jurisprudence:

(1) the contention that laws are commands of human beings.

(2) the contention that there is no necessary connection between law and morals, or law as it is and ought to be.

(3) the contention that the analysis (or study of the meaning) of legal concepts is (a) worth pursuing and (b) to be distinguished from historical inquiries into the causes or origins of laws, from sociological inquiries into the relation of law and other social phenomena, and from the criticism or appraisal of law whether in terms of morals, social aims, 'functions,' or otherwise.

(4) the contention that a legal system is a 'closed logical system' in which correct legal decisions can be deduced by logical means from predetermined legal rules without reference to social aims, policies, moral standards, and

(5) the contention that moral judgments cannot be established or defended, as statements of facts can, by rational argument, evidence, or proof ('noncognitivism' in ethics).

Bentham and Austin held the views described in (1), (2), and (3) but not those in (4) and (5). Opinion (4) is often ascribed to analytical jurists, but I know of no 'analyst' who held this view. ("Positivism and the Separation of Law and Morals," reproduced, infra.)

You may wish to reconsider Hart's final point after you have studied this chapter.

The divine laws and positive laws are properly so called.—Of positive moral rules, some are laws properly so called, but others are laws improper. The positive moral rules which are laws improperly so called, may be styled laws or rules set or imposed by opinion: for they are merely opinions or sentiments held or felt by men in regard to human conduct. A law set by opinion and a law imperative and proper are allied by analogy merely; although the analogy by which they are allied is strong or close. — Laws metaphorical or figurative, or merely metaphorical or figurative, are laws improperly so called. A law metaphorical or figurative and a law imperative and proper are allied by analogy merely; and the analogy by which they are allied is slender or remote.

• • •

By determining the essence or nature of a law imperative and proper, and by determining the respective characters of those four several kinds, I determine positively and negatively the appropriate matter of jurisprudence. I determine positively what that matter is; and I distinguish it from various objects which are variously related to it, and with which it not unfrequently is blended and confounded. I show moreover its affinities with those various related objects: affinities that ought to be conceived as precisely and clearly as may be, inasmuch as there are numerous portions of the rationale of positive law to which they are the only or principal key.

• • •

LECTURE 1

The matter of jurisprudence is positive law: law, simply and strictly so called: or law set by political superiors to political inferiors. But positive law (or law, simply and strictly so called) is often confounded with objects to which it is related by *resemblance,* and with objects to which it is signified, *properly* and *improperly,* by the large and vague expression *law.* To obviate the difficulties springing from that confusion, I begin my projected Course with determining the province of jurisprudence, or with distinguishing the matter of jurisprudence from those various related objects: trying to define the subject of which I intend to treat, before I endeavour to analyse its numerous and complicated parts.

A law, in the most general and comprehensive acceptation in which the term, in its literal meaning is employed, may be said to be a rule laid down for the guidance of an intelligent being by an intelligent being having power over him. Under this defintion are concluded, and without impropriety, several species. It is necessary, to define accurately the line of demarcation which separates these species from one another, as much mistiness and intricacy has been infused into the science of jurisprudence by their being confounded or not clearly distinguished. In the comprehensive sense above indicated, or in the largest meaning which it has, without extension by metaphor or analogy, the term law embraces the following objects: — Laws set by God to his human creatures, and laws set by men to men.

• • •

Laws set by men to men are of two leading or principal classes: classes which are often blended, although they differ extremely; and which, for that reason, should be severed precisely, and opposed distinctly and conspicuously.

Of the laws or rules set by men to men, some are establilshed by *political* superiors, sovereign and subject; by persons exercising supreme and subordinate *government,* in independent nations, or independent political societies. The aggregate of the rules thus established, or some aggregate forming a portion of that aggregate, is the appropriate matter of jurisprudence, general or particular. To the aggregate of the rules thus established, or to some aggregate forming a portion of that aggregate, the term *law*, as used simply and strictly, is exclusively applied. But, as contradistinguished to *natural* law, or to the law of *nature* (meaning, by those expressions, the law of God), the aggregate of the rules, established by political superiors, is frequently styled *positive* law, or law existing by *position*. As contradistinguished to the rules which I style *positive morality*, and on which I shall touch immediately, the aggregate of the rules, established by political superiors, may also be marked commodiously with the name of *positive law*. For the sake, then, of getting a name brief and distinctive at once, and agreeably to frequent usage, I style that aggregate of rules, or any portion of that aggregate, *positive law:* though rules which are not established by political superiors, are also *positive*, or exist by *position*, if they be rules or laws, in the proper signification of term.

Though *some* of the laws or rules, which are set by men to men, are established by political superiors, *others* are *not* established by political superiors, in the capacity or character.

Closely analogous to human laws of this second class are a set of objects frequently but *improperly* termed *laws*, being rules set and enforced by *mere opinion*, that is, by the opinions or sentiments held or felt by an indeterminate body of men in regard to human conduct. Instances of such a use of the term *law* are the expressions—'The law of honour;' The law set by fashions;' and rules of this species constitute much of what is usually termed 'International law.'

The aggregate of human laws properly so called belonging to the second of the classes above mentioned, with the aggregate of objects *improperly* but by *close analogy* termed laws, I place together in a common class, and denote them by the term *positive morality*. The name *morality* severs them from *positive law*, while the epithet *positive* disjoins them from the *law of God*. And to the end of obviating confusion, it is necessary or expedient that they *should* be disjoined from the latter by that distinguishing epithet. For the name *morality* (or *morals)*, when standing unqualified or alone, denotes indifferently either of the following objects: namely positive morality *as it would be*, if it conformed to the law of God, and were, therefore, deserving of *approbation*.

Beside the various sorts of rules which are included in the literal acceptation of the term law, and those which are by a close and striking analogy, though improperly, termed laws, there are numerous applications of the term law, which rest upon a slender analogy and are merely metaphorical or figurative. . . .

Having suggested the *purpose* of my attempt to determine the province of jurisprudence: to distinguish positive law, the appropriate matter of jurisprudence, from the various objects to which it is related by resemblance, and to which it is related, nearly or remotely, by a strong or slender analogy: I shall now state the essentials of *a law* or *rule* (taken with the largest signification which can be given to the term *properly*).

Every *law* or *rule* (taken with the largest signification which can be given the term *properly)* is a *command*. Or, rather, laws or rules, properly so called, are a *species* of commands.

Now, since the term *command* comprises the term *law*, the first is the simpler as well as the larger of the two. But, simple as it is, it admits of explanation. And, since it is the *key* to the sciences of jurisprudence and morals, its meaning should be analysed with precision.

• • •

If you express or intimate a wish that I shall do or forbear from some act, and if you will visit me with an evil in case I comply not with your wish, the *expression* or *intimation* of your wish is a *command*. A command is distinguished from other significations of desire, not by the style in which the desire is signified, but by the power and the purpose of the party commanding to inflict an evil or pain in case the desire be disregarded. If you cannot or will not harm me in case I comply not wish your wish, the expression of your wish is not a command, although you utter your wish in imperative phrase. If you are able and willing to harm me in case I comply not with your wish, the expression of your wish amounts to a command, although you are prompted by a spirit of courtesy to utter it in the shape of a request. . . .

A command, then, is a signification of desire. But a command is distinguished from other significations of desire by this peculiarity: that the party to whom it is directed be liable to evil from the other, in case he comply not with the desire.

Being liable to evil from you if I comply not with a wish which you signify, I am *bound* or *obliged* by your command, or I lie under a *duty* to obey it. If, in spite of that evil in prospect, I comply not with the wish which you signify, I am said to disobey your command, or to violate the duty which it imposes. Or (changing the expression) wherever a duty lies, a command has been signified; and whenever a command is signified, a duty is imposed.

Concisely expressed, the meaning of the correlative expressions is this. He who will inflict an evil in case his desire be disregarded, utters a command by expressing or intimating his desire: He who is liable to the evil in case he disregard the desire, is bound or obliged by the command.

The evil which will probably be incurred in case a command be disobeyed or (to use an equivalent expression) in case a duty broken, is frequently called a *sanction*, or an *enforcement of obedience*. Or (varying the phrase) the command or the duty is said to be *sanctioned* or *enforced* by the chance of incurring the evil.

Considered as thus abstracted from the command and the duty which it enforces, the evil to be incurred by disobedience is frequently styled a *punishment*. But, as punishments, strictly so called, are only a *class* of sanctions, the term is too narrow to express the meaning adequately.

• • •

The truth is, that the magnitude of the eventual evil, and the magnitude of the chance of incurring it, are foreign to the matter in question. The greater the eventual evil, and the greater the chance of incurring it, the greater is the efficacy of the command, and the greater is the strength of the obligation: Or (substituting expressions exactly equivalent), the greater is the *chance* that the command will be obeyed, and that the duty will not be broken. But where there is the smallest chance of incurring the smallest evil, the expression of a wish amounts to a command, and, therefore, imposes a duty. The sanction, if you will, is feeble or insufficient; but still there *is* sanction, and, therefore, a duty and a command.

By some celebrated writers (by Locke, Bentham, and, I think Paley), the term *sanction*, or *enforcement of obedience* is applied to conditional good as well as to conditional evil: to reward as well as to punishment. But, with all my habitual veneration for the names of Locke and Bentham, I think that this extension of the term is pregnant with confusion and perplexity.

Rewards are, indisputably, *motives* to comply with the wishes of others. But to talk of commands and duties as *sanctioned* or *enforced* by rewards, or to talk of rewards as *obliging* or *constraining* to obedience, is surely a wide departure from the established meaning of the terms.

If *you* expressed a desire that *I* should render a service, and if you proffered a reward as the motive or inducement to render it, *you* would scarcely be said to *command* the service, nor should *I*, in ordinary language, be *obliged* to render it. In ordinary language, *you* would *promise* me a reward, on condition of my rendering the service, whilst *I* might be *incited* or *persuaded* to render it by the hope of obtaining the reward.

Again: If a law held out a *reward* as an *inducement* to do some act, an eventual *right* is conferred, and not an *obligation* imposed, upon those who shall act accordingly: The *imperative* part of the law being addressed or directed to the many whom it requires to *render* the reward.

In short, I am determined or inclined to comply with the wish of another, by the fear of disadvantage or evil. I am also determined or inclined to comply with the wish of another, by the hope of advantage or good. But it is only by the chance of incurring *evil*, that I am *bound* or *obliged* to compliance. It is only by conditional *evil*, that duties are *sanctioned* or *enforced*. It is the power and the purpose of inflicting eventual *evil* and *not* the power and purpose of imparting eventual *good*, which gives to the expression of a wish the name of a *command*.

If we put *reward* into the import of the term *sanction*, we must engage in a toilsome struggle with the current of ordinary speech; and shall often slide unconsciously, notwithstanding our efforts to the contrary, into the narrower and customary meaning.

It appears, then, from what has been premised, that the ideas or notions comprehended by the term *command* are the following. 1. A wish or desire conceived by a rational being, that another rational being shall do or forbear. 2. An evil to proceed from the former, and to be incurred by the latter, in case the latter comply not with the wish. 3. An expression or intimation of the wish by words or other signs.

It also appears from what has been premised, that *command, duty,* and *sanction* are inseparably connected terms: that each embraces the same ideas as the others, though each denotes those ideas in a peculiar order or series.

A wish conceived by one, and expressed or intimated to another, with an evil to be inflicted and incurred in case the wish be disregarded, are signified directly and indirectly by each of the three expressions. Each is the name of the same complex notion.

But when I am talking *directly* of the expression or intimation of the wish, I employ the term *command:* The expression or intimation of the wish being presented *prominently* to my hearer; whilst the evil to be incurred, with the chance of incurring it, are kept (if I may so express myself) in the background of my picture.

When I am talking *directly* of the chance of incurring the evil, or (changing the expression) of the liability or obnoxiousness to the evil, I employ the term *duty,* or the term *obligation:* The liability or obnoxiousness to the evil being put foremost, and the rest of the complex notion being signified implicitly.

When I am talking *immediately* of the evil itself, I employ the term *sanction,* or a term of the like import: The evil to be incurred being signified directly; whilst the obnoxiousness to that evil, with the expression or intimation of the wish are indicated indirectly or obliquely.

• • •

Commands are of two species. Some are *laws* or *rules*. The others have not acquired an appropriate name, nor does language afford an expression which will mark them briefly and precisely. I must, therefore, note them as well as I can by the ambiguous and inexpressive name of '*occasional* or *particular* commands.'

The term *laws* or *rules* being not unfrequently applied to occasional or particular commands, it is hardly possible to describe a line of separation which shall consist in every respect with established forms of speech. But the distinction between laws and particular commands may, I think, be stated in the following manner.

By every command, the party to whom it is directed is obliged to do or to forbear.

Now where it obliges *generally* to acts or forbearances of a *class,* a command is a law or rule. But where it oblilges to a *specific* act or forbearance, or to acts or forbearances which it determines *specifically* or *individually,* a command is occasional or particular. In other words, a class or description of acts is determined by a law or rule, and acts of that class or description are enjoined or forbidden generally. But where a command is occasional or particular, the act or acts, which the command enjoins or forbids, are assigned or determined by their specific or individual natures as well as by the class or description to which they belong.

The statement which I have given in abstract expressions I will now endeavour to illustrate by apt examples.

If you command your servant to go on a given errand, or not to leave your house on a given evening, or to rise at such an hour on such a morning, or to rise at that hour during the next week or month, the command is occasional or particular. For the act or acts enjoined or forbidden are specially determined or assigned.

But if you command him *simply* to rise at the hour or to rise at that hour *always,* or to rise at that hour *till further orders,* it may be said, with propriety, that you lay down a *rule* for the guidance of your servant's conduct. For no specific act is assigned by the command, but the command obliges him generally to acts of a determined class.

If a regiment be ordered to attack or defend a post, or to quell a riot, or to march from their present quarters, the command is occasional or particular. But an order to exercise daily till further orders shall be given would be called a *general* order, and *might* be called a *rule*.

If Parliament prohibited simply the exportation of corn, either for a given period or indefinitely, it would establish a law or rule: a *kind* or *sort* of acts being determined by the command, and acts of that kind or sort being *generally* forbidden. But an order issued by Parliament to meet an impending scarcity, and stopping the exportation of corn *then shipped and in port,* would not be a law or rule, though issued by the sovereign legislature. The order regarding exclusively a specified quantity of corn, the negative acts or forbearances, enjoined by the command, would be determined specifically or individually by the determinate nature of their subject.

As issued by a sovereign legislature, and as wearing the form of a law, the order which I have now imagined would probably be *called* a law. And hence the difficulty of drawing a distinct boundary between laws and occasional commands.

Again: An act which is not an offence, according to the existing law, moves the sovereign to displeasure; and though the authors of the act are legally innocent or unoffending, the sovereign commands that they shall be punished. As enjoining a specific punishment in that specific case, and as not enjoining generally acts or forbearances of a class, the order uttered by the sovereign is not a law or rule.

Whether such an order would be *called* a law, seems to depend upon circumstances which are purely immaterial: immaterial, that is, with reference to the present purpose, though material with reference to others. If made by a sovereign assembly deliberately, and with the forms of legislation, it would probably be called a law. If uttered by an absolute monarch, without deliberation or ceremony, it would scarcely be confounded with acts of legislation, and would be styled an arbitrary command. Yet, on either of these suppositions, its nature would be the same. It would not be a law or rule, but an occasional or particular command of the sovereign One or Number.

To conclude with an example which best illustrates the distinction, and which shows the importance of the distinction most conspicuously, *judicial commands* are commonly occasional or particular, although the commands which they are calculated to enforce are commonly laws or rules.

For instance, the lawgiver commands that thieves shall be hanged. A specific theft and a specified thief being given, the judge commands that the thief shall be hanged, agreeably to the command of the lawgiver.

Now the lawgiver determines a class or description of acts; prohibits acts of the class generally and indefinitely; and commands, with the like generality, that punishment shall follow transgression. The command of the lawgiver is, therefore, a law or rule. But the command of the judge is occasional or particular. For he orders a specific punishment, as the consequence of a specific offence.

According to the line of separation which I have now attempted to describe, a law and a particular command are distinguished thus: —Acts or forbearances of a class are enjoined *generally* by the former. Acts *determined specifically,* are enjoyed or forbidden by the latter.

A different line of separation has been drawn by Blackstone and others. According to Blackstone and others, a law and a particular command are distinguished in the following manner: —A law obliges *generally* the members of the given community, or a law obliges *generally* persons of a given class. A particular command obliges a *single* person, or persons whom it determines *individually*.

That laws and particular commands are not to be distinguished thus, will appear on a moment's reflection.

For, *first,* commands which oblige generally the members of the given community, or commands which oblige generally persons of given classes, are not always laws or rules.

Thus, in the case already supposed; that in which the sovereign commands that all corn actually shipped for exportation be stopped and detained; the command is obligatory upon the whole community, but as it obliges them only to a set of acts individually assigned, it is not a law. Again, suppose the sovereign to issue an order, enforced by penalties, for a general mourning on occasion of a public calamity. Now, though it is addressed to the community at large, the order is scarcely a rule, in the usual acceptation of the term. For, though it obliges generally the members of the entire community, it obliges to acts which it assigns specifically, instead of obliging generally to acts or forbearances of class. If the sovereign commanded that *black* should be the dress of his subjects, his command would amount to a law. But if he commanded them to wear it on a specified occasion, his command would be merely particular.

And, *secondly,* a command which obliges exclusively persons individually determined, may amount, notwithstanding, to a law or rule.

For example, a Father may set *a rule* to his child or children: a guardian, to his ward: a master, to his slave or servant. And certain of God's *laws* were as binding on the first man, as they are binding at his hour on the millions who have sprung from his loins.

Most, indeed, of the laws which are established by political superiors, or most of the laws which are simply and strictly so called, oblige generally the members of the political community, or oblige generally persons of a class. To frame a system of duties for every individual of the community, were simply impossible: and if it were possible, it were utterly useless. Most of the laws established by poliltical superiors are, therefore, *general* in a twofold manner: as enjoining or forbidding generally acts of kinds or sorts; and is binding the whole community, or, at least, whole classes of it members.

But if we suppose that Parliament creates a grants an office, and that Parliament binds the grantee to services of a given description, we suppose a law established by political superiors, and yet exclusively binding a specified or determinate person.

• • •

It appears, from what has been promised, that a law, properly so called, may be defined in the following manner.

A law is a command which obliges a person or persons.

But, as contradistinguished or opposed to an occasional or particular command, a law is a command which obliges a person or persons, and obliges *generally* to acts or forbearances of a class.

In language more popular but less distinct and precise, a law is a command which obliges a person or persons to a *course* of conduct.

Laws and other commands are said to proceed from *superiors,* and to bind or oblige *inferiors*. . . .

Superiority is often synonymous with *precedence* or *excellence*. We talk of superiors in rank; of superiors in wealth; of superiors in virtue: comparing certain persons with certain other persons; and meaning that the former precede or excel the latter in rank, in wealth, or in virtue.

But, taken with the meaning wherein I here understand it, the term *superiority* signifies *might:* the power of affecting others with evil or pain, and of forcing them, through fear of that evil, to fashion their conduct to one's wishes.

For example, God is emphatically the *superior* of Man. For his power of affecting us with pain, and of forcing us to comply with his will, is unbounded and resistless.

To a limited extent, the sovereign One or Number is the superior of the subject or citizen: the master, of the slave or servant: the father, of the child.

In short, whoever can *oblige* another to comply with his wishes, is the *superior* of that other, so far as the ability reaches: The party who is obnoxious to the impending evil, being, to the same extent, the *inferior*.

The might or superiority of God, is simple or absolute. But in all or most cases of human superiority, the relation of superior and inferior, and the relation of inferior and superior, are reciprocal. Or (changing the expression) the party who is the superior as viewed from one aspect, is the inferior as viewed from another.

For example, To an indefinite, though limited extent, the monarch is the superior of the governed: his power being commonly sufficient to enforce compliance with his will. But the governed, collectively or in mass, are also the superior of the monarch: who is checked in the abuse of his might by his fear of exciting their anger; and of rousing to active resistance the might which slumbers in the multitude.

A member of a sovereign assembly is the superior of the judge: the judge being bound by the law which proceeds from that sovereign body. But, in his character of citizen or subject, he is the inferior of the judge: the judge being the minister of the law, and armed with the power of enforcing it.

It appears, then, that the term *superiority* (like the terms *duty* and *sanction)* is implied by the term *command*. For superiority is the power of enforcing compliance with a wish; and the expression or intimation of a wish, with the power and the purpose of enforcing it, are the constituent elements of a command.

'That *laws* emanate from *superiors'* is, therefore, an identical proposition. For the meaning which it affects to impart is contained in its subject.

•   •   •

. . . There are other objects improperly termed laws (not being commands) which yet may properly be included within the province of jurisprudence. These I shall endeavor to particularize:—

1. Acts on the part of legislatures to *explain* positive law, can scarcely be called laws, in the proper signification of the term. Working no change in the actual duties of the governed, but simply declaring what those duties *are,* they properly are acts of *interpretation* by legislative authority. Or, to borrow an expression from the writers on the Roman Law, they are acts of *authentic* interpretation.

But, this notwithstanding, they are frequently styled laws; *declaratory* laws, or declaratory statutes. They must, therefore, be noted as forming an exception to the proposition that laws are a species of commands. . . .

2. Laws to repeal laws, and to release from existing duties, which also be excepted from the proposition 'that laws are a species of commands.' In so far as they release from duties imposed by existing laws, they are not commands, but revocations of commands. They authorize or permit the parties, to whom the repeal extends, to do or to forbear from acts which they were commanded to forbear from or to do. And, considered with regard to this, their immediate or direct purpose, they are often named *permissive laws,* or, more briefly and more properly, *permissions*.

Remotely and indirectly, indeed, permissive laws are often or always imperative. For the parties released from duties are restored to liberties or rights; and duties answering those rights are, therefore, created or revised. . . .

3. Imperfect laws, or laws of imperfect obligations, must also be excepted from the proposition that laws are a species of commands.

4. An imperfect law (with the sense wherein the term is used by the Roman jurists) is a law which wants a sanction, and which, therefore, is not binding. A law declaring that certain acts are crimes, but *annexing* no punishment to the commission of the class, is the simplest and most obvious example.

Though the author of an imperfect law signifies a desire, he manifests no purpose of enforcing compliance with the desire. But where there is not a purpose of enforcing compliance with desire, the expression of a desire is not a command. Consequently, an imperfect law is not so properly a law, as counsel, or exhortation, addressed by a superior to inferiors.

•   •   •

The imperfect laws, of which I am now speaking, are laws which are imperfect, in the sense of the *Roman jurists:* that is to say, laws which speak the desires of political superiors, but which their authors (by oversight or design) have not provided with sanctions. . . .

. . . there are certain laws (properly so called) which may *seem* not imperative. Accordingly, I will subjoin a few remarks upon laws of this dubious character.

1. There are laws, it may be said, which *merely* create *rights:* And, seeing that every command imposes a *duty,* laws of this nature are not imperative.

But, as I have intimated already, and shall show completely hereafter, there are no laws *merely* creating *rights.* There are laws, it is true, which *merely* create *duties:* duties not correlating with correlating rights, and which, therefore may be styled *absolute.* But every law, really conferring a right, imposes expressly or tacitly a *relative* duty, or a duty correlating with the right. If it specify the remedy to be given, in case the right shall be infringed, it imposes the relative duty expressly. If the remedy to be given be not specified, it refers tacitly to pre-existing law, and clothes the right which it purports to create with a remedy provided by that law. Every law, really conferring a right, is, therefore, imperative: as imperative, as if its only purpose were the creation of a duty, or as if the relative duty, which it inevitably imposes, were merely absolute.

The meanings of the term *right,* are various and perplexed; taken with its proper meaning, it comprises ideas which are numerous and complicated; and the searching and extensive analysis, which the term, therefore, requires, would occupy more room than could be given to it in the present lecture. . . .

2. According to an opinion which I must notice *incidentally* here, though the subject to which it relates will be treated *directly* hereafter, *customary* laws must be excepted from the proposition that laws are a species of commands.

• • •

. . . According to the latter opinion, all judge-made law, or all judge-man law established by *subject* judges, is purely the creature of the judges by whom it is established immediately. To impute it to the sovereign legislature, or to suppose that it speaks the will of the sovereign legislature, is one of the foolish or knavish *fictions* with which lawyers, in every age and nation, have perplexed and darkened the simplest and clearest truths.

I think it will appear on a moment's reflection, that . . . customary law is *imperative,* in the proper signification of the term; and that all judge-made law is the creature of the sovereign or state.

At its origin, a custom is a rule of conduct which the governed observe spontaneously, or not in pursuance of a law set by a political superior. The custom is transmuted into positive law, when it is adopted as such by the courts of justice, and when the judicial decisions fashioned upon it are enforced by the power of the state. But before it is adopted by the courts, and clothed with the legal sanction, it is merely a rule of positive morality: a rule generally observed by the citizens or subjects; but deriving the only force, which it can be said to possess, from the general disapprobation falling on those who transgress it.

Now when judges transmute a custom into a legal rule (or make a legal rule not suggested by a custom), the legal rule which they establish is established by the sovereign legislature. A subordinate or subject judge is merely a minister. The portion of the sovereign power which lies at his disposition is merely delegated. The rules which he makes derive their legal force from authority given by the state: an authority which the state may confer expressly, but which it commonly imparts in the way of acquiescence. For, since the state may reverse the rules which he makes, and yet permits him to enforce them by the power of the political community, its sovereign will 'that his rules shall obtain as law' is clearly evinced by its conduct, though not by its express declaration.

•   •   •

The opinion of the party which abhors judge-made laws, springs from their inadequate conception of the nature of commands.

Like other significations of desire, a command is express or tacit. If the desire he signified by *words* (written or spoken), the command is express. If the desire be signified by conduct (or by any signs of desire which are *not* words), the command is tacit.

Now when customs are turned into legal rules by decisions of subject judges, the legal rules which emerge from the customs are *tacit* commands of the sovereign legislature. The state, which is able to abolish, permits its ministers to enforce them: and it, therefore, signifies its pleasure, by that [sic] its voluntary acquiescence, 'that they shall serve as a law to the governed.'

My present purpose is merely this: to prove that the positive law styled *customary* (and all positive law made judicially) is established by the state directly or circuitously, and, therefore, is *imperative*. I am far from disputing, that law made judicially (or in the way of improper legislation) and law made by statute (or in the properly legislative manner) are distinguished by weighty differences. I shall inquire, in future lectures, what those differences are; and why subject judges, who are properly ministers of the law, have commonly shared with the sovereign in the business of making it.

I assume, then, that the only laws which are not imperative, and which belong to the subject-matter of jurisprudence, are the following:—1. Declaratory laws, or laws explaining the import of existing positive law. 2. Laws abrogating or repealing existing positive law. 3. *Imperfect* laws, or laws of *imperfect* obligation.

NOTES

1. The preferred method of Positivist jurisprudence was human observation of the structure of the law, without, unfortunately, much consideration of what the appropriate focus was. But contrary to the natural law school, there were to be no a priori assertions other than that law was made by humans rather than emanating from a transcendental source. Austin posited that law is a rule laid down by a political superior for a political inferior. Is the foregoing statement accurately descriptive? Explain.

2. Among other things, Austin invoked Divine Law which was to be discovered by the application of Bentham's postulated Pleasure-Pain Principle and the Principle of Utility (see Chapter 12). Under the Pleasure-Pain Principle, actions are to be approved or disapproved according to whether they augment happiness or pleasure or prevent unhappiness or pain. The Utility Principle, briefly put, holds that choices are to be made so as to increase or optimalize the greatest pleasure of the greatest number. Do you think that the religions you are familiar with are based on pleasure-pain and utility principles? Discuss.

3. Many factors may have accounted for Austin's focus on rules and the painstaking analysis by him and other Positivists of the precise meaning of many terms in black letter law. Concern over the vagueness and diffusion of natural law may have stimulated an attempt to limit sharply the discretion of appliers of law at all levels, particularly of judges and to assure neutrality in decision and the avoidance of bias influencing outcomes. Psychological factors and acculturation should not be excluded. Austin's wife felt that he had been influenced by his years of army service as a young man. (See preface to J. Austin, *Lectures on Jurisprudence* 3 (5th ed. 1885). Do you think that certain jurisprudential frames may be attractive to certain personality types? Which ones? Why?

4. Compare Austin's view that law is a command backed by a sanction not by a reward, with the view of contemporary psychologists that such factors as trust, fairness, credibility and affiliation are more important factors than coercion in securing obedience to rules (see J. Piaget, *The Moral Judgment Of The Child*, (1932); E. Erikson, Identity and the Life Cycle, I *Psychologic Issues* (1959); Id., *Insight and Responsibility* (1964).

Why did Austin depart from the views of his mentor, Bentham and insist that the possibility of sanctions, not rewards, was the factor that transformed a command into law?

5. The Philosophical Radicalist movement in England and the tradition of Liberalism sought to limit the sphere of governmental intrusion into areas of private activity. On the continent, there may have been a distrust of judges who had been identified in the past with the aristocracy or the state religion, against the interests of a particular class, formerly powerless, but now with increased influence in the legislature. What protection could legislation give if judges could override frustrating expectations and plans based upon statutes? Hence the growing attraction of the notion that governemnt should be a "government of laws, not men" and a focus upon rules as a technique to limit the discretion of appliers of law. Does this have application to the United States? Discuss.

6. A key political strut underpinning positivism was the notion of the legislative supremacy of Parliament. This doctrine had come to reflect the enhanced political power of the class that had now won great influence in the House of Commons. Since this same group retained loyalty to certain moral principles, not shared by the majority, a dichotomy characteristic of modern positivism emerged: the conflict between law and morality. Does it arise in any of the schools of jurisprudence considered in preceding chapters? Discuss.

7. The notion of law as the command of the sovereign, binding upon all and superordinate to the power of judges, has been acknowledged by many. Blackstone commented, "I know of no power in the ordinary forms of the Constitution, that is vested with the authority to control it [Parliament]." 1 W. Blackstone, *Commentaries on the Law of England* 91 (1815). Consider the following:

> It is often said that it would be unconstitutional for the United Kingdom Parliament to do certain things, meaning that the moral, political and other reasons against doing them are so strong that most people would regard it as highly improper if Parliament did these things. But that does not mean that it is beyond the power of Parliament to do such things. If Parliament chose to do any of them the courts could not hold the Act of Parliament invalid. *Madzimbamuto v. Burke-Lardner* [1969] A.C. 710, 723.

How different is this from the notion of law as the incontestable order of a political superior, which binds all, including judges, and *ipso facto* is valid, applied in Nazi Germany? Consider the description of the Nuremberg Tribunal in the *Justice* case. (Case No. 3, Military Tribunal III, National Military Tribunal):

> We pass now . . . to a consideration of the law in action, and of the influence of the "Fuehrer principle" as it affected, the officials of the Ministry of Justice, prosecutors, and judges. Two basic principles controlled conduct within the Ministry of Justice. The first concerned the absolute power of Hilter in person or by delegated authority to enact, enforce, and adjudicate law. The second concerned the incontestability of such law. Both principles were expounded by the learned Professor Jahrreiss, a witness for all of the defendants. Concerning the first principle, Dr. Jahrreiss said:
>
> > If now in the European meaning one asks about legal restrictions, and first of all one asks about restrictions of the German law, one will have to say that restrictions under German Law did not exist for Hitler. He was *legibus solutus* in the same meaning in which Louis XIV claimed that for himself in France. Anybody who said something different expresses a wish that does not describe the actual legal facts.
>
> Concerning the second principle, Jahrreiss supported the opinion of Gerhard Anschuetz, "crown jurist of the Weimar Republic", who holds that if German laws were

enacted by regular procedure, judicial authorities were without power to challenge them on constitutional or ethical grounds. Under the Nazi system, and even prior thereto, German judges were also bound to apply German law even when in violation of the principles of international law . . . .

Compare *Madzimbamuto* and the description in the *Nuremberg* decision. Discuss.

HART'S CONCEPT

Professor H.L.A. Hart of Oxford is probably the foremost contemporary exponent of positivism. He claims to be in the tradition of John Austin. In his major work, *The Concept of Law* (1961), Hart indicates certain problems with the Austinian formula and suggests an alternative version of Positivism which addresses those problems.

The selections which follow reflect Hart's concern with the two strands of Positivism: the conception of law as composed of political orders and the moral dissonance produced by that theory.

HART, THE CONCEPT OF LAW 78-96 (1961)

. . . the elements out of which the theory was constructed, viz, the ideas of orders, obedience, habits, and threats, do not include, and cannot by their combination yield, the idea of a rule, without which we cannot hope to elucidate even the most elementary forms of law. It is true that the idea of a rule is by no means a simple one: we have already seen in Chapter III the need, if we are to do justice to the complexity of a legal system, to discriminate between two different though related types. Under rules of the one type, which may well be considered the basic or primary type, human beings are require to do or obstain from certain actions, whether they wish to or not. Rules of the other type are in a sense parasitic upon or secondary to the first; for they provide that human beings may by doing or saying certain things introduce new rules of the primary type, extinguish or modify old ones, or in various ways determine their incidence or control their operations. Rules of the first type impose duties; rules of the second type confer powers, public or private. Rules of the first type concern actions involving physical movement or changes; rules of the second type provide for operations which lead not merely to physical movement or change, but to the creation or variation of duties or obligations . . . . in the combination of these two types of rule there lies what Austin wrongly claimed to have found in the notion of coercive orders, namely, the key to the science of jurisprudence . . . . What we shall attempt to show, in this and the succeeding chapters, is that most of the features of law which have proved most perplexing and have both provoked and eluded the search for definition can best be rendered clear, if these two types of rule and the interplay between them are understood. We accord this union of elements a central place because of their explanatory power in elucidating the concepts that constitute the framework of legal thought. . . .

2. THE IDEA OF OBLIGATION

It will be recalled that the theory of law as coercive orders, notwithstanding its errors, started from the perfectly correct appreciation of the fact that where there is law, there human conduct is made in some sense non-optional or obligatory. In choosing this starting-point the theory was well inspired, and in building up a new account of law in terms of the interplay of primary and secondary rules we too shall start from the same idea. It is, however, here, at this crucial first step, that we have perhaps most to learn from the theory's errors.

Let us recall the gunman situation. A orders B to hand over his money and threatens to shoot him if he does not comply. According to the theory of coercive orders this situation illustrates the notion of obligation or duty in general. Legal obligation is to be found in this situation write large; A must be the sovereign habitually obeyed and the orders must be general, prescribing courses of conduct not single actions. The plausibility of the claim that the gunman situation displays the meaning of obligation lies in the fact that it is certainly one in which we would say that B, if he obeyed, was 'obliged' to hand over his money. It is, however, equally certain that we should mis-describe the situation if we said, on these facts, that B 'had an obligation' or a 'duty' to hand over the money. So from the start it is clear that we need something else for an understanding of the idea of obligation. There is a difference, yet to be explained, between the assertion that someone *was obliged* to do something and the assertion that he *had an obligation* to do it. The first is often a statement about the beliefs and motives with which an action is done: B was obliged to hand over his money, may simply mean, as it does in the gunman case, that he believed that some harm or other unpleasant consequences would befall him if he did not hand it over and he handed it over to avoid those consequences. In such cases the prospect of what would happen to the agent if he disobeyed has rendered something he would otherwise have preferred to have done (keep the money) less eligible.

Two further elements slightly complicate the elucidation of the notion of being obliged to do something. It seems clear that we should not think of B as obliged to hand over the money if the threatened harm was, according to common judgments, trivial in comparison with the disadvantage or serious consequences, either for B or for others, of complying with the orders, as it would be, for example, if A merely threatened to pinch B. Nor perhaps should we say that B was obliged, if there were no reasonable grounds for thinking that A could or would probably implement his threat of relatively serious harm. Yet, though such references to common judgments of comparative harm and reasonable estimates of likelihood, are implicit in this notion, the statement that a person was obliged to obey someone is, in the main, a psychological one referring to the beliefs and motives with which an action was done. But the statement that someone *had an obligation* to do something is of a very different type and there are many signs of this difference. Thus not only is it the case that the facts about B's action and his beliefs and motives in the gunman case, though sufficient to warrant the statement that B was obliged to hand over his purse, are not sufficient to warrant the statement that he had an obligation to do this; it is also the case that facts of this sort, i.e. facts about beliefs and motives, are not necessary for the truth of a statement that a person had an obligation to do something. Thus the statement that a person had an obligation, e.g. to tell the truth or report for military service, remains true even if he believed (reasonably or unreasonably) that he would never be found out and had nothing to fear from disobedience. Moreover, whereas the statement that he had this obligation is quite independent of the question whether or not he in fact reported or service, the statement that someone was obliged to do something, normally carries the implication that he actually did it.

Some theorists, Austin among them, seeing perhaps the general irrelevance of the person's beliefs, fears, and motives to the question whether he had an obligation to do something, have defined this notion not in terms of these subjective facts, but in terms of the *chance* or *likelihood* that the person having the obligation will suffer a punishment or 'evil' at the hands of others in the event of disobedience. This, in effect, treats statements of obligation not as psychological statements but as predictions or assessments of chances of incurring punishment or 'evil'. To many later theorists this has appeared as a revelation, bringing down to earth an elusive notion and restating it in the same clear, hard, empirical terms as are used in science. It has, indeed, been accepted sometimes as the only alternative to metaphysical conceptions of obligation or duty as invisible objects mysteriously existing 'above' or 'behind' the world of ordinary, observable facts. But there are many reasons for rejecting this interpretation of statements of obligation as predictions, and it is not, in fact, the only alternative to obscure metaphysics.

The fundamental objection is that the predictive interpretation obscures the fact that, where rules exist, deviations from them are not merely grounds for a prediction that hostile reactions will follow or that a court will apply sanctions to those who break them, but are also a reason or justification for such reaction and for applying the sanctions. We have already drawn attention in Chapter IV to this neglect of the internal aspect of rules and we shall elaborate it later in this chapter.

There is, however, a second, simpler objection to the predictive interpretation of obligation. If it were true that the statement that a person had an obligation meant that *he* was likely to suffer in the event of disobedience, it would be a contradiction to say that he had an obligation, e.g. to report for military service, but that owing to this fact that he had escaped from the jurisdiction, or had successfully bribed the police of the court, there was not the slightest chance of his being caught or made to suffer. In fact, there is no contradiction in saying this and such statements are often made and understood.

It is, of course, true that in a normal legal system, where sanctions are exacted for a high proportion of offences, an offender usually runs a risk of punishment; so, usually the statement that a person has an obligation and the statement that he is likely to suffer for disobedience will both be true together. Indeed, the connexion between these two statements is somewhat stronger than this: at least in a municipal system it may well be true that, unless *in general* sanctions were likely to be exacted from offenders, there would be little or no point in making particular statements about a person's obligations. In this sense, such statements may be said to presuppose belief in the continued normal operation of the system of sanctions much as the statement 'he is out' in cricket presupposes, though it does not assert, that players, umpire, and scorer will probably take the usual steps. Nonetheless, it is crucial for the understanding of the idea of obligation to see that in individual cases the statement that a person has an obligation under some rule and the prediction that he is likely to suffer for disobedience may diverge.

It is clear that obligation is not to be found in the gunman situation, though the simpler notion of being obliged to do something may well be defined in the elements present there. To understand the general idea of obligation as a necessary preliminary to understanding it in its legal form, we must turn to a different social situation which, unlike the gunman situation, includes the existence of social rules; for this situation contributes to the meaning of the statement that a person has an obligation in two ways. First, the existence of such rules, making certain types of behaviour a standard, is the normal, though unstated, background or proper context for such a statement; and, secondly, the distinctive function of such statement is to apply such a general rule to a particular person by calling attention to the fact that his case falls under it.

• • •

Rules are conceived and spoken of as imposing obligations when the general demand for conformity is insistent and the social pressure brought to bear upon those who deviate or threaten to deviate is great. Such rules may be wholly customary in origin: there may be no centrally organized system of punishments for breach of the rules; the social pressure may take only the form of a general diffused hostile or critical reaction which may stop short of physical sanctions. It may be limited to verbal manifestations of disapproval or of appeals to the individuals' respect for the rule violated; it may depend heavily on the operations of feelings of shame, remorse, and guilt. When the pressure is of this last-mentioned kind we may be inclined to classify the rules as part of the morality of the social group and the obligation under the rules as moral obligation. Conversely, when physical sanctions are prominent or usual among the forms of pressure, even though these are neither closely defined nor administered by officials but are left to the community at large, we shall be inclined to classify the rules as a primitive or rudimentary form of law. We may, of course, find both these types of serious social pressure behind what is, in an obvious sense, the same rule of conduct; sometimes this may occur with no indication that one of them is peculiarly appropriate as primary and the other secondary, and then the question whether we are confronted with a rule of morality or rudimentary law may not be susceptible of an answer. But for the moment the possibility of drawing the line between law and morals need not detain us. What is important is that the insistence on importance or *seriousness* of social pressure behind the rules is the primary factor determining whether they are thought of as giving rise to obligations.

Two other characteristics of obligation go naturally together with this primary one. The rules supported by this serious pressure are thought important because they are believed to be necessary to the maintenance of social life or some highly prized feature of it. Characteristically, rules so obviously essential as those which restrict the free use of violence are thought of in terms of obligation. So too rules which require honesty or truth or require the keeping of promises, or specify what is to be done by one who performs a distinctive role or function in the social group are thought of in terms of either 'obligation' or perhaps more often 'duty'. Secondly, it is generally recognized that the conduct required by these rules may, while be- nefiting others, conflict with what the person who owes the duty may wish to do. Hence obligations and duties are thought of as characteristically involving sacrifice or renunciation, and the standing possibility of conflict between obligation or duty and interest is, in all societies, among the truisms of both the lawyer and the moralist.

• • •

. . . The fact that rules of obligation are generally supported by serious social pressure does not entail that to have an obligation under the rules is to experience feelings of compulsion or pressure. Hence there is no contradicition in saying of some hardened swindler, and it may often be true, that he had an obligation to pay the rent but felt no pressure to pay when he made off without doing so. To *feel* obliged and to have an obligation are different though frequently concomitant things. To identify them would be one way of misinterpreting, in terms of psychological feelings, the important internal aspect of rules to which we drew attention in Chapter III.

Indeed, the internal aspect of rules is something to which we must again refer before we can dispose finally of the claims of the predictive theory. For an advocate of that theory may well ask why, if social pressure is so important a feature of rules of obligation, we are yet so concerned to stress the inadequacies of the predictive theory; for it gives this very feature a central place by defining obligation in terms of the likelihood that threatened punishment or hostile reaction will follow deviation from certain lines of conduct. The difference may seem slight between the analysis of a statement of obligation as a prediction, or assessment of the chances, of hostile reaction to deviation, and our own contention that though this statement presupposes a background in which deviations from rules are generally met by hostile reactions, yet its characteristic use is not to predict this but to say that a person's case falls under such a rule. In fact, however, this difference is not a slight one. Indeed, until its importance is grasped, we cannot properly understand the whole distinctive style of human thought, speech, and action which is involved in the existence of rules and which constitutes the normative structure of society.

The following contrast again in terms of the 'internal' and 'external' aspect of rules may serve to mark what gives this distinction its great importance for the understanding not only of the law but of the structure of any society. When a social group has certain rules of conduct, this fact afford an opportunity for many closely related yet different kinds of assertion; for it is possible to be concerned with the rules, either merely as an observer who does not himself accept them, or as a member of the group which accepts and uses them as guides to conduct. We may call these respectively the 'external' and the 'internal points of view'. Statements made from the external point of view may themseslves be of different kings. For the observer may, without accepting the rules himself, assert that the group accepts the rules, and thus may from outside refer to the way in which *they* are concerned with them from the internal point of view. But whatever the rules are, whether they are those of games, like chess or cricket, or moral or legal rules, we can if we choose occupy the position of an observer who does not even refer in this way to the internal point of view of the group. Such an observer is content merely to record the regularities, in the form of the hostile reaction, reproofs, or punishments, with which deviations from the rules are met. After a time the external observer may, on the basis of the regularities observed, correlate deviation with hostile reaction, and be able to predict with a fair measure of success, and to assess the chances that a deviation from the group's normal behavior will meet with hostile reaction or punishment. Such knowledge may not only reveal much about the group, but might enable him to live among them without unpleasant consequences which would attend one who attempted to do so without such knowledge.

If, however, the observer really keeps austerely to this extreme external point of view and does not give any account of the manner in which members of the group who accept the rules view their own regular behaviour, his description of their life cannot be in terms of rules at all, and so not in the terms of the rule-dependent notions of obligation or duty. Instead, it will be in terms of observable regularities of conduct, predictions, probabilities, and signs. For such an observer, deviations by a member of the group from normal conduct will be a sign that hostile reaction is likely to follow, and nothing more. His view will be like the view of one who, having observed the working of a traffic signal in a busy street for some time, limits himself to saying that when the light turns red there is a high probability that the traffic will stop. He treats the light merely as a natural *sign that* people will behave in certain ways, as clouds are a *sign that* rain will come. In so doing he will miss out a whole dimension of the social life of those whom he is watching, since for them the red light is not merely a sign that others will stop: they look upon it as a *signal for* them to stop, and so a reason for stopping conformity to rules which make stopping when the light is red a standard of behaviour and an obligation. To mention that is to bring into the account the way in which the group regards its own behaviour. It is to refer to the internal aspect of rules seen from their internal point of view.

The external point of view may very nearly reproduce the way in which the rules function in the lives of certain members of the group, namely those who reject its rules and are only concerned with them when and because they judge that unpleasant consequences are likely to follow violation. Their point of view will need for its expression, 'I was obliged to do it', I am likely to suffer for it if . . . ' . But they will not need forms of expression like 'I had an obligation' or 'You have an obligation' for these are required only by those who see their own and other persons' conduct from the internal point of view. What the external point of view, which limits itself to observable regularities of behaviour, cannot reproduce is the way in which the rules function as rules in the lives of those who normally are the majority of society. These are the officials, lawyers or private persons who use them, in one situation after another, as guides to the conduct of social like, as the basis for claims, demands, admissions, criticism, or punishment, viz., in all the familiar transactions of life according to rules. For them the violation of a rule is not merely a basis for the prediction that a hostile reaction will follow but a *reason* for hostility.

At any given moment the life of any society which lives by rules, legal or not, is likely to consist in a tension between those who, on the one hand, accept and voluntarily co-operate in maintaining the rules, and so see their own and other persons' behaviour in terms of the rules, and those who, on the other hand, reject the rules and attend to them only from the external point of view as a sign of possible punishment. One of the difficulties facing any legal theory anxious to do justice to the complexity of the facts is to remember the presence of both these points of view and not to define one of them out of existence. Perhaps all our criticisms of the predictive theory of obligation may be best summarized as the accusation that this is what it does to the internal aspect of obligatory rules.

3. THE ELEMENTS OF LAW

It is, of course, possible to imagine a society without a legislature, courts or officials of any kind. Indeed, there are many studies of primitive communities which not only claim that this possibility is realized but depict in detail the life of a society where the only means of social control is that general attitude of the group towards its own standard modes of behaviour in terms of which we have characterized rules of obligation. A social structure of this kind is often referred to as one of 'custom'; but we shall not use this term, because it often implies that the customary rules are very old and supported with less social pressure than other rules. To avoid these implications we shall refer to such a social structure as one of primary rules of obligation. If a society is to live by such primary rules alone, there are certain conditions which, granted a few of the most obvious truisms about human nature and the world we live in, must clearly be satisfied. The first of these conditions is that the rules must contain in some form restrictions on the free use of violence, theft, and deception to which human beings are tempted but which they must, in general, repress, if they are to coexist in close proximity to each other. Such rules are in fact always found in the primitive societies of which we have knowledge, together with a variety of others imposing on individuals various positive duties to perform services or make contributions to the common life. Secondly, though such a society may exhibit the tension, already described, between those who accept the rules and those who reject the rules except where fear of social pressure induces them to conform, it is plain that the latter cannot be more than a minority, if so loosely organized a society of persons, approximately equal in physical strength, is to endure: for otherwise those who reject the rules would have too little social pressure to fear. This too is confirmed by what we know of primitive communities where, though there are dissidents and malefactors, the majority live by the rules seen from the internal point of view.

More important for our present purpose is the following consideration. It is plain that only a small community closely knit by ties of kinship, common sentiment, and belief, and placed in a stable environment, could live successfully by such a regime of unofficial rules. In any other conditions such a simple form of social control must prove defective and will require supplementation in different ways. In the first place, the rules by which the group lives will not form a system, but will simply be a set of separate standards, without any identifying or common mark, except of course that they are the rules which a particular group of human beings accepts. They will in this respect resemble our own rules of etiquette. Hence if doubts arise as to what the rules are or as to the precise scope of some given rule, there will be no procedure for settling this doubt, either by reference to an authoritative text or to an official whose declarations on this point are authoritative. For, plainly, such a procedure and the acknowledgement of either authoritative text or persons involve the existence of rules of a type of different from the rules of obligation or duty which *ex hypothesi* are all that the group has. This defect in the simple social structure of primary rules we may call its *uncertainty*.

A second defect is the *static* character of the rules. The only mode of change in the rules known to such a society will be the slow process of growth, whereby courses of conduct once thought optional become first habitual or usual, and then obligatory, and the converse process of decay, when deviations, once severely dealt with, are first tolerated and then pass unnoticed. There will be no means, in such a society, of deliberately adapting the rules to changing circumstances, either by eliminating old rules or introducing new ones: for, again, the possibility of doing this presupposess the existence of rules of a different type from the primary rules of obligation by which alone the society lives. In an extreme case the rules may be static in a more drastic sense. This, though never perhaps fully realized in any actual community, is worth considering because the remedy for it is something very characteristic of law. In this extreme case, not only would there be no way of deliberately changing the general rules, but the obligations which arise under the rules in particular cases could not be varied or modified by the deliberate choice of any individual. Each individual would simply have fixed obligations or duties to do or abstain from doing certain things. It might indeed very often be the case that others would benefit from the performance of these obligations; yet, if there are only primary rules of obligation they would have no power to release those bound from performance or to transfer to others the benefits which would accrue from performance. For such operations of release or transfer create changes in the initial positions of individuals under the primary rules of obligations, and for these operations to be possible there must be rules of a sort different from the primary rules.

The third defect of this simple form of social life is the *inefficiency* of the diffuse social pressure by which the rules are maintained. Disputes as to whether an admitted rule has or has not been violated will always occur and will, in any but the smallest societies, continue interminably, if there is no agency specially empowered to ascertain finally, and authoritatively, the fact of violation. Lack of such final and authoritative determinations is to be distinguished from another weakness associated with it. This is the fact that punishments for violations of the rules, and other forms of social pressure involving physical effort or the use of force, are not administered by a special agency but are left to the individuals affected or to the group at large. It is obvious that the waste of time involved in the group's unorganized efforts to catch and punish offenders, and the smouldering vendettas which may result from self help in the absence of an official monopoly of 'sanctions', may be serious. The history of law does, however, strongly suggest that the lack of official agencies to determine authoritatively the fact of violation of the rules is a much more serious defect; for many societies have remedies for this defect long before the other.

The remedy for each of these three main defects in this simplest form of social structure consists in supplementing the *primary* rules of obligation with *secondary* rules which are rules of a different kind. The introduction of the remedy for each defect might, in itself, be considered a step from the pre-legal into the legal world; since each remedy brings with it many elements that permeate law: certainly all three remedies together are enough to convert the regime of primary rules into what is indisputably a legal system. We shall consider in turn each of these remedies and show why law may most illuminatingly be characterized as a union of primary rules of obligation with such secondary rules. Before we do this, however, the following general points should be noted. Though the remedies consist in the introduction of rules which are certainly different from each other, as well as from the primary rules of obligation which they supplement, they have important features in common and are connected in various ways. Thus they may all be said to be on a different level from the primary rules, for they are *about* such rules; in the sense that while primary rules are concerned with the actions that indivduals must or must not do, these secondary rules are all concerned with the primary rules themselves. They specify the ways in which the primary rules may be conclusively ascertained, introduced, eliminated, varied, and the fact of their volation conclusively determined.

The simplest form of remedy for the *uncertainty* of the regime of primary rules is the introduction of what we shall call a 'rule of recognition'. This will specify some feature or features possession of which by a suggested rule is taken as a conclusive affirmative indication that it is a rule of the group to be supported by the social pressure it exerts. The existence of such a rule of recognition may take any of a huge variety of forms, simple or complex. It may, as in the early law of many societies, be no more than that an authoritative list or text of the rules is to be found in a written document or carved on some public monument. No doubt as a matter of history this step from the pre-legal to the legal may be accomplished in distinguishable stages, of which the first is the mere reduction to writing of hitherto unwritten rules. This is not itself the crucial step, though it is a very important one: what is crucial is the acknowledgement of reference to the writing or inscription as *authoritative,* i.e. as the *proper* way of disposing of doubts as to the existence of the rule. Where there is such an acknowledgement there is a very simple form of secondary rule: a rule for conclusive identification of the primary rules of obligation.

In a developed legal system the rules of recognition are of course more complex; instead of identifying rules exclusively by reference to a text or list they do so by reference to some general characteristic possessed by the primary rules. This may be the fact of their having been enacted by a specific body, or their long customary practice, or their relation to judicial decisions. Moreover, where more than one of such general characteristics are treated as identifying criteria, provision may be made for their possible conflict by their arrangement in an order of superiority, as by the common subordination of custom or precedent to statute, the latter being a 'superior source' of law. Such complexity may make the rules of recognition in a modern legal system seem very different from the simple acceptance of an authoritative text: yet even in this simplest form, such a rule brings with it many elements distinctive of law. By providing an authoritative mark it introduces, although in embryonic form, the idea of a legal system: for the rules are now not just a discrete unconnected set but are, in a simple way, unified. Further, in the simple operation of identifying a given rule as possessing the required feature of being an item on an authoritative list of rules we may have the germ of the idea of legal validity.

The remedy for the *static* quality of the regime of primary rules consists in the introduction of what we shall call 'rules of change'. The simplest form of such a rule is that which empowers an individual or body of persons to introduce new primary rules for the conduct of the life of the group, or of some class within it, and to eliminate old rules. As we have already argued in Chapter IV it is in terms of such a rule, and not in terms of orders backed by threats, that the ideas of legislative enactment and repeal are to be understood. Such rules of change may be very simple or very complex: the powers conferred may be unrestricted or limited in various ways: and the rules may, besides specifying the persons who are to legislate, define in more or less rigid terms the procedure to be followed in legislation. Plainly, there will be a very close connexion between the rules of change and the rules of recognition: for where the former exists the latter will necessarily incorporate a reference to legislation as an identifying feature of the rules, though it need not refer to all the details of procedure involved in legislation. Usually some official certificate or official copy will, under the rules of recognition, be taken as a sufficient proof of due enactment. Of course if there is a social structure so simple that the only 'source of law' is legislation, the rule of recognition will simply specify enactment as the unique identifying mark or criterion of validity of the rules. This will be the case for example in the imaginary kingdom of Rex I depicted in Chapter IV: there the rule of recognition would simply be that whatever Rex I enacts is law.

We have already described in some detail the rules which confer on individuals power to vary their initial positions under the primary rules. Without such private power-conferring rules society would lack some of the chief amenities which law confers upon it. For the operations which these rules make possible are the making of wills, contracts, transfers of property, and many other voluntarily created structures of rights and duties which typify life under law, though of course an elementary form of power-conferring rule also underlies the moral institution of a promise. The kinship of these rules with the rules of change involved in the notion of legislation is clear, and as recent theory such as Kelsen's has shown, many of the features which puzzle us in the institutions of contract or property are clarified by thinking of the operations of making a contract or transferring property as the exercise of limited legislative powers by individuals.

The third supplement to the simple regime of primary rules, intended to remedy the *inefficiency* of its diffused social pressure, consists of secondary rules empowering individuals to make authoritative determinations of the question whether, on a particular occasion, a primary rule has been broken. The minimal form of adjudication consists in such determinations, and we shall call secondary rules which confer the power to make them 'rules of adjudication'. Besides identifying the individuals who are to adjudicate, such rules will also define the procedure to be followed. Like the other secondary rules these are on a different level from the primary rules: though they may be reinforced by further rules imposing duties on judges to adjudicate, they do not impose duties but confer judicial powers and a special status on judicial declarations about the breach of obligations. Again these rules, like the other secondary rules, define a group of important legal concepts: in this case the concepts of judge or court, jurisdiction and judgment. Besides these resemblances to the other secondary rules, rules of adjudication have intimate connexions with them. Indeed, a system which has rules of adjudication is necessarily also committed to a rule of recognition of an elementary and imperfect sort. This is so because, if courts are empowered to make authoritative determinations of the fact that a rule has been broken, these cannot avoid being taken as authoritative determinations of what the rules are. So the rule which confers jurisdiction will also be a rule of recognition, identifying the primary rules through the judgments of the courts and these judgments will become a 'source' of law. It is true that this form of rule of recognition, inseparable from the minimum form of jurisdiction, will be very imperfect. Unlike an authoritative text or a statute book, judgments may not be couched in general terms and their use as authoritative guides to the rules depends on a somewhat shaky inference from particular decisions, and the reliability of this must fluctuate both with the skill of the interpreter and the consistency of the judges.

It need hardly be said that in few legal systems are judicial powers confined to authoritative determinations of the fact of violation of the primary rules. Most systems have, after some delay, seen the advantages of further centralization of social pressure; and have partially prohibited the use of physical punishments or violent self help by private individuals. Instead they have supplemented the primary rules of obligation by further secondary rules, specifying or at least limiting the penalities for violation, and have conferred upon judges, where they have ascertained the fact of violation, the exclusive power to direct the application of penalities by other officials. These secondary rules provide the centralized official 'sanctions' of the system.

If we stand back and consider the structure which has resulted from the combination of primary rules of obligation with the secondary rules of recognition, change and adjudication, it is plain that we have here not only the heart of a legal system, but a most powerful tool for the analysis of much that has puzzled both the jurist and the political theorist.

Not only are the specifically legal concepts with which the lawyer is professionally concerned, such as those of obligation and rights, validity and source of law, legislation and jurisdiction, and sanction, best elucidated in terms of this combinationn of elements. The concepts (which bestride both law and political theory) of the state, of authority, and of an official require a similar analysis if the obscurity which still lingers about them is to be dissipated. The reason why an analysis in these terms of primary and secondary rules has this explanatory power is not far to seek. Most of the obscurities and distortions surrounding legal and political concepts arise from the fact that these essentially involve reference to what we have called the internal point of view: the view of those who do not merely record and predict behaviour conforming to rules, but *use* the rules as standards for the appraisal of their own and others' behaviour. This requires more detailed attention in the analysis of legal and political concepts than it has usually received. Under the simple regime of primary rules the internal point of view is manifested in its simplest form, in the use of those rules as the basis of criticism, and as the justification of demands for conformity, social pressure, and punishment. Reference to this most elementary manifestation of the internal point of view is required for the analysis of the basic concepts of oblilgation and duty. With the addition to the system of secondary rules, the range of what is said and done from the internal point of view is much extended and diversified. With this extension comes a whole set of new concepts and they demand a reference to the internal point of view for their analysis. These include the notions of legislation, jurisdiction, validity and, generally, of legal powers, private and public. There is a constant pull toward an analysis of these in the terms of ordinary or 'scientific', fact-stating or predictive discourse. But this can only reproduce their external aspect: to do justice to their distinctive, internal aspect we need to see the different ways in which the law-making operations of the legislator, the adjudication of a court, the exercise of the legislator, the adjudication of a court, the exercise of private or official powers, and other 'acts-in-the-law' are related to secondary rules.

NOTES

1. a. Positivism distinguished between the "is and the ought"—between what the law is, the province of jurisprudence, and what it should be. Bentham was largely concerned with "deontology," with what the law ought to be (see Chapter 12.) In the Positivist School's practical outlook, goal formulation and policy factors were disregarded. As one British judge expressed it, policy is "a very unruly horse, which can carry its rider he knows not where." (J. Burroughs, in *Richardson v. Mellish* 2 Bing. 229, 250 (1824), 130 Eng. Rep. 294, 302 (1824). This view led to criticism that the Positivists place an undue emphasis on derivational logic to solve problems and that they ignore the "ought" factors that are inevitably considered by decisionmakers (see Chapter 1). Discuss.

b. Recall the observation of Jhering in Chapter 6 that judges often have two contradictory legal precepts or lines of case precedent from which to choose, each of which will lead to a different decision. Are there things besides goals and policies on which the judge can and does base his choice? Discuss.

c. Both Bentham and Austin separated deontology, or the science of legislation (what the law should be), from "jurisprudence," the law as Austin thought it was. Both thought that the goals of law-making could be ascertained by resort to the Principle of Utility, or as Austin claimed, by reference to Divine Law, as ascertained by Bentham's Pleasure-Pain Principle. Was this principle used widely to ascertain specific goals or was it used merely as a device to infiltrate some elements of goal formulation into an allegedly autonomous rule system of law? Discuss.

2. Professor H.L.A. Hart, in the hope of avoiding the value neutralism of his predecessors, sought a "rational connexion between facts and the content of legal and moral rules" *(Concept of Law* 189-95, 196, reproduced at 282 supra). He did not, however, develop systematic criteria or a set of values to guide goal formulation, nor did he indicate just how the facts to which he alludes (such as the necessity of humans for survival) would be appllied in detail in concrete cases. Discuss.

3. a. Does authority play a role in Austin's conception of law as the command of a political superior backed with the power to inflict sanctions? Discuss the ways in which his conception is different from that of Thrasymachus (see Chapter 3).

b. Hart emphasizes the role of the "internal view" and "psychological" aspects of obedience to law. Does he leave any room for the notion of power as a component of a legal system? Is his position the converse of that of the exponents of the jurisprudence of naked power, examined in Chapter 2. Discuss.

4. a. Does the concept developed by Austin and Hart of law as rules (by political superiors to political inferiors) ignore much of what transpires in community-wide decisionmaking? In complex contemporary communities, what of the prescriptive or law-making roles of informal decisionmakers, such as labor leaders, religious leaders, information media personnel, the wealthy, university professors, etc.? What of the perspectives and acts of the members of the community?

b. In a democratic community, are legislators political superiors or are they also political inferiors subject to the will of the electorate? Is it more useful to conceive of decisionmaking as a two-way flow, rather than a hierarchy with ''orders'' flowing in only one direction?

5. Is Hart's analogy of the law of a community and the rules of a cricket game apt? Unlike the routinized, simple, and stable activity in a cricket game, the interactions, activities and conflicts in a changing, complex community are extraordinarily multifaceted. Discuss.

6. Even if one were to restrict one's concern with law to a focus on decision by judges—as Positivists often do—is it accurate to assume—as Positivists do—that such decisions are objective and simply entail applying a fixed rule to an objectively definable fact situation before the court? At the very least, a judge will be required to perform the following acts, all of which allow room for and even require substantial subjective discretion:

a) *Selecting the relevant facts.* The facts of every new case are different in some way from the facts of cases decided previously. A focus on one fact (or group of facts) rather than another, can greatly affect the decision.

b) *Selecting the relevant rule.* The rule actually applied must be selected from a huge reservoir of prior cases, statutes, doctrines, customary law, etc. Recall McDougal's observation in Chapter 6 that rules often travel in pairs of complementary opposites. Which of two equally applicable lines of precedent cases, rules, doctrines etc. should the judge apply to the case before him and why?

c) *Interpreting the law.* Since rules are usually phrased in general terms, the judge must decide what the rule ''means'' and what it was intended to accomplish, in applying it to the factually unique case at bar.

d) *Supplementing the rule.* Since no legislator can conceive in advance of every situation that may arise (especially, where conditions constantly change) rules cannot, and do not, provide for every possible situation and eventuality. The judge must then fill in the ''gaps'' in the law if he is not to return these cases to the legislature for enactment of additional legislation every time such cases arise.

e) *Formulating the remedy.* In formulating an appropriate remedy, the judge must take into account that certain remedies may not be effective because some of their effects may be undesirable or because they will stimulate too much resistance. Recall the statement of the U.S. Supreme Court in *Brown v. Board of Education* that its decision was to be carried out with ''deliberate'' speed, rather than at once, because of anticipated difficulties and resistance.

f) *Communicating the decision.* How the decision is to be worded can be crucial. Decisions in areas such as abortion and preferential treatment of minorities may arouse considerable emotional feelings in the community at certain times. A judge must accordingly be careful to formulate the decision in a manner calculated to minimize resistance and encourage compliance with the decision.

All the foregoing components of judicial decision (which by no means exhaust the steps required for decision) allow and require much subjectivity. Is the notion of law as rules applied objectively by a judge pertinent or useful to these functions? Discuss.

7. Refer to the Appendix at the end of Chapter 1. Aside from their falure to clarify goals adequately, do the theories of Austin and Hart give consideration to the study of any of the intellectual tasks outlined in the Appendix, i.e., the study of historial trends; the study of contexts and conditions of decision; the formulation of strategies to effect goals? Do they focus at all on patterns of actual control, including investigation of whether rules issued by political

superiors do, in fact, control behavior of those to whom the rules are directed? Is their study of law limited to decisions by those formally clothed with decisionmaking powers, such as judges and legislators, and does it include all others who may input into decisionmaking processes?

DWORKIN'S CONCEPT

Ronald Dworkin, a student of Hart and his successor at Oxford, carries even further than his mentor Positivism's focus on rules and on courts. But in his analysis Dworkin concedes that the model of rules as a technique of decision-making does not explain judicial behavior in many complex situations. To plug the gap, he incorporates the notion of "principles" to which judges may have resort in situations in which the rules available are not adequate for the decision. In reading the following selection, ask yourself whether Dworkin's conception of principles is sufficiently precise to fulfill the basic demands of positivistic jurisprudence.

DWORKIN, IS LAW A SYSTEM OF RULES?, IN THE PHILOSOPHY OF LAW
38-40, 42-52, 54-58, 60-65 (R. DWORKIN ed. 1977)

I. POSITIVISM

Positivism has a few central and organizing propositions as its skeleton, and though not every philosopher who is called a positivist would subscribe to these in the way I present them, they do define the general position I want to examine. These key tenets may be stated as follows:

(a) The law of a community is a set of special rules used by the community directly or indirectly for the purpose of determining which behaviour will be punished or coerced by the public power. These special rules can be identified and distinguished by specific criteria, by tests having to do not with their content but with their *pedigree* or the manner in which they were adopted or developed. These tests of pedigree can be used to distinguish valid legal rules from spurious legal rules (rules which lawyers and litigants wrongly argue are rules of law) and also from other sorts of social rules (generally lumped together as 'moral rules') that the community follows but does not enforce through public power.

(b) The set of these valid legal rules is exhaustive of 'the law', so that if someone's case is not clearly covered by such a rule (because there is none that seems appropriate, or those that seem appropriate are vague, or for some other reason) then that case cannot be decided by 'applying the law'. It must be decided by some official, like a judge, 'exercising his discretion', which means reaching beyond the law for some other sort of standard to guide him in manufacturing a fresh legal rule or supplementing an old one.

(c) To say that someone has a 'legal obligation' is to say that his case falls under a valid legal rule that requires him to do or to forbear from doing something. (To say he has a legal right, or has a legal power of some sort, or a legal privilege or immunity, is to assert, in a shorthand way, that others have actual or hypothetical legal obligations to act or not to act in certain ways touching him). In the absence of such a valid legal rule there is no legal obligation; it follows that when the judge decides an issue by exercising his discretion, he is not enforcing a legal obligation as to that issue.

This is only the skeleton of positivism. The flesh is arranged differently by different positivists, and some even tinker with the bones. Different versions differ chiefly in their description of the fundamental test of pedigree a rule must meet to count as a rule of law. . . .

H.L.A. Hart's version of positivism is more complex than Austin's, in two ways. First, he recognizes, as Austin did not, that rules are of different logical kinds (Hart distinguishes two kinds, which he call 'primary' and 'secondary' rules). Second, he rejects Austin's theory that a rule is a kind of command, and substitutes a more elaborate general analysis of what rules are. We must pause over each of these points, and then note how they merge in Hart's concept of law. . . . Primary rules are those that grant rights or impose oblilgations upon members of the community. The rules of the criminal law that forbid us to rob, murder, or drive too fast are good examples of primary rules. Secondary rules are those that stipulate how, and by whom, such primary rules may be formed, recognized, modified, or extinguished.

• • •

Hart's concept of law is a construction of these various distinctions. Primitive communities have only primary rules, and these are binding entirely because of practices of acceptance. Such communities cannot be said to have 'law', because there is no way to distinguish a set of legal rules from amongst other social rules, as the first tenet of positivism requires. But when a particular community has developed a fundamental secondary rule that stipulates how legal rules are to be identified, the idea of a distinct set of legal rules, and thus of law, is born.

• • •

In this way Hart rescues the fundamentals of positivism from Austin's mistakes. Hart agrees with Austin that valid rules of law may be created through the actions of officials and public institutions. But Austin thought that the authority of these institutions lay only in their monopoly of power. Hart finds their authority in the background of constitutional standards against which they act, constitutional standards that have been accepted, in the form of a fundamental rule of recognition, by the community which they govern. This background legitimates the decisions of government and gives them the cast and call of obligation that the naked commands of Austin's sovereign lacked. Hart's theory differs from Austin's also, in recognizing that different communities use different ultimate tests of law, and that some allow other means of creating law than the deliberate act of a legislative institution. Hart mentions 'long customary practice' and 'the relation (of a rule) to judicial decisions' as other criteria that are often used, though generally along with and subordinate to the test of legislation.

So Hart's version of positivism is more complex than Austin's, and his test for valid rules of law is more sophisticated. In one respect, however, the two models are very similar. Hart, like Austin, recognizes that legal rules have furry edges (he speaks of them as having 'open texture') and, again like Austin, he accounts for troublesome cases by saying that judges have and exercise discretion to decide these cases by fresh legislation. (I shall later try to show why one who thinks of law as a special set of rules is almost inevitably drawn to account for difficult cases in terms of someone's exercise of discretion.)

II. RULES, PRINCIPLES, AND POLICIES

I want to make a general attack on positivism, and I shall use H.L.A. Hart's version as a target, when a particular target is needed. My strategy will be organized around the fact that when lawyers reason or dispute about legal rights and obligations, particularly in those hard cases when our problems with these concepts seem most acute, they make use of standards that do not function as rules, but operate differently as principles, policies, and other sorts of standards. Positivism, I shall argue, is a model of and for a system of rules, and its central notion of a single fundamental test for law forces us to miss the important roles of these standards that are not rules.

I just spoke of 'principles, policies, and other sorts of standards'. Most often I shall use the term 'principle' generically, to refer to the whole set of these standards other than rules; occasionally, however, I shall be more precise, and distinguish between principles and policies. Although nothing in the present argument will turn on the distinction, I should stake how I draw it. I call a 'policy' that kind of standard that sets out a goal to be reached, generally an improvement in some economic, political, or social feature of the community (though some goals are negative, in that they stipulate that some present feature is to be protected from adverse change). I call a 'principle' a standard that is to be observed, not because it will advance or secure an economic, political, or social situation deemed desirable, but because it is a requirement of justice or fairness or some other dimension of morality. Thus the standard that automobile accidents are to be decreased is a policy, and the standard that no man profit by his own wrong is a principle. The distinction can be collapsed by construing a principle as stating a social goal (i.e., the goal of a society in which no man profits by his own wrong), or by construing a policy as stating a principle (i.e., the principle that the goal the policy embraces is a worthy one) or by adopting the utilitarian thesis that principles of justice are disguised statements of goals (securing the greatest happiness of the greatest number). In some contexts the distinction has uses which are lost if it is thus collapsed.

My immediate purpose, however, is to distinguish principles in the generic sense from rules, and I shall start by collecting some examples of the former. The examples I offer are chosen haphazardly: almost any case in a law school casebook would provide examples that would serve as well. In 1889 a New York court, in the famous case of *Riggs v. Palmer,* had to decide whether an heir named in the will of his grandfather could inherit under that will, even though he had murdered his grandfather to do so. The court began its reasoning with this admission: It is quite true that statutes regulating the making, proof and effect of wills, and the devolution of property, if literally construed, and if their force and effect can in no way and under no circumstances be controlled or modified, give this property to the murderer. But the court continued to note that all laws as well as all contracts may be controlled in their operation and effect by general, fundamental maxims of the common law. No one shall be permitted to profit by his own fraud, or to take advantage of his own wrong, or to found any claim upon his own iniquity, or to acquire property by his own crime. The murderer did not receive his inheritance.

In 1960, a New Jersey court was faced in *Henningsen v. Bloomfield Motors, Inc.* with the important question of whether (or how much) an automobile manufacturer may limit his liability in case the automobile is defective. Henningsen had bought a car, and signed a contract which said that the manufacturer's liabililty for defects was limited to 'making good' defective parts, 'this warranty being expressly in lieu of all other warranties, obligations or liabilities'. Henningsen argued that, at least in the circumstances of his case, the manufacturer ought not to be protected by this limitation, and ought to be liable for the medical and other expenses of persons injured in a crash. He was not able to point to any statute, or to any established rule of law, that prevented the manufacturer from standing on the contract. The court nevertheless agreed with Henningsen. At various points in the court's argument the following appeals to standards are made: (a) '[W]e must keep in mind the general principle that, in the absence of fraud, one who does not choose to read a contract before signing it cannot later relieve himself of its burdens.' (b) 'In applying that principle, the basic tenet of freedom of competent parties to contract is a factor of importance.' (c) 'Freedom of contract is not such an immutable doctrine as to admit of no qualification in the area in which we are concerned.' (d) 'In a society such as ours, where the automobile is a common and necessary adjunct of daily life, and where its use is so fraught with danger to the driver, passengers and the public, the manufacturer is under a special obligation in connection with the construction, pro- motion and sale of his cars. Consequently, the courts must examine purchase agree- ments closely to see if consumer and public interests are treated fairly.' (e) ' "[I]s there any principle which is more familiar or more firmly embedded in the history of Anglo-American law than the basic doctrine that the courts will not permit them- selves to be used as instruments of inequity and injustice?" ' (f) ' "More specifically, the courts generally refuse to lend themselves to the enforcement of a 'bargain' in which one party has unjustly taken advantage of the economic necessities of the other. . . ." '

The standards set out in these quotations are not the sort we think of as legal rules. They seem very different from propositions like 'The maximum legal speed on the turnpike is sixty miles an hour' or 'A will is invalid unless signed by three witnesses'. They are different because they are legal principles rather than legal rules.

The difference between legal principles and legal rules is a logical distinction. Both sets of standards point to particular decisions about legal obligation in particular circumstances, but they differ in the character of the direction they give. Rules are applicable in an all-or-nothing fashioin. If the facts a rule stipulates are given, then either the rule is valid, in which case the answer it supplies must be accepted, or it is not, in which case it contributes nothing to the decision. . . .

If we take baseball rules as a model, we find that rules of law, like the rule that a will is invalid unless signed by three witnesses, fit the model well. If the requirement of three witnesses is a valid legal rule, then it cannot be that a will has been signed by only two witnesses and is valid. The rule might have exceptions, but if it does it is inaccurate and incomplete to state the rule so simply, without enumerating the exceptions. In theory, at least, the exceptions could all be listed, and the more of them that are, the more complete is the statement of the rule.

But this is not the way the sample principles in the quotations operate. Even those which look most like rules do not set out legal consequences that follow automatically when the conditions provided are met. We say that our law respects the principle that no man may profit from his own wrong, but we do not mean that the law never permits a man to profit from wrongs he commits. In fact, people often profit, perfectly legally, from their legal wrongs. The most notorious case is adverse possession—if I trespass on your land long enough, some day I will gain a right to cross your land whenever I please. There are many less dramatic examples. If a man leaves one job, breaking a contract, to take a much higher paying job, he may have to pay damages to his first employer, but he is usually entitled to keep his new salary. If a man jumps bail and crosses state lines to make a brilliant investment in another state he may be sent back to jail, but he will keep his profits. . . .

A principle like 'No man may profit from his own wrong' does not even purport to set out conditions that make its application necessary. Rather, it states a reason that argues in one direction, but does not necessitate a particular decision. If a man has or is about to receive something, as a direct result of something illegal he did to get it, then that is a reason which the law will take into account in deciding whether he should keep it. There may be other principles or policies arguing in the other direction—a policy of securing title, for example, or a principle limiting punishment to what the legislature has stipulated. If so, our principle may not prevail, but that does not mean that it is not a principle of our legal system, because in the next case, when these contravening considerations are absent or less weighty, the principle may be decisive. All that is meant, when we say that a particular principle is a principle of our law, is that the principle is one which officials must take into account, if it is relevant, as a consideration inclining in one direction or another.

The logical distinction between rules and principles appears more clearly when we consider principles that do not even look like rules. Consider the proposition, set out under (d) in the excerpts from the *Henningsen* opinion, that the 'manufacturer is under a special obligation in connection with the construction, promotion and sale of his cars'. This does not even purport to define the specific duties such a special obligation entails, or to tell us what rights automobile consumers acquire as a result. It merely states—and this is an essential link in the *Henningsen* argument—that automobile manufacturers must be held to higher standards than other manufacturers, and are less entitled to rely on the competing principle of freedom of contract. It does not mean that they may never rely on that principle, or that courts may rewrite automobile purchase contracts at will; it means only that if a particular clause seems unfair or burdensome, courts have less reason to enforce the clause than if it were for the purchase of neckties. The 'special obligation' counts in favour, but does not in itself necessitate, a decision refusing to enforce the terms of an automobile purchase contract.

This first difference between rules and principles entails another. Principles have a dimension that rules do not—the dimension of weight or importance. When principles intersect (the policy of protecting automobile consumers intersecting with principles of freedom of contract, for example), one who must resolve the conflict has to take into account the relative weight of each. This cannot be, of course, an exact measurement, and the judgment that a particular principle or policy is more important than another will often be a controversial one. Nevertheless, it is an integral part of the concept of a principle that it has this dimension, that it makes sense to ask how important or how weighty it is.

Rules do not have this dimension. We can speak of rules as being *functionally* important or unimportant (the baseball rule that three strikes are out is more important than the rule that runners may advance on a balk, because the game would be much more changed with the first rule altered than the second). In this sense, one legal rule may be more important than another within the system of rules, so that when two rules conflict one supersedes the other by virtue of its greater weight. If two rules conflict, one of them cannot be a valid rule. The decision as to which is valid, and which must be abandoned or recast, must be made by appealing to considerations beyond the rules themselves. A legal system might regulate such conflicts by other rules, which prefer the rule enacted by the higher authority, or the rule enacted later, or the more specific rule, or something of that sort. A legal system may also prefer the rule supported by the more important principles. (Our own legal system uses both of these techniques.)

It is not always clear from the form of a standard whether it is a rule or a principle. 'A will is invalid unless signed by three witnesses' is not very different in form from 'A man may not profit from his own wrong', but one who knows something of American law knows that he must take the first as stating a rule and the second as stating a principle. In many cases the distinction is difficult to make—it may not have been settled how the standard should operate, and this issue may itself be a focus of controversy. The First Amendment to the United States Constitution contains the provision that Congress shall not abridge freedom of speech. Is this a rule, so that if a particular law does abridge freedom of speech, it follows that it is unconstitutional? Those who claim that the first amendment is 'an absolute' say that it must be taken in this way, that is, as a rule. Or does it merely state a principle, so that when an abridgement of speech is discovered, it is unconstitutional unless the context presents some other policy or principle which in the circumstances is weighty enough to permit the abridgement? That is the position of those who argue for what is called the 'clear and present danger' test or some other form of 'balancing'.

Sometimes a rule and principle can play the same role, and the difference between them is almost a matter of form alone. The first section of the Sherman Act states that every contract in restraint of trade shall be void. The Supreme Court had to make the decision whether this provision should be treated as a rule in its own terms (striking down every contract 'which restrains trade', which almost any contract does) or as a principle, providing a reason for striking down a contract in the absence of effective contrary policies. The Court construed the provision as a rule, but treated that rule as containing the word 'unreasonable', and as prohibiting only 'unreasonable' restraints of trade. This allowed the provision to function logically as a rule (whenever a court finds that the restraint is 'unreasonable' it is bound to hold the contract invalid) and substantially as a principle (a court must take into account a variety of other principles and policies in determining whether a particular restraint in particular economic circumstances is 'unreasonable').

· · ·

III. PRINCIPLES AND THE CONCEPT OF LAW

Once we identify legal principles as separate sorts of standards, different from legal rules, we are suddenly aware of them all around us. Law teachers teach them, lawbooks cite them, legal historians celebrate them. But they seem most energetically at work, carrying most weight, in difficult lawsuits like *Riggs* and *Henningsen*. In cases like these, principles play an essential part in arguments supporting judgments about particular legal rights and obligations. After the case is decided, we may say that the case stands for a particular rule (e.g. the rule that one who murders is not eligible to take under the will of his victim). But the rule does not exist before the case is decided; the court cites principles as its justification for adopting and applying a new rule. In *Riggs*, the court cited the principle that no man may profit from his own wrong as a background standard against which to read the statutes of wills, and in this way justified a new interpretation of that statute. In *Henningsen*, the court cited a variety of intersecting principles and policies as authority for a new rule respecting manufacturers' liability for automobile defects.

An analysis of the concept of legal obligation must therefore account for the important role of principles in reaching particular decisions of law. There are two very different tacks we might take.

(a) We might treat legal principles the way we treat legal rules and say that some principles are binding as law and must be taken into account by judges and lawyers who make decisions of legal obligation. If we took this tack, we should say that in the United States, at least, the 'law' includes principles as well as rules.

(b) We might, on the other hand, deny that principles can be binding the way some rules are. We would say, instead, that in cases like *Riggs* or *Henningsen* the judge reaches beyond the rules that he is bound to apply (reaches, that is, beyond the 'law') for extra-legal principles he is free to follow if he wishes.

• • •

The two lines of attack on principles parallel these two accounts of rules. The first tack treats principles as binding upon judges, so that they are wrong not to apply the principles when they are pertinent. The second tack treats principles as summaries of what most judges 'make it a principle' to do when forced to go beyond the standards that bind them. The choice between these approaches will affect, perhaps even determine, the answer we can give to the question whether the judge in a hard case like *Riggs* or *Henningsen* is attempting to enforce pre-existing legal rights and obligations. But if we take the second, we are out of court on that issue, and we must acknowledge that the murderer's family in *Riggs* and the manufacturer in *Henningsen* were deprived of their property by an act of judicial descretion applied *ex post facto*. This may not shock many readers—the notion of judicial discretion has percolated through the legal community—but it does illustrate one of the most nettlesome of the puzzles that drive philosophers to worry about legal obligation. If taking property away in cases like these cannot be justified by appealing to an established obligation, another justification must be found, and nothing satisfactory has yet been supplied.

In my skeleton diagram of positivism, previously set out, I listed the doctrine of judicial discretion as the second tenet. Positivists hold that when a case is not covered by a clear rule, a judge must exercise his discretion to decide that case by what amounts to a fresh piece of legislation. There may be an important connection between this doctrine and the question of which of the two approaches to legal principles we must take. We shall therefore want to ask whether the doctrine is correct, and whether it implies the second approach, as it seems on its face to do. *En route* to these issues, however, we shall have to polish our understanding of the concept of discretion: I shall try to show how certain confusions about that concept, and in particular a failure to discriminate different senses in which it is used, account for the popularity of the doctrine of discretion. I shall argue that in the sense in which the doctrine does have a bearing on our treatment of principles, it is entirely unsupported by the arguments the positivists use to defend.

IV. DISCRETION

• • •

I call both of these senses weak to distinguish them from a stronger sense. We use 'discretion' sometimes not merely to say that an official must use judgement in applying the standards set him by authority, or that no one will review that exercise of judgment, but to say that on some issue he is simply not bound by standards set by the authority in question. In this sense we say that a sergeant has discretion if he has been told to pick any five men for patrol he chooses or that a judge in a dog show has discretion to judge airedales before boxers if the rules do not stipulate an order of events. We use this sense not to comment on the vagueness or difficulty of the standards, or on who has the final word in applying them, but on their range and the decisions they purport to control. If the sergeant is told to take the five most experienced men, he does not have discretion in this strong sense because that order purports to govern his decision. The boxing referee who must decide which fighter has been the more aggressive does not have decretion, in the strong sense for the same reason.

• • •

We may now return, with these observations in hand, to the positivists' doctrine of judicial discretion. That doctrine argues that if a case is not controled by established rule, the judge must decide it by exercising discretion. We want to examine this doctrine and to test its bearing on our treatment of principles; but first we must ask in which sense of discretion we are to understand it.

• • •

It therefore seems that positivists, at least sometimes, take their doctrine in the third, strong sense of discretion. . . . It is the same thing to say that when a judge runs out of rules he has discretion, in the sense that he is not bound by any standards from the authority of law, as to say that the legal standards judges cite other than rules are not binding on them.

So we must examine the doctrine of judicial discretion in the strong sense. (I shall henceforth use the term 'discretion' in that sense.) Do the principles judges cite in cases like *Riggs* or *Henningsen* control their decisions, as the sergeant's orders to take the most experienced men or the referee's duty to choose the more aggressive fighter control the decisions of these officials?

• • •

. . . A positivist might argue that even though some principles are binding, in the sense that the judge must take them into account, they cannot determine a particular result. This is a harder argument to assess because it is not clear what it means for a standard to 'determine' a result. Perhaps it means that the standard *dictates* the result whenever it applies so that nothing else counts. If so, then it is certainly true that individual principles do not determine results, but that is only another way of saying that principles are not rules. Only rules dictate results, come what may. When a contrary result has been reached, the rule has been abandoned or changed. Principles do not work that way; they incline a decision one way, though not conclusively, and they survive intact when they do not prevail. This seems no reason for concluding that judges who must reckon with principles have discretion because a set of principles *can* dictate a result. If a judge believes that principles he is bound to recognize point in one direction and that principles pointing in other direction, if any, are not of equal weight, then he must decide accordingly, just as he must follow what he believes to be a binding rule. He may, of course, be wrong in his assessment of the principles, but he may also be wrong in his judgment that the rule is binding. The sergeant and the referee, we might add, are often in the same boat. No one factor dictates which soldiers are the most experienced or which fighter the more aggressive. These officials must make judgments of the relative weights of these various factors; they do not on that account have discretion.

• • •

Of course, if the positivists are right in another of their doctrines—the theory
that in each legal system there is an ultimate test for binding law like Professor Hart's
rule of recognition—it follows that principles are not binding law. But the incompatibility of principles with the Positivists' theory can hardly be taken as an argument
that principles must be treated any particular way. That begs the question; we are
interested in the status of principles because we want to evaluate the positivists'
model. The positivist cannot defend his theory of a rule of recognition by fiat; if
principles are not amenable to a test he must show some other reason why they
cannot count as law. Since principles seem to play a role in arguments about legal
obligation (witness, again, *Riggs* and *Henningsen*), a model that provides for that
role has some initial advantage over one that excludes it, and the latter cannot properly
be inveighed in its own support.

• • •

When, then, is a judge permitted to change an existing rule of law? Principles
figure in the answer in two ways. First, it is necessary, though not sufficient, that
the judge find that the change would advance some policy or serve some principle,
which policy or principle thus justifies the change. In *Riggs* the change (a new
interpretation of the statute of wills) was justified by the principle that no man should
profit from his own wrong; in *Henningsen* certain rules about automobile manufacturer's liability were altered on the basis of the principles and policies I quoted from
the opinion of the court.

But not any principle will do to justify a change, or no rule would ever be safe.
There must be some principles that count and others that do not, and there must be
some principles that count for more than others. It could not depend on the judge's
own preference amongst a sea of respectable extra-legal standards, any one in principle eligible, because if that wer the case we could not say that any rules were
binding. We could always imagine a judge whose preferences amongst extra-legal
standards were such as would justify a shift or radical re-interpretation of even the
most entrenched rule. Either of these implications, of course, treats a body of principles and policies as law in the sense that rules are; it treats them as standards
binding upon the officials of a community, controlling their decisions of legal right
and obligation.

• • •

Most rules of law, according to Hart, are valid because some competent institution
enacted them. Some were created by a legislature, in the form of statutory enactments.
Others were created by judges who formulated them to decide particular cases, and
thus established them as precedents for the future. But this test of pedigree will not
work for the *Riggs* and *Henningsen* principles. The origin of these as legal principles
lies not in a particular decision of some legislature or court, but in a sense of
appropriateness developed in the profession and the public over time. Their continued
power depends upon this sense of appropriateness being sustained. If it no longer
seemed unfair to allow people to profit by their wrong, or fair to place special burdens
upon oligopolies that manufacture potentially dangerous machines, these principles
would no longer play much of a role in new cases, even if they had never been
overruled or repealed. (Indeed, it hardly makes sense to speak of principles like these
as being 'overruled' or 'repealed'. When they decline they are eroded, not torpedoed.)

• • •

Yet we could not devise any formula for testing how much and what kind of institutional support is necessary to make a principle a legal principle, still less to fix its weight at a particular order of magnitude. We argue for a particular principle by grappling with a whole set of shifting, developing, and interacting standards (themselves principles rather than rules) about institutional responsibility, statutory interpretation, the persuasive force of various sorts of precedent, the relation of all these to contempoprary moral practices, and hosts of other such standards. We could not bolt all of these together into a single 'rule', even a complex one, and if we could the result would bear little relation to Hart's picture of a rule of recognition, which is the picture of a fairly stable master rule specifying some feature or features possession of which by a suggested rule is taken as a conclusive affirmative indication that it is a rule.

• • •

Hart does not say that a master rule might designate as law not only rules enacted by particular legal institutions, but rules established by custom as well. . . .

Hart, reversed Austin on this point. The master rule, he says, might stipulate that some custom counts as law even before the courts recognize it. But he does not face the difficulty this raises for his general theory because he does not attempt to set out the criteria a master rule might use for this purpose. It cannot use, as its only criterion, the provision that the community regard the practice as *morally* binding, for this would not distinguish legal customary rules from moral customary rules, and of course not all of the community's long standing customary moral obligations are enforced at law. If, on the other hand, the test is whether the community regards the customary practice as *legally* binding, the whole point of the master rule is undercut, at least for this class of legal rules. The master rule, says Hart, marks the transformation from a primitive society to one with law, because it provides a test for determining social rules of law other than by measuring their acceptance. But if the master rule says merely that whatever other rules the community accepts as legally binding are legally binding, then it provides no such test at all, beyond the test we should use were there no master rule. The master rule becomes (for these cases) a non-rule of recognition; we might as well say that every primitive society has a secondary rule of recognition, namely the rule that whatever is accepted as binding is binding. Hart himself, in discussing international law, ridicules the idea that such a rule could be a rule of recognition, by describing the proposed rule as 'an empty repetition of the mere fact that the society concerned . . . observes certain standards of conduct as obligatory rules.'

Hart's treatment of custom amounts, indeed, to a confession that there are at least some rules of law that are not binding because they are valid under standards laid down by a master rule but are binding—like the master rule—because they are accepted as binding by the community. This chips at the neat pyramidal architecture we admired in Hart's theory: we can no longer say that only the master rule is binding because of its acceptance all other rules being valid under its terms.

This is perhaps only a chip, because the customary rules Hart has in mind are no longer a very significant part of the law. But it does suggest that Hart would be reluctant to widen the damage by bringing under the head of 'custom' all those crucial principles and policies we have been discussing. If he were to call these part of the law and yet admit that the only test of their force lies in the degree to which they are accepted as law by the community or some part thereof, he would very sharply reduce that area of the law over which his master rule held any dominion. It is not just that all the principles and policies would escape its sway, though that would be bad enough. Once these principles and policies are accepted as law, and thus as standards judges must follow in determining legal obligations, it would follow that rules like those announced for the first time in *Riggs* and *Henningsen* owe their force at least in part to the authority of principles and policies, and so not entirely to the master rule of recognition.

So we cannot adapt Hart's version of positivism by modifying his rule of recognition to embrace principles. No tests of pedigree, relating principles to acts of legislation, can be formulated, nor can his concept of customary law, itself an exception to the first tenet of positivism, be made to serve without abandoning that tenet altogether. One more possibility must be considered, however. If no rule of recognition can provide a test for identifying principles, why not say that principles are ultimate, and *form* the rule of recognition of our law? The answer to the general question 'What is valid law in an American jurisdiction?' would then require us to state all the principles (as well as ultimate constitutional rules) in force in that jurisdiction at the time, together with appropriate assignments of weight. A positivist might then regard the complete set of these standards as the rule of recognition of the jurisdiction. This solution has the attraction of paradox, but of course it is an unconditional surrender. If we simply designate our rule of recognition by the phrase 'the complete set of principles in force', we achieve only the tautology that law is law. If, instead, we tried actually to list all the principles in force we would fail. They are controversial, their weight is all important, they are numberless, and they shift and change so fast that the start of our list would be obsolete before we reached the middle. Even if we succeeded, we would not have a key for law because there would be nothing left for our key to unlock.

I conclude that if we treat principles as law we must reject the positivists' first tenet, that the law of a community is distinguished from other social standards by some test in the form of a master rule. We have already decided that we must then abandon the second tenet—the doctrine of judicial discretion—or clarify it into triviality. What of the third tenet, the positivists' theory of legal obligation?

This theory holds that a legal obligation exists when (and only when) an established rule of law imposes such an obligation. It follows from this that in a hard case—when no such established rule can be found—there is no legal obligation until the judge creates a new rule for the future. The judge may apply that new rule to the parties in the case, but this is *ex post facto* legislation, not the enforcement of an existing obligation.

The positivists' doctrine of discretion (in the strong sense) required this view of legal obligation, because if a judge has discretion there can be no legal right or obligation—no entitlement—that he must enforce. Once we abandon that doctrine, however, and treat principles as law, we raise the possibility, that a legal obligation might be imposed by a constellation of principles as well as by an established rule. We might want to say that a legal obligation exists whenever the case supporting such an obligation, in terms of binding legal principles of different sorts, is stronger than the case against it.

Of course, many questions would have to be answered before we could accept that view of legal obligation. If there is no rule of recognition, no test for law in that sense, how do we decide which principles are to count, and how much, in making such a case? How do we decide whether one case is better than another? If legal obligation rests on an undemonstrable judgment of that sort, how can it provide a justification for a judicial decision that one party had a legal obligation? Does this view of obligation square with the way lawyers, judges, and laymen speak, and is it consistent with our attitudes about moral obligation? Does this analysis help us to deal with the classical jurisprudential puzzles about the nature of law?

These questions must be faced, but even the questions promise more than positivism provides. Positivism, on its own thesis, stops short of just those puzzling, hard cases that send us to look for theories of law. When we reach these cases, the positivist remits us to a doctrine of discretion that leads nowhere and tells nothing. His picture of law as a sytem of rules has exercised a tenacious hold on our imagination, perhaps through its very simplicity. If we shake ourselves loose from this model of rules, we may be able to build a model truer to the complexity and sophistication of our own practices.

NOTES

1. Professor Dworkin is aware of the unrealistic picture the Positivists paint of the structure of law—fixed, written rules, rigidly applied. In an attempt to break out of the Positivist prison, he purports to launch a "general attack on Positivism." But he criticizes Hart's notion of the discretion judges must resort to because of "gaps" in law. In place of discretion, Dworkin installs "principles" alongside rules in his framework of law. The principles are to be used when the rules prove inadequate. Compared to rules, Dworkin's principles have mysterious and even magical properties. Unlike rules, they do not necessarily determine how an issue should be decided; some, even, "do not count." These principles do not have their origin "in a particular decision of some legislature or court, but in a sense of appropriateness developed in the profession and the public over time." They are "controversial," they are numberless" and they "shift and change" rapidly. Is Dworkin's reliance upon these evanescent and ephemeral principles a reversion to historicism with another version of its mystical *volksgeist?* Is it use of a myth system? Discuss.

2. By including "principles" in the Positivist structure of law, Dworkin claims that he has denied the small amount of discretion that Hart was willing to concede to judges. But doesn't Dworkin, in fact, vest judges with a vast discretion, since judges can resort to changing and shifting principles to support a decision in any direction, without fear of contradiction? After all, these principles as Dworkin puts it, cannot even be listed, being so "controversial" and constantly shifting and changing? Is Dworkin really permitting use of the widest discretion while purporting to eliminate its use? Discuss.

3. A consensus on community goals could provide guidelilnes for judges and also act as some restraint on their discretion, if rules or "principles" are ambiguous. Note that Dworkin does not attempt to clarify or categorize goals in terms of various human aspirations, or otherwise, but leaves it to judges to reach their decisions by relying upon the mysterious and varied "principles."

4. The rule model can be a guideline for decision-makers only in the simplest and most routinized and limited of universes, for example, the universe of a clerk in which a superior determines that there will be a binary choice of only two possibilities. In most situations, the universe presented to the decision-maker is much more complicated and changing. Often it presents challenges which could not have been contemplated by those who framed policy. In these circumstances, the decision-maker, a judge or some functional equivalent, must innovate and engage in a process of making choices. The positivist jurist who must engage in this often conceals his de facto defection from Positivism by a variety of strategems. Professor Dworkin acknowledges the real impossibility of operating according to the positivist's model of rules. He seeks to use principles as a way of filling in the gaps in the rules. Professor Hart, as we saw, would resort to a certain discretion in circumstances of "open texture." In the United States, judges have referred to the "penumbra" of rules or statutory formulations or to general

principles. All of these formulae and their equivalents permit the judge to continue to pay lip service to Positivism while in fact using a jurisprudence which is much more creative and expansive. If this judicial discretion persists, what is the political effect of a doctrine which officially ignores it? Discuss.

AMERICAN JUDICIAL PRACTICE

Judicial review in the United States is a revealing test of the positivist theory. On the one hand, judicial review can be presented as an ultimate expression of Positivism. The court charged with judicial review scrutinizes the actions of legislatures and all other officials to confirm that secondary and tertiary legislation conform to the written constitution. If these examinations do in fact take the document called the Constitution and systematically test every secondary act of legislation or administration against it, they are true to Positivism. But if the document in question was drafted centuries before in a context quite different from the one in which it is currently being applied, it is plain that a good deal of myth is operating to obscure what is actually occurring. The court under the guise of loyalty to the Constitution is, in fact, creating law by determining whether certain innovations are to be deemed appropriate to contemporary goals or whether they should be struck down.

Another method by which judges and lower courts pay lip service to Positivism but engage in an entirely different jurisprudence is found in "extensive" interpretation. In purporting to interpret a statutory enactment, judges plainly go far beyond the language and in some cases against the manifest intention of the legislature. Nonetheless, this is done in solemn fashion as if it were an appropriate interpretation of the statute. For example, in the case of *State v. Shack,* 58 N.J. 297, 277 A.2d 369 (1971), a New Jersey statute provided in part that "any person who trespasses on any lands . . . after being forbidden so to trespass by the owner . . . is a disorderly person and shall be punished by a fine of not more than $50.00." The owner of a migrant labor camp refused admission to persons who were employed by private organizations funded by the United States government and who desired entry in order to render legal and medical services to migrant workers. The court, unwillilng to strike down the statute on the basis of the United States or New Jersey Constitution, instead "interpreted" the statute so that the word "trespass" did not include forbidden entry onto a migrant labor camp. In a selection which is hardly a paragon of lucidity, the court said ". . . under our State law the ownership of real property does not include the right to bar access to governmental services available to migrant workers and hence there was no trespass within the meaning of the penal statute. The policy considerations which underlie that conclusion may be much the same as those which would be weighed with respect with one or more of the constitutional challenges, but a decision in unconstitutional terms is more satisfactory, because the interests of migrant workers are more expansively served in that way than they would be if they had no more freedom than these constitutional concepts could be found to mandate if indeed they apply at all."

This technique is not uncommon. In *Edwards v. Habib* 397 F. 2d 687 (D.C. Cir. 1968), Judge Skelly Wright purported to rely on a section of the District of Columbia housing code, which *authorized* evictions by a landlord for nonpayment of rent. He interpreted the section to *bar* evictions when there was a retaliatory motive by the landlord in evicting the tenant who had complained to the authorities about housing code violations. A similar case of statutory "interpretation" is *Javins v. First National*

Realty Corp. 428 F. 2d 1071 (D.C. Cir. 1970 infra at p. 528), in which the court again interpreted a section of the Washington, D.C. code as providing a warranty of habitability for tenants, permitting them to sue the landlord in contract, though the section contained no such provision.

Another form of lip service to Positivism lies in the restraints placed upon the use of precedent cases by lawyers. In most federal circuit courts, particularly in the second circuit, many of the cases decided by the court are classified by it as having no binding value as precedents. These cases may not thereafter be cited or relied upon by attorneys. (See *N.Y. Times,* U.S. Appeals Court Restricts Use of Opinions by Lawyers, Feb. 21, 1983, at B-1; Judge Feinberg, Letter to the editor, *N.Y. Times,* Feb. 28, 1983, at A-14; *N.Y. Times,* Response to Judge Feinberg, Letter to the editor, March 9, 1983, at A-22).

More puzzling, indeed sometimes quite ludicrous, is Positivism's often rigid construction and distortion of the objectives of legislation. Consider the following examples.

McBOYLE v. UNITED STATES
283 U.S. 25 (1930)

[Mr. Justice Holmes delivered the opinion]. . . The petitioner was convinced of transporting from Ottawa, Illinois, to Guymon, Oklahoma, an airplane that he knew to have been stolen, and was sentenced to serve three years' imprisonment and to pay a fine of $2,000. The judgment was affirmed by the Circuit Court of Appeals for the Tenth Circuit. 43F. 2d 273. A writ of certiorari was granted by this Court on the question whether the National Motor Vehicle Theft Act applies to aircraft. . . . That Act provides: "Sec. 2. That when used in this Act: (a) The term 'motor vehicle' shall include an automobile, automobile truck, automobile wagon, motor cycle, or any other self-propelled vehicle not designed for running on rails;. . . Sec. 3. That whoever shall transport or cause to be transported in interstate or foreign commerce a motor vehicle, knowing the same to have been stolen, shall be punished by a fine of not more than $5,000, or by imprisonment of not more than five years, or both."

Section 2 defines the motor vehicles of which the transportation in interstate commerce is punished in Section 3. The question is the meaning of the word 'vehicle' in the phrase "any other self-propelled vehicle not designed for running on rails." No doubt etymologically it is possible to use the word to signify a conveyance working on land, water or air, and sometimes legislation extends the use in that direction, e.g., land and air, water being separately provided for, in the Tariff Act, September 22, 1922, c. 356, Section 401 (b, 42 Stat. 858, 948. But in everyday speech 'vehicle' calls up the picture of a thing moving on land. Thus in Rev. Stats. Section 4, intended, the Government suggests, rather to enlarge than to restrict the definition, vehicle includes every contrivance capable of being used "as a means of transportation on land." And this is repeated, expressly excluding aircraft, in the Tariff Act, June 17, 1930, c. 997, Section 401 (b); 46 Stat. 590, 708. So here, the phrase under discussion calls up the popular picture. For after including automobile truck, automobile wagon and motor cycle, the words "any other self-propelled vehicle not designed for running on rails" still indicate that a vehicle in the popular sense, that is a vehicle running on land, is the theme. It is a vehicle that runs, not something, not commonly called a vehicle, that flies. Airplanes were well known in 1919, when this statute was passed; but it is admitted that they were not mentioned in the reports or in the debates in Congress. It is impossible to read words that so carefully enumerate the different forms of motor vehicles and have no reference of any kind to aircraft, as including airplanes under a term that usage more and more precisely confines to a different class. The counsel for the petitioner have shown that the phraseology of the statute as to major vehicles follows that of earlier statutes of Connecticut, Delaware, Ohio, Michigan and Missouri, not to mention the late Regulations of Traffic for District of Columbia, Title 6c. 9 Section 242, none of which can be supposed to leave the earth.

Although it is not likely that a criminal will carefully consider the text of the law before he murders or steals, it is reasonable that a fair warning should be given to the world in language that the common world will understand, of what the law intends to do if a certain line is passed. To make the warning fair, so far as possible the line should be clear. When a rule of conduct is laid down in words that evoke in the common mind only the picture of vehicles moving on land, the statute should not be extended to aircraft, simply because it may seem to us that a similar policy applies, or upon the speculation that, if the legislature had thought of it, very likely broader words would have been used. *United States* v. *Thind,* 261 U.S. 204, 209.

THE NEW DEAL

A curious chapter in American judicial history is provided by the early New Deal. The Supreme Court struck down many legislative efforts designed to restructure the American system so that it could, in Congress' opinion, respond to contemporary challenges. The grounds for striking the legislation down were that they were inconsistent with the Constitution. For example, The Bituminous Coal Conservation Act of 1935, which attempted to regulate minimum wages and maximum hours in bituminous coal mines, was held by the court to be "so clearly arbitrary, and so clearly a denial of rights safeguarded by the due process clause of the Fifth Amendment that it is unnecessary to do more than refer to decisions of this court which foreclose the question. *Schechter Poultry Corp. v. United States . . .*" *(Carter v. Carter Coal Co.,* 298 U.S. 238 (1936). The positivist theory of the Supreme Court is, perhaps, best exemplified by the classic formulation of Justice Roberts in striking down the Agricultural Adjustment Act of 1933, one of the main props of the "New Deal."

> There should be no misunderstanding as to the function of this court in such a case. It is sometimes said that the court assumes a power to overrule or control the action of people's representatives. This is a misconception. The Constitution is the supreme law of the land ordained and established by the people. All legislation must conform to the principles it lays down. When an act of Congress is appropriately challenged in the courts as not conforming to the constitutional mandate the judicial branch of the government has only one duty—to lay the Articles of the Constitution which is invoked beside the statute which is challenged and to decide whether the latter squares with the former. All the court does or can do, is to announce its considered judgment on the question. The only power it has, if such it may be called, is the power of judgment. This court neighter approves nor condemns any legislative policy. Its delicate and difficult office is to ascertain and declare whether the legislation is in accordance with, or in contravention of, the provisions of the Constitution; and having done that, its duty ends . . . *(United States v. Butler,* 297 U.S. 1).

In a short time, the Supreme Court struck down as unconstitutional six major pieces of congressional legislation designed to help overcome the serious and unprecedented economic depression. President Franklin D. Roosevelt then proposed, on February 5, 1937, to add new justices to the Supreme Court—the so-called "Court-Packing" plan. Shortly thereafter, the Supreme Court ruled that the National Labor Relations Act was constitutional and distinguished its prior holdings essentially to the contrary (e.g. the *Schechter Poultry* and *Carterl* cases), saying without further explanation, "these cases are not controlling here." As one commentator noted, ". . . The court had in substance overruled cases decided less than one year before on major constitutional issues. No serious effort had been made to distinguish the *Carter* case. . . . There had been no change in the membership of the court. . . . But few attributed the difference in results between the decisions in 1936 and those in 1937 to anything in the cases themselves . . . their facts, the arguments presented, or the authorities cited." (Stern, The Commerce Clause and the National Economy, 1933-40, 59 *Har. L. Rev.* 645, 1946).

A spirited statement of positivist thought and its defense was made by Mr. Justice Hugo Black.

HARPER v. VIRGINIA
383 U.S. 663 (1966)

. . . Another reason for my dissent from the Court's judgment and opinion is that it seems to be using the old "natural-law-due-process formula" to justify striking down state laws as violations of the Equal Protection Clause. I have heretofore had many occasions to express my strong belief that there is no constitutional support whatever for this Court to use the Due Process Clause as though it provided a blank check to alter the meaning of the Constitution as written so as to add to it substantive constitutional changes which a majority of the Court at any given time believes are needed to meet present-day problems. Nor is there in my opinion any more constitutional support for this Court to use the Equal Protection Clause, as it has today, to write into the Constitution its notions of what it thinks is good governmental policy. If basic changes as to the respective powers of the state and national governments are needed, I prefer to let those changes be made by amendment as Article V of the Constitution provides. For a majority of this Court to undertake that task, whether purporting to do so under the Due Process or the Equal Protection Clause amounts, in my judgment, to an exercise of power the Constitution makers with foresight and wisdom refused to give the Judicial Branch of the Government. I have in no way departed from the view I expressed in *Adamson* v. *California,* 332 U.S. 46,90 decided June 23, 1947, that the "natural-law-due-process formula" under which courts make the Constitution means what they think it should at a given time "has been used in the past, and can be used in the future, to license this Court, in considering regulatory legislation, to roam at large in the broad expanses of policy and morals and to trespass, all too freely, on the legislative domain of the States as well as the Federal Government."

The Court denies that it is using the "natural-law-due-process formula." It says that its invalidation of the Virginia law "is founded not on what we think governmental policy should be, but on what the Equal Protection Clause requires." I find no statement in the Court's opinion, however, which advances even a plausible argument as to why the alleged discriminations which might possibly be effected by

Virginia's poll tax law are "irrational," "unreasonable," "arbitrary," or "invidious" or have no relevance to a legitimate policy which the State wishes to adopt.
The Court gives no reason at all to discredit the long-standing beliefs that making
the payment of a tax a prerequisite to voting is an effective way of collecting revenue
and that people who pay their taxes are likely to have a far greater interest in their
government. The Court's failure to give any reasons to show that these purposes of
the poll tax are "irrational," "unreasonable," "arbitrary," or "invidious" is a
pretty clear indication to me that none exist. I can only conclude that the primary,
controlling, predominant, if not the exclusive reason for declaring the Virginia law
unconstitutional is the Court's deep-seated hostility and antagonism, which I share,
to making payment of a tax a prerequisite to voting.

The Court's justification for consulting its own notions rather than following the
original meaning of the Constitution, as I would, apparently is based on the belief
of the majority of the Court that for this Court to be bound by the original meaning
of the Constitution is an intolerable and debilitating evil; that our Constitution should
not be "shackled to the political theory of a particular era," and that to save the
country from the original Constitution the Court must have constant power to renew
it and keep it abreast of this Court's more enlightened theories of what is best for
our society. It seems to me that this is an attack not only on the great value of our
Constitution itself but also on the concept of a written constitution which is to survive
through the years as originally writen unless changed through the amendment process
which the Framers wisely provided. Moreover, when a "political theory" embodied
in our Constitution becomes outdated, it seems to me that a majority of the nine
members of this Court are not only without constitutional power but are far less
qualified to choose a new constitutional political theory than the people of this country
proceeding in the manner provided by Article V.

The people have not found it impossible to amend their Constitution to meet new
conditions. The Equal Protection Clause itself is the product of the people's desire
to use their constitutional power to amend the Constitution to meet new problems.
Moreover, the people, in Section 5 of the Fourteenth Amendment, designated the
governmental tribunal they wanted to provide additional rules to enforce the guarantees of the Amendment. The branch of Government they choose was not the
Judicial Branch but the Legislative. I have no doubt at all that Congress has the
power under Section 5 to pass legislation to abolish the poll tax in order to protect
the citizens of this country if it believes that the poll tax is being used as a device
to deny voters equal protection of the laws. . . . But for us to undertake in the guise
of constitutional interpretation to decide the constitutional policy question of this case
amounts, in my judgment, to a plain exercise of power which the Constitution has
denied us but has specifically granted to Congress. I cannot join in holding that the
Virginia state poll tax law violates the Equal Protection Clause.

NOTES

1. Justice Black suggests that there are adequate opportunities for change of the Constitution
through formal amendment processes and through legislation. Recall the discontent expressed
by Professor Zinn about opportunities for such change in Chapter 4. Is Justice Black realistic
and practical? Compare Justice Black's position with that espoused by Justice Fortas in Chapter
4. How would you characterize Justice Fortas' approach to constitutional change by the
Supreme Court?

2. In a complex system which espouses power-sharing and effective democracy, is it practical to insist that changes in the law be pursued and effected only through the ponderous processes of the legislature? Is it practical to imagine changes made only by the even more cumbersome constitutional amendment process? Discuss.

3. Though their politics may have been different, there are some extraordinary parallels between the positivist theories expressed by Justices Roberts and Black. Is it possible to appraise statutory instruments for constitutionality by looking only at the language of the statute in question and a corresponding phrase in the Constitution? Is it possible to ignore social and economic as well as political implications in constitutional review? Discuss.

4. Is Justice Roberts' positivistic theory of judicial review possible when a document has been drafted for the ages and (i) has purposely been rendered in general and sweeping terms and, hence, often cannot provide clear guidelines for the more detailed items in the statute and (ii) the interpreters are confronted with problems that could not have been anticipated by the constitutional drafters? Discuss.

Consider, Justice Douglas' position, ''The decisions of yesterday or of the last century are only starting points. . . . A judge looking at a constitutional decision may have a compulsion to reveal the past history and accept what was once written. But he remembers above all else that it is the Constitution which he swore to support and defend, not the gloss which his predecessors may have put on it. So he comes to formulate his own laws, rejecting some earlier ones as false and embracing others. He cannot do otherwise unless he lets men long dead and unaware of the problems of the age in which he lives to do his thinking for him.'' (Justice William O. Douglas, Stare Decisis, *Record* N.Y. City B. Ass'n. May 1949 at 152).

5. When constitutional language is abstract or vague and courts or other decisionmakers are given authority to implement the document, what is the function of that vague language? Discuss.

6. If language is vague and provides few guidelines, what criteria are decisionmakers to bring to bear in making choices? Consider this question in relation to the material developed in Chapter 1 and the problems presented in Chapter 1 and 4.

7. Both Justices Roberts and Black are sympathetic to the notion of a system of ''rule of law'' rather than ''rule of men.'' Both, as a result are anxious to enhance the route of automatic application of text and to restrict the introduction of personal preference in choice by individual judges. What does ''rule of law'' mean? How does a law rule? Some wags have suggested that as law does not do anything by itself, the rule of law really means the rule of those specialized to giving effect, direction and shape to what the community accepts as law, in other words, rule of lawyers. Discuss.

C. K. Allen, *Law in the Making* (7th ed. 1964).

E. Bodenheimer, Analytical Positivism, Legal Realism and the Future of Legal Method, 44 *Va. L. Rev.* 365 (1958).

R. Dworkin, *Taking Rights Seriously* (1978); *The Philosophy of Law* (1977).

L. Fuller, *The Morality of Law* (1964).

H. L. A. Hart, *The Concept of Law* (1961); Analytical Jurisprudence in Mid-Twentieth Century: A Reply to Professor Bodenheimer, 105 *U. Pa. L. R.* 953 (1957).

W. Hohfeld, *Fundamental Legal Conceptions As Applied In Judicial Reasoning, and Other Legal Essays* (W. Cook & A. Corbin eds. 1946, 1964).

G. Hughes, *Law, Reason and Justice: Essays in Legal Philosophy* (1969).

H. Kantorowicz, *The Definition of Law* (A. Campbell ed. 1958).

H. Kelsen, *The Pure Theory of Law* (1967).

N. MacCormick, *H. L. A. Hart* (1981).

W. L. Morison, *John Austin* (1982).

H. Morris, Verbal Disputes and the Legal Philosophy of John Austin, 7 *U.S.L.A. L. Rev.* 27 (1959:60).

J. Raz, *The Concept of a Legal System* (1970).

W. Rumble, Divine Law, Utilitarian Ethics and Positivist Jurisprudence: A Study of the Legal Philosophy of John Austin, 24 *Amer. J. Juris,* 139 (1979); John Austin, Judicial Legislation and Legal Positivism, 13 *U. W. Austrl. L. J.* 77 (1977).

R. Summers, The New Analytical Jurists, 41 *N.Y.U. L. Rev.* 861 (1966); Professor H.L.A. Hart's Concept of Law, 4 *Duke L. J.* 629 (1963).

Note, Hart, Austin, and the Concept of a Legal System, 84 *Yale L. J.* 584 (1975).

CHAPTER 8

Law Without Morality:
The Jurisprudence of Neutral Principles

*I may be doing wrong but I'm doing
it in a proper and customary manner.*
George Bernard Shaw

A peculiarly American rendition of Positivism was offered by Professor Wechsler in his theory of "neutral principles" according to which courts were to render judgment. Judgments which could not be traced back systematically to these neutral principles are deemed to be political and as a result illicit exercises of judicial power.

WECHSLER, TOWARD NEUTRAL PRINCIPLES OF CONSTITUTIONAL LAW,
73 HARV. L. REV. 2, 5–12, 14–20, 22–35 (1959)

I. THE BASIS OF JUDICIAL REVIEW
• • •

You will not wonder now why I should be concerned about the way Judge Hand has read the text, despite his view that the judicial power was a valid importation to preserve the governmental plan. Here as elsewhere a position cannot be divorced from its supporting reasons; the reasons are, indeed, a part and most important part of the position. To demonstrate I quote Judge Hand:

> [S]ince this power is not a logical deduction from the structure of the Constitution but only a practical condition upon its successful operation, it need not be exercised whenever a court sees, or thinks that it sees, an invasion of the Constitution. It is always a preliminary question how importunately the occasion demands an answer. It may be better to leave the issue to be worked out without authoritative solution; or perhaps the only solution available is one that the court has no adequate means to enforce.

If this means that a court, in a case properly before it, is free—or should be free on any fresh view of its duty—either to adjudicate a constitutional objection to an otherwise determinative action of the legislature or executive, national or state, or to decline to do so, depending on "how importunately" it considers the occasion to demand an answer, could anything have more enormous import for the theory and practice of review? What showing would be needed to elicit a decision? Would anything suffice short of a demonstration that judicial intervention is essential to prevent the government from foundering—the reason, you recall, for the interpolation of the power to decide? For me, as for anyone who finds the judicial power anchored in the Constitution, there is no such escape from the judicial obligation; the duty cannot be attenuated in this way.

313

The duty, to be sure, is not that of policing or advising legislatures or executives, nor even, as the uninstructed think, of standing as an ever-open forum for the ventilation of all grievances that draw upon the Constitution for support. It is the duty to decide the litigated case and to decide it in accordance with the law, with all that that implies as to a rigorous insistance on the satisfaction of procedural and jurisdiction requirements.

• • •

It is true, and I do not mean to ignore it, that the courts themselves regard some questions as "political," meaning thereby that they are not to be resolved judicially, although they involve constitutional interpretation and arise in the course of litigation. Judge Hand alluded to this doctrine which, insofar as its scope is undefined, he labeled a "stench in the nostrils of strict constructionists." And Mr. Justice Frankfurter, in his great paper at the Marshall conference, avowed "disquietude that the line is often very thin between the cases in which the Court felt compelled to abstain from adjudication because of their 'political' nature, and the cases that so frequently arise in applying the concepts of 'liberty' and 'equality'. "

• • •

If I may put my point again, I submit that in cases of the kind that I have mentioned, as in others that I do not pause to state, the only proper judgement that may lead to an abstention from decision is that the Constitution has committed the determination of the issue to another agency of government than the courts. Difficult as it may be to make that judgment wisely, whatever factors may be rightly weighed in situations where the answer is not clear, what is involved is in itself an act of constitutional interpretation, to be made and judged by standards that should govern the interpretive process generally. That, I submit, is *toto caelo* different from a broad discretion to abstain or intervene.

The Supreme Court does have a discretion, to be sure, to grant or to deny review of judgments of the lower courts in situations in which the jurisdictional statute permits certiorari but does not provide for an appeal. I need not say that this is an entirely different matter. The system rests upon the power that the Constitution vests in Congress to make exceptions to and regulate the Court's appellate jurisdiction; it is addressed not to the measure of judicial duty in adjudication of a case but rather to the right to a determination by the highest as distinguished from the lower courts.

• • •

II. THE STANDARDS OF REVIEW

If courts cannot escape the duty of deciding whether actions of the other branches of the government are consistent with the Constitution when a case is properly before them in the sense I have attempted to describe, you will not doubt the relevancy and importance of demanding what, if any, are the standards to be followed in interpretation. Are there, indeed, any criteria that both the Supreme Court and those who undertake to praise or to condemn its judgments are morally and intellectually obligated to support?

• • •

I revert then to the problem of criteria as it arises from both courts and critics—by which I mean criteria that can be framed and tested as an exercise of reason and not merely as an act of willfulness or will. Even to put the problem is, of course, to raise an issue no less old than our culture. Those who perceive in law only the elements of fiat, in whose conception of the legal cosmos reason has no meaning or no place, will not join gladly in the search for standards of the kind I have in mind. I must, in short, expect dissent *in limine* from anyone whose view of the judicial process leaves no room for the antinomy Professor Fuller has so gracefully explored. So too must I anticipate dissent from those more numerous among us who, vouching no philosophy to warranty, frankly or covertly make the test of virtue in interpretation whether its result in the immediate decision seems to hinder or advance the interests or the values they support.

I shall not try to overcome the philosophic doubt that I have mentioned, although to use a phrase that Holmes so often used—"it hits me where I live." That battle must be fought on wider fronts than that of constitutional interpretation; and I do not delude myself that I can qualify for a command, great as is my wish to render service. The man who simply lets his judgment turn on the immediate result may not, however, realize that his position implies that the courts are free to function as a naked power organ, that it is an empty affirmation to regard them, as ambivalently he so often does, as courts of law. If he may know he disapproves of a decision when all he knows is that it has sustained a claim put forward by a labor union or a taxpayer, a Negro or a segregationist, a corporation or a Communist—he acquiesces in the proposition that a man of different sympathy but equal information may no less properly conclude that he approves.

You will not charge me with the exaggeration if I say that this type of *ad hoc* evaluation is, as it has always been, the deepest problem of our constitutionalism, not only with respect to judgments of the courts but also in the wider realm in which conflicting constitutional positions have played a part in our politics.

• • •

All I have said, you may reply, is something no one will deny, that principles are largely instrumental as they are employed in politics, instrumental in relation to results that a controlling sentiment demands at any given time. Politicians recognize this fact of life and are obliged to trim and shape their speech and votes accordingly, unless perchance they are prepared to step aside; and the example that John Quincy Adams set somehow is rarely followed.

That is, indeed, all I have said but I now add that whether you are tolerant, perhaps more tolerant than I, of the *ad hoc* in politics, with principle reduced to a manipulative tool, are you not also ready to agree that something else is called for from the courts? I put it to you that the main constituent of the judicial process is precisely that it must be genuinely principled, resting with respect to every step that is involved in reaching judgment on analysis and reasons quite transcending the immediate result that is achieved. To be sure, the courts decide, or should decide, only the case they have before them. But must they not decide on grounds of adequate neutrality and generality, tested not only by the instant application but by others that the principles imply? Is it not the very essence of judicial method to insist upon attending to such other cases, preferably those involving an opposing interest, in evaluating any principle avowed?

Here too I do not think that I am stating any novel or momentous insight. But now, as Holmes said long ago in speaking of "the unrest which seems to wonder vaguely whether law and order pay," we "need education in the obvious." We need it more particularly now respecting constitutional interpretation, since it has become a commonplace to grant what many for so long denied: that courts in constitutional

determinations face issues that are inescapably "political"—political in the third
sense that I have used the word—in that they involve a choice among competing
values or desires, a choice reflected in the legislative or executive action in question,
which the court must either condemn or condone.

• • •

Does not the special duty of the courts to judge by neutral principles addressed
to all the issues make it inapposite to contend, as Judge Hand does, that no court
can review the legislative choice—by any standard other than a fixed "historical
meaning" of constitutional provisions—without becoming a "third legislative chamber?" Is there not, in short, a vital difference between legislative freedom to appraise
the gains and losses in projected measures and the kind of principled appraisal, in
respect of values that can reasonably be asserted to have constitutional dimension,
that alone is in the province of the courts? Does not the difference yield a middle
ground between a judicial House of Lords and the abandonment of any limitation
on the other branches—a middle ground consisting of judicial action that embodies
what are surely the main qualities of law, its generality and its neutrality? This must,
it seems to me, have been in Mr. Justice Jackson's mind when in his chapter on the
Supreme Court "as a political institution" he wrote in words that I find stirring,
"Liberty is not the mere absence of restaint, it is not a spontaneous product of
majority rule, it is not achieved merely by lifting underprivileged classes to power,
nor is it the inevitable by-product of technological expansion. It is achieved only by
a rule of law." Is it not also what Mr. Justice Frankfurter must mean in calling upon
judges for "allegiance to nothing except the effort, amid tangled words and limited
insights, to find the path through precdent, through policy, through history, to the
best judgment that fallible creatures can reach in that most difficult of all tasks: the
achievement of justice between man and man, between man and state, through reason
called law"?

You will not understand my emphasis upon the role of reason and of principle
in the judicial, as distinguished from the legislative or executive, appraisal of conflicting values to imply that I depreciate the duty of fidelity to the text of the
Constitution, when its words may be decisive—though I would certainly remind you
of the caution stated by Chief Justice Hughes: "Behind the words of the Constitutional
provisions are postulates which limit and control." Nor will you take me to deny
that history has weight in the elucidation of the text, though it is surely subtle business
to appraise it as a guide. Nor will you even think that I deem precedent without
importance, for we surely must agree with Holmes that "imitation of the past, until
we have a clear reason for change, no more needs justification than appetite." But
after all, it was Chief Justice Taney who declared his willingness "that it be regarded
hereafter as the law of this court, that its opinion upon the construction of the
Constitution is always open to discussion when it is supposed to have been founded
in error, and that its judicial authority should hereafter depend altogether on the force
of the reasoning by which it is supported." Would any of us have it otherwise, given
the nature of the problems that confront the courts?

At all events, is not the relative compulsion of the language of the Constitution,
of history and precedent—where they do not combine to make an answer clear—itself
a matter to be judged, so far as possible, by neutral principles—by standards that
transcend the case at hand? I know, of course, that it is common to distinguish, as
Judge Hand did, clauses like "due process," cast "in such sweeping terms that their
history does not elucidate their contents," from other provisions of the Bill of Rights

addressed to more specific problems. But the contrast, as it seems to me, often implies an overstatement of the specificity or the immutability these other clauses really have—at least when problems under them arise.

• • •

Even "due process," on the other hand, might have been confined, as Mr. Justice Brandeis urged originally, to a guarantee of fair procedure, coupled perhaps with prohibition of executive displacement of established law—the analogue for us of what the barons meant in Magna Carta. . . .

So far as possible, to finish with my point, I argue that we should prefer to see the other clauses of the Bill of Rights read as an affirmation of the special values they embody rather than as statements of a finite rule of law, its limits fixed by the consensus of a century long past, with problems very different from our own. To read them in the former way is to leave room for adaptation and adjustment if and when competing values, also having Constitutional dimension, enter on the scene.

Let me repeat what I have thus far tried to say. The courts have both the title and the duty when a case is properly before them to review the actions of the other branches in the light of Constitutional provisions, even though the action involves value choices, as invariably action does. In doing so, however, they are bound to function otherwise than as a naked power organ; they participate as courts of law. This calls for facing how determinations of this kind can be asserted to have any legal quality. The answer, I suggest, inheres primarily in that they are—or are obliged to be—entirely principled. A principled decision, in the sense I have in mind, is one that rests on reasons with respect to all the issues in the case, reasons that in their generality and their neutrality transcend any immediate result that is involved. When no sufficient reasons of this kind can be assigned for overturning value choices of the other branches of the Government or of a state, those choices must, of course, survive. Otherwise, as Holmes said in his first opinion for the Court, "a Constitution, instead of embodying only relatively fundamental-speaking communities, would become the partisan of a particular set of ethical or economical opinions. . . . "

The virtue or demerit of a judgment turns, therefore, entirely on the reasons that support it and their adequacy to maintain any choice of values it decrees, or, it is vital that we add, to maintain the rejection of a claim that any given choice should be decreed. The critic's role, as T. R. Powell showed throughout so many fruitful years, is the sustained, disinterested, merciless examination of the reasons that the court advanced, measured by standards of the kind I have attempted to describe. I wish that more of us today could imitate his dedication to that task.

III. SOME APPRAISALS OF REVIEW

One who has ventured to advance such generalities about the courts and constitutional interpretation is surely challenged to apply them to some concrete problems—if only to make clear that he believes in what he says.

• • •

The second group of cases to which I shall call attention involves what may be called the progeny of the school-segregation ruling of 1954. Here again the Court has written on the merits of the constitutional issue posed by state segregation only once; its subsequent opinions on the form of the decree and the defiance in Arkansas deal, of course, with other matters. The original opinion, you recall, was firmly focused on state segregation in the public schools, its reasoning accorded import to the nature of the educational process, and its conclusion was that separate educational facilities are "inherently unequal."

What shall we think then of the Court's extension of the ruling to other public facilities, such as public transportation, parks, golf courses, bath houses, and beaches, which no one is obliged to use—all by per curiam decisions? That these situations present a weaker case against state segregation is not, of course, what I am saying. I am saying that the question whether it is stronger, weaker, or of equal weight appears to me to call for principled decision. I do not know and submit you cannot know, whether the per curiam affirmance in the *Dawson* case, involving public bath houses and beaches, embraced the broad opinion of the circuit court that all state-enforced racial segregation is invalid or approved only its immediate result and, if the latter, on what ground.

• • •

Is it not also true and of importance that some of the principles the Court affirmed were strikingly deficient in neutrality, sustaining, for example, national authority when it impinged adversely upon labor, as in the application of the Sherman Act, but not when it was sought to be employed in labor's aid? On this score, the contrast in today's position certainly is striking. The power that sustained the Wagner Act is the same power that sustains Taft-Hartley—with its even greater inroads upon state autonomy but with restraints on labor that the Wagner Act did not impose.

One of the speculations that I must confess I find intriguing is upon the question whether there are any neutral principles that might have been employed to mark the limits of the commerce power of the Congress in terms more circumscribed than the vital abandonment of limits in the principle that has prevailed. Given the readiness of President Roosevelt to compromise on any basis that allowed achievement of the substance of his program, might not the formulae of coverage employed in the legislation of the Thirties have quite readily embraced any such principles the Court had been able to devise before the crisis became so intense—principles sustaining action fairly equal to the need? I do not say that we would or should be happier if that had happened and the Court still played a larger part within this area of our federalism, given the attention to state interests that is so inherent in the Congress and the constitutional provisions governing the selection and the composition of the Houses, which make that attention very likely to endure. I say only that I find such speculation interesting. You will recall that it was Holmes who deprecated argument of counsel the logic of which left "no part of the conduct of life with which on similar principles Congress might not interfere."

• • •

If I am right in this it helps to make a further point that has more bearing upon current issues, that I believe it misconceives the problem of the Court to state it as the question of the proper measure of judicial self-restraint, with the resulting issue whether such restraint is only proper in relation to protection of a purely economic interest or also in relation to an interest like freedom of speech or of religion, privacy, or discrimination (ast least if it is based on race, origin, or creed). Of course, the courts ought to be cautious to impose a choice of values on the other branches of a state, based upon the Constitution, only when they are persuaded, on an adequate and principled analysis, that the choice is clear. That I suggest is all that self-restraint can mean and in that sense it always is essential, whatever issue may be posed. The real test inheres, as I have tried to argue, in the force of the analysis. Surely a stronger analysis may be advanced against a particular uncompensated taking as a violation of the fifth amendment than against a particular limitation of freedom of speech or press as a violation of the first.

In this view, the "preferred position" controversy hardly had a point—indeed, it never has been really clear what is asserted or denied to have a preference and over what. Certainly the concept is pernicious if it implies that there is any simple, almost mechanical basis for determining priorities of values having constitutional dimension, as when there is an inescapable conflict between claims to free press and a fair trial. It has a virtue, on the other hand, insofar as it recognizes that some ordering of social values is essential; that all cannot be given equal weight, if the Bill of Rights is to be maintained.

•   •   •

. . . Finally, I turn to the decisions that for me provide the hardest test of my belief in principled adjudication, those in which the Court in recent years has vindicated claims that deprivations based on race deny the equality before the law that the fourteenth amendment guarantees. The crucial cases are, of course, those involving the white primary, the enforcement of racially restrictive covenants, and the segregated schools.

The more I think about the past the more skeptical I find myself about predictions of the future. Viewed a priori would you not have thought that the invention of the cotton gin in 1792 should have reduced the need for slave labor and hence diminished the attractiveness of slavery? Brooke Adams tells us that its consequences were precisely the reverse; that the demand for slaves inncreased as cotton planting became highly lucrative, increased so greatly that Virginia turned from coal and iron, which George Washington envisaged as its future, into an enormous farm for breeding slaves—forty thousand of whom it exported annually to the rest of the South. Only the other day I read that the Japanese evacuation, which I thought an abomination when it happened, though in the line of duty as a lawyer I participated in the effort to sustain it in the Court, is now believed by many to have been a blessing to its victims, breaking down forever the ghettos in which they had previously lived. But skeptical about predictions as I am, I still believe the decisions I have mentioned—dealing with the primary, the covenant, and schools—have the best chance of making an enduring contribution to the equality of our society of any that I know in recent years. It is in this perspective that I ask how far they rest on neutral principles and are entitled to approval in the only terms that I acknowledge to be relevant to a decision of the courts.

The primary and covenant cases present two different aspects of a single problem—that it is a state alone that is forbidden by the fourteenth amendment to deny equal protection of the laws, as only a state of the United States is precluded by the fifteenth amendment from denying or abridging on the grounds of race or color the right of citizens of the United States to vote. It has, of course, been held for years that the prohibition of action by the state reaches not only an explicit deprivation by a statute but also action of the courts or of subordinate officials, purporting to exert authority derived from public office.

•   •   •

. . . Yet three years later *Classic* was declared in *Smith v. Allwright* to have determined in effect that primaries are a part of the election, with the consequence that parties can no more defend racial exclusion from their primaries than can the state, a result reaffirmed in 1953. This is no doubt a settled proposition in the Court. But what it means is not, as sometimes has been thought, that a state may not escape the limitations of the Constitution merely by transferring public functions into private hands. It means rather that the constitutional guarantee against deprivation of the franchise on the ground of race or color, has become a prohibition of party organization upon racial lines, at least where the party has achieved political hegemony. I ask with all sincerity if you are able to discover in the opinions thus far written in support of this result—a result I say again that I approve—neutral principles that satisfy the mind. I should suppose that a denial of the franchise on religious grounds is certainly forbidden by the Constitution. Are religious parties, therefore, to be taken as proscribed? I should regard this result too as one plainly to be desired but is there a constitutional analysis on which it can be validly decreed? Is it, indeed, not easier to project an analysis establishing that such a proscription would infringe rights protected by the first amendment?

The case of the restrictive covenant presents for me an even harder problem. Assuming that the Constitution speaks to state discrimination on the ground of race but not to such discrimination by an individual even in the use or distribution of his property, although his freedom may no doubt be limited by common law or statute, why is the enforcement of the private covenant a state discrimination rather than a legal recognition of the freedom of the individual? That the action of the state court is action of the state, the point Mr. Chief Justice Vinson emphasizes in the Court's opinion is, of course, entirely obvious. What is not obvious, and is the crucial step, is that the state may properly be charged with the discrimination when it does no more than give effect to an agreement that the individual involved is, by hypothesis, entirely free to make. Again, one is obliged to ask: What is the principle involved? Is the state forbidden to effectuate a will that draws a racial line, a will that can accomplish any disposition only through the aid of law, or is it a sufficient answer there that the discrimination was the testator's and not the state's? May not the state employ its law to vindicate the privacy of property against a trespasser, regardless of the grounds of his exclusion, or does it embrace the owner's reasons for excluding if it buttresses his power by the law? Would a declaratory judgment that a fee is determinable if a racially restrictive limitation should be violated represent discrimination by the state upon the racial ground? Would a judgment of ejectment?

• • •

Lastly, I come to the school decision, which for one of my persuasion stirs the deepest conflict I experience in testing the thesis I propose. Yet I would surely be engaged in playing Hamlet without Hamlet if I did not try to state the problems that appear to me to be involved.

The problem for me, I hardly need to say, is not that the Court departed from its earlier decisions holding or implying that the equality of public educational facilities demanded by the Constitution could be met by separate schools. I stand with the long tradition of the Court that previous decisions must be subject to reexamination when a case against their reasoning is made. Nor is the problem that the Court disturbed the settled patterns of a portion of the country; even that must be accepted as a lesser evil than nullification of the Constitution. Nor is it that history does not confirm that an agreed purpose of the fourteenth amendment was to forbid separate schools or that there is important evidence that many thought the contrary; the words are general and leave room for expanding content as time passes and conditions change. Nor is it that the Court may have miscalculated the extent to which its judgment would be honored or accepted; it is not a prophet of the strength of our national commitment to respect the judgments of the courts. Nor is it even that the

Court did not remit the issue to the Congress, acting under the enforcement clause of the amendment. That was a possible solution, to be sure, but certainly Professor Freund is right that it would merely have evaded the claims made.

The problem inheres strictly in the reasoning of the opinion, an opinion which is often read with less fidelity by those who praise it than by those by whom it is condemned. The Court did not declare, as many wish it had, that the fourteenth amendment forbids all racial lines in legislation, though subsequent per curiam decisions may, as I have said, now go that far. Rather, as Judge Hand observed, the separate-but-equal formula was not overruled "in form" but was held to have "no place" in public education on the ground that segregated schools are "inherently unequal," with deleterious effects upon the colored children in implying their inferiority, effects which retard their educational and mental development. So, indeed, the district court had found as a fact in the Kansas case, a finding which the Supreme Court embraced, citing some further "modern authority" in its support.

Does the validity of the decision turn then on the sufficiency of evidence or of judicial notice to sustain a finding that the separation harms the Negro children who may be involved? There were, indeed, some witnesses who expressed that opinion in the Kansas case, as there were also witnesses in the companion Virginia case, including Professor Garrett of Columbia, whose view was to the contrary. Much depended on the question that the witness had in mind, which rarely was explicit. Was he comparing the position of the Negro child in a segregated school with his position in an integrated school where he was happily accepted and regarded by the whites; or was he comparing his position under separation with that under integration where the whites were hostile to his presence and found ways to make their feelings known? And if the harm that segregation worked was relevant, what of the benefits that it entailed: sense of security, the absence of hostility? Were they irrelevant? Moreover, was the finding in Topeka applicable without more to Clarendon County, South Carolina, with 2,799 colored students and only 295 whites? Suppose that more Negroes in a community preferred separation than opposed it? Would that be relevant to whether they were hurt or aided by segregation as opposed to integration? Their fates would be governed by the change of system quite as fully as those of the students who complained.

I find it hard to think the judgment really turned upon the facts. Rather, it seems to me, it must have rested on the view that racial segregation is, in principle, a denial of equality to the minority against whom it is directed; that is, the group that is not dominant politically and, therefore, does not make the choice involved. For many who support the Court's decision this assuredly is the decisive ground. But this position also presents problems. Does it not involve an inquiry into the motive of the legislature, which is generally foreclosed to the courts? Is it alternatively defensible to make the measure of validity of legislation the way it is interpreted by those who are affect by it? In the context of a charge that segregation *with equal facilities* is a denial of equality, is there not a point in *Plessy* in the statement that if "enforced separation stamps the colored race with a badge of inferiority" it is solely because its members choose "to put that construction about it"? Does enforced separation of the sexes discriminate against females merely because it may be the females who resent it and it is imposed by judgments predominantly male? Is a prohibition of miscegenation a discrimination against the colored member of the couple who would like to marry?

For me, assuming equal facilities, the question posed by state-enforced segregation is not one of discrimination at all. Its human and its constitutional dimensions lie entirely elsewhere, in the denial by the state of freedom to associate, a denial that impinges in the same way on any groups or races that may be involved. I think, and I hope not without foundation, that the Southern white also pays heavily for segregation, not only in the sense of guilt that he must carry but also in the benefits he is denied. In the days when I was joined with Charles H. Houston in a litigation in the Supreme Court, before the present building was constructed, he did not suffer more than I in knowing that we had to go to Union Station to lunch together during the recess. Does not the problem of miscegenation show most clearly that it is the freedom of association that at bottom is involved, the only case, I may add, where it is implicit in the situation that association is desired by the only individuals involved? I take no pride in knowning that in 1956 the Supreme Court dismissed an appeal in a case in which Virginia nullified a marriage on this ground, a case in which the statute had been squarely challenged by the defendant, and the Court, after remanding once, dismissed per curiam on procedural grounds that I make bold to say are wholly without basis in the law.

But if the freedom of association is denied by segregation, integration forces an association upon those for whom it is unpleasant or repugnant. Is this not the heart of the issue involved, a conflict in human claims of high dimension, not unlike many others that involve the highest freedoms—conflicts that Professor Sutherland has recently described. Given a situation where the state must practically choose between denying the association to those individuals who wish it or imposing it on those who would avoid it, is there a basis in neutral principles for holding that the Constitution demands that the claims for association should prevail? I should like to think there is, but I confess that I have not yet written the opinion. To write it is for me the challenge of the school-segregation cases.

Having said what I have said, I certainly should add that I offer no comfort to anyone who claims legitimacy in defiance of the courts. This is the ultimate negation of all neutral principles, to take the benefits accorded by the constitutional system, including the national market and common defense, while denying it allegiance when a special burden is imposed. That certainly is the antithesis of law.

———

Wechsler's position was attacked from different angles by a number of writers. Professors Miller and Howell, for example, directed the force of their criticism at the very notion of the possibility of neutrality in the process of making choices.

MILLER & HOWELL, THE MYTH OF NEUTRALITY IN
CONSTITUTIONAL ADJUDICATION,
27 U. CHI. L. REV. 661–673 (1960)

The teleological conception of his function
must be ever in the judge's mind.
—Benjamin Nathan Cardozo

1. INTRODUCTION

In two recent papers, responsible students of the United States Supreme Court have dealt extensively with so-called "neutral principles" of constitutional adjudication. The first was Professor Herbert Wechsler's Holmes Lecture delivered at the

Harvard Law School in April 1959 and since published in the *Harvard Law Review,* the other, labeled "A Reply to Professor Wechsler," is authored by Professor Louis H. Pollak of the Yale Law School. A third essay, by another highly regarded observer, Professor Henry M. Hart, Jr., is somewhat peripherally correlated with the other two. Both Wechsler and Pollak profess credence in the notion that neutral principles of adjudication can be agreed upon and should be followed by the nine men whose fate it is to sit on the highest bench. Hart holds a similar view, although he speaks of principles which are "impersonal and durable" rather than neutral. Because this position states at best a half-truth, this commentary has been written, not to engage in contentious debate but to point up another dimension to the concept of neutrality in constitutional decision-making. What follows suggests that neutrality, save on a superficial and elementary level, is a futile quest; that it should be recognized as such; and that it is more useful to search for the values that can be furthered by the judicial process than for allegedly neutral or impersonal principles which operate within that process.

Let us begin with a brief recapitulation of what each of the commentators has said. The position of each is easily stated. Wechsler adheres to these ideas: (a) the Supreme Court has a "duty to decide the litigated case . . . in accordance with the law . . ."; (b) the products of the fulfillment of this duty are to be viewed, not as good or bad depending on the result, but in accordance with unstated other standards, these standards presumably to vary from factual situation to factual situation; (c) the Justices on the Court should employ a method which he described as follows: "the maine [sic] constituent of the judicial process is precisely that it must be genuinely principled, resting with respect to every step that is involved in reaching judgment on analysis and reasons quite transcending the immediate result that is achieved . . ."; and further: it is "the special duty of the courts to judge by neutral principles addressed to all the issue[s]." Finally, Wechsler tells us that the "virtue or demerit of a judgment turns, therefore, entirely on the reasons that support it and their adequacy to maintain any choice of values it decrees."

• • •

On one level these papers are exhortations to members of the Supreme Court to pull up their "judicial socks" and to act more as judges are alleged to act in an idealized view of the Anglo-American system of jurisprudence. This is the level of what can be called superficial or elementary neutrality. It seems to mean at least this: Decisions should be reached in constitutional cases, not in accordance with who the litigants were or with the nature or consequences of the results that flow from the decision, but by the application of known or ascertainable objective standards to the facts of the case. These standards are "neutral" because they have an existence independent of litigants; they are identifiable by Supreme Court Justices (and presumably by lawyers, although none of the three authors raises the specter of conflicting neutral principles); and they are usable in making decision and in writing opinions (though it should be said here that the three authors are never entirely clear whether it is the results or the opinion explaining those results that they are criticizing). In other words, the collective view of the three commentators is one of justice blindfolded, with even-handed application of known principles to known facts. So stated, the position is both an appealing and a familiar one. But it seems to ignore some basic elements of human activity and, accordingly, has at best only a very limited usefulness. Rather than providing any viable standards for gauging judicial decision-making, it merely restates the question.

Of the three, only Professor Pollak expresses any doubt about the principles of neutrality, and then only in passing. . . . He marks his adherence to the limited view of judicial neutrality, but notes in concluding his paper that Professor Wechsler's efforts "to capture and tame the concept are plainly unavailing," followed by a quotation from a recent address by Professor Myres S. McDougal:

> The essence of a reasoned decision by the authority of the secular values of a public order of human dignity is a disciplined appraisal of alternative choices of immediate consequences in terms of preferred long-term effects, and not in either the timid foreswearing of concern for immediate consequences or in the quixotic search for criteria of decision that transcend the world of men and values in metaphysical fantasy. The reference of legal principles must be either to their internal—logical—arrangement or to the external consequences of their application. It remains mysterious what criteria for decision a "neutral" system could offer.

It is on that note adumbrated but not developed by Professor Pollak that the following discussion is based.

● ● ●

The first point we want to make is this: Adherence to neutral principles, in the sense of principles which do not refer to value choices, is impossible in the constitutional adjudicative process. (We limit ourselves to constitutional adjudication at this time, although much of what is said here is applicable to litigation generally.) Strive as he might, no participant in that process can be neutral. Even though this should be thought of as being self-evident, it is desirable to set it out in some detail. Before doing so, however, it should be noted that neutrality of *principle,* as distinguished from neutrality of attitude, is an obviously fallacious way of characterizing the situation. Principles, whatever they might be, are abstractions, and it is the worst sort of anthropomorphism to attribute human characteristics to them. Neutrality, if it means anything, can only refer to the thought processes of identifiable human beings. Principles cannot be neutral or biased or prejudiced or impersonal—obviously. The choices that are made by judges in constitutional cases always involve value consequences, thus making value choice unavoidable. The principles which judges employ in projecting their choices to the future, or in explaining them, must also refer to such value alternatives, if given empirical reference. A principle might, in Professor Hart's term, be "durable," but only because enough human beings want it to be so. Can there be neutrality of attitude in constitutional adjudication?

II. NEUTRALITY IN OTHER DISCIPLINES

The process of judicial decision-making is a species of human thought and human choice and should be viewed against the background of what is known about human knowledge and thought processes. The study of the United States Supreme Court is a significant facet of the study of man, both metaphysically and epistemologically. Although this is neither the time nor the place to review all of what is accepted in the sociology of knowledge, it is desirable and relevant to indicate what some leading students of various other disciplines have concluded regarding neutrality or objectivity in thought and decision-making. In this section we shall set out, in very brief form, the opinions of a classical philosopher (Plato), a natural scientist (P.W. Bridgman), a physical chemist who is also a social philosopher (Michael Polanyi), a sociologist

(Karl Mannheim), a social scientist (Gunnar Myrdal), a political philosopher (Leo Strauss), a historian (Isaiah Berlin), and a theologian (Reinhold Neibuhr). The consistent teaching of these respected observers is that neutrality or objectivity is not attainable, either in the social sciences or in the natural sciences. (Needless to say, it is rarely pretended to in the humanities.) Knowledge, therefore, is primarily *decisional* in nature. This means that the human agency cannot be eliminated from any subject to which man addresses his attention, that value preferences inescapably intrude to guide decisions made among competing alternatives. Professor Wechsler agrees that a judge must make a choice among conflicting values, but maintains that such a choice itself can be guided by adherence to neutral principles. This we deny, and we begin our discussion of the students of other relevant disciplines with a statement by sociologist Louis Wirth:

> In studying what is, we cannot totally rule out what ought to be. In human life the motives and ends of action are part of the process by which action is achieved and are essential in seeing the relation of the parts to the whole. Without the end most acts would have no meaning and interest to us. But there is, nevertheless, a difference between taking account of ends and setting ends. Whatever may be the possibility of complete detachment in dealing with physical things, in social life we cannot afford to disregard the values and goals of acts without missing the significance of many of the facts involved. In our choice of areas for research, in our selection of data, in our methods of investigation, in our organization of materials, not to speak of the formulation of our hypotheses and conclusions, there is always manifest some more or less clear, explicit or implicit assumption or scheme of evaluation.

Plato stressed the distinction between rigorous apodictic knowledge and decisional knowledge, and believed the latter to be immensely more valuable than the former. . . . As theologian Robert Cushman recently commented:

> Plato . . . takes the position that there are various possible premises of thought because there are differing orders of reality with appropriately diverse avenues of apprehension. Therefore, what a man "knows," what he judges to be "real" is determined by which avenue he customarily employs and what data he usually accredits as actually "given" for reflections.

•   •   •

So far as the physical sciences are concerned—those which in the popular mind are devoid of the "human element"—recent testimony by one of the more notable scientists, P. W. Bridgman, points to similar conclusions. Writing in 1959, Bridgman, Nobel Prize winner in physics and long highly regarded as a thoughtful analyst of human behavior, tells us that "even in pure physics . . . it is becoming evident that the problem of the 'observer' must eventually deal with the observer as thinking about what he observes." Further, in a statement particularly relevant to the latter part of this paper, Bridgman states: "In my own case, pursuit of operational analysis has resulted in the conviction, a conviction which has increased with the practice, that it is better to analyze in terms of doings and happenings than in terms of objects or static abstractions." If a physicist cannot divorce the personal element of preferences from his study, it would seem to be an *a fortiori* proposition that the social scientist (including the lawyer and judge) cannot.

Bridgman is weightily supported by Michael Polanyi, who, in two recent books, argues that fact is inseparable from value and that the sciences cannot be severed from the humanities. How then does the personal factor manifest itself in the very structure of science? Polanyi discovers it wherever there is an act of appraisal, choice, or accreditation. Each science operates within a conceptual framework which it regards as the "most fruitful" for those facts it "wishes" to study because they are "important," and it thereby chooses to ignore other facts which are "unimportant," "misleading," and "of no consequence." Polanyi's position is aptly summed up in the following statement:

> The ideal of a knowledge embodied in strictly impersonal statements now appears self-contradictory, meaningless, a fit subject for ridicule. We must learn to accept as our ideal a knowledge that is manifestly personal.

Strong support for the views of Bridgman and Polanyi is found in actual laboratory "decision" in contemporary physics. In the theorem of uncertainty, Heisenberg's Principle of Indeterminacy, there is major substantiation for the hypothesis of dynamic "creativity" not merely in human interaction but also in the world of physical phenomena. Heisenberg's Principle is a "new law . . . regarding the behavior of those infinitesimal units of matter which are studied in micro-physics. Knowing the position and velocity of a body, we should be able to predict where it will be the next instant; but the particles in question do not behave in this way, as sober bits of matter should. Statistical laws governing their behavior we can safely formulate but not the behavior of the single particle." It does little good to retort that the failure is not that of the scientist but rather of his instruments, on the supposition that "some day" more reliable instruments will be invented to make exact predictablilty possible. Nor does it help to be told that completely reliable physical laws are lacking only because the observer adds something to the observed by the very act of observation. For, with Kant, that is precisely the point on which we would insist and will later apply to an analysis of the judicial process.

What Bridgman and Polanyi (and Heisenberg) find valid in the physical sciences and are willing to carry over to the social sciences is buttressed by the conclusions of Karl Mannheim in his study of the sociology of knowledge. In *Ideology and Utopia* Mannheim confronts the problem of objectivity and decides that the contextual pattern "colored by values and collective-unconscious, volitional impulses" is crucial, and then seeks a new type of objectivity in the social sciences not through the exclusion of evaluations but "through the critical awareness and control of them." This assertion, which coincides in concept with the "operational" thesis of Bridgman noted above, seems to show the way to a more meaningful analysis of the judicial function in constitutional adjudication. (We shall return to it in Section IV, below). Because constitutional law is for the most part political theory expressed in lawyers' language, the Justices of the Court in reaching their decisions manipulate juristic theories of politics. Mannheim's views of objectivity and neutrality in the area of politics thus are presently relevant:

> When . . . we enter the realm of politics, in which everything is in process of becoming and where the collective element in us, as knowing subjects, helps to shape the process of becoming, where thought is not contemplation from the point of view of a spectator, but rather the active participation and reshaping of the process itself, a new type of knowledge seems to emerge, namely, that in which decision and standpoint are inseparably bound together. In these realms, there is no such thing as a purely theoretical outlook on the part of the observer. It is precisely the purposes that a man has that give him his vision,

even though his interests throw only a partial and practical illumination on that segment of the total reality in which he himself is enmeshed, and towards which he is oriented by virtue of his essential social purposes.

Gunnar Myrdal, the Swedish political economist, places great importance on the idea that social scientists should work from explicit value premises; that is to say, a person should set out his personal preferences and predelictions as clearly as possible when dealing with social data. By so doing, he will enable one who reads his exposition to evaluate what he says in the light of those preferences. It is only in this way, according to Myrdal, that any manageability and real intelligibility may be attained in handling social phenomena. The idea has been set out with some particularity in a collection of his essays entitled *Value in Social Theory.* Myrdal adheres to "the fundamental thesis that value premises are necessary in research and that no study and no book can be *wertfrei,* free from valuations."

> Quite apart from drawing any policy conclusions from social research or forming any ideas about what is desirable or undesirable, we employ and we need value premises in making scientific observations of facts and in analysing their causal interrelation. Chaos does not organize itself into cosmos. We need viewpoints and they presume valuations. A "disinterested social science" is, from this viewpoint, pure nonsense. It never existed, and it will never exist. We can strive to make our thinking rational in spite of this, but only by facing the valuations, not by evading them.

"Analysis and prognosis," to Myrdal, "cannot be neutral, in the sense that they belong to a sphere of actual and possible causal relations which can be permanently separated from valuations and the programmes which they inspire."

Myrdal's point has two facets: first, value preferences cannot be divorced from the study of social phenomena; and second, it is desirable for one who works in the field to set out the preferences he is seeking to further, for in this way a greater degree of objectivity is attained. "Specification of valuation aids in reaching objectivity since it makes explicit what otherwise would be only implicit. . . . Only when the premises are stated explicitly is it possible to determine how valid the conclusions are."

Leo Strauss in *Natural Right and History,* along slightly different but contiguous lines, maintains that "historical objectivity" also is actually *abetted* by the retention of value-judgements:

> The rejection of value judgments endangers historical objectivity. In the first place, it prevents one from calling a spade a spade. In the second place it endangers that kind of objectivity which legitimately requires the forgoing [sic] of evaluations, namely, the objectivity of interpretation. The historian who takes it for granted that objective value judgments are impossible cannot take very seriously that thought of the past which was based on the assumption that objective value judgments are possible, i.e., practically all thought of earlier generations. Knowing beforehand that all thought was based on a fundamental delusion, he lacks the necessary incentive for trying to understand the past as it understood itself.

Moreover, in Strauss' assessment of the special positivism of Max Weber may be located the position of value judgments vis-à-vis the principle of neutrality. "Re-

ference to values is incompatible with neutrality: it can never be 'purely theoretical.'
But non-neutrality does not necessarily mean approval; it may also mean rejection.''

An additional dimension to the limitations which must be faced in any analysis
of human thought is set out by the historian, Isaiah Berlin, in this manner:

> For it is plainly a good thing that we should be reminded by social scientists
> that the scope of human choice is a good deal more limited than we used to
> suppose; that the evidence at our disposal shows that many of the acts too often
> assumed to be within the individual's control are not so; that man is an object
> in nature to a larger degree than has at times been supposed, that human beings
> more often than not act as they do because of characteristics due to heredity
> or physical or social environment or education, or biological laws of physical
> characteristics or the interplay of these factors with each other, and with the
> obscurer factors loosely called psychical characteristics; and that the resultant
> habits of thought, feeling and expression are as capable of being classified and
> made subject to hypotheses and systematic prediction as the behavior of material
> objects. And this certainly alters our ideas about the limits of freedom and
> responsibility.

Finally, Reinhold Niebuhr, without peer among native American theologians,
has firmly denied that science is now able, or ever will be able, completely and
perfectly, to analyze and predict the power and decisional factors in human relationships. His fundamental stricture against the ''scientific approach'' is that science
cannot understand human motives, for ''even the natural sciences are based on
metaphysical suppositions.'' The *human* world, furthermore, is too dimensionally
varied for any unilinear interpretation to have validity:

> The importance of hypotheses increases with the complexity and variability of
> the data into which they are projected. Every assumption is an hypothesis, and
> *human nature is so complex that it justifies almost every assumption and pre-
> judice with which either a scientific investigation or an ordinary human contact
> is initiated.*

• • •

Professor Wechsler admits that value choices are inevitable, but diverges on the
second point of *how* they are made. What we suggest is that his quest for neutrality
is fruitless. In the interest-balancing procedures of constitutional adjudication, neutrality has no place, objectivity is achievable only in part, and impartiality is more
of an aspiration than a fact—although certainly possible in some degree. In making
choices among competing values, the Justices of the Supreme Court are themselves
guided by value preference. Any reference to neutral or impersonal principles is,
accordingly, little more than a call for a return to a mechanistic jurisprudence and
for a jurisprudence of nondisclosure as well as an attempted denial of the teleological
aspects of any decision, wherever made. The members of the high bench have never
adhered to a theory of mechanism, whatever, their apologists and commentators may
have said, in the judicial decision-making process. Even in the often-quoted assertion
by Mr. Justice Roberts about the duty of the Court to lay the statute against the
Constitution to ascertain if the one squares with the other, one would indeed have
to be naive to believe that this statement in fact described the process. Some reference
to Supreme Court history will serve to substantiate the point.

• • •

A rundown of some of the better known constitutional decisions of the past will serve to underscore the proposition that non-neutrality has characterized the Court's decision-making. First, however, it is appropriate to point out that the rewriting of history is not merely the assumed prerogative of historians of the Soviet Union or of the fictional bureaucrats of George Orwell's *1984*. It has been the unconfessed though less flagrant practice of both historians since Thucydides and Justices of the Supreme Court. Historians must strive to be empirical while realizing they can never be "objective," Von Ranke not excluded. Herbert Butterfield in his masterful *Whig Interpretation of History* and Leo Strauss in his equally perceptive *Natural Right and History* have argued persuasively against the "historicist fallacy." That fallacy takes two forms. One is the pretense that history may be categorically outlined in accordance with discoverable "scientific" laws to permit its periodization and prognostication about its future. Proponents include Vico, Hegel, Marx, and Comte. The other is to appraise a former historical era by the criteria of values that have become important since, or conversely, to assume that the standards of an earlier epoch were good for all time, and thus the present is condemned, since the world commenced its decline with the disintegration of the supposed medieval synthesis, or earlier.

———

A different line of critique and an alternative program are offered by Professor McDougal.

McDougal, The Application of Constitutive Prescriptions: An Addendum to Justice Cardozo, Thirty-third Annual Benjamin J. Cardozo Lecture, Ass'n of the Bar of New York 16–23 (1978)

The most ambitious, and influential, recent effort to afford guidance for constitutive application is Professor Wechsler's now classic, "Toward Neutral Principles of Constitutional Law." In this essay Wechsler seeks to formulate "the minimal criteria of a defensible interpretative judgment." . . . In the introduction to the book reprint he offers further clarification:

> I certainly do not deny that constitutional provisions are directed to protecting certain special values or that the principled development of a particular provision is concerned with the value or the values thus involved. The demand of neutrality is that a value and its measure be determined by a general analysis that gives no weight to accidents of application, finding a scope that is acceptable whatever interest, group, or person may assert the claim.

Unhappily, neither Professor Wechsler nor any of his innumerable commentators has ever been able to suggest any criteria, other than syntactic, for distinguishing between principles of adequate and inadequate generality and neutrality. What are described as the "accidents" of "interest, group, or person" may be among the factors most relevant to decision. A rational concern for long-term interests in the real world commonly includes, further, a concern for the next steps, or immediate consequences. The effective accommodation of opposing interests must require, beyond verbal abstractions, the balancing and integration of value demands in social process.

The most uncompromising contemporary proponent of principled decision, only in measure after the fashion of Wechsler, is Professor, quondam Solicitor-General, Bork. In an article, "Neutral Principles and Some First Amendment Problems,"

Professor Bork explores the implications of Wechsler's concept and finds a deeper base for the requirement of principled decision in "the seeming anomaly of judicial supremacy in a democratic society." The power of the Supreme Court is, according to Bork, undemocratic, and our society has consented to be "ruled undemocratically" only "within defined areas by certain enduring principles believed to be stated in and placed beyond the reach of majorities, by the Constitution." This dilemma, Bork alleges, "imposes severe requirements upon the Court":

> For it follows that the court's power is legitimate only if it has, and can demonstrate in reasoned opinions that it has a valid theory derived from the Constitution, of the respective spheres of majority and minority freedom. If it does not have such a theory but merely imposes its own value choices, or worse if it pretends to have a theory but actually follows its own predilections the Court violates the postulates of the Madisonian model that alone justifies its power. It then necessarily abets the tyranny either of the majority or of the minority.

Bork, not surprisingly, has some difficulties in identifying and specifying an appropriate theory for the Court. He insists that "the determination of 'social value' cannot be made in a principled way" and that "the choice of 'fundamental values' by the Court cannot be justified." He summarizes:

> Where constitutional materials do not clearly specify the value to be preferred, there is no principled way to prefer any human value to any other. The judge must stick close to the text and the history, and their fair implications, and not construct new rights.

Bork makes his dependence upon syntactic derivation explicit. "Logic" he writes, "has a life of its own, and devotion to principle requires that we follow where logic leads." He adds:

> We have not carried the idea of neutrality far enough. We have been talking about neutrality in the *application* of principles. If judges are to avoid imposing their own values upon the rest of us, however, they must be neutral as well in the *definition* and *derivation* of principles.

The time was when professors in the Yale Law School were somewhat more dubious about the possibilities of obtaining new truth by syntactic derivation and were more wary of permitting themselves, or requiring others, to be coerced by such logic. The corridors still echo with Thurman Arnold's homely wisdom that he who snaps at a gnat does not necessarily have to swallow a camel. The blunt contraposition, further, of majority and minority interests minimizes the potentialities of genuine integration in common interest, and the notion that man can make no reasoned choice of values both indicates a barren conception of reason and underestimates man.

The most articulate and most productive of the proponents of principled decision was of course my late, and much respected, colleague, Professor Alexander Bickel. In a huge flow of books and articles he plead, most eloquently, for the "passive virtues" and judicial restraint. He shared the misconception that constitutional review is undemocratic and described "constitutional judgment" as "a high policy-making function performed in a political democracy by an institution that has to be regarded as deviant." Thus, he insisted that the "process of the coherent, analytically warranted, principled declaration of general norms alone justifies the Court's function." Yet in many moving passages he admitted defeat in his efforts to draw more than an imprecise line between principled and unprincipled decision, and in his appraisal of particular decisions his mellow humanity commonly seeped through syntactic constraints to a genuine concern for the value consequences of decision. In his most important book, *The Least Dangerous Branch,* he stated that by "principle" he meant "general propositions," that is, "organized ideas of universal validity in the given universe of a culture and a place, ideas that are often grounded in ethical and moral presuppositions." "Principle, ethics, morality" he added, "these are evocative, not definitional terms; they are attempts to locate meaning, not to enclose it." In his peroration in this book, in attempting to indicate what Mr. Justice Frankfurter meant by "fundamental presuppositions," he retreated finally to the words of a literary critic. This critic wrote that the "superiority of one writer over another (Faulkner over J. P. Marquand)

> cannot be proved, [but] it can be demonstrated, a quite different operation involving an appeal—by reasons, analysis, illustration, and rhetoric—to cultural values which critic and reader have in common, values no more susceptible of scientific statement then are the moral values-in-common to which Jesus appeals but which, for all that, exist as vividly and definitely as do mercy, humility, and love.

In some of his later work Bickel did not always seem to realize that the values upon which judges might draw for guidance in decision need not be confined to religious or metaphysical absolutes (whether Whig or Lockean) but could include the very secular demands of members of a particular community, and that such secular demands could be appraised, as decision-makers have immemorially appraised them, in terms of their relation to common interest.

. . . Similarly, Professor (long-time Dean and quandam Under-Secretary) Eugene Rostow has, in a series of articles later published in book form, written an eloquent, and powerful, defense of the democracy of constitutional review. . . . The basic assumption underlying the argument of the proponents of "principled" decision he gives short shrift:

> But universal manhood suffrage does not imply, in theory or in fact, that policy can properly be determined in a democracy only through universal popular elections, or that universal popular elections have or should have the capacity to make any and all decisions of democratic government without limits or delays of any kind. Representative government is, after all, a legitimate form of democracy, through which the people delegate to their elected representatives in legislatures, or in executive offices, some but not necessarily all of their powers, for a period of years. Neither the town meeting nor the Swiss referendum is an indispensable feature of democratic decision-making.

In similar vein, Professor Charles Black has written brilliantly, in refutation of many positions taken by the proponents of principled decision, most importantly in relation to the lawfulness of constitutional review itself and the racial desegregation decisions. He observes that the "precision of textual explication is nothing but specious in the areas that matter" and bases his own recommended applications primarily upon "the total structure that the text has created." He employs what others might call interpretation by "major purposes" in common interest and builds upon a "general consensus" in a continuing process of communication.

A more recent response to the advocates of principled decision is that of Judge Skelly Wright in his comprehensive and insightful article, "Professor Bickel, The

Scholarly Tradition, and the Supreme Court.'' Judge Wright offers telling description of the ambiguities and inconsistencies in the appeals for principled decision and concludes that its advocates cannot hope by sheer exercises in syntactic logic to achieve the ends to which they aspire. He notes that Bickel admits "his doubt that the Court has ever fully met the Wechslerian standards and recognizes that he does not know whether the Warren Court fell any further short than its predecessor" and inquires whether Bickel should not have "hesitated somewhat longer—whether he is not demanding the nearly impossible." He writes:

> If past Courts have also systematically failed to meet the requirements of prin-
> cipled decision-making, does this not suggest that the requirements them-
> selves—at least as applied by the scholarly critics—are fatally unrealistic?

He adds:

> How are we to evaluate the 'neutrality' of line-drawing except by reference to
> some sort of value choices?

On the constructive side, Judge Wright insists that many of the important value choices that an applier must make are already made in the basic flow of constitutive communication, but he offers no very precise recommendations about how these important choices can be specified and applied in particular instances. One of the authors upon whom Judge Wright builds, Professor Jan Deutsch, offers an even more devastating review of the inadequacies of the principled decision illusion and suggests a solution of the difficulties through the employment of "precedent" in context. The flow of precedents is, however, but one component of the total flow of constitutive communication and commonly speaks with an especially ambiguous and forked tongue. A rational performance of the application function must require procedures for evaluating precedents, along with other communications, in terms of probable future consequences and for relating complementary precedents to specific choices in the context in which such choices have to be made.

NOTES

1. Beyond these criticisms, does the Wechslerian view tend to sterilize the entire function of decisionmaking in complex and changing environments? What is the point of constantly trying to replicate the past with great fidelity, when the future may be quite different? Is decisionmaking an attempt to respond to new challenges in new environments with reference to contemporary as well as to past principles? Discuss.

2. Is the concept of "a government of laws, not of men" requiring decisions by courts based upon fixed rules, a viable one? Consider Justice Frankfurter:

> The meaning of "due process" and the content of terms like "liberty" are not revealed
> by the Constitution. It is the Justices who make the meaning. They read into the neutral
> language and the Constitution their own economic and social views. Let us face the fact
> that five Justices of the Supreme Court are the molders of policy rather than the impersonal
> vehicles of revealed truth. (F. Frankfurter, The Supreme Court and the Public, 83 *Forum*
> 332–34 (1930).

3. It was pointed out by von Jhering that in a difficult case a judge might have recourse to two groups of legal doctrines, or two different lines of decisions from which to choose, each one applicable with equal logical force to the case at hand but each leading to a different conclusion. Which one should the judge select? A doctrine of strict application of the written

rules expressed in prior legislation and cases would not help here. Can one decide without reference to values and the goals sought by the decision?

4. Is it possible for written rules to be sufficiently detailed and clear to cover every situation that may arise, especially in the constantly shifting kaleidescope of conditions in modern society? Is language susceptible to such precision? Assuming that it is, would the application of "fixed" rules result in undesired consequences, as conditions change in society or as perceptions of justice (e.g., "equality") and goals undergo revision?

5. Can and will legislatures act fast enough to amend written laws when the emergence of new conditions makes change desirable? According to one interpretation of recent history, the American Congress, under pressure and fear of voter reaction, did not pass important civil rights legislation until after the Supreme Court—not directly answerable to voters—decided *Brown vs. Board of Education,* a case which came out strongly against racial segregation and precipitated a change in popular attitudes. (See Chapter 10 and the references there for the contention that the Constitution and legislation should not be regarded as having a fixed determinant meaning for all time).

6. On the other hand, is it consistent with democratic ideals for the courts and other decision-makers, not directly answerable to the voting public, to be given wide discretion in applying law, whether by reference to articulated general goals or otherwise? If taxation without representation is tyranny, what of law-making by non-elected judges? This has been the contention of scholars such as R. Berger, *Government by Judiciary* (1977) and N. Glazer, *Towards an Imperial Judiciary?,* 41 *Pub. Interest* 104 (Fall, 1975). But see the spirited defense by A. Bickel, *The Least Dangerous Branch* (1962). The criticism of judicial discretion has sharpened of late in reaction to the expanded activities of some federal courts that have undertaken administrative functions for which they may be regarded as neither competent nor authorized. Such activities have included operating schools (including decisions as to what kind of basketballs to purchase for the school gymnasium), prisons, hospitals, etc. and also mandating expenditures of monies, thereby setting the level of taxation to be established by municipalities, fixing budget priorities and even threatening to jail municipal officials who would disobey such court mandates.

If courts and other decisionmakers are to have discretion to decide without being bound by rules with fixed meanings, will it result in arbitrary and capricious decisionmaking? Are there alternative methods of control? Discuss.

POSITIVISM AND MORALITY

The sharp distinction between law and morality created by the positivistic formula generates its own problems. Because positivism characterizes law as the order of a political superior to a subordinate, the legal relevance of the morality of the subordinate is substantially reduced. Members of the group to whom the commands are directed who have intense moral demands of their own will find that it is increasingly difficult or morally costly for them to comply with law even if they assume that law is entitled to some obedience. This distinction between law and morality, flowing from the very formulation of Positivism, has generated its own cottage industry of jurisprudence.

In the piece that follows, Professor H.L.A. Hart addresses at a theoretical level the basic problem of the distinction between law and morals in Positivism.

HART, POSITIVISM AND THE SEPARATION OF LAW AND MORALS, 71 HARV. L.R. 593, 615–620 (1958)

The third criticism of the separation of law and morals is . . . less an intellectual argument against the Utilitarian distinction than a passionate appeal supported not by detailed reasoning but by reminders of a terrible experience. For it consists of the testimony of those who have descended into Hell, and, like Ulysses or Dante, brought back a message for human beings. Only in this case the Hell was not beneath or beyond earth but on it; it was a Hell created on earth by men for other men.

This appeal comes from those German thinkers who lived through the Nazi regime and reflected upon its evil manifestation in the legal system. One of these thinkers, Gustav Radbruch, had himself shared the 'positivist' doctrine until the Nazi tyranny, but he was converted by this experience and so his appeal to other men to discard the doctrine of the separation of law and morals has the special poignancy of a recantation. What is important about this criticism is that it really does confront the particular point which Bentham and Austin had in mind in urging the separation of law as it is and as it ought to be. These German thinkers put their insistence on the need to join together what the Utilitarians separated just where this separation was of most importance in the eyes of the Utilitarians; for they were concerned with the problem posed by the existence of morally evil laws.

Before his conversion Radbruch held that resistance to law was a matter for the personal conscience, to be thought out by the individual as a moral problem, and the validity of a law could not be disproved by showing that its requirements were morally evil or even by showing that the effect of compliance with the law would be more evil than the effect of disobedience. Austin, it may be recalled, was emphatic in condemning those who said that if human laws conflicted with the fundamental principles of morality then they cease to be laws, as talking 'stark nonsense.'

> The most pernicious laws, and therefore those which are most opposed to the will of God, have been and are continually enforced as laws by judicial tribunals. Suppose an act innocuous, or positively beneficial, be prohibited by the sovereign under the penalty of death; if I commit this act, I shall be tried and condemned, and if I object to the sentence, that it is contrary to the law of God . . . the court of justice will demonstrate the inconclusiveness of my reasoning by hanging me up, in pursuance of the law of which I have impugned the validity. An exception, demurrer, or plea, founded on the law of God was never heard in a Court of Justice, from the creation of the world down to the present moment.

These are strong, indeed brutal words, but we must remember that they went along—in the case of Austin and, of course, Bentham—with the conviction that if laws reached a certain degree of iniquity then there would be a plain moral obligation to resist them and to withhold obedience. We shall see, when we consider the alternatives, that this simple presentation of the human dilemma which may arise has much to be said for it.

• • •

. . . But something more disturbing than naiveté is latent in Radburch's whole presentation of the issues to which the existence of morally iniquitous laws give rise. It is not, I think, uncharitable to say that we can see in his argument that he has only half digested the spiritual message of liberalism which he is seeking to convey to the legal profession. For everything that he says is really dependent upon an enormous overvaluation of the importance of the bare fact that a rule may be said to be a valid rule of law, as if this, once declared, was conclusive of the final moral question: Ought this rule of law to be obeyed? Surely the truly liberal answer to any sinister use of the slogan 'law is law' or of the distinction between law and morals is, 'Very well, but that does not conclude the question. Law is not morality; do not let it supplant morality.'

• • •

. . . If with the Utilitarians we speak plainly, we say that laws may be law but too evil to be obeyed. This is a moral condemnation which everyone can understand and it makes an immediate and obvious claim to moral attention.

NOTES

1. Why have Positivists drawn a line between law and morality? Many reasons have been suggested including: the fear that conflicting claims over what constitutes morality could lead to civil strife; the fear that a majority or an elite, acting through the government, would impose its own notions of morality upon others in the community and intrude upon "private" spheres of action; the "scientific" bent of Positivism which eschewed notions of morality since they supposedly could not be proven or established by empirical inquiry.

Hart has attempted to point out an additional advantage in distinguishing law from morality. A link between the two could, he claimed, permit reactionaries to argue that a law that "is," is *ipso facto* moral and hence should not be changed; this would obstruct necessary law reform. At the same time, those dissatisfied with existing law could invoke its "immorality" and claim that the law in its entirety should be superceded; this would undermine social stability. (Hart, *The Concept of Law* 206)

2. Positivism regards a law as valid even if it is immoral. Hart notes that a person who is under a legal duty to obey the law which is, by definition, valid, might still refuse to obey it on grounds of morality or individual conscience. If that person complied with a wicked law, should that person be punished? Is the distinction between law and morality here palpable or is there so much interstimulation that they are points on a continuum? Once it is postulated that a law is valid and that there is a "legal" duty to obey it, won't people in general tend to regard it as "moral" to obey the law? Where people have been trained to view law as a system conferring benefits on all of society, won't they tend to view it as an overriding good outweighing the lesser evil of the immoral content of a specific piece of legislation? What, after all, are the sources of the notion, encountered again and again that the law is something that should be obeyed, that it has an elevated almost sacred status. The notion of the good, "law-abiding" citizen, as contrasted with the evil "law-breaker" is deeply embedded in the social conscience. Recall the Socratic argument in *Crito* in Chapter 4.

3. The dilemma of "immoral" laws in nineteenth century America is reflected in the cases in which judges upheld the institution of slavery, although they deemed it immoral. As some of them expressed it, "You know full well that I have ever been opposed to slavery. But I take my standard of duty as a judge from the Constitution." (W. Wetmore, *Life and Letters of Joseph Story,* 2: 431 (1851)). "With the abstract principles of slavery, courts called to administer law have nothing to do. It is for the people, who are sovereign, and their representatives, in making consitutions and in the enactment of laws, to consider the laws of nature, and the immutable principles of right. This is a field which judges cannot explore. . . . They look to the law and to the law only." (*Miller v. McQuerry,* 17 F. Cas. 332 (No. 9583) (C.C.D. Ohio, 1853) at 339). "As a citizen and as a man, I may admit the injustice and immorality of slavery, . . . But as a jurist, I must look at that standard of morality, which the law prescribed." (*Jackson v. Bullock,* 12 Conn. 39 (1837)).

In the *Dred Scott* case (p. 234 supra) the Supreme Court upheld the institution of slavery although it indicated that it might be regarded as reprehensible.

4. Some, responsive to moral demands, argue that the Positivist view that morality has no place in law has resulted in the proliferation, in the United States, of legislation permitting "no fault" divorce, the failure in practice of local officials to prosecute violations of criminal laws consisting of consensual sexual activities of adults, such as adultery and bigamy. Discuss.

5. Morality still plays a role in legislative prohibitions and judicial interpretation concerning the sale or distribution of obscene materials. Why is morality relevant in this and not in other matters? Discuss.

WOLFENDEN AND THE CONTROVERSY ABOUT HOMOSEXUALITY

Not surprisingly, positivists have hardly carried the day in their rejection of a role for morality in decision and law. Many writers and judges continue to feel that fundamental moral principles should be and are expressed in the law and should in particular be used to supplement or temper the application of formal legal principles. In many cases these two positions are proxies for fundamental disagreements about key issues in the organization of society. In England, a debate over the appropriate legal response to adult consensual homosexuality generated a jurisprudence debate in precisely these terms. The *Wolfenden Report,* dealing with the problem of homosexual offenses and prostitution, was co-authored by H.L.A. Hart.

THE WOLFENDEN REPORT: HOME OFFICE REPORT ON HOMOSEXUAL OFFENSES AND PROSTITUTION 9–10, 21, 24, 79–80, (CMD 247 (1957))

. . . Our primary duty has been to consider the extent to which homosexual behavior and female prostitution should come under the condemnation of the criminal law, and this has presented us with the difficulty of deciding what are the essential elements of a criminal offense. There appears to be no unquestioned definition of what constitutes or ought to constitute a crime. To define it as "an act which is punished by the State" does not answer the question: What acts ought to be punished by the State? We have therefore worked with our own formulation of the function of the criminal law so far as it concerns the subjects of this enquiry. In this field, its function, as we see it, is to preserve public "order and decency," to protect the citizen from what is "offensive or injurious," and to provide sufficient safeguards against exploitation and corruption of others, particularly those who are especially vulnerable because they are young, weak in body or mind, inexperienced, or in a state of special physical, official or economic dependence.

It is not, in our view, the function of the law to intervene in the private lives of citizens, or to seek to enforce any particular pattern of behavior, further than is necessary to carry out the purposes we have outlined. It follows that we do not believe it to be the function of the law to attempt to cover all the fields of sexual behavior. Certain forms of sexual behavior are "regarded by many" as sinful, morally wrong, or objectionable for reasons of conscience, or of religious or cultural tradition; and such actions may be reprobated on these grounds. But the criminal law does not cover all such actions at the present time; for instance, adultery and fornication are not offenses for which a person can be punished by the criminal law. Nor indeed is prostitution as such.

We appreciate that opinions will differ as to what is offensive, injurious or inimical to the common good, and also as to what constitutes exploitation or corruption; and that these opinions will be based on moral, social or cultural standards. We have been guided by our estimate of the standards of the community in general, recognizing that they will not be accepted by all citizens, and that our estimate of them may be mistaken.

We have had to consider the relationship between the law and public opinion. It seems to us that there are two overdefinite views about this. On the one hand, it is held that the law ought to follow behind public opinion, so that the law can count on the support of the community as a whole. On the other hand, it is held that a necessary purpose of the law is to lead or fortify public opinion. Certainly it is clear that if any legal enactment is markedly out of tune with public opinion it will quickly fall into disrepute. Beyond this we should not wish to dogmatise, for on the matters with which we are called upon to deal we have not succeeded in discovering an unequivocal "public opinion," and we have felt bound to try to reach conclusions for ourselves rather than to base them on what is often transient and seldom precisely ascertainable.

•   •   •

It is also part of the function of the law to preserve public order and decency. We therefore hold that when homosexual behavior between males takes place in public it should continue to be dealt with by the criminal law. . . .

Besides the two categories of offence we have just mentioned, namely, offences committed by adults with juveniles and offences committed in public places, there is a third class of offence to which we have had to give long and careful consideration. It is that of homosexual acts committed between adults in private.

•   •   •

We have indicated . . . our opinion as to the province of the law and its sanctions, and how far it properly applies to the sexual behavior of the individual citizen. On the basis of the considerations there advanced we have reached the conclusion that legislation which covers acts in the third category we have mentioned goes beyond the proper sphere of the law's concern. We do not think that it is proper for the law to concern itself with what a man does in private unless it can be shown to be so contrary to the public good that the law ought to intervene in its function as the guardian of that public good.

•   •   •

. . . There remains one additional . . . argument which we believe to be decisive, namely, the importance which society and the law ought to give to individual freedom of choice and action in matters of private morality. Unless a deliberate attempt is to be made by society, acting through the agency of the law, to equate the sphere of crime with that of sin, there must remain a realm of private morality and immorality which is, in brief and crude terms, not the law's business. To say this is not to condone or encourage private immorality. On the contrary, to emphasize the personal and private nature of moral or immoral conduct is to emphasize the personal and private responsibility which a mature agent can properly be expected to carry for himself without the threat of punishment from the law.

•   •   •

Prostitution is a social fact deplorable in the eyes of moralists, sociologists and, we believe, the great majority of ordinary people. But it has persisted in many civilizations throughout many centuries, and the failure of attempts to stamp it out by repressive legislation shows that it cannot be eradicated through the agency of the criminal law. It remains true that without a demand for her services the prostitute could not exist, and that there are enough men who avail themselves of prostitutes to keep the trade alive. It also remains true that there are women who, even when there is no economic need to do so, choose this form of livelihood. For so long as these propositions continue to be true there will be prostitution, and no amount of legislation directed towards its abolition will abolish it.

It follows that there are limits to the degree of discouragement which the criminal law can properly exercise towards a woman who has deliberately decided to live her life in this way, or a man who has deliberately chosen to use her services. The criminal law, as the Street Offences Committee plainly pointed out, "is not concerned with private morals or with ethical sanctions." This does not mean that society itself can be indifferent to these matters, for prostitution is an evil of which any society which claims to be civilized should seek to rid itself; but this end could be achieved only through measures of sexual relationship and to a raising of the social and moral outlook of society as a whole. In these matters, the work of the churches and organizations concerned with mental health, moral welfare, family welfare, child and marriage guidance and similar matters should be given all possible encouragement. But until education and the moral sense of the community bring about a change of attitude towards the fact of prostitution, the law by itself cannot do so.

At the same time, the law has its place and functions in this matter. We cannot do better than quote the words of the Street Offences Committee—

> As a general proposition it will be universally accepted that the law is not concerned with private morals or with ethical sanctions. On the other hand, the law is plainly concerned with the outward conduct of citizens in so far as that conduct injuriously affects the rights of other citizens. Certain forms of conduct it has always been thought right to bring within the scope of the criminal law on account of the injury which they occasion to the public in general. It is within this category of offences, if anywhere, that public solicitation for immoral purpose finds an appropriate place.

Lord Devlin, on the other hand, argued that morals were an appropriate subject for regulation and enforcement by law.

DEVLIN, THE ENFORCEMENT OF MORALS 4–19 (1968)

. . . I must admit that I begin with a feeling that a complete separation of crime from sin (I use the term throughout this lecture in the wider meaning) would not be good for the moral law and might be disastrous for the criminal. But can this sort of feeling be justified as a matter of jurisprudence? And if it be a right feeling, how should the relationship between the criminal and the moral law be stated? Is there a good theoretical basis for it, or is it just a practical working alliance, or is it a bit of both? That is the problem which I want to examine, and I shall begin by considering the standpoint of the strict logician. It can be supported by cogent arguments, some of which I believe to be unanswerable and which I put as follows.

Morals and religion are inextricably joined—the moral standards generally accepted in Western civilization being those belonging to Christianity. Outside Christendom other standards derive from other religions. None of these moral codes can claim any validity except by virtue of the religion on which it is based. Old Testament morals differ in some respects from New Testament morals. Even within Christianity there are differences. Some hold that contraception is an immoral practice and that a man who has carnal knowledge of another woman while his wife is alive is in all circumstances a fornicator; others, including most of the English-speaking world, deny both these propositions. Between the great religions of the world, of which

Christianity is only one, there are much wider differences. It may or may not be right for the State to adopt one of these religions as the truth, to found itself upon its doctrines, and to deny to any of its citizens the liberty to practise any other. If it does, it is logical that it should use the secular law whenever it thinks it necessary to enforce the divine. If it does not, it is illogical that it should concern itself with morals as such. But if it leaves matters of religion to private judgement, it should logically leave matters of morals also. A State which refuses to enforce Christian beliefs has lost the right to enforce Christian morals.

If this view is sound, it means that the criminal law cannot justify any of its provisions by reference to the moral law. It cannot say, for example, that murder and theft are prohibited because they are immoral or sinful. The State must justify in some other way the punishments which it imposes on wrongdoers and a function for the criminal law independent of morals must be found. This is not difficult to do. The smooth functioning of society and the preservation of order require that a number of activities should be regulated. The rules that are made for that purpose and are enforced by the criminal law are often designed simply to achieve uniformity and convenience and rarely involve any choice between good and evil. Rules that impose a speed limit or prevent obstruction on the highway have nothing to do with morals. Since so much of the criminal law is composed of rules of this sort, why bring morals into it at all? Why not define the function of the criminal law in simple terms as the preservation of order and decency and the protection of the lives and property of citizens, and elaborate those terms in relation to any particular subject in the way in which it is done in the Wolfenden Report? The criminal law in carrying out these objects will undoubtedly overlap the moral laws. Crimes of violence are morally wrong and they are also offences against good order; therefore they offend against both laws. But this is simply because the two laws in pursuit of different objectives happen to cover the same area. Such is the argument.

• • •

Now, if the law existed for the protection of the individual, there would be no reason why he should avail himself of it if he did not want it. The reason why a man may not consent to the commission of an offence against himself beforehand or forgive it afterwards is because it is an offence against society. It is not that society is physically injured; that would be impossible. Nor need any individual be shocked, corrupted, or exploited; everything may be done in private. Nor can it be explained on the practical ground that a violent man is a potential danger to others in the community who have therefore a direct interest in his apprehension and punishment as being necessary to their own protection. That would be true of a man whom the victim is prepared to forgive but not of one who gets his consent first; a murderer who acts only upon the consent, and maybe the request, of his victim is no menace to others, but he does threaten one of the great moral principles upon which society is based, that is, the sanctity of human life. There is only one explanation of what has hitherto been accepted as the basis of the criminal law and that is that there are certain standards of behaviour or moral principles which society requires to be observed; and the breach of them is an offence not merely against the person who is injured but against society as a whole.

Thus, if the criminal law were to be reformed so as to eliminate from it everything that was not designed to preserve order and decency or to protect citizens (including the protection of youth from corruption), it would overturn a fundamental principle. It would also end a number of specific crimes. Euthanasia or the killing of another at his own request, suicide, attempted suicide and suicide pacts, duelling, abortion, incest between brother and sister, are all acts which can be done in private and without offence to others and need not involve the corruption or exploitation of others. Many people think that the law on some of these subjects is in need of reform, but no one hitherto has gone so far as to suggest that they should all be left outside the criminal law as matters of private morality. They can be brought within it only as a matter of moral principle. It must be remembered also that although there is much immorality that is not punished by the law, there is none that is condoned by the law. The law will not allow its processes to be used by those engaged in immorality of any sort. For example, a house may not be let for immoral purposes; the lease is invalid and would not be enforced. But if what goes on inside there is a matter of private morality and not the law's business, why does the law inquire into it at all?

I think it is clear that the criminal law as we know it is based upon moral principle. In a number of crimes its function is simply to enforce a moral principle and nothing else. The law, both criminal and civil, claims to be able to speak about morality and immorality generally. Where does it get its authority to do this and how does it settle the moral principles which it enforces? Undoubtedly, as a matter of history, it derived both from Christian teaching. But I think that the strict logician is right when he says that the law can no longer rely on doctrines in which citizens are entitled to disbelieve. It is necessary therefore to look for some other source.

In jurisprudence, as I have said, everything is thrown open to discussion and, in the belief that they cover the whole field, I have framed three interrogatories addressed to myself to answer:

1. Has society the right to pass judgment at all on matters of morals? Ought there, in other words, to be a public morality, or are morals always a matter for private judgement?
2. If society has the right to pass judgement, has it also the right to use the weapon of law to enforce it?
3. If so, ought it to use that weapon in all cases or only in some; and if only in some, on what principles should it distinguish?

I shall begin with the first interrogatory and consider what is meant by the right of society to pass a moral judgement, that is, a judgement about what is good and what is evil. The fact that a majority of people may disapprove of a practice does not of itself make it a matter for society as a whole. Nine men out of ten may disapprove of what the tenth man is doing and still say that it is not their business. There is a case for a collective judgement (as distinct from a large number of individual opinions which sensible people may even refrain from pronouncing at all if it is upon somebody else's private affairs) only if society is affected. Without a collective judgement there can be no case at all for intervention. Let me take as an illustration the Englishman's attitude to religion as it is now and as it has been in the past. His attitude now is that a man's religion is his private affair; he may think of another man's religion that it is right or wrong, true or untrue, but not that it is good or bad. In earlier times that was not so; a man was denied the right to practice what was thought of as heresy, and heresy was thought of as destructive of society.

• • •

This view—that there is such a thing as public morality—can also be justified by *a priori* argument. What makes a society of any sort is community of ideas, not only political ideas but also ideas about the way its members should behave and govern their lives; these latter ideas are its morals. Every society has a moral structure as well as a political one: or rather, since that might suggest two independent systems, I should say that the structure of every society is made up both of politics and morals. Take, for example, the institution of marriage. Whether a man should be allowed to take more than one wife is something about which every society has to make up its mind one way or the other. In England we believe in the Christian idea of marriage and therefore adopt monogamy as a moral principle. Consequently the Christian institution of marriage has become the basis of family life and so part of the structure of our society. It is there not because it is Christian. It has got there because it is Christian, but it remains there because it is built into the house in which we live and could not be removed without bringing it down. The great majority of those who live in this country accept it because it is the Christian idea of marriage and for them the only true one. But a non-Christian is bound by it, not because it is part of Christianity but because rightly or wrongly, it has been adopted by the society in which he lives. It would be useless for him to stage a debate designed to prove that polygamy was theologically more correct and socially preferable; if he wants to live in the house, he must accept it as built in the way in which it is.

We see this more clearly if we think of ideas or institutions that are purely political. Society cannot tolerate rebellion; it will not allow argument about the rightness of the cause. Historians a century later may say that the rebels were right and the Government was wrong and a percipient and conscientious subject of the State may think so at the time. But it is not a matter which can be left to individual judgement.

The institution of marriage is a good example for my purpose because it bridges the division, if there is one, between politics and morals. Marriage is part of the structure of our society and it is also the basis of a moral code which condemns fornication and adultery. The institution of marriage would be gravely threatened if individual judgements were permitted about the morality of adultery; on these points there must be a public morality. But public morality is not to be confined to those moral principles which support institutions such as marriage. People do not think of it as something that is good in itself and offering a good way of life and that it is for that reason that our society has adopted it. I return to the statement that I have already made, that society means a community of ideas; without shared ideas on politics, morals and ethics no society can exist. Each one of us has ideas about what is good and what is evil; they cannot be kept private from the society in which we live. If men and women try to creat a society in which there is no fundamental agreement about good and evil they will fail; if, having based it on common agreement, the agreement goes, the society will disintegrate. For society is not something that is kept together physically; it is held by the invisible bonds of common thought. If the bonds were too far relaxed the members would drift apart. A common morality is part of the bondage. The bondage is part of the price of society; and mankind, which needs society, must pay its price.

● ● ●

You may think that I have taken far too long in contending that there is such a thing as public morality, a proposition which most people would readily accept, and may have left myself too little time to discuss the next question which to many minds may cause greater difficulty: to what extent should society use the law to enforce its moral judgments? But I believe that the answer to the first question determines the way in which the second should be approached and may indeed very nearly dictate the answer to the second question. If society has no right to make judgements on morals, the law must find some special justification for entering the field of morality;

if homosexuality and prostitution are not in themselves wrong, then the onus is very clearly on the lawgiver who wants to frame a law treatment. But if society has the right to make a judgement and has it on the basis that a recognized morality is as necessary to society, as say, a recognized government, then society may use the law to preserve morality in the same way as it uses it to safeguard anything else that is essential to its existence. If therefore the first proposition is securely established with all its implications, society has a prima facie right to legislate against immorality as such.

• • •

All sexual immorality involves the exploitation of human weaknesses. The prostitute exploits the lust of her customers and the customer the moral weakness of the prostitute. If the exploitation of human weaknesses is considered to create a special circumstance, there is virtually no field of morality which can be defined in such a way as to exclude the law.

I think, therefore, that it is not possible to set theoretical limits to the power of the State to legislate against immorality. It is not possible to settle in advance exceptions to the general rule or to define inflexible areas of morality into which the law is in no circumstances to be allowed to enter. Society is entitled by means of its laws to protect itself from dangers, whether from within or without. Here again I think that the political parallel is legitimate. The law of treason is directed against aiding the king's enemies and against sedition from within. The justification for this is that established government is necessary for the existence of society and therefore its safety against violent overthrow must be secured. But an established morality is as necessary as good government to the welfare of society. Societies disintegrate from within more frequently than they are broken up by external pressures. There is disintegration when no common morality is observed and history shows that the loosening of moral bonds is justified in taking the same steps to preserve its moral code as it does to preserve its government and other essential institutions.[1] The

---

[1] It is somewhere about this point in the argument that Professor Hart in *Law, Liberty and Morality* discerns a proposition which he describes as central to my thought. He states the proposition and his objection to it as follows (p. 51). 'He appears to move from the acceptable proposition that *some* shared morality is essential to the existence of any society [this I take to be the proposition on p. 12] to the unacceptable proposition that a society is identical with its morality as that is at any given moment of its history, so that a change in its morality is tantamount to the destruction of a society. The former proposition might be even accepted as a necessary rather than an empirical truth depending on a quite plausible definition of society as a body of men who hold certain moral views in common. But the latter proposition is absurd. Taken strictly, it would prevent us saying that the morality of a given society had changed, and would compel us instead to say that one society had disappeared and another one taken its place. But it is only on this absurd criterion of what it is for the same society to continue to exist that it could be asserted without evidence that any deviation from a society's shared morality threatens its existence.' In conclusion (p. 82) Professor Hart condemns the whole thesis in the lecture as based on 'a confused definition of what a society is.'

I do not assert that *any* deviation from a society's shared morality threatens its existence. I assert that they are both activities which are capable in their nature of threatening the existence of society so that neither can be put beyond the law.

• • •

The proposition that I made in the text is that if (as I understand Professor Hart to agree, at any rate for the purrposes of the argument) you cannot have a society without morality, the law can be used to enforce morality as something that is essential to a society. I cannot see why this proposition (whether it is right or wrong) should mean that morality can never be changed without the destruction of society. If morality is changed, the law can be changed. Professor Hart refers . . . to the proposition as 'the use of legal punishment to freeze into immobility the morality dominant at a particular time in a society's existence.' One might as well say that the inclusion of a penal section into a statute prohibiting certain acts freezes the whole statute into immobility and prevents the prohibitions from ever being modified.

suppression of vice is as much the law's business as the suppression of subversive activities; it is no more possible to define a sphere of private morality than it is to define one of private subversive activity. It is wrong to talk of private morality or of the law not being concerned with immorality as such or to try to set rigid bounds to the part which the law may play in the suppression of vice. There are no theoretical limits to the power of the State to legislate against treason and sedition, and likewise I think there can be no theoretical limits to legislation against immorality. You may argue that if a man's sins affect only himself it cannot be the concern of society. If he chooses to get drunk every night in the privacy of his own home, is any one except himself the worse for it? But suppose a quarter or a half of the population got drunk every night, what sort of society would it be? You cannot set a theoretical limit to the number of people who can get drunk before society is entitled to legislate against drunkenness. The same may be said of gambling. The Royal Commission on Betting, Lotteries, and Gaming took as their test the character of the citizen as a member of society. They said: 'Our concern with the ethical significance of gambling is confined to the effect which it may have on the character of the gambler as a member of society. If we were convinced that whatever the degree of gambling this effect must be harmful we should be inclined to think that it was the duty of the state to restrict gambling to the greatest extent practicable.'

In what circumstances the State should exercise its power is the third of the interrogatories I have framed. But before I get to it I must raise a point which might have been brought up in any one of the three. How are the moral judgements of society to be ascertained? By leaving it until now, I can ask it in the more limited form that is now sufficient for my purpose. How is the law-maker to ascertain the moral judgements of society? It is surely not enough that they should be reached by the opinion of the majority; it would be too much to require the individual assent of every citizen. English law has evolved and regularly uses a standard which does not depend on the counting of heads. It is that of the reasonable man. He is not to be confused about anything and his judgement may be largely a matter of feeling. It is the viewpoint of the man in the street—or to use an archaism familiar to all lawyers—the man in the Clapham omnibus. He might also be called the right-handed man. For my purpose I should like to call him the man in the jury box, for the moral judgement of society must be something about which any twelve men or women drawn at random might after discussion be expected to be unanimous. This was the standard the judges applied in the days before Parliament was as active as it is now and when they laid down rules of public policy. They did not think of themselves as making law but simply as stating principles which every right-minded person would accept as valid. It is what Pollock called 'practical morality,' which is based not on theological or philosophical foundations but 'in the mass of continuous experience half-consciously or unconsciously accumulated and embodied in the morality of common sense'. He called it also 'a certain way of thinking on questions of morality which we expect to find in a reasonable civilized man or a reasonable Englishman, taken at random'.

Immorality then, for the purpose of the law, is what every right-minded person is presumed to consider to be immoral. Any immorality is capable of affecting society injuriously and in effect to a greater or lesser extent it usually does; this is what gives the law its *locus standi*. It cannot be shut out. But—and this brings me to the third question—the individual has a *locus standi* too; he cannot be expected to surrender to the judgement of society the whole conduct of his life. It is the old and familiar question of striking a balance between the rights and interests of society and those of the individual. This is something which the law is constantly doing in matters large and small. . . .

I do not think that one can talk sensibly of a public and private morality any more than one can of a public or private highway. Morality is a sphere in which there is a public interest and a private interest, often in conflict, and the problem is to reconcile the two. This does not mean that it is impossible to put forward any general statements about how in our society the balance ought to be struck. Such statements cannot of their nature be rigid or precise; they would not be designed to circumscribe the operation of the law-making power but to guide those who have to apply it. While every decision which a court of law makes when it balances the public against the private interest is an *ad hoc* decision, the cases contain statements of principle to which the court should have regard when it reaches its decision. In the same way it is possible to make general statements of principle which it may be thought the legislature should bear in mind when it is considering the enactment of laws enforcing morals.

I believe that most people would agree upon the chief of these elastic principles. There must be toleration of the maximum individual freedom that is consistent with the integrity of society. . . . But in all matters of conscience the principle I have stated is generally held to prevail. It is not confined to thought and speech; it extends to action, as is shown by the recognition of the right to conscientious objection in war-time; this example shows also that conscience will be respected even in times of national danger. The principle appears to me to be peculiarly appropriate to all questions of morals. Nothing should be punished by the law that does not lie beyond the limits of tolerance. It is not nearly enough to say that a majority dislike a practice; there must be a real feeling of reprobation. Those who are dissatisfied with the present law on homosexuality often say that the opponents of reform are swayed simply by disgust. If that were so it would be wrong, but I do not think one can ignore disgust if it is deeply felt and not manufactured. Its presence is a good indication that the bounds of toleration are being reached. Not everything is to be tolerated. No society can do without intolerance, indignation, and disgust; they are the forces behind the moral law, and indeed it can be argued that if they or something like them are not present, the feelings of society cannot be weighty enough to deprive the individual of freedom of choice. I suppose that there is hardly anyone nowadays who would not be disgusted by the thought of deliberate cruelty to animals. No one proposes to relegate that or any other form of sadism to the realm of private morality or to allow it to be practiced in public or in private. It would be possible no doubt to point out that until a comparatively short while ago nobody thought very much of cruelty to animals and also that pity and kindliness and the unwillingness to inflict pain are virtues more generally esteemed now than they have ever been in the past. But matters of this sort are not determined by rational argument. Every moral judgement, unless it claims a divine source, is simply a feeling that no right-minded man could behave in any other way without admitting that he was doing wrong. It is the power of a common sense and not the power of reason that is behind the judgements of society. But before a society can put a practice beyond the limits of tolerance there must be a deliberate judgement that the practice is injurious to society. There is, for example, a general abhorrence to homosexuality. We should ask ourselves in the first instance whether, looking at it calmly and dispassionately, we regard it as a vice so abominable that its mere presence is an offence. If that is the genuine feeling of the society in which we live, I do not see how society can be denied the right to eradicate it. Our feeling may not be so intense as that. We may feel about it that, if confined, it is tolerable, but that if it spread it might be gravely injurious; it is in this way that most societies look upon fornication, seeing it as a natural weakness which must be kept within bounds but which cannot be rooted out. It becomes then a question of balance, the danger to society in one scale and the extent of the restriction in the other. On this sort of point the value of an investigation by such a body as the Wolfenden Committee and its conclusions is manifest.

. . . I return therefore to the simple and observable fact that in matters of morals the limits of tolerance shift. Laws, especially those which are based on morals, are less easily moved. It follows as another good working principle that in any new matter of morals the law should be slow to act. By the next generation the swell of indignation may have abated and the law be left without the strong backing which it needs. But it is then difficult to alter the law without giving the impression that moral judgement is being weakened. This is now one of the facts that is strongly militating against any alteration to the law on homosexuality.

A third elastic principle must be advanced more tentatively. It is that as far as possible privacy should be respected. This is not an idea that has ever been made explicit in the criminal law. Acts or words done or said in public or in private are all brought within its scope without distinction in principle. But there goes with this a strong reluctance on the part of judges and legislators to sanction invasions of privacy in the detection of crime. The police have no more right to trespass than the ordinary citizen has; there is no general right of search; to this extent an Englishman's home is still his castle. . . .

This indicates a general sentiment that the right to privacy is something to be put in the balance against the enforcement of the law. Ought the same sort of consideration to play any part in the formation of the law? Clearly only in a very limited number of cases. When the help of the law is invoked by an injured citizen, privacy should be measured against injury criminally done to another. But when all who are involved in the deed are consenting parties and the injury is done to morals, the public interest in the moral order can be balanced against the claims of privacy. . . . I think that, as I have already suggested, the test of 'private behaviour' should be substituted for 'private morality' and the influence of the factor should be reduced from that of a definite limitation to that of a matter to be taken into account. Since the gravity of the crime is also a proper consideration, a distinction might well be made in the case of homosexuality between the lesser acts of indecency and the full offense, which on the principles of the Wolfenden Report it would be illogical to do.

The last and the biggest thing to be remembered is that the law is concerned with the minimum and not with the maximum; there is much in the Sermon on the Mount that would be out of place in the Ten Commandments. We all recognize the gap between the moral law and the law of the land. . . .

NOTES

1. While both Hart and Devlin refer to "morality" they appear to mean not fixed and unchangeable codes of morals regarded as having universal and permanent validity, but rather codes of rectitude followed by a particular community at a particular time. Note the reliance by both of them on public opinion. Is it appropriate for the shaping of laws to rely, as Devlin would have it, on the reaction of the "the man in the Clapham omnibus" who, "is not

expected to reason about anything,'' and whose, ''judgment may be largely a matter of feeling''?

While Hart feels the morality and law should be separate, note that he too, favors the shaping of law by public opinion in matters such as commonly held views regarding decency (e.g., ''homosexual behavior between males . . . in public'') or other areas of public opinion which are, ''based on moral, social or cultural standards.''* Is the distinction then, between Hart and Devlin on the role of morality in law, fundamental and theoretical, or confined largely to the prohibition by law of private consensual acts between adults and prohibitions on behavior which would be ineffectual in practice (e.g., prostitution)?

2. Lord Devlin makes frequent reference in his lecture to the morality or moral consensus shared by Englishmen. That consensus, he seems to feel, justifies using criminal and other law to maintain key aspects of community life. Yet most modern societies are extraordinarily heterogeneous. In addition to divisions into class, caste, gender, and religion, distinctions arising from region, occupation, sexual preference group and many other functional groupings serve to further fragment practice and preference. When Lord Devlin grandly invokes the ''Englishmen's view,'' to whom is he referring? Is there any empirical basis for his assumption that the views that he and the group that he is personally familiar with share are also accepted by large number of the rest of the population? If not, isn't the invocation of general group consensus as a basis for legal action a use of language akin to the structural naturalism we considered in the previous chapter? Consider, in this regard, the majority and dissenting opinion in the *Repouille* case infra.

3. Even assuming that Lord Devlin speaks for the majority, why is his majority or any majority entitled to insist that others not behave in ways that they consider offensive? Consider the *Reynold's* case (Chapter 4).

CASE LAW

In a number of disputes, courts have taken different positions regarding law and morality. Consider the following cases.

DYETT V. PENDLETON
8 COW. 727 (N.Y. 1826)

[Tenant vacated leased premises and refused to pay rent.] Sen. Crary: . . . The facts offered to be proved on the trial are, substantially, that in February, 1820, from time to time, and at sundry times, the plaintiff introduced into the house, (two rooms upon the second floor and two room upon the third floor whereof had been leased to the defendant,) divers lewd women or prostitutes, and kept and detained them in the said house all night, for the purpose of prostitution; that the said lewd women or prostitutes would frequently enter the said house in the day time, and after staying all night, would leave the same by daylight in the morning; that the plaintiff sometimes introduced other men into the said premises, who, together with him, kept company with the said lewd women or prostitutes during the night; that on such occasions, the plaintiff and the said lewd women or prostitutes, being in company in certain parts of the said house, not included in the lease to the defendant, but adjacent thereto, and in the occupation or use of the plaintiff, were accustomed to make a great deal of indecent noise and disturbance, the said women or prostitutes often

*Note too, that although Hart was a positivist, he was also a reformer in the tradition of Bentham (particularly with regard to criminal law). Despite his positivist stance, he held that one could disobey the law on the ground that the law was immoral. Additionally, despite the ''scientific'' bent of positivism, he felt that natural law had some place in a legal system (see page 204 supra.)

screaming extravagantly, and so as to be heard throughout the house, and by the near neighbors, and frequently using obscene and vulgar language so loud as to be understood at a considerable distance; that such noise and riotous proceedings, being from time to time continued all night, greatly disturbed the rest of persons sleeping in other parts of the said house, and particularly in those parts thereof demised to the defendent; that the practices aforesaid were matters of conversation and reproach in the neighborhood, and were of a nature to draw, and did draw, odium and infamy upon the said house, as being a place of ill fame, so that it was no longer respectable for moral and decent persons to dwell or enter therein; that all the said immoral, indecent and unlawful practices and proceedings were by the procurement or with the permission and concurrence of the plaintiff; that the defendant, being a person of good and respectable character, was compelled, by the repetition of the said indecent practices and proceedings, to leave the said premises, and did, for that cause, leave the same on or about the beginning of March, 1820, after which he did not return thereto, &c.

This evidence, being objected to by the plaintiff's counsel, was rejected by the court, and is now to be considered as true.

• • •

The whole science of law consists in the application of a few simple principles to the "affairs and bosoms of men." In *Collins v. Blantern,* (2 Wils. R. 350), it is said by lord chief justice *Wilmot,* that "all writers upon our law agree in this: no polluted hand shall touch the pure fountains of justice." I should lay hold upon this principle, if there was no other, for the purpose of chastising vice and impudence, on the one hand, and protecting virtue and innocence, on the other. When the defendant is told that every right, when withheld, shall have its remedy, and every injury its proper redress, and that personal security, which includes reputation, is one of his absolute rights, and then told he must live in a brothel, against his will, or, at least, pay rent for it, he cannot but see the disparity between the text and the comment, and if the one is right, the other is wrong.

If the evidence offered does not technically prove an eviction, yet, as there is no other plea under which the defence can be made, for the sake of giving effect to it, I should resort not to the statute law, nor to the common law, but to the great principles of morality, on which both are founded; and if, in the long tract of ages which are past, I could find no case parallel with the present, I should decide against the plaintiff, satisfied that if the same case had ever existed, the principal actor in it had not aspired to immortality by publishing his own infamy.

Colden, Senator. . . . It is conceded, on all hands, that to excuse the non-performance of a covenant to pay rent, an entry of the lessor and an eviction of the lessee must be pleaded. But the plaintiff in error contends that the evidence he offered, should have been received as proper proof of an entry and eviction. This doctrine appears to be entirely new, and no case was cited to shew that it was not so. Indeed, the counsel of the plaintiff in error seemed to appeal to the moral, rather than to the municipal law. And if we were to decide this case according to the dictates of morality, we might be disposed to pronounce a judgment in his favor. It is true that the moral law and the law of the land should not be at variance; but if they be so, it is not for us, in our judicial capacity, to reconcile them. We are, in rendering our judgments, not to determine as we may think the law of our country should be, but as we find it established; and the question now presented for our decision is, whether a lessee, finding himself temporarily disturbed in the enjoyment of the demised premises by the misconduct or immoral practices of the lessor, may abandon the tenement for the whole term, and be exonerated from the payment of rent. If this question were to be answered in the affirmative, it would, in my opinion, introduce a new and very extensive chapter in the law of landlord and tenant.

NOTES

1. In contemporary judicial usage, the notion of morality is often quite different from that espoused by John Austin and his successors. For Austin, morality or a moral decision was a decision that was derived from some fundamental principles or postulates, often of divine origin. It was thoroughly examined from a logical standpoint and once reached, defended with full commitment. Austin wished to separate this sharply from those prescripts that were produced by the apparatus of the state. Contemporary judges, in contrast, use the term morality in a comparatively debased fashion. Frequently it means no more than the syntax of contemporary prejudice or the "gut reactions" of a supposed community (which is rarely explored empirically). In matters such as euthanasia or unconventional sexual behavior, the judicial analysis is not whether it is inappropriate, in accordance with certain basic moral principles or demonstrably injurious to individuals or the community, but rather whether or not people in general would be outraged by it. Can the reactions of people who have not reflected on the matter and have not made clear their own moral calculus be considered morality in the sense in which the term has been used in the more formal literature?

Consider in this regard *Repouille v. U.S.* 165 F. 2d 152, (2d Cir. 1947). A father killed his thirteen year old son who had suffered from a brain injury which caused him "to be an idiot and a physical monstrosity." The majority held that the father did not, as a result, possess requisite "sound moral character" required by law to become a naturalized citizen. The majority ruled that the issue before it was whether the father's conduct conformed "to the generally accepted moral conventions current at the time," which were "now prevalent generally in the country." The court, admitting that "we are without means of verifying our conclusion," concluded that it felt "reasonably secure in holding that only a minority of virtuous persons would deem the practice morally justifiable." Judge Jerome Frank, in dissent, felt that "the correct statutory test . . . is the attitude of our ethical leaders," but that in any event the court should not "resort to our mere unchecked surmises."

Note that in *Repouille,* for both Judge Hand, speaking for the majority and for Judge Frank in dissent, the moral position is no more than the unexamined responses of members of the community. Which community? Which members? Is there no need for those members somehow or other to explain or justify their position?

2. Are the dilemmas of this case in any way comparable to those faced by Mr. Fedorenko (Chapter 4, page 159)? Discuss. In Hart's view, should Fedorenko had been excluded from the United States, since he "merely" obeyed the laws of Nazi Germany, which, according to Hart, were "valid laws"? Discuss.

3. The "Act of State" doctrine provides an example of judicial avoidance of moral problems. According to some interpretations of this doctrine, judges believe that they must refrain from exercising jurisdiction, otherwise well founded, if it would require them to review the governmental acts of another state done in its own territory. Some judges, in applying this doctrine, are willing to give effect in the United States to odious acts done abroad, which are repellent to our law and morality, simply because they are governmental acts. This concern with fidelity to formal law without regard to the social consequences would appear characteristic of positivism, despite Professor Hart's disavowal, noted earlier. Thus in *Bernstein v. Van Heyghen Freres S.A.,* 163 F.2d 246 (2d Cir. 1947), the court held that it was powerless to question the confiscation by Nazi Germany of the property of a Jew, who, after World War II, sued in an American court to recover for the confiscation. Yet the court found that confiscation, solely because the plaintiff was a Jew, "was utterly odious" and "abhorrent to . . . moral notions" and could be acted upon by an American court if the confiscator were a private person. See also *Holzer v. Deutsche Reichsbahn-Gesellschaft,* 277 N.Y. 474, 14

N.E. 2d 799 (1938), and generally, the discussion on the positivistic consequences of Act of State in McDougal & Reisman, *International Law in Contemporary Perspective* (1981).

4. In a decision by the International Court of Justice, [1969] International Court of Justice Reports 31, a majority held: ". . . Whatever the legal reasoning of a court of justice, its decisions must by definition be just, and therefore in that sense equitable. . . ." Discuss.

5. A common positivistic formulation acknowledges that a particular principle may be part of the moral universe and the general culture of the community concerned, but insists that decisionmakers should refuse to give effect to it because it has not been incorporated into law. In one case in Israel, the petitioners had gone through an unauthorized civil marriage ceremony, rather than a religious ceremony required by law. They sought to rely on a general principle of freedom of religion, expressed in the Declaration of Independence as well as in a variety of international documents. The court, acknowledged that freedom of religion was a principle of the state but noted that as parliament had not incorporated that principle into law and had in fact legislated in ways incompatible with it, the court had no choice but to deny the petitioners' claim. (*Rogozinsky et al. v. State of Israel* 26(1) P.D. 130 (1927)). As an exercise, try to justify the court's decision.

POSITIVISM AND THE PROTECTION OF MINORITIES

As will be recalled, part of the impulse for the installation of the doctrine of Positivism in nineteenth century England was the desire by the newly franchised schismatic Christian sects to ensure protection for themselves and the practice of their faith. This feature of minority protection continues to be closely related to modern positivistic jurisprudence. Minority leaders believe that the strict application of rules, and, in particular, the separation of the moral demands of the majority from those rules, can provide a greater degree of protection for minorities. In this conception, the notion of law as a body of rules with judges applying them with the strictest fidelity is thus thought to contribute to the realization of liberalist ideals, for a court would be counted on to apply nothing which was not made into formal law. The rule of law, as a result, is assumed to provide a degree of security for all peoples.

Recall in Chapter 2, Professor Pospisil's discussion of multiple legal systems in a single territorial community. In heterogeneous communities, there are also multiple moral systems. Minority groups are frequently concerned to establish a political and legal order which protects them from the potential tyranny of the majority morality. In such complex communities, the doctrines of positivism distinguishing between law and morality and admonishing judges to apply the law without deferring to majority notions of morality, are looked to as a great protection for the liberty of minority groups and even for the opportunities among majority members to experiment with alternative living styles. The ideal becomes the neutral and mechanical application of rules without any contamination by the personal preferences or morals or ethics of those applying them. This aspect of Positivism and its historic link with the rise of Liberalism has been explored by Professor Shklar in a sympathetic treatment of Positivism's distinction between law and morality.

SHKLAR, LEGALISM
1–3, 5–10, 12, 14–17
19–20, 22–26 (1964)

What is legalism? It is the ethical attitude that holds moral conduct to be a matter of rule following, and moral relationships to consist of duties and rights determined by rules. Like all moral attitudes that are both strongly felt and widely shared it expresses itself not only in personal behavior but also in philosophical thought, in political ideologies, and in social institutions. . . .

Legalism, so understood, is thus often an inarticulate, but nonetheless consistently followed, individual code of conduct. It is also a very common social ethos, though by no means the only one, in Western countries. To a great extent it has provided the standards of organization and the operative ideals for a vast number of social groups, from governmental institutions to private clubs. Its most nearly complete expression is in the great legal systems of the European world. Lastly, it has also served as the political ideology of those who cherish these systems of law and, above all, those who are directly involved in their maintenance—the legal profession, both bench and bar. The court in law and the trial according to law are the social paradigms, the perfection, the very epitome, of legalistic morality. They are, however, far from being its only expressions. Indeed, they are inconceivable without the convictions, mores, and ideologies that must permeate any society which wishes to maintain them.

• • •

. . . The urge to draw a clear line between law and non-law has led to the constructing of ever more refined and rigid systems of formal definitions. This procedure has served to isolate law completely from the social context within which it exists. Law is endowed with its own discrete, integral history, its own "science" and its own values, which are all treated as a single "block" sealed off from general social history, from general social theory, from politics, and from morality. The habits of mind appropriate, within narrow limits, to the procedures of law courts in the most stable legal systems have been expanded to provide legal theory and ideology with an entire system of thought and values. This procedure has served its own ends very well: it aims at preserving law from irrelevant considerations, but it has ended by fencing legal thinking off from all contact with the rest of historical thought and experience.

As an alternative to this unsatisfactory situation, it is suggested here that one ought not to think of law as a discrete entity that is "there," but rather to regard it as part of a social continuum. At one end of the scale of legalistic values and institutions stand its most highly articulate and refined expressions, the courts of law and the rules they follow; at the other end is the personal morality of all those men and women who think of goodness as obedience to the rules that properly define their duties and rights. Within this scale there is a vast area of social beliefs and institutions, both more and less rigid and explicit, which in varying degrees depend upon the legalistic ethos. This would provide an approach suitable to law as an historical phenomenon, and would replace the sterile game of defining law, morals, and politics in order to separate them as concepts both "pure" and empty, divorced from each other and from their common historical past and contemporary setting.

• • •

. . . The assumption throughout is that social diversity is the prevailing condition of modern nation-states and that it *ought* to be promoted. Pluralism is thus treated as a social actuality that no contemporary political theory can ignore without losing its relevance, and also as something that any liberal should rejoice in and seek to promote, because it is in diversity alone that freedom can be realized. A free society is not one in which people are merely allowed to make effective social choices among a variety of alternatives, but one in which they are encouraged to do so. The range and the number of choices available and the mutual tolerance among those who choose conflicting paths are what determine the degree of freedom that the members of any modern society can be said to enjoy. If one must be a hero, a saint, or at least enormously courageous and self-confident in order to pursue a manner of life or to express views other than those agreeable to the powers that be, both governmental and social, one cannot be said to live in a free society. These views are at least as old as John Stuart Mill, and hardly novel. No one today can claim, nor did Mill assume a hundred years ago, that everyone frantically yearns for personal liberty or regards tolerance as a virtue or finds the self-control it demands easy. It cannot even be said, as he did, that freedom is needed for "progress." What is evident, however, is that diversity and the burdens of freedom must be endured and encouraged to avoid the kinds of misery that organized repression now brings. This is a type of liberalism quite common among members of permanent social minority groups, and it surely reflects both the apprehensions and the positive experiences which their situation creates.

• • •

In the case of analytical positivism it undeniably is a criticism to show that political preferences have contrived to inspire and condition its whole development and inner character, often with unfortunate results—because this theory regards its ideological neutrality as the very core of its position. Imperviousness to ideology is regarded as the foremost condition of legal "science"; indeed, the latter is defined by its immunity to contamination. Moreover, the image of law that analytic positivism has devised consists of sets of rules carefully divorced from ideology. Its whole theory of the separation of law from morals is designed to achieve this end. This is also what leads it to an excessive formalism. For only thus can the neutrality of law as a concept and of legal science as an intellectual discipline be maintained. However, it will be shown that these efforts are themselves conditioned by ideology and that the failure to recognize this has made analytic positivism a far less persuasive theory than it might otherwise have been. This is not meant to be one of those jobs of debunking that try to expose the "real," and presumably unworthy, hidden tendencies of ideas with which one disagrees. Since the ideological inspiration of analytical positivism is liberalism and a skeptical view of ethics, it is obviously quite congenial to its present unmasker. It is not the aims of ideology, but the results of treating political preferences as the logical necessities of any valid theory of law, that are highly questionable.

• • •

Lastly, there is legalism itself. To say that it is an ideology is to criticize only those of its traditional adherents who, in their determination to preserve law from politics, fail to recognize that they too have made a choice among political values. In itself this would hardly be a new accusation, nor a very important one. What does matter is again the intellectual consequences of this denial, and the attendant belief that law is not only separate from political life but that it is a mode of social action superior to mere politics. This is what will later be discussed as "the policy of justice," for legalism as an ideology does express itself in policies, in institutional structures, and in intellectual attitudes. As a social ethos which gives rise to the political climate in which judicial and other legal institutions flourish, legalism is beyond reproach. It is the rigidity of legalistic categories of thought, especially in appraising the relationships of law to the political environment within which it functions, that is so deleterious. This is the source of the artificiality of almost all legal theories and is what prevents its exponents from recognizing both the strengths and weaknesses of law and legal procedures in a complex social world.

. . . Legalism is, above all, the operative outlook of the legal profession, both bench and bar. Moreover, most legal theory, whether it be analytical positivism or natural law thinking, depends on categories of thought derived from this shared professional outlook. The tendency to think of law as "there" as a discrete entity, discernibly different from morals and politics, has its deepest roots in the legal profession's views of its own functions, and forms the very basis of most of our judicial institutions and procedures. That lawyers have particularly pronounced intellectual habits peculiar to them has often been noticed, especially by historians and other students of society whose views differ sharply from those of the legal profession.

• • •

The dislike of vague generalities, the preference for case-by-case treatment of all social issues, the structuring of all possible human relations into the form of claims and counterclaims under established rules, and the belief that the rules are "there"—these combine to make up legalism as a social outlook. When it becomes self-conscious, when it challenges other views, it is a full-blown ideology. Since lawyers are engaged in their daily lives with political or social conflicts of some kind, they are bound to run up against perspectives radically different from their own. As law serves ideally to promote the security of established expectations, so legalism with its concentration on specific cases and rules is, essentially, conservative.

• • •

If many lawyers, in America especially, do recognize that the courts do legislate and make basic social choices, this is less true and even less accepted in other countries. Even in the United States, moreover, the public at large and important sections of the bar do not perceive their functions thus. The courts are expected to interpret the law, not to alter it. Professional ideology and public expectations, in fact, do mold the conduct of the judiciary and its perception of its role. To seek rules, or at least a public consensus that can serve in place of a rule, must be the judge's constant preoccupation, and it affects his choices in ways that are unknown to less constrained political agents. To avoid the appearance of arbitrariness is a deep inner necessity for him. The trouble is that the possibility of aloofness does not depend on the judge's behavior alone, but also on the public responses to it. In England, given the acceptance of Parliamentary sovereignty, the judiciary is not exposed to controversy as extensive as that in America. Here both the nature of the issues placed before the courts and the greater scope of choice available put the judiciary inevitably into the very midst of the great political battles of the nation. Elective state judiciaries, moreover, are bound to remain subject to public scrutiny, which the English judiciary is spared.

• • •

. . . This formalism makes for adaptability in the long run, but it also represents a rooted conservatism. When it comes to changes that affect the judicial establishemnt directly, moreover, conservatism becomes immobility. An A.B.A.-sponsored survey of the American legal profession concluded that when it came to reforming procedure, for instance, lawyers were unreasonably obstinate. Observers of the English bar have reached the same conclusion. . . .

The antiquity of legalism as an ideology is, in fact, one of the wonders of history. It is itself the expression of the continuity of the legal profession and its basic tasks. Whereas science has rendered the practice of modern medicine quite unlike the pre-nineteenth century profession of the same name, the heirs of Coke resemble him closely in vocabulary, outlook, and concerns. De Tocqueville's description of the legalistic ethos is as accurate today as it was when it was written. Order and formality being the marks of the legal mind, he wrote, it is natural for lawyers to support the established social order. As long as they are not deprived of the authority which they regard as their due they will rally to the regime of power. The radical village lawyer of the French Revolution was an aberration that the aristocracy foolishly brought upon itself. In the normal course of events conservatism is inseparable from legalism. "If they prize freedom much, they generally value legality still more: they are less afraid of tyranny, than of arbitrary power." . . .

Almost a hundred years after de Tocqueville wrote, Max Weber could still present a picture of the ideology of the legal profession that was virtually unaltered. Lawyers remained as wedded to formal justice as ever and so to all the interests that relied on permanence and predictability in social procedures. . .

What he and de Tocqueville saw was that a legal caste, once it had established the "rule of law" securely against threats from absolutist arbitrariness, was bound to prefer order to liberty. What de Tocqueville called aristocratic habits of thought, Weber believed (rightly) to be more a matter of "internal professional ideology." . . . Nevertheless, the main thrust of legalistic ideology is toward orderliness, and formalism can readily reinforce an inherent preference for authority. The ease with which German lawyers accepted "Adolf Legalite's" pretentions to legitimacy, the support they gave Nazism until its radical anti-legalistic tendencies revealed themselves (and even after), more than justify de Tocqueville's and Weber's suspicions. It cannot be repeated often enough that procedurally "correctly" repression is perfectly compatible with legalism. That is the cost of conservative adaptability.

● ● ●

If one is to treat legal thinking in ideological terms, one must also look at its relationships to other ideologies. Indeed, the complex relations between liberalism and legalism form one of the major themes of the present study. Some of the most obvious bearings of legalism upon both liberalism and conservatism are, of course, well known. "Freedom under law," "a government of law, not of men"—the limitation of private and public power through the vigorous application of general rules—is inseparable from liberalism.

● ● ●

Because the threat to "the West" is external at present and so more obviously non-Western in character, the ideological defense of the Western tradition has become increasingly rigid. It is no longer just a matter of emphasizing that legalism has been far stronger in the West than elsewhere, which is certainly true. The ideology of "the West" now goes well beyond that, insisting as it does upon a single Western political tradition. It always comes down to a political tradition of freedom under law or the rule of law. The difficulty with this self-congratulatory view of the Western past is that it flies in the face of the most obvious facts of history. There is no *one* Western tradition. It is a tradition of traditions. Moreover, political freedom has been the exception, a rarity, in Europe's past, remote and recent. It is indeed the very diversity of traditions and conditions that makes European history so turbulent and various. To say that *a* political tradition, "freedom under law," ties all that together into a neat pattern is an ideological abuse of the past. It falsifies the past, and renders the present incomprehensible. What it expresses is the nostalgia of a liberalism that has ceased to look to the future and which seeks to maintain itself not as a hope but as an ancient possession, to be valued more for its familiarity and age than for its intrinsic merits.

Conservative liberalism also inspires that ideology of the rule of law which has Professor Hayek as its most persuasive and consistent advocate. This indeed is grand ideology, with its own theory of history, or psychology, of epistemology, of economics, and of politics. History is seen as a battle between the healthy instincts of society and the destructive power urges of the state. The battle is fought essentially in terms of intellectual conceptions, especially in terms of economic theories, for it is economic policy that is fundamental. Once the free market is tampered with, even by such a policy as professional licensing, the swift decline of society into absolutionism and destruction is inevitable. The chief agents of this destructive urge in the modern world are the intellectuals who want to plan society, not grasping that this requires unobtainable total knowledge of society as a whole. Since their plans must fail, they end by becoming tyrants. The answer to these false political aspirations is the rule of law. The rule of law is the miracle of liberalism, government without coercion. By coercion, Professor Hayek does not mean any exercise of power, but only what occurs when one man issues a direct command to others to perform a specific action to serve his own ends. The chief source of coercion is government, for it is seen, essentially, as a military agency. Coercion can, however, be eliminated if men are governed entirely by general rules which are applied impersonally and equally to all. These rules must, moreover, be accepted by those to whom they apply directly, as well as by others. Such general rules, indeed, have the character of a natural necessity and, as such, people adjust to them spontaneously. It is, of course, not obvious that men do accept natural necessity. The very existence of technology argues against such a notion. It is even more difficult to imagine what laws other than traffic rules can possibly have the character that is ascribed to genuine law here. Certainly no other examples are offered.

It is not clear at all that the contrast between direct commands and general rules can be maintained. There are direct commands which are general: "Fasten your seatbelts," for example. There are general rules that are highly coercive: "No one may travel abroad," for instance. The difference is clearly not one of form at all, but of the ends served by both laws and commands. The purpose of this division is, in fact, to show that administrative action is not lawlike in character. Only general legislation providing for the barest needs of peace and order in society may truly be honored by the name of law. All else is not natural but coercive. Law, to be law, may merely articulate those standards that are already immanent in society, else it becomes destructive impositions. Although freedom is clearly the end of such a vision, it is also a deeply conservative one, for the natural is the prevalent. That is why law ought to have nothing to do with politics, with that, dangerous realm of purposive social action. It exists, rather, to limit politics. To be sure, rules of law do exist to ensure the security of expectations, but here security and freedom, tradition and legality are totally identified. As such, this too, like the ideology of "the West," is a liberalism that clings to legalism because of its conservative implications.

•　•　•

There is nothing inherently odd or silly about the passion for clarity and precison classifications and definitions. What is curious is that there should be endless disputes about the "true" meaning of words and phrases. Since these arguments tend to center on words which refer to subjects about which few of us are neutral, such as "law," "religion," "ideology," or "justice," it is of considerable practical importance to know exactly what friend and foe mean in using these explosive words. One might also assume that here the issues are basically ideological; they are semantic only in appearance. This can be seen in the effects created by that very fear of "bias" which is so widely shared among American social scientists and which tends to encourage exercises in definition and "methodology" as a means of "coming clean" about one's "values." For, however honest these efforts may be, they seem to be futile. Somehow the definition and categories remain only covert or open expressions of ideological preferences and as such inevitably become subjects of bitter dispute. Nor, on the other hand, is there any reason to believe that the elucidation of "common usage" as a means of evading "right" definitions can succeed in bringing even limited agreement. To say that to insist upon "true" meanings is a species of verbal self-righteousness misses the point. We protest because words arouse incompatible emotions in us. Until the unlikely event of our ceasing to be different from one another, even a complete analysis of how words in fact behave in our language will not diminish the tensions created by our responses to them. It is not the words but the feelings behind them that cause men to fight.

NOTES

1. Permanent minorities have found a special attraction, as we said, in Positivism and in its conception of a restrictive definition and strict application of law without regard to the precipitating events that bring the case to bar or to the social consequences flowing from decision. Is that protection actually vouchsafed by positivism? Consider the *Korematsu* case, 323 U.S. 214 (1944), which arose during the Second World War and involved the Supreme Court's review of the constitutionality and general lawfulness of the incarceration of one hundred and twenty thousand Japanese, many of them citizens of the United States, in camps more than a thousand miles away from home. The majority of the court found the establishment and operation of these concentration camps to be technically valid and constitutional. (Even from a technical standpoint, the issue of constitutionality was extremely controversial, as was eloquently stated by the dissenters from the opinion). *Korematsu* resonated to two aspects of positivistic jurisprudence. It applied the law in a very technical and textual sense, finding the questionable behavior constitutional and lawful, and it followed its textual interpretation by completely ignoring the social consequences, in particular, the enormous hardships imposed on people, not for things they had done, but simply because they were members of the suspect group.

If the Supreme Court had not followed positivism, is it likely that large numbers of Americans of Japanese extraction would have been incarcerated? The application of the law here, whether justified in context or not, is interesting in this jurisprudential setting because it represents a departure from a positivistic application of a constitutional principle designed to protect minorities and to limit governmental intrusion.

2. Does Rule of Law as Shklar describes it really provide the guarantee demanded? Can one formulate rules so that they do in fact limit the discretion of the appliers? Is this desirable? Consider *Korematsu* in your response.

3. Compare the rigidities of the Rule of Law as criticized by some of the earlier writers, with the doctrine of "Socialist Legality" as applied in a number of socialist and communist states:

> One must be . . . prepared for all and any sacrifice, even, if necessary, be ready to resort to every possible trick, ruse, illegal method, to conceal and falsify the truth in order to infiltrate the unions, to remain within them and to perform Communist activities inside the Unions at all costs. Lenin, 2 *Selected Works* 701 (1947).

4. Another aspect of the Rule of Law and Liberalism mentioned by Shklar is the belief that government intervention into the private affairs of individuals should be kept to a minimum.

This was expressed by the Supreme Court in *Griswold v. Connecticut,* 38 U.S. 479 (1965), which dealt with a state law banning the sale and prescription of contraceptives, as follows:

> The present case, then, concerns a relationship lying within the zone of privacy created by several fundamental constitutional guarantees. And it concerns a law which, in forbidding the *use* of contraceptives rather than regulating their manufacture or sale, seeks to achieve its goals by means having a maximum destructive impact upon that relationship. Such a law cannot stand in light of the familiar principle, so often applied by this Court, that a "governmental purpose to control or prevent activities constitutionally subject to state regulation may not be achieved by means which sweep unnecessarily broadly and thereby invade the area of protected freedoms." *NAACP v. Alabama.* Would we allow the police to search the sacred precincts of marital bedrooms for telltale signs of the use of contraceptives? The very idea is repulsive to the notions of privacy surrounding the marriage relationship.
>
> We deal with a right of privacy older than the Bill of Rights—older than our political parties, older than our school system. Marriage is a coming together for better or for worse, hopefully enduring, and intimate to the degree of being sacred. It is an association that promotes a way of life, not causes; a harmony in living, not political faiths; a bilateral loyalty, not commercial or social projects. Yet it is an association for as noble a purpose as any involved in our prior decisions.

For further elaboration of views emphasizing freedom from government interference, particularly in the economic sphere, see F. A. Hayek, *The Constitution of Liberty* (1960), *Law, Legislation and Liberty* (1973), *The Rule of Law* (1975), and M. Friedman & R. Friedman, *Free to Choose: A Personal Statement* (1980).

POSITIVISM IN PERSPECTIVE

A number of general observations may be made about the jurisprudential frame we have considered in this chapter.

Force, for Austin and Positivists, is a postulate, not a hypothesis or an empirically tested statement. There is no effort to apply the techniques of the natural sciences and to observe the operation of political power in context: its degree of effectiveness and the degree of conformity, if any, of behavior to regulations laid down by a sovereign. Nor are the contexts of such regulation—who, in fact, is expected by the public at large to make community-wide decisions and enforce them and how—examined by Positivists. The concept of decision is limited to legislation enacted by legislatures and applied by judges. The making of decisions and their affects are observed only obliquely through the filter of rules. Positivists do not have a notion of law as a continuous, active process of formal and informal decisionmaking. Law for the Positivist is little more than the verbalisms of legislators or judges. This constitutes a fraction of community decisions as discussed in Chapter 1.

The "facts" with which Austin and other Positivists deal are collections of legislation and court decisions—the communications of legislators and the pronouncements of judges. Is this an adequate factual picture? Does this limited selection of decisions from the past really control the current behavior of decisionmakers or of the general public? Are these decisions reliable indices of future decision and behavior? Are the conditions which existed when these decisions were made and their overall contexts (often ignored by Positivists) relevant to understanding what the "law" is at present or what it will be?

Austin and other Positivists assume that fixed rules, incorporated in verbal formulations in the past, have unequivocal and unchanging meaning when applied in a fixed manner and provide a frame for stable decisions to be rendered in the present and future. Is this notion realistic? Based upon contemporary studies in communications and linguistics, it has been argued that the past decisions of legislatures and courts are essentially communications from persons in the past to persons existing today and that such communications can only be considered in their overall contexts and can be understood only in accordance with the shared expectation of both the communicators and those to whom the communications are addressed, including the people today with regard to whom the decisions are to be applied. Discuss.

Does the Positivist view imply a perception that rules and notions of law have a metaphysical, autonomous and unchanging nature and constitute an independent entity which can be considered on its own without reference to the persons who laid down or applied the rule, the various circumstances surrounding such enunciations, or the actions and reactions to the rule of the persons affected by it? Is such a notion realistic? Is it useful?

P. Devlin, *The Enforcement of Morals* (1959).

L. Fuller, *The Majority of Law* (1969).

H.L.A. Hart, *Law, Liberty, and Morality* (1963).

L. Henkin, Morals and The Constitution: The Sin of Obscenity, 63 *Colum. L. R.* 391 (1963).

G. B. Hughes, Morals and The Criminal Law, in *Essays in Legal Philosophy* (R. Summers ed. 1968).

Law, Morality, and Society: Essays in Honor of H.L.A. Hart (P.M.S. Hacker & J. Raz eds. 1979).

B. Mitchell, *Law, Morality and Religion in a Secular Society* (1967).

J. Raz, *The Authority of Law: Essays on Law and Morality* (1979).

E. Rostow, The Enforcement of Morals, 18 *Cambridge L.J.* 174 (1960).

Williams Committee, Report of the Committee on Obscenity and Film Censorship (Command 7772, 1979).

Wolfenden Committee, Report of the Committee on Homosexual Offenses and Prostitution (Command 247, 1980).

CHAPTER 9

Legal Ethics in Leviathan:
The Jurisprudence of Bureaucracy

*We know enough if we know we are the King's subjects. If his cause
be wrong our obedience to the King wipes the crime of it out of us.*
Shakespeare

*One Covington and Burling associate explained that he didn't have
to worry about ethical issues because he's the low man on the totem
pole . . . [who] works for a great bunch of guys who really know
their stuff.*
Mark Green

DEAN, BLIND AMBITION 32–35 (1976)

The tests started that first day at the White House. After a brief explanation of my
meager quarters, I had sat down at my desk. I didn't have anything to do, but then
my secretary brought me a sealed envelope with a small red tag. I asked her what
it was. She had not opened it; it was stamped "CONFIDENTIAL," and the red tag
meant "priority." Someone had been planning work for the new counsel. The cover
memorandum was a printed form, with striking blue and red instructions filled in:

ACTION MEMORANDUM
FROM THE STAFF SECRETARY   LOG NO.: P523
Date: Friday, July 24, 1970   Time: 6:30 p.m.
Due Date: Wednesday, August 5, 1970   Time: 2:00 p.m.
SUBJECT: Request that you rebut the recent attack on the Vice-President.

An attached "confidential memorandum" said that a new muck-raking magazine
called *Scanlan's Monthly* had published a bogus memo linking Vice-President Agnew
with a top-secret plan to cancel the 1972 election and to repeal the entire Bill of
Rights. Agnew had publicly denounced the memo as "completely false" and "ridiculous," and the editors of *Scanlan's* had replied: "The Vice-President's denial
is as clumsy as it is fraudulent. The document came directly from Mr. Agnew's
office and he knows it." My instructions were clear: "It was noted that this is a
vicious attack and possibly a suit should be filed or a federal investigation ordered
to follow up on it."

"Noted" by whom? Since the memorandum was signed by John Brown, a
member of Haldeman's staff, I called him to find out. The "noter" was the President,
I was told: he had scrawled my orders in the margin of his daily news summary. No
one had to explain why the President's name was not used. He was always to be
kept one step removed, insulated, to preserve his "deniability."

So this is my baptism, I thought. I was astounded that the President would be
so angrily concerned about a funny article in a fledgling magazine. It did not square

359

with my picture of his being absorbed in diplomacy, wars and high matters of state. Was it possible that we *had* a secret plan to cancel the election and the Bill of Rights? I was embarrassed by the thought. Now I cannot look back on this episode without laughing, but then I was not at all loose about it. It was the President of the United States talking. Maybe he was right.

On the due date, I wrote my first memorandum to the President, explaining the hazards of a lawsuit and the wisdom of waiting to see what an FBI investigation produced. I thought the affair had been put to rest. Not so. Back came another action memorandum from the staff secretary. The President agreed with my conclusions, but he wasn't yet content. "It was requested," said the memorandum, "that as part of this inquiry you should have the Internal Revenue Service conduct a field investigation on the tax front."

This was the "old Nixon" at work, heavy-handed, after somebody. I began to fret. How could anything be at once so troubling and so absurd? The President was asking me to do something I thought was dangerous, unnecessary and wrong. I did nothing for several days, but the deadline was hard upon me. I couldn't simply respond, "Dean opposes this request because it is wrong and possibly illegal." I had to find some practical reason for doing the right thing or I would be gone. I called Bud Krogh several times, but he was out. Then I thought of my recent acquaintance, Murray Chotiner, and arranged to meet him.

"I need some counsel, Murray."

"You're the lawyer. You're the one who is supposed to give counsel around here," he said with a chuckle.

"I'm still trying to find the water fountains in this place," I said. "Murray, seriously, I need some advice. The President wants me to turn the IRS loose on a shit-ass magazine called *Scanlan's Monthly* because it printed a bogus memo from the Vice-President's office about cancelling the 'seventy-two election and repealing the Bill of Rights."

Murray laughed. "Hell, Agnew's got a great idea. I hope he has a good plan worked out. It would save us a lot of trouble if we dispensed with the 'seventy-two campaign." Murray wasn't taking my visit as seriously as I was. We joked about Agnew for a few minutes before I could get him to focus on my problem, and he had the answer. "If the President wants you to turn the IRS loose, then you turn the IRS loose. It's that simple, John."

"I really don't think it's necessary, Murray. The President's already got Mitchell investigating it. The FBI, I guess."

"I'll tell you this, if Richard Nixon thinks it's necessary you'd better think it's necessary. If you don't he'll find someone who does."

I was not convinced and said so, but nicely. "Okay, but let me ask you this, Murray. You're a lawyer. Isn't it illegal and therefore crazy to use IRS to attack someone the President doesn't like?"

"Not so," he snorted. He stopped and retrieved the calm he rarely lost. "John, the President is the head of the executive branch of this damn government. If he wants his tax collectors to check into the affairs of anyone, it's his prerogative. I don't see anything illegal about it. It's the way the game is played. Do you think for a second that Lyndon Johnson was above using the IRS to harass those guys who were giving him a hard time on the war? No sir. Nor was Lyndon above using IRS against some good Republicans like Richard Nixon. I'll tell you he damn near ruined a few."

Murray was testy, or maybe defensive—I couldn't decide. It was clear that he didn't want to discuss the matter further. I thanked him and left. If I was going to play ball in Richard Nixon's league, I would have to get over my squeamishness. I am not sure what I would have done if John J. Caulfield had not walked into my office.

Jack Caulfield could easily have been born in the mind of Damon Runyon instead of in New York City. He had moved up the ranks of the New York police force, from a street beat to detective, arriving at the White House after an assignment as candidate Nixon's personal bodyguard in 1968. Bob Haldeman had assigned him to me without telling me why. Caulfield explained that he was White House liaison with the Secret Service and the local police, but his principal assignment was to investigate Senator Edward M. Kennedy's conduct in the Chappaquiddick accident for John Ehrlichman.

Jack was a bountiful source of information. He knew what everybody was doing. He could tell you how to get a refrigerator or parking privileges and who was sleeping with whose secretary. And he wanted to help me find my bearings. He seemed a natural person to turn to with my IRS orders, and I decided to show him the memos. "How would you handle this assignment?" I asked.

"This isn't any problem. I'll take care of it for you with a phone call," he answered confidently. He returned the next day to report that a tax inquiry would be fruitless because the magazine was only six months old and its owners had yet to file their first return. Being resourceful, however, he had asked the IRS to look into the owners themselves. "You can tell the President everything is taken care of," he assured me.

"I've got a good one for you to pass along to the President," Jack added proudly. His Treasury Department sources had noticed an authoritative article on U.S.–Mexico drug traffic published by Scanlan's Monthly. It would make excellent background reading for the President's upcoming meeting with Mexican President Diaz Ordaz. I attached a copy of the article to my memo to the President, and I was amused to hear that the article was removed before the memo landed on the President's desk. No one in Haldeman's office wanted to be responsible for passing along anything from a magazine the President hated so much.

I summarized the tax situation in my report. "The fact that Scanlan's is a new entity does not make the tax inquiry very promising," I concluded. "Accordingly, I have also requested that the inquiry be extended to the principal organizers and promoters of the publication." Thus, within a month of coming to the White House, I had crossed an ethical line. I had no choice, as I saw it. The fact that I had not carried out the assignment myself eased my conscience slightly. I had no idea how Jack had done it so easily, nor did I ask, and I never found out what became of the IRS inquiry.*

---

*Lest one think Dean's experience a passing constitutional aberration, consider the following defense of a respected Democrat by Roswell Gilpatric, Deputy Secretary of Defense from 1961–1964, *N.Y. Times* June 17, 1979, at sec. 4, p. 18, col. 3.

David Halberstam's June 10 letter referring to Robert McNamara as "one of the most disturbingly flawed civil servants of this era" is the worst example of attempted character assassination I recall seeing published in your columns. . . .

Mr. Halberstam's central point about Mr. McNamara appears to be that the latter put his loyalty to the President above what Mr. Halberstam terms "a larger loyalty to the truth and to the democratic process." But under our Constitution any official in the executive branch, who is appointed by the

Chapter 3 hypothesized a coup d'etat in the United States in which military elements seize control of the government. The question there was how you would respond. In reviewing the lawfulness of such a coup in another country, Chief Justice Taft ruled that, at least from the perspective of outsiders, people who seized control of the government in violation of the constitution would be viewed as constituting the lawful government—if they were effective. Suppose you were a long-term employee of the Department of Justice when the hypothetical coup in the United States took place. The coup leaders would have announced over radio and television that all government officials were to continue to report to work and to discharge their legal functions; those who did not would be deemed in violation of martial law and would be severely punished. No doubt your deep commitment to the Constitution, to democracy and to the lawful transfer of the legitimate power would be profoundly offended. But what could you actually do to oppose this coup?

In reflecting on this hypothetical, some of you may have found yourselves unable to address the question because you were uncertain as to who or what now comprised the government. One of the peculiar aspects of modern society is the multicellular organism we call bureaucracy. In government, business (especially in large corporations), in universities, in the military, human beings are organized in complex, hierarchical systems. At each level, the primary responsibility is to discharge a limited task, to follow the directives of the superior level, to give clear directives to lower levels and to consider rarely, if at all possible, the overall purposes and consequences of the organization. In organizations such as these, a mid-level functionary, let us say an executive, is really unaffected by a take-over, a type of business coup which changes the top level of management, but leaves the rest of the organization intact. Practically speaking, the notion of Rule of Law and compliance with directives in such an organization is involved less with deference to the highest figure or to the entity as a whole than with loyalty to and compliance with the directives of the immediately superior level of organization. Hence such organizations, like tapeworms, have an extraordinary resilience to coups and other unauthorized changes. Like it or not, given the sort of coup we have hypothesized, mid-level functionaries in a bureaucratic organization may continue to operate with a very limited sense (if any) of violation of duty. For the bureaucrat, one of the attractions of this course of action is that since it can be characterized as technical, apolitical and legal it is, thus, the safest.

In this chapter, we consider some adaptations of certain doctrines of Positivism to the contemporary bureaucratic phenomenon. The resulting jurisprudence has improved the continuity of organizations and their capacity to operate in the face of unauthorized political changes. But not without costs. It has anesthetized the sense of personal and systematic responsibility of individuals.

THE NATURE OF THE BEAST

There are many descriptions of the bureaucratic phenomenon. In the selection below, Robert Presthus attempts to set out the most salient and recurring features of bureaucracy.

President and confirmed by the Senate, owes his supreme loyalty to the President. Such an official can only escape that loyalty by resigning his office. Whether Mr. McNamara should have resigned as Secretary of Defense earlier than he did is a question over which future historians of the war in Vietnam may differ. But under our system of government there can be no question of where a Cabinet officer's loyalty lies while he remains in office.

PRESTHUS, THE ORGANIZATIONAL SOCIETY 27–55 (1962)

We now turn to an analysis of the structural characteristics of the typical big organization. While such organizations obviously differ in size, product, age, and tradition, they are quite similar in form, procedure, and the claims they make upon their members for loyalty and consistency. Most of them have the following characteristics: large size, specialization, hierarchy, status anxiety, oligarchy (rule by the few), co-optation (selection of their successors by the organization's elite), "efficiency," and rationality. The bureaucratic model to be described here is an ideal type. It has no exact counterpart in the real world. However, although every big organization may not exhibit all these characteristics, we can safely assume that most of them will. While all big orgnizations may not be bureaucratic, most bureaucratic organizations will be big. Such organizations provide a distinctive psychological climate in which authority and status are nicely differentiated. As a result, behavioral expectations will be big. Such organizations provide a distinctive psychological climate in which authority and status are nicely differentiated. As a result, behavioral expectations are clearly prescribed; interpersonal relations occur in a structured context. Ideally, there is very little ambiguity in bureaucratic organizations.

Although all the characteristics of the bureaucratic model are actually reinforcing, size is among its most significant features . . . "size" refers here to organizations in which the number of members is large enough to prohibit face-to-face relations among most participants.

Durkheim has shown that as societies increase in size, density, and urbanization, the division of labor increases rapidly. Like suicide, specialization is a function of increasing civilization. This is because the members of the undifferentiated society find themselves in too intense competition. They therefore turn to a division of labor which will permit each segment to pursue its own goals with a minimum of conflict.

• • •

Some qualification of Durkheim's assumption that specialization is generally beneficial seems required. There is an inherent tension in organizations between those in hierarchical positions of authority and those who play specialized roles. Each feels that his role is more essential to the organization. The specialist deplores the fact that those in hierarchical roles have appropriated to themselves the definitions of success in our society. In the university, for example, the major rewards in prestige and income go to those in administrative (hierarchical) positions. The most eminent faculty member must become an administrator if he is to secure larger shares of these values. . . .

On the other hand, those in hierarchical positions often find the specialist difficult. Rarely can he be persuaded that his own department does not deserve the lion's share of the organization's resources. His "trained incapacity" makes it difficult for him to see that the administrator's role is inevitably one of achieving compromise among competing units within the organization. The conflict is often one between the organization-wide view of the administrator and the restricted, introverted perspective of the specialist. . . .

Size has other dysfunctions. We know that as size increases morale decreases. While the relationship is less consistent, lower productivity and absenteeism are also associated with organizational size. This is apparently because men find it difficult to identify with the large number of people found in the typical big organization. While small-group membership eases this problem, it does not necessarily improve the individual's rapport with the organization qua organization. Individuals tend to

feel unimportant and somewhat alienated by its size, anonymity, and power. They
do not seem to count. . . .

Hierarchy may be defined as a system for ranking positions along a descending
scale from the top to the bottom of the organization. . . . Hierarchy, which is as old
as history, is of religious origin where it referred to the ranking of the officialdom
set up to administer religious values. As Weber shows, the change from charismatic
authority, based upon revelation or magic, to *bureaucratic authority,* occurred in
both religion and politics. This "routinization of charisma" brought *rules and officials*
to administer them. The discretion of each official was necessarily limited, however,
and the power he exercised was not personal but legal. Therefore, "a hierarchy of
superiors, to which officials may appeal and complain in an order of rank, stands
opposite the citizen or member of the association. . . . This situation also holds for
the hierocratic association that is the church." Hierarchy, then, is the result of the
separation of personal, charismatic authority from official authority.

. . . It is well known that the farther away one is from those in high organizational
posts the greater the tendency to hold them in awe, to attribute to them charismatic
or magical powers. Hierarchical differences in status, power, and income reinforce
this perception. The higher one goes in the hierarchy the more his activities become
differentiated and unamenable to precise evaluation. Contrast this situation with the
role of the specialist who is assigned responsibility for a given functional task.
Communication barriers between elite and rank and file aggravate this condition. In
sum, the deference accorded organizational leaders is highly charged with charismatic
implications. Such deference validates the individual's need to impute superiority to
those above him. It also honors the American creed which holds that there are
significant personal differences in ability between those who succeed and those who
do not.

Hierarchy is nicely illustrated by military organization. Ranks and authority are
graded from the top to the bottom of the organization. Ideally, this apparatus provides
a chain of command extending throughout the entire system, in which each person
from commanding general to buck private is under the control of the man immediately
above him. At the same time he is himself the supervisor of the person directly below
him in the hierarchy. It is not only *positions* that are ranked in terms of authority,
but relative amounts of authority, status, deference, income, and other perquisites
of office are ascribed to each position. Such perquisites are allocated disproportion-
ately. They tend to cluster near the top and to decrease rapidly as one descends the
hierarchy. This inequitable distribution of scarce values is characteristic of all big
organizations; it provides a built-in condition of inequality and invidious differentiation. Hierarchical monopoly of the distribution system augments the power of
those at the top since rewards can be allocated to reinforce elite definitions of
"loyalty," "competence," and so on. A related objective of this inequality is to
reinforce the organization's status system, which in turn reinforces the authority and
legitimacy of its leaders. . . .

Hierarchy gives those at the top control of the formal communication system
whose channels follow hierarchical lines. Since information is obviously a prerequisite
for participation, this control enables the elite to manipulate both the issues and those
who help resolve them. Hierarchy permits elites to determine what kind of issues
will be raised for organizational consideration. Potential solutions can be delimited
by hierarchical control of meetings. By proposing only one or two alternatives and
by indicating his preference among them, the formal leader can exercise dispropor-

tionate influence. The conditions of individual participation, that is to say, are always affected by hierarchy. Often, the places that individuals take around a conference table are an accurate index of their rank and status in the organization. The ensuing discussion tends to follow such rankings, with senior members dominating. As in other contexts, the weight attached to propositions is often a function of the status of their originator. The informal groups that appear in organizations are similarly structured by the relative influence, skill, seniority, and conviviality of their members.

Perhaps the main function of hierarchy is to assign and to validate authority along a descending scale throughout the organization. The resulting allocations surely constitute the basic authority structure of the organization. . . .We have seen that hierarchical authority has charismatic elements. But the greatest deviation from the hierarchical system of authority is the authority that specialists enjoy by virtue of their technical skill and training. The steady accumulation of knowledge which characterizes modern Western society underlies this development. New skill groups arise and demand recognition of their expertise; . . .

The resulting competition often leads to considerable legerdemain whereby mock recognition is given to line authority when in fact a decision has been made by specialists. Such fictions permit the traditional image of hierarchical supremacy to remain unchallenged by the relentless advance of scientific knowledge. Perhaps the best current example . . . is the management of federal atomic weapons and missile research by high ranking military officers whose experience has been restricted to the command of an army division or a ship.

•   •   •

Despite the challenges of expertise and emotion, hierarchy remains a critical basis of organizational authority. From the human side, hierarchy is a graded system of interpersonal relationships, a society of unequals in which scarce values become even scarcer as one descends the hierarchy. Some tension inevitably results since freedom, rewards, and influence are unequally shared by those in the organization. This condition is aggravated because the career chances of any given individual rest in the hand of his immediate superior. This provides serious obstacles for those at lower ranks in the form of innumerable veto barriers which requests for rewards or promotion must penetrate. Not only can the request be denied at any level, but if such requests are negated some distance up the hierarchy, those concerned may never learn the reasons for the veto nor at what point it occurred. This condition tends to increase the common feelings of remoteness and powerlessness among members of big organizations.

Hierarchy has other functions. By delegating authority to the point where the skill necessary to carrying out tasks resides, hierarchy links authority with skill. By monopolizing the distribution system, elites increase their control of those in the organization. Big organizations therefore tend to exhibit an "upward looking" posture and a certain anxiety. When this atmosphere is set against democratic values of individual autonomy and self-realization, considerable tension may result. A serious operational dysfunction may occur as individuals, forced to choose between initiative and risk on the one hand and clearance and safety on the other, tend to choose the latter. They resist delegation. Those in higher positions are also reluctant to delegate because this makes them responsible for the potential error of others. Such resistance is explained by the organization's drive to increase control, but since control is achieved only by limiting delegation, the organization tends to slow down. This unanticipated consequence refutes the claim that power must be centralized if big organizations are to act expeditiously: there still remains the gap between those who make decisions and those who carry them out.

Closely articulated with hierarchy in big organizations is the *status* system. Status refers to the allocation of different amounts of authority, income, deference, rights, and privileges to the various positions in the hierarchy. Prestige is the deference attached to each position, and generally it follows hierarchy. The largest amounts of deference are assigned to those at the top of the hierarchy, and the relative amounts decrease at a disproportionate rate as one descends. Ideally, both status and prestige are accurate indexes of a person's contributions to the organization. As we have seen, however, the existing system of distribution insures that those in hierarchical "line" positions receive disproportionate rewards in comparison with those in specialist roles. The status system's functional consequences include concrete recognition of individual worth and achievement. Its dysfunctions include invidious comparisons of individual contributions, comparisons which are not always objectively based. Perhaps its main operational consequence is to reinforce the authority of those at each hierarchical level in the organization. Those in the upper levels of the organization are more highly reinforced because status indexes are skewed toward the top.

• • •

The social framework of status also suggests that its symbols become a substitute for values no longer attainable. The difficulty of achieving independence through owning one's business, a difficulty which reflects the trend toward bigness and concentration; the employment of the "independent" professions on a bureaucratic, salaried basis; the devaluation of the term "professional"—all seem conducive to increased status anxiety and striving. In a larger context, the whole trend toward big organization is involved, in the sense that size and anonymity result in sustained attempts by the individual to preserve status in compensation for the loss of autonomy. C. Wright Mills speaks of the "status panic" that characterizes life in the white-collar world.

Also related is the mock "professionalization" of ordinary jobs through increased educational requirements. Ludicrous efforts to borrow prestige by subsituting status-laden titles for socially devalued jobs: "news analyst" for reporter; "mortician" for undertaker; the crisp term "executive" for all sorts of routine jobs; the co-optation of the honored symbol, "professional"—all suggest the effort to achieve status by word magic. In a deeper sense this trend may reflect decreased occupational mobility. If one cannot ascend the ladder as easily as before, why not enhance the status of that which is obtainable?

The American assumption of upward-mobility generation by generation is thus related to status idealization. A comparison with class-bound European and Middle Eastern societies suggests that sheer age, the maturing of the economy, and declining personal autonomy in the U.S. will increase status consciousness, and that a greater emphasis will come to be placed upon artificial, bureaucratic distinctions as the more objective means to status become more difficult to achieve. A free and easy democracy requires a unique social and economic situation with relatively equal access to abundant natural resources. The organizational society checkmates this situation as the lessons of power are learned by many groups and as their countervailing power results in a rough equilibrium between major social interests. In this milieu big organizations naturally turn to subtle status rewards as compensation for economic and personal dependence and limited mobility. The honoring of seniority is an obvious example. The small gap between initial and upper-level incomes in the bureaucratized professions further encourages the use of psychic rewards such as graduated ranks, titles, name plates, and "atmosphere."

Members are clearly differentiated according to their role and status. Types of sanction, forms of communication, dress and conduct in off-work activities are determined by one's position in the organizational hierarchy. As a rule those who deal with the public enjoy exceptional status reinforcements, including large, well-appointed offices, expense accounts (and hence greater social mobility), more staff and secretarial assistance, and those mechanical and human props that formalize access, create an impression of preoccupation with important matters, and encourage attitudes of deference. . . .

The assignment of authority and status along hierarchical lines means that the conditions of participation in big formal organizations are determined by a minority. This characteristic of the bureaucratic model may be called *oligarchy,* which means "rule by the few." Although oligarchy has usually meant rule by the wealthy, modern oligarchs are often salaried employees whose status and powers are based upon their *control,* not their ownership of great organization resources. Although the power of such elites is limited in their external relations by the power of similar minorities elsewhere, our concern is with the *internal* aspects of organizations where oligarchy seems relatively unrestrained. This is not to say oligarchy is inevitable, but merely that it is a highly probable feature of big organization.

One must qualify the oligarchic generalizations in other ways. Constraints against oligarchy vary from one kind of organization to another. . . . The skills and interests required for true bargaining between leaders and led exist in different measure in different societies. Oligarchy, as a result, will be more probable in underdeveloped societies where political and organizational skills are the monopoly of relatively limited groups. There, in Pareto's phrase, the "circulation of elites" occurs within a small group. In Western society, on the other hand, relatively high literacy rates and greater participation in a greater number of associations means that the skills which make oligarchy possible are more widely distributed. As a result, its effects are somewhat modulated.

It is always necessary to add that while "oligarchy" means the power of the few over the many, this does not mean that the majority is powerless. Even Machiavelli's Prince was admonished to have due regard for popular myths. The important point is that such power is unequal. The concept of power assumes reciprocity, but there is always a difference between the power of one actor and another. Obviously all elites are to some extent limited by their assumptions about mass reactions to their politics, but an oligarchy is characterized by the *preponderance of power* it enjoys. Oligarchy, then, assumes inequality of power, nothing more.

Oligarchy is apparent in the fact that decisions in big organizations are usually made by a minority. When organizations become large, communication is difficult and the power of decision tends to be restricted to a few leaders. Some elites enhance their power by concealing information; but in any event the problems of disseminating information and of providing for widespread participation present almost unsuperable obstacles. The pressure of demands for quick decisions often makes consultation impracticable. The highly technical character of many decisions tends furthermore to limit participation to those who have the requisite skills and knowledge—this despite the fact that the ramifications of the decision may extend throughout the organization. Thus the intensity of oligarchy probably increase in some sort of geo-metric ratio to organizational size. We know, for example, that the atomization of stock ownership encourages oligarchy. The more dispersed the stockholders become, the greater the power of the controlling minority. And it is control, not ownership, that counts in modern organization.

Robert Michels, a very distinguished student of oligarchy, found that it was characteristic of *big* organizations rather than of all. In his view, organizations become oligarchic for technical and psychological reasons. The sheer number of members prohibits communication; and the resulting ignorance and inertia encourage direction by the few. Meanwhile, specialist claims increase the tendency toward oligarchy, because new skill groups gain access to strategic points in the hierarchy and acquire an impetus to rule. Public relations men, for example, are now among the top policy makers in most organizations. Thus size, numbers, and the need for expertise are among the technical reasons for minority control.

These "causes" of oligarchy are reinforced by psychological factors, including the desire for power encouraged by the dominant values of our society. Although oligarchy is often justified by the need for control and the pressure for action, it also reflects individual drives for power. The fulfillment of this drive is often encouraged, furthermore, by the "true believer's" need for some omnipotent leader or myth. That is to say, many subordinates need the man of power to displace the burden of individual responsibility and to receive in return the benefits of certainty. Although its psychic nuances cannot be treated here, a significant by-product of oligarchy must be mentioned: the selective process in big organizations brings the power seeker to the top. Moreover, power and its dividends increase as one ascends the hierarchy.

While the logic and rewards of organization encourage the drive for power, its criteria of selection ensure that those who rise possess an exceptional urge to dominate. The implications for responsibility are sharpened by Michels' conclusion that control of any elite can come only from *outside* the organization.

Michels developed his "iron law of oligarchy" by observing socialist political parties in western Europe. Despite their lip service to equality, he found them oligarchic in operation. Power was centered in a core of permanent officials who made policy and presented it full-blown to the members for ratification. It is similarly ironic that big organizations in the United States also exist in a democratic context and employ a liberal rhetoric, but are often nevertheless oligarchic. This is not only confusing but also somewhat inhibiting insofar as analysis is concerned. The problem of power if often ignored as an uncomfortable aberration. As a result, one must often cut through a haze of cheerful rationalizations concerning manifest power disequilibria. One such rationalization is the notion that authority in big organizations is essentially a matter of *consent,* depending upon the acceptance of those who are subject to it. This view must be qualified, however, mainly because it fails to ask *why* authority is accepted. When this question is asked, the problems of learned deference to authority, to influence, and to sanctions are raised, and the motives for "acceptance" become clearer.

Obviously, individuals "accept" authority for many reasons and many possible reactions exist, ranging from eager cooperation to reluctant obedience. Confronted with an order, the average individual will estimate the consquences of various alternatives and adopt the one that seems in his own interest, insofar as he is able to identify it. In this restricted sense authority is no doubt "accepted." But to suggest as this thesis does that it is commonly within the individual's range of discretion either to accept or to reject is misleading. Rejection is usually impractical. Moreover, such a view fails to recognize the propensity to obey induced by socialization and by hierarchy, both of which tend to institutionalize obedience and to redefine "acceptance" by creating an expectation of compliance.

Hunter's study of power in Atlanta, Georgia, suggests the locus and the tactics of oligarchy. While Atlanta may be unique, and while more recent research raises questions about elitist assumptions of community power structure, this remains an impressive study. He found a weblike pattern of power and influence ultimately residing in a half dozen members of an old-family elite. Viewed from the outside, power appeared to be more widely diffused, since many of its agents were obviously not members of the inner circle. But this illusion reflected the need to organize and to delegate power, particularly the need for a means of enlisting the energies and great expectations of those at the periphery. The vital decision to act or not to act remained in the inner circle, although the responsibility for organizing, articulating, and carrying it through was necessarily shared with others. The latter exercised influence, it is true, but theirs was a borrowed, temporary influence. In effect, this group *administered* the power of the industrial, banking, legal, and social elite, and enjoyed the facade of power that such participation gave them.

The structure of oligarchy thus consisted of an inner elite supported by an aspiring, co-opted outer circle which dealt with an apathetic ratifying majority. Although the inner elite remained behind the scenes, reaching policy decisions at informal meetings, respondents were apparently able to differentiate nicely between the "real" power holders and the contenders at various levels. . . . While an outsider might occasionally be co-opted, usually through a romantic or a pecuniary nexus (and these were not necessarily exclusive), admission to this circle was extremely limited.

A similar tendency toward oligarchy is visible in most large groups, regardless of their function and ideology. In Congress, for example, party control is much stronger in the House than in the Senate, in part because the House is five times as large. Within Congress the selection and the influence of committees encourage government by minority. . . .

Perhaps the most powerful of such committees is the House of Rules Committees which mainly determines the form and content of legislation that reaches the floor of the House of Representatives. Here again, the size variable is critical, for it is generally agreed that in the Senate, only one-fifth as large, committees are less powerful and legislation coming from them is subject to a much more incisive scrutiny.

● ● ●

Although the locus of their power is state and local rather than national, our political parties are similarly controlled by a professional minority. Even a casual appraisal of the preliminary tactics of presidential nominating conventions reveals the power of the active minority. Here again there is little despotism, although exhibitions such as the Democratic convention of 1960 suggest that the line is at times rather finely drawn. Ordinarily the will of the rank and file will not be flagrantly violated, and self-interest alone insures that the nominee will be broadly representative. Nevertheless, in the 1960 Democratic convention, a handful of big-city and state leaders in New York, Pennsylvania, Ohio, Illinois, and California were able to push through without serious opposition a candidate whose popular appeal was certainly less impressive than his campaign organization and unlimited resources. In sum, such conventions are often the mere formalization of extended, preliminary, behind-the-scenes caucusing by innumerable combinations of influence and interest, reflecting bargaining among big-city, state, and national party leaders. And such bargaining is almost entirely restricted to a professional party elite, however sensitive it may be to great social and economic interests. . . .

Similar behaviors appear in academic and professional associations, in labor unions, corporations, and universities. The "causes" are the same: the need for the organizing skills of permanent officials; the development of bureaucratic systems of leadership, before which the unorganized majority is virtually powerless; and the size and specialization of contemporary groups, reflecting modern innovations in political tactics and communication. The desire for power and the discipline of those who hope to rise, as well as the apathy or disenchantment of the majority, are also at work.

The role of *co-optation* in enhancing organizational discipline and continuity must also be emphasized. As Michels said, co-optation is the process by which those in power designate their successors. This prerogative is part of the monopoly of scarce values that hierarchy assigns to the organization's elite. Since such successors are chosen by existing elites, it can be assumed that they will personify traditional values. In this way sanctioned behaviors and expectations are transmitted through agents selected after what tends to be (given the remarkable tenure of oligarchs) a lengthy apprenticeship. Meanwhile the impact of co-optation extends beyond those immediately affected. Each promotion and its rituals provide an opportunity to dramatize the terms under which rewards are given. The indexes of success are reaffirmed, and the upward-mobiles receive another impetus to rise. For various reasons, including the desire to preserve internal unity and discipline, *loyalty* seems to have become the main basis for bureaucratic succession. Like seniority, loyalty enjoys the advantage of wide acceptance, for it is a quality almost everyone can aspire to.

Oligarchy and co-optation are apparent in union leadership, which becomes a sinecure despite periodic elections and an emphasis upon democratic values. Samuel Gompers served a thirty-eight-year term as president of the AFL. After his death in 1924 the reins were held by William Green for almost three decades. Daniel Tobin led the Teamsters for virtually half a century; Hutcheson led the Carpenters for thirty-five years and, upon retirement, was succeeded by his son. John I. Lewis was president of the UMW for over forty years. Such tenures and the resulting control of policy make possible tremendous concentrations of power. As Kermit Eby said:

> The modern trade union, like the modern corporation, is monolithic; one huge human shaft of power directed from the top. Its conventions are attended by professionals—"pork choppers"—whose present and future security depends on the maintenance of the power hierarchy. Decisions which affect the rank-and-file worker are increasingly removed from his hands in both time and space. The decisions which must be made are technically so complicated that only the expert or the leaders advised by the expert are competent to make them.

Oligarchy as an "organic necessity" is the result of technical demands for internal direction, unity and consistency, control of market conditions, leadership skills, public relations, and lobbying. It is rendered necessary, in short, by the need for someone to give coherence and continuity to the vague, often conflicting aspirations of the majority. Given the role of unanticipated consequences in human affairs, the implications of oligarchy may come as a shock to those who exercise it, assuming that such considerations ever arise. Doubts, however, are probably resolved by the assumptions of infallibility that characterize most oligarchs; self-images which are nourished by their isolation and power.

Power to initiate, to communicate, to reward, to sanction, to shape public opinions—these are the prerogatives and tactics of oligarchy. As a result, policy and orders flow from the top downward, limiting the rank and file to an essentially negative role. Having neither the power of initiation, which permits the oligarchy to decide what shall be done and when, nor of choosing the avenues of consultation, which can be used to ensure favorable reactions to their policies, nor the control of patronage, which ensures discipline, the majority can only ratify. When such actions sharply violate their expectations, the mass may exercise a veto power, but such contingencies are remote since they occur only if the majority loses the tactical skill that brought it to power in the first place.

In democratic societies the tendency toward oligarchy stands out most sharply in crises, when the use of arbitrary methods for democratic ends becomes acceptable. An obvious example is the way in which military and security imperatives are accepted during wartime. Most of us regard such invasions as a temporary inconvenience, a necessary tribute to national survival. Similarly, during wartime certain groups shelve ideals which previously had seemed irreducible. For example, physical scientists made great contributions during and after World War II through research on new weapons. It is well known that their professional ethic centers on individual independence, on the free exchange of information, and on a rigorous disavowal of authority as a basis for truth. These values, moreover, are not merely desirable; they are supposedly among the essentials of scientific progress. Yet apparently they could be set aside. We find, for example, that during World War II the 30,000 scientists in the Office of Scientific Research and Development were controlled by about "thirty-five men in senior positions." This minority assigned research, established policy via-a-vis the military and the public, and generally ran things according to "convenient, authoritarian military liaisons."

Hierarchy and oligarchy seek *rationality,* another common structural characteristic of large-scale organization. Rationality may be defined as the capacity for objective, intelligent action. It is usually characterized by a patent behavioral nexus between ends and means. While rationality is always limited by human error, inadequate information, and chance, within these limits the rational person applies intelligence, experience, and technical skills to solve his problems. In an ideal-typical organization rationality is sought by organizing and directing its many parts so that each contributes to the whole product. Specialization, careful recruitment, job analysis, and planning are among the obvious means to this end.

We assume that society tends to produce individuals who possess its dominant characteristics. The rationality of the big organization is similarly instilled in its members. Not only are its structure and procedures designed to enhance predictability, but individuals too become, insofar as possible, animated instruments. Individual discretion is limited by regulations and precedents that cover all anticipated events, and such regulations tend to become ends in themselves. As a result, individuals try to find written authority for every action and to avoid action when such cannot be found. The very interpretation of rules and the search for authority to act (or not to act) become valued skills. Knowledge of the rules and how they can be bent gives the individual security and a share of organized power. He thus develops a vested interest in preserving the rules against change.

Rationality is also sought through the division of labor and through recruitment on a scientific basis. Job requirements, including both technical skill and emotional qualities, are determined by men selected for their ability to determine such qualifications. . . .

Even the specialist's isolation contributes to his skill because he finds satisfaction in the complete mastery of his role. Denied an understanding of the larger scheme, he magnifies the limited insights and satisfactions that are within his grasp. He is, as it were, driven to this end. Objective, impersonal standards become all the more acquisitive because he is often unaware of their implications. He thinks everyone lives that way. One is reminded of the Prussian staff officer who spent a lifetime seeking ways to reduce mobilization time by one half-hour. As Merton and others have shown, certain dysfunctions follow, including a resistance and an inability to change.

Another significant by-product occurs: the decision-making process becomes highly diffused, the product of an organizational mind. Organized irresponsibility follows. Decision making in the big organization becomes vague and impersonal, and the instrument of an anonymous, fragmented intelligence. Each decision is the result of various technical and personal considerations, the sum of the contributions of everyone involved in the deciding process. This diffusion means that "everyone" (i.e., no one) is responsible. In extreme cases the condition may lead to arbitrary and immoral behavior, particularly when compounded by intense personal identification with the state, the party, the church, or the "organization." In every case, the probabilities that the organization may act unjustly are increased by the weakening of individual responsibility. Only "the system" is responsible.

The modern culmination of this system was seen in the Nazi apparatus. "The crime is handed down from chief to sub-chief until it reaches the slave who receives orders from above without being able to pass them on to anybody. One of the Dachau executioners weeps in prison and says, 'I only obeyed orders. The Fuhrer and the Reichsfuhrer, alone, planned all this and then they ran away. Gluecks received orders from Kaltenbrunner and, finally, I received orders to carry out the shootings. I have been left holding the bag because I was only a little *Hauptscharführer* and because I couldn't hand it on any lower down the line. Now they say that I am the assassin.' " This suggests why the big organization more often causes a crime of logic than one of passion, to use Camus' phrase.

Such procedures and attitudes are often necessary to handle the volume and diversity of activity in big organizations. Methods for handling each type of problem are prescribed, with each specialist contributing to the decision on the basis of his skill and jurisdiction. This overriding technical ethos increases the probability that personal factors will be minimized. Ideally, there is no way that such elements can affect the decision process. The specialist's loyalty is to the work process and to his own technical skill, rather than to any mitigating aspects of a case. As Weber shows, to do otherwise would evoke considerable anxiety, so strong are the demands of precedent and procedure.

The organization, in sum, is rationally planned to achieve its ends. Like the human organism, it has a directing center that transmits cues to the entire organization. Authority, rewards, and sanctions are allocated in ways that ensure that its members work together. As we have seen, hierarchy and oligarchy are perhaps the main instruments for so doing. The first assigns authority, responsibility, status, income, and deference in a descending scale from top to bottom, providing a chain of graded interpersonal relationships that insures the delegation of all sanctioned impulses.

Oligarchy makes its contribution by monopolizing power and the distribution of the organization's scarce values. Men work for status, recognition, and security; oligarchy permits the organization's elite to determine the conditions under which such values are allocated.

All this is highly idealized, of course. Informal centers of power compete with the elite for influence in determining how resources are to be distributed. Unanticipated consequences subvert the organization's formal goals. Individuals persist in giving their latent objectives priority over organizational claims. Nevertheless, in organizations with high morale, i.e., those in which the legitimacy of means and ends is widely endorsed, the image is generally accurate. The resulting bond between the elite and the rank and file ensures identification, consensus, and even a sense of real participation among the latter.

NOTES

1. Presthus inventories many of the acknowledged features of contemporary bureaucratic organization. But there are two features in particular which deserve special attention. The first is what we may call "task responsibility" as opposed to "outcome responsibility." The very complexity of the bureaucratic organization means that most individuals operating at lower levels are unlikely to know its major purposes or to be able to see or even conceive of its entire operation. They assume perforce that their superiors know what they are doing; hence they can hardly be deemed to be responsible for the "outcome-event" which the organization produces, be it a service, a product, a pattern of destruction or whatever, for in many cases they will not even know what it is. For example, it would be most unlikely that those working on an assembly line or in lower level clerical activities would appreciate the environmental impacts of some of the products they are producing. It is even more unlikely that they will appreciate long-term ecological effects on the other side of the planet on which even experts may disagree. Where production processes are complex, many workers may not even know, let alone understand the "outcome-events" or end products to which they are contributing. Where bureaucracy incorporates advanced technology, in the context of an industrial, science-based civilization, the difficulties for many of the people working in organizations even to understand *the implications* of the outcome-events to which they contribute increase enormously.

In such a setting, it is not surprising that a new ethic of responsibility takes hold: a responsibility to discharge the particular task which passes one's desk or one's factory space but not a responsibility for the final outcome which could not be concluded without the contribution of the particular task. This is the ethic of "task" rather than "outcome" responsibility.

2. The moral implications of this new ethic, particularly in a democracy, are obvious. People who would otherwise test the outcomes to which their acts contributed in terms of their own moral calculus and hence have the option of refraining from or changing those acts if that calculus was violated, need not even face that question. If the only ethic relevant is task responsibility, they may suspend their moral judgment. The implications of task responsibility were hauntingly captured in song-writer Tom Lehrer's parody of Dr. Werner von Braun, missile expert, who supposedly says, *pace* Lehrer, "Once the rockets go up, /who cares where they come down./ It's not my department,/says Werner von Braun."

———

Lest we think that that is exceptional, consider the following excerpts from a *New York Times* article describing perceptions of responsibility of Air Force officers during the Vietnam war.

TREASTER, ABOARD A B-52 BOMBER HIGH OVER VIETNAM A CREW TAKES
PART IN AN "IMPERSONAL WAR," N.Y. TIMES OCT. 13, 1972, AT 12.

Andersen Air Force Base, Guam, October 4—Six hours and 14 minutes after
taking off from this Pacific island base, Capt. Terry Jennings' B-52 shuddered and
32,500 pounds of high-explosive bombs plummeted toward South Vietnam.

A few seconds later a ground controller radioed, "good job,"—the bombs were
right on target.

There was not a flicker of reaction from one of the six crewmen, no sign of
satisfaction or any trace of excitement—an attitude, of course, that has been common
in bomber crews for years.

For the crewmen, sitting in their air-conditioned compartments more than five
miles above the steamy jungle of South Vietnam, the bomb run had been merely
another familiar technical exercise. The crew knew virtually nothing about their target
and they showed no curiosity.

Only the radar-navigator, who in earlier wars would have been called the bom-
bardier, saw the bombs exploding, and those distant flashes gave no hint of the
awesome eruption of flames and steel on the ground. No one in the plane, including
this correspondent, heard the deafening blast.

In many ways, Captain Jennings and his men are typical of the scores of crews
that have been sent to Guam since February in a build-up that has brought the number
of B-52's bombing Indochina to about 200—four times more than were in the theater
at the close of last year. Some of the big bombers are based at Utapao, Thailand.

They are intelligent, steady, family men doing a job they've been told to do.
Because they are professionals, they take pride in doing their work well. But neither
Captain Jennings' crew nor any of the numerous other pilots and crewmen interviewed
displayed the kind of enthusiasm for their assignment that bubbles through conversations with fighter pilots. "It's a job," the bomber men often say.

• • •

The maps used by the crews show almost no place names. One general said that
kept the maps uncluttered. It also keeps them impersonal. The targets are given code
numbers and are marked by intersecting map coordinates.

"For all you know," one pilot said, "you could be bombing New York City."

The pilot was joking. But he and his colleagues are disciplined men who have
taken an oath of service in the Air Force and they regard themselves foremost, as
professionals. Several crewmen were asked what they would do if they were ordered
to "take out Hanoi—not just the military installations but the whole city." All
answered that they would "jump in our planes and go." Their only concern, they
said, would be for personal safety.

Whether the war is right or wrong is not an issue with the crews, they say. They
do not make policy, but are instruments of policy. They have been trained to operate
the machinery of the B-52 and that is what they do. Where they put the bombs is
someone else's decision and someone else's responsibility, they feel.

"As far as losing any sleep over what we're doing, how many people we
kill . . . we never get to see the damage," said Captain Crook, whose home is in
Memphis.

At another point he said, "if we were killing anybody down there with our bombs
I have to think we were bombing the enemy and not civilians. I feel quite sure about
our targeting."

A pilot in another crew put it this way: "You don't consider that you're going out and killing somebody. You say, 'we've got a job to do and let's go out and do it.' The other part isn't considered."

————

Historians note that types of bureaucratic phenomena are to be found in some earlier empires and civilizations. Bureacracy, as we know it in this century, is particularly distinctive in that it has achieved a degree of power and a centrality in people's lives just as other traditional and potentially competing and balancing institutions—the family, religion, the state—have tended to decrease both in effectiveness and, perhaps as a consequence, personal importance. These traditional institutions used to be the enduring ones and hence the ones most worthy of personal investment and loyalty. But in the rapid changes and turbulences of life in modern industrial society, many of the traditional institutions now prove to be short-lived. Recall, in this regard, Pospisil's view in Chapter 2. In contrast, the corporation, the firm, the school or the government for which one works appear to have an extraordinary stability and endurance and may become the prime units for providing basic life support. Thanks to their "magical" properties, these new organizations become screens onto which many of the mystical attributes formerly attributed to smaller social organizations are now projected. Blau and Meyer write of this "mythicization" of the contemporary bureaucratic organization.

BLAU & MEYER,
BUREAUCRACY IN MODERN SOCIETY
51–52 (2d ed. 1971)

Large organizations tend to develop distinctive ideologies that glorify them and their members and exaggerate their virtues. The myths surrounding the U.S. Marines are a typical example. Such ideologies serve useful functions for the organization, by creating a sense of purpose among its members, strengthening their commitment and loyalty, and spurring them to greater efforts in behalf of the organization. Particularly significant is the role of these beliefs in transforming a collectivity of individuals with their separate goals into a working organization—something that exists apart from its members, which shapes their behavior, and which has overriding purposes. Philip Selznick describes this process as follows:

> To create an institution we rely on many techniques for infusing day-to-day behavior with long-run meaning and purposes. One of the most important of these techniques is the elaboration of socially integrating myths. These are efforts to state, in the language of uplift and idealism, what is distinctive about the aims and methods of the enterprise. Successful institutions are usually able to fill in the formula "What we are proud of around here is. . . ." Sometimes, a fairly explicit institutional philosophy is worked out; more often a sense of mission is communicated in more indirect but no less significant ways. The assignment of high prestige to certain activities will itself help to create a myth, especially if buttressed by occasional explicit statements. The specific ways of projecting a myth are as various as communication itself. For creative leadership, it is not the communication of a myth that counts; rather, creativity depends on having the will and the insight to see the necessity of the myth, to discover

a successful formulation, and above all to create the organizational conditions that will sustain the ideals expressed.

———

The mystique can sometimes overpower the rationality of actors subject to it. They begin unquestioningly to assume that whatever those higher in the organization do must be right. In *The Trial*, Kafka's guards, by their very trust in their superiors, explain how bureaucracies can generate weird evils.

> ". . . We are humble subordinates who can scarcely find our way through a legal document and have nothing to do with your case except to stand guard over you for ten hours a day and draw our pay for it. That's all we are, but we're quite capable of grasping the fact that the high authorities we serve, before they would order such an arrest as this, must be quite well informed about the reasons for the arrest and the person of the prisoner. There can be no mistake about that. Our officials, so far as I know them, and I know only the lowest grades among them, never go hunting for crime in the populace, but, as the Law decrees, are drawn toward the guilty and must then send out us warders. That is the Law. How could there be a mistake in that?" "I don't know this Law," said K. "All the worse for you," replied the warder. "And it probably exists nowhere but in your own head," said K.*

Another aspect of the bureaucratic environment on which Presthus does not remark should be noted in passing. Within complex organizations, there are compelling dynamics pressing participants toward a consensus and support of the group or organizational position. There are substantial latent sanctions to be directed against those who insist on pointing out the irrationality or reality-denying aspects of the group position. The comprehensiveness, the "totalistic" quality of the bureaucracy is such that deviant patterns of thinking become increasingly "unthinkable." Moreover, patterns of affection that are generated in many of the interactions in the bureaucracy raise the cost of disagreeing with what seems to be the group's consensus. The self-proclaimed rationality of the bureaucracy becomes self-evident and situational pressures on conformity limit the possibility of independent thinking and policy-correction. One consequence of this during the Vietnam War may have been patterns of reflexive, uncritical thinking at the elite level in the United States. This aspect of "groupthink" is discussed cogently by Professor Janis.

JANIS, GROUPTHINK, IN 2 SMALL GROUPS AND SOCIAL INTERACTION
39–44 (H.H. BLUMBERG, A.P. HARE, V. KENT & M. DAVIES EDS. 1983)**

One major source of defective decision making has been described in my analysis of fiascos resulting from foreign policy decisions made by presidential advisory groups. . . . I call attention to a *concurrence-seeking tendency* that occurs among moderately or highly cohesive groups. When this tendency is dominant, the members use their collective cognitive resources to develop rationalizations in line with shared illusions about the invulnerability of their organization or nation and display other symptoms of concurrence seeking (referred to as 'groupthink').

———

*F. Kafka, *The Trial* 6 (W. Muir trans. 1968).
**See also I. Janis, *Victims of Groupthink: A Psychological Study of Foreign Policy Decisions and Fiascos* (1972)

A number of historic fiascos appear to have been products of defective policy planning on the part of misguided government leaders who obtained social support from their ingroups of advisers. My analysis of case studies of historic fiascos suggests that the following groups of policy advisers were dominated by 'groupthink': (1) Neville Chamberlain's inner circle, whose members supported the policy of appeasement of Hitler during 1937 and 1938, despite repeated warnings and events indicating that it would have adverse consequences; (2) Admiral Kimmel's ingroup of Naval Commanders whose members failed to respond to warnings in the fall of 1941 that Pearl Harbor was in danger of being attacked by Japanese planes; (3) President Truman's advisory group, whose members supported the decision to escalate the war in North Korea despite firm warnings by the Chinese Government that United States entry into North Korea would be met with armed resistance from the Chinese; (4) President John F. Kennedy's advisory group, whose members supported the decision to launch the Bay of Pigs invasion of Cuba despite the availability of information indicating that it would be an unsuccessful venture and would damage public relations between the United States and other countries; (5) President Lyndon B. Johnson's 'Tuesday luncheon group,' whose members supported the decision to escalate the war in Vietnam despite intelligence reports and other information indicating that this course of action would not defeat the Viet Cong or the North Vietnamese and would entail unfavorable political consequences within the United States. In all these 'groupthink'—dominated groups, there were strong pressures toward uniformity, which inclined the members to avoid raising controversial issues, questioning weak arguments, or calling a halt to soft-headed thinking.

Other social psychologists . . . have noted similar symptoms of groupthink in the way Nixon and his inner circle handled the Watergate cover-up. Drawing on their work and my own detailed analyses of the unedited Nixon tapes, I have recently completed an additional case study of the Watergate cover-up and have used it to elaborate on the theory of concurrence seeking. . . .

Eight main symptoms of groupthink run through the case studies of historic decision-making fiascos. Each symptom can be identified by a variety of indicators, derived from historical records, observers' accounts of conversations, and participants' memoirs. The eight symptoms of groupthink are:

1. An illusion of invulnerability, shared by most or all the members, which creates excessive optimism and encourages taking extreme risks;
2. Collective efforts to rationalize in order to discount warnings which might lead the members to reconsider their assumptions before they recommit themselves to their past policy decisions;
3. An unquestioned belief in the group's inherent morality, inclining the members to ignore the ethical or moral consequences of their decisions;
4. Stereotyped views of rivals and enemies as too evil to warrant genuine attempts to negotiate, or as too weak and stupid to counter whatever risky attempts are made to defeat their purposes;
5. Direct pressures on any member who expresses strong arguments against any of the group's stereotypes, illusions, or commitments, making clear that this type of dissent is contrary to what is expected of all loyal members;
6. Self-censorship of deviations from the apparent group consensus, reflecting each member's inclination to minimize to himself the importance of his doubts and counterarguments;

7. A shared illusion of unanimity concerning judgments conforming to the majority view (partly resulting from self-censorship of deviations, augmented by the false assumption that silence means consent);

8. The emergence of self-appointed mindguards—members who protect the group from adverse information that might shatter their shared complacency about the effectiveness and morality of their decisions.

● ● ●

Janis and Mann have elaborated on the theory of concurrence seeking, or group-think, as a defective pattern of decision making. Their assumption is that the symp-toms of groupthink are behavioral consequences of a coping pattern of *defensive avoidance,* which is mutually supported by the group members. . . .

Not all cohesive groups suffer from groupthink, though all may display some of its symptoms from time to time. . . . A group whose members are highly competent and who have properly defined roles, with traditions and standard operating proce-dures that facilitate critical inquiry, is probably capable of making better decisions than any individual in the group who works on the problem alone. . . . And yet the advantages of having policy decisions made by groups are often lost because of psychological pressures that arise when the members work closely together, share the same values and, above all, face a crisis together in which everyone realizes at the outset that whatever action the group decides to take will be fraught with serious risks and that there is little hope for obtaining new information that will point to a satisfactory solution. In these circumstances, the leader and the members of his ingroup are subjected to stresses that, according to the groupthink hypothesis, generate a strong need for mutual social support.

As conformity pressures begin to dominate, according to Janis and Mann (1977), the striving for unanimity fosters the pattern of defensive avoidance, with charac-teristic lack of vigilance, unwarranted optimism, sloganistic thinking, and reliance on shared rationalizations that bolster the least objectionable alternative. That alter-native is often the one favored by the leader or other influential persons in the policy-making group on the basis of initial biases that remain uncorrected despite the availability of impressive evidence showing it to be inferior to other feasible courses of action.

● ● ●

I have reviewed the extensive literature on decision making and have extracted seven major criteria to use in judging whether a decision made by a person or group is of *high quality.* Such judgments pertain to the decision-making *procedures* that lead up to the act of commitment to a final choice. . . . As applied to policy-planning groups, the seven procedural criteria are as follows: The group (1) thoroughly can-vasses a wide range of policy alternatives; (2) takes account of the full range of objectives to be fulfilled and the values implicated by the choice; (3) carefully weighs whatever is found out about the costs or drawbacks and the uncertain risks of negative consequences, as well as the positive consequences, that could flow from each alternative; (4) intensively searches for new information relevant for further evaluation of the policy alternatives; (5) conscientiously takes account of any new information or expert judgment to which the members are exposed, even when the information or judgment does not support the course of action they initially prefer; (6) re-examines the positive and negative consequences of all known alternatives, including those originally regarded as unacceptable, before making a final choice; and (7) makes detailed recommendations or provisions for implementing and executing the chosen policy, with special attention to contingency plans that might be required if various known risks were to materialize.

NOTES

1. These criticisms notwithstanding, one cannot overlook the extraordinary amplification of power gained from coordinating the thinking and behavior of a vast number of people in a single enterprise. This has been fundamental to the rise of the industrial and scientific civilization of the West. Contemporary Japanese corporate life seems to have carried it a stage further with astonishingly effective results.

2. But should one assume that complex coordinations among vast numbers of people require the rigid hierarchicalization of the bureaucracy with its concomitant tendency toward suppression of dissent and alternative thinking? Recent experiments and studies indicate that in some complex organizations, it is possible to share both responsibility and decisionmaking competence at many levels, thereby increasing commitment and enthusiastic contribution to the organization and the ultimate product.

Bureaucracy is frequently presented as inherently antithetical to democracy and to systems of power sharing. But in the following selection, Blau and Meyer argue that bureaucracy and bureaucratic procedures may be *indispensable* to the maintenance of democracy, in large, complex organizations.

BLAU & MEYER,
BUREAUCRACY IN MODERN SOCIETY 164–67 (2d ed. 1971)

Bureaucracies endanger democratic freedoms, but at the same time they serve important functions in a democratic society that must not be ignored. Thus Weber points out that bureaucratic personnel policies—employment on the basis of technical qualifications—reduce the handicap of underprivileged groups in the competition for jobs. Blacks, for example, have a better chance of being hired when objective criteria rather than personal considerations govern the selection of candidates. Of course, the children of wealthier familes, who can more easily afford the education that qualifies them for the most desirable jobs, continue to have a distinct advantage over others. Bureaucratization does not produce complete equality of occupational opportunities. Nevertheless, the fact that it does minimize the direct effects of status privileges, such as noble birth or skin color, constitutes a democratizing influence.

• • •

. . . [T]he decisions of all enforcement agents should be governed by uniform standards and protected against being influenced by personal considerations. This is another way of saying that bureacratically organized enforcement agencies are necessary for all members of the society to be equal under the law.

Other contributions of bureaucracy have already been discussed. Democratic objectives would be impossible to attain in modern society without bureaucratic organizations to implement them. Thus, once the decision to provide free employment service to the public had been reached through democratic processes, a complex administrative system for this purpose had to be established. Furthermore, the high standard of living we enjoy today depends, in part, on the adoption of efficient bureaucratic methods of organization in private industry. . . . [On the other hand,] bureaucracies create profound inequalities of power. They enable a few individuals, those in control of bureaucratic machinery, to exercise much more influence than others in the society in general and on the government in particular.

The prevalence of bureaucracies in a society also undermines democracy in more subtle ways. . . . We generally no longer govern our voluntary associations: we simply join them, pay our dues, and let experts run them. As a result, we have less and less opportunities for acquiring experiences that are essential for effective participation in a democratic government.

. . . In a community the size of the United States, however, the individual's voice is lost, and only organized groups have the strength to make themselves heard. By joining democratic organizations and helping to decide their policies, people have a chance to exert some influence on the larger community. . . .

NOTES

1. The phenomenon of bureaucratic jurisprudence is part-and-parcel of substantial power changes that have occurred within the past century, some of which were mentioned briefly above. Loyalty is not an abstract concept but is a social relationship in which the loyal party pays fealty to a particular entity or person for many reasons, but in part because he expects protection and a variety of other value indulgences. For a time, the power of the state apparatus was unsurpassed within its territorial bounds. Claims for loyalty could be made with the implied promise that they would be repaid by an organization with the capacity to deliver. In liberal democracies, in the past fifty years, many other organizations have come to play the most important roles in peoples' lives. The corporation, whether in the United States, West Germany or Japan, is, for many, the agency which in fact will provide work, health care, educational opportunities, vacation and recreation, educational opportunities for children, retirement protection, even burial. In these circumstances, is it surprising that there is a subtle shift of loyalty from the apparatus and symbol system of the state to the apparatus and symbol system of the organization most critical to the life of the individual?

2. Liberal democracy is a system which encourages the formation of entities that coexist with the state apparatus and compete for the loyalties of individuals. Authoritarian and totalitarian systems permit no such organizations to flourish, precisely because they may compete with the loyalties demanded exclusively by the state apparatus and the elite that manages it. Thus, in a socialist system, even the church will enjoy only the most tenuous tolerance, and that conditional on its not becoming too effective. But in democratic systems, the technological revolution of communications provides greater opportunities for private groups to maintain constant communication with constituencies, further enhancing their capacity to rival the apparatus of the state.

3. The previous comments have focused on a ''system'' rather than the people composing it. There is a tendency at the present time to attribute asocial or unacceptable behavior not to individual personal defects or a certain mild weakness in the accused individual, but rather to blame it on the structure of society as a whole. In considering the John Dean case ask yourself—if you think Dean behaved improperly—whether the cause derived from the structure of a society and, in particular, the style of bureaucratic organization or from weaknesses in Dean's moral fiber. Did events like Watergate and a complex of cases not unlike the one described by Dean occur because there is something wrong with the way the United States is organized or because there is something wrong with a number of people who secured power at a particular time? In the case of the U.S. Air Force pilots over Vietnam, is there something wrong with the system or was there something deficient in their own way of looking at and reacting to events?

HANS KELSEN AND THE "PURE THEORY"

The jurisprudence of Hans Kelsen almost seems to have been designed for the bureaucratic universe. Kelsen's earliest work, done with Rudolf Stammler, developed some basic notions of administrative law in Europe. Thereafter Kensen, still quite a young scholar, refined his conceptions of jurisprudence. The theory he developed, often called the "pure theory", has been associated with the German philosopher Kant. But unlike Kant's philosophy, it would appear to be amoral and an-ethical, primarily concerned with understanding and providing guidelines for behavior in complex organizations. Consider the following excerpts.

KELSEN, GENERAL THEORY OF LAW AND STATE
xiii–xviii, 110–136, 175–177 (A. WEDBERG TRANS. 1945)

The theory which will be expounded in the main part of this book is a general theory of positive law. Positive law is always the law of a definite community: the law of the United States, the law of France, Mexican law, international law. To attain a scientific exposition of those particular legal orders constituting the corresponding legal communities is the design of the general theory of law here set forth. This theory, resulting from a comparative analysis of the different positive legal orders, furnishes the fundamental concepts by which the positive law of a definite legal community can be described. [The subject matter of a general theory of law is the legal norms, their elements, their interrelations, the legal order as a whole, its structure, the relationship between different legal orders, and, finally, the unity of the law in the plurality of positive legal orders.]

Since the aim of this general theory of law is to enable the jurist concerned with a particular legal order, the lawyer, the judge, the legislator, or the law-teacher, to understand and to describe as exactly as possible his own positive law, such a theory had to derive its concepts exclusively from the contents of positive legal norms. It must not be influenced by the motives or intentions of lawmaking authorities or by the wishes or interests of individuals with respect to the formation of the law to which they are subject, except in so far as these motives and intentions, these wishes and interests, are manifested in the material produced by the lawmaking process. What cannot be found in the contents of positive legal norms cannot enter a legal concept. The general theory, as it is presented in this book, is directed at a structural analysis of positive law rather than at a psychological or economic explanation of its conditions, or a moral or political evaluation of its ends.

When this doctrine is called the "pure theory of law," it is meant that it is being kept free from all the elements foreign to the scientific method of a science whose only purpose is the cognition of law, not its formation. A science has to describe its object as it actually is, not to prescribe how it should be or should not be from the point of view of some specific value judgments. The latter is a problem of politics, and, as such, concerns the art of government, an activity directed at values, not an object of science, directed by reality.

The reality, however, at which a science of law is directed, is not the reality of nature which constitutes the object of natural science. If it is necessary to separate the science of law from politics, it is no less necessary to separate it from natural science. One of the most difficult tasks of a general theory of law is that of determining the specific reality of its subject and of showing the difference which exists between legal and natural reality. The specific reality of the law does not manifest itself in the actual behavior of the individuals who are subject to the legal order. This behavior may or may not be in conformity with the order the existence of which is the reality in question. The legal order determines what the conduct of men ought to be. It is a system of norms, a normative order. The behavior of individuals as it actually is, is determined by laws of nature according to the principle of causality. This is natural reality. And in so far as sociology deals with this reality as determined by causal laws, sociology is a branch of natural science. Legal reality, the specific existence of the law, manifests itself in a phenomenon which is mostly designated as the positiveness of law. The specific subject of legal science is positive or real law in contradistinction to an ideal law, the goal of politics. Just as the actual behavior of the individuals may or may not correspond to the norms of positive law regulating this behavior, positive law may or may not correspond to an ideal law presented as justice or "natural" law. It is in its relation to the ideal law, called justice or "natural" law, that the reality of positive law appears. Its existence is independent of its conformity or nonconformity with justice or "natural" law.

The pure theory of law considers its subject not as a more or less imperfect copy of a transcendental idea. It does not try to comprehend the law as an offspring of justice, as the human child of a divine parent. The pure theory of law insists upon a clear distinction between empirical law and transcendental justice by excluding the latter from its specific concerns. It sees in the law not the manifestation of a super-human authority, but a specific social technique based on human experience; the pure theory refuses to be a metaphysics of law. Consequently it seeks the basis of law—that is, the reason of its validity—not in a meta-juristic principle but in a juristic hy-pothesis—that is, a basic norm, to be established by a logical analysis of actual juristic thinking.

Much traditional jurisprudence is characterized by a tendency to confuse the theory of positive law with political ideologies disguised either as metaphysical speculation about justice or as natural-law doctrine. It confounds the question of the essence of law—that is, the question of what the law actually is—with the question of what it should be. It is inclined more or less to identify law and justice. On the other hand, some theories of jurisprudence show a tendency to ignore the borderline separating a theory of legal norms regulating human behavior from a science causally explaining actual human behavior, a tendency resulting in confusing the question as to how men legally ought to behave with the question as to how men actually behave and how they probably will behave in the future. The latter question can be answered, if at all, only on the basis of a general sociology. To become merged in this science seems to be the ambition of modern jurisprudence. Only by separating the theory of law from a philosophy of justice as well as from sociology is it possible to establish a specific science of law.

The orientation of the pure theory of law is in principle the same as that of so-called analytical jurisprudence. Like John Austin in his famous *Lectures on Juris-prudence,* the pure theory of law seeks to attain its results exclusively by an analysis of positive law. Every assertion advanced by a science of law must be based on a positive legal order or on a comparison of the contents of several legal orders. It is by confining jurisprudence to a structural analysis of positive law that legal science is separated from philosophy of justice and sociology of law and that the purity of its method is attained. In this respect, there is no essential difference between ana-lytical jurisprudence and the pure theory of law. Where they differ, they do so because the pure theory of law tries to carry on the method of analytical jurisprudence more consistently than Austin and his followers. This is true especially as regards such fundamental concepts as that of the legal norm on the one hand, and those of the legal right and the legal duty on the other, in French and German jurisprudence presented as a contrast between law in an objective and law in a subjective sense; and, last but not least, as regards the relationship between law and the State.

Austin shares the traditional opinion according to which law and State are two different entities, although he does not go so far as most legal theorists who present the State as the creator of the law, as the power and moral authority behind the law, as the god of the world of law. The pure theory of law shows the true meaning of these figurative expressions. It shows that the State as a social order must necessarily be identical with the law or, at least, with a specific, a relatively centralized legal order, that is, the national legal order in contradistinction to the international, highly decentralized, legal order. Just as the pure theory of law eliminates the dualism of law and justice and the dualism of objective and subjective law, so it abolishes the dualism of law and State. By so doing it establishes a theory of the State as an intrinsic part of the theory of law and postulates a unity of national and international law within a legal system comprising all the positive legal orders.

The pure theory of law is a monistic theory. It shows that the State imagined as a personal being is, at best, nothing but the personification of the national legal order, and more frequently merely a hypostatization of certain moral-political postulates. By abolishing this dualism through dissolving the hypostatization usually connected with the ambiguous term ''State,'' the pure theory of law discloses the political ideologies within the traditional jurispurdence.

It is precisely by its anti-ideological character that the pure theory of law proves itself a true science of law. Science as cognition has always the immanent tendency to unveil its object. But political ideology veils reality either by transfiguring reality in order to conserve and defend it, or by disfiguring reality in order to attack, to destroy, or to replace it by another reality. Every political ideology has its root in volition, not in cognition; in the emotional, not in the rational, element of our consciousness; it arises from certain interests, or rather, from interests other than the interest in truth. This remark, of course, does not imply any assertion regarding the value of the other interests. There is no possibility of deciding rationally between opposite values. It is precisely from this situation that a really tragic conflict arises: the conflict between the fundamental principle of science, Truth, and the supreme ideal of politics, Justice.

The political authority creating the law and, therefore wishing to conserve it, may doubt whether a purely scientific desirable. Similarly, the forces tending to destroy the present order and to replace it by another one believed to be better will not have much use for such a cognition of law either. But a science of law cares neither for the one nor for the other. Such a science the pure theory of law wishes to be.

The postulate of complete separation of jurisprudence from politics cannot sincerely be questioned if there is to be anything like a science of law. Doubtful only is the degree to which the separation is realizable in this field. A marked difference does indeed exist in this very feature between natural and social science. Of course, no one would maintain that natural science runs no danger at all of attempts by political interests to influence it. History demonstrates the contrary, and shows clearly enough that a world power has sometimes felt itself threatened by the truth concerning the course of the stars. But the fact that in the past natural science had been able to achieve its complete independence from politics is due to the powerful social interest in this victory: the interest in that advance of technique which only a free science can guarantee. But social theory leads to no such direct advantage afforded by social technique as physics and chemistry produce on the acquisition of engineering knowledge and medical therapy. In social and especially in legal science, there is still no influence to counteract the overwhelming interest that those residing in power, as well as those craving for power, have in a theory pleasing to their wishes, that is, in a political ideology.

This is especially true in our time, which indeed "is out of joint," when the foundations of social life have been shaken to the depths by two World Wars. The ideal of an objective science of law and State, free from all political ideologies, has a better chance for recognition in a period of social equilibrium.

It seems, therefore, that a pure theory of law is untimely today, when in great and important countries, under the rule of party dictatorship, some of the most prominent representatives of jurisprudence know no higher task than to serve—with their "science"—the political power of the moment. If the author, nevertheless, ventures to publish this general theory of law and State, it is with the belief that in the Anglo-American world, where freedom of science continues to be respected and where political power is better stabilized than elsewhere, ideas are in greater esteem than power; and also with the hope that even on the European continent, after its liberation from political tyranny, the younger generation will be won over to the ideal of an independent science of law; for the fruit of such a science can never be lost.

•   •   •

A. The Unity of a Normative Order

A. THE REASON OF VALIDITY: THE BASIC NORM

The legal order is a system of norms. The question then arises: What is it that makes a system out of a multitude of norms? When does a norm belong to a certain system of norms, an order? This question is in close connection with the question as to the reason of validity of a norm.

In order to answer this question, we must first clarify the grounds on which we assign validity to a norm. When we assume the truth of a statement about reality, it is because the statement corresponds to reality, because our experience confirms it. The statement "A physical body expands when heated" is true, because we have repeatedly and without exception observed that physical bodies expand when they are heated. A norm is not a statement about reality and is therefore incapable of being "true" or "false," in the sense determined above. A norm is either valid or non-valid. Of the two statements: "You shall assist a fellowman in need," and "You shall lie whenever you find it useful," only the first, not the second, is considered to express a valid norm. What is the reason?

The reason for the validity of a norm is not, like the test of the truth of an "is" statement, its conformity to reality. As we have already stated, a norm is not valid because it is efficacious. The question why something ought to occur can never be answered by an assertion to the effect that something occurs, but only by an assertion that something ought to occur. In the language of daily life, it is true, we frequently justify a norm by referring to a fact. We say, for instance: "You shall not kill because God has forbidden it in one of the Ten Commandments"; or a mother says to her child: "You ought to go to school because your father has ordered it." However, in these statements the fact that God has issued a command or the fact that the father has ordered the child to do something is only apparently the reason for the validity of the norms in question. The true reason is norms tacitly presupposed because taken for granted. The reson for the validity of the norm, You shall not kill, is the general norm, You shall obey the commands of God. The reason for the validity of the norm, You ought to go to school, is the general norm, Children ought to obey their father. If these norms are not presupposed, the references to the facts concerned are not answers to the questions why we shall not kill, why the child ought to go to school. The fact that somebody commands something is, in itself, no reason for the statement that one ought to behave in conformity with the command, no reason for considering the command as a valid norm, no reason for the validity of the norm the contents of which corresponds to the command. The reason for the validity of a norm leads back not to reality, but to another norm from which the first norm is derivable in a sense that will be investigated later. Let us, for the present, discuss a concrete example. We accept the statement ''You shall assist a fellowman in need,'' as a valid norm because it follows from the statement, ''You shall obey the commandments of Christ.'' The statement ''You shall lie whenever you find it useful,'' we do not accept as a valid norm, because it is neither derivable from another valid norm nor is it in itself an ultimate, self-evidently valid norm.

A norm the validity of which cannot be derived from a superior norm we call a ''basic'' norm. All norms whose validity may be traced back to one and the same basic norm form a system of norms, or an order. This basic norm constitutes, as a common source, the bond between all the different norms of which an order consists. That a norm belongs to a certain system of norms, to a certain normative order, can be tested only by ascertaining that it derives its validity from the basic norm constituting the order. Whereas an ''is'' statement is true because it agrees with the reality of sensuous experience, an ''ought'' statement is a valid norm only if it belongs to such a valid system of norms, if it can be derived from a basic norm presupposed as valid. The ground of truth of an ''is'' statement is its conformity to the reality of our experience; the reason for the validity of a norm is a presupposition, a norm presupposed to be an ultimately valid, that is, a basic norm. The quest for the reason of validity of a norm is not—like the quest for the cause of an effect—a *regressus ad infinitum;* it is terminated by a highest norm which is the last reason of validity within the normative system, whereas a last or first cause has no place within a system of natural reality.

B. THE STATIC SYSTEM OF NORMS

According to the nature of the basic norm, we may distinguish between two different types of orders or normative systems; static and dynamic systems. Within an order of the first kind the norms are ''valid'' and that means, we assume that the individuals whose behavior is regulated by the norms ''ought'' to behave as the norms prescribe, by virtue of their contents: Their contents has an immediately evident quality that guarantees their validity, or, in other terms, the norms are valid because of their inherent appeal. This quality the norms have because they are derivable from a specific basic norm as the particular is derivable from the general. The binding force of the basic norm is itself self-evident, or at least presumed to be so. Such norms as ''You must not lie,'' ''You must not deceive,'' ''You shall keep your promise,'' follow from a general norm prescribing truthfulness. From the norm ''You shall love your neighbor,'' one may deduce such norms as ''You must not hurt your neighbor,'' ''You shall help him in need,'' and so on. If one asks why one has to love one's neighbor, perhaps the answer will be found in some still more general norm, let us say the postulate that one has to live ''in harmony with the universe.'' If that is the most general norm of whose validity we are convinced, we will consider it as the ultimate norm. Its obligatory nature may appear so obvious that one does not feel any need to ask for the reason of its validity. Perhaps one may also succeed in deducing the principle of truthfulness and its consequences from this ''harmony'' postulate. One would then have reached a norm on which a whole system of morality could be based. However, we are not interested here in the question of what specific norm lies at the basis of such and such a system of morality. It is essential only that the various norms of any such system are implicated by the basic norm as the particular is implied by the general, and that, therefore, all the particular norms of such a system are obtainable by means of an intellectual operations, viz., by the inference from the general to the particular. Such a system is of a static nature.

C. THE DYNAMIC SYSTEM OF NORMS

The derivation of a particular norm may, however, be carried out also in another way. A child, asking why it must not lie, might be given the answer that its father has forbidden it to lie. If the child should further ask why it had to obey its father, the reply would perhaps be that God has commanded that it obey its parents. Should the child put the question why one has to obey the commands of God, the only answer would be that this is a norm beyond which one cannot look for a more ultimate norm. That norm is the basic norm providing the foundation for a system of dynamic character. Its various norms cannot be obtained from the basic norm by an intellectual operation. The basic norm merely establishes a certain authority, which may well in turn vest norm-creating power in some other authorities. The norms of a dynamic system have to be created through acts of will by those individuals who have been authorized to create norms by some higher norm. This authorization is a delegation. Norm creating power is delegated from one authority to another authority; the former is the higher, the latter the lower authority. The basic norm of a dynamic system is the fundamental rule according to which the norms of the system are to be created. A norm forms part of a dynamic system if it has been created in a way that is—in the last analysis—determined by the basic norm. A norm thus belongs to the religious system just given by way of example if it is created by God or orginates in an authority having its power from God, ''delegated'' by God.

B. THE LAW AS A DYNAMIC SYSTEM OF NORMS

A. THE POSITIVITY OF LAW

The system of norms we call a legal order is a system of the dynamic kind. Legal norms are not valid because they themselves or the basic norm have a content the binding force of which is self-evident. They are not valid because of their inherent appeal. Legal norms may have any kind of content. There is no kind of human behavior that, because of its nature, could not be made into a legal duty corresponding to a legal right. The validity of a legal norm cannot be questioned on the ground that its contents are incompatible with some moral or political value. A norm is a valid legal norm by virtue of the fact that it has been created according to a definite rule and by virtue thereof only. The basic norm of a legal order is the postulated ultimate rule according to which the norms of this order are established and annulled, receive and lose their validity. The statement "Any man who manufactures or sells alcoholic liquors as beverages shall be punished" is a valid legal norm if it belongs to a certain legal order. This it does if this norm has been created in a definite way ultimately determined by the basic norm of that legal order, and if it has not again been nullified in a definite way, ultimately determined by the same basic norm. The basic norm may, for instance, be such that a norm belongs to the system provided that it has been decreed by the parliament or created by custom or established by the courts, and has not been abolished by a decision of the parliament or through custom or a contrary court practice. The statement mentioned above is no valid legal norm if it does not belong to a valid legal order—it may be that no such norm has been created in the way ultimately determined by the basic norm, or it may be that, although a norm has been created in that way, it has been repealed in a way ultimately determined by the basic norm.

Law is always positive law, and its positivity lies in the fact that it is created and annulled by acts of human beings, thus being independent of morality and similar norm systems. This constitutes the difference between positive law and natural law, which, like morality, is deduced from a presumably self-evident basic norm which is considered to be the expression of the "will of nature" or of "pure reason." The basic norm of a positive legal order is nothing but the fundamental rule according to which the various norms of the order are to be created. It qualifies a certain event as the initial event in the creation of the various legal norms. It is the starting point of a norm-creating process and, thus, has an entirely dynamic character. The particular norms of the legal order cannot be logically deduced from this basic norm, as can the norm "Help your neighbor when he needs your help" from the norm "Love your neighbor." They are to be created by a special act of will, not concluded from a premise by an intellectual operation.

B. CUSTOMARY AND STATUTORY LAW

Legal norms are created in many different ways: general norms through custom or legislation, individual norms through judicial and administrative acts or legal transactions. Law is always created by an act that deliberately aims at creating law, except in the cases when law has its origin in custom, that is to say, in a generally observed course of conduct, during which the acting individuals do not consciously aim at creating law; but they must regard their acts as in conformity with a binding norm and not as a matter of arbitrary choice. This is the requirement of so-called *opinio juris sive necessitatis*. The usual interpretation of this requirment is that the individuals constituting by their conduct the law-creating custom must regard their acts as determined by a legal rule; they must believe that they perform a legal duty or exercise a legal right. This doctrine is not correct. It implies that the individuals concerned must act in error: since the legal rule which is created by their conduct cannot yet determine this conduct, at least not at a legal rule. They may erroneously believe themselves to be bound by a rule of law, but this error is not necessary to constitute a law-creating custom. It is sufficient that the acting individuals consider themselves bound by any norm whatever.

We shall distinguish between statutory and customary law as the two fundamental types of law. By statutory law we shall understand law created in a way other than

by custom, namely, by legislative, judicial, or administrative acts or by legal transactions, especially by contracts and (international) treaties.

C. THE BASIC NORM OF A LEGAL ORDER

A. THE BASIC NORM AND THE CONSTITUTION

The derivation of the norms of a legal order from the basic norm of that order
is performed by showing that the particular norms have been created in accordance
with the basic norm. To the question why a certain act of coercion—e.g., the fact
that one individual deprives another individual of his freedom by putting him in
jail—is a legal act, the answer is: because it has been prescribed by an individual
norm, a judicial decision. To the question why this individual norm is valid as part
of a definite legal order, the answer is: because it has been created in conformity
with a criminal statute. This statute, finally, receives its validity from the constitution,
since it has been established by the competent organ in the way the constitution
prescribes.

If we ask why the constitution is valid, perhaps we come upon an older constitution. Ultimately we reach some constitution that is the first historically and that
was laid down by an individaul usurper or by some kind of assembly. The validity
of this first constitution is the last presupposition, the final postulate, upon which
the validity of all the norms of our legal order depends. It is postulated that one ought
to behave as the individual, or the individuals, who laid down the first constitution
have ordained. This is the basic norm of the legal order under consideration. The
document which embodies the first constitution is a real constitution, a binding norm,
only on the condition that the basic norm is presupposed to be valid. Only upon this
presupposition are the declarations of those to whom the constitution confers norm-
creating power binding norms. It is this presupposition that enables us to distinguish
between individuals who are legal authorities and other individuals whom we do not
regard as such, between acts of human beings which create legal norms and acts
which have no such effect. All these legal norms belong to one and the same legal
order because their validity can be traced back—directly or indirectly—to the first
constitution. That the first constitution is a binding legal norm is presupposed, and
the formulation of the presupposition is the basic norm of this legal order. The basic
norm of a religious norm system says that one ought to behave as God and the
authorities instituted by Him command. Similarly, the basic norm of a legal order
prescribes that one ought to behave as the "fathers" of the constitution and the
individuals—directly or indirectly—authorized (delegated) by the constitution command. Expressed in the form of a legal norm; coercive acts ought to be carried out
only under the conditions and in the way determined by the "fathers" of the constitution or the organs delegated by them. This is, schematically formulated, the
basic norm of the legal order of a single State, the basic norm of a national legal
order. It is to the national legal order that we have here limited our attention. Later,
we shall consider what bearing the assumption of an international law has upon the
question of the basic norm of national law.

B. THE SPECIFIC FUNCTION OF THE BASIC NORM

That a norm of the kind just mentioned is the basic norm of the national legal
order does not imply that it is impossible to go beyond that norm. Certainly one may

ask why one has to respect the first constitution as a binding norm. The answer might be that the fathers of the first constitution were empowered by God. The characteristic of so-called legal positivism is, however, that it dispenses with any such religious justification of the legal order. The ultimate hypothesis of positivism is the norm authorizing the historically first legislator. The whole function of this basic norm is to confer law-creating power on the act of the first legislator and on all the other acts based on the first act. To interpret these acts of human beings as legal acts and their products as binding norms, and that means to interpret the empirical material which presents itself as law as such, is possible only on the condition that the basic norm is only the necessary presupposition of any positivisitc interpretation of the legal material.

The basic norm is not created in a legal procedure by a law-creating organ. It is not as a positive legal norm is—valid because it is created in a certain way by a legal act, but it is valid because it is presupposed to be valid; and it is presupposed to be valid because without this presupposition no human act could be interpreted as a legal, especially as a norm-creating, act.

By formulating the basic norm, we do not introduce into the science of law any new method. We merely make explicit what all jurists, mostly unconsciously, assume when they consider positive law as a system of valid norms and not only as a complex of facts, and at the same time repudiate any natural law from which positive law would receive its validity. That the basic norm really exists in the juristic conscious-ness, is the result of a simple analysis of actual juristic statements. The basic norm is the answer to the question: how—and that means under what condition—are all these juristic statements concerning legal norms, legal duties, legal rights, and so on, possible?

C. THE PRINCIPLE OF LEGITIMACY

The validity of legal norms may be limited in time, and it is important to notice that the end as well as the beginning of this validity is determined only by the order to which they belong. They remain valid as long as they have not been invalidated in the way which the legal order itself determines. This is the principle of legitimacy.

This principle, however, holds only under certain conditions. It fails to hold in the case of a revolution, this word understood in the most general sense, so that it also covers the so-called *coup d'Etat*. A revolution, in this wide sense, occurs whenever the legal order of a community is nullified and replaced by a new order in an illegitimate way, that is in a way not prescribed by the first order itself. It is in this context irrelevant whether or not this replacement is affected through a violent uprising against those individuals who so far have been the "legitimate" organs competent to create and amend the legal order. It is equally irrelevant whether the replacement is effected through a movement emanating from the masss of the people, or through action from those in government positions. From a juristic point of view, the decisive criterion of a revolution is that the order in force is overthrown and replaced by a new order in a way which the former had not itself anticipated. Usually, the new men whom a revolution brings to power annul only the constitution and certain laws of paramount political significance, putting other norms in their place. A great part of the old legal order "remains" valid also within the frame of the new order. But the phrase "they remain valid," does not give an adequate description of the phenomenon. It is only the contents of these norms that remain the same, not the reason of their validity. They are no longer valid by virtue of having been created in the way the old constitution prescribed. That constitution is no longer in force; it is replaced by a new constitution which is not the result of a constitutional alteration of the former. If laws which were introduced under the old constitution "continue to be valid" under the new constitution, this is possible only because validity has expressly or tacitly been vested in them by the new constitution. The phenomenon is a case of reception (similar to the reception of Roman law). The new order "receives," i.e., adopts, norms from the old order; this means that the new order gives validity to (puts into force) norms which have the same content as norms of the old order. "Reception" is an abbreviated procedure of law-creation. The laws which, in the ordinary inaccurate parlance, continue to be valid are, from a juristic viewpoint, new laws whose import coincides with that of the old laws. They are not identical with the old laws, because the reason for their validity is different. The reason for their validity is the new, not the old, constitution, and between the two continuity holds neither from the point of view of the one nor from that of the other. Thus, it is never the constitution merely but always the entire legal order that is changed by a revolution.

This shows that all norms of the old order have been deprived of their validity by revolution and not according to the principle of legitimacy. And they have been so deprived not only *de facto* but also *de jure*. No jurist would maintain that even after a successful revolution the old constitution and the laws based thereupon remain in force, on the ground that they have not been nullified in a manner anticipated by the old order itself. Every jurist will presume that the old order—to which no political reality any longer corresponds—has ceased to be valid, and that all norms, which are valid within the new order, receive their validity exclusively from the new constitution. It follows that, from this juristic point of view, the norms of the old order can no longer be recognized as valid norms.

D. CHANGE OF THE BASIC NORM

It is just the phenomenon of revolution which clearly shows the significance of the basic norms. Suppose that a group of individuals attempt to seize power by force, in order to remove the legitimate government in a hitherto monarchic State, and to introduce a republican form of government. If they succeed, if the old order ceases, and the new order begins to be efficacious because the individuals whose behavior the new order regulates actually behave, by and large, in conformity with the new order, then the order is considered as a valid order. It is now according to this new order that the actual behavior of individuals is interpreted as legal or illegal. But this means that a new basic norm is presupposed. It is no longer the norm according to which the old monarchical constitution is valid, but a norm according to which the new republican constitution is valid, a norm endowing the revolutionary government with legal authority. If the revolutionaries fail, if the order they have tried to establish remains inefficacious, then, on the other hand, their undertaking is interpreted, not as a legal, a law-creating act, as the establishment of a constitution, but as an illegal act, as the crime of treason, and this according to the old monarchic constitution and its specific basic norm.

E. THE PRINCIPLE OF EFFECTIVENESS

If we attempt to make explicit the presupposition on which these juristic considerations rest, we find that the norms of the old order are regarded as devoid of validity because the old constitution and, therefore, the legal norms based on this constitution, the old legal order as a whole, has lost its efficacy; because the actual behavior of men does no longer conform to this old legal order. Every single norm loses its validity when the total legal order to which it belongs loses its efficacy as a whole. The efficacy of the entire legal order is a necessary condition for the validity of every single norm of the order. A *conditio sine qua non,* but not a *conditio per quam.* The efficacy of the total legal order is a condition, not the reason for the validity of its constituent norms. These norms are valid not because the total order is efficacious, but because they are created in a constitutional way. They are valid, however, only on the condition that the total order is efficacious; they cease to be valid, not only when they are annulled in a constitutional way, but also when the total order ceases to be efficacious. It cannot be maintained that, legally, men have to behave in conformity with a certain norm, if the total legal order, of which that norm is an integral part, has lost its efficacy. The principle of legitimacy is restricted by the principle of effectiveness.

• • •

The relation between validity and efficacy thus appears to be the following: A norm is a valid norm if (a) it has been created in a way provided for by the legal order to which it belongs, and (b) if it has not been annulled either in a way provided for by that legal order or by way of desuetudo or by the fact that the legal order as a whole has lost its efficacy.

• • •

D. THE STATIC AND THE DYNAMIC CONCEPT OF LAW

If one looks upon the legal order from the dynamic point of view, as it has been expounded here, it seems possible to define the concept of law in a way quite different from that in which we have tried to define it in this theory. It seesm especially possible to ignore the element of coercion in defining the concept of law.

It is a fact that the legislator can enact commandments without considering it necessary to attach criminal or civil sanction to their violation. If such norms are also called legal norms, it is because they were created by an authority which, according to the constitution, is competent to create law. They are law because they issue from a law-creating authority. According to this concept, law is anything that has come about in the way the constitution prescribes for the creation of law. This dynamic concept differs from the concept of law defined as a coercive norm. According to the dynamic concept, law is something created by a certain process, and everything created in this way is law. This dynamic concept, however, is only apparently a concept of law. It contains no answer to the question of what is the essence of law, what is the criterion by which law can be distinguished from other social norms. This dynamic concept furnishes an answer only to the question whether or not and why a certain norm belongs to a system of valid legal norms, forms a part of a certain legal order. And the answer is, a norm belongs to a certain legal order if it is created in accordance with a procedure prescribed by the constitution fundamental to this legal order.

It must, however, be noted that not only a norm, i.e., a command regulating human behavior, can be created in the way prescribed by the constitution for the creation of law. An important stage in the law-creating process is the procedure by which general norms are created, that is, the procedure of legislation. The constitution may organize this procedure of legislation in the following way: two corresponding resolutions of both houses of parliament, the consent of the chief of State, and publication in an official journal. This means that a specific form of law creation is established. It is then possible to clothe in this form any subject, for instance, a recognition of the merits of a statesman. The form of a law—a declaration voted by parliament, consented to the chief of State, published in the official journal—is chosen in order to give to a certain subject, here to the expression of the nation's gratitude, the character of a solemn act. The solemn recognition of the merits of a statesman is by no means a norm, even if it appears as the content of a legislative act, even if it has the form of a law. The law as the product of the legislative procedure, a statute in the formal sense of the term, is a document containing words, sentences; and that which is expressed by these sentences need not necessarily be a norm. As a matter of fact, many a law—in this formal sense of the term—contains not only legal norms, but also certain elements which are of no specific legal, i.e. normative, character, such as, purely theoretical views concerning certain matters, the motives of the legislator, political ideologies contained in references such as "justice" or "the will of God," etc., etc. All these are legally irrelevant contents of the statute, or, more generally, legally irrelevant products of the law-creating process. The law-creating process includes not only the process of legislation, but also the procedure of the judicial and administrative authorities. Even judgments of the courts very often contain legally irrelevant elements. If by the term "law" is meant something pertaining to a certain legal order, then law is anything which has been created according to the procedure prescribed by the constitution fundamental to this order. This does not mean, however, that everything which has been created according to this procedure is law in the sense of a legal norm. It is a legal norm only if it purports to regulate human behavior, and if it regulates human behavior by providing an act of coercion as sanction.

XI. THE HIERARCHY OF THE NORMS

A. THE SUPERIOR AND THE INFERIOR NORM

The analysis of law, which reveals the dynamic character of this normative system and the function of the basic norm, also exposes a further peculiarity of law: Law regulates its own creation inasmuch as one legal norm determines the way in which another norm is created, and also, to some extent, the contents of that norm. Since a legal norm is valid because it is created in a way determined by another legal norm, the latter is the reason of validity of the former. The relation between the norm regulating the creation of another norm and this other norm may be presented as a relationship of super- and sub-ordination, which is a spatial figure of speech. The norm determining the creation of another norm is the superior, the norm created according to this regulation, the inferior norm. The legal order, especially the legal order the personification of which is the State, is therefore not a system of norms coordinated to each others, standing, so to speak, side by side on the same level, but a hierarchy of different levels of norms. The unity of these norms is constituted by the fact that the creation of one norm—the lower one—is determined by another—the higher—the creation of which is determined by a still higher norm, and that this *regressus* is terminated by a highest, the basic norm which, being the supreme reason of validity of the whole legal order, constitutes its unity.

B. THE DIFFERENT STAGES OF THE LEGAL ORDER

A. THE CONSTITUTION

1. CONSTITUTION IN A MATERIAL AND A FORMAL SENSE; DETERMINATION OF THE CREATION OF GENERAL NORMS

The hierarchical structure of the legal order of a State is roughly as follows: Presupposing the basic norm, the constitution is the highest level within national law. The constitution is here understood, not in a formal, but in a material sense. The constitution in the formal sense is a certain solemn document, a set of legal norms that may be changed only under the observation of special prescriptions, the purpose of which it is to render the change of these norms more difficult. The constitution in the material sense consists of those rules which regulate the creation of the general legal norms, in particular the creation of statutes. The formal constitution, the solemn document called "constitution," usually contains also other norms, norms which are no part of the material constitution. But it is in order to safeguard the norms determining the organs and the procedure of legislation that a special solemn document is drafted and that the changing of its rules is made especially difficult. It is because of the material constitution that there is a special form for constitutional laws or a constitutional form. If there is a constitutional form, then constitutional laws must be distinguished from ordinary laws. The difference consists in that the creation, and that means enactment, amendment, annulment, of constitutional laws is more difficult than that of ordinary laws. There exists a special procedure, a special form for the creation of constitutional laws, different from the procedure for the creation of ordinary laws. Such a special form for constitutional laws, a constitutional form, or constitution in the formal sense of the term, is not indispensable, whereas the material constitution, that is to say norms regulating the creation of general norms and—in modern law—norms determining the organs and procedure of legislation, is an essential element of every legal order.

A constitution in the formal sense, especially provisions by which change of the constitution is made more difficult than the change of ordinary laws, is possible only if there is a written constitution, if the constitution has the character of statutory law. There are States, Great Britain for instance, which have no "written" and hence no formal constitution, no solemn document called "The Constitution." Here the (material) constitution has the character of customary law and therefore there exists no difference between constitutional and ordinary laws. The constitution in the material sense of the term may be a written or an unwritten law, may have the character of statutory or customary law. If, however, a specific form for constitutional law exists, any contents whatever may appear under this form. As a matter of fact, subject matters which for some reason or other are considered especially important are often regulated by constitutional instead of by ordinary laws. An example is the Eighteenth Amendment of the Constitution of the United States, the prohibition amendment, now repealed.

The material constitution may determine not only the organs and the procedure of legislation, but also, to some degree, the contents of future laws. The constitution can negatively determine that the laws must not have a certain content, e.g., that the parliament may not pass any status which restricts religious freedom. In this negative way, not only the contents of statutes but of all the other norms of the legal order, judicial and administrative decisions likewise, may be determined by the constitution. The constitution, however, can also positively prescribe a certain content of future statutes; it can, as does, for instance the Constitution of the United States of America, stipulate "that in all criminal prosecutions the accused shall enjoy the right to a speedy and public trial, by an impartial jury of the State and district wherein the crime shall have been committed, which district shall have been previously ascertained by law, etc. . . ." This provision of the constitution determines the contents of future laws concerning criminal procedure. The importance of such stipulations from the point of view of legal technique will be discussed in another context.

• • •

B. GENERAL NORMS ENACTED ON THE BASIS OF THE CONSTITUTION; STATUTES, CUSTOMARY LAW

The general norms established by way of legislation or custom form a level which comes next to the constitution in the hierarchy of law. These general norms are to be applied by the organs competent thereto, especially by the court, but also by the administrative authorities. The law-applying organs must be instituted according to the legal order, which likewise has to determine the procedure which those organs shall follow when applying law. Thus, the general norms of statutory or customary law have a two-fold function: (1) to determine the law-applying organs and the procedure to be observed by them and (2) to determine the judicial and administrative acts of these organs. The latter by their acts create individual norms, thereby applying the general norms to concrete cases.

C. SUBSTANTIVE AND ADJECTIVE LAW

To these two functions correspond the two kinds of law, which are commonly distinguished: material or substantive and formal or adjective law. Beside the substantive criminal law there is an adjective criminal law of criminal procedure, and the same is true also of civil law and administrative law. Part of procedural law, of course, are also those norms which constitute the law-applying organs. Thus two kinds of general norms are always involved in the application of law by an organ: (1) the formal norms which determine the creation of this organ and the procedure it has to follow, and (2) the material norms which determine the contents of its judicial or administrative act. When speaking of the "application" of law by courts and administrative organs, one usually thinks only of the second kind of norms; it is only the substantive civil, criminal, and administrative law applied by the organs one has in mind. But no application of norms of the second kind is possible without the application of norms of the first kind. The substantive civil, criminal, or administrative law cannot be applied in a concrete case without the adjective law regulating the civil, criminal, or administrative procedure being applied at the same time. The two kinds of norm are really inseparable. Only in their organic union do they form the law. Every complete or primary rule of law, as we have called it, contains both the formal and the material element. The (very much simplified) form of a rule of criminal law is: If a subject has committed a certain delict, then a certain organ (the court), especially on the motion of another organ (the public prosecutor), direct against the delinquent a certain sanction. As we shall show later, a more explicit statement of such a norm is: If the competent organ, that is the organ appointed in the way prescribed by the law, has established through a certain procedure prescribed by the law, that a subject has committed a delict, determined by the law, then a sanction prescribed by the law shall be directed against the delinquent. This formulation clearly exhibits the systematic relation between substantive and adjective law, between the determination of the delict and the sanction, on the one hand, and the determination of the organs and their procedure, on the other.

D. DETERMINATION OF THE LAW-APPLYING ORGANS BY GENERAL NORMS

The general norms created by legislation or custom bear essentially the same relation to their application through courts and administrative authorities as the constitution bears to the creation of these same general norms through legislation and custom. Both functions—judicial or administrative application of general norms, and the statutory or customary creation of general norms—are determined by norms of a higher level, formally and materially, with respect to the procedure and with respect to the contents of the function. The proportion, however, in which the formal and the material determination of both functions stand to one another, is different. The material constitution chiefly determines by what organs and through what procedure the general norms are to be created. Usually, it leaves the contents of these norms undetermined or, at least, it determines their contents in a negative way only. The general norms created by legislation or custom according to the constitution, especially the statutes, determine, however, not only the judicial and administrative organs and the judicial and administrative procedure but also the contents of the individual norms, the judicial decisions and administrative acts which are to be issued by the law-applying organs. In criminal law, for instance, usually a general norm very accurately determines the delict to which the courts, in a concrete case, have to attach a sanction, and accurately determines this sanction, too; so that the content of the judicial decision—which has to be issued in a concrete case—is predetermined to a great extent by a general norm. The degree of material determination may of course vary. The free discretion of the law-applying organ is sometimes greater, sometimes less. The courts are usually much more strictly bound by the substantive civil and criminal laws they have to apply than are the administrative authorities by the administrative statutes. This, however, is besides the point. Important is the fact that the constitution materially determines the general norms created or its basis to a far less extent than these norms materially determine the individual norms enacted by the judiciary and the administration. In the former case, the formal determination is predominant; in the latter case, formal and material determination balance one another.

• • •

F. THE "SOURCES" OF LAW

The customary and the statutory creation of law are often regarded as the two "sources" of law. In this context, by "law" one usually understands only the general norms, ignoring the individual norms which, however, as just as much part of law as are the general ones.

"Source" of law is a figurative and highly ambiguous expression. It is used not only to designate the above-mentioned methods of creating law, custom and legislation (the latter terms understood in its widest sense comprising also creation of law by judicial and administrative acts and legal transactions) but also to characterize the reason for the validity of law and especially the ultimate reason. The basic norm is then the "source" of law. But, in a wider sense, every legal norm is a "source" of that other norm, the creation of which it regulates, in determining the procedure of creation and the contents of the norm to be created. In this sense, any "superior" legal norm is the "source" of the "inferior" legal norm. Thus, the constitution is the "source" of statutes created on the basis of the constitution, a statute is the "source" of the judicial decision based thereon, the judicial decision is the "source" of the duty it imposes upon the party, and so on. The "source" of law is thus not, as the phrase might suggest, an entity different from and somehow existing independently from law; the "source" of law is always itself law: a "superior" legal norm in relation to an "inferior" legal norm, or the method of creating an (inferior) norm determined by a (superior) norm, and that means a specific content of law.

The expression "source of law" is finally used also in an entirely non-juristic sense. One thereby denotes all those ideas which actually influence the law-creating organs, for instance, moral norms, political principles, legal doctrines, the opinions of juristic experts, etc. In contradistinction to the previously mentioned "sources" of law, these "sources" do not as such have any binding force. They are not—as are the true "sources of law"—legal norms of a specific content of legal norms. It is, however, possible for the legal order, by obliging the law-creating organs to respect or apply certain moral norms of political principles or opinions of experts, to transform these norms, principles, or opinions into legal norms and thus into true sources of law.

The ambiguity of the term "source of law" seems to render the term rather useless. Instead of a misleading figurative phrase one ought to introduce an expression that clearly and directly describes the phenomenon one has in mind.

G. CREATION OF LAW AND APPLICATION OF LAW

1. MERELY RELATIVE DIFFERENCE BETWEEN LAW-CREATING AND LAW-APPLYING FUNCTION

The legal order is a system of general and individual norms connected with each other according to the principle that law regulates its own creation. Each norm of this order is created according to the provisions of another norm, and ultimately according to the provisions of the basic norm, constituting the unity of this system of norms, the legal order. A norm belongs to this legal order only because it has been created in conformity with the stipulations of another norm of the order. This *regressus* finally leads to the first constitution, the creation of which is determined by the presupposed basic norm. One may also say that a norm belongs to a certain legal order if it has been created by an organ of the community constituted by the order. The individual who creates the legal norm is an organ of the legal community because and insofar as his function is determined by a legal norm of the order constituting the legal community. The imputation of this function to the community is based on the norm determining the function. This explanation, however, does not add anything to the previous one. The statement "A norm belongs to a certain legal order because it is created by an organ of the legal community constituted by this order'' and the statement ''A norm belongs to a legal order because it is created according to the basic norm of this legal order'' assert one and the same thing.

A norm regulating the creation of another norm is ''applied'' in the creation of the other norm. Creation of law is always application of law. These two concepts are by no means, as the traditional theory presumes, absolute opposites. It is not quite correct to classify legal acts as law-creating and law-applying acts; for, setting aside two borderline cases of which we shall speak later, every act is, normally, at the same time a law-creating and a law-applying act. The creation of a legal norm is—normally—an application of the higher norm, regulating its creation, and the application of a higher norm is—normally—the creation of a lower norm determined by the higher norm. A judicial decision, e.g., is an act by which a general norm, a statute, is applied but at the same time an individual norm is created obligating one or both parties to the conflict. Legislation is creation of law, but taking into account the constitution, we find that it is also application of law. In any act of legislation, where the provisions of the constitution are observed, the constitution is applied. The making of the first constitution can likewise be considered as an application of the basic norm.

2. DETERMINATION OF THE LAW-CREATING FUNCTION

As pointed out, the creation of a legal norm can be determined in two different directions: the higher norm may determine: (1) the organ and the procedure by which a lower norm is to be created, and (2) the contents of the lower norm. Even if the higher norm determines only the organ, and that means the individual by which the lower norm has to be created, and that again means authorizes this organ to determine at his own discretion the procedure of creating the lower norm and the contents of this norm, the higher norm is ''applied'' in the creation of the lower norm. The higher norm must at least determine the organ by which the lower norm has to be created. For a norm the creation of which is not determined at all by another norm cannot belong to any legal order. The individual creating a norm cannot be considered the organ of a legal community, his norm-creating function cannot be imputed to the community, unless in performing the function he applies a norm of the legal order constituting the community. Every law-creating act must be a law-applying act, i.e., it must apply a norm preceding the act in order to be an act of the legal order of the community constituted by it. Therefore, the norm-creating function has to be conceived of as a norm-applying function even if only its personal element, the individual who has to create the lower norm, is determined by the higher norm. It is this higher norm determining the organ which is applied by every act of this organ.

That creation of law is at the same time application of law, is an immediate consequence of the fact that every law-creating act must be determined by the legal order. This determination may be of different degrees. It can never be so weak that the act cease to be an application of law. Nor can it be so strong that the act ceases to be a creation of law. As long as a norm is established through the act, it is a law-creating act, even if the function of the law-creating organ is in a high degree determined by the higher norm. This is the case when not only the organ and the law-creating procedure but also the contents of the norm to be created are determined by a higher norm. However, in this case, too, an act of law-creating exists. The question whether an act is creation or application of law is in fact quite independent of the question as to the degrees to which the acting organ is bound by the legal order. Only acts by which no norm is established may be merely application of law. Of such a nature is the execution of a sanction in a concrete case. This is one of the two borderline cases mentioned above. The other is the basic norm. It determines the creation of the first constitution; but being presupposed by juristic thinking, its presupposition is not itself determined by any higher norm and is therefore no application of law.

H. INDIVIDUAL NORMS CREATED ON THE BASIS OF GENERAL NORMS

1. THE JUDICIAL ACT AS CREATION OF AN INDIVIDUAL NORM

As an application of law traditional doctrine considers above all the judicial decision, the function of courts. When settling a dispute between two parties or when sentencing an accused person to a punishment, a court applies, it is true, a general norm of statutory or customary law. But simultaneously the court creates an individual norm providing that a definite sanction shall be executed against a definite individual. This individual norm is related to the general norms as a statute is related to the constitution. The judicial function is thus, like legislation, both creation and application of law. The judicial function is ordinarily determined by the general norm both as to procedure and as to the contents of the norm to be created, whereas legislation is usually determined by the constitution only in the former respect. But that is a difference in degree only.

2. THE JUDICIAL ACT AS A STAGE OF THE LAW-CREATING PROCESS

From a dynamic standpoint, the individual norm created by the judicial decision is a stage in a process beginning with the establishment of the first constitution, continued by legislation and custom, and leading to the judicial decisions. The process is completed by the execution of the individual sanction. Statutes and customary laws are, so to speak, only semi-manufactured products which are finished only through the judicial decision and its execution. The process through which law constantly creates itself anew goes from the general and abstract to the individual and concrete. It is a process of steadily increasing individualization and concretization.

The general norm which, to certain abstractly determined conditions, attaches certain abstractly determined consequences, has to be individualized and concretized in order to come in contact with social life, to be applied to reality. To this purpose, in a given case it has to be ascertained whether the conditions, determined *in abstracto* in the general norm, are present *in concreto,* in order that the sanction, determined *in abstracto* in the general norm, may be ordered and executed *in concreto.* These are the two essential elements of the judicial function. This function has, by no means, as is sometimes assumed, a purely declaratory character. Contrary to what is sometimes asserted, the court does not merely formulate already existing law. It does not only "seek" and "find" the law existing previous to its decision, it does not merely pronounce the law which exists ready and finished prior to its pronouncement. Both in establishing the presence of the conditions and in stipulating the sanction, the judicial decision has a constitutive character. The decision applies, it is true, a preexisting general norm in which a certain consequence is attached to certain conditions. But the existence of the concrete conditions in connection with the concrete consequence is, in the concrete case, first established by the court's decision. Conditions and consequences are connected by judicial decisions in the realm of the concrete, as they are connected by statutes and rules of customary law in the realm of the abstract. The individual norm of the judicial decision is the necessary individualization and concretization of the general and abstract norm. Only the prejudice, characteristic of the jurisprudence of continental Europe, that law is, by definition, only general norms, only the erroneous identification of law with the general rules of statutory and customary law could obscure the fact that the judicial decision continues the law-creating process from the sphere of the general and abstract into that of the individual and concrete.

3. THE ASCERTAINMENT OF THE CONDITIONING FACTS

The judicial decision is clearly constitutive as far as it orders a concrete sanction to be executed against an individual delinquent. But it has a constitutive character also, as far as it ascertains the fact conditioning the sanction. In the world of law, there is no fact "in itself," no "absolute" fact, there are only facts ascertained by a competent organ in a procedure prescribed by law. When attaching to certain facts certain consequences, the legal order must also designate an organ that has to ascertain the facts in the concrete case and prescribe the procedure which the organ, in so doing, has to observe. The legal order may authorize this organ to regulate its procedure at its own discretion; but organ and procedure by which the conditioning facts are to be ascertained must be—directly or indirectly—determined by the legal order, to make the latter applicable to social life. It is a typical layman's opinion that there are absolute, immediately evident facts. Only by being first ascertained through a legal procedure are facts brought into the sphere of law or do they, so to speak, come into existence within this sphere. Formulating this in a somewhat paradoxically pointed way, we could say that the competent organ ascertaining the conditioning facts legally "creates" these facts. Therefore, the function of ascertaining facts through a legal procedure has always a specifically constitutive character. If, according to a legal norm, a sanction has to be executed against a murderer, this does not mean that the fact of murder is "in itself" the condition of the sanction. There is no fact "in itself" that A has killed B, there's only my or somebody else's belief or knowledge that A has killed B. A himself may either acquiesce or deny. From the point of view of law, however, all these are not more than private opinions without relevance. If the judicial decision has already obtained the force of law, if it has become impossible to replace this decision by another becauses there exists the status of *res judicata*—which means that the case has been definitely decided by a court of last resort—then the opinion that the condemned was innocent is without any legal significance. As already pointed out, the correct formulation of the rule of law is not "If a subject has committed a delict, an organ shall direct a sanction against the delinquent," but "If the competent organ has established in due order that a subject has committed a delict, then an organ shall direct a sanction against this subject."

•   •   •

L. SOCIOLOGICAL JURISPRUDENCE PRESUPPOSES THE NORMATIVE CONCEPT OF LAW

A. DIFFERENCE BETWEEN THE LEGAL AND THE ILLEGAL ACT

The value of a description of positive law in sociological terms is further diminished by the fact that sociology can define the phenomenon of law, the positive law of a particular community, only by having recourse to the concept of law as defined by normative jurisprudence. Sociological jurisprudence presupposes this concept. The object of sociological jurisprudence is not valid norms—which form the object of normative jurisprudence—but human behavior. What human behavior? Only such human behavior as is, somehow or other, related to "law." What distinguishes such behavior, sociologically, from behavior which falls outside the field of the sociology of law? An example may serve to illuminate the problem. Somebody receives a notice from the taxation authorities, requesting him to pay an income tax of $10,000, in default whereof a punishment is threatened. The same day, the same person receives a notice from the head of a notorious gang requesting him to deposit $10,000 in a designated place, failing which he will be killed, and a third letter in which a friend asks for a large contribution toward his support. In what respect does the taxation notice differ, sociologically, from the blackmail letter, and both from the letter of the friend? It is obvious that there exists three different phenomena, not only from a juristic, but also from a sociological point of view, and that at least the friend's letter with its effect on the receiver's behavior is not a phenomenon which falls within the field of a sociology of law.

B. MAX WEBER'S DEFINITION OF SOCIOLOGY OF LAW

The most successful attempt so far to define the object of a sociology of law has been made by Max Weber. He writes: "When we are concerned with 'law,' 'legal order', 'rule of law', we must strictly observe the distinction between a juristic and a sociological point of view. Jurisprudence asks for the ideally valid legal norms. That is to say . . . what normative meaning shall be attached to a sentence pretending to represent a legal norm. Sociology investigates what is actually happening in a society because there is a certain chance that its members believe in the validity of an order and adapt [orientieren] their behavior to this order." Hence, according to this definition, the object of a sociology of law is human behavior which the acting individual has adapted (oreintiert) to an order because he considers that order to be "valid"; and that means, that the individual whose behavior forms the object of sociology of law considers the order in the same way as normative jurisprudence consider the law. In order to be the object of a sociology of law, the human behavior must be determined by the idea of a valid order.

C. LEGAL AND DE FACTO AUTHORITY

From the point of view of normative jurisprudence, the order to pay taxes differs from the gangster's threat and the request made by the friend by the fact that only the tax order is issued by an individual who is authorized by a legal order assumed to be valid. From the standpoint of Max Weber's sociological jurisprudence, the difference is that the individual who receives the notice to pay his tax interprets this notice in such a way. He pays the tax considering the command to pay it as an act issued by an individual authorized by an order which the taxpayer considers to be valid. Outwardly, he may act in an identical manner with respect to the notice from the taxation authorities, the threat from the gangster band, and the letter from his friend. He may, for instance, pay the required amount in all three cases. From a juristic point of view, there is, however; still a difference. The one payment is fulfillment of a legal obligation, the others are not. From a sociological point of view, a difference between the three cases can be maintained only by considering the juristic concept of law as it is, in fact, present in the minds of the individuals involved. Sociologically, the decisive difference between the three cases is the fact that the behavior of the taxpayer is determined—or at least accompanied—by the idea of a valid order, of norm, duty, authority, whereas his behavior in the other cases is not determined or accompanied by such an idea. If the behavior in case of the gangster threat is at all the object of a sociology of law, it is because it represents a crime, legally determined as blackmail. The third case doubtless fails outside the field of a sociology of law, because the human behavior in question has no relation to the legal order as a system of norms.

Llewellyn explains that, from the point of view of a sociology of law, "authority does not refer to an efflux of a 'normative system' but to the basic situation which exists when Jones says 'Go' and Smith goes, as distinct from that in which Smith does not go; and the drive of *de facto* authority of this sort to provide itself with felt rightness or rightfulness is regarded, again, as a behavior drive observable among men-in-groups." The "rightness or rightfulness" can be nothing but an idea which accompanies the behavior of Jones and Smith. This idea, too, is "observable." For observable is not only the external but also the internal behavior of individuals, their ideas and feelings which accompany their external behavior. The psychologist observes only the internal behavior, and sociology is, to a great extent, social psychology. Ideas are psychic acts which are distinguishable by their contents. The individuals living within the State have an idea of law in their minds, and this idea is—as a matter of fact—the idea of a body of valid norms, the idea of a normative system. Some of their actions are characterized by the fact that they are caused or accompanied by ideas the contents of which is the law as a normative system. Sociological jurisprudence cannot describe the difference existing between the behavior of Smith in case he considers Jones to be a gangster, without referring to the contents of certain ideas which accompany the behavior of Smith. The difference of his behavior in the two senses consists essentially in the difference which exists between the contents of the ideas accompanying Smith's behavior. In the one case, Smith interprets the command issued by Jones as the act of an authority authorized by the normative system of positive law, in the other cases he interprets Jones' command according to the normative system of positive law as a crime. In the third case, he does not refer Jones' request to the legal order at all. It is exactly by these different interpretations—in the mind of Smith—that his behavior is sociologically different in the three cases. A sociology cannot describe the difference between the first two cases without referring to law as a body of valid norms, as a normative system. For law exists as such a body of valid norms in the minds of individuals, and the idea of a law causes or accompanies their behavior, which is the object of a sociology of law. The sociology of law can eliminate the third case from its special field only because there is no relation between Smith's behavior and the law.

Sociology of law, as described by Max Weber, is possible only by referring the human behavior which is its object to the law as it exists in the mind of men as contents of their ideas. In men's minds, law exists, as a matter of fact, as a body of valid norms, as a normative system. Only by referring the human behavior to law as a system of valid norms, to law as defined by normative jurisprudence, is sociological jurisprudence able to delimit its specific object from that of general sociology; only by this reference is it possible to distinguish sociologically between the phenomenon of legal and the phenomenon of illegal behavior, between the State and a gang of racketeers.

NOTES

1. Compare Kelsen's and Austin's conceptions of the legal status of judge-made law and of customary law. What accounts for the difference between them?

2. In our discussison of positivism in the preceding chapter, we noted the attraction it has held at different times for permanent minorities, those who view a rigidly applied neutral law as an artifact that can protect them from the potentially tyrannical moral views of a majority. Kelsen's conception of jurisprudence presents a certain parallel to this. One must bear in mind that Kelsen's work was rooted in the Astro-Hungarian empire, a complex of many different and discrete ethnic and language groups, each with its own authority dynamic and its own exclusive moral code. Within this reticulate network, the attraction (to lawyer and official) of a "pure" conception of law whose character as such had nothing to do with content, but was characterized only by the power to back up its rules, is obvious; it opens the way for compromise by suspending the operation of group myth, religion, racial doctrine, etc. Do you think this strategem can work? Explain.

3. Some followers of Kelsen assumed that his basic norm or *grundnorm* actually exists in every system. It was "hypothesized" and scholars would then try to track back to it. But if the *grundnorm* does exist, heavy responsibilities lie on all those at lower levels of authority. Before they comply with a particular order, they too would be obliged to check back to ascertain whether the superior giving that order had himself been properly authorized and whether his order itself was within the limits of his mandate and not as *excès de pouvoir*. Of course, in the complex bureaucracies we are considering here, such an investigation would be impractical if not impossible. Joseph Heller writes sardonically:

> . . . ."Who do you work for? My superiors. Do you have any authority? Oh yes. A great deal. Over who? My subordinates. I can do whatever I want once I get permission from my superiors. I'm my own boss. After all, I'm not really my own boss." J. Heller, *Good as Gold* 124 (1979).

In real circumstances, the most one can expect is a rather quick check as to the superior position of the person issuing the order. If he "checks out," you comply.

It is now clear that Kelsen never took the basic norm or *grundnorm* as something real or even hypothesized but only as a fiction. In a lecture delivered in Austria in 1964*, Kelsen made it quite clear that the basic norm or *grundnorm* was merely hypothesized and hence it was not to be traced empirically to determine whether it exists. Insofar as this view is accepted, there is no need for the person receiving an order to determine the appropriateness of the authority.

4. Recall *Presthus'* observation that oligarchy (rule by an elite) is a nearly universal feature of bureaucratic organizations. Can the United States too, be viewed as one large (or even a composite of a number of) bureaucratic organization(s) ruled largely by elites, with decisions made and controlled by higher-ups along the lines outlined by Kelsen?

5. Kelsen, it would appear, had an extraordinary insight into the reality of complex bureaucracy and seems to have designed a jurisprudence appropriate to it. In keeping with this, Kelsen quite explicitly disavows any moral mission or dimension or concern for social

*Republished in 2 *Osterreichischen Juristentages Verhandlungen* Part VII, at 65 and 71 (1964).

consequences. They are appropriate considerations for other disciplinary orders but not for law. Recall, in this regard, the observation in the preceding chapter about the effect that law has in shaping popular moral notions. Is the distinction Kelsen seeks to draw cogent?

6. Kelsen's conception of the origin of authority and indeed the origin of law can be contrasted with a number of the writers considered earlier. For natural law writers, the ultimate authority for law and the ultimate source of obedience is some transempirical or supernatural source. For the religious person, for example, one starts with an obligation to obey God; one obeys the king because the king rules by the grace of God and with divine authority. For a positivist such as Austin one obeys because of the naked power at the disposal of the political superior. Law is an exercise of naked power and its chief characteristic is that the deviation from the norm would occasion a sanction or "evils" in Austin's terms. Kelsen may be contrasted with both of these approaches. He reacts sharply to the natural law tradition and, as his writings in other areas show, to the historicist source of authority as well. He is a positivist in that in his conception, law is a secular creation. But Kelsen is unlike Austin who examined authority's origin in naked power and unlike Jefferson who finds the root of authority in the consent of those subjected to it. Kelsen held that, in a system of norms which was viewed as binding, there must be a norm holding that one ought to comply with other norms and that that norm constitutes the basis of authority. You may incline to view this as a classic "cop-out" but its very existential approach and the curious way that it resonates with the reality of contemporary bureaucratic organization makes it an extraordinarily effective doctrine, enhancing organizational continuity.

7. Lon Fuller felt that the differences between Kelsen and Austin are "largely those of emphasis and expression rather than of substance." L. Fuller, *The Problems of Jurisprudence* 105 (1949). There are, indeed, may apparent similarities in theory shared by Austin, Hart, who places himself in Austin's School, and Kelsen: a conception of law as rules and a consequent focus and emphasis upon rules; a view of law as an autonomous essence; a separation between the "is" and the "ought" and between law and morals etc. But there are some important differences between their theories and their implications.

(a) Hart views the ordinary man as a prime mover and a key element in the legal system. Attitudes of people (without considering the adequacy of Hart's empirical investigation of them), the so-called "internal view" of the law are crucial to the existence of a legal system. For Kelsen, on the other hand, the ordinary man often seems to be a little more than a cog in the machinery of the legal system. His attitudes, even his actions, only rarely affect the validity or existence of a legal system. Kelsen's emphasis is on officials.

(b) For Kelsen, the primary form of law is a norm authorizing the imposition of sanctions by those in authority for specified acts or delicts. Secondarily, the norm imposed a duty regarding behavior for the ordinary person. For Hart, law primarily sets out what ordinary persons are required to do or refrain from doing. Only secondarily are there norms for officials to impose sanctions.

(c) Hart regards a legal system as requiring the existence of secondary rules, particularly, a "rule of recognition." For Kelsen, a norm is valid law if it derives ultimately from a *grundnorm*. Is this compatible with Hart's "rule of recognition"?

(d) Hart, accepting a separation of law and morals, believes that there is a "rational connexion between 'natural facts' and the content of legal and moral rules." Law may, moreover, take account of public notions of morality. Kelsen's "Pure Law" eschews any predicate of facts or values for the validity or existence of law.

(e) Hart explicitly stated that one had the right on moral grounds to disobey an immoral but valid law. Kelsen regarded moral issues as extralegal, beyond the pale of legal consideration. Many have taken Kelsen's view as implying that one ought to obey a "valid" law, especially since, in the eyes of many persons, "valid" laws often import that one is "morally" obligated to obey them and, if necessary, to disregard the moral issues involved. Hence, Kelsen's theory can be employed as a technique of bureaucratic survival in the face of orders from those higher up.

(f) In terms of comparative method, Hart seems to place greater emphasis and importance than Kelsen on the analysis of the implications and precise meanings of terms and language employed in norms or in language talking about law.

8. Many of the apparent similarities between the view of Kelsen and Hart are derived from totally different premises:

(a) Both seek to limit individual choice and exercise of discretion by officials. Hart (and Austin) arrive at this goal because of an intense concern with order and a decided preference for decision conforming to precedent. The exercise of wide individual discretion by decision-makers stirs fears and threatens stability of expectations. For Kelsen, however, limitation on individual discretion flows from the view that each person, whether in the hierarchical line of state officials or a member of the public, is bound by valid norms and decisions from superiors in the hierarchy.

(b) It has been suggestsed that the Positivist's (particularly Austin's) focus on rules and obedience to superior orders derives in part from a psychologial predilection to submit to external authority. Hans Kelsen, on the other hand, indicates that he has an emotional preference for the ideal of peace (achieved by obedience and avoidance of strife) over that of justice (See his Die Idee des Naturrechtes, 7 *Zeitschrift für Offentliche Recht* 221, 248 (1928); cf. Fuller, *Problems of Jurisprudence* 110 (1949). This is based in part on his belief that order (and peace), unlike justice, are attainable ideals.

(c) Both Hart and Kelsen ignore the policy content of authoritative decisions and the relations between the perspectives and actions of all persons which affect the process and outcome of authoritative decision. In Kelsen, this may stem in part from reluctance to assume the responsibility of choice. In Hart, does it flow to some extent from satisfaction with the status quo?

9. Compare Kelsen's strict unilinear hierarchy of norms and Hart's exclusive focus on norms and decisions of state officials, particularly courts, on the one hand, with Pospisil's theory of interpenetrating and simultaneous systems of law, including unofficial and informal systems, on the other.

Which do you think provides a more accurate framework for inquiry? Which is more useful for performing decision tasks?

10. Consider Judge Hardy Dillard's observation:

> To ask, however tentatively, 'what *are* rules?' is unwittingly to endow them with a kind of reality or existence even a metaphysical existence, which is illusory. Rules of law do not 'exist' in the sense in which a tree or a stone or the planet Mars might be said to exist. True, they may be articulated and put on paper and in that form they exist, but, whatever their form, they are expressed in words which are merely signs mediating human subjectives. They represent and arouse expectations which are capable of being explored scientifically. The 'law' is thus not a 'something' impelling obedience; it is a constantly evolving process of decision making and the way it evolves will depend on the knowledge and insights of the decision makers. So viewed, norms of law should be considered less as compulsive commands than as tools of thought or instruments of analysis. Their impelling quality will vary greatly depending on the context of application, and, since the need for stability is recognized, the norms may frequently provide for a high order of predictability. But this is referable back to the expectations entertained and is not attributable to some existential quality attaching to the norms themselves. In other words, our concept of 'law' needs to be liberated from the cramping, assumption that it 'exists' as a kind of 'entity' imposing restraints on the decision makers. The Policy-Oriented Approach to Law, 40 *Va.Q. Rev.* 626, 629 (1964).

Discuss.

11. Are the foci of attention of Hart and Kelsen too restricted? Both seem to focus on hierarchical sources and formulation of norms, and on derivational logic applied to legislation and court decisions. They consistently ignore authoritative and controlling decisions by those

who do not fit into the formal hierarchical mold of superiors and inferiors or who do not occupy official positions in the state.

For what purposes, is it sufficient to concentrate on written norms, court decisions, or even decisions not reflected in public verbal pronouncements without considering whether these decisions can be carried out in practice?

12. Are the verbal pronouncements of courts and legislatures reliable indicators of future decisions? Consider, for example, the New Deal cases (p. 308) or *Brown v. Board of Education* (p. 489) in which decisions were made contrary to past precedent, without decisionmakers stating that the rules or the "law" had changed, or that social conditions had undergone extensive transformation. Is a view of law as a collection of static rules, rather than an ongoing decision process, appropriate for a changing world?

13. For Austin, the command of a political superior is law even if there is only the smallest chance that a sanction will be applied to enforce it. Force for him is a logical postulate, not an empirically referential term. Kelsen and Hart have tended to follow Austin's lead in this respect and largely to ignore actual distributions of effective power.

One commentator had defended Kelsen's failure to deal with social realities by claiming, "Kelsen disclaims any pretension of dealing with 'sociological' phenomena; his theory is not an attempt to describe how men actually behave in matters having to do with law and government. Rather it is an attempt to analyze the notions that are necessarily contained in a point of view that is commonly taken toward law. . . . Thus interpreted the philosophy of positive law is analyzing not an external reality of the physical world, but an internal reality of men's thinking . . .''. L. Fuller, *Problems of Jurisprudence* 112 (1949. Discuss.

14. Of what relevance, if any, is the positivist frame of jurisprudence for resolving basic problems facing contemporary communities? Does it consider effects of decisions on all values? Does it consider decisionmaking by non-official persons or groups and decisions other than verbal formulations by courts or legislative bodies?

Recall the tasks required to resolve problems: clarification of goals, study of past trends, analysis of existing conditions, projections as to what conditions are likely to be in the relevant future, and invention of strategies necessary to achieve the desired social results. Are any of these tasks aided by the positivist mode of thought? Discuss. Would you agree that Positivism is essentially "an exercise in applied semantics"? (L. Fuller, *The Problems of Jurisprudence* 113 (1949).

15. Kelsen's theory that a new *grundnorm* comes into effect with a successful revolution, has been cited by courts in Pakistan, Rhodesia, and Uganda to justify the recognition by the courts of new governments that come into power by coups. (*State v. Dosso* (1958)) 2 Pakistan S.C.R. 180 at 185, 195; *Uganda v. Commissioner of Prisons, ex parte Matovu* (1966) E.A. 514 at 535.

In the wake of the unilateral declaration of independence of the white minority government in Rhodesia (now known as Zimbabwe), the British government continued to insist that *it* was the proper authority in Rhodesia; the independent white government, however, insisted that *it* was the only authority. In the well-known case of *Madzimambuto v. Burke-Lardner*, courts relied on Kelsen's theory to support the break-away government in both Rhodesia and in the House of Lords. 39 *Int'l L. Rep.* 61 (1970). Recall *Tinocco* in Chapter 3. Is Kelsen's jurisprudence essentially a theory of naked power?

LEGAL ETHICS AND BUREAUCRATIC JURISPRUDENCE

Whatever the origins of the bureaucratic style of organization, it has become one of the basic techniques of organizing human beings in our civilization. For everyone who lives in its shadow, it becomes a fact of life one takes account of in virtually every decision. The bureaucratic organization thus becomes a particularly problematic phenomenon when it is examined in the light of the lawyer's role, a specialized social role with its own ethical responsibilities.* Recall the case of John Dean at the beginning of the chapter. To whom was Dean required to pay loyalty? Is the lawyer operating in a large corporation responsible to the community at large in his capacity as an officer of the court, is he responsible to the corporation as a whole, or is he responsible to particular superiors who may have hired him and whose decisions will probably determine his general career opportunities?

The problems we are considering may be examined by reference to two contrasting examples.

A. Because of a perceived disparity between the defense capability of the United States and its major political adversary, a decision has been taken to resume atmospheric nuclear testing. As lawyer and a member of the task force considering this, you are privy to information showing that the resumption of testing is likely to lead to increased Strontium 90 in the air and increased leukemia among children between the ages three to ten. Congress has passed general legislation prohibiting governmental activities likely to cause environmental deterioration. However you are under a variety of administrative regulations which prohibit you from expressing this information publicly. For what it is worth, you assume that the United States does indeed require the testing lest its security position be seriously jeopardized.

B. Imagine, now, that you are counsel to a large corporation. The corporation, which is going through a difficult economic phase, has the option of either closing down and as a result laying off several thousand employees, causing a small depression in the entire region in which it operates or of producing a line of items which in all likelihood will have long-term negative environmental effects and possibly negative effects on a certain statistically as yet undetermined number of workers in the plant. If the company produces the product, it is likely that it will survive and may then be in a position to suspend these operations in a better economic time. If it does not, it is clear that it will fail.

What would you do in each of the two cases hypothesized? Is your answer any different because in one you are working for the government directly and in the other for a private organization? If so, why?

How would you respond to a request from your client in comparable circumstances? Do you think that the original lawyer for *The New York Times* in the case discussed below behaved properly and professionally?

Consider the comments of Abe Krash.

KRASH, PROFESSIONAL RESPONSIBILITY TO CLIENTS AND THE PUBLIC INTEREST: IS THERE A CONFLICT?, 55 CHI. B. REC. 31 (SPECIAL CENTENNIAL ISSUE, 1974)

. . . . I insist upon the proposition that lawyers best serve the public interest when they faithfully and competently represent the private interests of their clients. This is not to say that lawyers—individually and as a group—do not have responsibilities to the social welfare. I most certainly believe the bar does have such obligations—especially to improve the administration of justice. But in an adversary system which proclaims the right of everyone to counsel, a lawyer's paramount responsibility is to his client.

• • •

*In some ways analogous to the role of the lawyer in this respect is the role of the physician, especially the psychiatrist, the accountant and virtually any other professional who is certified and one of whose functions involves providing authoritative services to the public at large.

The traditional point of view on the lawyer's obligations to his client is reflected in a recently published biography of John W. Davis. As his biographer points outs, Davis adhered "absolutely to the principle that the lawyer's duty was to represent his client's interests to the limit of the law, [and] not to moralize on the social and economic implications of the client's lawful action." Subject to certain qualifications, which I shall indicate, I too subscribe to that position.

During the past decade, however, that philosophy of legal practice has been sharply challenged by a number of parties . . . Lawyers, it was said, have devoted their talents to aiding corporations who degrade the environment, who advertise and distribute products hazardous to consumers, and who monopolize the economy. "The problem with the legal profession today, [it was claimed] contrary to the current fashion, is not Watergate lawyers, but lawyers."

•   •   •

My first thesis is that the "public interest," unless it is defined more precisely, is a concept too nebulous—it is too ambiguous a standard—to serve as a basis for any practical action or judgment regarding a lawyer's professional conduct.

What is the "public interest" to which lawyers allegedly owe a duty? Who decides what the "public interest" is? What is the scope of these obligations to society's welfare? And what are the consequences if a lawyer does not discharge this responsibility?

. . . . [A] recent book on the Wall Street bar entitled Lions In the Street . . . illustrates some of the extremely subtle and complex factors which are involved.

For many years, the outside General Counsel for the New York Times was an old and distinguished New York law firm. In 1971, the editors of The Times informed their General Counsel that they had obtained possession of secret documents involving America's involvement in Vietnam—the Pentagon papers—and the editors asked counsel for an opinion as to whether the materials could be published. Counsel reportedly advised The Times that if they published the documents before they were declassified there was a risk of criminal prosecution. The law firm reportedly advised the editors not to publish on the grounds, among others, that it would be contrary to the "public interest" to do so. The Times editors determined to publish notwithstanding this advice. When the Department of Justice notified The Times that it would seek a preliminary injunction to restrain further publications, the law firm informed The Times that the firm could not represent the newspaper. The Times was represented by other counsel in the litigation which followed. The rest, of course, is history.

•   •   •

This incident raises a number of important questions. Was counsel's personal view of the "public interest" a relevant factor in his advice? Or was it the responsibility of counsel to state only the legal consequences which would flow from publication, and, to paraphrase John W. Davis, not to moralize about the implications of printing the secret documents? Let it be assumed that counsel's view had been that the public interest called for publication of the documents. Should that opinion have influenced his advice? Anyone who has every given advice in a matter in which his personal feelings are deeply engaged knows how difficult it is to detach his private views from his professional advice. But that is the responsibility of a legal adviser. Lawyers are not precluded from expressing their personal views to their clients of what the public interest requires, but counsel do have the responsibility, candidly and meticulously, to segregate that aspect of their advice. It seems to me that they have the duty to state to their clients: "I will give you my personal view of the public interest if you are interested in knowing it." I may add that I distinguish such an expression of personal views from advice to a client concerning the probable public repercussions or reaction to particular conduct—obviously such advice may be of the utmost relevance and importance.

• • •

The criticism of lawyers based on the theory that their clients are engaged in conduct which some people feel is pernicious to society's welfare seems to me both wrong and dangerous. . . . But no one who practiced in Washington in the early 1950's, as I did, will ever forget the dreadful problems in finding lawyers willing and able to help them faced by government employees who were driven from their jobs on loyalty and security charges.

• • •

My second thesis is that an individual lawyer, as a general rule is privileged to accept or reject the representation of a particular client on the basis of counsel's personal predilections or his views of the public interest. However, once a lawyer has agreed to represent a party, he has a duty, to the best of his ability to advocate a position, if his client's interest so requires, which counsel may personally regard as contrary to the public interest.

• • •

. . . [T]he idea that a lawyer will represent, with all of his dedication, those persons with whose views he may profoundly disagree, seems to me basic to our system.

It has been suggested that a distinction should be made between acting as an advocate for a client with respect to past conduct and advising a client as to his future conduct.

• • •

In practice, it is extremely difficult to apply this distinction. Many firms represesnt clients as a General Counsel, defending their clients' past conduct and rendering advice as to future transactions. Moreover, as The New York Times case makes clear, it may be exceedingly difficult in a situation involving proposed conduct to assert with confidence that the public interest requires one thing but not another. To take another example: Assume that an opinion is requested of counsel concerning the legality of a proposed merger under the antitrust laws. If the client determines to proceed with the transaction notwithstanding counsel's opinion that the merger is likely to be adjudged illegal, the lawyer who rendered the opinion is certainly not disabled from representing the client in the event the merger is challenged. A competent adviser would, of course, point out to his client that not all that is legal is wise; and that short term profits may lead to long-term difficulties. Moreover, I suspect that most lawyers feel freer than the lawyers of a generation ago to point out to a client the public policy implications of a proposed course of conduct. However, I remain of the view that the ultimate policy decision must be made by the client. Further, I am of the view that the solution to this problem is not to impose on counsel the burden of representing interests other than those of his client, but rather to take appropriate steps to insure that all interests are effectively represented.

NOTES

1. Dr. Johnson, in a remark lawyers often cite, said, "You do not know it to be good or bad till the judge determines it. . . . An argument which does not convince yourself may convince the judge to whom you urge it. . . ." What does the notion of "good or bad" or right or wrong mean in this selection?

2. Krash argues similarly that given the difficulty of determining what the public interest will be held to by some authoritative decisionmakers, the lawyer retained by someone should make no effort whatsoever to determine that beforehand, but should simply take the case and develop the best argument he or she can for the client. Do you think that the Krash position is adequate? Why? Why not?

―――――――

In contrast with Krash's laissez-faire approach, Mark Green, in the following selection, insists that the lawyer does have an affirmative obligation to determine the compatability of a client's interest with the public interest.* Moreover, Green suggests that lawyers *can* determine what the public interest is.

GREEN, THE OTHER GOVERNMENT 270–288 (1975)

. . . .[A]lthough most lawyers assume themselves to be in "private practice," they are, in fact, members of a public profession.

•   •   •

This public status entails a scale of obligations. . . . [T]he Code of Professional Responsibility says that "when an action in the best interest of his client seems to him to be unjust, he may ask his client for permission to forgo such action." ABA Formal Opinion Number 155 prohibits a lawyer from aiding or tolerating the "commission of an unlawful act, even if received in confidence. . . . He should, if unable to get the client to cease the conduct, make such disclosures as may be necessary to protect those against whom the conduct is threatening or working illegal harm." Thus, a lawyer can restrain, refuse, or even disclose a client's activities if sufficiently harmful.

The Code imposes more affirmative obligations yet on its adherents. It states that "a lawyer should assist in improving the legal system," and that "in assisting his client to reach a proper decision, it is often desirable for a lawyer to point out those factors which may lead to a decision that is usually just as well legally permissible." Federal judge Charles Wyzanski has elaborated this obligation. "The modern lawyer almost invariably advises his client upon not only what is permissible, but also what is desirable, he wrote. "And it is in the public interest that the lawyer should regard himself as more than a predictor of legal consequences. His social duty to society as well as to his client involves many relevant social, economic and philosophical considerations."

[But one may argue] *It is up to the adversary system, not the lawyer, to uncover the truth*. This is largely true where the adversary system exists. But what of where it doesn't?

The adversary process is more the exception than the rule in Washington. At the agencies . . . corporate lawyers "descend like locusts," whereas opposing consumer lawyers make only an occasional appearance.

*See, however, Model Rules off Professional Conduct adopted in August, 1983, sec. 1.6 and 1.13 infra.

In Congress, the absence of any formal adversary system is obvious. Thousands of corporate lobbyists, often lawyers, patrol Capitol Hill corridors to watch out for hostile legislation.

• • •

Who can say what the "public interest" really is? There is some merit in this question.

• • •

But that line-drawing is difficult does not mean that no line can ever be drawn. Otherwise, scrambling into the safety hatch of "who can say," lawyers would cease to function as independent professionals.

• • •

It is guilt by association to tar a lawyer with the views of his client. Thus, when the ACLU defends Nazis or Communists from unconstitutional infringements, it is wrong to perceive the lawyer as endorsing his clients' policies; rather, he is upholding constitutional safeguards due any citizen.

Yet this contrasts with a corporate lawyer who on a continuing basis advises his client not merely on constitutional safeguards but also on policy matters. As Lloyd Cutler has written, the Washington lawyer "is not limited, as in the courts, to defending what has already occurred. He has the opportunity of advising his client what ought to be done—how best to accommodate its practical problems to the emerging demands of the public interest." What if the client ignores its lawyer's counsel, or what if the lawyer advises not what ought to be done but what the client can get away with? It seems illogical to criticize say, a corporate polluter but not the Washington lawyer whose perennial strategies may *permit* the pollution.

Does Green in fact suggest criteria and procedures for determining the public interest? In the *Dean* case, the *Nuclear Testing* case and the *Corporate Violation of Law* case, is the public interest clear? If not, how does one determine public interest?

A slightly different approach to the problem, closer to that espoused by Krash than Green, is offered by Dam.

DAM, THE SPECIAL RESPONSIBILITY OF
LAWYERS IN THE EXECUTIVE BRANCH,
55 CHI B. REC. 4 (SPECIAL CENTENNIAL ISSUE, 1974)

Let us assume that a lawyer employed in the Executive Branch of the Federal Government learns that a fellow employee has committed a Federal crime. Does this lawyer have a duty to report the crime and, if so, to whom? And under what statute or ethical code provision would he have such a duty? There are, of course, crimes and crimes. For example, some crimes are no doubt rarely enforced standards of some long departed legislature that was struggling with conditions that no longer exist. To avoid transgressions, I shall assume that the crime in question is serious and would normally be enforced by the competent authorities if the illegal acts were known.

• • •

Although I shall limit myself to this single situation, the answer—or at least the analysis of the problem—may turn on several subsidiary facts. Let us therefore distinguish the case of the lawyer working *qua* lawyer from the case of the lawyer as policy maker or administrator. As we all know, many of the top policy officials in Government are lawyers by profession. This has always been true, and all that has changed is that we are no longer so proud of it. So we shall want to know not only whether the lawyer who takes such a job remains subject to the ethical standards of the practicing bar, but also whether the attorney-client privilege is relevant to his duty to report crimes.

• • •

But perhaps he has been guilty of misprision of felony. . . .

Misprision of felony remains in the common-law category in England and many states, but the United States Code does contain a misprision provision. Under this statute, "whoever, having knowledge of the actual commission of a felony cognizable by a court of the United States, conceals and does not as soon as possible make known the same to some judge or other person in civil or military authority under the United States" has himself thereby committed a felony. The few decisions that we do have, most of quite recent vintage, emphasize that concealment and disclosure are two separate requirements and that the concealment must involve an affirmative act.

• • •

A positive duty to disclose can be found in Section 535 of Title 28. Where criminal violations involving Government officers and employees are involved, there is such a duty. But let us examine that duty closely: "Any information, allegation, or complaint received in a department of agency of the executive branch of the government relating to violations of Title 18 involving Government officers and employees *shall* be expeditiously reported *to the Attorney General by the head of the department or agency.*" Let us note several things about this provision. First, it is not itself a criminal statute and hence a failure to report is not itself an offense. Second, the duty to report to the Attorney General lies with the "head of the department or agency." Nothing in this provision imposes any duty on subordinates of the agency head to report to him. And even if there were an independent duty to report to the agency head, the design of the statute indicates that the subordinate has thereby absolved himself and the decision of the agency head to take the matter no further would in no way require the subordinate himself to seek out the Attorney General.

• • •

. . . [Could an employee of the White House Office be required to report a crime to his superior?] A 1958 Concurrent Resolution, which Civil Service Commission regulations require each employee to become acquainted with, provides that "[a]ny person in the Government service should . . . [e]xpose corruption wherever discovered." Quite aside from the fact that as a concurrent resolution it was not signed by the President and hence cannot be regarded as having the force of law, the legislative history itself states that it "creates no new law; imposes no penalties; identifies no new type of crime; and establishes no legal restraints on anyone."

From the statutes and judicial decisions reviewed thus far, it is difficult though not impossible to conclude that the Government lawyer has a duty to report a crime if he merely learns of it and takes no affirmative action to conceal the crime.

• • •

. . . [T]he ABA's Code of Professional Responsibility . . . is designed primarily with the private practitioner and the private client in mind. Nevertheless, a member of the bar working in the Government, whether as lawyer or otherwise, is still a member of the bar and an officer of the court. As such, he not only may not ''[e]ngage in illegal conduct involving moral turpitude'' but he is also forbidden to ''[e]ngage in conduct involving dishonesty, fraud, deceit, or misrepresentation.'' While these are worthy standards, they suggest that failure to report a crime, which surely by itself falls short of fraud, deceit and the like, would not be misconduct justifying disciplinary action. Indeed, if criminal activity is a ground for disciplinary action only when it involves ''moral turpitude,'' then surely the mere failure to report a crime is not punishable. Nor can one easily derive a specific duty to report a crime from the general injunction not to ''[e]ngage in conduct that is prejudicial to the administration of justice.'' Of course, where concealment is added to silence, this latter standard becomes directly in point but then, as we have seen, the criminal law itself becomes operable.

The Code of Professional Responsibility does contain in Canon 8 special rules for the ''lawyer who holds public office'' but these rules have to do more with conflict of interest than with our problem.

. . . .[A]n ethics opinion adopted in November by the National Council of the Federal Bar Association . . . left open the case not only of the policy or administrative official but more specifically the case of most of the lawyers who were implicated in Watergate matters. Nonetheless, the Committee did draw an important distinction between ''willful or knowing disregard of or breach of law'' and ''conduct . . . about which the lawyer may hold a firm position as to its illegality but which he nevertheless recognizes is in an area subject to reasonable differences of professional opinion as to its legality.'' If I am correct in believing that a substantial portion of the activities lumped together under the general heading of ''Watergate'' fall in the latter category, then this distinction is crucial. With respect to this latter category the Federal Bar Ethics Committee concluded:

> Ordinarily there is no need for disclosure of such conduct beyond the personnel of the agency where it arises. Differences of opinion as to the legality of action are often unavoidable in the process of arriving at a course of action to be recommended or adopted. The lawyer may not deem the decision reached or the action taken to be legally sound, but in the situation in which the question arises it may not be misconduct at all.

In an extended discussion of this point, the Committee went on to point out that the lawyer's duty of confidentiality to those who confide in him would vary with the subject matter and, specifically, the duty of confidentiality would be greater where ''national security or the conduct of foreign affairs'' were involved.

The Committee concluded that ''disclosure beyond the confines of the agency or other law enforcing or disciplinary authorities of the Government is *warranted* only in the case when the lawyer as a reasonable and prudent man, conscious of his professional obligation of care, confidentiality and responsibility, concludes that these authorities have without good cause failed in the performance of their own obligation to take remedial measures required in the public interest.''

This conclusion underlines a curious yet instructive point about the Committee decision. Throughout the opinion the issue is whether the Government lawyers *may* disclose, not whether he *must* disclose. Even where an agency employee had engaged in corrupt conduct and there was no doubt in the lawyer's mind that the conduct was illegal, the committee was simply concerned to say that there were no circumstances where the criminal conduct could not be reported outside the agency.

What these formulations mean to me is that any rule *requiring* disclosure of all crimes would go well beyond the general ethical understanding and professional expectation of Government lawyers as a class. On the question of the expectations of lawyers, it is worth noting that four of the nine members of the Ethics Committee were judges, and that the opinion was unanimous.

• • •

. . . [O]ur Government lawyer, particularly of the second category, will often find himself consulted by agency employees about bureaucratic issues, about personal legal problems, about Congressional relations, and about a host of other issues that he cannot easily duck and still pretend he is doing his job, but which create grave questions as to who the client is the moment that any admission of criminal activity comes into the conversation. What is the lawyer to do? Terminate the conversation at the first inkling of what is coming and thereby lose an opportunity to serve the public interest by cleaning up an unwholesome situation? Is he to warn the consulting employee that he shall have to report whatever is admitted? Or is he to mislead the consulting employee, who after all is consulting one whom he knows to be a lawyer, by remaining silent and then in effect become the prosecutor against him by reporting the crime? In a special interpretation of Canon 4 of the Code of Professional Responsibility, the Federal Bar Association has established as a Federal Ethical Consideration (rather than as a disciplinary rule) the following rule for this situation: "[T]he lawyer should inform the employee that a federal lawyer is responsible to the department or agency concerned and not the individual employee and, therefore, the information is not privileged."

• • •

. . . [T]he lawyer who holds a policy-making position rather than a legal position . . . will sometimes be consulted on legal issues. It seems to me that his position is in fact not much different from that of my second and third lawyers. It may, however, be expedient to treat him differently and deny the attorney-client privilege. But also how is he to be treated? Like a layman and therefore subject only to the criminal laws and not to bar disciplinary procedures? Or are we to hold him, since he is a member of the bar, to the same standards as a Government lawyer to whom the privilege would be available? More generally, the attorney-client privilege aside, what are to be the standards applicable to the lawyer, member of the bar, officer of the court, who assumes policy-making responsibilities? Is he to be treated in the political quagmire of Washington to a higher standard than his collegues who come from other professions? Granted that a crime involving moral turpitude is ground for disbarment, is he to be disbarred for non-criminal conduct which does not meet the high *ex post* standards of his state bar?

One easy answer is, of course, that if he doesn't like it, let him resign from the bar upon entering Government service. This is a logically correct conclusion, but one which could turn out to rob the Government of much of its best and most ethical talent. I have pointed to the great tradition of this country of members of the bar entering the Government for limited periods; surely we should not make Government an even more hazardous occupation than it inevitably is.

NOTES

1. On a moral scale of 1–10, appraise the approaches sketched by Krash, Green and Dam. Which of them do you think is most likely to lead to a set of practices conducive to high ethical behavior in government? Which is most convenient for the practicing bar?

2. Take the theories developed by Dam and apply them to the dilemma posed to John Dean at the beginning of the chapter. On the basis of Dam's analysis, how would you advise Dean were he to have consulted you?

3. The problem of multiple and incompatible loyalties is, if anything, exacerbated when the corporation in question is a multinational. In those circumstances, its employees are loyal to the company but may have little or no loyalty to a host state in which they happen to be stationed for several years, because they understand that their career prospects rest with the company. Draft a memorandum for senior executives in such a company, providing appropriate guidelines for their behavior.

————————

Those who feel that some burden of private decision is incumbent on the lawyer faced with the dilemma of the general counsel for the *New York Times* must develop some criteria and some procedures for making those choices in actual contexts. One effort at this problem takes as its starting point the question of determining the lawfulness of paying a bribe in a particular context in which there are a number of legal systems, some of which would appear to authorize the bribe while others prohibit it.

REISMAN, FOLDED LIES 128–131 (1979)

THE RELEVANCE OF EVALUATIVE CRITERIA

Few people would gainsay the proposition that it is appropriate to bribe when (1) the official policy being subverted is one that is deemed grossly immoral and (2) the object of the bribe is to secure a result that is generally deemed to be moral or right and, for practical purposes, otherwise unattainable. One would have to be a pathological positivist to assume that Bertolt Brecht's bribe tendered to an immigration official in order to escape the Nazis during the Third Reich was wrong. Though certain moral philosophers might insist that any act of disobedience ought to be public if it is to be deemed to be moral, this seems both impractical and unrealistic. In the more ruthless of our modern autocracies that prescription virtually assures that dissent will be a once-in-a-lifetime event. Irrational demands for publicity may derive from deep superstitions about the ultimate authority or sovereignty of the state or ruling elite. For people who believe that, whatever the merits, the state is ultimately right, it is quite plain that tolerated acts of civil disobedience should be followed either by voluntary exposure to personal dangers or by the initiation of acts inviting or assuring self-destruction. Socrates, for example, took on the state and, having made his point, participated in his own destruction; Socrates is not unlike the young Japanese who strikes a superior and then commits hara-kiri.

Evaluation presupposes criteria. Do you accept the idea that it is right to evade the incidence of a norm that requires immoral behavior or whose application would lead to consequences that are morally repugnant? Is it right to subvert a system that is basically "wrong"? If you accept such propositions, you must face the broader question of the content of the "higher," or, at least, other, code that justifies "illegal" acts. The important point here is that assessments of when it is appropriate to bribe will always be based upon a "higher," often unstated, code of preferences from which the state official who is the target of the bribe is allegedly deviating. From the standpoint of the moralist or his latter-day incarnation, the policy scientist, any attempt to develop a systematic code for evaluating the lawfulness of bribery must clarify a broader, transcending code of behavior against which the official behavior that is the target of subversion can be treated. Let us call this larger test one of general goal clarification.

In circumstances in which the briber is animated by natural law doctrines or by belief in supernatural laws reliably communicated by a divinity, goals and code are ready-made. There are tactical, but few moral, problems. A comparable function is implicitly performed by a highly ethnicized environment in which it is taken for granted that loyalty and substantially moral behavior are owed only to members of the family, tribe, race, dialect group, or sex group—whatever the unit of identification may be. In aristocracies, in which there are significant cleavages between rulers and the ruled, the notion of primary loyalty to one's class simplifies the act of lying and bribing on behalf of the class; the act may, however, be just as complex when engaged in for other purposes. The operational code of the elite in popular democracies is less clear-cut, as we have seen, for "vertical identifications," that is, identifications between ruler and ruled, may be more significant influences on behavior.

Where loyalties are clearly owed to your own state, bribing officials of another state on its behalf may expose you to personal dangers, but it is not wrong or unlawful under the terms of the effective loyalty system. The same "exemption" may apply with regard to bribes on behalf of one's corporation, though here bribers may encounter more internal dissonance, for apparently that social formation has yet to achieve a status fully comparable to the state's.

In command systems, what one's superior orders is, by definition, right; at the very least, responsibility for the rightness or wrongness of the command is his alone. "We know enough," say the soldiers in *Henry V*, "if we know we are the king's subjects. If his cause be wrong, our obedience to the king wipes the crime of it out of us." For command systems in modern bureaucracies, staffed by less assured moralists, Hans Kelsen developed a more involved jurisprudential version. It essentially held that in the bureaucratic context, the only pertinent legal course was the command of a properly authorized superior.

Some elites justify bribery, as we have seen, by shifting to a technological rather than logical derivation of authorization. The bribe, though a violation of part of the formal code, is actually necessary to fulfill the larger objectives of the entire normative code. Here and in circumstances in which the briber operates from more secure perspectives, the challenge is the creation or postulation of a set of principles or preferences that identify ultimate group or individual purposes and would warrant defections from the formal code when they are necessary to achieve these higher ends.

Instances of bribery that at first glance seem lawful or appropriate in their particular context are often deemed so because they effectuate a normative or loyalty system to which the observer is most committed. In highly ethnicized environments such as India, parts of Africa, the Middle East, or in any place or sector where the nation-state remains only an incipient social organization, the most intense loyalties relate to extended family, tribe, ethnic, or dialect group. For actors in such a system, nepotism imports laudable loyalty and not opprobrium. Individual members of a particular loyalty group (for example, the tribe) will view as lawful bribes paid to government officials to secure the application of tribal norms rather than discrepant national norms. What we encounter here are normative prescriptions more intensely demanded than the formal law. Individuals on the scene should, under the terms of *their* normative code, apply that code's pertinent norms, even though application might violate the formal law; but they cannot be applied because of the total political situation. The bribe vindicates people's deeper loyalties and the preferred normative system.

COMMUNITY EVALUATION

In examples such as these, the notion of morality is that of the moral syntax of particular group members and not necessarily the code that an outsider or someone committed to a larger or more inclusive community would deploy to evaluate the propriety of particular bribes or of bribery in general. Within a particular legal viewpoint, bribery may be condemned absolutely, but it is more likely that the lawfulness of particular bribes will be evaluated, as we have mentioned earlier, in context: who bribed whom, how, where, for how much, for what purpose, with what result, and with what consequences flowing from refusal to pay the bribe. Even those who condemn bribery are likely to find that variations in the answers to some of these questions will influence their conclusions about lawfulness or, indirectly but equivalently, the severity of the sanction that they demand. In multiple code situations, whether or not a particular event is right or lawful depends on your legal viewpoint. But are there inclusive viewpoints with more transcending and durable standards by which anyone can recognize the violence and deceit of a bribe?

Crusaders and reformers usually insist that such standards exist. But many students of bribery question such faith. . . .

NOTES

1. Considering the procedures suggested by Reisman, recall the discussison in Chapter 4 and, in particular, the notion of obedience to the state. In Chapter 3, you will recall, proponents of naked power suggested that one should focus on the holders of real power and completely ignore the dictates of the apparatus of the state. To what extent are those views relevant and cogent in this discussion?

2. Krash's contention may be influenced by the difficulty of gaining adequate information about the options available, not to speak of determining the likely response of some public authority which must determine what the content of "public interest" will be in the particular case. To what extent is that relevant to the dilemma faced by the professional in cases like these?

———

In addressing new problems, lawyers always look for analogies. Some of the difficulties faced by lawyers in determining the appropriate loyalties in corporate legal practice bear similarities to the problems of other professionals who must distinguish between their loyalty to their patients or clients and their commitments to community welfare. Consider in this regard two cases that address these problems in different ways.

TARASOFF V. REGENTS OF THE UNIVERSITY OF CALIFORNIA
SUPREME COURT OF CALIFORNIA, 1976
17 Cal. 3d 425, 551 P. 2d 334, 131 Cal. Rptr. 14

Tobriner, Justice: On October 27, 1969, Prosenjit Poddar killed Tatiana Tarasoff. Plaintiffs, Tatiana's parents, allege that two months earlier Poddar confided his intention to kill Tatiana to Dr. Lawrence Moore, a psychologist employed by the Cowell Memorial Hospital at the University of California at Berkeley. They allege that on Moore's request, the campus police briefly detained Poddar, but released him when he appeared rational. They further claim that Dr. Harvey Powelson, Moore's superior, then directed that no further action be taken to detain Poddar.

• • •

. . . No one warned plaintiffs of Tatiana's peril.

Concluding that these facts set forth causes of action against neither therapists and policeman involved, nor against the Regents of the University of California their employer, the superior court sustained defendant's demurrers to plaintiffs second amended complaints without leave to amend. This appeal ensued.

• • •

The second cause of action can be amended to allege that Tatiana's death proximately resulted from defendants' negligent failure to warn Tatiana or others likely to apprise her of her danger. Plaintiffs contend that as amended, such allegations of neglience and proximate causation, with resulting damages, establish a cause of action. Defendants, however, contend that in the circumstances of the present case they owed no duty of care to Tatiana or her parents and that, in the absence of such duty, they were free to act in careless disregard of Tatiana's life and safety.

In analyzing this issue, we bear in mind that legal duties are not discoverable facts of nature, but merely conclusory expressions that, in cases of a particular type, liability should be imposed for damage done. As stated in Dillon v. Legg (1968) 68 Cal. 2d 728, 734,: ''The assertion that liability must . . . be denied because defendant bears no 'duty' to plaintiff 'begs the essential question—whether the plaintiff's interests are entitled to legal protection against the defendant's conduct. . . . [Duty] is not sacrosanct in itself, but only an expression of the sum total of those considerations of policy which lead the law to say that the particular plaintiff is entitled to protection.' (Prosser, Law of Torts [3d ed. 1964] at pp. 332–333.)''

In the landmark case of Rowland v. Christian (1968) 69 Cal. 2d 108, Justice Peters recognized that liability should be imposed ''for an injury occasioned to another by want of his ordinary care of skill'' as expressed in section 1714 of the Civil Code. Thus, Justice Peters, quoting from Heaven v. Pender (1883) 11 Q.B.D. 503, 509 stated: '' 'whenever one person is by circumstances placed in such a position with regard to another . . . that if he did not use ordinary care and skill in his own conduct . . . he would cause danger of injury to the person or property of the other, a duty arises to use ordinary care and skill to avoid such danger.' ''

We depart from ''this fundamental principle'' only upon the ''balancing of a number of considerations''; major ones ''are the foreseeability of harm to the plaintiff, the degree of certainty that the plaintiff suffered injury, the closeness of connection between the defendant's conduct, the policy of preventing future harm, the extent of the burden to the defendant and consequences to the community of imposing a duty to exercise care with resulting liability for breach, and the availability, cost and prevalence of insurance for the risk involved.''

The most important of these considerations in establishing duty is foreseeability. As a general principle, a "defendant owes a duty of care to all persons who are foreseeably endangered by his conduct, with respect to all risks which make the conduct unreasonably dangerous." As we shall explain, however, when the avoidance of foreseeable harm requires a defendant to control the conduct of another person, or to warn of such conduct, the common law has traditionally imposed liability only if the defendant bears some special relationship to the dangerous person or to the potential victim. Since the relationship between a therapist and his patient satisfies this requirement, we need not here decide whether foreseeability alone is sufficient to create a duty to exercise reasonable care to protect a potential victim of another's conduct.

Although, as we have stated above, under the common law, as a general rule, one person owed no duty to control the conduct of another the courts have carved out an exception to this rule in cases in which the defendant stands in some special relationship to either the person whose conduct needs to be controlled or in a relationship to the foreseeable victim of that conduct (see Rest. 2d Torts, (315–320). Applying this exception to the present case, we note that a relationship of defendant therapists to either Tatiana or Poddar will suffice to establish a duty of care; as explained in section 315 of the Restatement Second of Torts, a duty of care may arise from either "(a) a special relation . . . between the actor and the third person which imposes a duty upon the actor to control the third person's conduct, or (b) a special relation . . . between the actor and the other which gives to the other a right of protection."

Although plaintiffs' pleadings assert no special relation between Tatiana and defendant therapists, they establish as between Poddar and defendant therapists the special relation that arises between a patient and his doctor or psychotherapist. Such a relationship may support affirmative duties for the benefit of third persons. Thus, for example, a hospital must exercise reasonable care to control the behavior of a patient which may endanger other persons. A doctor must also warn a patient if the patient's condition or medication renders certain conduct, such as driving a car, dangerous to others.

Although the California decisions that recognize this duty have involved cases in which the defendant stood in a special relationship *both* to the victim and to the person whose conduct created the danger, we do not think that the duty should logically be constricted to such situations. Decision of other jurisdictions hold that the single relationship of a doctor to his patient is sufficient to support the duty to exercise reasonable care to protect others against dangers emanating from the patient's illness. The courts hold that a doctor is liable to persons infected by his patient if he negligently fails to diagnose a contagious disease (Hofmann v. Blackmon (Fla. App. 1970) 241 So. 2d 752), or, having diagnosed the illness, fails to warn members of the patient's family.

Since it involved a dangerous mental patient, the decision in Merchants Nat. Bank & Trust Co. of Fargo v. United States (D.N.D. 1967) 272 F. Supp. 409 comes closer to the issue. The Veterans Administration arranged for the patient to work on a local farm, but did not inform the farmer of the man's background. The farmer consequently permitted the patient to come and go freely during nonworking hours; the patient borrowed a car, drove to his wife's residence and killed her. Notwithstanding the lack of any "special relationship" between the Veterans Administration and the wife, the court found the Veterans Administration liable for the wrongful death of the wife. . . .

Defendants contend, however, that imposition of a duty to exercise reasonable care to protect third persons is unworkable because therapists cannot accurately predict whether or not a patient will resort to violence. In support of this argument amicus representing the America Psychiatric Association and other professional societies cites numerous articles which indicate that therapists, in the present state of the art, are unable reliably to predict violent acts; their forecasts, amicus claims, tend consistently to overpredict violence, and indeed are more often wrong than right. Since predictions of violence are often erroneous, amicus concludes, the courts should not render rulings that predicate the liablility of therapists upon the validity of such predictions. . . .

We recognize the difficulty a therapist encounters in attempting to forecast whether a patient presents a serious danger of violence. Obviously, we do not require that the therapist, in making that determination, render a perfect performance; the therapist need only exercise "that reasonable degree of skill, knowledge, and care ordinarily possessed and exercised by members of [that professional specialty] under similar circumstances." Within the broad range of reasonable practice and treatment in which professional opinion and judgment may differ, the therapist is free to exercise his or her own best judgment without liability; proof, aided by hindsight, that he or she judged wrongly is insufficient to establish negligence.

In the instant case, however, the pleadings do not raise any questions as to failure of defendant therapists to predict that Poddar presented a serious danger of violence. On the contrary, the present complaints allege that defendant therapists did in fact predict that Poddar would kill, but were negligent in failing to warn.

• • •

The risk that unnecessary warnings may be given is a reasonable price to pay for the lives of possible victims that may be saved. We would hesitate to hold that the therapist who is aware that his patient expects to attempt to assassinate the President of the United States would not be obligated to warn the authorities because the therapist cannot predict with accuracy that his patient will commit the crime.

We recognize the public interest in supporting effective treatment of mental illness and in protecting the rights of patients to privacy (see In re Liftschutz, 2 Cal. 3d at p. 432), and the consequent public importance of safeguarding the confidential character of psychotherapeutic communication. Against this interest, however, we must weigh the public interest in safety from violent assault. The Legislature has undertaken the difficult task of balancing the countervailing concerns. In Evidence Code section 1014, it established a broad rule of privilege to protect confidential communications between patient and psychotherapist. In Evidence Code section 1024, the Legislature created a specific and limited exception to the psychotherapist-patient privilege: "There is no privilege . . . if the psychotherapist has reasonable cause to believe that the patient is in such mental or emotional condition as to be dangerous to himself or to the person or property of another and that disclosure of the communication is necessary to prevent the threatened danger."

We realize that the open and confidential character of psychotherapist dialogue encourages patients to express threats of violence, few of which are ever executed. Certainly a therapist should not be encouraged routinely to reveal such threats; such disclosures could seriously disrupt the patient's relationship with his therapist and with the persons threatened. To the contrary, the therapist's obligations to his patient require that he does not disclose a confidence unless such disclosure is necessary to avert danger to others, and even then that he do so discreetly, and in a fashion that would preserve the privacy of his patient to the fullest extent compatible with the prevention of the threatened danger. (See Fleming & Maximov, The Patient or His Victim: The Therapist's Dilemma (1974) 62 Cal. L. Rev. 1025, 1065–1066.)

The revelation of a communication under the above circumstances is not a breach of trust or a violation of professional ethics; as stated in the Principles of Medical Ethics of the American Medical Association (1957), section 9: "A physician may not reveal the confidence entrusted to him in the course of medical attendance . . . *unless he is required to do so by law or unless it becomes necessary in order to protect the welfare of the individual or of the community.*" (Emphasis added.) We conclude that the public policy favoring protection of the confidential character of patient-psycho-therapist communications must yield to the extent to which disclosure is essential to avert danger to others. The protective privilege ends where the public peril begins.

Our current crowded and computerized society compels the interdependence of its members. In this risk-infested society we can hardly tolerate the further exposure to danger that would result from a concealed knowledge of the therapist that his patient was lethal. If the exercise of reasonable care to protect the threatened victim requires the therapist to warn the endangered party or those who can reasonably be expected to notify him, we see no sufficient societal interest that would protect and justify concealment. The containment of such risks lies in the public interest. For the foregoing reasons, we find that plaintiffs' complaints can be amended to state a cause of action against defendants Moore, Powelson, Gold, and Yandell and against the Regents as their employer, for breach of a duty to exercise reasonable care to protect Tatiana.

•   •   •

NOTES

The bureaucratic mode of thinking, placing loyalty to one's organization or client above duty to others and one's community, is widespread. Numerous instances have come to light in which lawyers, accountants and other professionals have acted in accordance with this patern. Many courts have echoed the reasoning of the *Tarasoff* Court and have held professionals liable for large sums—sometimes, many millions of dollars, for their actions in attempting to further the interests of their firms or clients in unethical ways. (See e.g., N.Y. Times, Sept. 11, 1982, at 37; N.Y. Times, Sept. 14, 1982, at D-1; Wall Street J., Sept. 14, 1982, at 1; cf. *Berkey Photo, Inc. v. Eastman Kodak Co.*, 603 F, 2d 263 (2d Cir. 1979)).

Would a lawyer who does not reveal that his client intends to murder somebody be liable under the theory of the Tarasoff case, or could the lawyer legitimately claim that there is no duty to disclose pursuant to the express provisions of the Model Rules of Professional Conduct? What of massive fraud which the client intends to perpetrate? In the OPM case, attorneys who learned of fraud by their clients, which eventually aggregated many millions of dollars, continued to act as attorneys for OPM, thereby (unwittingly) assisting the commission of additional frauds. Eventually, they resigned as counsel for the clients, but failed to disclose to the clients' new counsel that the clients apparently intended to continue their fraudulent activities, or even to reveal the reasons for their resignation as attorneys. This was done upon the advice of experts in legal ethics. Subsequently, the clients, with the unwitting assistance of new counsel, committed additional frauds of many millions of dollars. (*Report of the Trustee,* in Re OPM Leasing Services, Inc. Southern District of NY #81-B-10533, April 25, 1983).

MEYERHOFER V. EMPIRE FIRE AND MARINE INSURANCE COMPANY
497 F. 2d 1190 (2d Cir. 1974)

Empire Fire and Marine Insurance Company on May 31, 1972, made a public offering of 500,000 shares of its stocks, pursuant to a registration statement filed with the Securities and Exchange Commission (SEC) on March 28, 1972. The stock was offered at $16 a share. Empire's attorney on the issue was the firm of Sitomer, Sitomer & Porges. Stuart Charles Goldberg was an attorney in the firm and had done some work on the issue.

Plaintiff Meyerhofer, on or about January 11, 1973, purchased 100 shares of Empire stock at $17 a share. He alleges that as of June 5, 1973, the market price of his stock was only $7 a share—hence, he has sustained an unrealized loss of $1,000. Am'd Compl. P9a. Plaintiff Federman, on or about May 31, 1972, purchased 200 shares at $16 a share, 100 of which he sold for $1,363, sustaining a loss of some $237 on the stock sold and an unrealized loss of $900 on the stock retained.

On May 2, 1972, plaintiffs, represented by the firm of Bernson, Hoeniger, Freitag & Abbey (the Bernson firm), on behalf of themselves and all other purchases of Empire common stock, brought this action alleging that the registration statement and the prospectus under which the Empire stock had been issued were materially false and misleading. Thereafter, an amended complaint, dated June 5, 1973 was served. The legal theories in both were identical, namely, violations of various sections of the Securities Act of 1933, the Securities Exchange Act of 1934, Rule 10b-5, and common law negligence, fraud and deceit. Damages for all members of the class of rescission were alternatively sought.

The lawsuit was apparently inspired by a Form 10-K which Empire filed with the SEC on or about April 12, 1973. This form revealed that the "The Registration Statement under the Securities Act of 1933 with respect to the public offering of the 500,000 shares of Common Stock did not disclose the proposed $200,000 payment to the law firm as well as certain other features of the compensation arrangements between the Company [Empire] and such law firm [defendant Sitomer, Sitomer and Porges)]." Later that month Empire disseminated to its shareholders a proxy statement and annual report making similar disclosures.

The defendants named were Empire, officers and directors of Empire, the Sitomer firm and its three partners, A.L. Sitomer, S.J. Sitomer and R.E. Porges, Faulkner, Dawkins & Sullivan Securities Corp., the managing underwriter, Stuart Charles Goldberg, originally alleged to have been a partner of the Sitomer firm, and certain selling stockholders of Empire shares.

On May 2, 1973, the complaint was served on the Sitomer defendants and Faulkner. No service was made on Goldberg who was then no longer associated with the Sitomer firm. However, he was advised by telephone that he had been made a defendant. Golderg inquired of the Bernson firm as to the nature of the charges against him and was informed generally as to the substance of the complaint and in particular the lack of disclosure of the finder's fee arrangement. Thus informed, Goldberg requested an opportunity to prove his non-involvement in any such arrangement and his lack of knowledge thereof. At this stage there was unfolded the series of events which ultimately resulted in the motion and order thereon now before us on appeal.

Goldberg, after his graduation from Law School in 1966, had rather specialized experience in the securities field and had published various books and treatises on related subjects. He became associated with the Sitomer firm in November 1971.

While there Goldberg worked on phases of various registration statements including Empire, although another associate was responsible for the Empire's registration statement and prospectus. However, Goldberg expressed concern over what he regarded as excessive fees, the nondisclosure or inadequate disclosure thereof, and the extent to which they might include a "finder's fee," both as to Empire and other issues.

The Empire registration became effective on May 31, 1972. The excessive fee question had not been put to rest in Goldberg's mind because in middle January 1973 it arose in connection with another registration (referred to as "Glacier"). Goldberg had worked on Glacier. Little purpose will be served by detailing the events during the critical period January 18 to 22, 1973, in which Goldberg and the Sitomer partners were debating the fee disclosure problem. In summer Goldberg insisted on a full and complete disclosure of fees in the Empire and Glacier offerings. The Sitomer partners apparently disagreed and Goldberg resigned from the firm on January 22, 1973.

On January 22, 1973, Goldberg appeared before the SEC and placed before it information subsequently embodied in his affidavit dated January 26, 1973, which becomes crucial to the issues now to be considered.

Some three months later, upon being informed that he was to be included as a defendant in the impending action, Goldberg asked the Bernson firm for an opportunity to demonstrate that he had been unaware of the finder's fee arrangement which, he said, Empire and the Sitomer firm had concealed from him all along. Goldberg met with members of the Bernson firm on at least two occasions. After consulting his own attorney, as well as William P. Sullivan Special Counsel with the Securities and Exchange Commission, Division of Enforcement, Goldberg gave plaintiffs' counsel a copy of the January 26th affidavit which he had authored more than three months earlier. He hoped that it would verify his nonparticipation in the finder's fee omission and convince the Bernson firm that he should not be a defendant. The Bernson firm was satisfied with Goldberg's affidavit, the Bernson firm amended plaintiffs' complaint. The amendments added more specific facts but did not change the theory or substance of the original complaint.

By motion date June 7, 1973, the remaining defendants moved "pursuant to Canons 4 and 9 of the Code of Professional Responsibility, the Disciplinary Rules and Ethical Considerations applicable thereto, and the supervisory power of the Court" for the order of disqualification now on appeal.

By memorandum decision and order, the District Court ordered that the Bernson firm and Goldberg be barred from acting as counsel or participating with counsel for plaintiffs in this or any future action against Empire involving the transactions placed in issue in this lawsuit and from disclosing confidential information to others.

The complaint was dismissed without prejudice. The basis for the Court's decision is the premise that Goldberg had obtained confidential information from his client Empire which, in breach of relevant ethical canon, he revealed to plaintiffs' attorneys in their suit against Empire. The Court said its decision was compelled by "the broader obligations of Canons 4 and 9."*

*Code of Professional Responsibility
Canon 4
A lawyer Should Preserve the Confidence and Secrets of a Client; Ethical Considerations
EC 4–1 Both the fiduciary relationship existing betwen lawyer and client and the proper functioning of the legal system require the preservation by the lawyer of confidences and secrets of one who had employed or sought to employ him.

• • •

There is no proof—not even a suggestion—that Goldberg had revealed any information, confidential or otherwise, that might have caused the instigation of the suit. To the contrary, it was not until after the suit was commenced that Goldberg learned that he was in jeopardy. The District court recognized that the complaint had been based on Empire's—not Goldberg's—disclosures, but concluded because of this that Goldberg was under no further obligation "to reveal the information or to discuss the matter with plaintiffs' counsel."

Despite the breadth of paragraphs EC 4–4 and DR 4–101 (B), DR 4–101 (C) recognizes that a lawyer may reveal confidences or secrets necessary to defend himself against "an accusation of wrongful conduct." This is exactly what Goldberg had to face when, in their original complaint, plaintiffs named him as a defendant who wilfully violated the securities laws.

The charge, of knowing participation in the filing of a false and misleading registration statement, was a serious one. The complaint alleged violation of criminal statutes and civil liability computable at over four million dollars. The cost in money of simply defending such an action might be very substantial. The damage to his

---

EC4–4 The attorney-client privilege is more limited than the ethical obligation of a lawyer to guard the confidences and secrets of his client. The ethical precept, unlike the evidentiary privilege, exists without regard to the nature or source of information or the fact that others share the knowledge. A lawyer should endeavor to act in a manner which preserves the evidentiary privilege. . . .

EC 4–5 A lawyer should not use information acquired in the course of the representation of a client to the disadvantage of the client and a lawyer should not use, except with the consent of his client after full disclosure, such information for his own purposes. . . .

EC 4–6 The obligation of a lawyer to preserve the confidences and secrets of his client continues after the termination of his employment. . . .

Disciplinary Rules

DR 4–101 Preservation of Confidences and Secrets of a Client

(A) "Confidence" refers to information protected by the attorney-client privilege under applicable law, and "secret" refers to other information gained in the professional relationship that the client has requested be held inviolate or the disclosure of which would be embarrassing or would be likely to be detrimental to the client.

(B) Except when permitted under DR 4–101 (C), a lawyer shall not knowingly:

(1) Reveal a confidence or secret of his client.

(2) Use a confidence or secret of his client to the disadvantage of the client.

(3) Use a confidence or secret of his client for the advantage of himself or of a third person, unless the client consents after full disclosure.

(C) A lawyer may reveal:

(4) Confidences or secrets necessary to establish or collect his fee or to defend himself or his employees or associates against an accusation of wrongful conduct.

Canon 9

A Lawyer Should Avoid Even the Appearance of Professional Impropriety; Ethical Considerations

EC 9–1 Continuation of the American concept that we are to be governed by rules of law requires that the people have faith that justice can be obtained through our legal system. A lawyer should promote public confidence in our system and in the legal profession.

EC 9–6 Every lawyer owes a solemn duty to uphold the integrity and honor of his profession; to encourage respect for the law and for the courts and the judges thereof; to observe the Code of Professional Responsibility; to act as a member of a learned profession, one dedicated to public service; to cooperate with his brother lawyers in supporting the organized bar through the devoting of his time, efforts, and financial support as his professional standing and ability reasonably permit; to conduct himself so as to reflect credit on the legal profession and to inspire the confidence, respect, and trust of his clients and off the public; and to strive to avoid not only professional impropriety but also the appearance of impropriety.

professional reputation which might be occasioned by the mere pendency of such a charge was an even greater cause for concern.

Under these circumstances Goldberg had the right to make an appropriate disclosure with respect to his role in the public offering. Concomitantly, he had the right to support his version of the facts with suitable evidence.

The problem arises from the fact that the method Goldberg used to accomplish this was to deliver to Mr. Abbey, a member of the Bernson firm, the thirty page affidavit, accompanied by sixteen exhibits, which he had submitted to the SEC. This document not only went into extensive detail concerning Goldberg's efforts to cause the Sitomer firm to rectify the nondisclosure with respect to Empire but even more extensive detail concerning how these efforts had been precipitated by counsel for the underwriters having come upon evidence showing that a similar nondisclosure was contemplated with respect to Glacier and their insistence that full corrective measures should be taken. Although Goldberg's description reflected seriously on his employer, the Sitomer firm and, also, in at least some degree, on Glacier, he was clearly in a situation of some urgency. Morever, before he turned over the affidavit, he consulted both his own attorney and a distinguished practitioner of securities law, and he and Abbey made a joint telephone call to Mr. Sullivan of the SEC. Moreover, it is not clear that, in the context of this case, Canon 4 applies to anything except information gained from Empire. Finally, because of Goldberg's apparent intimacy with the offering, the most effective way for him to substantiate his story was for him to disclose the SEC affidavit. It was the fact that he had written such an affidavit at an earlier date which demonstrated that his story was not simply fabricated in response to plaintiffs' complaint.

The District Court held: "All that need be shown . . . is that during the attorney-client relationship Goldberg had access to his client's information relevant to the issues here. *See Emle Industries, Inc. v. Patentex, Inc.*, 478 F.2d 562 (2d Cir. 1973). However, the irrebutable presumption of *Emle Industries* has no application to the instant circumstances because Goldberg never sought to "prosecute litigation," either as a party . . . or as counsel for a plaintiff party. . . . At most the record discloses that Goldberg might be called as a witness for the plaintiffs but that role does not invest him with the intimacy with the prosecution of the litigation which must exist for the *Emle* presumption to attach.

In addition to finding that Goldberg had violated Canon 4, the District Court found that the relationship between Goldberg and the Bernson firm violated Canon 9 of the Code of Professional Responsibility which provides that:

> EC 9–6 Every lawyer [must] strive to avoid not only professional impropriety but also the appearance of impropriety.

The District Court reasoned that even though there was no evidence of bad faith on the part of either Golderg or the Bernson firm, a shallow reading of the facts might lead a casual observer to conclude that there was an aura of complicity about their relationship. However, this provision should not be read so broadly as to eviscerate the right of self-defense conferred by DR4–101 (C)(4).

Nevertheless, Emle Industries, Inc. v. Patentex, Inc., *supra,* requires that a strict prophylactic rule be applied in these cases to ensure that a lawyer avoids representation of a party in a suit against a former client where there may be the appearance of a possible violation of confidence. To the extent that the District Court's order prohibits Goldberg from *representing* the interest of these or any other plaintiffs in this or similar actions, we affirm that order. We also affirm so much of the District Court's order as enjoins Goldberg from disclosing material information except on discovery or at trial.

The burden of the District Court's order did not fall most harshly on Goldberg; rather its greatest impact has been felt by Bernson, Hoeniger, Freitag & Abbey, plaintiffs' counsel, which was disqualified from participation in the case. The District Court based its holding, not on the fact that the Bernson firm showed bad faith when it received Golderg's afffidavit, but rather on the fact that it was involved in a tainted association with Goldberg because his disclosures to them inadvertently violated Canons 4 and 9 of the Code of Professional Responsibility. Because there are no violations of either of these Canons in this case, we can find no basis to hold that the relationship between Goldberg and the Bernson firm was tainted. The District Court was apparently unpersuaded by appellees' salvo of innuendo to the effect that Goldberg "struck a deal" with the Bernson firm or tried to do more than prove his innocence to them. Since its relationship with Goldberg was not tainted by violations of the Code of Professional Responsibility, there appears to be no warrant for its disqualification from participation in either this or similar actions. A fortiori there was no sound basis for disqualifying plaintiffs or dismissing the complaint.

NOTES

1. Did the court follow the bureaucratic mode of thinking in deciding this case? Would the community be better served if lawyers and other professionals were required to disclose the wrongful acts of their clients?

2. Was the court being unduly protective of lawyers instead of the public interest, by requiring the lawyer in this case to withhold the information regarding the client's wrongful act?

In response to an indication by the SEC that its thinking ran in this direction, the American Bar Association issued a statement of policy in 1975 regarding the responsibilities and liabilities of lawyers advising clients.

STATEMENT OF POLICY ADOPTED BY AMERICAN BAR ASSOCIATION
REGARDING RESPONSIBILITIES AND LIABILITIES OF LAWYERS
IN ADVISING WITH RESPECT TO THE COMPLIANCE BY CLIENTS
WITH LAWS ADMINISTERED BY THE SECURITIES AND EXCHANGE
COMMISSION, AUGUST 12, 1975.
REPRINTED IN 31 BUS. LAW 543 (1975)

Be it resolved, that this Association adopts the following Statement of Policy regarding responsibilities and liabilities off lawyers in advising with respect to the compliance by clients with laws administered by the Securities and Exchange Commission ("SEC"):

1. The confidentiality of lawyer-client consultations and advice and the fiduciary loyalty of the lawyer to the client, as prescribed in the American Bar Association's Code of Professional Responsibility ("CPR"), are vital to the basic function of the lawyer as legal counselor because they enable and encourage clients to consult legal counsel freely, with assurance that counsel will respect the confidentiality of the

client's communications and will advise independently and in the client's best interest
without conflicting loyalties or obligations.

2. This vital confidentiality of consultation and advice would be destroyed or
seriously impaired if it is accepted as a general principle that lawyers must inform
the SEC or others regarding confidential information received by lawyers from their
clients even though such action would not be permitted or required by the CPR. Any
such compelled disclosure would seriously and adversely affect the lawyer's function
as counselor, and may seriously and adversely affect the ability of lawyers as advocates to represent and defend their clients' interests.

3. In light of the foregoing considerations, it must be recognized that a lawyer
cannot, consistently with his essential role as legal advisor, be regarded as a source
of information concerning possible wrong-doing by clients. Accordingly, any principal of law which, except as permitted or required by the CPR, permits or obliges
a lawyer to disclose to the SEC otherwise confidential information, should be established only by statute after full and careful consideration of the public interests
involved, and should be resisted unless clearly mandated by law.

4. Lawyers have an obligation under the CPR to advise clients, to the best of
their ability, concerning the need for or advisability of public disclosure of a broad
range of events and circumstances, including the obligation of the client to make
appropriate disclosures as required by various laws and regulations administered by
the SEC. In appropriate circumstances, a lawyer may be permitted or required by
the Disciplinary Rules under the CPR to resign his engagement if his advice concerning disclosures is disregarded by the client and, if the conduct of a client clearly
establishes his prospective commission of a crime or the past or prospective perpe-
tration of a fraud in the course of the lawyer's representation, even to make the
disclosures himself. However, the lawyer has neither the obligation nor the right to
make disclosure when any reasonable doubt exists concerning the client's obligation
of disclosure, i.e., the client's failure to meet his obligation is not clearly established,
except to the extent that the lawyer should consider appropriate action, as required
or permitted by the CPR; in cases where the lawyer's opinion is expected to be relied
on by third parties and the opinion is discovered to be not correct, whether because
it is based on erroneous information or otherwise.

5. Fulfillment by attorneys of their obligations to clients under the CPR best
serves the public interest of assisting and furthering clients' compliance with legal
requirements. Efforts by the government to impose responsibility upon lawyers to
assure the quality of their clients' compliance with the law or to compel lawyers to
give advice resolving all doubts in favor of regulatory restrictions would evoke serious
and far-reaching disruption in the role of the lawyer as counselor, which would be
detrimental to the public, clients and the legal profession. In fulfillment of their
responsibility to clients under the CPR, lawyers must be free to advise clients as to
the full range of their legitimately available courses of action and the relative attendant
risks involved. Furthermore, it is often desirable for the lawyer to point out those
factors which may suggest a decision that is morally just as well as legally permissible.
However, the decision as to the course to be taken should be made by the client. The
client's actions should not be improperly narrowed through the insistence of an
attorney who may perhaps unconsciously, eliminate available choices from consideration because of his concern over possible personal risks if the position is taken
which, though supportable, is subject to uncertainty or contrary to a known, but
perhaps erroneous, positions of the SEC or a questionable lower court decision.

Public policy, we strongly believe, is best served by lawyers acting in conformance with their obligations to their clients and others as prescribed under the CPR. Accordingly, liability should not be imposed upon lawyers whose conduct is in conformance with the CPR.

NOTES

1. Courts have been extremely "understanding" of the burdens on lawyers in circumstances like these. In many cases they have effectively prevented government agencies from punishing attorneys for alleged violations of obligations under the law, by establishing a very high threshold of proof or by viewing the obligations of the attorneys very technically so they can be discharged in perfunctory documents. See, in this regard *SEC v. National Student Marketing Corp.,* 457 F. Supp. 682 (Dist. Ct. D.C. 1976).

2. In the last decade, a number of the largest and most prestigious law and accounting firms in the country have been found guilty of serious violations of law in attempting to further their own interests and the interst of their clients. Some of them have been forced to pay many millions of dollars by courts or in settlement of suits by defrauded members of the public. (See, e.g. N.Y. Times, September 11, 1982, page 37; Wall Street Journal, September 14, 1982, page 1; N.Y. Times, September 14, 9182, D1, D8. Wall Street Journal, June 21, 1983, page 1). A suit for $300 million dollars in damages was instituted against three of the most prominent accounting firms in the U.S.A., charging fraud *(Anderson v. Schacht,* See N.Y. Times, November 29, 1983, page D-1).

3. Note how heavily the District Court came down on Goldberg for his violations of law by the client. This is consistent with the viewpoint adopted by the American Bar Association in their Model Rules of Professional Conduct. The court's treatment of Goldberg should be compared with its "understanding" treatment of lawyers who violate the law to further interest of clients. The lawyers of OPM were not brought up for disbarment proceedings.

SELF-REGULATION: THE A.B.A.

Is the lawyer, like all the other officers of the corporation, primarily responsible for the success and continuity of the organization itself or singularly responsible for its conformity to the norms of the more general legal system? Consider, in this regard, the American Bar Association's *Model Rules* adopted in August, 1983. Among other things, the rules addressed the question of the proper loyalty of a lawyer working for an organization who learns that an offficer, employee or other person is engaged in an action which may be a violation of a legal obligation of the organization or a violation of the law. The meeting at which the Rules were considered was reportedly stormy.

MODEL RULES OF PROFESSIONAL CONDUCT

RULE 1.13 ORGANIZATION AS CLIENT

(a) A lawyer employed or retained by an organization represents the organization acting through its duly authorized constituents.

(b) If a lawyer for an organization knows that an officer, employee or other person associated with the organization is engaged in action, intends to act or refuses to act in a matter related to the representation that is a violation of a legal obligation to the organization, or a violation of law which reasonably might be imputed to the organization, and is likely to result in substantial injury to the organization, the lawyer shall proceed as is reasonably necessary in the best interest of the organization. In determining how to proceed, the lawyer shall give due consideration to the seriousness of the violation and its consequences, the scope and nature of the lawyer's representation, the responsibility in the organization and the apparent motivation of the person involved, the policies of the organization concerning such matters and any other relevant considerations. Any measures taken shall be designed to minimize disruption of the organization and the risk of revealing information relating to the representation to persons outside the organization. Such measures may include among others:

(1) asking reconsideration of the matter;

(2) advising that a separate legal opinion on the matter be sought for presentation to appropriate authority in the organization; and

(3) referring the matter to higher authority in the organization, including, if warranted by the seriousness of the matter, referral to the highest authority that can act in behalf of the organization as determined by applicable law.

(c) If, despite the lawyer's efforts in accordance with paragraph (b), the highest authority that can act on behalf of the organization insists upon action, or a refusal to act, that is clearly a violation of law and is likely to result in substantial injury to the organization, the lawyer may resign in accordance with Rule 1.16.

(d) In dealing with an organization's directors, officers, employees, members, shareholders or other constituents, a lawyer shall explain the identity of the client when it is apparent that the organization's interests are adverse to those of the constitutents with whom the lawyer is dealing.

(e) A lawyer representing an organization may also represent any of its directors, officers, employees, members, shareholders or other constituents, subject to the provisions of Rule 1.7. If the organization's consent to the dual representation is required by Rule 1.7, the consent shall be given by an appropriate official of the organization other than the individual who is to be represented, or by the shareholders.

COMMENT:
THE ENTITY AS THE CLIENT

An organizational client is a legal entity, but it cannot act except through its officers, directors, employees, shareholders and other constituents.

Officers, directors, employees and shareholders are the constituents of the corporate organizational client. The duties defined in this Comment apply equally to unincorporated associations. "Other constituents" as used in this Comment means the position equivalent to officers, directors, employees and shareholders held by persons acting for organizational clients that are not corporations.

When one of the constituents of an organizational client communicates with the organization's lawyer in that person's organizational capacity, the communication is protected by Rule 1.6 [infra]. Thus, by way of example, if an organizational client requests its lawyer to investigate allegations of wrongdoing, interviews made in the course of that investigation between the lawyer and the client's employees or other constituents are covered by Rule 1.6. This does not mean, however, that constituents of an organizational client are the clients of the lawyer. The lawyer may not disclose to such constituents information relating to the representation except for disclosures explicitly or impliedly authorized by the organizational client in order to carry out the representation or as otherwise permitted by Rule 1.6.

When constituents of the organization make decisions for it, the decisions ordinarily must be accepted by the lawyer even if their utility or prudence is doubtful. Decisions concerning policy and operations, including ones entailing serious risk, are not as such in the lawyer's province. However, different considerations arise when the lawyer knows that the organization may be substantially injured by action of a constituent that is in violation of law. In such a circumstance, it may be reasonably necessary for the lawyer to ask the constituent to reconsider the matter. If that fails, or if the matter is of sufficient seriousness and importance to the organization, it may be reasonably necessary for the lawyer to take steps to have the matter reviewed by a higher authority in the organization. Clear justification should exist for seeking review over the head of the constituent normally responsible for it. The stated policy of the organization may define circumstances and prescribe channels for such review, and a lawyer should encourage the formulation of such a policy. Even in the absence of organization policy, however, the lawyer may have an obligation to refer a matter to higher authority, depending on the seriousness of the matter and whether the constituent in question has apparent motives to act at variance with the organization's interest. Review by the chief executive officer or by the board of directors may be required when the matter is of importance commensurate with their authority. At some point it may be useful or essential to obtain an independent legal opinion.

In an extreme case, it may be reasonably necessary for the lawyer to refer the matter to the organization's highest authority. Ordinarily, that is the board of directors or similar governing body. However, applicable law may prescribe that under certain conditions highest authority reposes elsewhere; for example, in the independent directors of a corporation.

RELATION TO OTHER RULES

. . . .this Rule does not limit or expand the lawyer's responsibility under Rule 1.6. . . .

RULE 1.6 CONFIDENTIALITY OF INFORMATION

(a) A lawyer shall not reveal information relating to representation of a client unless the client consents after consultation, except for disclosures that are impliedly authorized in order to carry out the representation, and except as stated in paragraph (b).

(b) A lawyer may reveal such information to the extent the lawyer reasonably believes necessary:

(1) to prevent the client from committing a criminal act that the lawyer believes is likely to result in imminent death or substantial bodily harm; or

(2) to establish a claim or defense on behalf of the lawyer in a controversy between the lawyer and the client, to establish a defense to a criminal charge or civil claim against the lawyer based upon conduct in which the client was involved, or to respond to allegations in any proceeding concerning the lawyer's representation of the client.

COMMENT:

The lawyer is part of a judicial system charged with upholding the law. One of the lawyer's functions is to advise clients so that they avoid any violation of the law in the proper exercise of their rights.

The observance of the ethical obligation of a lawyer to hold inviolate confidential information of the client not only facilitates the full development of facts essential to proper representation of the client but also encourages people to seek early legal assistance.

Almost without exception, clients come to lawyers in order to determine what their rights are and what is, in the maze of laws and regulations, deemed to be legal and correct. The common law recognizes that the client's confidences must be protected from disclosure. Based upon experience, lawyers know that almost all clients follow the advice given, and the law is upheld.

A fundamental principle in the client-lawyer relationship is that the lawyer maintain cofidentiality of information relating to the representation. The client is thereby encouraged to communicate fully and frankly with the lawyer even as to embarrassing or legally damaging subject matter.

The principle of confidentiality is given effect in two related bodies of law, the attorney-client privilege (which includes the work product doctrine) in the law of evidence and the rule of confidentiality established in professional ethics. The attorney-client privilege applies in judicial and other proceedings in which a lawyer may be called as a witness or otherwise required to produce evidence concerning a client. The rule of client-lawyer confidentiality applies in situations other than those where evidence is sought from the lawyer through compulsion of law. The confidentiality rule applies not merely to matters communicated in confidence by the client but also to all information relating to the representation, whatever its source. A lawyer may not disclose such information except as authorized or required by the Rules of Professional Conduct or other law. See also Scope.

The requirement of maintaining confidentiality of information relating to representation applies to government lawyers who may disagree with the policy goals that their representation is designed to advance.

AUTHORIZED DISCLOSURE

A lawyer is impliedly authorized to make disclosures about a client when appropriate in carrying out the representation, except to the extent that the client's instructions or special circumstances limit that authority. In litigation, for example, a lawyer may disclose information by admitting a fact that cannot properly be disputed, or in negotiation by making a disclosure that facilitates a satisfactory conclusion.

Lawyers in a firm may, in the course of the firm's practice, disclose to each other information relating to a client of the firm, unless the client has instructed that particular information be confined to specified lawyers.

DISCLOSURE ADVERSE TO CLIENT

The confidentiality rule is subject to limited exceptions. In becoming privy to information about a client, a lawyer may foresee that the client intends serious harm to another person. However, to the extent a lawyer is required or permitted to disclose a client's purposes, the client will be inhibited from revealing facts which would enable the lawyer to counsel against a wrongful course of action. The public is better protected if full and open communication by the client is encouraged than if it is inhibited.

Several situations must be distinguished. First, the lawyer may not counsel or assist a client in conduct that is criminal or fraudulent. See Rule 1.2(d). Similarly, a lawyer has a duty under Rule 3.3(a)(4) not to use false evidence. This duty is essentially a special instance of the duty prescribed in Rule 1.2(d) to avoid assisting a client in criminal or fraudulent conduct.

Second, the lawyer may have been innocently involved in past conduct by the client that was criminal or fraudulent. In such a situation the lawyer has not violated Rule 1.2(d), because to "counsel or assist" criminal or fraudulent conduct requires knowing that the conduct is of that character.

Third, the lawyer may learn that a client intends prospective conduct that is criminal and likely to result in imminent death or substantial bodily harm. As stated in paragraph (b)(1), the lawyer has professional discretion to reveal information in order to prevent such consequences. The lawyer may make a disclosure in order to prevent homicide or serious bodily injury which the lawyer reasonably believes is intended by a client. It is very difficult for a lawyer to "know" when such a heinous purpose will actually be carried out, for the client may have a change of mind.

The lawyer's exercise of discretion requires consideration of such factors as the nature of the lawyer's relationship with the client and with those who might be injured by the client, the lawyer's own involvement in the transaction and factors that may extenuate the conduct in question. Where practical, the lawyer should seek to persuade the client to take suitable action. In any case, a disclosure adverse to the client's interest should be no greater than the lawyer reasonably believes necessary to the purpose. A lawyer's decision not to take preventive action permitted by paragraph (b)(1) does not violate this Rule.

WITHDRAWAL

If the lawyer's service will be used by the client in materially furthering a course of criminal or fraudulent conduct, the lawyer must withdraw, as stated in Rule 1.6(a)(1).

After withdrawal the lawyer is required to refrain from making disclosure of the clients' confidences, except as otherwise provided in Rule 1.6 Neither this rule nor Rule 1.8(b) nor Rule 1.16(d) prevents the lawyer from giving notice of the fact of withdrawal, and the lawyer may also withdraw or disaffirm any opinion, document, affirmation, or the like.

Where the client is an organization, the lawyer may be in doubt whether contemplated conduct will actually be carried out by the organization. Where necessary to guide conduct in connection with this Rule, the lawyer may make inquiry within the organization as indicated in Rule 1.13(b).

•   •   •

NOTES

1. What are the actual obligations of the lawyer in the circumstances contemplated by Rule 1.13?

2. Under the tentative draft of Rule 1.3(c) a lawyer had a restricted option to reveal violations of law if this would be in the best interest of the organization. Under the rules presently in effect, adopted in August, 1983, the lawyer may not reveal the violation of law in any case, but "may" simply resign. Note that the lawyer is not *required* to resign.

3. After the rules were accepted, the *Wall Street Journal* remarked:

> The image of lawyers wasn't helped by the American Bar Association's recent fight over a new code of ethics. Debated in February and adopted in August, the code weighs heavily on the side of lawyers preserving their clients secrets—at almost all costs. Approval of the code, which isn't binding unless adopted in individual states, heaped negative publicity on lawyers. In addition to requiring lawyers to keep quiet about clients committing fraud, the code permits them to remain silent if they believe their clients are going to commit violent crimes. Wall Street J., August 15, 1983, at 16, col. 1.

Discuss.

4. Under Rule 1.6, may a lawyer reveal that a client is about to commit massive fraud? Are lawyers *required* to reveal that a client is about to commit murder? Discuss whether this view of the lawyer's obligation is analogous to the limited view of "task responsibility" prevalent in bureaucratic organizations and to the notion there of primary loyalty to one's group.

5. Characterize and discuss the ABA's basic conception of the relationship between lawyers working in an organization and their obligation to the community at large.

6. In the light of the cases considered above and the draft proposals of the American Bar Association, do you think the bar has responded adequately and that there is a sufficient protection of the public interest through legal ethics? Discuss.

C. Bernard, *The Functions off the Executive* (1938).

E. Berne, *The Structure and Dynamics of Organizations and Groups* (1963).

T. Eckhoff and N. K. Sunby, The Notion of Basic Norms in Jurisprudence, 19 *Scandinavian Studies in Law* 123 (1975).

A. Etzioni, *A Comparative Analysis of Complex Organizations* (1961).

M. P. Golding, Kelsen and the Concept of "Legal System." in *More Essays in Legal Philosophy* (R. Summers ed. 1971).

J. W. Harris, Kelsen's Concept of Authority, 36 *Cambridge L.J.* 353 (1977).

H. L. A. Hart, Kelsen Visited, 16 *U.C.L.A. L.R.* 709 (1963).

G. Hughes, Validity and the Basic Norm, 59 *Cal. L. R.* 695 (1971); *Law, Reason and Justice; Essays in Legal Philosophy* (1969).

H. Kelsen, *The Pure Theory of Law* (1967); *General Theory of Law and State* (1945).

J. Mashaw, *Bureaucratic Justice: Managing Social Security Disability Claims* (1983).

W. H. McNeil, *The Great Frontier: Freedom and Hierarchy in Modern Times* (1983).

H. Simon, *Administrative Behavior, A Study of Decision-Making Processes in Administrative Organizations* (1947).

J. Stone, *Legal System and Lawyers' Reasonings* (1964), esp. Ch. 3.

Symposium, The Legacy of The New Deal: Problems and Possibilities in the Administrative State, Part I, 92 *Yale L.J.* 1080 (1983); Part II, 92 *Yale L.J.* 1357, (1983).

L. Von Mises, *Bureaucracy* (1945).

CHAPTER 10

Telling It Like It Is: American Legal Realism

Law . . . a high class racket.
Fred Rodell

A student unconcerned about learning or personal growth but only with "psyching out" his teacher to determine which combination of words and behavior will get a high mark, might be called a "Student Realist." Anything that will accomplish his goal is deemed appropriate. As learning is synonymous with what the teacher wants, the requisite skill involves mastering whatever is necessary to winning a certain reward from the teacher.

Notions akin to these are central to a characteristically American jurisprudence which has come to be referred to as legal Realism. A key part of the folklore of lawyers who specialize in litigation is that the outcome of a case depends largely on who the judge is. Statutes and centuries of precedent fade in importance. The records and political biographies of individual judges likely to be judging the case are studied carefully for indications of their ways of thinking and for their biases and preferences. Docketing becomes a major factor in decision and judicial appointments are examined with great care. Realism's distinctive feature is the assumption that the key if not the only factor in decision is the judge; the judge and the complexities of individual personality rather than rules actually account for decisions. In the United States, Legal Realism infuses the entire process of judicial appointments. From the lowest courts to the highest courts of the land, candidates are scrutinized for their political preferences, their biases, their alliances and any other factors likely to influence the decisions they will make. All of these inquiries assume that whatever the rules may say, the key element in the particular application will be the judge.

While this jurisprudence is largely an American product, there are analogies in other legal systems. In France, early in the century, François Geny developed a jurisprudence emphasizing the central role of the judge and the comparatively fictitous function of rules in making choices. In Germany, the so-called Free Law movement made comparable arguments though it took them in quite different directions. In the Scandinavian countries, a type of legal realism created largely by Olivecrona, Ross and Lundstadt, yielded cognate insights.

From ancient Hebrew and Roman law on, one tradition has rested on the notion that if the rules are clear, any judge with minimum skill in juridical science can apply those rules to reach a proper and predictable conclusion. So heavy was the reliance on rules as the key factor in decision that Roman law forbade a judge to render a decision in circumstances in which there was a gap in the rules. Should a gap occur, the judge was obliged to return a judgment of *non liquet,* meaning it is not clear. A number of European systems influenced by Roman law were forced to depart somewhat, from this conclusion. In the Swiss civil code, for example, when there is a gap in the rules, the judge is instructed to act as a legislator and to fill the gap in as he thinks the legislature would have done. But this is exceptional. For most of the European systems, the belief continues that it is the rules that make decisions; the judge is no more than an artisan applying them in predetermined method.

The radical, even revolutionary feature of American Legal Realism has been its rejection of rules as a way of controlling behavior and in particular providing effective guides for judges. Oliphant and Hewitt led the assault by attacking the fundamental notions of rules as key factors in making choices.

OLIPHANT & HEWITT,
INTRODUCTION TO J. RUEFF, FROM THE PHYSICAL
TO THE SOCIAL SCIENCES: INTRODUCTION TO A STUDY
OF ECONOMIC AND ETHICAL THEORY
x–xxi, xxv–xxvii (H. GREEN TRANS. 1929)

So far as most lawyers, judges and legal scholars are conscious of methods employed in their work, they avow three types of approach to the legal problems with which they deal. For convenience let them be called the *transcendental,* the *inductive* and the *practical* methods respectively. The first two types purport to be wholly methodical and it is the absence of the methodlogy thus professed which is a differentiating characteristic of the third type. It is an interesting excursion to take some concrete legal problem of general interest and to watch the application of each of these three methods to it.

It is necessary to use some caution in choosing the problem thus to be studied in order not to miss the whole point to the matter. The problem in a case before a court for solution may be covered and determined by the explicit language of some valid statute. Again it may be, so far as its facts are concerned, all but wholly identical with some previous case which the court has already decided. This prior decision binds the court under the Anglo-American doctrine of following precedents. In either case the court will decide the question quickly. Indeed, cases whose outcomes is thus clearly predestined by some statute or prior decision often have a way of never getting into the courts at all, which is natural enough, and they are not the cases upon which legal scholars and judges spend their time and efforts. Such cases present no real problems at all and are not good cases to study in order to get an understanding of these three prevalent types of method used on legal problems. We need a case presenting some features of real novelty.

Of the all but infinite number of such cases that might be chosen as an example for study, one as good as any other is that which recently arose in Seattle, Washington. A group of the teachers in the public schools of Seattle were members of a teachers' union and others were being solicited to join. When the time came for re-hiring these teachers for the coming year, the Board of Education is reported to have called upon the teacher, as a condition to being re-employed, to sign a contract to the effect that he would not become a member of this union, and, if already a member, would promptly withdraw.

Has the School Board the privilege to refuse to hire a teacher who will not sign such a contract? Suppose this question reaches the court in the form of an appropriate action or suit to compel the School Board to proceed with the hiring of teachers without the imposition of this condition. How should the court decide the case?

Or suppose the matter comes before the court in a different way. Suppose one of these teachers signs this contract but later joins the union in violation of his promise not to do so and is then sued by the School Board for breach of this contract. Is the contract valid in the sense that the teacher is liable in damages for his breach of it?

Assuming that there is no statute applicable to these questions and that no cases all but identical with these two supposed cases have ever been decided by the courts, how is the court to go about solving these two novel problems?

One approach, and, indeed, one most commonly employed, is what is here called, the "transcendental" approach. It starts by assuming the existence of some general "principles" within which the solution of these and most concrete problems is hidden away. The theory of this approach seems to be that such a general "principle" can, in some way, be evolved out of one's inner consciousness or sensed as enveloping heat is. Thus obtained, it is then set down as the major premise of a deductive syllogism, the subject of whose minor premise is the case which we are examining. The solution of the problem is then brought forth in the conclusion which is drawn from these two premises by the operation of the inexorable laws of deductive logic.

One such general principle, which, according to this method, is pregnant with the solution of the first of our two questions, is as follows:

One who is under no duty to enter into a contract with another may stipulate anything which he pleases as a condition to entering such a contract. The appropriate minor premise is: The Seattle School Board was under no legal duty to enter into a new contract with any of these teachers. It follows as a conclusion that the Seattle School Board may impose, as a condition to entering into new contracts with these teachers, anything which it pleases, including, of course, the stipulation that the teachers shall agree not to become or to remain members of the teachers' union.

Similarly, as to our second question, involving the validity of the teachers' contract not to become or to remain a member of the teachers' union, a broad general principle which can serve as a major premise is to the effect that *persons of full age and of normal mental competency have the legal power freely to determine the terms of any contract which they may enter into, and, when they have so determined them, they are bound by the contract which they have thus made.* The appropriate minor premise for the syllogism is: These Seattle school teachers were persons of full age and of normal mental competency. By the operation of the inexorable laws of deductive logic, the conclusion follows that these school teachers are bound by a valid contract not to become or to remain members of the teachers' union.

One difficulty with this approach is that equally valid lines of argument leading to the exactly opposite result in each case can be constructed. Thus, instead of laying down as a major premise the general principle that one who is under no duty to enter into a contract with another may stipulate anything which he pleases as a condition to entering into such a contract, an equally well authenticated "principle" may be laid down as follows: *Officials administering the trust of public office are bound to distribute the benefits and emoluments of government with impartiality and may not unreasonably discriminate in the appointment of those to discharge public duties and to receive public funds therefor.* The appropriate minor premise to accompany this major one is: To deny employment to a teacher merely because he refuses to agree not to join a particular organization of teachers is an unreasonable discrimination. The wheels of the deductive machine turn and out comes the conclusion that the Seattle School Board does not have the privilege of refusing to hire teachers because of their refusal to sign a contract not to become or to remain a member of the teachers' union.

Or take our second case as to the validity of the contract not to join the teachers' union. Here again, instead of starting with the major premise to the effect that a sane adult may determine for himself the terms of his contract, we can start with an acceptable major premise to the effect that *freedom of association, whether for social or economic purposes, being one of the primary liberties guaranteed by our form of government, any contract to deprive oneself of this freedom is opposed to public policy and void.* An appropriate minor premise would be: The contrast of a Seattle teacher not to become or to remain a member of the teachers' union represents an attempt to surrender his inalienable freedom of association. It follows as a conclusion that his contract not to become or remain a member of the teachers' union is unenforcible.

Upon reflection, it must be clear that, for any case wherein there is a clash of two groups having conflicting interests, two conflicting major premises can always be formulated, one embodying one set of interests, the other embodying the other. Each group has had its advocate to formulate its interests into general propositions and our novel cases all involve some such conflict of interest.

That two such conflicting major premises can always be found is but the result of the fundamental futility of this approach as a method of determining how novel cases should be decided. This futility resides in the way such major premises are obtained. We "create" them, as this book makes abundantly clear, for the very purpose of serving as the bases of our explanation of that totality of social phenomenon which makes up our selected experience, including also what we want to see come about. Of course, they are formulated in such a manner as to include that decision of the case before us which we desire. Those of us who have different and conflicting interests know social "reality" differently. Different factors were operative to determine our respective views of the totality of social pheonomena. Moreover, different ones of us desire different things to come about, including different decisions of the case before the court. In consequence, we "created" different causes to account for social "reality" present or desired. These causes so "created" are the conflicting major premises of this method of approach to legal problems. They are the rational, not the empirical side of the shield.

This being so, it seems clear that this approach, as a method for ascertaining how any novel case should be decided, is not a certain guide. As Mr. Rueff's book so clearly shows, the deductive syllogism is merely a machine which, if run backward, will produce major premises constituting useful stenographic expressions of the totality of our experience and, for law, this totality means the totality of (*inter alia*) previously decided cases and decisions desired.

Nevertheless, if one is to judge from many of the opinions being turned out by our courts today in the decision of cases, the confidence in the validity of this approach is still widespread. This confidence is rooted in an articulate or inarticulate belief in a "natural law" made up of abiding "principles" of right and justice whose existence transcends change in time, place and circumstance. There is neither space nor occasion to write here the history of this school of thought but it is worth while to note how persistent and vigorous it still is in the field of law at least.

The second method of approach to the solution of legal problems is what has been called the "inductive" one. This approach, like the one already described, employs the deductive syllogism, in which syllogism, as before, the case to be decided constitutes the subject of the minor premise. The outstanding difference between the two approaches has to do only with the theory as to the source of major premises.

The "inductive" approach does not assume a system of fundamental and change-less general "principles" existing apart from cases decided in the past. It purports to derive them from an examination of a number of such particular decisions.

Any one of the four hypothetical major premises already set out will serve to illustrate how this is done. Consider the first, which is to the effect the one who is under no duty to enter into a contract with another is at liberty to stipulate anything which he pleases as a condition to entering into such a contract. The method of inductively deriving such a premise consists of examining a number of cases, in which persons other than teachers entering into contracts relating to matters other than union membership have been held free to stipulate contractual terms of varying content. Cases thus examined will include other stipulations insisted upon both by persons not in public office and by those in public office. Such other stipulations will relate to matters of more or of less vital concern to the other party than a teacher's freedom of organization is to him. The cases so examined may thus have the widest range as to their practical similarity to the case up for decision. From all of these cases there is "induced" a principle which becomes the major premise of a deductive syllogism, the subject of whose minor premise is the case to be decided.

If the principle thus "induced" is no broader than the sum of the previous cases which it summarizes, it obviously does not and cannot include the case to be decided, which, by hypothesis, is a new and an undecided case, and, hence, can form no part of the generalization made from previous cases only. If it does not include the case to be decided, it is powerless to produce and determine a decision of it. If it is taken to include the case to be decided, it assumes the very thing that is supposed to be up for decision.

Just as was true with reference to the first approach so also as to this second approach, for each general principle induced from one set of cases, a conflicting general principle leading to an opposite result can usually be "induced" by selecting a different group of past decisions to serve as the basis of the induction and the same variety of factors governs that choice.

To sum up thus far, both of these two approaches have these two weaknesses in common. Each can be used with equal validity by both parties to the litigation and thus be made to "prove" exactly opposite propositions. Each approach must assume that the major premise is broad enough to cover the case to be decided.

Both of these two logical approaches, the "transcendental" and the "inductive," beg the question they are set to solve, and are, therefore, inadequate for the solution of new cases. In each case, the decision reached will depend on the major premise adopted. This in turn will depend upon which of two conflicting interests is to be served.

•   •   •

Under the guise of logic, then, we have methods purely arbitrary, everything depending on the choice of the major premise. This is not objectionable as method; the abuse lies in applying logic in the proper sphere of the empirical. When so applied, there is nothing to insure that the major premise chosen bears any useful relation to prevalent social values—the essence of justice. It is quite as likely to be the dogma of a medieval ghost still ruling as from the mists of antiquity.

•   •   •

To return to the methods of approach to legal problems, the third is the one here called the "practical" approach. Typically it is resorted to only when there arises a case for which no appropriate major premise is apparent (either as a matter of sheer assumption or of induction from prior decisions) or for which evenly competing major premises are so obviously present that this fact cannot be ignored. When so driven to it, the orthodox technique of the judge is to consider the question, as he says, "not on principle but on policy," i.e., explicitly to consider which way, as a practical matter, the case ought to be decided.

When the third method is resorted to, there is seldom any informed and exhaustive marshalling of the practical considerations *pro* and *con*. The court typically reaches its practical solution by reliance upon "common sense"—a sort of intuition of experience which assumes to know how to decide the practical questions of life merely as a result of having lived in life. In exceptional and rare cases where the judge's "common sense" experience is quite obviously inadequate because of the technical character of the question in issue, resort is had to the expert judgment of others as to the practical effects of deciding the case one way or another.

It is, of course, true that to apply to a novel case, the first and second approaches already discussed means that that case must be decided by the operation of sheer chance or by the operation of practical factors. It is really the court's conscious or unconscious consideration of the latter that determines which major premise shall be chosen when either of the first two methods is being pursued. In practical effect, therefore, the difference betwen the first and second method on the one hand and the third method on the other is that the weighing of practical considerations is *consciously* done in the latter only. It is not *methodically* done in either.

• • •

. . . Moreover, a misplaced confidence in the power of logic, whether deductive or inductive, in some mysterious fashion, to coerce the human mind into sure paths leading to sound answers to novel practical questions has resulted in an all but complete absence of any testing of conclusions by observation or experimentation, even by those who scorn "natural law" and profess rigidly to follow inductive processes in passing upon new cases.

There has been such complete absence of effort methodically to develop the empirical side of law and such an over-elaboration of its rational side that scholarshsip in law tends more and more to neglect how courts actually decide cases and more and more to consider what they say about why they decide as they do, which, after all, is stating the same thing in another way.

Unless, therefore, one is prepared to call a body of learning which has substantially no empirical branch or techniques a science, there is no science of law.

FREUDIAN ADAPTATIONS

Jerome Frank confirmed the assault on rules but from a psychological perspective. Any law student knows by the end of the first year of law school—even without the benefit of the Oliphant and Hewitt selection—that he or she can write an equally cogent majority or dissenting opinion and reach virtually any decision dictated in a reasonably persuasive and suitably legalistic fashion. Frank puzzled over the fact that at one level of consciousness, all lawyers knew this, but almost always refused to acknowledge it explicitly. Using some Freudian psychology, he attempted to explain the phenomenon of the persistence of belief in rules in terms of what he conceived to be the central issues of that approach. Anyone familiar with Freud's work will, of course, appreciate that Frank's presentation is a simplification and distortion of what Freud was trying to do. That notwithstanding, *Law and the Modern Mind* proved to be a best seller in jurisprudence.

FRANK, LAW AND THE MODERN MIND
6–10, 18–20, 118–122, 125–131, 133 (1930)

Even in a relatively static society, men have never been able to construct a comprehensive, eternized set of rules anticipating all possible legal disputes and settling them in advance. Even in such a social order no one can foresee all the future permutations and combinations of events; situations are bound to occur which were never contemplated when the original rules were made. How much less is such a frozen legal system possible in modern times. New instruments of production, new modes of travel and of dwelling, new credit and ownership devices, new concentrations of capital, new social customs, habits, aims and ideals—all these factors of innovation make vain the hope that definitive legal rules can be drafted that will forever after solve all legal problems. When human relationships are transforming daily, legal relationships cannot be expressed in enduring form. The constant development of unprecedented problems requires a legal system capable of fluidity and pliancy. Our society would be strait-jacketed were not the courts, with the able assistance of the lawyers, constantly overhauling the law and adapting it to the realities of ever-changing social, industrial and political conditions; although changes cannot be made lightly, yet law must be more or less impermanent, experimental and therefore not nicely calculable. *Much of the uncertainty of law is not an unfortunate accident; it is of immense social value.*

•   •   •

Since legal tentativeness is inevitable and often socially desirable, it should not be considered an avoidable evil. But the public learns little or nothing of this desirability of legal tentativeness from the learned gentlemen of the law. Why this concealment? Have the lawyers a sinister purpose in concealing the inherent uncertainty of law? Why, it may fairly be asked, do they keep alive the popular belief that legal rules can be made predictable? If lawyers are not responsible for legal indefiniteness, are they not guilty, at any rate, of duping the public as to the essential character of law? Are they not a profession of clever hypocrites?

There is no denying that the bar appears to employ elaborate pretenses to foster the misguided notions of the populace. Lawyers do not merely sustain the vulgar notion that law is capable of being made entirely stable and unvarying; they seem bent on creating the impression that, on the whole, it is already established and certain.

•   •   •

. . . Each week the courts decide hundreds of cases which purport to turn not on disputed "questions of fact" but solely on "points of law." If the law is unambiguous and predictable, what excuses can be made by the lawyers who lose these cases? They should know in advance of the decisions that the rules of law are adverse to their contentions. Why, then, are these suits brought or defended? In some few instances, doubtless, because of ignorance or cupidity or an effort to procure delay, or because a stubbornly litigious client insists. But in many cases, honest and intelligent counsel on both sides of such controversies can conscientiously advise their respective clients to engage in the contest; they can do so because, prior to the decisions, the law is sufficiently in doubt to justify such advice.

It would seem, then, that the legal practitioners must be aware of the unsettled condition of the law. Yet observe the arguments of counsel in addressing the courts, or the very opinions of the courts themselves: they are worded as if correct decisions were arrived at by logical deduction from a precise and pre-existing body of rules.

•   •   •

Here we arrive at a curious problem: Why do men crave an undesirable and indeed unrealizable permanence and fixity in law? Why in a modern world does the ancient dream persist of a comprehensive and unchanging body of law? Why do the generality of lawyers insist that law should and can be clearly knowable and precisely predictable although, by doing so, they justify a popular belief in an absurd standard of legal exactness? Why do lawyers, indeed, themselves recognize such an absurd standard, which makes their admirable and socially valuable achievement—keeping the law supple and flexible—seem bungling and harmful?

• • •

This, then is our partial explanation of the basic legal myth: The filial relation is clearly indicated as one important unconscious determinant of the ways of man in dealing with all his problems, including the problem of his attitude towards the law. The several components of this explanation may be summarized thus:

(1) The infant strives to retain something like pre-birth serenity. Conversely, fear of the unknown, dread of chance and change, are vital factors in the life of the child.

(2) These factors manifest themselves in a childish appetite for complete peace, comfort, protection from the dangers of the unknown. The child, "unrealistically," craves a steadfast world which will be steady and controllable.

(3) The child satisfies that craving, in large measure, through his confidence in and reliance on his incomparable, omnipotent, infallible father.

(4) Despite advancing years, most men are at times the victims of the childish desire for complete serenity and the childish fear of irreducible chance. They then will to believe that they live in a world in which chance is only an appearance and not a reality, in which they can be free of the indefinite, the arbitrary, the capricious. When they find life distracting, unsettling, fatiguing, they long to rise above the struggle for existence; to be rid of all upsetting shifts and changes and novelties; to discover an uninterrupted connection between apparently disjunctive events; to rest in an environment that is fundamentally stable. They revert, that is, to childish longings, which they attempt to satisfy through "the rediscovery of father," through father-substitutes. Even where the fear factor is absent, the desire for father-substitutes may persist; father-dependence, originally a means of adaptation, has become an end-in-itself.

(5) The Law can easily be made to play an important part in the attempted rediscovery of the father. For, functionally, the law apparently resembles the Father-as-Judge.

(6) The child's Father-as-Judge was infallible. His judgments and commands appeared to bring order out of the chaos of conflicting views concerning right conduct. His law seemed absolutely certain and predictable. Grown men, when they strive to recapture the emotional satisfaction of the child's world, without being consciously aware of their motivation, seek in their legal systems the authoritativeness, certainty and predictablity which the child believed that he had found in the law laid down by the father.

(7) Hence the basic legal myth that law is, or can be made, unwavering, fixed and settled.

• • •

Many more are the unfortunate sequels or corollaries of the fundamental error. Notably, there is the insistent effort to achieve predictability by the attempt to mechanize law, to reduce it to formulas in which human beings are treated like identical mathematical entities. Under such influences, there is proclaimed the ideal of "a

government of laws and not of men.'' The law is dealt with as if it were settled once
and for all; its rules are supposed to operate impartially, inflexibly: justice must be
uniform and unswerving. In other words, the stress is on generalizations, not on
concrete happenings; on averages, not on details. Little allowance can be made for
justice in the particular case; thus the law is written and thus it must be applied.
Novelty and creativeness must not be permitted. Adaptation of the rules to peculiar
individual circumstances is frowned upon. Discretion in the judge must be avoided
for fear that it would lead to dangerous arbitrariness. Individualization of controversies, response to the unique human facts of the particular case, would make the
law uncertain, unpredictable.

    . . . [E]ven so enlightened a thinker as Salmond [comments]:

• • •

    "The law is impartial. It has no respect of persons. Just or unjust, wise or
    foolish, it is the same for all, and for this reason men readily submit to its
    arbitrament. Though the rule of law may work injustice to the individual case,
    it is nevertheless recognized that it was not made for the individual case and
    that it is alike for all. 'Durum sed ita scriptum est' is allowed as a sufficient
    justification for its imperfect operation in the individual instance. The law-
    abiding spirit so created in a community is a public advantage that far outweighs
    the benefits which may accrue in particular cases by allowing to courts the
    opportunity of substituting what they conceive to be natural justice in lieu of
    justice according to law. An elaborate and technical system of law is doubtless
    in many respects an evil but it is the only road to freedom from greater evils.
    We are in bondage to the law,' said Cicero, '*in order that we may be free.*'
    'Legibus servimus ut liberi esse possimus.' ''

    . . . The law is not a machine and the judges not machine-tenders. There never
was and there never will be a body of fixed and predetermined rules alike for all.
The acts of human beings are not identical mathematical entities; the individual
cannot be eliminated as, in algebraic equations, equal quantities on the two sides can
be cancelled. Life rebels against all efforts at legal over-simplications. New cases
ever continue to present novel aspects. To do justice, to make any legal system
acceptable to society, the abstract preestablished rules have to be adapted and adjusted, the static formulas made alive. It is impossible to do as Salmond would have
judges do, that is, eliminate "the influence of illegitimate considerations applicable
to the particular instance."

    Note that Salmond significantly calls these considerations "illegitimate." There
we touch the nerve of the vice in the conventional attitude expressed by him. For
these considerations "applicable to the particular instance" must and do make themselves felt. And, because they are considered "illegitimate" these influences are
buried and concealed.

    The judges, that is, are asked to perform in the dark what is the very essence of
the judicial function. He must balance conflicting human interests and determine
which of several opposing individual claims the law should favor in order to promote
social well-being. As each case comes before him, he must weigh the claim of the
parties. He must determine whether to fit a particular case into the terms of some
old rules (either because they are working well, or because men have acted in reliance
upon them and he considers the protection of such reliance socially valuable) or to
"legislate" by revising and adjusting the preexisting rules to the circumstances of

the instant controversy. If these powers of the judiciary are unwisely exercised, the community will suffer.

Now, the task of judging calls for a clear head. But our judges, so far as they heed the basic myth, can exercise their power with only a muzzy comprehension of what they are doing. When they make "new rules," they often sneak them into the *corpus juris;* when they individualize their treatment of a controversy, they must act as if engaged in something disreputable and of which they themselves can not afford to be aware. But the power to individualize and to legislate judicially is of the very essence of their function. To treat judicial free adaptation and law-making as if they were bootlegging operations, renders the product unnecessarily impure and harmful.

To do their intricate job well our judges need all the clear consciousness of their purpose which they can summon to their aid. And the pretense, the self-delusion, that when they are creating they are borrowing, when they are making something new they are merely applying the commands given them by some existing external authority, cannot but diminish their effficiency. They must rid themselves of this reliance on a non-existent guide, they must learn the virtue, the power and the practical worth of self-authority.

While the majority of lawyers deny that judges make law, a vigorous minority assert, realistically, that they do. But when does a judge make law? The minority here splits into two groups.

John Chipman Gray is typical of the first group. His contribution to hard-headed thinking about law was invaluable. He compelled his readers to differentiate between *law* and *sources* of law. "The Law of the State," he wrote, "is composed of the rules which the courts, that is the judicial organs of that body, lay down for the determination of legal rights and duties." He felt it absurd to affirm the existence of law which the courts do not follow: "The Law of a State . . . is not an ideal, but something which actually exists." His thesis was that "the Law is made up of the rules for decision which the courts lay down; that all such rules are Law; that *rules for conduct which the courts do not apply are not Law; that the fact that courts apply rules is what makes them Law; that there is no mysterious entity "The Law" apart from these rules; and that the judges are rather the creators than the discoverers of the Law."*

According to Gray, the "law of a great nation" means "the opinons of a half-a-dozen old gentlemen, . . . " For, "if those half-a-dozen old gentlemen form the highest tribunal of a country, then no rules or principle which they refuse to follow is Law in that country." Of course, he added, "those six men seek the rules which they follow not in their own whims, but they derive them from *sources* . . . to which they are directed, by the organized body (the State) to which they belong, to apply themselves."

And those sources of law—i.e., sources of "the rules for decision which the courts lay down"—are statutes, judicial precedents, opinions of experts, customs and principles of morality (using the term morality to include "public policy").

● ● ●

Holmes's description of law can be stated as a revision of Gray's definition, thus: Law is made up not of rules for decision laid down by the courts but of the decision themselves. All such decisions are law. The fact that courts render these decisions makes them law. There is no mysterious entity apart from these decisions. If the judges in any case come to a "wrong" result and give forth a decision which is disordant with their own or any one else's rules, their decision is none the less law.

The "law of a great nation" means the decisions of a handful of old gentlemen, and whatever they refuse to decide is not law. Of course those old gentlemen in deciding cases do not follow their own whims, but derive their views from many sources. And among those sources are not only statutes, precedents, customs and the like, but the rules which other courts have announced when deciding cases. Those rules are no more law than statutes are law. For, after all, rules are merely words and those words can get into action only through decisions; it is for the courts in deciding any case to say what the rules mean, whether those rules are embodied in a statute or in the opinion of some other court. The shape in which rules are imposed on the community is those rules as translated into concrete decisions. Your bad man doesn't care what the rules may be if the decisions are in his favor. He is not concerned with any mysterious entity such as the Law of Massachusetts which consists of the rules usually applied by the courts; he regards only what a very definite court decides in the very definite case in which he is involved; what is the "usual rule" is a matter of indifference to him. To paraphrase Bishop Hoadly, whoever has an absolute authority to translate rules into specific judgments, it is he who is truly the law-giver to all intents and purposes, and not the persons—be they legislators or other judges—who first wrote or spoke the rules. What lawyers are engaged in is predicting or procuring determinations of concrete problems. Clients want those concrete determinations rather than generalizations. Judges are called on not to make rules, but to decide which side of some immediate controversy is to win. The rules are incidental, the decisions are the thing.

Whenever a judge decides a cases he is making law; the law of that case, not the law of future cases not yet before him. What the judge does and what he says may somewhat influence what other judges will do or say in other cases. But what the other judges decide in those other cases, as a result of whatever influences, will be the law in those other cases. The law of any case is what the judge decides.

Often when a judge decides a case he simultaneously publishes an essay, called an opinion, explaining that he used an old rule or invented a new rule to justify his judgment. But no matter what he says, it is his decision which fixes the legal positions of the litigants. If Judge Brilliant decides that Mr. Evasion must pay the federal government $50,000 for back taxes or that Mrs. Goneril is entitled to nothing under the will of her father, Mr. Lear, the contents of the judge's literary effusion makes not one iota of practical difference to Mr. Evasion or Mrs. Goneril. Opinion or no opinion, opinion-with-a-new-rule-announced or opinion-with-old-rules-proclaimed—it is all one to the parties whose contentions he adjudicated.

To be sure, this opinion may affect Judge Conformity who is later called on to decide the case of Rex vs. Humpty Dumpty. If Judge Brilliant in Mr. Evasion's case describes a new legal doctrine, his innovation may be *one* of the factors which actuates Judge Conformity to decide for Humpty Dumpty, if Judge Conformity thinks the facts in Humpty Dumpty's case are like those in Mr. Evasion's cass. But—need it be reiterated?—the new doctrine will be but one of the factors actuating Judge Conformity.

The business of the judges is to decide particular cases. They, or some third person viewing their handiwork, may choose to generalize from these decisions, may claim to find common elements in the decisions in the cases of Fox vs. Grapes and Hee vs. Haw and describe the common elements as "rules." But those descriptions of alleged common elements are, at best, some aid to lawyers in guessing or bringing about future judicial conduct or some help to judges in settling other disputes. The rules will not directly decide any other case in any given way, nor authoritatively compel the judges to decide those other cases in any given way; nor make it possible for lawyers to bring it about that the judges will decide any other cases in any given way, nor infallibly to predict how the judges will decide any other cases. Rules, whether stated by judges or others, whether in statutes, opinions or text-books by learned authors, are not the Law, but are only some among many of the sources to which judges go in making the law of the cases tried before them. Because Gray was still obsessed by the belief that the essence of law is generality, he refused to see that rules formulated by judges are, like statutes, only one of the sources of law. As Edmund Burke put it: "No rational man ever did govern himself by abstractions and universals. The major (premise) makes a pompous figure in the battle, but victory depends upon the little minor of circumstances."

There is no rule by which you can force a judge to follow an old rule or by which you can predict when he will verbalize his conclusion in the form of a new rule, or by which he can determine when to consider a case as an exception to an old rule, or by which he can make up his mind whether to select one or another old rule to explain or guide his judgment. His decision is primary, the rules he may happen to refer to are incidental.

The law, therefore, consists of *decisions* not of rules. If so, then *whenever a judge decides a case he is making law*. The most conservative or timid judge, deny it though he may, is constantly engaged in law-making; if he were to see himself objectively he would doubtless feel like Moliere's M. Jourdain who was astonished to learn that all his life he had been talking prose.

Many a case is decided without the writing of an opinion. The trial judge usually does not bother to tell why he thinks John Doe should lose to Richard Roe. But does he any the less make the law of the case because he has not tried to tell the story of his reactions to the evidence in the shape of legal formulas? Surely law does not come into being only in those cases that are appealed to an upper court which will write an opinion reciting some rules.

Holmes has convinced but a small part of the bar, for his statement of the nature of law is a frontal attack on the basic legal myth and all the sub-myths. But he has some brilliant disciples. Perhaps the hardest-hitting is Professor Walter Wheeler Cook. He expresses the realistic view of law thus:

> "We as lawyers," writes Cook, "like the physical scientists, are engaged in the study of objective physical phenomena. Instead of the behavior of electrons, atoms or planets, however, we are dealing with the behavior of human beings. As lawyers we are interested in knowing how certain officials of society—judges, legislators, and others—have behaved in the past, in order that we may make a prediction of their probable behavior in the future. Our statements of the 'law' of a given country are therefore 'true' if they accurately and as simply as possible describe the past behavior and predict the future behavior of these societal agents. . . . 'Right,' 'duty,' and other names for legal relations are therefore not names of objects or entities which have an existence apart from the behavior of the officials in question, but merely terms by means of which we describe to each other what prophecies we make as to the probable occurrence of a certain sequence of events—the behavior of the officials."
> "The practicing lawyer . . . is engaged in trying to forecast future events. What he wishes to know is . . . what a number of more or less elderly men who compose some court of last resort will do when confronted with the facts of

his client's case. He knows how they or their predecessor have acted in the past in more or less similar situations. He knows that if without reflection the given situation appears to them as not differing substantially from those previously dealt with, they will, as lawyers say, follow precedent. This past behavior of the judges can be described in terms of certain generalizations we call rules and principles of law. If now the given situation appears to the court as new, i.e., as one which calls for reflective thinking, the lawyer ought to know, but usually does not, because of his unscientific training, that his case is 'new' because these rules and principles of law do not yet cover the situation. . . . As it is the lawyer finds competing analogies or principles which are possibly applicable. A familiarity with modern studies of human thinking would reveal to him that his job is not to find the preexisting meaning of the terms in the rules and principles which he wishes the court to apply, but rather to induce the court to give those terms for the first time a meaning which will reach the desired result. If we shift our point of view from that of the practicing lawyer to that of the judge who has to decide a new case, the same type of logical problem presents itself. The case is by hypothesis new. This means there is no compelling reason of pure logic which forces the judge to apply any one of the competing rules urged on him by opposing counsel. His task is not to find the preexisting but previously hidden meaning in these rules; it is to give them a meaning. . . . The logical situation confronting the judge in a new case being what it is, it is obvious that he must legislate, whether he will or no."

What then is the part played by legal rules and principles? We have seen that one of their chief uses is to enable the judges to give formal justifications—rationalizations —of the conclusions at which they otherwise arrive. From that point of view these formulas are devices for concealing rather than disclosing what the law is. At their worst they hamper the clear thinking of the judges, compelling them to shove their thoughts into traditional forms, thus impeding spontaneity and the quick running of ideas; they often tempt the lazy judge away from the proper task of creative thinking to the easier work of finding platitudes that will serve in the place of robust cerebration.

. . . The conscientious judge, having tentatively arrived at a conclusion, can check up to see whether such a conclusion, without unfair distortion of the facts, can be linked with the generalized points of view theretofore acceptable. If none such are discoverable, he is forced to consider more acutely whether his tentative conclusions is wise, both with respect to the case before him and with respect to possible implications for future cases.

But it is surely mistaken to deem law merely the equivalent of rules and principles. The lawyer who is not moderately alive to the fact of the limited part that rules play is of little service to his clients. The judge who does not learn how to manipulate these abstractions will become like that physician, described by Mill, "who preferred that patients should die by rule rather than live contrary to it." The number of cases which should be disposed of by routine application of rules is limited. To apply rules mechanically usually signifies laziness, or callousness to the peculiar factors presented by the controversy.

Viewed from any angle, the rules and principles do not constitute law. They may be aids to the judge in tentatively testing or formulating conclusions; they may be positive factors in bending his mind towards wise or unwise solutions of the problem before him. They may be the formal clothes in which he dressed up his thoughts.

But they do not and cannot completely control his mental operations and it is therefore unfortunate that either he or the lawyers interested in his decision should accept them as the full equivalent of that decision. If the judge so believes, his thinking will be the less effective. If the lawyers so believe, their opinions on questions of law (their guesses as to future decisions) will be unnecessarily inaccurate.

• • •

The unwisdom of confining attention to rules and principles can perhaps be made more clear by such questions as these: Will these rules and principles suffice as the sole or chief bases of predicting future decisions? Are they the only mode of describing all future probabilities for the purpose of predicting future decisions? Do they, in other words, constitute sufficient explanations of past decisions or causes or indications of the course of future decisions? Are they adequate as records of what has heretofore happened in the courts and of what will happen? To what extent are they helpful as histories of past law or as guides to the law that is to come?

An answer to these questions must lead to a vision of law as something more than rules and principles, must lead us again to the opinion that the personality of the judge is the pivotal factor. Where, then, is the hope for complete uniformity, certainty, continuity in law? It is gone except to the extent that the personalities of all judges will be substantially alike, to the extent that the judges will all have substantially identical mental and emotional habits.

NOTES

1. Jerome Frank would have us believe that judges do not apply rules, supposed expressions of community policy derived from certain authoritative sources, but in fact make choices based upon their own preferences. If Frank is correct, what is the source of the content of the choice made by the judges?

2. If Frank's view is correct, what is the authority or legitimacy of a judge's choice? Empirically, law derives from community process; is the judge's decision based on that? How is it determined? Recall in this regard Dworkin's policies and principles in Chapter 7.

3. If Frank is correct in his view, are judicial decisions from the many different courts and court systems in the United States likely to be consistent or will they be a chaotic babble in which each judge does what is right in his own eyes?

4. You will note that Frank addresses judges as if they were the sole sources and appliers of law. In view of the materials developed in Chapters 1 and 2 and the discussions in subsequent chapters, is this an adequate focus? Does the focus itself introduce certain distortions in Frank's theory?

An even more extreme skepticism about rules and about law in general was expressed by Frank's colleague, Thurman Arnold.

ARNOLD, THE SYMBOLS OF GOVERNMENT
31–36, 44–45 (1935)

Far older than economics as a way of thinking about society, stands the "Law." It is perhaps the most mysterious and most occult of all branches of learning, because both the student and the layman are constantly warned that there is so much more here than meets the eye—something above and beyond any particular set of books or institutional habits.

• • •

. . . In spite of all the irrefutable logic of the realists, men insist upon believing
that there are fundamental principles of law which exist apart from any particular
case, or any particular human activity; that these principles must be sought with a
reverent attitude; that they are being improved constantly; and that our sacrifices of
efficiency and humanitarianism in their honor are leading us to a better government.
The truth of such a philosophy cannot be demonstrated or proved. It exists only
because we seem unable to find comfort without it.

The thing which we reverently call "Law" when we are talking about government
generally, and not predicting the results of particular lawsuits, can only be properly
described as an attitude or a way of thinking about government. It is a way of writing
about human institutions in terms of ideals, rather than observed facts. It meets a
deep-seated popular demand that government institutions symbolize a beautiful dream
within the confines of which principles operate, independently of individuals.

• • •

Of course, there are countless rules, institutional habits, and various kinds of
social compulsions in every society. These are often called law. It is not with these
that we are dealing when we study "law" in Western civilization. The fundamental
principles of law do not represent what we do, but what we ought to do. The science
of the law is not the method which judges actually use, but the method which they
ought to use. It is a sort of Heaven which man has created for himself on earth. It
is a characteristic of all paradises that they should be different from what we actually
experience in everyday affairs. Otherwise there would be no object in creating them.
Therefore no one should be surprised because there is so little similarity between the
ideals of the law and what the courts actually do. It is part of the function of "Law"
to give recognition to ideals representing the exact opposite of established conduct.
Most of its complications arise from the necessity of pretending to do one thing,
while actually doing another. It develops the structure of an elaborate dream world
where logic creates justice. It permits us to look at the drab cruelties of business
practices through rose-colored spectacles.

The principles of law are supposed to control society, because such an assumption
is necessary to the logic of the dream. Yet the observer should constantly keep in
mind that the function of law is not so much to guide society, as to comfort it. . . .

"Law" is primarily a great reservoir of emotionally important social symbols.
It develops, as language develops, in spite of, and not because of, the grammarians.
Though the notion of a "rule of Law" may be the moral background of revolt, it
ordinarily operates to induce acceptance of things as they are. It does this by creating
a realm somewhere within the mystical haze beyond the courts, where all our dreams
of justice in an unjust world come true. Thus in the realm of law the least favored
members of society are comforted by the fact that the poor are equal to the rich and
the strong have no advantage over the weak. The more fortunately situated are
reassured by the fact that the wise are treated better than the foolish, that careless
people are punished for their mistakes. The trader takes heart by learning that the
law ignores the more profitable forms of dishonesty in deference to the principle of
individual freedom from governmental restraint. The preacher, however, is glad to
learn that all forms of dishonesty which can be curbed without interfering with
freedom or with economic law are being curbed. The dissatisfied minority is cheered
by the fact that the law is elastic and growing. The conservative is convinced that
it is becoming more and more certain. The industrial serf is told that no man, not
even his own employer, is above the law. His employer, however, feels secure in

the fact that his property is put above ordinary legislative law by the Constitution, which is the highest form of law there is. It protects us on the one hand from regulation, on the other hand from arbitrary power exercised without regulations. It saves us from the mob, and also from the dictator. It prevents capitalism from turning into communism, democracy from becoming the rule of an unthinking people. It gives all people an equal chance for success, and at the same time protects those who have been born in more favored positions of privilege and power.

From a practical point of view it is the greatest instrument of social stability because it recognizes every one of the yearnings of the underprivileged, and gives them a forum in which those yearnings can achieve official approval without involving any particular action which might joggle the existing pyramid of power. It permits the use of an argumentative technique by which powerful institutions can be defended on the ground that taking away privileges from them would take away freedom from the poor.

• • •

Thus we see that "Law" represents the belief that there must be something behind and above government without which it cannot have performance or respect. Even a dictator cannot escape this psychology of his time. He does not quite believe in his own government unless he is able to make gestures toward this prevailing idea. It is child's play for the realist to show that law is not what it pretends to be and that its theories are sonorous, rather than sound; that its definitions run in circles; that applied by skillful attorneys in the forum of the courts it can only be an argumentative technique; that it constantly seeks escape from reality through alternate reliance on ceremony and verbal confusion. Yet the legal realist falls into grave error when he believes this to be a defect in the law. From any objective point of view the escape of the law from reality constitutes not its weakness but its greatest strength. Legal institutions must constantly reconcile ideological conflicts, just as individuals re-concile them by shoving inconsistencies back into a sort of institutional subconscious mind. If judicial institutions become too "sincere," too self-analytical, they suffer the fate of ineffectiveness which is the lot of all self-analytical people. They lose themselves in words, and fail in action. They lack that sincere fanaticism out of which great governmental forces are welded.

The abstract ideals of the law require for their public acceptance symbolic conduct of a very definite pattern by a definite institution which can be heard and seen. In this way only can they achieve the dramatic presentation necessary to make them moving forces in society. Any abstract ideal which is not tied up with a definite institution or memorialized by particular ceremonies, becomes relegated to the limbo of metaphysics and has little social consequence. The institutions which throw about the law that atmosphere of reality and concreteness so necessary for its acceptance are the court and the law school. The one produces the ceremonial ritualistic trial; the other produces a theoretical literature which defends the ideal from attack by absorbing and weaving into its mystical pattern all the ideas of all of the critics. In other words, trials today are the product of courts; books the product of law schools.

LLEWELLYN'S THEORY OF THE CONSTITUTION

Karl Llewellyn, in many ways the dean of American Legal Realism, directed a major part of his early attack on Positivism to the constitutional problem. Llewellyn insisted that the Constitution was not a document but in fact a complex process or institution, an artifact created and maintained over time by human beings, quite conscious of their objectives.

LLEWELLYN, THE CONSTITUTION AS AN INSTITUTION,
34 COLUM. L. REV. 1 (1934)

The argument of this paper runs somewhat as follows: The existing theory of our constitutional law once had some point and value; as applied to a code some century and a half old, it has ceased to serve. It covers perhaps half of what the Court actually does, but covers the half in such manner as to throw the other half into Stygian black. A theory which suffers from any such misrepresentation of the facts confuses and distorts issues. It cannot help but lead, repeatedly, to purblind action. And action which is intellectually purblind, even when it is informed by considerable intuition, registers an unfortunate number of misses on occasions when bull's-eyes are needed. A recanvass of the nature of any working constitution, and especially of ours, as being in essence not a document, but a living institution built (historically, genetically) in first instance *around* a particular Document, would make clear both the fact of and the reasons for the major vagaries of the Court's action. It would lay the foundation for an intelligent reconstruction of our constitutional law theory. The practice of the Court to date offers indication that such reconstruction would be healthy. Indeed, the times make it rather clear that *some* reconstruction is on the way; they call for getting clear the issues involved, before the reconstruction occurs.

• • •

The framework of orthodox constitutional theory consists of a number of propositions which to a new Adam or the well-known sudden visitor from Mars would seem appalling. Indeed, save for the blinders of familiarity, they would appall the thinking man of here and now.

(1) There is the notion that the primary source of information as to what our Constitution comes to, is the language of a certain Document of 1789, together with a severely select coterie of additional paragraphs called Amendments. Is this not extraordinary? The Document was framed to start a governmental experiment for an agricultural, sectional, seaboard folk of some three millions. Yet it is supposed to control and describe our Constitution to give basic information about the government of a nation, a hundred and thirty millions strong, whose population and advanced industrial civilization have spread across a continent.

(2) There is the notion that rulings of the Supreme Court on constitutional points *interpret,* or *apply,* seldom do more than *merely* interpret or apply, this Document as Amended. This notion is a corollary of the first.

(3) From the two flows a third: that the next best source of information as to what the Constitution is, lies in the aforementioned rulings of the Supreme Court.

(4) Related to these notionss are two others. One, that the only amendments to the Constitution are the Amendments.

(5) The other—a sort of premise to the theory at large—that "written" and unwritten constitutions are different in their fundamental nature.

. . . [S]uch propositions or notions . . . are hopelessly misdescriptive of the facts about our constitutional life; . . . they are seriously ill-adapted to achieve the major purposes to which constitutional law theory is designed.

• • •

. . . [A] code purports to be exclusive and all-inclusive, for present and future. Which means that in due course it will be made to "contain" what it does not contain. . . .

When we turn to our Document in the light of this, we find (with surprise) that certain of its phrasings still state portions of the working Constitution with some accuracy. We have in fact a legislature in two houses. It bears the name Congress. The first of these facts has significance. We have a president. That also has significance. The Senate contains two Senators from each state; each sits for six years. That has significance as well. There is more. The Government borrows money upon the credit of the United States. There are heads of departments. The pocket veto is expressly foreseen and provided. Over and above the very considerable number of matters of vital moment (Congressional privilege of debate; federal control over interstate commerce) there are a number of minor rule-of-the-road provisions still more or less in force; entitulations, qualifications for office, and the like. There are, moreover, provisions of rare incidence, such as impeachment, which have perhaps a prophylactic value even when they do not come into actual use. Such a one as succession of the Vice-President enjoys the curious distinction of being regularly applied when the contingency arises, without ever being seriously reckoned with beforehand—unless by the wives of vice-presidential candidates. All of these things, and the rarity of Amendments, make a lasting tribute to the skill of the experimenting Framers. The thought that the nation could work on indefinitely with little more than the original language as its sacred Code has proved correct. The device of enumerating blanket powers leaves the Document, in appearance, still "controlling," despite range or mass of concrete action taken "under" them.

Yet the appearance cheats. Wherever there are today established practices "under" or "in accordance with" the Document, *it is only the practice which can legitimize the words as being still part of our governing Constitution*. It is *not* the words which legitimize the practice. This is the first principle of a sane theory of our constitutional law. Its necessity is patent wherever practice has flatly abrogated a portion of this "supreme law of the land." Discretion in the electoral college is the classic instance; can any doubt that if that college should today disregard their mandate, such action would be contrary to our Constitution? Yet "vote by ballot"—the original language, repeated in the Twelfth Amendment—is a strange way of saying "act as rubber stamps."

• • •

At the beginning of a code experiment, intent of the language has a clear and proper bearing on men's actions. Some changes are toward, some older things are to be carried forward. The words have as their function to guide action. The words are thus—at the beginning—best read in terms of the legislative history. Cases already have been put in the debate. But even here, intent cannot rule purely. Some cases have *not* been put in the debate. Resort must then be had to language and circumstance, to "obvious" rather than to real intent. Forthwith sets in the overwhelming tendency of clear-cut words, in law as in life, to usurp exclusive attention whenever they are met with. And all of this is buttressed by the traditions of our law. Hence the rise of orthodox constitutional theory was, if not inevitable, almost so. A good code being, as indicated, a successful experiment, and one reaching some distance out into so much of the future as wise men might foreguess, the treatment in terms of real plus "necessary" intent does little harm—for some good time. Indeed it furthers mightily the standing of the code while the latter is working its way into traditional acceptance. Such treatment has, that is to say, political value. While the code is young, "intent" contributes to stability.

But the older the code, the less the need for such treatment, and the greater the need for departing from it. Some cases, as has been mentioned, were *not* put in the debate. The "glass" in which the future shows is metal none too highly polished. The outward sign of the newer inward grace is Marshall's word: "We must remember that it is a *Constitution* which we are expounding." Thus is signalled a treatment of the Document in which the vital element becomes the need and circumstances of the case. This also, however, and most unfortunately, darkly. The language is still: "which we are *expounding*." The voice of Jacob speaks over psuedo-hands of Esau: *pseudo*-interpretation. The present need is thus served *as if* by ancient meaning; more recent wisdom clothes itself in ancient words; the road over fiction has begun. More, and worse; it is not conscious fiction. Clothed as it is in the language of original intent and language of the Document, the newer method of dealing does not overthrow or displace the old. Rather does it creep in silently, alongside, but leave the old still nominal master of the house. By its own phrasing it invites confusion. By its own verbal expression it invites its own inventors, in any subsequent case, to overlook it, or to throw it out.

In curiously similar fashion the working Constitution creeps in beside the Document, always in deference, always in nominal subjection. Not being clothed in words, it can be unobtrusive—so much so that even in the occasional instances (electoral college; the President's power over war-making, or dependence on him to initiate legislation, appropriation or other) in which practice flouts the Document, no man sees the flouting, thanks to the observance of the form—thanks also to the now ingrown *institution* of simply *taking* the Document, without thought or inquiry, as being *the* dominant factor.

But the President's position as head of his party, as dispenser of patronage, as limited by the "courtesy of the Senate" as long as administration Senators are good—are these not basic to the framework of our government? Or the expected second term? Or the unconstitutionality of a third? There is only one reason for considering such matters extra-constitutional; the no-longer-reasoned, creaking, ideology which simply *takes* the Document as both dominant and all-containing. Do I mean that the Supreme Court would, on demand, declare the third election of a president to be void? Of course not. I mean that institutions which sit so firmly that the Supreme Court never gets a chance to pass on variations from them attain the zenith of fundamental law's perfection.

Neither, as has been indicated, would I deny the shaping influence of the Document—which is to say, of men's ways and attitudes with reference to the Document—upon the going Constitution. The argument is, that there is only one way of knowing whether, and how far, any portion of the Document is still alive; and that is to watch what men are doing and how men feel, in the connection. If their doing and feeling squares more or less roughly with the language, so much the luckier for the language; if not, so much the worse. Whether the one or the other, it is the action and the attitude which give the light. The argument is, further, that most of the going framework of our Leviathan is hardly adumbrated in the Document. As a criterion of what our working Constitution is, the language fails in both directions. It affords neither a positive nor a negative test.

Here and there the two are square. Some instances above. But, to repeat, the working Constitution is in good part utterly extra-Documentary (the privilege of

Senatorial filibuster; the powers of the Conference Committee; the President's power of removal; the Supreme Court's power of review; the party system; the campaign fund). This, plus the less frequent fact of abrogation, ought to be enough in itself to kill the Cock Robin of orthodox theory (who cares who did it, if it be done?) and to dethrone the Words. But the Words put forward a cover first to be disposed of.

• • •

An institution is in first instance a set of ways of living and doing. It is not, *in first instance*, a matter of words or rules. The existence of an institution lies first of all and last of all in the fact that people do behave in certain patterns *a, b* and *c*, and do not behave in other conceivable patterns *d* to *w*. And the probability that an institution will continue coincides with whatever probability there is that people will continue so to behave. Every living constitution is an institution; it *lives* only so far as that is true. And the difference between a "written" and an "unwritten" constitution lies only in the fact that the shape of action in the former case is *somewhat* influenced by the presence of a particular document, and of particular attitudes toward it, and particular ways of dealing with its language.

A national constitution is a somewhat peculiar institution in that it involves in one phase or another the ways of a huge number of people—well-nigh the whole population. If, like ours, it is a firmly established constitution, it involves ways of behavior deeply set and settled in the make-up of these people—and it involves not patterns of doing (or of inhibition) merely, but also accompanying patterns of thinking and of emotion—attitudes, e.g., potent and largely predictable, toward the verbal symbol "Constitution" and toward any person supposed to be attacking "It."

As an institution of major size, then, our working constitution embraces the interlocking ways and attitudes of different groups and classes in the community—*different* ways and attitudes of *different* groups and classes, but all cogging together into a fairly well organized whole.

• • •

. . . [T]*he working Constitution is amended whenever the basic ways of government are changed* . . . Indeed, *amendment occurs typically by action of the relevant specialists alone,* and without alteration of the language of the Document. Of their own motion they can, and of their own motion or under pressure from interested groups they do, change the manner of government in vital aspects, widen it startlingly, ring out old pieces of the Constitution as bells ring out an Old Year. It is they who have remade the pattern of government as we have passed from a dominantly agricultural into a dominantly industrial and on into a dominantly financial economy. It is they who have tinkered, twisted, invented, on the governmental side, either to further shifts in economic institutions or to catch up with such shifts; to attempt some adjustment of the emergent new to the persistent old. By legislation. By executive or administrative practice. By building the wherewithal to elect or control executives or legislators. Under their hands the Document had been blotted out like the original text upon a double palimpsest.

"By action of the relevant specialists alone." Often a single person (a President), or a single group; more often several groups in active or passive concert. Occasionally, as mentioned, one peculiar group intrudes a veto; the judges. Their power so to do, if called upon, is the most vital reason for invoking the cumbersome machinery of Amendment. It is not the only reason. Neither, thanks to the awkwardness of the machinery, is their veto often an occasion for its invocation. In the main, when the judges interpose their Nay, men shrug and suffer. Yet this much is patent; unless the judges have vetoed, or unless it is confidently believed that if called upon they will veto, Amendment is in the main unnecessary, and is rarely resorted to. Where their veto occurs or is anticipated, the *working* Constitution (which includes judicial review) prescribes Amendment as the sole available process of amending. This not because the Document so says, nor is it because the proposed amendment varies from the Document, or from its judicial "interpretation." *It is because one body of the relevant specialists happen to be unwilling to let the proposed amendment pass.* Why else are we concerned about the personnel of the Court?

• • •

. . . [A] constitution is not the governmental machine at large, but rather its *fundamental* frameword. . . . Hence there remains the problem, within the totality of going government, of marking off how much and which portions are to be regarded as basic to the whole, and therefore, as the working Constitution. . . .

. . . [W]hatever one takes as being this working Constitution, he will find the edges of his chosen material not sharp, but penumbra-like. And the penumbra will of necessity be in constant flux. New patterns of action develop, win acceptance (sometimes suddenly), grow increasingly standardized among an increasing number of the relevant persons, become more and more definitely and consciously "the thing to do," proceed to gain value as honored in tradition—i.e., become things to be accepted in and of themselves without question of their utility—until they take on finally, to more and more of the participants, the flavor of the "Basic."

• • •

The manner of framing the question is psychologically of huge importance. "Is this within the powers granted by the Document?" throws the base-line of inquiry back a century and a half, constricts the vision to the static word, turns discussion into the channels of logomachy. It invites, and too often produces, artificial limitation of attention to the nonessential, the accidental: to wit, what language happens to stand in the Document, or in some hoary—or beardless—test of its "interpretation." . . .

Contrast the effect of framing the question thus: "Is this within the leeway of change which our going governmental scheme affords? And even if not, does the nature of the case require the leeway to be widened to include it?" The base-line then becomes so much of the past only *as is still alive,* and the immediate future comes to bear as well. The tone and tendency of the very question is dynamic. The "nature of the case" invites attention to explicit policy. While that continuity with the past which, if not a duty, is wisdom quite as well as a necessity, is carefully preserved—only that the past concerned is that embodied not in an ancient Text, but in a living Government.

• • •

Four things appear, I trust, from the foregoing.

First, that there is no disposition, under this approach by way of practice and institution, to disregard the normative and ideal element in constitutional law. As stated, in the penumbra the only guidance lies in idealizations. The quarrel is with turning to the Document as their source, in any case in which living practice with a function, or formative practice with a function, exist to serve as better base-lines.

Second, that there is no quarrel to be had with judges *merely* because they disregard or twist Documentary language, or "interpret" it to the despair of original intent, in the service of what those judges conceive to be the inherent nature of our institutions. To my mind, such action is their duty. To my mind, the judge who builds his decision to conform with his conception of what our institutions must be if we are to continue, roots in the deepest wisdom. . . .

The third point is therefore, obviously, that a sane theory of constitutional law would no more be a substitute for adequate personnel than is the prevalent modified and halfway reworking of the ancient orthodoxy. The only guarantee of judicial wisdom will remain the judge.

• • •

There is, in a word, one reason, and one only, for turning in this day to the Text. A "written constitution" is a system of unwritten practices in which the Document in question, by virtue of men's attitudes, has *a little influence. Where it makes no important difference which way the decision goes,* the Text—in the absence of countervailing practice—is an excellent traffic-light. Aside from such cases, any Text of fifty years of age is an Old Man of the Sea. For the rest, the Constitution is an institution. . . .

. . . The view advanced here *sounds* unorthodox. It sounds unorthodox only because it puts into words the *tacit* doing of the Court, and draws from that doing conclusions not to be avoided by a candid child. Whatever the Court has *said,* it has repeatedly made concessions to governmental practice and governmental need. Whatever the Court has *said,* it has repeatedly turned to established governmental practice in search of norms. Whatever the Court has *said,* it has shaped the living Constitution to the needs of the day as it felt them. The whole expansion of the due process clause has been an enforcement of the majority's ideal of government-as-it-should-be, running free of the language of the Document. Whatever the Court has *said,* it has departed from its own precedents whenever it saw fit to do so. It has refined and whittled precedents into unrecognizability, or shifted the line of their development from East to West. Whatever the Court has *said,* it has in deciding repeatedly weighed policy to a degree exceedingly unusual in private law decision. But all of this has, in the main, been *sub silentio.* . . . All of this undermining of the ancient orthodox approach had taken place in prudery, with averted eyes. It minds one of some Victorian virgin tubbing in a nightgown.

RODELL'S INTUITIONISM

Not surprisingly, many devotees of Realism spent much time trying to predict what courts would, in fact, do. Rather than predict on the basis of rules or the formal jurisprudence expressed in past decisions, this branch devised a variety of non-rule or anti-rule approaches to predict future behavior. Fred Rodell developed a romantic but uncannily effective intuitionism, in which he drew heavily on his assumptions about the personalities and values of key judges and possible alignments in collegiate tribunals, to predict outcomes in key cases.

RODELL, NINE MEN: A POLITICAL HISTORY OF
THE SUPREME COURT FROM 1790 TO 1955
6–7, 28–32, 328–330 (1955)

. . . He [Justice Stone] also said: "Courts are not the only agency of government that must be assumed to have capacity to govern." This statement, while true on its face, is essentially and subtly—though of course not deliberately—misleading. No "agency of government" governs; no "court" governs; only the men who run the agency of government or the court or the Supreme Court do the governing. The power is theirs because the decisions are theirs; decisions are not made by abstractions like agencies or courts. Justice Stone, who knew what he meant, might a little better have said: "Five or six of the nine men who make up this Court are not the only men in our government who must be assumed to have the capacity to govern." And he might have added: "Nor are they necessarily the wisest in their judgments; I work with them and have reason to know."

For the old saw, beloved of history textbooks and political speeches, that "ours is a government of laws, not of men," is an insult and an undemocratic canard. Laws are words, nothing more. Laws do not write or enforce or interpret themselves. Even constitutions are no more than words except as men give them flesh and muscle and meaning in action; then the flesh and muscle are molded and the meaning in action is directed by men. The words of the Soviet constitution are in many ways more democratic than those of ours—as are the words of the constitutions of several Latin-American countries now run by dictators. And the cold truth about "laws, not men" was never better put than by one of the Founding Fathers, John Mercer of Maryland, who said that all of them were wise enough to know as they hammered out the U.S. Constitution back in 1787: "It is a great mistake to suppose that the paper we are to propose will govern the United States. It is the men whom it will bring into the government and interest in maintaining it."

Among those men, and most powerful of all of them for the past century and a half, are the Justices of the U.S. Supreme Court. They may say—and often do—that it is not *they* who make the decisions, lay down the rules, give orders to every other governing official in the land; they may say they do nothing but "interpret" the laws, including the Constitution; they may talk at times as though they neither had nor need human minds, as though they might almost as well be a nine-headed calculating machine, intricately adjusted to the words of the constitution and of lesser laws, and ready to give automatic answers to the attorneys who drop their briefs in the proper slot and push the button. But even non-lawyers have come to find a trifle naive and unconvincing the old fantasy that our government, especially its judicial branch, is mechanically controlled by laws, not by men. If it were, how explain split Supreme Court decisions (5–4, 6–3, 7–2, even 8–1); how explain dissenting opinions that too often make more sense than the majority "opinions of the Court"; how explain the "overruling" of past decisions—a term which means that the same question, decided one way before, is now decided exactly the opposite way?

• • •

. . . (One Justice recently rebuked a lawyer who referred, in argument, to "your former opinion, Mr. Justice," by snapping: "You don't mean *my* opinion; you mean the opinion of the *Court*.") The myth has also been fostered by almost all legal scholars who write about the Court; the more naive discuss "the Court's" work, "its" philosophy, "its' shifting points of view, as though "it" were a strange creature with eighteen legs and one brain; the more sophisticated deplore, particularly of late, the Court's failure to act as they think "it" ought to act—that is, as a single-purposed, predictable, and perforce mono-minded institution, for all its being made up of nine men.

• • •

The second and related myth, even more deeply imbedded in our folklore of government, has it that the men who become Justices become simultaneously—or ought to become if they don't—politically sterile; that they put on, or should put on, with their robes a complete impartiality or indifference toward the nation's social and economic problems; that they switch, or should switch, their minds to neutral in dealing with every issue outside the verbal needlework of the law.

• • •

. . . The idea that a human being, by a conscious act of will, can rid his mind of the preferences and prejudices and political slants or values that his whole past life has accumulated in him, and so manage to think in the rarefied atmosphere of simon-pure objectivity, is simply a psychological absurdity. . . . Myths or no myths, solemn show or no solemn show, the Supreme Court is nothing more than nine sometimes wise, sometimes unwise, but always human, men.

And so it is superficial, however technically true, to say, for example, that "the Supreme Court," in 1935, declared unconstitutional the New Deal's railroad retirement act (under which all railroads would have had to chip in to a compulsory insurance fund to pay annuities to retired railroad workers over the age of 65). It is somewhat more accurate, more meaningful, and more revealing to say that five Supreme Justices—one of whom made the legal reputation that led to his Justiceship as a lawyer for the Great Northern, the Northern Pacific, and the Chicago, Burlington, and Quincy railroads (Butler); one of whom was kicked upstairs to the Court because of his cantankerousness as Attorney-General, including his reluctance to prosecute the New York, New Haven, and Hartford Railroad on anti-trust charges (McReynolds); one of whom had made a small fortune and a large legal name for himself by representing, in government and out, the Union Pacific Railroad (Van Devanter); one of whom had been a close senate friend of a certain Senator Harding who later, as President, named him to the Court, after the voters of Utah had refused to re-elect him because of his reactionary Senate record in behalf of corporations, including railroads (Sutherland); and one of whom, as a former Philadelphia lawyer, had counted among his several large corporate clients the Pennsylvania Railroad plus its affiliates (Roberts)—that these five Justices outvoted their four considerably abler colleagues (Hughes, Brandeis, Cardozo, and Stone—who dissented) and thus negated the will of Congress, the will of the country, as well as, quite coincidentally of course, saving money for the railroads. Not all of the Supreme Court's constitutional decisions are as easy to explain as this one, or as crystal-clear in meaning and in motive. But none of those decisions can be explained or analyzed or understood on any other than a sheerly superficial, legalistic level, except in terms of the justices, the *men*, who made them.

Hence, any attempt to explore and evaluate the Court's role in our national history—past, present, and future—must stem from and come constantly back to the men who really play that role in the Court's name. It must cut through all the folderol of ceremony and sanctimony; it must not be taken in by the quaint notion that words, whether of constitution or statute, can govern, without men to use the words as the men see fit to use them; it must be kept straight that the so-called reasons the Justices give for what they do, in their long and legal-languaged opinions, are as often self-justifying excuses, wittingly or unwittingly made, as they are genuine sources of decision. Any such attempt must recognize too, in a realistic way, that the overwhelming political power held by the Justices is triply an irresponsible power—in that they are accountable to no one but themselves; in that they never take, nor can they take, responsibility for affirmative government action; and in that they can either use or refuse to use their power as they please, without ever so much as telling why.

And last—and first—any such attempt must consider the proper part, if any, to be played by a small and autocratic group of men who make authoritarian decisions within the framework of a constitutional democracy.

• • •

Prediction in print is a preoccupation for the foolhardy. And yet, if the prior lives of Justices help shape, and so help foretell, what their slants and bents on the Court will be, a rough guess—to be checked ten years hence—can be made about Harlan. Too conventional in background, too conformist in career, ever to match the fiery independent thinker and liberal dissenter who was his grandfather, Harlan may yet prove not so orthodox a Justice as many suppose; indeed, he is a new breed of cat on the Court. Though born in Chicago, he is a Princeton-to-Oxford-to-Wall-Street-law-practice product—the Court's first Ivy League "white-shoe boy," its first Rhodes Scholar, its first full-fledged Eastern Dewey Republican. That he has always been well-to-do and upper-crust does not necessarily betoken automatic conservatism; so was Holmes. Politically closer to Warren than to any other present Justice, despite major differences in their pre-Court work and lives, Harlan is also apt to be *judicially* closer, but without the Westerner's strength and simplicity. Like his Chief, he has never held federal office—except for a brief apprenticeship on a federal court of appeals—and his stints of public service (odd jobs of investigating or prosecuting) have been for the state; the national government will get from him no special preference. Again like Warren, his prosecuting was tempered with humanity, and the few criminal cases he heard as a court of appeals judge display concern for the fair treatment of defendants; he will be no Vinson at kicking the Bill off Rights around.

In all likelihood, the general slant of the new Justice will be just about the opposite of Reed's—except for a similarly super-lawyerlike over-attention to detail. On economic issues, where the country-bred boy tended anti-business, the big-city boy will tend pro-business; where the rural small-town lawyer tended pro-labor, the Wall Street financial lawyer will tend anti-labor; where the federal government servant tended strongly pro-national and somewhat anti-state on taxes and regulation, the private practitioner and occasional state servant will tend strongly anti-national and somewhat pro-state. It is on civil liberties that Harlan may turn the tables the other way; for where Reed, ex-Solicitor-General of the U.S., came close to thinking that government, especially the federal government, could not be wrong—no matter how it treated the Bill of Rights—Harlan may have that sense of *noblesse oblige* on such matters which so often goes with born-and-bred economic conservatism. True, Harlan, during the court-of-appeals prelude to his Justiceship, did deliver the decision that sent a dozen second-string Communist leaders to jail under the Smith Act; but it was not his job to question the Smith Act's constitutionality, so recently upheld by the Vinson Court in the Dennis case; and his patient, painstaking, sixty-page opinion reads almost as though he were seeking some way to set the poor fools free. It is far more meaningful that, in 1940, Harlan served as special counsel to New York City's Board of Higher Education in its futile effort, blocked by local judicial Philistines, to bring to the City College faculty the famous if unconforming philosopher, Bertrand Russell. Just possible, if hopefully, the appointment of Harlan may give the court one more and badly-needed vote for freedom of the mind.

BEHAVIORAL JURISPRUDENCE: JURIMETRICS

Rodell's prediction by romantic intuitionism was rejected by a number of scholars who sought a more systematic and scientific approach. Glendon Shubert, the leader of a school known as Behavioral Jurisprudence and called by some "Jurimetrics," built on the work of Underhill Moore. He sought to develop a systematic, behavioral method for predicting judgments.

SCHUBERT, BEHAVIORAL JURISPRUDENCE,
2 LAW & SOC'Y REV. 407 (1968).

For over two thousand years, the science of law has been a dull esoteric subject, with traditional logic its long suit and the syllogism its ace in the hole. . . . Throughout these two millennia, jurisprudence was a "science" only in the sense of "moral science," that is to say, it was a branch of philosophy. It was concerned with prescriptive norms rather than with descriptions of human action, and therefore, it dealt almost exclusively with ideals for, rather than with the realities of, the behavior of judges, lawyers, jurors, and litigants.

The emergence of social science during the nineteenth century was both the precursor and the cause of significant changes in the "scientific" component of legal science.

• • •

The realist movement in American jurisprudence, like the social science of its day, was highly pragmatic and empirical in its orientation, but not overly burdened or concerned with the development of systematic theory. More recently, as one of the fruits of the shift in emphasis (and in scope) that is involved in the difference between social and behavioral science, a really new approach to jurisprudence has evolved. . . . All have agreed, however, that the proper subject of study is not "law" in the classical sense of verbal statements purporting to rationalize the content of constitutional and statutory documents, or appellate court opinions. Inquiry has instead focused on what human beings, cast in socially defined roles in certain characteristic types of decision-making sequences which traditionally have been identified as "legal," do in their interactions and transactions with each other.

• • •

The new approach defines its data on the basis of observations of what kinds of factors influence adjudicatory decisions, what kinds of values are preferred in such decisions, and how the decisions affect the behavior of other people. The old approach defines as its data the verbal statements of opinions that are written to justify the decisions of appellate court majorities, and seeks to discover the effect of such opinions upon a metaphysical essence which is called "the law."

The new approach focuses upon humans who act in adjudicatory roles, and is interested in understanding judges as people—or, better put, people as judges. The old approach studies institutions which it calls courts, and what courts do purports to be the objective of investigation.

The new approach is very much concerned with understanding the effect that cultural—and subcultural—differences have upon adjudicatory behavior.

• • •

Figure 1 depicts in an elementary way the kinds of structures, functions, and interrelationships that from a behavioral standpoint are important to the understanding of the judicial system, and indeed, to any other kind of political system.

• • •

Relationships among other persons with whom an individual comes into contact constitute the social system. . . . These are represented by the residual social space

"C." The cultural system represents widely accepted patternings of beliefs and social values, such as myths, customs, and law. The content of this system is ideational rather than any directly observable activity.

The sociopsychological segment (2), which represents the overlap between the personality system and the social system, is concerned with the individual's socialization and recruitment, and with his attributes and attitudes; the psychocultural segment (3), where the personality and cultural systems overlap, represents the individual's conception of his role(s), and the ideologies which he accepts. The sociocultural segment (4) of overlap between the social and cultural systems represents the patterning of institutional roles, and the output functions of accommodation and regulation of the behavior of others.

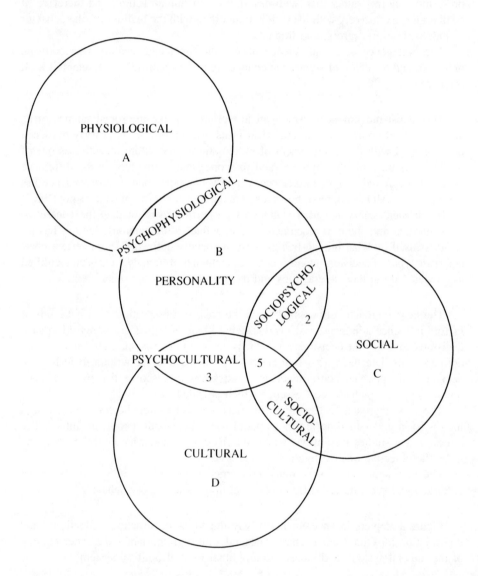

Figure 1. A BEHAVIORAL VIEW OF THE SUBSYSTEMS OF ANY POLITICAL
(INCLUDING ANY JUDICIAL) SYSTEM

An individual's physiological system will affect his political relationships with other persons and their ideas only indirectly, through the functioning of his personality. Therefore, only the three subsystems, personality, social, and cultural, share a space of mutual intersection (which is also, necessarily, the area of mutual intersection among the three joint segments of sociopsychological, psychocultural and sociocultural functions). This central space, segment 5, represents the individual's decision-making, i.e., his choices among political alternatives.

One can infer from Figure 1 that when any individual is cast in a political role, his choices among alternative possibilities for action will depend upon complex (and doubtless shifting, through time) interdependencies among several different sets of variables. In order to understand, and perhaps ultimately to be able to predict with some accuracy, how any individual acts or is likely to act in such a role, it is necessary that we observe and examine data which bear upon operations involving each of the relevant variables. It should be emphasized, however, that each of the concepts denoted in the figure (e.g., "attributes" and "institutional roles") is itself a complex configuration of subvariables. Anyone who has ever attempted to do either field or experimental research involving an attempt to measure the effect of any *one* of these subvariables upon behavior is well aware of the magnitude, complexity, and long-range implications of the research task that Figure 1 implies.

• • •

Psychological rationality is in a modal position between the other two types of rationality. According to this theory, judges receive certain information concerning cases they are expected to decide, as a consequence of social input functions of interest articulation and aggregation, and of interaction and communication. (These correspond to argument between counsel, the examination of witnesses in trials, and the sequence of interim decisions, by the judge, on questions of procedure that arise during the course of the trial; or also, in appellate courts, to briefs filed by counsel and to discussions among the judges.) To be distinguished from this proximate information about the pending case is the more stable and enduring kind of information which the judge has accepted, at earlier stages of his career, as the result of his socialization and recruitment experience. Sociopsychological structures such as judge's attributes and his attitudes are causally related to, and dependent upon, the input functions of socialization and recruitment. Both kinds of information—the proximate data about the case, and his predisposition or bias toward the kind of policy question that it raises for decisions—are of critical importance to the choice that he will make, and both kinds of information are produced primarily as the result of his interaction with other people.

Perception, cognition, and choice-making are personality function concepts which purport to distingiush sequential states in a continuous and continuing process. Their utility is for purposes of analysis. For example, both the logical and the non-logical types of rationality also assume—although usually with no discussion of the matter—that perception takes place before, in the first instance, skill can be exercised or, in the second instance, displacement can occur. But neither cognition nor choice-making are necessary elements in the logical, or in the non-logical, theories of personality. The personality structures which will affect one's choice-making are ideology and role. The former is his pattern of beliefs, expectations, obligations and related knowledge about life and the world and the latter is his understanding of others' expectations, and his own expectations, concerning how he shall make his choices and what they should be. The latter point in particular—the psychocultural concept of role, in comparison to the logical concept of stare decisis, and the non-logical concept of rationalization—illustrates the advantages that the psychological theory offers, even if we speak for the moment only in terms of greater flexibility. There is nothing to preclude either stare decisis or rationalization from supplying the group of justices; but both stare decisis and rationalization are limiting cases, and the psychological theory does not require that *either* of these provide a monistic definition of judicial role.

The output functions of a judge's decisions are, from a cultural point of view, the policy norms associated with his choices, and, from a sociological point of view, output functions include the accommodation and regulation of the interests of the litigants, and of other persons directly affected.

• • •

. . . .The present difficulty in testing the utility of the model is that most of the relevant empirical data remain to be observed, analyzed, and reported. But, however inadequate it might prove to be when data become available to appraise its "goodness of fit," the theory of psychological rationality may in the meantime be of some use in guiding the very research efforts which can result in its disconfirmation. At least, it offers two considerable advantages over the conventional wisdom about judges: it is not fettered with the idiosyncratic parameters of the American politico-legal culture; and it offers some promise of forging a theory about judges and courts which can articulate with what otherwise is known scientifically about human behavior.

NOTES

1. The attempts of jurimetricians to predict the behavior of judges is fraught with difficulties. Although Schubert once stated, "The number of basic attitudinal dimensions that are relevant to the decision-making of the United States Supreme Court is very small," *Judicial Behavior* 552 (G. Schubert ed. 1964), he still admitted the complexity of the task he had set himself.

"Out of the entire situation (including the record, briefs, oral argument, conversation with colleagues, newspaper and television commentary, law review articles, the competence of his clerk, the current state of mental and physical health of himself and his family, perhaps the war news from Viet Nam, et cetera and infinitem, plus the remembered and the sublimated historical antecedents of all these events) a judge defines the issue to which he will react in his decisions . . ." *Judicial Decision-Making* 61 (G. Schubert ed. 1963).

2. Predictions of judicial decisions by behavioralists are often based upon defining the problem in terms of legal doctrine, or in such crude political terms as whether a particular judge is "liberal" or "conservative"; those formulae must be oblivious to the numerous complex factors actually entering into a decision. Often ignored or downplayed are the effects on decision of the identity of the litigant, the arenas or contexts in which the disputes arose, the values of goals which the judge may seek to achieve or enhance, the class and culture of a particular judge, the existence or degree of crisis which prevails in a particular case, psychological factors in the judge's personality and many other factors which influence a particular decision. Failure to take adequate account of such factors can seriously distort predictions.

3. The attitudes of a judge, which jurimetricians attempt to isolate and measure, are often not based upon, or even consistent with findings of psychology, but rather, are confined to political science concepts. This is exemplified by the attempt to label judges as "conservative," or "liberal," or to test alleged "sympathy" judges may have for particular rights. Thus, Schubert has attempted to measure attitudes of judges in terms of social liberalism and social conservatism, economic liberalism and economic conservatism, and attitudes regarding judicial

activism versus judicial restraint. Schubert, Prediction from a Psychometric Model, in *Judicial Behavior* 569 (G. Schubert ed. 1964). Similar attempts have been made to measure attitudes or sympathy toward labor unions and toward government regulation of business. (See Spauth, Warren Court Attitudes Toward Business, in *Judicial Decision-Making* 79 (G. Schubert ed., 1963)).

4. The attempt at "scientifically" based prediction of judicial decisions has led to the claim that by the use of Boolean Algebra and simultaneous equations, one can "obtain a *precise and exhaustive* distinction between combinations of facts that lead to decisions in favor of one party and combinations of facts that lead to decisions in favor of the opposing party." (Cort, Simultaneous Equations and Boolean Algebra in the Analysis of Judicial Decisions, in *Judicial Behavior* 477 (G. Schubert ed., 1964)). Others have urged the use of symbolic logic and coefficients of correlation. (See Nagel, Using Simple Calculations to Predict Judicial Decisions, 4 *Am. Behav. Sci.* 24 (1960); Lawlor, Foundations of Logical Decision-Making, *Mod. Uses Logic & L.* 98 (1963); *idem,* Stare Decisis and Electronic Computers, in *Judicial Behavior,* 492 (G. Schubert ed. 1964). Such methodology presumes that judges will apply the same legal doctrine and case precedents to similar facts and that all will have the same visceral reaction to certain fact patterns. It ignores the numerous complex factors which may affect a decision. More fundamental, however, is the complete failure even to attempt to clarify and postulate goals and to study the past and existing predicted conditions, in order to determine the decision which will most effectively enhance the goals desired. As one harsh critic put it, "What is wrong with these studies, of course, is not that they use statistics. We shall never be able to dispense with counters and verifiers. But it is wrong to suppose that merely by compiling figures we can arrive at science. There is something twisted about the practice. During the last war the natives of New Guinea became accustomed to receiving goods from the sky. After the war the planes came no more. Then there developed a new form of the 'Cargo Cult': The natives built landing strips and fascimiles of airplanes on the ground in the hope that they would attract planes loaded with cargo from the sky. Mathematical behavioralists admire the natural scientist. They have built their facsimiles on the ground. But they have not drawn down bounty from the sky." Wormuth, Matched-Dependent Behavioralism: The Cargo Cult in Political Science, 20 *W. Pol. Q.* 809, 849 (1967).

CRITICAL LEGAL THEORY

A contemporary efflorescence of Legal Realism is to be found in a movement generally called the Critical Legal Studies. Adherents of this group identify themselves with the Realist movement and continue their often polemical style.

GORDON, NEW DEVELOPMENTS IN LEGAL THEORY, IN THE POLITICS OF LAW: A PROGRESSIVE CRITIQUE 281 (D. KAIRYS ED. 1982)

This will be a composite biography, partly imaginary and partly autobiographical. It will not tell the story of any particular person involved in the "critical legal studies" movement; nor could it, because we have come from so many different starting points—some of us law teachers with humanist intellectual concerns and liberal (civil rights and antiwar) political involvements in the 1960s and 1970s; others radical activists of the 1960s who identified with neo-Marxist versions of socialist theory or feminism or both; still others primarily practitioners, many of whom are associated with the National Lawyers Guild and who work in collective law practices, legal service offices, or a variety of other progressive jobs. Yet for all the diversity in background of this collection of people, and the perpetual, sharp conflicts over issues of method within it, there is an amazing amount of convergence in the work of this group, which suggests that there may be some common features to our common disenchantment with liberal legalism.

So, imagine someone who first started thinking seriously about law as a student in law school in the late 1960s.

•   •   •

Basically, the teachers taught us to do two things: doctrinal analysis and policy analysis. Doctrinal analysis was (as I now recognize) a kind of toned-down legal realism; we learned how to take apart the *formal* arguments for the outcome of a case and to find the underlying layer of "principles" and "purposes" behind the rules. Policy analysis was a kind of quickie utilitarian method for use in close cases—it was supposed to enable us to argue for outcomes that could efficiently serve social policies somehow inhering in the legal system. The policies were derived either by appeal to an assumed general consensus of values (personal security, economic growth), or to an assumed (and assumed to be good) trend of historical development (such as from protecting producers to protecting consumers). Sometimes there would be competing policies, representing conflicting "interests"; here the function of policy analysis was to provide an on-the-spot rapid-fire "balancing" of interests.

•   •   •

Outside politics must have made it easier for law students of the late 1960s and early 1970s than it had been for those who had graduated just before them to see what was wrong with this vision of law as neutrally benevolent technique. The appeal to a deep social consensus was hardly a winner in a society apparently splintering every day between blacks and whites, hawks and doves, men and women, hippies and straights, parents and children. The appeal to the underlying march of historical progess was in trouble for the same reason. The vision of law as a technocratic policy science administered by a disinterested elite was tarnished, to say the least, for anyone who watched the "best and the brightest" direct and justify the war in Vietnam. The fluent optimistic jargon of policy science in the middle of such unspeakable slaughter and suffering seemed not only absurdly remote from any real world of experience but literally insane.

Under these conditions young lawyers became desperate for a more plausible and less compromised view of the social uses of law;

•   •   •

. . . The greatest contribution was probably an eduation in all the myriad ways in which the system was not a set of neutral techniques available to anyone who could seize control of its levers and pulleys but a game heavily loaded in favor of the wealthy and powerful. Procedure was so expensive and slow that one's side could be exhausted in a single engagement with an enemy who could fight dozens. One was likely to obtain the most favorable rule outcomes just where enforcement of them seemed most hopeless. And even the doctrinal victories peaked all too early; just as a promising line of rules opened up, it would be qualified before it became truly threatening (e.g., antidiscrimination doctrine became quagmired at sanctioning intentional state action against groups; equal protection doctrine flirted briefly with remedies for wealth inequalities, then scurried into retreat).

At this point, the felt need for a theory that would help explain what was going on became acute; and the kind of theory that seemed called for was one that connected what happened in the legal system to a wider political-economic context. Here orthodox legal thought had almost nothing to offer because even though liberal lawyers had learned from the legal realists that all law was social policy, their working methods kept technical (narrowly legal) issues at the forefront of legal analysis; the conventions of scholarship dictated that if social context were to be discussed at all, it had to be done casually and in passing. Liberal activist lawyers in the process of radical disillusionment had to reach back to the sources of social and political theory, which law school had pushed out of focus. When they did, it was like discovering that what had happened to them was something they had known about all along but had partially suppressed.

The main kinds of common-sense explanations available to them were what are sometimes called instrumental theories of the relationship between law and society. In the *liberal* version, law is a response to social "demands." These demands are frequently those of specific interest groups that want some advantage from the state; law represents the compromise bargains of multiple conflicting interest groups. Other times the demands are more generally expressed as those of the functional "needs" of "the society" or "the economy"; e.g., "the market" needs stable frameworks for rational calculation, which the legal system responds to with contract enforcement, security devices, recording of land titles, etc. In the *orthodox Marxist* version of instrumentalism, of course, bourgeois law is a product not of just any group's demands but specifically those of the capitalist ruling class. In both versions, a "hard" world of economic actions (or "material base") determines what happens in the "soft" world of legal rules and processes (as part of the ideological "superstructure"). Also common to both versions is a deep logic theory of historical change. In the liberal version, this is usually: feudalism $\lozenge$ mercantilism $\lozenge$ industrial capitalism $\lozenge$ organized capitalism $\lozenge$ modern welfare capitalism; in the Marxist version, much the same with slightly different terms. Both versions assume that legal systems go through different stages that are necessary functions of the prevailing economic organization. Liberals, for example, explained nineteenth-century tort rules that put all the risks of accidents or product defect on workers and consumers either as functional to that stage of industrial development (because infant industries needed to keep their costs down) or as the result of a temporary (and soon remedied) imbalance of political power in favor of capitalists; the instrumentalist Marxist said much more straightforwardly that capitalists just imposed these costs on workers.

• • •

Nonetheless, anyone who thought about it would begin to see a great many problems with crude instrumentalist theory. The capitalists did not seem to win all the time through state policy and law; workers had been granted rights to organize and bargain collectively out of it, blacks had received the abolition of slavery and some affirmative government action promoting their rights, radicals had been granted some rights to teach and write, the poor had received some welfare entitlements, etc. Obviously, all this could be rerationalized as serving the long-term interests of the capitalist ruling class, but that would take considerable refinements of the theory. Some writers spoke of the strategy of "corporate liberalism"—the ruling class promotes government social-welfare programs and regulation of business in order to prevent political (through popular risings) and economic (through chaotic competition) destabilization of the social order. Other writers, borrowing from European neo-Marxist sources, began to speak of law as a means of "legitimating" class society; in order to be bearable to those who suffer most from it, law must be perceived to be approximately just, so the ruling class cannot win all the time. Still others, extending the point, saw the "legitimacy" of capitalist society as importantly inhering in (among a number of other factors, such as a certain degree of social mobility, social security for everyone, and apparently meritocratic criteria for determining people's shares of income and wealth) the legal system's promises to protect rights of freedom and security for everyone in the society equally—promises that must sometimes be made good. So, since the legal system must at least appear universal, it must operate to some extent independently (or with "relative autonomy," as the saying goes) from concrete economic interests or social classes. And this need for legitimacy is what makes it possible for other classes to use the system against itself, to try to entrap it and force it to make good on its utopian promises. Such promises may therefore become rallying points for organization, so that the state and law become not merely instruments of class domination but "arenas of class struggle."

Once leftist lawyers became accustomed to thinking this way, a whole new set of problems and questions opened up. One was that given this view of the matter, hard-won struggles to achieve new legal rights for the oppressed began to look like ambiguous victories. The official legal establishment had been compelled to recognize claims on its utopian promises. But these real gains may have deepened the legitimacy of the system as a whole; the labor movement secured the vitally important legal rights to organize and strike, at the cost of fitting into a framework of legal regulation that certified the legitimacy of management's making most of the important decisions about conditions of work.

In any case, once one begins to focus closely on problems such as these, one begins to pay much more attention to what instrumentalists think of as the "soft" or "superstructural" aspects of the legal system. If what is important about law is that it functions to "legitimate" the existing order, one starts to ask *how* it does that. And for the purposes of this project, one does not look only at the undeniably numerous, specific ways in which the legal system functions to screw poor people—though it is always important to do that too, to point it out as often and as powerfully as possible—but rather at all the ways in which the system seems at first glance basically uncontroversial, neutral, acceptable. This is Antonio Gramsci's notion of "hegemony," i.e., that the most effective kind of domination takes place when both the dominant and dominated classes believe that the existing order, with perhaps some marginal changes, is satisfactory, or at least represents the most that anyone could expect, because things pretty much have to be the way they are. So Gramsci says, and the "critical" American lawyers who have accepted his concept agree, that one must look closely at these belief-systems, these deeply held assumptions about politics, economics, hierarchy, work, leisure, and the nature of reality, which are profoundly paralysis-inducing because they make it so hard for people (including the ruling classes themselves) even to *imagine* that life could be different and better.

Law, like religion and television images, is one of these clusters of belief—and it ties in with a lot of other nonlegal but similar clusters—that convince people that all the many hierarchical relations in which they live and work are natural and necessary. A small business is staffed with people who carry around in their heads mixed clusters of this kind: "I can tell these people what to do and fire them if they're not *very* polite to me and quick to do it, because (a) I own the business; (b) they have no right to anything but the minimum wage; (c) I went to college and they didn't; (d) they would not work as hard or as efficiently if I didn't keep after them; a business can't run efficiently without a strong top-down command structure; (e) if they don't like it they can leave," etc.—and the employees, though with less smugness and enthusiasm, believe it as well. Take the ownership claim: the employees are not likely to think they can challenge that because to do so would jeopardize their sense of the rights of ownership, which they themselves exercise in other aspects of life ("I own this house, so I can tell my brother-in-law to get the hell out of it"): they are locked into a belief-cluster that abstracts and generalizes the ownership claim.

•   •   •

Now, the point of the work (usually called anti-positivist or interpretive) that some of the "critical" lawyers are doing is to try to describe—to make maps of—some of these interlocking systems of belief. Drawing here on the work of such "structuralist" writers are Levi-Strauss and Piaget, they claim that legal ideas can be seen to be organized into structures, i.e., complex cultural codes. The way human beings experience the world is by collectively building and maintaining systems of shared meanings that make it possible for us to interpret one another's words and actions. Positivist social scientists (who would include both liberal and Marxist "instrumentalist" legal theorists) are always trying to find out how social reality objectively works, the secret laws that govern its action; they ask such questions as, "Under what economic conditions is one likely to obtain formal legal rules?" Anti-positivists assert that such questions are meaningless, since what we experience as "social reality" is something that we ourselves are constantly constructing; and that this is just as true for "economic conditions" as it is for "legal rules." If I say, "That's a bus taking people to work," I'm obviously doing much more than describing a physical object moving through space; my statement makes no sense at all except as part of a larger cultural complex of shared meanings; it would mean little or nothing to you if your culture were unfamiliar with bus technology, with "work" as an activity performed in a separate place outside the family compound, or indeed with "work" as distinct from "play" or "prayer."

"Law" is just one among many such systems of meaning that people construct in order to deal with one of the most threatening aspects of social existence; the danger posed by other people, whose cooperation is indispensable to us (we cannot even have an individual identify without them to help define it socially), but who may kill us or enslave us. It seems essential to have a system to sort out positive interactions (contracts, taxation to pay for public goods) from negative ones (crimes, torts, illegal searches, unconstituional seizure of property). In the West, legal belief-structures, together with economic and political ones, have been constructed to accomplish this sorting out. The systems, of course, have been built by elites who have thought they had some stake in rationalizing their dominant power positions, so they have tended to define rights in such a way as to reinforce existing hierarchies of wealth and privilege.

Even more important, such system building has the effect of making the social world as it is come to seem natural and inevitable. Though the structures are built, piece by interlocking piece, with human intentions, people come to "externalize" them, to attribute to them existence and control over and above human choice; and, moreover, to believe that these structures must be the way they are. Recall the example given earlier of the person who works in a small business for the "owner" of the business. It is true that the owner's position is backed up by the ultimate threat

of force—if she does not like the way the people behave on her property, she can
summon armed helpers from the state to eject them—but she also has on her side
the powerful ideological magic of a structure that gives her the "rights" of an
"employer" and "owner," and the worker the "duties" of an "employee" and
"invitee" on the "owner's property." The worker feels he cannot challenge the
owner's right to eject him from her property if she does not like the way he behaves,
in part because he feels helpless against the force she can invoke, but also because
in part he accepts her claim as legitimate; he respects "individual rights of ownership"
because the powers such rights confer seem necessary to his own power and freedom;
limitations on an "owner's" rights would threaten him as well. But the analogy he
makes is possible only because of his acquiescence in a belief structure—liberal
legalism—that abstracts particular relationships between real people (this man and
the woman he "works for"; this man and the brother-in-law he wants to eject from
his house) into relations between entirely abstract categories of "individuals" playing
the abstract social roles of "owner," "employee," etc. This process of allowing the
structures we ourselves have built to mediate relations among us so as to make us
see ourselves as performing abstract roles in a play that is produced by no human
agency is what is usually called (following Marx and such modern writers as Sartre
and Lukacs) reification. It is a way people have of manufacturing necessity; they
build structures, then act as if (and genuinely come to believe that) the structures
they have built are determined by history, human nature, economics, law.

Perhaps a promising tactic, therefore, of trying to struggle against being demo-
bilized by our own conventional beliefs is to try to use the ordinary rational tools
of intellectual inquiry to expose belief-structures that claim that things as they are
must necessarily be the way they are. There are many varieties of this sort of critical
exercise, whose point is to unfreeze the world as it appears to common sense as a
bunch of more or less objectively determined social relations and to make it appear
as (we believe) it really is; people acting, imagining, rationalizing, justifying.

One way of accomplishing this is to show that the belief-structures that rule our
lives are not found in nature but are historically contingent; they have not always
existed in their present form.

This discovery is extraordinarily liberating, not (at least not usually) because
there is anything so wonderful about the belief-structures of the past, but because
uncovering those structures makes us see how arbitrary our categories for dividing
up experience are, how nonexhaustive of human potentiality. Another useful exercise
is just simply empirical disproof of the claim of necessity. When it is asserted that
strict, predictable rules of private property and free contract are necessary to protect
the functioning of the market, maintain production incentives, etc., it can be shown
that the actual rules are not at all what they claim to be, that they can be applied
quite differently in quite different circumstances, sometimes "paternalistically,"
sometimes strictly, sometimes forcing parties to share gains and losses with each
other, and sometimes not at all. Or it may be asserted that certain hierarchical ways
of organizing are necessary for efficient realization of economics of scale. One can
use historical (nineteenth-century worker-organized steel production) or comparative
(Japanese, for instance) examples to demonstrate that "efficient" production can
occur under all sorts of conditions. Or one can try to show that even at the level of
theory, the claim of necessity is, on its own terms, incoherent or contradictory; this
approach is currently being practiced on the various forms of "legal economics":
that claim that certain regimes of legal rules are "efficient." One can bring similar

critiques to bear on claims that things must be the way they are because of some long-term logic of historical change (''modernization,'' what is, after all, an inevitable consquence of social life in industrialized societies,'' ''the price of living in a modern pluralistic society,'' ''an inevitable consequence of the declining rate of profit under monopoly capitalism,'' etc.). It turns out that these theories of development cannot be applied to the concrete histories of particular societies without being so qualified, refined, or partially repudiated that they lose all their force as determining theories—at best, they are only helpful insights or ways of organizing thinking about the world.

If we start to look at the world this way—no longer as some determined set of ''economic conditions'' or ''social forces'' that are pushing us around but rather as in the process of continuous creation by human beings, who are constantly reproducing the world they know because they (falsely) believe they have no choice—we will obviously bring a very different approach to the debate over whether legal change can ever effect real (''social and economic'') change, or whether law is wholly dependent on the real, ''hard'' world of production. For if social reality consists of reified structures, ''law'' and ''the economy'' are *both* belief-systems that people have externalized and allowed to rule their lives. Moreover, if the critiques of legal belief-structures are accurate—that even in their theoretically ideal forms they are contradictory and incoherent, and that in practical application they depart constantly from the ideal in wildly unpredictable fashion—it follows that no particular regime of legal principles *could* be functionally necessary to maintain any particular bunch of legal rules, except of course those that may be part of the *definition* of that economic order, as ''private property'' of some sort is to most people's definition of capitalism.

So—if one were to adopt this approach—one would no longer be inclined to look for ''scientific'' or ''positivist'' explanations of how the world works in large-scale theories of historical interrelations between states, societies, and economics (one would actually be trying to knock down such theories). It may be that the place to look is somewhere quite different—in the smallest, most routine, most ordinary interactions of daily life in which some human beings dominate others and they acquiesce in such domination. It may be, as Foucault's work suggests, that the whole legitimating power of a legal system is built up of such myriad tiny instances.

I do not want to give the impression that everyone in the critical legal-studies movement has adopted the approaches I have just described. On the contrary, these approaches are hotly debated. Some of those who most fiercely dispute the validity of these approaches do so in part on political grounds.

• • •

The notion that there are no objective laws of social change is in one way profoundly depressing. Those who have come to believe it have had to abandon the most comforting hopes of socialism: that history was on its side, and that history could be accelerated through a scientific understanding of social laws. It no longer seems plausible to think that organization of the working class or capture of the state appartus will *automatically* bring about the conditions within which people could begin to realize the utopian possibilities of social life. Such strategies have led to valuable if modest improvements in social life, as well as to stagnation, cooptation by the existing structures, and nightmare regimes of state terror. Of course, this does not mean that people should stop trying to organize the working class or to influence the exercise of state power; it means only that they have to do so pragmatically and experimentally, with full knowledge that there are no deeper logics of historical

necessity that can guarantee that what we do now will be justified later. Yet, if the
real enemy is us—*all* of us, the structures we carry around in our heads, the limits
on our imagination—where can we even begin? Things seem to change in history
when people break out of their accustomed ways of responding to domination, by
acting as if the constraints on their improving their lives were not real and that they
could change things; and sometimes they can, though not always in the way they
had hoped or intended; but they never knew they could change them at all until they
tried.

NOTES

1. Have the exponents of the Critical Legal Studies movement, as exemplified by the
selection, adequately clarified and systematically developed the goals they would like to effect?
Have they developed strategies to effect necessary changes? Have they thought through which
goals should receive priority over others in the event that discrete goals clash in given situations?
If not, does the movement have an essentially destructive thrust similar to the negative tendencies of the American Legal Realist Movement?

2. While emphasizing a focus on the overall structure of society, do Critical Legal students
"zero in" on details to make meaningful recommendations for change?

3. Does the Critical Legal Studies Movement reject or accept any particular structure or
form of society as right or "natural"? What of a socialist society? Discuss. Recall the ex-
ploration of Structural Naturalism in Chapter 5.

PRACTICAL CONSEQUENCES OF REALISM

Some of Legal Realism's iconoclastic impulses did serve to clear the way for
more positive contributions. Foremost among them was the comparatively *realistic*
focus that Realism encouraged. Rather than looking at rules and decisions in a
sentimental fashion, the Realist tried to look at what was actually transpiring in courts
and in the community and what effects a particular decision would have. From there,
it was a very short step to testing those effects against the more general preferences
or politics held by his group, class or the community. When judges adopted this
perspective, it sometimes forced them to introduce changes by judicial fiat precisely
because they concluded the system of rules was yielding social results inconsistent
with community goals.

CONSTITUTIONAL LAWS

Reynolds v. Sims can be viewed, for better or worse, as a consequence of the
Realist perspective. In that case, the Supreme Court intervened in the political processes by which members of the legislature are chosen. This had a major political
effect. The Court's justification was that there was a need to synchronize practice
with what the court felt were basic national values.

REYNOLDS V. SIMS
377 U.S. 533 (1961)

Mr. Chief Justice Warren delivered the opinion: Involved in these cases are an
appeal and two cross-appeals from a decision of the Federal District Court for the
Middle District of Alabama holding invalid, under the Equal Protection Clause of

the Federal Constitution, the existing and two legislatively proposed plans for the apportionment of seats in the two houses of the Alabama Legislature, and ordering into effect a temporary reappointment plan comprised of parts of the proposed but judicially disapproved measures. . . .

. . . The state of similar cases filed and decided by lower courts since our decision in [Baker v. Carr] amply shows that the problem of state legislative malapportionment is one that is perceived to exist in a large number of the States. . . . We intimated no view [in Baker] as to the proper constitutional standards for evaluating the validity of a state legislative apportionment scheme.

• • •

Wesberry [v. Sanders] clearly established that the fundamental principle of representative government in this country is one of equal representation for equal numbers of people, without regard to race, sex, economic status, or place of resident within a State. Our problem, then, is to ascertain, in the instant case, whether there are any constitutionally cognizable principles which would justify departures from the basic standard of equality among voters in the apportionment of seats in state legislatures. . . .

Legislators represent people, not trees or acres. Legislatures are elected by voters, not farms or cities or economic interests. As long as ours is a representative form of government, and our legislatures are those instruments of government elected directly by and directly representative of the people, the right to elect legislators in a free and unimpaired fashion is a bedrock of our political system. It could hardly be gainsaid that a constitutional claim has been asserted by an allegation that certain otherwise qualified voters had been entirely prohibited from voting for members of their state legislature. . . . And it is inconceivable that a state law to the effect that, in counting votes for legislators, the votes of citizens in one part of the State would be multiplied by two, five, or 10, while the votes of persons in another area would be counted only at face value, could be constitutionally sustainable. Of course, the effect of state legislative districting schemes which give the same number of representatives to unequal numbers of constituents is identical. Overweighting and overevaluation of the votes of those living here has the certain effect of dilution and underevaluation of the votes of those living there. The resulting discrimination against those individual voters living in disfavored areas is easily demonstrable mathematically. Their right to vote is simply not the same right to vote as that of those living in a favored part of the State. Two, five, or 10 of them must vote before the effect of their voting is equivalent to that of their favored neighbor. Weighting the votes of citizens differently, by any method or means, merely because of where they happen to reside, hardly seems justifiable. . . .

. . . Full and effective participation by all citizens in state government requires . . . that each citizen has an equally effective voice in the election of members of his state legislature. Modern and viable state government needs, and the Constitution demands, no less.

Logically, in a society ostensibly grounded on representative government, it would seem reasonable that a majority of the people of a State could elect a majority of that State's legislators. To conclude differently, and to sanction minority control of state legislative bodies, would appear to deny majority rights in a way that far surpasses any possible denial of minority rights that might otherwise be thought to result. Since legislatures are responsible for enacting laws by which all citizens are to be governed, they should be bodies which are collectively responsive to the popular will. And the concept of equal protection has been traditionally viewed as requiring the uniform treatment of persons standing in the same relation to the governmental action questioned or challenged. With respect to the allocation of legislative representation, all voters, as citizens of a State, stand in the same relation regardless of where they live. Any suggested criteria for the differentiation of citizens are insufficient to justify any discrimination, as to the weight of their votes, unless relevant to the permissible purposes of legislative apportionment. Since the achieving of fair and effective representation for all citizens is concededly the basic aim of legislative apportionment, we conclude that the Equal Protection Clause guarantees the opportunity for equal participation by all voters in the election of state legislators. Diluting the weight of votes because of place of residence impairs basic constitutional rights under the Fourteenth Amendment just as much as invidious discriminations based upon factor's such as race . . . or economic status. . . .

. . . .Our constitutional system amply provides for the protection of minorities by means other than giving them majority control of state legislatures. And the democratic ideals of equality, and majority rule, which have served this Nation so well in the past, are hardly of any less significance for the present and the future.

We are told that the matter of apportioning representation in a state legislation is a complex and many-faceted one. We are advised that States can rationally consider factors other than population in apportioning legislative representation. We are admonished not to restrict the power of the States to impose differing views as to political philosophy on their citizens. We are cautioned about the dangers of entering into political thickets and mathematical quagmires. Our answer is this: a denial of constitutionally protected rights demands judicial protection; our oath and our office require no less of us. . . . To the extent that a citizen's right to vote is debased, he is that much less a citizen. The fact that an indivdual lives here or there is not a legitimate reason for overweighting or diluting the efficacy of his vote. The complexions of societies and civilizations change, often with amazing rapidity. . . . But the basic principle of representative government remains, and must remain, unchanged—the weight of a citizen's vote cannot be made to depend on where he lives. Population is, of necessity, the starting point for consideration and the controlling criterion for judgment in legislative apportionment controversies. A citizen, a qualified voter, is no more nor no less so because he lives in the city or on the farm. This is the clear and strong command of our Constitution's Equal Protection Clause. This is an essential part of the concept of a government of laws and not men. This is at the heart of Lincoln's vision of "government of the people, by the people, [and] for the people." The Equal Protection Clause demands no less than substantially equal state legislative representation for all citizens, of all places as well as of all races. . . .

We hold that, as a basic constitutional standard, the Equal Protection Clause requires that the seats in both houses of a bicameral state legislature must be apportioned on a population basis. Simply stated, an individual's right to vote for state legislators is unconditionally impaired when its weight is in a substantial fashion diluted when compared with votes of citizens living in other parts of the State.

• • •

Since we find the so-called federal analogy inapposite to a consideration of the constitutional validity of state legislative apportionment schemes, we necessarily hold that the Equal Protection Clause requires both houses of a state legislature to be apportioned on a population basis. The right of a citizen to equal representation and to have his vote weighted equally with those of all other citizens in the election of members of one house of a bicameral state legislature would amount to little if States could effectively submerge the equal-population principle in the apportionment of seats in the other house. If such a scheme were permissible, an individual citizen's ability to exercise an effective voice in the only instrument of state government directly representative of the people might be almost as effectively thwarted as if neither house were apportioned on a population basis. . . . In summary, we can perceive no constitutional difference, with respect to the geographical distribution of state legislative representation between the two houses of a bicameral state legislature.

• • •

. . . So long as the divergence from a strict population standard are based on legitimate considerations incident to the effectuation of a rational state policy, some deviations from the equal-population principle are constitutionally permissible with respect to the apportionment of seats in either or both of the two houses of a bicameral state legislature. But neither history alone, nor economic or other sorts of group interests, are permissible factors in attempting to justify disparities from population-based representation. Citizens, not history or economic interests, cast votes. Considerations of area alone provide an insufficient justification for deviations from the equal-population principle. Again, people, not land or trees or pastures, vote. Modern developments and improvements in transportation and communications make rather hollow, in the mid-1960s, most claims that deviations from population-based representation can validly be based solely on geographical considerations. Arguments for allowing such deviations in order to insure effective representation for sparsely settled areas and to prevent legislative districts from becoming so large that the availability of access of citizens to their representatives is impaired are today, for the most part, unconvincing.

• • •

We find . . . that the action taken by the District Court in this case, in ordering into effect a reapportionment of both houses of the Alabama Legislature for purposes of the 1962 primary and general elections, by using the best parts of the two proposed plans which it had found, as a whole, to be invalid, was an appropriate and well-considered exercise of judicial power. [After finding that Legislatures had been "unconstitutionally" apportioned in Alabama, Colorado, Delaware, Maryland, New York, and Virginia, the Court, the following week, held that the Legislatures of nine other states had also been unconstitutionally apportioned.]

CRIMINAL LAW

Realism has had comparable consequences in the criminal law area. It is disquieting to realize that more than 90% of convictions in the American system of criminal justice result, not from trials, but from "plea bargaining" or privately negotiated agreements between the prosecutor and the defense attorney in which the accused pleads guilty in return for a reduction of the charge. Being entitled to a jury trial, in which the state is obliged to prove its case beyond reasonable doubt, means very little if 90% of those cases are actually resolved in processes anterior to the court—especially if those processes were coercive. In the past, confessions were sometimes extracted from defendants who were subjected to enormous pressures of various kinds while in the hands of the police, making a mockery of the constitutional privilege against self-incrimination. Where courts have pierced the myth of the way the law is supposed to work and explored what is actually happening, they have sometimes been able to mitigate some of the evils by insisting that constitutional principles apply even to the pre-court stages. Consider, in this regard, the *Miranda* decision.

MIRANDA V. ARIZONA
384 U.S. 436 (1966)

Mr. Chief Justice Warren delivered the opinion: The cases before us raise questions which go to the roots of our concepts of American criminal jurisprudence: the restraints society must observe consistent with the Federal Constitution in prosecuting individuals for crime. More specifically, we deal with the admissibility of statements obtained from an individual who is subjected to custodial police interrogation and the necessity for procedures which assure that the individual is accorded his privilege under the Fifth Amendment to Constitution not to be compelled to incriminate himself.

• • •

The constitutional issue we decide in each of these cases is the admissibility of statements obtained from a defendant questioned while in custody or otherwise deprived of his freedom of action in any significant way. In each, the defedant was questioned by police officers, detectives, or a prosecuting attorney in a room in which he was cut off from the outside world. In none of these cases was the defendant given a full and effective warning of his rights at the outset of the interrogation process. In all the cases, the questioning elicited oral admissions, and in three of them, signed statements as well which were admitted at their trials. They all thus share salient features—incommunicado interrogation of individuals in a police-dominated atmosphere, resulting in self-incriminating statements without full warnings of constitutional rights. . . .

Again we stress that the modern practice of in-custody interrogation in psychologically rather than physically oriented. . . . Interrogation still takes place in privacy. Privacy results in secrecy and this in turn results in a gap in our knowledge as to what in fact goes on in the interrogation rooms. A valuable source of information about present police practices, however, may be found in various police manuals and texts which document procedures employed with success in the past, and which recommend various other effective tactics. These texts are used by law enforcement agencies themselves as guides. It should be noted that these texts professedly present the most enlightened and effective means presently used to obtain statements through custodial interrogation. By considering these texts and other data, it is possible to describe procedures observed and noted around the country.

• • •

From these representative samples of interrogation techniques, the setting prescribed by the manuals and observed in practice becomes clear. In essence, it is this: To be alone with the subject is essential to prevent distraction and to deprive him of any outside support. The aura of confidence in his guilt undermines his will to resist.

. . . He merely confirms the preconceived story the police seek to have him describe. Patience and persistence, at times relentless questioning, are employed. To obtain a confession, the interrogator must "patiently maneuver himself or his quarry into a position from which the desired objective may be attained." When normal procedures fail to produce the needed result, the police may resort to deceptive statagems such as giving false legal advice. It is important to keep the subject off balance, for example, by trading on his insecurity about himself or his surroundings. The police then persuade, trick, or cajole him out of exercising his constitutional rights.

Even without employing brutality, the "third degree" or the specific stratagems described above, the very fact of custodial interrogation exacts a heavy toll on individual liberty and trades on the weakness of individuals.

• • •

In these cases, we might not find the defendants' statements to have been involuntary in traditional terms. Our concern for adequate safeguards to protect precious Fifth Amendment rights is, of course, not lessened in the slightest. In each of the cases, the defendant was thrust into an unfamiliar atmosphere and run through menacing police interrogation procedures. The potentiality for compulsion is forcefully apparent, for example, in *Miranda*, where the indigent Mexican defendant was a seriously disturbed individual with pronounced sexual fantasies, and in *Stewart*, in which the defendant was an indigent Los Angeles Negro who had dropped out of school in the sixth grade. To be sure, the records do not evince overt physical coercion or patent psychological ploys. The fact remains that in none of these cases did the officers undertake to afford appropriate safeguards at the outset of the interrogation to insure that the statements were truly the product of free choice.

It is obvious that such an interrogation environment is created for no purpose other than to subjugate the individual to the will of his examiner. This atmosphere carries its own badge of intimidation. To be sure, this is not physical intimidation, but it is equally destructive of human dignity. The current practice of incommunicado interrogation is at odds with one of our Nation's most cherished principles—that the individual may not be compelled to incriminate himself. Unless adequate protective devices are employed to dispel the compulsion inherent in custodial surroundings, no statement obtained from the defendant can truly be the product of his free choice.

From the foregoing, we can readily perceive an intimate connection between the privilege against self-incrimination and police custodial questioning. It is fitting to turn to history and precedent underlying the Self-Incrimination Clause to determine its applicability in this situation.

II.

[The policies of the privilege against self-incrimination] point to one overriding thought: the constitutional foundation underlying the privilege is the respect a government—state or federal—must accord to the dignity and integrity of its citizens. . . . In sum, the privilege is fulfilled only when the person is guaranteed the right "to remain silent unless he chooses to speak in the unfettered exercise of his own will." *Malloy v. Hogan*. . . .

The question in these cases is whether the privilege is fully applicable during a period of custodial interrogation. . . . We are satisfied that all the principles embodied in the privilege apply to informal compulsion exerted by law-enforcement officers during in-custody questioning. An individual swept from familiar surroundings into police custody, surrounded by antagonistic forces, and subjected to the techniques of persuasion described above cannot be otherwise than under compulsion to speak. As a practical matter, the compulsion to speak in the isolated setting of the police station may well be greater than in courts or other official investigations, where there are often impartial observers to guard against intimidation or trickery.

• • •

Today, then, there can be no doubt that the Fifth Amendment privilege is available outside of criminal court proceedings and serves to protect persons in all settings in which their freedom of action is curtailed in any significant way from being compelled to incriminate themselves. We have concluded that without proper safeguards the process of in-custody interrogation of persons suspected or accused of crime contains inherently compelling pressures which work to undermine the individual's will to resist and to compel him to speak where he would not otherwise do so freely. In order to combat these pressures and to permit a full opportunity to exercise the privilege against self-incrimination, the accused must be adequately and effectively apprised of his rights and the exercise of those rights must be fully honored.

• • •

The circumstances surrounding in-custody interrogation can operate very quickly to overbear the will of one merely made aware of his privilege by his interrogators. Therefore, the right to have counsel present at the interrogation is indispensable to the protection of the Fifth Amendment privilege under the system we delineate today. Our aim is to assure that the individual's right to choose between silence and speech remains unfettered throughout the interrogation process. A once-stated warning, delivered by those who will conduct the interrogation, cannot itself suffice to that end among those who might require knowledge of their rights. A mere warning given by the interrogators is not alone sufficient to accomplish that end. Prosecutors themselves claim that the admonishment of the right to remain silent without more "will benefit only the recidivist and the professional." . . . Thus, the need for counsel to protect the Fifth Amendment privilege comprehends not merely a right to consult with counsel prior to questioning, but also to have counsel present during any questioning if the defendant so desires.

• • •

If an individual indicates that he wishes the assistance of counsel before any interrogation occurs, the authorities cannot rationally ignore or deny his request on the basis that the individual does not have or cannot afford a retained attorney. The financial ability of the individual has no relationship to the scope of the rights involved here. The privilege against self-incrimination secured by the Constitution applies to all individuals. The need for counsel in order to protect the privilege exists for the indigent as well as the affluent. In fact, were we to limit these constitutional rights to those who can retain an attorney, our decisions today would be of little significance. The cases before us as well as the vast majority of confession cases with which we have dealt in the past involve those unable to retain counsel. While authorities are not required to relieve the accused of his poverty, they have the obligation not to take advantage of indigence in the administration of justice. Denial of counsel to the indigent at the time of interrogation while allowing an attorney to those who can afford one would be no more supportable by reason or logic than the similar situation at trial and on appeal struck down in *Gideon* and *Douglas*.

• • •

The principles announced today deal with the protection which must be given to the privilege against self-incrimination when the individual is first subjected to police interrogation while in custody of the state or otherwise deprived of his freedom of action in any way. It is at this point that our adversary system of criminal proceedings commences, distinguishing itself at the outset from the inquisitorial system recognized in some countries. Under the system of warnings we delineate today or under any other system which may be devised and found effective, the safeguards to be erected about the privilege must come into play at this point.

• • •

The experience in some other countries also suggests that the danger to law enforcement in curbs on interrogation is overplayed. The English procedure since 1912 under the Judge's Rules is significant. As recently strengthened, the Rules require that a cautionary warning be given an accused by a police officer as soon as he has evidence that affords reasonable grounds for suspicion; they also require that any statement made be given by the accused without questioning by police. The right of the individual to consult with an attorney during this period is expressly recognized.

PRODUCTS LIABILITY AND CONSUMER PROTECTION

A comparable development attributable to the Realist perspective, can be found in the fields of consumer protection and products liability. As industrial civilization spread through all parts of the country and national distribution of goods produced in different locales increased, many of the traditional rules which had served to provide a degree of protection to consumers in earlier contexts proved inadequate. For example, the old requirement that there be a certain "privity" or contractual relationship between the manufacturer and the injured party seeking to sue will rarely be fulfilled because of the interposition between manufacturer and consumer of numerous parties who play a role in the complex national marketing and distribution process. The consumer's practical lack of opportunity and expertise to detect defects in the product to be purchased has compelled reliance on the manufacturer; the potential danger inherent in the product made a mockery of limitations of warranties imposed by manufacturers. Even if this problem did not arise, the manufacturer could self-liberate from certain foreseeable injuries caused to the users of his product by a narrowly drafted warranty.

A Realist perspective has permitted courts to expose the obsolescence and counter-utility of the older doctrines by looking at what is actually happening. It has acted as a spur toward the creation, through judicial legislation, of new and more appropriate doctrines, crafted to provide a greater degree of consumer protection in the new context.

Consider the following cases.

HENNINGSEN V. BLOOMFIELD MOTORS, INC.
SUPREME COURT OF NEW JERSEY, 1960
32 N.J. 358, 161 A.2d 69

[This was an action against an automobile manufacturer and dealer to recover for injuries from defects in the car.]

. . . Judicial notice may be taken of the fact that automobile manufacturers, including Chrysler Corporation, undertake large scale advertising programs over telelvision, radio, in newspapers, magazines and all media of communciations in order to persuade the public to buy their products. As has been observed above, a number of jurisdictions, conscious of modern marketing practices, have declared that when a manufacturer engages in advertising in order to bring his goods and their ability to the attention of the public and thus to create consumer demand, the representations made constitute an express warranty running directly to a buyer who purchases in reliance thereon. The fact that the sale is consummated with an independent dealer does not obviate that warranty. . . .

In view of the cases in various jurisdictions suggesting the conclusion which we have now reached with respect to the implied warranty of merchantability, it becomes apparent that manufacturers who enter into promotional activities to stimulate consumer buying may incur warranty obligations of either or both the express or implied character. These developments in the law inevitably suggest the inference that the form of express warranty made part of the Henningsen purchase contract was devised for general use in the automobile industry as a possible means of avoiding the consequences of the growing judicial acceptance of the thesis that the described express or implied warranties run directly to the consumer.

In the light of these matters, what effect should be given to the express warranty in question which seeks to limit the manufacturer's liability to replacement of defective parts, and which disclaims all other warranties, express or implied? In assessing its significance we must keep in mind the general principles that, in the absence of fraud, one who does not choose to read a contract before signing it, cannot later relieve himself of its burdens. . . . And in applying that principle, the basic tenet of freedom of competent parties to contract is a factor of importance. But in the framework of modern commercial life and business practices, such rules cannot be applied on a strict, doctrinal basis. The conflicting interests of the buyer and seller must be evaluated realistically and justly, giving due weight to the social policy evinced by the Uniform Sales Act, the progressive decisions of the courts engaged in administering it, the mass production methods of manufacture and distribution to the public, and the bargaining position occupied by the ordinary consumer in such an economy. This history of the law shows that legal doctrines, as first expounded, often prove to be inadequate under the impact of later experience. In such cases, the need for justice has stimulated the necessary qualifications or adjustments. . . .

In these times, an automobile is almost as much a servant of convenience for the ordinary person as a household utensil. For a multitude of other persons it is a necessity. Crowded highways and filled parking lots are a commonplace of our existence. There is no need to look any further than the daily newspaper to be convinced that when an automobile is defective, it has great potentiality for harm.

No one spoke more graphically on this subject than Justice Cardozo in the landmark case of MacPherson v. Buick Motor Co., 217 N.Y. 382, . . .

"Beyond all question, the nature of an automobile gives warning of probable danger if its construction is defective. This automobile was designed to go 50 miles per hour. Unless its wheels were sound and strong, injury was almost certain. It was as much a thing of danger as a defective engine for a railroad. . . . The dealer was indeed the one person of whom it might be said with some approach to certainty that by him the car would not be used. . . . Precedents drawn from the days of travel by stagecoach do not fit the conditions of travel today. The principle that the danger must be imminent does not change, but the things subject to the principle do change. They are whatever the needs of life in a developing civilization require them to be."

In the 44 years that have intervened since that utterance, the average car has been constructed for almost double the speed mentioned; 60 miles per hour is permitted on our parkways. The number of automobiles in use has multiplied many times and the hazard of the user and the public has increased proportionately. The Legislature has intervened in the public interest, not only to regulate the manner of operations on the highway but also to require periodic inspection of motor vehicles and to impose a duty on manufacturers to adopt certain safety devices and methods in their construction. R.S. 39:3–43 et. seq. N.J.S.A. It is apparent that the public has an interest not only in the safe manufacture of automobiles, but also, as shown by the Sales Act, in protecting the rights and remedies of purchasers, so far as it can be accomplished consistently with our system of free enterprise. In a society such as ours, where the automobile is a common and necessary adjunct of daily life, and where its use is so fraught with danger to the driver, passengers and the public, the manufacturer is under a special obligation in connection with the construction, promotion and sales of his cars. Consequently, the courts must examine purchase agreements closely to see if consumer and public interests are treated fairly.

What influence should these circumstances have on the restrictive effect on Chrysler's express warranty in the framework of the purchase contract? As we have said, warranties originated in the law to safeguard the buyer and not to limit the liability of the seller or manufacturer. It seems obvious in this instance that the motive was to avoid the warranty obligations which are normally incidental to such sales. The language gave little and withdrew much. In return for the delusive remedy of replacement of defective parts at the factory, the buyer is said to have accepted the exclusion of the maker's liability for personal injuries arising from the breach of the warranty, and to have agreed to the elimination of any other express or implied warranty. An instinctively felt sense of justice cries out against such a sharp bargain. But does the doctrine that a person is bound by his signed agreement in the absence of fraud, stand in the way of any relief? . . .

The traditional contract is the result of free bargaining of parties who are brought together by the play of the marker, and who meet each other on a footing of approximate economic equality. In such a society there is no danger that freedom of contract will be a threat to the social order as a whole. But in present-day commercial life the standardized mass contract has appeared. It is used primarily by enterprises with strong bargaining power and position. "The weaker party, in need of the goods or services, is frequently not in a position to shop around for better terms, either because the author of the standard contract has a monopoly (natural or artificial) or because all competitors use the same clauses. His contractual intention is but a subjection more or less voluntary in terms dictated by the stronger party, terms whose consequences are often understood in a vague way, if at all." Kessler, "Contracts of Adhesion—Some Thoughts About Freedom of Contract," 43 Colum. L. Rev. 629, 632 (1943); . . . Such standardized contracts have been described as those in which one predominant party will dictate its law to an undetermined multiple rather than to an individual. They are said to resemble a law rather than a meeting of the minds. Siegelman v. Cunard White Star, 221 F. 2d 189, 206 (2 Cir. 1955). . . .

———

Creative adjudication and the clarification and application of innovative policy by courts in particular cases has gone even further. Consider the following revolutionary case.

SINDELL V. ABBOTT LABORATORIES
SUPREME COURT OF CALIFORNIA, 1980
26 Cal. 3d 588, 607 P. 2d 924, 163 Cal. Rptr. 132

Mosk, Justice: This case involves a complex problem both timely and significant: may a plaintiff, injured as the result of a drug administered to her mother during pregnancy, who knows the type of drug involved but cannot identify the manufacturer of the precise product, hold liable for her injuries a maker of a drug produced from an identical formula?

Plaintiff Judith Sindell brought an action against eleven drug companies and Does 1 through 100, on behalf of herself and other women similarly situated. The complaint alleges as follows:

Between 1941 and 1971, defendants were engaged in the business of manufacturing, promoting, and marketing diethylstilbesterol (DES), a drug which is a synthetic compound of the female hormone estrogen. The drug was administered to plaintiff's mother and the mothers of the class she represented,[1] for the purpose of preventing miscarriage. In 1947, the Food and Drug Administration authorized the marketing of *DES* as a miscarriage preventative, but only on an experimental basis, with a requirement that the drug contain a warning label to that effect.

DES may cause cancerous vaginal and cervical growths in the daughters exposed to it before birth, because their mothers took the drug during pregnancy. The form of cancer from which these daughters suffer is known as adenocarcinoma, and it manifests itself after a minimum latent period of 10 to 12 years. It is a fast-spreading and deadly disease, and radical surgery is required to prevent it from spreading. DES also causes adenosis, precancerous vaginal and cervical growths which may spread to other areas of the body. The treatment for adenosis is cauterization, surgery, or cryosurgery. Women who suffer from this condition must be monitored by biopsy or colposcopic examination twice a year, a painful and expensive procedure. Thousands of women whose mothers received DES during pregnancy are unaware of the effects of the drug.

In 1971, the Food and Drug Administration ordered defendants to cease marketing and promoting DES for the purpose of preventing miscarriages, and to warn physicians and the public that the drug should not be used by pregnant women because of the danger to their unborn children.

During the period defendants marketed DES, they knew or should have known that it was a carcinogenic substance, that there was a grave danger after varying periods of latency it would cause cancerous and precancerous growths in the daughters of the mothers who took it, and that it was ineffective to prevent miscarriage. Nevertheless, defendants continued to advertise and market the drug as a miscarriage preventative. They failed to test DES for efficacy and safety; the tests performed by others, upon which they relied, indicated that it was not safe or effective. In violation of the authorization of the Food and Drug Administration, defendants marketed DES on an unlimited basis rather than as an experimental drug, and they failed to warn of its potential danger.[2]

[1]The plaintiff class alleged consists of "girls and women who are residents of California and who have been exposed to DES before birth and who may or may not know that fact or the dangers" to which they were exposed. Defendants are also sued as representatives of a class of drug manufacturers which sold DES after 1941.

[2]It is alleged also that defendants failed to determine if there was any means to avoid or treat the effects of DES upon the daughters of women exposed to it during pregnancy, and failed to monitor the carcinogenic effects of the drug.

Because of defendants' advertised assurances that DES was safe and effective to prevent miscarriage, plaintiff was exposed to the drug prior to her birth. She became aware of the danger from such exposure within one year of the time she filed her complaint. As a result of the DES ingested by her mother, plaintiff developed a malignant bladder tumor which was removed by surgery. She suffers from adenosis and must constantly be monitored by biopsy or colposcopy to insure early warning of further malignancy.

. . . We begin with the proposition that, as a general rule, the imposition of liability depends upon a showing by the plaintiff that his or her injuries were caused by the act of the defendant or by an instrumentality under the defendant's control. The rule applies whether the injury resulted from an accidental event . . . or from the use of a defective product. . . .

There are, however, exceptions to this rule. Plaintiff's complaint suggests several bases upon which defendants may be held liable for her injuries even though she cannot demonstrate the name of the manufacturer which produced the DES actually taken by her mother. . . . We shall conclude that these doctrines, as previously interpreted, may not be applied to hold defendants liable under the allegations of this complaint. However, we shall propose and adopt a fourth basis for permitting the action to be tried, grounded upon an extention of the *Summers* doctrine.

• • •

If we were confined to the theories of *Summers* and *Hall,* we would be constrained to hold that the judgment must be sustained. Should we require that plaintiff identify the manufacturer which supplied the DES used by her mother or that all DES manufacturers be joined in the action, she would effectively be precluded from any recovery. As defendants candidly admit, there is little likelihood that all the manufacturers who made DES at the time in question are still in business or that they are subject to the jurisdiction of the California courts. There are, however, forceful arguments in favor of holding that plaintiff has a cause of action.

In our contemporary complex industrialized society, advances in science and technology create fungible goods which may harm consumers and which cannot be traced to any specific producer. The response of the courts can be either to adhere rigidly to prior doctrine, denying recovery to those injured by such products, or to fashion remedies to meet these changing needs. Just as Justice Traynor in his landmark concurring opinion in *Escola v. Coca Cola Bottling Company* (1941) 24 Cal. 2d 453, 467–468, 150 P.2d 436, recognized that in an era of mass production and complex marketing methods the traditional standard of negligence was insufficient to govern the obligations of manufacturer to consumer, so should we acknowledge that some adaptation of the rules of causation and liability may be appropriate in these recurring circumstances. The Restatement comments that modification of the *Summers* rule may be necessary in a situation like that before us. (see fn. 16, *ante.*)

The most persuasive reason for finding plaintiff states a cause of action is that advanced in *Summers*: as between an innocent plaintiff and negligent defendants, the latter should bear the cost of the injury. Here, as in *Summers,* plaintiff is not at fault in failing to provide evidence of causation, and although the absence of such evidence is not attributable to the defendants either, their conduct in marketing a drug the effects of which are delayed for many years played a significant role in creating the unavailability of proof.

From a broader policy standpoint, defendants are better able to bear the cost of injury resulting from the manufacture of a defective product. As was said by Justice

Traynor in *Escola*, "[t]he cost of an injury and the loss of time or health may be an overwhelming misfortune to the person injured and a needless one, for the risk of injury can be insured by the manufacturer and distributed among the public as a cost of doing business." (24 Cal. 2d p. 462, 150 P.2d p. 441); . . . The manufacturer is in the best position to discover and guard against defects in its products and to warn of harmful effects; thus, holding it liable for defects and failure to warn of harmful effects will provide an incentive to product safety. . . . These considerations are particularly significant where medication is involved, for the consumer is virtually helpless to protect himself from serious, sometimes permenant, sometimes fatal, injuries caused by deleterious drugs.

Where, as here, all defendants produced a drug from an identical formula and the manufacturer of the DES which caused plaintiff's injuries cannot be identified through no fault of plaintiff's, a modification of the rule of *Summers* is warranted. As we have seen, an undiluted *Summers* rationale is inappropriate to shift the burden of proof of causation to defendants because if we measure the chance that any particular manufacturer supplied the injury-causing product by the number of producers of DES, there is a possibility that none of the five defendants in this case produced the offending substance and that the responsible manufacturer, not named in the action, will escape liability.

But we approach the issue of causation from a different perspective: we hold it to be reasonable in the present context to measure the likelihood that any of the defendants supplied the product which allegedly injured plaintiff by the percentage which the DES sold by each of them for the purpose of preventing miscarriage bears to the entire production of the drug sold by all for that purpose. Plaintiff asserts in her briefs that Eli Lilly and Company and 5 or 6 other companies produced 90 percent of the DES marketed. If at trial this is established to be the fact, then there is a corresponding likelihood that this comparative handful of producers manufactured the DES which caused plaintiff's injuries, and only 10 percent likelihood that the offending producer would escape liability.

If plaintiff joins in the action the manufacturers of a substantial share of the DES which her mother might have taken, the injustice of shifting the burden of proof to defendants to demonstrate that they could not have made the substance which injured plaintiff is significantly diminished. While 75 to 80 percent of the market is suggested as the requirement by the Fordham Comment (at p. 996), we hold only that a substantial percentage is required.

The presence in the action of a substantial share of the appropriate market also provides a ready means to apportion damages among the defendants. Each defendant will be held liable for the proportion of the judgment represented by its share of that market unless it demonstrates that it could not have made the product which caused plaintiff's injuries. In the present case, as we have seen, one DES manufacturer was dismissed from the action upon filing a declaration that it had not manufactured DES until after plaintiff was born. Once plaintiff has met her burden of joining the required defendants, they in turn may cross-complaint against other DES manufacturers, not joined in the action, which they can allege might have supplied the injury-causing product.

Under this approach, each manufacturer's liability would approximate its responsibility for the injuries caused by its own products. Some minor discrepancy in the correlation between market share and liability is inevitable; therefore, a defendant may be held liable for a somewhat different percentage of the damage than its share of the appropriate market would justify. It is probably impossible, with the passage of time to determine market share with mathematical exactitude. But just as a jury cannot be expected to determine the precise relationship between fault and liability in applying the doctrine of comparative fault . . . or partial indemnity . . . the difficulty of apportioning damages among the defendant producers in exact relation to their market share does not seriously militate against the rule we adopt. As we said in *Summers* with regard to the liability of independent tortfeasors, where a correct division of liability cannot be made "the trier of fact may make it the best it can." (33 Cal. 2d at p. 88, . . .)

We are not unmindful of the practical problems involved in defining the market and determining market share, but these are largely matters of proof which properly cannot be determined at the pleading stage of these proceedings. Defendants urge that it would be both unfair and contrary to public policy to hold them liable for plaintiff's injuries in the absence of proof that one of them supplied the drug responsible for the damage. Most of their arguments, however, are based upon the assumption that one manufacturer would be held responsible for the products of another or for those of all other manufacturers if plaintiff ultimately prevails. But under the rule we adopt, each manufacturer's liability for an injury would be approximately equivalent to the damages caused by the DES it manufactured.

Richardson, J., dissenting.

• • •

The foregoing result is directly contrary to long established tort principles. Once again, in the words of Dean Prosser, the applicable rule is: "[Plaintiff] must introduce evidence which affords a reasonable basis for the conclusion that it is more likely than not that the product of the defendant was a substantial factor in bringing about the result. A mere possibility of such causation is not enough; and when the matter remains one of pure speculation or conjecture, or the probabilities are at best evenly balanced, it becomes the duty of the court to direct a verdict for the defendant." *(Prosser,* supra, sec. 41, at p. 241, italics added, fns. omitted.) Under the majority's new reasoning, however, a defendant is fair game if it happens to be engaged in a similar business and causation is *possible* even though remote.

In passing, I noted the majority's dubious use of market share data. It is perfectly proper to use such information to assist in proving, circumstantially, that a particular defendant probably caused plaintiffs' injuries. Circumstantial evidence may be used as a basis for proving the requisite probable causation. (Id., at . 242.) The majority, however, authorizes the use of such evidence for an entirely different purpose, namely, to impose and allocate liability among multiple defendants only one of whom may have produced the drug which injured plaintiffs. Because this use of market share evidence does not implicate any particular defendant, I believe such data are entirely irrelevant and inadmissible, and that the majority errs in such use. . . .

———

In style, Legal Realism tended to be flamboyant and dramatic. In orientation, it often was avowedly and openly concerned with advocating change and securing its implementation. But for all of its contributions, Realism had serious deficiencies. It could open the eyes of its acolytes to what was actually happening, escorting them from Socrates' figurative cave where one saw only dim shadows of what was actually occurring, but it did not equip the student or decisionmaker with any systematic way of observing, determining how things should be changed or how one ought to design strategies for implementing preferences. Despite its concern for bringing about reform, clarification of goals, the inescapable first step of reform, was never performed systematically by the Realists. As Professor Ackerman has observed:

> Realists did relatively little to formulate new criteria by which substantive legal outcomes could be evaluated. At the core of Realism was an extraordinary optimism, a belief that once men were free from all the damaging myths of the past, they would have little difficulty understanding the proper shape of a just society.*

The Realists were proud of the fact that they alone could "tell it like it is." Yet the real test of the viability of their theory was not the constant invocation of the word reality, but whether they developed a method for describing it in ways that could improve the effectiveness of th lawyer in the performance of the intellectual tasks we discussed in Chapter 1. In this regard, the Realist contribution was ultimately disappointing. Many did no more than describe in a very intuitionistic fashion what they thought social process to be. Others become captive to stereotypes, rather than conducting detailed empirical inquiry. Even Glendon Schubert, a self-conscious social scientist working the Realist mode, used terms of reference so general that they could not be made operational. Many of these failings have been exposed by American sociological jurisprudence, whose efforts to remedy them will be considered in the following chapter.

---

*B. Ackerman, Book Review, 103 *Daedalus* 119, 122 (1974) (review of J. Frank, *Law and the Modern Mind* (1930)).

T. Arnold, *The Folklore of Capitalism* (1937): *The Symbols of Government* (1935).

E. Bodenheimer, Modern Analytic Jurisprudence and the Limits of Its Usefulness, 104 *U. Pa. L. R.* 1080 (1955–56).

F. Cohen, *The Legal Conscience* (1960): Toward Realism in Jurisprudence, 59 *Yale L. J.* 886 (1949–50).

W. W. Cook, Scientific Method and the Law, 13 *A.B.A. Jour.* 303 (1920).

B. Cordozo, *The Nature of the Judicial Process* (1921); *The Growth of the Law* (1924); *Paradoxes of Legal Science* (1927).

J. Frank, *Law and the Modern Mind* (1930; *What the Courts Do In Fact* (1932).

L. Fuller, American Legal Realism, 82 *U. Pa. L. R.* 429 (1934); *The Morality of Law* (1964).

W. Hohfeld, *Fundamental Legal Conceptions As Applied In Judicial Reasoning, and Other Legal Essays* (W. Cook & A. Corbin eds. 1946, 1964).

O. W. Holmes, The Path of the Law, 10 *Harv. L. R.* 457 (1897); Law in Science and Science in Law, 12 *Harv. L. R.* 443 (1899); *Collected Legal Papers* (1920).

D. Kairys, *The Politics of Law: A Progressive Critique* (1980).

L. Kalman, *Legal Realism at Yale, 1927-1960* (1986).

K. Llewellyn, A Realistic Jurisprudence—The Next Step, 30 *Colum. L. R.* 431 (1930); *Jurisprudence: Realism in Theory and Practice* (1962).

K. Llewellyn and E. A. Hoebel, *The Cheyenne Way: Conflict and Case Law in Primitive Jurisprudence* (1941).

M. McDougal, Fuller versus American Legal Realism: An Intervention, 50 *Yale L. J.* 828 (1940).

U. Moore, *My Philosophy of Law* (1941).

U. Moore & G. Sussman, The Lawyer's Law, 41 *Yale L. J.* 566 (1930).

H. Oliphant, A Return to Stare Decisis, 14 *A.B.A. Jour.* 71, 159 (1928).

K. Olivecrona, *Law as Fact* (1971).

R. Pound, The Call for a Realist Jurisprudence, 44 *Harv. L. R.*697 (1931).

M. Radin, Legal Realism, 31 *Colum. L. R.* 824 (1931).

A. Ross, *On Law and Justice* (1958); *Directives and Norms* (1968).

W. Rumble, *American Legal Realism* (1968).

G. Schubert, *Judicial Policy-making: the Political Role of the Courts* (rev. ed. 1974).

R. S. Summers, *Instrumentalism and American Legal Theory* (1982).

Symposium, Critical Legal Studies, 36:1 *Stanford L.R.* 1 (1984).

W. Twining, *Karl Llewellyn and the Realist Movement* (1973).

R. Unger, The Critical Legal Studies Movement, 96 *Harv. L. R.* 561 (1983); *The Critical Legal Studies Movement* (1986).

S. M. Verdun-Jones, The Jurisprudence of Karl Llewellyn 1 *Dalhousie L. J.* 441 (1974); Studies in American Legal Realism (J.S.D. thesis at Yale Law School, 1977).

H. Yntema, American Legal Realism in Retrospect, 9 *Vand. L. R.* 317 (1960).

CHAPTER 11

Using Social Sciences: Sociological Jurisprudence

Much of what passes as social science is just exercise in technical vocabulary or mere plausible impressionism.
Morris Raphael Cohen

Imagine that you are the judge of a federal district court, sitting in a city racked by severe racial tensions. The law of the land is committed to a system of racial justice based on personal equality. Racial integration has been identified as an indispensable step for achieving this goal. One of the principal modalities chosen is school integration. In your district, it is clear that such integration will arouse tremendous resistance.

Given the distribution of races about the city, integrationists claim that busing in the only method for systematically securing integrated interactions in one of the few sectors of society in which the government has sufficient control. Opponents argue that busing and school integration not only do not achieve the larger social goal of racial justice, but may actually work against it. Moreover, they contend that where busing has been imposed, the effects on education have been disastrous; hence they argue that in lowering the quality of education, not only minority members but the entire country and its future security interests suffer.

In arguing this case, counsel for both sides have relied on "Brandeis briefs," a method of pleading in which, in place of or in addition to statutory and case material, substantial amounts of what is considered scientific data about our society, either general or prepared for the particular case, are presented to the court.

MULLER V. OREGON
208 U.S. 412, 419–21 (1908)

[Louis D. Brandeis filed a "very copious collection." Those were described in the margin of the Court's opinion as including]:

> extracts from over ninety reports of committees, bureaus of statistics, commissioners of hygiene, inspectors of factories, both in this country and in Europe, to the effect that long hours of labor are dangerous for women, primarily because of their special physical organization. The matter is discussed in these reports in different aspects, but all agree as to the danger. . . . Following them are extracts from similar reports discussing the general benefits of short hours from an economic aspect of the question. In many of these reports individual instances are given tending to support the general conclusion. Perhaps the general scope and character of all these reports may be summed up in what an inspector for Hanover says: "The reasons for the reduction of the working day to ten hours—(a) the physical organization of women, (b) her maternal func-

486

tions, (c) the rearing and education of the children, (d) the maintenance of the home—are all so important and so far reaching that the need for such reduction need hardly be discussed.''

[Mr. Justice Brewer, delivering the opinion of the court, remarked]:

The legislation and opinions referred to in the margin may not be, technically speaking, authorities, and in them is little or no discussion of the constitutional question presented to us for determination, yet they are significant of a wide-spread belief that woman's physical structure, and the functions she performs in consequence thereof, justify special legislation restricting or qualifying the conditions under which she should be permitted to toil. Constitutional questions, it is true, are not settled by even a consensus of present public opinion, for it is the peculiar value of a written constitution that it places in unchanging form limitations upon legislative action, and thus gives a permanence and stability to popular government which otherwise would be lacking. At the same time, when a question of fact is debated and debatable, and the extent to which a special constitutional limitation goes is affected by the truth in respect to that fact, a widespread and long continued belief concerning it is worthy of consideration. We take judicial cognizance of all matters of general knowledge.

How do you, as a lawyer and judge, evaluate this data? How do you determine what part (if any) is credible? How do you deal with apparent contradictions between scientists? How do you determine whether or not the projections about probable consequences, argued by each side, are accurate?

The Common Law's method of gathering information for a case presupposed a small community and questions of sufficient simplicity so that information presented to 12 laymen in an ordinary adversarial process would yield an answer which could be expected to be accurate. In a mass industrial society of some 250 million people, spread over an entire continent, in which many developments are innovative and cannot be projected from past experience, is it still practicable to assume that ordinary assumptions about reality and routine procedures of presentation of data will yield an accurate presentation? The intuitive images of reality that each of us have are based on such fragmentary and anecdotal exposure to this mass and complex society that no single one of us can simply rely on those images and hope to have an accurate representation of what is occurring in the United States or a similarly developed society. Beyond a certain level of development and complexity, there is no escape from the use of statistical reductions in presentations of trends and, even more, no escape from the use of such methods for projections of what is likely to happen under certain circumstances in the future. Whether we are presenting data to a judge in an antitrust case, trying to persuade a regulatory agency, or providing information for a company planning a national advertising campaign for a new product, we must perforce use many of the techniques of the social sciences to describe and project the aggregate behavior of a mass society so large that no single individual can apprehend it in a personal sense.

In the complexities of the advanced industrial and science-based civilization of America, it has become increasingly difficult to transform high-level policy into social practice. Inevitably, those charged with the implementation of law have turned to scientific experts in social organization and phenomena and to experts on the way the law actually operates in society for guidance in implementation.

In 1953, Morris Raphael Cohen noted:

> When we come, however, to the appellate work of higher courts, in which new public policies are decided under the guise of their legality or constitutionality, we find courts making all sorts of factual generalizations without adequate information. The facilities of our courts for acquiring information as to actual conditions are very limited. Courts have to decide all sorts of complicated issues after a few hours of oral argument and briefs of lawyers. Are ten hours per day in the old-type bakery a strain on the baker's health? Will a workmen's compensation act or a minimum wage law take away the property of the employer or of the worker that receives less than the minimum of subsistence? It is not to the credit of any system that its chief exponents can put their amateurish opinions against those of physicians or economists who have given these questions careful scientific study. Yet the law cannot simply and uncritically accept all the opinions of economists or sociologists. After all, on many important points social scientists are not agreed among themselves; and certainly the social sciences do not demonstrate their results as rigorously as do the natural sciences.*

Sociological jurisprudence has come to refer to quite different branches of endeavor. The first has been the use of sociological techniques of inquiry to examine the institutions of the law themselves. This older focus was largely a scientific effort with little explicit policy relevance. The second branch of the sociological enterprise has been the use of contemporary sociological techniques by the institutions of law as a way of making their own efforts more effective in changing or stabilizing different sectors of social order.

Sociological jurisprudence in this second sense has been directly and openly concerned with making decisionmaking more efficient by incorporating some of the insights of the systematic study of society. A key question in reviewing this material is whether sociological jurisprudence has in fact been helpful. Has it identified goals clearly? Has it been more efficient than other more intuitive methods of the law in reviewing trends to see whether or not goals have been achieved? Has it been able to identify the factors that accounted for decisions and to formulate rules? Has it been more effective in making matter-of-fact predictions about future trends and how they will approximate preferred goals? And finally, most central to the law, has it been able to aid in the development of alternative methods for achieving goals?

In using or adapting social science methods for legal functions, it is important to be precise as to which intellectual task is being performed. Obviously social science methods are useful if not indispensable for describing what has gone on in the past. Similarly, social science methods will be useful for determining the conditioning factors that accounted for those trends. And there is little doubt but that scientific methods of projecting or extrapolating likely future behavior will be important for the task of projection of likely future decisions (prediction). On the other hand, the task of clarification of goals as well as the taks of invention of alternative methods to achieve goals rely more on ingenuity and creativity on the part of the lawyer and much less on rigorous scientific methods. In the material that follows, try to identify which intellectual task is being performed and whether apparent disputes about the appropriateness of scientific method or data are concerned with methodology or are actually with conflict about goals.

*M. R. Cohen, Law and Scientific Method, in *Law and the Social Order: Essays in Legal Philosophy* 184 (1953).

SCIENCE AND DESEGREGATION

A use of sociological data which precipitated one of the major revolutions in twentieth century America was the Supreme Court's apparent reliance on a variety of social science conclusions in *Brown v. Board of Education*.

BROWN V. BOARD OF EDUCATION
347 U.S. 483 (1954)

Mr. Chief Justice Warren delivered the opinion[:] These cases come to us from the States of Kansas, South Carolina, Virginia and Delaware. . . .

In each of the cases, minors of the Negro race, through their legal representatives, seek the aid of the courts in obtaining admission to the public schools of their community on a nonsegregated basis. In each instance, they had been denied admission to schools attended by white children under laws requiring or permitting segregation according to race. This segregation was alleged to deprive the plaintiffs of the equal protection of the laws under the Fourteenth Amendment. In each of the cases other than the Delaware case, a three-judge federal district court denied relief to the plaintiffs on the so-called "separate but equal" doctrine announced by this Court in *Plessy* v. *Ferguson,* 163 U.S. 537. Under that doctrine, equality of treatment is accorded when the races are provided substantially equal facilities, even though these facilities be separate. In the Delaware case, the Supreme Court of Delaware adhered to that doctrine, but ordered that the plaintiffs be admitted to the white schools because of their superiority to the Negro schools.

Reargument was largely devoted to the circumstances surrounding the adoption of the Fourteenth Amendment in 1868. It covered exhaustively consideration of the Amendment in Congress, ratification by the states, then existing practices in racial segregation, and the views of proponents and opponents of the Amendment. This discussion and our own investigation convince us that, although these sources cast some light, it is not enough to resolve the problem with which we are faced. At best, they are inconclusive. The most vivid proponents of the post-War Amendments undoubtedly intended them to remove all legal distinctions among "all persons born or naturalized in the United States." Their opponents, just as certainly, were antagonistic to both the letter and the spirit of the Amendments and wished them to have the most limited effect. What others in Congress and the state legislature had in mind cannot be determined with any degree of certainty.

An additional reason for the inconclusive nature of the Amendment's history, with respect to segregated schools, is the status of public education at that time. In the South, the movement toward free common schools, supported by general taxation, had not yet taken hold. Education of white children was largely in the hands of private groups. Education of Negroes was almost nonexistent, and practically all of the race were illiterate. In fact, any education of Negroes was forbidden by law in some states. Today, in contrast, many Negroes have achieved outstanding success in the arts and sciences as well as in the business and professional world. It is true that public school education at the time of the Amendment had advancd further in the North, but the effect of the Amendment on Northern States was generally ignored in the congressional debates. Even in the North, the conditions of public education did not approximate those existing today. The curriculum was usually rudimentary; ungraded schools were common in rural areas; the school term was three months a years in many states; and compulsory school attendance was virtually unknown. As a consequence, it is not surprising that there should be so little in the history of the Fourteenth Amendment relating to its intended effect on public education.

In the first cases in this Court construing the Fourteenth Amendment, decided shortly after its adoption, the Court interpreted it as proscribing all state-imposed discriminations against the Negro race. The doctrine of ''separate but equal'' did not make its appearance in this Court until 1896 in the case of *Plessy* v. *Ferguson, supra,* involving not education but transportation. American courts have since labored with the doctrine for over half a century.

• • •

In the instant cases, that question is directly presented. Here, unlike *Sweatt* v. *Painter,* there are findings below that the Negro and white schools involved have been equalized, or are being equalized, with respect to buildings, curricula, qualifications and salaries of teachers, and other ''tangible'' factors. Our decisions therefore, cannot turn on merely a comparison of these tangible factors in the Negro and white schools involved in each of the cases. We must look instead to the effect of segregation itself on public education.

In approaching this problem, we cannot turn the clock back to 1868, when the Amendment was adopted, or even to 1896, when *Plessy* v. *Ferguson* was written. We must consider public education in the light of its full development and its present place in American life throughout the Nation. Only in this way can it be determined if segregation in public schools deprives these plaintiffs of the equal protection of the laws.

Today, education is perhaps the most important function of state and local governments. Compulsory school attendance laws and the great expenditures for education both demonstrate our recognition of the importance of education to our democratic society. It is required in the performance of our most basic public responsibilities, even service in the armed forces. It is the very foundation of good citizenship. Today it is a principal instrument in awakening the child to cultural values, in preparing him for later professional training, and in helping him to adjust normally to his environment. In these days, it is doubtful that any child may reasonably be expected to succeed in life if he is denied the opportunity of an education. Such an opportunity, where the state has undertaken to provide it, is a right which must be made available to all on equal terms.

We come then to the question presented: Does segregation of children in public schools solely on the basis of race, even though the physical facilities and other ''tangible'' factors may be equal, deprive the children of the minority group of equal educational opportunities? We believe that it does.

In *Sweatt* v. *Painter, supra* in finding that a segregated law school for Negroes could not provide them equal educational opportunites, this Court relied in large part on ''those qualities which are incapable of objective measurement but which make for greatness in a law school.'' In *McLaurin* v. *Oklahoma State Regents, supra,* the Court, in requiring that a Negro admitted to a white graduate school be treated like all other students, again resorted to intangible considerations: ''. . . his ability to study, to engage in discussions and exchange views with other students, and, in general, to learn his profession.'' Such considerations apply with added force to children in grade and high schools. To separate them from others of similar age and qualifications solely because of their race generates a feeling of inferiority as to their status in the community that may affect their hearts and minds in a way unlikely ever to be undone. The effect of this separation on their educational opportunities was well stated by a finding in the Kansas case by a court which nevertheless felt compelled to rule against the Negro plaintiffs:

> "Segregation of white and colored children in public schools has a detrimental effect upon the colored children. The impact is greater when it has the sanction of the law; for the policy of separating the races is usually interpreted as denoting the inferiority of the negro group. A sense of inferiority affects the motivation of a child to learn. Segregation with the sanction of law, therefore, has a tendency to retard the educational and mental development of negro children and to deprive them of some of the benefits they would receive in a racial[ly] integrated school system."

Whatever may have been the extent of psychological knowledge at the time of *Plessy* v. *Ferguson*, this finding is amply supported by modern authority.[11] Any language in *Plessy* v. *Ferguson* contrary to this finding is rejected.

We conclude that in the field of public education the doctrine of "separate but equal" has no place. Separate educational facilities are inherently unequal. Therefore, we hold that the plaintiffs and others similarly situated for whom the actions have been brought are, by reason of the segregation complained of, deprived of the equal protection of the laws guaranteed by the Fourteenth Amendment. This disposition makes unnecessary any discussion whether such segregation also violates the Due Process Clause of the Fourteenth Amendment.

In *Brown v. Board of Education,* the Supreme Court precipitated a revolution in American social organization and mores. The court purported to reach its judgment by relying on the social science data invoked before it. To what extent are courts, staffed by people with the special training given to lawyers, competent to interpret and appraise social science data? To what extent was the social science data submitted to the court correct or correctly appraised?

Brown generated both intense resistance in the streets and in the schools and intense resistance among scholars. Many of the latter contended that either the data on which the court purported to rely were unsound or that in general the reliance on social science data had no place in the law. An enormous literature formed in the wake of *Brown*.

Data itself means nothing unless it is subjected to interpretations and to projections into what may be quite different situations from those in which it originated. A number of critics directed their remarks to the mechanical use and more general abuse which they alleged, *Brown* and subsequent courts were making of this data. The next selection of articles treats these issues and indicates by their very vehemence the breadth and intensity of the controversy. In the selection that follows, we will consider some of the strategic imperatives that *Brown* and subsequent courts purported to draw from the data submitted to them.

---

[11] K. B. Clark, Effect of Prejudice and Discrimination on Personality Development (Midcentury White House Conference on Children and Youth, 1950); Witmer and Kotinsky, Personality in the Making (1952), c. VI; Deutscher and Chein, The Psychological Effects of Enforced Segregation; A Survey of Social Science Opinion, 26 J. Psychol. 259 (1948); Chein, What are the Psychological Effects of Segregation Under Conditions of Equal Facilities? 3 Int. J. Opinion and Attitude Res. 229 (1949); Brameld, Education Costs, in Discrimination and National Welfare (MacIver, ed., 1949), 44–48; Frazier, The Negro in the United States (1949), 674–681. And see generally, Myrdal, An American Dilemma (1944.)

WOLF, SOCIAL SCIENCE AND THE COURTS:
THE DETROIT SCHOOLS CASE,
42 PUB. INTEREST 102 (1976)

The role of the social sciences in judicial decision-making has received considerable attention from the field of law, and in recent years much of this attention has focused on issues related to school segregation. Social scientists have not paid nearly so much attention—few, for example, have chosen to make a detailed study of a single case. Yet many of the Northern school cases—involving, as they do, issues of greater complexity and ambiguity than the cases concerning the openly dual systems of the pre-1954 South—have used substantial amounts of social-science materials. In addition, the significance of a single case in law is somewhat different than is generally true in the social sciences because of the controlling effects of precedent.

In April of 1971, the National Association for the Advancement of Colored People (NAACP) brought a lawsuit before a federal district court, charging *de jure* segregation within the Detroit school system. This case led to a decision upholding the charges of the NAACP, and subsequently to an order for inter-district busing. The decision was upheld by the 6th Circuit Court of Appeals, but the inter-district busing remedy was reversed by the Supreme Court in a 5–4 decision in 1974. I undertook a study of all the testimony presented in the course of the landmark Detroit case [Bradley v. Millikan, 338 F. Supp. 582 (E.D. Mich. 1971)] in order to discover what kinds of social-science materials were introduced, and to evaluate their quality and comprehensiveness. I wanted to learn whether there were crucial omissions of evidence that otherwise might have supported, contradicted, or modified the testimony that was introduced. I also wanted to discover how the court dealt with the considerable and sometimes conflicting array of demographic data presented and to evaluate the extent to which the judicial decisions, at various levels, accurately reflected the weight of the social-science evidence that had been offered. Finally, if the study revealed (as I anticipated, from preliminary investigation, that it might) certain problems and inadequacies in the use of social-science materials in the courtroom, I hoped to indicate some possible avenues for improvement.

The basic material for analysis was the verbatim transcript of the 41-day trial, held in 1971, as well as many of the exhibits offered in evidence, plus the transcript of the court hearings conducted the following year on alternative plans for desegregation. The chief areas of social-science concern, broadly classified, were 1) the extent, nature, and causes of racial separation in urban neighborhoods: 2) the economic, social, and psychological factors—both in and out of school—believed to be associated with various aspects of learning; and 3) the allegations and refutations of segregative practices within the school system. I had not foreseen the extent to which social-sciences materials would be involved in this last category, but there proved to be many references to demographic, sociological, and psychological factors in the course of disputed testimony concerning the reasons for and consequences of various school system policies and practices. A completely unexpected category was the rather considerable amount of testimony (and controversy) about methodology, some of it in response to challenges to the validity of evidence that had been introduced.

The decision of the Federal District Court on September 27, 1971, declaring Detroit schools to be segregated *de jure* was marked by the unusual prominence given to consideration of demographic trends and to an extended discussion of the nature and causes of racially segregated housing. That portion of the decision concerned with those matters opened with these words: ''In considering the present racial complexion of the City of Detroit and its public school system we must first look to the past and view in perspective what has happened in the last half century.'' This was followed by almost seven pages (about one third of the text) on housing, population movements, demographic characteristics, and their effects on the schools. These findings were a largely accurate reflection of the testimony that had been presented on a wide range of specific topics in this general subject area; the measurement of segregation in housing; comparisons between the housing patterns of blacks and white ethnics; practices and policies, past and present, of the real estate industry; economic factors in residential choices of blacks; the impact upon housing patterns of government policy in urban renewal, public housing, FHA, and other federal programs; and the earlier judicial enforcement of restrictive convenants. Both the trial and the remedy hearings were marked by frequent references to ''white flight'' and its alleged causes; and school policy decisions, past and projected, were frequently rationalized by references to ''white flight'' and to the operation of a ''tipping point'' in schools and in housing.

Judge Roth's decision drew the following conclusions about the causes of residential segregation:

> While the racially unrestricted choice of black persons and economic factors may have played some part in the development of this pattern of residential segregation it is, in the main, the result of past and present practices and customs of racial discrimination both public and private, which have and do restrict the housing opportunities of black people. On the record, there can be no other finding.

The record, however, was entirely the presentation of the plaintiffs. Because the defendants took the legal position that testimony about housing was irrelevant to the charge that Detroit's schools were segregated *de jure,* they offered no evidence on this subject. Regardless of the legal aspects, the fact that all of the housing witnesses were selected by one side tended to restrict the range of issues and narrow the perspective offered in this testimony. As a basis for understanding the relative impact of a variety of factors involved in fashioning social policy (which was what was happening here) the court was not well served by this method of presentation. This became even more apparent during the discussions of remedies, when plans for desegregation were developed, to a large extent, on the basis of inadequately verified hypotheses concerning residential behavior.

Since legal advantage, rather than sociological relevance, governed the choice of materials to be presented, there was no testimony that reflected the studies of scholars who attribute greater importance to the economic ability of blacks or who stress the significance of the social class distribution of blacks in accounting for the residential preferences of *whites*. There was no testimony that emphasized the similarities, rather than the differences, between the residential behavior of blacks and that of other ethnic groups; indeed, no expert who testified appeared to define black Americans in these terms. There was no reference to research revealing the continuing strength of social relationships among ethnic groups (including blacks) despite cultural assimilation. The testimony on the causes of racial transition in urban neighborhoods was very sparse, consisting of references to solicitation by real-estate agents and the racial prejudice of whites. No testimony challenged the assertion that there is a ''corresponding effect'' between the racial composition of a school and that of a neighborhood—the phrase suggests a force of comparable magnitude in either direction.

The effect of omissions of content was compounded by the style of presentation. The limitations of the adversary mode in the presentation of social-science evidence were accentuated by the fact that most of the expert witnesses on housing were from social action agencies rather than the academic disciplines. Karl Taeuber, the notable demographer, who offered the best testimony during the trial, was virtually the only scholar. The background and customary responsibilities of civil rights professionals involve the use of knowledge to persuade and convert. Speakers exaggerate certainty, omit contrary evidence, and fail to acknowledge gaps in the data or in causal linkages. They do not reveal or perhaps are not aware of, methodological weaknesses that require many conclusions to be held quite tentatively.

From the record of housing segregation established in the trial the Federal District Court proceeded to the declaration that there was an "affirmative obligation of the defendant Board . . . to adopt and implement pupil assignment practices and policies that compensate for and avoid incorporation into the school system the effects of residential racial segregation." In view of this emphasis, it is surprising to discover that the 6th Circuit Court of Appeals, while upholding the finding that Detroit schools were segregated *de jure,* specifically rejected this contention, which had figured so largely in the District Court's chain of reasoning, and removed all of the references to housing that had been so prominent in Judge Roth's decision. . . . Comments (in the transcript) from the defendants' counsel and the reports of observers at the trial suggests that this material also made a deep impression upon the listeners, and especially upon Judge Roth.

The message of the housing testimony was that racial segregation arose from discrimination based on prejudice, aided and abetted by government, and that it was severe, widespread, unresponsive to economic improvement, worsened by the passage of time, and impervious to the assimilative processes that had dispersed other groups. So said the housing experts. If traditional pupil-assignment practices continued, there was no hope for the emergence of the mixed schools which, in the virtually unanimous opinion of the education experts who were to follow, were indispensable for educational achievement.

A considerable amount of expert testimony on education was offered during both the trial in 1971, and the hearing on desegregation plans conducted by Judge Roth in 1972. A wide range of issues was covered, some at great length, some briefly; the relationship between a child's background and academic achievement; the definition and measurement of socio-economic status; the class-linked differences in attitudes, values, and overt behavior; and various problems in the definition and measurement of intelligence. There was a great deal of testimony on the effect of varying degrees of race and social-class mixture upon academic achievement, and upon other outcomes such as self-concept, motivation, aspirations, racial attitudes, and race relations. There was testimony on the effects of "tracking," ability-grouping, and the validity of tests used for such placement. There were presentations on the allocation of a variety of educational resources, with much emphasis on teachers' training, experience, skills, attitudes, and expectations.

During the remedy hearings, as the comparative merits of the several proposals for desegregation were considered, there was a great deal of additional testimony on the presumed effects of certain proportions of race and social-class mixture. These hearings also included much testimony on the expected effects of all of these factors on residential behavior. New social-science issues also emerged during these hearings: how large a proportion black would be needed to protect what was terms "identity," or sometimes "self-identity"; the effects on children of more frequent changes in school assignment; and the effects of distance upon parental involvement in school affairs and on "community control" (a form of which had recently been introduced in Detroit).

Taken as a whole, the expert testimony about education was characterized by a number of serious omissions. There were no references to the differences in educational achievement between ethnic groups at similar income levels, although such differences are widely known and reasonably well documented. Although erroneous testimony by the plaintiffs' chief education witness (who asserted that, for the most part, entry-level differences between pupils are minimal) was corrected by the defendants' education experts almost two months later, it was never revealed that the capacity of schools to eradicate these differences has not thus far been demonstrated. No social-science expert challenged, modified, or even questioned assertions about educational and psychological harm from grouping by scholastic proficiency or more general aptitudes. No expert questioned the many exaggerated assertions made by both sides concerning research findings on the effects of teacher attitudes (the so-called "expectancy hypothesis") on student achievement, despite a considerable array of critical material on this work. No social-science testimony systematically evaluated the incompatibility seen by many analysts between community control of schools and large-scale programs of pupil dispersion for the purpose of integration.

Perhaps most crucial of all, there was no serious challenge to the exaggerated claims, made by expert witnesses on both sides, of the power of racial and social-class mixture of classmates to improve the educational performance of low-achieving students. Yet there was, even by the time of the trial, a substantial literature on this matter, including material by the often-cited James Coleman, written in apparent response to unwarranted assertions about the power of classroom heterogeneity. At many points the (strong) effects of the *individual child's* socio-economic background on academic performance was confused with the weak (and doubtful) effects of his *classmates'* socio-economic status. The general import of the testimony on education was such as to persuade a reasonable man without research training or academic background that the proper kind of race-class mix in the classroom would heighten aspirations, improve motivation, raise self-esteem, and improve the academic performance of low-achieving black children. Simultaneously, contact with these children would reduce the prejudices and correct the stereotypes of whites, thus improving race relations. But there is little support in the professional literature for this dubious set of propositions.

There were virtually no references in the rulings of the Federal District Court or the 6th Circuit Court of Appeals to educational harm stemming from predominantly one-race schools, or to the educational benefits from mixture, despite the very substantial amount of testimony on these subjects. Research findings on these effects appear increasingly inconclusive in recent years. In the light of much criticism and uncertainty, there is a new reluctance to rely upon such data on the part of some who were previously enthusiastic about utilizing such data. Paul Dimond (NAACP co-counsel) expressed a current appraisal in a recent article: "I do not believe the evidence on educational advantage proves much of anything." This is a striking contrast to many past claims, and one must note that no such admission was made during the trial.

Why, then, in the light of this increased skepticism, was material on educational effects offered by the plaintiffs? Two reasons come to mind: 1) Since the legal basis for findings on Northern-style school segregation is still not completely established, it is prudent to be as inclusive as possible; and 2) such material has an important role in persuading a judge that equal educational opportunity requires racially-mixed schools. In the Detroit case this conviction was apparently shared by both sides, who often seemed to be vying with each other in expressing their ideological commitment to this goal. The board of education expert witnesses would yield to no one in their devotion to integration; they differed mainly in contending that by the time the system had acquired a strongly pro-integration leadership, the demography of the Detroit public schools (already a majority of blacks before Norman Drachler became superintendent in 1966) made overall success impossible.

The expert testimony, then, on both housing and education, was marked by a high degree of consensus. Although the defendants presented no witnesses of their own on residential patterns, at some points they indicated their unwillingness to be associated with any attempt to rebut or minimize the evidence about discrimination in housing. We have already noted that there appeared to be genuine agreement between the adversaries on the benefits of integration, the harm of racial isolation in schools, and the moral and ideological imperatives of the goal of integration.

If the contrast in statements made by Judge Roth before and after the trial is an indication of his beliefs, this high degree of consensus by experts was not without effect. The judge was a conservative among Democrats and had not been associated with civil-rights efforts. His pre-trial ruling in favor of voluntary integration plan (backed by more conservative members of the Detroit school board) and against the rather limited "April 7 Plan"—the rejection of which resulted in the Detroit case—indicates his original orientation. In that ruling he praised the "magnet plan" because "it is voluntary," whereas "the April Plan's principal aim is to improve integration by the numbers—it does not offer incentive . . . or provide motivation. . . . Instead of a change of diet it offers forced feeding." He concluded: "It is our belief that in this way [the "magnet plan"] the students, in their quest for identity and in their inherited drive for realizing their potential, will bring about such integration as no coercive method could possibly achieve."

From this disinclination to select a mildly "coercive" plan involving a limited number of high school students, the judge moved to the following declaration of aim shortly after the conclusion of the trial: " . . . the task we are called upon to perform is a social one which society has been unable to accomplish. In reality, our courts are called upon in these school cases to attain a goal through the education system by using the law as a lever."

The instrument eventually chosen to attain this goal was a metropolitan plan of unprecedented dimensions, involving the reassignment and dispersion over a considerable area of a large proportion of the 780,000 students, of all ages, from 53 school systems. The legal basis cited for this remedy, however, was not the social-science testimony, but the evidence of constitutional violations within the school system.

• • •

[Professor Owen] Fiss has said only that the theory [for attributing responsibility] "seems contrived." What about the evidence? My original intention in studying the school violations testimony was to learn how a judge went about the task of evaluating the validity and assessing the significance of great masses of factual data concerning unfamiliar subjects. I approached the testimony on recent school violations with skepticism, on three counts: First, from a sociologist's perspective, if schools were already completely segregated as a consequence of residential patterns, the "principle of parsimony" seemed to argue against further "explanations" for this condition. Second, my own research in changing neighborhoods suggested that the school system had been trying to maintain integrated schools, albeit with inadequate and ineffective tools. Third, it did not seem likely that a pro-integration superintendent and school board president (both winners of NAACP awards) and a deputy superintendent (who had spent much of his career as a local executive of the NAACP) whose responsibility it was to study and approve changes in boundaries, feeder patterns, and transportation would countenance racial discrimination. If the courts' assessments concerning recent school violations had been accurate, it was important to learn if the testimony revealed the ways in which their supervision had been evaded, their orders disobeyed, and their aims frustrated.

The school-violations testimony is voluminous—and formidable. In addition to hundreds of hours of oral presentations there are maps, charts, racial counts (since 1961), data on present and anticipated population movements and on school building and room capacity, considerations of local geography and traffic arteries, problems of changing parochial school enrollments—plus the whole problem of school organization, at times clearly confusing to the judge. Some of this testimony covered a period of almost 20 years.

• • •

. . . But the line between facts and their interpretation is unclear: Could a school have been erected in a different spot to create a mixed enrollment? Facts about racial composition and residential trends in an area are needed, as well as the weighing of certain values (the choice between a small neighborhood primary school with a homogeneous enrollment and a larger and more distant one which is heterogeneous) and legal interpretations that are not reducible to facts. If, for example, population facts indicate that the race mixture of a neighborhood will be quite temporary (how temporary?), is such a site choice "segregation"?

• • •

A third category of school offenses had to do with boundary changes, feeder patterns, and the exercise of parental choice on some blocks between boundaries (the so-called "optional zones"). This subject involves both a mass of factual data and possible alternative explanations offered for these events. Each instance requires a separate investigation to check fact-accuracy, greatly complicated by the fact that a single change in a feeder pattern often has a "domino" or ripple effect. Some of these violations of 15 or more years ago, as well as some more recent, were admitted by the defendants to have indeed taken place under earlier administrations.

I had not anticipated the extent to which (ill-defined) concepts and assumptions from the social sciences would be involved in this testimony. For example, the plaintiffs' expert witness often declared that a certain change in student assignments "increased" or "decreased" the "community's perception of segregation," and thus contributed to segregation generally, presumably because of an eventual impact on residential behavior. No evidence was offered to support these assertions. Beyond the fact that competing values and interpretations intrude at so many points, it is difficult for a court to assess the accuracy and evaluate the significance of such data in adversary proceedings—an important problem, not restricted, of course, to school segregation cases. Among the difficulties in this case were the following:

1. The lack of public disclosure constituted an obstacle to the fair evaluation of the data. Little of the testimony about recent school violations appeared in the newspapers during the course of the trial, so that people who had contrary information to that being presented were not aware of what was being reported to the courts. School principals with direct knowledge of how many children from their own schools were being bused to other schools did not know the exact nature of testimony given about busing until long after the ruling. Some still do not know.

2. Public relations considerations played such a large part in the testimony of school board staff members that the free flow of information was inhibited. Most scholars minimize the power of site-selection to alter the pattern of racial imbalance in large cities with substantial black populations. But the assertion that site-selection was a powerful influence was scarcely challenged directly—mainly, one guesses, because the Detroit board was officially committed to a platitudinous policy on this subject, originated by the state board of education. Nobody was willing to say publicly what most said privately; that the policy was virtually meaningless and, for the City of Detroit, incapable of contributing to the aim of promoting integration from the time it was adopted.

3. The commitment to racial integration on the part of the leadership of the school system was such that testimony on school practices was marked by some lack of candor, distinct from public-relations considerations. I refer to a seeming reluctance to make statements which might weaken the fragile support of existing public opinion for the cherished goal of integration. In this broad sense, the two sides in the Detroit case were not adversaries.

In the course of these several thousand pages there were many disputes and explanations (some brief, some lengthy) concerning various techniques and methods of research; the validity and adequacy of sampling procedures and questionnaire results; the use of census data to make inferences about school populations; the meaning of sampling error; the difference between cross-sectional and longitudinal analysis; the statistical significance of differences in samples and differences in total-enumeration procedures; the identification of variables as dependent or independent; the problems of regression-analysis; the ascertainment of item-reliability in an index; the appropriate indices for the measurement of socio-economic status; the association of variables and the correlation—versus causation distinction; the selection and use of polar categories; the problems of demographic prediction and trend-extrapolation; the meaning of the scattergram; the standard error and cultural bias in testing; the computation of indices of segregation in schools and in housing; the meaning of the normal curve; the interpretation of scale differences; and, finally, the meaning and use of the chi-square test.

Some of these controversies and explanations illustrate the problems faced by courts in cases where scientific materials are offered. There were some explanations which required a fair amount of knowledge of quantitative techniques—which as it appears from the record, some of those present, including the judge, did not have. (Here, as in the substantive areas, there was enormous advantage on the side of the plaintiffs, whose counsel had been specializing in school-segregation cases for years and had the help of academic consultants well acquainted with the professional literature.)

The layman's problems in following technical discussions of quantitative research procedures were only a minor obstacle to the court's understanding, however. The truly serious problem was the failure of the experts to convey to the judge the basic logic of scientific inquiry. In a recent article on the use of scientific experts in a product-liability case the authors concluded:

> . . . the presentation of evidence was such that this most significant question of . . . causation, pivotal to the litigation on any premise, was dispersed and never clearly and coherently addressed in the lengthy trial. Irrelevancies dominated, and the treatment of this major . . . issue was sporadic and shallow. . . . The analogy to the blind leading the blind is not inappropriate.

This is what happened in Detroit, although there was more than one issue of causation involved. For example: There were lengthy statistical presentations on educational-resource allocations to predominantly black and white schools presented along with school achievement levels, but no explanation of how to discover what causal relationship, if any, exists between variations in school-inputs and variations in learning. Indeed, during the remedy hearings (after the trial ended) the judge revealed that he had thought all along that the child's socio-economic status was "part of input."! What had he made of all those discussions about resources and social class? It seems clear that much of the significance of this key causal controversy somehow escaped him, yet his intelligence and conscientious interest are clear from the record.

A second key causal controversy centered around the impact of racial concentration on achievement; and again, graphic presentations showing school achievement levels and school racial composition were offered. But since academic achievement scores are not disaggregated by race in Detroit there is no way even to begin to study the "effects" of the variations in school racial composition. In all of the hundrends of pages of testimony on the "effects" of a variety of factors on Detroit's black students, the absence of data classified by race within schools was not discussed, nor the implications of this deficiency explained to the judge.

In some instances issues of central importance vanished during elaborate presentations which had the form, but not the substance, of "social science." For example, in the presentation of various calculations of the proper social-class mix for desegregation plans, the white children were collapsed into polar categories: They were either "middle-class" (often described as "high-status") or "poor" whites—and the white working class virtually disappeared from one of the world's great industrial centers. Much of the testimony on educational topics was not far above the level of "pop" sociology. Terms were not clearly defined nor consistently used. Anecdotal material was offered, without challenge, to establish general propositions. Hypotheses—concerning, e.g., the "tipping point"—were presented as if they were verified generalizations. Sources were sometimes cited incorrectly; some "facts" were inaccurate, some accounts of research were garbled. (Several important references to data in the Coleman report, for example, were erroneous or distorted.)

What is the appropriate role for social science in the courtroom? The growing reluctance to use research findings and scholarly opinion as grounds for desegregation orders seem a proper recognition of the "revisionist" character of scientific knowledge. (Some of the most important reanalyses of the data used in the study by Coleman et al., as well as other research on the effects of pupil heterogeneity on achievement, for example, appeared after the Detroit trial.) In the future new knowledge may support, question, or reverse earlier findings. Social-science testimony performs a useful and necessary function when, as Michael Katz has noted, such material reveals erroneous assumptions and conclusions by "disclosing the inadequacies or insufficiencies in method, loosenenss in reasoning, or paucity of evidence relied upon to construct the causal model upon which a policy rests." The removal of these insubstantial foundations should compel greater judicial reliance upon clear constitutional principles.

Regardless of the extent to which the social-science evidence offered in a de-segregation case is used as legal underpinning for the court's decision, such material appears to have an important influence upon the general perspective of judges. Many pages of the transcript in the Detroit case read like a one-student-seminar session. The expert-witness/teacher instructs and explains: the judge/student asks a question, and verifies his understanding by a comment or example: the teacher then assesses and indicates (much too timidly) the accuracy of his pupil's understanding. But there are many aspects of courtroom procedural tradition which are educationally disad-vantageous; the long time lapse between opposing witnesses testifying on the same topic; the absence of direct confrontation between experts who offer contradictory evidence, especially concerning the nature of factual material; the extreme deference shown to the court's remarks, which allows half-truths to stand uncorrected; the extent to which the adversary system controls the production of evidence; and the extent to which the emergence of the best approximation of scientific "truth" is jeopardized (just as in criminal cases) when the two sides are very unequal in expertise and experience. The court is a poor classroom. It is the only place where we can decide if a man is guilty of murder, but it is not a good place to study the causes of homicide. The source of some of these problems is in the very nature of the adversary system, and this raises the question whether matters of educational policy are appropriately handled by judicial proceedings.

The adversary mode in the presentation of evidence always tends to offend our most basic notions of scientific inquiry. Barrington Moore has observed:

> If a defense lawyer is suddenly surprised by a piece of evidence as an argument turned up by the prosecution he is never supposed to say: "My, I had never thought of that! It is a good point and my client must be guilty." On the other hand, that is exactly what an intellectually honest scholar is supposed to do under the circumstances.

The law literature contains many procedural suggestions aimed at modifying some of those aspects of adversary proceedings that most academic witnesses find so distasteful. Among these suggestions are proposals for court-appointed masters to evaluate evidence, panels of consultants, joint committees of legal and behavioral-science scholars to prepare written submissions and other materials, and "devil's advocates" (a title peculiarly appropriate for these school-segregation cases) to argue unpopular positions. No single reform would be more helpful than to make trial records readily available. Their inaccessibility is a serious problem for scholars, and a barrier to citizen review. The cost per page varies from $.50 to $1.50, making a copy of a lengthy trial record virtually unobtainable.

Social-science testimony *is* being used in these school cases, and it should be of better quality than much that was offered during the Detroit case. (A reading of some other rulings makes me suspect that this case was not unique.) Most academics are quite unaware of the level of some of the scientific evidence offered in such cases. How could they know? Media coverage of the testimony during the landmark Detroit case was surprisingly sparse. It might be useful for the professional societies of the academic disciplines involved to monitor trials on important social issues.

Perhaps it is because so many scholars shun adversary proceedings that some of the expert witnesses are not very expert. The professional societies would do well to develop lists of highly qualified people in various fields and to support strongly those willing to undergo the rigors of courtroom appearances—especially on behalf of those litigants willing to have the expert witness present as much of the "whole truth" as he thinks he knows at the time. The "whole truth," of course, will actually be only partial, and it will be tentative—and it is always subject to change.

NOTES

1. Wolf raises questions about the capacity of courts to appraise and correctly act upon social science data which may have been collected for entirely different purposes. Are you persuaded by the argument?

2. In cases like those involving racial integration, if courts do not rely on social science data lodged by the parties, what can they use to guide them in making choices and devising strategies? Discuss.

3. In cases in which courts are obliged to appraise the behavior of large-scale and complex institutions and their compliance with national law, can the courts avoid using social science data which tries to generalize the behavior of aggregates and project likely future behavior? What are the alternatives?

4. If courts are not equipped to deal with this sort of information, what other agencies in government should be charged with overseeing compliance with such statutory programs?

5. If courts will inevitably have a role in such programs, whether direct, as in school desegregation, or indirect, as in numerous reviews of complex federal regulatory agency action, what steps are available to improve courts performance in relying on social science data?

Brown was no more than a clarion call. Courts and other governmental agencies about the country were then required to implement the basic policy it had expressed. One technique—some would say it was an imperative of *Brown*—involved busing students from *de facto* segregated neighborhoods to schools that had not been integrated, thereby achieving a racial balance in the schools and overcoming the effects that the Supreme Court had denounced in *Brown*. Busing itself was designed and justified by reference to social science data. It gave rise to great national controversy. Proponents and opponents of the technique relied heavily on social scientific data to support their position or to undermine the position of their opponents.

Consider one case ordering busing.

SWANN ET AL. V. CHARLOTTE-MECKLENBURG BOARD OF EDUCATION
402 U.S. 1 (1971)

[Chief Justice Burger delivered the opinon]. . . . We granted certiorari in this case to review important issues as to the duties of school authorities and the scope of powers of federal courts under this Court's mandates to eliminate racially separate public schools established and maintained by state action. Brown v. Board of Education, 347 U.S. 483 (1954). . . .

This case and those argued with it arose in States having a long history of maintaining two sets of schools in a single school system deliberately operated to carry out a governmental policy to separate pupils in schools solely on the basis of race. That was what Brown v. Board of Education was all about. These cases present

us with the problem of defining in more precise terms than heretofore the scope of
the duty of school authorities and district courts in implementing Brown I and the
mandate to eliminate dual systems and establish unitary systems at once. Meanwhile
district courts and courts of appeals have struggled in hundreds of cases with a
multitude and variety of problems under this Court's general directive. Understand-
ably, in an area of evolving remedies, those courts had to improvise and experiment
without detailed or specific guidelines. This Court, in Brown I, appropriately dealt
with the large constitutional principles; other federal courts had to grapple with the
flinty, intractable realities of day-to-day implementation of those constitutional commands. Their efforts, of necessity, embraced a process of "trial and error," and our
effort to formulate guidelines must take into account their experience. . . .

I

The Charlotte-Mecklenburg school system, the 43d largest in the Nation, encompasses the city of Charlotte and surrounding Mecklenburg County, North Carolina.
The area is large—550 square miles—spanning roughly 22 miles east-west and 36
miles north-south. During the 1968–1969 school year the system served more than
84,000 pupils in 107 schools. Approximately 71% of the pupils were found to be
white and 29% Negro. As of June 1969, there were approximately 24,000 Negro
students in the system, of whom 21,000 attended schools within the city of Charlotte.
Two-thirds of those 21,000—approximately 14,000 Negro students—attended 21
schools which were either totally Negro or more than 99% Negro.

This situation came about under a desegregation plan approved by the District
Court at the commencement of the present litigation in 1965 . . . based upon geographic zoning with a free-transfer provision. The present proceedings were initiated
in September 1968 by petitioner Swann's motion for further relief based on Green
v County School Board, 391 US 430 . . . (1968), and its companion cases. All
parties now agree that in 1969 the systems fell short of achieving the unitary school
system that those cases require.

The District Court held numerous hearings and received voluminous evidence.
In addition to finding certain actions of the school board to be discriminatory, the
court also found that residential patterns in the city and county resulted in part from
federal, state, and local government action other than school board decisions. School
board action based on these patterns, for example, by locating schools in Negro
residential areas and fixing the size of the schools to accommodate the needs of
immediate neighborhoods, resulted in segregated education. These findings were
subsequently accepted by the Court of Appeals.

In April 1969, the District Court ordered the school board to come forward with
a plan for both faculty and student desegregation.

• • •

The Finger Plan. The plan submitted by the court-appointed expert Dr. Finger,
adopted the school board zoning plan for senior high schools with one modification:
it required that an additional 300 Negro students be transported from the Negro
residential area of the city to the nearly all-white Independence High School.

The Finger plan for the junior high schools employed much of the rezoning plan
of the board, combined with the creation of nine "satellite" zones. Under the satellite
plan, inner-city Negro students were assigned by attendance zones to nine outlying

predominately white junior high schools, thereby substantially desegregating every junior high school in the system.

The Finger plan departed from the board plan chiefly in its handling of the system's 76 elementary schools. Rather than relying solely upon geographic zoning, Dr. Finger proposed use of zoning, pairing, and grouping techniques, with the result that student bodies throughout the system would range from 9% to 38% Negro.

The District Court described the plan thus:

"Like the board plan, the Finger plan does as much by rezoning school attendance lines as can reasonably be accomplished. However, unlike the board plan, it does not stop there. It goes further and desegregates all the rest of the elementary schools by the technique of grouping two or three outlying schools with one black inner city school; by transporting black students from grades one through four to the outlying white schools; and by transporting white students from the fifth and sixth grades from the outlying white schools to the inner city black school."

Under the Finger plan, nine inner-city Negro schools were grouped in this manner with 24 suburban white schools.

• • •

II

Nearly 17 years ago this Court held, in explicit terms, that state-imposed segregation by race in public schools denies equal protection of the laws. At no time has the Court deviated in the slightest degree from that holding or its constitutional underpinnings. None of the parties before us challenges the Court's decision of May 17, 1954, that "in the field of public education the doctrine of 'separate but equal' has no place. Separate educational facilities are inherently unequal. Therefore, we hold that the plaintiff and others similarly situated . . . are, by reason of the segregation complained of, deprived of the equal protection of the laws guaranteed by the Fourteenth Amendment.

• • •

Over the 16 years since Brown II, many difficulties were encountered in implementation of the basic constitutional requirement that the State not discriminate between public school children on the basis of their race. Nothing in our national experience prior to 1955 prepared anyone for dealing with changes and adjustments of the magnitude and complexity encountered since then. Deliberate resistance of some to the Court's mandates has impeded the good-faith efforts of others to bring school systems into compliance. The detail and nature of these dilatory tactics have been noted frequently by this court and other courts.

• • •

The problems encountered by the district courts and courts of appeals make plain that we should now try to amplify guidelines, however incomplete and imperfect, for the assistance of school authorities and courts. The failure of local authorities to meet their constitutional obligations aggravated the massive problem of converting from the state-enforced discrimination of racially separate school systems. This process has been rendered more difficult by changes since 1954 in the structure and patterns of communities, the growth of student populations, movement of families, and other changes, some of which had marked impact on school planning, sometimes neutralizing or negating remedial action before it was fully implemented. Rural areas accustomed for half a century to the consolidated school systems implemented by bus transportation could make adjustments more readily than metropolitan areas with dense and shifting population, numerous schools, congested and complex traffic patterns.

• • •

In seeking to define even in broad and general terms how far this remedial power extends it is important to remember that judicial powers may be exercised only on the basis of a constitutional violation. Remedial judicial authority does not put judges automatically in the shoes of school authorities whose powers are plenary. Judicial authority enters only when local authority defaults.

School authorities are traditionally charged with broad power to formulate and implement educational policy and might well conclude, for example, that in order to prepare students to live in a pluralistic society each school should have a prescribed ratio of Negro to white students reflecting the proportion for the district as a whole. To do this as an educational policy is within the broad discretionary powers of school authorities; absent a finding of a constitutional violation, however, that would not be within the authority of a federal court. As with any equity case, the nature of the violation determines the scope of the remedy. In default by the school authorities of their obligation to proffer acceptable remedies, a district court has broad power to fashion a remedy that will assure a unitary school system.

• • •

The record in this case reveals the familiar phenomenon that in metropolitan areas minority groups are often found concentrated in one part of the city. In some circumstances certain schools may remain all or largely of one race until new schools can be provided or neighborhood patterns change. Schools all or predominantly of one race in a district of mixed population will require close scrutiny to determine that school assignments are not part of state-enforced segregation.

• • •

The scope of permissible transportation of students as an implement of a remedial decree has never been defined by this Court and by the very nature of the problem it cannot be defined with precision. No rigid guidelines as to student transportation can be given for application to the infinite variety of problems presented in thousands of situations. Bus transportation has been an integral part of the public education system for years, and was perhaps the single most important factor in the transition from the one-room schoolhouse to the consolidated school. Eighteen million of the nation's public school children, approximately 39% were transported to their schools by bus in 1969–1970 in all parts of the country.

The importance of bus transportation as a normal and accepted tool of educational policy is readily discernible in this and the companion case, Davis, supra. The Charlotte school authorities did not purport to assign students on the basis of geographically drawn zones until 1965 and then they allowed almost unlimited transfer privileges. The District Court's conclusion that assignment of children to the school nearest their home serving their grade would not produce an effective dismantling of the dual system is supported by the record.

Thus, the remedial techniques used in the District Court's order were within that court's power to provide equitable relief; implementation of the decree is well within the capacity of the school authority.

The decree provided that the buses used to implement the plan would operate on direct routes. Students would be picked up at schools near their homes and transported to the schools they were to attend. The trips for elementary school pupils average about seven miles and the District Court found that they would take "not over 35 minutes at the most." This system compares favorably with the transportation plan previously operated in Charlotte under which each day 23,600 students on all grade levels were transported an average of 15 miles one way for an average trip requiring over an hour. In these circumstances, we find no basis for holding that the local school authorities may not be required to employ bus transportation as one tool of school desegregation. Desegregation plans cannot be limited to the walk-in school.

An objection to the transportation of students may have validity when the time or distance of travel is so great as to either risk the health of the children or significantly impinge on the educational process. District courts must weigh the soundness of any transportation plan in light of what is said . . . above. It hardly needs stating that the limits on time of travel will vary with many factors, but probably with none more than the age of the students. The reconciliation of competing values in a desegregation case is, of course, a difficult task with many sensitive facets but fundamentally no more so than remedial measures courts of equity have traditionally employed. . . .

———

A sense of the tenor of the debate about the social science data used in assessing the pertinence of the busing strategy and its effects can be gained from the following selections from *The Public Interest,* Winter, 1973.

PETTIGREW, SMITH, USEEM & NORMAND, BUSING: A REVIEW OF "THE EVIDENCE", PUB. INTEREST, WINTER, 1973, AT 88

[In this selection, the authors respond to an article by David Armor entitled The Evidence on Busing, 28 *Pub. Interest,* Summer, 1972, at 90. On the basis of the evidence his tests produced, Armor concluded that busing as a technique of integration fails on four out of five counts; it does not lead to improvements in achievement, grades, aspirations and racial attitudes for black children.]

David Armor's "The Evidence on Busing," (*The Public Interest,* No. 28, Summer 1972) presented a distorted and incomplete review of this politically charged topic. We respect Armor's right to publish his views against "mandatory busing." But we challenge his claim that these views were supported by scientific evidence. . . . We must limit ourselves here to outlining and discussing briefly our principal disagreements with Armor, which center on four major points.

First, his article begins by establishing unrealistically high standards by which to judge the success of school desegregation. "Busing," he claims, works only if it leads—in *one* school year—to increased achievement, aspirations, self-esteem, interracial tolerance, and life opportunities for black children. And "busing" must meet these standards in *all* types of interracial schools; no distinction is made between *merely desegregated* and *genuinely integrated* schools.

This "integration policy model," as it is labeled, is *not* what social scientists who specialize in race relations have been writing about over the past generation. Indeed, Armor's criteria must surely be among the most rigid ever employed for the evaluation of a change program in the history of public education in the United States.

Second, the article presents selected findings from selected studies as "*the* evidence on busing." The bias here is twofold. On the one hand, the few students mentioned constitute an incomplete list and are selectively negative in results. Unmentioned are at least seven investigations—from busing programs throughout the nation—that meet the methodological criteria for inclusion and report *positive* achievement results for black students. These seven studies are widely known.

On the other hand, only cursory descriptions are provided of the few investigations that are reviewed. Mitigating circumstances surrrounding black responses to dese-gregation are not discussed. For example, we are not told that educational services for the transported black pupils were actually *reduced* with the onset of desegregation in three of the cited cities. In addition, negative findings consistent with the paper's anti-busing thesis are emphasized, while positive findings from these same cities are either obscured or simply ignored. Newer studies from three of the cited cities showing more positive results are not discussed.

Positive findings are also obscured by the utilization of an unduly severe standard. The achievement gains of black students in desegregated schools are often compared with white gains, rather than with the achievement of black students in black schools. But such a standard ignores the possibility that *both* racial groups can make more meaningful educational advances in interracial schools. Indeed, this possibility ac-tually occurs in three of the cities mentioned by Armor. Yet he does not inform us of this apparent dual success of desegregation; instead, "busing" is simply rated a failure because the black children did not far outgain the improving white children.

Third, the paper's anti-busing conclusions rest primarily on the findings from one short-term study conducted by Armor himself. This investigation focused on a vo-luntary busing program in metropolitan Boston called METCO. Yet this study is probably the weakest reported in the paper. Our re-examination of its data finds that it has extremely serious methodolgical problems.

Two major problems concern deficiencies of the control group. To test the effects of "busing" and school desegregation, a control group should obviously consist exclusively of children who neither are "bused" nor attend desegregated schools. But our check of this critical point reveals that this is not the case. . . .

Incredible as it sounds, then, Armor compared a group of children who were bused to desegregated schools with another group of children which included many who also were bused to desegregated schools. Not surprisingly, then, he found few differences between them.

• • •

Serious, too, is an enormous non-response rate in the second test administration, a problem alluded to by Armor only in a footnote. For the elementary students, only 51 percent of the eligible METCO students and 28 percent of the eligible "control" students took part in both of the achievement test sessions. The achievement results for junior and senior high students are also rendered virtually meaningless by the participation of only 44 percent of the eligibile METCO students and 20 percent of the eligible "control" students. . . .

There are other problems in the METCO study. Some children were included who initially performed as well as the test scoring allowed and therefore could not possibly demonstrate "improvement"; in fact, these pupils comprise one sixth of all the junior high pupils tested for achievement gains in reading. Moreover, the con-ditions for the third administration of the attitude tests were different for the METCO students and the "controls": The former took the tests at school and the latter took them at home with their parents or proctors. Even apart from the severe control group problems, then, the faulty research design makes any conclusion about differences in racial attitudes between the two groups hazardous.

The inadequate discussion of the METCO study in Armor's article makes it virtually impossible for even the discerning reader to evaluate it properly. We uncovered its many errors only from unpublished earlier materials and from reanalyzing the data ourselves. Differential statistical standards are employed, with less rigorous standards applied to findings congruent with the article's anti-busing thesis; attitude difference among METCO schools are not shown; and misleading claims of consistency with other research findings are made.

•　•　•

The picture is considerably more positive, as well as more complex, than Armor paints it. For example, when specified school conditions are attained, research has repeatedly indicated that desegregated schools improve the academic performance of black pupils. Other research has demonstrated that rigidly high and unrealistic aspirations actually deter learning; thus, a slight lowering of such aspirations by school desegregation can lead to beter achievement and cannot be regarded as a failure of "busing." Moreover, "militancy," and "black consciousness and solidarity" are not negative characteristics, as Armor's article asserts, and their alleged development in desegregated schools could well be regarded as a further success, not a failure, of "busing." Finally, the evidence that desegregated education sharply expands the life opportunities of black children is more extensive than he has indicated.

Consequently, Armor's sweeping policy conclusion against "mandatory busing" is neither substantiated nor warranted. Not only does it rely upon impaired and incomplete "evidence," but in a real sense his paper is not about "busing" at all, much less "mandatory busing." Three of the cities discussed—among them Boston, the subject of Armor's own research—had *voluntary,* not "mandatory busing." "Busing" was never cited as an independent variable, and many of the desegregation studies discussed involved some children who were not bused to reach their interracial schools. Indeed, in Armor's own investigation of METCO, some of the METCO children were not bused while many of the controls were.

Fourth, objections must be raised to the basic assumptions about racial changes that undergird the entire article. Public school desegregation is regarded as largely a technical matter, a matter for social scientists more than for the courts. Emphasis is placed solely on the adaptive abilities of black children rather than on their constitutional rights. Moreover, the whole national context of individual and institutional racism is conveniently ignored, and interracial contact under any conditions is assumed to be "integration". . . .

AMOR, THE DOUBLE DOUBLE STANDARD: A REPLY
PUB. INTEREST, WINTER, 1973, AT 119

The essential requirement for sound reasoning in this matter is observance of the distinction among the findings of science, the results of policy and the dictates of law or morality. I studied the results of existing policies of induced school integration (all of which used, of necessity, varying amounts of busing). I was *not* studying the scientific issue of what *might* happen under various conditions (other than those in effect in the program studied), nor the legal question of whether it *should* have happened according to various constitutional interpretations. My task was far simpler. I asked only the question: What *has* happened? My critics have confused the *has* with the *might* and the *should*. This confusion is further compounded by their application of two double standards for the evaluation and use of the evidence on busing.

• • •

One expectation stands out above all others; Integrated education will enhance the academic achievement of minority groups, and thereby close (or at least substantially reduce) the achievement gap. There is good reason for the prominence of this belief. The Coleman study revealed a large and consistent achievement gap between white students and most minority groups (with the notable exception of Oriental students). . . .

They have presented no convincing evidence that any programs—even those fulfilling their conditions—are having an important effect. There is no clear evidence in the studies mentioned that they fulfilled their conditions, nor is there *any* evidence in these studies—regardless of the conditions—that school integration will close the achievement gap by "approximately a fourth". . . .

Their belief in the possibility of educational benefits rests upon their highly questionable rejection of black and white achievement comparisons and upon a variety of small and inconsistent fluctuations in the achievement of bused students. This leads them to hold that my "firm policy conclusion against 'mandatory busing' is not substantiated by the evidence presented." Apparently, then, their view is that mandatory busing (or induced integration), whether ordered by the courts or by a local school board, is strictly a moral and constitutional issue and does not require any justification involving educational benefits. They have therefore placed the burden of proof not upon those who back the social intervention but upon those who object to the intervention.

I cannot agree with the assumptions behind this reasoning, with the kind of morality it represents, or with the implicit suggestion that social science should be used only when it favors the values of the social scientist. . . .

The second double standard is applied by the critique's assertion that the whole matter is really a constitutional issue, to be decided by "the Court's interpretation of the 14th Amendment." The double standard here is obvious. One willingly applies social science findings to public policy if they are in accordance with one's values, but declares them irrelevant if they contradict one's values. Pettigrew's resort to this tactic recalls a press conference reported in the *New York Times* on June 11, 1972, in which Dr. Kenneth Clark—whose scientific research and assistance was so important in the 1954 Supreme Court decision—was quoted as saying that "courts and political bodies should decide questions of school spending and integration, not on the basis of uncertain research findings, but on the basis of the constitutional and equity rights of human beings." The double standard could not be expressed more graphically.

It will be disastrous for the social sciences if they allow themselves to be used in this way. We social scientists depend upon society for our existence; our credibility is undermined if we do not present and use our findings in a consistent manner. The responsible use of social science in policy matters requires that we state the facts as they occur, no matter how painful their implications. And if we are willing to use facts to initiate policy reform, we must likewise use them to question existing policy. I believe that in the long run society will benefit more from decisions based on facts than from ideology contradicted by facts.

I do not want to imply that we should engage in social intervention only when it is supported by social science or stop any social intervention when the findings of science question its support. Social science cannot be brought to bear on all issues of policy, sometimes for technical reasons and sometimes for ethical reasons. Some policies cannot be researched, and some policies are demanded by constitutional principles or by common morality. But when policies are based upon empirical considerations that social science can study, there is a way that policy and science can proceed in concert. That way utilizes the method of social experimentation and evaluation—a method that has long been prominent in the medical sciences. We would not think of prescribing a new drug without first obtaining sound evidence of both its efficiency and its harmlessness by experimental evaluation of its actual effects on human subjects (usually volunteers). Why should not a similar standard be applied to proposed remedies for curing social ills? Our assumptions about social behavior have been proven wrong in the past, and they will be proven wrong in the future. The only way to make reasonably sure that the remedy is not worse than the malady is to engage in careful research under realistic conditions. That our government is beginning to adopt the principle of social experimentation is shown by Congress's recent decision to perform a large-scale, long-term experiment to test the efficiency of a guaranteed income plan before implementing it for the whole nation. This is a welcome sign for those who want to see a closer connection between social science and public policy.

WILSON, ON PETTIGREW AND ARMOR: AN AFTERWORD, PUB. INTEREST, WINTER, 1973, AT 132

The circumstances under which social science can produce non-obvious, non-trivial, valid findings are unfortunately not as commonplace as we would like. One must be able to define and measure with some precision the factors under consideration, to study or manipulate them without changing them in unknown ways, and to isolate them either experimentally or statistically from the influence of other factors. When these circumstances occur and where there exists financial support for such inquiries, social science prospers—as it has in voting studies and market research. The effects to be explained (a vote, a consumer purchase) are unambiguous and easily measured, the factors generally thought to produce these effects (the income, education, religion, or occupation of the voter or consumer) are also easily measured, the carrying out of the study (at least after the fact) does not alter the decision, and political candidates and business firms are willing to pay for the results.

Studies of the effects of segregated or desegregated schools (or even studies of schools, period) rarely meet all of these criteria; neither do efforts to understand the causes of crime, of persistent unemployment, of broken families, of drug addiction, and of racial differences (if any) in intelligence. Either the effects to be studied are hard to measure (as with educational attainment or true crime rates), or the possible causes are hard to define and detect (as with most habits of mind and of personality), or the possible explanatory factors are hard to disentangle (as with race, class, and education), or the act of studying the situation alters it (as when persons who are part of an experiment come to like or dislike the special attention that is being paid to them).

• • •

. . . [O]n what grounds can anyone defend such policy-evaluating social science as exists? In part, because some studies *do* provide answers, even when judged by the most rigorous standards—it is a sad but clear fact, for example, that the reading scores of black children in big-city elementary schools lag significantly behind white scores. (What is at issue is not the difference, but what causes it and what may be done about it.) But in large part social science evaluations and the debates over them, are useful because they expose the complexities of a problematic situation, extend the range of possible explanations for those conditions, increase our awareness of the unintended as well as intended outcomes of any policy intervention, and stimulate us to reflect on the inadequacies of our own preconceptions about the matter. In short, serious social science, seriously debated, can be a civilizing influence, despite the fact that some of its critics regard the very effort to be scientific as uncivilized.

Social science begins by attempting to simplify human affairs in order that they can be more easily explained, but it often ends by making them even more complex than originally supposed. It is perhaps this tendency that leads some persons, impatient for change, to charge social scientists with being "conservative" (an otherwise hilarious accusation, given the political predisposition of most social scientists). The more complex a situation is thought to be and the greater the importance of subjective, as opposed to material, conditions in explaining it, the more intractable it will seem to be. . . . But in the long run policy will be made whatever social science may say and, indeed, the commitment to policy change is in many cases a necessary precondition for an evaluative study.

SOCIOLOGICAL JURISPRUDENCE AND VALUE COMMITMENT

In Chapter 6, we considered von Jhering's insight; in a heterogeneous community, with groups of roughly equal power, each group may succeed in having a norm or law prescribed that favors its own position. Because the norms will be contradictory, each party may repair to a decisionmaker claiming that its position is in fact the law. The complementarity of norms has a curious counterpart in the legal use of social science data. In the previous selections, you will have observed that each side is able to invoke social scientific research and findings supporting its own position. In some cases, you may have suspected that the outcome of the study, as Wilson tartly observes, is predetermined by the preferences of the investigator. These questions touch on one of the sorest points in contemporary social science and its use by law; the extent to which personal preference, policy or value as it is sometimes referred to, has a role in scientific inquiry. The effect of value on social science inquiry (and by implication on its use by law) is the focus of the following selection.

DAHRENDORF, VALUES AND SOCIAL SCIENCE: THE VALUE DISPUTE IN PERSPECTIVE, IN ESSAYS IN THE THEORY OF SOCIETY 1, 6–7, 9–17 (1968)

. . . [V]alue judgments cannot be derived from scientific insights. The assertions of social science and value judgments may legitimately be seen as two distinct types of statement. We may ask, therefore, at which points in the sociologist's research he encounters value judgments, and how he should act in these encounters. . . .

Scientific inquiry begins, at least in temporal terms, with the choice of a subject, and it is here that we find the first possible encounter between social science and value judgments. That the process of inquiry begins with the choice of a subject is rather a trivial statement; but if we advance one step further and ask on what basis a scholar chooses the themes of his research, we have left the realm of triviality . . . value judgments are often a factor in choosing a subject.

. . . the choice of subject is made in what may be called the antechamber of science, where the sociologist is still free from the rules of procedure that will later govern his research. It is probably unrealistic to insist that value judgments be eliminated from the choice of subjects; in any case it is quite unnecessary, since the reason why a subject is regarded as worth investigating is irrelevant in principle to its scientific treatment.

• • •

. . . . Must value judgments be radically eliminated from the formulation of scientific theories?

Popper's argument is convincing:

> All scientific descriptions of facts are highly selective. . . . It is not only impossible to avoid a selective point of view, but also wholly undesirable to attempt to do so; for if we could do so, we should get not a more "objective" description, but only a mere heap of entirely unconnected statements. But, of course, a point of view is inevitable; and the naive attempt to avoid it can only lead to self-deception, and to the uncritical application of an unconscious point of view.

I think we may go even further and assert that selectivity of this sort, even if based on a value judgment, is not only inevitable but also no threat to scientific inquiry. To see this, we need only distinguish between two aspects of scientific inquiry that are often misleadingly confused; the logic and the psychology of scientific discovery.

A selective point of view, such as the conservative bias of the sociologist described above, does cause a scholar to see what he wants to see and be blind to other things. However, this merely tells us how the scholar has come to formulate a given hypothesis X; it does not tell us whether hypothesis X is true or false, tenable or untenable. Neither the values nor the thought processes of a scientist determine the validity of his hypotheses; their validity is determined only by empirical test. Nor can empirical tests as such affect the values and thought processes of the scientist in any way. In short, the psychological motives behind the formulation of any scientific theory or hypothesis are irrelevant to its truth or validity. It follows that the encounter between social science and value judgments at the stage of theory formation cannot have harmful consequences.

• • •

. . . . [T]he problem of values as subjects of inquiry . . . [and] the study of the normative aspects of social action [have] occupied a prominent place in scientific sociology. This theme has been even more prominent in recent social anthropology. . . .

. . . When Weber's opponents interpreted his insistence on a value-free sociology as an effort to eliminate the subject matters of social values from sociological research, . . . Weber replied, "if the normatively valid becomes a subject of empirical investigation, it loses, as a subject of investigation, its normative character; it's treated as 'existing,' not as 'valid'." Indeed, it is neither necessary nor sensible to renounce the attempt to study the normative elements of social structure with the tools of empirical social science. Although there are numerous difficulties in such research, it involves no serious confusion of science and value judgments.

• • •

. . . [C]onfusing social science and value judgments—that is, presenting in the guise of scientific propositions what are demonstrably value statements unsupported by evidence—I shall call ideological distortion. In sociology we encounter time and again two kinds of such ideologically distorted statements. The first is the kind of overextension of specific propositions that is illustrated in our example. All so-called "single-factor theories," theories that assign absolute determining force to a single factor like race, nationality, or the relations of production, belong in this group; so does the familiar contemporary theory that the tendency toward a leveling-in of certain status symbols in present-day Western societies is transforming them into "classless" societies without structurally generated group conflicts. The second is the presenting of untestable and thus speculative propositions as scientific. An example is the thesis of the alienation of the industrial worker. However much sense this thesis may make in philosophical terms, it has no place in empirical social science, since no amount of empirical research can either confirm or refute it.

All distortions of this kind contain implicit value judgments. Moreover, it is evident that if statements are alleged to be based on scientific investigation when they are in fact drawn from other sources, we are faced with a serious confusion of values and social science. But how is the sociologist to avoid ideological distortions, or to perceive and correct them where they have occurred? Three suggested answers to this question are offered in the literature. The first is the one recommended by Rumney and Maier; training in objectivity with the assistance of psychoanalysis and the sociology of knowledge. More than other scholars, the sociologist, himself inseparably a part of the subject of his research, is in danger of confusing his professional statements with his personal value judgments. The only way to avoid this confusion is by instituting a permanent process of self-observation and self-criticism, in which all propositions are systematically scrutinized for traces of ideological distortion. Another suggestion is that the sociologist explicitly declare the values that have guided him in his research, so that his readers or listeners will be in a position to analyze any ideological distortions that he might unwittingly be guilty of.

It seems to me, however, that a third suggestion is considerably more promising and effective than the first two. Science is always a concert of many. The progress of science rests at least as much on the cooperation of scholars as it does on the inspiration of the individual. This cooperation must not be confined to the all too popular "teamwork"; rather, its most indispensable task is mutual criticism. Wherever scientific criticism gives way to a careless or quietistic tolerance, the gate is open to dishonest and worthless research. Let us not forget that ideologically distorted statements are always bad scientific statements. And it seems to me that it is the main task of scientific criticism, to expose such statements and correct them. In the long run, this procedure alone can protect sociology—though not the individual sociologist—against the danger of ideological distortion.

•   •   •

Obviously, the application of scientific results to practical problems involves an encounter between science and value judgments. . . . Two utterly different ways of thinking meet here; systematic empirical observation leading to insights into what is, and the strictly meta-empirical conviction of what should be. The latter, the value judgment, is in no way implicit in the former, the scientific insight. It is an additional and different matter; it is above all a matter removed from the domain of the social scientist as such. The application of scientific results, involving as it does an implicit or even explicit decision about goals and purposes, cannot be considered part of the social scientist's professional activity. At this point, science and value judgments have to be strictly separated.

Is there such a thing, then, as a scientific social policy? Or does the sociologist have to renounce all intention of intervening in the destiny of the society he investigates? . . . If by "intervening" (the concept of "social engineering" often used in England and the United States comes to mind here) we mean action related to goals determined by the sociologist himself, then such action lies outside his strictly scientific competence. He can, however, use the scientific knowledge at his disposal to suggest promising ways of realizing goals formulated by someone else.

•   •   •

. . . Should the social scientist profess both of them in his teaching and writing, or does his calling confine him to strictly scientific matters?

. . . I want to advance the thesis that whereas sociology as a value-free science in Weber's sense may be desirable, the sociologist as such must always be morally committed if he is to protect himself and others from unintended consequences of his actions.

. . . At many points the encounter of social science and value judgments is harmless, and at others the concert of scholarly opinion may exert a corrective influence. . . . [T]he sociologist has to be more than a man who works at sociology. Whatever he does, says, and writes has potentially far-reaching effects on society. It may be true, generally speaking, that sociologists are neither better nor worse than the societies they live in. But even if sociological research merely helps strengthen such tendencies as are already present in society, the sociologist remains responsible for the consequences of his actions. . . .

NOTES

1. Dahrendorf and others reserve a role for value or policy in social science inquiry. They could hardly have done otherwise. How can one use social science techniques (or indeed any techniques at all) for reviewing past trends, identifying conditions, assaying projections, if one does not know what objectives are being sought? It is impossible even to establish a focus, to determine what is a problem, to identify discrepancies between preference and projection, without having decided what one wants. In other words, it is impossible even to find problems unless one has established a certain set of preferences expressed with sufficient precision to be called policies. Interestingly enough, even those social science theorists who allow for the role of value in inquiry do not suggest a systematic method for determining it. It is viewed, as Dahrendorf put it, as the antechamber of science. Are you satisfied with this conclusion?

2. Do you think that the clarification of goals, particularly for large communities, is a matter which can be done in a spasmodic, capricious fashion or is it, like many of the other intellectual tasks, susceptible to a systematic and rational procedure? Sociological jurisprudence, like legal realism, has contributed little to this central point. Other jurisprudential frames have also failed to confront it.

———————

Sociological jurisprudence has been tantalizing but has as yet failed to fulfill much of its promise. While it has generated a good deal of anecdotal description of some interesting areas of the law and some criticisms and suggestions for reform, it has not yet been expressed in a systematic policy—oriented fashion that would make it pointedly relevant to the decision specialist in the twentieth or twenty-first century. Some sociological jurisprudence has been able to identify conditions, future

trends and suggests alternatives in limited areas. But by and large, this is a jurisprudence which is more of a view from Pisgah than an actual crossing of the Jordan
River. Interestingly enough, the most telling criticisms of its shortcomings have come
from writers who are closest to it but who departed from it precisely because they
felt that it tended to sterilize some of the most important contributions it promised.
We will consider some of their criticisms in Chapter 12.

D. Black, The Boundaries of Legal Sociology, 81 *Yale L. J.* 1088 (1972).

N. Caplan, A. Morrison, & R. J. Stambaugh, *The Use of Social Science Knowledge in Policy Decision at the National Level: a Report to Respondents* (1975).

J. Dewey, Liberating the Social Scientist: A Plea to Unshackle the Story of Man, 4:4 *Commentary,* Oct. 1947, at 378.

L. Duguit, *Law in the Modern State* (F. Laski transl. 1970).

E. Durkheim, *Division of Labor in Society* (G. Simpson transl. 1952).

E. Ehrlich, *Fundamental Principles of the Sociology of Law* (1962).

L. Godwin, *Can Social Science Help Solve National Problems? Welfare: A Case in Point* (1975).

I. L. Horowitz, *The Use and Abuse of Social Science* (1975).

C. W. Mills, *The Sociological Imagination* (1959).

J. Monahan & L. Walker, Social Authority: Obtaining, Evaluating, and Establishing Social Science in Law, 134:3 *U. Pa. L. Rev.* 477 (1986); *Social Science in Law: Cases & Materials* (1985).

P. Nonet, For Jurisprudential Sociology, 10 *Law & Soc. Rev.* 525 (1970).

L. J. Petrazycki, *Law and Morality* (1955).

R. Pound, A Theory of Social Interests, 15 *Papers & Proc. Amer. Soc. Society* 16 (1921): *Outline of Lectures on Jurisprudence* (5th ed. 1943); Sociology of Law and Sociological Jurisprudence, 5 *U. Toronto L.J.* 1 (1943); The Scope and Purpose of Sociological Jurisprudence, 24 *Harv. L. Rev.* 591 (1911); 25 *Harv. L. Rev.* 140 (1911); 25 *Harv. L. Rev.* 489 (1912).

P. Selznick, *Law, Society and Industrial Justice* (1969).

The Sociology of Georg Simmel (K. H. Wolff ed. & transl. 1964).

P. Sorokin, *Contemporary Sociological Theories* (1928).

R. Stammler, *The Theory of Justice* (I. Husik transl. 1925).

J. Stone, Problems Confronting Sociological Enquiries Concerning International Law, 85 *Rec. des Cours* 96 (1956).

N. S. Timasheff, *An Introduction to the Sociology of Law* (N. Babb transl. 1955).

U.S. National Science Foundation, *Knowledge Into Action: Improving the Nation's Use of the Social Sciences* (1968).

Max Weber, *The Theory of Social and Economic Organization* (A. M. Henderson & T. Parsons transl. 1947).

CHAPTER 12

Policy: Contemporary Approaches

I mean to include under critical, or teleological, jurisprudence proper the systematic testing or critique of our principles and rules of law according to considerations extrinsic or external to the principles and rules as such, that is, according to the psychological, ethical, political, social, and economic bases of the various doctrines and the respective purposes or ends sought to be achieved thereby.
Wesley Newcomb Hohfeld

From the very first example in this book, each real or hypothetical case has demonstrated that law, in all but the most trivial cases, involves a process of choice and that decisions in complex societies like ours cannot be made in any satisfactory fashion by reference to rules alone. Strict application of rules must presuppose that the rules will be implemented in a stable and routinized environment in which they will achieve the outcomes rule-makers sought. This is a supposition of questionable reliability. Alternatively, strict rule-appliers must simply ignore social consequences, a course whose costs could be too high to be acceptable. In fact, the contemporary decisionmaker operates in a universe in which the immediate and longer-term consequences of many choices are the issues at stake for a heterogeneous constituency which often cannot agree about basic policies, desired results or methods of implementation. A formalistic and retroactive application of rules *after* a choice has been made—rules as a ritual—will not add legitimacy to an otherwise politicially unacceptable decision. No one is fooled and, in any case, contending groups have their own rules, for rules as we have seen, travel in complementary pairs. The jurisprudences of rules are obsolete. Events, rather than philosophical preferences have driven contemporary decisionmakers to develop methods of making and appraising decisions that respond to contemporary reality and needs.

The broad but varied jurisprudential movements that emerged in the United States in response to these changes are eclectic in that they draw on many of the insights of the traditional schools of jurisprudence and the insights and skills of a range of social and natural sciences. Curiously, contemporary progressive approaches sometimes try to conceal themselves in the traditional verbiage of the law. Hence the persistence of some of the manifest features of many of the theories considered in the previous chapters and, as a result, the odd coexistences of modern and atavistic doctrines in a single decision. But no matter how artful the camouflage, pleading, deliberations and the actual process of making decisions increasingly pay little more than lip-service to traditional jurisprudence myths.

The new jurisprudential approaches tend, after the Legal Realists, to view law as a process of making decisions. As a result, they seek to develop procedures and guidelines for making choices in complex situations rather than rote acceptance and detailed application of rules by derivational logic. They have, perforce, addressed

516

the clarification and implementation of policy as a fundamental legal task. Many have come to call these jurisprudences the "policy science" approach, since common to all of the different sub-schools in this frame is (i) a concern with the shaping and implementation of policy and (ii) a conception of decision which views the formation and implementation of policy as its central task. It is appropriate to refer to these approaches as a science because, by-and-large, an effort has been made to develop systematic methods for clarifying and implementing policy and, in addition, for incorporating aspects of the physical or natural sciences which are deemed relevant.*

In this chapter we will examine several of the major currents of policy science jurisprudence.** In line with the critical approach taken throughout the book, we are concerned not simply with the invocation of the words "policy" or "social science" as talismans, but rather with the extent to which those purporting to use the methods referred to, do in fact, develop a systematic, comprehensive and socially responsible jurisprudence. The reader will recall from Chapter 1 and its Appendix and the discussions in previous chapters that a systematic approach to making social choices involves the discharge of five intellectual tasks. We will examine the diverse approaches to policy science for the adequacy of their performance of these tasks, and for their compliance with the requirements of a clear observational standpoint, an appropriate set of conceptions, a detailed model of the social process which they are trying to influence and some systematic way of making choices. But we will concentrate primarily on the task of goal clarification, for it is central, even quintessential to a policy-oriented approach and, from the legal-ethical standpoint, may well be its most important contribution. It should be plain, however, that its execution invariably requires a coordinate performance of the other intellectual tasks, for the quest for policy is much more than feverish cogitation in an ivory tower. After clarification of policy, one must design the procedures for its implementation, taking account of the costs, disruptions, necessary ameliorations and even the compromises and temperings of preferred policy which may be necessary to secure its realization.

JUDICIAL APPLICATIONS: "INTUITIVE" POLICY AND ITS PROBLEMS

While legislatures increasingly resort to methods of social and policy sciences for the determination and justification of public policy, American courts, even when they rely on these methods, frequently retain precedents and their logical manipulation as a way of justifying their decisions. In cases such as *Baker v. Carr,*† *Reynolds v.*

---

*The trend is not limited to law. The policy science approach has become a virtual paradigm in American intellectual development. It is to be found, with broad similarities in approach, in economics, sociology, psychology, the specialized area called systems analysis, military science and even in public health and medicine. Our discussion will focus on policy sciences in the law. For general references about the adaptation of these ideas in other fields, the reader may consult the suggested reading at the end of the chapter.

**The proliferation of sub-schools of policy-oriented approaches precludes a comprehensive treatment of each. For example, the refined analyses of behavior in two person and multi-person games, which has been adapted for some legal research, appear to be policy relevant. But on closer analysis, much seems primarily concerned with tactics and without a clear clarification of goals. Moreover, it does not examine the full range of institutions within which people operate and, most important, fails to distinguish a "constitutional" or structural dimension, that special process by which the institutions for decisionmaking are established and maintained, what Llewellyn (in the selection in Chapter 10) called the "Constitution as an Institution" or what might more accurately be called the "constitutive process."

†369 U.S. 186 (1962)

*Sims** and others considered in previous chapters, it is clear that the judges were engaged in creative law-making. Nonetheless they chose to present their conclusions as if they were completely consonant with prior precedents. (Can this incongruity be explained by looking to the larger, often latent political functions which courts perform and the need to satisfy a very diverse constituency? What are the costs of this technique?)

Yet courts can sometimes be extraordinarily candid about the fact that they are stating the law for a particular case and for future cases not in terms of congruence with past decisions but in terms of a policy that will lead to a congruence in the future between goals and social consequences. Consider, for example, the question of which institutions in the United States should be relieved from the obligations to pay taxes. Ordinarily, this is a benefit which is given to certain charitable or educational institutions because they are assumed to be performing important functions for the community or are engaged in matters of essentially personal liberty. To what extent should charitable or educational institutions which discriminate on the basis of religion or race because they feel this is compelled by religious dictates, be denied such benefits? In the *Bob Jones University* case, the Supreme Court grappled with this problem. In the selection that follows, note that the Court's analysis does not purport to justify itself by reference to previous decisions but rather by reference to securing desirable social consequences.

BOB JONES UNIVERSITY V. UNITED STATES
461 U.S. 574 (1983)

[Chief Justice Burger delivered the opinion of the Court]. . . . Until 1970, the Internal Revenue Service granted tax-exempt status to private schools, without regard to their racial admissions policies, under Sec. 501(c)(3), of the Internal Revenue Code, 26 U.S.C. Sec. 501(c)(3),[1] and granted charitable deductions for contributions to such schools under Sec. 170 of the Code, 26 U.S.C. Sec. 170.[2]

• • •

The revised policy on discrimination was formalized in Revenue Ruling 71–447, 1971–2 Cum. Bull. 230:

Both the courts and the Internal Revenue Serivce have long recognized that the statutory requirement of being 'organized and operated exclusively for religious, charitable, . . . or educational purposes' was intended to express the basic

---

*377 U.S. 533 (1967)

[1]Section 501(c)(3) lists the following organizations, which, pursuant to Sec. 501(a), are exampe from taxation unless denied tax exemptions under other specified sections of the Code:

"Corporations, and any community chest, fund, or foundation, *organized and operated exclusively for religious, charitable,* scientific, testing for public safety, literary, *or educational purposes,* or to foster national or international amateur sports competition (but only if no part of its activities involve the provision of athletic facilities or equipment), or for the prevention of cruelty to children or animals, no part of the net earnings of which inures to the benefit of any private shareholder or individual, no substantial part of the activities of which is carrying on propaganda, or otherwise attempting, to influence legislation . . . and which does not participate in, or intervene in (including the publishing or distributing of statements), any political campaign on behalf of any candidate for public office." (Emphasis added).

[2]Section 170(a) allows deductions for certain "charitable contributions." Section 170(c)(2)(B) includes within the definition of "charitable contribution" a contribution or gift to or for the use of a corporation "organized and operated exclusively for religious, charitable, scientific, literary, or educational purposes. . . ."

POLICY 519

common law concept [of 'charity']. . . . All charitable trusts, educational or otherwise, are subject to the requirements that the purpose of the trust may not be illegal or contrary to public policy. *Id.,* at 230.

Based on the "national policy to discourage racial discrimination in education," the IRS rules that "a private school not having a racially nondiscriminatory policy as to students is not 'charitable' within the common law concepts reflected in sections 170 and 501(c)(3) of the Code." *Id.,* at 231.

The application of the IRS construction of these provisions to petitioners, two private schools with racially discriminatory admissions policies, is now before us.

• • •

Bob Jones University is a nonprofit corporation located in Greenville, South Carolina. Its purpose is "to conduct an institution for learning . . . giving special emphasis to the Christian religion and the ethics revealed in the Holy Scriptures.". . . . The corporation operates a school with an enrollment of approximately 5,000 students, from kindergarten through college and graduate school. Bob Jones University is not affiliated with any religious denomination, but is dedicated to teaching and propagation of its fundamentalist Christian religious beliefs. It is both a religion and educational institution. Its teachers are required to be devout Christians, and all courses at the University are taught according to the Bible. Entering students are screened as to their religious beliefs, and their public and private conduct is strictly regulated by standards promulgated by University authorities. [These standards provide in part:]

• • •

THERE IS TO BE NO INTERRACIAL DATING

1. Students who are partners in an interracial marriage will be expelled.
2. Students who are members of or affiliated with any group or organization which holds as one of its goals or advocates interracial marriage will be expelled.
3. Students who date outside their own race will be expelled.
4. Students who espouse, promote, or encourage others to violate the University's dating rules and regulations will be expelled. . . .

The University continues to deny admission to applicants engaged in an interracial marriage or known to advocate interracial marriage or dating. . . .

Until 1970, the IRS extended tax-exempt status to Bob Jones University under Sec. 501(c)(3). By the letter of November 30, 1970, that followed the injunction issued in *Green v. Kennedy, supra.* the IRS formally notified the University of the change in IRS policy, and announced its intention to challenge the tax-exempt status of private schools practicing racial discrimination in their admissions policies.

After failing to obtain an assurance of tax exemption through administrative means, the University instituted an action in 1971 seeking to enjoin the IRS from revoking the school's tax-exempt status.

• • •

In Revenue Ruling 71–477, the IRS formalized the policy first announced in 1970, that Sec. 170 and Sec. 501(c)(3) embrace the common law "charity" concept. Under that view, to qualify for a tax exemption pursuant to Sec. 501(c)(3), an institution must show, first, that it falls within one of the eight categories expressly set forth in that section, and second, that its activity is not contrary to settled public policy.

Section 501(c)(3) provides that "[c]orporations . . . organized and operated exclusively for religious, charitable . . . or educational purposes" are entitled to tax exemption. Petitioners argue that the plain language of the statute guarantees them tax-exempt status. They emphasize the absence of any language in the statute expressly requiring all exempt organizations to be "charitable" in the common law sense, and they contend that the disjunctive "or" separating the categories in Sec. 501(c)(3) precludes such a reading. Instead, they argue that if an institution falls within one or more of the specified categories it is automatically entitled to exemption, without regard to whether it also qualifies as "charitable." The Court of Appeals, rejected that contention and concluded that petitioners' interpretation of the statute "tears section 501(c)(3) from its roots." *United States v. Bob Jones University, supra* 639 F. 2d., at 151.

It is a well-established canon of statutory construction that a court should go beyond the literal language of a statute if reliance on that language would defeat the plain purpose of the statutes:

> The general words used in the clauses . . . taken by themselves, and literally construed, without regard to the object in view, would seem to sanction the claim of the plaintiff. But this mode of expounding a statute has never been adopted by any enlightened tribunal—because it is evident that in many cases it would defeat the object which the Legislature intended to accomplish. And it is well settled that, in interpreting a statute, the court will not look merely to a particular clause in which general words may be used, *but will take in connection with it the whole statute . . . and the objects and policy of the law. . . . Brown v. Duchesne,* 19 How. 183, 194 (1857) (emphasis added).

Section 501(c)(3) therefore must be analyzed and construed within the framework of the Internal Revenue Code and against the background of the Congressional purposes. Such an examination reveals unmistakable evidence that, underlying all relevant parts of the Code, is the intent that entitlement to tax exemption depends on meeting certain common law standards of charity—namely, that an institution seeking tax-exempt status must serve a public purpose and not be contrary to established public policy.

This "charitable" concept appears explicitly in Sec. 170 of the code. That section contains a list of organizations virtually identical to that contained in Sec. 501(c)(3). It is apparent that Congress intended that list to have the same meaning in both sections. In Sec. 170, Congress used the list of organizations in defining the term "charitable contributions." On its face, therefore, Sec. 170 reveals that Congress' intention was to provide tax benefits to organizations serving charitable purposes. The form of Sec. 170 simply makes plain what common sense and history tells us: in enacting both Sec. 170 and Sec. 501(c)(3), Congress sought to provide tax benefits to charitable organizations, to encourage the development of private institutions that serve a useful public purpose or supplement or take the place of public institutions of the same kind.

Tax exemptions for certain institutions thought beneficial to the social order of the country as a whole, or to a particular community, are deeply rooted in our history, as in that of England. The origins of such exemptions lie in the special privileges that have long been extended to charitable trusts.

• • •

. . . These statements clearly reveal the legal background against which Congress enacted the first charitable exemption statute in 1894: charities were to be given preferential treatment because they provide a benefit to society.

• • •

In enacting the Revenue Act of 1938, ch. 289, 52 Stat. 447 (1938), Congress expressly reconfirmed this view with support to the charitable deduction provision:

> The exemption from taxation of money and property devoted to charitable and other purposes is based on the theory that the Government is compensated for the loss of revenue by its relief from financial burdens which would otherwise have to be met by appropriations from other public funds, and by the benefits resulting from the promotion of the general welfare. H.R. Rep. No. 1860, 75th Cong., 3d Sess. 19 (1938).

A corollary to the public benefit principle is the requirement, long recognized in the law of trusts, that the purpose of a charitable trust may not be illegal or violate established public society. In 1861, this Court stated that a public charitable use must be "consistent with local laws and public policy," *Perin v. Carey, supra.* 24 How., at 501. Modern commentators and courts have echoed that view. See *e.g.* Restatement (Second) of Trusts, Sec. 377, comment c (1959); 4 Scott, Sec. 377, and cases cited therein; Bogert, Sec. 378, at 191–192.

When the Government grants exemptions or allows deductions all taxpayers are affected; the very fact of the exemption or deduction for the donor means that other taxpayers can be said to be indirect and vicarious "donors." Charitable exemptions are justified on the basis that the exempt entity confers a public benefit—a benefit which the society or the community may not itself choose or be able to provide, or which supplements and advances the work of public institutions already supported by tax revenues. History buttresses logic to make clear that, to warrant exemption under Sec. 501(c)(3), an institution must fall within a category specified in that section and must demonstrably serve and be in harmony with the public interest. The institution's purpose must not be so at odds with the common community conscience as to undermine any public benefit that might otherwise be conferred.

We are bound to approach these questions with full awareness that determinations of public benefit and public policy are sensitive matters with serious implications for the institutions affected; a declaration that a given institution is not "charitable" should be made only where there can be no doubt that the activity involved is contrary to a fundamental public policy. But there can no longer be any doubt that racial discrimination in education violates deeply and widely accepted views of elementary justice. Prior to 1954, public education in many places still was conducted under the pall of *Plessy v. Ferguson,* 163 U.S. 537 (1896); racial segregation in primary and secondary education prevailed in many parts of the country. See *e.g.,* Segregation and the Fourteenth Amendment in the States (B. Reams & P. Wilson, eds. 1975). This Court's decision in *Brown v. Board of Education,* 347 U.S. 483 (1954), signalled an end to that era. Over the past quarter of a century, every pronouncement of this Court and myriad Acts of Congress and Executive Orders attest a firm national policy to prohibit racial segregation and discrimination in public education.

An unbroken line of cases following *Brown v. Board of Education* established beyond doubt this Court's view that racial discrimination in education violates a most fundamental national public policy, as well as rights of individuals.

The right of a student not to be segregated on racial grounds in schools . . . is indeed so fundamental and pervasive that it is embraced in the concept of due process of law. *Cooper v. Aaron, 1 358 U.S., 1, 19 (1958).*

• • •

Congress, in Titles IV and VI of the Civil Rights Act of 1964, Pub. L. 88–352, 78 Stat. 241, 42 U.S.C. subsection 2000c et seq., 2000c–6, et seq., clearly expressed its agreement that racial discrimination in education violates a fundamental public policy. Other sections of that Act, and numerous enactments since then, testify to the public policy against racial discrimination. . . .

The Executive Branch has consistently placed its support behind eradication of racial discrimination. . . .

Few social or political issues in our history have been more vigorously debated and more extensively ventilated than the issue of racial discrimination, particularly in education. Given the stress and anguish of the history of efforts to escape from the shackles of the "separate but equal" doctrine of *Plessy v. Ferguson, supra.* it cannot be said that educational institutions that, for whatever reasons, practice racial discrimination, are institutions exercising "beneficial and stabilizing influences in community life," *Walz v. Tax Comm'n,* 397 U.S. 664, 673 (1970), or should be encouraged by having all taxpayers share in their support by way of special tax status.

There can thus be no question that the interpretation of Sec. 170 and Sec. 501(c)(3) announced by the IRS in 1970 was correct. That it may be seen as belated does not undermine its soundness. It would be wholly incompatible with the concepts underlying tax exemption to grant the benefit of tax-exempt status to racially discriminatory educational entities, which "exer[t] a pervasive influence on the entire educational process." *Norwood v. Harrison, supra.* 413 U.S., at 469. Whatever may be the rationale for such private schools' discrimination in education is contrary to public policy. Racially discriminatory educational institutions cannot be viewed as conferring a public benefit within the "charitable" concept discussed earlier, or within the Congressional intent underlying Sec. 170 and Sec. 501(c)(3).

Petitioners contend that, regardless of whether the IRS properly concluded that racially discriminatory private schools violate public policy, only Congress can alter the scope of Sec. 170 and Sec. 501(c)(3). Petitioners accordingly argue that the IRS overstepped its lawful bounds in issuing its 1970 and 1971 rulings.

Yet ever since the inception of the tax code, Congress has seen fit to vest in those administering the tax laws very broad authority to interpret those laws. In an area as complex as the tax system, the agency Congress vests with administrative responsibility must be able to exercise its authority to meet changing conditions and new problems. . . .

Congress, the source of IRS authority, can modify IRS rulings it considers improper; and courts exercise review over IRS actions. In the first instance, however, the responsibility for construing the Code falls to the IRS. Since Congress cannot be expected to anticipate every conceivable problem that can arise or to carry out day-to-day oversight, it relies on the administrators and on the courts to implement the legislative will. Administrators, like judges, are under oath to do so.

In Sec. 170 and Sec. 501(c)(3), Congress has identified categories of traditionally exempt institutions and has specified certain additional requirements for tax exemption. Yet the need for continuing interpretation of those statutes is unavoidable. For more than 60 years, the IRS and its predecessors have constantly been called upon to interpret these and comparable provisions, and in doing so have referred consistently to principles of charitable trust law. . . .

Guided, of course, by the Code, the IRS has the responsibility, in the first instance, to determine whether a particular entity is "charitable" for purposes of Sec. 170 and Sec. 501(c)(3). This in turn may necessitate later determinations of whether given activities so violate public policy that the entities involved cannot be deemed to provide a public benefit worthy of "charitable" status. We emphasize, however, that these sensitive determinations should be made only where there is no doubt that the organization's activities violate fundamental public policy.

• • •

Petitioners contend that, even if the Commissioner's policy is valid as to non-religious private schools, that policy cannot constitutionally be applied to schools that engage in racial discrimination on the basis of sincerely held religious beliefs. As to such schools, it is argued that the IRS construction of Sec. 170 and Sec. 501(c)(3) violates their free exercise rights under the Religion Clauses of the First Amendment. This contention presents claims not heretofore considered by this Court in precisely this context.

. . . However, "[n]ot all burdens on religion are unconstitutional. . . . The state may justify a limitation on religious liberty by showing that it is essential to accomplish an overriding governmental interest." . . .

On occasion this Court has found certain governmental interests so compelling as to allow even regulations prohibiting religiously based conduct. In *Prince v. Massachusetts*, 321 U.S. 158 (1944), for example the Court held that neutrally cast child labor laws prohibiting sale of printed materials on public streets could be applied to prohibit children from dispensing religious literature. The Court found no constitutional infirmity in "excluding [Jehovah's Witness children] from doing there what no other children may do."*Id.* at 170. See also *Reynolds v. United States*, 98 U.S. 145 (1878); *United States v. Lee, supra; Gillete v. United States, supra*. Denial of tax benefits will inevitably have a substantial impact on the operation of private religious schools, but will not prevent those schools from observing their religious tenets.

The governmental interest at stake here is compelling. As discussed in Part II, *supra,* the Government has a fundamental, overriding interest in eradicating racial discrimination in education—discrimination that prevailed, with official approval, for the first 165 years of this Nation's history. That governmental interest substantially outweighs whatever burden denial of tax benefits places on petitioners' exercise of their religious beliefs. The interests asserted by petitioners cannot be accommodated with that compelling governmental interest, see *United States v. Lee, supra,* 455 U.S., at 250–260, and no "less restrictive means," see *Thomas v. Review Board, supra,* 450 U.S., at 718, are available to achieve the governmental interest.

• • •

The judgments of the Court of Appeals are, accordingly, *Affirmed.*

Justice Powell concurring in part and concurring in the judgment.

• • •

I

Federal taxes are not imposed on organizations "operated exclusively for religious, charitable, scientific, testing for public safety, literary, or educational purposes. . . ." 26 U.S.C. Sec. 501(c)(3). The Code also permits a tax deduction for contributions made to these organizations. Sec. 170(c). It is clear that petitioners, organizations incorporated for educational purposes, fall within the language of the statute. It also is clear that the language itself does not mandate refusal of tax-exempt status to any private school that maintains a racially discriminatory admissions policy. Accordingly there is force in Justice Rehnquist's argument that Secs. 170(c) and 501(c)(3) should be construed as setting forth the only criteria Congress has established for qualification as a tax-exempt organization. See *post,* at 1–4 (Rehnquist, J., dissenting). Indeed, were we writing prior to the history detailed in the Court's opinion, this could well be the construction I would adopt. But there has been a decade of acceptance that is persuasive in the circumstances of this case, and I conclude that there are now sufficient reasons for accepting the IRS's construction of the Code as proscribing tax exemptions for schools that discriminate on the basis of race as a matter of policy.

• • •

With all respect, I am unconvinced that the critical question in determining tax-exempt status is whether an individual organization provides a clear "public benefit" as defined by the Court. Over 106,000 organizations filed Sec. 501(c)(3) returns in 1981. Internal Revenue Service, 1982 Exempt Organization Business Master File. I find it impossible to believe that all or even most of those organizations could prove that they "demonstrably serve and [are] in harmony with the public interest" or that they are "beneficial and stabilizing influences in community life." Nor am I prepared to say that petitioners, because of their racially discriminatory policies, necessarily contribute nothing of benefit to the community. It is clear from the substantially secular character of the curricula and degrees offered that petitioners provide educational benefits.

Even more troubling to me is the element of conformity that appears to inform the Court's analysis. The Court asserts that an exempt organization must "demonstrably serve and be in harmony with the public interest," must have a purpose that comports with "the common community conscience," and must not act in a matter "affirmatively at odds with [the] declared position of the whole government." Taken together, these passages suggest that the primary function of a tax-exempt organization is to act on behalf of the Government in carrying out governmentally approved policies. In my opinion, such a view of Sec. 501(c)(3) ignores the important role played by tax exemptions in encouraging diverse, indeed often sharply conflicting, activities and viewpoints. As Justice Brennan has observed, private, non-profit groups receive tax exemptions because "each group contributes to the diversity of association, viewpoint, and enterprise essential to a vigorous, pluralistic society." *Walz, supra,* at 689 (Brennan J., concurring). Far from representing an effort to reinforce any perceived "common community conscience," the provision of tax exemptions to nonprofit groups is one indispensable means of limiting the influence of governmental orthodoxy on important areas of community life. Given the importance of our tradition of pluralism, "[t]he interest in preserving an area of untrammeled choice for private philanthropy is very great." *Jackson v. Statler Foundation,* 496 F. 2d 623, 639 (CA2 1974) (Friendly, J., dissenting from denial of reconsideration en banc).

• • •

I would emphasize however, that the balancing of these substantial interests is for *Congress* to perform. I am unwilling to join any suggestion that the Internal Revenue Service is invested with authority to decide which public policies are sufficiently "fundamental" to require denial of tax exemptions. Its business is to administer laws designed to produce revenue for the Government, not to promote "public policy." As former IRS Commissioner Kurtz has noted, questions concerning religion and civil rights "are far afield from the more typical tasks of tax administrators—determining taxable income." Kurtz, Difficult Definitional Problems in Tax Administration: Religion and Race, 23 Catholic Lawyer 301, 301 (1978). This Court often has expressed concern that the scope of an agency's authorization be limited to those areas in which the agency fairly may be said to have expertise, and this concern applies with special force when the asserted administrative power is one to determine the scope of public policy.

• • •

Justice Rehnquist, dissenting.

The Court points out that there is a strong national policy in this country against racial discrimination. To the extent that the Court states that Congress in furtherance of this policy could deny tax-exempt status to educational institutions that promote racial discrimination, I readily agree. But, unlike the Court, I am convinced that Congress simply has failed to take this action and, as this Court has said over and over again, regardless of our view on the propriety of Congress' failure to legislate we are not constitutionally empowered to act for them.

In approaching this statutory construction question the Court quite adeptly avoids the statute it is construing. This I am sure is no accident, for there is nothing in the language of Sec. 501(c)(3) that supports the result obtained by the Court. . . . With undeniable clarity, Congress has explicitly defined the requirements for Sec. 501(c)(3) status. An entity must be (1) a corporation, or community chest, fund, or foundation, (2) organized for one of the eight enumerated purposes, (3) operated on a nonprofit basis, and (4) free from involvement in lobbying activities and political campaigns. Nowhere is there to be found some additional, undefined public policy requirement.

The Court first seeks refuge from the obvious reading of Sec. 501(c)(3) by turning to Sec. 170 of the Internal Revenue Code which provides a tax deduction for contributions made to Sec. 501(c)(3) organizations. In setting forth the general rule, Sec. 170 states:

> There shall be allowed as a deduction any charitable contribution (as defined in subsection (c) payment of which is made within the taxable year. A charitable contribution shall be allowable as a deduction only if verified under regulations prescribed by the Secretary. 26 U.S.C. Sec. 170 (a)(1).

The Court seizes the words "charitable contribution" and with little discussion concludes that "[on] its face, therefore, Sec. 170 reveals that Congress' intention was to provide tax benefits to organizations serving charitable purposes," intimating that this implies some unspecified common law charitable trust requirement *Ante,* at 2026.

. . . Plainly, Sec. 170(c) simply tracks the requirements set forth in Sec. 501(c)(3). Since Sec. 170 is no more than a mirror of Sec. 501(c)(3) and, as the Court points out, Sec. 170 followed Sec. 501(c)(3) by more than two decades, *ante,* at 11. n. 10, it is at best of little usefulness in finding the meaning of Sec. 501(c)(3).

Making a more fruitful inquiry, the Court next turns to the legislative history of Sec. 501(c)(3) and finds that Congress intended in that statute to offer a tax benefit to organizations that Congress believed were providing a public benefit. I certainly agree. But then the Court leaps to the conclusion that this history is proof Congress intended that an organization seeking Sec. 501(c)(3) status "must fall within a category specified in that section, *and must demonstrably serve and be in harmony with the public interest." Ante,* at 17 (emphasis added). To the contrary, I think that the legislative history of Sec. 501(c)(3) unmistakably makes clear that *Congress has decided* what organizations are serving a public purpose and providing a public benefit within the meaning of Sec. 501(c)(3) and has clearly set forth in Sec. 501(c)(3) the characteristics of such organizations. In fact, there are few examples which better illustrate Congress' effort to define and redefine the requirements of a legislative act.

• • •

One way to read the opinion handed down by the Court today leads to the conclusion that this long and arduous refining process of Sec. 501(c)(3) was certainly a waste of time, for when enacting the original 1894 statute Congress intended to adopt a common law term of art, and intended that this term of art carry with it all of the common law baggage which defines it. Such a view, however, leads also to the unsupportable idea that Congress has spent almost a century adding illustrations simply to clarify an already defined common law term.

Another way to read the Court's opinion leads to the conclusion that even though Congress has set forth *some* of the requirements of a Sec. 501(c)(3) organization, it intended that the IRS additionally require that organization meet a higher standard of public interest, not stated by Congress, but to be determined and defined by the IRS and the courts. This view I find equally unsupportable. Almost a century of statutory history proves that Congress itself intended to decide what Sec. 501(c)(3) requires. Congress has expressed its decision in the plainest of terms in Sec. 501(c)(3) by providing that tax-exempt status is to be given to any corporation, or community chest, fund, or foundation that is organized for one of the eight enumerated purposes, operated on a nonprofit basis, and uninvolved in lobbying activities or political campaigns. The IRS certainly is empowered to adopt regulations for the enforcement of these specified requirements, and the courts have authority to resolve challenges to the IRS's exercise of this power, but Congress has left it to neither the IRS nor the courts to select or add to the requirements of Sec. 501(c)(3).

The Court suggests that unless its new requirement be added to Sec. 501(c)(3), nonprofit organizations acquire tax exempt status. . . . Since the Court does not challenge the characterization of *petitioners* as "educational" institutions within the meaning of Sec. 501(c)(3), and in fact states several times in the course of its opinion that petitioners *are* educational institutions, . . . it is difficult to see how this argument advances the Court's reasoning for disposing of petitioners' cases.

But simply because I reject the Court's heavy-handed creation of the requirement that an organization seeking Sec. 501(c)(3) status must "serve and be in harmony with the public interest," *ante,* at 17, does not mean that I would deny to the IRS the usual authority to adopt regulations further explaining what Congress meant by the term "educational." The IRS has fully exercised that authority in 26 CFR Sec. 1.501(c)(3)–1(d)(3). . . . I have little doubt that neither the "Fagin School for Pickpockets" nor a school training students for guerrilla warfare and terrorism in other countries would meet the definitions contained in the regulations.

Prior to 1970, when the charted course was abruptly changed, the IRS had continuously interpreted Sec. 501(c)(3) and its predecessors in accordance with the view I have expressed above. This, of course, is of considerable significance in determining the intended meaning of the statute. *NLRB v. Boeing Co.,* 412 U.S. 67,

75 (1973); *Power Reactor Development Co. v. Electricians,* 367 U.S. 396, 408 (1961).

• • •

The Court next asserts that "Congress affirmatively manifested its acquiescence in the IRS policy when it enacted the present Sec. 501(i) of the Code," a provision that "denies tax exempt status to social clubs whose charters or policy statements provide for" racial discrimination. *Ante,* at 26. Quite to the contrary, it seems to me that in Sec. 501(i) Congress showed that when it wants to add a requirement prohibiting racial discrimination to one of the tax-benefit provisions, it is fully aware of how to do it. Cf. *Commissioner v. Tellier,* 383 U.S. 687, 693 N. 10 (1966).

• • •

I have no disagreement with the Court's finding that there is a strong national policy in this country opposed to racial discrimination. I agree with the Court that Congress has the power to futher this policy by denying Sec. 501(c)(3) status to organizations that practice racial discrimination. But as of yet Congress has failed to do so. Whatever the reasons for the failure, this Court should not legislate for Congress.

Petitioners are each organized for the "instruction or training of the individual for the purpose of improving or developing his capabilities," 26 CFR Sec. 1.501(c)(3)–1(d)(3), and thus are organized for "educational purposes" within the meaning of Sec. 501(c)(3). Petitioners' nonprofit status is uncontested. There is no indication that either petitioner has been involved in lobbying activities or political campaigns. Therefore, it is my view that unless and until Congress affirmatively amends Sec. 501(c)(3) to require more, the IRS is without authority to deny petitioners Sec. 501(c)(3) status. For this reason, I would reverse the Court of Appeals.

NOTES

1. Is it appropriate for the courts and the Internal Revenue Service to use income tax laws, as in the *Bob Jones University* case, to achieve public policy goals in non-tax activities (e.g., racial integration)?

2. When the Internal Revenue Code exemption for charitable and educational organizations was first enacted, the belief was pervasive that "separate but equal" schools were permissible. (See, for example, the United States Supreme Court's decision in *Plessy v. Ferguson,* 163 U.S. 537 (1896)). Note that the majority in the *Bob Jones* case, in denying that the Code should be interpreted today to continue the exemption for segregationist educational institutions and in stressing the need for "continuing interpretation of those statutes," rejects a historicist approach of deferring to and perpetrating views that were authoritative in the past (See Chapter 6, supra). What is the source of the majority's decision? McDougal, Lasswell and Miller, *Interpretation of Agreements and World Public Order* (1967), contend that a constitution is an ongoing communication which should be interpreted in accordance with the shared contemporary expectations of communicators and communicatees, and that heavy emphasis should, accordingly, be placed upon *current* views of the community. Does the Court by its holding adopt that view? Discuss.

3. Would it be more appropriate, or more "legal" to act directly in the legislative mode to prohibit undesirable activities? In the *Bob Jones* case, direct action against Bob Jones University could not avail because of conflicting views leading to a deadlock in Congress; should that situation have been taken as a national consensus that no action should be taken? If direct governmental action might violate the "establishment of religion" clause in the Constitution, should courts act instead? If the activities of Bob Jones University might be

constitutionally protected "private action" rather than "state action" amenable to governmental prohibition, should courts act?

4. Congress had not acted to amend specifically the Internal Revenue Code so as to deny exemptions to segregationist institutions like Bob Jones University. Should bureaucratic agencies establish and clarify policy where the legislature has not acted? Does it matter that such officials are not chosen by the public directly, are not answerable to it and may not reflect prevailing public opinion? Do the same considerations apply to courts? Discuss.

In the *Javins* case, a distinguished judge relied entirely on preferred policy to overrule a settled body of law and to install in its place innovative institutional arrangements.

JAVINS V. FIRST NATIONAL REALTY CORPORATION
428 F. 2d 1071 (D.C. Cir. 1970)

[Wright, J.] . . . The facts revealed by the record are simple. By separate written leases, each of the appellants rented an apartment in a three-building apartment complex in Northwest Washington known as Clifton Terrace. The landlord, First National Realty Corporation, filed separate actions in the Landlord and Tenant Branch of the Court of General Sessions on April 8, 1966, seeking possessison on the ground that each of the appellants had defaulted in the payment of rent due for the month of April. The tenants, appellants here, admitted that they had not paid the landlord any rent for April. However, they alleged numerous violations of the Housing Regulations as "an equitable defense of [a] claim by way of recoupement or set-off in an amount equal to the rent claim," as provided in the rules of the Court of General Sessions. They offered to prove

> [t]hat there are approximately 1500 violations of the Housing Regulations of the District of Columbia in the building of Clifton Terrace, where Defendant resides, some affecting the premises of this Defendant directly, others indirectly, and all tending to establish a course of conduct of violation of the Housing Regulations to the damage of Defendants.

• • •

Since, in traditional analysis, a lease was the conveyance of an interest in land, courts have usually utilized the special rules governing real property transactions to resolve controversies involving leases. However, as the Supreme Court has noted in another context, "the body of private property law . . . , more than almost any other branch of law, has been shaped by distinctions whose validity is largely historical. Courts have a duty to reappraise old doctrines in the light of the facts and values of contemporary life—particularly old common law doctrines which the courts themselves created and developed. As we have said before, "[T]he continued vitality of the common law . . . depends upon its ability to reflect contemporary community values and ethics."

The assumption of landlord-tenant law, derived from feudal property law, that a lease primarily conveyed to the tenant an interest in land may have been reasonable in a rural, agrarian society; it may continue to be reasonable in some leases involving farming or commercial land. In these cases, the value of the lease to the tenant is the land itself. But in the case of the modern apartment dweller, the values of the lease is that it gives him a place to live. The city dweller who seeks to lease an apartment on the third floor of a tenement has little interest in the land 30 or 40 feet below, or even in the bare right to possession within the four walls of his apartment. When American city dwellers, both rich and poor, seek "shelter" today, they seek a well-known package of goods and services—a package which includes not merely walls and ceilings, but also adequate heat, light and ventilation, serviceable plumbing facilities, secure windows and doors, proper sanitation, and proper maintenance.

• • •

. . . Ironically, however, the rules governing the construction and interpretation of "predominantly contractual" obligation in leases have too often remained rooted in old property law.

Some courts have realized that certain of the old rules of property law governing leases are inappropriate for today's transactions. In order to reach results more in accord with the legitimate expectations of the parties and the standards of the community, courts have been gradually introducing more modern precepts of contract law in interpreting leases. Proceeding piecemeal has, however, led to confusion where "decisions are frequently conflicting, not because of a healthy disagreement on social policy, but because of the lingering impact of rules whose policies are long since dead."

In our judgment, the trend toward treating leases as contracts is wise and well considered. Our holding in this case reflects a belief that leases of urban dwelling units should be interpreted and construed like any other contract.

III

Modern contract law has recognized that the buyer of goods and services in an industrialized society must rely upon the skill and honesty of the supplier to assure that goods and services purchased are of adequate quality. In interpreting most contracts, courts have sought to protect the legitimate expectations of the buyer and have steadily widened the seller's responsibility for the quality of goods and services through implied warranties of fitness and merchantability.

• • •

IV

A. In our judgment the common law itself must recognize the landlord's obligation to keep his premises in a habitable condition. This conclusion is compelled by three separate considerations. First, we believe that the old rule was based on certain factual assumptions which are no longer true; on its own terms, it can no longer be justified. Second, we believe that the consumer protection cases discussed above require that the old rule be abandoned in order to bring residential landlord—tenant law into harmony with the principles on which those cases rest. Third, we think that the nature of today's urban housing market also dictates abandonment of the old rule.

The common law rule absolving the lessor of all obligations to repair originated in the early Middle Ages. Such a rule was perhaps well suited to an agrarian economy; the land was more important than whatever small living structure was fully capable of making repairs himself. These historical facts were the basis on which the common law constructed its rules; they also provided the necessary prerequisites for its application.

• • •

It is overdue for courts to admit that these assumptions are no longer true with regard to all urban housing. Today's urban tenants, the vast majority of whom live in multiple dwelling houses, are interested, not in the land, but solely in "a house suitable for occupation." Furthermore, today's city dweller usually has a single, specialized skill unrelated to maintenance work; he is unable to make repairs like the "jack-of-all-trades" farmer who was the common law's model of the lessee. Further, unlike his agrarian predecessor who often remained on one piece of land for his entire life, urban tenants today are more mobile than ever before. A tenant's tenure in a specific apartment will often not be sufficient to justify efforts at repairs. In addition, the increasing complexity of today's dwellings renders them much more difficult to repair than the structures of earlier times. In a multiple dwelling repair may require access to equipment and areas in the control of the landlord. Low and middle income tenants, even if they were interested in making repairs, would be unable to obtain any financing for major repairs since they have no long-term interest in the property.

Our approach to the common law of landlord and tenant ought to be aided by principles derived from the consumer protection cases referred to above. In a lease contract, a tenant seeks to purchase from his landlord shelter for a specified period of time. The landlord sells housing as a commercial businessman and has much greater opportunity, incentive and capacity to inspect and maintain the condition of his building. Moreover, the tenant must rely upon the skill and bona fides of his landlord at least as much as a car buyer must rely upon the car manufacturer. In dealing with major problems, such as heating, plumbing, electrical or structural defects, the tenant's position corresponds precisely with "the ordinary consumer who cannot be expected to have the knowledge or capacity or even the opportunity to make adequate inspection of mechanical instrumentalities, like automobiles, and to decide for himself whether they are reasonably fit for the designed purpose." Henningsen v. Bloomfield Motors, Inc., 32 N.J. 358, 375, 161 A.2d 69, 78 (1960).

Since a lease contract specifies a particular period of time during which the tenant has a right to use his apartment for shelter, he may legitimately expect that the apartment will be fit for habitation for the time period for which it is rented. . . .

Even beyond the rationale of traditional products liability law, the relationship of landlord and tenant suggests further compelling reasons for the law's protection of the tenants' legitimate expectations of quality. The inequality in bargaining power between landlord and tenant has been well documented. Tenants have very little leverage to enforce demands for better housing. Various impediments to competition in the rental housing market, such as racial and class discrimination and standardized form leases, mean that landlords place tenants in a take it or leave it situation. The increasingly severe shortage of adequate housing further increases the landlord's bargaining power and escalates the need for maintaining and improving the existing stock. Finally, the findings by various studies of the social impact of bad housing has led to the realization that poor housing is detrimental to the whole society, not merely to the unlucky ones who must suffer the daily indignity of living in a slum.

Thus we are led by our inspection of the relevant legal principles and precedents to the conclusion that the old common law rule imposing an obligation upon the lessee to repair during the lease term was really never intended to apply to residential urban leaseholds. Contract principles established in other areas of the law provide a more rational framework for the apportionment of landlord-tenant responsibilities; they strongly suggest that a warranty of habitability be implied into all contracts for urban dwellings.

B. We believe, in any event, that the District's housing code requires that a warranty of habitability be implied in the leases of all housing that it covers.

Is the use of legal doctrine by the courts adequate to decide such cases? Some courts have adopted with approval the view expressed by one commentator that, "The courts recognize that they cannot, through the enunciation of doctrines which decide cases, adequately stake out the limits of fair treatment; that if the quest for fairness is left to a series of occasional encounters between courts and public administrators it can but partially be fulfilled; and that the political branches, accordingly, labor under their own obligations to avoid unfairness regardless of what the courts may require." Michelman, Property, Utility, and Fairness: Comments on the Ethical Foundations of "Just Compensation" Law, 80 *Harv. L. Rev.* 1165, 1252 (1967), cited with approval by the court in *Community Redevelopment Agency vs. Abrams,* 15 Cal. 3d. 813, 543 P.2d. 905, 126 Cal. Rptr. 473 (1975).

But an effective policy approach cannot be so spontaneous and intuitive. In a case such as *Javins,* the failure to consider in a systematic and comprehensive fashion the aggregate consequences of the different options led the court to choose a course of action which may have discouraged investment in housing and thus frustrated the court's goal. An efficient policy approach requires a more systematic and comprehensive method.

McDOUGAL & LASSWELL, LEGAL EDUCATION AND PUBLIC POLICY, 52 YALE L.J. 203, 212–213 (1943)

. . . Effective policy-making (planning and implementation) depends on clear conception of goal, accurate calculation of probabilities, and adept application of knowledge of ways and means. We submit that adequate training must therefore include experiences that aid the developing lawyers to acquire certain skills of thought: goal-thinking, trend-thinking, and scientific-thinking. The student needs to clarify his moral values (preferred events, social goals); he needs to orient himself in past trends and future probabilities; finally, he needs to acquire the scientific knowledge and skills necessary to implement objectives within the context of contemporary trends.

Goal-thinking requires the clarification of values. In a democratic society it should not, of course, be an aim of legal education to *impose* a single standard of morals upon every student. But a legitimate aim of education is to seek to promote the major values of a democratic society and to reduce the number of moral mavericks who do not share democratic preferences. The student may be allowed to reject the morals of democracy and embrace those of despotism; but his education should be such that, if he does so, he does it by deliberate choice, with awareness of the consequences for himself and others, and not by sluggish self-deception.

How can incipient lawyers be trained in the clarification of values? Whatever the difficulties of communication, any statement of values must begin with words of high-level abstraction, of ambiguous reference. No brief definition can convey to anyone else much of what the definer means. Too many persons jump to conclusions about the meaning of terms, regardless of the rules of intepretation intended by the speaker. At the risk of misconstruction, we offer our brief statement of democratic morals. The supreme value of democracy is the dignity and worth of the individual; hence a democratic society is a commonwealth of mutual deference—a commonwealth where there is full opportunity to mature talent into socially creative skill, free from discrimination on grounds of religion, culture, or class. It is a society in which such specific values as power, respect, and knowledge are widely shared and are not concentrated in the hands of a single group, class, or institution—the state—among the many institutions of society. This formula is not new. On the contrary, it states the implicit or explicit assumptions of most of the traditional moralists of democracy. But such a statement of democratic values—and this is the point of our present emphasis—cannot be understood, or implemented, unless it is amplified by rules of interpretation, of varying degrees of generality, that show how observers of specific situations can validly use the terms in describing concrete reality and promoting the occurrence of relatively specific events in harmony with the definition. This task of spelling out values in terms of consistent propositions of varying degrees of generality or of relating general propositions to operational principles is a long and arduous process. But it is indispensable to clarity and, hence, to the education of policy-makers.

Clarification of values, by relating general propositions to operational principles in representative and specific contexts, must for effective training be distinguished from the traditional, logical, *derivation* of values by philosophers. Such derivation—that is, exercises by which specialists on ethical philosophy and metaphysics take sentences that define moral standards and deduce from them more inclusive propositions or vice versa—is a notorious blind alley. Divorced from operational rules, it quickly becomes a futile quest for a meaningless *why*, perpetually culminating in "some inevitably circular and infinitely regressive logical justification" for ambiguous preferences. From any relatively specific statements of social goal (necessarily described in a statement of low-level abstraction) can be elaborated an infinite series of normative propositions of ever-increasing generality; conversely, normative statements of high-level abstraction can be manipulated to support any specific social goal. Prospective lawyers should be exposed, by way of warning and sophistication, to the work of representative specialists in derivation; relatively little time should be required, however, to teach them how to handle, and how to achieve emotional freedom from, the ancient exercises.

NOTES

1. Professors Lasswell and McDougal have developed detailed procedures which, they contend, will help decisionmakers to act in an effective and efficient manner. Some are set out in other parts of this Chapter and in the Appendix to Chapter 1. Consider, for example, the usefulness for the lawyer of their value categories. Do you think that merely making explicit that the activities and aspirations of humans encompass varied value sectors such as power, wealth, enlightenment, skill, well-being, affection, respect and rectitude can be of aid to the lawyer or any other participant in decisionmaking? Why? Would it help broaden the focus of decisionmakers and lessen the likelihood of overlooking important factors in making social choices? Are there costs to this type of analysis?

2. Consider whether the court in the *Javins* case, supra, would have been inclined to consider the wider possible ramifications of its decision in that case and whether it might have decided the case differently had it tried to consider explicitly the possible effects of its decision on each of the value categories developed by Professors Lasswell and McDougal?

THE CENTRALITY OF PROBLEM AND GOAL

All approaches to jurisprudence which place the issue of policy center-stage must begin with a method for formulating problems. From a policy standpoint, a problem is an anticipated discrepancy between a preference and a projected flow of decisions. This formulation of a problem, presupposing both a clarification of goals and a method of extrapolating or making certain assumptions about future decisions, creates the tension between preference and prediction that motivates the policy scientist and decisionmaker to try to intervene in social process in ways likely to increase approximation to goals in the future. This conception of problem generates the policy-science method.

The policy-oriented approach may be compared to the much more intuitionistic problem formulations in the other jurisprudential schools we have considered. In many, a problem is anything (or everything) the writer does not understand. The implicit syllogism is on the order of: I do not understand X; therefore it is important; therefore it is a problem. In others, a problem is how certain people use a term. Recall, for example, H.L.A. Hart for whom a question on the order of "What do people mean when they say 'law'," becomes the key problem. While these formulations may be useful as a way of stimulating research, it is clear that they can have only accidental relevance to the policy process of the community. They will not acquire such relevance until a statement of preference is established, projections about the probable failure to achieve that preference in the future are made and an effort is mounted to invent alternative solutions.

Central to this notion of problem is the recognition that law involves making key choices that, over time, will influence patterns of production and distribution of all values in a community, with radiating effects on each of its members. One of the first to introduce this consideration explicitly into jurisprudence in a non-natural law format was Jeremy Bentham whom we encountered earlier in our discussion of the rise of Positivism in England. Bentham insisted that law be conceived of as a process of decision designed to realize certain social ends. His efforts to develop a scientific method for determining what those ends or goals should be were systematic and explicit. He rejected the analogical approach of Blackstone which found "new" propositions in law by drawing analogies and, instead, resorted to a teleological approach, according to which one determines what the law should be (and by implication, what it will be) by reference to what social purposes are at stake; trying to secure the greatest possible happiness for the greatest number of people. But rather than expressing his (or his class', group's, religion's) social purposes as choices, could Bentham either consciously or unconsciously have been caching his preferences behind what he called the Principle of Utility?

The Utility Principle, itself, incorporates a natural law notion of a "natural" right of all individuals to equality; one man's happiness is equal to another's (whether nobleman or peasant, saint or sinner, good or wicked, wise or feeble-minded, a person with long life-expectancy or one with almost none at all). The implementation of the principle depends on one being able to quantify pleasure and pain and measure them in units, and to determine the quality of pleasure or pain in each unit in order to decide if any proposed decision should be made or course of action taken. Consequences, in terms of aggregate pleasures and pains to all the persons who would be affected, could then be measured with accuracy. A moment's reflection should indicate that the opportunities for infiltrating subjective preferences into this formula are great indeed. For one thing, what is meant by happiness will determine the outcome of the application of the formula.

Consider in this regard a selection from Bentham.

BENTHAM, AN INTRODUCTION TO THE PRINCIPLES
OF MORALS AND LEGISLATION 33–41, 44–48, 50, 59, 64–66, 68–77
(LONDON, 1780)

CHAPTER 1

OF THE PRINCIPLE OF UTILITY

I. Nature has placed mankind under the governance of two sovereign masters, *pain* and *pleasure*. It is for them alone to point out what we ought to do, as well as to determine what we shall do. On the one hand the standard of right and wrong, on the other the chain of causes and effects, are fastened to their throne. They govern us in all we do, in all we say, in all we think: every effort we can make to throw off our subjection, will serve but to demonstrate and confirm it. In words a man may pretend to abjure their empire: but in reality he will remain subject to it all the while. The *principle of utility* recognises this subjection, and assumes it for the foundation of that system, the object of which is to rear the fabric of felicity by the hands of reason and of law. Systems which attempt to question it, deal in sounds instead of sense, in caprice instead of reason, in darkness instead of light.

But enough of metaphor and declamation: it is not by such means that moral science is to be improved.

II. The principle of utility is the foundation of the present work: it will be proper therefore at the outset to give an explicit and determinate account of what is meant by it. By the principle of utility is meant that principle which approves or disapproves of every action whatsoever, according to the tendency which it appears to have to augment or diminish the happiness of the party whose interest is in question; or, what is the same thing in other words, to promote or to oppose that happiness. I say of every action whatsoever; and therefore not only of every action of a private individual, but of every measure of government.

III. By utility is meant that property in any object, whereby it tends to produce benefit, advantage, pleasure, good, or happiness (all this in the present case comes to the same thing), or (what comes again to the same thing) to prevent the happening of mischief, pain, evil, or unhappiness to the party whose interest is considered: if that party be the community in general, then the happiness of the community: if a particular individual, then the happiness of that individual.

IV. The interest of the community is one of the most general expressions that can occur in the phraseology of morals: no wonder that the meaning of it is often lost. When it has a meaning, it is this. The community is a fictitious *body,* composed of the individual persons who are considered as constituting as it were its *members.* The interest of the community then is, what?—the sum of the interests of the several members who compose it.

V. It is in vain to talk of the interest of the community without understanding what is the interest of the individual.* A thing is said to promote the interest, or to

*Interest. Interest is one of those words, which not having any superior genus, cannot in the ordinary be defined.

be *for* the interest, of an individual, when it tends to add to the sum total of his pleasures; or, what comes to the same thing, to diminish the sum total of his pains.

VI. An action then may be said to be conformable to the principle of utility, or, for shortness sake, to utility (meaning with respect to the community at large), when the tendency it has to augment the happiness of the community is greater than any it has to diminish it.

VII. A measure of government (which is but a particular kind of action, performed by a particular person or persons) may be said to be conformable to or dictated by the principle of utility, when in like manner the tendency which it has to augment the happiness of the community is greater than any which it has to diminish it.

VIII. When an action, or in particular a measure of government, is supposed by a man to be conformable to the principle of utility, it may be convenient, for the purposes of discourse, to imagine a kind of law or dictate, called a law or dictate of utility: and to speak of the action in question, as being comformable to such law or dictate.

IX. A man may be said to be a partisan of the principle of utility when the approbation or disapprobation he annexes to any action, or to any measure, is determined, by and proportioned to the tendency, which he conceives it to have to augment or to diminish the happiness of the community: or in other words, to its conformity or unconformity to the laws or dictates of utility.

• • •

XI. Has the rectitude of this principle been ever formally contested? It should seem that it had, by those who have not known what they have been meaning. Is it susceptible of any direct proof? It should seem not: for that which is used to prove everything else, cannot itself be proved: a chain of proofs must have their commencement somewhere. To give such proof is as impossible as it is needless.

• • •

XIV. To disprove the propriety of it by arguments is impossible; but, from the causes that have been mentioned, or from some confused or partial view of it, a man may happen to be disposed not to relish it. Where this is the case, if he thinks the settling of his opinions on such a subject worth the trouble, let him take the following steps, and at length, perhaps, he may come to reconcile himself to it.

1. Let him settle with himself, whether he would wish to discard this principle altogether: if so, let him consider what it is that all his reasonings (in matters of politics especially) can amount to?

2. If he would, let him settle with himself, whether he would judge and act without any principle, or whether there is any other he would judge and act by?

3. If there be, let him examine and satisfy himself whether the principle he thinks he has found is really any separate intelligible principle: or whether it be not a mere principle in words, a kind of phrase, which at bottom expresses neither more nor less than the mere averment of his own unfounded sentiments: that is, what in another person he might be apt to call practice?

4. If he is inclined to think that his own approbation or disapprobation, annexed to the idea of act, without any regard to its consequences, is a sufficient foundation for him to judge and act upon, let him ask himself whether his sentiment is to be a standard of right and wrong, with respect to every other man, or whether every man's sentiment has the same privilege of being a standard in itself?

5. In the first case, let him ask whether his principle is not despotical, and hostile to all the rest of [the] human race?

6. In the second case, whether it is not anarchical, and whether at this rate there are not as many different standards of right and wrong as there are men? and whether even in the same man, the same thing, which is right to-day, may not (without the least change in its nature) be wrong to-morrow? and whether the same thing is not right and wrong in the same place at the same time? and in either case, whether all argument is not at an end? and whether, when two men have said, ''I like this,'' and ''I don't like it,'' they can (upon such a principle) have any thing more to say?

• • •

CHAPTER II

OF PRINCIPLES ADVERSE TO THAT OF UTILITY

• • •

II. A principle may be different from that of utility in two ways: 1. By being constantly opposed to it: this is the case with a principle which may be termed the principle of *ascetism*. 2. By being sometimes opposed to it, and sometimes not, as it may happen: this is the case with another, which may be termed the principle of *sympathy* and *antipathy*.

III. By the principle of asceticism I mean that principle, which, like the principle of utility, approves or disapproves of any action, according to the tendency which it appears to have to augment or diminish the happiness of the party whose interest is in question; but in an inversive manner: approving of actions in as far as they tend to diminish his happiness: disapproving of them in as far as they tend to augment it.

• • •

IX. The principle of asceticism seems originally to have been the reverie of certain hasty speculators, who having perceived, or fancied, that certain pleasures, when reaped in certain circumstances, have, at the long run, been attended with pains more than equivalent to them, took occasion to quarrel with every thing that offered itself under the name of pleasure. Having then got thus far, and having forgot the point which they set out from, they pushed on, and went so much further as to think it meritorious to fall in love with pain. Even this, we see, is at bottom but the principle of utility misapplied.

• • •

XI. Among principles adverse to that of utility, that which at this day seems to have most influence in matters of government, is what may be called the principle of sympathy and antipathy. . . . By the principle of sympathy and antipathy, I mean that principle which approves or disapproves of certain actions, not on account of their tending to augment the happiness, not yet on account of their tending to diminish the happiness of the party whose interest is in question, but merely because a man finds himself disposed to approve or disapprove of them: holding up that approbation or disapprobation as a sufficient reason for itself, and disclaiming the necessity of looking out for any extrinsic ground. Thus far in the general department of morals; and in the particular department of politics, measuring out the quantum (as well as determining the ground) of punishment, by the degree of the disapprobation.

• • •

XIV. The various systems that have been formed concerning the standard of right and wrong, may all be reduced to the principle of sympathy and antipathy. One account may serve for all of them. They consist all of them in so many contrivances for avoiding the obligation of appealing to any external standard, and for prevailing upon the reader to accept of [sic] the author's sentiment or opinion as a reason, and that a sufficient one, for itself. The phrases different, but the principle the same.

CHAPTER III

OF THE FOUR SANCTIONS OR SOURCES OF PAIN AND PLEASURE

I. It has been shown that the happiness of the individuals, of whom a community is composed, that is, their pleasures and their security, is the end and the sole end which the legislator ought to have in view: the sole standard, in conformity to which each individual ought, as far as depends upon the legislator, to be *made* to fashion his behaviour. But whether it be this or any thing else that is to be *done,* there is nothing by which a man can ultimately be *made* to do it, but either pain or pleasure. Having taken a general view of these two grand objects (viz. pleasure, and what comes to the same thing, immunity from pain) in the character of *final* causes; it will be necessary to take a view of pleasure and pain itself, in the character of *efficient* causes or means.

II. There are four distinguishable sources from which pleasure and pain are in use to flow: considered separately, they may be termed the *physical,* the *political,* the *moral,* and the *religious:* and inasmuch as the pleasures and pains belonging to each of them are capable of giving a binding force to any law or rule of conduct, they may all of them be termed *sanctions.*

• • •

CHAPTER IV

VALUE OF A LOT OF PLEASURE OR PAIN, HOW TO BE MEASURED

I. Pleasures then, and the avoidance of pains are the *ends* which the legislator has in view: it behoves him therefore to understand their *value.* Pleasures and pains are the *instruments* he has to work with: it behoves him therefore to understand their force, which is again, in another point of view, their value.

II. To a person considered *by himself,* the value of a pleasure or pain considered *by itself,* will be greater or less, according to the four following circumstances:

1. Its *intensity.*
2. Its *duration.*
3. Its *certainty* or *uncertainty.*
4. Its *propinquity* or *remoteness.*

III. These are the circumstances which are to be considered in estimating a pleasure or a pain considered each of them by itself. But when the value of any pleasure or pain is considered for the purpose of estimating the tendency of any *act* by which it is produced, there are two other circumstances to be taken into the account; these are,

5. Its *fecundity,* or the chance it has of being followed by sensations of the *same* kind: that is, pleasures, if it be a pleasure: pains, if it be a pain.

6. Its *purity,* or the chance it has of not being followed by sensations of the *opposite* kind: that is, pains, if it be a pleasure: pleasures, if it be a pain.

These two last, however, are in strictness scarcely to be deemed properties of the pleasure of the pain itself; they are not, therefore, in strictness to be taken into the account of the value of that pleasure or that pain. They are in strictness to be deemed properties only of the act, or other event, by which such pleasure or pain has been produced; and accordingly are only to be taken into the account of the tendency of such act or such event.

IV. To a *number* of persons, with reference to each of whom the value of a pleasure or a pain is considered, it will be greater or less, according to seven circumstances: to wit, the six preceding ones: *viz.*

1. Its *intensity*.
2. Its *duration*.
3. Its *certainty* or *uncertainty*.
4. Its *propinquity* or *remoteness*.
5. Its *fecundity*.
6. Its *purity*.

And one other, to wit:

7. Its *extent; that is, the number of persons to whom it extends;* or (in other words), who are affected by it.

V. To take an exact account, then, of the general tendency of any act, by which the interests of a community are affected, proceed as follows. Begin with any one person of those whose interests seem most immediately to be affected by it: and take an account,

1. Of the value of each distinguishable *pleasure* which appears to be produced by it in the *first* instance.

2. Of the value of each *pain* which appears to be produced by it in the *first* instance.

3. Of the value of each pleasure which appears to be produced by it *after* the first. This constitutes the *fecundity* of the first *pleasure* and the *impurity* of the first *pain*.

4. Of the value of each *pain* which appears to be produced by it after the first. This constitutes the *fecundity* of the first *pain,* and *impurity* of the first pleasure.

5. Sum up all the values of all the *pleasures* on the one side, and those of all the pains on the other. The balance, if it be on the side of pleasure, will give the *good* tendency of the act upon the whole, with respect to the interests of that *individual* person; if on the side of pain, the *bad* tendency of it upon the whole.

6. Take on account of the *number* of persons whose interests appear to be concerned; and repeat the above process with respect to each. *Sum up* the numbers expressive of the degrees of *good* tendency, which the act has, with respect to each individual, in regard to whom the tendency of it is *good* upon the whole; do this again with respect to each individual, in regard to whom the tendency of it is *bad* upon the whole. Take the *balance;* which, if on the side of *pleasure,* will give the general *good tendency* of the act, with respect to the total number of community of individuals concerned; if on the side of pain, the general *evil tendency,* with respect to·the same community.

• • •

CHAPTER V

PLEASURES AND PAINS, THEIR KINDS

I. Having represented what belongs to all sorts of pleasures and pains alike, we come now to exhibit, each of itself, the several sorts of pains and pleasures. Pains and pleasures may be called by one general word, interesting perceptions. Interesting perceptions are either simple or complex. The simple ones are those which cannot any one of them be resolved into more: complex are those which are resolvable into divers simple ones. A complex interesting perception may accordingly be composed either: 1. Of pleasures alone: 2. Of pains alone: or, 3. Of a pleasure or pleasures, and a pain or pains together. What determines a lot of pleasures, for example, to be regarded as one complex pleasure, rather than as divers simple ones, is the nature of the exciting cause. Whatever pleasures are excited all at once by the action of the same cause, are apt to be looked upon as constituting all together but one pleasure.

II. The several simple pleasures of which human nature is susceptible, seem to be as follows: 1. The pleasures of sense. 2. The pleasures of wealth. 3. The pleasures of skill. 4. The pleasure of amity. 5. The pleasures of a good name. 6. The pleasures of power. 7. The pleasures of piety. 8. The pleasures of benevolence. 9. The pleasures of malevolence. 10. The pleasures of imagination. 11. The pleasures of memory. 12. The pleasures of expectation. 13. The pleasures dependent on association. 14. The pleasures of relief.

III. The several simple pains seem to be as follows: 1. The pains of privation. 2. The pains of the senses. 3. The pains of awkwardness. 4. The pains of enmity. 5. The pains of an ill name. 6. The pains of piety. 7. The pains of benevolence. 8. The pains of malevolence. 9. The pains of the memory. 10. The pains of the imagination. 11. The pains of expectation. 12. The pains dependent on association. . . .

IV. 1. The pleasures of sense seem to be as follows: 1. The pleasures of the taste or palate; including whatever pleasures are experienced in satisfying the appetites of hunger and thirst. 2. The pleasure of intoxication. 3. The pleaures of the organ of smelling. 4. The pleasures of the touch. 5. The simple pleasures of the ear; independent of association. 6. The simple pleasures of the eyes; independent of association. 7. The pleasure of the sexual sense. 8. The pleasure of health; or, the internal pleasureable feeling or flow of spirits (as it is called), which accompanies a state of full health and vigour; especially at times of moderate bodily exertion. 9. The pleasures of novelty: or, the pleasures derived from the gratification of the appetite of curiosity, by the application of new objects to any of the senses.

V. 2. By the pleasures of wealth may be meant those pleasures which a man is apt to derive from the consciousness of possessing any article or articles which stand in the list of instruments of enjoyment or security, and more particularly at the time of his first acquiring them; at which time the pleasure may be styled a pleasure of gain or a pleaure of acquisition; at other times a pleasure of possession.

3. The pleasures of skill, as exercised upon particular objects, are those which accompany the application of such particular instruments of enjoyment to their uses, as cannot be so applied without a greater or lesser share of difficulty or exertion.

VI. 4. The pleasures of amity, or self-recommendation, are the pleasures that may accompany the persuasion of a man's being in the acquisition or the possession of the good-will of such or such assignable person or persons in particular: or, as the phrase is, of being upon good terms with him or them: and as a fruit of it, of his being in a way to have the benefit of their spontaneous and gratuitous services.

VII. 5. The pleasures of a good name are the pleasures that accompany the persuasion of a man's being in the acquisition or the possession of the good-will of the world about him; that is, of such members of society as he is likely to have concerns with; and as a means of it, either their love or their esteem, or both: and as a fruit of it, of his being in the way to have the benefit of their spontaneous and gratuitous services. These may likewise be called the pleasures of good repute, the pleasures of honour, or the pleasures of the moral sanction.

VIII. 6. The pleasures of power are the pleasures that accompany the persuasion of a man's being in a condition to dispose people, by means of their hopes and fears, to give him the benefit of their services: that is, by the hope of some service, or by the fear of some disservice, that he may be in the way to render them.

IX. 7. The pleasures of piety are the pleasures that accompany the belief of a man's being in the acquisition or in possession of the good-will or favour of the Supreme Being: and as a fruit of it, of his being in a way of enjoying, pleasures to be received by God's special appointment, either in this life, or in a life to come. These may also be called the pleasures of religion, the pleasures of a religious disposition, or the pleasures of the religious sanction.

X. 8. The pleasures of benevolence are the pleasures resulting from the view of any pleasures supposed to be possessed by the beings who may be the objects of benevolence; to wit, the sensitive beings we are acquainted with; under which are commonly included, 1. The Supreme Being. 2. Human beings. 3. Other animals. These may also be called the pleasures of goodwill, the pleasures of sympathy, or the pleasures of the benevolent or social affections.

XI. 9. The pleasures of malevolence are the pleasures resulting from the view of any pain supposed to be suffered by the beings who may become the objects of malevolence: to wit, 1. Human beings. 2. Other animals. These may also be styled the pleasures of ill-will, the pleasures of the irascible appetite, the pleasures of antipathy, or the pleasures of the malevolent or dissocial affections.

XII. 10. The pleasures of the memory are the pleasures which, after having enjoyed such and such pleasures, or even in some case after having suffered such and such pains, a man will now and then experience, at recollecting them exactly in the order and in the circumstances in which they were actually enjoyed or suffered. These derivative pleasures may of course be distinguished into as many species as there are of original perceptions, from whence they may be copied. They may also be styled pleasures of simple recollection.

XIII. 11. The pleasures of the imagination are the pleasures which may be derived from the contemplation of any such pleasures as may happen to be suggested by the memory, but in a different order, and accompanied by different groups of circumstances. These may accordingly be referred to any one of the three cardinal points of time, present, past, or future. It is evident they may admit of as many distinctions as those of the former class.

XIV. 12. The pleasures of expectation are the pleasures that result from the contemplation of any sort of pleasure, referred to time *future,* and accompanied with the sentiment of *belief.* These also may admit of the same distinctions.

XV. 13. The pleasures of association are the pleasures which certain objects or incidents may happen to afford, not of themselves, but merely in virtue of some association they have contracted in the mind with certain objects or incidents which are in themselves pleasurable. Such is the case, for instance, with the pleasure of skill, when afforded by such a set of incidents as compose a game of chess. This derives its pleasurable quality from its association partly with the pleasures of skill, as exercised in the production of incidents pleasurable of themselves; partly from its association with the pleasures of power. Such is the case also with the pleasure of good luck, when afforded by such incidents as compose the game of hazard, or any other game of chance, when played at for nothing. This derives its pleasurable quality from its association with one of the pleasures of wealth; to wit, with the pleasure of acquiring it.

XVI. 14. Farther on we shall see pains grounded upon pleasures; in like manner may we now see pleasures grounded upon pains. To the catalogue of pleasures may accordingly be added the pleasures of *relief:* or, the pleasures which a man experiences when, after he has been enduring a pain of any kind for a certain time, it comes to cease, or to abate. These may of course be distinguished into as many species as there are of pains: and may give rise to so many pleasures of memory, of imagination, and of expectation.

XVII. 1. Pains of privation are the pains that may result from the thought of not possessing in the time present any of the several kinds of pleasures. Pains of privation may accordingly be resolved into as many kinds as there are of pleasures to which they may correspond, and from the absence whereof they may be derived.

XVIII. There are three sorts of pains which are only so many modifications of the several pains of privation. When the enjoyment of any particular pleasure happens to be particularly desired, but without any expectation approaching to assurance, the pain of privation which thereupon results takes a particular name, and is called the pain of *desire* or of unsatisfied desire.

XIX. Where the enjoyment happens to have been looked for with a degree of expectation approaching to assurance, and that expectation is made suddenly to cease, it is called a pain of disappointment.

XX. A pain of privation takes the name of a pain of regret in two cases: 1. Where it is grounded on the memory of a pleasure, which having been once enjoyed, appears not likely to be enjoyed again; 2. When it is grounded on the ideas of a pleasure, which was never actually enjoyed, nor perhaps so much as expected, but which might have been enjoyed (it is supposed,) had such or such a contingency happened, which, in fact, did not happen.

XXI. 2. The several pains of the senses seem to be as follows: 1. The pains of hunger and thirst; or the disagreeable sensations produced by the want of suitable substances which need at times to be applied to the alimentary canal. 2. The pains of the taste: or the disagreeable sensations produced by the application of various substances to the palate, and other superior parts of the same canal. 3. The pains of the organ of smell: or the disagreeable sensations produced by the application of various substances to the skin. 5. The simple pains of the hearing: or the disagreeable sensations excited in the organ of that sense by various kinds of sounds: independently (as before,) of association. 6. The simple pains of the sight; or the disagreeable sensations if any such there be, that may be excited in the organ of that sense by visible images, independent of the principle of association. 7. The pains resulting from excessive heat or cold, unless these be referable to the touch. 8. The pains of disease: or the acute and uneasy sensations resulting from the several diseases and indispositions to which human nature is liable. 9. The pain of exertion, whether bodily or mental: or the uneasy sensation which is apt to accompany any intense effort, whether of mind or body.

XXII. 3. The pains of awkwardness are the pains which sometimes result from the unsuccessful endeavor to apply any particular instruments of enjoyment or security to their uses, or from the difficulty a man experiences in applying them.

XXIII. 4. The pains of enmity are the pains that may accompany the persuasion of a man's being obnoxious to the ill-will of such or such an assignable person or persons in particular: or, as the phrase is, of being upon ill terms with him or them: and, in consequence, of being obnoxious to certain pains of some sort or other, of which he may be the cause.

XXIV. 5. The pains of an ill-name, are the pains that accompany the persuasion of a man's being obnoxious, or in a way to be obnoxious to the ill-will of the world about him. These may likewise be called the pains of ill-repute, the pains of dishonour, or the pains of the moral sanction.

XXV. 6. The pains of piety are the pains that accompany the belief of a man's being obnoxious to the displeasure of the Supreme Being: and in consequence to certain pains to be inflicted by his especial appointment, either in this life or in a life to come. These may also be called the pains of religion; the pains of a religious disposition; or the pains of the religious sanction. When the belief is looked upon as well-grounded, these pains are commonly called religious terrors; when looked upon as ill-grounded, superstitious terrors.

XXVI. 7. The pains of benevolence are the pains resulting from the view of any pains supposed to be endured by other beings. These may also be called the pains of good-will, of sympathy, or the pains of the benevolence or social affections.

XXVII. 8. The pains of malevolence are the pains resulting from the view of any pleasure supposed to be enjoyed by any beings who happen to be the objects of a man's displeasure. These may also be styled the pains of ill-will, of antipathy, or the pains the malevolent or dissocial affections.

XXVIII. 9. The pains of the memory may be grounded on every one of the above kinds, as well of pains of privation as of positive pains. These correspond exactly to the pleasures of the memory.

XXIX. 10. The pains of the imagination may also be grounded on any one of the above kinds, as well of pains of privation as of positive pains: in other respects they correspond exactly to the pleasures of the imagination.

XXX. 11. The pains of expectation may be grounded on each one of the above kinds, as well as pains of privation as of positive pains. These may be also termed pains of apprehension.

XXXI. 12. The pains of association correspond exactly to the pleasures of association.

XXXII. Of the above list there are certain pleasures and pains which suppose the existence of some pleasure or pain of some other person, to which the pleasure or pain of the person in question has regard: such pleasures and pains may be termed *extra-regarding*. Others do not support any such thing: these may be termed *self-regarding*. The only pleasures and pains of the extra-regarding class are those of benevolence and those of malevolence: all the rest are self-regarding.

XXXIII. Of all these several sorts of pleasures and pains, there is scarce any one which is not liable, on more accounts than one, to come under the consideration of the law. Is an offence committed? It is the tendency which it has to destroy, in such or such persons, some of these pleasures, or to produce some of these pains, that constitutes the mischief of it, and the ground for punishing it. It is the prospect of some of these pleasures, or of security from some of these pains, that constitutes the motive or temptation, it is the attainment of them that constitutes the profit of the offence. Is the offender to be punished? It can be only by the production of one or more of these pains, that the punishment can be inflicted.

• • •

Of the Principle of Utility. Wherein then consists the good of the community? A question this which is to be answered not by vague declamation, not by point and metaphor, but by minute analysis and sober estimation. We shall endeavour then to travel on slowly and circumspectly, not with Rhetoric, but rather with Metaphysics and Mathematics for our guides. We shall endeavor to catch, as much as possible, the spirit of the two last-named sciences, and, as much as possible, to avoid the language.

• • •

. . . This then I assume as a *postulatum.* If it be denied me, I confess I shall be altogether at a loss to prove it. Nor will I go about to prove it in this essay: which is but a small part detached from an entire system of legal policy of which, were it finished, this axiom would form the bases. I will not, I say, in this place go about to prove it: nor shall I easily be brought to think it necessary. I could not easily have thought it had been new to anyone, if I did not remember that before I had read Helvetius it was new even to myself. I could not have thought it possible when once announced to contravert it: if I had not seen those by whom it has been contraverted. Two short questions may in this place answer the purpose of all argument. Supposing (without any foundation) that any other than the happiness of the community ought to be the end of legislative policy, what motive has the community to pursue it?

This then is the postulatum I set out with. To enable me to apply it with advantage it will be necessary before I enter upon the particular subject of Punishment, to go through the following operations:

1st, to distinguish the several sources from whence Pain and Pleasure are in use to flow:

2d, to mark out and describe the serveral species of pains and pleasures I shall have occasion to distinguish:

3dly, to show how the value of a pain or pleasure is to be measured:

4thly, to point out how such value may in every case be expressed:

5thly, to show the various proportions in which pain or pleasure, according as they are applied are apt to follow from the operations which are their causes: by enumerating the causes fo the different degrees of *sensibility* that are observable among men.

6thly, I shall mark out the station occupied by the business of Punishment in the general map or Plan of Jurisprudence. These several operations will form the business of as many chapters.

A reader who comes fresh to the subject and untinctured with any technical prejudices would be apt I imagine to wonder how a principle like this should ever have lain unobserved; how when once observed it should ever after have been neglected, much more how it should ever have been opposed; how any other should ever have been set up, and of what nature such other could possibly have been. He would conceive it impossible that any writer either on morals or what is called Natural Jurisprudence should ever have neglected or opposed it; and if compelled by the evidence of his eyes to acknowledge that such writers have existed, his next wonder would be what it is their speculations could consist of.

Of moralists it does not fall in the way of the present design to take any special notice any further than just to observe that it is to the open opposition or neglect with which the generality of them have treated this principle, that their works are held in such general and deserved neglect, and are acknowledged to be of so little use for the guidance of men in either their political or domestic conduct.

NOTES

1. Bentham was one of the early proponents of the view that decisionmaking should consciously seek those options most likely to bring about desired consequences. Systematically, he identified this as the greatest amount of pleasure. As Bentham himself recognized, the "correctness" of his value of the greatest happiness cannot be proven empirically. Discuss the implications of this admission in a heterogeneous society like the United States or in a multi-cultured world.

2. Where decisions can have multifaceted effects and ramifications, is it necessary, as some have argued, to place "weights" on different pleasures and pains in order to ascertain which acts will produce the greatest net aggregate of pleasure? Who determines these weights? How?

3. Bentham was one of the pioneers in refining the specification of the values for which humans strive. Thus he specified "pleasures" of power, wealth, piety and others, which were susceptible to comparison over time and between different societies. Bentham's Utilitarian Pleasure-Pain Principle assumes that there are units of pleasures and pains which can be measured. Bentham included measuring factors such as intensity, duration and propinquity of pleasures and pains. Are they adequate refinements for choice-making? Are pleasures and pains quantifiable in this way?

4. Is a decription of what people want the same as clarifying and specifying goals in the various areas of human activity?

5. Does goal specification and clarification require the use of other values, in addition to "happiness"? William Godwin believed that promises could be broken or one's mother left to perish in a fire, if these promoted the general happiness. Other theorists, such as Hastings, Rashdell and G. E. Moore, suggested the alternative utilitarian formula of "the greatest *good* of the greatest number" instead of the greatest *happiness* of the greatest number" (the so-called "School of Ideal Utilitarianism"). They insisted, for example, that the happiness of a drunkard in breaking crockery is not to be equated with the happiness of a hungry man in obtaining bread. H. Sidgwick insisted that there had to be an equal distribution of happiness, not simply the creation of greater aggregate amounts if these would be limited to some people only. Cf. Rawls' proposal of decisions for the benefit of the least favored in society, supra.

6. Would Bentham's Pleasure-Pain Principle permit the majority to enslave the minority if this would lead to a net return of pleasure (assuming that the pleasure of the majority of slave-holders would exceed the pain of the minority of slaves)? Under the utilitarian calculus, could an innocent person be executed or even lynched if his death could prevent a riot which would lead to many deaths? Does the utilitarian end always justify the means?

7. Does Bentham indicate satisfactory ways for determining means of reaching goals, how to ascertain the conditions which presently exist and those likely to exist which may impede or aid in reaching specified goals, how to take advantage of past experiences in attempting to reach goals, how to determine the likely effects of specific decisions with regard to achieving goals, how to devise alternative means to attain them? Why are questions like these important?

8. Some of Bentham's followers, attempting to accommodate the rule-oriented jurisprudence of Positivism with the more radical teleological approach of Bentham's Utilitarianism,

created a dichotomy between what they called rule-utilitarianism and act-utilitarianism (whether following *rules* optimalizes utility, or whether ignoring them and addressing the utility of each *act* is preferable). Having established this dichotomy, writers spent a good deal of time trying to determine which was the appropriate course to adopt. Is the entire distinction consistent with a strict utilitarian approach? Is the proper question one about rules or is it about a set of policies about the production and distribution of values one is trying to achieve? In a utilitarian approach, in any context, one tries to design a response which optimalizes as many of the policies at stake as possible, in ways compatible with minimum order. In the utilitarian calculus, is the distinction between act and rule, so dear to this school of Utilitarianism, factitious? Discuss.

9. The utilitarian approach has recently been attacked by a group of scholars who commit themselves to the primacy of rights. (See, for example, H. L. A. Hart, Between Utility and Right, in *The Ideas of Freedom* 79 (1979), and other essays there.) ''Rightists'' feel that Utilitarianism, in its search for choices that increase the benefits for the community as a whole, must be inconsiderate if not ruthless in dealing with the claims and expectations of some individuals. The antidote, they believe, is to eschew Utilitarianism and instead to limit substantially the options available to decisionmakers by creating certain entrenched rights which always ''trump,'' so-to-speak, utilitarian considerations. The exact content of those rights varies according to the political predilection of the writer concerned.

Not surprisingly, this particular academic debate mirrors and in turn influences a political debate in our civilization. A rights approach is essentially conservative, preserving a value allocation—whether it be power, wealth, respect, skill, enlightenment or any other value—against any redistributions, even if it can be demonstrated that they will yield net advantages to the entire community. A utilitarian approach, in its many guises, always has a potential for value redistribution, even radical change, as its fundamental policy is to find or design arrangements which produce the maximum of benefits for members of a class or community.

Though the debate seems uniquely contemporary, a moment's reflection will indicate that these two patterns of thought may be found, in different guises, in many different periods. Wherever there is conflict between those who wish change and those who wish to conserve some value allocation, a version of rightist language recommends itself. The industrial revolution and the rise of a technological and science-based civilization has aggravated the tension. As long as the basic pattern of life was one of stability, rights could always be invoked as a way of limiting authoritative power. After the advent of the industrial revolution, however, some measure of utilitarian planning was always required. Elites had to consider which choice options would lead to a net increase in national power, national wealth and so on. As long as those who were politically relevant felt that structural changes and value increases promised to maintain or improve their position, they were happy to adopt such a utilitarian calculus. But at the point at which further value increase was deemed unlikely and that, rather than a perpetually increasing pie, future redistributions meant a smaller slice of the pie for them and their constituents, the threatened ''haves'' ineluctably move toward a ''rights'' theory. (See, in this regard, the contrasting views of Lester C. Thurow, *The Zero-Sum Society: Distribution and the Possibilities for Economic Change* (1980). Recall also the comparison of Savigny and von Jhering discussed in Chapter 6.) What do you think of the logic of this argument?

THE LASSWELL-MCDOUGAL APPROACH TO POSTULATION

An early effort at addressing the goal postulation aspect of jurisprudence at the macro-political level was developed by Harold Lasswell in his innovative notion of ''preventive politics.''

LASSWELL, PSYCHOPATHOLOGY AND POLITICS
197–203 (1930)

This redefinition of the problem of politics may be called the idea of preventive politics. The politics of prevention draws attention squarely to the central problem of reducing the level of strain and maladaptation in society. In some measure it will proceed by encouraging discussions among all those who are affected by social policy, but this will be no iron-clad rule. In some measure it will proceed by improving the machinery of settling disputes, but this will be subordinated to a comprehensive program, and no longer treated as an especially desirable mode of handling the situation.

The recognition that people are poor judges of their own interest is often supposed to lead to the conclusion that a dictator is essential. But no student of individual psychology can fail to share the conviction of Kempf that "Society is *not* safe . . . when it is forced to follow the dictations of one individual, of one automatic apparatus, no matter how splendidly and altruistically it may be conditioned." Our thinking has too long been misled by the threadbare terminology of democracy versus dictatorship, of democracy versus aristocracy. Our problem is to be ruled by the truth about the conditions of harmonious human relations, and the discovery of the truth is an object of specialized research; it is no monopoly of people as people, or of the ruler as ruler. As our devices of accurate ascertainment are invented and spread, they are explained and applied by many individuals inside the social order. Knowledge of this kind is a slow and laborious accumulation.

The politics of prevention does not depend upon a series of changes in the organization of government. It depends upon a reorientation in the minds of those who think about society around the central problems: What are the principle factors which modify the tension level of the community? What is the specific relevance of a proposed line of action to the temporary and permanent modification of the tension level?

The politics of prevention will insist upon a rigorous audit of the human consequences of prevailing political practices. How does politics affect politicians? One way to consider the human value of social action is to see what the form of social action does to the actors. When a judge has been on the bench thirty years, what manner of man has he become? When an agitator has been agitating for thirty years, what has happened to him? How do different kinds of political administrators compare with doctors, musicians, and scientists? Such a set of inquiries would presuppose that we were able to ascertain the traits with which the various individuals began to practice their role in society. Were we able to show what certain lines of human endeavor did to the same reactive type, we would lay the foundation for a profound change in society's esteem for various occupations.

Any audit of the human significance of politics would have to press far beyond the narrow circle of professional politicians. Crises like wars, revolutions, and elections enter the lives of people in far-reaching ways. The effect of crises on mental attitude is an important and uncertain field. Thus it is reported that during the rebellion of 1745–46 in Scotland there was little hysteria (in the technical pathological sense). The same was true of the French Revolution and of the Irish Rebellion. Rush reported in his book *On the Influence of the American Revolution on the Human Body* that many hysterical women were "restored to perfect health by the events of the time." Havelock Ellis, who cites these instances, comments that "in such cases the emotional tension is given an opportunity for explosion in new and impersonal channels, and the chain of morbid personal emotions is broken.''

The physical consequences of political symbolism may be made the topic of investigation from this point of view:

> When the affect can not acquire what it needs, uncomfortable tensions or anxiety (fear) are felt, and the use of the symbol or fetish, relieving this anxiety, has a marked physiological value in that it prevents the adrenal, thyroid, circulatory, hepatic and pulmonic compensatory strivings from becoming excessive.

Political programs will continually demand reconsideration in the light of the factors which current research discloses as bearing upon the tension level. Franz Alexander recently drew attention to the strains produced in modern civilization by the growing sphere of purposive action. He summed up the facts in the process of civilized development in the following way: "Human expressions of instinct are subject to a continual tendency to rationalization, that is, they develop more and more from playful, uncoordinated, purely pleasure efforts into purposive actions." The "discomfort of civilization" of which Freud . . . wrote . . . is characteristic of the rationalized cultures with which we are acquainted. Life is poor in libidinal gratifications of the primitive kind which the peasant, who is in close touch with elementary things, is in a position to enjoy. Modern life furnishes irrational outlets in the moving picture and in sensational crime news. But it may be that other means of relieving the strain of modern living can be invented which will have fewer drawbacks.

Preventive politics will search for the definite assessment, then, of cultural patterns in terms of their human consequences. Some of these human results will be deplored as "pathological," while others will be welcomed as "healthy." One complicating factor is that valuable contributions to culture are often made by men who are in other respects pathological. Many pathological persons are constrained by their personal difficulties to displace more or less successfully upon remote problems, and to achieve valuable contributions to knowledge and social policy. Of course the notion of the pathological is itself full of ambiguities. The individual who is subject to epileptic seizures may be considered in one culture not a subnormal and diseased person, but a supernormal person. Indeed, it may be said that society depends upon a certain amount of pathology, in the sense that society does not encourage the free criticism of social life, but establishes taboos upon reflective thinking about its own presuppositions. If the individual is pathological to the extent that he is unable to contemplate any fact with equanimity, and to elaborate impulse through the processes of thought, it is obvious that society does much to nurture disease. This leads to the apparent paradox that successful social adjustment consists in contracting the current diseases. If "health" merely means a statistical report upon the "average," the scrutiny of the individual ceases to carry much meaning for the modification of social patterns. But if "health" means something more than "average," the intensive study of individuals gives us a vantage ground for the revaluation of the human consequences of cultural patterns, and the criticism of these patterns.

If the politics of prevention spreads in society, a different type of education will become necessary for those who adminster society or think about it. This education will start from the proposition that it takes longer to train a good social scientist than it takes to train a good physical scientist. The social administrator and social scientist must be brought into direct contact with his material in its most varied manifestations.

He must mix with rich and poor, with savage and civilized, with sick and well, with old and young. His contacts must be primary and not exclusively secondary. He must have an opportunity for prolonged self-scrutiny by the best-developed methods of personality study, and he must laboriously achieve a capacity to deal objectively with himself and with all others in human society.

This complicated experience is necessary since our scale of values is less the outcome of our dialectical than of our other experiences in life. Values change more by the unconscious redefinition of meaning than by rational analysis. Every contact and every procedure which discloses new facts has its repercussions upon the matrix of partially verbalized experience, which is the seeding ground of conscious ideas.

One peculiarity of the problem of the social scientist is that he must establish personal contact with his material. The physical scientist who works in a laboratory spends more time adjusting his machinery than in making his observations, and the social scientist who works in the field must spend more time establishing contacts than in noting and reporting observations. What the instrumentation technique is to the physicist, the cultivation of favorable human points of vantage is for most social scientists. This means that the student of society as well as the manager of social relations, must acquire the technique of social intercourse in unusual degree, unless he is to suffer from serious handicaps, and his training must be directed with this in mind.

The experience of the administrator-investigator must include some definite familiarity with all the elements which bear importantly upon the traits and interests of the individual. This means that he must have the most relevant material brought to his attention from the fields of psychology, psychopathology, physiology, medicine, and social science. Since our institutions of higher learning are poorly organized at the present time to handle this program, thorough curricular reconstructions will be indispensable.

What has been said in this chapter may be passed in brief review. Political movements derive their vitality from the displacement of private affects upon public objects. Political crises are complicated by the concurrent reactivation of specific primitive motives which were organized in the early experience of the individuals concerned. Political symbols are particularly adapted to serve as targets for displaced affect because of their ambiguity of reference, in relation to individual experience, and because of their general circulation. Although the dynamic of politics is the tension level of individuals, all tension does not produce political acts. Nor do all emotional bonds lead to political action. Political acts depend upon the symbolization of the discontent of the individual in terms of a more inclusive self which champions a set of demands for social action.

Political demands are of limited relevance to the changes which will produce permanent reductions in the tension level of society. The political methods of coercion, exhortation, and discussion assumes that the role of politics is to solve conflicts when they have happened. The ideal of a politics of prevention is to obviate conflict by the definite reduction of the tension level of society by effective methods, of which discussion will be but one. The preventive point of view insists upon a continuing audit of the human consequences of social acts, and especially of political acts. The achievement of the ideal of preventive politics depends less upon changes in social organization than upon improving the methods and the education of social administrators and social scientists.

The preventive politics of the future will be intimately allied to general medicine, psychopathology, physiological psychology, and related disciplines. Its practitioners will gradually win respect in society among puzzled people who feel their responsibilities and who respect objective findings. A comprehensive functional conception of political life will state problems of investigation, and keep receptive the minds of those who reflect at length upon the state.

In a later work, Lasswell suggested in more detail some of the methods for clarifying goals in heterogeneous societies.

LASSWELL, CLARIFYING VALUE JUDGMENT:
PRINCIPLES OF CONTENT AND PROCEDURE,
1 INQUIRY 87, 93–98 (1958)

CONFIGURATIVE THINKING AND REPRESENTATIVE EXPOSURE

Procedural principles appear to concern two problems: One, how to employ the assets in hand in the task of judgment; two, how to enlarge the range and quantity of assets at one's disposal. I refer to the use of current assets as "configurative thinking," and the expansion of scope as "representative exposure."

Configurative thinking is goal oriented. It is contextually oriented in the sense that not one but all goals are considered. It is also oriented in time, since value judgments are choices in the emerging process of history. It is oriented toward knowledge, since all available information is taken into account. In a word: configurative thinking is goal oriented, time oriented, knowledge oriented; and it can best proceed by employing five interconnected though distinguishable patterns of thought.

GOAL THINKING

The proper emphasis in goal thinking is upon the *contextual whole*. We do an insufficient job of clarifying a *specific* commitment to the UN, for instance, if we fail to assess it in relation to *all* of our *general* goals. We do an inadequate job if we fail to appraise *each general* statement in reference to *all*. A commitment to world unity, for instance, requires qualification if we are also committed to political freedom. *Unless tentative value judgments are reviewed in the context of a total conception of the preferred form of social order, unnecessary inconsistencies and omissions occur.*

Goals are long range, mid-range, and immediate. The long range ("Utopian" goals) are almost independent of timing. But little of any consequence can be said about mid-range and immediate objectives without giving full weight to temporal ordering.

TREND THINKING

Herewith the time dimension is brought directly to the thinker's focus of attention. He asks himself in regard to a given context to what extent preferred goals have been approximated? How much sacrifice has been made in order to achieve them?

SCIENTIFIC THINKING

Although trend knowledge is helpful in obtaining preliminary estimates of value cost and gain, scientific analysis is essential to refine the initial estimates. It is customary of scientific thought to include the construction of explanatory descriptive models, and the gathering and processing of data. It is well known that historical trends may create misleading impressions of the strength of various factors that condition change. Perhaps great results appear to have been achieved by personal leadership and negotiating skill. Scientific analysis may show that in the concrete circumstances these factors were of trivial importance when compared with the impact of "atomic stalemate."

PROJECTIVE THINKING

Trend and factor (scientific) thinking are requisite to projective thinking, which is concerned with future events. The question is, if we assume that no policy changes will be introduced, how will things turn out? Projective thinking is carried on by the use of "developmental constructs," which we characterize as theoretical models of significant cross-sections of past and future. Goals (preferred events) are taken as points of departure for these constructs. Hence one may begin with world unity as exemplified in the UN, starting with the inauguration of the UN after World War II and selecting ten or twenty-year intervals in the future which are then characterized in terms of a strengthened or weakened UN.

A developmental construct is formulated on the basis of all information at the disposal of the thinker; and it is subject to critical reconsideration as information improves. For developmental purposes information is of three kinds: systematic historical (trend) knowledge; scientific propositions (with a specifiable degree of empirical confirmation); unsystematic information about the past and present.

Obviously it is not enough to extrapolate historical trends into the future, since in many cases the curves come into conflict at future points; and trend knowledge provides no method by which the result can be forecast.

Further, it is not enough to project scientific generalizations into the future. Scientific propositions avoid time; they treat time, where it enters, as a factor whose routine of interaction with other variables (at a specified magnitude) is *invariant*. Thus time is considered in order to escape from its role in the "natural order" of past and prospective history. In this perspective the mystic and the scientist share a curious ultimate bias against time. Developmental thinking, on the contrary, stresses "natural order," and refers to the future in terms open to validation by future observers. Since scientific propositions are formulated as invariant relations the task of projective thought is to estimate the likelihood that the stipulated conditions of invariance will appear at specific future times.

Often, when one turns to available knowledge about the past, it appears that scholarship and science have failed to provide much that is directly in point. But a large amount of unsystematic information is at hand with which to fill out the current picture as best one can.

POLICY THINKING

We come to policy thinking, or the invention and assessment of alternative courses of action. Instead of assuming "no influence," as was done in projective thinking, the situation is examined to disclose ways and means of influencing the future as it unfolds. Here projective thinking is continued in a different frame of reference. Stress is laid upon inventiveness, upon permitting new ideas to enter into the historical process through the subjective life of the thinker.

For relatively circumscribed problems it is feasible to draw up maps of preference and expectation, after the manner recommended in game theory. We are, however, concerned with the social context as a whole, and it is beyond the present range of possibility to draw comprehensive maps of preference and expectation. Sufficiently precise operational indexes are not now obtainable. Also, the computations required by the army of potential variables are not practicable for existing equipment.

A cautionary note: The impression may have been given in the present discussion that configurative thinking is like a ceremonial dance that follows a strict progression through a series of regular figures called goal, trend, scientific, projective, and policy thinking. However, no "once and for all" implication is intended. Procedural flexibility improves the chances of clarity, since it is possible to employ each method until the marginal probability of further contributions by each is estimated to be the same.

REPRESENTATIVE EXPOSURE

We have said that the configurative method can be employed to utilize the knowledge accessible to the thinker at a given time. We turn now to procedures whose principle role is to prepare the thinker to endure or attain a higher level of rationality. Once more the key conception is contextuality. We speak of representativeness; the intention is to emphasize that the ideal program is a sampling of all human experience. We know enough of learning to realize that learning is largely situational. It occurs in networks of interaction. Much of what purports to be social learning is exceedingly superficial because there has been no full participation, no saturation in the culture, the class, the interest group, the crisis situation, or even the type of personality about which the learning is presumably taking place.

The exposure program is designed with two lines of intensification in view: One, *understanding* of people; two, *insight* into the Self. The latter factor places a formidable limitation upon the degree of penetration possible in efforts at understanding. In this connection we are using the technical conception of insight; we refer to the discovery of attributes of the Self that are ordinarily excluded from the focus of full waking attention by smooth working mechanisms of "resistance" and "repression." The anxieties are the cover forces that stand in the way of rationality.

INDIVIDUAL AND COLLECTIVE PROJECTS

I have been describing the pursuit of clarified values as a project for individual thinkers. So it is. But individual thinkers need not try to restrict themselves to the Robinson Crusoe role which has been a favorite image of the Self among thinkers. It is out of the question for a solitary thinker to accomplish as much alone as when he is functioning as part of a system in which social intelligence operates effectively. Estimates of the future depend upon access to a current flow of information that is comprehensive, representative, concise and reliable. To the extent that the agencies of enlightenment are malfunctioning, the mind of every thinker suffers handicap. Some intellectual tasks cannot be performed.

The thinker depends upon more than the current flow of intelligence; he is nurtured in the antecedent process by which he obtains skills and motivations to pursue enlightenment as a major value.

Today the thinking group—that is, the specialists who pursue an inclusive and tested image of the whole of human history—have a more formidable task than ever. There is a need of an *intermediate stratum* of thinkers to function between specialists on "truth by definition" and men of action—or desperation—who are the responsible makers of value judgments in every sphere. The intermediate role calls for the life-long cultivation of the thinker's potential for rationality.

There is continuity in such a life. At any cross-section the individual finds himself "seized" by a host of value preferences; the technique of choosing among them is improvable. The principal lines of improvement appear to be in the methods of configurative thinking and of exposure to representative occasions of understanding and insight.

The task of clarification does not come to an end in the career line of individuals or collectivities. It continues as long as time exposes a new visage in history. The act of judgment is rationally performed when further reflection would, in all probability, add no gains comparable with the losses of postponement. We are suggesting that the value commitments of the individual need not be arbitrary, even though they are empirically rather than transempirically grounded. The primary reliance of the thinker in this operation needs to be upon procedures rather than upon the analysis of the content of definitions or propositions. The procedures themselves are two-fold, one addressed to the effective use of the intellectual assets at hand, the other to the improvement of the thinker's fundamental equipment. In the effective use of available knowledge the configurative patterns increase the contextuality of goal, the historical sweep of information, the scientific thoroughness of analysis, the imaginative anti-cipation of the future, and the inventive appraisal of policy that increase the likelihood of an optimally rational result. In the enlargement of range and diversity of under-standing and insight the individual—and the group—has an opportunity for stretching human capability to its uttermost limit in an unending search for clarity of judgment.

LAW AND ECONOMICS AS POLICY SCIENCE

One of the current policy-science approaches, with advocates on many law fa-culties, involves the use of micro-economics for clarifying policy and for the appraisal of earlier decisions. A leader and pioneer in this area is *quondam* professor and now Judge Richard Posner.

POSNER, ECONOMIC ANALYSIS OF LAW
16–23, 101–104, 179–187, 190
(2d ed. 1977)

. . . [T]he hallmark of the "new" law and economics—the law and economics that is almost entirely new within the last decade and a half is the application of the theories and empirical methods of economics to the legal system across the board—to common law fields such as tort, contract, and property, to the theory and practice of punishment, to civil, criminal, and administrative procedure, to the theory of legislation, and to law enforcement and judicial administration. Whereas the "old" law and economics confined its attention to laws governing explicit economic relationships, and indeed to laws governing limited subset of such laws (the law of contracts, for example, was omitted), the "new" law and economics recognizes no such limitation on the domain of economic analysis of law. (The terms "old" and "new" are used to indicate sequence, not relative value or promise.).

The new law and economics date from the early 1960's, when Guido Calabresi's first article on torts and Ronald Coase's article on social cost were published. These were the first attempts to apply economic analysis in a *systematic* way to areas of law that did not avowedly regulate economic relationships. . . .

Coase's article established a framework for analyzing the assignment of property rights and liability in economic terms. This opened up a vast field of legal doctrine to fruitful economic analysis,. . . . A very important, although for a time neglected, feature of Coase's article was its implications for the positive analysis of legal doctrine. Coase suggested that the English law of nuisance had an implicit economic logic. Later writers have generalized this insight and argued that many of the doctrines and institutions of the legal system are best understood and explained as efforts to promote the efficient allocation of resources. This is, indeed, a major theme of the present book.

• • •

NORMATIVE AND POSITIVE ECONOMIC ANALYSIS OF LAW
• • •

[T]he economist is not the ultimate arbiter of social choice. Although he cannot tell society whether it should seek to limit theft, he can show that it would be inefficient to allow unlimited theft; he can thus clarify a value conflict by showing how much of one value—efficiency, surely an important, if not necessarily paramount, value in any society—must be sacrificed to achieve another. Or, taking a goal of limiting theft as a given, the economist may be able to show that the means by which society has attempted to attain that goal are inefficient—that society could obtain more prevention, at lower cost, by using different methods. If the more efficient methods did not impair any other values, then presumably they would be considered socially desirable even if efficiency were assigned a relatively low place in the hierarchy of values. In short, it would seem that a significant normative role must be conceded to economics even if no attempt is made to derive efficiency from some more basic ethical postulate.

While the normative role of economic analysis in the law is thus an important one, the positive role—that of explaining the rules and outcomes in the legal system as they are—is, in this writer's view, even more important. As we shall see in subsequent chapters, many areas of the law, especially—but by no means only—the great common law fields of property, torts, crimes and contracts, bear the stamp of economic reasoning. Few legal opinions, to be sure, contain explicit references to economic concepts, and few judges have a substantial background in economics. But the true grounds of legal decision are often concealed rather than illuminated by the characteristic rhetoric of judicial opinions (why should this be so?) Indeed, legal education consists primarily of learning to dig beneath the rhetorical surface to find those grounds. It is an advantage of economic analysis as a tool of legal study rather than a drawback that it does not analyze cases in the conceptual modes employed in the opinions themselves.

. . . Not only are justice and fairness not economic concepts, but the economist is not interested in the one question that concerns the victim and his lawyer; who should bear the costs of *this* accident? To the economist, the accident is a closed chapter. The costs that it inflicted are "sunk" costs that cannot be retrieved by a transfer payment from the injurer to the victim (why?) The economist is interested in methods of preventing future accidents and thus reducing accident costs but the parties to the litigation have no interest in the future. Their concern is limited to the financial consequences of a past accident.

But this dichotomy is overstated. The decision in the case will affect the future, and so should interest the economist, becauses it will establish or confirm a rule for the guidance of people engaged in dangerous activities. The decision is a warning that if one behaves in a certain way and an accident results, he will have to pay a judgment (or will be unable to obtain a judgment, if the victim). By thus altering the prices that confront people, the warning may affect their behavior and therefore accident costs.

● ● ●

Once the frame of reference is thus expanded beyond the immediate parties to the case, justice and fairness assume broader meanings than what is just or fair as between this plaintiff and this defendant. The issue becomes what is a just and fair result for a class of activities, and cannot be resolved without at least some consideration of the impact of alternative rulings on the frequency of accidents and the cost of accident precautions. The legal and economic approaches are not so divergent after all.

CRITICISMS OF THE ECONOMIC APPROACH

The economic approach to law has aroused considerable antagonism. . . .

. . . Because economics is an incomplete and imperfect science, it is easy to poke fun at, just as it is easy to poke fun at medicine for the same reason (e.g., its failure to cure the common cold). But no one proposes to write off medicine.

. . . A more intelligenct version of this criticism attacks the use of economics in normative analysis of law by challenging the validity of the philosophical basis of economics, which is utilitarianism. No doubt there is a close relationship between normative economics and utilitarianism, though there are also important differences. However, the proper normative uses of economics, mentioned earlier—to clarify value conflicts and to show how to achieve given social ends by the most efficient means—are quite untouched by any debate over the philosophical merits of utilitarianism. Even more clearly, the ability of economic analysis to enlarge our understanding of how the legal system actually operates is not undetermined by the attacks on utilitarianism. If the participants in the legal process act as rational maximizers of their satisfactions, if the legal process itself has been shaped by a concern with maximizing economic efficiency, the economist has a rich field of study whether or not a society in which people behave in such a way or institutions are shaped by such concerns is a good society.

Another common criticism of the economic approach to law is that the attempt to explain the behavior of legal institutions, and of the people operating or affected by them, on economic grounds must fail because, surely, much more than rational maximizing is involved in such behavior: the motivations of the violent criminal cannot be reduced to income maximization or the goals of the criminal justice system to minimization of the costs of crime and of its control. Not only does this criticism reflect a fundamental misunderstanding of the nature of scientific inquiry, but it is not really a criticism; it is a prediction that the economic approach will ultimately turn out to be barren. Readers of this book can make their own predictions.

• • •

Another common criticism of the "new" law and economics—though it is really not a criticism but rather a reason for the distaste with which the subject is regarded in some quarters—is that it manifests a strongly conservative political bias. Its practitioners have found for example, as we shall see in subsequent chapters, that capital punishment has a deterrent effect, and that legislation designed to protect the consumer frequently ends up hurting him. Findings such as these provide ammunition to the supporters of capital punishment and the opponents of consumer legislation. Yet economic research that provides support for liberal positions is rarely acknowledged—at least by liberals—as manifesting political bias. . . .

The economic approach is also criticized for ignoring "justice"—which surely should be the central concern of the legal system and those who study it. In evaluating this criticism, we must distinguish carefully between different senses in which the term is used in legal settings. It is sometimes used to mean "distributive justice," which can be defined crudely as the "proper" degree of economic inequality. Although, as mentioned earlier, economists cannot tell the society what that degree is, they have much to say that is highly relevant to the debate over inequality—about the actual amounts of inequality in different societies and in different periods about the difference between real economic inequality and inequalities in pecuniary income that merely offset cost differences or reflect different positions in the life cycle, and about the costs of achieving greater real or nominal equality.

• • •

. . . [T]he primary role of economic analysis would appear to be one of dispelling certain pseudojustice issues which seem to be based on sheer intellectual confusion and even more important, to assist in value clarifiction by showing the society what it must give up to achieve some noneconomic ideal of justice.

• • •

THE THEORY OF HOUSEHOLD PRODUCTION

The economic analysis of the family is founded on the perception that the household is not merely a consuming, but more importantly a producing, unit in society. The food, clothing, furniture, medicines, and other market conditions that the household purchases are really inputs into the production of nourishment, warmth, affection, children, and the other tangible and intangible goods that constitute the output of the household. A most important input into this productive process is not a market commodity at all, but is the time of the household members, in particular (in the traditional family) of the wife.

• • •

Declining marriage and birth rates, and rising divorce rates, suggest that the traditional family is in decline. Economic theory provides an explanation for the underlying trends. The demand for and relative wages of women employed in the market have grown dramatically in recent decades. This has increased the opportunity costs of being a housewife, which are simply the market income (net of tax and other costs of market versus household work) forgone by staying at home. The household commodity that places the greatest demands on the wife's time is rearing children, so an increase in the opportunity costs of the wife's time is immediately translated into an increase in the price that the household must pay to have children. A rise in the price of children can be expected to reduce the quantity of children demanded; and since rearing children is not only one of the most important activities of the household but also the one most difficult to conduct at comparable cost outside of the household, a decline in the demand for children should result—and evidently has resulted—in a decline in the demand for marriage, the standard method of household formation.

Because so much of family law is based on a concern with the welfare of children, the motivations for producing children must be explored. Children may be produced (1) as an unintended by-product of sexual activity, (2) as an income-producing investment, (3) as a source of other services to the parents, and (4) (really a subset of (3) out of an instinct or desire to preserve the species, or possibly to perpetuate the genetic characteristics, the name, or the memory of the parents. In an age of widely available contraception and abortion, (1) has become unimportant. (2) was once important in our society (as it is in very poor societies today); at common law, the parents owned the child's market earning until his majority and were entitled to support from the child in their old age. The outlawing of child labor, and the prevalence of public and private pension schemes, have obsoleted (2) and prompted a search for less tangible services that parents might derive from a child (for example, respect). (3) and (4) thus emerge as the most plausible explanations for the desire to have children in contemporary society.

•   •   •

Cursory as the above survey of the economics of the family is, it enables us to explain some, and criticize other, important features of family law. It also provides, as we shall see, both an opportunity to review in a different context the principles developed in the last two chapters, and a basis for analyzing, in the next chapter, important issues of tort damage law. That is why a largely statutory body of law appears as a branch of the common law in the organization of this book.

FORMATION AND DISSOLUTION OF MARRIAGE

Commercial partnerships are voluntary contractual associations, and so, up to a point, are marriages. Even (otherwise) totalitarian states respect freedom of choice in marriage. And the "marriage market" is an apt metaphor for the elaborate process of search by which individuals seek marital partners with whom to form productive households. To be sure, explicit marrage contracts are rare, but that may be because the law, by a process now familiar to the reader, saves the parties the trouble of negotiation by defining the rights and obligations that they automatically assume when they enter into marriage.

•   •   •

THE IMPLICIT ECONOMIC LOGIC OF THE COMMON LAW

Our survey of the major common law fields suggests that the common law exhibits a deep unity that is economic in character. The differences among the law of property, the law of contracts (including implied contracts), the law of torts (and the parts of the criminal law that overlap tort law), and (to a lesser extent) family law are primarily differences in vocabulary, detail, and specific subject matter rather than in method of policy. (To this list could be added another branch of the judge-made law, admirality law.) The common law method is to allocate responsibilities between people engaged in interacting activities in such a way as to maximize the joint value, or, what amounts to the same thing, minimize the joint cost of the activities. It may do this by redefining a property right, by devising a new rule of liability, or by recognizing a contract right, but nothing fundamental turns on which device is used. . . .

. . . If the law fails to allocate responsibilities between the parties in such a way as to maximize value, the parties will, by an additional and not costless transaction, nullify the legal allocation. This is the economic reason why the common law does not recognize a right to be free from competition. It is a right that the successful competitor would always buy (why?), so its only economic effect would be to increase the number and hence costs of transactions. Clearly, however, the economic importance of the common law is smaller in the areas where transaction costs are low than in areas where they are high. The presumption in such areas is that existing customs and practices are efficient and rules intended to alter them both inefficient and, worse, futile.

The stamp of economics is also strongly evident in the remedial aspects of the common law, including the rules examined in the last chapter relating to the application of the criminal sanction, themselves a branch of judge-made law. And in Part VI of this book we shall see that the procedural and institutional, as well as substantive and remedial, dimensions of the common law reveal the stamp of economics.

The reader may wonder whether it is plausible to attribute economic insight to common law judges, especially since litigants rarely couch their arguments in economic terms. However, the character of common law litigation virtually compels a confrontation with economic issues. The typical common law case involves a dispute between two parties over which one should bear a loss. In searching for a reasonably objective and impartial standard, as the traditions of the bench require him to do, the judge can hardly fail to consider whether the loss was the product of wasteful, uneconomical resource use. In a culture of scarcity, this is an urgent, an inescapable question. And in most cases, at least an approximation to the answer is reasonably accessible to intuition and common sense.

THE COMMON LAW AND ECONOMIC GROWTH

Economic analysis can help to clarify the controversial role of the common law in the economic growth of this country. The usual view is that the common law, by the permissiveness toward economic activity that it displayed during the nineteenth century, helped to foster rapid economic development. A variant is that the common law subsidized growth by failing to make industry bear all of the costs that an efficiency standard would have required that it bear. The permissiveness of the common law in the nineteenth century is contrasted with the many restrictions imposed on economic activity by the law in both the preceding and following periods.

It is necessary to clarify the concepts of growth and of subsidy. The rate of economic growth is the rate at which the output (or output per capita) of a society increases. Since growth is fostered by efficient resource use, there is a sense, but a rather uncontroversial one, in which the common law, insofar as it has been shaped by a concern with efficiency, may be said to have fostered growth. Society can force the pace of growth by compelling people to consume less and save more and by increasing the returns to capital investment. If the common law played any role in accelerating economic growth, it must have been by making capital investment more profitable.

In this vein, it has been argued that nineteenth-century contract law consistently favored the performing over the paying party in order to encourage entrepreneurship. But every business firm is simultaneously, and more or less equally, performer and payer: it is the performer with respect to contracts for the sale of its output; it is payer with respect to contracts for the purchase of its inputs. It derives no clear gain from having the law tilted in favor of performers.

It has been suggested that the common law of industrial accidents favored industry. But we have seen that, as between parties already in a contractual relationship, the efficient level of safety would be achieved (or approximated) even if the law imposed *no* liability for accidental injury. . . .

The area in which the argument that the law favored growth seems most plausible is that of accidents to strangers. Consider two alternative rules of law, one that a railroad is liable to travelers injured at railroad crossings only if the railroad was negligent, the other that the railroad is strictly liable to them (unless, perhaps they were contributorily negligent). The accident rate is similar under both rules, but the railroad's costs will be higher under the second and this will lead to an increase in its prices and a fall in its output and profits. The first rule encourages and the second rule discourages railroading, although perhaps trivially.

•   •   •

As a final example of how economic analysis can be used to evaluate the claims of legal historians, consider the recent suggestion that the development of impossibility and related doctrines in the law of contracts demonstrates the decline of free-market principles of law since the nineteenth century. No doubt those principles are in general less influential than they once were but the specific illustration is inapt; as we have seen, impossibility and related excuses are necessary to make the law of contracts efficient; they are implicit in the positive economic theory of contract law. This mistake is an especially puzzling one in view of the same author's assertion that nineteenth-century contract law consistently favored the performing party, who might be expected to favor a liberal doctrine of excuses.

THE MORAL CONTENT OF THE COMMON LAW

The view of the common law as a system for promoting economic efficiency will strike many readers as an incomplete—if not severely impoverished—theory of the common law, particularly in its disregard of the moral dimension of law. Surely, it will be argued, the true purpose of law, especially of those fundamental principles of law embodied in the common law of England and the United States, is to correct injustices and thereby vindicate the moral sense.

In fact, there appears to be no fundamental inconsistency between morality and efficiency. Moral principles—honesty, truthfulness, trustworthiness (for example, keeping promises), selflessness (for example, consideration for others), charity, neighborliness, avoidance of negligence and coercion—serve in general to promote efficiency. That such principles have survived—as cherished, if not always observed, social and personal values—for thousands of years suggests they are traits that by and large enrich rather than impoverish the society that cultivates them. Their economic value will be apparent to the careful reader of the previous chapters. Honesty, trustworthiness, and love reduce the costs of transactions; avoidance of coercion promotes the voluntary costs (sometimes in economics called, indeed ''neighborhood effects''); selflessness reduce free-riders problems, charity reduces the demand for administratively costly public welfare programs; carefulness reduces social waste.

• • •

The common law may be viewed as an effort to attach costs to the violation of moral principles—principles that we have suggested operate to enhance the efficiency of a market (as of most other types of) economy. Yet one observes that the law does not in general incorporate *any* moral principle to its fullest extent. For example, the law of contracts enforces only a limited subset of promises; many morally objectionable breaches of promise do not give rise to a cause of action. The explanation may be that the substantive principles of the law are limited by the costs of administering the law. The costs of enforcing all promises would be disproportionate to the gains, since many promises do not enhance value significantly, and some that do may occur in circumstances where the costs of legal error outweigh the benefits from enforcing the promise in the form made (for example, a contract rendered unenforceable by the Statute of Frauds because oral rather than written). Even more fundamentally, the law take no cognizance of breaches of the moral code that do not affect other people—for example, the slander uttered in solitude. Here the cost of enforcing morality would be great and the benefits in enhanced efficiency small. Yet one can see how a habit of refraining from slander regardless of the circumstances could be viewed (and hence inculcated) as morally desirable because it reduced the likelihood that an injurious slander would be uttered.

The economic nature of the relationship between law and morals can be illustrated with reference to the question of punishing homosexual relations between consenting adults. The costs of punishing any sort of victimless crime are great. The benefits in this case may be small. The disapprobation of homosexuality may, as suggested in Chapter 5, stem from an era in which there were considerable external benefits from population increase. These benefits may be much less today, or even negative. This may explain why conventional moral feelings about homosexuality are also changing—and why legal sanctions against homosexual conduct are eroding.

Why, then, are some apparently efficient transactions forbidden in the name of morality? Suppose that when I get married I ask my wife to agree, when I die, to fling herself on my funeral pyre. I pay her what she considers fair consideration for this promise, which both of us fully intend to be legally enforceable, knowing that she may want to renege when the time for performance arrives. No court would enforce such a contract. No court would enforce Shylock's contract with Antonio. No court would enforce a voluntary contract to become another's slave. A convicted criminal is not permitted to substitute a lashing that would impose on him pain slightly less than his prison sentence even if he showed that the cost savings to the state would greatly exceed the reduction in the severity of punishment that was his motive for proposing the transaction. These examples are puzzling from an economic standpoint, but some less so than others. The fact that people have very different, and very hard to measure, thresholds of pain makes it difficult (i.e., costly) to impose a desired level of cost or pain by means of ''afflictive punishment.'' The differences in the pecuniary costs of imprisonment (due to income differences) and in the nonpecuniary costs of imprisonment (due to social status, standard of living, previous imprisonment, etc.) are somewhat more easily measurable.

• • •

The basic function of law, in an economic perspective, is to alter incentives. This implies that law does not command the impossible, since a command impossible to fulfill will not alter behavior. The impossible command is to be distinguished from the legal sanction that is unavoidable only because the cost of avoidance is greater than the cost of the sanction. There is no incongruity in making the party who breaches a contract liable in damages in a case where he had no real choice because the cost of performing the contract would have greatly exceeded the damages from nonperformance (or even because performance would have been literally impossible). The law has simply placed the risk of nonperformance on the party who fails to perform. The proper criticism of the various pockets of strict liability in the criminal law (for example, reasonable mistake [is] no defense in a prosecution for bigamy or statutory rape) is not that they are inconsistent with the idea of law but that the risk imposed is greater than the circumstances warrant.

The requirement that law must treat equals equally is another way of saying that the law must have a rational structure, for to treat differently things that are the same is irrational. Economic theory is a system of deductive logic; when correctly applied, it yields results that are consistent with one another. Insofar as the law has an implicit economic structure, it must be rational: it must treat like cases alike.

Law, viewed in the economic perspective as a system for altering incentives and thus regulating behavior, must also be public. If the content of a law became known only after the events to which it was applicable occurred, the existence of the law could have no effect on the conduct of the parties subject to it. Stated otherwise, the economic theory of law is a theory of law as deterrence, and a threat that is not communicated cannot deter.

Finally, the economic theory of law presupposes machinery for ascertaining the existence of the facts necessary to the correct application of a law.

NOTES

1. Does Posner conceive of the law as consisting of doctrines and rules, often made not in accordance with a purposive design to achieve certain manifest goals, but rather intuitively shaped to attain the efficient allocation of economic resources? Posner adumbrates his "economic approach to law" by stating, "A very important, although for a time neglected, feature of [Ronald H.] Coase's article was its implications for the positive analysis of legal doctrine. Coase suggested the English law of nuisance had an implicit economic logic. Later writers have generalized this insight and argued that many of the doctrines and institutions of the legal system are best understood and explained as efforts to promote the efficient allocation of resources. This is, indeed, a major theme of the present book. (p. 17). . . . The reader indeed, may wonder whether it is plausible to attribute economic insight to common law judges, especially since litigants rarely couch their arguments in economic terms. . . ." (p. 180) Do you think economic efficiency is all the English law of nuisance has been about? Do you think the "efficient allocation of resources" is the key to understanding a legal system? Discuss.

2. Consider Posner's " . . . view of the common law as a system for promoting economic efficiency . . . " (p. 185). "(I)t may be possible to deduce the basic formal characteristics of law itself from economic theory" (1st edition, p. 393). Even assuming that economic theory can explain the various ways the many different elements of wealth have been treated by common law, what of the other values involved in decisionmaking, such as power, well-being, enlightenment, etc.?

3. Posner all but disregards the use for law studies of scholarly disciplines other than economics, e.g. sociology, psychology, anthropology, communications study, etc. In some cases, this leads to simplistic explanations. Consider his statement about laws dealing with

homosexuality. "The disapprobation of homosexuality may stem from an era in which there were considerable external benefits from population increase. These benefits may be much less today, or even negative. This may explain why conventional moral feelings about homosexuality are also changing—and why legal sanctions against homosexual conduct are eroding." (p. 186). Does this explanation strike you as cogent? Discuss.

4. Does Posner address the need for the systematic clarification and specification of goals on a level of abstraction lower than "economic efficiency" in the single value he examines? Does he consider it relevant to study past trends to see what has been accomplished in the past in a particular area or activity and why (or why not)? Is he concerned to devise alternative strategies to achieve postulated goals? Is the reason why Posner does not engage in these tasks to be found in his view of law as consisting of rules and doctrines, rather than a process of decision by which a community attempts to clarify and secure its common interest? Discuss.

5. Posner appears to lack a conception of the elements of authority and control (whether or not expressed in formal rules and doctrines) and the need for a balanced emphasis on operations and perspectives. What effect does that have on his descriptions and prescriptions?

6. Consider Posner's statement that, "The common law may be viewed as an effort to attach costs to the violation of moral principles—principles that we have suggested operate to enhance the efficiency of a market (as of most other types of) economy." . . . (p. 185) "The basic function of law, in an economic perspective, is to alter incentives." (p. 190). The latter thought has also been expressed by Arrow, whose work is considered in the following section. Is this an accurate statement of social goals, whether with regard to rectitude (morality) or the seven other values?

————

A more systematic effort to look at the larger problems of choice-making in law, which has influenced many lawyers, is to be found in the work of Kenneth Arrow, a leading economic theorist and recent Nobel Laureate.

Arrow, Social Choice and Individual Values
2–3, 22–23, 106–107 (2d ed. 1963)

It should be emphasized here that the present study is concerned only with the formal aspects of the . . . question . . . if it is formally possible to construct a procedure for passing from a set of known individual tastes to a pattern of social decision-making, the procedure in question being required to satisfy certain natural conditions. An illustration of the problem is the following well-known "paradox of voting." Suppose there is a community consisting of three voters, and this community must choose among three alternative modes of social action (e.g., disarmament, cold war, or hot war). It is expected that choices of this type have to be made repeatedly, but sometimes not all of the three alternatives will be available. In analogy with the usual utility analysis of the individual consumer under conditions of constant wants and variable price-income situations, rational behavior on the part of the community would mean that the community orders the three alternatives according to its collective preferences once for all, and then chooses in any given case that alternative among those actually available which stands highest on this list. A natural way of arriving at the collective preference scale would be to say that one alternative is preferred to another if a majority of the community prefer the first alternative to the second, i.e., would choose the first over the second if those were the only two alternatives. Let A, B, and C be the three alternatives, and 1, 2, and 3 the three individuals. Suppose individual 1 prefers A to B and B to C (and therefore A to C), individual 2 prefers B to C and C to A (and therefore B to A), and individual 3 prefers C to A and A to B (and therefore C to B). Then a majority prefer A to B, and a majority prefer

B to C. We may therefore say that the community prefers A to B and B to C. If the community is to be regarded as behaving rationally, we are forced to say that A is preferred to C. But in fact a majority of the community prefer C to A. So the method just outlined for passing from individual to collective tastes fails to satisfy the condition of rationality, as we ordinarily understand it. Can we find other methods of aggregating individual tastes which imply rational behavior on the part of the community and which will be satisfactory in other ways?

If we continue the traditional identification of rationality with maximization of some sort (to be discussed at greater length below), then the problem of achieving a social maximum derived from individual desires is precisely the problem which has been central to the field of welfare economics.

• • •

I will largely restate Professor Bergson's formulation of the problem of making welfare judgments in the terminology here adopted. The various arguments of his social welfare function are the components of what I have here termed the social state, so that essentially he is describing the process of assigning a numerical social utility to each social state, the aim of society then being described by saying that it seeks to maximize the social utility or social welfare subject to whatever technological or resource constraints are relevant or, put otherwise, that it chooses the social state yielding the highest possible social welfare within the environment. As with any type of behavior described by maximization, the measurability of social welfare need not be assumed; all that matters is the existence of a social ordering satisfying Axioms I and II. As before, all that is needed to define such an ordering is to know the relative ranking of each pair of alternatives.

The relative ranking of a fixed pair of alternative social states will vary, in general, with changes in the values of at least some individuals; to assume that the ranking does not change with the changes in individual values is to assume, with traditional social philosophy of the Platonic realist variety, that there exists an objective social good defined independently of individual desires. This social good, it was frequently held, could best be apprehended by the methods of philosophic inquiry. Such a philosophy could be and was used to justify government by the elite, secular or religious, although we shall see below that the connection is not a necessary one.

To the nominalist temperament of the modern period, the assumption of the existence of the social ideal in some Platonic realms of being was meaningless. The utilitarian philosophy of Jeremy Bentham and his followers sought instead to ground the social good on the good of individuals. The hedonist psychology associated with utilitarian philosophy was further used to imply that each individual's good was identical with his desires. Hence, the social good was in some sense to be a composite of the desires of individuals. A viewpoint of this type serves as a justification of both political democracy and laissez-faire economics or at least an economic system involving free choice of goods by consumers and of occupations by workers.

The hedonist psychology finds its expression here in the assumption that individual's behavior is expressed by individual ordering relations Ri. Utilitarian philosophy is expressed by saying that for each pair of social states the choice depends on the ordering relations of all individuals, i.e., depends on $R1, \ldots Rn$ where n is the number of individuals in the community. Put otherwise, the whole social ordering relation R is to be determined by the individual ordering relations for social states, $R1, \ldots ,Rn$. We do not exclude here the possibility that some or all of the choices between pairs of social states made by society might be independent of the preferences of certain particular individuals, just as a function of several variables might be independent of some of them.

DEFINITION 4: *By* a social welfare function *will be meant a process or rule which, for each set of individual orderings R1, . . . Rn for alternative social states (one ordering for each individual), states a corresponding social ordering of alternative social states, R.*

As a matter of notation, we will let *R* be the social ordering corresponding to the set of individual orderings *R1, . . . , Rn*, the correspondence being that established by a given social welfare function; if primes or seconds are added to the symbols for the individual orderings, primes or seconds will be added to the symbol for the corresponding social ordering.

•   •   •

2. THE SOCIAL DECISION PROCESS

Little has argued cogently that a rule for social decision-making is not the same as a welfare judgment. A welfare judgement requires that some one person is judge; a rule for arriving at social decisions may be agreed upon for reasons of convenience and necessity without its outcomes being treated as evaluations by anyone in particular.

This distinction is well taken. I would consider that it is indeed a social decison process with which I am concerned and, not strictly speaking, a welfare judgment by any individual. That said, however, I am bound to add that in my view a social decision process serves as a proper explication for the intuitive idea of social welfare. The classical problems of formulating the social good are indeed of the metaphysical variety which modern positivism finds meaningless; but the underlying issue is real. My own viewpoint towards this and other ethical problems coincides with that expressed by Popper: "Not a few doctrines which are metaphysical, and thus certainly philosophical, can be interpreted as hypostatizations of methodological rules." All the writers from Bergson on agree on avoiding the notion of a social good not defined in terms of the values of individuals. But where Bergson seeks to locate social values in welfare judgments by individuals, I prefer to locate them in the actions taken by society through its rules for making social decisions. This position is a natural extension of the ordinalist view of values; just as it identifies values and choices for the individual, so I regard social values as meaning nothing more than social choices.

In fact, the Bergson formulation cannot be kept distinct from the interpretation of social welfare in terms of social decisions processes. In the first place, the argument of paragraph 1 shows that the Bergson social welfare function is necessarily a constitution, that is, a potential social decision process; the body of welfare judgments made by a single individual are determined, in effect, by the social decision process which the individual would have society adopt if he could. In the second place, the location of welfare judgments in any individual, while logically possible, does not appear to be very interesting. "Social welfare" is related to social policy in any sensible interpretation; the welfare judgments formed by any single individuals are unconnected with action and therefore sterile. Bergson recognizes the possible difficulty in his 1954 paper: I quote the passage at length since it displays the issue so well.

"I have been assuming that the concern of welfare economics is to counsel individual citizens generally. If a public official is counseled, it is on the same basis as any other citizen. In every instance reference is made to some ethical values which are appropriate for the counseling of the individual in question. In all this I believe I am only expressing the intent of welfare writings generally; or if this is not the intent, I think it should be. But some may be inclined nevertheless to a different conception, which allows still another interpretation of Arrow's theorem. *Accordig to this view the problem is to counsel not citizens generally but public officials* [emphasis added]. Furthermore, the values to be taken as data are not those which might guide the official if he were a private citizen. The official is envisaged instead as more or less neutral ethically. His one aim in life is to implement the values of other citizens as given by some rule of collective decision-making. Arrow's theorem apparently contributes to this sort of welfare economics the negative finding that no consistent social ordering could be found to serve as a criterion of social welfare in the counseling of the official in question.''

NOTES

1. Kenneth Arrow operates with a basic conception: ''The social choice from any given environment is an aggregation of individual preferences'' (p. 103) or '' . . . the aggregation of individual choices into collective ones . . . '' (p. 93). These statements raise a number of questions:

a. Do these statements approximate goal clarification as we have been considering it? Goal clarifications; as we have seen, requires the systematic and disciplined consideration of the basic goals and policies (i) for which the constitutive process, that process concerned with the establishment and maintenance of fundamental power institutions in a community, would operate and (ii) for the basic structure of the public order, including all other value processes concerned with the production and distribution of specific values. Goal clarification necessarily requires a very comprehensive and systematic approach which must be animated by a conception of those common interests likely to contribute to the realization of the aspirations of all members of the community. In considering writers such as Arrow and Posner, assess the extent to which they do address these questions.

b. Arrow is concerned with the choices or preferences made separately by each individual, including those made on impulse or without thought. Contrast that conception with purposive and explicit goal postulation on behalf of the community concerning basic values, in conjunction with examining trends of past decisions, the conditions which shaped them, present and projected conditions which might inhibit or facilitate action to achieve desired goals and formulation of alternative strategies to attain goals. Do individuals who express their preferences in a host of often small, separate actions under widely varying conditions and pressures and diverse time frames, explore goals deliberately? Do they profess their preferred method of achieving such goals?

c. Do Bentham, Posner, Arrow *et al* assume that what individuals want is *per se* good, in other words, what *is,* is *good?* Do they, thus, deal with ''is'' or ''ought''? Is the ascertainment of preferences made by each individual for his own selfish benefit to be equated with the postulation of goals for the overall benefit of an interdependent society or of all individuals? (Some account of this latter point has been taken by Bergson and Pareto). Discuss.

d. Indeed, does Professor Arrow really engage in goal clarification? Surely there is a great difference between adding up the sum total of human choices in one limited sector—let us say a department store—and determining the appropriate goals for a longer-term, far more encompassing constitutive process and public order system. Is part of the attraction of a work such as Professor Arrow's to be found in its legitimization of a method of non-decisionmaking, its celebration of the operation of the "free market," and the careful evasion of fundamental problems of making choices about the structure and objectives of the polity, which necessarily excite great disagreement? We will take this matter up below. Consider in this regard the parallels between Arrow and writers in the structural naturalist frame, supra.

It is worth emphasizing that goal clarification as used by policy scientists is more than spasmodic and impulsive choices made by human beings acting alone or in aggregate to meet immediate demands. The fact that a large number of people seem to prefer video games to investing money in schools does not mean that the rise of stocks in video game corporations is indicative of a public policy choice in favor of those over education. Goal clarification does not take place unless there has been an explicit examination of longer-term interests and longer-term consequences tested against a variety of goals. In this respect, does the use of the word "market" and the short-term choice resorted to by writers such as Arrow obscure the necessity for goal clarification? One justification for this is that it is supposedly most expressive of genuine democracy. Discuss.

2. A second question arising from the quotations in 1. above, concerns the comprehensiveness of goal clarification as expressed there. In the first and second chapters supra and in the Appendix to Chapter 1, we pointed out that persons concerned with either description or intervention in contemporary social process must identify a range of institutions specialized to producing different things. We adopted Lasswell's eight-value spectrum, in which he examines the things that people want, their activities in pursuit of those objectives and the institutionalized arrangements for producing and distributing them in terms of eight categories: power, wealth, enlightenment, skill, well-being, affection, respect and rectitude. Lasswell, in other work, pointed out that both goal clarification and description of what is happening in any setting must look at the full range of these value institutions. In goal clarification, in particular, it is important to examine the aspirations of human beings not simply for wealth but for power, health, affection, respect, opportunity and so on. Micro-economic analysis tends to look only at wealth. Does this address the issue of goal clarification? Consider one value, affection. Can one determine, for example, in purely economic terms the appropriate social goals for the shaping and sharing of affection, including attitudes toward premarital sexual relations, extramarital sexual relations, the easy termination of marital unions, the practice of homosexuality among adults, and sexual relations between adults and minors and so on?

3. Individual personal freedom is apparently an overriding issue with Posner, Arrow et al, and it becomes the fulcrum of their analyses. But by ignoring the actual distribution of power and wealth and the differential distribution of access to the market, for whom does it achieve those objectives in a meaningful and not a taunting way? Recall *Lochner v. New York*, supra, which held a statute that limited the long hours of bakery employees to be unconstitutional because it violated their constitutionaly guaranteed "freedom" to contract to work for long hours? Shall we abrogate child labor laws for comparable reasons? Discuss.

4. In general, when writers such as Arrow state they are concerned with optimalizing personal freedom, which they take to be the ability of human beings to make choices in a market place, that market place is taken as a given. But the market place is not natural, but is an ongoing human creation. It is a very complex and delicate socio-political artifact, created and maintained by official and un-official elites. It is only within this artifact that the choice-making that Arrow and others talk about is possible. Yet, goal clarification must address the fundamental structure of choice-making. It is this constitutive dimension, in this case the establishment and maintenance of the market (and, perhaps seven other value situations as Lasswell would contend) over time, that should be part of its central focus. In the United States, for example, we cannot imagine the market without official maintenance of a currency, a complex process that (i) assigns and changes the value of that currency over time and, in doing so, changes patterns of employment and employment-opportunity for millions, (ii)

maintains through a variety of incentives and subsidies, a banking system and a set of financial institutions, (iii) maintains an infra-structure for the movement of goods and services about the country and (iv) over time, through an ensemble of political and legal instruments, tries to ensure a degree of stability that favors the production and distribution of certain items and discourages production and distribution of others. All of these constitutive decisions establish, maintain and change the market place within which the individual appears to be making his "free" choice. Goal clarification in a systematic policy-oriented approach is concerned with the establishement, maintenance over time, change and appraisal in terms of fundamental goals of this larger constitutive process.

5. Arrow's conception imports an inherent, structural democracy. Does it invite inquiry into the possible dominance of some individuals or groups, thanks to their control of power or some other value, to make choices which are effectively imposed on others? Discuss.

Consider the problem of unrecorded amplification of power in the market, Arrow's sole prism for determining people's choices. The application of principles of economic analysis to the power process licenses those endowed with power or with wealth to amplify their power and increase their choice-making potential as against a variety of others. Fundamental to the ideal of popular democracy, developed in the past two centuries, has been the effort to restrain and temper the operation of wealth in the power arena by establishing a single vote for a single person. Does Arrow's approach, using economics in the power arena, achieve this?

6. Arrow has concluded that there is no satisfactory general method for decisionmaking in a society very rich in possibilities and preferences. (See his Values and Collective Decison Making, in *Philosophy, Politics, and Society* 25 (P. Laslett & W. Runcimen eds. 1967). Perhaps we have here a clue as to why a non-method was chosen. Professor Arrow has developed a notion of goals which is little more than the sum total of the wishes expressed and recorded by human beings in a particular social sector. Arrow chooses the market place, a highly institutionalized part of the wealth process, access to which is based upon having a certain amount of money, and in which desires are expressed by choosing or rejecting those limited number of items available in the particular sector of the market. But this method, while obviating some problems, creates others. The conception of goal clarification tends to validate the basic system found in the United States, but from a more disengaged perspective, does it approximate an adequate process of goal clarification?

Consider the market place in social context.* If we deal with a population of 10,000 people, 6,000, let us say, will have the entry ticket—adequate money—to participate in the market place and express their choices there. Four thousand others may not have adequate money and as a result their choices cannot be recorded. Moreover, even many of the participants within the market place will be expressing other critical choices in non-market settings: the family, friendship units, the church or synagogue, the power process and so on. The problem with choosing a limited and restricted social sector, access to which requires a certain accumulation of values neither democratically nor equally shared is twofold: it reflects only the choices of those who have the wherewithal to enter and it distorts actual terms of the portions made available to them by the market place.

7. Even Adam Smith was unwilling to extend the principles of the invisible hand and the market place to the fundamental structures of government. He was sensitive to its limitations and aware of the need for a process capable of the more explicit projection of common interest. Only von Jhering, whom we considered earlier, (p. 236), was willing to extend the market place to the power arena; his work, you will recall, was little more than a paean to the operation of naked power. While Arrow does not address this issue directly, does his fundamental approach put him close to von Jhering?

8. Even when micro-economics purports to look at other value sectors, it is obliged to translate values sought there into the language of mathematics. This is done often by assigning

---

*The term "market" is often used to refer to the aggregate of wealth transactions, but in fact treats only certain measurable exchanges. Hence it ignores exchanges taking place above or below it. See, in this regard, F. Braudel, *The Structures of Everyday Life: Civilization and Capitalism 15th–18th Century* 27–29 (Eng. Trans. 1981).

numerical valences that have not been expressed either socially or in scholarly fashion in
numerical value, so that the single mensurative technique used in micro-economic analysis
can be brought to bear. The assignment is frequently arbitrary, assuming, in particular, a
homogenous community; once accomplished, its arbitrary origin is then ignored. The result
is that intricate "number-crunching" may be performed on a set of quantifications that may
have no relation whatsoever to the valence human beings attribute to them. Is this fascination
with method and concern with refinement in its use, of any utility to the clarification and
implementation of policy?

"MUDDLING THROUGH" AS POLICY METHOD

Critics of the policy sciences approach frequently cite the additional costs required
for gathering, processing, retrieving and using data about the self or the environment
for policy choices. In the work by Braybrooke and Lindblom considered below, this
becomes a major justification for their preference for "muddling through."

BRAYBROOKE & LINDBLOM,
A STRATEGY OF DECISION, POLICY EVALUATION AS A
SOCIAL PROCESS 38–48, 50–51, 54–56 (1963)

[The authors characterize as "synoptic"] the following procedures for an ideal
analytical process: (1) The policy-maker should pursue an agreed-upon set of values. . . ; (2) the aims of policy should be clearly formulated in advance of choosing
among alternative policies. . . ; (3) the policy-maker should attempt a comprehensive
overview of policy problems and of alternative policies. . . ; (4) co-ordination of
policy should be made the explicit function of the policy maker. . . ; (5) economists
as policy analysts should be comprehensive in considering economic variables and
values. . . . Such a conception of ideal policy analysis is not unusual; its prescriptions
are so "obvious" as to be the first things that come to anyone's mind.

This conception appeals not only to economists like Tinbergen. Writing about
problem solving in public administration, Marshall Dimock endorses fundamentally
the same ideal method:

> First, there are always the problem and the issues. Second, there are the facts
> and analyses that need to be applied to the issues. Third, there is the setting
> forth of alternatives and the pros and cons applicable to each possible solu-
> tion—all this in the light of larger institutional goals and objectives. Fourth,
> there is the decision proper, which depends upon choosing among alterna-
> tives. . . .

If Tinbergen and Dimock differ in emphasis and even on some particular points,
they nevertheless appear to be endorsing processes that are fundamentally alike. Both
call for a systematic canvassing of possible alternative policies, for a similarly systematic analysis of the consequences of each possible alternative possibility, and for
policy choices to serve goals or objectives somehow separately established.

• • •

Comprehensiveness is often seen as logically necessary for rational choice; in
fact, rational choice comes close to being defined as a choice that, *inter alia,* responds
to a comprehensive consideration of all relevant variables. Herbert A. Simon has
written, "Rational choice will be feasible to the extent that the limited set of factors

upon which decision is based corresponds, in nature, to a closed system of varia- bles—that is, to the extent that significant indirect effects are absent.''

It is generally conceded, of course, that such comprehensiveness is an ideal rather than an achievement. This qualification is sometimes partly recognized in models of problem solving, as, for example, when it is specified that not all alternative policies but only all important alternative policies are to be canvassed. Similarly, the impossibility of achieving a completely full account of the consequences of each alternative policy under analysis is sometimes conceded. Still, the ideal remains, and the policy analyst is still told: Be comprehensive!

As for separation of fact and value, although everyone recognizes that in problem solving the choice of subjectives is in fact influenced to some degree by the choice of means, we have seen, especially in Tinbergen's statement, an insistence that as an ideal the specification of objectives precedes the final choice of means. To solve a problem, it is generally believed, its conditions must be finally fixed. Hence even if for a time fact suggests value and vice versa, at some point values must be fixed so that choice can then be made.

• • •

Note further that under this conception of problem solving, ideal policy-making, rational decision-making, policy analysis, and rational problem solving are synony- mous. The ideal way to make policy is to choose among alternatives after careful and complete study of all possible courses of action and all their possible consequences in the light of one's values. That is to say, ideally one treats the policy question as an intellectual problem; one does not look upon a policy question as calling for the exercise of something called ''political'' forces. Although it would be a mistake to identify policy-making, policy analysis and decision-making in every case with prob- lem solving, it is nevertheless conventional to equate them in their ideal forms.

In this study, we shall call this method of problem solving ''synoptic,'' for the sake of convenience, although it has generally borne no specific name, being accepted almost everywhere not merely as one of several types of rational decision-making but as *one* process of rational decision-making. This acceptance is not surprising, for almost everyone takes it for granted that one cannot be rational about a problem without understanding it, and, as we observed, understanding requires comprehen- siveness of information and analysis. Similarly, one cannot be rational without first knowing what one wants and proceeding from there to a systematic examination of alternative means of attaining these wants. Moreover, this method of decision-making is consistent with scientific canons, including the prescription that purely scientific analysis must be kept free from contamination by ethical components of the problem- solving process. In every respect, what we call ''synoptic analysis'' appears to correspond to good sense, fundamental notions of rationality, and scientific proce- dure.

• • •

J. S. Brunner, J. J. Goodnow, and G. A. Austin report an experiment in problem solving that throws light on the presumed virtues of the synoptic method as an ideal. The experimenter tells the subject that, with respect to a specially printed deck of cards, he (the experimenter) has in mind a subset whose characteristics he would like the subject to discover. For example, the subset might be all the red cards, all the cards with borders, or all the black cards with borders. All the cards in the deck are displayed simultaneously to the subject, and the subject is permitted to select single cards in any order he wishes and to ask wheether or not they are members of the subset.

In their report, Bruner, Goodnow, and Austin identify four possible strategies chosen by the subjects for solving the problem:

1. *Simultaneous scanning*. The subject attempts to develop all possible hypotheses identifying the subset, to keep in mind as he proceeds just which hypotheses have been validated and which remain, and to estimate which of all possible requests for information about a particular card would test a maximum number of remaining hypotheses. In the language of this chapter, the experimenter is synoptic in his attempt to be comprehensive and systematic.

2. *Successive scanning*. The subject tests a series of hypotheses one at a time by asking his question each time about a card that bears on the one hypothesis then under test. Inevitably, the subject will finally identify the subset, but he may be a long time in doing so. In the language of this chapter, he is synoptic in the exhaustiveness with which he examines "the pros and cons of each alternative possibility."

3. *Conservative focusing*. The subject finds a positive instance, a card to which the experimenter responds affirmatively; he then makes a sequence of choices each of which alters only one attribute of the first positive instance to see whether the change yields a second instance or not. It will be noticed that this strategy focuses exclusively on the kind of increment or margin of difference that . . . rational-deductive method and the method of the welfare function do not facilitate. This is a nonsynoptic strategy in its incremental, noncomprehensive features.

4. *Focus gambling*. This strategy is like number three except that the subject takes risks by altering more than one attribute at a time. Although risky, it is worth attempting if time is short. It too, in our language, is nonsynoptic.

The experimenters report that scanning imposes a great cognitive strain and that simultaneous scanning imposes so great a strain that it is not feasible. It requires the subject to grasp and calculate beyond his capacities. In focusing, they report, subjects achieve great cognitive economy. The results are that scanners' performance degenerate under conditions of increasing difficulty while focusers show little or no change. These conclusions hold for such changes in conditions as shortening the time allowed, increasing the number of alternatives, and reducing redundancy.

Thus, at least under the circumstances of this experiment, it is not true that the best way to solve a problem is to be comprehensive; and, at least in some circumstances—when time is short, for example—it may be best to trust to a degree to luck. The experiment also suggests not only that scanning is less successful than focusing but also that it is not a serviceable ideal—one would not advise a subject who wished to improve his performance to push scanning to the maximum. The experiment therefore challenges synopsis as an ideal.

The results are not at all surprising. Despite the prestige of the synoptic method as an ideal, all of us have long known that, in a number of respects, the ideal is vulnerable. It is well known, for example, that the mind flees from comprehensiveness, that an "object of perception, or judgment, is referred, not to the whole world, but to a specific background or framework." Fully developed, such a proposition leads to the position that our minds do more than merely throw out what is unaffected by their activity and irrelevant to present difficulties—if that were all, there would be no challenge to the synoptic ideal. Rather, our minds determine what is relevant and irrelevant, by imposing a structure upon the problem situation. This structure tends to vary from mind to mind; and though it is true that on occasion people can

be brought to adopt similar structures, it usually occurs at the expense of comprehensiveness and may mean that the most useful insights are abandoned together with
the structures of assumption and interpretation that furnished them.

In a study of research on agricultural problems, Charles M. Hardin documents
the fact—hardly unfamiliar—that different research groups have quite different insights and that this phenomenon is not merely an occasional intellectual aberration
but is both desirable and in many ways inevitable. . .

It may be contended that the use of frames of reference, preliminary structuring,
habitual modes—whatever they are called—does not seriously challenge the synoptic
ideal. Everyone knows, it may be said, that we all have to organize our minds;
organization means selection, and selection means noncomprehensiveness. The comprehensiveness called for in the synoptic ideal, it may be added, means comprehensiveness only within such an intellectual organization as every man must achieve.
It is not a foolish call for omniscience.

To this argument, we reply that it is either a foolish call or a very uncertain one.
If the synoptic ideal does not call for omniscience, what degree of comprehensivenss
does it call for? . . .

There are other strands of antisynoptic thought. In an amusing example, Michael
Polanyi calls attention to the difference between specification of a problem-solving
strategy, on the one hand, and of a solved problem, on the other. To ride a bicycle,
he says it is necessary at any given angle of unbalance for the rider to give a turn
to the front wheel that is by some measure inversely proportional to the square of
the speed at which he is proceeding. If this method specifies a solution for the cyclist,
would anyone try to ride by making these calculations? At its best, the synoptic
method is roughly analogous to riding by Polanyi's formula. It states conditions
whose attainment would imply that a solution was at hand, but it gives no clue as
to how people actually deal with problems. What is worse, those who advocate the
ideal have not often drawn even Polanyi's distinction.

• • •

Karl Popper sounds still another antisynoptic note. Many of his objections to
large-scale social reform or as he calls it, utopian engineering, constitute criticisms
of the synoptic method, which utopian reformers implicitly assume to be both necessary and possible. He stresses the limitations both of man's intellectual capacities
and of his available knowledge and argues that both preclude comprehensiveness in
analysis. Similarly, he argues that the close interplay between fact and value precludes
the separation of factual and evaluative parts of analysis to the degree required in
utopian reform. Above all, he insists that a decision-making system must be adapted
to the experimental nature of social reforms, in which ends are as much adjusted to
means, through reappraisal of objectives in the light of success or failure with policies,
as means are to ends.

. . . On still another track, Richard C. Snyder and Glenn D. Paige, on the basis
of an intensive study of the American decision to fight in Korea, suggest that analysis
should ideally sometimes revolve around single policy alternatives to the exclusion
of others. . . .

> . . . One possible consequence of the single alternative process may
> be . . . to provide a way of *simplifying a situation to the point where action
> is possible,* thus avoiding the complexities of estimate involved in discussing
> multiple alternatives.

It would be a mistake to dismiss Snyder and Paige's suggestion as a make-shift method suitable only for emergencies, when a single possible alternative may be a better focus than multiple alternatives because time is short. In public policy-making, time is never a free good; it is always short to some degree. Ideals, as well as practices, need to be adapted to that fact.

For a last illustrative dissent from the synoptic ideal, Martin Meyerson and Edward C. Banfield make a persuasive case against thoroughgoing examination of the problem situation, of alternative courses of action, and of consequences in their case study of policy-making with respect to the location of public housing in Chicago. Of the Chicago Housing Authority, they write,

> As the case study shows, the Authority made little use of social science or of any technical knowledge regarding social phenomena. . . . No one, for example, had precise or systematic knowledge of the ends that people entertained regarding public housing. . . . It might be that the clearance of slums in one place created new slums or worsened old ones somewhere else. No one knew. . . .
> To have assembled a useful amount of information on even these few matters would have required a large staff of highly trained researchers . . . more of a staff certainly than it would be reasonable to expect the Authority to employ.

In short, information is extremely costly and is not always worth its cost. Hence, comprehensive analysis is not always worth its cost.

Nor can this fundamental, if obvious, criticism of the synoptic system be dismissed on the ground that, costs aside, one should still aspire to comprehensiveness as an ideal. One should never ever be "as comprehensive as possible," whatever that means. For in fact one cannot now or in any calculable future put costs aside; the costliness of analysis is a fundamental fact that all analytical strategies should face up to. What Meyerson and Banfield's point suggests is that we need an analytical strategy of decision making method that would give some guidance as to what steps to take in the light of the costliness of the analysis, whether in terms of the analyst's own time and energy or in terms of a research budget.

• • •

These dissents from one or another point of the synoptic ideal are no less persuasive than the outline of the ideal itself. What is to be inferred from the conflict between the two? Simply that one should try to realize the ideal as fully as possible? The dissents suggest very strongly that analysts do in fact find alternative strategies that can sometimes be exploited with great skill. Thus, in the experiment with the cards, the subjects adapted to unreasonable demands on their cognitive faculties by "focusing" rather than "scanning." Simon's "satisficing" model is another adaptation to limited cognitive faculties and costliness of search, just as Popper's now familiar "piecemeal engineering" is an adaptation to the discrepancy between the complexity of the problem and the capacity of the human mind.

The key concept here is adaptation, adaptation of the problem-solving method to certain troublesome characteristics of problems and problem-solving situations. A decision-making method is adapted to a specified difficulty in decision-making only if it contains some prescriptions that give specific guidance in overcoming such difficulty. And the conclusion that we urge at this stage of the argument is that the synoptic ideal, like the rational deductive and welfare function methods, is distinguished by its failure to incorporate adaptive features. To expose the poverty of this ideal more fully with respect to adaptive features, we can summarize the dissenting notes in the form of a list of failures of adaptation, at the same time extending the list to identify still other failures.

In all these failures of adaptation, the snyoptic ideal displays the same confusion between conceivability and practicability, or between operability in principle and operability in practice, that we found in the rational-deductive method and the method of the social welfare function. The following propositions can be read as applicable both to the synoptic methods taken as a whole and to the two evaluative methods considered by themselves. . . .

1. The synoptic ideal is not adapted to man's limited problem-solving capacities.

• • •

2. The synoptic ideal is not adapted to inadequacy of information.
3. The synoptic ideal is not adopted to the costliness of analysis.

• • •

4. The synoptic ideal is not adapted to failures in constructing a satisfactory evaluative method (whether a rational deductive system, a welfare function, or some other).

[After three other criticisms, the authors conclude]

8. The synoptic ideal is not adapted to the diverse forms in which policy problems actually arise.

• • •

Public policy problems like inflation, unemployment, social security, reform of the judiciary, relief of urban congestion, and segregation are single "synthetic" problems each of which encompasses a host of disparate but interlocked individual and group problems. We might add that they quickly lose their synthetic character in practice; once formulated, they become deeply felt problems to those individuals and groups whose own important goals include reconciliation and a wide sharing of satisfactions in society. To these people (the group includes many policy analysts) these problems are no less real than the sub-problems out of which they were constructed.

The consequence of focusing on a synthetic problem is that the problem is no longer a simple situation in which goal achievement is thwarted but an extremely complex adjustment-of-interests situation. This fact is familiar, but its implications are not always perceived. Problem solving becomes a more continuous process than is ordinarily thought. Whether or not a possible reconciliationn today is satisfactory will depend not solely on the characteristic of today's problem but also on what yesterday's pattern of reconciliation was and what tomorrow's might be.

• • •

On the other hand, however, a continuous attack on a synthetic problem also creates new difficulties in analysis. A problem of reconciliation of interests is not a stable, well-formed problem that retains its outlines so firmly that "all consequences of all alternatives" can be investigated. The public policy problem, is highly fluid. The synoptic ideal, as we have already seen, is even less well adapted to this fluid problem than to a static one.

NOTES

1. Obviously a principle of economy applies to the use of any tool. The tool is used only insofar as it contributes to the achievement of goals; the consideration of parsimony—how much should be invested in either using or refining the use of a tool—must be addressed with

respect to its deployment in any matter. But allowing this point, does it mean that all decisions should be made spontaneously, intuitively or by "seat of the pants" or "gut reaction"? Many critics (perhaps even Braybrooke and Lindblom, despite explicit disavowal) of complex decision schemes tend to assume that problems are simple. Some are: should I, as a young and impecunious lawyer, buy a brown suit or a blue suit? Psychologists tell me that the color brown is much more reassuring. I could wear the suit in addressing juries and stroking the delicate egos of clients. On the other hand, blue is a decisive "leadershp" color. A blue suit would be useful for bar association functions, lectures and for social purposes. Plainly a choice such as this is not worth the installation and operation of an entire policy science method. But are the major choices with which our profession and decisionmakers in complex civilizations are concerned on the order of a blue or a brown suit?

2. As for the more complex decision, Braybrooke and Lindblom, like many others who have criticized what they call the synoptic method, overlook the fact that decisionmaking is an ongoing process and that decisions of concern to the policy scientist are complex social choices which have to be made over a period of years, in some cases decades! What appears to be unmanageably complex in an hour is manageable in a week, a month, a year. What is unmanageable for a single person is manageable with a staff, especially one with computer resources. As for the appearance of unexpected variables, obviously, decisions must be constantly made, re-evaluated and re-made to take them into account. For such decisions, vast staffs are established to gather and process information and bring it to the attention of decisionmaking teams which then incorporate it in their reasoning. Ongoing assessments of changes in the environment are constantly made and are themselves incorporated in future choice-making. For choices such as these, the establishment of large teams and complex computer systems of data—for processing, storage and retrieval—make economic sense.

THE NEW HAVEN SCHOOL AS POLICY SCIENCE

In an article synthesizing their approach, Professors Myres S. McDougal and Harold D. Lasswell set out the basic elements of a policy-oriented jurisprudence.

LASSWELL & McDOUGAL, CRITERIA FOR A THEORY ABOUT LAW, 44 S. CAL. L. REV. 362, 374–394 (1971)

The inference we draw from our examination of past theories about law is, that a jurisprudence which would serve the purposes of a free society must seek both a more comprehensive and a more penetrating frame of references, after the aspiration of the most advanced modern theories in other fields of inquiry about social process. The formidable challenge to legal scholars today is, in the language much abused by repetition, to create a jurisprudence which is "relevant": such a jurisprudence will find authority, not in theological or metaphysical or autonomous abstractions, but rather, in a conception known since at least six centuries before Christ, in the perspectives of living community members—their demands for values, their identifications with others, and their expectations about the requirements of decision for securing their demanded values in all their communities—and it will provide, and apply, theory and procedures appropriate to implementing this conception of authority. From this man-centered, universalist and equalitarian perspective, the challenge is not merely to seek to resolve issues connected with law by "definition," but rather to relate authoritative decision to preferred public order. Though definitions are a part of life, by themselves they tell us nothing about life. Properly managed definitions are tools of discovery, since they guide attention to the social process itself where human beings are perpetually engaged in the never-ending transactions by which values are shaped and shared. Legal institutions, which are a part of the process of value shaping and sharing, must be appraised according to the contributions which they make to value outcomes and institutions. In any community, the legal system is but a part of a more inclusive system, the system of public order, which includes a preferred pattern for the distribution of values and a preferred pattern of basic institutions. The appropriate scope of inquiry into any legal system is, therefore, to appraise its significance for the system of public order which it expected to protect and fulfill. A relevant jurisprudence will define the full breadth and depth of this undertaking and identify the methods by which the pertinent tasks can be performed. In the aggregate, a legal system is to be appraised in terms of the values to be maximized in the total context of public order. The overall task of inquiry is, hence, to assess the degree of success or failure of the system, to account for the factors that condition these results, and to clarify the goals and the policy alternatives available in the emerging future. The indispensable function of a relevant jurisprudence must be to assist this inquiry by delimiting an economic frame of reference for studying the interrelations of law and social process and by specifying in detail the intellectual tasks by which such study can be made and applied to the solution of the exigent problems it reveals. A jurisprudence which would effectively serve the needs of both scholars and specialists in decision, and indeed of all who would understand and affect the social processes in which they live, must, accordingly, be comprised of a systematic, flexible, and configurative approach, exhibiting at least four major emphases:

> 1. It must achieve clarity in distinguishing the observational standpoints of the scholar and decision-maker, and in aid of enlightenment, as well as of decision, develop a theory *about* law, and not merely *of* law.
>
> 2. It must establish a focus of attention both comprehensive and selective, effectively relating authoritative decision to the larger social and community processes by which it is affected and which it in turn affects.
>
> 3. It must identify the whole range of intellectual tasks relevant to problem-solving about the interrelations of law and social process, and it must specify economic and effective procedures for the performance of each of these tasks.
>
> 4. It must make explicit, in all necessary degrees of abstraction and precision, the values which are postulated, or assumed, to be at stake in decision and inquiry.

Clarity about observational standpoint is important because the objectives of the scholar and those of the authoritative decision-maker, the professional advocate, the effective power holder, and the community member may be very different. The primary concern of the scholar must be, as we have indicated, for *enlightenment* about the aggregate interrelationships of authoritative decision and other aspects of community process, while the authoritative decision-maker and others may be more interested in *power*, in the making of effective choices in conformity with demanded public order. If the scholarly observer does not adopt perspectives different from those either of the community member making claims or of the authoritative decision-maker who responds to such claims, he can have no criteria for appraising the rationality in terms of community interest of either claims or decision. Hence, what the scholarly observer requires is a theory *about* law, designed to facilitate performance of the pertinent tasks in inquiry about decision, as distinguished from the theories *of* law which are employed by decision-makers and others for obtaining and justifying outcomes within the decision process and are, thus, among the variables about which the scholar seeks enlightenment. Good theory about law may of course on occasion be found useful by decision-makers and, hence, also become in the course of time a part of theories of law; similarly, good theories of law may sometimes be sufficiently precise and relevant to serve particular purposes of the scholar in his more comprehensive inquiry. Yet it can only compound confusion if the very different observational standpoints and purposes attending the use of the same or comparable signs are not kept in mind.

The comprehensiveness and realism with which an observer conceives his major focus of attention—what he regards as law and how he locates it in its larger community context—are important because they determine how he conceives every detailed part of his study: his framing of problems, his choice of tools and procedures, and his recommendation of alternatives. When inquiry is focused only upon rules of law—perspectives—to the exclusion of actual choices or practices—operations—there can be no assurance that it will have any relevance to what is actually happening in a community. When considerations of authority are overemphasized, with relative neglect of control or effective power, the outcomes of inquiry may have little bearing upon the future course of law and public order; similarly, when naked power is overemphasized at the expense of authority, inquiry may not be appropriately creative. When law is conceived only as rules applied by courts or other agencies, there may be disastrous neglect of how rules are made, as well as of other important aspects of the comprehensive process of authoritative decision. When law is regarded as something mystical or autonomous and distinct from community policy, no inquiry is admitted, or tools afforded, for relating decisions to the events in social process to which they are a response and, in turn, affect. When neat distinctions are made between the characteristics of national and international law, and national law is regarded as isolated from the larger world about it, it becomes impossible either to account for many important factors which affect decision or rationally to clarify policies for the various interpenetrating communities which in fact embrace the activities of man. A relevant jurisprudence must, in sum, seek a comprehensiveness and realism in focus which will encourage both a systematic, configurative examination of all the significant variables affecting decision and the rational appraisal of the aggregate value consequences of alternatives in decision.

The appropriate specifications of a comprehensive set of intellectual tasks, or skills, is important because it is the range of tasks performed, as well as the quality of performance, which determines the relevance of inquiry for policy. The most deliberate attempts to clarify general community policy which do not at the same time systematically pursue other tasks, such as the description of past trends in decision and the analysis of factors affecting decision, may achieve only Utopian exercises. The description of past trends in decision, which is not guided by policy priorities and explicitly related to social processes, affords a most meager basis for drawing upon the wisdom of the past. The scientific study of factors affecting decision, which is not oriented by reference to problems in basic community policy, may be of no more than incidental relevance, despite enormous cost. The effort to predict future trends in decision by the mere extrapolation of past trends, without considering whether the factors that affect decisions will remain the same, may produce destructive illusion rather than genuine forecast. In confusion about the character of, and appropriate procedures for, the different relevant intellectual tasks, the creativity in the invention and evaluation of policy alternatives, which is indispensable to rational decision, may be lost. For traditional exercises in derivational logic and the sterile pursuit of meaningless questions, a relevant jurisprudence will substitute the systematic and disciplined employment of a whole series of distinguishable but interrelated intellectual tasks.

The explicit postulation of a comprehensive set of goal values is important, finally, not merely for the promotion of a preferred public order, but also as affecting the economic performance of the various relevant intellectual tasks. It is seldom questioned today that authoritative decision, in both particular and aggregate, has important impacts upon the distribution of values in a community; conversely, it is equally common knowledge that perspectives about value distribution, entertained by both authoritative decision-makers and community members, are among the most significant variables affecting decision. The scholarly observer is, further, inextricably a part of community process; he, like other community members, is incurably affected by preferences about value distribution, and the enlightenment (or obscurantism) which he achieves in inquiry must have inescapable effects upon community process. Just as there can be no neutral or autonomous theories about law, in the sense of rules devoid of policy content, so also there can be no indifferent theories about law, in the sense of knowledge or ignorance, without policy consequences. In the context of these exigencies, it is the unique opportunity of observers specialized to inquiry about law not merely to relate law to its past policy content, but rather, and further, to clarify and promote the policies best designed to serve the particular kind of public order for which they are willing to commit themselves with their fellow community members. It is only by the deliberate clarification of, and explicit commitment to, basic community goals—at all levels of abstraction and from both short-term and long-term time perspectives—that dependable, creative, and economic guidance can be given to the examination of past trends, the allocation of effort to the assessment of factors affecting decision, and the evaluation of future possibilities and alternatives.

When jurisprudence is conceived in this recommended broad reach, it scarcely requires argument that everyone seriously concerned with inquiry about law—established official, effective decision-maker, advocate, community member, or scholarly observer—employs some kind of jurisprudence, however effective or ineffective and however consciously or unconsciously it may be held. Just as the human being tends to place any perception of the environment or of the self within a whole set of assumptions which give such perception meaning and significance, so also an observer of matters legal tends to locate these in a larger context of assumption about causes and consequences. Thus, the experienced lawyer may have a rich and varied body of expectations about the probable responses of different judges to different doctrines, styles of argument, and types of parties involved in controversies. He may predict that one judge is heavily disposed to side with the prosecutor, while another seems to regard the defendant in actions to which the government is party as a weak and tragic figure who stands alone. Whether these perspectives are true or false, they are part of a significant set of assumptions about legal processes which can be distinguished from the conventional language of legal doctrine. The more skilled the observer or practitioner the more comprehensive and explicit his assumptions about the larger context in which he operates are likely to be. One task of a relevant jurisprudence must of course be to bring all these vague assumptions—of varying degrees of comprehensiveness, consciousness, explicitness, and realism—to a clear focus of attention for rational evaluation and, perhaps, for renovation into more systematic and dependable knowledge.

• • •

For elaborating the goal criteria we recommend for a more relevant theory about law, it will be convenient to organize our discussion about the four major emphases indicated above:

1. The establishment of observational standpoint.
2. The delimitation of the focus of inquiry.
3. The performance of intellectual tasks.
4. The explicit postulation of public order goals.

The recommendations we make are addressed to all who are concerned to improve our theory about law, to increase our knowledge of the reciprocal impacts of legal and social process, and thereby to enhance the quality of both law and public order in all our communities.

A. THE ESTABLISHMENT OF OBSERVATIONAL STANDPOINT

The principal distinction which requires to be made is, as we have seen, that between the scholarly observer, whose primary concern is for enlightenment, and the authoritative decision-maker and others whose ultimate interest is in power, in the making of effective choices. It must of course be recognized that the scholar, the authoritative decisionmaker, the advocate or counsellor, and the interested community member may all require the same enlightenment and may all find it necessary to engage in the same or comparable intellectual tasks in the course of rational inquiry and rational decision. The enlightenment which the scholarly observer achieves and communicates must, further, have inevitable effects upon the intelligence and pro- motion functions of authoritative decision, and the scholarly may on occasion deli- berately assume active decision-making roles in the gathering of intelligence and promotion of policy. Yet it remains that for dependable, realistic, and effective inquiry and knowledge the scholar must distinguish himself and his purposes and procedures from the events which he has under observation, including the purposes and procedures of the participants in those events. It is of the utmost importance that the scholar create and maintain a *functional* theory which enables him realistically to perform the indispensable intellectual tasks in reference to the flow of authoritative decisions and the accompaniment of *conventional* theories employed to explain and justify decisions. If he permits the perspectives and communicative signs of the participants in legal and social process, which are a part of the data he is observing, to dominate his own perspectives and instruments of inquiry and communication, the consequences can only be intellectual confusion, distortion in perception and report, and loss of the enlightenment toward which his scholarly specialization is directed.

In emphasizing the importance of clarity in the scholar's perception of his unique standpoint and role, it is not our suggestion that he can, or should, completely isolate himself from participation in social and community process. On the contrary, it is our strong recommendation that the scholar should be as conscious as possible of the different communities with which he identifies, of which he is a member, and upon which he has unavoidable impacts. His most appropriate identifications are with the whole of the different communities, often concentric in their territorial reach and interprenetrating in their functional value processes, in which he participates, and the enlightenment he seeks should be that relevant to clarifying and implementing the common interests of all the members of these communities. It is the special role of the scholar—seeking to make appropriate discount for the biases of his cultural background, class and group memberships, personality formation, and previous experience—to assume a vantage point different from that either of the active community participants who make claims before processes of authoritative decision or of the authoritative decision-makers who respond to such claims, and from this vantage point to clarify and identify for the different participants in community process the common interests which they themselves may not have been able to perceive.

For discounting the biases conditioned by culture, class, interest, personality, and so on, and previous exposure to crisis, the contemporary scholar may, when necessary, take advantage of the broad knowledge and specialized procedures made available by modern psychological and behavioral science.

The establishment and maintenance of an appropriate scholarly standpoint does not necessarily require the development of some esoteric meta-language, employing words different from those ordinarily employed by lawyers and social scientists. What is required, however, is a set of words or system of signs, including more than words or word-substitutes, both sufficiently comprehensive and sufficiently precise, to make reference to all the significant features of the total context of legal and social process, and that these words or signs be employed in a functional, rather than conventional, sense. It is futile to hope, as so many scholars have hoped, that the confusions which so readily arise from multiple usage can be avoided by attempting to coin new terms as the exclusive idiom of jurisprudential theory. Systematic writers are part of society and as such are in more or less direct communication with practitioners who are concerned with the legal process of a local community or of the world community as a whole. Even systems of expression that contain many new words may succeed in making certain conceptions so articulate that these initial idiosyncracies are incorporated within written codes, opinions and briefs. In the process of dissemination these words are likely to become detached from the original definitions put forward by the systematizer. If confusions are to be kept at a minimum, the prophylaxis is neither the adoption of esoteric vocabularies nor timidity in introducing new terms in order to sharpen distinctions which are dimly perceived in ordinary usage. The appropriate strategy is to propagate intellectual skill in maintenance of observational standpoint and performance of relevant intellectual tasks. The pertinent skill enables a word-user to locate his position in the total context of communication, and deliberately to choose whether to employ particular terms in a sense that is conventional within a given legal system, or according to definitions that are chosen to perform the distinctive functions of jurisprudence. The well-instructed manipulator of language has intellectual tools enabling him to hold his vocabulary at arm's length and to select the label appropriate to the role which he has chosen to play. Hence the same label may be employed—quite deliberately—in several senses; and different labels may be attached to the same conceptual frame. These choices will depend upon a host of factors connected with the many forums in which the individual scholar finds himself participating.

B. THE DELIMITATION OF THE FOCUS OF INQUIRY

The most important criteria for delimiting the focus of inquiry are comprehensiveness and appropriate selectivity. The comprehensiveness and the realism in detail with which a focus is delimited affect both how particular problems are formulated and the dependability and economy with which the different relevant intellectual tasks can be brought to bear upon such problems. The broadest reach of an appropriately contextual, configurative jurisprudence must extend to the whole of the social and community processes in which authoritative decision is an interacting component; yet a viable theory must offer concepts and procedures which will facilitate a focus in whatever precision may be necessary upon particular decisions and particular flows of decisions.

The principal emphases of a focus of the required comprehensiveness and selectivity are not difficult to formulate. The central spotlight in such a focus will be empirically and explicitly upon *authoritative decision*. Decision will be observed as effective choice, composed of both perspectives and operations. Perspectives will be seen to include expectations about both authority and control, and inquiry will be made about both patterns of authority and patterns of control in fact. Law will be regarded not merely as rules or as isolated decision, but as a continuous *process* of authoritative decision, including both the constitutive and public order decisions by which a community's policies are made and remade. The processes of authoritative decision in any particular community will be seen to be an integral part, in an endless sequence of causes and effects, of the whole social process of that community. Every particular community will, finally, be observed to affect, and be affected by, a whole complex of parallel and concentric, interpenetrating communities, from local through regional to global.

If it be questioned whether a focus of this comprehensiveness is really necessary, some of the imperatives for effective performance of the different relevant intellectual tasks may be recalled. The clarification of community policies can scarcely proceed rationally without taking into account, in so far as economy permits, the *aggregate* consequences of alternative choices; small gains with respect to one value or in the short run may be offset by large losses with respect to another value or in the long run. The description of past trends in decision will not produce dependable knowledge if not made in terms of comparisons across boundaries and through time, in a context of causes and consequences; without an examination of the larger social and community context one cannot know, further, whether all relevant past experience has been observed. The effective performance of the scientific task of identifying significant environmental and predispositional variables must require, because of the interdependence of social and community processes, a map of the larger context of such processes. The forecast of future decisions, in whatever degree it can be made effective, is obviously dependent upon the prior effective performance of the descriptive and scientific tasks. The greater the range of alternatives considered in the management of social and decision processes, the greater of course the chances of creativity and success in the invention and evaluation of new alternatives in policy.

Each of the emphases specified for appropriate comprehensiveness and selectivity in focus may be briefly developed.

1. A BALANCED EMPHASIS UPON PERSPECTIVES AND OPERATIONS

Our recommended theory will, as indicated, characterize law as including both perspectives and operations, without exaggerated emphasis upon either technical rules of law (ambiguously assumed to describe perspectives) or bare physical operations (what decision-makers can be observed to do). A central focus will be sought explicitly upon *decision*, as including both perspectives (the subjectivities attending choice)

and operations (the choices actually made and enforced by threats of severe deprivations or promises of extreme indulgences). Inquiry will be directed in balanced
emphasis toward the patterns in subjectivities and operations, and the interrelations
of these patterns, which prevail in a continuous flow of decision.

By this emphasis the formal, manifest content of the perspectives expressed in
conventional rules of law may be pierced for detailed examination of the choices in
fact made through their invocation and application. Yet perspectives may still be
studied, perhaps even more realistically, as among the several factors importantly
affecting choice.

It will be observed that in a pluralistic community, such as exhibited in most
organized groupings of men and even in the largest earth-space community, technical
rules of law are commonly created in sets of complementary opposites to express all
pluralistic interests, and that the quality of the public order a particular community
achieves is determined by the aggregate flow of the specific choices by which such
complementary rules are related to specific instances. Inquiry which would be con-
sequential must extend beyond mere concern for the complementary rules alone to
identification of the facts that affect the detailed relation in specific instances and to
evaluation of the consequences of alternative choices.

2. CLARITY IN CONCEPTION OF BOTH AUTHORITY AND CONTROL

Our recommended theory will characterize law, further, not merely as decision,
but as *authoritative* decision, in which elements of both authority and control are
combined. By authority we mean participation in decision in accordance with community perspectives about who is to make what decisions and by what criteria; the
reference is empirical, to a certain frequency in the perspectives of the people who
constitute a given community. By control we mean effective participation in decision-
making and execution—that choice in outcome is realized in significant degree in
practice. When decisions are authoritative but not controlling, they are not law but
pretense; when decisions are controlling but not authoritative, they are not law but
naked power.

Our recommended theory will make inquiry about perspectives of authority both
establishing certain decision-makers (who is authorized to make what decisions, with
respect to whom, and by what procedures) and indicating appropriate criteria for
decision, relating to the scope, range, and domain of the values authorized to be
affected and to the detailed shaping and sharing of values regarded as appropriate
for particular contexts. It will observe whether these conceptions are empirically or
transempirically grounded, whether regarded as a part of the social process or transcendent of the social process, and whether presented as demand or non-demand.
When the perspectives of authority observed are demand conceptions (formulated in
terms of the volition or preference of participant conceiving them), it will be noted
whether they relate to social process values, asserted "autonomous oughts" of legal
prescription, the lessons of history, consistency in logical or syntactical operations,
ethical norms, or other undefined rectitude norms.

Our recommended theory will regard control as a function of many interrelated
variables and will project empirical inquiry about the factors which in fact affect
decision. It will be concerned with traditional notions of "obligation" and "binding"
only insofar as these notions realistically reflect the subjectivities of participants in
an arena. It will systematically investigate the role of non-official groups, including
political parties, pressure groups and private associations.

In this conception, it is not necesary to stipulate some single ratio of coincidence of authority and control as necessary for ''law.'' When different ratios are discovered, they can be compared with one another for scholarly and policy purposes. The critical task is not to fix upon a preferred ratio but to ascertain the patterns in the relation between authority and control that have occurred, probably will occur, can be made to occur, and are recommended to occur in particular contexts.

By these emphases, both authority and control can be subjected to systematic and disciplined inquiry through employment of all the techniques of modern science.

3. COMPREHENSIVENESS IN CONCEPTION OF PROCESSES OF AUTHORITATIVE DECISION

Our recommended theory will, in still further detail, extend its focus beyond occasional or isolated authoritative decisions, to the whole continuous *process* of authoritative and controlling decision by which the community shapes and shares its values. In any community, this process of authoritative and controlling decision, as an integral part of a more comprehensive process of effective power, can be seen to be composed of two different kinds of decisions; first, the decisions which establish and maintain the most comprehensive process of authoritative decision and, secondly, the flow of particular decisions which emerge from the process so established for the regulation of all the other community value processes. The first of these types of decision may be conveniently described as ''constitutive,'' and the second as ''public order.''

For the comprehensive and economic description of a process of decision, as of other social processes, it is necessary to employ some systematic set of terms (the precise words do not matter if equivalences can be made clear) to refer to the participants in the process, their perspectives (demands, identifications, expectations), the situations of intersection, the base values at the disposal of participants, the strategies employed in management of base values, and the immediate outcomes and long-term effects achieved.

In the terms we find convenient, the ''constitutive process'' of a community may be described as the decisions which identify and characterize the different authoritative decision-makers, specify and clarify basic community policies, establish appropriate structures of authority, allocate bases of power for sanctioning purposes, authorize procedures for making the different kinds of decision, and secure the continuous performance of all the different kinds of decision functions (intelligence, promotion, prescription, etc.) necessary to making and administering general community policy.

In complementary terms, the ''public order'' decisions of a community may be described as those, emerging in continuous flow from the constitutive process, which shape and maintain the protected features of the community's various value processes. These are the decisions which determine how resources are allocated and developed, and wealth produced and distributed; how human rights are promoted and protected or deprived; how enlightenment is encouraged or retarded; how health is fostered, or neglected; how rectitude and civil responsibility are matured; and so on through the whole gamut of demanded values.

It will be obvious in any community that an intimate relationship exists between constitutive process and public order. The economy and effectiveness of the constitutive process a community can achieve vitally affects the freedom, security, and abundance of its public order, while the quality of the public order a community attains, in turn affects the viability of the constitutive process it can maintain. By distinguishing, however, between these two different types of decisions, and seeking systematic coverage of both, inquiry may avoid destructive fixation upon the mere application of allegedly given rules and vacuous controversies about the differences between "political" and "legal" decision, and may appropriately extend its concern to all relevant features of the processes by which law is made and applied and their consequences for preferred public order.

The conventional description of the different phases in authoritative decision which we describe as "authority functions" is in such terms as "legislative," "executive," "judicial," and "administrative," but these terms would appear to refer more to authority structures than functions. Inquiry seeking both greater precision and comprehensiveness in describing authority functions might distinguish the following (or their equivalents):

Intelligence: Obtaining information about the past, making estimates of the future, planning.

Promoting: Urging proposals.

Prescribing: Projecting authoritative policies.

Invoking: Confronting concrete situations with provisional characterization in terms of a prescription in a concrete situation.

Applying: Final characterization and execution of a prescription in a concrete situation.

Terminating: Ending a prescription or arrangement within the scope of a prescription.

Appraising: Comparison between goals and performance.

Careful delimitation of the flow of decision in social process may enable the scientific observer and the decision-making participant to distinguish between two interacting realms of social order, the *public order* and the *civic order*. The total public order, as the analyst can make explicit, includes the relatively stable features of the power process (the constitutive patterns) and the protected and encouraged features of all value-institution processes other than power. Since public order is characterized by severely sanctioned commitments (in expectations and realization), civil order is the realm of milder sanction. Irrespective of the terminology employed, equivalent distinctions must be made articulate in a theory that is adequately fashioned to meet the issues pertinent to a comprehensive system of jurisprudence.

4. THE RELATION OF LAW TO SOCIAL PROCESS

A theory about law which would even approximate relevance will relate authoritative decision not merely explicitly, but systematically, to the larger social process that envelops such decision. It is changes in the distribution of values in social process, when values are conceived as demanded relations among human beings, which stimulate claimants to appeal to processes of decision and invoke the prescription and application of authoritative policy. Every phase in the process of authoritative decision is affected both by the past distribution of values and by the perspectives (demands, identifications, and expectations) of participants about future distribution. The outcomes of processes and authoritative decision, in turn, not only directly affect the future distribution of values among the claimants and others but, in total impact and in the long run, determine and secure a community's public order.

For comprehensive and precise description of the social process context of decision, any categorizations of values and institutional practices which can be given detailed operational indices in terms of specific, empirical relations between human beings can be made to serve the purposes of policy-oriented inquiry. The most general conceptualization we recommend is in terms of eight value-institution categories made familiar by contemporary social science:

Power:	government, law, politics.
Wealth:	production, distribution, consumption.
Respect:	social class and caste.
Well-being:	health, safety, comfort arrangements.
Affection:	family, friendship circles, loyalty.
Skill:	artistic, vocational, professional training and activity.
Rectitude:	churches and related articulators and appliers of standards of responsible conduct.
Enlightenment	mass media, research.

When these or equivalent value-institutional categories are employed, in appropriately detailed phase analysis, to describe the events in social process which precipitate claims to authoritative decision, the claims which participants make about such precipitating events and relevant policies in their appeals to decision, and the choices which the established decions-makers actually make in their prescriptions and applications of policy, then effective comparisons can be made through time within single communities, and across the boundaries of communities, for study of the factors that affect decision and of the public order consequences of decision.

5. THE RELATION OF LAW TO ITS LARGER COMMUNITY CONTEXT

A completely contextual, configurative theory about law will recognize that today mankind interacts on a global, and even earth-space scale. In the sense of interdetermination with respect to all values, the whole of mankind presently constitutes a single community, however primitive. One component of this largest community is a process of *effective* power in the sense that decisions are in fact taken and enforced, by severe deprivations and high indulgences, which are inclusive in their research and effects. Similarly, within this comprehensive process of effective power, may be observed an integral, transnational process of authoritative decision in the sense of a continuous flow of decisions made from perspectives of authority—that is, made by the people who are expected to make them, in accordance with community expectations about how they should be made, in established structures, and by authorized procedures. This transnational process of authoritative decision, like its embracing transnational social processes, is maintained at many different community levels and in many different interpenetrating patterns of perspectives and operations, in affecting and being affected by, the value processes in all the component communities of the larger earth-space community. A global public order, thus, affects the internal public order of its many constituent communities and the internal public order of each constitutent community, in turn, affects the global public order.

Unintimidated by monists who posit an as yet non-existent universality, or dualists who insist upon an impossible separation of national and transnational law, or neo-realists who suggest that international law is a form of fraudulent moralizing of little consequence, proponents of a relevant theory about law will seek an accurate empirical account of the reciprocal impact or interaction, in the distribution of inclusive and exclusive decisions and in consequences for values, of the interpenetrating processes of national and transnational authority. Inquiry will be directed not toward hierarchies of normative-ambiguous rules but toward the interdeterminations of communities and value processes of many differing degrees of geographic reach, including the contemporary emerging regional communities. Inclusive and exclusive decisions will be conceived not as dichotomous absolutes but as expressing a continuum in degrees of shared participation in the making of decisions, with reference not only to the number of participants but to degrees or sharing in all detailed phases, including clarification of common interests, access to arenas, control over base values, management of strategies, and determination of outcomes. All important arenas, whether external or internal to particular communities under observation, will be brought within inquiry. Sepcial consideration will be given to appraising, in terms of their consequences for preferred values, the contentions of rival systems of public order, of incompatible value orientation, aspiring toward completion on a global or earth-space scale.

C. THE PERFORMANCE OF INTELLECTUAL TASKS

The intellectual tasks for whose performance provision must be made in a relevant jurisprudence have already been indicated to extend, beyond traditional exercises in derivational logic and even the activities designated by more restrictive conceptions of "science," to a whole complex of interrelated activities, indispensable both to effective inquiry and to rational choice in decision. The tasks we recommend include the clarification of goals, the description of past trends in decision, the analysis of conditions affecting decision, the projection of future trends in decision, and the invention and evaluation of policy alternatives. It is believed that this itemization is comprehensive in that it embraces all the necessary tasks, and economic in that it excludes or deemphasizes wasteful or unnecessary tasks, such as derivational exercises with syntactic or transempirical or other ill-defined premises. Similarly, it is designed to avoid the confusion and inefficiency inherent in the normative-ambiguity of conventional legal concepts which purport in one undifferentiated stroke simultaneously to serve all relevant tasks.

By this emphasis upon the deliberate, systematic, and differentiated performance of each of a comprehensive set of intellectual tasks, it is not our suggestion that these different tasks can be economically performed in some set order or complete isolation from each other. It is rather our recommendation that all tasks be employed configuratively, in relation to specified problems in context. The rational employment of any particular task requires both the disciplined location of specific problems in their larger context and the systematic testing of formulations and findings achieved in the performance of that particular task against the formulations and findings achieved by the other tasks with respect to every significant feature of the context. The performance of all tasks must, thus, relate to the same events and in measure to go forward concurrently, but with clear discrimination in purpose of observation and particular skill employed.

It remains briefly to indicate what is involved in each of the recommended tasks.

1. THE CLARIFICATION OF COMMUNITY POLICIES

The most relevant clarification will explicitly and deliberately seek the detailed specification of postulated goals, whatever the level of abstraction of their initial formulation, in terms which make clear empirical reference to preferred events in social process. To the degree that economy permits, every choice in alternatives recommended will be related to its larger community context and to all important community interests which may be affected. The time dimensions of clarification will be made explicit by distinguishable immediate or short-term, middle-range, and long-range objectives. The most secure clarification will build upon the concurrent and systematic performance of all the other relevant intellectual tasks and employ the knowledge so acquired about past trends in decision, past conditioning factors, future probabilities, and possible alternative solutions.

2. THE DESCRIPTION OF PAST TRENDS IN DECISION

The most relevant description of past trends in decisions will be, not anecdoctal [sic] in terms of isolated tidbits of doctrine and practice, but rather systematic in terms of degrees of approximation to clarified policies for constitutive process and public order. For the more effective comparison of decisions and their consequencs both through time and across community boundaries, the events which precipitate recourse to authoritative decision, the detailed claims which participants made to such decision, the factors which appear to condition decision, and the immediate and longer-term consequences of decision for the participants and others will all be categorized ''factually'' in terms of value-institution processes, including all the different detailed phases of such processes. In supplement of the conventional summaries of complementary rules and concepts, comprehensive maps in value-institutional terms will be designed for both constitutive process and other protected features of public order, and the flow of decision will be observed in relation to specific, detailed types of claims. Procedures will be devised for relating specific types of claims to their total context and for appraising the responses by authoritative decision-makers to such claims in terms of their conformity to clarified policies.

3. THE ANALYSIS OF FACTORS AFFECTING DECISION

In policy-relevant performance of the scientific task, inquiry will be made for the interplay of the multiple factors affecting decision, and overwhelming importance will not be ascribed to any one factor or category of factors, such as those relating to wealth or to ''taught tradition'' or the rectitude perspectives. Comprehensive theories about the factors affecting decision will be formulated and tested by the appropriate procedures of contemporary science. Formulations will be inspired by the ''maximization postulate,'' that all responses are, within the limits of capabilities, a function of net value expectation and emphasis will be placed upon both predispositional and environmental variables. The significance of factors deriving from culture, class, interest, personality and previous exposure to crisis will be explicitly examined. Rigor will be sought in theoretical models, but not by an over-emphasis upon the importance of mathematical measurement or experiment. Many different vantage points and both extensive and intensive procedures will be employed in data gathering and processing.

4. THE PROJECTION OF FUTURE TRENDS

In a policy-relevant jurisprudence, expectations about the future will be made as conscious, explicit, comprehensive, and realistic as possible. Developmental constructs, embodying varying alternative anticipations of the future, will be deliberately formulated and tested in the light of all available information. The simple linear or chronological extrapolations made in conventional legal theory will be subjected to the discipline of knowledge about conditioning factors and past changes in the composition of trends.

5. THE INVENTION AND EVALUATION OF POLICY ALTERNATIVES

In a policy-relevant jurisprudence, creativity will be encouraged by demand for the deliberate invention and assessment of new alternatives in policy, institutional structures, and procedures. Every phase of decision process, whether of constitutive process or relating to public order, and every facet of conditioning context, will be examined for opportunities in innovation which may influence decision toward greater conformity with clarified goals. Assessment of particular alternatives will be made in terms of gains and losses with respect to all clarified goals and disciplined by the knowledge acquired of trends, conditioning factors, and future possibilities. All the other intellectual tasks will be synthesized and brought to bear upon search for integrative solutions characterized by maximum gains and minimum losses. Special procedures for encouraging creativity will be employed, including expansions and contractions of the focus of attention, alternation of periods of intensive concentration and inattention, free association, and experiment with random combinations.

D. THE EXPLICIT POSTULATION OF BASIC PUBLIC ORDER GOALS

A relevant jurisprudence will recognize that policy choices are ineradicable components of any process of authoritative decision and that there are today rival systems of public order aspiring toward completion both internally within states and on a global scale. For everyone concerned with inquiry about law, one insistent question must be: what basic policy goals is he, as a responsible citizen of the larger community of mankind and of various lesser component communities, willing to recommend to other similarly responsible citizens as the primary postulates of public order, infusing and transcending all particular communities?

We emphasize the postulation and clarification of public order goals in contradistinction to their derivation. Infinitely regressive logical derivations from premises of transempirical or highly ambiguous inference contribute little to the detailed specification of values, in the sense of demanded relations between human beings, which is required for rational decision. Peoples subscribing to very different styles in derivation have long demonstrated that they can cooperate for promotion of the values of human dignity, irrespective of the faiths or creeds which they employ for justification. Expressions of preference among different derivations can only divide potential co-workers, without contributing to creativity.

The comprehensive set of goal values which, because of many heritages, we recommend for clarification and implementation are, as already suggested, those which are today commonly characterized as the basic values of human dignity, or of a free society. These are the values bequeathed to us all by the great democratic movements of mankind and being very more insistently expressed in the rising common demands and expectations of peoples everywhere. As demanded in the United Nations Charter, the Universal Declaration of Human Rights, the proposed covenants on human rights, regional agreements and programs, national constitutions, political party platforms, and other official and unofficial pronouncements, these values are of course formulated at many different levels of abstraction and in many different cultural and institutional modalities. The basic thrust of all formulations is, however, toward the greatest production and widest possible distribution of all important values, and the appropriate task for both scholarly observers and authoritative decision-makers, who accept and seek to implement these rising common demands, is that of effectively performing all the various intellectual tasks outlined above for the better relation of broad general preferences for shared power, shared respect, shared enlightenment, and so on to all the specific choices which must be made in different specific contexts in the prescription and application of law.

The basic goal values postulated for preferred public order cannot of course be representative only of the exclusive, parochial values of some particular segment of the larger community of mankind, but such values can admit a very great diversity in the institutional practices by which they are sought and secured. In different particular communities and cultures very different institutional practices may contribute equally to overriding goals for the increased production and sharing of values. When overriding goals are accepted, experiment and creativity may be encouraged by the honoring of a wide range of functional equivalents in the institutional practices by which values are sought.

It will be noted that the postulation of basic goal values we recommend differs from a mere exercise in faith. We do not expect to acquire new knowledge by postulation alone. It is only by the systematic and disciplined exercise of the various relevant intellectual skills that new knowledge can be acquired.

———

An early effort to translate the insights in the previous selection into a curriculum, an on-going institutionalized program for the training of lawyers designed to impart both the skills necessary for the clarification and implementation of public policy and a commitment to the principles of democracy, was spelled out in a classic piece by McDougal and Lasswell.

MCDOUGAL & LASSWELL, LEGAL EDUCATION AND PUBLIC POLICY,
52 YALE L.J. 203, 213–216 (1943)

Implementation of values requires, first, trend-thinking. This considers the shape of things to come regardless of preferences. His goals clarified, a policy-maker must orient himself correctly in contemporary trends and future probabilities. Concerned with specific features of the future that are ever emerging from the past, he needs to be especially sensitive to time, and to forecast with reasonable accuracy passage from one configuration of events to the next. For this purpose he must have at his disposal a vast array of facts properly organized and instantly accessible. No one, much less a policy-maker, can do without expectations about the future—expectations about the probability of a short or a long-drawn-out war, of mounting or diminishing taxes, of rising or falling standards of living. To think developmentally is to be explicit about these anticipations of the shape of things to come. Every policy proposal and decision, including our recommendations about legal training, turns in part upon a picture of significant changes in the recent past, and expectations about significant changes in the emerging future. The nature of our picture of recent trends, together with our interpretation of the principal cross-currents of the near future, have been briefly indicated in our description of the wane of democratic values and of the unrealistic orientation of contemporary policy-makers. The results of trend-thinking must continually be evaluated by the policy-maker in the light of his goals; the task is to think creatively about how to alter, deter, or accelerate probable trends in order to shape the future closer to his desire.

Implementation of values requires, next, scientific-thinking. While trend information is indispensable, it is not sufficient to enable us to mold the future. Trends have a way of changing direction; and often we can contribute to these changes by the skilful management of factors that condition them. A trend is not a cause of social changes; it is a register of the relative strength of the variables that produce it. We do not learn about causal factors by passively observing trend; we must compare many examples of trend before we can build up a body of scientific knowledge. The laws and propositions of science state invariant interrelations. We do not have scientific knowledge when we know, for example, that there was a trend toward world war in 1939; it is only when we can, by comparing war periods, relate war to conditioning factors that we have science. When we look toward the future our aim is not to draw a fatalistic series of trend curves in the direction they have been moving in the past. To extrapolate in this way is necessary but it is a prelude to the use of creative imagination and of available scientific knowledge in deciding how to influence the future. The very act of taking thought and of acting on the basis of thought are among the factors that determine the future trend of events. In a democratic society a policy-maker must determine which adjustments of human relationships are in fact compatible with the realization of democratic ideals. Which procedures actually aid or hamper the realization of human dignity? How can the institutions of legislation, adjudication, administration, production, and distribution be adjusted to democratic survival? What are the slogans and doctrines—in which contexts of experience—that create acceptance of democratic ideals and inspire effort to put them into practice? In short, the policy-maker needs to guide his judgment by what is scientifically known and knowable about the causal variables that condition the democratic variables.

Effective training in scientific thinking requires that students become familiar with the procedures by which facts are established by planned observation. Most of our sources of information about human experience are not deliberately created records. For the most part we must rely upon whatever inferences can be drawn from accidental residue of the past. In recent decades, and especially with the rapid expansion of the social and psychological sciences the observing of human conduct has become progressively more technical and exhaustive. It is not too much to say that the great contribution of modern specialists on the human sciences is less in the realm of general theory than in the perfecting of method by which ancient speculations can be confirmed, modified or rejected. From the laboratory of the psychologist, the field expedition of the ethnologist, and the clinic of the physician have come illuminating bodies of data; and the procedures of observation invented in these special situations have stimulated the development of ways of studying men and women under normal circumstances in our own civilization. The effect of many kinds of human environment—in family, factory, school, army, prison, market—have been subjected to careful scrutiny. The results are continually applied and retested in the selecting of personnel in business, government, army, and other social structures. Systems of incentive (the granting of indulgence or the inflicting of deprivation) are explored for their efficacy in raising production and reducing disciplinary problems. Modes of phrasing are pretested to evaluate their effectiveness as modifiers of buying, giving, voting. Throughout the length and breadth of modern society decisions are modified on the basis of what is revealed by means of intensive or extensive observation of human life, the procedures varying all the way from the prolonged interviews of a psychoanalytic psychiatrist to the brief questions of the maker of an opinion poll.

Acquaintance with various methods of observation not only furnishes a sound basis for policy planning—it contributes directly to skill in the practical management of human affairs. Another glance at the job analysis of the modern lawyer set forth above indicates something of the range of management problems with which he must grapple. Success calls for skill in direct personal contact with client, partner, clerk, opposing counsel, investigator, witness, jurymen, judge (to name some conspicuous examples); likewise, there is need of skill in public relations (in the handling of grand jury investigations, conducting trials, conducting legislative hearings).

From all the emphasis which we have placed upon certain ways of thinking, observing, and managing, it should not be inferred that we propose to discard or neglect the traditional skills and knowledge of the lawyer. It is the lawyer's mastery over constitutions, statutes, appellate opinions, and textbooks of peculiar idiom, and his skill in operating the mechanics (procedure) of both governmental institutions (courts, legislatures, administrative boards, executive offices) and private associations (corporations, partnerships, trade associations, labor unions, consumers' cooperatives) that set him apart from, and give him a certain advantage over, such other skill groups in our society as diplomats, economists, social psychologists, social historians, and biologists. But much of what currently passes for instruction in law schools is a waste of time because it consists of the reiteration of a limited list of ambiguous terms cut asunder from any institutional context that would set a limit to their ambiguities. Thus a student may learn that if discussion begins with "contract," it must then proceed by rearrangement of certain meanings to be assigned to a small list of well-known words, such as "offer and acceptance," "consideration," "mistake," "performance," "condition," and so on; but he knows very little unless he has also learned to complete the meaning of these terms by reference to representative institutional contexts and important social values. What we propose is that training and the distinctive core of the lawyer's repertory of skills and information be given a new sense of purpose and new criteria of relevance. It is a fundamental truth of practical and scientific psychology that purpose increases ease of learning; students can be expected to acquire more rather than less mastery of legal technicality when the comparatively small repertory of key legal terms is considered in relation to the goals and the vital problems and processes of democracy rather than in a formalistic framework, unoriented toward policy. The lawyer's traditional storehouse of learning is already too tightly stuffed with legacies from the past to be thoroughly mastered by anyone in a lifetime of devoted scholarship; a student must, if he is not to choke on triviality, have extrinsic criteria of relevance. There comes a time, as Mr. Justice Holmes long ago remarked, when energy can be more profitably spent than in the reading of cases. Given a new sense of purpose and trained in the skills and information which should be common to all policy makers, the lawyer cannot escape becoming a better lawyer. Schools which prepare themselves to emphasize such purposes and to offer such training may succeed in becoming more truly vocational even as they grow more genuinely professional.

NOTES

1. Does the McDougal and Lasswell view which emphasizes the necessity of decisions based upon policy and designed to achieve desired outcomes, reserve any place in law for rules and legal doctrines? Is there any purpose to having rules if decisions (by courts as well as other decisionmakers) are tailored by and shaped to achieve policy goals rather than determined by norms and legal doctrines? Are rules and legal doctrines appropriate subjects for intensive study in law schools?

2. Is there a clash between the views of McDougal and Lasswell that decisons (even of judges and bureaucrats) should be made to effectuate policy goals and their view of maximum feasible sharing of power (decisionmaking) as a prime goal? After all, judges and bureaucrats are often appointed for life and are not answerable to the community for their decisions? How is such a clash, if any, to be resolved?

3. Whose policy goals are public officials supposed to implement? Don't rules express or reflect policy goals? Discuss.

4. Recall the criticism made by Braybrooke and Lindblom. As a practical matter, is it possible to examine adequately all the relevant variables relating to each of the values set forth by McDougal and Lasswell in postulating and clarifying goals, studying trends and conditions, making projections and devising alternative strategies? Recall that these require the examination of participants, their perspectives, situations, base values, etc. as well as study of authority and control, perspectives and operations and many other matters. If it is not practical to do all this, is it worthwhile, or even misleading, to look only at some of these matters? Discuss.

5. Is it necessary to quantify values in order to decide which goals to pursue when, in particular instances, goals clash as they are likeley to do in complex systems? (e.g., rewarding merit v. assuring equal sharing of all values, or the latter v. maximum freedom of action and opportunity.) If quantification is required, how is this to be done and by what criteria?

6. If goal specification is a question of choice to be made, without quantification of the various values, on what basis is choice to be made and one value preferred over another? If choice is to be made without empirical proof that a particular value is inherently more desirable or likeley to yield more general benefits, does this expose policy sciences to some of the same criticisms aimed at natural law and other transempirical theories? Discuss.

7. Will the steps which must be taken to assure the McDougal-Lasswell postulated goal of human dignity, requiring the widest possible production and maximum feasible sharing of all values, mean that equality of result, not simply of opportunity, must be assured? If so, will this require so much constant governmental supervision and intervention in social processes that it will result in a serious loss of individual liberty? Discuss.

8. What do McDougal and Lasswell mean by "merit" when they call for a system of public order in which there is a maximum distribution of all values but also considerations of merit? Does "merit" include effort expended by an individual? Ability? Need, including need based on *lack* of ability?*

9. Meritocracy seems to underpin the goal postulation of McDougal and Lasswell. Meritocracy, as a set of social doctrines, was firmly installed about two centuries ago, largely as a way of legitimizing the acquisition of power by the new middle class, non-aristocratic men who would otherwise have been barred from office by an inherited myth that made lineage and aristocracy the prerequisite for power; when that was supplanted by "merit," the way was open for their entry and consolidation of power.

It is sometimes claimed that meritocracy is not a natural or absolute system and should not be conceived of in Social Darwinian terms. The self-made person is relatively rare. A large component of "merit" is the result of opportunities to develop made possible by power, money, enlightenment, health, respect and so on. Those who have access to these values are more likely to demonstrate "merit." Unless there are very strict controls about the transmission of wealth and other values from generation to generation, meritocracy can be easily distorted, ceasing to serve as a doctrine of opportunity and becoming a doctrine of validation of existing elites. Discuss.

*See McDougal, Lasswell & Chen, *Human Rights and World Public Order* 381 (1980).

POLICY SCIENCE

K. Arrow, *Social Choice and Individual Values* (1951).

W. Ascher, *Forecasting: An Appraisal for Policy-Makers and Planners* (1978).

W. Ascher & W. Overholt, *Strategic Planning and Forecasting: Political Risk and Economic Opportunity* (1983).

The Study of Policy Formation (R. A. Bauer & K. J. Gergen eds. 1968).

W. J. Baumol, *Economic Theory and Operation Analysis* (1961).

D. Braybrooke & C. Lindblom, *A Strategy of Decision: Policy Evaluation as a Social Process* (1963).

G. Brewer & R. Brunner, *Organized Complexity, Empirical Theories of Political Development* (1971).

G. Brewer & P. deLeon, *The Foundations of Policy Analysis* (1983).

S. Brown, *Political Subjectivity: Applications of Q-Methodology in Political Science* (1980).

R. Brunner, The Policy Sciences as Science. 15 *Policy Sciences* 115 (1982).

J. M. Buchanan & G. Tullock, *The Calculus of Consent* (1961).

N. Caplan, A. Morrison, & R. J. Stambaugh, *The Use of Social Science Knowledge in Policy Decision at the National Level: a Report to Respondents* (1975).

Y. Dror, *Design for Policy Sciences* (1971).

O. Duncan, Social Forecasting: The State of the Art, 17 *Pub. Interest* 88 (1969).

Controversies and Decisions: The Social Sciences and Public Policy (C. Frankel ed. 1976).

H. Kahn, *On Thermonuclear War* (1967).

H. Lasswell & A. Kaplan, *Power and Society: A Framework for Political Inquiry* (1950).

H. Lasswell, *A Pre-view of Policy Sciences* (1971); *Psychopathology and Politics* (1930; reprinted with Afterthoughts, 1960); *Politics: Who Gets What, When, How?* (1936, reprinted 1951).

C. Lindblom, Decision-making: The Science of Muddling Through, 19 *Pub. Ad. Rev.* 79 (1959).

C. Lindblom & D. K. Cohen, *Usable Knowledge: Social Science and Social Problem Solving* (1979).

R. D. Luce & H. Raiffa, *Games and Decisions: Introduction and Critical Survey* (1957).

O. Morgenstern, *The Question of National Defense* (2d ed. 1961).

S. S. Nagel, *Policy Studies and the Social Sciences* (1975).

F. S. C. Northrop, *The Logic of the Sciences and the Humanities* (1947).

The Policy Sciences (D. Lerner & H. Lasswell eds. 1951).

Political Development and Change, A Policy Approach (G. Brewer & R. Brunner eds. 1975).

K. Popper, Prediction and Prophecy in the Social Sciences, in *Theories of History* 276 (P. Gardiner ed. 1959).

W. H. Riker, *Theory of Political Coalitions* (1962).

M. Shubik, *Game Theory in the Social Sciences: Concepts and Solutions* (1982).

R. C. Snyder, Game Theory and the Analysis of Political Behavior, in S. Bailey *Research Frontiers in Politics and Government* 70 (1955).

J. von Neumann & O. Morgenstern, *Theory of Games and Economic Behavior* (1944).

A. Wildavsky, *Speaking Truth to Power: The Art and Craft of Policy Analysis* (1979).

INFORMATION THEORY

H. Alker, Jr., *Mathematics and Politics* (1965).

W. R. Ashby, *An Introduction to Cybernetics* (1956).

R. B. Braithwaite, *Theory of Games as a Tool for the Moral Philosopher* (1955).

C. Cherry, *On Human Communication* (1957).

C. W. Churchman, *Prediction and Optimal Decision: Philosophical Issues of a Science of Values* (1961).

K. Deutsch, *The Nerves of Government: Models of Political Communication and Control* (1963).

K. Deutsch, *Nationalism and Social Communication* (1953).

A. Downs, *An Economic Theory of Democracy* (1957).

The Integration of Political Communities (P. Jacob & J. Toscano eds. 1964).

C. A. Miller, *Language and Communication* (1951).

A. Rapoport, *Strategy and Conscience* (1964).

W. Riker, *The Theory of Political Coalitions* (1962).

B. Russett et al., *World Handbook of Political and Social Indicators* (1964).

T. Schelling, *The Strategy of Conflict* (1960).

S. Vajda, *An Introduction to Linear Programming and the Theory of Games* (1960).

JURIMETRICS

F. Cort, Predicting Supreme Court Decisions Mathematically: A Quantitative Analysis of the 'Right to Counsel' Cases, 51 *Am. Pol. Sci. Rev.* 1 (1957).

F. Fisher, The Mathematical Analysis of Supreme Court Decisions: The Use and Abuse of Quantitative Methods, 52 *Am. Pol. Sci. Rev.* 321 (1958).

Judicial Decision-making (G. Schubert ed. 1963).

R. Lawlor, Stare Decisis and the Electronic Computers, in *Judicial Behavior* 492 (G. Schubert ed. 1964); Foundations of Logical Legal Decision-making, *Mod. Uses Logic & L.,* June, 1963, at 98.

L. Lovinger, Jurimetrics, in *Judicial Behavior* 72 (G. Schubert ed. 1964).

S. Nagel, Statistical Prediction of Verdicts and Awards, *Mod. Uses Logic & L.,* Sept., 1963, at 135: Using Simple Calculations to Predict Judicial Decisions, 4 *Am. Behav. Sci.* 24 (1967).

R. B. Perry, *General Theory of Value* (1950).

W. Riker & F. Schap, Disharmony in Federal Government 2 *Behav. Sci.* 276 (1957).

G. Schubert, The Study of Judicial Decision-Making as an Aspect of Political Behavior, 52 *Am. Pol. Sci. Rev.* 1007 (1958); *Quantitative Analysis of Judicial Behavior* (1959); A Psychometric Model of the Supreme Court, 4 *Am. Behav. Sci.* 14 (1961); Ideologies and Attitudes, Academic and Judicial, in *Judicial Policy-making: the Political Role of the Courts* (rev. ed. 1974).

S. Ulmer, The Anlaysis of Behavior Patterns on the United States Supreme Court, 22 *J. Pol.* 629 (1960).

LAW AND ECONOMICS

B. Ackerman, *Private Property and the Constitution* (1977).

K. Arrow, *Social Change and Individual Values* (1951, 1963).

C. E. Baker, The Ideology of the Economic Analysis of Law, 5 *J. Phil. & Pub. Aff.* 3 (1975).

G. S. Becker, *The Economic Approach to Human Behavior* (1976).

A. Bergson, A Reformulation of Certain Defects of Welfare Economics, 52 *Q. J. Econ.* 310 (1938).

D. Black, On the Rationale of Group Decision-Making, 56 *J. Pol. Econ.* 23 (1948).

D. Black, *The Theory of Committees and Elections* (1958).

D. Braybrooke & C. E. Lindblom, *A Strategy of Decision: Policy Evaluation as a Social Process* (1963).

J. M. Buchanan, An Individualistic Theory of Political Process, in *Varieties of Political Theory* 25 (D. Easton ed. 1966); Good Economics—Bad Law, 60 *Va. L. Rev.* 483 (1974).

G. Calabresi, *The Costs of Accidents* (1970); Transaction Costs, Resource Allocation and Liability Rules: A Comment, 11 *J.L. & Econ.* 67 (1968).

G. Calabresi & P. Bobbitt, *Tragic Choices* (1978).

G. Calabresi & D. Malamed, Property Rules, Liability Rules, and Inalienability: One View of the Cathedral, 85 *Harv. L. Rev.* 89 (1972).

R. Coase, The Problem of Social Cost, 3 *J. L. & Econ.* 1 (1967).

R. A. Dahl & C. E. Lindblom, *Politics, Economics and Welfare: Planning and Politico-economic Systems Resolves Into Basic Social Processes* (1953).

A. Downs, *An Economic Theory of Democracy* (1957).

R. Epstein, A Theory of Strict Liability, 2 *J. Legal Stud.* 151 (1973).

C. Fried, The Value of Life, 82 *Harv. L. Rev.* 415 (1969): *An Anatomy of Values* (1972).

M. Friedman, *Capitalism and Freedom* (1962).

W. M. Landes & R. A. Posner, The Independent Judiciary in an Interest Group Perspective, 1 *J. L. & Econ.* 875 (1975); The Private Enforcement of Law, 4 *J. Legal Stud.* 1 (1975).

A. Leff, Economic Analysis of Law: Some Realism About Nominalism, 60 *Va. L. Rev.* 451 (1974).

C. E. Lindblom, *The Intelligence of Democracy: Decision-Making Through Mutual Adjustments* (1965).

Mathematical Methods in the Social Sciences (K. Arrow, S. Carlin & P. Suppes eds. 1959).

F. Michelman, Property, Utility, and Fairness: Comments on the Ethical Foundations of "Just Compensation" Law, 80 *Harv. L. Rev.* 1165 (1967).

E. Mishan, *Pareto Optimality and the Law,* 19 *Oxford Econ. Papers* 255 (1967).

P. Munch, An Economic Analysis of Eminent Domain, 84 *J. Pol.* 473 (1976).

W. Nutter, The Coase Theorem on Social Cost: A Footnote, 11 *J. L. & Econ.* 503 (1968).

V. Pareto, *Selected Sociological Writings* (F. Feiner transl. 1976).

R. A. Posner, *Economic Analysis of Law* (2d ed. 1977); The Economic Approach to Law, 53 *Tex. L. Rev.* 757 (1957); The Rights of Creditors of Affiliated Corporations, 43 *U. Chi. L. Rev.* 499 (1976).

A. Smith, *An Inquiry into the Nature and Causes of the Wealth of Nations* (London 1776).

J. Tobin, On Limiting the Domain of Inequality, 13 *J. L. & Econ.* 263 (1970).

Towards a General Theory of Action (T. Parsons & E. A. Shils eds. 1951).

G. Tullock, *The Logic of the Law* (1971).

F. A. von Hayek, *The Road to Serfdom* (1944).

L. Von Mises, *Bureaucracy* (1945).

SYSTEMS ANALYSIS AND THEORY

L. Apostel, Can Metaphysics Be a Science? in *Studia Philosophica Gandensia*, 1, T. 7 (1963).

C. W. Churchman, *Prediction and Optimal Decision, Philosophical Issues of a Science of Values* (1961); *The Systems Approach and Its Enemies* (1979).

K. Deutsch, Toward an Inventory of Basic Trends and Patterns in Comparative and International Politics, 54 *Am. Pol. Sci. Rev.* 34 (1960).

D. Easton, *The Political System* (1953); *A System Analysis of Political Life* (1965).

F. A. von Hayek, *The Counter-Revolution of Science: Studies on the Abuse of Reason* (1952).

M. Kaplan, The New Great Debate: Traditionalism vs. Science in International Relations, 19 *World Pol.* 1 (1966).

M. J. Levy, Jr., *The Structure of Society* (1952).

R. MacIver, *Social Causation* (1942).

J. G. Miller, Living Systems: Structure and Process, *Behav. Sci.* 10 (1965).
Modern Systems Research for the Behavioral Scientist, A Sourcebook (W. Buckley ed. 1968).
T. Parsons, *The Social System* (1951); *The Structure of Social Action* (1937).
L. Von Bertalanffy, *General System, Theory: Foundations, Development, Applications* (rev. ed. 1969).

USES OF MATHEMATICS IN LAW

P. Bridgman, *The Nature of Physical Theory* (1936); Some General Principles of Operational Analysis 52 *Psych. Rev.* 246 (1945).
R. Dahl, The Concept of Power, 2 *Behav. Sci.* 2 (1957).
O. Davis & M. Hinich, A Mathematical Model of Policy Formulation in a Democratic Society, in *Mathematical Applications in Political Science* (J. L. Bernd ed. 1966).
R. Dowse, A Functionalist's Logic, 18 *World Pol.* 607 (1966).
C. Farris, A Scale Analysis of Ideological Factors in Congressional Voting, in *Legislative Behavior; A Reader in Theory and Research* 399 (J. Wahlke & H. Eulau eds. 1959).
J. March, An Introduction to the Theory of Measurement of Influence, 49 *Am. Pol. Sci. Rev.* 431 (1955); Measurement Concepts in the Theory of Influence, 19 *J. Pol.* 202 (1957).
W. N. McPhee, Survival Theory and Culture, in *Formal Theories of Mass Behavior* 26 (1963).
W. Riker, A Test of the Adequacy of the Power Index, 4 *Behav. Sci.* 120 (1959).
W. Riker, A Method for Determining the Significance of Roll Call Votes in Voting Bodies, in *Legislative Behavior: A Reader in Theory and Research* 377 (J. C. Wahlke & H. Eulau eds. 1959).
L. Shapley & M. Shubik, A Method for Evaluating the Distribution of Power in a Committee System, in *Legislative Behavior* (J. C. Wahlke & H. Eulau eds. 1959).
H. Simon, *Models of Man: Social and Rational: Mathematical Essays on Rational Human Behavior in a Social Setting* (1957).
The State of the Social Sciences (L. D. White ed. 1956).
L. Tribe, Trial Mathematics: Precision and Ritual of the Legal Process, 84 *Harv. L. Rev.* 329 (1971).
A. A Tschuprow, *Principles of the Mathematical Theory of Correlation* (1939).

MISCELLANEOUS

A. Bickel, *The Supreme Court and the Idea of Progress* (1970); *The Least Dangerous Branch* (1962).
R. Dahl, The Behavioral Approach in Political Science: Epitaph for a Monument to a Successful Protest, 55 *Am. Pol. Sci. Rev.* 763 (1965).
J. Deutsch, Neutrality, Legitimacy and the Supreme Court: Some Intersections Between Law and Political Science, 20 *Stan. L.Rev.* 169 (1968).
G. Gunther, The Subtle Vices of 'Passive Virtues'—A Comment on Principle and Expediency in Judicial Review, 64 *Colum. L. Rev.* 1 (1964).
H. Lasswell, *The Future of Political Science* (1963).
F. Michelman, The Supreme Court and Litigation Access Fees: The Right to Protect One's Right—Part I, 1973 *Duke L. J.* 1153.
J. Mill, Bentham, in *The Philosophy of John Stewart Mill* 18 (M. Cohen ed. 1961).
J. Miller, Toward a General Theory for the Behavioral Sciences, 10 *Am. Psychol.* 513 (1955).
J. O'Shaughnessy, *Inquiry and Decision, A Methodology for Management and the Social Sciences* (1972).
J. J. C. Smart and B. Williams *Utilitarianism, For and Against* (1973).

Afterword

Twelve chapters have presented a spectrum of jurisprudential frames which the contemporary lawyer can adopt or adapt to help in the performance of legal tasks. Whichever of those frames, in whole or in part, you decide is useful to you, one thing should be clear: basic theories about law or jurisprudence are indispensable for the performance of legal tasks. In a subtle fashion, a theory of jurisprudence influences how you locate yourself in the processes of which you are a part and which you are trying to influence, and to identify the effective decisionmakers, who need not necessarily be the formal decisionmakers, in differnt situations. Even when the lawyer is not aware of them, theories, like "forms of action" in Maitland's lapidary expression, rule us from the graves.

In appraising jurisprudence and deciding which of the approaches here is most useful to you, you may wish to refer back to the cases and hypotheticals presented in Chapters 1 and 2. Jurisprudence, as we said then, is a very practical subject. If a particular school of thought is not helpful to you in solving problems like those, its "theoretical" or "abstract" value is inconsequential. Whatever the judgment on it, it certainly does not deserve much attention in law school.

We hope that these materials have sensitized you to the important relation between the practice of law and the quality of our democracy and the very special responsibilities that the American lawyer shoulders in it. Law is a process of human beings making choices and the quality of mind and the character of those who are the contemporary custodians of that process—people like yourself—will largely determine what is finally produced.

Jurisprudence, you should now appreciate, is not a subject that is learned and then put on a shelf. It is an ongoing process of self-discovery and discovery of the key features of the processes in which you operate and the environment which you wish to change. An afterword in any book on jurisprudence is not conclusion but commencement.

Index

Abortion, 189, 190, 195
  see also Roe v. Wade
  decision up to physician and mother, 195
  now relatively safe, 190
  reasons why prohibited, 190
  regulation by state in first trimester, 194
  state's interest in, 190
Aquinas, Thomas, 118, 155, 208, 222
Admissions and hiring dilemmas, 10
"Act of State," 348, 349
Adamson v. California, 309
American legal realists, 470
American legal realism
  see Legal realism, 449
Analytical jurisprudence
Analytical jurisprudence
  as distinguished from deontological jurisprudence, 270
Analytical positivism
  see also Positivism,
    excessively formalistic, 351
    inspired by liberalism, 351
Anarchism, 67
  critics of, 109
  Godwin as exponent of, 99
  Godwin as naive, 109
Anarchist, 99
Aristotle, 45, 170, 173
  Politics, 197
Armor, David, 505
Arnold, Thurman, 247, 330
  The Symbols of Government, 447
Arrow, Kenneth, 66
  basic conceptions of, 564
  Social Choice and Individual Values, 561
Austin, John, 270, 283, 292, 295, 296, 334, 348, 382, 383, 403
  compared with Kelsen, H., 402
  failure to consider intellectual tasks, 294
  force viewed as logical postulate, not an empirically referential term, 404
  The Province of Jurisprudence Determined, 270
  views compared with those of psychologists, 281

Authoritative decision
  as part of effective power process, 581
  comprehensiveness in conception of, 581
Authority, 3, 106, 108, 247, 289
  (and) control, not always congruent, 3
  critics, 109
  done his duty, 98
  defined, 580
  effect on power, 52
  ethics of applying systems of, 247
  found in perspectives of living community members, 573
  giving rise to restraints, 52
  in Austin's conception of law, 292
  legal and *de facto,* 400
  obedience to, viewed as duty, 98
  political, 105
  required for collective life, 109
  submission to because of psychological attitude to one's duty, 98
Authority and control
  processes of, 14
Authority, hierarchical
  difficult to disobey, 93
  the Milgram experiments, 93

Baker v. Nelson, 175, 176, 178
Basic norm, 402
  is presupposed as valid, 385
  see also Grundnorm,
Behavior
  internal compared with external, 401
Behavioralists
  predictions of judicial decisions by, 462
Behavioral Jurisprudence, 458
Bentham, Jeremy, 24, 233, 270, 273, 292, 334
  An Introduction to the Principles of Morals and Legislation, 534
  as exponent of utilitarianism, 534
  conceived of law as process of decision designed to achieve certain goals, 533
Bernstein v. Van Heyghen Freres S.A., 348
Besserman, Heinrich
  hypothetical case of, 82

Bickel, Alexander
   neutrality, 330
Bill of Rights
   entirely principled, 317
Black, Charles
   views on neutral principles, 331
Blacks
   generations required to repair oppression
      of, 136
   power of, 78
Blau & Meyer
   Bureaucracy in Modern Society, 375,
      379
Bob Jones University v. U.S. 518
Bradwell v. The State, 169
"Brain dead", 181
   see Death, 181
Brandeis, Louis D., Justice, 486
Braybrooke and Lindblom
   A Strategy of Decision, 567
Bribery
   lawfulness of, 23
   "spice boxes", 23
   to public officials, 23
Brown v. Board of Education, 489
Buck v. Bell, 192
   sterilization, 192
Bureaucracy
   characteristics of modern society, 363
   complex hierarchical system, 362
   endangers democratic freedom, 379
   in modern science, 375
   jurisprudence of, 359
   rule of law in, 362
   serves important functions in democratic
      society, 379
   task responsibility in, as opposed to out-
      come responsibility, 373
Bureaucratic jurisprudence, 380
   see Jurisprudence, of bureaucracy,
Bureaucratic model
   characteristics of, 363
   described, 363
   hierarchical structure of, 363
Burke, 231, 237
   *Reform of Representation in the House of
      Commons,* 231
Busing
   to overcome racial segregation, 501, 502,
      505
Busing: A Review of the Evidence
   Pettigrew, Smith, Useem & Normand,
      505

Calabresi, Guido, 553
Calley, Lieutenant
   His Own Story, 91
Charitable deductions
   not available with regard to segregated
      schools, 518
Civic order
   differentiated from public order, 582
Civil disobedience, 99, 109, 134, 139, 141,
      145, 166, 334
   See also, Conscientious objection; Con-
      scientious objectors
   accepting punishment of, 143
   and violence, 145
   as defined by Rawls, John, 121
   as fostering disrespect for law, 141
   defined, 121, 134
   degree of violence related to importance
      of issues, 145
   depends on importance of issues and laws,
      144, 145
   distinguished from revolution, 134
   does not lead to general disorder, 142
   distinguished from conscientious refusal,
      123
   endemic to democratic societies, 109
   for equal liberty, 123
   Gandhi, 145
   in unjust government, the true place for
      just men is prison, 115
   involves conflict of duties, 121
   is result, not cause of violence, 142
   justification for, 123
   limited, 125
   limited in nearly just society, 119
   limitations on, 119
   may provide outlet for rebellion, 142
   naive, 109
   non-payment of taxes, 115
   not violent, 122, 135, 145
   of laws that are not wrong, 143
   principle of fair equality of opportunity,
      123
   refusal to serve in Viet Nam War, 137,
      150
   restrictions on, 123
   role of, 127
   serious infringements, 123
   Thoreau, 145
   violations, 123
   violence to people distinguished from vio-
      lence to property, 145
Civil rights

ascerbic comments about demonstrators, 92

comparison of civil rights protesters with demonstrators, 91

penalties of law accepted by Socrates, 91

Class struggle, 251

Cleaver, E. 75, 78, 79

Domestic Law and International Order, 75

schizophrenic view about nature of people, 80

Code, 198, 199, 200

drafting of, 198

Code of Hammurabi, 32

as myth system, 24

Code of Professional Responsibility, 409

see Legal ethics,

Codification, see Code

Cohen, Morris R., 232, 247

four dogmas of historicism, 233

Psychology and Scientific Methods, 232

rationalism and historicism compared, 232

complementarity of legal principles, 247

Command, 273, 274, 275

as creating duty, 273

connection with duty and sanction, 274

defined, 273

ideas comprehended by, 274

requires power to inflict evil for disobedience, 273

Commands

general as distinguished from particular, 275

generally determined, 275

species of, 275

Common law

economic analysis of, 556

Communication

as a central principle of natural law, 209

as a way of being alive, 209

Concentration camps,

murder of Jewish civilians, 159

service of armed guard at, 159

Confessions

see Criminal law

Confidentiality

duty of lawyer to client, 417

Configurative thinking

defined, 549

Conscience,

placing American people above, 91

Conscientious objection, 150, 151

based on ethical commitments, 150

Conscientious objectors, 137, 152, 153

see also Dissent

conscription for non-combat service, 154

religious and non-religious, 155

Conscientious refusal, 127

defined, 123

justification for, 125

see Civil disobedience, 123

to serve in armed forces, 127

Conscription, 152

see also Draft,

power of Congress, 152

when permissible, 126

Constitution, United States, 154, 308

see also Judicial review; constitutional law,

amendment of, 310

appropriate for judges to "twist" language, 454

as a living institution, not as a document, 450

designed to survive for many years, 310

determines content of general norms, 394

due process clause,

fifth amendment, 150, 153, 155

fourth amendment, 189

establishment of religion clause, 152

first amendment, 150, 151, 153, 155, 157

fourteenth amendment, 176, 177, 178, 190, 191

free exercise of religion clause, 150, 152

how actually amended, 453

innovations in by judges, 306

Justice Douglas' view of

interpretation of, 311

interpretations of, 306, 314

lip service to, 306

Llewellyn's theory of, 449

ninth amendment, 176, 189

only practice legitimizes words of the Constitution, 451

original meaning of, 310

segregation, 317

Constitutional law

myth of neutrality in adjudication, 322

neutral principles of, 313

principles of interpretation of, 313

Constitutional laws,

see also Constitution,

affected by legal realism, 470

Constitutional objections

power of Congress to draft, 152

Constitutive prescriptions, 329

Constitutive process
  defined, 14, 581
  dynamic conception, 14
  ongoing decision process, relationship with
      public order, 581
Control, 4
  defined, 580
  effective power, 4
Consumer protection
  affected by legal realism, 477
Contract, Social
  see Social contract, 102
Cook, Walter Wheeler, 445
Country
  see also State, 87
  argument of "love it or leave it", 90
Courts
  decisionmaking by, 329
  independent of government, 133
  function of in interpreting Constitution,
      308
Court system
  restraints on elites, 52
Crime, 254
  see Criminal Law
  and sin, 254
  difficult to determine which acts should
      constitute crime, 336
  not diminished by punishment, 74
  separate from sin, 338
Crime against nature, 175
  is vague term, 175
Crimes, 257
  changing definitions of, 257
Criminal law
  affected by legal realism, 473
  and moral principles, 340
  and offenses against society as a whole,
      339
  confessions, 474
  goals of, 336
  most convictions result from "plea bar-
      gaining", 473
  relation to moral law, 339
Critical legal studies
  development of, 463
  drawing on "structuralist" writers, 467
  failure to clarify and systematically de-
      velop goals, 470
  similarities to Americal Legal Realist
      Movement, 470
  views similar to Gramsci's, 79
Critical legal theory

  see, Critical legal studies,
Crito, 79, 143, 146
Cultural system, 460
  see Jurisprudence,
Custom
  distinguished from law, 287
  Hart's treatment of, 303
Customary law, 280, 387, 394
Customary rules
  distinguished from law, 287
Cyclical historicism, 253
  see Historicism, 253

Dahl, R. 52
  *Who Governs: Democracy and Power in
      an American City,* 44
  Government by: economic and social elites,
      44, 47
  interest groups, 45, 46
  masses and leaders, 47
  political parties, 45, 46
Dahrendorf, Ralf, 64, 65, 510
  In Praise of Thrasymachus, 64
Dam, K.
  *The Special Responsibility of Lawyers
      in the Executive Branch,* 410
Dean, John
  Blind Ambition, 539
Death
  "brain dead", 181
  determination of, 179
  determination of cannot be produced from
      religious or moral principle, 183
  easing of, 186
Decision
  see also, Decision-makers, Decision-mak-
      ing, Decisions
  definition of, 7
  intellectual tasks of, described,
  social decision-making, 563
  strategy of, 567
Decisionmaking
  components, 12, 461
  definition of problem in, 16
  intellectual tasks of -
      goal clarification, 16, 20
      trend analysis, 16, 20
  non-neutrality in decisions of the Supreme
      Court, 329
  tools for, 12
Decision, rational, 215
Decision
  a variety of distinct functions or oper-

ations, 7
definition, 7
Decisions
    analysis of factors affecting, 585
    application, 15
    appraisal, 15
    components of, 14
    description of past trends, 585
    different phases of, described, 582
    intellectual tasks of, described, 584
    intelligence, 15
    interpretation by political, economic and
        military spheres, 50
    invocation, 15
    made by appraisal of alternative choices,
        324
    prescription, 15
    projection of future trends, 585
    promotion, 15
    resort to general principles, 436
    termination, 15
Decisionmakers
    means of power have increased, 50
Decisionmaking
    elements of making law, applying law,
        terminating law, 7
    general terms of, described, 8
    summarized, 7
Democracy
    and equality, 45
    and unequal distribution of resources, 45
Desegregation, 489
De Tocqueville, A., 353
Detroit Schools case, 492
    see also Legal education; social science
        and the courts,
Devlin, Patrick, Lord, 338, 345
Dewey, John,
    Freedom and Culture, 250
Dillard, H., 404
Discrimination,
    see also Segregation
    national policy to discourage racial dis-
        crimination, 519
    power of Congress, 155
Disobedience,
    see Civil disobedience, 140
    Disobedience and Democracy, 140
Displaced Persons Act,
    see also Concentration camps; Fedorenko
        v. U.S., 159
    bars assisting in persecuting civilians, 160
Dissent, 128

see also Civil disobedience;
    Fortas, Abe,
    by causing physical injury, 130
        or interfering with others,
    by trespass, 130
    by unlawfully preventing movement of
        traffic, 130
    conscientious objectors, 137
    limitations of, 129
    protected by Constitution, 132
    right to, 129
    right to be protected, by state, 133
    to cause injury by, violating valid laws,
        132
    when possible, 153
Divine law, 253, 292
DNR ("Do not resuscitate")
    applied to the terminally ill, 181
Doctrine,
    analysis of, 464
Dred Scott v. Sanford, 234, 266, 335
Drugs, 157
    see also Peyote,
Due process clause, 150
Durkheim, E., 363
Duty, 203
    see also Command, 274
    defined, 273, 283, 285
    to obey laws, 202
    none to eradicate evil, 112
    problematic for permanent minorities, 121
Dworkin, Ronald
    and positivism, 294
    attack on positivism, 296
    definition of "obligation", 294
    Is Law a System of Rules?, 294
    key propositions of positivism, 294
    theory of principles available to judges to
        fill in gaps in rules, 294
Dyett v. Pendleton, 346

Economic analysis of law
    criticism of, 554
    explains rules and outcomes of legal sys-
        tem, 553
    legal doctrines as promoting efficient al-
        location of resources, 552
    use to clarify value conflicts, 555
    use to determine most efficient means to
        achieve desired ends, 555
Economic elements
    as ultimately determining element in
        history, 249

Economics
   see Economic analysis of law,
Economy, 248, 270
   see also Marx, Karl,
   as real basis of legal structure of society, 248
Economy, United States
      dominated by giant corporations, 49
Edginton v. Fitzmaurice, 154
Education, 531
   see Detroit schools case,
   see Legal education,
Edwards v. Habib, 306
Ehrlich, Eugene, 5, 38, 39
   "living law", 37
   association, 36
   not be created by the state, 37
Eisenhower, President, 26
Eisenstadt v. Baird, 190
Elites, 23, 26, 31, 58, 79
   clash with democratic myth, 48
   concentration of power in, 47
   defined, 25
   derive power from state, corporation and army, 49
   how accommodated to constitutional principles, 48
   interchanging roles, 51
   monopolize power, 44
   rule of media, 52
Empirical Studies
      see, Legal Realism; Policy Science; Social Science; Sociology of Law,
Engels, F., 248
   correspondence of, 249
Equality
   and democracy, 45
Equilibrium model
   of social life, 66
Ethics,
   devaluation of, 257
   of applying systems of authority, 247
Ethics, Nichomachean, 170
Euthanasia, 184
   see Matter of Quinlan, 179
Expert testimony
   see also Social science and the courts,
   flaws in usage in courts, 494
   use in courts characterized as "blind leading the blind", 499
Evil
      in return for evil is not just, 86
Factors,

analysis of, 17
Facts, 491
   see also Social science data,
   descriptions of are highly selective, 511
   inseparable from values, 325, 326
   unclear line between facts and interpretation, 497
Fairness
   defined, 213
   for individuals, 217
   principles of, 217
Family,
   economic analysis of, 555
   established by nature, 171
Fedorenko
   appeals, 92
   social consequences, 92
Fedorenko v. United States, 92, 159
Females,
      see Natural law, 171
Fetus
   as a person, 193
   fourteenth amendment, 193
   viability of, 196
   viability outside womb, 194
Fifth amendment, 191
   see Constitution, U.S.,
First amendment, 157, 158, 191
   see Constitution, U.S.,
Focus of inquiry,
   delimitation of, 578
   on authoritative decision, 579
   on both authority and control, 579
   on both perspectives and operations, 579
   on civic order, 14
   on comprehensiveness and selectivity, 579
   on phase analysis:
      participants
      perspectives
      situations
      bases of power
      strategies
      outcomes, 14
   phase, description of and interaction, 14
   public order, 14
Fortas, Abe, 128
   Concerning Dissent and Civil Disobedience, 128
   views of as compared with views of Rawls, 128
Force,
   see Austin, John; Control; Jurisprudence of naked power; Positivism,

Fourth amendment, 191
   due process clause,
Frank, Jerome, Judge
   Law and the Modern Mind, 439
Freedom and Culture, 250
Freedom of speech, 129
   limitations of,
Freud, Sigmund, 547
Fuller, Lon, 24, 197, 204, 210, 403
  natural law, minimum content of, 208
  the morality of laws, 208

Ghandhi, M., 134, 135, 145
Gangster
  order of, distinguished from legal norm,
    by Kelsen, and by Hart, 401
General will
  when supercedes private judgment, 101
Germany, situation in, 282
  see also, Hart, H. L. A.; *Concept of Law,*
Goals
  clarification of, 513
  contributions of sociological jurisprudence
    to goal clarification, 513
  explicit postulation of, 586
  is not simply a given, 10
Goal clarification
  see also Decisionmaking,
  requirements of, 564
  intellectual tasks of, 17
Goal thinking
  defined, 549
  requires clarification of values, 531
  training in should be goal of legal edu-
    cation, 531
Godwin, William, 99, 544
  *An Enquiring Concerning Political Jus-
    tice,* 99
  exponent of primacy of individual judg-
    ment, 99
  universal exercise of private judgment,
    101
Gordon, R. W., 463
Gorgias, 63, 79
Government
  as inexpedient, 102
  authority of, 117
  bound by laws, 135
  duty to obey, 107, 111
  evils of, 102
  is best if governs least, 102
  justice, 105
  majority rule because are strongest, 110

  nature and object of, 99
  object of, 107
  origins of, 105
  purpose of, 105
Government of laws, 353, 442
  as an insult and undemocratic canard, 456
  as naive fantasy, 456
  as neutral, 332
Government and laws
    interrogation by, 87
Gramsci, Antonio, 466
  theory of hegemony, 79
Gray, John Chipman, 443
Green, Mark
    The Other Government, 409
Griswold v. Connecticut, 177, 190
Groupthink
  cause of numerous errors by government
    leaders, 377
  pressures for conformity in small groups,
    377
  symptoms of, 377
Group-will, 37
Grundnorm
  see also Basic Norm,
  is merely hypothesized, and does not ne-
    cessarily exist, 402

Harper v. Virginia, 309
Harris v. State, 173
Hart, H. L. A. 175, 182, 204, 295, 345,
    533, 545
  alternate version of positivism, 282
  aptness of analogy of law to rules of cricket
    game, 292
  concept of law, 204, 208
  failure to consider intellectual tasks, 294
  law and morality, 333
  minimum content of natural law, 204
  notion of power as component of legal
    system, 292
  The Concept of Law, 282
  two types of rules—primary and second-
    ary, defined, 282
Hegel, F., 248, 250, 329
Hegemony
    theory of, 79, 466
Hierarchy
  as relationship of super- and sub-ordina-
    tion, 392
  characteristic of bureaucratic organiza-
    tions, 364
  functions and features of, 364

hierarchical structure described, of norms, 392
patterns in governance, 82
ways of organizing in, 468
Higher law
appeals to constitute a fundamental problem of democratic society, 92
see Law, Higher, 92
Historicism, 222, 224, 253
assumptions about law, 224
assumptions of, 224
based upon belief in determinism, 233
belief in individualized, attributes of nations, 226
belief that law is determined by spirit of a people, 233
conservative exponents, 225
cyclical, 253
fallacy of, 329
four main dogmas of, 233
in American constitutional theory, 266
jurisprudence of, 224
notion of law as according with "spirit" of a people, 232
Historicism, Radical, 248
Historicist
approach rejected by Supreme Court, 527
Historicist jurisprudence
appraisal of, 266
History
as a series of conflicts between classes, 250
Hitler, A.
laws in Germany under, 201
obligation to obey, 201
Hobbes, T., 65
Hoebel, E. A., 38, 39
Holzer v. Deutsche Reichsbahn-Gesellschaft, 253, 348
Homosexuality
see also Wolfenden Report,
as criminal offense, 336
as natural or unnatural, 178
Henningsen v. Bloomfield Motors, Inc., 477
Howell, R. F.,
in constitutional adjudication, 322
Hughes, Chief Justice, 137
Human dignity, 324

Immigration and Nationality Act, 159
Immorality,
impossibility of setting limits to power of

state to control, 342
Incompatibility of principles, 302
Incompetent,
terminating life of, 179
Inequalities
in resources, 46, 48
Injustice,
see also, Justice
should be evenly distributed, 120
Institutions,
how regenerated, 261
self-replicating character of, 263, 264, 265
Intellectual tasks,
analysis of factors affecting decisions, 575
clarifying goals, 575
description of past trends, 575
evaluation of policy alternatives, 575
factor analysis, defined, 16
goal clarification, defined, 16
importance of, 575
invention of alternatives, 17
defined,
prediction of future trends, 575
prediction, defined, 17
trend analysis, defined, 16
Intellectual tasks of decision,
described, 584
International law,
a de facto government may exist even if it does not conform to its constitution, 57
relation to national law, 583
Interpretation,
extensive, 306
function of court in, 308
going against intention of legislature, 306
of Constitution, 313
unclear line between facts and interpretation, 497
Irrational,
in human behavior, 166

Jacobson v. Massachusetts, 192
Janis, M.,
cause of numerous errors by government leaders, 376
Groupthink, 376
tendency to seek concurrence among members of group, 376
Javins v. First National Realty Corp., 306, 528
Jews,
as law abiding, 92

murdered in Treblinka, 159, 161, 162, 166
Jhering, R., 24, 236, 266
  Struggle for Law, 236
  view of law as media tool between competing claimants, 246
  applicability of contradictory precepts or procedures, 292
Judges,
  areas in which they exercise subjective discretion, 293
  attacks notion of rules as key factors in making choices, 434
  decisions by as focus of concern by positivists, 293
  key role in determining outcome of a case, 434
  subjective discretion as inherent in function of, 293
Judicial decision,
  difficulties in predicting, 462
  predictions about, 463
  use of Boolean Algebra to predict, 463
Judicial discretion, 294, 300
  and legal principles, 305
  view of positivists, 301
Judicial practice, 306
Judicial process
  see Judges; Judicial decisions
Judicial restraint, 318, 330
Judicial review, 308, 313
  positivist theory of, 311
  as expression of positivism, 306
  judging by neutral principles, 316
  judgment based on immediate result, 314
  need to be genuinely principled and transcending immediate results, 315
  obligation of courts to rule unconstitutionality of statute, 314
  political questions, 314, 316
  should be based on reason and principles, 316
  standards of, 314
Jurimetrics, 459
  difficulties in predicting behavior of judges, 462
  see, Behavioral jurisprudence,
Jurisprudence, 1, 220, 271
  see also, Behavioral jurisprudence; Justice; Law
  as a science, 459
  as positive law, 271
  as separate from politics, 383
  behavioral, 459

new approaches to, 459
importance only if it contributes to problem-solving, 11
includes certain laws not imperative, 280
inherited literature, 10
is it relevant? 1
must be realistic and must encourage systematic and configurative examination of significant variables affecting decision, 574
must clarify observational standpoint, 574
must comprise four major emphases to be relevant, 574
must have comprehensive focus, 574
must specify values postulated or assumed, 574
needs to specify intellectual tasks to study interrelations of law and social process, 574
New Haven School, seeks more comprehensive and penetrating frame of reference—view of authority, 573
as bureaucracy, see "Pure theory" of law, 359, 381
of naked power, 56
of natural law, 82
of obedience—definition, 82
of obedience
  —independent moral
  —value in obeying
  —authority, 82
province of, 270
solving social problems, 10-11
study of cultural system, 459
study of relationships in social system, 459
Jurisprudence of bureaucracy, 359
Jurisprudence, Sociological, presuppositions of, 400
Justice, 107-108, 170, 210
  see also, Law
  all are bound to conform to principles of, 107
  as the basic structure of society, 211
  concept of as distinguished from conception of, 211, 212
  concerns major social institutions, 211
  consists in superior ruling over and having more than inferior, 63
  definition of, 104
  (is) dependent on how rights and duties are assigned, 212
  distinguished from just, 170
  duty, 104

(as) fairness, 214, 220
(as) fairness, requirement of, 214
(as) first virtue of social institutions, 210
(as) the interest of the stronger, 59
intuitive convictions regarding, 210
main idea of theory of, 213
moral, 104
more important than life or children, 90
as natural, 170
natural justice as distinguished from justice by convention,
political, 170
principles apply to inequalities, 212
principles of, 210
role of, 210
structural nature of, 209
theory of, 209
various conceptions of, 215
Jurisprudential "frames", 8
Justice as fairness, 221
duty to comply with just institutions, 221
duty to do justice, 221
Justices
Rawls' principles of, 119
The Justice's dilemma
alternatives available to Chief Justice,
8
Just society, 210
rights not subject to political bargaining,
210
Just war, 126

Kafka, F.
The Trial, 376
Kairys, D., 463
Kelsen, Hans, 381
see "pure theory" of law, 381
compared with Austin, 402
General Theory of Law and State, 381
his conception of origin of law and of au-
thority contrasted with others, 403
roots of his conception of jurisprudence,
402
views of compared with those of Hart and
Austin, 403
Kennedy, President John
lies of, 26
King, Jr., Martin Luther, 99, 134, 143
accepting jail sentence, 135
Letter from Birmingham City Jail, 118
Krash, A., 406, 409
Kropotkin, Prince Piotr, 75, 78
Revolutionary Pamphlets, 67

schizophrenic view about nature of people,
80
views compared with those of Gorgias and
of Nietzsche, 79
Language, Naturalist, 180, 196
Lasswell, Harold., 14, 52
Clarifying Value Judgment: Principles of
Content and Procedure, 549
Criteria for a Theory about Law, 573
Legal Education and Public Policy, 587
policy-oriented jurisprudence, 573
and "preventive politics", 546
Psychopathology and Politics, 546
Lasswell, H. D. and McDougal M.S.
Criteria for a Theory About Law, 573
Lasswell, H. and McDougal M.S.
Criteria for a Theory About Law, 573
Law, xiii, 202, 203
see also Civil disobedience; Laws; Norms;
Obedience; Positivism, Rules
agreement, 87
agreement of with individual, 87
all achievements of are achieved by struggle, 237
appearances and reality, 23
of associations, 36
belief in certainty of is legal myth, 441
as a belief system, 469
bequeathed by slavery, serfdom, feudalism and royalty, 67
brings citizens into existence, 87
changes in, 200
character of, 271
(as) cluster of beliefs, 466
(as) command, 272, 273
command by political superior to inferior,
277
(as a) continuous process of problem-solving, xiii
continuous process of authoritative decision, 579
(as) creating duty, 273
creation and application of, 397
of criminal gang, 41
criteria for a theory about, 573
critical studies in, see Critical legal studies
decisions cannot be made by rules alone,
516
(as) the decisions of courts, 443
(as) decisions that are both authoritative
and controlling, 580-83
defined, 134, 271
defined as a command which obliges, 277

development of compared to language, 227

difference between creating and applying law, 396

distinct from morals, 333

does not consist simply of mental exercises about abstract notions or rules, 9

duty to disobey, 128
— genocide laws, 128
— segregation laws, 129

duty to obey, 128, 129

duty to obey evil law, 334

as dynamic system of norms, 386

(and) economics, 552

in early history, 226

educates citizens, 87

elements of, 287

ends of, 543

established by lawyers, middle class and priests to protect own interests, 67

existing without political authority, 37

exists among subgroups, 38

exists where there are coercive means, 37

expectations of the effective and relevant actors, 6

expectations shared about the right way of doing things, 6

Freudian reasons for belief in certainty of law, 441

functions of, 337

higher than law of state, 92

idealistic, defined, 253

ideational, defined, 256

as identical with state, 383

an inquiry into a social process, 6

inner morality of, 203

(as) instrument of social stability, 449

(as) instrument to order and change society, 246

instrumentalist theory of relation with society, 465

involves process of choice, 516

little to do with the official rules, 5

the living law, 5

long term consequences of breaking, 91

(as) made by a judge whenever he decides a case, 443

made by weak majority, 63

major portion is to protect property, 71

(as) making choices, 533

(as) a means of "legitimizing" class society, 465

means "the opinions of a half-a-dozen old gentlemen", 494

misdeeds accomplished in the name of, 68

(and) morality, 155, 313

moral obligation to obey, 201

(and) morals, 204

nature of structural, 197

necessary criteria of law, 38

need to maintain order, 132

neutral, criticism of, 464

not necessary to be credited by state, 36

(as) nothing more than words, 456

obedience to, 129, 254

obedience to immoral law, 141

obligation to obey, 201

observation of actual behavior, 5

operates to induce acceptance of things as they are, 448

operational code, 25

(as) order of political superior to political inferior, 269, 270

organic connection of with character of people, 227

origin in ruling class for their advantage, 70

origin of, see Savigny, K. F., 236, 237

paradox of, 128

persistent discrepancies in, 24

personnel and procedures as important as the content, 6

(and) policy, 4

of political superior to political inferior, 271

politics of, 463

power sometimes in sub-group, 41

(a) practical guide to the law in context, 4

principles of bound up with interests of individuals and classes, 237

private systems of, 25

procedure for creating, 392

(as) process of continuous creation by humans, 469

(as) process of shaping and sharing values, 574

(as) a product of conflict, 246

(a) product of modern times, 69

provisions for interpretation of, 288

provisions for mode of change in, 288

public law, 25

and the "real world", 24

related to larger community context, 583

relation to public opinion, 337

relation to social process, 582

requires struggle, 236
as rooted in material conditions, 248
as rule by one with power, 271
rule of has intrinsic value, 140
rules, drawbacks of law as, 305
(as) rules, ignores much that transpires in
    decisionmaking, 293
(as) rules which are actually applied by
    judge, 443
sanctioned by priest and warriors, 69
science of, 383, 459
sensate, defined, 255
(and) social process, 266
sources of, 68, 445
sources of—defined, 395
statements of are true if they describe past
    behavior and predict future behavior
    of law officials, 446
static and dynamic concept of, 391
struggle for, 236
structures in, 197
subgroups of, 38
substantive and adjective, 394
survival as aim of, 204
symbolizes a dream, 448
systems of
    —ideational, idealistic, 253
uncertainty in is not an accident, 440
accident, 440
useless and hurtful, 72
valid because derived from a basic norm,
    382
viewed as a continuous process of author-
    itative decision, 579
viewed as having autonomous essence,
    404
viewed as organized into structures, 466,
    467
viewed as part of a social continuum, 350
violation of unconstitutional law, 132
(as a) way of thinking about government,
    448
ways to fail to make, 198
ways to make, 197
worship of, 65
Law, higher
    social consequences of appeals to, 92
Law and economics
    defined, 552
Law and morality
    reasons for distinction by positivists, 335
    Law, Morality of, 197
Law practice,

much transacted outside of the adver-
    sary process, 1
Law, rule of
    defined, 134, 353
Law, sources of
    rules are only some of sources of law,
        445
Laws
    see also, Justice, Norms
    brings humans into the world, 88
    character of different kinds of, 270
    (as) creating duties, 279
    (as) commands, 270
    educates humans, 88
    implied contract to obey law if citizen re-
        mains in state, 88
    implied contract with citizen that he may
        leave if unsatisfied with state, 88
    improperly called, 270
    may go where he pleases, 88
    may interfere with actions not beliefs, 149
    in Nazi Germany, 282
    properly called, distinguished from im-
        properly called, 270
    as rules by political superiors, 271
    should not be destroyed, 87
    slave of, 87
    violation of as a means of public pressure,
        134
    violation of is punishable regardless of
        motivation, 134
Lawyers, xiii, 222, 352
    see also Legal profession
    architects of the law, 10
    bring about the future, 1
    called upon to make policy judgments, 2
    charged with failing to discharge respon-
        sibilities for welfare of society, 408
    Code of Professional Responsibility, 412
    commercial and political functions, 1
    contributions to the clarification of the
        common interest, 10
    "critical", 467
    decisionmaking, predicting and influenc-
        ing, 3
    difficult to find existence of duty to report
        a crime by a client, 411
    duty of confidentiality according to policy
        of American Bar Association, 425
    duty of confidentiality to clients under
        Model Rules of American Bar Asso-
        ciation, 427
    duty to clients of confidentiality, 412

duty to disclose crimes of client, 410
duty to disclose false securities registration statement, 424
engaged in study of objective physical phenomena; behavior of human beings, 445
engaged in trying to forecast behavior of judges, 445
functions of, 222
(as) intellectual jobbers and contractors, 10
leftist, 466
make value judgments, 1
members of a public profession, 409
non-court problem, 2
(as) policy makers or administrators, 8, 411
prefer order to liberty, 353
as problem-solvers, xiii
responsibilities and liabilities of, 425
restraining influence of, 52
serve public interest best by faithfully representing private interests of clients, 408
should assist in improving legal system, 409
special responsibility of in executive branch, 410
special skills relevant to responsibilities in the body politic, 10
spend most of their time out of courts, 1
strategist for high finance, cluster of banks, 10
time in courts, 1
trial lawyer not prototype of the legal profession, 1
Leases
issues decided by use of contract law, rather than property law, 528
are made in a different context than formerly, 530
Legal
see, Law, Laws, Positivism, Rules,
Legal decisions
features of, 41
induced by resort to prior decisions, 437, 438
by resort to "common sense", 439
Legal doctrines
travel in pairs of opposites, 247
Legal education
aim of, 1
aim to turn students into better citizens and

community leaders, 2
conceived in terms of courts, 2
focus on courts, 1
and public policy, 531
requires training in goal-thinking, trend-thinking, and scientific-thinking, 531, 532
training to perform intellectual tasks of decision, 587
Legal ethics, 359
American Bar Association's *Model Rules*, 427
core of professional responsibility, 409
duty to represent client whose interest is contrary to that of the public, 408
statement of policy of American Bar Association, 425
Legal fictions
definition of, 24
not synonymous with myth systems, 24
Legal history
see, Historicism; Historical jurisprudence
Legalism,
defined, 314
elements of, 351
as operative outlook of the legal profession, 352
Legal levels
and multiplicity of legal levels, 35
within a single society, 35
Legal norms
see Norms
Legal obligation, 304
relating to principles, 300
Legal order
see "Pure theory of law"
all legal norms are derived from same basic norm, 388
Constitution, 393
different stages of, 393
as system of norms, 384, 386
Legal Philosophy
see Jurisprudence
Legal positivism, 459
see Positivism,
Legal principles, 237, 247
applicability determined by set of shifting standards, 303
bound up with interests of individuals and classes, 237
can not be determined by test of pedigree, 304
cannot be listed, 304

distinguished from legal rules, 297

distinguished from rules and policies defined, 296

do not constitute law, 446

equally valid conflicting principles exist, 436

magical and mysterious properties of, 305

as not binding in law, 302

are numerous, 304

shift and change, 304

travel in pairs of complementary opposites, 247

Legal problems

three types of approaches to resolve, 435

Legal profession, 352

as conservative, 352

problem-solving, 7

supports established social order, 352

Legal realism

assumes that the judge is the key factor in decision, 434

Freudian adaptations, 439

deficiencies of, 483

induces judges to change laws to yield desired social results, 470

practical consequences of, 470

rejection of rules as providing effective guides for judges, 435

view of law as process of making decisions, 516

Legal realists, 266

Legal right, 241

ideal value of, 242

struggle for, is duty to oneself and to society, 242

Legal rule

does not have dimension of weight, 298

Legal rules, 199, 246

see Law, Laws

see also McDougal, M.

distinguished from legal principles, 297

master rule, 303

need for clarity of, 199

need to know in advance, 199

need to be reasonable, 199

requirements of, 201

travelling in pairs of opposites, 247

Legal science, 351

Legal system

appraised in terms of values to be maximized, 574

balanced opposites of, 247

combination of primary and secondary rules, 291

example of multiplicity of among Chinese, 40

(as) game loaded in favor of wealthy and powerful, 464

hierarchy of systems, 39

includes Cosa Nostra, 40

includes family, 40

legitimizing power of, 469

(as) part of system of public order, 574

required primary and secondary rules, 289

Legal theory

important only if it contributes to problem-solving, 11

Legislation

appropriateness of, 228

nature of, 106

Legitimacy

achieved by preponderance of power over resistance, 66

Lex imperfecta, 33, 35

to protect operational code, 31

Lex simulata, 33, 35

discrepancy between myth system and operational code, 34

examples of, 31

imperfect law, 33

to protect operational code, 32

Liberalism

based on free market, 354

Lies

insulate leaders from responsibility for, 25

by public officials, 26

Life

divergence of opinion on when life begins, 194

fourteenth amendment, 193

question of when life begins not resolved by court, 193

prenatal, protection of, 191

prolongation of by artificial means, 179

right of doctor to terminate, 183

right to terminate one's own life, 185

use of extraordinary means to preserve, 185

view of Catholic Church on termination of life, 183

Life support

see Matter of Quinlan

Liberty, 189

protected by Constitution, 190

Limited altruism

as natural fact, 205
Limited resources
  as natural fact, 205
Limited strength of will
  as natural fact, 206
Limited understanding
  as natural fact, 206
Llewellyn, Karl, 401
  The Constitution as an Institution, 449
  multiple legal systems within our society,
    38
Local institutions
  as part of a process of shaping and shar-
    ing values, 573
Lochner v. New York, 189
Locke, John, 273
Logic
  difficulty of resort to logic in making de-
    cisions, 438
  syntactic derivation, 330
  use in law, 330
Lopez-Alcalde, Justice, 8
Loving v. Virginia, 177
Loyalty
  see Jurisprudence of bureaucracy, 380

MacPherson v. Buick Motor Co., 478
Machiavelli, N., 47
Maine, Henry, Sir, 233, 267
Marriage
  by two persons of same sex, refusal to
    issue license to, 176
  economic analysis of, 176, 556
  as fundamental to human race, 177
  involves procreation and rearing of chil-
    dren, 177
  as involving politics and morals, 341
Marx, Karl, 250, 267, 329
  the class struggle
    *A Contribution to Critique of Politi-
      cal Economy*, 248
  correspondence of, 249
Marxist theory, 251, 266
  criticism of, 251
  criticism of, as based on single cause, 251
  "dated", 253
  as non-scientific, 251
Masses
  governing society, 47
Matter of Quinlan, 179, 232
McBoyle v. United States, 307
McDougal, Myres, S., xiv, 324, 329
  authority, ethics of applying systems of,
    247

Criteria for a Theory about Law, 573
Ethics of Applying Systems of Authority,
  247
Legal Education and Public Policy, 531,
  587
policy-oriented jurisprudence, 573
McDougal and Reisman
  *International Law in Contemporary
    Perspective*, 348
Meyerhofer v. Empire Fire and Marine Insurance Company, 421
Milgram, experiments
  actions of subjects compared with actions
    of Socrates and Martin Luther King,
    98
  few people can resist authority, 97
  ordinary people can become agents of de-
    struction, 97
Milgram, Stanley
  the perils of obedience, 93
  the Milgram experiments, 93
Miller, J. C.
  constitutional adjudication, 322, 527
Mills, C. Wright, 10, 52, 66
  The Power Elite, 48, 366
Miranda v. Arizona, 474
Morality, 202
  of aspiration, 202
  as distinguished from positive law, 272
  duty of, 104
  of duty, 208
  excludes obedience, 108
  (and) justice, 105
  (and) law, 155, 313
  public, 340, 342
  (and) positivism, 333
  source of, 348
Moral law
  relation to criminal law, 339
Moral obligation to obey law, 201
Morals
  enforcement of, 338
  and law, 204
  of society judged by viewpoint of man on
    Clapham omnibus, 343
Mormons, 148
  see Polygamy, 158
Mosca, G., 44
Muddling through
  as policy method, 567
Muller v. Oregon, 486
Multiple legal systems, 36, 53
  idea expressed by Max Weber, 37
  in a particular territorial area individual

exposed to several simultaneously, 42

multiple levels in stable society, 35

Myrdal, Gunnar, 324

values necessary in research, 327

Myths

myth systems and law, 23

that government of United States is one of laws, not men, 456

that one who becomes a justice of the court becomes politically sterile, 456, 457

Myth system,

code discrepant from the myth system, 27

discrepancies with law on books, 52

discrepancy with norms applied in practice, 24

discrepant from operational code, 26, 27

not legal fiction, 24

operational code, 24

and operational codes, 23

symbiotic relationship with operational code, 34

Naked power

see Power

Narcotics

see Peyote,

Nation

idea of, 231

Natural

see Naturalist language,

effect of use of this term, 170

sexual behavior, 173

usefulness of the term, 209

use of term can obscure thinking, 173

Natural duty, 221

see Natural law; Rawls, John

to uphold just institutions, 120

Natural duties

see Law, Duty to obey; Natural Law; Rawls, John

characteristics of, 221

examples of, 220

of individuals, 220

Natural facts, 206

as a basis of law, 205

detailed, 205

Natural justice

defined, 64

Natural law,

see Nature, belief structures, Physical naturalism, Structural naturalism,

based upon natural facts, 205

based on religious beliefs, 175

communication as a central principle of, 175, 209

difference between men and women, 169

different meanings of, 82

distinction from positive law, 387

distinguished from learned law, 227

(and) due process, 309

equality of people as basis of, 204

fails to provide standard to classify act as crime, 175

fundamental problem of democratic society, 92

helps to legitimize role of governing elite but also constitutes threat to them, 92

human vulnerability as a basis of, 204

jurisprudence of, 82

legitimizing the role of the governing elite, 92

made up of abiding principles of right and justice, 437

minimal content of, 175, 204, 208

natural facts as basis of, 207

natural legitimate content of law, 118

natural necessity, 207

opposing, 92

perils of obedience, 94

and positivists, 197

postulates true but unverifiable, 82

and rebellion, 92

simple truisms as core of, 207

sources of, 175

used to restrain government action, 92

Natural necessity

see Natural law, 207

Natural rights

term used to obstruct attempts to decide and clarify goals, 91

Naturalism

see Nature, 197

see Naturalist language, 197

distinguished from obedience as natural law, 170

jurisprudence of physical and structural naturalism, 169, 170

physical and structural, definition of, 169, 170, 178

structural, 169

Naturalist language

see Nature; Natural law

Nature, 166, 169, 174

see Natural law,
belief structures not found in, 468
crime against, 173, 174
crime against nature, 173
difference between men and women, 166
formation of family, 171
formation of state, 171
formation of villages, 171
intimates that powerful should have more
    than weaker, 63
thing fully developed, 171
as unchangeable, 170
Nazi, 197
concentration camps, 159
actions of, 159, 160
binding in United States, 58
Nazi Germany, 269
Nazis
see Concentration camps
activities as, 159
concealment of, 160
evil laws of, led some to reject positivism,
    334
laws of, 201
obligation to obey, 201
validity of law of, 334
Nearly just society, 128
see Civil disobedience, 119
requirement to obey law in, 119
Negroes
see Blacks
see Dred Scott v. Sandford
see Racial discrimination
entitlement to constitutional rights, 234
Neutrality
in constitutional adjudication, 322, 329
myth of, 322, 323
in non-law disciplines, 324
in other disciplines, 324
Neutral principles, 322
of constitutional interpretation, 313
difficulty of formulating criteria for, 329
distinguished from value choices, 329
impossibility of, 324
New Deal, The
legislation under stricken down by courts,
    308
Nicomachean ethics, 170
Nietzsche, F.W., 170
Ninth amendment, 191
Non-neutrality, 329
Norm
creation and contents determined by higher

norm, 397
is not a statement about reality, 384
is valid if derived from basic norm, 385
Normative order
see Norms
Normative systems
lip service, 24
Norms
devaluation of, 257
discrepancies, 24
hierarchy of, 392
static and dynamic systems, 385, 386
system of, 382
valid even if incompatible with moral or
    political value, 386
Norms, Basic
see Grundnorm
change of, 389
defined, 388
legitimacy of as based on effectiveness,
    389
Nuremberg doctrine,
covers only extreme outrages, 138
obedience to superior orders, 138
Nuremberg principles, 269, 282
Nuremberg trials, 92, 166
obligation to refuse to obey, 92, 166

Obedience
see also Civil disobedience; Obligation to
    obey laws,
argument for, 83
entails not regarding oneself as responsible
    for actions, 98
essence is to view oneself as instrument
    of another, 98
ethic of, 82
jurisprudence, 82
limited, 109
mechanical obedience to state illustrated
    by Lt. Calley, 93
Obedience to laws, 120
problematic for permanent minority, 121
Obedience to orders of authority figures
the Milgram experiments, 93
Objectivity
and values, 327
Obligation, 274
see also Duty,
defined, 283
distinguished from "obliged", 283
as prediction, 283
primary rule of, 287

Observational standpoint, 20, 574
  comprehensive focus, 13
  elements of, 12
  focal requirements, 13
  focus, as "lenses", 13
  of scholar as compared to decisionmaker,
      577
  and self scrutiny, 12
  social process, 12
  sources of distortion, 13
Oligarchy
  causes of, 368
  defined, 367
  feature of bureaucracies and large orga-
      nizations, 371
  "iron law" of, 368
  perogatives and tactics of, 371
Oligphant and Hewitt
  Introduction to J. Rueff, From the Physical
      to the Social Sciences: Introduction
      to a Study of Economic and Ethical
      Theory, 435
Operational code, 197
  by-product of social complexity, 26
  defence of, 29
  discrepant from myth system, 26
  examples of, 29
  illegality of, 26
  (and) myth systems, 24
  perceived as illegal, 24
  protected by public officials, 30
  view them as lawful, 29
  viewed as lawful examples, 29
  requirement for, 220
Obedience to rules
  when required, 218
Observation
  focus of, 12
  balanced emphasis required on authority
      and control, 12
  targets of, 14
Operations
  expectations of what is right, 13
  what people actually do, 13, 14
Opinions
  of some persons to be disregarded, 84
  regard only opinions of men of under-
      standing, 85
Organizations, Large
  characteristics of, 371
  ideologies developed in, 375
Original agreement
  see Original position

Original position, 119, 121, 125, 127, 210,
    213, 222
  see Rawls, A Theory of Justice, 210
  concept of, defined, 215
  conditions of persons in, 215
  defined, 213
  as expository device, 215
  insures justice and fairness, 215
  most philosophically favored interpreta-
      tion, 215
  not a historical occurrence, 213
  parties choose principles for concepts of
      right, 218
  principles chosen in, 218

Pain
  see also Bentham, J.,
  and pleasure, 534, 537
Paley, W., 111, 112
Paradoxes of Legal Science
    Cardozo, B. N., 247
Penal Law,
  see Criminal Law
Penntown, 2
  ask who the boss is, 3
  information needed to fashion a course of
      action, 3
People, the
  nowhere consulted, 76
People v. Woody, 156
Persecution,
  see Fedorenko v. United States, 165
Person
  in due process clause, 193
  in equal protection clause, 193
  fetus as, 193
  not defined in Constitution, 193
Personality
  system overlaps with social system, 460
Perspectives
  what people say, 13
Peyote
  use of in religious ceremonies, 156, 157
Phase analysis
  components of, 14
Philosophical radicalists, 281
  influence on rise of positivism, 281
Plato, 25, 58, 63, 64, 67, 90, 143, 222, 324,
    325
  dialogues of, 83
Pleasure
  see Bentham, J.
  and pains, 534

—different types of, 539
—sources of, 539
Pleasure and pain
    how measured, 537
Pleasure-pain principle, 292, 544
    see Bentham, J., Utilitarianism
    defined, 280
Policies
    clarification of, described, 584
    compared with rules and principles de-
        fined, 296
Policy
    analysis of, 464
    considerations of in judicial decisions, 306
    contemporary approaches, 516
    evaluation of as a social process, 567
    goals achieved by use of income tax laws,
        527
    intuitive judicial application, 517, 518
    invention and evaluation of alternatives,
        586
    (and) law, 4
    (and) legal education, 531, 587
    molded by justices in Supreme Court, 332
    often made in a series of informal meet-
        ings, 4
    as version of utilitarian method, 464
    requires method of formulating problems,
        533
    role of in social science inquiry, 513
    should be based on empirical considera-
        tions, 509
    use of to override law, 528
    and values, 327
Policy science
    jurisprudence of, 517
    (the) "New Haven School", 573
    requires performance of many intellectual
        tasks, 517
    view of role of policy as central to deci-
        sionmaking, 516, 517
    view of law as process of making deci-
        sions, 516, 517
Policy thinking
    defined, 550
Political economy, 248
    see Marx, K., 248
Political justice, 99, 170
    enquiry into by W. Godwin, 99
    as natural, 170
Political questions, 150
Politicians
    influence in governing, 47

Politics, 171
    of Aristotle, 171
    "preventive politics" defined, 546
    and psychopathology, 546
Polygamy, 158
    as offense against society, 149
    not protected by Constitution, 148
    see Reynolds v. U.S., 158
Popper, Karl, 511, 570
Positive law, 226, 271, 272
    as distinguished from morality, 272
    as jurisprudence, defined, 271
    origin of, 226
    is positive because it is created and an-
        nulled by acts of human beings, 387
Positivism, 197, 269, 294
    see also, "Pure Theory" of law as adapted
        to contemporary bureaucracy, 362,
        363
    analytical, 351
    as "an exercise in applied semantics", 404
    assumes force as a postulate, not empiri-
        cally tested, 356
    attractive to permanent minorities, 355
    definition of law, 269
    disregards goal formulation and policy fac-
        tors, 292
    distinguishes the "is and the "ought", 292
    distortion of objectives of legislation, 307
    five meanings of, 270
    focus on acts of judges, 356
    (as) not focusing on decisions of non-of-
        ficials, 404
    (as) jurisprudence of rules, 269
    key underpinning of, 281
    key propositions of as set by Dworkin, R.,
        294
    key propositions of as set by Hart, H.L.A.,
        294
    lip service to by judges, 306
    and morality, 333
    and naked power theories, 269
    observation as method of, 280
    (and the) protection of minorities, 349
    rescued by Hart from Austin's mistakes,
        295
    restricted focus of attention by Hart and
        Kelsen, 404
    rigid construction of statutes, 307
    rules identified by pedigree, 294
    (and) separation of law and morality, 270
    (and) validity of Nazi laws, 334
    value for resolving problems of society,
        405

versions of Hart and Austin compared, 295
view of Dworkin, R. on, 294
Positive morality, 272
see also Positivism, 197, 280
assume that rules have unequivocal and unchanging meanings, 356
focus on decisionmaking by judges, 293
place undue emphasis on derivational logic, 292
reasons for focus on rules, 280
seeking unitary principle governing social and moral life, 280
views regarding Nazi laws, 334
Posner, Richard, Judge
Economic Analysis of *Law*, 552
Pospisil, Leopold, 35, 349
legal levels, 35
Multiplicity of Legal Systems, 35
Potential life
compelling interest, 194
viability, 194
Power, 261
activities of holders, 262
control by sanctions, 65
definition of effective power, 583
(and) democracy, 45
exercised on behalf of society, 65
holders of, 261
role of authority in, 52
Power elite
consists of heads of political, corporate and military spheres, 50
inner core consists of leaders in legal, economic and military spheres, 51
interchange of leadership between military, political and economic orders, 51
Power structure
police department and armed forces are two arms of, 75
Precedents
restrictions by courts on use of, 307
Prediction, 17
see also, Judicial decision
of judicial decisions, see, 463
Presthus, Robert
The Organizational Society, 363, 376
Primary rules
conditions required for existence of, 288
defects of, 287
inefficiency, as defect, 288
of obligation, 287

procedures for interpretation of required, 288
requirement for changes in, 288
static character of, as defect, 288
uncertainty, as defect of, 287
Principle of fairness, 220
see Rawls, John,
Principle of utility, 292, 533
see Bentham, J., Utilitarianism
defined, 280, 534
Principles of law, 237
bound up with interests of individuals, 237
neutral principles, 316, 322
use of neutral principles, 318
Principles
see also Legal principles; Neutral principles
and the concept of law, 299
definition of, 331
of content and procedure, 549
neutral, 322
Privacy, 179
see also Griswold v. Connecticut; Matter of Quinlan; Roe v. Wade
fourteenth amendment, 192
includes abortion decision, 192
ninth amendment, 192
right of, 177, 179, 185, 345
right to, may be superceded by other interests, 193
right to, not absolute, 191
right to, of women, 193
Private judgment, 166
see Civil disobedience,
Problem
definition of from policy standpoint, 533
Problem solving
see also Braybrooke and Lindblom, *A Strategy of Decision*, 567
comprehensiveness in, 568
comprehensiveness in may not be worthwhile, 571
difficulties of, 569
possible strategies for, 569
"synoptic" method, 568
Process of decision
need for systematic set of terms to describe, 581
Products liability, 477
Projective thinking
defined, 550
Promises
nature of obligation to observe, 104

Property, 240
   as extension of the person, 241
Prostitution, 178
   see also Wolfenden Report, 336
   as a crime, 336
Protests
   see also Civil disobedience; Dissent
   protected by Constitution, 132
   by violating reasonable laws, 131
Psychology
   rationality theory, 461, 462
Psychopathology and Politics, 546
   see also Lasswell, Harold,
Public interest
   difficulty of determining, 407, 408
   too nebulous a standard to guide lawyer's
      conduct, 407
Public order, 574
   decisions of defined, 581
   differentiated from civic order, 582
   of human dignity, 324
Puchta, 238
"Pure theory" of law
   defined, 381
   general theory of law is connected to po-
      sitive law, not to psychological, eco-
      nomic, moral or political evaluations,
      381
   focuses exclusively on analysis of positive
      law, 382
   is oriented like analytical jurisprudence,
      382

Racial segregation
   use of busing to overcome, 501, 502
Radbruch, Gustav, 334
Radical historicism, 248
Rational choice, 567
   see also Problem solving
Rawls, John, 27, 120, 128, 210, 222
   A Theory of Justice, 119
   principles of, 222
Realism, 459
   see also Legal realism,
Realist movement
   highly pragmatic and empirical, 459
   new approach to jurisprudence, 459
Realists, 459
   see also Legal realism
Reason
   See Decisionmaking
Riesman, David, 8, 10
Reisman, W.M. *A Theory of Law and Policy*,
   4

Folded Lies, 23
   myth system and operational code, 23
   policy perspective, 4
Religion
   establishment clause in United States Con-
      stitution, 150
   freedom of belief distinguished from free-
      dom of action, 148
   free exercise of, 150, 157
Religious freedom
   abridgement of, 158
Religious Liberty
   see also Conscientious objection; Consti-
      tution; United States; Reynolds v.
      United States
Replication
   of the past, 261
Repouille v. United States, 348
Republic, The, 25, 58, 64
Revolution
   as right of all men, 111
Reynolds v. Sims, 470
Reynolds v. United States, 158
Rex, 198, 199, 200, 202
Right
   defined, 279
Rights, 240
   duty to struggle for, 240
Rodell, Fred, 434
   intuitionism of, 455
   *Nine Men: A Political History of the Su-
      preme Court from 1790 to 1955*, 455
Roe v. Wade, 189
Rogozinsky et al. v. State of Israel, 349
Rostow, Eugene, 331
Rousseau, J. J., 67, 103, 104, 105, 213
   responsibility for rise of totalitarian de-
      mocracy, 65
Rule of law
   see also Law, Rule of, 134, 353
   based on free market, 354
   in bureaucracy, 362
   contrasted with rule of men, 311
   criticized as rigid, 355
   implies minimum intervention of govern-
      ment, 355
   profoundly immoral law, 141
Rules, 197, 199, 269
   see Positivism,
   are not mere predictions, 284
   see Local rules, 199
   (of) adjudication, 291
   basic character of, 204

of change, 290

compared with principles and policies, 296

conceived as imposing obligations, 285

difficulty of applying without reference to values and goals, 333

difficulty of providing for all situations, 333

do not constitute law, 446

human vulnerability as basis of, 204

internal and external points of view, 286

need for public to know, 197

no fixed and predetermined body of rules exists, 442

play limited role in judicial decisions, 446

(as) predictive, 285

premised on sanctions, 284

primary and secondary, 282

reasons for obedience to, 204

of recognition, 289

require serious social pressure to obey, 285

rule of recognition, 291

union of primary and secondary rules required for existence of legal system, 289

serve as justifications of judges' decisions, 446

Rules of law, 141

do not constitute law, 446

Sanction, 273, 274

see Command, 274

Savigny, K. F., 226, 231, 232, 233, 236, 238, 246, 266, 267

exponent of mythical group consciousness, 246

On The Vocation Of Our Age For Legislation and Jurisprudence, 226

Savigny-Puchta, 237

theory regarding origins of law, 237

Schubert, Glendon, 484

Behavioral Jurisprudence, 484

Science

descriptions of facts, are selective, 511

Science of law

see also Law, science of, 383

directed at a system of norms, 382

Scientific thinking

defined, 550

Segregation

court decisions regarding, 317, 319

restrictive covenants, 320

in schools, 320

(and) science, 489

racial, 486

segregated schools not tax exempt, 518

unconstitutionality of, 317

Selective service, 155

see also Conscription; Conscientious objection,

discrimination against non-religious conscientious objection, 155

first amendment, 155

Sex discrimination, 169

see Natural law, difference between men and women, 169

Sexual behavior, 173

natural and unnatural, 173

Shklar, J., 349

Sin, 254

and crime, 254

Sindell v. Abbott Laboratories, 480

Skinner v. Oklahoma, 177

ex rel. Williamson,

Slavery, 172

expedient and right for some, 172

Social change

no objective laws of, 469

Social choice

see also Arrow, Kenneth and individual values, 561

Social contract, 105, 119, 213, 231

as partnership between those in past, present and future, 231

conflicts with concepts of equality and justice, 102

difficulties of the concept, 102

two conflicting notions of, 65

Social control,

see Social process

Social justice, 211, 212

see also Justice

conception of provides standards, 212

Social Process, 266

and law, 266

collection of people with conflicting perspectives interacting, 6

relationship to law described, 582

social, psychological, biological, ecological features of human behavior, 6

Social Processes, 266

community process, 15

constitutive process, defined, 15

effective power, 15

making and applying of policy, 15

Social science, 486
  and the courts, 492, 493
  failure to use expert testimony effectively,
     493
  problems of usage in courts, suggestions
     for overcoming, 499
  provides data for decisionmaking, 491
  role in judicial decisionmaking, 492
  stating facts regardless of how painful, 508
  values and value judgments, 510, 512
Social science data, 491
  detrimental effect of, 491
Social system, 459, 460
  see Jurisprudence, study of relationships
     in social system,
Social theories, 261
  construction of, 261
Social welfare
    problem of making judgments regard-
     ing, 562
Society, 210, 212
  as contract, 232
  stages in formation of, 249
  well-ordered, definitions of, 210, 212
  well-ordered principles regarding, 210,
    212
Sociological jurisprudence, 486
  see Jurisprudence, Sociological,
  different branches of, 488
  distinguishing external from internal be-
    havior, 401
  presuppositions of, 400
  value commitment, 510
Sociology
    as value free, 511
Sociology of law
  as defined by Max Weber, 400, 401
  investigates what is really happening in
    regard to a valid order, 400
Socrates, 25, 59, 65, 66, 90, 99, 143, 147,
  166, 232
  breaking covenant with state if he flees,
    89
  trial of, 83
Socratic, 65
Sorokin, P.
  Crisis of Our Age, 253
  cyclical historicism, 253
Standards
  distinct from rules,
  principles and policies, 296, 297
  may be difficult to distinguish from rules,
    299

State, 171
  agreement of with individual, 87
  disturbs peace on internal and doctrinal
    levels, 142
  distinguished from the people, 78, 146
  external level of, 142
  (as) identical with law, 383
  identity of interests with society, 90
  implied contract that citizen may leave if
    dissatisfied, 87
  individual not justified in destroying, 87
  interests of different from interests of peo-
    ple, 146
  law of is higher than "natural rights" of
    individuals, 91
  may defend its existence against acts, 133
  natural form of society, 172
  (as) parent or master of its citizens, 87
  position in international law not affected
    by changes in government, 57
  to be valued more than parents, 87
State, The
    distinguished from the people, 49, 78
Sterilization, 192
Stinchcombe, A.
    Constructing Social Theories, 261, 266
Storey, Robert, 10
Strauss, Leo, 324, 327, 329
Structural
  see law, structural nature of
Struggle for Law, 236
  see Jhering, R.,
Suicide
  see Matter of Quinlan, 179
Superior orders
  as exonerating immoral behavior, 92
  refusal to obey at risk of death, 92
Supreme Court, 308, 309
  can be understood only in terms of its
    members, 457
  political history of, 455
Survival
  as necessary condition for human achieve-
    ment, 208
Swann et al. v. Charlotte-Mecklenburg Board
  of Education, 501
Symbolic logic
    use of in predicting judicial decisions,
    463
System, in Law,
  see Legal system

Taft, W.H., Chief Justice, 55, 58, 362
Tarasoff v. Regents of the University of California, 417
Theft
    of motor vehicles, 307
The Justice's Dilemma, 8
Theory *about* law
    as distinguished from theory *of* law, 574
The Republic, 58
Theta Fraternity, 5
Thoreau, Henry David, 118, 145, 147, 154
    Civil Disobedience, 109
Thrasymachus, 58, 64, 66, 79
Thurow, Lester C., 545
Tinoco case
    (Great Britain v. Costa Rica), 56
Tocqueville, A., 45, 47
Totalitarian democracy
    responsibility for by Rousseau, 65
Treblinka, 161, 162, 166
    see Concentration camps, 159, 161
    several hundred thousand Jewish civilians murdered there, 159
Trend thinking
    defined, 549

Unnatural
    see Natural law,
United States v. Sisson, 150
Unjust law
    see also Civil disobedience,
    binding in a reasonably just society, 120
    defined, 118
    duty to comply with, 120
Unjust laws
    duty to disobey, 113
    not in harmony with moral law, 119
    reasons why unjust, 118
    segregation laws, 119
    should not be obeyed, 118
    so classified if degrades human personality, 119
Utilitarianism, 544
    see also, Bentham, J.
    act-utilitarianism distinguished from role-utilitarianism, 545
    attacked by scholars committed to primacy of rights, 545
    (and) economic analysis of law, 554
Utilitarians, 534
    see Bentham, J.; Utilitarianism,
Utility
    see also, Bentham, J.; Utilitarianism

incompatible with justice and fairness, 214
principle of, 214, 219, 533

Values
    clarification of distinguished from derivation of, 532
    clarification of and training in, 53
    clarifying judgments regarding, 549
    "correctness" of, cannot be proven empirically, 544
    defined per Lasswell, H., 14
    describe any process, 15
    different categories of, described, 583
    human dignity is supreme value of democracy, 532
    inseparable from facts, 325, 326
    judgments on values cannot be derived from scientific insights, 510
    necessary in research, 327
    need to spell out in specific situations, 531, 532
    (and) social choice, 561
    (and) social science, 510
    useful to describe processes, 14
    use of is not threat to scientific inquiry, 511
    value judgments cannot be eliminated from scientific theories, 510, 511
Veil of ignorance
    see Rawls; *A Theory of Justice*,
Vietnam, War in, 137, 150, 154, 156
Violence
    see Civil disobedience, 145
    to persuade, 136
    not productive, 136
    not protected by law, 134
    not successful where alternative means exist, 136
    romanticization of, 236
Volksgeist
    see Savigny, K. F.
von Gierke, Otto, 36, 38, 39
von Jhering, R., 510
    goal clarification, 566
    The Struggle for Law, 236
Voting
    paradox of, 561

War
    impersonal, 374
    just, 126
    power to draft, 152
    public and private interests in, 153

Weber, Max, 39, 41, 234, 327, 353, 379, 400, 401, 511
  definition of sociology of law, 400
  existence of legal systems with a given society, 37
Wechsler, H., 313, 329
Wilson, E., 509
Wolf E.P.
  social science and the courts, 492
Wolfenden Report
  see Homosexuality,

Women
  treatment in common law, 169
Wright, Skelly, Judge
  see, Javins v. First National Realty Corp.
  views on neutral principles, 331

Youth
  causes of revolt, 136
  revolt of, 136

Zinn, Howard, 140, 151, 166